10/00

Newsmakers®

ISSN 0899-0417

Newsmakers®

The People Behind Today's Headlines

Geri Koeppel

Edited by
Aaron J. Oppliger

2000
Issue 4

Includes Nationality, Occupation
Subject, and Newsmakers Indexes

GALE GROUP

Detroit
New York
San Francisco
London
Boston
Woodbridge, CT

STAFF

Edited by Aaron Oppliger, *Associate Editor*

Geri Koeppel, *Writer and Main Researcher*

Bridget Travers, *Managing Editor, General Biography/Genealogy*

Maria Franklin, *Permissions Team Leader*
Margaret Chamberlain, *Permissions Specialist*
Julie Juengling, *Permissions Assistant*

Stacy Melson, *Buyer*
Mike Logusz, *Macintosh Artist*

Mary Beth Trimper, *Manager, Composition and Electronic Prepress*
Carolyn A. Fischer, *Composition Specialist*

Theresa Rocklin, *Manager, Technical Support Services*
Edward J. David, *Programmer/Analyst*

Dean Dauphinais, *Senior Editor, Imaging & Multimedia Content*
Randy Bassett, *Image Database Supervisor*
Robert Duncan and Dan Newell, *Imaging Specialists*
Pamela A. Reed, *Imaging Coordinator*

Victoria B. Cariappa, *Research Manager*
Barbara McNeil, *Research Specialist*

Cover Photos: Erykah Badu (AP/Wide World Photos)
and Joaquin Phoenix (The Kobal Collection)

ISBN 0-7876-3070-5 (this volume)
ISBN 0-7876-3066-7 (complete 2000 set)
ISSN 0899-0417

v

Contents

Obituaries

Introduction

Newsmakers provides informative profiles of the world's most interesting people in a crisp, concise, contemporary format. Make *Newsmakers* the first place you look for biographical information on the people making today's headlines.

Important Features

- **Attractive, modern page design** pleases the eye while making it easy to locate the information you need.

- **Coverage of all the newsmakers** you want to know about people in business, education, technology, law, politics, religion, entertainment, labor, sports, medicine, and other fields.

- **Clearly labeled data sections** allow quick access to vital personal statistics, career information, major awards, and mailing addresses.

- **Informative sidelights essays** include the kind of in-depth analysis you're looking for.

- **Sources for additional information** provide lists of books, magazines, newspapers, and internet sites where you can find out even more about *Newsmakers* listees.

- **Enlightening photographs** are specially selected to further enhance your knowledge of the subject.

- **Separate obituaries section** provides you with concise profiles of recently deceased newsmakers.

- **Publication schedule and price** fit your budget. *Newsmakers* is published in three paperback issues per year, each containing approximately 50 entries, and a hardcover cumulation, containing approximately 200 entries (those from the preceding three paperback issues plus an additional 50 entries), *all at a price you can afford!*

- And much, much more!

Indexes Provide Easy Access

Familiar and indispensable: The *Newsmakers* indexes! You can easily locate entries in a variety of ways through our four versatile, comprehensive indexes. The Nationality, Occupation, and Subject Indexes list names from the current year's *Newsmakers* issues. These are cumulated in the annual hardbound volume to include all names from the entire *Contemporary Newsmakers* and *Newsmakers* series. The Newsmakers Index is cumulated in all issues as well as the hardbound annuals to provide concise coverage of the entire series.

- **Nationality Index**—Names of newsmakers are arranged alphabetically under their respective nationalities.

- **Occupation Index**—Names are listed alphabetically under broad occupational categories.

- **Subject Index**—Includes key subjects, topical issues, company names, products, organizations, etc., that are discussed in *Newsmakers*. Under each subject heading are listed names of newsmakers associated with that topic. So the unique Subject Index provides access to the information in *Newsmakers* even when readers are unable to connect a name with a particular topic. This index also invites browsing, allowing *Newsmakers* users to discover topics they may wish to explore further.

- **Cumulative Newsmaker Index**—Listee names, along with birth and death dates, when available, are arranged alphabetically followed by the year and issue number in which their entries appear.

Available in Electronic Formats

Diskette/Magnetic Tape. *Newsmakers* is available for licensing on magnetic tape or diskette in a fielded format. The database is available for internal data processing and nonpublishing purposes only. For more information, call 1-800-877-GALE.

Online. *Newsmakers* is available online as part of the Gale Biographies (GALBIO) database accessible through LEXIS-NEXIS, P.O. Box 933, Dayton, OH 45401-0933; phone: (937) 865-6800; toll-free: 1-800-227-9597.

Suggestions Are Appreciated

The editors welcome your comments and suggestions. In fact, many popular *Newsmakers* features were implemented as a result of readers' suggestions. We will continue to shape the series to best meet the needs of the greatest number of users. Send comments or suggestions to:

The Editor
Newsmakers
The Gale Group
27500 Drake Rd.
Farmington Hills, MI 48331-3535

Or, call toll-free at 1-800-877-GALE

Christina Aguilera

Singer

Born Christina Maria Aguilera,December 18, 1980, in New York, NY; daughter of Fausto Aguilera (an Army sergeant) and Shelly Kearns.

Addresses: *Home*—Wexford, PA, and Manhattan, NY. *Record company*—RCA Records, 1133 Avenue of the Americas, New York, NY 10036.

Career

Began singing at block parties around Pittsburgh, PA, 1980s; appeared on *Star Search,* c. 1988; joined cast of the New Mickey Mouse Club, 1993–95; sang national anthem for local sports teams in Pittsburgh, c. 1990; recorded "Reflections" for *Mulan* soundtrack, 1998; signed contract with RCA Records, 1998; released debut album, *Christina Aguilera,* 1999.

Awards: ALMA Award and Grammy Award for best new artist, 2000.

Sidelights

In August of 1999, teen singer Christina Aguilera stole the musical spotlight with her self– titled debut album and hit single, "Genie in a Bottle." Arriving on the charts at number one, *Christina Aguiler a* later spawned another hit single, "What a Girl Wants," and had many critics insisting that she was not just another fleeting pop icon. David E. Thigpen in *Time* called her "one of the most strikingly gifted singers to come along since Mariah Carey." Aguil-era has also been praised for her R&B influences such as Etta James, which lends a maturity to her sounds beyond typical bubblegum dance tunes. In 2000, she won a Grammy Award for best new artist, beating out Britney Spears and Macy Gray.

Aguilera was born on December 18, 1980, on New York City's Staten Island. Her father, Fausto Aguilera, was born in Ecuador and served as an Army sergeant in New York, Texas, and Japan when his daughter was small. Aguilera's mother, Shelly, is Irish American. They met in college and had a troubled marriage. "I think that the reason that my drive was so strong and I was so passionate about music was because I grew up in an environment of domestic violence," Aguilera told Neil Strauss in *Rolling Stone.* "Music was my release to get away from it all. I would seriously run up to my bedroom an put on that *Sound of Music* tape." Aguilera went on to say that her father has since apologized for the abuse.

Aguilera's parents divorced when she was six, and she and her mother and younger sister, Rachel, soon moved in with her grandmother, Delcie Fidler, in Wexford, Pennsylvania. Fidler was the first person to recognize Aguilera's vocal talents and give her encouragement. In elementary school talent shows,

Aguilera began singing Whitney Houston tunes. Soon she started appearing at block parties around the Pittsburgh area. At age eight, Aguilera appeared on *Star Search* singing Whitney Houston's "Greatest Love of All," but did not win. She was performing the national anthem at Pittsburgh Steelers and Penguins games by age ten.

When Aguilera was 14, her mother married Jim Kearns, a paramedic who had a son and daughter of his own. Aguilera resented her new father. "Here was a male telling me what to do," she related to Strauss. "And that was the last thing I wanted to hear, after my other situations." However, the singer adapted to her new family, and noted that her mother and stepfather "have a beautiful marriage, and I'm really happy." Aguilera's mom and stepfather later had another son, Robert Michael, who was born in the mid–1990s.

Meanwhile, with no formal acting or singing lessons behind her, Aguilera auditioned for the cast of the *New Mickey Mouse Club* at age ten. The producers did not feel she was old enough at the time, so they asked her back when she was 12. From 1993 to 1995 she appeared on the show, commuting back and forth from Pittsburgh to Orlando, Florida, for tapings. On the *New Mickey Mouse Club*, Aguilera was called "Little Diva" or "Mini– Diva" because of her "little strut," as she told Strauss. She donned ears alongside the likes of future teen singer Britney Spears, actor Keri Russell of *Felicity*, and Justin Timberlake and J.C. Chasez of N'Sync. Richard Harrington of the *Washington Post* wrote, "Of those, Aguilera would seem to have the most musical potential, thanks to a genuinely powerful voice that's evoked comparisons to the younger Mariah Carey and Whitney Houston, though it for the most part avoids those singers' ornamental mannerisms."

After the demise of the *New Mickey Mouse Club*, Aguilera traveled the world, performing in countries like Japan and Romania. Then, in 1998, her manager sent Disney executives a tape of her singing Houston's "I Wanna Run to You," recorded at home on a portable stereo. They were looking for someone who could hit a high "E" note above a middle "C," and after hearing the tape, signed her up to sing "Reflections" on the soundtrack to 1998's *Mulan*. It reached the top 15 on the charts and was nominated for a Golden Globe award for best original song in a motion picture.

The same week that Aguilera was recording for Disney, RCA Records got a hold of her demo tape and called her in to audition *a cappella*. She landed a

contract with them, and after a year and half, released her self–titled debut album in August of 1999. It was anchored by the dance–pop hit "Genie in a Bottle," which had taken just a few weeks to reach the top of the charts, and stayed there for five weeks. Rob Sheffield in *Rolling Stone* wrote that "the lyrics...boast enough sexual innuendo to make 'Little Red Corvette' sound like a nice song about changing your oil filter."

Aguilera admitted to Chris Willman in *Entertainment Weekly* that she and executive producer Ron Fair disagreed about the album's first single, because she wanted a tune that better showcased her wide vocal range. But she also noted that Fair taught her "how to not let the cat out of the bag too soon, how to keep it soft at first." After its strong opening, *Christina Aguilera* sold eight million copies by the following summer. This came right on the heels of Spears' hot debut, and thus sparked rumors that the two were fierce rivals. Aguilera informed Kristen Baldwin in *Entertainment Weekly*, "I get a lot of the Britney questions. 'Is there a rivalry? Is there catfighting?' I'm like, 'Noooooo.' If anything, we'll probably do a collaboration." She also remarked to Evelyn McDonnell in *Interview* that the speculation is "really, really hurtful to me because Britney and I were close in the Mickey Mouse Club. We were the two little girls of the show, so we bonded."

Other songs on Aguilera's first release featured other dance–pop numbers like a cover of Whitney Houston's "So Emotional" and power ballads such as "I Turn to You," written by the same person who penned the similar–sounding Celine Dion tune "Because You Loved Me." The effort also included two tracks—"Love Will Find a Way" and "Love for All Seasons"—produced by Carl Sturken and Evan Rogers, who also worked with teen groups N'Sync and Boyzone. Aguilera had another hit single off the album with "What a Girl Wants, "produced by Guy Roche, who also worked with singers Brandy and Aaliyah. In addition to winning the Grammy for best new artist in 2000, Aguilera was also nominated for best female pop vocal performance.

Once Aguilera's album came out, she embarked on a 45–day cross–country promotional tour. The label boosted her profile as well by hiring Electric Artists, an Internet marketing firm, to go into newsgroups and message boards in order to stir up interest in the singer. Later, she remade the single "Genie in a Bottle" in Spanish to highlight her Latina heritage, riding on the coattails of Hispanic singers such as Ricky Martin, Jennifer Lopez, and Marc Anthony. After that became a hit, Aguilera, who speaks little

Spanish, began working with a speech coach in order to put out an all–Spanish album in fall of 2000 that would include some previously recorded cuts and some new Latin–flavored ones.

Some of Aguilera's other accomplishments included singing a duet with B.B. King and belting a solo rendition of "The Christmas Song" for President Bill Clinton on the television special *Christmas at the White House*. After that, the president asked her to sing the opening tune on his *Millenium* special, broadcast from Washington, D.C. Aguilera also performed a duet with Enrique Iglesias at the Super Bowl halftime show in 2000 and was named best new artist at that year's ALMA awards, which recognizes Hispanic entertainment figures.

Rising to such heights at such a young age occasionally brought conflict into Aguilera's life. As she mentioned to McDonnell in *Interview,* "Whenever anyone wants to label you a role model, it's difficult to do normal nineteen–year–old girl things. Dennis Rodman gave me good advice. I was talking about feeling like I'm under a microscope, so I can't just have fun because everybody wants to make such a big deal out of it. And he said, 'Controversy never hurt anybody.'"

Nevertheless, Aguilera was frank in several interviews about her resentment of the double standard in the treatment of male and female stars. She pointed out that when boy bands like N'Sync and Backstreet Boys do pelvic thrusts on stage or attend strip clubs, it is macho, but if she or Spears bare their tummies or sing suggestive lyrics, they are lambasted for being overly sexual. Aguilera was skewered in the media at one point when it was reported that she had attended a strip club with some male performers. She remarked to Strauss in *Rolling Stone,* "They totally overlook the fact that Backstreet Boys cuss during their interviews, go to strip clubs all the time and do normal things for their age. It's not a dis to them, but it's so unfair."

Aguilera, though, is no stranger to criticism. By the time she was in middle school, she was growing weary of taunts from other students jealous of her budding musical success. She had changed elementary schools after *Star Search* and began home schooling in the eighth grade. At 18, she returned to her hometown to attend a friend's senior prom, but the other students left the floor when "Genie in a Bottle" was played. "It was kind of sad," Aguilera commented in *People* . "All I want to do is be normal. But really, it's other people who won't let me be that way."

Aguilera has an apartment on the Upper West Side of Manhattan but considers her basement bedroom in Wexford her true home. Though her flat–as–a–board abdomen has been the focus of many a photograph, she insist she has never been to a gym, and admits to eating junk food, albeit in small doses. "Wendy's is my favorite," she remarked to Anthony Bozza in *Rolling Stone,* "but McDonald's will do."

Sources

Periodicals

Entertainment Weekly, August 20, 1999, p. 126; September 17, 1999, p. 31; March 31, 2000, p. 20.
In Style, June 2000, p. 356.
Interview, April 2000, p. 112.
People, September 27, 1999, p. 75.
Rolling Stone, August 19, 1999, pp. 36, 118; October 28, 1999, p. 52; July 6, 2000, p. 80.
Time, August 16, 1999, p. 69; March 6, 2000, p. 70.
Toronto Sun, May 18, 2000, p. 61; July 7, 2000, p. 53.
TV Guide, August 21, 1999, p. 20.
Washington Post, September 8, 1999, p. C1.

Online

Christina Aguilera Official Web Site, http://www.christina–a.com (August 1, 2000).

Pedro Almodovar

Director

Born September 25, 1951, in Calzada de Calatrava, Ciudad Real, Spain; son of a bookkeeper.

Addresses: *Office*—El Deseo S.A., Ruiz Perello 15, Madrid, Spain; c/o Ministry of Culture, Motion Picture Division, Avenida de Burgos 5, 28036 Madrid, Spain.

Career

Screenwriter and director. Worked for Telefonica telephone company, 1970–c.1980; singer in rock band, Almodovar and McNamara; actor with independent theater troupe, Los Goliardos; writer of comic strips and columns for underground newspaper, all in Madrid, Spain, all c. 1970s. Director of films and writer of screenplays, including *Pepi, Luci, Bom y otras chicas del monton* (*Pepi, Luci, Bom and Other Girls on the Heap*), 1980; *Laberinto de pasiones* (*Labyrinth of Passion*), 1982; *Entre tinieblas* (*Dark Habits*), 1983; *Que he hecho yo para merecer esto?!!* (*What Have I Done to Deserve This?*), 1984; *Matador*, 1986; *La ley del deseo* (*Law of Desire*), 1987; *Mujeres al borde de un ataque de nervios* (*Women on the Verge of a Nervous Breakdown*), 1988; *Atame!* (*Tie Me Up! Tie Me Down!*), 1990; *Tacones lejanos* (*High Heels*), 1991; *Kika*, 1993; *La flor de mi secreto* (*Flower of My Secret*), 1995; *Carne tremula* (*Live Flesh*), 1997; *Todo sobre mi madre* (*All About My Mother*), 1999.

Awards: Berlin International Film Festival, Teddy Award for best feature film, 1987, for *Law of Desire;* Fantasporto international fantasy film special jury award, 1986, and award for best director, 1987, both

for *Matador;* Los Angeles Film Critics Association "New Generation" Award, 1987; Venice International Film Festival best screenplay award, European Film Award for best young film, National Board of Review of Motion Pictures best foreign film award, and New York Film Critics Circle best foreign film award, all 1988, all for *Women on the Verge of a Nervous Breakdown;* National Society of Film Critics special citation for originality, 1988, for *Matador* and *Women on the Verge of a Nervous Breakdown;* Goya Award (Spain) for best original screenplay, and Italian National Syndicate of Film Journalists Silver Ribbon award, both 1989, for *Women on the Verge of a Nervous Breakdown;* named Man of the Year by Spanish magazine *Cambio 16,* 1989; Cesar Award (France) for best foreign film, 1993, for *High Heels;* Italian National Syndicate of Film Journalists Silver Ribbon award, 1998, for *Live Flesh;* Cesar Honorary Award (France), 1999; People's Choice Award for best European director, 1999; International Film Critics Federation Fipresci Award, grand prize, Cannes Film Festival best director award, European Film Award, audience award, Ft. Lauderdale International Film Festival People's Choice award, and New York Film Critics Circle Award for best foreign language film, all 1999, for *All About My Mother;* Academy Award for best foreign film, Bodil Award for best non–American film, British Academy Award for best non–English language film, British Academy Award David Lean Award for direction, Cesar Award for best foreign film, Chicago Film Critics Association Award for best foreign language film, Cinema Brazil Grand prize for best foreign film, Goya Award for best director, and Palm Springs International Film Festival international filmmaker award, all 2000, for *All About My Mother.*

Sidelights

Spanish filmmaker Pedro Almodovar is an intriguing figure whose works are known for their eccentric cast of characters, sense of kitsch, and tendency to probe into cultural and moral issues. Renowned for his bent toward the surreal and his use of stunning imagery, Almodovar's trademark is perhaps his ability to make the outrageous seem ordinary. He began making films in 1980, five years after the death of Generalissimo Francisco Franco, who ruled Spain under his fascist dictatorship for 36 years. Upon his death, a new cultural openness flourished in the country that had been repressed under harsh censorship, and Almodovar emerged as one of the most prominent creative voices. After being a colorful member of Madrid's subculture in the 1970s, he made his first professional film in 1980, and went on to gain acclaim for works like *Woman on the Verge of a Nervous Breakdown* and *Tie Me Up! Tie Me Down!* In 1999 and 2000, Almodovar was showered with praise and awards for his feature *All About My Mother.*

Stephen Schaefer in *Harper's Bazaar* summed up Almodovar's films by stating, "Mostly his movies serve up a funky, punky mixture of romanticism and sleaze, horror and comedy, high melodrama and low camp." Vito Russo in *Film Comment* noted, "Almodovar fears government and church repression, Franco and the Ophus Dei (a right–wing Catholic cult popular in Spain and Italy), but also any group–think from sex roles to manners to well–meaning radicals who would overthrow both." Russo related that the filmmaker once noted, "I don't like any kind of militancy, and I don't like telephones. Passion has its own irrational rules, and like indifference, it can drive people to sublime or dangerous extremes. Society is preoccupied with controlling passion because it's a disequilibrium, but for the individual it is undeniably the only motor that gives sense to life."

Almodovar ("ahl–moh–DOH–vahr") was born on September 25, 1951, in the poor village of Calzada de Calatrava, Ciudad Real, in southwestern Spain. His father worked as a bookkeeper at a gas station and made wine at home for extra income, and his mother, a domineering homemaker, raised Almodo-

var and his two older sisters and younger brother. In a *Vanity Fair* interview with Ben Brantley he called her "a very possessive woman." When Almodovar was eight, his family moved to the interior region of La Mancha, a cold and isolated rural region where he felt like "an astronaut in the court of King Arthur," as he noted in *GQ*. There, his mother urged him to earn money for the family by teaching the locals how to read. "As a result of having seen my mother fight it out always, it's the women who end up running life in my films," Almodovar noted to Brantley. As he grew older, however, he became very close to his mother, who has appeared in cameos in some of his films (credited as Francisca Caballero), although she never goes to see them. His father died in 1980.

When he was ten, Almodovar was offered a scholarship to a Catholic school run by Salesian priests. He told Brantley that he experienced sexual abuse by the priests and demanded that his parents remove him. Later, yearning for city life, at age 17 Almodovar ran away to Madrid, "with the intention of becoming Madrid's most modern person," as he mentioned to Brantley. There, he joined the underground arts scene. Almodovar took college courses, made and sold jewelry and crafts on the street, and lived as a hippie, enjoying the swinging "free love" atmosphere of the day.

Meanwhile, Almodovar took a job with Telefonica, the state phone company, in 1970, and would work there for about a decade while pursuing his creative endeavors on the side. "I led a double life," he told Hal Hinson in the *Washington Post*. He saved up money to buy a super–8 film camera, which was used to make amateur movies before the advent of video, and produced a series of short silent works featuring his friends in the acting roles. They often spoofed pornographic films, and were similar to the early works of cult favorites Andy Warhol and John Waters. However, Almodovar told Brantley that his main inspiration was from American underground movies and comics; he also wrote his own X–rated comic books as well. By the late 1970s, he was shooting on the more professional 16–mm format.

In addition, Almodovar became known around Madrid for his punk rock band, Almodovar and McNamara. In this project, he would strut on stage dressed in drag, sporting fishnet stockings, platform shoes, and a leather miniskirt. An old friend related to Brantley that he looked like "a cross between Bette Midler, Divine, and the New York Dolls." Almodovar also wrote a series of sham autobiographical articles for the Spanish periodical *La luna* under the guise of being an international porn star,

Patti Diphusa (*patidifusa* means "flabbergasted" in Spanish). He also worked with an experimental theater group called Los Goliardos, where he met Carmen Maura, who would go on to become one of his regular female actors.

In 1980, Almodovar produced his first feature film, *Pepi, Luci, Bom y otras chicas del monton,* on a budget of $5,000. The title means, "*Pepi, Luci, Bom, and Other Girls on the Heap.* " He shot it over the course of a year and a half, on weekends and during paid sabbaticals from the phone company. He told David Leavitt in the *New York Times Magazine* that it was his "dirtiest movie." The year of its release, the movie was screened at the San Sebastian Film Festival, where it shocked patrons with its kinky and brutal scenes. He has compared it to John Waters's notorious *Pink Flamingos.*

Almodovar's next film, *Laberinto de pasiones* (*Labyrinth of Passions*), was released in Spain in 1982 and in the United States in 1990. It is a low–budget musical for which Almodovar also composed and performed the score, and it deals with a group of young people in Madrid trying to break away from repressive fathers in order to find pleasure. It involves, among other characters, a bisexual punk singer involved with a nymphomaniac feminist, and a dry cleaner's daughter who suffers chronic incestuous rape. Still, the film is permeated by a sense of humor and gaiety.

With his third film, 1983's *Dark Habits,* Almodovar began to attract attention on an international level. The picture was shown at the Venice and Miami film festivals in 1984 and featured a cast of drug–addict nuns who keep a pet tiger. But it was his fourth project, 1984's *Que he hecho yo para merecer esto? (What Have I Done to Deserve This?)* that earned him his first box–office hit in Spain. It concerns a suburban homemaker who works as a maid on the side to supplement the family's income. If this sounds a tad tame for Almodovar, the mother is hooked on speed, sells her 12–year–old son to a lecherous dentist, and kills her husband with a frozen ham. The rest of the screen family includes a teenage heroin dealer, a husband who is involved with a plot to forge Adolf Hitler's memoirs, a mother–in–law who is fixated on her pet lizard, and a neighbor who is a prostitute.

Although *What Have I Done to Deserve This?* was Almodovar's first major hit, his earlier movies did well, too, and this success was even more notable at a time when home– grown films in Spain were declining in popularity. As Marsha Kinder reported in

Film Quarterly, Spanish films accounted for only 17.5 percent of the market in their own country in 1985, as opposed to 30 percent in 1970. In addition, Almodovar's 1986 effort, *Matador,* was the third–largest grossing film that year. It was released in the United States in 1988. Kinder called the film "an exercise in excess, a stylish psychological thriller with extravagant costumes, lush visuals, and the narrative logic of erotic fantasy." The picture, which lambastes the Spanish ideal of machismo, centers on a former matador who was gored in the ring and now teaches bullfighting. But to satisfy his ongoing blood lust, he kills young girls. Antonio Banderas appeared in this film as one of the matador's students.

After this, in 1986 Almodovar formed his own production company, El Deseo, with his producer brother, Agustin. They released *La ley del deseo,* which opened the next year in the United States as *Law of Desire.* It was his first project that was not partially state– subsidized. Like *Matador,* it is a psychological thriller, and again featured Banderas as a jealous homosexual lover who murders his boyfriend after mistakenly believing he has had an affair. The picture also involves two brothers, one of whom suffers from amnesia and the other of whom is a transsexual actor who lives with a lesbian lover. *La ley del deseo* was the most popular film in Spain in 1986.

In 1988, Almodovar reached the highest point of his career to date with *Mujeres al borde de un ataque de nervios* (*Women on the Verge of a Nervous Breakdown*). It revolves around a pregnant television soap opera actress. Pepa, whose lover, Ivan, a married man, dumps her. The picture, modeled after 1950s American comedies such as *How to Marry a Millionaire,* has a zany, fast–paced feel with underpinnings of sadness and loneliness. This was Spain's second–largest box office draw the year of its release, and it became an international hit as well, reaping several awards and nominations, including an Academy Award nomination for best foreign film.

Almodovar's next project, 1990's *Atame!,* was released the same year in the United States as *Tie Me Up! Tie Me Down!* It received an X rating, much to his consternation. The picture focuses on a former porno film star who is abducted by a recently released mental patient (Banderas, again) and ties her to a bed, then waits for her to fall in love with him. Though some criticized the work for its violence against women, Almodovar pointed out that the ropes were only symbols of the problems inherent in getting to know someone and a metaphor for the emotional ties in any relationship. In addition, the kidnapper shops specifically for the softest ropes he can find. Some critics found this film to be medio-cre, while others thought it was Almodovar's best work. As he explained to Leavitt in the *New York Times Magazine*, the female character in *Tie Me Up! Tie Me Down!* "cannot live without this passion, but at the same time she has to accept everything that goes with it. She doesn't say 'I love you'; she says 'tie me up.'"

Then, in 1991 Almodovar released *High Heels*, which won the 1993 Cesar Award in France for best for-eign film, beating out works by Woody Allen, Rob-ert Altman, and James Ivory. The movie is about a singer–actress who returns from 15 years away from Madrid to discover that her daughter, an anchor-woman, has married one of her former lovers. When the husband is found dead, both become suspects. Next came 1993's *Kika*, a satire on reality– based television, and then *La flor de mi secreto* (*The Flower of My Secret*) in 1995, which came out the following year in the United States. It is a melodrama about a romance novelist. Then, in 1997, Almodovar re-leased *Carne tremula* (*Live Flesh*), an adaptation of a crime novel by Ruth Rendell.

Almodovar's greatest success came in 1999, with *Todo Sobre Mi Madre* (*All About My Mother*). As al-ways, it featured an unconventional cast of charac-ters, including a young nun, Sister Rosa, who has become pregnant and contracted AIDS from a drag queen, and the transvestite's former wife, Manuela, who has come looking for him to tell him that their son whom he never knew was born has been killed in a tragic accident. Their lives intersect with sev-eral other quirky personalities, including a haughty stage actress and a transsexual. *All About My Mother* received 14 nominations for Goya Awards, Spain's equivalent of the Oscars, which had often shut Almodovar out of the running. He ended up receiv-ing the Goya for best director, in addition to a slew of other international honors, including an Acad-emy Award in 2000 for best foreign film.

Almodovar is a burly man with a broad face and thick black hair. He cites as his major influences the filmmakers Luis Bunuel, Alfred Hitchcock, and Billy Wilder. He is openly gay, but it seems that Almodovar's main love interest is his career. As he remarked to Hinson in the *Washington Post*, film-making "is a kind of obsession. When I am making a movie I feel absolutely possessed, and that pos-session is the most intense feeling I have ever known. Some people say that a film director is like a god, and, in fact, it is a little like that. It's an ex-traordinary gift to be able to represent your own fantasies and give them life. Not just your dreams, but everything that excites you and interests you. It gives your life a lot of meaning."

Sources

Books

Dictionary of Hispanic Biography, Gale Research, 1996.
Gay & Lesbian Biography, St. James Press, 1997.
International Dictionary of Films and Filmmakers, Vol-ume 2: Directors, St. James Press, 1996.

Periodicals

Advocate, February 3, 1998, p. 49.
American Film, March 1988, p. 72; January/February 1992, p. 38.
Entertainment Weekly, May 4, 1990, p. 19.
Film Comment, November–December 1988, p. 13.
Film Quarterly, Fall 1987, p. 33.
GQ, November 1989, p. 104.
Harper's Bazaar, December 1988, p. 82.
Hispanic, May 1998, p. 32.
Interview, April 1996, p. 48.
Newsweek, December 5, 1988, p. 88.
New York Times Magazine, September 12, 1999, p. 67.
Time International, December 13, 1999, p. 48.
Vanity Fair, April 1990, p. 182.
Variety, April 20, 1998, p. 39; September 13, 1999, p. 24; December 13, 1999, p. 42; January 3, 2000, p. 10.
Vogue, June 1990, p. 124.
Washington Post, June 30, 1990, p. G1.

Online

"Pedro Almodovar," *Contemporary Authors Online*, Gale Group web site, http://www.galenet.com (February 22, 2000).
"Pedro Almodovar," Internet Movie Database web site, http://us.imdb.com (May 5, 2000).

Wally Amos

AP/Wide World Photos

Business entrepreneur

Born Wallace Amos Jr., July 1, 1936, in Tallahassee, FL; son of Wallace (a gas company employee) and Ruby Amos; married three times; married third wife, Christine Harris (a flight attendant and product designer), July 1, 1979; children: three sons by first two marriages, (with third wife) Sarah Kapiolani.

Addresses: *Home*—P.O. Box 897, Kailua, Hawaii 96734.

Career

Saks Fifth Avenue, New York City, stockroom clerk, promoted to supply manager, 1958–61; William Morris Agency, New York City, mailroom clerk, promoted to executive secretary, became talent agent, 1961–67; ran own management business, Los Angeles, CA, 1967–74; Famous Amos Chocolate Chip Cookies, founder, owner and president, 1975–85, vice chairman, 1985–89; motivational speaker, 1989–91; Wally Amos Presents Chip & Cookie, founder and owner, 1992; Uncle Noname cookie company, founder and owner, 1992—; promoter of Famous Amos cookies for Keebler, 1999—. Author of autobiographical and inspirational books; motivational speaker. *Military service* U.S. Air Force, 1953–57.

Awards: Award for Entrepreneurial Excellence from President Ronald Reagan, 1986; Horatio Alger Association citation, 1987. Sidelights

In the mid–1970s, Wally Amos founded the first gourmet cookie company under the brand name Famous Amos, offering up a special recipe sold in chic retail outlets and favored by various celebrities. Although he was soon rolling in the dough thanks to his relentless promotion and enthusiasm for his product, by the mid–1980s Amos found that he had no nose for business. His company came under control of a succession of investors, until finally he had no stake in the firm. Complaining that the recipe had been altered and the quality had declined once the new investors began to mass–market the cookies in vending machines and other low–end outlets, Amos founded another cookie company, only to find that he no longer owned the right to use his name or likeness in promotions. Though the chips were down, Amos persevered by marketing his goods as Uncle Noname. Though he has had rocky times with that venture as well, he is seeking success with a line of no–fat muffins and has signed on with Keebler, the new owner of Famous Amos, to help them market his old brand. They have even agreed to let him use his name on his products now, so the muffins can be found under the name Uncle Wally's.

Amos was born on July 1, 1936, in Tallahassee, Florida, the son of Wallace Amos, who worked for the local gas company, and Ruby Amos. Neither of his parents could read or write, and they raised Amos with little affection. They separated when Amos was 12 and later divorced. Amos was then sent to live in Harlem, New York City, with his Aunt Della who was the first person to give him chocolate chip cookies. As he told Ron Harris in *Ebony* , "Since I was 12, I have had a fetish for chocolate chip cookies."

In 1951, Amos began living with his mother and grandmother, who had also moved to New York City, and his love of food led him to enroll at the Food Trades Vocational High School. Through the school, he landed a job in a hotel kitchen, but he soon found it tedious to work long hours at a hot stove; he dropped out of school six months before graduation. Amos joined the Air Force in 1953 and served a four–year stint, during which time his aunt faithfully sent him her homemade cookies. He earned his high school equivalency degree while in the military.

Once discharged, Amos attended secretarial school in New York City and then landed a job as a stock clerk at Saks Fifth Avenue. Although he was promoted to supply manager in 1961, he remained unhappy with the salary—$85 a week—and moved on to join the William Morris Agency, which represents many top stars. Amos started in the mailroom and in janitorial work, but showed initiative right away. As he mentioned to J. Gregory Clemons in *Black Enterprise,* "I was doing things I wasn't told to do. I saw a need for things to be done and did them." Within two months, he was promoted to substitute secretary, and it was not long before he permanently became the personal secretary to the firm's executive vice president, Howard L. Hausman. Amos impressed Hausman with his motivation and knack for spotting talent. He once took Hausman to a club to see a pair of singers, Paul Simon and Art Garfunkel, and they were signed to the agency soon after.

Subsequently, Amos was put in charge of the company's newly formed rock–and–roll department, where he helped further the careers of Diana Ross, Marvin Gaye, Sam Cooke, the Temptations, and more. In 1967, he decided to venture out on his own and left William Morris to manage trumpeter Hugh Masakela, but the relationship soured. He moved to Los Angeles and began signing other entertainers, but he soon grew impatient with the pretensions of the business. In the meantime, Amos had grown fond of baking chocolate chip cookies as a way to relax and often used them as calling cards when contacting Hollywood bigwigs. Eventually, as he told Clemons, "I couldn't deal with show business anymore. A series of client difficulties put me in a financial bind. I wasn't making any money, so I said to myself that I'm going to have to find something else to do."

Though many aficionados of his cookies had urged him to begin a baked goods operation, Amos never thought it a serious possibility until a friend suggested she might know an investor. That person fell through, but Amos was excited about the idea by this point and came up with a business proposal. Singer Helen Reddy and her manager/husband, Jeff Wald, put up the first $10,000, and other big names like Marvin Gaye later invested as well. Although Amos's first inspiration had been his Aunt Della, he based his recipe on one by Ruth Wakefield of Lowell, Massachusetts, but added more nuts and chips. A neighbor, Tony Christian, designed the look of the first store, which opened in March of 1975 on the corner of Sunset Boulevard and Formos Avenue. The kickoff party tempted a crowd of 1,500 with free champagne.

Calling his goods "Famous Amos" chocolate chip cookies, Amos worked long days baking and delivering the cookies himself, as well as tirelessly promoting them. They became hot items at upscale department stores and retail outlets, and many celebrities touted them. His picture, featuring him wearing a Hawaiian–print shirt and Panama straw hat, graced each bag and tin. He soon opened production facilities in Nutley, New Jersey, and Van Nuys, California, and more stores in Los Angeles and Hawaii, where he moved in 1977. The first year in business, Famous Amos brought in $300,000, and by 1982, revenues reached $12 million. Amos's original store became a tour bus attraction, and the shirt and hat he wore in his picture were admitted to the Smithsonian Institution. In addition, Amos sparked off a gourmet cookie craze that spread from the West Coast to supermarkets across the nation, and soon firms like Otis Spunkmeyer, Mrs. Fields, and others got into the market as well.

In November of 1983, Amos published his autobiography, *The Famous Amos Story: The Face that Launched a Thousand Chips,* which related the tale of his rise. In 1986, he received one of President Ronald Reagan's Awards for Entrepreneurial Excellence. By that time, however, Amos's fortunes were flagging. In 1985, on a trip to Salt Lake City, he discovered his home in Hawaii was being auctioned off because he was 15 months late on his mortgage, though he later managed to reclaim his house. That year, his business had lost $300,000 on sales of $10 million as competitors gained on him. Admitting to Gail Buchalter in *Forbes* that he was "not a businessman," Amos sold a majority of the stock in 1985 to the Bass Brothers of Texas, an investment group. A former California senator, John Tunney, eventually bought out the Bass Brothers, but the firm ended up going through the hands of several investors in rapid succession. Amos, meanwhile, had retained a slot as vice–chairman, but his responsibilities were whittled away until he was basically a figurehead. In addition, he lost all equity in the firm.

In 1989, even though he was still drawing a healthy salary as a spokesperson, Amos left the Famous Amos company altogether and signed a two–year agreement not to compete with the brand he founded. He made money giving motivational speeches and filtered off of his retirement funds when times were lean. Once the two years had expired, he was back in business in 1992 with Wally Amos Presents Chip & Cookie, using his original recipe. The new Famous Amos owners, the Shansby Group, in the meantime, had changed his recipe and downscaled the product to sell in vending machines, grocery stores, and warehouse food clubs. Amos also plugged merchandise such as dolls, books, cookie jars, and T–shirts for his new brand.

Before long, the owners of the Famous Amos brand name sued Amos over trademark infringement. Although he countersued, when they settled, he was not allowed to use his own name or likeness on the packaging of any food products, but he could use them in promotions. However, Amos turned around and opened the Uncle Noname (pronounced "no–NAHM–ay") Cookie Company and installed a professional management team. He parlayed his misfortunes into a marketing ploy: Each Uncle Noname cookie bag included a tale about making lemonade out of lemons, as well as a recipe for lemonade. The brand was designed this time to compete in vending machines and at grocery stores and food clubs, rather than with the high–end cookie business, which had become overloaded.

Amos continued to be inspired by his spiritual side and his contributions to charity, pledging that one percent of all sales from Uncle Noname would benefit Cities in Schools, a program to prevent dropouts. In addition, Amos kept up his motivational talks and once told an audience, according to Linda Eardley of the St. Louis Post–Dispatch, "Cookies are more than flour, sugar, eggs, and vanilla. There is a secret ingredient—the person making the cookies. The attitude, values, personality, morals, spirit, energy of the person. Who you are is transferred to what you are doing."

In 1994, Amos cowrote another autobiography, titled Man with No Name: Turn Lemons into Lemonade, which included generous doses of inspirational passages. However, sales of his bulk bags were soon canceled by stores like Price Club/Costco. "It started like a ball of fire and then fizzled out," Amos

noted to Ron Trujillo in USA Today. By 1995, though, convenience chain 7–Eleven signed a distribution deal for two–ounce grab bags, so Uncle Noname began production of that size only. Despite this break and his unrelenting optimism, Amos eventually found himself mired in debt. "It was just an uphill battle, looking to establish a new cookie company without having the resources and still in the minds of everybody being Famous Amos," he explained to Dana Canedy in the New York Times.

Trading in his chips, Amos began selling fat–free and sugar–free muffins under the Uncle Noname brand by 1996 and, also that year, churned out a new book, Watermelon Magic: Seeds of Wisdom, Slices of Life. His upbeat attitude did not protect the company from filing for Chapter 11 bankruptcy protection in 1997, but he and president Lou Avignone kept the faith. Meanwhile, Keebler acquired Famous Amos in 1998, becoming the fifth owner since Amos originally let it go. The next year, 1999, they extended an offer, asking Amos to promote his former brand in exchange for an undisclosed salary and, in addition, letting him use his own name and likeness on his new products. After asking them to alter their recipe to improve the quality, he agreed.

Under the deal with Keebler, Amos shows up at airports, supermarkets, and trade shows to push Famous Amos cookies and has started calling his muffin brand name Uncle Wally's. Since he has no ownership in Famous Amos, he has indicated that Uncle Wally's muffins will remain his main priority, although he conceded to Canedy in the New York Times, "I will always be Famous Amos." Amos has three sons from his first two marriages and was married for the third time to Christine Harris on July 1, 1979. She was a flight attendant for TWA airlines and later helped design Famous Amos paraphernalia like key rings, T–shirts, jewelry, and posters. The couple has a daughter, Sarah Kapiolani, and still lives on the island of Oahu, Hawaii. Amos has often donated his time to work for various charities and has been a longtime national spokesperson for the Literacy Volunteers of America.

Selected writings

Amos, Wally and Leroy Robinson, The Famous Amos Story: The Face that Launched a Thousand Chips, Doubleday, 1983.

Amos, Wally and Camilla Denton, The Power in You: Ten Secret Ingredients for Inner Strength, Nightingale–Conant, 1988.

Amos, Wally and Camilla Denton, Man with No Name: Turn Lemons into Lemonade, Aslan, 1994.

Amos, Wally and Stu Glauberman, *Watermelon Magic: Seeds of Wisdom, Slices of Life*, Beyond Words, 1996.

Sources

Books

Business Leader Profiles for Students, Gale Research, 1999.

Contemporary Black Biography, volume 9, Gale Research, 1995.

Periodicals

Black Enterprise, January 1981, p. 34; January 1995, p. 22.
Ebony, September 1979, p. 52.
Forbes, March 10, 1986, p. 176.
Miami Times, July 28, 1994.
Newsday, December 29, 1997, p. C4.
Newsweek, November 14, 1983, p. 16.
New York Times, July 3, 1999, p. B1.
Parade, May 22, 1994, p. 4.
People, February 17, 1992, p. 101.
Record (Bergen, NJ), August 21, 1996, p. F3.
St. Louis Post–Dispatch, March 17, 1993, p. 3A; September 7, 1994, p. 1C; July 25, 1997, p. 1C.
USA Today, October 9, 1995.
Washington Afro–American, November 23, 1996.

Laurie Anderson

Photo by Gert Krautbauer

Performance artist

Born in 1947 in Glenn Ellyn (some sources say Wayne), IL; daughter of Arthur T. (a paint dealer) and Mary Louise (a homemaker; maiden name, Rowland) Anderson. *Education:* Barnard College, B.A. (magna cum laude) in art history, 1969; Columbia University, M.F.A. in sculpture, 1972.

Addresses: *Office*—530 Canal St., New York, NY 10013. *Agent*—Monterey Peninsula Artists, 509 Hartnell St., Monterey, CA 93940.

Career

Performance artist, musician, director, music composer, and writer. City College of New York, New York City, instructor in art history, 1973–75; artist–in–residence at ZBS Media, New York, 1974. Work represented in various exhibitions at galleries and museums, including Harold Rivkin Gallery, Holly Solomon Gallery, and Museum of Modern Art. Work also featured in traveling exhibitions, including "Women Conceptual Artists," 1974, and as one– woman installations, including *Story Show* and *Automotive,* both 1972; *O– Range* and *Duets on Ice,* both 1973; *Songs and Stories for the Insomniac,* 1975; *Refried Beans for Instants,* 1976; *For Instants, Part V,* 1977; *Handphone Table,* 1978; and *Americans on the Move,* 1979.

Has toured with multi-media performance pieces, including *United States, Parts I- IV,* 1983; *Mister Heartbreak,* 1984-85; *Home of the Brave,* 1986; *Natural History,* 1986; *Empty Places,* 1990; *Stories from the Nerve Bible,* 1995; *The Ugly One with the Jewels,* 1995;

Dal Vivo (*Life*), 1998; and *Moby Dick,* 1999. Recordings include *It's Not the Bullet that Kills You, It's the Hole,* 1977; *Airwaves,* 1977; *New Music for Electronic and Recorded Media,* 1978; *Big Ego,* 1979; *O Superman,* 1981; (contributor) *You're the Guy I Want to Share My Money With,* Giorno Poetry Systems, 1981; *Big Science,* Warner Bros., and *Let X=X,* both 1982; *Mister Heartbreak,* 1984; *United States Live,* 1985; *Home of the Brave,* Warner Bros., 1986; *Strange Angels,* Warner Bros., 1989; *Bright Red,* 1994; *The Speed of Darkness,* 1997; and *Songs and Stories from Moby Dick,* 2000.

Awards: Grants from National Endowment for the Arts, 1974, 1977, and 1979, and New York State Council on the Arts, 1974 and 1977; Villager Award, 1981; Guggenheim fellowship, 1983.

Sidelights

Nearly all accounts of Laurie Anderson sum her up as a performance artist, but for those who have experienced her work firsthand, it is clear that this quick tag line does not do her justice. Combining music, vocal manipulation, stunning visuals, observations about popular culture, and witty, incisive social commentary, she brings together a world of media in order to showcase her various talents in a seamless production. After becoming an art–world superstar in Europe, by the early 1980s, her star climbed in the United States as well, making her the first performance artist to become a popular mainstream name. After her song "O Superman" became a hit in England, she landed a recording contract with Warner Bros. in 1981 and began touring nationally and internationally.

During Anderson's rise, many other performance artists' work often ended up as fodder for widespread mockery by those who considered it devoid of anything other than shock value. Critics debated the meaning of someone inviting audience members to examine her cervix and call it art, as Annie Sprinkle did; they also wondered whether there was anything redeeming, for example, in Chris Burden's work *Shoot,* in which a friend actually fired a bullet into his arm from a distance of 15 feet. Anderson's efforts, on the other hand, were entertaining, featuring enjoyable compositions that fused violin and electronic beats, not to mention an early use of spoken "samples;" intriguing imagery using film, video and photography; and a cerebral quality that was not so highbrow as to be exclusive. In *Esquire,* John Rockwell summed up Anderson's work by stating that it "is a compendium of pop culture and homey observations of day–to–day life, freed from high-culture pretensions and any overt attempt to express the ineffable." He added, "What lifts her texts beyond pop pastiche is her abrupt, glancing intimations of the erotic, the political, and the cosmic. She presents a landscape of the ordinary made extraordinary through unexpected juxtaposition."

Anderson was born in 1947 in Glenn Ellyn, Illinois (some sources say in Wayne, Illinois), the second of eight children —four boys, four girls—of Arthur T. and Mary Louise (Rowland) Anderson. Her father was a well–off paint dealer and her mother a homemaker, and she grew up in the affluent suburbs west of Chicago. As a child, she studied violin and played with the Chicago Youth Symphony and in a chamber ensemble with other members of her family. "I was a goody–goody kid," she revealed to Jack Kroll in *Newsweek.* "I wanted to be a librarian until I began to realize that there was a dark side to librarians. They were like jailers, putting books out on parole."

At age 16, Anderson gave up the violin, because, as she told Kroll, "I was becoming a real technocrat, trying to play fast with lots of technique." After high school, she went off to New York City's Barnard College in 1966, where she earned a bachelor of arts degree in art history in 1969, graduating magna cum laude and Phi Beta Kappa. Around that

time, she began keeping company with conceptual artists, and displayed a distinct political streak in her work. Ann Jarmusch in *ARTNews* noted that one of her early pieces, *The Street Wall Journal: Hanoi, Haiphong Strike Back,* from about 1969, "bears a riveting caricature of Richard Nixon as a fanged eagle gleefully excreting bombs on a pile of skulls."

Subsequently, Anderson earned a master of fine arts in sculpture at Columbia University in 1972, and studied privately with renowned minimalist artist Sol Le Witt. Her works by the early 1970s had "moved quickly from agitprop art to whimsically inventive performance pieces," as Frank Rose observed in the *Nation.* In 1972 Anderson staged her first performance art pieces, *Automotive* and *Story Show.* The former featured her conducting a "symphony" of car, truck, and motorcycle horns in a bandshell in Rochester, Vermont; the latter was a multimedia installation featuring her own photographs. Renewing her earlier enthusiasm for music, her 1974 effort, *Duets on Ice,* featured Anderson wearing ice skates frozen in blocks of ice as she played violin in a duet with her own prerecorded violin performance. Throughout, she spoke of the parallels of ice skating and violin playing, especially the aspect of balance. The show ended when the ice melted.

In the meantime, while building up her reputation, Anderson supported herself as a freelance art critic and interviewer for publications such as *ARTnews* and *Artforum.* She also taught classes at New York's City College, where, drifting off in the darkened room while showing slides, "she began to forget what she was supposed to tell the students about the works and made up stories about them instead—a habit that continued until she quit, shortly before being fired," as Jennifer Allen reported in *New York.* She also taught poetry for a time at the notorious Riker's Island prison in New York City, telling Germano Celant in *Interview,* "I did a lot of projects like that. We were revolutionaries. We really thought we could change things through concentrated communal actions."

Beginning in 1974, Anderson began to attract grants from the National Endowment of the Arts, the New York State Council on the Arts, and others, which allowed her to devote all her attention to her art. On one of these grants, she became an artist–in–residence at an audio production company in upstate New York called ZBS Media. There, she became more intrigued with recording techniques, which led to the creation of one of her most well-known pieces, *Handphone Table (When You Were Here).* This is an interactive sculpture consisting of a pine table with alternating layers of rubber and lead insulation. Viewers place their elbows in two depressions on the table and their hands over their ears in order to hear hidden tape–recorded music carried through the wood and through their own arms.

Since the mid–1970s, Anderson's music has figured prominently in her performances. However, she increasingly added narrative to her works, realizing that words added a much– needed dimension. As Kurt Loder commented in *Rolling Stone*, Anderson "*talks* more eloquently that many singers *sing.* " Her words combined with her visuals made for an overall storytelling experience which often featured quirky tales of everyday modern life, elements of pop culture, and social satire. Much of her material was autobiographical. Some early examples of this kind include *Songs and Stories for the Insomniac*, 1975; and *Refried Beans for Instants*, 1976.

In addition, Anderson physically adapted her violin by replacing the bow's horsehair with an audio tape and putting a tape–playback head at the bridge so that she could play sections of tape with her instrument. She also has mounted a turntable onto the violin and put a needle in the bow so she could play records. By the late 1970s, she was also experimenting with manipulating her voice electronically, being able to make it sound older, younger, or even like a man or like a chorus of children.

Anderson eventually began to record some of her works. Selections were collected on two anthology albums in the 1970s, *Airwaves*, 1977, and *New Music for Electronic and Recorded Material*, 1977. Then in 1981, the single "O Superman" soared up the British pop charts and sold 800,000 copies, transforming her from an art world sensation to a pop icon. This featured Anderson's manipulated voice blending together common expressions in a way that becomes both funny and disturbing. She sold copies by mail order from her loft until she found she could not keep up with the orders. Soon, she landed an eight–record deal with Warner Bros., and in 1982 released *Big Science,* a melange of excerpts from her live performance piece, *United States I–IV,* which toured the following year. The bulk of the album was recorded in a 16–track studio in Anderson's loft in the Soho district of Manhattan.

Anderson's inspiration for *United States I–IV,* as she told Don Shewey in the *New York Times Magazine,* began when she was touring in Europe: "I've frequently found myself sitting across the dinner table from people who ask me, 'How can you live in a country like that?' I really am on the defensive a lot of the time, and I need to have some way to deal with that." She added, "The idea was to make a big portrait of the country, and I divided it up sort of arbitrarily into four parts, transportation, politics, money and love. If there's any throughline, it's some question about America as Utopia and trying to understand how people really feel about living here."

United States I–IV opened on February 3 and 4, 1983, at the Brooklyn Academy of Music (BAM), in a two–evening, six–hour extravaganza. An audience of more than 85,000 flocked to it, and she followed up this premiere with widespread tours in the United States and Europe. The work featured a cornucopia of symbols and text strung together with a word-play that highlighted her sharp wit and keen ear for the language, including, as in one instance, ironic snippets of phone conversations, messages from answering machines, and other disembodied voices such as over loudspeakers. As she told Michael Walsh in *Time,* "The genius of American English is inflection. I place phrases in different spots so they can resonate differently and leave lots of room for people to make connections." Despite the good turnout, some critics were not impressed with the effort, and as Kroll noted, "Some Laurie watchers think she's gotten too big, too Las Vegas." Many others raved, however, and Walsh concluded that *United States I–IV* "is the biggest, most ambitious and most successful example to date of the avant– garde hybrid known as performance art."

In 1984, the University of Pennsylvania's Institute of Contemporary Art organized a mid– career summary of Anderson's works that also traveled to Los Angeles, Houston, and Flushing, New York. That same year, Harper & Row released a book documenting her Brooklyn performance of the United States, and also that year, she also released her second album, *Mister Heartbreak*. It included the lead song "Sharkey's Day," an ethereal examination of American life that centers on a middle–aged store manager with a mediocre life and strange dreams; it featured the voice of late Beat poet William Burroughs.

Anderson premiered a new performance, *Empty Places,* in 1989, preparing for the piece by taking photographs of desolate New York City neighborhoods at night. Concerning the misery of homelessness rampant during the lavish, consumer–oriented 1980s, it opened, once again, to standing–room only crowds at BAM. The next year, her album *Strange Angels* came out, which included some typically arranged pop songs, despite her reputation as one of the reigning queens of the avant–garde. She followed up her next album, 1994's *Bright Red,* with the *Stories from the Nerve Bible* tour in 1995, and that same year put out the acclaimed CD–ROM, *Puppet Motel.* In 1997, she created an installation that transmitted an image of a longtime inmate at San Vittore Prison in Milan, Italy, to the Fondazione Prada gallery in order to exhibit a work about being confined.

In October of 1999, Anderson returned to BAM to mount *Songs and Stories from Moby Dick,* which "bills itself as the Herman Melville novel reinvented as a 'postmodern musical' and Anderson's most ambitious project since her 1983 epic, *United States,*" according to Peter G. Davis in *New York.* It was also her first large–scale multimedia event since the *Nerve Bible,* and marked the first time in her career that other performers were onstage with her. In addition, the show featured the Talking Stick, which Roselee Goldberg in the *New York Times* described as "a microphone filled with digital processing equipment capable of producing a full orchestra of sounds." More philosophical than many of her other works, which tended to be topically oriented, *Songs and Stories from Moby Dick* examines greater themes such as authority, insanity, and the search for life's meaning. Debra Jo Immergut in the *Wall Street Journal* applauded the effort, commenting, "Anderson's sense of humor is as nimble as her intellect is fierce."

A small–built woman with short, spiky hair, Anderson possesses a "waifish folksiness," as John Leland described in *Vogue,* and is romantically linked with rocker Lou Reed. She lives in what Bill Van Parys in *Rolling Stone* dubbed "a corporate–esque TriBeCa duplex loft." In addition to composing music for her own projects, she has contributed music to films by directors Jonathan Demme and Wim Wenders, and to dance pieces by Trisha Brown, Melissa Fenley, Bill T. Jones, and others. At London's Royal Festival Hall in 1997, she curated the two– week Meltdown festival. In 1999, Anderson signed a contract with Nonesuch Records, which also carries the works of Philip Glass, Kronos Quartet, Gipsy Kings, Bill Frisell, and other artists. Despite the high–tech accompaniment that Anderson uses in her works,

she once noted in a lecture, according to Ann Jarmusch in the *Nation,* "I think of the work that I do as the most ancient in the world: storytelling."

Sources

Books

Contemporary Musicians, volume one, Gale Research, 1989.
Contemporary Theatre, Film and Television, volume 18, Gale Research, 1998.

Periodicals

ARTNews, May 1984, p. 128.
Down Beat, October 1984, p. 22.
Entertainment Weekly, February 24, 1995, p. 125.
Esquire, December 1982, p. 136.
Interview, March 1997, p. 144;August 1998, p. 52.
Nation, September 8, 1984, p. 185.
New Statesman, June 20, 1997, p. 41.
Newsweek, February 21, 1983, p. 77.
New York, February 14, 1983, p. 18; September 13, 1999, p. 90.
New York Times, October 3, 1999, sec. 2, p. 29; October 7, 1999, p. E1.
New York Times Magazine, February 6, 1983, p. 27.
People, March 21, 1983, p. 107; May 7, 1990, p. 137.
Rolling Stone, July 8, 1982, p. 22; April 20, 1995, p. 33.
Time, February 21, 1983, p. 68.
Vogue, January 1990, p. 90.
Wall Street Journal, October 13, 1999, p. A28.

Online

"Laurie Anderson," *Contemporary Authors Online,* Gale Group web site, http://www.galenet.com (December 1, 1999).
Laurie Anderson official web site, http://www.laurieanderson.com (January 12, 2000).

Natalie Angier

Journalist and author

Born February 16, 1958, in New York City; daughter of Keith (a machinist) and Adele Bernice (a meatpacking worker, indexer, and schoolteacher; maiden name, Rosenthal) Angier; married Richard Steven Weiss, 1990; children: Katherine Ida. *Education:* Attended the University of Michigan; Barnard College, B.A., 1978.

Addresses: *Home*—Takoma Park, MD. *Office*—c/o *New York Times,*—229 W. 43rd St., New York, NY 10036.

Career

Texas Instruments, technical writer, c. 1979; *Discover* magazine, New York City, researcher, then staff writer, 1980–83; *Savvy* magazine, editor, 1983–84; *Time* magazine, New York City, staff writer, 1984–86; New York University, New York City, journalism teacher, 1987–89; *New York Times,* Washington, D.C. office, began as reporter, became science correspondent, 1990 .

Awards: Marine Biology Labs, Lewis Thomas award for writing about the life sciences, 1990, for *Natural Obsessions: The Search for the Oncogene;* Pulitzer Prize for reporting, 1991; General Motors International Award, 1991; American Association for the Advancement of Science award for excellence in journalism, 1992; Barnard College distinguished alumna award, 1993.

Photograph by Jerry Bauer

Sidelights

Natalie Angier, a science writer for the *New York Times,* is a standout in the journalism field for imparting detailed information in specific language while managing to construct readable prose that expresses her fascination with a variety of topics. As Ann Darby wrote in *Publishers Weekly,* "Whereas it's enough for many science writers just to get their facts straight, Angier has pushed the bounds of science writing. Tackling unusual, sometimes even repugnant topics in vivid, playful and acrobatic prose, she has developed a style and an approach to stories that are distinctly hers." Also, May Berenbaum commented in *BioScience,* "Angier is renowned for the breadth of her interests, the accuracy of her reporting, and the clarity of her prose." In addition to working at the newspaper, Angier is a talented author whose books on scientific subjects are also penned in her trademark entertaining manner. In 1999, she attracted a great deal of attention for *Woman: An Intimate Geography,* which combined an assortment of disciplines including medicine, psychology, history, and literature to examine the female body from a variety of angles, all from a feminist perspective.

Angier was born on February 16, 1958, in the Bronx borough of New York City, the third of four siblings. Her father, Keith, worked as a machinist, and her mother, Adele Bernice (Rosenthal) Angier, worked in a meatpacking plant and as an indexer in Time Warner's library before becoming a schoolteacher. They met in the Communist Youth Party and were both anti–establishment idealists, but they had many differences, too. They divorced when Angier was 12. In *Ms.* magazine, she recalled that her father was "a sexist pig," but she also noted that he had a feminine side to him that made him emotional, and her mother had a rational side to her that would normally be considered masculine. "So I think that I saw in both of them a certain degree of androgyny is such a boring word but there was this kind of maleness and femaleness that would express itself in complex and always changing ways." In addition, she noted, the children in her family did not adhere to strict prescriptions of gender activities. Girls did not always play with dolls, and they often played sports.

After the divorce, Angier and her younger brother moved with their mother to rural New Buffalo, Michigan. By age 13, she was already a feminist who helped her mother organize consciousness–raising groups. After skipping two grades, she entered the University of Michigan at age 16, then transferred to Barnard College. Long before cross–disciplinary studies were common, Angier enrolled in a combination of courses in literature, physics, and astronomy, hoping to merge her two passions science and creative writing.

While in college, Angier became exposed to the British magazine the *New Scientist,* which approached the field with a sense of humor and an openness that she had not seen in American publications. Subsequently, she dreamed of starting up a magazine like it. Angier got her bachelor of arts degree from Barnard in 1978, and then spent a couple years at the City University of New York doing graduate work in medieval literature. She left in 1979 and landed a job as a technical writer for Texas Instruments. However, the area of the company in which she worked was soon shut down, just about the time that *Time* magazine began to publish a new science magazine.

Discover, which published its first issue in 1980, was tailor–made for Angier and her interests. She found a job there as a researcher, but was soon promoted to staff writer. There, she began to cover biology, writing in particular about animal behavior and evolutionary biology. She left in 1983 to work for the women's magazine *Savvy,* then moved to *Time*

magazine as a science writer in 1984. She left in 1986 and later taught journalism at New York University in New York City from 1987 to 1989.

In the meantime, Angier had been mulling over ideas for a book. In 1984 while on vacation in Italy, she met a scientist who told her about oncogenes. These genes regulate cell development when healthy, but when they are defective, they cause cancer. Angier proposed a book on the topic that would delve into the day–to–day world of scientific investigation, with all its false leads and dead–end roads, instead of the usual offering on some new breakthrough. She ended up shadowing scientists in the research laboratory of Robert Weinberg at the Whitehead Institute, a biomedical institute affiliated with the Massachusetts Institute of Technology (MIT). She also ended up also covering Weinberg's rival, Michael Wigler, based at the Cold Springs Harbor Laboratory on Long Island, New York.

In 1988, Angier published *Natural Obsessions: The Search for the Oncogene.* The book was applauded for not only spelling out the scientific process, but also for its keen profiles of the quirky scientists and for its ability to impart the excitement involved in scientific research. As Eric Lax wrote in the *New York Times Book Review,* "One does not have to be a molecular biologist or follow every step to enjoy the fun and appreciate the beauty, or to share in the frustration of a promising hypothesis that hits a dead end after months of work and hope." In the end, though, Angier was in fact present for a breakthrough when the scientists isolated the gene for a type of cancer of the eye called retinoblastoma.

After this, Angier joined the *New York Times* in 1990 when its longtime science writer, Harold Schmeck, retired. Just a year later, she won a Pulitzer Prize for science writing, and in 1992 she received a Science Journalism Award from the American Association for the Advancement of Science. After a few years, she revised a selection of her *New York Times* articles and published them as *The Beauty of the Beastly: New Views on the Nature of Life,* 1995. In this work, Angier explores some of the paradoxes of the natural world, such as how seemingly repulsive creatures, like dung beetles, can harbor a kind of beauty, and how appealing animals, like dolphins and birds, often exhibit behavior that would repel humans if we understood it. For example, male dolphins have a seedy habit of ganging up on a lone female for sexual domination.

Commenting on *The Beauty of the Beastly,* Derek Bickerton in the *New York Times* wrote, "For those who revel in bizarre oddities of nature, Ms. Angier's book is a gold mine." He also praises her "gift for lively metaphor and insistence on rendering abstract ideas and complex processes in familiar, concrete terms." Berenbaum in *BioSicence*, meanwhile, pointed out, "Angier's writing is enormously entertaining; she makes no apologies for anthropomorphism and uses analogies, stories, figures of speech, and wonderful world play to explain a breathtaking range of phenomena . For example, in describing the structure of a cell, Angier marvels how efficiently three–foot–long strands of DNA are packed into a space only a hundred–thousandth of an inch across 'too tiny to qualify even as a Manhattan closet.'"

In 1999, Angier created a flurry of media interest with her next book, *Woman: An Intimate Geography.* In this, she uses biology as a springboard to examine the female body and then expands her scope to include a wide–ranging investigation about the essence of being a woman. For example, she includes a great deal of "did–you–knows," such as the fact that the clitoris has twice as many nerve endings as the penis. The book received generally positive reviews, many of which praised Angier's wit along with her approach of challenging many of the beliefs about women and their bodies. Specifically, Angier targets evolutionary psychology, a branch of study that tries to explain human behavior by using Darwinian principles. The author believes this has led to a spate of sexual myths. For example, she argues against the commonly held ideas that men are more promiscuous for biological reasons, and she tries to offer practical, rather than biological, explanations for why men value youth and beauty and women prefer a partner with money and status. She also personalizes many of the topics; for example, she confides that she and her husband had trouble with conception, and notes that she finally got pregnant only after they relaxed.

In addition to questioning what has been reported previously about women and their bodies, Angier in *Woman: An Intimate Geography* also delves into areas that have been discussed rarely, if at all. Her work not only addresses topics like why the vagina smells the way it does, but also why women can be fiercely aggressive toward each other. She finds no subject taboo, and sometimes interjects an enthusiasm for sexuality that provided titillating passages. In discussing the work, JoAnn C. Gutin remarked in *Newsday,* "What makes 'Woman' such fun to read is Angier's attitude: She reveals herself here as the Sandra Bernhard of science journalism. Her pulsating prose could make Madonna blush."

Some critics, however, quarreled with Angier's reasoning in some areas, and some prominent researchers, including Steven Pinker, claimed that Angier's political beliefs too heavily influenced her science in the work. And though some griped about the over–the–top language in some of her more colorful passages, many reviewers still applauded the effort. For instance, Abraham Verghese in the *New York Times Book Review* commented, "Angier's prose can sometimes get too exuberant, but at least it never sounds textbookish and it always keeps the reader engaged." *Woman* was a best–seller and named to several best– books–of–the–year lists, in addition to receiving a nomination for a 1999 National Book Award.

Angier married Richard Steven Weiss, a science reporter for the *Washington Post,* in 1990. They have a daughter, Katherine Ida Weiss Angier, and live in Takoma Park, Maryland, a suburb of Washington, D.C.

Sources

BioScience, April 1996, p. 297.
Discover, May 1999, p. 96.
Journal of the American Medical Association, December 1, 1999, p. 2083.
Library Journal, February 1, 1999, p. 115.
Ms., February/March 2000, p. 48.
National Review, June 14, 1999, p. 52.
Natural History, July 1999, p. 58.
Newsday, April 18, 1999, p. B9.
Newsweek, April 12, 1999, p. 69.
New York Times, June 14, 1995, p. C19.
New York Times Book Review, July 10, 1988, p. 7; May 23, 1999, p. 10.
Publishers Weekly, March 15, 1999, p. 38; March 22, 1999, p. 64.

Jennifer Aniston

AP/Wide World Photos

Actor

Born February 11, 1969, in Sherman Oaks, CA; daughter of John (an actor) and Nancy (a model–actor and photographer) Aniston.

Addresses: *Home*—Los Angeles, CA. *Agent*—Creative Artists Agency, 9830 Wilshire Blvd., Beverly Hills, CA 90212.

Career

Actor. Stage appearances include off–Broadway plays *For Dear Life,* 1988–89, and *Dancing on Checker's Grave.* Television appearances include episodes of *Herman's Head,* 1992;*Quantum Leap,* 1992; and *Burke's Law,* 1994; series *Ferris Bueller,* 1990; *Molloy,* 1990; *The Edge,* 1992; *Muddling Through,* 1994; and *Friends,* 1994 ; and movie *Camp Cucamonga,* 1990. Film appearances include *Leprechaun,* 1993; *She's the One,* 1996; *Picture Perfect,* 1997; *'Til There Was You,* 1997; *Waiting for Woody,* 1998; *The Object of My Affection,* 1998; *Dream for an Insomniac,* 1998; *Office Space,* 1999; and *The Iron Giant* (voice), 1999.

Sidelights

Jennifer Aniston became a household name in the mid–1990s with the success of the NBC sitcom *Friends,* about a tight–knit group of twentysomething pals living in Manhattan. As Rachel Green, the suburban princess turned ditzy coffeehouse waitress, Aniston won fans for her ability to show the human side of a slightly snotty yet spunky underachiever. In addition, she spawned imitators in salons across the globe thanks to her ultra–popular shag hairstyle. Though Rachel eventually grew out her hair and graduated from waiting tables to working at Ralph Lauren headquarters, she never lost her scatterbrained charm or her hard abs and attractive features that drew many male viewers. The show continued to post strong ratings several seasons into its run, and some wondered what would happen once the *Friends* contract expired in 2000, especially since the entire cast had also been pursuing feature films. Aniston told Nancy Collins *in Rolling Stone,* "We're all with *Friends* until *Friends* dies. If one of us goes, we all go." It is no secret that Aniston's future aspirations include making more movies, although she has expressed a desire to break away from lighter fare. "It's not that I don't enjoy romantic comedies," she commented to Collins. "But give me a shot at something different."

Aniston was born on February 11, 1969, in Sherman Oaks, California. However, she grew up in an apartment in Manhattan with her actor father, John Aniston, her actor–model mother, Nancy Aniston (now a photographer), and her older half–brother, Johnny Melick, from her mother's first marriage. Her father got his start on the daytime drama *The Days of Our Lives* in 1969, and since 1985, has played the villainous Victor Kiriakis almost continuously except for a period of time in 1998. He was born in Greece, and his family surname was originally Anastassakis. His close pal, Telly Savalas, the late actor who played Kojak on television, was Aniston's godfather.

When Aniston was about nine or ten, her father left her mother for another woman (whom he eventually married), and the divorce was hard on her. She told Rich Cohen in *Rolling Stone,* "I felt so totally responsible. I know it sounds cliché, but I really felt it was because I wasn't a good enough kid." To Mal Vincent of the *Knight–Ridder Tribune News Service,* she recalled, "I was always a little troublemaker. Nothing really criminal, but I'd always get reported for clowning or talking. I'd do things just to get both parents together in the principal's office."

At a young age, after seeing a Broadway production of *Children of a Lesser God,* Aniston decided to become an actor. "My father did not want me to be in this business," she noted to Cohen. "It's so full of rejection." Nevertheless, she was accepted to New York's High School of Performing Arts (better known as the school in the film *Fame*). After graduating in 1987, she lived with her mother for about a year, going to auditions and working at Jackson Hole, an eatery on the Upper West Side of Manhattan. Her father wanted her to enroll in college, but Aniston was determined to begin her acting career. She landed some off–Broadway parts, in *For Dear Life* in 1988–89 and *Dancing on Checker's Grave.*

At age 20, Aniston moved to Los Angeles to try to break into the business there. She worked in telemarketing while trying to land parts, and became part of a close–knit community of actors and writers in Laurel Canyon, where "everybody watched out for everybody," as she related to Cohen. She recalled fondly the women's support group that formed out of that circle, and during that time she met some of the people who would remain her long–time friends. But her resume was not expanding, though her waistline was. Her agent advised her to shed some pounds. She remarked to Susan Korones Gifford in *Redbook,* "I didn't even know I was overweight until someone told me. I hate it that your self–worth is metered by how much you weigh." After going on the Nutri/System plan and giving up her favorite dish, mayonnaise–on– white–bread sandwiches, she lost weight and began to win roles.

In 1990, Aniston showed up on the short–lived series *Ferris Bueller,* playing Jeannie Bueller, and on *Molloy,* playing Courtney Walker. Later, she appeared on *The Edge,* 1992, and *Muddling Through,* 1994, in addition to landing guest spots on shows like *Herman's Head, Quantum Leap,* and *Burke's Law.*

But she was terrified of going on movie auditions, as she mentioned to Watson, because her agent insisted that she would become a television celebrity. "I hated him for that," Aniston stated to Watson, "because I thought, You have no faith in me." She did, however, manage a starring part in 1993's hokey horror flick *The Leprechaun.*

As predicted, Aniston's big break came when she tried out for a part on a pilot called *Friends Like These.* Initially asked to read for the part of Monica, she declined, insisting that she was "so much more Rachel," as she mentioned to Watson, adding, "more neurotic than Monica, a bit offbeat." The series began airing in 1994 as *Friends,* and immediately became one of the hottest new shows, thanks to the quirky and likable characters and their on– screen chemistry. The sitcom also stars Courtney Cox, Lisa Kudrow, Matt LeBlanc, Matthew Perry, and David Schwimmer.

Before long, Aniston emerged as the "sexiest" friend, appearing on camera in tight–fitting, midriff–baring clothes and showing up on dozens of magazine covers even in the buff on one issue of *Rolling Stone.* She also made more waves than her costars for her signature hairdo, a layered and fluffy shoulder–length style with ends curled toward the face. It became the envy of women nationwide, who poured into salons asking their stylists for the "Rachel" look. It was the biggest hair fad since Farrah Fawcett's feathered locks on the 1970s cheesecake cop show *Charlie's Angels.* And despite her plea to be recognized for her talent and not her hair, she snagged a lucrative contract in Western Europe and Russia to model for L'Oreal shampoo.

Though Aniston's tresses attracted much attention, all of the *Friends* actors were extremely popular, and the cast remained close even off–screen. Their camaraderie led them to stick together and all negotiate a higher salary, given the show's phenomenal success. In 1996, they all asked for a raise and were harshly criticized for their request. As Aniston noted in *Cosmopolitan,* "We never threatened to strike. The six of us wanted to be paid the same amount because we all work the same amount as each other." But, she added, "It was twisted into 'Look at these brats demanding all this money.'" The final deal was that they received an increase from $35,000 to $75,000 an episode, increasing incrementally each season to $120,000 by their sixth year. As the program continued, the ratings remained high thanks to an on–again, off–again romance between Rachel and the character of Ross, a cerebral, soft–hearted anthropologist.

Meanwhile, the other *Friends* cast members were parlaying their small–screen celebrity into film roles, with varying degrees of success. Aniston posted one of the best critical receptions of any of them in *She's the One*, 1996. She started small, with a minor role as a neglected wife. It was the first big–budget work by director Ed Burns, who gained acclaim for *The Brothers McMullen*. Following that, she took the bigger step of a starring role in 1997's *Picture Perfect*, about a junior advertising executive who concocts a fictional fiancé when she realizes that her single status has a negative impact on her chances of getting ahead at work. This serves to draw the attention of a "bad boy" coworker, played by Kevin Bacon. Also that year she took a supporting role in the romantic comedy *'Til There Was You*. As with her character of Rachel, many accounts pointed out that one of Aniston's main strengths as an actor lie in her ability to come across as perky and just insecure enough to make her human without being irritating.

The next year, Aniston appeared in two more features. *The Object of My Affection* required her to flex her dramatic muscles a bit more than earlier projects, portraying an unwed pregnant woman who falls in love with her gay best friend. For the part, she wore a pad that made her look and feel pregnant. Also in 1998, she costarred with Ione Skye in *Dream for an Insomniac*, about a coffee house employee (Skye) who moves to Los Angeles with a friend (Aniston) in hopes that the man she is after will follow her. And in 1999, she appeared in the corporate–rebellion comedy *Office Space*, written and directed by Mike Judge of *Beavis and Butthead* fame. Also that year, she provided a voice–over for animation in *The Iron Giant*.

Being one of the most popular stars out there, Aniston, like many celebrities, has had to endure constant probing into her personal life. When she was starting out, she dated actor Charlie Schlatter, her costar on the sitcom *Ferris Bueller*. After that, she briefly saw Counting Crows lead singer Adam Duritz, but she reported that too much publicity too soon ended up extinguishing any hopes for that. Then, her high–profile two–and–a–half year relationship with actor Tate Donovan ended in March of 1998.

Subsequently, Aniston was seen out and about with actor Brad Pitt, who was coming off of a breakup with actor Gwyneth Paltrow. Though they insisted they were just friends for a long stretch, the media continued to hound them. They finally went public with their relationship by early 1999, making them a much–sought after photo opportunity, since both have been considered two of the most beautiful people in Hollywood. In addition, rumors immediately surfaced that the two were already married,

but they were apparently false, even though Aniston seemed to sport a flashy engagement ring by late that year. She continued to try to elude the press on the topic, telling Collins in *Rolling Stone*, "My responsibility to the public is my work not what goes on in my private life. To talk about a relationship trivializes something that's nobody's business."

In other personal news about Aniston, she became estranged from her mother in 1996 after the latter spoke about her daughter to a tabloid television show. They spoke once during the next few years but parted ways again after her mother penned a tell–all book in 1999 titled *From Mother and Daughter to Friends: A Memoir*. It included tales of Aniston's childhood antics and the family's poverty–stricken days when her father was a struggling actor. Nancy Aniston told Charles Laurence of the *Daily Telegraph* that writing the book was "therapy."

At five feet, five inches tall, Aniston has kept her weight down to a willowy 112 pounds, though she told Gifford in *Redbook* that she does not monitor her diet as closely as she used to when she was trying to slim down. "I watch what I eat, but I don't not eat a cheeseburger, because life is no fun living on salads and fruit." She keeps fit with yoga and a personal trainer. She owns a three–bedroom home in the Hollywood Hills and loves to shop for antiques, and is known to be generous, often splurging on friends and family. She once bought her brother a Bronco as a gift, and another time picked up the whole tab for a ski trip to Aspen with a dozen pals.

Sources

Books

Contemporary Theatre, Film and Television, volume 15, Gale Research, 1996.

Periodicals

Cosmopolitan, August 1997, p. 172.
Daily Telegraph, January 11, 2000. *Entertainment Weekly*, December 15, 1995, p. 29; August 16, 1996, p. 15; June 6, 1997, p. 11.
Knight–Ridder/Tribune News Service, August 4, 1997.
Mademoiselle, April 1998, p. 174.
People, December 25, 1995, p. 92; November 18, 1996, p. 82; August 11, 1997, p. 98; November 16, 1998, p. 10; March 8, 1999, p. 120; May 10, 1999, p. 192; October 25, 1999, p. 10; December 6, 1999, p. 72.

Redbook, October 1998, p. 132; August 1999, p. 80.
Rolling Stone, March 7, 1996, p. 34; March 4, 1999, p. 54.
Seventeen, April 1998, p. 122.
TV Guide, February 10, 1996, p. 48; July 26, 1997, p. 16.
US, February 1996, p. 36.

Online

"Jennifer Aniston," Internet Movie Database web site, http://us.imdb.com (April 21, 2000).
"Jennifer Aniston," Mr. Showbiz web site, http://mrshowbiz.go.com (April 21, 2000).

Marc Anthony

Singer, songwriter, and actor

Born Marco Antonio Muniz, September 16, 1969, in New York, NY; son of Felipe (a lunchroom worker and guitarist) and Guillermina (a homemaker) Muniz; children: (with Debbie Rosado) Arianna.

Addresses: *Office*—Marc Anthony Productions, 1385 York Ave., Ste. 6F, New York, NY 10021.

Career

Wrote songs and sang backup for Sa–Fire, The Latin Rascals, and Menudo; released debut album, *When the Night Is Over,* Atlantic Records, 1991. Actor; stage appearances include *Capeman,* New York City, 1998; film appearances include *Natural Causes,* 1994; *Hackers,* 1995; *Big Night,* 1996; *The Substitute,* 1996; and *Bringing Out the Dead,* 1999.

Awards: *Billboard* award for best new artist, 1994; Grammy Award for best tropical Latin performance, 1998, for *Contra la Corriente;* Tu Musica Award for best tropical album of the year for *Todo a su Tiempo;* Lo Nuestra Award, Ace Award, Diplo Award (Puerto Rico).

Sidelights

Though he began riding a wave of popularity among Latin recording artists in the United States in the late 1990s, Marc Anthony has been a mainstay in the salsa genre for years. By blending in pop and spicing up his songs with a healthy dose of romance, he had been a star in Spanish–speaking areas long before the release of his English–language salsa album, *Marc Anthony,* hit the shelves in 1999. His slightly smoky tenor is lush and expressive, and he has been known to start crying on stage during love songs. Women swoon and throw undergarments on stage during his concerts, and his balladeering style has earned him comparisons to Frank Sinatra. In 1998, before Ricky Martin had burst on the scene, Anthony took home the Grammy Award for best tropical Latin performance, for his 1997 album *Contra la Corriente.* The singer has started drawing raves for his acting talents as well, most notably with a turn as a deranged transient man in 1999's *Bringing Out the Dead.*

Anthony was born Marco Antonio Muniz on September 16, 1969, in New York City. He was raised in Spanish Harlem, the youngest of five boys and three girls. His father, Felipe, worked in a hospital lunchroom, and Guillermina ("Jenny"), was a homemaker. They are now divorced. Anthony was exposed to jibaro music and salsa beginning at a tender age. His father had moved from Puerto Rico in the 1950s and played guitar; he also enjoyed listening to Ruben Blades, Hector Lavoe, and Willie Colon. Anthony would climb up on the kitchen table and sing along during his dad's jam sessions. By the time he was three, he was able to draw tears from female family members with his soulful renditions.

When Anthony was six or seven, he sang "El Zolsar" at a social club where his father was playing, and a man gave his mother a dollar, telling her that her child would make it big someday. It was the first money Anthony ever earned for his talent. However, like many children, Anthony considered his parents' music and the Latin image uncool. "I couldn't relate to the suits, the chains and the pinky rings, so it didn't interest me," he remarked to Cristina Veran in *Newsday*. Instead, he started getting into rock and roll, rap, and dance music. "I was raised in New York during the Seventies and Eighties," he mentioned to Clark Collis in the *Daily Telegraph*. "So I was exposed to everything. Jimi Hendrix. Motown. Disco. Salsa. You name it." He has also claimed the light–as–their–name pop group Air Supply as an influence.

At age 12, Anthony and his sister began singing background vocals for commercials, including one for Bumble Bee tuna. At 15, he was a water boy for one of his idols, Ruben Blades. "I used to pray for him to be thirsty, just to be onstage," Anthony reminisced to Collis in the *Daily Telegraph*. By high school, Anthony was writing music, which caught the attention of the dance–pop singer Sa–Fire. He ended up penning two songs, "You Said You Love Me" and "I Better Be the Only One," for her album, as well as singing backup. Another single he wrote, "Boy I've Been Told," became a Top 40 hit. He went on to sing background for The Latin Rascals, who worked with Little Louis Vega. In the meantime, Anthony was also writing songs in both English and Spanish for Menudo, as well as serving as a backup singer and vocal coach for them.

In the early 1990s, Vega became a producer for Atlantic Records and asked Anthony to sing for him. He recorded a dance album in English, *When the Night Is Over*, and had a number one *Billboard* dance hit with "Ride on the Rhythm," but failed to make waves beyond that. Though he was performing house music at clubs in New York City, he found it encouraging if audiences numbered even in the triple digits. Then he and Vega opened for Tito Puente at Madison Square Garden in New York City. Anthony's manager subsequently prodded him to begin recording salsa music, but he resisted. Not long after that, though, he was listening to the radio and heard the Juan Gabriel ballad, "Hasta Que Te Conoci" (which means "Until I Met You" in English). Inspired, he came up with an upbeat salsa version of the tune, and it became his ticket to stardom.

In 1993, Anthony released his first salsa album, *Otra Nota*, on Soho Latino/RMM Records. Soon, his manager sent him to perform at Radio y Musica, a Latin–music convention in Los Angeles. Most of the attendees were disk jockeys. Highly intimidated and wearing borrowed clothes because his financial situation was tight, he sang a song backed only by instrumentals from a DAT player. He recalled to Alec Wilkinson in the *New Yorker*, "I'm trembling up a storm. I walk up to the mike and think, 'Make believe you're in your living room singing to your mom.'" Afterward, he darted off the stage so fast that until his manager grabbed him, he did not notice he was getting a standing ovation. He told Wilkinson that he then heard disk jockeys making calls, saying, "Find this kid's CD. I threw it out this morning it's in the trash. Find it and play it."

Later that same day, Anthony was booked on a Spanish–language television program called *Carnaval Internacional*, which is broadcast internationally. "That changed my life forever," he stated to Wilkinson, adding, "It seemed like years before I was ever in New York again." He began to tour constantly, playing Puerto Rico, Argentina, Colombia, Ecuador, even Tokyo. Some traditionalists disliked his romantic take on salsa and dismissed it an inauthentic, but many critics delivered accolades. He also won support from fellow musicians like Blades and Placido Domingo, who began to call and ask about doing projects together.

In 1995, Anthony followed up with *Todo a Su Tiempo* (which means "All in Due Time" in English). Touring to promote the work, he spent 50 weeks on the road. Though his energy level on stage is cranked up as he struts through his dance moves, unlike salsa stars of old, Anthony projects a more down–to–earth appearance, favoring simple apparel in lieu of the "hot Latin lover" image with sleek suits and slick hair. "It is an appeal that is real, accessible and trustworthy," observed Veran in *Newsday*. Anthony in 1996 was nominated for a Grammy Award in 1996 for *Todo a Su Tiempo*, sharing the category with three of his idols Blades, Colon, and Celia Cruz.

As his music career was reaching new heights, Anthony was gearing up an acting career as well. He made his debut in 1995's *Hackers*, playing a Secret Service agent in a thriller about cybersleuths trying to foil an evil genius planning to unleash a crippling computer virus. The next year, he was cast as a waiter in *Big Night*, starring Minnie Driver, Isabella Rossellini, and Stanley Tucci, about a family trying to save their Italian restaurant. He also had a minor role as a high school gang member in *The Substitute* that same year.

Anthony's next album, *Contra la Corriente* ("Against the Current") came out in fall of 1997. But he did not have the opportunity to embark on a promotional tour, because he had been cast in Paul Simon's *Capeman,* which opened on Broadway in early 1998. This turned out to be a boon, though, when Anthony's new manager, Bigram Zayas–also his half–brother and best friend–suggested he play an "Off to Broadway" megaconcert at Madison Square Garden. Though no salsa solo act had ever headlined there, Anthony sold out two concerts at the venue. He then took the stage in *Capeman,* a musical about a murder case. In it, he played teenager Salvador Algron, a Puerto Rican who killed two other teens in a New York park in 1959 after a gang misunderstanding. Blades, incidentally, portrayed the killer as an older man. Although *Capeman* was praised for its song sequences and Anthony was applauded for his vocal talents, the play closed after two months.

By this time, Anthony was so famous that an architect refused payment for his work in building a home in Puerto Rico for the singer, claiming that working for him was payment enough, as Wilkinson reported in the *New Yorker.* In fact, he is something of a saint in Puerto Rico for committing to build 100 homes for families displaced by Hurricane Georges. In addition, he sold out a 60,000–seat stadium in Colombia, and is popular throughout Europe, Japan, and Central America as well. He became so well–known in Spanish–speaking areas that he needs escorts to accompany him, and he became the only salsa singer with a gold album in America.

However, Anthony did not get major crossover exposure until fellow Latin crooner Ricky Martin hit the scene and reached number one on the pop charts with his first all–English release. In addition, Jennifer Lopez with whom he recorded the radio hit "No Me Ames" was beginning to attract attention as well. Around that time, amid disputes with music mogul Ralph Mercado with whom he had signed a contract in 1992 Anthony managed to cut his own English album as well, the first since his 1991 dance effort. He signed a deal with Columbia Records estimated to be worth more than $30 million, and in 1999 released *Marc Anthony.* Featuring Latin–tinged pop tunes, it spawned the top ten hit "I Need to Know." But he bristled at the term "crossover," explaining to Chris Willman in *Entertainment Weekly,* "I started out singing in English, so what am I crossing over to? That makes it sound like I'm trying my hand at someone else's music. But I'm just as American as I am Puerto Rican. This is my music as much as anybody else's."

Also in 1999, Anthony was seen in his biggest film role to date, playing the erratic homeless man Noel in Martin Scorsese's *Bringing Out the Dead.* Though the film stars Nicolas Cage as a troubled New York City ambulance driver, Noel is a centerpiece of the tale. Disheveled and dreadlocked, the character of Noel provides "sort of the backbone of the morality of the story," according to Scorsese in a *People* article. "Ultimately the whole film comes together around him." Critics were receptive to his wild and violent performance, which countered his usual persona of the sensitive, sensual singer.

Though Anthony has been linked with various starlets including Lopez and actor Mira Sorvino he announced his engagement to Dayanara Torres, a former Miss Universe, in October of 1999. From a previous relationship with police officer Debbie Rosado, which ended in 1995, he has a daughter, Arianna, with whom he spends much of his time. Anthony, who favors wearing Prada designs, is about five feet, eight inches tall, with a slender build, black hair, jutting cheekbones, and a strong jaw. He told Mim Udovitch in *Rolling Stone* that he is the tallest in his family, and revealed, "My father is five feet two and weighs, like, 100 pounds wet."

Although *People en Espanol* magazine once named Anthony one of the most beautiful people alive, he was not always such a looker. As he mentioned to Dennis Hensley in *Cosmopolitan,* "I was ugly and skinny growing up, and one time my dad said, 'You look like me, so you better work on your personality." His fame and accolades apparently have not affected his ego. As he told Udovitch, "I don't need other people to validate me. I'm pretty hard on myself, so if I feel good, then I know there's something to feel good about."

Selected discography

When the Night Is Over, Atlantic, 1991.
Otra Nota, Soho Latino/RMM, 1993.
Todo a Su Tiempo, Soho Latino/RMM, 1995.
Contra la Corriente, RMM, 1997.
Marc Anthony, Columbia, 1999.

Sources

Books

Contemporary Musicians, volume 19, Gale Research, 1997.

Periodicals

Cosmopolitan, February 2000, p. 204.
Daily Telegraph, January 6, 2000, p. 25.
Entertainment Weekly, October 8, 1999, p. 32.

Interview, February 1999, p. 84.

Latin Beat, December 1997, p. 40.

Newsday, July 20, 1995, p. B3; June 13, 1999, p. D10.

New Yorker, December 8, 1997, p. 96.

New York Times Magazine, August 29, 1999, p. 42.

People, October 4, 1999, p. 45; December 13, 1999, p. 185.

Rolling Stone, April 27, 2000, p. 33.

Time, September 20, 1999, p. 80.

TV Guide, February 12, 2000, p. 46.

Variety, February 2, 1998, p. 39.

Online

Marc Anthony Official Web Site, http://www.marcanthonyonline.com (April 12, 2000).

"Marc Anthony," Internet Movie Database web site, http://us.imdb.com (April 12, 2000).

Christina Applegate

Actor

Born November 25, 1972, in Los Angeles, CA; daughter of Robert Applegate (a record company executive) and Nancy Priddy (an actor).

Addresses: *Home*—Laurel Canyon, CA. *Agent*—International Creative Management, 8942 Wilshire Blvd., Beverly Hills, CA 90211.

Career

Began appearing on television at age three months; acted in radio and television commercials as a youth. Television appearances include episodes of *Father Murphy*, 1981; *Mama's Family*, 1983; *Quincy*, 1983; *Charles in Charge*, 1984; *All Is Forgiven*, 1986; *Still the Beaver*, 1986; *Amazing Stories*, 1986; *Silver Spoons*, 1986; *Family Ties*, 1987; *21 Jump Street*, 1988; *Top of the Heap*, 1991; *Mad TV*, 1996; and *Pauly*, 1997; series *Heart of the City*, 1986; *Married...With Children*, 1987–97; and *Jesse*, 1998–2000; and movies *Grace Kelly*, 1983; and *Dance 'Til Dawn*, 1988.

Film appearances include *Jaws of Satan*, 1981; *Beatlemania*, 1981; *Streets*, 1990; *Don't Tell Mom the Babysitter's Dead*, 1991; *Across the Moon*, 1994; *Wild Bill*, 1995; *Vibrations*, 1995; *Mars Attacks!*, 1996; *Vibrations*, 1996; *Nowhere*, 1997; *Claudine's Return*, 1998; *The Big Hit*, 1998; *Jane Austen's Mafia!*, 1998; *Out in Fifty*, 1999; and *The Giving Tree*, 1999.

Awards: Young Artist Award for best young television actress, 1987, for *Heart of the City*, and 1989, for *Married...With Children*; Ft. Lauderdale International Film Festival President Award for "Star on the Horizon," 1998; People's Choice Award for favorite female performer in a new series and *TV Guide* Award for favorite star of a new series, both 1999, for *Jesse*.

Sidelights

Christina Applegate began acting almost as soon as she was born, showing up with her actor mother on sets and getting cast in commercials. In her teens, she became synonymous with her provocative character, Kelly Bundy, on the popular Fox television show *Married...With Children,* a controversial show that delivered a dysfunctional twist to the typical family sitcom. With her skin–tight outfits, cherry–red lipstick, and dim–bulb persona, the promiscuous Kelly was object of uncountable bimbo jokes on the program, but nevertheless held great sex appeal for many male viewers. Applegate spent 11 years on the show before branching into new territory as a sweet single mother on the NBC sitcom *Jesse,* which allowed her to become much more multi–dimensional. Applegate has also appeared in numerous film roles, but she is best known for her memorable small–screen characters.

Applegate was born on November 25, 1972, in Los Angeles, California. Her father, Robert Applegate, is a former record company executive, and her mother,

Nancy Priddy, is an actor. "I was born and raised in Hollywood," Applegate told Bob Thomas in the *Washington Times.* "I've always been in the picture business. My mom was an actress, and after she gave birth to me, she'd go on a lot of calls for mothers with kids." Applegate began acting at the age of three months, when she appeared in her mother's arms on *The Days of Our Lives.* At five months old, Applegate showed up in a Playtex nursers commercial, and as soon as she could talk, she began doing radio commercials. Her parents divorced soon after she was born, but the split was amicable. Her father remarried and had two more children, and she became best friends with her step–sister.

By age seven, Applegate had earned enough money to buy a house, by age ten, she began working steadily in television and film. Some of her early parts included guest spots on the shows *Mama's Family, Charles in Charge, Silver Spoons,* and *Family Ties.* Her movie debut came in 1981, working with her mother in the horror flick *Jaws of Satan.* Also that year she had a role in *Beatlemania: The Movie* and then in 1983 played a young Grace Kelly in the television biopic about the actor–turned–princess. In 1986, she landed a starring role in the ABC series *Heart of the City.*

At age 16, Applegate left school to start acting full–time when she landed the role of Kelly Bundy in *Married...With Children,* which premiered in 1987. Dressed in revealing outfits each week, she steamed up the screen while bearing the brunt of the punch lines delivered from her parents and brother. The show was innovative because of its unconventional take on the traditional nuclear family. Family members continuously insulted each other; all were mean– spirited, foul–mouthed personalities. Bruce Fetts in *Entertainment Weekly* even dubbed the show "smutcom." But it attracted viewers, despite—or more likely, because of—a national campaign sparked by a Michigan housewife to boycott the show because she felt it lambasted family values. The show ran until the spring of 1997, and continues to be seen in syndication.

After several seasons of *Married...With Children,* Applegate still enjoyed working on the program, but began to openly long for a more well–rounded character. "I think over the last couple years Kelly's gotten dumber and dumber and dumber," she noted to Lisa Schwarzbaum in *Entertainment Weekly* in 1991, "and she's on her way to being a complete vegetable. I'd love to see her turn her whole life around, do something progressive." While Kelly Bundy would never change, Applegate looked to new projects to stretch her acting range.

During breaks from *Married...With Children,* Applegate began to work her way into feature films. Her first starring role was as a heroin–addicted hooker in *Streets,* 1990, and then she played a clean–cut teen in *Don't Tell Mom the Babysitter's Dead,* 1991. She also appeared in the western *Wild Bill,* 1995, and the spoof *Mars Attacks!,* 1996, and had major parts in 1994's *Across the Moon* and 1995's *Variations.* However, Applegate was not exactly a blockbuster star, probably because she was typecast for so many years as the ditzy and slutty Kelly Bundy. As she told Elaine Warren in *TV Guide,* "When you're on a television show, people start thinking that's what your personality is in real life. They can't see you as anything different, and they don't respect you as an actress."

But after *Married...With Children* had run its course after 11 years, Applegate snagged the lead role on a new NBC sitcom, *Jesse,* which featured her in a completely new light. On it, she played Jesse Warner, a single mother of a ten–year–old son making her way by working at her grizzled father's German–themed restaurant while studying to be a nurse. Applegate told Bruce Fetts in *Entertainment Weekly,* "It's not about a young career woman in her late 20s to early 30s who's neurotic," referring to a spate of similar shows. "It's more of a family–oriented comedy." She drew upon her mother's experiences as a single mom in order to flesh out the character.

Jesse premiered in September of 1998 in the ratings at number four, the highest–rated show of the new season. Without a doubt, its success was largely due to its place in NBC's winning Thursday night lineup. But critics were receptive as well, and Applegate won a *TV Guide* Award and People's Choice Award in 1999 for her role. The show continued to win viewers over with its on–again, off–again love story between Jesse and her Chilean neighbor, Diego, played by Bruno Campos. Nevertheless, the show's ratings dropped and it was cancelled in May of 2000. Chances are, though, that Applegate will continue to appear on the big and small screen. In 1998 she appeared in the comedy *Jane Austen's Mafia!* and in *The Big Hit* starring Mark Wahlberg and Lou Diamond Philips, and in 1999 she starred in the movies *The Giving Tree* and in *Out in Fifty.*

In addition to acting, Applegate enjoys jazz dance, which helps her stay slim for the camera. Schwarzbaum reported in *Entertainment Weekly* that the actor spends 60 to 70 percent of her time keeping in shape, and Applegate expressed to her, "I think it's sick that we have to do that, because acting is from the soul, not from the body, but this business is all about appearance." She also enjoys reading and writing poetry, and she practices meditation and attends regular church services. Applegate has lived in Laurel Canyon, California, all of her life, and enjoys the location because it is so close to the city yet feels far removed. She is involved with the AIDS Project Los Angeles and in charities for breast and ovarian cancer, and has marched in support of the homeless in Washington, D.C.

Sources

Periodicals

Entertainment Weekly, September 13, 1991, p. 61; September 11, 1998, p. 68.
Gannett News Service, September 4, 1998.
GQ, July 1992, p. 132.
In Style, November 1998, p. 370.

People, December 4, 1989, p. 129; May 10, 1999, p. 164; June 26, 2000, p. 134.
St. Louis Post–Dispatch, October 8, 1998, p. G6.
Teen, July 1989, p. 42.
TV Guide, May 25, 1991, p. 10.
USA Today, October 1, 1998, p. 3D.
USA Weekend, September 20, 1998, p. 19.
Washington Times, September 18, 1998, p. C12.

Online

"Christina Applegate," Internet Movie Database web site, http://us.imdb.com (July 11, 2000).
"Christina Applegate," Mr. Showbiz.com, http://mrshowbiz.go.com (July 11, 2000).
"Christina Applegate," NBC web site, http://www.nbc.com/jesse (July 11, 2000).

Lance Armstrong

Reuters/Archive Photos

Professional cyclist

Born September 18, 1971, in Plano, TX; son of Linda Walling (a secretary); married Kristin Richard (a former public relations executive), 1998; children: Luke David.

Addresses: *Home*—Austin, TX, and Nice, France.

Career

Signed with Subaru–Montgomery team as amateur, 1991; signed with Motorola team as amateur, 1992, turned professional, signing with Motorola team, 1992; signed with Cofidis team (France), 1996; signed with U.S. Postal Service team, 1997. Competed with U.S. Olympic team, 1992, 1996.

Awards: *Triathlete* magazine, named rookie of the year, 1988; national sprint–course triathlon champion, 1988, 1989; U.S. national amateur champion cyclist, 1991; won First Union Grand Prix, Thrift Drug Classic, and a stage in Tour of Galicia, 1992; won U.S. National Road Race Championship, World Road Race Championship, Thrift Drug Triple Crown, and a stage in Tour de France, 1993; won Thrift Drug Classic, 1994; won Tour DuPont, San Sebastian Classic, and stage of Tour de France, 1995; named *Velonews* male cyclist of the year, 1995; won Tour DuPont and Fleche Wallone, 1996; won Cascade Classic, Rheinland Pfalz Rundfardt, Spring 56K Criterium, and Tour of Luxembourg, 1998; won Tour de France, 1999. Also numerous other top–five finishes in various races.

Sidelights

As winner of the 1999 Tour de France, Lance Armstrong is not only an American success story for his cycling talents, but also because of the seemingly insurmountable obstacles he overcame on his way to achieving this goal. After chalking up several notable victories at events like the World Road Race Championship, Thrift Drug Triple Crown, and Tour DuPont, Armstrong was dubbed the "Golden Boy" of American cycling and credited with restoring national pride in the sport, long dominated by Europeans. However, in 1996, at age 25, he was stricken with cancer in the prime of his career. Remarkably, Armstrong used the same determination in fighting the disease as he had in his competitions in order to beat back the tumors in his testicles, lungs, abdomen, lymph nodes, and brain. He managed to overcome the odds not only to survive, but also to return to his career and ride to victory at several more contests, including the world's most respected cycling event.

Armstrong was born on September 18, 1971, in Plano, Texas, a suburb of Dallas. His parents split up when he was very young, and his mother Linda— who had her only child when she was just 17 years old—then married Terry Armstrong. They later divorced as well, and Armstrong's mother married technical recruiter John Walling in 1992. His mother, whom Alexander Wolff in *Sports Illustrated* cribed as a "5 ft. 3 in., 100–pound steel magnolia," worked as a secretary to provide for her son when her marriages did not work out, displaying a tenacity that rubbed off on her son. As Armstrong told Wolff, "She instilled all her drive, motivation and toughness in me."

Athletic from a tender age, when Armstrong was in fifth grade, he began running six miles a day after school and entering weekend races with a mix of youth and adults. Throughout the years he would amass several ribbons and trophies for his age groups. He later took up swimming. He tried sports like baseball, football, and basketball, but he was better at endurance events than those requiring coordination. At age 13, Armstrong began competitive cycling and combined his three favorite activities to begin entering triathlons, contests which include a 1,000–meter swim, 15–mile bike ride, and three–mile run. Also at 13, he won the Iron Kids Triathlon and became a professional triathlete at age 16. In high school, he twice became the national sprint–course triathlon champion back–to–back in 1989 and 1990, and in 1988 *Triathlete* magazine named him rookie of the year.

Soon, Armstrong realized that his favorite part of triathlons was being on the bike—it was his strongest activity, and others noticed this as well. When he was a senior at Plano East High School, the U.S. Olympic development team invited Armstrong to train with them in Colorado Springs, Colorado. This required taking six weeks off of school to train, and he was told he could not graduate if he did so. Risking his diploma for the time being, Armstrong joined the Subaru– Montgomery team coached by Eddie Borysewicz, who had led the 1984 Olympic team. Armstrong eventually took private classes and graduated from high school in 1989.

The summer following his graduation, Armstrong qualified for the 1990 junior world team and subsequently placed eleventh in the World Championship Road Race, posting the best time of any American since 1976. He also earned second place at the national team time trials that year. In 1990, before turning 19, he moved to Austin, Texas, mainly because he enjoyed the lively music scene there. Also that year, he became the U.S. national amateur champion, in addition to winning the First Union Grand Prix and the Thrift Drug Classic, both of which are usually won by professionals. In 1991, Armstrong competed in the Tour DuPont, then the

longest and most difficult stage race, covering 1,085 miles over 11 days. He finished in the middle of the pack, but many held high hopes for the newcomer. That same year, Armstrong won the Italy's 11–day Settimana Bergamasca race. Although Italian fans threw tacks on the road to slow him down, he won by more than a minute, defeating an Italian competitor.

In 1992, Armstrong finished second in the U.S. Olympic time trials and raced in the Summer Olympics in Barcelona, Spain. Though he was favored to win, in a rare slump, he came in a disappointing fourteenth in that 115–mile road race. Undeterred, he turned professional immediately after the Olympics, joining the Motorola team on a paid basis. In his first pro event, the San Sebastian Classic, in Spain, he came in dead last out of 111 competitors in the daylong event, but insisted on finishing. Though he was crushed, he signed up for a World Cup race in Zurich, Switzerland, two weeks later, in which he placed second and stunned the European racing world.

Armstrong continued to put in a strong showing in 1993, winning several titles, including cycling's coveted "Triple Crown" with victories at the Thrift Drug Classic, the Kmart West Virginia Classic, and the CoreStates Race (the U.S. Professional Championship). For this accomplishment, he received a $1 million bonus, which he shared with his Motorola teammates, who were ranked among the top five in the world. This was the first time ever that an American team had reached this high of a position in cycling.

In July of 1993, Armstrong started off powerfully in his first Tour de France, considered by many to be the world's most prestigious race. He won the eighth stage of the 21–stage race, only the fifth American and the third–youngest to win a stage, but then sunk to 62nd place and eventually pulled out. Earlier that year, he came in second in May at the Tour DuPont, a 12–stage race, which was a respectable showing, especially for a 21–year–old racer. Most cyclists are thought to be in their prime in their mid–twenties, because they have had more time to hone their mental skills by this point, in addition to developing their physical strength.

The following month, August of 1993, in the most important success of his career up to that point, Armstrong prevailed at the World Road Race Championship in Oslo, Norway. This one–day event covered 161 miles and was rendered more difficult and dangerous that year by pouring rain. The slick roads caused Armstrong—now the leader of the Motorola—team to crash twice, but his teammates drafted him for a while and allowed him to restore his composure and strength. (Drafting is when a rider takes the rear position in a team, thus obtaining the benefit of wind blockage.) By the end of the race he broke away from the lead pack and finished in 6 hours, 17 minutes, and 10 seconds.

Armstrong's performance at the World Road Race Championship made him the youngest person ever, and the second American, to win this contest. "The day changed my life," Armstrong told Leigh Montville in *Sports Illustrated*. "The expectation levels grew." In an unorthodox move, the new world champion brought his mother onto the victory stand with him. The achievement also prompted Norway's King Harland to invite Armstrong to pay him a visit. However, the king did not extend the courtesy to the cyclist's mother, so he turned down the offer. King Harland later changed his mind, and both Armstrong and his mother attended the reception.

At his next Tour DuPont in 1994, Armstrong again placed second and came in seventh in the world championship road race. He also took second place at the San Sebastian Classic in Spain as well as a race in France. Before the 1995 Tour DuPont, according to Montville in *Sports Illustrated*, Armstrong stated, "I don't want to finish second again." In the past, his weakness in this contest was in the time trials, when riders race against the clock alone, rather than competing against others. This time, Armstrong noted to Montville, "I think I'm stronger. I've never felt better. I just hope I can keep this form for as long as it takes." Sure enough, Armstrong pulled through this time, winning three of 12 individual stages and coming in two minutes ahead of his closest rival in the race, Viatcheslav Ekimov of Russia, who had defeated him the previous year.

After this victory, Motorola teammate Fabio Casartelli hit a wall in the 1995 Tour de France and died from head injuries, prompting Armstrong to ride even harder. He again won a stage of the race this time, although he later came in 36th, but it marked the first time he had finished. He also won the San Sebastian Classic that year, making him the first American to win a World Cup road race. He took this contest again in 1996, in addition to the Fleche Wallone in Belgium.

Also in 1996, Armstrong won his second Tour DuPont with the Motorola team and set records for 10 career stage victories, 5 stage wins, 14 top–three finishes, 11 consecutive days as race leader, largest margin of victory (at 3 minutes, 15 seconds), and fastest average speed in a time trial (at 32.9 miles per hour). In addition, he rode again for the 1996 U.S. Olympic team in Atlanta, Georgia, placing sixth in the time trials and 12th in the road race. The races seemed to fatigue him more than usual, and earlier that summer he was unable to finish the Tour de France, as he came down with bronchitis.

Despite these disappointments, Armstrong remained seventh–ranked in the world and in 1996 signed a contract with France's Team Cofidis. That October, though, in a shock to cyclist and athletes everywhere, he was diagnosed with testicular cancer that had spread to his abdomen, lungs, and lymph nodes. After experiencing severe pain in a testicle and coughing up blood, he saw the doctor and had the testicle removed the next day. Armstrong then gave up red meat, dairy products, and coffee, and began aggressive chemotherapy. Even with as far as the cancer had spread, he was given a 65 to 85 percent chance of survival. "I might have a bald head and not be as fast," he commented in *Sports Illustrated*, "but I'll be out there. I'm going to race again."

In yet another blow, however, doctors soon discovered tumors on Armstrong's brain. His odds of survival dipped to 50–50, then to 40 percent. The surgery to remove them was a success, though, and, after more chemotherapy treatment, Armstrong was declared cancer–free in February of 1997. Though his lungs were scarred, he was determined to get back on his bike. When Cofidis canceled his contract and yanked his $600,000 annual salary, he became a free agent but did not attract any interest. Finally he managed to snag a position worth about $200,000 with the United States Postal Service team; he called the pay cut "an 80–percent cancer tax," reported Todd Balf in Bicycling.

By 1998, Armstrong was back in competition and looked to be in good condition. He took fourth place at the World Road Race Championships and won the Cascade Classic, the Rheinland Pfalz Rundfardt, the Spring 56K Criterium, and the Tour of Luxembourg. He also placed second at the First Union Invitational. By the summer of 1999, Armstrong was ready to compete again in the Tour de France, made up of 2,290 miles of exhausting terrain. Though it was a victory for Armstrong to even be competing in the event, he captured even more attention when it began to look like he was going to win. He was not demoralized by rumors, circulated in the French press, that his amazing comeback was assisted by performance–enhancing drugs, especially since frequent blood and urine tests showed no trace of such substances.

In an awe–inspiring finish, Armstrong ended up winning the Tour de France 7 minutes and 37 seconds ahead of his nearest rival, Alex Zulle of Switzerland. He dominated the race from the start, becoming only the second American to win the contest, and posted an average speed of 40.2 kilometers an hour, or 25 miles per hour, breaking the record of 39.9 kilometers per hour set in 1998. The victory was not only uplifting due to Armstrong's cancer fight, but also as a matter of national pride, since he was riding with an American–sponsored team—the U.S. Postal Service team, which had not even won a stage in its first two Tour de France outings in 1997 and 1998—and seven of the nine members were American. Greg LeMond, the other American Tour de France champion, had ridden with French teams when he won in 1986, 1989, and 1990.

At five feet, ten inches and 158 pounds, Armstrong is broad–shouldered and has short brown hair. He owns a million–dollar home in Austin named "Casa Linda" after his mother. He helped design the Mediterranean–style home, which took two years to plan and build, and splits his time between there and a house in Nice, France. Armstrong established the Lance Armstrong Junior Olympic Race Series in 1995 in order to promote cycling and racing among American youth, and in 1996 he founded the Lance Armstrong Foundation for Cancer, to benefit cancer research and promote early cancer detection and awareness. In 1998, Armstrong married Kristin Richard, a former public relations executive he met through his cancer foundation. They had their first child, Luke David, on October 12, 1999, using sperm that was frozen before Armstrong began chemotherapy. His autobiography is due out from Putnam in 2000, and a film based on his life is in the works as well.

Sources

Periodicals

Bicycling, July 1995, p. 50; August 1996, p. 28; February 1997, p. 44; July 1997, p. 86; January–February 1998, p. 52; May 1998, p. 21.

Men's Fitness, October 1998, p. 102.

New York Times, July 25, 1999, sec, 2, p. 23; July 26, 1999, p. D1.

People, October 28, 1996, p. 56; August 9, 1999, p. 62.

Publisher's Weekly, August 30, 1999, p. 12.

Sporting News, August 9, 1999, p. 63.

Sports Illustrated, May 24, 1993, p. 50; July 4, 1994, p. 52; May 15, 1995, p. 32; May 20, 1996, p. 48; October 21, 1996, p. 19; August 9, 1999, p. 68.

Texas Monthly, December 1996, p. 116.

Time, July 22, 1999, p. 66.

U.S. News & World Report, August 9, 1999, p. 60.

Online

Lance Armstrong Online! (official web site), http://lancearmstrong.com (October 25, 1999).

United States Postal Service Pro Cycling Team (official web site), http://uspsprocycling.com (October 25, 1999).

Bernard Arnault

Corbis Corporation

Business executive

Born March 5, 1949, in Roubaix, France; son of Jean and Marie Jo (Savinel) Arnault; married Anne Dewavrin (divorced); married Helene Mercier (a classical pianist); children: (from first marriage) Delphine, Antoine; (from second marriage) Alexandre, Frederic, Jean.

Addresses: *Home*—Paris, France; St. Tropez, France; London, England; and northern France. *Office*—LVMH, 30 ave. Hoche, 75008 Paris, France.

Career

Ferret–Savinel construction (later real estate) firm, France, 1971–81; developed real estate in U.S., 1981–84; Boussac Saint Freres textile firm, owner, 1984–88; LVMH, president, chair, and CEO, 1989—.

Sidelights

One of the world's richest and most influential business executives, Bernard Arnault is the head of LVMH Moet Hennesy Louis Vuitton, a French producer of a wide line of luxury goods. In addition to owning Moet and Chandon and Dom Perignon champagnes, Hennessy cognac, and Louis Vuitton luggage, it is also the umbrella firm for the fashion houses of Givenchy, Christian Dior, Christian Lacroix, and Kenzo; the cosmetics and perfume seller Sephora; the fragrance line of Guerlain; Le Bon Marche department stores, and more. Then, in 1999 LVMH also acquired the winery of Chateau d'Yquem, known for producing the sumptuous Sauternes wines. Arnault holds 33 percent of the stock in LVMH and is worth roughly $19 billion.

Though Arnault has been derided as a corporate raider and is often reviled in labor– friendly France, he has built up an empire that is admired for its profitability. From 1998 to 1999 alone, the firm's sales increased 23 percent, to $8.5 billion, and profits were up 160 percent, to $700 million. But Arnault has not only attracted the reputation of the ruthless businessperson; he has also cultivated an image as a connoisseur himself. "I have always been interested in creativity," Arnault remarked to Jennifer Steinhauer in the *New York Times*. "Even when I was working in construction, what I liked was to work with architects. I have always liked very much creators, and in luxury you are in a sense working with artists, those who have the capacity to transform creative ideas in reality."

Arnault was born on March 5, 1949, in Roubaix, near Lille in northern France, to Jean and Marie Jo (Savinel) Arnault. His family owned a profitable construction business, and Arnault picked up on commerce from his father while cultivating a love of music from his mother, who played piano. In fact, Arnault as a youth harbored a desire to become a concert pianist, but eventually decided he was not talented enough. Instead, he studied engineering at the prestigious Ecole Polytechnique in Paris, graduating in 1971.

Subsequently, instead of following the bulk of his classmates into government posts or engineering, Arnault went to work at his father's company, Ferret–Savinel. "I was considered a heretic for going into business," Arnault told David Lawday in *U.S. News & World Report.* By the mid–1970s, the firm had grown to include about 1,500 employees and roughly $100 million in revenues, and had expanded into building vacation homes in southern France. Arnault asked for shares, and his father gave him about a third of the business. Four years after joining the company, he made steep changes, making a deal to sell it to the Rothschild family's Societe Nationale de Construction. Arnault laid the plan before telling his father, but managed to convince him after the fact that it was a good idea. Within a year, the firm was more profitable than ever.

Though Arnault's real estate business was one of the top sellers in France as of the early 1980s, political issues left him concerned. When Francois Mitterand became president in 1981, he introduced sweeping socialist reforms that called for the nationalization of some private industry. Real estate was not expected to be affected, but Arnault was exasperated nevertheless. He set off for New Rochelle, New York, and built condos in Florida. Though the venture did not turn into anything big, the experience made a strong impression on him. Arnault was exposed to Wall Street and capitalism, and also, as he commented to Per–Henrik Mannson in the *Wine Spectator*, "I realized that France was very small compared to the rest of the world."

However, while in New York earlier for the first time on a vacation, Arnault also began to get an idea of France's strengths. As he related to Holly Brubach in the *New York Times Magazine*, "When you ask a cab driver in New York, 'What do you know about Franc—do you know who is the President?,' the answer is, 'No.' But he knows Christian Dior. Dior was in his day on the cover of Time magazine. He was already part of French culture, like the Eiffel Tower. To build a name that transcends the individual and becomes a symbol of France—it's a phenomenon that happens very rarely. That's what got me into the luxury business."

While working in America, Arnault instructed his company's attorney to watch out for any business opportunities that looked good. When the lawyer called with an idea, Arnault returned to France in 1984 and made a bid for Boussac Saint Freres, a troubled textile firm owned by the government. Though it was bankrupt, one of its assets was the fashion house of Dior. In addition, his first wife was a cousin of one of the owners, so he had an inside edge.

After he gained ownership of Boussac, Arnault exhibited the kind of tactic that angered labor groups as he laid off thousands of workers (some sources reported about 5,000, others have said 8,000) and sold off almost all of its manufacturing assets for about $500 million. This made him one of the wealthiest men in the nation while also earning him the nickname "the Terminator." The government, irate that he broke his promise to preserve jobs, made him repay around $60 million of the money it had invested. Despite this rocky start, Arnault soon attracted the admiration of fellow business executives, as Boussac began turning a profit again within two years. It was restructured under the name Financiere Agache, and by 1991 was worth more than $1 billion on the French stock market.

Meanwhile, Arnault in 1988 began to buy stock in LVMH, which was formed in 1987 after the merger of Louis Vuitton and Moet Hennessy. Vuitton had been an obscure leather– goods firm that was transformed into a worldwide status brand thanks to the efforts of the company president, Henry Racamier. Moet Hennessy produced fine champagne and liquor. Soon after the merger, though, internal struggles began at the top. Racamier battled against Alain Chevalier, Moet Hennessy's president, for control. Chevalier had joined up with Anthony Tennant of Great Britain's Guinness brewing company. Racamier then sought to bring Arnault on board in order to shift the balance of power, and saw him as a sort of protégé.

However, little did Racamier know that Arnault had been eyeing LVMH, and began purchasing stock even before joining the company. Christian Dior had earlier sold LVMH the right to its name to use on perfumes, and Arnault had thought it wise to join the two operations. He struck a deal with Racamier to become a decision–maker in LVMH interests. Shortly after joining the enterprise, though, Arnault shifted alliances to pair with Tennant and form a holding company with Guinness which became LVMH's largest shareholder with about a 37 percent stake. By this point, Arnault held 60 percent of LVMH, enough to take control of the firm. He became president and chair of LVMH in January of 1989 when Chevalier resigned, and Racamier was also edged out in April of 1990. This earned him the nicknames "Le Raider" and "the wolf in cashmere."

In the meantime, Arnault had continued to expand his empire of luxury goods by hiring designer Christian Lacroix away from the Jean Patou couture house in 1987. He planned to build up Lacroix's name into as well–known a brand as Dior, and to capitalize on it by producing not only clothing, but also perfume, accessories, and cosmetics. Later, Patou won an unfair– competition lawsuit in the French courts against Arnault for this move. Also in 1987, Arnault acquired Celine, which manufactured luggage, shoes, and suits and was well–established in Asia. In 1988, he bought the Givenchy couture and fragrance lines from Count Hubert de Givenchy, who rose to fame in 1961 when he designed the outfits worn by Audrey Hepburn in the film *Breakfast at Tiffany's.*

While building up a French luxury empire, though, Arnault shook up not only the business community but also the fashion world as he introduced several foreign designers to head some of the most well–known couture houses. In the mid–1990s he fired Givenchy and appointed controversial British designer John Galliano to head up the line. Then, Arnault moved Galliano to the more prestigious Dior line and named Alexander McQueen, another fashion iconoclast from Britain, to take charge at Givenchy. He later signed American Michael Kors, known for his clean, contemporary styling, to rejuvenate the house of Celine, and appointed American Marc Jacobs, known for his "grunge" looks, to design accessories and a ready–to–wear line for Vuitton.

These moves shocked the French, who felt that foreigners could not do justice to the chic styles they were known for. But Arnault did not let the criticism bother him, telling Martha Duffy in *Time,* "I'm not interested in anything else but the youngest, the brightest, and the very, very talented." Indeed, seeking out the top names, regardless of national origin, seemed to be working. Nicholas Moss and Charles Masters wrote in a 1997 *European* article, "In less than a decade, Arnault has revitalised the French luxury goods sector from a disparate collection of venerable but underperforming industries into a formidable international powerhouse. LVMH's brands are more sought after than ever, and the company's financial performance is better than satisfactory."

However, some saw this success as a cheapening of luxury, and accused Arnault of providing elite goods to the masses. In Holly Brubach's piece for the *New York Times Magazine* titled "And Luxury for All," she stated, "A new market has emerged one made up of people who, though they can't afford a house in Paris's 16th arrondissement or an apartment of New York's Park Avenue, have enough disposable income to buy a Vuitton handbag (if not a trunk) or a bottle of Dior perfume."

Continuing to acquire high–end companies, Arnault throughout the 1990s purchased the Bon Marche department store chain, changing its name to Le

Bon Marche. But one of his biggest coups came in 1996 with the acquisition of DFS, the Duty Free Shoppers chain that has tony boutiques in airports and upscale shopping sites worldwide. In the late 1990s he began to try fervently to acquire Gucci, but the firm fought back, and lawsuits and counter–suits flew through the courts. Gucci finally took advantage of the fact that it was registered in the Netherlands in order to shield itself from a takeover. It ended up selling a 42 percent stake to PPR, a firm controlled by Francois Pinault, Arnault's fiercest business rival.

Though the Asian crisis of the late 1990s hit LVMH hard and sent shares tumbling, the company recovered as Arnault bought up even more businesses, from Tag Heuer Swiss watches to American cosmetics firms like Hard Candy. It also expanded its Sephora cosmetic and perfume stores into the United States. He also began to invest in Internet start–ups, pouring $500 million into operations like eBay, LibertySurf (a European Internet–service provider), and Nomade, Europe's top web portal. He also tried to gear up a site integrating a variety of companies called Europ@web, but as of the summer of 2000, that venture was troubled.

Meanwhile, in yet another major move, in November of 1996 Arnault acquired a 55 percent stake in the 400–year–old Chateau d'Yquem winery in Sauternes, located in Bordeaux, France. The white wine produced there is one of the most sought–after sweet wines among collectors. Believing the respected, family–owned business would be another the "undisputed jewel" in the LVMH crown, as he remarked to Mannson in the *Wine Spectator,* Arnault took advantage of internal strife to purchase the controlling interest. However, the head of Yquem, Count Alexandre de Lur Saluces, had for years bitterly resisted suggestions that the winery be sold, and fought against Arnault vehemently, filing lawsuits and preventing him from actually taking over even though he was a majority owner. In fact, Arnault could not even set foot on the grounds for the first couple of years or so of owning the stake.

By April of 1999, though, Arnault had won the war and took possession of Yquem. After all the dissidence, Arnault named Lur Saluces president of the firm, and the two maintain a strong working relationship. "We have excellent relations," Arnault commented to Mannson in the *Wine Spectator.* "Deep down, I've always gotten along with the creators or with the men who represented a tradition in business."

Though he puts in 10 to 12 hours daily at the office, Arnault finds time to exercise regularly, keeping his six–foot–two–inch frame trim at 170 pounds. He was married to Anne Dewavrin and divorced, and from that relationship has two children, Delphine and Antoine. In 1991, he married Helene Mercier, a French–Canadian classical pianist, and they have three sons, Alexandre, Frederic, Jean. Arnault's wife performs around the globe and continues to record under her maiden name. He and his family live in a Paris mansion in the upscale sixteenth arrondissement, and he also has homes in northern France, London, and the Mediterranean resort town of St. Tropez, all equipped with wine cellars. Arnault's passion for music has never waned; he enjoys Chopin and once played in concert with his wife.

Sources

Business Week, July 30, 1990, p. 48; July 5, 1999, p. 71; January 10, 2000, p. 67; July 31, 2000, p. 18.
Economist, July 15, 2000, p. 66.

European, July 31, 1997, p. 8.
Forbes, June 7, 1997, p. 80.
Fortune, January 2, 1989, p. 40; March 20, 2000, p. 163.
Gourmet, September 1998, p. 52.
Newsweek, August 7, 1989, p. 40.
New York, April 26, 1999, p. 24.
New York Times, January 14, 1989, p. 34; January 22, 1996, p. D2; October 31, 1996, p. D9; August 17, 1997, sec. 3, p. 1; May 15, 2000, p. C1.
New York Times Magazine, July 12, 1998. Time, April 21, 1997, p. 112; May 1, 2000, p. 48.
U.S. News & World Report, September 26, 1988, p. 45.
Vanity Fair, July 1999, p. 94.
Wall Street Journal, May 26, 1999, p. A18; May 27, 1999, p. A21.
Wine Spectator, June 30, 2000, p. 40.

Erykah Badu

AP/Wide World Photos

Singer and songwriter

Born Erica Wright, February 26, 1971, in Dallas, TX; daughter of William "Toosie" Wright, Jr. and Kolleen Gipson Wright; children: (with rap artist Andre "Dre" Lauren Benjamin) son, Seven Sirius. *Education:* Attended Grambling State University (Louisiana), 1989–93; studied theater.

Addresses: *Record company*—Universal Records, 1755 Broadway, 7th Fl., New York, NY 10019.

Career

Worked at Steve Harvey's Comedy House in Oak Cliff, TX, late 1980s–early 1990s, began waiting tables and selling tickets, promoted to booking acts and stage managing; taught dance and theater at the South Dallas Cultural Center and waited tables at a coffeehouse, early 1990s; worked with performing arts group Soul Nation, early 1990s; formed Erykah Free (with cousin, Robert "Free" Bradford), 1994, opened for touring hip–hop acts in Dallas, TX; signed with Kedar Entertainment, 1995, and released debut album, *Baduizm,* 1997. Acting credits include films *Blues Brothers 2000,* 1998; and *The Cider House Rules,* 1999.

Awards: Grammy Awards for best R&B album and best female R&B performance, 1998; four Soul Train awards; two NAACP Image awards; American Music Award.

Sidelights

Erykah Badu's music has been given called "neo–soul" or "alternative R&B," because it blends rhythm–and–blues with hip–hop, jazz, and funk, but Badu herself prefers to call it soul music. "No one asks a bird the explanation for the song; they just enjoy it," she remarked to Joy Bennett Kinnon in *Ebony.* As soon as her debut album, *Baduizm,* came out in 1997, her voice was likened to that of Ella Fitzgerald, Sarah Vaughn and Nina Simone, and other greats, though she has said that her biggest influences include classic soul and R&B greats. In late 1999, Badu shed her ubiquitous towering headwraps and long, slinky gowns to appear in a prominent supporting role in the acclaimed film *The Cider House Rules.*

Badu was born Erica Wright about 1971 in Dallas, Texas. She was mainly raised by her mother, Kolleen Gipson Wright, and her grandmother, Thelma Gipson, both of whom acted in local theater. Her father, William "Toosie" Wright, was often gone or in jail, but his mother, Viola "Ganny" Wilson, kept involved in her grandchildren's lives. (Badu has a younger sister, Koryan, or "Koko," and younger brother, Eevin.) Badu loved music from the time she was a toddler, pounding on her great–grandmother's piano at age two and commanding others to sing. As a child, she acted in the summer recreation program run by her godmother, Gwen Hargrove, and she also sang in the choir of the First Baptist Church of Hamilton Park.

In school, Badu was always on stage, performing in dancing and acting competitions and usually winning the top prize. She took dance lessons with the troupe Mahogany and later studied ballet. Both groups practiced at the Martin Luther King Recreation Center. Badu told Joyce Saenz Harris in the *Dallas Morning News,* "I never left the building! I was always there."

As a teen, Badu auditioned to attend Dallas' Booker T. Washington High School for the Performing and Visual Arts, the same school that produced jazz trumpeter Roy Hargrove and singer Edie Brickell. She was accepted in all areas of the school and enrolled in the theater program, but later decided to focus on dance and music. "I wasn't the best dancer," she admitted to Harris in the *Dallas Morning News.* "I was pigeon–toed! But I could feel it. And that's what stood out to the teacher. I could close my eyes and feel the music and let my body do what it was supposed to do."

While in high school, Badu decided to change her name because, as she told Chuck Arnold in *People,* "I didn't want to have the slave name anymore." However, her mother insisted that she, and not a slave owner, had named her daughter, so they compromised on the unique spelling. As Badu explained to Arnold, "'Kah' is Kemetic [ancient Egyptian] for 'the inner self.' And I came up with the name Badu because it's one of the jazz–bebop riffs that I sing." Later her father told her that Badu means 'to manifest truth' in Arabic.

After graduating in 1989, Badu wanted to go to Howard University, but her grade point was not high enough. Instead, she enrolled at Grambling State University in Louisiana, where she majored in theater. Badu enjoyed the small, wooded campus and the melting pot of people from all over. She told Harris, "I learned so much there that had nothing to do with scholastics." Though she went to college from 1989 to 1993, she left a few credits shy of her degree.

Returning to Dallas, Badu landed a job at Steve Harvey's Comedy House in Oak Cliff, where she waited tables and sold tickets. One night she bounded up on stage to join Harvey's act, and he made her a regular part of the routine. Badu was eventually promoted to booking acts and stage managing. When Harvey left town, she taught dance and theater at the South Dallas Cultural Center and waited tables at a coffeehouse. In addition, she began to work with the performing arts group Soul Nation, cofounded by her friend Trisha Crear.

In 1994 Badu joined up with her cousin, Robert "Free" Bradford, and formed the band Erykah Free, which fused hip–hop, soul, and R&B. She mentioned to Natasha Stovall in the *New York Times* that they "opened for every hip–hop group that came through Dallas. We were hometown celebrities." They put together a demo package to shop to record labels. In 1995, after opening for soul singer D'Angelo, they were discovered by his manager, Kedar Massenburg, who was in the process of opening his own division of Universal Records called Kedar Entertainment.

However, Massenburg was only interested in signing Badu, not the duo. Though this caused a rift, she later dedicated her first album to her cousin, and he received producing and songwriting credits on it as well. During each concert, she would light a candle in his honor to signify their connection. Badu, in fact, makes a point of surrounding herself with candles and incense on stage as well as at home and in hotel rooms because it helps keep her at peace.

By late 1995, Badu had a contract and had traded in her long braids, jeans, and T–shirt for an Afrocentric style anchored by distinctive headwraps. She insisted on keeping close tabs on her career from the start. "You can't go into [the music business] and say, 'Aw, I just want to sing; I don't care,'" Badu noted to Michael A. Gonzales in *Essence.* "If you're not prepared, you'll get jacked . It's beautiful and new to be spiritual, but I'm going to take advantage as well. Since I'm in demand and I'm the boss, I'm going to get everything that's due me."

In January of 1997, Badu's first single, "On and On," became a Top 40 hit even before the release of her debut album, *Baduizm,* the following month. The song and CD reached number one on the *Billboard* R&B charts and the album crossed over to hit number two on the pop charts as well. The accompanying video, an homage to the film *The Color Purple,* was also praised. It was written and directed by Badu and featured several of her friends and family members. Part of her early success was due to avid marketing by Massenburg. He had pumped out 10,000 cassettes of "On and On" to the crowds at the 1996 Soul Train Music Awards, and heavily pushed it to radio stations and clubs, thus generating a buzz around Badu before her CD hit the shelves. He also gained exposure for her by having her sing a duet of "Your Precious Love" with D'Angelo on the soundtrack for *High School High.*

Critical reception to *Baduizm* was warm, as many compared Badu's voice to legendary soul and jazz singers of the past. Kevin Powell of *Rolling Stone* remarked, "There is an old soul within Badu's honey–coated voice, and she sounds eerily like a modern–day version of [Billie Holiday]." Badu told Powell that like Holiday, she tries to make her voice sound like jazz horns. But, she has also noted that other big influences include Stevie Wonder, Marvin Gaye, and Chaka Khan. Christopher John Farley wrote in *Time*, "Badu's voice isn't cuddly or cozy; it's sharp and metallic at points, wounded and sad at others. Most of the songs on *Baduizm* are slow, supple and subtle." Morthland, describing the singer's sound in *Texas Monthly*, wrote, "Her voice is the aural equivalent of dry ice: hot and cold, smooth but thin, with a brittle edge."

The cuts on *Baduizm* showcased diverse musical styles. "Otherside of the Game," for example, is a hip–hop tune dedicated to prisoner Mumia Abu–Jamal. The song centers on a pregnant woman who is afraid authorities are going to come and claim her lover. Though he is involved in an unsavory occupation, he provides for his family. On the other hand, a remake of "Touch a 4–Leaf Clover" was rooted in classic soul, and "Appletree" prominently featured sounds of the 1940s and 1950s. The latter was inspired by the singer's paternal grandmother. Badu noted to John Morthland in *Texas Monthly*, "She's always putting proverbs on me. One of 'em is you pick your friends like you pick your fruit, 'cause you don't want no rotten fruit." The second single off the CD, the R&B–sounding "Next Lifetime," was also a hit. It concerned a love triangle where two of the parties decide they will meet again in another lifetime.

Within two months of hitting the shelves, *Baduizm* went platinum. By the end of 1997, the singer also released *Erykah Badu Live,* and in 1998 she was nominated for four Grammy Awards best new artist, best R&B album, best female R&B performance, and best R&B song. She walked away with awards for best R&B album and best female R&B performance. In addition, Badu was honored with four Soul Train awards, two NAACP Image awards, and an American Music Award.

After scoring this coup with her first CD, Badu decided to move into acting, landing a small role in the 1998 film *Blues Brothers 2000*. She also played herself on episodes of the soap opera *One Life to Live* and the drama *New York Undercover*. Then, Badu was cast in the critically lauded film *The Cider House Rules* in 1999. In it, she portrays Rose Rose, the daughter of an incestuous migrant worker (played by veteran actor Delroy Lindo). "When I started out in this business, I had a whole master plan," Badu related to Gonzales in *Essence.* "I said, 'Okay, I'm going to be a superstar. I'll start as a singer so I can be individually recognized and have a whole persona. Then I'll go on to acting, because everyone wants to see a recording star on film. Then after film, I'll direct, and after directing I'll write movies and have my own corporation and then have a dance school and then an acting school and ultimately a whole arts foundation.'"

Badu is single and in late 1997 had a son, Seven; she liked the name because seven is a prime number, meaning it cannot be divided except by itself or the number one. The father is rap artist Andre "Dre" Lauren Benjamin, a member of the group OutKast. The two first met in New York City in late 1996. Badu told Harris in the *Dallas Morning News* that they are "real good friends." The singer moved to Brooklyn from her native Dallas after signing her record contract so she could be closer to the music industry. Badu deals with pressures of life with her spiritual beliefs and ties to family and friends. She noted to Gonzales in *Essence,* "I create my own calm. And I keep my balance, because I know that it's not really me, by myself…. The Creator always gives me the energy." She also remarked to Kinnon in *Ebony,* "It's good to have real good people and energy around you to make sure that you stay grounded and to make sure that they keep your ego up and to stay confident and keep your creative juices flowing."

Sources

Dallas Morning News, February 22, 1998, p. 1E.

Ebony, July 1997, p. 36; July 1998, p. 68.

Essence, August 1997, p. 90.

Jet, December 8, 1997, p. 38; December 27, 1999, p. 15.

New York Times, April 6, 1997, sec. 2, p. 37.

People, June 2, 1997, p. 146; July 14, 1997, p. 72.

Philadelphia Tribune, February 28, 1997.

Premiere, February 1999, p. 39.

Rolling Stone, March 20, 1997, p. 23; December 25, 1997, p. 155.

Seventeen, June 1997, p. 108.

Texas Monthly, May 1997, p. 58.

Time, February 10, 1997, p. 77.

Washington Afro–American, March 22, 1997.

Amiri Baraka

Archive Photos

Author

Born Everett Leroy Jones, later changed to LeRoi Jones; changed to Imamu Ameer Baraka in 1968, later modified to Amiri Baraka; born October 7, 1934, in Newark, New Jersey; son of Coyette Leroy (a postman and elevator operator) and Anna Lois (a seamstress and later administrative professional; maiden name, Russ) Jones; married Hettie Cohen, October 13, 1958 (divorced, August 1965); married Sylvia Robinson (Bibi Amina Baraka), August 1966; children: (first marriage) Kellie Elisabeth, Lisa Victoria Chapman; (second marriage) Obalaji Malik Ali, Ras Jua Al Aziz, Shani Isis, Amiri Seku, Ahi Mwenge. *Education:* B.A., Howard University; graduate courses at Columbia University.

Addresses: *Home*—Newark, NJ. *Office*—Department of Africana Studies, State University of New York, Long Island, NY 11794. *Agent*—Joan Brandt, Sterling Lord Agency, 660 Madison Ave., New York, NY 10021.

Career

Writer. Founded *Yugen* magazine and Totem Press publishing company, 1958; New School for Social Research, New York City, instructor, 1961–64; State University of New York at Stony Brook, assistant professor, 1980–83, associate professor, 1983–85, professor of Afro–American studies, 1985 . Visiting professor, University of Buffalo, summer, 1964, Columbia University, fall, 1964, and 1966–67, San Francisco State University, 1967, Yale University, 1977–78, George Washington University, 1978–79, and Rutgers University, 1988. Founded Black Arts Repertory Theatre School, 1964, director, 1964–

66; director of Spirit House community theater, Newark, NJ, 1965–75, and head of advisory group at Treat Elementary School, Newark. Member, All–African Games, Pan African Federation, Black Academy of Arts and Letters, National Black Political Assembly (secretary general; co–governor), National Black United Front, Congress of African People (co–founder, chairperson), Black Writers' Union, League of Revolutionary Struggle, United Brothers (Newark), Newark Writers Collective. *Military service:* U.S. Air Force, 1954–57.

Awards: John Hay Whitney fellowship, 1960–61; Longview Award for best essay of the year, 1961, for "Cuba Libre;" Obie Award, 1964, for *Dutchman;* Guggenheim fellowship, 1965–66; Yoruba Academy fellow, 1965; second prize at the First World Festival of Negro Arts, Dakar, Senegal, 1966, for *The Slave;* Doctorate of Humane Letters, Malcolm X College, 1972; Rockefeller Foundation fellow, 1981; National Endowment for the Arts poetry award, 1981; New Jersey Council for the Arts award, 1982; American Book Award, 1984, for *Confirmation: An Anthology of African–American Women;* Drama Award, 1985; PEN–Faulkner Award, 1989; Langston Hughes Medal for outstanding contribution to literature, 1989; American Book Awards Lifetime Achievement Award,

1989; Ferroni Award, Italy, and Foreign Poets Award, 1993; Black Drama Festival, Winston– Salem, SC, Playwright's Award, 1997.

Sidelights

One of the most influential and controversial contemporary American writers, Amiri Baraka became a vanguard of the Black Arts movement in the 1960s and throughout the decades has produced a prolific output of poetry, drama, fiction, and non-fiction. He catapulted to fame with his 1964 play *Dutchman,* an openly political work on race issues, and has continued to inject his often–changing political beliefs in his art. Though he aligned himself with the black nationalist movement in the 1960s, which scorned integration, he later became a Marxist and socialist. In addition to his literature, Baraka has harbored a lifelong fascination with the contribution of black musicians to American culture, and has written several scholarly works on that subject. He has also contributed to music periodicals as well as general–interest publications, and is a professor at the State University of New York at Stony Brook.

Baraka was born Everett Leroy Jones–in college, he modified the spelling to LeRoi–on October 7, 1934, in Newark, New Jersey, the son of Coyette Leroy ("Roy")and Anna Lois (Russ) Jones. He has one sister, Elaine. Baraka's father worked as a barber and then a postal worker, eventually reaching the position of supervisor, and his mother worked as a seamstress and later as an office worker for a government bureau. Baraka's uncle and maternal grandparents also lived with his family, and his grandfather was actually "the head of our household, and without a doubt, my earliest role model," according to Baraka in an *Essence* interview with Audreen Buffalo. He added, "He was very dignified and very strong a race man, like they say.... He was high up in the Bethany Baptist Church, president of the Sunday school, and he sat on the board of trustees." His grandfather and grandmother had formerly owned grocery stores, but later in life his grandfather became paralyzed in an accident and was never the same. Baraka's mother had attended Fisk and Tuskegee universities, and gave her children lessons in singing, dancing, drums, piano, and art.

As a youth, Baraka was an excellent and creative student, penning his own comic strip, "The Crime Wave," by seventh grade. He also wrote short stories. He attended McKinley Junior High School and Barringer School, a college preparatory school populated mostly by Italian students. Though Baraka's parents were proud that he was one of only a few blacks at his high school, he felt alienated, and later he would harshly criticize the concept of assimilation that his parents embraced.

Baraka was offered scholarships to many colleges, and in 1951 began attending Rutgers University. But he continued to feel isolated, so he transferred to the predominantly black Howard University the next year. Eventually, however, he wrote about Howard as the epitome of the black bourgeoisie which he despised. Nevertheless, the experience gave Baraka access to prominent scholars such as Sterling A. Brown, E. Franklin Frazier, and Nathan Scott, Jr. He also was exposed to learning about black history and culture, thanks to a series of "unofficial" courses on African American music taught in the dormitory.

But Baraka lost interest in his studies and began to spend the bulk of his time socializing and frequenting jazz clubs. He flunked out, and considered it to be one of the defining moments of his life. As he noted to Buffalo in *Essence,* "Once I got thrown out, I was forced to deal with myself in a real way.... I went into the air force; it was the worst period of my life. I finally found out what it was like to be disconnected from family and friends. I found out what it was like to be under the direct jurisdiction of people who hated black people. I had never known that directly." He began basic training at Sampson Air Force Base in Geneva, New York, on October 6, 1954, a day before his nineteenth birthday. Later, though, after leaving the service, he would obtain his bachelor's degree from Howard and take graduate courses at Columbia University.

In spite of his negative experience with the military, Baraka excelled. He was the only African American selected for weather training school, and was sent to Chanute Field in Rantoul, Illinois, for this schooling. He was an outstanding student there, graduating with the highest grade point average in his class, and was elected class leader. Thanks to his performance, he was allowed first choice of his tour of duty. He asked to be sent to Puerto Rico, thinking that the base there would be akin to a country club.

When military life did not meet his expectations, Baraka began to read extensively. Some of the authors he enjoyed included Ernest Hemingway, Franz Kafka, Thomas Hardy, and Marcel Proust. Due in large part to this intellectual stimulation, Baraka began to write poetry and keep a journal. However, after he was accused of Communist leanings due to some of the literature he kept on hand, Baraka was undesirably discharged from the air force in 1957 just 30 days before he was due to be honorably discharged.

At the time, the Beat movement in literature was beginning its ascent, which challenged literary and social conventions. Baraka moved to New York's bohemian East Village and became aligned with this group. He fell in with a group of white intellectuals and married a white Jewish woman, Hettie Cohen, who worked for the *Partisan Review.* Baraka saw his first piece published in that journal in 1958, the same year they married. Also that year, he and his wife started up the magazine *Yugen,* which showcased up–and–coming Beat poets such as Allen Ginsberg, Gregory Corso, Jack Kerouac, and others. It came out sporadically until 1962. Baraka in 1959 launched the publishing company Totem Press, which published his first poetry collection, *Preface to a Twenty–Volume Suicide Note,* in 1961. Baraka and Cohen had two children together, Kellie Elisabeth and Lisa Victoria Chapman.

During a trip to Cuba in 1960, Baraka met the nation's Communist leader, Fidel Castro, as well as several politically committed young artists and writers who urged him to take a more activist role with his writing. He later penned the award–winning essay "Cuba Libre" about his experiences there. Eventually, Baraka drifted away from the Beats and became more aligned with artists of the Third World. He formed a political group, the Organization of Young Men, and joined several groups as well, including On Guard, the Fair Play for Cuba Committee (he eventually became the chair and lecturer of the New York Chapter), and the League of Revolutionary Struggle, a Marxist organization.

In 1964, Baraka published his second poetry collection, *The Dead Lecturer,* which deals with his changing emotions regarding his social circle. Also that year, he became a celebrity with his off–Broadway play, *Dutchman,* which is his best–known work. It concerns two people who meet on the subway: a young, middle–class black man, Clay, and a white counter–culture woman named Lula. She taunts him about his repressed racial identity and goads him to display his black persona. He finally releases a tirade against her and all whites, and she stabs him to death. In the play, Baraka used symbolism and experimental techniques to delve into stereotypes about race and gender. Widely praised, *Dutchman* won the 1964 Obie Award for best American play.

By this point, Baraka was immersed in black nationalist thought, and he began to fully separate himself from whites, believing that an integrated society was impossible. He moved to Harlem in the mid–1960s and founded the Black Arts Repertory Theatre School, a haven not only for performance and art but also for revolution. But the place was

shut down in 1966 by police, reportedly because an arms cache was stored there. Though short–lived, the influential project shaped black drama around the nation. Meanwhile, Baraka divorced his wife in 1965.

Baraka returned to Newark, his home town, and started another arts project, Spirit House. In 1968 he changed his name to Imamu Ameer Baraka, the words being Bantu Muslim for "spiritual leader," "blessed," and "prince." He later changed "Ameer" to "Amiri" and dropped "Imamu." Also, in August of 1966 he married Sylvia Robinson, later known as Bibi Amina Baraka, and they have five children: Obalaji Malik Ali, Ras Jua Al Aziz, Shani Isis, Amiri Seku, and Ahi Mwenge.

In the 1970s, Baraka was established as a black nationalist leader, and he helped organize the Congress of African People in 1970 and the National Black Political Assembly in 1972. In the meantime, he published the poetry collection *Black Magic,* and continued to write essays on race as well. By the mid–1970s, his ideology took a turn, and he disassociated himself from black nationalism and instead grasped socialism, declaring himself a follower of Karl Marx, Vladimir Lenin, and Chairman Mao. His first Marxist–Leninist poetry collection, *Hard Facts,* came out in 1975, and a collection of Marxist plays, *The Motion of History,* was released in 1978.

Into the 1990s, Baraka continued to write poetry, composing "Y's, Why's, Wise: The Griot's Tale," an epic poem that some compared to the works of Walt Whitman, William Carlos Williams, and Charles Olson. (A griot is a traditional African oral storyteller.) A 30–year anthology titled *Transbluesency: Selected Poetry 65–95* came out in 1995, and a collection of new poetry, *Funk Lore,* was also released that year. Baraka is active in the arts and culture scene around Newark, and has submitted proposals to the city government there suggesting the creation of an arts district which would reflect the multinational diversity of the area. In 1998, he made a cameo appearance as a truth– telling street poet in the Warren Beatty film *Bulworth.*

Throughout Baraka's life, music has been a keen interest. In the 1960s, he wrote for several music publications, including *Downbeat, Metronome,* and *Jazz.* He also held a job for a time at the jazz magazine the *Record Trader.* His repertoire includes volumes of scholarship on African American music and musicians, including the classic 1963 work *Blues People: Negro Music in White America,* which has been translated into various languages. Also, with his wife, he co–wrote *The Music: Reflections on Jazz and Blues,* 1987, which combined his Marxist ideology with music criticism discussing the works of artists like Miles Davis, Chico Freeman, and Woody Shaw.

In 1972 and 1973, Baraka was sentenced to 48 consecutive weekends in a halfway house for an alleged dispute with his wife, and while there, he penned *The Autobiography of LeRoi Jones,* which was published in 1984. In addition to writing, Baraka is an educator. He lectures and gives readings from his work frequently, and has been a visiting professor at several institutions. In addition to teaching at the New School for Social Research in New York City from 1961 to 1964, he joined the State University of New York at Stony Brook as an assistant professor in 1980. In 1983 he was promoted to associate professor, and became a professor of Afro–American studies in 1985. He is now a professor emeritus in the department of Africana studies. In 1988, Baraka worked on Jesse Jackson's presidential campaign, and in 1989, he was given the American Book Awards Lifetime Achievement Award, the Langston Hughes Medal, and the PEN–Faulkner Award.

Selected writings

Plays

A Good Girl Is Hard to Find (produced Montclair, New Jersey, 1958; New York, 1965).

Dante (produced New York, 1961; as *The 8th Ditch,* produced New York, 1964). Included in *The System of Dante's Hell,* 1965.

The Baptism (produced New York, 1964; London, 1971). With *The Toilet,* Grove Press, 1967.

Dutchman (produced New York, 1964; London, 1967). With *The Slave,* Morrow, 1964; London, Faber, 1965; in *Black Theatre USA,* Free Press, 1996.

The Slave (produced New York, 1964; London, 1972). With *Dutchman,* Morrow, 1964; Faber, 1965.

The Toilet (produced New York, 1964), published with *The Baptism,* Grove Press, 1967.

Experimental Death Unit £1, also director; produced New York, 1965; included in *Four Black Revolutionary Plays,* 1969.

Jello (produced New York, 1965), Third World Press, 1970.

A Black Mass (also director; produced Newark, 1966). Included in *Four Black Revolutionary Plays,* 1969.

Arm Yrself or Harm Yrself (produced Newark, 1967), Jihad, 1967.

Slave Ship: A Historical Pageant (produced Newark, 1967; New York, 1969), Jihad, 1967.

Madheart (also director: produced San Francisco, 1967). Included in *Four Black Revolutionary Plays,* 1969.

Great Goodness of Life (A Coon Show), also director; produced Newark, 1967; New York, 1969. Included in *Four Black Revolutionary Plays,* 1969.

Home on the Range (produced Newark and New York, 1968). Published in *Drama Review,* Summer 1968.

Police, published in *Drama Review,* Summer 1968.

The Death of Malcolm X, in *New Plays from the Black Theatre,* edited by Ed Bullins, Bantam, 1969.

Rockgroup, published in *Cricket,* December 1969.

Four Black Revolutionary Plays, Bobbs Merrill, 1969; Calder and Boyars, 1971.

Insurrection (produced New York, 1969).

Junkies Are Full of (SHHH . . .) and *Bloodrites* (produced Newark, 1970); published in *Black Drama Anthology,* edited by Woodie King and Ron Milner, New American Library, 1971.

BA–RA–KA, in *Spontaneous Combustion: Eight New American Plays,* edited by Rochelle Owens, Winter House, 1972.

Black Power Chant, published in *Drama Review,* December 1972.

Columbia the Gem of the Ocean (produced Washington, D.C., 1973).

A Recent Killing (produced New York, 1973).

The New Ark's a Moverin (produced Newark, 1974).

The Sidnee Poet Heroical (also director; produced New York, 1975), Reed, 1979.

S–1 (also director; produced New York, 1976); included in *The Motion of History and Other Plays,* 1978.

(With Frank Chin and Leslie Marmon Silko) *America More or Less,* music by Tony Greco, lyrics by Arnold Weinstein (produced San Francisco, 1976).

The Motion of History (also director; produced New York, 1977); included in *The Motion of History and Other Plays,* 1978.

The Motion of History and Other Plays (includes *S–1* and *Slave Ship*); Morrow, 1978.

What was the Relationship of the Lone Ranger to the Means of Production? (produced New York, 1979).

At the Dim'crackr Convention (produced New York, 1980).

Boy and Tarzan Appear in a Clearing (produced New York, 1981).

Weimar 2 (produced New York, 1981).

(With George Gruntz) *Money: A Jazz Opera,* music by Gruntz (produced New York, 1982).

Primitive World, music by David Murray (produced New York, 1984).

General Hag's Skeezag: A Play. In Black Thunder New York, Mentor, 1992.

The Election Machine Warehouse, Simon & Schuster, 1997.

Screenplays

Dutchman, 1967.
Black Spring, 1967.
A Fable, 1971.
Supercoon, 1971.

Novel

The System of Dante's Hell, Grove Press, 1965; MacGibbon and Kee, 1966.

Short Stories

Tales, Grove Press, 1967; MacGibbon and Kee, 1969.

Poetry

April 13, Penny Poems, 1959.
Spring and Soforth, Penny Poems, 1960.
Preface to a Twenty Volume Suicide Note, Totem–Corinth, 1961.
The Disguise, privately printed, 1961.
The Dead Lecturer, Grove Press, 1964.
Black Art, Jihad, 1966.
A Poem for Black Hearts, Broadside Press, 1967.
Black Magic: Collected Poetry 1961–1967, Bobbs Merrill, 1969.
It's Nation Time, Third World Press, 1970.
(With Fundi [Billy Abernathy]), *In Our Terribleness: Some Elements and Meaning in Black Style*, Bobbs Merrill, 1970.
Spirit Reach, Jihad, 1972.
Afrikan Revolution, Jihad, 1973.
Hard Facts, Peoples War, 1976.
Selected Poetry, Morrow, 1979.
AM/TRAK, Phoenix Book Shop, 1979.
Spring Song, privately printed, 1979.
Reggae or Not!, Contact Two, 1981.
Thoughts for You!, Winston Derek, 1984.
LeRoi Jones Amiri, Thunder's Mouth Press, 1991.
An Amiri Baraka/LeRoi Jones Poetry Sampler, Satori Press, 1991.
Transbluesency: The Selected Poems of Amiri Baraka/LeRoi Jones (1961–1995), Marsilio, 1995.
Wise, Why's, Y's, Third World Press, 1995.
Funk Lore: New Poems, 1984–1995, Sun & Moon Press, 1996.

Other

Cuba Libre (essay), New York, Fair Play for Cuba Committee, 1961.

Blues People: Negro Music in White America, Morrow, 1963; MacGibbon and Kee, 1965; Payback Press, 1995.
Home: Social Essays, Morrow, 1966; MacGibbon and Kee, 1968.
Black Music, Morrow, 1968; MacGibbon and Kee, 1969.
(With Larry Neal and A.B. Spellman) *Trippin': A Need for Change*, Cricket, 1969(?).
A Black Value System, Jihad, 1970.
Gary and Miami: Before and After, Jihad, n.d.
Raise Race Rays Raze: Essays since 1965, Random House, 1971.
Strategy and Tactics of a Pan African Nationalist Party, National Involvement, 1971.
Beginning of National Movement, Jihad, 1972.
Kawaida Studies: The New Nationalism, Third World Press, 1972.
National Liberation and Politics, Congress of Afrikan People, 1974.
Crisis in Boston!!!!, Vita Wa Watu–People's War Publishing, 1974.
Afrikan Free School, Jihad, 1974.
Toward Ideological Clarity, Congress of Afrikan People, 1974.
The Creation of the New Ark, Howard University Press, 1975.
Selected Plays and Prose, Morrow, 1979.
The Autobiography of LeRoi Jones, Freundlich, 1983.
Daggers and Javelins: Essays 1974–1979, Morrow, 1984.
The Artist and Social Responsibility, Unity, 1986. (With Amina Baraka) *The Music: Reflections on Jazz and Blues*, Morrow, 1987.
The LeRoi Jones/Amiri Baraka Reader, edited by William J. Harris, Thunder's Mouth Press, 1991.
A Race Divided, New York, Emerge Communications, 1991.
The Afro American National Question, New Jersey, Unity & Struggle, 1992.
Heathens and Revolutionary Art: Poems and Lecture, White Fields Press, 1994.
(Edited by Charlie Reilly) *Conversations with Amiri Baraka*, University of Mississippi, 1994.
Eulogies, Marsilio Publishers, 1996.
Home: Social Essays, Ecco Press, 1998.
(Editor) *Four Young Lady Poets*, Totem–Corinth, 1962.
(Editor) *The Moderns: New Fiction in America*, Corinth, 1963; MacGibbon and Kee, 1965.
(Editor, with Larry Neal) *Black Fire: An Anthology of Afro–American Writing*, Morrow, 1968.
(Editor) *African Congress: A Documentary of the First Modern Pan–African Congress*, Morrow, 1972.
(Editor, with Diane di Prima) *The Floating Bear: A Newsletter, Numbers 1–37*, Laurence McGilvery, 1974.
(Editor, with Amina Baraka) *Confirmation: An Anthology of African American Women*, Morrow, 1983.

Sources

Books

Baraka, Amiri, *The Autobiography of LeRoi Jones*, Freundlich Books, 1984.
Contemporary Black Biography, volume 1, Gale Research, 1992.
Contemporary Dramatists, sixth edition, St. James Press, 1999.
Contemporary Popular Writers, St. James Press, 1997.
Notable Black American Men, Gale Research, 1998.

Periodicals

Chicago Citizen, January 21, 1999, p.1.
Essence, May 1985, p. 82.
New York Beacon, October 7, 1998, p. 30.

Online

"Amiri Baraka," *Contemporary Authors Online*, Gale Group web site, http://www.galenet.com (February 22, 2000).

Charlene Barshefsky

U.S. trade representative

Born c. 1951 in Illinois; daughter of a chemical engineer and a schoolteacher; married Edward Cohen; children: daughters Mari and Devra. *Education:* University of Wisconsin, B.A., 1972; Catholic University, J.D., 1975.

Addresses: *Office*—Office of the U.S. Trade Representative, 600 17th St. NW, Washington, DC 20508–0001.

Career

Steptoe & Johnson law firm, partner, 1975–93; Executive Office of the President, Washington, DC, deputy U.S. trade representative, 1993–96, U.S. trade representative, 1996 .

Sidelights

As the U.S. Trade Representative, Charlene Barshefsky became a high–profile member of President Bill Clinton's cabinet due to the influence that post has on business in an increasingly global marketplace. With such rapid growth throughout the 1990s in computers and telecommunications, it became much more possible for a company to expand into international arenas. With this came more complex relationships with other countries, however, and Barshefsky has treaded these waters skillfully. Not only is she a shrewd negotiator, but she is also known for her uncanny ability to gauge the reactions of the people with whom she is working and tailor her strategies to them. As Barshefsky put

it to Mary D'Ambrosio in *Working Woman*, "At times, one must be tough, bullheaded, and stubborn. But catching a fly with honey works, too."

Barshefsky was born about 1951 in Illinois and grew up in Chicago. Her parents, immigrants from Russia and Poland, moved to the United States as adolescents and did not speak English. Her father trained to become a rabbi, then became a chemical engineer in Chicago. Her mother worked as a substitute teacher. Both prized education and were disappointed when Barshefsky chose to pursue a law degree, which they considered to be a trade, instead of getting an advanced degree in an academic field as her old brother and sister had done. Only Barshefsky's maternal grandmother, who lived with the family, was pleased because she considered it important for women to support themselves.

After receiving her bachelor's degree with honors from the University of Wisconsin in 1972, Barshefsky enrolled at the Columbus School of Law at Washington, D.C.'s Catholic University. There, she obtained her juris doctorate in 1975, graduating seventh in her class. Thanks to her excellent record, she landed a job at Steptoe & Johnson, one of Washington's most prominent law firms.

At Steptoe & Johnson, Barshefsky worked in the trade division, which was a budding area of law and, unusually, not male–dominated. Her career took off immediately, and in 1990 she was named co–chair of the firm's international division. Her salary was about half a million dollars a year at this point. Then, in 1993, the new U.S. trade representative, Mickey Kantor, offered Barshefsky the post as the deputy in charge of trade to Asia and Latin America.

Even though Barshefsky had never been to Asia and had no political experience, she knew she was a quick learner and could handle the job. However, she was concerned about the effect on her family, since the job required a great amount of travel time. Despite her high–powered law career, Barshefsky served as room mother to both of her young daughters' classes and assisted in the older ones' art class a couple of times a month. "The notion then of throwing routine aside and plunging into something new was very threatening to me," she remarked to Elsa Walsh in the *New Yorker*.

Barshefsky's husband, Edward Cohen, was excited about the idea. He was keen on politics, being a lawyer himself and having grown up in a suburb of Washington, D.C. However, he, too, had some reservations about the effect the job would have on the family. Barshefsky's daughters, Mari and Devra, ages nine and four at the time of the job offer, also did not like the idea of their mother traveling so much, but Devra said, "If there's any chance you can meet the President, you should do it," Barshefsky related to Walsh.

In February of 1993, Barshefsky accepted the position and by June was back from Japan, where she had tried to convince the government to accept more imports from the United States. Immediately, she appeared to be a natural negotiator; her hard bargaining stances caused colleagues to nickname her "Stonewall." Though talks broke down and she returned home, the Japanese Prime Minister soon called her back in hopes of establishing a common ground. When she went back, Barshefsky decided to deal with the Japanese on a product–by–product basis instead of sweeping agreements, and thus managed to free up barriers to exporting paper, glass, wood, semiconductors, and agricultural products. Barshefsky also landed agreements for Japan to purchase telecommunications services, medical equipment, and insurance.

However, enforcing agreements with foreign powers is often more problematic than forging them, and Barshefsky was diligent in this area. When Ja-

pan failed to keep up their promises, she consulted the World Trade Organization (WTO), which monitors global trade. This was a politically savvy move, because the WTO is a multilateral body and thus the decision was not seen as an American attack on Japan.

In one of her most high–profile accomplishments, Barshefsky dealt with China regarding copyright laws. U.S. foreign policy dictated that the Chinese had to honor copyrights on films, music, and software, but many companies there were obviously flouting the rules and pirating videos, CDs, and computer programs. By 1995, American firms estimated this was costing them $2 billion a year, and as a result, the U.S. government was considering imposing $1 billion in sanctions. This, however, was undesirable for both nations, since many U.S. businesses were hoping to soon reach China as a new market.

Working with Chinese Foreign Trade Minister Wu Yi, Barshefsky managed to put together a 22–page document ten hours past the original deadline in February of 1995. It called for China to raid factories and retailers where pirated goods were made and sold, to set up task forces to keep closer tabs on violators, and to give greater authority to customs officials to stop exporting the pirated merchandise. In addition, the nation opened its doors to American software and audiovisual goods, and agreed to set up joint ventures for producing wares in China.

However, as many suspected, it was difficult to enforce the agreement. Barshefsky returned to China later in 1995 and outlined several points where the government had not lived up to its end of the bargain. Chinese officials admitted that pirating problems continued, but noted that it was much more problematic to control than they had figured. Barshefsky then explained tactfully that China had to become more responsible for its actions if it wanted to operate in a global marketplace and eventually join the WTO. She also pointed out that the government there had virtually eliminated pornography in Guangdong Province in a heartbeat and that she felt they could do the same for piracy.

In April of 1996, Kantor became secretary of commerce and President Bill Clinton named Barshefsky acting U.S. trade representative. She took over the post permanently when Kantor's term was officially up in 1997. In order to approve her nomination, Congress had to pass a waiver to a law that stated that no one who had ever acted on behalf of a foreign government in a trade dispute could be instituted as a trade representative or deputy trade representative. When Barshefksy had practiced law, she worked on behalf of the Canadian Embassy and Province of Quebec in a lumber–related case. Most legislators opposed the law and overwhelmingly supported Barshefsky's nomination.

In 1997, Barshefsky lobbied hard to get "fast–track" trade authority, which would require legislators to vote on trade issues without adding any amendments. She felt this would help "increase access to foreign markets and shift trade conditions in our favor," as she noted, according to a *Congressional Digest* of a speech given to the House Ways and Means Committee's Subcommittee on Trade. However, many congresspeople were against it because they wanted the ability to put in statements against practices like child labor and environmental protections.

After this, Barshefsky made waves in Europe over bananas. Though neither the United States nor Europe grows or exports bananas, some American businesses, such as Chiquita, operate out of Latin America, and the European Union (E.U.) for years refused to buy from there, instead purchasing them form former European colonies in the Pacific, Caribbean, and Africa. In response, Barshefsky supported 100 percent taxes on luxury goods like gourmet foods and cashmere, shocking the Europeans and dismaying many Americans with rich taste.

In addition, Barshefsky was involved with the controversy over hormone–treated beef. The E.U. since 1989 had refused to import beef treated with hormones, citing possible health risks. The WTO in 1998 deemed the ban illegal, saying there was scant proof of this, but the E.U. ignored the ruling. Then, in fact, the E.U. decided to start banning all American beef after it found 12 percent of 258 samples contained traces of hormones. Barshefsky tried to broker a deal to label all hormone–treated beef, but European officials rejected the offer. By April of 1999, though, the E.U. began accepting hormone–free beef.

In late 1999, Barshefsky headed further dealings with China. After the talks, the two nations signed an historic deal that would pave the way for China to join the WTO. The agreement stated that China would cut tariffs on a variety of products, from wheat to cars and more; eliminate middlemen, who are licensed importers and exporters that have long been a detriment to foreign investment; allow Hollywood and other foreign film enterprises to distribute 40 films per year; and open up the nation to foreign banks, insurance companies, and telecom-

munications industries. However, the Chinese negotiators at the last minute, after the deal was done, wanted to fine–tune some of the points. Barshefsky related her characteristically blunt reaction in *Time International*: "I said, 'Oh, please. Too complicated. Can't possibly deal with it. What time is the signing?' And that was the end of the negotiation."

Barshefsky's name was often in the news in late 1999 and early 2000 as well for her involvement in the WTO Ministerial Conference held in Seattle, Washington. She had much optimism that the talks would smooth the way for negotiating more open global commerce, insisting that initial rounds were hopeful. Other leaders, though, disagreed with her assessment, saying they had reached little common ground in early sessions. In the end, the conference was a disaster, with talks disintegrating as the E.U. accused the United States of calling for too many concessions, specifically in terms of agriculture. In addition, many observers felt that the conference came at a bad time, since U.S. elections were scheduled for 2000 and several foreign negotiators figured that U.S. delegates would not want to appear weak by making concessions.

Above all, though, the WTO talks were marred by high–profile protests by groups ranging from unions to environmentalists to anarchists. Some activists concentrated on specific sore spots, such as genetically modified foods, while others espoused their views that America's labor force would be edged out by cheaper employees abroad. Though thousands protested peacefully, a select few thugs decked out in bandanas and ski masks also joined the scene and wreaked havoc, vandalizing property and looting stores. The mayor of Seattle ended up imposing a curfew and calling in the National Guard, further embarrassing U.S. interests at the talks. Nevertheless, Barshefsky clung to hopes that future talks would hold greater promise, since earlier negotiations with nations like China came together after dismal beginnings and false starts.

Known just as much for her silk scarves as for her iron will, Barshefsky has earned the name "Dragon Lady" from Japanese negotiators. She described the crux of her successful negotiating techniques to Ann Scott Tyson in the *Christian Science Monitor,* noting that they included "knowing what you want, which sounds rather elementary but is so critical. Persistence. And a recognition that there are 1,000 points to the same goal.... So there's a certain agility you need as a negotiator, the ability to see the opportunity, and the ability to think through the thousand variations and permutations so that you can get to where you want to go." When traveling, Barshefsky rarely sightsees, preferring to do business and get back home to Washington, D.C. to her family. To relax, she enjoys listening to the music of Bob Dylan.

Sources

Business Week, July 21, 1997, p. 34; January 31, 2000, p. 50.

Christian Science Monitor, April 30, 1999, p. 1. *Congressional Digest,* December 1997, p. 298.

Congressional Quarterly Weekly Report, February 1, 1997, p. 290; March 1, 1997, p. 529.

New Yorker, March 18, 1996, p. 86.

New York Times, February 27, 1995, p. A1; May 17, 1996, p. D1.

Time International, November 29, 1999, p. 18.

USA Today, September 19, 1995; November 7, 1997, p. 2A.

Wall Street Journal, November 16, 1999, p. A1.

Washington Post, December 2, 1999, p. A40.

Working Woman, June 199, p. 17.

Warren Beatty

Archive Photos

Actor

Born Henry Warren Beatty; March 30, 1937, in Richmond, VA; son of Ira O. (an educational psychologist and public school administrator) and Kathlyn (a drama teacher and homemaker; maiden name, MacLean) Beatty; brother of Shirley MacLaine (an actress, dancer, director, producer, and writer); married Annette Bening (an actress), March 3, 1992; children: Kathlyn, Benjamin, Isabel Ira Ashley. *Education:* Attended the Stella Adler Theatre School, 1957; graduated from Northwestern University, 1959.

Addresses: *Agent*—Creative Artists Agency, 9830 Wilshire Blvd., Beverly Hills, CA 90212.

Career

Actor, director, and producer. Member, Screen Actors Guild, Writers Guild of America, Directors Guild of America, Sigma Chi. Stage appearances include *A Loss of Roses*, New York City, 1960, and stock productions in Connecticut, New Jersey, and New York. Television appearances include series *Love of Life*, c. 1957; *The Many Loves of Dobie Gillis*, 1959–60; episodes of *Kraft Television Theatre*, 1957; *Studio One*, 1957; *Alcoa Presents*, 1960; *Wagon Train*, 1964; *What's My Line*, 1965; *Vibe*, 1998; and various appearances on talk shows, specials, and awards presentations.

Film appearances include *Splendor in the Grass*, 1961; *The Roman Spring of Mrs. Stone*, 1961; *All Fall Down*, 1962; *Lilith*, 1963; *Mickey One*, 1965; *Promise Her Anything*, 1966; *Kaleidoscope*, 1966; *Bonnie and Clyde*, 1967;

The Only Game in Town, 1970; *McCabe and Mrs. Miller*, 1971; *Dollars*, 1972; *Year of the Woman*, 1973; *The Parallax View*, 1974; *The Fortune*, 1975; *Shampoo*, 1975; *Heaven Can Wait*, 1978; *Reds*, 1981; *George Stevens: A Filmmaker's Journey* (documentary), 1984; *Ishtar*, 1987; *Dick Tracy*, 1990; *Bugsy*, 1991; *Truth or Dare*, 1991; *Love Affair*, 1994; and *Bulworth*, 1998.

Other film work includes executive producer, *The Pick-Up Artist*, 1987; producer, *Bonnie and Clyde*, 1967; *Ishtar*, 1987; and *Bugsy*, 1991; producer and cowriter, *Shampoo*, 1975; *Heaven Can Wait*, 1978; *Reds*, 1981; *Dick Tracy*, 1990; *Love Affair*, 1994; and *Bulworth*, 1998; and director, *Heaven Can Wait*, 1978; *Reds*, 1981; *Dick Tracy*, 1990; and *Bulworth*, 1998.

Awards: Theatre World Award, 1960; Golden Globe Award, new star of the year, 1962; Hasty Pudding Man of the Year, Hasty Pudding Theatricals, Harvard University, 1975; National Association of Theatre Owners (NATO) star of the year, 1975; National Society of Film Critics Award (with Robert Towne), best original screenplay, 1975, for *Shampoo*; NATO director of the year and NATO producer of the year, both 1978; Golden Globe Award, best actor in a musical/comedy, 1979, for *Heaven Can Wait*; Academy Award, Golden Globe Award, and Los Angeles Film Critics Association Award, all for best director, and Directors Guild of America citation for outstanding directorial achievement for feature films, all 1981, for *Reds;* also numerous nominations for Academy Awards, Golden Globe Awards, and others.

Sidelights

One of the most multitalented people in Hollywood, Warren Beatty has excelled as an actor, writer, director, and producer, and is the only person to have been nominated for an Academy Award in all four categories on two separate occasions, for *Heaven Can Wait* and *Reds.* After beginning his career as a cocky sex symbol known just as much for his off–screen exploits with women as for his acting prowess, he became a leading star in the 1960s and matured into a respected member of the entertainment world. In 1998, Beatty was the creative force behind the intriguing film *Bulworth,* an extended political commentary about a crooked senator who finds redemption in the truth. The reaction to the work was mixed, but served to stir up attention to Beatty's long–time political involvement with the Democratic party. In 1999, he made headlines not for his performances or romantic encounters (he married actor Annette Bening in 1992 and soon settled into family life), but because he began hinting that he might seek nomination for the 2000 presidential run.

Henry Warren Beatty was born on March 3, 1937, in Richmond, Virginia, to Ira O. and Kathlyn (MacLean) Beatty. His father, was an educational psychologist and public school administrator, and his mother was a homemaker who also taught drama and directed plays with local community theater groups. They gave him and his sister, now famous actor Shirley MacLaine, a relatively typical middle–class upbringing in Arlington, Virginia. McLaine always showed a propensity for entertaining, but Beatty was more introverted, preferring solitary pursuits such as reading and playing the piano.

By the time Beatty attended Washington and Lee High School in Arlington, where his father was the principal, he had developed an interest in athletics and became a football star and president of his senior class. However, by that time his passion for theater had been sparked. He declined a number of football scholarships in order to enroll at Northwestern University in Evanston, Illinois, where he started to study drama. "I stopped playing football," he remarked to Lynn Hirschberg in the *New York Times Magazine.* "I was in the process of consigning myself to a more effete way of life." After

his freshman year, he traveled to New York City and enjoyed it so much, he dropped out of college to devote himself to acting. He began studying with renowned drama coach Stella Adler, who encouraged him.

After working a series of odd jobs, including as a bricklayer's assistant, dishwasher, and cocktail lounge pianist in order to pay the bills, Beatty found jobs in television in 1957, acting in soap operas and movies for programs like *Kraft Television Theatre* and *Studio One.* He also worked in stock theater productions around the Northeast. Eventually, he caught the eye of a director and was offered a five–year, $400–a–week contract with MGM, an impressive sum for a struggling actor at the time. "I liked L.A. from the get–go," Beatty told Hirschberg.

Beatty's first film was supposed to be *Strike Heaven in the Face,* but MGM eventually canceled it. Subsequently, he took a part on the television situation comedy series *The Many Loves of Dobie Gillis,* playing the wealthy, snooty Milton Armitage. Before his work on that program had aired, however, Beatty decided to return to New York to do plays, and borrowed $2,600 from the agency representing him in order to buy out his contract with MGM. "I wasn't doing anything that meant anything" in Hollywood, he explained to Hirschberg. The major item that had caught everyone's attention was his romance with British–born actor Joan Collins, which provided a seemingly endless stream of gossip and began his longstanding image as a playboy.

In New York, Beatty saw his Broadway debut in *A Loss of Roses,* 1960. Though the play was generally panned, most critics commended Beatty's performance. After this, he was recommended to star in the 1961 film *Splendor in the Grass,* as the handsome, adolescent son of a well–to–do family and his doomed relationship with his high school sweetheart, played by Natalie Wood. This sentimental tale established Beatty as a new heartthrob, and led to another high–profile part the same year in *The Roman Spring of Mrs. Stone,* an adaptation of the Tennessee Williams novella about a rich widow (Vivien Leigh) and the young gigolo who leeches off of her. Continuing to play seductive yet troubled characters, Beatty then starred in *All Fall Down,* 1962, about an unstable narcissist who embarks on one love affair after another.

After a two–year hiatus, Beatty returned to the screen with 1964's *Lilith,* playing a psychiatrist who falls in love with one of the patients in a mental institution and eventually declines into illness himself. Though the effort was a disaster, Beatty's anti-hero persona led him to be cast in *Mickey One*, 1965, an artsy thriller about a standup comedian who changed his identity to protect himself from mobsters. Though some critics initially praised it, the effort failed at the box office. Looking for a vehicle to please fans, Beatty made *Promise Her Anything*, a comedy about two laid-back lovers in Greenwich Village, which illustrated his talent for lighter material. During the filming, he began living with his costar, Leslie Caron, and was named in her divorce lawsuit brought about by her husband, Peter Hall, then the artistic director of Britain's Royal Shakespeare Company.

Concerned about the quality of his projects, Beatty took matters into his own hands, finding his next script on his own and producing the effort. In 1967's *Bonnie and Clyde*, he starred as ruthless Depression-era killer Clyde Barrow, while Faye Dunaway played his cohort Bonnie Parker. The work sealed Beatty's reputation as an innovator and made him a millionaire, since he agreed to a slice of the profits in lieu of a set salary. Though some critics originally balked at the graphic violence, the stylized way it was presented came to be seen as having an enormous impact on film techniques. The movie racked up ten Academy Award nominations, including best actor and actress. Beatty's next project, *The Only Game in Town*, 1970, costarring Elizabeth Taylor, did not fare nearly as well. In 1971 he starred in Robert Altman's *McCabe and Mrs. Miller*, about a gambler on the frontier who builds a brothel for his girlfriend.

After a few more minor projects, Beatty returned to producing with 1975's *Shampoo*, which he cowrote with Robert Towne. This story of a Beverly Hills hair stylist who tries to achieve success with his sexual exploits was misunderstood by many to be mainly an autobiographical, semi-pornographic tale of womanizing, but some realized that it was a sociopolitical satire. Set during election time in 1968, when Richard Nixon became president, the movie examined the subsequent changing moral atmosphere in the United States. By this point, Beatty had developed a reputation as being keenly attuned to politics and active in the Democratic party. He had worked on the 1968 campaign for Robert Kennedy, and served as a fund-raiser and entertainment chairman for Senator George McGovern during his 1972 presidential bid, at one point convincing Paul Simon and Art Garfunkel to reunite for a concert at Madison Square Garden which reaped a million dollars for the cause. Later, he served as a top adviser to presidential hopeful Gary Hart in 1984 and 1988.

In 1978, Beatty not only cowrote, produced, and starred in a film, he also ventured into directing for the first time, sharing the credit with Buck Henry in *Heaven Can Wait*, a remake of the 1941 classic romantic comedy *Here Comes Mr. Jordan*, about a man who is reincarnated. It was a huge popular success and was nominated for nine Academy Awards (but only won one, for best art direction); Beatty also received a 1979 Golden Globe Award for best actor in a musical/comedy for his acting. His next effort, *Reds*, was even more ambitious. Not only did Beatty produce, cowrite, direct, and star in it, but the subject matter and budget exceeded anything he had tried previously. The work deals with American journalist John Reed, one of the founders of the Communist Labor party in the United States and author of *Ten Days That Shook the World*—a first-hand account of the 1917 Russian Revolution—and his stormy relationship with his wife, Louise Bryant, a free-thinking writer. This epic was nominated for 12 Oscars, but only received three, including one for Beatty for best direction.

Coming off of *Reds*, however, Beatty experienced a huge debacle with 1987's *Ishtar*, which tried to capture the spirit of the old "road" movies that starred Bing Crosby and Bob Hope. In it, he and Dustin Hoffman teamed as a pair of washed-up lounge singers who mistakenly get involved in international intrigue. The budget spiraled to make it the costliest comedy ever made at the time, but it bombed at the box office. Beatty was back in fan's good graces as the title character in *Dick Tracy*, though some complained he was getting too old for the role. Then came *Bugsy*, 1991, about gangster Bugsy Siegel, who made over the slow-paced desert town of Las Vegas into the exciting gambling capital nicknamed "Sin City." Beatty excelled in this gritty part.

Throughout his career, Beatty carried a reputation as a Casanova *Esquire* even ran an article titled "Beds," a takeoff of his film Reds, that was mainly a compilation of testimonies about his personality and charm from his numerous past lovers and friends, some anonymous, others not. So it was a bit of a surprise when he married fellow actor Bening in 1992 and settled into domesticity. They had secretly become involved while filming *Bugsy*, and she announced she was pregnant with his child in July of 1991. In a case of art imitating life, in 1994 they starred together in the picture *Love Affair*, regarding a bed-hopping celebrity jet-setter who finally meets the right woman.

Fully meshing his political beliefs with his film career, Beatty in 1998 released *Bulworth*, which he cowrote from his own original idea. It focuses on a Democratic senator, depressed due to the corruption of politics and his role in the game, who hires a hit man to kill him during his reelection campaign. Freed from the shackles of answering to big business, he begins compulsively telling the grim truth to his constituents, openly explaining that politicians only give favors to those who contribute big money, for example. During a speech at a black church, he meets a young woman, Nina, and is exposed to hip–hop and rap music, as well as the lifestyle of those harshly affected by dirty politics. He begins to rap his messages about the deep pockets of the health care industry, race relations, the situation in the Middle East, and more. The rhymes allow Beatty to get his liberal political commentary across in an entertaining manner. "If I'd done it straight it would have been C–Span," he remarked to Jonathan Alter in *Newsweek.* "And everyone would be asleep."

While critics delivered a mixed bag of reactions to *Bulworth,* the film drew attention once more to Beatty's political activism, which had been rather dormant in the 1990s as far as getting involved with the Democratic party. Many admired the strong opinions he revealed in the story and subsequent interviews, to which he readily agreed in order to strongly promote the project. Some began to ask if he was interested in a real–life political seat. Initially, he shrugged off the idea, but in the summer of 1999, as others began throwing their hats in the ring for the 2000 presidential bid, Beatty remarked that he might consider running as well. Though most considered him a long shot, his comments generated a flurry of press.

Gossip columns have chronicled Beatty's actions since his first days in Hollywood, but the actor is generally quiet about his private life, and at one point, refused to give interviews for 12 years. For many years, Beatty lived out of a suite in the Beverly Wilshire hotel, even staying there often after building a home in the mid–1970s in Los Angeles. After it was destroyed in the 1992 earthquake, he found new quarters in a large Spanish–style home in the hills above Beverly Hills, where he lives with his wife, Bening, and his children, Kathlyn, Benjamin, and Isabel Ira Ashley.

Sources

Books

Contemporary Theatre, Film and Television, volume 22, Gale Group, 1999.
International Dictionary of Films and Filmmakers, Volume 3: Actors and Actresses, third edition, St. James Press, 1996.

Periodicals

Entertainment Weekly, December 17, 1993, p. 8; May 22, 1998, p. 42.
Esquire, May 1990, p. 151.
GQ, April 1996, p. 76.
Newsweek, May 18, 1998, p. 66; August 23, 1999, p. 4.
New York Times, March 17, 1974; December 9, 1991; August 12, 1999, p. A14; August 15, 1999, sec. 4, p. 15; October 1, 1999, p. A21.
New York Times Magazine, May 10, 1998, p. 20.
People, May 25, 1998, p. 126.
Rolling Stone, May 31, 1990, p. 44.
St. Louis Post–Dispatch, June 1, 1998, p. D3.
Time, December 9, 1991, p. 90; August 23, 1999, p. 35.
USA Today, May 22, 1998, p. 5E.

Online

"Warren Beatty," Internet Movie Database web site, http://us.imdb.com (November 8, 1999).
"Warren Beatty," Mr. Showbiz web site, http://mrshowbiz.go.com (November 8, 1999).

Beck

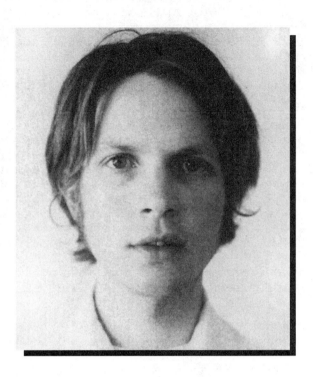

Singer, songwriter, and musician

Born July 8, 1970, in Los Angeles, CA; son of David Campbell (a street musician) and Bibbe Hansen (an office worker and singer).

Addresses: *Record company*—DGC Records, 9130 Sunset Blvd., Los Angeles, CA 90069.

Career

Began as street musician, c. 1986; released first single, "Loser," on Bong Load Custom Records, 1993; signed with DGC label, 1994, and released debut album, *Mellow Gold,* 1994. Toured with Lollapalooza Festival, 1995. First art exhibition opened May, 1998, at the Santa Monica Museum of Art.

Awards: Grammy Awards for best male rock vocal performance, for "Where It's At," and for best alternative music performance, for *Odelay,* both 1997; five MTV Video Music Awards, 1997; Grammy Award for alternative music performance, 2000.

Sidelights

When singer songwriter Beck surged onto the musical horizon in 1993 with the enigmatic yet catchy "Loser," he was hailed by some as an innovator, while numerous others derided him as a flash in the pan with a gimmick that would soon wear thin. When his first major follow–up, *Odelay,* came out in 1997, however, most seemed to recognize him as a new talent with a head–spinning ability to combine several musical genres in a listenable and intelligent manner. In addition, though some still termed his lyrics nonsense, others discerned irony and homage. Beck has often been compared to Bob Dylan because of his literary vocals, but some say he is closer to Frank Zappa the way he imports pop culture into his songs. The musician himself often refers back to early blues and folk icons as his inspiration. In any event, the combination of styles and influences has produced an entirely new sound. When Beck released *Midnite Vultures* in 1999, he once again stunned and pleased many critics with his inventiveness.

Beck Hansen was born on July 8, 1970, in Los Angeles, California. He was influenced early on by his father, David Campbell, a bluegrass street musician. His mother, Bibbe Hansen, an office worker, raised Beck and his younger half–brother, Channing, in some shady but character–laden areas of Los Angeles. She, too, was drawn to entertaining, joining a mostly–transvestite underground punk band called Black Fag. In ninth grade, Beck dropped out of school, telling Jancee Dunn in *Rolling Stone,* "I'm sure there's something good about high school, but not any of the ones I went to."

For a short time during his childhood, Beck lived with his grandparents in Kansas, where his grandfather was a Presbyterian minister. There, he says he was subconsciously influenced by church hymns. In addition, he spent time in Europe with his other grandfather, artist Al Hansen, a member of the Fluxus avant–garde movement of the 1950s and 1960s. As Beck related in *Rolling Stone*, "He collects cigarette butts and glues them together and makes pictures of naked ladies, then sprays everything silver. His stuff was taking trash and making it art. I guess I try to do that, too."

Subsequently, Beck worked various odd jobs, once working as a stock boy at Sears until he was fired. Meanwhile, he spent much of his youth pedaling around Hollywood Boulevard, checking out the punk and hip–hop scene. At age 16, he got a guitar and began his career as a street musician, taking after his father. Although he once admitted that his first musical recording purchase was probably the soundtrack to *Xanadu*, he was also greatly inspired by folk and blues legends Woody Guthrie and Mississippi John Hurt.

In addition to playing near Lafayette Park where he would confuse the local Salvadoran soccer players with his covers of Leadbelly, Beck would play guitar and sing on city buses. "Some drunk would start yelling at me, calling me Axl Rose," he recalled in *Rolling Stone*. "So I'd start singing about Axl Rose and the levee and bus passes and strychnine, mixing the whole thing up."

When he was 17, Beck took a bus to New York City, where he slept on friends' couches while he hunted for work and his own place. During that time, he hung out in the East Village and became exposed to the anti–folk acoustic punk scene happening there. However, he eventually wore out his welcome and returned to Los Angeles.

Back in California, Beck eked out a living working at a video store in Silverlake. On the side, he would perform at coffeehouses and small clubs in between the main acts. He eventually piqued the interest of the partners at Bong Load Custom Records as well as a talent director at BMG Music Publishing. Hearing that Beck would like to try some rap, Bong Load put him in touch with Karl Stephenson, a producer known for his work in hip–hop. Together they cut the 12–inch single "Loser" in a friend's living room, releasing it in March of 1993.

Cutting–edge radio stations around the country were instantly enthused with "Loser," and MTV played his quirky video repeatedly. The song features an entirely original blend of funk, folk, rap, country, and blues on top of an infectious beat.

Many reviewers dismissed the experimental lyrics as convoluted, and it was not difficult to see why, as the song opens, "In the time of chimpanzees I was a monkey, butane in my veins so I'm out to get the junkie with the plastic eyeballs, spray–paint the vegetables, dog food stalls with the beefcake pantyhose." However, as Beck explained to Mark Kemp in *Rolling Stone*, "I couldn't sing my songs every night if I thought, 'Oh, I just scribbled this down—it doesn't really mean anything. It's got to have some connection to me…. I've written hundreds of songs, and I got bored of saying things the same way. I wanted to use the language differently."

Soon, the self–deprecating refrain of "I'm a loser, baby, so why don't you kill me?" became a wry anthem for disaffected youth, and the media dubbed Beck the slacker poster boy. Mark Lewman in *Entertainment Weekly*, for instance, called him "Generation X's latest Pied Piper." However, as Beck retorted in *Rolling Stone*, "I *never* had any slack. I was working a $4 an hour job trying to stay alive. I mean, that slacker kind of stuff is for people who have the time to be depressed about everything." He also noted to Mark Brown of the *Knight–Ridder/ Tribune News Service*, "People have this image of me as a pot–smoking, channel–surfing teen. I didn't even own a TV for most of my adult life."

Subsequently, major labels courted Beck for a contract. He ended up signing with the Geffen subsidiary DGC, even though their deal did not offer the most money, because they allowed him a remarkable level of creative freedom as well as letting him continue to record with independent labels on the side if he wished. Though some dismissed Beck as a one–hit wonder, he would soon disprove the criticism. In 1994 he released his first full album, *Mellow Gold*, which contained "Loser" and a slew of other creative gems that left many critics impressed.

Next, instead of issuing the much–anticipated big follow–up, Beck put out two independent albums. He issued the noise–laden *Stereopathic Soul Manure* on the punk label Flipside and the folk– and blues–heavy *One Foot in the Grave* on the label K, both in 1994. Then, in 1995 he toured with the Lollapalooza Festival, where he remembered seeing "blue plastic seats. Empty. Very empty," as he told Dunn in *Rolling Stone*. Though his live shows usually attracted a contingent of admirers, he did not pander to them. Instead of faithfully replaying "Loser," he might change the lyrics, or not play it at all. He was also known to launch into an extended bluegrass or blues riff—or even stand on stage and chant one word repeatedly—as crowds buzzed in heated anticipation of hearing his big hit.

Meanwhile, Beck had met some of his blues idols, such as Junior Kimbrough, and won admiration from the likes of Johnny Cash and Tom Petty, who recorded cover versions of his songs on their 1996 albums. He then went back into the studio and concentrated on putting together a more focused work, working with the acclaimed Dust Brothers (John King and Michael Simpson). In 1996, he released *Odelay*, a stunning effort that Brown deemed a "finely textured, hip–hop/rock masterpiece." Most critics were similarly smitten, as were fans: Though the effort had only sold about 750,000 copies by the end of the year, it was voted album of the year by *Rolling Stone* readers and critics, and Beck was voted artist of the year by *Spin* magazine. *Odelay* eventually reached platinum status.

Beck went on to win two Grammy Awards in 1997, for the cut "Where It's At" (best male vocal performance) and for best alternative music performance, for the entire *Odelay* album, which was also nominated in the best album category. He also won five MTV Video Music Awards. One of the biggest tracks on *Odelay*, "Where It's At" is a tribute to the entrepreneur–like quality of rap; another hit, "Devil's Haircut," criticizes the stifling level of physical vanity in America. Beck told Ray Rogers in *Interview* that the album title *Odelay* "comes from Chicano slang—orale! It's sort of an exclamation of 'all right, things are all right.'" In the *New York Times Magazine*, Gerald Marzorati wrote, "Beck can go from the Donovan psychedelic–folk thing to the Beastie Boys hip–hop thing to the Keith Richards honky–tonk thing like *that*, which is funny but not *only*, and not in a cynical way." He also noted Beck's ability "to be sincere *and* ironic."

After this success, Beck toured frequently, but also found time to express himself in a non–musical format. In May of 1998 he staged his first art exhibit, consisting of collages not unlike his grandfather's works. Unfortunately, his grandfather died in 1995 and though he was proud of the success of "Loser," did not get to see Beck collect his Grammy awards or view his creations at the opening at the Santa Monica Museum of Art. The Thread Waxing Space gallery in New York City hosted the exhibit beginning that September. Also there, Beck's brother Channing Hansen staged one of his grandfather's performance pieces, which consisted of reading a list of names then wrapping his head in masking tape.

Also in 1998, Beck veered in a new direction musically with *Mutations*. Cutting out the hip–hop and samples, the low–key work consisted of country waltzes, slow ballads, and a bossa nova tune, "Tropicalia," influenced by the Brazilian movement of the same name of the 1960s. Other tunes included sitar music or harpsichord. Beck still stamped all songs with his unconventional lyrics, but he did not consider this laid–back work to be the true follow–up to *Odelay*, and did not tour to promote it. Instead, he returned to the studio to start on the next project even before releasing *Mutations*, which won a Grammy for best alternative music performance in 2000.

By the end of 1999, Beck was again embraced wholeheartedly by critics with his released *Midnite Vultures*, which was billed as his "party record." "Laughter is the immediate response to most of the songs on *Midnite Vultures* so much so that it could be called a comedy record," wrote Ben Ratliff in the *New York Times*. He added, "Here, at last, is a rock star who is using irony the right way. His appropriations from pop history are so precise that he forces you to admire, rather than snicker at, the materials he is working with." Ratliff summed up, "This record will be a favorite at parties for a long time; some of its choruses are as strong as any in pop." However, the effort was not dismissed as a lightweight joke album. David Gates in *Newsweek* observed, "Each track here is a record in itself, with an almost Ellingtonian wealth of detail, color and texture; on "Peaches & Cream," several themes get stated separately, disappear, then come together at the end." Featuring Beck's now–expected mixture of genres, the tunes included blues, rap, country, and a healthy dose of soul and funk. However, he managed to meld them together in a unique way, deftly sidestepping any charges that he was beginning to sound familiar.

Often described as baby–faced, two of Beck's most distinguishing features are his wide eyes and pouty mouth. This, along with his messy hair, provide a stark contrast to his preferred stage garb: oddly formal ill–fitting suits. He noted in *Rolling Stone* that he began donning that style of apparel one day after a clothing company for no apparent reason sent him two free suits in the mail. On stage, he has been known to perform the moonwalk or robot dance, providing even more of a weird juxtaposition to his appearance. It all seems to work in conjunction, however, with his quirky lyrics and jumble of musical forms. Beck and his longtime girlfriend, fashion stylist Leigh Limon, live in Los Angeles.

Sources

Books

Contemporary Musicians, volume 18, Gale Research, 1997.

Periodicals

Entertainment Weekly, April 8, 1994, p. 14; February 14, 1997, p. 32; May 28, 1999, p. 110.

Interview, August 1996, p. 92.

Knight–Ridder/Tribune News Service, October 9, 1996; November 16, 1998.

Newsweek, November 29, 1999, p. 102.

New York Times, November 21, 1999, p. AR33.

New York Times Magazine, February 23, 1997, p. 32.

People, December 29, 1997, p. 70; May 25, 1998, p. 11.

Rolling Stone, April 21, 1994, p. 79; July 11, 1996, p. 51; January 23, 1997, p. 42; April 17, 1997, p. 58; November 26, 1998, p. 39; September 30, 1999, p. 62.

Time, January 20, 1997, p. 74; September 28, 1998, p. 101; November 29, 1999, p. 83.

USA Today, December 2, 1999, p. 4D.

Art Bell

Radio show host

Born June 17, 1945; son of military officers; divorced first wife; married, wife's name, Ramona; children: (from first marriage) Art Bell IV. *Education:* Attended the University of Maryland.

Addresses: *Home*—Pahrump, NV. *Office*—P.O. Box 4755, Pahrump, NV 89041–4755.

Career

Worked as a radio station board operator and chief engineer; employed as a disk jockey, including at KENI, Anchorage, AK; XTRA, Tijuana, Mexico; and KSBK, an English–language station in Okinawa, Japan; Times Mirror company, Las Vegas, NV, television station chief engineer; KDWN, Las Vegas, talk show host, beginning mid–1980s; host of syndicated shows *Coast to Coast AM* and *Dreamland*. *Military service:* U.S. Air Force.

Sidelights

Syndicated radio host Art Bell, who broadcasts from a studio in his trailer home in the desert just outside Nevada's legendary Area 51, is a beacon for anyone interested in the paranormal, such as UFOs and aliens, but his topics include politics and current events as well. His five–hour show, *Coast to Coast AM,* has been on the air since the mid–1980s, and he also hosts a Sunday program called *Dreamland. Coast to Coast AM* is the highest–rated late–night show in the country (airing at 1 a.m. Eastern time) and the fourth–most popular overall after Rush Limbaugh, Dr. Laura Schlessinger,

AP/Wide World Photos

and Howard Stern. It airs on more than 400 stations to roughly 15 million listeners. Much of his show's appeal lies in the callers, many of whom are eccentric, to put it mildly. However, unlike other talk show hosts who often mock and belittle their fans over the airwaves, Bell lets callers voice their opinions and relate often outrageous anecdotes while he comments in a soothing and generally uncritical manner. "The traditional formula in talk radio has been contention," Bell explained to Joshua Hammer in *Newsweek*. " 'Call 'em idiots. Tell them they're screwed up.' That's not my style."

Bell was born on June 17, 1945, the son of military officers in the Marines. He moved frequently around the Northeast as a child, and to form friends, he became an avid ham radio operator. The Art Bell web site notes that he developed a taste for news as a boy, and as an Air Force enlistee, he and a friend built a pirate radio station on the Amarillo Air Force base in order to play rock and roll. Later, he attended the University of Maryland, where he learned his way around the sound board and became a radio station chief engineer. This led to on–air stints; his first experience behind the microphone was on KENI in Anchorage, Alaska. There, he once embarked on a 116–hour solo broadcast, earning a place in the *Guinness Book of World Records.* Bell's web site biography also notes that he lived in Okinawa, Japan, for a time, where he worked for KSBK, the only English–language station in Asia. There, he became more interested in international news and was exposed to a different perspective on political issues. Also, he crossed the border for a while to host a radio show on station XTRA, broadcasting from Tijuana, Mexico.

Though Bell left radio for a time to work in television as the chief engineer for the Times Mirror company in Las Vegas, he soon returned to the air when station KDWN in Vegas gave him a nighttime talk show broadcast over 13 states in the West. It started in the mid–1980s with a conservative political theme, but he gradually began inviting colorful personalities to the studio, and the format evolved. Later the show moved to a studio in his home in the Nevada desert. One of his early guests was John Lear, son of the Lear Jet inventor. He also happened to be a UFO conspiracy theory enthusiast. "It drove [my station manager] up a tree," Bell told Hammer in Newsweek. "She called me on the hot line and said, 'What the hell are you doing?' But the audience loved it."

However, Bell drew fire for letting one guest have his say. In November of 1996, an amateur astronomer called to say he had photographed the Hale–Bopp comet, and there appeared to be a large object about four times as large as the Earth trailing it. The next night, professor Courtney Brown of Emory University and director of the Farsight Institute in Atlanta, Georgia, went on the show to say that the object photographed was an alien spaceship. Later, Bell posted the picture on his web site, and the next day, two professors from the University of Hawaii called the show to say that it was a fake; the photograph had been altered. Bell then barred Brown—previously a frequent guest—from ever appearing on his radio show again.

Unfortunately, when 39 members of the Heaven's Gate cult committed suicide in 1997, some felt that Bell's earlier promotion of the so–called spaceship photo fueled their belief that a craft tagging along the Hale–Bopp comet was their ticket to the "next level" of existence. They thought that this ship was reachable only through killing themselves, or leaving their "vehicles," as they put it. Bell, on the other hand, insisted that the Heaven's Gate members were well aware that the picture had been proven to be a human–created image and knew that experts debunked the theory that Hale–Bopp had any kind of "companion" craft. "I'm not going to stop presenting my material because there are unstable people," he remarked, according to Thomas C. Genoni Jr. in Skeptical Inquirer. "That's what the First Amendment is all about."

Indeed, Bell continued to allow callers to phone in with bizarre stories about mysterious black helicopters, alien sightings, crop circles, doomsday predictions, and more. One fan built a time machine and later electrocuted himself with stolen transformers; another confessed to enjoying sex with iguanas more than with humans. Some think they are immortal, others believe they are the antichrist. Bell himself told Hammer that in the mid–1990s, he saw an huge triangular craft with red and white lights coming up behind him while he was driving on the road to his house. His studio, housed in his double–wide mobile home, is located in Pahrump, Nevada, 45 miles from Area 51, a top–secret Air Force base that is ground zero for government and alien conspiracy theorists. One popular hypothesis is that Area 51 is where the government took the alien bodies from the supposed spaceship crash in Roswell, New Mexico, in the 1940s.

In March of 1998, Premiere Communications, the third–largest radio syndicate in the nation, purchased a package of shows for $10 million that included Coast to Coast AM. However, in an enigmatic move even for him, on October 13, 1998, Bell announced on his show, "A threatening, terrible event occurred to my family, which I could not tell you about. Because of that event and a succession of other events, what you're listening to right now is my final broadcast," according to an article in the Washington Times. His fans, many of them conspiracy theorists, were abuzz with ideas of what may have happened, even though local police went to his home and found him there unharmed.

Bell returned to the airwaves on October 28 and chastised the rumor–mongers, but did not offer any explanation about the situation. He then made a special appearance as himself on the January 22, 1999, episode of the television series Millennium, but still no word emerged about the incident. Finally, in May of 1999, Frank Ahrens in the Washington Post reported that Bell was under stress due to a slander campaign that accused him of being a child molester, pornographer, pimp, and convict. Bell filed suit in Los Angeles against radio host David Oates and another man, Robert A.M. Stephens, whose web site states that he is a contractor for NASA. They were both former guests on Bell's show. One of the allegations involved a 20–year–old case in which Bell was running a video dating service in San Diego that was the subject of a police raid, because the law suspected he was making adult films. They soon discovered that Bell was just allowing his clients to videotape themselves talking so that potential suitors could view the tapes. He filed suit against the police department and won $50,000.

On June 1, 1999, more information was unveiled when it was revealed that Bell had filed suit against the Nevada school district and a former substitute teacher who was convicted on drug charges and also of molesting his son, Art Bell IV, whom he had with his first wife. "My own son had been molested and then I was accused of child molestation," Bell revealed to Jeffrey Ressner in *Time.* "I couldn't open my mouth because that would reveal my son's situation. The impact on me was profound." Bell filed charges against the school district using various "John Does" for anonymity, but when Bell IV turned 18, the case became public knowledge. In addition, the man who molested Bell's son tested positive for HIV, the virus that causes AIDS. Bell's son tested negative, but did not heal from the psychological trauma.

After Bell became wrapped up in the litigation, he trimmed the frequency of *Coast to Coast AM* from five nights a week to three. Although the slogan for Bell's program may be "The truth is in the night," many are skeptical of the outlandish tales of alien abductions, inexplicable cattle mutilations, and other such events that dominate the discussions. However, as witnessed by the popularity of television shows like *The X–Files,* audiences seem to love the tales whether they are real or fiction. Ressner in *Time* summed up, "A typical *Coast to Coast* is an all–night ghost story disguised as a talk show. The story being told may be the truth; it may be a crock. But it's great radio."

Sources

Periodicals

Economist, October 17, 1998, p. 33.
Entertainment Weekly, January 15, 1999, p. 9.
Newsday, November 1, 1998, p. B15.
Newsweek, July 13, 1998, p. 62.
Skeptical Inquirer, July–August 1997, p. 22; January–February 1999, p. 8.
Time, August 9, 1999, p. 64.
Washington Post, May 29, 1999, p. C1; June 1, 1999, p. C7.
Washington Times, October 14, 1998, p. A10.

Online

Art Bell web site, http://www.artbell.com (September 27, 1999).

Sandy Berger

U.S. National Security Adviser

Born Samuel Richard Berger, October 28, 1945, in Sharon, CT; married Susan Harrington; children: Deborah, Sarah, Alexander. *Education:* Cornell University, B.A., 1967; Harvard Law School, J.D., 1971.

Addresses: *Office*—National Security Council, 17th & Penn N.W., Washington, DC 20504.

Career

Speechwriter for George McGovern, 1972; legislative aide to New York City Mayor John V. Lindsay, 1972–73; Hogan & Hartson law firm, Washington, DC, international trade lawyer, 1973–77, 1980–92; U.S. State Department, deputy director of policy planning, 1977–80; speechwriter for President Jimmy Carter, then Secretary of State Cyrus Vance, 1977–80; U.S. deputy national security adviser, 1993–96, national security adviser, 1996—. Also served as adviser to Gary Hart, Walter Mondale, and Michael Dukakis.

Sidelights

Appointed the U.S. national security adviser in 1996, Sandy Berger brought to the job a wide breadth of knowledge about foreign affairs stemming from his long tenure in international law. Generally known as being the closest foreign–policy aide to President Bill Clinton, Berger is "perhaps the most influential national security adviser since Henry A. Kissinger," according to R. W. Apple Jr. in the *New York Times*. However, unlike most others who have held the post, Berger earned his title not due to his reputation for brilliant strategy, but by his knack for using his personality to forge integral political ties. "It is difficult to find anyone who knows him who does not like Mr. Berger," wrote Apple. "You might as well try to find someone who doesn't like Sara Lee." By all accounts, Berger is unpretentious and a gentleman, with a strong sense of personal ethics, though he can be blunt at times. However, Apple noted that "Berger gets very mixed reviews as a security adviser from those outside his immediate circle" and quoted some who criticized his inability to foresee events and develop strategies for them. Nevertheless, Berger is respected in political circles as being a highly–organized and analytical hard worker as well as a strong consensus–builder who is able to get the job done.

Samuel Richard Berger, known as "Sandy," was born on October 28, 1945, in Sharon, Connecticut, but grew up in the small town of Millerton (population about 900 at the time) in upstate New York, northeast of Poughkeepsie. When he was eight, his father died, and his mother supported the family with meager profits from an Army–Navy surplus store. His mother taught him a strict work ethic and the value of being organized. Each Sunday, Berger still hand– writes an intricate "to–do" list for the entire week.

As Democrats and Jews in an area that was mainly Protestant and Republican, Berger's family was different, but the sense of small–town community left an important imprint. After high school, he left his rural roots for Cornell University, where his charm made him a popular campus figure. He headed up the interfraternity council and lobbied the students to support civil rights. He organized a trip for African American students in Brooklyn to come to Cornell to display an art project on black history and sponsored a series of speakers including black activist Stokely Carmichael.

In addition to his student activities, Berger was an ace at his classwork and was highly influenced by some professors who became intellectual mentors, including George McTurnan Kahin, Walter LeFerber, and Andrew Hacker. After graduating in 1967 with a bachelor of arts degree, Berger earned a juris doctorate *cum laude* from Harvard Law School in 1971. Subsequently, Berger turned down a job in the office of a district judge and instead went to Washington, D.C., to work as a summer intern in the office Senator Harold Hughes, who had plans to run for the presidency. However, after the senator changed his mind regarding his candidacy, Berger landed a job with Representative Joseph Resnick of Iowa. The congressman had begun an investigation into the American Farm Bureau Federation, an advocacy group that had riled controversy. When Resnick abandoned his research due to political pressure, Berger picked up where he left off and published his only book, *Dollar Harvest: The Story of the Farm Bureau*, 1971, an expose of the harm the organization had done to family farms. In addition, while in law school, Berger volunteered on the campaigns of Robert F. Kennedy and Eugene McCarthy.

In 1972 Berger became a speechwriter for George McGovern, an old friend of Kahin's who was running for president against Richard Nixon. Though his candidate lost the race, Berger forged integral ties at this time, becoming friends with the likes of Bill Clinton and Gary Hart. Subsequently, he became a legislative aide to New York City Mayor John V. Lindsay, but when he left office a year later, Berger joined the liberal, Democratic law firm of Hogan & Hartson in Washington, D.C. There, he specialized in international trade, representing the governments of Japan, Poland, and China, among other clients. This would later raise the issue of a possible conflict of interest when Berger became national security adviser.

Berger left the law firm in 1977 to work for the U.S. State Department as deputy director of policy planning under President Jimmy Carter. He was also in-

volved with speechwriting for the president and for Secretary of State Cyrus Vance. Carter lost his reelection bid in 1980, and Berger returned to Hogan & Hartson, where he became a partner and director of the firm's international trade group. In the meantime, he was also keeping his finger in politics throughout the 1980s, acting as an adviser to the presidential campaigns of Walter Mondale, Gary Hart, and Michael Dukakis, and maintaining a friendly relationship with Pamela Harrington, a wealthy socialite known as a mover and shaker around Washington. He was also a member of a core group of friends who convinced Bill Clinton to run for the office of president; he helped Clinton prepare for his debate against President George Bush.

When Clinton won the 1992 election, he asked Berger to ensure a smooth transition from Bush's tenure in regards to national security and foreign affairs. At this point, Berger was offered the job of national security adviser, but he declined, stating he did not feel he had enough experience. He recommended Anthony Lake instead, who took the post, and Berger stepped in as his deputy. After Clinton won reelection in 1996, he moved around his cabinet members, naming Berger as national security adviser. As John F. Harris reported in the *Washington Post*, Berger "ordered a review of the principles guiding Clinton's second–term foreign policy. Among the goals he identified were integrating Eastern and Western Europe without provoking new tensions with Russia; encouraging more open trade; improved shared defenses against 'transnational threats' like terrorism and drug trafficking; and encouraging a 'strong, stable Asia Pacific community,' a policy Clinton seeks to promote by stressing cooperation with China over trade rather than confrontation over human rights."

After his appointment, two of Berger's biggest achievements were to convince the Senate to pass a ban on chemical weapons and to lobby the House of Representatives to extend China's most–favored–nation status in regard to trade, a controversial move that provoked an outcry among human rights activists. He was also influential in smoothing tensions between Secretary of State Madeline Albright and Secretary of Defense William S. Cohen concerning the United States' involvement in Bosnia. In addition, Berger, despite his background as vehemently anti–war during the Vietnam era, proposed that America bomb weapons arsenals in Iraq, a highly unpopular move among some dovish facets of society as well as among others who simply felt there was no good strategy in place for the move. Berger was also criticized for what some saw as an overly cautious stance on the involvement in Kosovo. Many disagreed with his reticence to use ground troops, insisting that an air–only war would not be successful. And, he came under fire for not reacting more quickly when he learned of suspicions regarding Chinese theft of nuclear secrets. Despite the controversial opinions about his performance, Berger was one of the most influential people in the U.S. government during Clinton's term.

In keeping with his down–to–earth ego, Berger, a plump man, is often rumpled, eschewing slick suits and designer eyeglasses, his conventionality starkly contrasting with other Clinton cabinet members such as Albright and Cohen. Berger met his wife, the former Susan Harrington, while they were both students at Cornell. They have three children, Deborah, Sarah and Alexander. Berger is known for putting in 15–hour days, and has six "in" boxes on his desk. On the infrequent occasions when he goes out of the office, he takes two cellular phones with him, just in case one fails.

Sources

Economist, February 21, 1998, p. 32.

New Republic, April 13, 1998, p. 19.

New York Times, December 6, 1996, p. D6; May 18, 1998, p. A9; August 25, 1999, p. A1.

Time, January 11, 1993, p. 20.

U.S. News & World Report, November 11 1996, p. 26.

Washington Post, July 7, 1997, p. A1; May 16, 1999, p. A1.

Andre Bishop

AP/Wide World Photos

Theater director

Born Andre Bishop Smolianinoff, November 9, 1948, in New York, NY; son of Andre V. (an investment banker) and Felice (Fay) Smolianinoff. *Education:* Harvard University, theater degree, 1970.

Addresses: *Home*—New York, NY. *Office*—c/o Lincoln Center Theater, 150 West 65th St., New York, NY 10023.

Career

Worked with the New York Shakespeare Festival and as a production associate on *Ghost Dance* for the New Dramatists Incorporated, New York City, 1973; Playwrights Horizons, New York City, volunteer and literary manager, 1975–77, artistic director, 1977–91; appeared in *Old Glory*, American Place Theater, 1976; Lincoln Center Theater, New York City, director, 1992—. Hunter College of New York University, instructor. Harvard University, Loeb Drama Center and Opera Musical Theatre, member of board of overseers; National Endowment for the Arts, member of theater panel; CAPS Playwrighting Program, consultant.

Awards: Margo Jones Award (with Playwrights Horizons), 1983; Lucille Lortel Award for Outstanding Achievement for a Body of Work (with Playwrights Horizons), 1989; Drama Desk Award, 1992.

Sidelights

One of the most influential members of the New York City theater community is Andre Bishop. As artistic director of Lincoln Center Theater, one of the best–respected drama organizations in the country, he guides productions of classics as well as new plays and musicals. In order to nurture original works, Bishop founded the Lincoln Center Playwrights and Directors Program, which sponsors workshops, symposia, and readings for up–and–coming artists. He went to Lincoln Center Theater after spending a decade and a half shaping the fledgling Playwrights Horizons theater group into a polished, professional troupe. Under his guidance, that organization became an influential force in contemporary drama, churning out several prize– winning new efforts including *The Heidi Chronicles* and *Driving Miss Daisy*.

Known for being a force in supporting the artistic growth of those with whom he works, Bishop commented to Laurie Winer in the *New York Times*, "While a lot of good work in the theater does come out of fear, I like working with people who need positive energy. Artists are very vulnerable. You have to create an atmosphere where they can listen and hear the criticisms that you do have, where they don't feel threatened constantly. They need to know you're on their side." As for how he chooses such intriguing and innovative works, Bishop remarked to Douglas McGill in the *New York Times*, "I like plays that are lucidly framed, but within that frame, I'm drawn to writing that is unpredictable, that comes at you in strange ways, that astonishes you verbally by expressing strange thoughts."

Bishop was born Andre Bishop Smolianinoff on November 9, 1948, in New York City. His father, Andre V. Smolianinoff, had immigrated to the United States from Belarus and became an investment banker, and his mother, the former Felice Fay, was a relative of the Harrimans, a prominent family in the New York area. However, she never flaunted her connections, telling David Richards in the *New York Times Magazine*, "We were the poor branch." In 1954, when Bishop was five years old, his parents separated (this was his mother's second marriage) and his father died of a coronary occlusion the following year. Subsequently, his mother officially changed her son's name to Andre S. Bishop, since she felt the old surname was too cumbersome.

In 1956, Bishop's mother married for a third time to Dwight Francis, a well–to–do New Englander who was distressed that his stepson showed no talent for sports. At age seven, Bishop was sent to the Swiss boarding school La Clairiere, where he found his fellow students rough and intimidating. Later he attended the Fay School in Massachusetts and St. Paul's in New Hampshire, which were more up-scale but still did not suit his personality. His brightest moments throughout childhood came when he experienced the theater. Bishop recalled to Richards, "The first stage show I ever saw was the Mary Martin 'Peter Pan,' of course. My aunt had got tickets in the front row." He sat close enough to see the light reflecting off the wires that allowed Martin to look as if she was flying, but was still entranced with the show. "I both believed in the illusion and I saw it for what it was," he explained to Richards.

Thereafter, Bishop was consumed by the stage. He would read *Theater Arts Magazine* and produce puppet shows. He befriended actress Katherine Cornell while vacationing with his family on Martha's Vineyard. He graduated from Harvard University in 1970, then moved to New York City to become an actor. Like numerous others, he took a variety of jobs while waiting for his big break. Bishop worked in the box office of the Delacorte Theater in Central Park and took tickets at Joseph Papp's Public Theater. He also worked at a record company and then for five years at a publishing house, reading gothic novels. He summed up that experience to McGill in the *New York Times* as "dismal." He also worked

with the New York Shakespeare Festival and as a production associate on *Ghost Dance* for the New Dramatists Incorporated in 1973.

In 1975, Bishop offered to help out at the Playwrights Horizons, a not–for–profit group that staged plays at a run–down former pornography theater on West 42nd Street. For a while, he performed mundane tasks such as sharpening pencils and running errands. However, as Bishop related to McGill, "The theater seemed to me to be very, very alive, and I remember thinking, 'I believe—at least I *think* I believe—in what they're doing.'" Soon, he began reading scripts that were sent in for consideration and wrote up reports about them for Robert Moss, who had founded Playwrights Horizons in 1971. In this way, he more or less created the job of literary manger for himself. In the meantime, Bishop tried acting classes with Wynn Handman, the artistic director of the American Place Theater. Though Handman cast him in a few bit parts in a revival of Robert Lowell's *Old Glory* in 1976, he knew Bishop was not a talented enough actor to shine.

The experience with Handman taught Bishop more about the theater and what constituted good drama, which he parlayed into his volunteer role at Playwrights Horizons. He began producing works, and by 1977 he was named artistic director of the Manhattan branch of the theater, which produced all kinds of works from young American playwrights, including classical tragedies, musical comedies, and modern farces. (The Queens branch of Playwrights Horizons, on the other hand, concentrated on classics and revivals.) "The emphasis was on developing plays, and not necessarily on achieving a polished final production," Bishop explained to McGill. "We put on staged readings and workshops, held playwrights' hands, and did a lot of what I call 'artistic social work.'" Eventually, Bishop became more choosy about who he wanted to work with and which efforts to produce.

In 1981, Moss left Playwrights Horizons to pursue work in regional theaters, and Bishop succeeded him as artistic director of the group. Under his leadership, the organization became one of the most widely respected theaters of that decade. His first year alone saw three mega–hits, including *The Dining Room* by A. R. Gurney, *Sister Mary Ignatius Explains It All for You* by Christopher Durang, and *Geniuses* by Jonathan Reynolds. Later, Bishop would go on to oversee Stephen Sondheim and James Lapine's *Sunday in the Park with George*, Alfred Uhry's *Driving Miss Daisy*, and Wendy Wasserstein's *The Heidi Chronicles*. All three of those works won Pulitzer Prizes; *The Heidi Chronicles* also won the 1989 Tony Award for best play and *Driving Miss Daisy* was adapted for film and won the 1989 Academy Award for best picture.

In addition to these larger plays, Bishop in 1988 founded the New Theater Wing, an outcropping of Playwrights Horizons dedicated to lower–budget productions and affordable seats. Costs for each play ran only about $30,000 and ticket prices were held to $5 in order to deflect criticism that the theater had become an elite institution. This approach allowed unknown playwrights, directors, and actors to get a foot in the door. Bishop told Wilborn Hampton in the *New York Times,* "Everybody cries, 'The theater is too expensive; there are no directors; the critics are killing the theater.' A lot of people are sitting around moaning, and I hate that. There are always answers to problems." To raise funds for this unprofitable effort, in addition to receiving grants and donations, Bishop enlisted some established playwrights, including Durang and Wasserstein, to teach an assortment of drama classes in conjunction with New York University. Bishop also earned money for this project by establishing Ticket Central, a box–office service for several Broadway theaters, in addition to running a scenery and costume shop.

Moving on to new opportunities, Bishop was named artistic director of the Lincoln Center Theater in January of 1992 when Gregory Mosher stepped down. At this point, he doubled his salary to somewhere in the low six figures, according to Richards, and increased his responsibility by leaps and bounds. At the two Playwrights Horizons theaters combined, seating capacity did not reach 250 and the annual budget was held at about $4 million. There were 6,000 annual subscribers when Bishop departed. The Lincoln Center Theater boasts a capacity of 1,050 in its Vivian Beaumont Theater and 300 in the Mitzi Newhouse Theater, in addition to budgets of $20 million and up and a subscriber list of 48,000 people, as of 1999. Though Bishop was sacrificing some of the good points of directing with a small theater, such as the ability to take chances and not worry about occasional failures, he was eager to work on a larger scale.

Right away, Bishop brought the works of a greater number of playwrights to Lincoln Center Theater, particularly featuring new works by colleagues from his days with Playwrights Horizons. Some of his first productions included Wasserstein's *The Sisters Rosensweig,* Jon Robins Baitz's *The Substance of Fire,* and the musical *My Favorite Year,* by Lynn Ahrens and Stephen Flaherty. He also staged *Carousel,* 1994, which won a Tony Award for best revival of a musical, as well as *The Heiress,* 1995, and *A Delicate Balance,* 1996, which both won Tony Awards for best revival of a play. In 1999, *Parade* was nominated for a Tony for best musical and Shakespeare's *Twelfth Night* starring Helen Hunt was nominated for best revival.

By his eighth season with Lincoln Center, Bishop was coming under fire for not being adventurous enough with staging new plays. Many critics, according to Robin Pogrebin in the *New York Times,* claimed that instead of bringing up innovative new voices, he was content to stick with proven playwrights that gained their reputation with him at Playwrights Horizons. Others pointed out that Bishop's loyalty to established colleagues was laudable and noted that he provided a logical step for maturing writers. In addition, though some felt that the small Mitzi Newhouse Theater would be a perfect space for up–and–coming shows, others chimed in that repertory theaters like the Lincoln Center should be dedicated to established works, rather than speculate on untested productions. Bishop, meanwhile, insisted that the decisions rested with his instincts. "Someone once said that being an artistic director is the intelligent exercise of one's own taste," he related to Pogrebin. "And that is what I believe with all my heart and soul."

Bishop lives in Greenwich Village in Manhattan and owns a vacation home on the island of Vinalhaven off the coast of Maine. In 1983, under his direction, Playwrights Horizons won the Margo Jones Award and in 1989 was granted the Lucille Lortel Award for outstanding achievement for a body of work, recognizing the development of new plays. Individually, Bishop won a 1992 Drama Desk Award for his work with Playwrights Horizons. He has also taught at Hunter College of New York University and serves as a member of the board of overseers at Harvard University's Loeb Drama Center and Opera Musical Theatre. In addition, Bishop is a consultant for the CAPS Playwrighting Program and a member of the theater panel for the National Endowment for the Arts.

Sources

Books

Contemporary Theatre, Film and Television, volume 9, Gale Research, 1991.

Periodicals

New York Times, January 3, 1982, sec. 2, p. 4; April 10, 1988, sec. 2, p. 22; August 19, 1990, sec. 2, p. 5; August 23, 1999, p. B1.
New York Times Magazine, September 13, 1992, p. 53.
Opera News, April 5, 1997, p. 40.
Variety, June 30, 1997, p. 69.

Manolo Blahnik

Corbis Corporation

Designer

Born November 27, 1942, in Santa Cruz, Canary Islands, Spain; son of Stefan (a banana plantation businessman) and Emmanuela Blahnik. *Education:* Attended University of Geneva, Switzerland, 1960s; also studied art in Paris.

Addresses: *Office*—49–51 Old Church St., London SW3, England.

Career

Feathers Boutique, London, jeans buyer, early 1970s; began designing shoes for Zapata Boutique and designer Ossie Clark, 1972; opened shop in London, 1973, later opened shops in New York, NY, Hong Kong, and inside Neiman–Marcus in Beverly Hills, CA.

Awards: Fashion Council of America Award, 1988, 1991; British Fashion Council Award, 1991; Balenciaga Award, 1991; American Leather Award, New York, 1991; Hispanic Institute, Antonion Lopez Award, Washington, DC, 1991.

Sidelights

Shoe designer Manolo Blahnik has become the feted name in upscale footwear with his elegant and often quirky offerings. "Manolo Blahnik is to shoes what [George] Gershwin is to tunes, [Italian director Luchino] Visconti to film, Rolls–Royce to engines, and the Swiss to cuckoo clocks," wrote Michael Roberts in *Interview*. With an unmistakable style that is known for elongating the leg while functioning as comfortably as stilettos possibly can feel, Blahnik infuses soul into his soles, with creations featuring hand–sewn embroidery and beading, lush materials, colors in rich jewel tones, carefully detailed stitching, and an ethereal quality made possible by the thinnest of straps and slimmest of spike heels. Some come in baroque fabrics or satin lined with crushed velvet, others in iguana skin.

Blahnik's delicate designs have become a favorite among many of the world's richest and most famous, including Madonna, Cher, Naomi Campbell, Anjelica Huston, Winon Ryder, Sandra Berhard, Kate Moss, Jerry Hall, Ivana Trump, and the late Princess Diana. Bianca Jagger was one of his first and most loyal customers ever since he started up his little London shop in the 1970s. These and numerous other women with a generous amount of disposable income pay roughly $450 to $2,600 per pair for their footwear in his boutiques and through high–end retailers. Many are ardent and vocal supporters of his craftmanship, purchasing closets full of his goods. Fashion designers clamor for Blahniks for their models on the catwalk, and the Metropolitan Museum in New York has even featured them in its galleries. According to Deborah Ross in the *Independent,* Jagger once summed up, "Manolo is not a shoemaker. He is a great artist."

Born in Santa Cruz de la Palma in Spain's Canary Islands, Blahnik was raised by a Czech father, Stefan, and Spanish mother, Emmanuela, on a banana plantation that his mother's family owned. His father, whose family owned a pharmaceutical firm in Prague, entered the plantation business after marrying her. Blahnik inherited his love of footwear from his mother, who passed along her passion for brocade and satin fabrics; she would purchase custom creations from the island's premier shoemaker, Don Cristino, when she was not making her own designs.

Blahnik was also greatly inspired by Spanish and American cinema, devouring the movies and committing to memory the cast and crew. In addition, he would also amuse himself by capturing lizards and costuming them in dresses he fashioned out of foil wrappers from chocolate or cigarettes. His first forays into footwear came with designs for his pet dogs and monkey. "I made shoes for all of them, out of muslin and pink cotton ribbons," Blahnik recalled to Amy Fine Collins in *Vanity Fair.* "I put shoes on everybody! One dog would lie on his back and stick his paws up in the air for me while I tied the bows."

Until Blahnik was 14, he and his younger sister Evangeline—who would later run his London boutique—were tutored at home. They were then sent to boarding schools in Switzerland, where he became multilingual and immersed himself in books and film. Attending the University of Geneva during the 1960s, Blahnik studied international law, but changed his major to literature after fainting at the sight of a cadaver in a forensics class. He also spent a year in Paris studying stage design at the Ecole de Louvre and worked in an apparel shop called GO, which Collins in *Vanity Fair* called "a swinging, quintessentially 60s boutique on the Rue Bonaparte." There, Blahnik became something of a local celebrity, a handsome and exotic attraction whom women admired.

In 1970, Blahnik moved to London. "I was possessed by London," he related in *Vogue.* "It was post–Beatles and all that nonsense, and to me the city seemed very exotic." With help from his previous employer at GO, he landed a job as a jeans buyer for Feathers, a trendy London shop at the time. Since he had a fondness for film and theatrics, he toyed with the idea of becoming a set designer, and worked briefly as a party decorator. However, in 1971 on a trip to New York, American *Vogue* editor Diana Vreeland examined his portfolio and was impressed with the style of footwear on all of the people in his set designs. She encouraged him to make shoes instead.

Meanwhile, Blahnik had, in fact, churned out a few pairs of men's shoes for Zapata, a small store owned by a few friends in London's Chelsea district. He returned to London and created a new line of shoes for Ossie Clark, one the hippest designers of the moment in London, and Blahnik saw his name soar. The designer's early products were constructed with a flair for style over substance, as displayed at that first fashion event. "They were shoes with high heels and crepe soles," he explained in *Vogue.* "The heels were rubber. Of course, they had metal spines [he pronounces it "speens"], but they weren't what I call very safe. They wobbled a bit. Those girls at Ossie Clark's show were teetering in those high rubber shoes and falling off, and it was hys–*ter*–ia."

Before long, Blahnik bought out Zapata and transformed it to the Manolo Blahnik boutique in 1973, a psychedelic refuge bedecked with Astro–Turf, fake flowers, and gingham cow murals on the walls. It became the hot spot to shop in no time. Since the fashion mood of the time was wild, customers flocked to his zany designs that were showcased nicley by the miniskirts and "leggy" look of the early 1970s. His offerings included a good deal of purple, which was the color du jour, and featured cutout shapes, appliques, and small, chunky heels. He also incorporated a "wet–look" leather that was popular. Though Blahnik's shoes continued to be more aesthetically appealing than actually wearable for the first few years, he eventually began to create more comfortable offerings. Nevertheless, his signature style remains the wispy mule with a stiletto heel that can reach five–and–a–half inches in height.

In 1981, Blahnik officially went international when he opened a shop on New York City's Madison Avenue. Due to some unsavvy business dealings, though, he almost lost rights to his own name. The shop was in disarray when George Malkemus, a young advertising copywriter with a decent trust fund, bought the licensing agreement from Blahnik's partners and entered an arrangement that allowed the designer much more participation. Other shops later followed in Hong Kong and inside Neiman–Marcus in Beverly Hills, California. Also, Bergdorf Goodman, Barneys, and other upscale retailers sell his wares. Though Blahnik's company is privately held, it is known to be a multimillion–dollar operation, and it has been reported that in North and South America alone, he sells anywhere from 60,000 to 70,000 pairs annually.

Blahnik finds inspiration for his fanciful designs from his travels, films, or books; many ideas come to him when he visits museums. His shoes are made with precision in Italy where everything is done by hand every bead is even stitched on individually. The designer himself cuts and carves the wooden the prototype, and even the largest of the four factories produce only about 40 to 60 pairs per day. Often, he can be found strolling through the work tables, overseeing the stitching and demonstrating how he wants things done. "It breaks my heart when people say these shoes are expensive," he noted in *Vogue*. "I try to convey a feeling of opulence, of abundance. You know, ribbons, wonderful silk satin, crushed velvet, pleating, embroidery, jewels. You have to have everything with generosity."

Reaching out to a new market, in 1998 Blahnik began offering men's shoes as well. For quite a while, he had been creating custom pairs for certain customers, but he finally decided to take it to a mass scale, with 15 types of shoes and sandals in a wide range of colors. Unlike his women's selection, though, he based most of the men's line on classics such as Oxfords and brogues. Though he admitted that men are more concerned with cut and comfort in a shoe, Blahnik expressed the hope that his male clientele would eventually reach out to more daring items. "For next season," he expressed to Damian Foxe in the *Independent*, "we will incorporate even more unusual style, perhaps even using brocade for evening, and introducing colours such as dusty pink and acid green for day."

Still, Blahnik is most highly regarded for his women's line, about which some become fanatical, collecting dozens of pairs. His works complement the fashions of legions of designers, including Yves Saint Laurent, Calvin Klein, Perry Ellis, Bill Blass, and Isaac Mizrahi. Designer Caroline Herrera swears by Blahnik both personally and in her shows, claiming to Collins, "Manolo's shoes give me legs. You can tell when a woman is wearing Manolos by the legs, by the way she stands and walks. The shoes are feminine and sexy, but never, ever vulgar." Similarly, designers Mark Badgley and James Mischka, renowned for their elegant gowns, told Collins, "They change the anatomy by drawing the legs out." And Richard Tyler's wife, Lisa Trafficante, insisted to Collins, "They take off five pounds."

Although Blahnik's shoes are regaled for their sexiness, the designer himself is also interested in their whimsy. The delicate beading, the ribbons that wind up legs, the crushed velvet lining, all appeal to his sense of theatrics. As he stated in *Vogue*, "My biggest kick in life, if I only achieve one thing, is to entertain people." Blahnik, a dapper man who is perennially outfitted in a tailored suit and tie, scoffs at unkempt hair and eschews the heavy, clunky look of footwear in vogue in the late 1990s. He also despises athletic shoes, telling Deborah Ross in the *Independent*, "Look at children from the United States. They have big deformed duck feet through wearing trainers."

Blahnik has several homes around the globe, including a flat in Kensington, England; a nineteenth-century house in Bath; and two sites in the Canary Islands. An avid reader, he helps deal with his incessant insomnia through books. Blahnik is fastidious about being clean; he bathes three times daily, and buys his 100 percent linen sheets from Ghidoli in Milan, which also supplies the Vatican. Not surprisingly, Blahnik is a stickler about well-kept feet, though he professes to get no sexual rise from them. When Roberts asked Blahnik, "Do you ever get sick of looking at feet?" he replied, "Ugly feet, yes. Nice feet, no." He noted to Collins in *Vanity Fair* that some of people with the best feet he has seen include Racquel Welch, Ryan O'Neal, and Diana Ross. When Collins asked him to recall some of the worst feet, he concluded, "I don't remember ugly feet. I erase it." He then added, however, "Maybe in L.A.—a hobo in Jesus sandals, with long, black, round nails. I think this is what evil looks like."

Sources

Books

Contemporary Fashion, St. James Press, 1995.

Periodicals

Harper's Bazaar, July 1997, p. 110.
Independent, November 12, 1997, p. 17; February 9, 1998, p. 13.
Interview, September 1991, p. 100.
Knight–Ridder/Tribune News Service, March 14, 1996.
New York Times Magazine, February 15, 1981, p. 74.
Town & Country Monthly, December 1998, p. 218.
Vanity Fair, May 1995, p. 148.
Vogue, March 1992, p. 310.

Gunter Blobel

Scientist

Born in 1936 in Waltersdorf, Silesia, Germany (now part of Poland); became U.S. citizen, 1980s; son of a veterinarian; married Laura Maioglio (a restaurateur). *Education:* University of Tubingen, Germany, M.D., 1960; University of Wisconsin, Ph.D. in oncology, 1967.

Addresses: *Office*—Rockefeller University, Cell Biology Lab, 66th and York Ave. New York, NY 10021–6339.

Career

Intern, Germany, 1960–62; Rockefeller University, New York City, laboratory fellow in cellular biology, 1967–69; assistant professor of cell biology, 1969–73; associate professor, 1973–76; professor, 1976 ; Howard Hughes Medical Institute, investigator, 1986 . Founder and president, Friends of Dresden, Inc. Contributor of articles to professional journals and chapters to books. Member of American Society of Cell Biology (president, 1990), American Philosophical Society, National Academy of Sciences, American Academy of Arts and Sciences.

Awards: National Academy of Sciences, U.S. Steel Award in molecular biology, 1978; Gairdner Foundation award, 1982; National Academy of Sciences, Richard Lounsbery Award, 1983; German Biochemistry Society, Warburg medal, 1983; American. Society of Cell Biology, Wilson medal, 1986, Roche Institute of Molecular Biology, U.D. Mattia award, 1986; Columbia University, Louisa Gross Horwitz prize, 1987; Waterford Biomedical Sciences award, 1989;

Albert Lasker Basic Medical Research award, 1993; King Faisal international prize for science, 1996; Mayor's award for Excellence in Science and Technology, 1997; Massry Prize, 1999; Nobel Prize in Physiology or Medicine, 1999, for the discovery that proteins have intrinsic signals that govern their transport and localization in the cell.

Sidelights

In 1999, Gunter Blobel, a cell biologist at Rockefeller University and an investigator at the Howard Hughes Medical Institute, won the Nobel Prize for physiology or medicine for his lifelong studies on the transport of cell proteins. Howard Hughes Medical Institute president Purnell W. Choppin noted on the organization's web site, "Through a historic series of experiments, Gunter revealed that each protein has its own 'molecular bar code,' which the cell reads and then guides the protein to the correct location." Blobel's findings on protein synthesis in cells had important ramifications for the study and treatment of a variety of illnesses ranging from Alzheimer's disease, cystic fibrosis, and kidney stones to familial hypercholesterolemia, in which cholesterol levels are extremely high due to a genetic disorder. Since Blobel's findings hold true for plant and yeast cells in addition to animal cells, his research has bearing on genetic engineering of plants, bacteria, and animals in order to produce pharmaceuticals. His current work includes the effort to unfurl the communication between a cell's nucleus and cytoplasm, with the hope of discovering what goes wrong in cancerous cells.

Blobel was born in 1936 in Waltersdorf, Silesia, Germany, which is now part of Poland. When he was eight, Allied bombings drove his family from their home. He and his seven siblings and his parents watched from the hillsides as the city of Dresden burned as the passed through. "You could read a newspaper by it," he told Carol Ezzell in *Scientific American*. In 1960 Blobel received a medical degree from the University of Tubingen in Germany, expecting to become a doctor. Medicine of all sorts runs in his family: His father was a veterinarian for large animals who cared for livestock, two brothers are also veterinarians, and one brother is a physician.

After finishing his medical internship at German hospitals in 1962, Blobel decided to change his course and focus on research. "When I was doing my internship, I realized that lots of diseases were treated symptomatically," he told Ezzell. "I wanted to treat the cause." With help from a brother who was a professor of veterinary medicine at the University of Wisconsin at Madison, he moved to the United States to study, obtaining his doctorate in oncology there in 1967.

Though Blobel always planned to return to Europe, he ended up staying in America and landing a post–doctoral fellowship at Rockefeller University in New York City in 1967. He was hired as an assistant professor of cell biology at Rockefeller University in 1969, and went on to spend his entire career there, becoming an associate professor in 1973 and a professor in 1976. He became a U.S. citizen in the 1980s. In 1986, he also joined the Howard Hughes Medical Institute as an investigator. The medical research organization is one of the largest philanthropies in the world, and boasts five other current Nobel Prize–winning members, as well as one former member.

Starting out at Rockefeller University, Blobel worked in the laboratory of George Palade, who would go on to receive the Nobel Prize in physiology or medicine in 1974 for his work on how cells excrete proteins. Palade was able to determine that to do this, cells use a folded membrane resembling a deflated beach ball, called the endoplasmic reticulum (ER),

which laces through the cell. However, he was not sure exactly how the mechanism actually transported the proteins.

In 1971, Blobel, along with another researcher, David Sabatini, put together a model of how these proteins flow through the cell even before experiments proved it. In effect, they hypothesized that the first few amino acids in a protein chain have a code, similar to an address or ZIP code, to tell the cell whether or not it is supposed to be secreted. If so, it is then placed into the ER. "At first it was just a wonderful thing to say because nothing hinted at a signal sequence," Blobel explained to Michael Hagmann in *Science*. "But it was by far the best thing we could come up with." Describing the idea, Hagmann wrote, "Just as people try to organize their belongings by devising filing systems, cells have to sort newly synthesized proteins and send them wherever they are needed: into different internal compartments called organelles or even out of the cell altogether."

Indeed, Blobel's best guess panned out. The next year, researchers at Cambridge University in England found the "ZIP code," or signal sequence, in one of the protein chains, thereby proving the model true. Though Sabatini moved on to other areas of research, Blobel forged ahead with cell proteins. By 1975 he had decoded the first signal sequence, and expanded his original hypothesis to say that ER membranes contain a tunnel–like pore, or "protein channel," in order to transport the proteins tagged for secretion into the ER.

Continuing their research, Blobel and his colleagues in the early 1980s discovered more specifically how the cells locate and transport proteins. First of all, they figured out that the cell reads the address of a protein by use of a "signal recognition protein" (SRP) that is attached to the cytoplasm. This is how the protein knows to "dock" on an ER membrane. The ER membrane, in turn, contains a receptor that allows the docking process. In addition, Blobel displayed that similar "ZIP codes" are used to steer proteins to other areas of the cell, such as the mitochondria. Later, in the 1990s, in a series of experiments of which he is proudest, Blobel and his team demonstrated the existence of the ER protein channel. Until then, many biologists had resisted the idea of both signal sequences and protein channels, believing that the explanation was too simple.

After winning the Nobel Prize in 1999, Blobel announced that he would donate the accompanying purse of $960,000 to the restoration of European buildings. Much of it went to a nonprofit foundation, Friends of Dresden, which he founded in 1995 devoted to restoring the Frauenkirche, an ornate church in Dresden, Germany, which he saw destroyed by bombings during World War II. It dates from 1743 and features a 300–foot–high bell–shaped stone cupola, and was in need of $200 million for the restoration. The church is the final building of Dresden's baroque skyline to be rebuilt, and the only one to be privately financed. With his prize funds, Blobel also donated money to restore a Dresden synagogue and a historic building in the village of Fubine, Italy.

Though Blobel was baptized Lutheran, he is not a regular churchgoer and has admitted that his passion for restoring the Frauenkirche was more aesthetic than religious, given that he is an architecture buff. In addition, he is an opera enthusiast and noted that the church reminds him of an opera house. Blobel is a tall man with a shock of thick, white hair. He is married to Laura Maioglio, owner of the Barbetta restaurant in midtown Manhattan. They live in a Park Avenue apartment and have no children. In addition to the Nobel Prize, Blobel has been honored with several other awards, including the National Academy of Sciences' Richard Lounsbery Award and the Warburg Medal of the German Biochemistry Society in 1983; the Louisa

Gross Horwitz prize from Columbia University in 1987; the Waterford Biomedical Sciences award in 1989, and the Albert Lasker Basic Medical Research award in 1993.

Sources

Periodicals

Daily Telegraph, October 12, 1999.
Independent, October 15, 1999, p. 9.
Lancet, October 16, 1999, p. 1363.
St. Louis Post–Dispatch, October 30, 1999, p. 29.
Science, October 22, 1999, p. 666.
Science News, October 16, 1999, p. 246.
Scientific American, January 2000, p. 16; May 2000, p. 38.
Star Tribune (Minneapolis, MN), October 12, 1999, p. 4A.

Online

"Gunter Blobel Wins 1999 Nobel Prize for Physiology or Medicine," October 11, 1999, Howard Hughes Medical Institute web site, http://www/hhmi.org (July 14, 2000).

Bill Bradley

AP/Wide World Photos

Politician

Born William Warren Bradley, July 28, 1943, in Crystal City, MO; son of Warren W. (a banker) and Susan (a schoolteacher; maiden name, Crowe) Bradley; married Ernestine Schlant, January 14, 1974; children: Theresa Anne. *Education:* Princeton University, B.A. in history, 1965; Oxford University, M.A. (cum laude), 1968.

Addresses: *Office*—c/o Bill Bradley for President, Inc., 395 Pleasant Valley Way, West Orange, NJ 07052. *Agent*—Paul Gitlin, 7 W. 51st St., New York, NY 10009.

Career

New York Knicks basketball team, New York City, player, 1967–77; U.S. Senate, senator from New Jersey, 1979–96; visiting scholar at Stanford University, Notre Dame, and the University of Maryland, c. 1996–98; author. *Military service* U.S. Air Force Reserve, 1967–78; became first lieutenant.

Awards: Olympic gold medal with U.S. basketball team, 1964; Rhodes Scholar, Oxford University, 1965–68; Truman Award, 1996, for public service.

Sidelights

From his days on the basketball court with the New York Knicks to his tenure in the U.S. Senate, Bill Bradley developed a reputation for tenacity and teamwork. Building a name as a diligent and trustworthy consensus–builder, he was respected on both sides of the political spectrum, though his own views leaned more to the left. As a former Rhodes scholar and a professional athlete, he brought with him to the job an impressive resume and one that embodied the American ideal of balancing the mental and physical. As Matt Bai summed up in *Newsweek*, "He was Jimmy Stewart in satin shorts: the small–town son of a banker, self– effacing and studious, clean–cut and Christian, dazzling on the court but so gifted award from it that he put off the pros for Oxford." After stepping down from three terms in the Senate, during which time he became known as a champion of tax reform, Bradley made the decision to run for president in the 2000 race.

Bradley was born on July 28, 1943, in Crystal City, Missouri, a small town 36 miles south of St. Louis on the Mississippi River. He was the only child of Warren and Susan (Crowe) Bradley, who had their son later in life (his father was 43 and his mother 35). His father was a staunchly Republican banker and his mother taught school for a time in a St. Louis suburb. They gave their son a disciplined and well–rounded upbringing, with lessons in a variety of musical instruments and sports, including swimming, boxing, and basketball. He also was an all–A student.

Though politics did not figure prominently in Bradley's early life, he noted to John L. Phillips in the *New York Times Magazine,* "Local politicians were always in the house or were discussed at dinner, so I was always aware of politics as a profession." However, as Bradley wrote in his memoir, *Time Present, Time Past,* "My mother always wanted me to be a success. My father always wanted me to be a gentleman. Neither wanted me to be a politician."

Above all other influences, Bradley loved to play basketball. He started the sport at age nine and would remain in Crystal City with relatives during the summer months to play while his parents vacationed in Palm Springs, Florida. Though his parents never actively encouraged this pursuit, he joined the Crystal City High School varsity team as a freshman in 1959, where he became a star player. By the time he graduated, he had twice been named an All-American, but he was also a leader scholastically as well, serving as president of the Missouri Association of Student Councils.

After high school, Bradley was deluged with scholarship offers from more than 75 schools, and initially chose Duke University in North Carolina for its balanced approach to academics and athletics. However, after a summer trip to Europe, he decided to attend Princeton instead, even though it did not offer him paid tuition, because it held a greater possibility of earning a Rhodes scholarship to attend Oxford later, as he noted in his memoir. At Princeton, the six-foot, five-inch Bradley led the Tigers to the National Collegiate Athletic Association (NCAA) semifinals in 1965, though they fell to the University of Michigan. Again, he was twice named All-American, and he was on the U.S. Olympic team that won a gold medal in Tokyo in 1964.

Besides honing his basketball skills at Princeton, Bradley's intellect was fine-tuned as well. Though he was a good student, he was not a deep thinker until he became intrigued by his college courses, especially history. "One was taught by H. H. Wilson, who'd been attacked by [Senator Joseph] McCarthy in the witch hunts of the 50's," he told Phillips. "A lot of stuff I read under him—*The Politics of Oil,* Eisenhower's speech on the military–industrial complex—outraged me. The American people were getting screwed. I'd leave class and wander around campus in a fog."

In addition, during the stormy 1960s, Bradley became aware of social issues, race relations, the Vietnam War, and the like. He graduated from Princeton in 1965 with honors as a history major, writing his senior thesis on Harry Truman's re–election to the Senate in 1940. In the meantime, had spent time in college dipping his toe into politics in Washington, D.C. He spent the summer of 1964 as a summer intern for U.S. Representative Richard Schweiker of Pennsylvania, then on the presidential campaign of William Scranton, the former Pennsylvania governor.

After Princeton, although Bradley could have entered the lucrative world of professional sports, he won his Rhodes scholarship and spent two years in England. There, he read European literature and history, particularly devouring the works of Albert Camus, Joseph Conrad, Fyodor Dostoevsky, and Leo Tolstoy. Upon his return in 1967, he joined the U.S. Air Force Reserve, and was on active duty for about six months. He stayed in the service until 1978, becoming a first lieutenant.

When his active duty was up, Bradley joined the New York Knicks basketball team in mid–season in 1967, becoming one of the highest–paid rookies at the time with a salary of half a million dollars over four years. Though the media fanfare was large, he kept to himself, shunning the flashy cars and wardrobe that professional athletes often purchase. Instead, he developed a reputation for frugality, shopping at the Army–Navy store and using paperclips if a button gave out. Teammates jokingly dubbed him "Dollar Bill," explaining that he probably had the first greenback he ever earned. On his time off, instead of signing rich endorsement offers, Bradley worked as an advisor to young African Americans looking toward college; he took up campaigning for environmental causes; and he worked for prison and welfare reform. He even spent a summer working at the Office of Economic Opportunity in Washington, D.C.

Though Bradley obviously had his sights set on an eventual political career, his basketball days were nothing to scoff at. He started out slow, not living up to the expectations set during his college days, but soon learned to adapt his style to become more of a team player. By the late 1960s, he was the starting shooting forward on the Knicks, and was part of a formidable group that included forward Dave DeBusschere, Willis Reed at center, Walt Frazier and Dick Barnett at guard, and reserves like Jerry Lucas and Phil Jackson on hand as well. In 1970, they beat the Los Angeles Lakers, led by Wilt Chamberlain, Elgin Baker, and Jerry West, to take the championship. Then, in 1973, they defeated the Lakers again in a dramatic series. By the mid– 1970s, the Knicks were starting to fizzle out, though, and Bradley retired from the game in 1977. He was elected to the basketball Hall of Fame in 1983.

Immediately, Bradley set his sights on running for public office. Many encouraged him to try local or state politics first, but the media guessed that he had something bigger in mind, and wondered if he was considering a presidential bid, or perhaps wanted to be secretary of state. Instead, Bradley cast his name in the hat for a U.S. Senate seat representing New Jersey, and won with 56 percent of the vote. When he took office as a Democrat in 1978 at age 35, he was the youngest sitting U.S. senator. At the time, it was highly unusual for a politician to come from a field other than law, and though his fame undoubtedly opened doors for his during the election, Bradley downplayed it once in office. "For nearly two years I refused virtually all non–New Jersey media interviews, because they obviously arose from my earlier celebrity," Bradley explained in *Time Present, Time Past.* "I wanted to be a U.S. senator, not a star."

During the campaign and after, Bradley made his name as a proponent of tax reform. In 1982, he wrote a treatise on the subject that suggested tax rates could be slashed if loopholes were taken away. Though considered a pipe dream by many Washington insiders who assumed special interest groups held too much control over the issue, Bradley saw his some of ideas come to fruition in 1986 when Congress passed a massive overhaul of the tax system. It was a testament to his ability to reach a common ground with political opponents; perhaps part of a legacy from his team–building years on the basketball courts. Throughout his 18 years in the senate, Bradley, a liberal, was also respected for his ethics. As an example of his stance on some topics, he stood for a woman's right to an abortion and the Equal Rights Amendment, he supported more investment in solar power and other environmental issues, and was against capital punishment. He also helped extend Medicaid benefits to more women and children, and also expanded the Earned Income Tax Credit, which assists the poor. In addition, he championed the right of women to stay in a hospital for at least 48 hours after giving birth.

In 1996, Bradley announced he was retiring from the Senate when his third term expired, stating famously, according to Liz Trotta in the *Washington Times,* that "politics is broken." But he noted in an interview in *Psychology Today* that he would remain involved in causes, stating, "The mistake is to assume that to be in public life today you have to be in elected office. I'm leaving the Senate. I'm not leaving public life. Only from the outside can you step back to project a larger vision of where the country should go and then use your efforts to further that vision." The next year, he became a contributor for the news division at CBS, and later also served as a

visiting scholar at various universities. Right after he announced his resignation, a bevy of pundits surmised he had his eye on a presidential campaign, but he denied it.

Later, Bradley admitted that he had been considering a run as early as 1988, but decided he was not experienced enough. In 1992, he mulled it over again, telling Chris Heath in *Rolling Stone,* "I thought I was ready, but there was something in me that said, 'Don't do it,' and I honored that inner voice. In retrospect, I'm glad I did." As it happened, his wife was diagnosed with breast cancer later that year and had to undergo a mastectomy.

By 1998, it seemed apparent that Bradley was planning to run for president, and by 1999 he made it official. He had a formidable challenge: As a Democrat, he was up against Vice President Al Gore, and would have to wrest the party's nomination away from him. Late that year and into the next, the two squared off in various debates along with the various Republican contenders, in which Bradley's key issues were campaign finance reform, universal health care, racial harmony, gun control, and fighting child poverty. Some commentators noticed that Bradley preferred to take a low–key approach to campaigning as opposed to going for the jugular, and pointed out that this could lead to his downfall. Steve Lopez in *Time,* for example, wrote, "Restraint at the dessert cart can be a healthy thing. In politics, it can crush you." As public opinion polls were tallied again and again throughout the race, it appeared he was at least gaining ground on Gore, though his numbers continued to lag in most cases.

On January 14, 1974, Bradley married German–born Ernestine Schlant, a professor of comparative literature at Montclair State College, and they have a daughter, Theresa Anne. His wife also has an adult daughter from a previous marriage. Notoriously secretive, Bradley did not reveal his wedding plans but to one close teammate, and then only a scant few days before the date. The rest of them read about it in the newspaper. In addition to *The Fair Tax* and his 1996 memoir *Time Present, Time Past,* Bradley in 1976 wrote *Life on the Run,* about the world of professional sports, and in 1998 released *Values of the Game,* in which he discusses themes of leadership, respect, and responsibility.

Selected writings

Life on the Run (autobiography), Quadrangle, 1976, new edition, Vintage Books, 1995.
The Fair Tax, Pocket Books, 1982.

Time Present, Time Past: A Memoir, Knopf, 1996.
Values of the Game, Artisan, 1998.

Sources

Books

Contemporary Heroes and Heroines, Book I, Gale Research, 1990.
Time Present, Time Past: A Memoir, Knopf, 1996.

Periodicals

Dallas Morning News, January 3, 1997, p.1C.
Newsweek, May 10, 1976, p. 115; September 13, 1999, p. 26.

New York Times Magazine, June 18, 1978, p. 16.
People, February 19, 1996, p. 27.
Psychology Today, March–April 1996, p. 34.
Rolling Stone, October 14, 1999, p. 53.
Time, November 20, 1978, p. 30; June 30, 1986, p. 37; April 14, 1997, p. 101; October 4, 1999, pp. 44, 52; December 20, 1999, p. 64.
US News & World Report, April 19, 1999, p. 39.
Washington Post, January 11, 2000, p. A17.
Washington Times, September 29, 1998, p. A1.

Online

"William Warren Bradley," Contemporary Authors Online, Gale Group web site, http://www.galenet.com (December 6, 1999).

Tom Brokaw

Broadcast journalist and author

Corbis Corporation

Born February 6, 1940, in Webster, SD; son of Anthony Orville "Red" (a construction worker) and Eugenia "Jean" (a clerk; maiden name, Conley) Brokaw; married Meredith Lynn Auld (a toy store chain proprietor), August 17, 1962; children: Jennifer Jean, Andrea Brooks, Sarah Auld. *Education:* Attended University of Iowa; University of South Dakota, B.A., 1962.

Addresses: *Home*—New York City and Montana. *Office*—National Broadcasting Co., 30 Rockefeller Plaza, New York, NY 10022.

Career

KYNT, Yankton, SD, disk jockey, late 1950s; WNEX, Yankton, newscaster, late 1950s; KTIV, Sioux City, Iowa, newscaster, weatherman, and staff announcer, 1960–62; KMTV, Omaha, NE, morning news editor, 1962–65; WSB–TV, Atlanta, GA, news editor and anchor, 1965–66; KNBC–TV, Los Angeles, CA, reporter and anchor, 1966–73; National Broadcasting Co. (NBC–TV), White House correspondent and anchor of Saturday evening news, 1973–76, co-host of *Today* show, 1976–81, co–anchor, then sole anchor, of *NBC Nightly News*, 1982 . Lecturer in television news at Yale University, New Haven, CT, 1978–79. Member of board of trustees of Norton Simon Museum of Art, Pasadena, CA. Author of *The Greatest Generation*, Random House, 1998; contributor of articles to newspapers and magazines, including *New York Times*, *New York Daily News*, *Los Angeles Times*, and *Family Weekly*. Author of introductions to various volumes, including *NBC News/Rand McNally World Atlas and Almanac*.

Awards: Golden Mike Award from Radio and Television News Association of Southern California; alumni achievement award from University of South Dakota.

Sidelights

Tom Brokaw's clean–cut Midwestern looks and easygoing nature have helped make him one of the top news anchors on television. Whether talking to heads of state or middle class Americans, he has gained a reputation for a cozy charm and an ability to ad–lib that are the basis of successful interviews. Though he has seen his ratings swell and fall, Brokaw has remained a vital force in NBC's news coverage, not only as the handsome face on camera, but also in managing the content, display, and coverage as well. After four decades in broadcasting, Brokaw turned his hand to the print medium, publishing the book *The Greatest Generation* in 1998. It topped the best–seller lists and brought an added measure of respect to an already distinguished career.

Brokaw was born on February 6, 1940, in Webster, South Dakota. His father, Anthony Orville Brokaw, who was known as "Red," worked at a government munitions depot in Igloo, South Dakota, and later was a foreman on the construction of the Fort Randall Dam and the Gavins Point Dam. Due to his father's job, the family relocated a couple of times during Brokaw's childhood, moving from Igloo to Pickstown, where the Fort Randall Dam was being built in the late 1940s, then to Yankton in 1955 before his second year in high school. His mother, Eugenia "Jean" (Conley) Brokaw, worked as a clerk in the Pickstown post office and then in a shoe store in Yankton. She had to work to help support the family, which included Brokaw's younger brothers, William and Michael.

When the family moved to Yankton, it was the biggest town Brokaw had ever seen, and he was a bit anxious about going to school with a crowd of about 800 students. He joined the football, basketball, and track teams, though he was never a standout athlete. He also acted in the school play and was selected as one of eight representing Yankton High School at Boys' State, a nationwide program to introduce youth to the workings of the American political system. Even then, his classmates knew Brokaw was bound for greatness. "From the word 'go,' Tom was going to be governor," stated his football coach, Don Allen, to Robert Goldberg and Gerald Jay Goldberg in *Anchors: Brokaw, Jennings, Rather and the Evening News.*

In high school, Brokaw worked after school at a clothing store and in the summers gave tours at the Gavins Point Dam, even writing his own guide descriptions. In 1955, he landed a job at a new local radio station, KYNT, where he spun records by the likes of Elvis Presley and Fats Domino. In his high school yearbook, he listed his hobbies as dancing and records, as Goldberg and Goldberg reported. After graduation, he went to the University of Iowa and planned to become a lawyer, but he was overly tempted by socializing and not by his books. "Lots of girlfriends, lots of good times, lots of missed classes," he admitted in *People.* "I assumed that I would get what I wanted just by showing up."

Returning home, Brokaw took a semester off. His mother—formerly an aspiring journalist whose dreams were thwarted over lack of tuition—then encouraged her son to apply for a job at a television station. He began earning a living as a newscaster at the CBS affiliate WNEX in Yankton, doing everything from cooking shows to weather reports. At the time, Lawrence Welk headed the house band there. Soon, Brokaw enrolled at the University of South Dakota at Vermillion.

After getting fired from WNEX for being out of town at an inopportune moment, Brokaw then dropped out of school as well. He went back to

KYNT, where he crossed paths again with Meredith Lynn Auld, a girl he dated in his junior year. She had gone to a different college and they temporarily parted ways, but she was back in Yankton for the summer. She entered the Miss Yankton beauty pageant–devised as a Republican fund–raiser–then went on to become Miss South Dakota 1959. Brokaw interviewed her for the radio station when she was in the Yankton contest, and after she won the state pageant, she called to tell him. Thinking his microphone was off, Brokaw told her he loved her, but in fact it was on, and the entire town heard the declaration.

However, Auld soon broke it off with Brokaw because of his lack of seriousness. This caused him to reassess his life, and he returned to the University of South Dakota and studied political science. By his senior year in 1960, he was working weekends at KTIV, the NBC television affiliate in Sioux City, Iowa. He and Auld married on August 17, 1962, and would go on to have three daughters: Jennifer Jean, Andrea Brooks, and Sarah Auld. Brokaw's wife later opened a chain of upscale toy stores in Manhattan called the Penny Whistle, and eventually became a writer.

In 1962, Brokaw graduated from college with a bachelor's degree in political science, although he was obviously entrenched in journalism by that point. As he noted to Toby Thompson in *Rolling Stone,* "If television hadn't existed, I'd probably have been a newspaperman." But he liked television much better, so right away he landed a job as a morning news editor and newscaster with KMTV, the NBC station in Omaha, Nebraska. "They initially offered me $90 a week, and I turned them down after having begged for the job," Brokaw recalled, according to Goldberg and Goldberg. "But I was the first college graduate in my family, just married, with a doctor father–in–law a bit unsure about his new son–in–law's future. I needed $100. They finally agreed on the condition that I never be given a raise. And I never was." At KMTV, Brokaw learned every facet of broadcasting, from applying his own makeup to writing scripts and editing film.

Moving to Atlanta in 1965, Brokaw worked for WSB–TV as editor and anchor of the 11 p.m. news. He gained national exposure there for contributing reports on racial issues to the *Huntley–Brinkley Report.* The next year, he started as a reporter for KNBC–TV in Los Angeles, and became an anchor on the 11 p.m. news. There, he covered top stories such as the 1966 California governor's race, in which Ronald Reagan defeated incumbent Edmund G. "Pat" Brown; the anti–Vietnam war movement; Robert

Kennedy's assassination; and the 1971 Sylmar earthquake. He burnished his appearance and demeanor to fit in with the upscale Southern California style, and began to hobnob with mover and shakers. In 1971, he was named to anchor an episode of *First Tuesday*, a monthly prime–time news magazine show on NBC, and the next year, he gained attention for his coverage of the California delegation at the Democratic National Convention.

In 1973, Brokaw was invited to join the NBC News as a White House correspondent and anchor on the Saturday evening news. He was just 33, and took the job despite a hefty pay cut. His timing was perfect, since the Watergate scandal involving President Richard Nixon was breaking, and he was in the thick of it. By this time, although some took note of his charisma and good looks and dismissed him, the former college dropout had become an avid reader and was highly regarded by many for his intellect and reporting skills. He was especially noted for his ability to deliver hard–hitting interview questions without being outwardly confrontational.

Soon, Brokaw was offered a rich three– to five–year contract as host of NBC's *Today* show after Barbara Walters left to join ABC News, and he took the air in August of 1976. The popularity of the morning news, weather, and chat program had been lagging behind *Good Morning America.* Along with cohost Jane Pauley and some other lively talent like Gene Shalit and Willard Scott, the show rose to the top in the ratings. During this time Brokaw earned the nickname "Duncan the Wonder Horse" for his tendency to work long hours and throw his all into the program. However, when five years was up, he wanted to move on. As he noted to Goldberg and Goldberg, he felt that "the long curve of my career was always serious journalism. The 'Today' show was kind of a left turn."

After the *Today* show stint, in 1982 Brokaw was offered multimillion dollar deals from all three networks. He stayed with NBC, though, to co–anchor the *NBC Nightly News* with Roger Mudd. Though NBC hoped that Brokaw and Mudd could compete with Dan Rather at CBS, the program's ratings dropped from second to third, behind ABC. As a result, Mudd was taken off the show, and some critics "complained that the pretty boy had beaten out the real reporter," as Gioia Diliberto put it in *People.* Brokaw was also criticized for not having the most precise diction. However, he soon established himself as an influential creative talent behind the scenes, first as managing editor, and later as chief of correspondents.

By the mid–1980s, Brokaw, Rather, and Peter Jennings at ABC were the heavyweight news anchors on the major networks. With his boyish looks and easygoing charm, Brokaw's ratings steadily rose from 1984 to 1986, as he gained roughly two million viewers and Rather lost about 400,000. Though there are many other factors that affect television news ratings, including which shows are positioned around it, Edwin Diamond in *Rolling Stone* suggested that Brokaw was becoming a force because his "kind of news is centrist." He explained, "The iconographic Dan, of course, is country & western, appealing to an older, idealized America of the imagination. Peter is urban, projecting an image with which a more youthful market can identify. Tom positions himself somewhere in between, in the middle an avatar of suburban values."

However, for about the next decade, Brokaw's *Nightly News* floundered. There was an occasional coup, such as his all–night on–the–scene coverage when a bomb went off at the 1996 Olympics in Atlanta, Georgia. That backfired, though, when Brokaw reported based on FBI data that security guard Richard Jewell had set off the device. Jewell later sued NBC and settled out of court for an undisclosed sum. And even though Brokaw was not involved, NBC also had lost much of its luster in 1992 when *Dateline* staged explosions in General Motors pickup trucks to illustrate safety concerns. In addition, polls and critical opinions in general for some time found Brokaw to be the least popular of the three major anchors.

In the mid–1990s, though, with direct input from Brokaw, NBC overhauled their coverage, and he began to run neck–in–neck with Jennings for the top spot. Charles Kaiser in New York gave him much of the credit for the turnaround, stating, "It is Brokaw himself who has played the most important role in his own redemption." Among other things, Kaiser noted that Brokaw lobbied for covering fewer stories in a more in–depth manner, and for moving out from behind the traditional anchor desk to stand in from of a 7–by–12–foot video board. "I've always hated the anachronistic idea of a white man, middle–aged, sitting there at a desk reading to America," Brokaw commented to Kaiser. From September 1996 to September 1997, the *NBC Nightly News* finally toppled *ABC World News Tonight* from its number–one ratings slot, which it had gripped since 1989. In the summer of 1997, Brokaw signed a new deal with NBC that reportedly paid him $7 million annually plus $3 million in stock. This came after cable news giant CNN tried to pry him away with a similarly sweet deal.

Though he had contributed several articles to publications such as the *New York Times* and *Los Angeles Times*, Brokaw became a full–fledged author in 1998 when Random House released *The Greatest Generation*. He got the idea in 1984 while covering the fortieth anniversary of D–Day. This collection of about 50 profiles of Americans who grew up during the Great Depression and experienced World War II sold two million copies by spring of 1999. In the work, Brokaw wrote, "I hope the book will in some small way pay tribute to those men and women who have given us the lives we have today." Brokaw also noted in *People*, "This generation had impact well beyond their own shores and their own interests. It was a privilege to tell their stories." Incidentally, his effort surpassed Jenning's *The Century* in January of 1999 to top the best–seller charts.

Admired by both major political parties, Brokaw was once offered a job as White House press secretary during the Nixon administration and as director of the National Park Service under President Bill Clinton's administration, though he passed on both. Avid socializers, Brokaw and his wife are known for their dinner parties, where they have hosted luminaries such as former Soviet leader Mikhail Gorbachev and architect I. M. Pei. He also counts actors Robert Redford and Harrison Ford among his circle of friends. A devoted fitness fan, Brokaw is a runner, and fights insomnia by working out in his Park Avenue building's gym; he was named one of *People* magazine's 50 most beautiful people in the world in 1999. In addition to having a home base in New York City, Brokaw and his wife own a 4,000–acre ranch in Montana. An enthusiastic outdoorsman, he also enjoys backpacking, skiing, softball, and mountain climbing.

Sources

Books

Contemporary Theater, Film and Television, volume 6, Gale Research, 1988. Goldberg, Robert and Gerald Jay Goldberg, *Anchors: Brokaw, Jennings, Rather and the Evening News*, Carol Publishing, 1990.

Periodicals

Esquire, March 1986, p. 90.
Good Housekeeping, January 1999, p. 24; January 2000, p. 77.
Newsweek, August 5, 1996, p. 34.
New York, January 6, 1997, p. 32.
People, April 28, 1986, p. 92; May 10, 1999, p. 143; January 18, 1999, p. 91.
Rocky Mountain News, October 26, 1997, p. 20D.
Rolling Stone, May 13, 1982, p. 26; October 9, 1986, p. 60.
Saturday Evening Post, May/June 1978, p. 78; May 1999, p. 12.
TV Guide, October 24, 1987, p. 6; January 9, 1999, p. 5.
Washington Post, July 22, 1981, p. B1.

Pierce Brosnan

The Kobal Collection

Actor

Born May 16, 1952 (some sources say 1953), in County Meath, Ireland; married Cassandra Harris (a model and actor), 1977 (died, 1991); children (with Harris): stepdaughter Charlotte, stepson Christopher, son Sean William; (with Keely Shaye Smith) Dylan Thomas.

Addresses: *Home*—Malibu, CA. *Agent*—Michael Menchol, Creative Artists Agency, 9830 Wilshire Blvd., Beverly Hills, CA 90212.

Career

Actor. Stage appearances include *Wait Until Dark*, London, 1976; *The Red Devil Battery Sign*, London, 1977; and various repertory productions. Television appearances include episodes of *The Professionals*, 1980; *Hammer House of Horror*, 1980; and *Moonlighting*, 1985; series *Remington Steele*, 1982–87; miniseries *The Manions of America*, 1981; *Nancy Astor*, 1984; *Noble House*, 1988; and *Around the World in 80 Days*, 1989; and movies *The Heist*, 1989; *Murder 101*, 1991; *Victim of Love*, 1991; *Death Train*, 1993; *The Broken Chain*, 1993; *Dangerous Pursuit*, 1994; *Don't Talk to Strangers*, 1994; and *Night Watch*, 1995.

Film appearances include *The Mirror Crack'd*, 1980; *The Long Good Friday*, 1980; *Nomads*, 1986; *The Fourth Protocol*, 1987; *Taffin*, 1998; *The Deceivers*, 1988; *Mister Johnson*, 1991; *The Lawnmower Man*, 1992; *Live Wire*, 1992; *Mrs. Doubtfire*, 1993; *Entangled*, 1993; *Love Affair*, 1994; *GoldenEye*, 1995; *Robinson Crusoe*, 1996; *The Disappearance of Kevin Johnson*, 1996; *The Mirror Has Two Faces*, 1996; *Mars Attacks!*, 1996; *Dante's Peak*, 1997; *Tomorrow Never Dies*, 1997; *Quest for Camelot* (voice), 1998; *The Nephew*, 1998; *The World Is Not Enough*, 1999; *The Thomas Crown Affair*, 1999; *The Match*, 1999; and *Grey Owl*, 1999.

Sidelights

The name is Brosnan, Pierce Brosnan but he is probably better known as James Bond, the legendary martini–drinking master spy created by author Ian Fleming. As the fifth actor to play Agent 007, Brosnan succeeded Sean Connery, George Lazenby, Roger Moore, and Timothy Dalton, and managed to update the part for more contemporary sensibilities while simultaneously re–injecting some of Bond's masculine bravado. The tall, handsome actor first stepped into the role with 1995's *GoldenEye*, and also performed in *Tomorrow Never Dies*, 1997, and *The World Is Not Enough*, 1999. Thanks to his chiseled features and dapper persona, Brosnan has played a variety of other sophisticated men on screen as well, ranging from scientists to a presidential aide. He first made his name in 1980s as a charming detective on the television series *Remington Steele*.

Brosnan was born on May 16, 1952 or 1953 (sources vary) in County Meath, Ireland. His father left the family when he was only a year old, and the two would not meet again until Brosnan was in his thirties and got a call from a cousin letting him know his father's whereabouts. He did not call for about a year, but then decided he wanted his children to know their grandfather and about two years later, they met. However, they did not see each other again, and his father died in about 1985.

After Brosnan's parents split up, his mother left him with grandparents so that she could go to London and study nursing. When his grandparents died, Brosnan went to live with an aunt and uncle. His mother married again, to a Scottish mechanic, and sent for her son when he was 11. He had attended strict Catholic schools in Ireland, and found that London schools offered much more freedom. "I kept waiting to get hit," Brosnan noted in a *People* article, "and when I found out I wouldn't be, I had a whale of a time." Still, he earned all A's in art and English, and dropped out of school to begin training as a commercial artist for Harrod's department store.

At age 18, Brosnan joined an experimental theater group and then launched into formal training at the Drama Centre of London for three years. He graduated in 1976, and that same year landed a role in the London premiere of the play *Wait Until Dark*. Six months later, playwright Tennessee Williams chose him to star in the role of McCabe in *The Red Devil Battery Sign*. The production soon closed, but Brosnan got good reviews. He noted in *People*, "From then on, I was never out of work." In addition to appearing with various repertory companies, he took the stage for a year and a half in the Franco Zeffirelli production of *Filumena*. However, as he mentioned to Diane DeDubovay in *McCall's*, "I knew I didn't want to strut around the boards doing 'Henry the Fifth' or Ibsen the rest of my life. I wanted to be a movie star."

Meanwhile, Brosnan began living with Australian supermodel and actor Cassandra "Cassie" Harris. She brought two children to the relationship Charlotte and Christopher, whom she had with her first husband, British actor Dermot Harris (brother of Richard Harris). The actor's Catholic upbringing began to weigh on his conscience, and they married in 1977 and he adopted the children. Later, in the early 1980s, they had a son, Sean William. Harris only had a couple of minor roles before her final appearance as a "Bond girl" in the 1981 film *For Your Eyes Only*.

Brosnan broke into film with an uncredited role in 1980's *The Mirror Crack'd*, playing in a scene with Elizabeth Taylor. That same year, he had a bit part in *The Long Good Friday*. Finally, in 1981, he landed a lead role in the miniseries *The Manions of America*, which was filmed in Ireland. After that, Brosnan borrowed money to go to Los Angeles so he and his wife could go on auditions. Within a few weeks, he had captured the role that would be his ticket to fame, playing a suave detective (and the title character) on the television series *Remington Steele*. Though the true sleuth of the operation was his boss and romantic partner, Laura Holt (played by Stephanie Zimbalist), Brosnan began to dominate the series thanks to his popularity with female viewers, who were attracted to his attractive features and debonair demeanor. He openly disdained his stature as a sex symbol, but his fate was sealed.

For a few years after its first airing in 1982, *Remington Steele* posted top 20 ratings, despite jabs from critics. However, by May of 1986, ratings had sunk, and NBC canceled the program, to the delight of Brosnan. He remarked in *People*, "It was too much like a job. I had just had enough. I'd had enough after two years, but I'd signed a seven–year contract." Subsequently, he signed on to play the jet–setting spy James Bond in the film *The Living Daylights*, scheduled to begin production in August of 1986.

However, once news about Brosnan's new film gig came out, NBC decided to un–cancel *Remington Steele*, figuring it could capitalize on the promotional possibilities. In addition, ratings for the summer reruns had jumped, and 10,000 fans wrote and called to protest the show's demise. The renewed interest in the show tethered Brosnan once again to his contract. The producers offered to find a way to allow him to work on both projects, but the film's producer, Albert "Cubby" Broccoli, shot down the plan, saying he was unwilling to allow the television show to ride on the coattails of Brosnan's fame in the Bond film. Instead, Broccoli hired Timothy Dalton for the part.

Less than a year later, in 1987, *Remington Steele* was canceled for good, and Brosnan launched his movie career. Earlier, he had earned a Golden Globe nomination for the 1984 miniseries *Nancy Astor*, about the first woman elected to the British House of Commons. In it, he portrayed the title character's first husband, Robert Gould Shaw. In addition, Brosnan appeared in the 1986's *Nomads*, but it was a dud. He then bucked typecasting when he took a part as a villain in 1987's *The Fourth Protocol*, playing a Soviet agent working undercover as a British spy and planning to detonate a nuclear bomb in England. Though it received some good reviews, the film flopped at the box office, as did Brosnan's next effort, *Taffin*, 1988, in which he starred as the title character.

Brosnan went on to work in another television miniseries, 1988's *The Noble House*, which got decent reviews, then showed up in theaters again as a British officer who infiltrates a cannibalistic religious cult in nineteenth–century India in *The Deceivers*. This effort was panned, however. He fared better in the miniseries version of the Jules Verne classic *Around the World in 80 Days*, which featured a stellar cast of notables, including Peter Ustinov and Eric Idle. After that, he had yet another turn as a Brit, in *Mister Johnson*, 1991, and then starred in Stephen King's *The Lawnmower Man*, about a scientist who turns a mentally slow gardener into a super–genius. It was considered a dog but did well at the box office. He also appeared in a couple more television movies in 1991.

In 1993, Brosnan performed in a more well–regarded blockbuster hit in the comedy *Mrs. Doubtfire*, although his character was minor. In it, Robin Williams portrayed a man who dons a disguise to get hired as a female nanny for his own children after his marriage splits up. Brosnan appeared as Stu, the mother's new boyfriend. Following that, he made some more television movies, then played a boyfriend again in 1994's *Love Affair*.

Finally, in 1995, Brosnan made his debut in the role of Agent 007 in *GoldenEye*. He was surprised when the opportunity presented itself again, though he noted to Bonnie Churchill in the *Christian Science Monitor*, "My Irish mother says, 'What's good for you, won't go by you,' and so here I am playing this coveted part. I'm a bit more lived–in now. I think in heart, soul, and mind, I'm better suited to play the role." Indeed, Dalton had not fit the bill for the debonair Bond, and Brosnan managed to refresh his appeal. Though he also revived the macho persona that had fallen by the wayside, the agent's image was updated with less smoking and drinking. Women also fared much better than they did in past efforts. The film brought in box office receipts of $28.1 million at its opening more than double what *The Living Daylights* made and went on to earn $340 million worldwide, one of the best–grossing pictures of the series.

In addition, Brosnan signed a three–picture deal to play Bond at the outset, going on to star in *Tomorrow Never Dies*, 1997, and *The World Is Not Enough*, 1999. However, when he signed the deal, he did not have enough clout to refuse promotional appearances. Upon the release of *Tomorrow Never Dies*, Brosnan was seen in tie–ins for BMW automobiles, Smirnoff vodka, Visa, Omega watches, and other products.

Outside of Bond, Brosnan's notable roles include a supporting part in *The Mirror Has Two Faces*, 1996, starring Barbra Streisand, who also directed the picture. In *McCall's*, she called him a "doll" and added, "He's generous, easy–going and fun to work with." In the film, he plays her slick, three–piece–suit–wearing dream lover. Then, he showed up that same year in an all–star cast in Tim Burton's wacky *Mars Attacks!* as a presidential advisor. The cast list included Jack Nicholson, Glenn Close, Martin Short, and Rod Steiger. His first day on the shoot, he admitted to Lawrence Grobel in *Cosmopolitan*, "I don't think I've ever been so scared or nervous or in awe on a set as I was that day." The next year, Brosnan was regularly doused with faux ashes for his work on *Dante's Peak*, a film about an exploding volcano in which he again played a scientist.

In addition to his busy acting career, Brosnan started up his own production company, Irish DreamTime, in the 1990s. However, the first film to be produced by his firm, *The Nephew*, went straight to video in 1998. In 1999, he produced and starred as the title character in *The Thomas Crown Affair*, costarring Rene Russo. It is a remake of the 1968 crime film of the same name starring Steve McQueen and Faye Dunaway. Once again, he portrayed a cool, powerful man, playing a bored billionaire who resorts to being a thief of fine artworks in order to inject spice in his life. After that, he also appeared in *Grey Owl*, about a Canadian conservationist. Despite being directed by Oscar winner Richard Attenborough, this picture also went directly to video.

When making *Remington Steele*, Brosnan split his time between homes in Los Angeles, in a rented home in the Hollywood Hills, and England. Later, with his acting career established in Hollywood, he bought a Spanish–style villa on six acres in Malibu, California. Brosnan's wife, Harris, died after a four–year battle with ovarian cancer at age 39 in 1991, and he talked openly in interviews about the loss and gave her the bulk of credit for his success. Her last words to him, according to Kahn in *McCall's*, were "Always an actor." He subsequently testified before Congress about cancer research and also headed several events to raise millions for the cause. In addition, he took up painting to help him cope with the loss, and also donated money to cancer research from the sale of his artworks.

Brosnan eventually began dating again, and met Keely Shaye Smith, an environmental reporter and gardening journalist, at an ecological fund–raiser. She got pregnant in 1996, and they had a son, Dylan Thomas, the next year, but did not make a commitment to the relationship at the time. As Brosnan commented to Grobel in *Cosmopolitan*, "I don't want to be tied down to just one woman . I have no plans to get married. Neither does she." However, they announced their engagement in the fall of 1999.

Sources

Books

Contemporary Theatre, Film and Television, volume 13, Gale Research, 1995.

Periodicals

Christian Science Monitor, November 20, 1995, p. 13.
Cosmopolitan, September 1996, p. 202.
Entertainment Weekly, February 18, 2000, p. 88.
Esquire, November 1995, p. 72.
Interview, August 1999, p. 100.

McCall's, August 1984, p. 32; December 1996, p. 51; August 1987, p. 148.
People, October 31, 1983, p. 48; August 11, 1986, p. 86; April 27, 1992, p. 76.
Redbook, May 1989, p. 36; December 1995, p. 63; December 1997, p. 80; December 1999, p. 64.
Time, December 15, 1997, p. 34.
USA Today, November 17, 1995.
World of Hibernia, Autumn 1997, p. 78.

Online

"Pierce Brosnan," Internet Movie Database web site, http://us.imdb.com (April 28, 2000).
"Pierce Brosnan," Mr. Showbiz web site, http://mrshowbiz.go.com (April 27, 2000).

Gro Harlem Brundtland

Physician, public health director, and political leader

Born April 20, 1939, in Oslo, Norway; daughter of Gudmund (a Norwegian cabinet member) and Inga Harlem; married Arne Olav Brundtland (a research director), December, 1960; children: Knut, Kaga, Ivar, and Jorgen. *Education:* University of Oslo, medical degree, 1963; Harvard University, master of public health degree, 1965.

Addresses: *Office*—c/o World Health Organization, Avenue Appia 20, 1211 Geneva 27, Switzerland.

Career

National Directorate of Health, Norway, medical officer with the office of hygiene, 1966–68; Oslo Board of Health, assistant medical director, 1968–74; national spokesperson for abortion rights, 1970; began representing Norway at international conferences and became active in the Labour party, 1970s; minister of the environment, 1974–79; Labour party vice chairman, 1975–81, and Labour party leader, 1981–92; elected to the Storting (parliament) for the city of Oslo, 1977–81, served as head of finance committee and foreign affairs committee, led committee on foreign and constitutional affairs, 1980–81, 1981–86, and 1989–90; Prime Minister of Norway, 1981, 1986–89, 1990–96; director general of World Health Organization, 1998.

Awards: Third World Prize, 1988; Indira Gandhi Prize, 1988; Onassis Foundation's Delphi Prize, 1992; Charlemagne Prize, 1994; Grawemeyer Award for ideas improving world order.

Sidelights

As the first female director general of the World Health Organization, Gro Harlem Brundtland brought to the position an ambitious plan for restoring credibility to the group and for engaging in wide–ranging but specific initiatives for improving the picture of international health. She had a wealth of experience to draw from when she began her five–year term in July 1998, as she had an impressive resume consisting of four terms as the first female prime minister of Norway, as well as experience working in high–profile positions with the United Nations. In all of her posts, Brundtland has been open about her dedication to women's rights and her commitment to environmental issues, while balancing her belief that a strong economy plays an important part in the well–being of everyone. In addition to holding two important firsts for women, Brundtland has received a number of other honors, including the Third World Prize and the Indira Gandhi Prize, both in 1988, the Delphi Prize from the Onassis Foundation in 1992, the Charlemagne Prize in 1994, and the Grawemeyer Award for ideas improving world order.

Brundtland was born on April 20, 1939, in Oslo, Norway, to Gudmund and Inga Harlem. Her family was highly connected in Norwegian politics, as her father served as a personal physician to Labor party prime ministers and was later a cabinet member from 1955 to 1965. He served as minister of social affairs from 1955 to 1961 and then as minister of defense from 1961 to 1965. When Nazi Germany occupied Norway during World War II, Brundtland was sent to Sweden while her parents worked in Norway for the resistance. After the war, she became politically active like her parents, joining the Norwegian Labour Movement at the age of seven.

When Brundtland was ten, the family moved to the Prospect Park section of Brooklyn after her father earned a position as a Rockefeller Fellow at New York University. She knew no English upon arrival, but was a fast learner. A few years later, they moved to Egypt, where her father worked for the United Nations as an expert on rehabilitation. This increased her international outlook. At the same time, while Brundtland's parents did not push her to excel, they did not set limits either. As Brundtland noted to Fred Hauptfuhrer in *People*, "From when I was very small, both [parents] gave me very clear indications that a girl has the same abilities and responsibilities as a boy. So I had this background of equality between the sexes instilled in me from the very beginning."

While in college, Brundtland in December of 1960 married political scientist Arne Brundtland, who had a political career of his own in Norway, albeit for the Conservative party. He served on the Oslo city council and was nominated for a seat in the parliament, which resulted in colorful coverage in the press concerning the fact that his wife was a leader for the opposing party. He later entered academia, becoming a senior research fellow at Norway's Institute of International Affairs, but continued to write a syndicated column as a Conservative advocate.

After earning her degree in medicine from the University of Oslo in 1963, Brundtland lived in the United States for a year when her husband was serving as a visiting scholar at Harvard University's Center for International Affairs. She, meanwhile, earned a scholarship to Harvard and earned her master's degree in public health in 1965. There, her interest in environmental issues was spawned, as she made the connection between personal health and environmental factors like pollution. This, in turn, stirred up her political activism. Arne Brundtland related to Hauptfuhrer, "She was doing so extremely well at Harvard that I told her, 'Since you're so damned clever, why don't you go home and join the government?'"

Returning to Norway in 1965, Brundtland worked as a pediatrician and as a consultant to the Ministry of Health. There, her main concerns included children's issues such as breast feeding, cancer prevention, and other diseases. In 1966, she became a medical officer with the office of hygiene at the National Directorate of Health, then from 1968 to 1974 served as assistant medical director to Oslo's Board of Health. Concurrently, she began representing Norway at international conferences and became active in the Labour party. In 1970, she successfully argued for abortion rights as the national spokesperson for the cause.

Brundtland's first major foray into politics came in 1974, when Norwegian Prime Minister Trygve Brattelishe named her minister of the environment. This was at a time when interest in the ecology was keen, and Brundtland became popular for advocating a respected program that instituted nature reserves. She was also involved in the international discussion on acid rain. She earned the nickname "green goddess" for her efforts. In addition, throughout the decade, the Labour party was strong and Brundtland rose quickly. She served as vice chairman of the Labour party from 1975 to 1981. In 1977, she was elected to the Norwegian parliament, called the Storting, for the city of Oslo, and in that position headed the finance committee and foreign affairs committee, two integral standing committees. She also led the committee on foreign and constitutional affairs for 1980–81, 1981–86, and 1989–90. She stepped down as minister of the environment in 1979.

The government of Norway experienced a major shake–up in 1981, stemming from a faltering economy that cast a pall on Labour's tenuous grip in the parliament. Also, citizens were split in a heated debate on the nation's security policy, precipitated by an accord signed in January of 1981 that let the United States stockpile arms, equipment, and ammunition in Norway in case of an invasion by the Soviet Union. Prime Minister Odvar Nordli was forced to resign early that year, and Brundtland—the most well–liked figure in her party, according to polls—stepped in as prime minister, making her the country's first female leader and, at age 41, the youngest woman to run a modern government.

Brundtland's seat was short–lived, however. In the general election held in September of 1981, a Conservative coalition ousted Labour and Brundtland handed the reins to Kare Willoch in October. Subsequently, she continued as the opposition party leader until she was reelected prime minister in May of 1986, serving until another Conservative victory in 1989. During this time, she named 8 women to her 18–member cabinet, giving it the highest proportion of females in the top echelon of government of any nation. It was not difficult to find them, because 41 percent of Labour party members, and 34 percent of Storting members, at the time were women, due to a Labour party drive in the 1980s to get more women involved in politics.

The advances for women did not always come easy. Brundtland had faced her share of male critics along the way who liked to call her "Chatterbox" and "Mother." Eventually, though, her gender became mostly a non–issue. In fact, when she was first named leader of her country in 1981, the newspapers did not play up the event to any real extent, placing the story of her succession on page one alongside articles on an Elton John concert and travel prices. Brundtland was instead regaled for her conflict resolution skills as well as her analytical mind. These strong suits served her well when she took the responsibility in 1983 of creating and chairing the United Nations World Commission on Environment and Development. In this job, Brundtland researched international environmental issues, concluding in the commission's 1987 report *Our Common Future* that global ecology could be best accomplished by a combination of environmental protection and economic growth. The recommendations within led to the Earth Summit, the United National Conference on Environment and Development, held in Rio de Janeiro in 1992.

After its win in 1989, the Conservative coalition government slid into trouble due to internal conflict among the factions. One of the major issues concerned whether Norway should join the European Community. Their coalition fell in October of 1990, and Brundtland rose to prime minister for the third time. In this term, she had to form a coalition with some minor parties to hold a majority in the 165–seat parliament. She began her fourth term as Norway's leader in 1993 and resigned abruptly in October of 1996. During her later time in office, she was lauded for her continuing concern for the environment and for the strong economy, though she drew criticism at times for not paying enough attention to strictly domestic affairs. In addition, despite her determination, she could not convince Norwegians to approve entry into the European Union, a setback that represented her greatest political failure.

Going back to her roots in medicine, in January of 1998 Brundtland was elected director general of the Geneva, Switzerland–based World Health Organization (WHO), the first woman ever to hold the post. Chosen from five candidates in a secret ballot, she was considered the heavy favorite among Western nations, especially the United States, which supports about one–quarter of the agency's budget and was unhappy with the previous WHO leader. Brundtland took over from Hiroshi Nakajima of Japan, who was plagued with accusations of trading favors for votes and chided for mismanaging the organization.

Upon her election to the five–year stint, Brundtland immediately pledged internal reform to clear up WHO's reputation, and after being confirmed by the World Health Assembly in May, she officially stepped into the position in July of 1998. Bringing her political background to the job, right away she stated that some of the main targets for WHO would include poverty, social inequality, and under-development, indicating her belief in a strong connection between health and economic prosperity. She indicated her desire to make health care available and affordable and to focus on disease prevention. In addition, she penned an editorial in Science in June of 1998 vowing to place an emphasis on international research efforts. Reports following Brundtland's election also frequently noted that she had caused a flap at a United Nations population conference in Cairo, Egypt, in 1994 when she suggested that abortion be decriminalized on a worldwide basis.

In her acceptance speech, Brundtland outlined that she wanted to make WHO "more effective, more accountable, more transparent and more receptive to a changing world," according to a *World Health* article. In addition, she announced her intent to increase the number of female employees at WHO. After a year in office, two of her first big projects were the drive to "Roll Back Malaria," a menace that has spiraled particularly in Africa since about the mid– 1980s, and the "Tobacco Free Initiative," to address tobacco as the cause of many premature deaths and to effect programs to convince people not to smoke. Also, Brundtland had reorganized more than 50 programs into 10 divisions, each focused on broad subject areas such as communicable diseases, mental health, social change, healthy environments, and sustainable development. Of course, she did not forget her belief that all are intertwined. As she explained to Sasha Nemecek in *Scientific American*, "If you chose the right pattern of development, you take care of health, the environment and economics."

Brundtland's hobbies include outdoor activities, particularly sailing and cross–country skiing. She and her husband had four children, Knut, Kaja, Ivar and Jorgen, though one son committed suicide in the early 1990s. At the outset of her marriage and career, Brundtland once commented to Gloria Steinem in *Ms.*, "I said, 'Look, I'm going to be a doctor and I'm going to have four children.' Any thinking about future society which presupposes, directly or indirectly, that there is not sufficient room for being a mother, for having children, for fulfilling the potential of life both for women and for men, because that's important for both is a dangerous sidetrack."

Sources

Books

Current Leaders of Nations, Gale Research, 1998.
Encyclopedia of World Biography, second edition, Gale Research, 1998.

Periodicals

Economist, October 26, 1996, p. 65.
Europe, September 1994, p. 16.

Journal of the American Medical Association, February 18, 1998, p. 491.
Lancet, February 7, 1998, p. 381; February 6, 1999, p. 477.
Ms., January 1988, p. 74.
New York Times, February 4, 1981, p. A6; January 28, 1998.
People, April 20, 1981, p. 34.
Public Health Reports, January 1999, p. 30.
Science, June 26, 1998, p. 2027.
Scientific American, June 1999, p. 28.
Time, October 6, 1986, p. 40.
UN Chronicle, Spring 1999, p. 12.
World Health, July 1998, p. 3.

Online

"Office of the Director–General," World Health Organization web site, http://www.who.org (October 19, 1999).

Carol Burnett

AP/Wide World Photos

Actor, singer, and comedian

Born April 26, 1933, in San Antonio, TX; daughter of Joseph "Jody" (a salesman and theater manager) and Ina Louise (a writer; maiden name, Creighton) Burnett; married Don Saroyan (an actor), December 17, 1955 (divorced, 1962); married Joe Hamilton (a producer), 1963 (divorced, 1983); children: (with Hamilton) Carrie Louise, Jody Ann, Erin Kate; eight stepchildren. *Education:* Attended the University of California, Los Angeles, 1953–55.

Addresses: *Home*—Santa Fe, NM, and Honolulu, HI. *Agent*—International Creative Management, 8942 Wilshire Blvd., Beverly Hills, CA 90211. *Publicist*—Kelman & Burditch Public Relations, 118 [00ab] S. La Brea Ave., Los Angeles, CA 90036.

Career

Actor, singer, and comedian. Began singing in cabarets and musical comedies; achieved national recognition with parody song "I Made a Fool of Myself over John Foster Dulles," 1957. Franklin D. Murphy Associate and board member, Emerson College, Boston, MA; established the "Carol Burnett Musical Competition Award," University of California, Los Angeles, Theatre Arts School, and established scholarships for the study of journalistic ethics at the University of Hawaii and the University of California at Berkeley. Author of autobiography, *One More Time*, Random House, 1986.

Stage appearances include *Once upon a Mattress*, New York City, 1959-60; *Fade Out Fade In*, New York City, 1964; *Plaza Suite*, Los Angeles, 1970; *I Do! I Do!*, Los Angeles, 1973; *Same Time, Next Year*, Los Angeles, 1977, and Jupiter, FL, 1980; *Love Letters*, Los Angeles, 1990; *Moon over Buffalo*, 1995; and *Putting It Together*, Los Angeles, 1998, and New York City, 1999-2000.

Television work includes guest appearances on numerous shows during the 1950s, including *The Ed Sullivan Show, The Dinah Shore Show,* and *The Tonight Show;* regular performer on *The Garry Moore Show,* 1959-62; star of own series, *The Carol Burnett Show,* 1967-78 and 1991, and *Carol & Company,* 1990. Other notable television appearances include movies *The Grass Is Always Greener over the Septic Tank,* 1978; *The Tenth Month,* 1979; *Friendly Fire,* 1979; *Life of the Party: The Story of Beatrice,* 1982; *Between Friends,* 1983; *The Laundromat,* 1985; *Follies in Concert,* 1986; *Hostage,* 1988; *Men, Movies & Carol* (also writer), 1994; and *Grace,* 1998; series *Stanley,* 1956-57; *The Entertainers,* 1964; *All My Children,* 1976; *Mama's Family,* 1983-85; *Mad about You,* 1994-96; and *Hollywood Squares,* 1998; and numerous specials and awards shows.

Other television work includes director, *Starring Katharine Hepburn* (also producer),1981; *Judy Garland: The Concert Years* (also producer), 1985; *James Stewart: A Wonderful Life* (also producer), 1987; *Ba-*

call on Bogart (also producer), 1988; *The Fred Astaire Songbook* (also producer), 1991; *Katharine Hepburn: All about Me* (also writer and producer), 1992; *The Universal Story* (also writer), 1995; and *Southern Star: A Portrait of Atlanta* (also writer and producer), 1996; producer, *Fred Astaire: Puttin' on His Top Hat*, 1980; *Fred Astaire: Change Partners and Dance*, 1980; and executive producer, *Plaza Suite*, 1987.

Film appearances include *Who's Been Sleeping in My Bed?*, 1963; *Pete 'n' Tillie*, 1972; *The Front Page*, 1974; *A Wedding*, 1978; *Health*, 1980; *Chu Chu and the Philly Flash*, 1981; The *Four Seasons*, 1981; *Annie*, 1982; *Noises Off*, 1992; *Wisecracks* (documentary), 1992. Also executive producer (with Marcia Brandwynne and Nadine Schiff), *Made in America*, 1993.

Awards: American Guild of Variety Artists Award, Outstanding Comedienne, and Theatre World Award, both 1960, for *Once upon a Mattress*; TV Guide Awards, outstanding female performer, 1961, 1962, and 1963, all for *The Garry Moore Show*; Emmy Award, outstanding performance in a variety or musical program or series, 1962, for *The Garry Moore Show*; Emmy Award, outstanding performance in a variety or musical program or series, 1963, for *Julie and Carol at Carnegie Hall*; Golden Globe Award, best female television star, 1968, and best TV actress in a musical/comedy, 1970, 1972, for *The Carol Burnett Show*; Antoinette Perry Special Award, 1969; Hasty Pudding Woman of the Year,1969; named Hollywood Women's Press Club Golden Apple Star of the Year, 1970; People's Choice Awards, best variety show, 1975, for *The Carol Burnett Show*; People's Choice Awards, favorite all–around female entertainer, 1975, 1976, 1977, 1978, 1979, 1980, and 1981; People's Choice Awards, favorite female television performer, 1976; voted Favorite All– Around Female Entertainer by the public in A.C. Nelson Company polls, 1976, 1977, 1978, and 1979; People's Choice Award, best musical variety show, 1977, for *The Carol Burnett Show*; Golden Globe Awards, best actress in a musical/comedy television series, 1977, 1978, for *The Carol Burnett Show*; Christopher Award and Bronze Rose Award from the Montreaux Television Contest, both 1977, for *Sills and Burnett at the Met*; National Critics' Circle Award, outstanding performance, 1977–78; San Sebastian Film Festival, best actress award, 1978, for *A Wedding*; Hollywood Women's Press Club, Louella Parsons Award, 1979; People's Choice Awards, favorite female television performer, 1979, 1980, and 1981; Women in Film Crystal Award, 1980; honorary Doctor of Humane Letters, Emerson College, 1980; American Guild of Variety Artists Award, favorite television performer, 1981; Jack Benny Humanitarian Award from the March of Dimes, 1981; Humanitarian of the Year Award from Variety Clubs International, 1983;

named one of the world's ten most admired women by *Good Housekeeping* magazine, 1983; Gold Medal Award from the International Radio and Television Society, 1984; Annual Cable Excellence Award, best actress in a dramatic or theatrical program, 1984, for *Between Friends*; inducted into the Academy of Television Arts and Sciences Hall of Fame, 1985; American Comedy Award, Lifetime Achievement Award, 1987; Horatio Alger Distinguished Americans Award from the Horatio Alger Association, 1988; People's Choice Award, favorite female performer in a new program, 1991; American Comedy Award, funniest female performer in a television special, 1990, for *Julie and Carol: Together Again!*; American Comedy Award for funniest female guest appearance in a TV series, 1997, 1998, for *Mad About You*; Emmy Award for outstanding guest actress in a comedy series, 1997, for *Mad About You*; American Comedy Award for funniest female performer in a TV special, 1999, for *The Marriage Fool*; *Entertainment Weekly* named her one of "The 100 Greatest Entertainers," 1999; Woman of the Year Award from the Los Angeles Times; Woman of the Year Award from the Academy of Television Arts and Sciences; three additional Golden Globe Awards; five Gold Medals from *Photoplay* magazine as Most Popular Television Star; four Entertainer of the Year Awards from the American Guild of Variety Artists, Best Female Comedienne; named Most Popular Television Star by the Newspaper Enterprise Association; Variety Club Award, Top Female Star; New York Friars Award, Entertainer of the Year; named one of the world's 20 most admired women in a Gallup Poll.

Sidelights

One of the most recognizable faces in entertainment, the multitalented Carol Burnett has been in the spotlight since her debut on a children's television show in the mid–1950s. Before that, she was a struggling acting student armed with a fervent desire to succeed and lift herself out of the cramped one–room apartment where she practiced singing with her mother in the bathroom. Ironically, a move from Hollywood where she where she spent most of her youth to New York City was her ticket to stardom. Soon, she had a long, successful run as host of her own variety series, where she delighted audiences with her zany characters in comedy skits, from inept secretaries to pretentious royalty. She was the driving creative force behind the show. Later, she turned to drama, proving that she was just as skilled at serious acting. However, musical theater was her first love, and in 1998, she was winning praise for her turn on Broadway in *Putting It Together*, which ran through early 2000.

Perhaps Burnett's strongest appeal lies in her ability to understand the human tragedy underneath the joke while not ruining the gag. Her own ability to laugh at her weaknesses and troubles and learn from them shines through in her characters. She has had her share of personal turmoil, but has remained dedicated to making others laugh. As she once commented to Susan Dworkin in *Ms.*, "Success is whipped cream. I have always grown from my problems and challenges, from the things that don't work out, that's when I've really learned."

Burnett was born on April 26, 1933, in San Antonio, Texas, to Jody and Louise (Creighton) Burnett. Both parents were alcoholics. Though her father worked at times as a portrait salesman and movie theater manager, he was often unemployed, and the family relied on welfare. However, since her parents moved to southern California when she was young, Burnett was basically raised by her maternal grandmother, Mabel Eudora White, whom she called Nanny. Her parents split up when she was in elementary school, and she and Nanny moved to Hollywood to live with Burnett's mother in a grim and cluttered one-room apartment. When Burnett was 11, her mother had another daughter, Christine, by a married man she had been seeing. Her mother continued to drink excessively, and even had a parakeet that drank too much.

While attending Selma Avenue Grammar School growing up, Burnett often feigned illness because she hated to be separated from Nanny. Though she was not big on school, she was a devoted filmgoer, seeing all the classics at the many movie houses around Hollywood. Meanwhile, her mother landed occasional freelance work interviewing stars like Rita Hayworth and Bob Hope. In addition, Burnett lived just a few blocks from Grauman's Chinese Theater, and enjoyed looking at the impressions of celebrities' hands and feet in the cement. She and Nanny would sometimes attend premieres at Grauman's and other major theaters in Hollywood. This all contributed to her starstruck nature.

Burnett attended Le Conte Junior High School and then graduated from Hollywood High School in 1951. In her teens, she and Nanny worked part-time at night cleaning offices at the Warner Brothers building, even though they were risking getting cut off of welfare. The offices they cleaned housed the artists who created posters and billboards advertising movies. Since Burnett was a good artist who enjoyed cartooning, she once left one of her drawings on one of the artists' tables, hoping to get discovered. Instead, she found a note asking her to stick to cleaning.

After high school, Burnett attended the University of California at Los Angeles (UCLA). By this time she had decided to pursue journalism, after work-

ing on her student newspapers in junior high and high school. One of her first big stories was interviewing actor Joel McCrea. However, UCLA did not offer a major in journalism, and while thumbing through the course catalog, she decided to major in theater arts and become an actor. Her only role up to that point had been playing a maid in a junior high play that one of the school's English teachers had written.

In college, Burnett got her start in a small student-written play titled *Keep Me a Woman Grown*, playing a hillbilly. She earned raves and was named "most outstanding newcomer" in the drama department after her first year. That summer, she got her first full-time job as an usher at the Warner Brothers Theater, but she was soon fired for refusing to seat a couple during the last ten minutes of the Alfred Hitchcock film *Strangers on a Train*. The next summer, while working in the box office of a different movie theater, she was invited to join the Stumptown Players, an elite group of UCLA graduate students who set up their own production company north of San Francisco. Over Nanny's protestations, she left, and became an immediate hit there. They asked her to return the next summer.

Meanwhile, Burnett began dating fellow acting student Don Saroyan, and the two were each given $1,000 to kick-start their careers by a benefactor she has refused to name. They met the man after performing a duet from *Annie Get Your Gun* for a private party. He was so impressed with their talent and ambition that loaned them the money to go to New York City to find fame in musical theater, on the conditions that they repay him in five years, they never reveal his identity, and they promise to help out other people in need once they became successful. She and Saroyan quit school and moved to New York, and her father died soon after. She found work as a hat check girl and doggedly pursued auditions for more than a year while living at the Rehearsal Club, a hotel for hopeful female actors. Soon she landed an agent and began working in summer stock and nightclubs.

On December 17, 1955, Burnett and Saroyan married. That day also marked her first television appearance, on the *Winchell-Mahoney Show* for children on Saturday mornings on NBC. She played the girlfriend of a ventriloquist's dummy. When she landed the job and phoned Nanny to tell her, she asked Burnett to say hello to her over the air. Burnett explained that she was not allowed to do this, but she told Nanny that she would tug on her earlobe as a secret signal to tell her she loved her. That started a career-long trademark.

After this start, Burnett landed a role opposite Buddy Hackett on the sitcom *Stanley* from 1956 to 1957. Also in 1956 she began appearing occasionally on the *Garry Moore Show*. Then, in 1957, she earned a name on the cabaret and nightclub circuit in New York, mainly for performing "I Made a Fool of Myself over John Foster Dulles," which parodied maudlin teenage love songs. She was thus invited to sing the tune on the *Tonight Show*, then hosted by Jack Paar, and Ed Sullivan's *Toast of the Town*. Her youngest sister came to live with her in 1958, and her mother died shortly afterward, in January of 1959.

By now, Burnett's career was taking off. In 1959, she became a regular on the *Garry Moore Show*, and in April of that year made her off–Broadway debut in *Once Upon a Mattress,* based on the fairy tale "The Princess and the Pea" and directed by George Abbott. It was such a success that it moved to Broadway by that November. She won several theater awards for her acting in the work. In 1962, Burnett earned her first Emmy Award for her appearances on the *Garry Moore Show,* then the next year she won another for *Julie and Carol Live at Carnegie Hall,* with Julie Andrews. Meanwhile, though, her success had cast a pall over her marriage, and she parted amicably from Saroyan in 1960. The divorce was final in 1962.

Also in 1962, Burnett signed a ten–year deal with CBS. She began starring in the variety series *The Entertainers* in 1964, but it was a dud and canceled the next year. She married Joe Hamilton, the producer of the *Garry Moore Show,* in 1963, and the couple raised three daughters Carrie Louise, Jody Ann, and Erin Kate in addition to Hamilton's eight children from a previous marriage. Hamilton ended up producing Burnett's highly popular and long–running variety series, *The Carol Burnett Show,* from 1967 to 1978.

On her show, Burnett endeared herself to viewers with a rollicking repertoire of characters, from cleaning women to Hollywood starlets. She was also talented at spoofing hit movies, and one of her specialties was mimicking wives of politicians. The show wavered at first but soon became a hit, featuring costars Harvey Korman, Tim Conway, and Vicki Lawrence (who strongly resembled Burnett) in their own range of wacky roles that complemented Burnett's. The program's popularity was also based on the star's folksy manner; she would open the show by gabbing amiably and closed it by answering questions from the audience. In its 11– year run, *The Carol Burnett Show* nabbed 22 Emmy Awards. In 1978, CBS asked Burnett for another year, but just

as Jerry Seinfeld would do a couple of decades later, she opted to bow out while she was on top. "My view is leave before they ask you to," she remarked in *Entertainment Weekly.*

Instead, Burnett moved into dramatic roles. She acted in films, including 1978's *The Wedding,* by director Robert Altman, and in the 1984 movie version of *Annie,* playing the greedy orphanage superintendent, but she was known more for her stage and television work. In 1979, she was noted for the television movie *Friendly Fire,* in which she played a mother who tries to find out the true cause of her son's death in Vietnam. In addition, Burnett toured with Rock Hudson in the play *I Do! I Do!* during the 1970s, and appeared in several Stephen Sondheim musicals during the 1980s.

Returning to comedy, Burnett appeared on Lawrence's series *Mama's Family* from 1983 to 1985, and launched her own show, *Carol & Company,* in 1990. It featured her performing with a theater repertory company in front of a live studio audience. The next year, she produced and starred in a new but short–lived incarnation of *The Carol Burnett Show.* In 1992, she took a recurring guest role on the hit sitcom *Mad About You,* starring Paul Reiser and Helen Hunt, as the mother of Hunt's character. She won another Emmy in 1997 for this part. Also in the 1980s and 1990s, Burnett directed and produced a number of television specials, mainly biographical works on stars like Jimmy Stewart, Katharine Hepburn, and Fred Astaire.

Back on stage, Burnett performed on Broadway in 1995's *Moon over Buffalo.* Then in 1998, she began starring in the musical collage *Putting It Together,* which opened at the Mark Taper Forum in Los Angeles before moving to Broadway. It featured a collection of songs from various past Stephen Sondheim efforts, laced together with a new narrative about the ups and downs of a middle–class married couple. Though some reviews were lukewarm on the material, Burnett was applauded for her work. David Mermelstein, for example, wrote in *Variety,* "Burnett, of course, is a performer of star quality who alternates between the comic and the tragic with rare grace." The curtain closed in February of 2000, but the production was later scheduled to be broadcast as a pay–per–view television special. In 1999, *Entertainment Weekly* dubbed her one of "The 100 Greatest Entertainers," adding to an extensive list of honors which include numerous People's Choice and Golden Globe awards, and recognition for her humanitarian efforts.

Burnett's private life through the years has been rocky and highly public. She broke up with Hamilton in 1982 and divorced two years later. He died in

1991. Her oldest daughter, Carrie, who starred with her mother in the 1987 television movie *Hostage,* battled drugs on and off. And Burnett was involved in a bitter dispute with the *National Enquirer* after they published a 1976 article claiming that she was obviously drunk in a Washington restaurant, spilling her wine on other patrons and arguing with Henry Kissinger. She sued and won $1.6 million, although the award was later reduced to $800,000. The case was a landmark in celebrity libel cases. With her settlement, Burnett established scholarships for the study of journalistic ethics at the University of Hawaii and the University of California at Berkeley. In 1986, she penned her autobiography, *One More Time,* which covers her life up to age 26. She lives in Santa Fe, New Mexico, and Honolulu, Hawaii.

Sources

Books

Burnett, Carol, *One More Time,* Random House, 1986.
Contemporary Musicians, volume 6, Gale Research, 1991.
Contemporary Theater, Film and Television, volume 16, Gale Research, 1997.

Periodicals

Entertainment Weekly, November 8, 1991, p. 40; November 1, 1999, p. 133.
Ms., September 1983, p. 43.
Saturday Evening Post, September 1976, p. 54; November 1986, p. 47.
Time, December 6, 1999, p. 120.
Washington Post, April 19, 1979, p. 81.
Variety, November 2, 1998, p. 65.

Online

"Carol Burnett," Biography web site, http://www.biography.com (April 5, 2000).
"Carol Burnett," *Contemporary Authors,* Gale Group web site, http://www.galenet.com (April 5, 2000).
"Carol Burnett," Internet Movie Database web site, http://us.imdb.com (April 5, 2000).

Michael Caine

Actor

Born Maurice Joseph Micklewhite in London, England, March 14, 1933; son of Maurice Joseph (a fish market porter) and Ellen Francis Marie (a cleaning woman; maiden name, Burchell) Micklewhite; married Patricia Haines (an actress), 1955 (divorced, c. 1958); married Shakira Khatoon Baksh (a model and jewelry designer), January 8, 1973; children: (first marriage) Dominique; (second marriage) Natasha.

Addresses: *Agent*—Dennis Selinger, International Creative Management, 76 Oxford St., London W1R 1RB, England.

Career

Actor. South Beach Brasserie, South Miami Beach, FL, restaurant owner, beginning in 1996; owner of five restaurants in London. *Military service*— British Army, 1951–53; served in Germany and Korea.

Stage appearances include *The Room*, Royal Court Theatre, London, 1960; *The Dumbwaiter*, Royal Court Theatre, 1960; *Next Time, I'll Sing for You*, Arts Theatre, London, 1963; *The Night of 100 Stars II*, Radio City Music Hall, New York City, 1985; and *The Night of 100 Stars III*, Radio City Music Hall, 1990. Also appeared with the Westminster Repertory Company, Horsham, England, 1953, with the Lowestoft Repertory Company, Lowestoft, England, 1954-55, and with the Theatre Workshop, London, 1955.

Television appearances include more than one hundred roles in British television movies between 1957 and 1963, including *The Compartment, Funny Noises with Their Mouths, Hobson's Choice, Luck of the Draw, The Other Man, The Playmates,* and *The Way with Reggie;* also appeared in various television episodes and specials; miniseries include *Jack the Ripper*, 1988; *World War II: When Lions Roared* (also known as *World War II: When There Were Giants*), 1994; and *20,000 Leagues Under the Sea*, 1997; television films include *The Ship That Couldn't Stop*, 1961; *Dr. Jekyll and Mr. Hyde*, 1990; *King Midas and the Golden Touch*, 1991; *Blue Ice*, 1993; *Midnight in St. Petersburg*, 1995; *Bullet to Beijing* (also known as *Len Deighton's Bullet to Beijing*), 1995; and *Mandela and de Klerk*, 1997.

Film appearances include *A Hill in Korea* (also known as *Hell in Korea*), 1956; *Sailor Beware!* (also known as *Panic in the Parlor*), 1956; *The Steel Bayonet*, 1957; *How to Murder a Rich Uncle*, 1958; *Carve Her Name with Pride*, 1958; *Blind Spot*, 1958; *The Key*, 1958; *A Woman of Mystery*, 1958; *Room 43* (also known as *The Girl in Room 43* and *Passport to Shame*), 1959; *Two-Headed Spy*, 1959; *Breakout* (also known as *Danger Within*), 1959; *The Bulldog Breed*, 1960; *Foxhole in Cairo*, 1960; *The Day the Earth Caught Fire* (also known as *The Day the Sky Caught Fire*), 1961; *The Wrong Arm of the Law*, 1962; *Zulu*, 1964; *The Ipcress File*, 1965; *Alfie*, 1966; *The Wrong Box*, 1966; *Gambit*, 1966; *Solo for Sparrow*, 1966; *Funeral in Berlin*, 1967; *Hurry Sundown*, 1967; *Billion Dollar Brain*, 1967; *Woman Times Seven* (also known as *Sept Fois Femme*

), 1967; *Tonite Let's All Make Love in London* (also known as *The London Scene*), 1967; *Deadfall*, 1968; *The Battle of Britain*, 1968; *The Magus*, 1969; *Play Dirty* (also known as *Written on the Sand*), 1969; *The Italian Job*, 1969; *Too Late the Hero* (also known as *Suicide Run*), 1970; *Simon, Simon*, 1970; *The Last Valley*, 1971; *Kidnapped*, 1971; *Get Carter*, 1971; *Pulp*, 1972; *Sleuth*, 1972; *X, Y, and Zee* (also known as *Zee and Co* .),1972; *The Black Windmill*, 1974; *The Marseilles Contract* (also known as *The Destructors*), 1974; *The Wilby Conspiracy*, 1975; *Peeper* (also known as *Fat Chance*), 1975; *The Man Who Would Be King* (also known as *Rudyard Kipling's The Man Who Would Be King*), 1975; *The Romantic Englishwoman*, 1975; *Harry and Walter Go to New York*, 1976; *The Eagle Has Landed*, 1976; *A Bridge Too Far*, 1977; *Silver Bears*, 1977; *The Swarm*, 1978; *California Suite* (also known as *Neil Simon's California Suite*), 1978; *Ashanti* (also known as *Ashanti, Land of No Mercy*), 1979; *Beyond the Poseidon Adventure*, 1979; *The Island*, 1980; *Dressed to Kill*, 1980; *The Hand*, 1981; *Victory* (also known as *Escape to Victory*), 1981; *Deathtrap*, 1982; *Jigsaw Man*, 1982; *Beyond the Limit* (also known as *The Honorary Consul*), 1983; *Educating Rita*, 1983; *Blame It on Rio*, 1984; *The Holcroft Covenant*, 1985; *Water*, 1986; *Sweet Liberty*, 1986; *Hannah and Her Sisters*, 1986; *Mona Lisa*, 1986; *Half Moon Street* (also known as *Escort Girl*), 1987; *Jaws: The Revenge*, 1987; *The Whistle Blower*, 1987; *Surrender*, 1987; *The Fourth Protocol*, 1987; *Hero*, 1987; *Dirty, Rotten Scoundrels*, 1988; *Without a Clue* (also known as *Sherlock and Me*), 1988; *A Shock to the System*, 1990; *Mr. Destiny*, 1990; *Bullseye!*, 1991; *The Muppet Christmas Carol*, 1992; *Noises Off*, 1992; *On Deadly Ground*, 1994; *Blood and Wine*, 1997; *Shadow Run*, 1998; *Little Voice*, 1998; *Curtain Call* (also known as *Later Life*), 1998; *The Debtors*, 1999; *The Cider House Rules*, 1999.

Awards: National Society of Film Critics Award for best actor, 1966, for *Alfie*; British Academy Award, best actor in a leading role, British Academy of Film and Television Arts, and Golden Globe Award, best actor in a film, all 1983, for *Educating Rita*; Academy Award, best supporting actor, 1986, for *Hannah and Her Sisters*; Variety Club Award, film actor of the year, 1988; Golden Globe Award, best actor in a miniseries or motion picture made for television, 1989, for *Jack the Ripper*; commander, Order of the British Empire, 1992; Silver Seashell, San Sebastian International Film Festival, 1996, for *Blood and Wine*; National Board of Review Career Achievement Award, 1998; Golden Globe Award for best actor in a comedy or musical, 1999, and London Critics Circle Award for supporting actor, 2000, both for *Little Voice*; Academy Award, best actor in a supporting role, and Screen Actors Guild best supporting actor award, both 2000, for *The Cider House Rules*; knighted by Queen Elizabeth II, 2000.

Sidelights

One of the most prolific actors of the past few decades has been Michael Caine, who seems to have a capacity for portraying virtually any role. As a leading man, he has covered stiff military types, sensuous romancers, and murderous schemers. But his two Academy Awards came from supporting parts, in 1986 for *Hannah and Her Sisters* and again in 2000 for *The Cider House Rules*. But though he also takes smaller roles as well as character parts and cameos, Caine always manages to remain a star and often steals the scene. In addition, he has often won good notices even when the productions have been panned.

Caine was born Maurice Joseph Micklewhite in London, England, on March 14, 1933, and later changed his name when he became an actor. His father, Joseph, like his grandfather and great–grandfather, was a fish market porter, and his mother, Ellen Francis Marie (Burchell) Micklewhite, worked as a cleaning woman when the Depression put her husband on unemployment. She also gave birth to a son, David Burchell, out of wedlock before she met Caine's father, but kept him a secret her entire life. He suffered from epilepsy and it was misdiagnosed as mental illness, so he spent his life in an asylum on the outskirts of London, where she visited every Monday without fail. Caine's mother died in 1989, and in 1991, he found out about the half–brother from a tabloid reporter who had discovered the information. He later went to meet Burchell, who died in 1992.

Caine was raised in poverty in South London, and he and his brother Stanley would work alongside their father on days they were not in school. The family lived in a run–down two–room apartment with gas light. During World War II, when London suffered nightly bombing raids by the Germans, Caine's mother handed her sons over to a child–safety program, where they were looked after by a foster mother out of town for six weeks. However, she beat Caine and locked him in a cupboard when she went out shopping, and gave him only one can of fish per day to eat. A teacher discovered sores on his legs and summoned the National Society for the Prevention of Cruelty to Children, who returned him to his parents. Throughout his life, Caine would give donations to the organization and other children's charities.

Afterward, Caine and his brother were relocated to a country mansion, and because his father was serving in the war, his mother came to help with caretaking as well. They lived comfortably in the servants' quarters, and he developed rich tastes by drinking leftover wine and smoking stubs of cigars. He also came to appreciate art and antiques. When the war ended, Caine moved back to London, where he was a loner, dreaming of the idyllic conditions he had experienced. "I didn't want to be who I was," Caine told Pat Jordan in *Mademoiselle*. "I wanted to be somebody else and something else."

As an adolescent, Caine won a scholarship to the prestigious Wilson's Grammar School, and later attended a Jewish school as well. He became an avid reader and also was enthralled with films. In high school, he joined the drama society "because there were all those pretty girls," he remarked to Natalie Gittelson in *McCall's*. "I liked one particularly. If I get the right part, I may be able to kiss her, I said to myself. So that's how I became an actor."

Unlike most young British actors, Caine did not pattern himself after big stage names. Instead, he looked to American cinema, admiring personalities such as Humphrey Bogart, James Cagney, Marlon Brando, and Cary Grant. "American actors were more realistic," Caine explained to Jordan. He added, "When I was a boy, half the British theater was about kings. The other half was about the upper class . And I had this thick cockney accent, see, and everyone else talked posh. I couldn't talk like that, so I felt there was no place for me in the British theater. But American movie actors had accents. Their movies were about the working class. In America, it didn't matter what class you were from."

Despite his love of acting, Caine dropped out of school at 16 and worked a number of dead–end jobs, even though his family was quite well off by then because his father's fish business had grown. Caine has blamed his lack of education on his belief that the British working class does not place enough value on schooling. Meanwhile, he continued to act with a local youth club, then from 1951 to 1953, did his compulsory service in the British Army, serving in Germany and Korea. Afterward, he worked briefly in a butter warehouse and a steelyard, then decided to try acting, despite his father's negative contention that it was a profession for homosexuals.

Answering an advertisement, Caine in 1953 went to work as an assistant stage manager at a repertory theater in the Sussex town of Horsham. He sometimes landed small parts as well, and gradually worked into bigger roles. The next year he found work in the Lowestoft Theater in Suffolk, where he played the juvenile lead in nearly every production. In 1955, he married one of the leading women, Patricia Haines, and they had a daughter, Dominique, in 1956.

However, the union was troubled from the start, and further stress came about when Caine and his wife moved to London to try to break into bigger theaters. When they had no luck, he resorted to working in a laundry. Unwilling to give in to his wife's ultimatum that he abandon acting in lieu of more steady work, Caine was divorced in 1958. He was soon arrested for not paying child support, but got back on his feet by working in factories at night in order to seek acting jobs during the day. Meanwhile, his father died at age 53 in the mid–1950s of liver cancer, never seeing his son achieve success.

After appearing in plays throughout this time billed as Michael Scott, Caine had to find a new identity when he began to pursue television and film work, because the name was already in use. Sitting in London's Leicester Square drinking tea, he looked up and noticed a marquee advertising the Bogart film *The Caine Mutiny*. Thus, his new surname was born, and he subsequently began to land small screen parts. By 1963, he had appeared in more than 100 television roles. His first film part came in *A Hill in Korea*, 1956, playing Private Lockyear.

After a string of bit parts in television and film over the next few years, with the occasional stage tour, Caine had his breakthrough in 1964's *Zulu*. He earned the part after snagging the lead in a production of *Next Time, I'll Sing for You*, which was moved from an obscure playhouse to the West End, where the director and star of the upcoming film caught his act. They figured Caine would make a decent Cockney soldier, but then decided to cast him as an upper–crust officer. His performance won him international acclaim. The next year, Caine played his first lead as spy Harry Palmer in *The Ipcress File*. He was critically hailed for capturing the essence of the character, a deadpan, working–class agent with horn–rimmed glasses who was the antithesis to the glamorous James Bond. He went on to make more Harry Palmer films, but none were as successful.

In 1966, Caine firmly established his star reputation in 1966's *Alfie*, about a charming cockney Casanova in swinging London. He earned his first Oscar nomination for the part, and the film became the highest–ever British box–office earner in the United States. Subsequently, Caine posted appearances in dozens of films, quite often as the sensitive seducer. However, though that image stuck, he also landed many military roles, playing lieutenants, captains, majors, and the like. Caine won another Oscar nomination for 1972's *Sleuth,* in which he costarred with Sir Laurence Olivier (who also earned an Oscar bid) in the tale of a mystery writer's game of wits with his wife's lover.

In the late 1970s and into the 1980s, Caine seemed to be involved with several duds, including *Silver Bears, The Swarm, The Hand, Ashanti, The Island,* and *Jaws: The Revenge.* However, throughout this time he was also acclaimed for roles in vehicles such as the 1978 comedy *California Suite* and the 1980 Brian DePalma thriller *Dressed to Kill.* He also attracted his third Oscar nomination for his part as Dr. Frank Bryant in 1983's *Educating Rita,* about an alcoholic English literature professor who takes on the job of expanding the intellectual horizons of a cockney homemaker.

In 1986, Caine finally earned his first Academy Award for best supporting actor for Woody Allen's *Hannah and Her Sisters,* playing a man who is infatuated with his wife's sister. After that, he won a Golden Globe award for his turn as the title character in the 1988 television miniseries *Jack the Ripper.* His work load eased up greatly after that, as he made a succession of television movies and appeared in a couple of documentaries about himself. There was also an unusual stint as Ebenezer Scrooge in 1992's *The Muppet Christmas Carol.*

In 1998, though, Caine re–emerged with *Little Voice,* about a sleazy agent who tries to mine the talent of an intensely withdrawn woman who can imitate the voices of famous singers. His role as the hustler was similar to the one in *Alfie,* and earned him another Golden Globe Award and a London Critics Circle Award. In 1999, Caine was firmly back in the spotlight again for his part as the dedicated director of a Maine orphanage in *The Cider House Rules,* an adaptation of the John Irving novel. In it, he plays Dr. Wilbur Larch, a stubborn, loving man who cares for his otherwise unwanted brood with a zeal, despite his unfortunate ether addiction. He also performs safe, illegal abortions in order to prevent women from dying at the hands of lesser–trained operators. Larch becomes particularly attached to one young boy, Homer Wells (Tobey Maguire), who seems destined to never be successfully adopted out of the institution, and teaches him everything he knows of the medical profession. At the 2000 Academy Awards, Caine earned his second supporting actor nod for this dramatic part.

In 1992, Caine published his autobiography, *What's It All About?,* reportedly to counter previous life stories written by others of which he disapproved.

"There's this perception of me being this incredibly lucky Cockney moron," he commented in *People.* He has also penned a few volumes of trivia and a book on acting.

Caine married again in 1973, to Shakira Baksh, a Guyanese–born fashion model who once placed third in the Miss World pageant. He saw her on television in a Maxwell House coffee commercial and later got her phone number from a friend. They eventually began living together, and though he did not plan to remarry, she became pregnant. A few weeks after the discovery, they were wed in Las Vegas. They have a daughter, Natasha, and Caine's wife later became a jewelry designer.

According to Caine, he moved from England to America after the British government taxed him at a 98 percent rate. In 1979, he bought a home in Beverly Hills overlooking the Pacific Ocean, and learned to drive in California at age 50. However, he noted to Gittelson in *McCall's,* "Then I took the car out and couldn't find anywhere to go."

Clearly preferring his native country, Caine also purchased a country home in Oxfordshire in the mid–1980s, after British leader Margaret Thatcher relaxed the tax laws. Then, in 1999, Caine moved again, purchasing a 10,000–square foot renovated barn on 22 acres just outside of London. It has six bedrooms and six bathrooms as well as its own theater and a 39–foot–long breakfast–kitchen area. In addition to being an avid gardener, Caine is a lifelong gourmet who loves fine cuisine and wine, and he owns several London restaurants as well as the South Beach Brasserie in South Miami Beach, Florida. Caine was named to the Order of the British Empire in 1992 and was knighted by Queen Elizabeth II in 2000.

Selected writings

Not Many People Know That: Michael Caine's Almanac of Amazing Information (published in the United States as *Michael Caine's Almanac of Amazing Information*), Robson Books (London), 1985.

And Not Many People Know This Either!: Michael Caine's Second Collection of Amazing Information, Robson Books, 1985.

Not Many People Know It's 1988!, Robson Books, 1987.

Michael Caine's Moving Picture Show, St. Martin's, 1988.

Acting in Film: An Actor's Take on Moviemaking, Applause Theatre Book Publishers, 1990.

What's It All About? (autobiography), Turtle Bay Books, 1992.

Sources

Books

Contemporary Theatre, Film and Television, volume 22, Gale Group, 1999.
International Dictionary of Films and Filmmakers, Volume 3: Actors and Actresses, St. James Press, 1996.

Periodicals

Entertainment Weekly, March 1, 2000, p. 67.
Knight–Ridder/Tribune News Service, December 22, 1998.

Ladies' Home Journal, January 1992, p. 38.
Mademoiselle, May 1982, p. 52.
McCall's, June 1986, p. 139.
New York Times, July 26, 1981, sec. 2, p. 1; October 16, 1983.
People, May 4, 1987, p. 104; December 7, 1992, p. 93; January 18, 1999, p. 11; March 27, 2000, p. 105.
TV Guide, October 16, 1988, p. 8.
Vanity Fair, August 1986, p. 98; December 1992, p. 150.
Variety, September 13, 1999, p. 48.

Online

"Michael Caine," *Contemporary Authors Online*, Gale Group web site, http://www.galenet.com (June 6, 2000).
"Michael Caine," Internet Movie Database web site, http://us.imdb.com (August 30, 2000).

Naomi Campbell

AP/Wide World Photos

Model and actor

Born in 1970 (sources variously cite May 20, May 21, or May 26), in Streatham, London, England; daughter of Valerie Campbell (a ballet dancer). *Education:* Studied classical ballet at Italia Conti Stage School, London; attended Academy of Performing Arts, London, c. 1985.

Addresses: *Office*—c/o Elite Model Management, 40 Parker St., London, WC2B 5PH, England. *Agent*—International Creative Management, 8942 Wilshire Blvd., Beverly Hills, CA, 90211.

Career

Model and actor. Elite Model Management, New York City, model, 1987– 93, and with Elite Premier, London; Ford Models, Inc., worked in Paris, 1991 , and New York City, 1993—. Co–owner (with models Elle MacPherson, Claudia Schiffer, and Christy Turlington) of Fashion Café; (a restaurant and coffee house), with locations in New York City, New Orleans, London, Jakarta, Barcelona, Mexico City, and Manila. Author of novel, *Swan*, Heinemann, 1996. Involved with efforts for underprivileged children, the Red Cross, and UNESCO.

Film appearances include *Quest for Fire*, 1982; *The Wall*, 1982; *Cool as Ice*, 1991; *The Night We Never Met*, 1993; *Pret-a-Porter* (*Ready to Wear*), 1994; *Catwalk*, 1995; *Miami Rhapsody*, 1995; *To Wong Foo, Thanks for Everything, Julie Newmar*, 1995; *Unzipped*, 1995; *Girl 6*, 1996; *An Alan Smithee Film: Burn Hollywood Burn*, 1997; *Beautopia*, 1998;

Television appearances include episodes of *The Cosby Show*, 1988; *The Fresh Prince of Bel-Air*, 1990; *Hi-Octane*, 1995; *Absolutely Fabulous*, 1995; *New York Undercover*, 1995; and *Model*, 1997; movie *Invasion of Privacy*, 1996; and numerous specials and awards shows. Has also appeared in music videos for George Michael's "Freedom" and Michael Jackson's "In the Closet."

Sidelights

With her almond–shaped eyes, high cheekbones, full lips, and satin–smooth skin, Naomi Campbell became a superstar almost immediately after launching her international modeling career. Her name was then catapulted into the top echelon of her field in August of 1989, when she became the first black woman to grace the cover of French *Vogue* an accomplishment she cites as one of her proudest moments. The next month, her face appeared on issues of American *Vogue* as well. Sometimes compared to legendary dancer and singer Josephine Baker, Campbell has also been called a black Marilyn Monroe or Brigitte Bardot, thus grouping her with sex symbols of eras past. She is definitely a contemporary star, however, crossing genres to dabble in acting, singing, and even business, opening the Fashion Café, a worldwide venture, in the mid–1990s with a few of her modeling colleagues. Despite her reputation as demanding and temperamental, which has caused upheaval with her modeling agency, Campbell remains much in demand for her exquisite looks.

Campbell was born in 1970 in Streatham, London, England. Her birth date has been cited in various sources as May 20, 21, or 26, and her father, a Jamaican immigrant who was part Chinese, left the family before she was born and was not named on her birth certificate, according to Jonathan Van Meter in *Vogue*. She and her brother were raised by their mother, Valerie Campbell—who was born in Jamaica but grew up in London—and by a nanny when their mother was traveling throughout Europe with the dance troupe Fantastica. Her mom sent home money for her daughter's dance classes, and when Campbell was ten, she was accepted to London's prestigious Italia Conti Stage School to study ballet. She also attended the London Academy of Performing Arts.

As a youth, Campbell landed bit parts in the films *Quest for Fire*, 1981, and Pink Floyd's *The Wall*, 1982, then was discovered at age 15 by a model scout. As she recalled to Van Meter in *Vogue*, "I was in the Covent Garden. I was going home after school, and I stopped off at my girlfriend's to have some ice cream, and this lady, Beth Boldt, tapped me on the shoulder and said, 'Do you want to model?'" Initially, Campbell did not believe the woman was an agent, but later read an interview with her in a British magazine, *Tatler*. She began to hound her mother to let her pursue the opportunity, and after the school year ended, she was allowed to contact Boldt.

In 1986, just before turning 16, Campbell posed for her first photographs and was signed to the Elite modeling agency in 1987. There, she befriended Christy Turlington, and ended up sharing an apartment with her in New York for a year. In no time, Campbell went from being a teenager in a school uniform to one of the top supermodels of the world, strutting down the catwalks for designers like Isaac Mizrahi, Calvin Klein, and Azzedine Alaia, and earning more than $1 million a year. Her face was emblazoned on the French, Italian, American, and British editions of *Vogue* in the late 1980s, and she also found her way onto some episodes of the hugely successful television series *The Cosby Show* in 1988. She played Julia, the girlfriend of Theo's friend Howard.

Campbell's rise to megastardom was even more noteworthy because of her color. At a time when the racial mix of the United States and other nations was changing, multiculturalism became hip. Bob Colacello in *Vanity Fair* quoted journalist George Wayne as saying, "It's chic to be global. And Naomi's got the whole nineties blend. She's got a Jamaican mother and a Chinese grandmother, she's European, she's American—she's it." Campbell has credited her popularity with helping to break the color barrier for other models as well.

Not surprisingly, with the benefits of celebrity came the pitfalls. Campbell became one of the biggest names in the gossip columns. In 1990, she was linked to boxer Mike Tyson, but insisted in *Interview* that they were just friends. However, she also initially denied that she was romantically involved with actor Robert De Niro, and later admitted that they had a four- year relationship. In addition, Colacello in *Vanity Fair* reported that Tyson was her "first love," and that they dated before and after his marriage to Robin Givens. Other possible suitors included actor Sylvester Stallone and Irish rock musician Adam Clayton of U2.

By the early 1990s, Campbell was diversifying her career, contributing vocals to a track on Vanilla Ice's soundtrack *Cool as Ice* and appearing in that movie as well as music videos. She showed up in Michael Jackson's "In the Closet" video and George Michael's "Freedom." Michael Musto in *Harper's Bazaar* mused in 1992 that Campbell would parlay this experience into film roles, but she told him, "I'm not banking on being an actress." However, she popped up the next year as a cheese shopper in *The Night We Never Met*, and in 1994 played a model in Robert Altman's *Pret–a–Porter* (*Ready to Wear*). The following year, she had parts in *Catwalk; To Wong Foo, Thanks for Everything, Julie Newmar*; and *Miami Rhapsody*, with Sarah Jessica Parker and Mia Farrow, which garnered her some good reviews. She also showed talent in a cameo in Spike Lee's *Girl 6*, 1996. Campbell continued to work in television as well, making cameos on *The Fresh Prince of Bel–Air* and the British comedy series *Absolutely Fabulous*, as well as appearing in a recurring role on the police drama *New York Undercover*.

Forays into other media, however, have not been as kind to Campbell. In *Vogue*, Van Meter concluded, "Her ghostwritten novel, *Swan*, was a laughing-stock, and her 1994 album, *Babywoman*, was a critical and commercial failure." In fact, *Seventeen* magazine gave *Swan* its "Super–cheesy award," noted Guy Trebay in the *New York Times Magazine*. On the other hand, in another attempt at singing, she recorded "La, La, La Love Song" with Japanese singer Toshi, which reached number one in Japan. Campbell continued to model as well, reaping fees of $10,000 a day, but also found lucrative work in advertisements. She was reportedly paid a six–figure sum to appear in Madonna's book *Sex,* which featured erotic photographs, and she handpicked all of the pictures for another photo book simply called *Naomi,* consisting of favorite shots of herself by top-name photographers such as Herb Ritts and Richard Avedon.

In 1995, Campbell became an entrepreneur as well, starting up the Fashion Cafe on a consultancy basis with her modeling pals Elle MacPherson, Claudia Schiffer, and Christy Turlington, along with Italian restaurateur Tommaso Buti, the major shareholder. The first location of the restaurant and coffee house opened in New York City, followed by branches in London, Jakarta, Barcelona, Mexico City, New Orleans, and Manila. This venture rode the trend of celebrity-themed eateries, such as Planet Hollywood, backed financially by Arnold Schwarzenegger and other stars. The first Fashion Caf[0082] was situated in Rockefeller Center, where patrons entered through a giant camera lens and serving staff parade to tables carrying cuisine down a catwalk. The decor included the requisite collection of memorabilia, from Madonna's famous Jean-Paul Gaultier bustier to one of Elizabeth Taylor's wedding gowns.

By 1997, however, Turlington pulled out of the company, and the next year, the Fashion Cafe was accused of mismanagement by its investors. Two of its franchises, in New Orleans and Barcelona, were shut down, and Buti resigned after selling his stake in the firm. New management was called in to restore order, though, and the endeavor continued at its other locations. Meanwhile, Planet Hollywood saw serious financial troubles as well, indicating that the boom in big-name bars and restaurants was coming to a close. John Willcock in the *Independent* reported that the supermodels involved with the Fashion Cafe were not going to lose money from the project, since their major role was to make appearances and they were paid fees for their time.

Though she can look charming in the pages of magazines, throughout her career, Campbell has developed a reputation for being notoriously difficult to work with, which supposedly led to her temporary dismissal from the Elite agency. Other reports, however, indicate that she quit (they later hired her back). She reportedly has a fiery temper and an addiction to her cellular phone, and is perpetually late to nearly any assignment or appointment. In addition, she is known for making selfish demands, such as insisting on being the first as well as last to appear on the runway at fashion shows.

In addition, according to Joe Warmington in the *Toronto Sun,* during a movie shoot there in September of 1998 while starring in the film *Prisoner of Love,* several crew members called Campbell "a 'nightmare' to work with," and one anonymous employee summed up by saying, "This is a spoiled child." While on the shoot, a Canadian assistant who worked for Campbell for nine days claimed the model grabbed her by the throat and assaulted her with a telephone. She was arrested and charged with assault causing bodily harm, and in February of 2000 pleaded guilty in absentia to the lesser charge of assault. Afterward, though, she was given an absolute discharge, which meant she would have no criminal record in Canada.

Despite all of the reports of nasty behavior, it is no secret that Campbell can be extremely generous as well. All of the proceeds from her book *Naomi,* for example, have been donated to the Red Cross Somalia Relief Fund, and she has worked with the Dalai Lama to raise money to build kindergartens for poor communities around the globe, the first being located in Jamaica. In February of 1998, she was involved with a fund raising event in Johannesburg, South Africa, for the Nelson Mandela Children's Fund. For that gala, she helped organize a fashion show. Campbell also pledged to donate to the fund one dollar from each item of clothing sold from her designer jeans line.

However, another nonprofit cause that Campbell was closely associated with ended badly. In 1994, People for the Ethical Treatment of Animals (PETA) hired her and four other top models to appear in the ad campaign featuring the tag line, "We'd rather go naked than wear fur." In March of 1997, though, Campbell strutted in a Fendi fashion show wearing a fur coat, and PETA responded by firing her as a spokeswoman and calling her "a disgrace," according to a *Maclean's* account.

As for her personal life, Campbell hobnobs with the elite of the fashion and entertainment world. She claims to still be good friends with De Niro, and keeps company with actors Joe Pesci and Jack Nicholson. In *Vogue,* she told Van Meter, "I'm not in the same boat as them, because they're legends, and sometimes I say to myself, 'God, I'm just shocked that these people like me.' They're all older than me. It's weird. I can talk to them and get advice from them, and I tell them how I feel . And they're not 'yes' people: I can ask them a question and get an honest answer."

Campbell, at five feet, nine-and-a-half inches tall and 122 pounds, wears a size 6 and once claimed, according to Trebay in the *New York Times Magazine,* "I don't watch my weight and I don't own a scale."

In fact, she boasts that her diet includes McDonald's burgers, fried chicken, and chocolate candy. She travels frequently for her work but keeps an apartment in New York City's TriBeCa neighborhood. Off the catwalk, she has a penchant for mixing designer clothes with items found at thrift stores. As for any future ambitions, she remarked to Van Meter, "Somewhere at one point in my life I'd love to just once do some type of dance performance because that was something that I studied from three years old to sixteen, every single day. And then I got discovered as a model and I didn't dance anymore and it was something that I really loved doing. When I listen to a great piece of music, I fantasize, Wouldn't it be great to do a really great routine to this?"

Sources

Books

Contemporary Theatre, Film and Television, Gale Research, 1999.

Periodicals

Entertainment Weekly, April 4, 1995, p. 6.
Harper's Bazaar, June 1992, p. 90.
Independent, October 21, 1998, p. 7.
Interview, May 1990, p. 52; February 1998, p. 56.
Maclean's, March 24, 1997, p. 12.
Mademoiselle, February 1989, p. 122.
New York Times Magazine, November 24, 1996, p. 60.
People, June 11, 1990, p. 44; December 30, 1991, p. 82; November 23, 1998, p. 132.
Toronto Sun, December 13, 1998, p. 4.
Vanity Fair, December 1990, p. 194.
Vogue, March 1999, p. 438.

Online

Fashion Cafe web site, http://www.fashion-cafe.com (January 5, 2000).
"Naomi Campbell Pleads Guilty, Seeks Rest," Mr. Showbiz web site, February 2, 2000, http://mrshowbiz.go.com (February 8, 2000).

Arthur L. Caplan

AP/Wide World Photos

Scholar and author

Born Arthur Leonard Caplan, March 31, 1950, in Boston, MA; son of Sidney D. (a pharmacist) and Natalie (a homemaker) Caplan; married Janet Stojak (a psychologist), June 6, 1971; children: Zach. *Education:* Brandeis University, B.A., 1971; Columbia University, M.A. in philosophy, 1973, M.A. in history and philosophy of science, 1975, Ph.D. in philosophy, 1979.

Addresses: *Office*—Department of Bioethics, University of Pennsylvania, 3401 Market St., Ste. 320, Philadelphia, PA 19104–3308.

Career

Columbia University College of Physicians and Surgeons, department of medicine and school of public health, instructor, 1977–81; Hastings Institute, associate for the humanities, 1977–84, associate director, 1985–87; University of Pittsburgh, visiting associate professor, 1986; University of Minnesota, professor of philosophy, professor of surgery, and director of the center for biomedical ethics, 1987–94; University of Pennsylvania, trustee professor of bioethics and director of Center for Bioethics, 1994—. Author of more than 475 journal articles and reviews; contributor of regular column to MSNBC web site.

Chairman, Department of Health and Human Services' Advisory Committee on Blood Safety and Availability; previous member of Presidential Advisory Committee on Gulf War Veterans' Illnesses and President Clinton's Health Care Advisory Panel. Also first president of the American Association of Bioethics, 1993-95. Frequent media commentator.

Awards: Hero of Public Health award, Columbia University; Philadelphia College of Textiles & Science Centennial Medal, 1995; Brandeis University Alumni Achievement Award, 1995; UTNE 100 Visionaries, 1995; McGovern Medal, American Medical Writers Association, 1998; various honorary degrees.

Sidelights

In an age of rapid scientific advances in health care, Arthur L. Caplan is considered one of the top experts on the sensitive ethical issues that come with procedures such as organ transplants, embryo implantation, cloning, artificial hearts, assisted suicide, and more. The author of more than 475 journal articles and reviews for the discipline known as bioethics, he has spearheaded public debate on these kinds of topics. Rather than remaining a detached academic, however, Caplan has devoted himself to formulating opinions on how to ethically deal with certain situations as well as trying to change the behavior of medical specialists, or legal policy, or both. He became known for his ability to reach out to learned scholars as well as laypeople with lively books such as *If I Were a Rich Man Could I Buy a Pancreas?* and *Am I My Brother's Keeper?: The Ethical Frontiers of Biomedicine.*

Immersing himself in building awareness of bioethics, Caplan became a staple in the popular media, interviewed in newspapers and magazines, as well as on radio and television. "I've probably been the person to make bioethics a public event, and I deliberately did it," he remarked in the *Chronicle of Higher Education*. "Not for the fame of it, but because that's the way you get the ears of the politicians who live and die by the media." He added that the public tends to pay more attention to subjects covered extensively in the media as well. Also, advances in medical technology caused a natural outcropping of ethical questions. "When I got started in this field, I think it was regarded as a fad," Caplan noted in the *Chronicle of Higher Education*. "But during the 1980s, we began to see and hear everybody talking about medical ethics. Things that were once relegated to the back pages became front-page news."

Caplan was born on March 31, 1950, in Boston, Massachusetts, and grew up in Framingham, the son of Sidney D. Caplan and Natalie Caplan. His father, a pharmacist, and mother, a homemaker, were not religious, but enrolled their son at Jewish schools. In first grade, he contracted polio and was sent to Children's Hospital in Boston. This strongly shaped his desire to investigate health care issues. Recalling his experience as a child, Caplan noted in the *Chronicle of Higher Education,* "People didn't tell the truth if a kid died. Parents couldn't stay overnight with their kids, and that seemed cruel. I remember, to, that we got a lot of information from other kids instead of from the nurses or doctors."

After graduating from North High School in Framingham, Caplan went on to receive a bachelor's degree in philosophy from Brandeis University in 1971. Back then, the field of bioethics was in its infancy. He went on to obtain master's degrees in philosophy (1973) as well as history and the philosophy of science (1975) from Columbia University. During this time, his mentors included Ernest Nagel and Sidney Morgenbesser, two of the great minds in the area of the philosophy of science. He later earned a doctorate in philosophy from Columbia in 1979.

While still a graduate student, in 1976 Caplan began teaching ethics to medical students at Columbia University's College of Physicians and Surgeons, which stirred his interest in subjects like organ transplants and in vitro fertilization (more commonly known by the jargon "test tube babies," this procedure involves growing embryos in a laboratory setting, then implanting them into a woman's uterus). This sealed Caplan's desire to make bioethics his full-time profession. At the time, the field was starting to bud due to news coverage of cases like that of Karen Ann Quinlan, a young woman in a coma whose parents went to the Supreme Court to have her removed from a respirator. Meanwhile, at a national conference on bioethics, one of the founders of the field, Daniel Callahan, offered Caplan a job at the Hastings Institute, a respected think tank devoted to bioethics. Caplan started there in 1977 and served as the center's associate director from 1985 to 1987.

In the meantime, Caplan also continued teaching at the Columbia as an associate for social medicine from 1978 to 1981, and was a visiting associate professor at the University of Pittsburgh in 1986. In 1987, the University of Minnesota offered him the opportunity to run his own center for biomedical ethics, as well as holding the posts of professor of philosophy and professor of surgery. He stayed until 1994, when the University of Pennsylvania recruited him to head their Center for Bioethics. They gave him a handsome salary of $200,000 a year and a budget for the center of $500,000, and gave him access to advanced research going on in the school's genetics labs as well. This piqued his interest, since he felt that gene therapy was going to be the big issue of the future; as he told Robert Leiter in the *Jewish Exponent*, "Minnesota didn't have that. Their expertise was in transplants."

A leader in the field, the University of Minnesota started on of the first master's programs in bioethics in 1997. As of 1999, there were roughly 50 bioethics centers among the United States' 125 medical schools. In addition to his duties at the University of Pennsylvania, sitting on 13 committees, running the center, and holding posts in the departments of philosophy and molecular engineering, Caplan is often in demand by journalists seeking his opinions. A much- requested guest on television shows like *Nightline* and programs on National Public Radio, he also contributes articles to publications such as the *New York Times, Washington Post, Los Angeles Times,* and *Philadelphia Inquirer.*

Caplan's status as a semi-celebrity has drawn fire from colleagues, who accuse him of slacking on his scholarly pursuits in favor of giving sound bites. He rejects the notion as sniping from ivory-tower types who do not believe that a complex academic topic such as bioethics can be addressed in the popular realm. In addition to appearing in the media, Caplan has also gone far in opening debate by publishing various books on bioethics that are readable and clear. They put forth his opinions on a range of topics, from surrogate mothers to whether alcoholics should receive liver transplants. In his works, he summarizes each issue and the related arguments, then delves into the expansive gray areas of each with his own theories. As he told Claudia Dreifus in the *New York Times Magazine*, "That's what philosophy ought to be: about real people, speaking to human concerns—not armchair fantasies about right and wrong."

In 1971 Caplan, known informally as "Art," married Janet Stojak, a psychologist, and they have a son, Zach. He lectures frequently around the world, writes a regular column on bioethics for the MSNBC web site, and serves as a paid consultant to pharmaceutical companies. Caplan is also an adviser to various nonprofit groups and government task forces, including acting as chairman of the Department of Health and Human Services' Advisory Committee on Blood Safety and Availability. Previously, he was a member of Presidential Advisory Committee on Gulf War Veterans' Illnesses and President Clinton's Health Care Advisory Panel.

Selected writings

(Editor) *The Sociobiology Debate: Readings on Ethical and Scientific Issues,* Harper, 1978.

(With Bernard Rosen) *Ethics in the Undergraduate Curriculum,* Hastings Center, 1980.

(Editor, with H. Tristram Engelhardt, Jr.) *Concepts of Health and Disease: Interdisciplinary Perspectives,* Addison–Wesley, 1981.

(Editor with Daniel Callahan) *Ethics in Hard Times,* Plenum, 1981.

(Editor, with Ronald Bayer and Norman Daniels) *In Search of Equity: Health Needs and the Health Care System,* Plenum, 1983.

(Editor, with Bruce Jennings) *Darwin, Marx, and Freud: Their Influence on Moral Theory,* Plenum, 1984.

(Editor, with Thomas H. Murray) *Which Babies Shall Live?: Humanistic Dimensions of the Care of Imperiled Newborns,* Humana, 1985.

(Editor, with others) *Applying the Humanities,* Plenum, 1985.

(Editor, with Engelhardt) *Scientific Controversies: Case Studies in the Resolution and Closure of Disputes in Science and Technology,* Cambridge University Press, 1987.

(Editor, with Rosalie A. Kane) *Everyday Ethics: Resolving Dilemmas in Nursing Home Life,* Springer, 1990.

(Editor, with others) *Compelled Compassion: Government Intervention in the Treatment of Critically Ill Newborns,* Humana Press, 1992.

(Editor) *When Medicine Went Mad: Bioethics and the Holocaust,* Humana Press, 1992.

If I Were a Rich Man Could I Buy a Pancreas?: And Other Essays on the Ethics of Health Care, Indiana University Press, 1992.

(Editor, with Kane) *Ethical Conflicts in the Management of Home Care: The Case Manager's Dilemma,* Springer, 1993.

(Editor, with others) *Prescribing our Future: Ethical Challenges in Genetic Counseling,* Aldine de Gruyter, 1993.

Moral Matters: Ethical Issues in Medicine and the Life Sciences, Wiley, 1995.

Am I My Brother's Keeper?: The Ethical Frontiers of Biomedicine, Indiana University Press, 1997.

Due Consideration: Controversy in the Age of Miracles, Wiley, 1998.

(Editor, with Daniel H. Coelho) *The Ethics of Organ Transplants: The Current Debate,* Prometheus, 1998.

Sources

Periodicals

Biography, April 1998, p. 38.
Chronicle of Higher Education, April 2, 1999, p. A40.
Commonweal, April 9, 1993, p. 34.
Futurist, November 1998, p. 10.
Issues in Science and Technology, Summer 1998, p. 86.
JAMA, Journal of the American Medical Association, July 22, 1998, p. 389.
Jewish Exponent, August 19, 1994.
Library Journal, November 15, 1997, p. 70; March 15, 1999, p. 102.
New York Times Magazine, December 15, 1996, p. 41.

Online

"Arthur L(eonard) Caplan," *Contemporary Authors,* Gale Group web site, http://www.galenet.com (December 1, 1999).

University of Pennsylvania Center for Bioethics web site, http://www.med.upenn.edu/bioethic/center (December 21, 1999).

Chris Carter

AP/Wide World Photos

Screenwriter and producer

Born in Bellflower, CA, in 1956; son of William (a construction worker) and Catherine (a homemaker; maiden name, Mulder) Carter; married Dori Pierson (a screenwriter), 1987. *Education:* California State University at Long Beach, degree in journalism, 1979.

Addresses: *Home*—Pacific Palisades, CA. *Office*—Fox Broadcasting Company, 10201 West Pico Blvd., Los Angeles, CA 90064.

Career

Surfing magazine, writer and editor, beginning 1979; Walt Disney Studios, screenwriter for television, including several television movies and pilots for *Cameo by Night* and *The Nanny*, co–producer of the comedy series *Rags to Riches*; creator and executive producer of comedy series *Brand New Life*, 1989; creator, executive producer, and occasional director of the drama series *The X–Files*, 1993—, creator and executive producer of the drama series *Millennium*, 1996–99, and *Harsh Realm*, 1999—.

Awards: Numerous awards for *The X– Files*, including the Environmental Media Award, outstanding episodic television (drama) for "Darkness Falls," 1994; Parent's Choice Honors for best series, 1994; Golden Globe Award for best dramatic series, 1995; Academy of Science Fiction, Fantasy and Horror, Saturn Award for outstanding television series, 1995; International Monitor Award for best director for "The List," 1996; and Golden Globe Award for best dramatic series, 1997; also named one of *Time*

magazine's 25 most influential Americans, 1997; also numerous nominations, including several Emmy Award nominations.

Sidelights

In real life, Chris Carter, the creative force of *The X–Files* and *Millenium*, is not a conspiracy theorist, UFO abductee, or any other label that people might confer on him after watching his shows. "People would be surprised to learn that I'm really the guy next door, not a paranoid, kook or crank," he mentioned to Michael A. Lipton in *People*. "I have no reason to believe in paranormal phenomena." However, the wildfire success of his programs has led many to believe that he has a magic touch. Comparing him to Rod Serling, the mind behind *The Twilight Zone*, and Gene Rodenberry, creator of *Star Trek*, a *Time* article observed, "To every generation, there is a visionary.... Today's seer is Chris Carter... creator of *The X–Files*, a show that takes America's obsession with the occult and cover– ups, with truths impossible to ignore but too terrible to be told, and transforms that paranoia into a compelling amalgam of hipness and horror—proving it possible to be both cool and unnerved." In addition to dreaming up *The X–Files*, a genre–defying program that premiered in 1993 and promises that "The truth is out there" as it sends two FBI agents chasing enigmatic happenings and curious creatures, Carter is responsible for the doomsday series *Millenium*, which ran from 1996 to 1999. In 1999, he sparked off yet another project, Harsh Realm, a series set inside a computer game.

Carter was born on October 13, 1956, in Bellflower, California, a middle–class suburb of Los Angeles. His father, William, who died in 1995, worked in construction while his mother, Catherine, also deceased, was a homemaker. He has one brother, Craig, who works as a physicist in Washington, D.C. All in all, Carter had a rather normal childhood, consisting of pitching in Little League games and surfing. However, he did enjoy classic science fiction television shows like *Mysterious Island*, which he watched three times a day for a full week while it was in re–runs, as well as *The Outer Limits, The Twilight Zone,* and *Night Gallery.* Also, he had an attraction to haunted houses. But his tendency to be paranoid was spawned from his relationship with his mother, as he explained to David Lipsky in *Rolling Stone:* "My mother, who I loved dearly, could never keep a secret. So if as a kid you go to your mother and she can't keep it secret, it develops in you, you know, a sense that nothing is safe."

Though Carter admitted to Lipsky that he "was not a great high school student," recalling that he was probably bored, he noted that he became more studious in college. He obtained a journalism degree in 1979 at California State University at Long Beach, where he worked his way through school making pottery. His wife told Benjamin Svetkey in *Entertainment Weekly,* "He would make 100 casserole dishes in a single night. With tops that fit!" Carter had a talent for making all kind of things. He recalled to Lipsky, "When I was a sophomore, I built a house from the ground up with a carpenter."

Right after college, Carter got a job at *Surfing* magazine in San Clemente, California, where he led an idyllic life of traveling, surfing, and writing. In 1983, he met Dori Pierson, a screenwriter who penned the 1988 film *Big Business,* and they married in 1987. She encouraged him to write a script. "I had never really had any ambition to be a screenwriter," he told Lipsky. "But I had an idea…. I mean, everybody has an idea for a movie." He cranked out a story called *National Pastime,* about three blue–collar kids going to fight in Vietnam, and gave it to his cousin's wife, who was an agent. Though it stirred some interest, the project sputtered out. He tried his hand again, this time with a comedy, and Jeffrey Katzenberg, who was then head of production at Disney studios, saw it and hired Carter to write for

television and produce some television movies. In one move, he went from making about $18,000 a year at Surfing to earning $40,000, with his own office and secretary, at Disney in Burbank.

In addition to frequently penning scripts for the *Disney Sunday Movie,* Carter worked on episodes of *The Nanny* and wrote a pilot for *Cameo by Night* for NBC. Then, in 1988 he worked as coproducer of the series *Rags to Riches* on NBC. Returning to Disney in 1989, he created the show *Brand New Life* and also acted as executive producer. This comedy series, strongly reminiscent of *The Brady Bunch,* appeared on a rotating basis with other shows on Disney's Sunday night lineup. At that point, "I was about as far from *The X–Files* as you could get," Carter commented to Michael A. Lipton in *People.*

In 1992, Carter signed a deal with Twentieth Century–Fox television to create a new project for the network. His first idea was for a scary show, and he drew from various sources for the premise. One of his main inspirations was a show from his childhood called *Kolchak: The Night Stalker,* which centered on a reporter who investigated a new monster each week. But as he commented to Lipsky, the world of science and technology changed so dramatically in the two decades since he watched the program, he was able to go much farther with The X–Files. He also drew ideas from the film *The Silence of the Lambs,* in which the main character is an FBI agent. Incidentally, Carter insists he has never watched a single episode of *Star Trek,* which is remarkable considering that the programs have a large common audience due to the science–fiction aspects present in each.

After coming up with the basis for the show, Carter saw an FBI agent being interviewed on the *Larry King Live* show about his investigations into satanic cults. "He said that he had found not one ounce of truth in any of those things," Carter told Lipsky. "But I found it interesting that they had somebody specifically investigating something like that." Thus, he melded all of his ideas into the concept of two FBI agents investigating the paranormal. However, having long been a science buff, he wanted the plots to be somewhat based on fact, instead of hinging on incredulous situations involving fictitious monsters and the like. He even has a science advisor he calls on at the University of Massachusetts to make sure that his information on topics such as virus replication is solid.

In addition, Carter devised his characters based on his own desire to believe in the paranormal while acknowledging his doubt. Thus, he came up with the idea to have one agent represent the skeptical, scientific side of the mind, while the other personified the more emotional, intuitive aspect. However, in order to break stereotypes, he decided the female agent would be the more fact–oriented of the two. Carter came up with the female character's name, Dana Scully, in homage to Los Angeles Dodger baseball announcer Vin Scully; agent Fox Mulder's surname was Carter's mothers' maiden name. The pair team up to travel the country digging into the explanations behind mysterious happenings, and each project is labeled an "X" file at the FBI, thus the title, *The X–Files*. Though many stories center on monsters, ghosts, spaceships, and the like, special effects are kept to a minimum—most of the eerie atmosphere on the program comes from the unique mood created by the lighting, style of shots, and music. In addition, much of the popularity of the show stems from the chemistry between Scully (Gillian Anderson) and Mulder (David Duchovny), not to mention a sly brand of wit that is injected into the scripts.

Carter, who is also the executive producer of *The X–Files*, often comes up with ideas for plots based on actual tales from the news media. For example, after hearing on National Public Radio about suicides on a military base in Haiti, he wrote a show about voodoo cults. Other shows have dealt with crop dusting, repressed memories, Gulf War syndrome, vaccinations as a tracking device, and heavily inbred families. Though these kind of story lines are wrapped up neatly in one hour of air time, many of the shows weave an ongoing tale of a global conspiracy involving an extraterrestrial race. Known as the "mythology" episodes, these reveal bits and pieces at a time, giving the program more of a sci–fi soap opera feel and providing cliff–hangers that keep viewers tuning in season after season. Higher–ups at Fox initially balked at this serial idea. Carter in 1995 pointed out to Dana Kennedy in *Entertainment Weekly*, "We have long, tedious arguments about the network's desire for 'closure.' But it's hard to put handcuffs on aliens every week and throw them in the slammer."

Before long, *The X–Files* became a hit among viewers and critics, with the requisite merchandising to go along with it. Devoted X–Philes could stock their homes with key chains, T–shirts, Mulder and Scully dolls, and so on. Many fans were just as enamored of minor charactersas well, including the mysterious "Smoking Man" and the Lone Gunmen, a trio of quirky and kind–hearted hackers and government conspiracy theorists who often lend a surreptitious hand to Mulder and Scully in times of need.

The X–Files was nominated for several Emmy Awards, and won Golden Globe Awards for best dramatic series in 1995 and 1997, among other honors.

In 1998, after five years of the series, Carter released *The X–Files: Fight the Future,* a full–length movie dealing with the alien race conspiracy. Some saw it as a big risk, due to the fact that much of the show's appeal was based on unanswered questions that would undoubtedly have to be resolved to some degree in a feature film. Carter remarked to Matt Roush in *TV Guide,* "I think it will be rejuvenating for the series and hopefully bring more viewers to the show." Indeed, the film was a blockbuster, earning $83 million at the box office, though it did not appear to attract legions of new fans. However, though one of the criticisms of the series had been that it was sometimes confusing to follow if a viewer missed an episode or two, the film stood on its own, while still managing to tie into the ongoing story line.

Meanwhile, in 1996, Carter had launched another series, *Millenium,* about a former FBI agent, now a private investigator in Seattle, who has the psychic ability to see into the minds of deranged killers. The show was based on the premise that all violence in the world is part of an organized evil plan that will culminate in mass horror as the calendar reaches the year 2000. It kicked off its first season with the highest debut Neilsen ratings of any show in the history of the Fox network, but was canceled in 1999. That same year, Carter came out with yet another series, *Harsh Realm,* named after an obscure comic book from the early 1990s. As he noted to Ken Tucker in *Entertainment Weekly,* the program is about "a world that's a duplicate of ours, set inside a computer game, in which real people are sent into the game to play, sometimes at the peril of their lives." Some of the characters enter the game and decide not to return. Carter was excited about the potential of this new show because the premise allows for far fewer boundaries in story–telling.

One of the top–paid writer–producers in the business, Carter's Fox contract pays him roughly $20 to $25 million a year. His production company is called Ten–Thirteen, after his birthdate. He is five feet, eleven inches tall with blond hair, and lives in Pacific Palisades, California, with his wife. He used to spend a great deal of time in Vancouver, Canada, where *The X–Files* was originally shot, but in 1998, the show moved to Los Angeles. Though he has never had a paranormal experience and is thus skeptical of such occurrences, Carter's views on government tend to have much in common with those of character Fox Mulder. As he revealed to Lipsky in *Rolling Stone,* "I have a basic mistrust of people. And because people are government, I have a basic mistrust of government. I think this government doesn't care about the individual. The government cares about government, and that's a problem. There's an interesting quote that one of the editors keeps on top of his keyboard: 'Perfect paranoia is perfect awareness.' I think if I'm adding static to the collective awareness, that's a good thing. Paranoia is good. It creates smart people."

Sources

Books

Authors and Artists for Young Adults, volume 23, Gale Research, 1998.

Contemporary Theatre, Film and Television, volume 16, Gale Research, 1997.

Periodicals

Entertainment Weekly, March 10, 1995, p. 18; October 18, 1996, p. 42; November 29, 1996, pp. 26, 38; June 12, 1998, p. 22; October 30, 1998, p. 24; September 10, 1999, p. 92.

GQ, April 1997, p. 107.

Newsweek, June 22, 1998, p. 73.

People, June 19, 1995, p. 117; April 29, 1996, p. 26; September 2, 1996, p. 48.

Rolling Stone, May 16, 1996, p. 38; February 20, 1997, p. 35.

Star Tribune (Minneapolis, MN), February 4, 1998, p. 12A.

Time, April 21, 1997, p. 40; May 25, 1998, p. 89.

TV Guide, November 16, 1996, p. 14; June 20, 1998, p. 18.

Online

"Chris Carter," *Contemporary Authors Online,* Gale Group web site, http://www.galenet.com (August 26, 1999).

Rubin Carter

Activist

Born May 15, 1937, in Clifton, NJ; married; wife's name, Mae Thelma (divorced, 1984); married Lisa Peters (separated); children: (by first marriage) one daughter; son, Raheem Rubin Carter.

Addresses: *Home*—Toronto, Ontario, Canada. *Office*—Association in Defense of the Wrongly Convicted; 438 University Ave., 19th Floor, Toronto, Ontario, Canada M5G 2K8.

Career

Professional boxer, 1961–67; author of autobiography, *The Sixteenth Round: From Number 1 Contender to Number 45472,* Viking, 1974; Association in Defense of the Wrongly Convicted (AIDWYC), Toronto, Ontario, Canada, executive director.

Sidelights

Rubin "Hurricane" Carter had a promising boxing career ahead of him when he and a friend were imprisoned in 1967 for a bar shooting that killed three. He vehemently maintained his innocence, and in the 1970s he was granted a second trial. Though scores of celebrities lined up to back him, the courts convicted him again. His morale was deflated until a black boy living in a commune of Canadians read Carter's autobiography, which he wrote in prison. The boy moved the group to act on behalf of this jailed American, and thanks to their efforts, Carter was finally freed on a writ of habeas corpus in 1985. Two of the Canadians, Sam Chaiton and Terry Swinton, later wrote a book about the or-

deal, *Lazarus and the Hurricane.* It was made into a Hollywood film in 1999, renewing interest in Carter's tale and thus bringing him into the spotlight once again. As Carter remarked to David Rakoff in the *New York Times Magazine,* "See how miraculous my life is? For 20 years, I was in solitary confinement, reviled as a racist triple murderer, just narrowly escaping the electric chair. And then, just last month, I found myself sitting in the White House with the president of the United States."

Rubin Carter was born on May 15, 1937, in Clifton, New Jersey. His introduction to the criminal justice system began early, when he was 11 years old and living in Paterson, New Jersey. As Chaiton and Swinton related in *Lazarus and the Hurricane,* Carter threw a bottle at a man's head and stabbed him while trying to protect his friends and himself from the man's sexual advances. The man charged Carter with assault, and in court, no one believed a young black man over a white man, even though Carter said that police knew the man was had assaulted other young boys.

Subsequently, Carter was sentenced to correctional home for boys for ten years, until age 21. His autobiography, according to Chaiton and Swinton, related the horrors of incarcerated life, including physical abuse by guards and sexual abuse of some of the younger, smaller inmates by older ones. When the abused boys complained, they received shock treatments. Carter was promised early release at age 17, in 1954, for good behavior, but when it failed to happen, he ran away and joined the army.

In the military, Carter continued to experience racism, but he managed to become one of the first blacks to win acceptance into the elite Rangers, the "Screaming Eagles" of the 101st Airborne. Stationed in Germany, he boasted to a friend about his fighting skills, and the man arranged a match with the army's heavyweight champion. Carter knocked him out in the first round and thus joined the army boxing team, wining the European light–welterweight championship for two consecutive years. He was invited to the 1956 Olympic trials, but his two years were up and he would have had to re–enlist. Eager to return home, he left the army.

Back in New Jersey at his parents' home, Carter found a job, bought a car, and had a girlfriend. But he was still a fugitive, and police raided the house one night and arrested him. He went to the Annandale Reformatory prison, and his G.I. benefits were cut off because he had entered the service illegally. After his release, for reasons beyond his explanation, Carter stole a woman's purse and was sentenced to three to nine years. He got out of Trenton State Prison after four years, in 1961.

While locked up, Carter began to prepare for becoming a professional boxer. He would do five thousand pushups each morning starting at 4 a.m., according to Chaiton and Swinton. When he was released, his Fu Manchu mustache, shaved head, and piercing stare helped make him a feared contender, and he started to win most of his fights by quick knockout. This earned him the nickname "Hurricane." Before long, he was the top middleweight contender and a public figure, appearing regularly in televised meets at Madison Square Garden. In 1963, he was admired for knocking out welterweight champion Emile Griffith in the first round, and the next year, amid controversy, he lost a split decision for the middleweight title to Joey Giardello.

Meanwhile, Carter had gotten married. He was also active in civil rights and an outspoken critic of racial issues in America. Unlike many activists of the time, though, he did not believe in passive resistance, which marked him as a troublemaker with law enforcement. Police harassed him often. In addition, Carter kept a high profile: He was a flashy dresser who drove a Cadillac that boasted his name

in silver on the side. All this came at a time when racial violence was brewing many of the nation's cities as African Americans were arguing for social equity. Focused on his career, which was 51–5 to that point, Carter was training for a match with middleweight title holder Dick Tiger.

It was at this time that Carter was picked up by police on the night of June 16, 1966, for questioning in a shooting at a Paterson bar that resulted in the deaths of the bartender and two customers. Then 29, he and a young fan, 19–year–old John Artis, who had never been in any trouble with the law, were riding in Carter's white Dodge after a night of dancing in a local club. Though they did not meet the description of the two black men wanted for the murders, they were taken to the police station and given lie–detector tests, which they passed. In addition, they were taken to the hospital to visit another victim who had been wounded, who told police that the two were not the men who shot him. Later, at a grand jury hearing, the investigator noted that not only did Carter and Artis not approximate the physical characteristics of the killers, but they also wore light clothing, whereas the killers had on dark apparel. The grand jury thus did not indict them.

However, four months later, Carter and Artis were arrested again, on October 14. Two witnesses, Alfred Bello and Arthur Dexter Bradley, who had committed a breaking–and–entering earlier that night nearby, testified that they saw Carter and Artis leaving the bar. Although other witnesses placed them elsewhere at the time of the murders, an all–white jury convicted them. In the spring of 1967, Carter was given one concurrent and two consecutive life sentences and Artis was given three concurrent life terms. In prison, he maintained his innocence in vain, and became respected among the other inmates for his honesty. He also began to read philosophical works by Plato and Socrates, and joined the Inmates Council to strive for better medical conditions after he lost an eye in an operation to fix a detached retina.

Carter wrote his autobiography in prison, detailing his life at the hands of what he perceived as a racist and unjust system. *The Sixteenth Round: From Number 1 Contender to Number 45472* was published by Viking in 1974, the title alluding to his bout with being locked up as an innocent man (a fight goes 15 rounds). Carter would later tell George Johnson in the *Calgary Sun* that prison is the "closest a body can come to being dead without a funeral. It's hard for anybody. But man, when you are innocent, it's 10 times harder." Meanwhile, each year, he told Johnson, the authorities would let Artis see his family right before Christmas and tell him that if he lied and said that Carter was the killer, they would let him go free. He refused and remained imprisoned; Carter told Johnson that Artis was "my always hero."

In 1974, a few weeks before Carter's book came out, Bello and Bradley recanted their testimony about Carter and Artis, saying that Paterson police had coerced them into lying with offers of reward money and lenient treatment of their own crimes. The case provoked the outrage of liberals and civil rights activists, and Carter found support from numerous celebrities and luminaries such as activist Coretta Scott King, singer Joan Baez, boxer Muhammed Ali, and several journalists and politicians. And in 1975, folk artist Bob Dylan came out with a new song, "Hurricane," commenting on Carter's situation and expressing his belief in the boxer's innocence. Carter and Artis got a new trial in the fall of 1976, but in the meantime, Bello had recanted his recantation. Despite the publicity and stream of support, the two were convicted a second time, on an old theory that they were exacting revenge for the earlier murder of a black bar owner. Their sentences were reinstated.

After this defeat, Carter withdrew from all prison activities. "I wanted to die," he told William Nack in Sports Illustrated. He would not see anyone or accept any gifts, and only ate one can of soup every three days. As he remarked to Brian D. Johnson in Maclean's, "I refused everything, because if I didn't have anything, the prison couldn't take anything away." But in 1980, he got a letter from a 17–year–old black man, Lesra Martin, who had read Carter's autobiography and felt compelled to write to him. Martin, whose first name was a modified version of "Lazarus," the Biblical figure who rose from the dead, was a disadvantaged boy who had been taken under the wing of a group of Canadian entrepreneurs. They had met him in Brooklyn, where he lived in the ghetto and was illiterate despite being in high school, and had taken him to their luxurious Toronto home to educate him.

Over the next four–and–a–half years, Martin and his Canadian mentors made frequent visits to Carter, and some of them eventually moved to New Jersey to be closer to him. They researched the case and helped Carter's and Artis's attorneys with their briefs. Martin, meanwhile, graduated with all A's and enrolled at the University of Toronto. Finally, in November of 1985, a federal judge reviewed the case and ordered Carter and Artis to be released. Though the case dragged on for 26 more months of appeals, the Supreme Court formally dismissed the

1966 indictment in February of 1988. Carter ended up moving to Canada and marrying one of the Canadians, Lisa Peters. He spent his time reading, writing, and lecturing at colleges and law firms.

In 1991, Chaiton and Swinton first published their book in Canada, and it was reissued in 1999 when a movie came out based on it. Hurricane, directed by Norman Jewison and starring Denzel Washington (who was nominated for an Academy Award for his role as Carter) renewed interest in the case. Some, however, criticized the film for taking liberties with the true story. Selwyn Raab, for instance, who reported on Carter's trial earlier, wrote in the New York Times, "The film sterilizes Mr. Carter's history before his arrest for murder." He also griped that the movie failed to give enough attention to Artis.

Raab also complained about the film's lack of attention to issues that arose after where its story left off. Unlike the feel–good ending in the movie, real life was not as tidily wrapped up, and it was more complex. Carter eventually split with the Canadians in 1994 and separated from his Canadian wife. An authorized biography, Hurricane: The Miraculous Journey of Rubin Carter, by former Wall Street Journal reporter James S. Hirsch, was released shortly after the film. In it, Carter accused the group of treating him "as a trophy horse to fill the coffers," according to a report by Johnson in Maclean's. In early 2000, Carter joined Hirsch on a book tour, although Chaiton and Swinton were simultaneously touring to promote the re–issue of their book. Some accounts characterized the split as a kind of divorce case, where the parties simply grew apart. According to Raab, Carter did not have any qualms about the film because of his continuing gratitude for Chaiton and Swinton's help, despite the fact that they parted ways.

Martin, incidentally, obtained a law degree and was called to the British Columbia bar in May of 1999. He was expelled from the commune earlier for dating a woman the group did not approve of him seeing. Ironically, he became a Crown attorney (equivalent to a county prosecutor in the United States), and his first case was a murder conviction. However, as Martin noted to Chris Wood in Maclean's, "I hope that we can eliminate wrongful prosecutions and convictions entirely. Where better to ensure they don't happen than at the opening gate, where you can still decide not to proceed if something's wrong." Carter attended Martin's call to the bar.

Carter was divorced from his first wife, Mae Thelma, in 1984. With her, he had a daughter and a son, Raheem Rubin, who was jailed in April of 1999 awaiting trial for assaulting his ex–girlfriend, a charge he denies. By 2000, though still legally married, Carter was living with a woman he met in Reno in 1998. He is the executive director of the Toronto–based Association in Defense of the Wrongly Convicted and gives frequent lectures. Remarkably, the man imprisoned for 19 years for a crime he did not commit harbors no ill will toward those who prosecuted him. "My story isn't about justice or injustice," he explained to Johnson in the *Calgary Sun*. "It had to do with black people in America, and all over the world for that matter, standing up for themselves, fighting for the right to be free, to express their opinions and the 'system' reacting to a challenge to its power, wanting to crush that challenge." Furthermore, he noted to Bob Minzesheimer in *USA Today*, "There is no bitterness. If I was bitter, it would mean they won."

Sources

Books

Chaiton, Sam, and Terry Swinton, *Lazarus and the Hurricane*, St. Martin's Griffin, 1999.

Periodicals

Calgary Sun, June 19, 1999, p. S12.
Christian Science Monitor, January 7, 2000, p. 15.
Entertainment Weekly, February 4, 2000, p. 40.
Maclean's, December 6, 1999, pp. 66, 70.
New York Times, October 15, 1974, p. 37; December 28, 1999, p. E1; December 29, 1999, p. E1; January 17, 2000, p. C9; January 18, 2000, p. E1.
New York Times Magazine, January 16, 2000, p. 17.
Publishers Weekly, January 31, 2000, p. 20; February 7, 2000, p. 19.
Record (Bergen County, NJ), January 8, 2000.
Sports Illustrated, April 13, 1992, p. 80; January 17, 2000, p. 18.
USA Today, December 29, 1999, p. 1D.
Washington Post, January 6, 2000, p. C1.

Online

"Rubin Carter," *Contemporary Authors Online*, Gale Group web site, http://www.galenet.com (February 22, 2000).

Ana Castillo

Author

Born Ana Hernandez Del Castillo, June 15, 1953, in Chicago, IL; daughter of Raymond and Rachel Rocha Castillo; children: son, Marcel Ramon Herrera. *Education:* Northern Illinois University, B.A. in art education, 1975; University of Chicago, M.A. in Latin American and Caribbean studies, 1979; University of Bremen, Ph.D. in American studies, 1991.

Addresses: *Office*—P.O. Box 408680, Chicago, IL 60640–8680.*Agent*—Susan Bergholz, 17 West 10th St. £5, New York, NY 10011.

Career

Writer, 1975—. Santa Rosa Junior College, Santa Rosa, CA, instructor in ethnic studies, 1975; Illinois Arts Council, writer–in–residence, 1977; Northwestern University, lecturer in history, 1980–81; Urban Gateways of Chicago, poet–in–residence, 1980– 81; San Francisco State University, instructor in women's studies, 1986–87; California State University at Chico, visiting professor of creative writing and fiction, 1988–89; University of New Mexico, Department of English, instructor, 1989, 1991–92; Mount Holyoke College, professor of bilingual creative writing, 1994.

Awards: Before Columbus Foundation American Book Award, 1987, for *The Mixquiahuala Letters;* Women's Foundation of San Francisco Award, 1988; California Arts fellowship for fiction, 1989; National Endowment for the Arts fellowship, 1990, 1995; New Mexico Arts Commission Grant, 1991; Carl Sandburg Literary Award, 1993, for *So Far from God;* Gustaves Myers Award, 1995, for *Massacre of the Dreamers;* Mexican Fine Arts Center Museum, Chicago, IL, Sor Juana Achievement Award, 1998.

Sidelights

Author Ana Castillo is acclaimed for her highly political feminist Chicana poetry, fiction, and essays. While her work often deals with racism and sexism and includes acerbic sociopolitical commentary, at the same time, it offers ironic humor and a universally appealing sense of storytelling. Still, the works generally have the most importance to women of color who have had similar experiences as the author. As Castillo told Elsa Saeta in *Melus,* "Most people usually say, 'Well, I wasn't really thinking about anybody when I was writing this.' And what I usually say is that 'When I'm writing, I'm thinking about a woman who is very much like me reading it.' Because that is the void that we have had in literature: a void in the representation in the literature of women who look and think and feel like me and who have had similar experiences in society. I wanted to fill that void."

Castillo was born on June 15, 1953, in Chicago, Illinois. Her parents, Raymond and Rachel Rocha Castillo, were Mexican American. They moved to the Midwest from the Southwest, where she had an upbringing very different from Hispanics there. As a teen, Castillo lived in an Italian neighborhood of the city and rented an apartment upstairs from "racist Italian landlords," as she recounted in *Essence.* She went on to add, "As part of the condition for our living in that building, my mother had to scrub on her knees the front–entrance stairs every Saturday morning for nearly ten years." Castillo also noted that her mother, who spoke scant English, was darker–skinned and could not "pass" for Italian the way her father sometimes did. In fact, she stated, he later changed his surname to Costello while the rest of the family kept the name Castillo.

Castillo's parents had opposite personalities. Her father, an outgoing man who also loved to play congas and bongos, "would talk to everybody and it didn't matter if you wouldn't talk back," as Castillo noted to Janet Jones Hampton in *Americas*. "He was very self– confident, a very attractive man. My mother was mostly Indian, Mexican Indian. True to that background, she was also very stoic, was uncomfortable with non–Spanish–speaking people." Her mother was also an orphan and was quite shy.

However, both of Castillo's parents were skilled storytellers. Her father would regale listeners with his repertoire of tried–and–true favorites, and her mother would spin intimate yarns around the table with close friends or family. She also had a lovely singing voice. Castillo, though, was never comfortable as a public speaker, so her creative side came out in writing and drawing. Ever since she was a child, she composed stories and poetry, and would draw or paint on any surface available. She dreamed of becoming an artist, never intending to seriously pursue writing.

Nevertheless, as a teen Castillo was sent to a girls' secretarial school. "That was what I was supposed to be according to my family and my background—be a file clerk," she told Elsa Saeta in *Melus*. "I suppose I couldn't have been a secretary because I'm a lousy typist and I've always had this aversion to authority, so I knew that I wouldn't get far in that atmosphere."

Afterward, Castillo worked to obtain scholarships and grants so that she could attend college and study art. She started at Chicago City College, a junior college, then after two years enrolled in Northern Illinois University, where she received her bachelor of arts degree in art education. During her college career, racism and sexism wore her down to the point where, as she told Saeta, "I was really convinced that I had no talent. I couldn't draw and I had no right to be painting. And, I couldn't draw anymore—I literally did not draw or paint anymore."

Instead, in her junior year, Castillo began to write poetry, and gave her first public reading while still a student at age 20. Her group of friends in the arts community encouraged her, and she was getting published by age 21, before she had even graduated. Early on, she contributed to the literary journal *Revista Chicano–Riquena,* now called the *Americas Review.* In 1977, Castillo published her first poetry chapbook, *Otro Canto,* with a grant from the Illinois Arts Council. Her second collection, *The Invitation,* came out in 1979 as she was graduating from the University of Chicago with a master of arts degree in Latin American and Caribbean studies. In 1991, she received a doctorate from the University of Bremen in Germany.

As Castillo embarked on her writing career, she was also becoming an activist. The times were the early– to mid–1970s, at the beginning of the Chicano and feminist movements. As such, she explained to Saeta in *Melus,* "I started out very consciously as a Latina poet, a political poet, or what is sometimes called a protest poet talking about the economic inequality of Latino people in this country." Oddly enough, Castillo admitted to Saeta that while she loved reading fiction, she did not enjoy reading poetry very much and yet she ended up becoming a poet for just about the first decade of her writing career.

In 1984, Castillo published her third book of poetry, *Women Are Not Roses,* which delves heavily into the idea of women who feel disenfranchised in a male–dominated culture. She later focused on feminism specifically in the context of the Chicana experience in her 1994 work *Massacre of the Dreamers: Essays on Xicanisma,* a collection of cultural criticism which was also her dissertation. For this, she received the 1995 Gustaves Myers Award. Castillo also focused strongly on feminist themes in her 1988 poetry collection *My Father Was a Toltec,* which mixes in her heritage by juxtaposing Spanish and English poems without translation.

Castillo's first major recognition came in 1986 with the publication of her first novel, *The Mixquiahuala Letters.* It is constructed as a series of correspondences between a California poet named Teresa and her college pal Alicia, a New York artist. The work centers on the changing roles of Latina women in the United States during the 1970s and 1980s and the resentment by white and Chicano males to their liberation. The book earned Castillo an American Book Award from the Before Columbus Foundation in 1987. Her next novel was *Sapogonia: An Anti–Romance in 3/8 Meter,* 1990. This work, about conflict in relationships, centers on the male narrator, Maximo Madrigal, and his obsession with Pastora Ake, the only woman he has not been able to seduce.

In 1993 Castillo published *So Far from God,* which was her most visible work to that point. Some reviewers commented that it held the most mass appeal of all her efforts to date. The story traces the life of a Latina woman, Sofi, and her four very different daughters. Esperanza is a successful newscaster but leads a shallow life; Caridad is beautiful but wastes her life with promiscuous encounters; Fe, apparently the most well–adjusted, falls into a trance when her fiance abandons her; and the youngest, "La Loca" ("The Crazy One"), died on her third birthday but was resurrected and was recognized thereafter as a saint.

Critics noted that *So Far from God* fits in the genre of magic realism, which is connected with South American writers such as Gabriel Garcia Marquez, Isabel Allende, and others. But many also pointed out that Castillo's style is more humorous and reads more easily than most in that category. Some reviewers, however, pointed out that the book is too crowded with characters, though overall the work was favorably received. It was honored with the Carl Sandburg Literary Award in 1993.

In 1996 Castillo's first short story collection, *Loverboys,* came out to positive reaction. A *Publishers Weekly* reviewer praised its "earthy eroticism and zesty humor," and a *Booklist* critic called Castillo "tirelessly inventive." The tales explore facets of love and friendship and feature a cast of quirky characters, including plenty of creative and strong–willed women. After that, Castillo commissioned several Latino artists and writers to compose essays about the Virgin of Guadalupe, which she collected in *Goddess of the Americas: Writings on the Virgin of Guadalupe.*

In 1999, Castillo published another novel, *Peel My Love like an Onion,* centering on a tough female protagonist, Carmen Santos. Like Castillo, Carmen was raised in Chicago and was not expected to make much of her life, but she overcame a childhood bout with polio and a subsequently damaged leg to become a flamenco dancer, and later, a successful singer. But then, in a bad run of luck, she is forced to eke out a living at menial jobs and return home to live with her grouchy mother. Meanwhile, her lover of 17 years has not committed to her, and she begins an affair with her lover's godson, who leaves her. Still, her spirit prevails. A *Publishers Weekly* reviewer commented that in this work, "Castillo's trademark feminist and border– crossing concerns acquire a new depth and complexity."

Outside of her books, Castillo has been published in several anthologies, and she frequently pens essays and columns for newspapers and magazines nationwide. In addition to writing, Castillo is constantly in demand for touring and speaking, and frequently appears at universities and conferences. She has also taught throughout her career. In 1975 she started out teaching ethnic studies at Santa Rosa Junior College in Sonoma County, California, and served as a writer–in–residence at the Illinois Arts Council in 1977. Then, in 1980 and 1981, she was a history at Northwestern University and a poet–in–residence at Urban Gateways of Chicago. She has also served as an instructor in women's studies at San Francisco State University in 1986–87; a visiting professor of creative writing and fiction at California State University at Chico in 1988–89; an instructor at the University of New Mexico's Department of English in 1989 and 1991–92; and a professor of bilingual creative writing at Mount Holyoke College in 1994.

Unlike many other writers, Castillo does not participate in writers' workshops; instead, she relies on her own eye for assessing her work as well as drawing from authors whose work she enjoys reading. Some of her influences as a teen were Latin American writers, African Americans such as Toni Morrison, and Anais Nin. As Castillo remarked to Saeta, Nin "had Spanish ancestry and Latin influence with French and Spanish in her language. And she was Catholic. Those things were very important to me. I stopped following the Catholic Church when I was eighteen, but Catholicism is embedded in our culture, in our psyche so she was a great teacher for me. Fifty years before I was writing, she was writing in the 1930s about issues that were very similar to the issues that I was writing about in the context of being Mexican."

Also, Castillo cited Gabriel Garcia Marquez and Jorge Amado as inspirations, as well as the book *The Three Marias.* "You see that influence in *The Mixquiahuala Letters* —the communication, the challenging of the church, the sexuality—all of those things come from *The Three Marias* ," Castillo told Saeta. "[The authors] were punished, castigated in Portugal for doing those things. When that book came out they were jailed and these were successful middle class journalists."

Castillo has also served as a contributing editor for *Humanizarte* and *Third Woman* magazines, and founded the Premio Ana Castillo, a literary prize for aspiring poets. In April of 2000, she was honored with other native Chicagoans such as blues legend Buddy Guy at a reception to launch a city history mural on the Skydeck of the Sears Tower. The mural's section on writers features her along with other hometown figures such as Studs Terkel,

Carl Sandburg, and Gwendolyn Brooks. Castillo lives on Chicago's north side with her son, Marcel Ramon Herrera.

Selected works

Otro canto (poems), Alternitiva Publications, 1977.
The Invitation (poems), privately printed, 1979.
Women Are Not Roses, Arte Publico, 1984.
The Mixquiahuala Letters (novel), Bilingual Press, 1986. (Editor with Cherrie Morgan) *This Bridge Called My Back,* ISP Press, 1988.
My Father Was a Toltec: Poems, West End Press, 1988.
Sargonia: An Anti–Romance in 3/8 Meter (novel), Bilingual Press, 1990.
So Far From God (novel), Norton, 1993.
Massacre of the Dreamers: Essays on Xicanisma, University of New Mexico Press, 1994.
My Father Was a Toltec and Selected Poems 1973–1988, Norton, 1995.
(Editor) *Goddess of the Americas: Writings on the Virgin of Guadalupe,* Riverhead Books, 1996.
Loverboys, Plume, 1997.
Peel My Love Like an Onion (novel), Doubleday, 1999.
My Daughter, My Son, the Eagle the Dove: An Aztec Chant, illustrated by S. Guevara, Dutton Books, 2000.

Sources

Books

Contemporary Women Poets, St. James Press, 1998.
Dictionary of Hispanic Biography, Gale Research, 1996.
Notable Hispanic American Women, Book 2, Gale Research, 1998.

Periodicals

Americas (English Edition), January 2000, p. 48.
Arizona Republic, October 10, 1999, p. E19.
Booklist, August 1996, p. 1881.
Commonweal, March 14, 1997, p. 24.
Essence, June 1993, p. 42.
Melus, September 22, 1997, p. 133.
Publishers Weekly, July 8, 1996, p. 73; August 12, 1996, p. 59; August 9, 1999, p. 342.

Online

"Ana (Hernandez Del) Castillo," *Contemporary Authors Online,* Gale Group web site, http://www.galenet.com (June 6, 2000).
Ana Castillo Personal Home Page, http://www.anacastillo.com (August 1, 2000).

Joan Chen

Actor

Born Chen Chong, April 26, 1961, in Singapore, China; daughter of physicians; married Jimmy Lau (a filmmaker; divorced); married Peter Hui (a doctor), 1991; children: (with Hui) Angela Frances. *Education:* California State University at Northridge, degree in filmmaking, 1991.

Addresses: *Home*—San Francisco, CA.

Career

Actor. Television appearances include series *Twin Peaks*, 1990–91; movies *Steel Justice*, 1992; *Shadow of a Stranger*, 1992; and *In a Class of His Own*, 1999; and episodes of *Miami Vice*, 1985; *MacGyver*, 1985; *Wiseguy*, 1989; *Nightmare Café*, 1989; *Tales from the Crypt*, 1993; *Strangers*, 1996; *Homicide: Life on the Street*, 1997; and *The Outer Limits*, 1998.

Film appearances include *Youth*, 1977; *The Little Flower*, 1980; *Awakening*, 1981; *Su xing*, 1981; *Dim Sum: A Little Bit of Heart*, 1984; *Tai-Pan*, 1986; *The Night Stalker*, 1987; *The Last Emperor*, 1987; *Heartbeat*, 1988; *The Blood of Heroes*, 1988; *Turtle Beach*, 1991; *Strangers*, 1991; *Deadlock*, 1991; *You Seng*, 1993; *Heaven & Earth*, 1993; *Red Rose, White Rose*, 1994; *On Deadly Ground*, 1994; *Golden Gate*, 1994; *The Wild Side*, 1995; *The Hunted*, 1995; *Judge Dredd*, 1995; *Precious Find*, 1996; and *Ziyu fengbao*, 1999. Other film work includes associate producer, *The Wild Side*, 1995; and director, coproducer, and cowriter, *Xiu-Xiu: The Sent-Down Girl*, 1998.

Awards: Golden Rooster award (China) for best actress, c. 1980, for *Little Flower*; Golden Horse award (Taiwan) for best actress, c. 1994, for *Red Rose, White*

Rose; Hong Kong Film Critics Society Award for best actress, 1995, for year–round performances; Fort Lauderdale International Film Festival Jury Award and Golden Horse award for best director, best picture (with Allison Liu and Cecile Shah Tsuei), and best screenplay (with Geling Yan), all 1998, National Board of Review Freedom of Expression Award, and Paris Film Festival Special Jury Prize, both 1999, all for *Xiu–Xiu: The Sent–Down Girl.*

Sidelights

Actor Joan Chen's real life has a more fascinating story line than most of the films in theaters. After her parents were whisked away for "re–education" during the Cultural Revolution in China, she was tapped by the government–run film studios to act in propaganda films. After her first big part made her a star, she only made three more films before heading to the United States—not to find fame in Hollywood, but so that she could enjoy a normal life and study medicine. The lure of the cameras drew her to California, though, and she was eventually discovered in a parking lot by director Dino de Laurentiis. After playing various stereotypical "China doll" roles, Chen's status was raised in the television series *Twin Peaks* and the film *Heaven & Earth.* Her real goal, though, was to crate her own stories. After releasing *Xiu–Xiu: The Sent–Down Girl* in major cinemas in 1999, Chen was widely applauded for her directorial talents.

Born Chen Chong on April 26, 1961, in Singapore, China, Joan Chen is the youngest of two children of prominent Chinese doctors. However, their opulent lifestyle ended during the Cultural Revolution under Mao Zedong in the late 1960s, when the educated were sent to labor on farms and in factories. Her parents were sent away, and Chen and her brother, Chase, now a painter in Los Angeles, were separated from them for long stretches. Due to Communist oppression, when she was five, her grandfather committed suicide by drinking cyanide in public. However, Chen's fortunes improved when Mao's wife, Jiang Qing, chose the 14–year–old Chen out of her school rifle squad to become an actor. As she explained to Susan Morgan in *Interview*, "The film studio just picks: 'You! You look like you could be an actress!'"

Leaving school, Chen worked on a film about the Long March that was never released. Her first appearance came in *Youth*, 1977, about a deaf–mute cured by acupuncture treatments. She was immediately hailed as the Chinese Elizabeth Taylor. When she was not on shoots, like all actors, Chen traveled around China to observe the working people and understand different places and situations. During this time, she learned more about politics and cultivated her public image as being humble and innocent. "I wasn't really calculating," Chen mentioned to Morgan, "but I began to know what people wanted."

Later, Chen attended a boarding school run by the studio, and began acting classes, although she had not finished high school. Still a teenager, Chen won the Golden Rooster award the equivalent of the Academy Award for her second film, *Little Flower*. Worried about neglecting her education, however, Chen studied with a tutor for a year and graduated. She was then accepted to an elite college for training diplomats. However, her education was interrupted again by her career. Though she only starred in four films before leaving China, Chen became a superstar, so huge that fans once rioted when she was spotted out shopping.

Weary of the fame, Chen longed for a challenge. "In a sense, everything came too easily to me," she told *In Style'* s Alison Dakota Gee. "I was happy to walk away from it all." In 1981, at age 20, Chen went to the United States, where no one knew her and she had to adjust to a completely different world. "I had seen death," she told Margy Rochlin in *Harper's Bazaar*. "I knew about survival. But I knew nothing about sex, drugs, or English."

At her parent's wishes, Chen enrolled at the State University of New York at New Platz, intending to study medicine, just as they had on fellowships in New York in the late 1970s. Soon, however, she decided to study filmmaking at California State University at Northridge. After a couple of years, struggling to pay the bills by hostessing at a restaurant, she wanted to begin acting again, and took the name "Joan" because it sounded like "Chong." Edging her way back in to the business, she landed a few small parts on television shows like *Miami Vice* and *MacGyver* before director Dino De Laurentiis spotted her one day walking through a parking lot. Discovering her qualifications, he cast her as the lead in the 1986 television epic *Tai–Pan*, based on the novel by James Clavell.

The role of May–May in *Tai–Pan* required Chen to return to China for shoots, which angered authorities there due to the character she played. They viewed her part, as a concubine to a foreign man, to be demeaning, and Chinese fans were cold to her. In addition, the production was a critical disaster. The next year, 1987, Chen appeared in Bernardo Bertolucci's *The Last Emperor*, as an empress addicted to opium. Both of these roles cast her as the sexy Asian female. She later commented to Melanie Rehak in the *New York Times Magazine*, "I knew there was one version of Chineseness that America wanted from me: exotic, slant–eyed, long–haired, sexy, vulnerable China doll. I was eager to adapt and conform. I regret that."

In 1990, Chen was cast as Josie Packard in David Lynch's edgy and successful television series *Twin Peaks* as a calculating widow with an evil streak, then branched out away from the glamour in the violent 1988 action flick *The Blood of Heroes* with Rutger Hauer. Her profile received an even bigger boost in Oliver Stone's *Heaven & Earth*, 1993, playing the mother of a Vietnamese girl. However, Chen followed this with some poor choices of projects, including *Judge Dredd*, 1994, and *On Deadly Ground*, 1995. Still, her reputation remained intact thanks to films like director Stanley Kwan's 1994's *Hong meigui, bai meigui* (*Red Rose White Rose*), which won her a Golden Horse award in Taiwan for best actress.

Meanwhile, Chen graduated from film school at California State University in 1991 and was eager to work on the other side of the camera for once. In 1998, she made her directorial debut with *Xiu Xiu: The Sent–Down Girl*, based on a novella by Yan Geling. The story is about a teenage girl who is "sent down" to the countryside, like more than seven million other youth, to perform manual labor during the Cultural Revolution. The film was acclaimed worldwide, winning seven Golden Horse awards in Taiwan, including for best director, best picture, and best screenplay adapted from another source; a Jury Award at the Fort Lauderdale International Film Festival; a Freedom of Expression award from the National Board of Review; and a Special Jury Prize at the Paris Film Festival. It was also nominated for a Berlin International Film Festival Award and for the Grand Prix in Paris.

Despite the honors, Chinese authorities frowned on *Xiu–Xiu* (pronounced sho–sho) and banned it from playing in the country. Part of their ire was due to the subject matter, but they were also displeased that Chen filmed in the nation without a legal permit. She shot it in the mountains between China and Tibet at an elevation of 13,000 feet. China banned her from working there for a year and ordered her to pay a fine worth ten percent of the film's budget, which was $1 million. This added further expense to a project that Chen had financed mostly by herself. The film saw major release in the United States in 1999.

In 1984, Chen married a Hong–Kong born filmmaker, Jimmy Lau, but they divorced in 1988. Later, she met Peter Hui, a San Francisco cardiologist, on a blind date in 1991 and they married after just six months. She settled with him in the Pacific Heights area of San Francisco. Though she was slightly concerned about leaving Los Angeles due to her acting career, Chen enjoys the environment of northern California as opposed to the Hollywood hustle and bustle, because, she remarked to Candy Kit Har Chan in *AsianWeek,* "You can have a quiet, private life in this town." However, she still considers Shanghai her home. "Every time I leave [Shanghai], it is hard. It is always a bit sad," she noted to Chan,

but later added, "But I think if I am in China long enough, I would miss the United States too." Chen and her husband have a daughter, Angela Frances, who was born in October of 1998.

Sources

Books

Contemporary Theatre, Film and Television, volume 13, Gale Research, 1995
Notable Asian Americans, Gale Research, 1995.

Periodicals

American Film, May 1990, p. 32.
AsianWeek, May 12, 1995.
Harper's Bazaar, December 1990, p. 156.
In Style, March 1999, p. 314.
Interview, December 1987, p. 146; August 1990, p. 76.
New York Times Magazine, May 23, 1999, p. 17.
People, November 17, 1986, p. 93; June 21, 1999, p. 91.
Time, April 5, 1999, p. 60.
Variety, March 2, 1998, p. 86.
Washington Times, June 16, 1999, p. C13.

Online

"Joan Chen," Internet Movie Database web site, http://us.imdb.com (December 22, 1999).

Mary Higgins Clark

Author

Born December 24, 1929, in New York, NY; daughter of Luke Joseph (a restaurant owner) and Nora C. (a buyer; maiden name, Durkin) Higgins; married Warren F. Clark (an airline executive), December 26, 1949 (died, September 26, 1964); married Raymond Charles Ploetz (an attorney), August 8, 1978 (marriage annulled, 1984); married John Conheeney (a business executive), November 30, 1996; children (from first marriage): Marilyn, Warren, David, Carol, Patricia. *Education:* Attended Villa Maria Academy, Ward Secretarial School, and New York University; Fordham University, B.A. (summa cum laude), 1979.

Addresses: *Home*—2508 Cleveland Ave., Washington Township, NJ 07675; and 210 Central Park S., New York, NY 10019. *Agent*—Eugene H. Winck, McIntosh & Otis, Inc., 475 Fifth Ave., New York, NY 10017.

Career

Writer. Remington Rand, New York City, advertising assistant, 1946–48; Pan American Airlines, flight attendant, 1948–49; radio scriptwriter and producer for Robert G. Jennings, 1965–70; Aerial Communications, New York City, vice president, partner, creative director, and producer of radio programming, 1970–80; David J. Clark Enterprises, New York City, chairman of the board and creative director, 1980—. Chair, International Crime Writers Conference, 1988. Member, Mystery Writers of America (president, 1987, member of board of directors); Authors Guild, Authors League of America; American Academy of Arts and Sciences; American Society of Journalists and Authors; American Irish Historical Society (member of executive council).

Awards: New Jersey Author Award, 1969, for *Aspire to the Heavens: A Biography of George Washington,* 1977, for *Where Are the Children?,* and 1978, for *A Stranger Is Watching;* Grand Prix de Literature Policiere (France), 1980; Deauville Film Festival (France) literary prize, 1998.

Sidelights

Best–selling author Mary Higgins Clark has become rich and famous for her suspenseful tales that have earned her comparisons to Agatha Christie. Her success is due in large part to her likable characters that readers love to root for. "I write about strong, nice people—they're ordinary people whose lives have been invaded," Clark explained to Elizabeth Hill O'Neill in *Publishers Weekly.* "The danger comes from outside. They're not looking for trouble, not walking down Eighth Avenue at 3 a.m."

Although readers can more easily identify with Clark's heroes and heroines because they are everyday people, the author herself has had a remarkable life. With five children under age 13, she was widowed from a husband she dearly loved. She started getting up at 5 a.m. to begin writing fiction at her kitchen table before going to her day job as a radio scriptwriter, and by her second novel was earning seven figures for her books. In 2000, Clark signed a new contract with her longtime publisher, Simon & Schuster, for a $64 million advance for four more novels and a memoir. Industry experts concluded that it set a record for the richest per–book contract given to a female writer.

Clark was born on December 24, 1929, in New York City. She is the middle child of Luke Joseph Higgins and Nora C. (Durkin) Higgins, and had a

Catholic upbringing in the Bronx. Her father owned and managed the Higgins Bar and Grille, an Irish–American pub, and her mother was a buyer for the B. Altman department store in Manhattan, which later went out of business. Growing up, Clark was an avid reader, and entertained her friends at pajama parties by spinning spooky stories. "I always knew I was going to be a writer," she told Patti Thorn in the *Rocky Mountain News.* "There was never a question in my mind. Ever since I could hold a pencil, I wrote poems, skits, plays. We put a velvet curtain up in the garage and the garage was our stage and people sat in the driveway. We'd charge two cents admission. I always kept a journal. It was just always there."

During the Depression years, Clark's father worked 20 hours a day at his business, hoping to prevent it from failing. When she was ten years old, he died in his sleep, leaving her mother with a pile of debt and two sons and a daughter to support. They tried to keep ahead by renting rooms, but they finally were forced to relocate into a small three–room apartment. After graduating from the Roman Catholic Villa Maria Academy in 1945, Higgins Clark attended Ward Secretarial School. She started working at Remington Rand as an advertising assistant in 1946, but a flight attendant friend awoke her spirit of adventure one day by announcing, "God, it was beastly hot in Calcutta," as Clark related to Roy Hoopes in *Modern Maturity.* The career sounded so exotic that she enrolled in a training school soon after.

In 1949 Clark got a job with Pan American Airlines, and around the same time she became engaged to Warren Clark, an airline executive whom she had known since childhood. They delayed the nuptials for a year so that she could travel and see the world, and they were married on December 26, 1949. The couple settled in the Stuyvesant Town area of New York, and within eight years, the Clarks had five children: Marilyn, Warren, David, Carol, and Patricia.

Meanwhile, Clark began to take creative writing courses at New York University. After dozens of rejection letters she finally sold a romantic fiction piece about and airline attendant. She told Hoopes, "I called my mother up and she said, 'Oh grand, but put the money in the bank.' I told her I was going to spend it and write more. She said, 'But Mary, you've used up your idea.'" Still, Clark continued to churn out stories even while raising her kids.

However, after ten happy years of marriage, Clark's husband began to experience numbness in his arms and chest. They soon learned that he was suffering from hardening of the arteries, a heart condition, and did not have long to live. But as Clark recalled in a *Redbook* article, "Of the fifteen years of our marriage, those five were the best. We did exactly what we wanted to do and saw only people we liked. We gave all our free time to each other and to the children." They traveled, and her husband took a dream job at another airline even though his condition made it impossible for him to sign up for health insurance or a pension.

In 1964 Clark's husband had his fourth heart attack in five years, and though she tried to revive him with mouth–to–mouth resuscitation, he could not be saved. At the same time, her mother–in–law, who was visiting at the time, also collapsed and died. Adding to the tragedy of her life, one of her brothers had died at age 18 from meningitis and the other was killed in an accident. Not to mention, after her husband's death, Clark was left to raise her five children ages 5 through 13 on her own with nothing but 18 months of his salary in savings.

But Clark had warning that she was going to have to work, so she had contacted a friend who had once contributed to radio shows. The week after her husband died, she began to write syndicated radio programs while her mother babysit her kids. Each show was four minutes long, and that included two commercials. It taught Clark to be concise. Soon, though, she yearned to write books. After working for a year on a biographical radio program called *Portrait of a Patriot,* she set out to pen a novel about George Washington, which was published in 1968 as *Aspire to the Heavens.* Although it won the 1969 New Jersey Author Award, the book sold dismally, which Clark attributed to its regrettable title. It was sold mainly in religious bookstores and inspirational sections, and thus did not get wide exposure.

Afterward, Clark became determined to write a work that would sell well, since she had children in college and private schools by this time and needed the income. To ensure a success, she mulled over the kinds of books she herself enjoyed reading, and realized she liked suspense thrillers. Around this time, the case of Alice Crimmins had been in the papers. She was a New York–area mother convicted of manslaughter of her daughter and murder of her son. The murder conviction was later overturned, and the manslaughter conviction was overturned but then upheld.

This struck a chord with Clark, and she knew it would intrigue others as well, since the fear of having something happen to a child is universal and deep–seated. In *Where Are the Children?*, she developed a lead character who was accused of murdering her children, but was innocent. The plot was very different from the real–life Crimmins case, and was unique to the suspense genre at the time because the villain was identified early on. But Clark's masterful style kept readers engaged. After two other publishers rejected the work, Simon & Schuster picked it up and it became a best–seller in 1975.

Subsequently, Clark's career took off. She earned $100,000 for the paperback rights to *Where Are the Children?*, and for her next thriller, 1978's *A Stranger Is Watching*, she reaped a $500,000 advance and $1 million for the paperback rights. It, too, played on a woman's fear, this time peering into the question of how much someone can trust a helpful stranger. Much of the tale is set beneath New York City's Grand Central Station, where a woman and a child are being held captive by a psychopath. In these two novels, Clark established her storytelling style of edgy suspense in a limited time frame: *Where Are the Children?* takes place over the course of just one day, and *A Stranger Is Watching* occurs over three days.

In the meantime, Clark returned to school, and obtained her bachelor of arts degree summa cum laude from Fordham University in 1979. The next year, she had another hit with *The Cradle Will Fall*, which was filmed as a CBS "Movie of the Week" in 1984. In fact, most of Clark's works have been adapted. Among others, *A Stranger is Watching* was released as a film in 1982 and her first novel was made into a film in 1986. However, her works in general do not earn as much for film rights as say, those of Stephen King or John Grisham, because they "are neither violent enough nor sexy enough for Hollywood," according to Alex Kuczynski in the *New York Times*. Though Clark does not write the screenplays for any of her books made into television movies or films, she was awarded the literary prize from France's Deauville Film Festival in 1998.

Clark's third novel, *The Cradle Will Fall*, published in 1980, revealed a more sophisticated plot than her first two because of the extent of medical information. It concerns a woman who is briefly hospitalized following a minor car accident, and while she is sedated, believes she sees a murder. When Clark began to pen the story, the heroine was married to a judge, but she soon felt something was awry. She concluded that her main character has to be vulnerable, and someone married to a judge would give readers the idea that he would protect her. In addition, Clark figured a single woman would leave room for a love interest, and romance thus became one of the cornerstones of her books.

In fact, most of Clark's stories follow a general pattern, which has proven popular with readers, if not critics, who tend to dismiss her tales as pat. The main character is usually an independent–minded female professional, often a reporter, attorney, or photographer. Roughly 50 pages into the book, the bad guy—always a male—enters and commits a vile crime. By the end, the heroine rights the wrong by convicting the killer, saving an imperiled child, avenging her husband's death, or whatever the case may be, and justice is served.

All of Clark's suspense novels have been best–sellers, and she is also wildly popular internationally, especially in Europe. John Baker, the editorial director of *Publishers Weekly*, told Kuczynski in the *New York Times*, "For authors who are enormously successful but generally critically spurned, as I am afraid poor Mary tends to be, there is a lot of money to be made overseas. I mean, they name streets after her in France. It's a sort of Jerry Lewis syndrome, I think."

Meanwhile, Clark's daughter Carol embarked on a writing career as well, and her first novel, *Decked*, hit the best–seller list in 1993 just as Clark's *I'll Be Seeing You* was fading from the hardcover list after 17 weeks. Carol Higgins Clark has also acted in supporting roles in film and of–Broadway, and in 1992 starred in the television movie *A Cry in the Night*, based on one of her mother's novels.

Since the death of her first husband, Clark has married again twice. On August 8, 1978, she wed attorney Raymond Charles Ploetz, but after six years, the marriage was annulled. She called the union a "colossal mistake," according to Kim Hubbard in *People*. Then, she married John Conheeney on November 30, 1996. Clark's daughter, Patty Derenzo, while working at the New York Mercantile Exchange, met Conheeney, the former CEO of Merrill Lynch Futures Inc., when he stopped by to say hello to her boss. In addition to being attractive, he had a lot in common with her mother. He was also Irish–American and was widowed in 1994 when he lost his wife of 40 years to cancer, and he lived in Ridgewood, New Jersey, near Clark's home in Saddle River. Conheeney has four adult children, and together the pair has 15 grandchildren.

Selected writings

Where Are the Children?, Simon & Schuster, 1975.
A Stranger Is Watching, Simon & Schuster, 1978.
The Cradle Will Fall, Simon & Schuster, 1980.
A Cry in the Night, Simon & Schuster, 1982.

Stillwatch, Simon & Schuster, 1984.
(With Thomas Chastain and others) *Murder in Manhattan* , Morrow (New York City), 1986.
Weep No More, My Lady, Simon & Schuster, 1987.
While My Pretty One Sleeps, Simon & Schuster, 1989.
Loves Music, Loves to Dance, Simon & Schuster, 1991.
All Around the Town, Simon & Schuster, 1992.
I'll Be Seeing You, Simon & Schuster, 1993.
Remember Me, Simon & Schuster, 1994.
Let Me Call You Sweetheart, Simon &Schuster, 1995.
Mary Higgins Clark: Three Complete Novels (contains *Where Are the Children?, A Stranger Is Watching,* and *The Cradle Will Fall*), Wings (New York City), 1995.
Silent Night, Simon &Schuster, 1995.
Moonlight Becomes You, Simon & Schuster, 1996.
Pretend You Don't See Her, Simon & Schuster, 1997.
All Through the Night, Simon & Schuster, 1998.
You Belong to Me, Simon & Schuster, 1998.
We'll Meet Again, Simon & Schuster, 1999.
Before I Say Goodbye, Simon & Schuster, 2000.

Short Story Collections

(Editor) *Murder on the Aisle: The 1987 Mystery Writers of America Anthology,* Simon & Schuster, 1987.
(With others) *Caribbean Blues,* J. Curley, 1988.
The Anastasia Syndrome and Other Stories, Simon & Schuster, 1989.
The Lottery Winner: Alvirah and Willy Stories, Simon & Schuster, 1994.
(Editor and author of introduction) *The International Association of Crime Writers Presents: Bad Behavior,* Harcourt Brace, 1995.

Other

Aspire to the Heavens: A Biography of George Washington, Meredith Press, 1969.
(Contributor) *I, Witness,* Times Books, 1978.

(Contributor) *Family Portraits,* edited by Carolyn Anthony, Doubleday, 1989.
Also contributor of stories to periodicals, including *Saturday Evening Post, Redbook, McCall's,* and *Family Circle.*

Sources

Books

Contemporary Popular Writers, St. James Press, 1997.
St. James Guide to Crime & Mystery Writers, fourth edition, St. James Press, 1996.
St. James Guide to Horror, Ghost & Gothic Writers, first edition, St. James Press, 1998.

Periodicals

Good Housekeeping, November 1996, p. 23.
Modern Maturity, August–September 1989, p. 52.
New York Times, May 22, 2000, p. C1.
People, November 2, 1992, p. 79; December 16, 1996, p. 54.
Publishers Weekly, May 19, 1989, p. 64; July 15, 1996, p. 20; May 1, 2000, p. 9.
Readers Digest, December 1989, p. 92.
Redbook, March 1991, p. 102.
Rocky Mountain News, June 11, 2000, p. 1E.
Variety, August 31, 1998, p. 88.

Online

"Mary Higgins Clark," *Contemporary Authors Online,* Gale Group web site, http://www.galenet.com (June 6, 2000).

Ward Connerly

AP/Wide World Photos

Activist and businessperson

Born June 15, 1939, in Leesville, LA; married Ilene Crews, 1962; children: one son, one daughter. *Education:* Attended American River Junior College; Sacramento State College, B.A. in political science, 1962.

Addresses: *Office*—Connerly & Associates, 2215 21st St., Sacramento, CA 95818.

Career

Worked as civil servant for state housing agencies, 1962–69 and served as deputy director of California's department of housing and urban development, 1971–73; chief consultant to California State Assembly committee on urban affairs, 1969–70; Connerly & Associates, president and chief executive officer, 1973—; chair and main spokesperson for California Civil Rights initiative, 1995—, and American Civil Rights Initiative, 1997—. Member of University of California Board of Regents, 1993—.

Sidelights

As one of the most visible leaders in the fight against affirmative action in the United States, Ward Connerly has stirred a great deal of controversy. Developed to offer women and minorities the same opportunities as white males, affirmative action laws often establish quotas in areas such as college admission, hiring and promotions, and government contracts arenas in which they have widely suffered discrimination in the past. Connerly, however, believes that such programs hamper the moti-

vation to succeed and are thus more of a detriment than a boon to those people it intends to assist. Thus, he has worked diligently to repeal affirmative action, starting with admissions and hiring rules at the University of California, where he serves on the Board of Regents. Subsequently, through his efforts, the entire state passed a proposition to end any kind of preferential treatment based on race, gender, or national origin, and Connerly is trying to expand his crusade into other states as well.

What makes Connerly even more of a volatile figure in this battle is the fact that he himself is African American. Despite outcries from other prominent black leaders who feel he is doing a disservice, he insists that he is looking out for fellow blacks, rather than trying to stifle their success. Explaining his position to B. Drummond Ayres Jr. in the *New York Times,* he stated, "Nobody ever gave me any race or sex preferences....And I made it anyway—high school, college, my own big business, important friends. If I could make it, anybody can, because the playing field is a lot closer to level now. The truth is that preferences at this point are not just reverse discrimination, they're degrading to people who accept them. They've got to go."

Connerly was born on June 15, 1939, in Leesville, Louisiana. His father left the family when he was two years old, and his mother died two years later. Raised by relatives, he lived in Washington state, then moved to Sacramento, California, to live with an uncle. By age 12 his grandmother obtained legal custody of him, but had little means to raise him. He has said that she raised chickens and sold eggs to help feed the family, and sometimes had nothing to eat but sweet potatoes. He once related that when he was 13, a representative from the welfare office paid a visit and made him so embarrassed of living on public funds that he landed a job as a janitor making 65 cents an hour in order to support the household.

Later, however, extended family members came forward to dispute Connerly's memories of an impoverished childhood. One uncle, according to A. Lin Neumann in the *Nation,* said that Connerly lied about having nothing to eat, and a first cousin in the same article recalled, "There were no chickens. Nobody sold eggs." However, Eric Pooley in *Time* suggested that Connerly's family was contradicting his anecdotes about his poor childhood because they disagreed with his politics, and Pooley interviewed an aunt who corroborated his stories. Connerly, meanwhile, insisted his personal history was accurate.

After high school, Connerly commuted to American River Junior College, where he was voted student president. Later he enrolled at Sacramento State College, again serving as student body president there. He was the first in his family to earn a college degree, graduating with a bachelor of arts in political science with honors in 1962. While a student, in 1959 he led a protest concerning housing discrimination, which captured the attention of lawmakers. They asked him to testify during debates on a fair-housing bill, which later passed.

Immediately after graduation, Connerly went to work at Sacramento's re-development agency, then moved to the state department of housing and urban development, rising to a managerial position. There, he became friends with legislator Pete Wilson, who was just about to become chair of the housing committee for the California State Assembly. Wilson hired Connerly in 1969 as the chief consultant for a new State Assembly committee on urban affairs, and the two remained close ever since. After the Republicans lost their majority in the Assembly, Connerly returned to work at the state housing department, where he was promoted to deputy director.

By 1973, on advice from Wilson, Connerly decided to step away from his stable government employment and open his own consulting and land-use planning company. It thrived, and by 1990, employed 15 people. Though some of his critics believed that Wilson contributed to his success, others disagreed. In addition, a *Jet* article cited a story in the *San Francisco Chronicle* which stated that he had accepted $140,000 over the years in affirmative action contracts from the government. Though roughly half of his business did indeed come from the government, Connerly disputed that it was affirmative action money, telling Donna St. George of the *Knight–Ridder/Tribune News Service,* "I don't think there's a minority around who hasn't benefited from the climate of inclusion that affirmative action has fostered. But I have never gone after the preference." He mentioned that he never listed himself on minority rosters, nor did he apply for minority "set-asides." However, Ayres in the *New York Times* reported that Connerly had indeed listed his firm as minority–owned in order to "keep all the benefits of a government contract." Pooley in *Time,* on the other hand, noted that Connerly had only disclosed his race after it was required.

Meanwhile, Connerly raised funds for the Republican party and was a generous donor himself, contributing $120,000 to Wilson's gubernatorial campaigns from 1990 to 1995. However, he was not in the political spotlight by any means, and held moderate views on such topics as abortion and gay rights. In 1993, Wilson appointed Connerly to the University of California Board of Regents, a 26–member group. In that position, he became aware of racial issues at the institution, and began to believe that racial quotas in hiring and admissions were a form of reverse racism against whites. His opinion was sealed in the summer of 1994, when a couple named Jerry and Ellen Cook approached him to say that their son had been rejected by the university's medical school, even though he had won acceptance at a number of higher–prestige institutions. Jerry Cook, a statistician, offered proof to Connerly that whites and Asians were often turned down, despite having better grades and test scores, to make way for other minorities.

Subsequently, Connerly developed a proposal that would base admissions solely on academic merit. However, he later amended his plan to acknowledge social and economic factors in admissions, but not race. In July of 1995, the University of California Board of Regents debated this plan in the midst of a tumultuous protest by activist Jesse Jackson that drew several hundred peaceful demonstrators. In the end, the board voted 15–10 to end racial preferences in hiring and contracting by January of 1996, and 14–10 to end preferences in admissions.

Meanwhile, a statewide movement was growing to abolish racial preferences. A group of academics in 1994 had formed the California Civil Rights Initiative (CCRI), which was pushing a ballot measure called Proposition 209. It read, "The state shall not discriminate against, or grant preferential treatment to, any individual or group on the basis of race, sex, color, ethnicity or national origin in the operation of public employment, public education or public contracting." This would effectively end affirmative action programs in the state. However, as of 1995, this group was suffering from lack of funding and poor management.

Connerly previously had hesitated to join CCRI, fearing a backlash against his family or business, because he had received phone threats after his involvement at the university. "I knew I would have to contend with the characterizations of 'sellout' and 'Uncle Tom' and 'traitor,'" he remarked to Michael Lynch in Reason. But by the end of 1995 he agreed to join them, and with help from Wilson, managed to gather the extra 700,000 signatures and then some to add to the existing 200,000 in order to get Proposition 209 on the ballot in November of 1996. As a result, he was accused of riding the issue for the sake of helping the political career of Wilson, who was planning to run for the presidency in 1996. Others, however, vouched for his sincerity. Indeed, he weathered severe criticism from those who opposed his position. Even total strangers in public would sometimes point accusing fingers at him, and one scathing editorial cartoon compared him to a Ku Klux Klan member.

However, Connerly remained devoted to his cause. In an interview for Black Enterprise, Connerly compared affirmative action to slavery, claiming that it leaves blacks dependent on, and dominated by, whites, who make the decisions on whether to allow them special consideration in matters of education and employment. He noted in the article, "There is absolutely no reason for black Americans to believe that they cannot succeed on the strength of their own talents, hard work, and initiative," adding that "affirmative action, which served this nation well for many years, has outlived its usefulness." As a counterpoint, Willie Brown, who was running to become mayor of San Francisco at the time, in the same interview suggested that affirmative action programs needed to be expanded, not eliminated. He felt this was necessary in order to continue "to move as many women and minorities as possible into the economic mainstream," citing the economic health of the state of California as a concern.

In spite of high–stakes backing to defeat the measure from groups like the Carnegie, Ford, and Rockefeller foundations, Proposal 209 passed in 1996, 54

to 46 percent. Immediately, though, the American Civil Liberties Union filed suit and won a temporary restraining order to prevent it from being enacted. In December, the Clinton administration announced it would also challenge the constitutionality of the proposition, claiming that it violated the 14th Amendment. But in spring of 1997, an appeals court lifted the injunction banning enforcement of the proposition, moving the fight to the California Supreme Court. It became law that summer.

Also in 1997, Connerly founded the American Civil Rights Initiative to take his battle against affirmative action nationwide. A similar referendum to California's in Washington later won with 58 percent of the vote. By 1999, Connerly had taken up the cause wholeheartedly in Florida, hoping to gather enough signatures for a ballot proposal in 2000 elections. However, Republican and Democrat leaders in the state were opposed to his efforts. A writer for Time suggested that in an election year, the hot–button issue scared off politicians, especially in a climate that seemed to favor moderates and eschew such polarizing issues. Still, some polls showed strong support for the measure.

In the meantime, Connerly also made news for supporting a platform that seemed to run counter to his affirmative action opposition. In 1998 he became a staunch supporter of the University of California's proposal to offer health benefits to domestic partners of gay employees. This was an even more volatile subject than race, as he explained to Louis Freedberg in Washington Monthly: "Blacks will get in your face and get angry with you, but the level of debate doesn't begin to compare with this one. People start talking about morals, the Bible, degenerates, and before you know it, you're off in a terrible debate in which you just can't reason with people." The proposal to offer the benefits at the university barely squeaked by on a vote of 13–12. Connerly explained that his position stemmed from his libertarian viewpoint that government should not infringe on personal liberties.

Connerly also attributed his empathy for gay partners to his own interracial union. According to Freedberg in Washington Monthly, he once wrote that when he was married, "There were those who said that such unions were immoral, unnatural, contrary to the Bible, and would lead to the deterioration of society," and added, "The ignorance and nonsense about interracial marriages 35 years ago is just as absurd today with reference to sexual union." His wife, on the other hand, who is white, told Tharp in U.S. News & World Report regarding her marriage, "We've had very few bad experiences." Connerly met his wife, the former Ilene Crews, in college, and they have a son and daughter. In addition to his black heritage, Connerly has a grandmother of Native American and Irish background and a white grandfather of French descent. Connerly runs his business out of a restored Victorian home in Sacramento, and earns up to $450 an hour for his consulting services.

Sources

Books

Contemporary Black Biography, volume 14, Gale Research, 1997.

Periodicals

Black Enterprise, November 1995, p. 156.
Christian Science Monitor, November 16, 1999, p. 2.
Chronicle of Higher Education, July 28, 1995, p. A27.
Economist, March 29, 1997, p. 34.
Forbes, May 5, 1997, p. 90.
Jet, August 7, 1995, p. 12.
Knight–Ridder/Tribune News Service, April 3, 1996.
Mother Jones, November–December 1997, p. 71.
Nation, July 21, 1997, p. 6.
National Review, September 2, 1996, p. 24; December 23, 1996, p. 39.
New York Times, April 18, 1996, p. A1; December 21, 1996, p. A1.
Reason, February 1998, p. 32.
Time, June 23, 1997, p. 32; August 2, 1999, p. 58.
U.S. News & World Report, March 25, 1996, p. 22.
Washington Monthly, March 1998, p. 20.

David Crosby

AP/Wide World Photos

Singer, songwriter, and guitarist

Born David Van Cortlandt Crosby, August 14, 1941, in Los Angeles, CA; son of Floyd Delafield Crosby (a cinematographer) and Aliph Van Cortlandt Crosby (a salesperson; maiden name, Whitehead); married Jan Dance, May 16, 1987; children: (with Debbie Donovan) Donovan Anne Crosby; (with Dance) Django. *Education:* Attended Santa Barbara City College, late 1950s.

Addresses: *Record company*—Reprise Records, P.O. Box 6868, Burbank, CA 91510.

Career

Folk singer in coffeehouses and small clubs, early 1960s; founding member, with Roger McGuinn, Gene Clarke, Chris Hillman, and Mike Clark, of the Byrds, 1964–68; with Stephen Stills and Graham Nash, formed Crosby, Stills and Nash, 1969, added member Neil Young to become Crosby, Stills, Nash and Young, 1970; has recorded solo and with other members of CSNY. Author (with Carl Gottleib), *Long Time Gone: The Autobiography of David Crosby,* 1988; and (with David Bender) *Stand and Be Counted: Making Music, Making History: The Dramatic Story of the Artists and Causes that Changed America,* 2000.

Awards: Grammy Award for best new artist, 1969, for album *Crosby, Stills and Nash;* inducted into the Rock and Roll Hall of Fame twice with the Byrds, and with Crosby, Stills and Nash.

Sidelights

Veteran folk rock artist David Crosby has been making music for about three decades, many of them with the classic rock groups Crosby, Stills and Nash and Crosby, Stills, Nash and Young (often known by the acronym CSNY). However, at many points in his career Crosby has been known more for his troubled personal life than for his musical talents. He was in the news regularly during the 1980s for repeated arrests stemming from drug charges, and these altercations finally landed him in prison. Subsequently, it appeared that his life was back on track, but then his liver failed and he was on the brink of death until a donor was located. Since then, Crosby, who still sports his trademark walrus mustache and tangled mass of long hair, has enjoyed a drug–free life.

In 1999, CSNY released a new album, *Looking Forward,* and embarked on another tour in January of 2000. In addition, Crosby in 2000 wrote a book with David Bender, *Stand and Be Counted,* which includes interviews with more than 40 of his friends and colleagues in order to exhibit the influence that musicians have had on activism over the previous five decades. It was scheduled to be broadcast as a four–

hour documentary on The Learning Channel cable network. Of course, Crosby also made the news prominently in 2000 when he was revealed as the biological father of two children born to Julie Cypher and singer–musician Melissa Etheridge.

Crosby was born on August 14, 1941, in Los Angeles, California. His father, Floyd Delafield Crosby, worked as a documentary cinematographer in the 1930s, and his mother, Aliph Van Cortlandt (Whitehead) Crosby, earned money as a salesperson at Macy's department store to help make ends meet. His older brother, Ethan, was born in 1937. Just after Crosby was born his father went to serve during World War II as a photographer, and afterward, the family moved to the Los Angeles community of Westwood. His father ended up working in Hollywood, except for a time during the 1950s when he was "blacklisted" as a suspected Communist, like many in the industry. His father later asked for a divorce and married Betty Cormack.

As a child, Crosby attended University Elementary School, run by the University of California at Los Angeles, for bright or advantaged children. He picked up a love of music early on, enjoying everything from classical to folk groups like the Weavers and Josh White. Thanks to his older brother, he also got hooked on jazz during its "golden age" of artists like Dave Brubeck, Chet Baker, Gerry Mulligan, and others. In fact, his entire family was musical. As Crosby wrote in his autobiography, *Long Time Gone*, "They tell me I was singing harmony when I was six years old and I'm not the one to contradict them because the experience that sticks in my memory is the way my family would sing at home. My father would play the mandolin, my older brother the guitar, and my mother sang. I'd do the harmony parts, all of us singing from a book called *The Fireside Book of Folk Songs.*" He also mentioned that although rock–and–roll was on the rise at the same time and the hits of Elvis Presley were perennially heard on the radio, he "wasn't into it."

When Crosby was still a youth, his family moved north to Santa Barbara and he began attending the exclusive Crane and then Cate prep schools. He also took up the hobby of sailing. Despite this seemingly genteel existence, Crosby's family was not part of Santa Barbara "society" and they were regularly strapped for money. This made him feel like an outsider, and probably as a result, he became "a disruptive influence and a troublemaker," as he wrote in *Long Time Gone*. The Cate administration asked him not to return, so he finished out his education at a public high school.

After high school, Crosby attended classes at Santa Barbara City College but was suspended after an arrest for breaking–and–entering. His parents paid

for counseling in lieu of a stiffer sentence, and he returned to college, where he studied mass communications, language, and sociology. Soon, though, Crosby dropped out to go to Los Angeles to study acting. In 1960 for a brief time he apprenticed at the Pasadena Playhouse. However, he got kicked out of acting classes for tardiness.

In the early 1960s, Crosby and his brother Ethan began to play folk music in clubs around Los Angeles. Before long, though, he left town, abandoning a pregnant girlfriend. He traveled to Arizona and Colorado, then to New York City, where he settled in the folk hub of Greenwich Village. By 1962, he had moved again, to Miami, Florida, where he began recording. After a few years as an itinerant musician, he joined up with Roger McGuinn, and they began to use amplification. In 1964, they had added Gene Clarke, Chris Hillman, and Mike Clark to the group, and called themselves the Byrds.

In May of 1965, the Byrds topped the charts with a remake of Bob Dylan's "Mr. Tambourine Man." Afterward, they had hits with another Dylan tune, "All I Really Want to Do," and Pete Seeger's "Turn! Turn! Turn!" That year they were one of the biggest musical acts in the nation along with the Beatles and the Rolling Stones. Their blend of folk music with electric instruments gave rise to the term "folk rock" and spawned a new genre. Crosby was admired for his clear, pure vocal quality, and his songwriting was integral to the band's success. However, he was thrown out in 1967 after an internal power struggle.

With a cash settlement he obtained from the Byrds after leaving the group, Crosby bought a sailing yacht, dubbed the Mayan, and moved to Florida. He would later live on it for many years off the coast of San Francisco, but by the 1980s it fell into disrepair and its caretaker sold off many of its parts. In the meantime, in the winter of 1967, with the money running out, Crosby met folk star Joni Mitchell and produced her first album. She introduced him to musician Graham Nash, who had played with the Hollies, as well as Stephen Stills and Neil Young of the Buffalo Springfield, which was about to break up. Though Young would not join them at first, the others formed Crosby, Stills and Nash in 1969 and released their self–titled debut album, which won a Grammy Award that year for best new artist. The record was a chart hit for more than two years, featuring songs like "Marrakesh Express" and "Suite: Judy Blue Eyes."

Before long, though Young continued to work with his group Crazy Horse, he also joined Crosby and the others to make the band Crosby, Stills, Nash and Young. This lineup played to half a million people at the legendary Woodstock festival in August of 1969 as well as the Big Sur Folk Festival a couple weeks later. Though his professional life was reaching new heights, around the end of September that year Crosby's girlfriend, Christine Hinton, was killed in a car accident. Afterward, he retreated a bit and allowed Nash to be the focal point of the band.

By the time CSNY shipped their second album, *Déjà Vu*, at the end of 1969, there were two million advance orders in place. They then kicked off their Carry On Tour, becoming the first major group to travel with their entire stage setup, from monitors and speakers to microphones and stage carpeting. Despite the group's success, they disbanded in 1970 due to personal and creative reasons. However, they would reunite sporadically over the next few decades to record and tour. In fact, their 1971 double-live album *Four Way Street*, put out by request of the record company, hit number one and stayed on the charts for a year even though it introduced very little new material. They also held a Reunion Tour in 1974 that was extravagantly marketed.

Crosby also recorded four albums with Nash during the 1970s; the first one, titled *Graham Nash and David Crosby*, stayed on the chart for four months. Crosby also released a solo album in 1971 titled *If I Could Only Remember My Name*. (Another solo album, *Oh Yes I Can*, came out in 1988.) Eventually, though, Crosby began to attract more attention for his addiction to drugs than for his musicianship. He had started smoking marijuana early in his career and over the years expanded his habit to include psychedelic drugs and cocaine. By the 1970s he was suffering from a perforated septum in his nose from snorting cocaine, so he switched to freebasing, or smoking, it.

Meanwhile, after Crosby's girlfriend, Hinton, was killed, he began a relationship with Debbie Donovan in the early 1970s and they had a daughter, Donovan Anne Crosby. While she was pregnant, though, he began a relationship with another woman, though he stayed friends with Donovan and was present at the childbirth. Just after his daughter's birth, Donovan moved out and Crosby's new girlfriend, Nancy Brown, moved in. She eventually left him, though, because she was tired of the drug scene and because Crosby had taken up with a new woman, Jan Dance. They lived together in Mill Valley, a town in California's affluent Marin County, and would stay together through his roughest days. They eventually married on May 16, 1987.

As Crosby plunged further and further into drug abuse, his friends became sincerely worried that he was killing himself. They attempted "interventions," in which they got together with doctors and therapists in a group to confront him to get treatment. He tried entering hospitals and treatment programs, but it did not work. As of the mid–1980s Crosby was freebasing cocaine daily and was addicted to heroin. As he stated in his book, *Long Time Gone*, "Heroin has always been the big villain, the bottom–line worst drug of all time. It's not. In my opinion, cocaine is more dangerous than heroin because you can kick heroin faster You get sick, but you can beat it. Freebase cocaine is more addictive on a more dangerous level."

In 1982, Crosby, Stills and Nash got together to put out a new album, *Daylight Again*—their first since 1977's *CSN* . They released another new album, *Allies*, in 1983, and toured Europe. However, also in the early 1980s, Crosby was arrested various times on charges of drug and weapons possession. On one occasion, he had suffered a seizure while driving, resulting from prolonged drug use, and crashed his car. He was bloated and disheveled, and his friends and bandmates had given his girlfriend, Dance, the morbid nickname "Death" because of her ghostly appearance.

Though Crosby was admitted to a court–mandated stay in a drug treatment center in 1985, he skipped out and continued to attract legal trouble for drugs and weapons. He went to jail in March of 1985, but was released in late spring on appeal. While out, he embarked on another successful Crosby, Stills and Nash tour, and later spent time in a halfway house. By the year's end, though, he was back in prison. He ended up being forced to go "cold turkey" in jail in solitary confinement at the Dallas County Jail before going to the Texas Department of Correction. After a total of 11 months of incarceration, he got out on parole in August of 1986 and went to a halfway house in Houston.

After Crosby's release, he told Todd Gold in *People*, "The prospect of going to prison was devastating. I was so afraid. But I was more afraid of having to kick the drugs. I thought I would die if I didn't have them." He subsequently appeared to be a changed person; he went on a diet and started working out. He lost weight and managed to stay off drugs. In 1994, Crosby embarked on yet another reunion tour with the band.

However, though he was in the best shape he had been in for many years, Crosby began to suffer debilitating abdominal pains and soon found out his liver was giving out. He was admitted to the UCLA Medical Center in November of 1994 and waited for a matching donor. Around this same time, his wife, Dance, found out she was pregnant. By the end of the month Crosby had a new liver, and the next year he had a son, Django.

In 1997, Crosby found out about another son, James Raymond, whom he never knew existed. Raymond was born in 1964 and given up for adoption by his mother, and had been a musician for 20 years before seeking out his biological father. The two collaborated, and began recording and touring under the name CPR.

Of course, the most fascinating element about Crosby's paternity came in early 2000, when a *Rolling Stone* article by Jancee Dunn revealed that he had donated sperm to father two children for Etheridge and her partner, Cypher. After much public speculation, the two women finally decided to disclose the information, feeling that the kids, Bailey and Beckett, would be better off if the secret was aired before they started school. The couple met Crosby and his wife while vacationing in Hawaii, and Dance suggested her husband as a donor. Cypher became pregnant via artificial insemination. Though the families are friends, Crosby does not share parental duties, nor is he the godfather of the children. But, as he told Dunn, "If, you know, in due time, at a distance, they're proud of who their genetic dad is, that's great."

Selected discography

With the Byrds

Mr. Tambourine Man, Columbia, 1965.
Turn! Turn! Turn!, Columbia, 1966.
Fifth Dimension, Columbia, 1966.
Younger than Yesterday, Columbia, 1967.
Greatest Hits, Columbia, 1967.
The Byrds, Asylum, 1973.
History of the Byrds, Columbia, 1973.
The Byrds Play Dylan, Columbia, 1980.
Never Before, Re-Flyte, 1988.

With Crosby, Stills and Nash

Crosby, Stills and Nash, Atlantic, 1969.
So Far, 1974.
CSN, Atlantic, 1977.
Replay, Atlantic, 1980.

Daylight Again, Atlantic, 1982.
Allies, Atlantic, 1983.
Live It Up, Atlantic, 1990.
After the Storm, Atlantic, 1994.

With Crosby, Stills, Nash and Young

Déjà Vu, Atlantic, 1970.
Four-Way Street, Atlantic, 1972.
American Dream, Atlantic, 1989.
Looking Forward, Reprise, 1999.

With Graham Nash

Crosby and Nash, Atlantic, 1972.
Wind on the Water, ABC, 1975.
Whistle Down the Wire, ABC, 1976.
Live, ABC, 1977.
Best of Crosby and Nash, ABC, 1977.

Solo

If I Could Only Remember My Name, Atlantic, 1971.
Oh Yes I Can, A&M, 1988.

Sources

Books

Contemporary Musicians, volume three, Gale Research, 1990.
Crosby, David and Carl Gottlieb, *Long Time Gone: The Autobiography of David Crosby*, Doubleday, 1988.

Periodicals

Booklist, February 1, 2000, p. 1002.
Entertainment Weekly, March 29, 1996, p. 78.
Knight-Ridder/Tribune News Service, July 11, 1997.
People, August 29, 1983, p. 22; September 8, 1986, p. 30; April 27, 1987, p. 52; November 21, 1994, p. 105; December 5, 1994, p. 87; February 20, 1995, p. 34.
Rolling Stone, December 23, 1982, p. 81; April 11, 1985, p. 10; November 21, 1985, p. 46; February 3, 2000, p. 40.
Toronto Star, March 30, 2000.
Toronto Sun, March 30, 2000, p. 54.

Russell Crowe

Actor and musician

Born April 7, 1964, in Wellington, New Zealand; son of Alex (a caterer and hotel manager) and Jocelyn (a caterer) Crowe.

Addresses: *Home*—Coffs Harbour, Australia. *Agent*—International Creative Management, 8942 Wilshire Blvd., Beverly Hills, CA 90211.

Career

Worked as a waiter, bartender, and bingo caller, 1980s; sang in rock band, Roman Antix, c. early 1980s, and 30 Odd Foot of Grunts, 1980s—; began acting on stage and television, c. 1970. Stage appearances include *The Rocky Horror Picture Show,* 1986–88; *Grease;* and *Blood Brothers.* Television appearances include episode of *Spyforce,* c. 1970; *Police Rescue,* 1990; and *The Late Show,* 1992; and miniseries *Brides of Christ,* 1993. Film appearances include *Prisoners of the Sun* (also known as *Blood Oath*), 1990; *The Crossing,* 1990; *Proof,* 1991; *Spotswood,* 1991; *Hammers Over the Anvil,* 1991; *Romper Stomper,* 1992; *The Silver Brumby,* 1993; *Love in Limbo,* 1993; *The Sum of Us,* 1994; *For the Moment,* 1994; *The Quick and the Dead,* 1995; *Virtuosity,* 1995; *Rough Magic,* 1995; *No Way Back,* 1996; *L.A. Confidential,* 1997; *Heaven's Burning,* 1997; *Breaking Up,* 1997; *Mystery, Alaska,* 1999; *The Insider,* 1999; and *The Gladiator,* 2000.

Awards: Australian Film Institute Award for best supporting actor, 1991, for *Proof;* Australian Film Institute Award for best actor and Australian Film Critics Circle Award for best actor, both 1992, and Seattle International Film Festival Award for best actor, 1993, all for *Romper Stomper;* Broadcast Film Critics Association Award, Los Angeles Film Critics Association Award, National Board of Review Award, and National Society of Film Critics Award, all for best actor, 1999, for *The Insider.*

Sidelights

Australian actor Russell Crowe was catapulted into stardom with his role as the corporate whistle–blower Jeffrey Wigand in 1999's *The Insider,* for which he was nominated for an Academy Award. It took him nearly a decade to go from being a promising new talent to a full– fledged Hollywood star, but throughout the journey, there had been many who predicted his success. By the time he made *Romper Stomper* in 1992, he was already likened to a young, steamy Marlon Brando, and he would also earn comparisons to James Dean, Mickey Rourke, and Nick Nolte. But then for a time, he began to attract attention for his respected art–film work instead of ending up in box–office hits. Crowe, meanwhile, told Jil Derryberry in *Interview,* "I want to play strong characters in movies that are clever, smart, and driven by an individual with something to say. Whether those films end up in cinema A or cinema B is not my concern."

Crowe was born on April 7, 1964, in Wellington, New Zealand, but moved to Australia when he was four. His parents, Alex and Jocelyn Crowe, were film–set caterers, so they relocated often. Crowe's maternal grandfather was a cinematographer. "My family's been in the business for three generations," he mentioned to Frank Lovece in *Newsday*. "I'm just the first one stupid enough to stand in from of the cameras!" Crowe also has an older brother, Terry.

At about the age of six, Crowe landed his first acting gig in the Australian television show *Spyforce*, playing an orphan. His parents catered the set, and the producer of the show was his mother's godfather. On the show, Crowe appeared with Jack Thompson, who would later costar with him in the 1994 film *The Sum of Us*.

When Crowe was about 14, his family moved back to New Zealand, where his parents managed a hotel called the Potter's Wheel, though it earned the nickname the Flying Jug for all the fights that occurred there. At 16, Crowe adopted the stage name Russ Le Roc and began singing in a rock band. With friend Dean Cochran he formed the group Roman Antix and in 1980 released the somewhat prophetic single, "I Want to Be Like Marlon Brando." The band eventually became 30 Odd Foot of Grunts, for which Crowe still sings, plays guitar, and writes songs.

In his late teens, Crowe started performing in musical theater. In addition to working on *Grease* and *Blood Brothers*, from 1986 to 1988, played the transvestite Frank N. Furter in a stage version of *The Rocky Horror Picture Show*. To supplement his income he waited tables, sold insurance, detailed cars, picked fruit, called bingo numbers, and wrangled horses.

Crowe snagged his first film role at age 25 in the love triangle story *The Crossing*, directed by George Ogilvie, who also did *Mad Max Beyond Thunderdome*. Even before shooting that film, Crowe was cast in the World War II drama *Prisoners of the Sun*, also known as *Blood Oath*. Both films were released in 1990. After casting Crowe in *The Crossing*, Ogilvie paid to have the actor's front tooth fixed; it had been chipped in a rugby game when he was ten.

After that, Crowe appeared as a dishwasher in the 1991 film *Proof*, winning a best supporting actor award from the Australian Film Institute for the effort. This would open another important door for him. When Australian director Geoffrey Wright saw him in the picture, he immediately considered him

for the part of a violent neo–Nazi in an upcoming film. As Wright commented to Amruta Slee in the *New York Times*, "I thought he was the most *menacing* dishwasher I'd ever seen. There's always something threatening about him on screen."

Crowe's turn as the skinhead gang leader Hando in 1992's *Romper Stomper* would be the turning point in his career. A desperate portrait of life among Australia's white supremacist gangs amid a backdrop of growing multiculturalism, it included scenes of Crowe's character committing violent racist acts and reading Adolf Hitler's *Mein Kampf* to his girlfriend. *Romper Stomper* was compared to Stanley Kubrick's *A Clockwork Orange* and was similarly both praised and condemned. In Australia, the film was accused of glorifying fascism. The country's prime minister, Paul Keating, denounced it as being devoid of morality. However, others deemed it a masterpiece, and it broke box office records on the continent. For the project, Crowe won best actor awards from the Australian Film Institute and Australian Film Critics Circle in 1992 and the Seattle International Film Festival in 1993.

After *Romper Stomper*, Crowe's next role was quite the opposite: He played a lovesick gay plumber in 1994's *The Sum of Us*, based on the play by David Stevens. Though the producers originally wanted to recruit a well–known American actor for the part, Crowe aggressively campaigned for the role and earned critical accolades for the effort. When Kim Basinger later asked him in *Interview* if he had any reservations about playing a gay character, Crowe replied, "There are many questions I'd ask a character—for instance, 'Do you believe in the death penalty?'—before I ever got round to 'What's your sexuality?' I think other factors are more important in terms of human relationships and the way society operates than what someone's sexuality is."

The same month *The Sum of Us* opened in theaters, he also showed up on screens in *The Quick and the Dead*, 1995, directed by Sam Raimi and costarring Sharon Stone. Crowe initially auditioned for a supporting part in the picture, but Stone actively pushed to bump him up to a lead role. As she told Jamie Diamond in the *New York Times*, "When I saw 'Romper Stomper,' I thought Russell was not only charismatic, attractive and talented, but also fearless. And I find fearlessness very attractive. I was convinced I wouldn't scare him."

Also in 1995, Crowe appeared in the science–fiction thriller *Virtuosity* playing a computer–generated psychopath named Sid 6.7. In the film, his character is created as a training simulation program for the police, and contains the personality traits of 183 of the world's most vile people, from Hitler to Charles Manson. When the program is unleashed from the computer, it takes a human form and begins to wreak havoc. He is pursued by a rogue cop, played by Denzel Washington, whose wife and child were murdered by a terrorist that is part of Sid 6.7's composition. Though the film was generally a disappointment, Crowe's performance received some good reviews.

In 1997, Crowe stirred more attention with his turn as crusty Los Angeles Police Department detective Bud White in the contemporary film noir *L.A. Confidential,* based on the novel by James Ellroy. The multilayered story revolves around three cops and involves several seemingly unrelated elements including a multiple shotgun killing and a brothel where the prostitutes all resemble famous movie stars. Its stylized cinematography enhanced the film's examination of moral issues. Crowe's characterization of the brutish yet complex detective earned him accolades, and the film overall was highly acclaimed. Subsequently, Crowe appeared in *Breaking Up* with Salma Hayek in 1997, and then in 1999's *Mystery, Alaska,* about a small–town hockey team that takes on an exhibition game with the New York Rangers. Crowe played the town sheriff and captain of the team.

Inarguably, Crowe's biggest role came in 1999's *The Insider,* directed by Michael Mann. In it, he portrayed Jeffrey Wigand, a former tobacco company executive who went on *60 Minutes* to tell the public that tobacco companies purposely put additives in cigarettes to make them more addictive, and lied about it under oath. Based on a true story recounted in a *Vanity Fair* article by Marie Brenner, the saga begins when Wigand is fired from his top– level research post at Brown & Williamson, one of the nation's largest tobacco firms. What follows is his hesitant decision to work with Lowell Bergman at *60 Minutes* and break his confidentiality agreement in order to reveal the company's secret.

In the meantime, however, Brown & Williamson tries to threaten and discredit Wigand, his personal life collapses, and CBS higher–ups decide to kill the story anyway because they fear that Brown & Williamson's certain legal action jeopardizes a sale of the network which would mean that many of them would lose great sums of money. Al Pacino as Bergman, a journalist guided by a high moral standard, provides a perfect complement to Crowe's Wigand. Thus, *The Insider* is just as much about the two ordinary men and their extraordinary drive to

do what is right as it is about corrupt tobacco companies and a media network blinded by profits and personal gains. It was roundly applauded by critics and nominated for a best picture Academy Award, and it thrust Crowe into a new echelon of Hollywood stardom.

On the surface, the young (then 34) and trim Crowe would seem an unlikely choice to play an overweight, white–haired man in his fifties, but Mann specifically chose him for the part. To prepare for his portrayal, Crowe gained 50 pounds and dyed his hair seven times before shaving his head in order to wear a wig. He also affected a realistic Bronx accent and adopted a waddling walk to complete the transformation. In fact, Crowe watched so many videotapes of Wigand that he did not even feel he needed to meet the real man in order to capture his essence. "I had so much footage on tape," he recounted to Claudia Puig in *USA Today.* "I had him walking, talking, sitting. I had him in relaxed mode. I had him under pressure." But after meeting Wigand in person, he told Puig, "I realized there's a whole emotional impact that I couldn't get from the volumes of research."

In the end, Crowe and Wigand spent less than two days together playing golf in South Carolina, but even the writer of the magazine article, Brenner, was convinced when she saw Crowe on the set that he had accurately summed up the tension Wigand was going through at the time. Wigand himself was pleased with the portrayal as well. Ironically, though, Crowe is a lifelong smoker. "It just proves how addictive nicotine is," he noted to Cathy Booth in *Time.* "I'm smart enough to acknowledge it but too stupid to stop." He added, "If I've contributed in some way to the next generation of kids not becoming addicted to nicotine, well, that's fine by me, mate."

In a remarkable turnaround, Crowe in just a few months shed the extra weight from *The Insider* and hardened up for his next project, Ridley Scott's *Gladiator,* 2000, in which he played Maximus, a Roman general turned gladiator. Though the film was not as critically lauded as his prior effort, it was a blockbuster at the box office and firmly established Crowe as not only a top actor but also a Hollywood sex symbol. David Ansen in *Newsweek* wrote, "In 'Gladiator,' he radiates an un–self–conscious, dyed–in–the–wool masculinity that seems to belong to another era. Is there an American actor Crowe's age who would look at home in a sword–and–sandal epic? Johnny Depp? John Cusack? Sean Penn? Don't think so." After that, Crowe seemed poised to take over from fellow Aussie Mel Gibson as the action hero du jour, but instead, he was scheduled to play a hostage negotiator in *Proof of Life* and then a circus freak in a Jodie Foster film.

In real life, Crowe lives up to the rugged image of many of his onscreen characters. He lives on a 560–acre farm near Coffs Harbour, Australia, about 340 miles north of Sydney, about a seven–hour drive. There, he raises cows and chickens, though he does not allow any of them to be killed for any reason. In his spare time he enjoys long motorcycle trips and playing guitar and singing for his rock band. "It's the things I do between acting jobs that inform my acting," Crowe explained to Puig in *USA Today.* "It's the real–life stuff that keeps what I do—in my own mind, anyway—fresh."

Sources

Periodicals

Biography Magazine, May 2000, p. 82.

Entertainment Weekly, November 5, 1999, p. 46; March 1, 2000, p. 17; May 12, 2000, p. 26.

GQ , March 1999, p. 238.

Interview, August 1995, p. 26; September 1997, p. 92.

Los Angeles Magazine, November 1999, p. 50.

Newsday, August 6, 1995, p. 17.

Newsweek, May 1, 2000, p .66.

New York Times, June 6, 1993, sec. 2, p. 26; March 26, 1995, sec. 2, p. 24; May 5, 2000, p. E1.

People, October 6, 1997, p. 154; May 22, 2000, p. 95.

Premiere, December 1999, p. 59.

St. Louis Post–Dispatch, October 12, 1997, p. 3E.

Time, November 1, 1999, p. 95.

USA Today, January 10, 2000, p. 1D.

Online

"Russell Crowe," Internet Movie Database web site, http://us.imdb.com (June 30, 2000).

"Russell Crowe," Mr. Showbiz web site, http://mrshowbiz.go.com (June 30, 2000).

Tom DeLay

Politician and businessperson

Born Thomas Dale DeLay, April 8, 1947, in Laredo, TX; son of an oil drilling contractor; married Christine Ann Furrh; children: Danielle. *Education:* Attended Baylor University; University of Houston, degree in biology, 1970.

Addresses: *Home*—Sugar Land, Texas. *Office*—341 Cannon House Office Bldg., Washington, DC 20515; 12603 Southwest Freeway, Ste. 285, Stafford, TX 77477.

Career

Albo Pest Control, Sugar Land, TX, proprietor, 1973–84; served in the Texas House of Representatives, 1979–84; U.S. Representative, Texas, 22nd district, 1984—, serves as House Majority Whip and on Appropriations Committee, has also served as chairman of Republican Study Committee, Deputy Whip, and Republican Conference Secretary.

Awards: National Taxpayers Union's Taxpayer's Friend award; Watchdog of the Treasury's Golden Bulldog Award; Peace through Strength's National Security Leadership award.

Sidelights

Tom DeLay, the Majority Whip in the U.S. House of Representatives, is nicknamed "the Hammer" for his tenacity and what some deem a heavy–handed approach to politics. To underscore his job title and reputation, he even keeps a bull whip in his office. As whip, his main duties are to count votes and to ensure that fellow Republicans adhere to the party line. But the lawmaker has emerged from the boundaries of that title to become considered one of the most important players in American politics, with many claiming that he even wields more control than Speaker of the House J. Dennis Hastert. A Republican from Texas, DeLay "embodies both strains of contemporary conservatism those focused on moral issues as well as those who want to foster a pro–business climate," according to Jeffrey L. Katz in *Congressional Quarterly Weekly Report.* DeLay is thus a champion of business, aiming to slash government spending and deregulate controls, while he is a foe of environmentalists who feel that anti–pollution legislation and other rules are a necessity. Admired by many conservatives, especially the religious right, he is often assailed by liberals of all types. In any case, he is a driving force in Republican campaigns, although as he geared up for the 2000 elections, he was coming under scrutiny for some of his fundraising efforts.

Thomas Dale DeLay was born on April 8, 1947, in Laredo, Texas, into a devout Baptist family, but grew up mostly in Venezuela due to his father' job as an oil drilling contractor. DeLay ended up working with his father on the rigs as he grew older. Some of the other men on the job would try to intimidate him, but DeLay's father insisted he not give up. This taught him the value of persistence and gave him the tools for sticking up for himself. After graduating from high school in 1965, he attended Baylor University, a Baptist institution, for two years, but was expelled for "dancing and for painting buildings green at rival Texas A&M," according to Fred Barnes in the *New Republic*. He then transferred the University of Houston, receiving his degree in 1970.

In college, DeLay studied biology because his father hoped he would become a doctor. But when he graduated, he began working for a company that formulated pesticides, and, after working there a few years, decided to run his own extermination business beginning in 1973. Though he did not care for the name of the firm he purchased, Albo Pest Control, he did not change it because market research surveys found that it made consumers think of a popular brand of dog food. He operated the company in Sugar Land, Texas, an upscale suburb of Houston, where he sprayed expensive homes and became "the Cadillac" of pest control firms, as he told Michael Weisskopf and David Maraniss in the *Washington Post.*

As his company grew and thrived, DeLay became more frustrated with what he saw as government meddling in business. First of all, after a prolonged dispute with the trade association, the state of Texas finally began to regulate and license exterminators. In addition, the federal Environmental Protection Agency (EPA) began to regulate pesticides as well in order to ensure that substances were not harmful to humans and the environment. In addition to finding the government rules costly, confusing, and difficult to follow, DeLay also disagreed with certain federal safety rules, such as requiring workers to wear hardhats when tunneling under buildings, as Weisskopf and Maraniss reported. "I was really angry," he remarked to Hanna Rosin in the *New Republic.* "It got me thinking that the government was the cost of doing business, so I got involved."

With support from other businesspeople, DeLay ran for a seat in the Texas House of Representatives in 1978 from his home county of Fort Bend and won. He established himself with the nickname "Mr. DeReg" (for deregulation), as Weisskopf and Maraniss noted, and after serving in state government until 1984, DeLay decided to run for a seat in the U.S. House of Representatives. In 1985 he was appointed freshman representative on the Republican Committee on Committees, and in his second term, snagged a seat on the powerful Appropriations Committee.

Also in the House, DeLay continued to forge his reputation of being pro–business and anti–big government by handing out Red Tape Awards for what he considered to be silly regulations. His drive to deregulate was generally overlooked by his colleagues, though, as the Democratic–controlled House at that time felt that government control of business practices had led to important benefits, including safer cars, a cleaner environment, and a resurgence in populations of some formerly protected species, like the bald eagle.

Other businesspeople were taking note of DeLay's efforts, though, and throughout the 1994 election campaign, DeLay hired a political consultant to monitor Republican candidates nationwide who had a good hope of winning. Using his support among the business community, he then helped raise funds for their campaigns, ensuring their loyalty. As it turned out, the elections that November marked the first time that Republicans had control of the House in 40 years. In turn, a great number of the House newcomers supported DeLay's bid for Majority Whip, helping him defeat Robert S. Walker, a close ally of Speaker of the House Newt Gingrich.

In the meantime, DeLay had organized a conglomeration of business lobbies that he dubbed Project Relief. The purpose of this assembly of groups was to put the brakes on some 4,000 regulations scheduled to be rolled out in the months after the 1994 elections, before the Republicans would have time to introduce legislation to combat them. One of the rules concerned clean air standards in California that would required United Parcel Service and other businesses with automotive fleets to replace all of their vehicles. DeLay and the business lobbyists pressed President Bill Clinton to demand a 100–day waiting period on federal rules, but it was rejected. He then created a bill that would place a 13–month hold on such regulations, and even though 51 Democrats defected from their party's stance to support the legislation, it was not enough to override a veto by the president. Later, DeLay's drive to deregulate suffered another blow when 51 Republicans joined House Democrats in July of 1995 to vote to keep in place key functions of the EPA.

By this time, DeLay had incurred the wrath of environmentalists, but it became worse when he introduced a bill that would cause the United States to withdraw from the Montreal Protocol. This international agreement, signed by 160 countries, banned the use of chlorofluorocarbons (CFCs), used in air conditioning coils, refrigerators, the making of plastic, and more. Scientists argued that CFCs broke down the protective ozone layer in the atmosphere, leading to the "greenhouse effect," which would cause a higher rate of skin cancer and the loss of many coastal areas. DeLay, on the other hand, called the research "debatable," according to Michael D. Lemonick in *Audubon,* even though the scientists were awarded the Nobel Prize in chemistry in 1995 and the public showed overwhelming support for retaining the ban. DeLay insisted that the prohibition would be expensive for industry, and has also called the EPA "the Gestapo of government," according to Rosin.

In contrast to his stance on environmental regulations, DeLay, who is against abortion, believes wholeheartedly that the government should become involved in reproductive regulation. Staunchly religious, he has received 100 percent ratings from the *New American* and *Christian Voice* magazines, as he mentioned on his official web site. DeLay admitted that he uses his political seat to further his personal views, telling Rosin, "I'm not just there to be a whip. I'm there to advance an agenda. And I win." In another break from his own free–market philosophies, in 1996, prompted by football's Houston Oilers' proposal to move to Nashville, Tennessee, he cosponsored a resolution that would have put limits on the ability of professional sports teams to relocate to other cities.

Among his associates in Congress, DeLay displayed a forcefulness that made him known as "more of an arm–twister than a sweet–talker," according to a *Congressional Quarterly Weekly Report* article. In that same piece, he remarked, "I'm a hard–working, aggressive, persistent whip. That's why I'm whip. I worked harder than anyone else. I raised more money than anyone else. I was smarter than anybody else in the race. I won because I worked hard and I don't give up." However, many suggested that DeLay's tactics included giving legislative favors to financial supporters, as well as family and friends. Gary Ruskin, director of the Ralph Nader watchdog group the Congressional Accountability Project, tried to force the House Ethics Committee to investigate him and Bud Shuster of Pennsylvania, but the charges were dismissed in November of 1997.

One of DeLay's most high–profile moves as whip came in July of 1997 when he led an unsuccessful coup to force Speaker of the House Gingrich out of his post. However, after Republicans lost five House seats during the 1998 elections, Gingrich resigned, and DeLay then helped orchestrate Robert L. Livingston's appointment as Speaker. When Livingston stepped down amid a scandal regarding extramarital affairs, DeLay then helped with J. Dennis

Hastert's transition into the post. However, since Gingrich's departure, DeLay is often considered the real leader of House. After the elections, he considered himself a key member in effecting the impeachment of the president. He came under fire in the media, though, because of continuing allegations implicating him in illegal fundraising affairs (the case was closed with no action taken against DeLay) and for allegations that he lied under oath in testimony regarding whether or not he continued to be involved with the Albo Pest Control business. That accusation was thrown out of court because the district attorney in DeLay's district said his testimony was evasive but not necessarily untruthful, and because the statute of limitations on perjury had expired in the case.

In 1999 DeLay helped spearhead a controversial plan to hamper union efforts to help Democratic candidates in 2000. Aiming to raise $25 million, he set up a fund–raising body as a nonprofit organization so that it can amass unlimited funds and will not have to reveal the names of the contributors. This group, the Republican Majority Issues Committee (ReMIC), was founded by one of DeLay's former aides, and while DeLay does not run it, Alison Mitchell and Marc Lacey in the *New York Times* noted that he "has been unabashedly helping it raise money." He defended the lack of disclosure of donors to them by stating that groups like the American Civil Liberties Union and other left–wing organizations do not have to disclose their contributors. Democrats have challenged ReMIC before the Federal Election Commission because of its obvious ties to DeLay, even though the group has stated it will not give directly to campaigns or work directly with elected officials. In addition, the House ethics committee in spring of 1999 issued a warning to DeLay regarding his role in trying to retaliate against a trade group for hiring a Democrat as its president by blocking a vote on a treaty that affected the organization.

Just after his sophomore year of college, DeLay married Christine Ann Furrh, and they have a daughter, Danielle. Their home base is Sugar Land, Texas, and DeLay often uses his auctioneer skills to raise funds for charity and community groups in the area. He also serves on the Advisory Board of Child Advocates of Fort Bend County.

Sources

Periodicals

Audubon, January–February 1996, p. 110.
Business Week, December 7, 1998, p. 36.

Congressional Quarterly Weekly Report, April 13, 1996, p. 977; July 4, 1998, p. 1827; May 15, 1999, p. 1141.

Mother Jones, September/October 1996, p. 40.

Nation, February 5, 1996, p. 6; November 2, 1998, p. 5.

New Republic, March 13, 1995, p. 23; October 9, 1995, p. 6; February 19, 1996, p. 17; February 15, 1999, p. 11.

New York Times, November 18, 1998, p. A26; November 19, 1998, p. A1; October 16, 1999, p. A1.

Texas Monthly, September 1996, p. 128; April 1999, p. 122.

Washington Monthly, June 1997, p. 8.

Washington, Post, March 12, 1995, p. A1.

Washington Times, February 3, 1999, p. A7; February 4, 1999, p. A3.

Online

"Tom DeLay," *Biography Resource Center Online,* Gale Group web site, http://www.galenet.com (August 27, 1999).

Tom DeLay Home Page, http://tomdelay.house.gov (October 27, 1999).

Taye Diggs

Actor

Born Scott Diggs, c. 1971, in New Jersey. *Education:* Syracuse University, B.F.A. in musical theater.

Addresses: *Agent*—Creative Artists Agency, 9830 Wilshire Blvd., Beverly Hills, CA 902112.

Career

Actor. Stage appearances include Broadway plays *Carousel* and *Rent*. Television appearances include episodes of *New York Undercover*, 1996; and *Law & Order*; and series *The Guiding Light*, 1997–98. Film appearances include *How Stella Got Her Groove Back*, 1998; *The Wood*, 1999; Go, 1999; and *The Best Man*, 1999.

Sidelights

When actor Taye Diggs made his big–screen debut in 1998, he had tongues wagging, both literally and figuratively. Though he described himself to Elizabeth Snead in *USA Today* as being "small and geeky" in high school, it is difficult to picture, especially since he was named one of *People* magazine's 50 most beautiful people in the world for 1999. It is unusual for a Hollywood newcomer to garner such attention, but Diggs's laid–back charm and undeniable good looks caused a stir in the press and sent women swooning after his premiere film performance in the island romance, *How Stella Got Her Groove Back*. Diggs started on Broadway, most notably in the hit play *Rent*, and only had a few other credits to his name when he hit the

theaters in the adaptation of Terry McMillan's best–selling novel. Immediately after his movie breakthrough, Diggs indicated that he would not mind returning to the stage, but nevertheless, he quickly lined up several more film roles in rapid succession, appearing in *Go* and *The Wood*, among others, throughout 1999.

Diggs was born around 1971 in New Jersey and raised in Rochester, New York. His real name is Scott Diggs, but when he was young, he had a friend who transformed his name into "Scott–taye," and the nickname stuck. The oldest of five children—three boys and two girls—Diggs was encouraged to enter the arts by his mother, who decided after her children were born to go back to college and take classes in dance and theater (his father is deceased). She also taught acting at a community theater. Further inspired by the movie *Fame*, Diggs soon discovered he, too, had a knack for performance, and transferred from a general public school to the High School of the Arts in Rochester. He then went on to study acting at Syracuse University and received a bachelor of fine arts degree in musical theater.

During his senior year at Syracuse, Diggs snagged an agent who had noticed him in a talent show. He moved to New York City and was set to start a job at a pizza restaurant in 1995 when he got word that he had been hired as an understudy in the Tony Award–winning Broadway play *Carousel*. After his stint as an understudy, he got the urge for a new challenge and left for Japan, where he sang and danced in the Caribbeanland exhibit at Disneyland in Tokyo for nine months. Subsequently, Diggs returned to New York and went to auditions, landing a spot in "a little play called *Rent*," as he remarked to Allison Samuels in *Newsweek*. "I had no idea it would become the hit it did, but it was a heck of an experience." In the musical *Rent*, Diggs played the bad guy, Benny the landlord, and stayed with the production for close to two years. The play earned a Pulitzer Prize and several Tony awards, thus opening more doors for Diggs, who began to line up auditions in Hollywood.

While working on *Rent* from 1996 to 1998, Diggs also began to appear on television in small parts on shows like *New York Undercover* and *Law & Order*, and he had a recurring role on the soap opera *The Guiding Light* in 1997–98 as Adrian "Sugar" Hill. However, most audiences first glimpsed his athletic physique and chiseled features when he showed up as the young Jamaican love interest in the film *How Stella Got Her Groove Back*, 1998. Based on the semi–autobiographical Terry McMillan novel, *Stella*, as it was commonly called, is about a high–powered stockbroker (played by Angela Bassett) who is financially successful but has no love life. She lets a friend talk her into flying on a whim to enjoy the resort pleasures of Jamaica, and there, as she learns to loosen up, she is approached by an island native named Winston Shakespeare, who is 20 years her junior. Despite Stella's concerns about their age difference and the disapproval of Winston's parents, they decide to parlay their tropical fling into a serious relationship.

Overjoyed at winning this meaty role for his debut, Diggs, who was still performing in *Rent* when he was cast, commented in a *Jet* article, "When I found out that I got the part, I wanted to find a way to relay to my friends and my co–actors how excited I was. So, I took off all my clothes and streaked around the theater, screaming at the top of my lungs, 'I got the part! I got the part!'" Actually, McMillan's first choice to play Winston reportedly was the model Tyson, known particularly for his Ralph Lauren ads; in addition, Diggs himself was not sure he was right for the part. "I wasn't tall and muscular with dreads," he told Snead in *USA Today*. "But I figured I'd go in and do my best because these were probably people I'd need to meet and,

hopefully, they'd remember me in the future." However, after Diggs gave off sparks in an initial reading with Bassett, he won the role.

Though Diggs found it a challenge to switch from live theater to making films, he found himself working on a string of projects after *Stella*. In 1999 he starred in *The Wood*, about a groom who gets cold feet, gets drunk, and ends up reminiscing with friends about past relationships with girlfriends, their families, and each other. "It took me a while to adjust [to filmmaking], and there was a lot of adjusting," he commented to Bob Thompson in the *Toronto Sun*. "By the time *The Wood* came around I realized it could be fun." Diggs enjoyed making a wedding movie so much that he signed on to headline in another one, *The Best Man*, written and directed by Malcolm Lee, cousin of Spike (who also helped produce it). Explaining the plot, Diggs related to Thompson, "I play a writer who has written a tell–all book about his friends at college, then ends up going to a wedding that they go to." Also In 1999, he appeared in a minor role in *Go*, a fast–paced tale of drugs and sex. Diggs is single but lives with girlfriend Idina Menzel, and singer who appeared with him in *Rent* and also toured on the Lilith Fair in 1998. The couple share an apartment in Manhattan.

Sources

Periodicals

Arizona Republic , July 15, 1999, The Rep, p. 23.
Atlanta Journal and Constitution, July 16, 1999, p. 14; July 23, 1999, p. 11.
Calgary Sun, July 17, 1999, p. 36.
Dallas Morning News, August 17, 1998, p. 6C; July 30, 1999, p. 5C.
Essence, August 1998, p. 86.
Gannett News Service, August 13, 1998.
Jet, August 17, 1998, p. 28.
Newsweek, August 24, 1998, p. 58.
New York Beacon, September 16, 1998, p. 27.
People, September 7, 1998, p. 37; May 10, 1999, p. 125; August 2, 1999, p. 116.
Record (Bergen County, NJ), July 17, 1999.
Toronto Star, July 11, 1999, p. S3.
USA Today, August 24, 1998, p. 3D.
Variety, September 20, 1999, p. 83.

Online

"Taye Diggs," Internet Movie Database web site, http://us.imdb.com (October 11, 1999).

Carl Djerassi

Scientist, author, and educator

Born October 29, 1923, in Vienna, Austria; son of Samuel and Alice (Friedmann) Djerassi; married Virginia Jeremiah (divorced, 1950); married Norma Lundholm (divorced, 1976); married Diane W. Middlebrook (a professor), June 21, 1985; children: (from second marriage) Dale, Pamela (deceased). *Education:* Kenyon College, A.B., 1942; University of Wisconsin, Ph.D., 1945.

Addresses: *Office*—Department of Chemistry, Stanford University, Stauffer I, Room 105, Stanford, CA, 94305–5080. *Agent*—Ed Victor Ltd., 162 Wardour St., London W1V 3AT, England.

Career

CIBA Pharmaceuticals, Summit, NJ, research chemist, 1942–43 and 1945– 49; Syntex S.A., Mexico City, Mexico, associate director of chemical research, 1949–52, vice president of research, 1957–60; Wayne State University, Detroit, MI, associate professor, 1952– 53, professor of chemistry, 1953–59; Stanford University, Stanford, CA, professor of chemistry, 1959—. President of Syntex Research, Palo Alto, CA, 1968–72; chairman and chief executive officer of Zoecon Corp., Palo Alto, 1968–83 and 1988; member of board of directors of Cetus Corp., Vitaphore, Inc., and Monoclonal Antibodies, Inc. Founder and president of resident artists' colony, Djerassi Foundation, Woodside, CA, 1979.

Awards: American Chemical Society: Award in Pure Chemistry, 1958, Baekland Medal, 1959, Fritsche Award, 1960, Award for Creative Invention, 1973, Award in the Chemistry of Contemporary Technological Problems, 1983, Priestly Medal, 1992, and the Willard Gibbs Medal, 1997; American Institute of Chemists Freedman Foundation Patent Award, 1970, and Chemical Pioneer Award, 1973; National Medal of Science, 1973, for synthesis of first oral contraceptive; Award for Creative Invention, 1973; Perkin Medal, 1975; Wolf Prize in Chemistry, 1978; inducted into National Inventors Hall of Fame, 1978, for steroid oral contraceptive patent; Bard Award in Medicine and Science, 1983; Discoverer's Award of the Pharmaceutical Manufacturer's Association, 1988; Roussel Prize, 1988; Gustavus John Esselen Award for Chemistry in the Public Interest, 1989; National Academy of Sciences award, 1990, for industrial application of science; National Medal of Technology, 1991, for contributions in the insect control field; Nevada Medal, 1992; International Mass Spectrometry Society Thomson Gold Medal, 1994; Prince Mahidol Award in Medicine (Thailand), 1995; Sovereign Fund Award, 1996; Sigma Xi William Proctor Prize for Scientific Achievement, 1998; Austrian Cross of Honor for Science and Art, 1999; and Chemical Heritage Foundation Othmer Gold Medal, 2000.

Sidelights

Chemist Carl Djerassi is often called the father of the birth control pill for his development of the steroid chemical that made the "Pill" possible. On October 15, 1951, he and fellow researchers at the Syntex corporation in Mexico synthesized norethindrone, a compound that could be used to treat menstrual disorders and infertility. More than a decade later, the Pill was also marketed for contraception. It works more than 99 percent of the time, when taken properly, by inhibiting ovulation. The substance that Djerassi created was revolutionary because it worked when ingested by mouth. It had already been discovered that the female sex hormone progesterone was a "natural" contraceptive, but it was rendered inactive when taken orally. Other birth control compounds were later developed, but norethindrone continues to be used in many pills today. In early May of 2000, around the fortieth anniversary of the Food and Drug Administration's approval of the Pill, Djerassi's name popped up in the media as various publications looked back on the historic moment and reviewed what the Pill meant in a larger sense beyond its reproduction-curbing capabilities.

By the end of 1961, almost half a million women were using the Pill, and the number grew to nearly nine million by 1970. As of 2000, the Pill was the most popular method of birth control other than sterilization, with 16 million women taking the drug. Despite, or perhaps because of, its widespread use, controversy surrounded the Pill. As with most new drugs, questions of safety arose. Though some animal testing was done on the Pill, many years of women taking the substance would need to elapse before its effects could be studied, and some people became irate that humans were being used as "guinea pigs." Djerassi vehemently argued in his autobiography, *The Pill, Pygmy Chimps, and Degas' Horse*, that it was extremely difficult to extrapolate meaningful findings from studies on other creatures, since their reproductive cycles and systems were so different. Incidentally, pills with much lower and supposedly safer doses of hormones were introduced as time went on. Studies on potential cancer risks continue, and it is believed that women over 35 and smokers are more susceptible to serious and even fatal complications, including blood clots and heart attacks.

In addition, throughout the 1960s and the 1970s, the Pill was both condemned and applauded for its role in societal changes. Many regarded the Pill as women's key to many kinds of freedoms, since it allowed control over their fertility. By being able to choose if and when they became pregnant, many reasoned, women could exercise more control over their personal and economic fates as well. However, others saw the Pill as contributing to a new era in sexual freedoms, which some considered to be a positive occurrence, but others saw as leading to moral decay and a breakdown in relationships and families. Even some feminists denounced the Pill as a way to coerce them into being more sexually active for the benefit of men.

Djerassi once remarked to Flametta Rocco in the *Daily Telegraph*, "When I look back, I am very proud of that invention. The Pill liberated women. It gave

them decision–making power and enormous independence." And, he stated in his autobiography, "I have no regrets that the Pill has contributed to the sexual revolution of our time and perhaps expedited it, because most of those changes in sexual mores would have happened anyway." In addition, he has also spoken out against the lack of new research into birth control, and has mentioned that he never expected the Pill to remain on the market as long as it has. When it was first developed, he told Tom Siegfried of the *Dallas Morning News*, "I said because the way things move now, within 10 years we're going to have much more sophisticated, more interesting, different approaches. But the same chemical is still used for millions of women…. To me that is a sad commentary about the state of advances in practical birth control." In addition to his scientific activities, Djerassi is a poet, fiction writer, and playwright.

Djerassi was born in Vienna, Austria, on October 29, 1923, the only child of Samuel and Alice (Friedmann) Djerassi. His father was Bulgarian and his mother was Austrian, and both were doctors. They separated when Djerassi was six. Being Jewish, however, Djerassi's parents remarried temporarily in 1938 so that his mother could obtain a Bulgarian passport to flee Vienna when Adolf Hitler annexed their nation for Germany. The family went to Sofia, Bulgaria, where the couple divorced again, then Djerassi and his mother arrived in America in December of 1939.

Because Djerassi left Bulgaria two years before completing high school, he sought advice on how to finish his education once he arrived in New York City. However, his contact, a friend of one of his former teachers in Europe, misunderstood the word "college" on his grade sheet, which refers to secondary education in Europe, and assumed he had taken university–level courses. He helped Djerassi enroll at Newark Junior College, telling him it was already too late in the year for an application to New York University.

Though Djerassi always expected to take after his parents and become a physician, a chemistry instructor at the junior college convinced him to switch his major from pre–med. After a semester on scholarship at Missouri's Tarkio College, he transferred to Kenyon College in Ohio in 1941, which also provided him a scholarship as well as room and board. He obtained his A.B. in chemistry there the next year. Afterward, still just 18 years old, he went back to New Jersey and landed a job as a junior chemist at the Swiss pharmaceutical firm CIBA. There, he worked under another Austrian immigrant, Charles Huttrer. The two of them within a year discovered one of the first antihistamines, tripelennamine, which cold and allergy sufferers could use to alleviate symptoms.

After a year with CIBA, Djerassi went on leave to continue his education. He applied for a research fellowship, and in less than three years, he finished his doctorate in chemistry at the University of Wisconsin in 1945. (He was excused from duty during World War II because of a bad knee.) While at Madison, Djerassi embarked on a study of steroids that would fascinate him throughout his life.

Returning to CIBA in 1945 to continue his work on antihistamines, Djerassi continued to pursue his research on steroids on the side. His eventual goal was to move from an industrial setting back into academia. After four years, a friend suggested him for the position of associate director of research at Syntex, a small drug firm in Mexico City. As Djerassi wrote in his autobiography, "I was convinced that the best route to the academic job still eluding me was to establish a scientific reputation in the literature. Even though my friends thought me mad for trying to do this in Mexico, I felt intuitively that this was the right place."

Syntex, Djerassi noted, was also interested in cementing their reputation, and they were involved in the cutting–edge field of developing synthetic cortisone from plant material. Also, they agreed to his unconventional request that they publish his scientific findings in the journals immediately, without the patent attorneys deciding what would or would not be run. Thus, Djerassi was able to publish prolifically, staking his claim as a notable scientist while also building his company's profile.

While working at Syntex, Djerassi and his team in 1951 ended up successfully synthesizing cortisone for commercial use from a giant local yam. It was thought, incorrectly, that the substance would be useful in treating arthritis. Still, this feat landed them on the cover of *Time* and *Newsweek,* and their coup was even more remarkable because the group hailed from a small firm in Mexico, which was not seriously regarded by most of the scientific community.

Meanwhile, Djerassi had also been working on a way to synthesize norethindrone, which mimicked the female sex hormone progesterone. The patent application was filed in November of 1951, and other scientists began using it to study the treatment of menstrual disorders and fertility problems.

Soon, researchers Gregory Pincus and John Rock who are both also sometimes referred to as "the father of the Pill"—began to investigate the steroid as a possible contraceptive. Fearing a potential controversy from the Catholic Church, the Searle company began to market the substance in 1960 as a means of "menstrual regulation," even though the FDA approved it that year for contraceptive use. It was finally advertised specifically as a means of birth control in 1962 by Ortho, a division of Johnson & Johnson. Incidentally, Djerassi in his autobiography pointed out that he made no royalties from the sales of norethindrone, since Syntex owned the patent. However, he did own stock in the firm.

While the Pill was actually being developed, Djerassi had left Syntex and snagged his desired teaching position, at Wayne University (later, Wayne State University) in Detroit, Michigan. He became an associate professor of chemistry in 1952 and was promoted to professor in 1953. While there, he continued to work with steroids, and developed the spectropolarimeter, a device to conduct measurements on steroids. In 1959, Djerassi moved to California with all of his research staff in order to take a position at Stanford University, where he has remained since.

Meanwhile, Djerassi acted as a consultant to Syntex during the 1950s, and later, from 1968 to 1972, served as the company's president of research. In 1968 he helped form his own firm, Zoecon Corporation, which was concerned with finding new approaches to controlling insects. He was its chief executive officer until 1983, and its chairman of the board until 1988. Also, Djerassi throughout the 1970s and 1980s was involved in research on marine sterols, which are solid steroid alcohols in animal and plant lipids.

In an unusual turn of events, late in his career Djerassi broadened his resume to include not only the science field but also literature. In fact, though he told Josie Glausiusz in *Discover* that his writing is a way to "smuggle important scientific ideas out to the general public," Rocco in the *Daily Telegraph* wrote, "He feels his new work is so important that he now calls himself, 'an author and fledgling playwright who also does chemistry.'" He took up creative writing in his sixties, after his second marriage dissolved and his new female partner, Diane Middlebrook, a professor much younger than he, had left him for a younger man. "All I knew was that he was in the literary field," Djerassi told Rocco. "So, I said, 'By God, I'm going to show her.'"

Indeed, Djerassi penned a novel about a scientist in love with a younger woman. After he sent her the manuscript, she was impressed, and they reunited.

They married in 1985. Since then, he has published short stories in literary magazines, a book of short stories, three novels, a scientific autobiography, a book of memoirs, and several novels, including *Cantor's Dilemma*, 1989, and *Menachem's Seed*, 1997. In addition, the first of a planned trilogy of plays, *An Immaculate Misconception*, was opened at the Edinburgh Fringe Festival in 1998 and performed in London, San Francisco, and Vienna in 1999. In May of 2000, it was broadcast on the BBC World Service. The work "deals with the ethical dilemmas we face as sex and reproduction become increasingly separate," he explained to Glausiusz in *Discover*, referring to methods such as in vitro fertilization.

Djerassi has encouraged others in the arts as well by founding an artists colony near Woodside, California in 1979. It provides studio space and residencies for about 70 artists each year in literature, the visual arts, music, and choreography. Since its inception, over a thousand artists have enjoyed its use. He set up the program in memory of his daughter, Pamela, who committed suicide in 1978 at age 28. In addition to Middlebrook, Djerassi was married in his late teens to a woman named Virginia, and they divorced in 1950 so that he could marry the woman carrying his first child. With his second wife, Norma Lundholm, he had Pamela and a son, Dale. Djerassi and his second wife divorced in 1976.

For his various contributions to science, Djerassi has received a rich collection of awards, including the American Institute of Chemists Freedman Foundation Patent Award in 1970 and Chemical Pioneer Award in 1973; the National Medal of Science in 1973, the Wolf Prize in Chemistry in 1978; the Roussel Prize in 1988; the National Academy of Sciences award in 1990, the National Medal of Technology in 1991, the Austrian Cross of Honor for Science and Art in 1999, and the Chemical Heritage Foundation Othmer Gold Medal in 2000. Also, he was inducted into National Inventors Hall of Fame, 1978, and holds several honorary doctorates. He continues to teach undergraduate courses at Stanford.

Selected writings

Optical Rotatory Dispersion, McGraw, 1959.
(Editor) *Steroid Reactions*, Holden–Day, 1963.
With Herbert Budzikiewicz and D. H. Williams) *Interpretation of Mass Spectra of Organic Compounds*, Holden–Day, 1964.
(With Budzikiewicz and Williams) *Structure Elucidation of Natural Products of Mass Spectrometry*, two volumes, Holden–Day, 1964.

(With Budzikiewicz and Williams) *Mass Spectrometry of Organic Compounds*, Holden–Day, 1967.
The Politics of Contraception: Birth Control in the Year 2001, Norton, 1979.
The Futurist, and Other Stories, Macdonald Futura, 1988.
Cantor's Dilemma (novel), Doubleday, 1989.
Steroids Made It Possible (scientific autobiography), American Chemical Society, 1990.
The Pill, Pygmy Chimps, and Degas' Horse: The Remarkable Autobiography of Carl Djerassi, Macmillan, 1991.
The Clock Runs Backward, Story Line Press, 1991.
The Bourbaki Gambit: A Novel, University of Georgia Press, 1994.
From the Lab into the World: A Pill for People, Pets, and Bugs, American Chemical Society, 1994.
Marx, Deceased: A Novel, University of Georgia Press, 1996.
Menachem's Seed: A Novel, University of Georgia Press, 1997.
NO: A Novel, University of Georgia Press, 1998.
An Immaculate Misconception (play), produced at Edinburgh Fringe Festival, 1998, broadcast on BBC World Service, 2000.

Sources

Books

Djerassi, Carl, *The Pill, Pygmy Chimps, and Degas' Horse: The Remarkable Autobiography of Carl Djerassi*, Basic Books, 1992.
Notable Twentieth–Century Scientists, Gale Research, 1995.

Periodicals

Chemical & Engineering News, June 3, 1991, p. 28.
Daily Telegraph, March 2, 1998.
Dallas Morning News, October 19, 1998, p. 5F; June 7, 2000, p. 5C.
Discover, June 2000, p. 24.
New York Times, May 9, 2000, p. D1.

Online

Carl Djerassi Official Home Page, http://www.djerassi.com (June 28, 2000).
"Carl Djerassi," *Contemporary Authors Online*, Gale Group web site, http://www.galenet.com (June 6, 2000).

Minnie Driver

Archive Photos

Actor

Born Amelia Driver, January 31, 1971, in London, England; daughter of Ronnie Driver (a businessman) and Gaynor Churchward (a model and designer); *Education:* Graduated from the Webber–Douglas Academy of Dramatic Art, London, 1991.

Addresses: *Home*—Los Angeles, CA. *Agent*—Endeavor, 9701 Wilshire Blvd., 10th Floor, Beverly Hills, CA 90212.

Career

Actor. Television appearances include episodes of *Casualty*, 1986; *Lovejoy*, 1986; *Peak Practice*, 1994; *The Day Today*, 1994; *Knowing Me Knowing You with Alan Partridge*, 1994; and *Murder Most Horrid*, 1996; series *My Good Friend*; miniseries *Mr. Wroe's Virgins*, 1993; and *The Politician's Wife*, 1995; and movies *God on the Rocks*, 1990; *That Sunday*, 1994; and *Cruel Train*, 1995. Film appearances include *Circle of Friends*, 1995; *GoldenEye*, 1995; *Big Night*, 1996; *Baggage*, 1996; *Sleepers*, 1996; *Grosse Pointe Blank*, 1997; *Good Will Hunting*, 1997; *The Governess*, 1998; *At Sachem Farm*, 1998; *Hard Rain*, 1998; *Tarzan* (voice–over for animation), 1999; *South Park: Bigger, Longer, and Uncut* (voice–over for animation), 1999; and *An Ideal Husband*, 1999.

Awards: ShoWest Award for female star of tomorrow, 1998; London Critics Circle Award, 1999, for British supporting actress of the year for *Good Will Hunting*.

Sidelights

Throughout her career, British actor Minnie Driver has played a diverse range of characters. Although American audiences got their first look at her as the chunky but lovable Benny in 1995's feel–good hit *Circle of Friends*, she soon returned to the screen as a sexy singer in a James Bond movie. Subsequently, Driver, who got her start in British television, established herself as a leading contender in Hollywood. She landed a likable role as the abandoned high–school sweetheart in *Grosse Pointe Blank*, then went on to earn major praise as Matt Damon's girlfriend in the blockbuster *Good Will Hunting*. She then flip–flopped between action pictures like *Hard Rain* to period pieces like *The Governess* within the same year, and showed up in an adaptation of Oscar Wilde's *The Ideal Husband* in 1999. Perhaps her unique image—strong jaw, broad–shouldered frame, and mass of curly dark locks—allows her to play differing parts in a business known for its similar looking leading actors.

Driver was born on January 31, 1971, in London, England. Her real first name is Amelia, but as she explained to Michael Musto in *Interview*, "My sister took one look at me in the hospital and said,

'Minnie.' Thanks a lot my whole future was determined by a two–year–old." Early on, she showed a penchant for performance, writing in *Vogue,* "My childhood was always a three–act play: the melodrama of bedtime, my delight in making my parents and their friends laugh, and of course, my cavernous need for attention." She also revealed that she wrote poetry and liked to read it aloud.

Raised mainly in Barbados, Driver's parents, financial tycoon Ronnie Driver and model–turned– designer Gaynor Churchward, broke up when Driver was almost seven years old. She was then sent to the Bedales boarding school in Hampshire, England, where Princess Anne once attended; it was not too far from the family's estate in Petersfield. Part of Driver's chameleon–like ability to affect different accents stems from the fact that she has moved around a lot.

Continuing on the path to acting, Driver attended the Webber–Douglas Academy of Dramatic Art in London, where she noted in *Vogue,* "I played no one under 50 in my three years there and was furious only the boys got to play Hamlet." After getting her degree in drama in 1991, she found an agent and began landing parts on the stage and on British television in between moonlighting as a jazz singer and guitar player in clubs around London. One of her television roles was in her own series, *My Good Friend,* and another was in a BBC miniseries, *The Politician's Wife,* in addition to numerous other BBC television movies in which she often played feisty women.

When Driver was 23, she received a copy of the script for the film *Circle of Friends,* asking her to consider the part of the chubby "ugly duckling." Instead of seeing it as her big break, she quipped to Paula S. Bernstein in the Minneapolis *Star Tribune,* "I was furious that the casting director had sent me a script that was for a fat girl." However, after reading the part, Driver felt she could identify with the character: "I had a very, very beautiful sister," she commented to Bernstein, adding, "I was always the dumpy younger sister." Though she pursued the job, the producers were uncomfortable hiring an unknown, and were not convinced that Driver could get the look they wanted. "I had the script for over a year before I got the role," she told Colin Lacey in *Irish America.* "The producers weren't too keen on me because I didn't look right, they said."

Set in Dublin in 1957, *Circle of Friends* was based on an autobiographical novel by Maeve Binchy about an overweight, dowdy girl who falls hard for the charming, attractive captain of the rugby team at college. The little, upbeat film, made in rural Ireland, was a surprise hit that year. Driver called upon her vocal skills and also trained with a voice coach in order to convincingly effect an Irish brogue, and ended up gaining 20 pounds in order to transform herself into the pudgy Benny. She also had to stand in ditches so that she would appear short and frumpy next to her costar, Chris O'Donnell. The five–foot, ten–inch actor once noted to Harper Barnes in the *St. Louis Post–Dispatch,* "I've lost three jobs because I'm tall. A lot of actors have such insecurity, they don't want to act with someone taller."

Although carrying extra weight and being cast in such an unglamorous part should have worried an up–and–coming actor like Driver, she quickly shattered any possible typecasting with her next role. In *GoldenEye,* 1995, her normally svelte figure had returned, and she was cast as a Russian country and western lounge singer, and the girlfriend of one of the bad guys. In it, she was all but unrecognizable in a red cowboy hat and outrageous dress. "I look so cheap, it's absolutely cool," she commented to Malissa Thompson in *Seventeen.* In fact, she was so far from her image in *Circle of Friends* that later, a Hollywood studio executive did not believe her when she told him she had been in *GoldenEye.* Further smashing any perception of her as Benny, Driver appeared on the runway as a celebrity model for Nicole Miller in New York's fall fashion shows in 1995.

In 1996, Driver showed up in a couple of smaller films, *Big Night* and *Baggage,* then entered a new realm with *Sleepers.* Based on Lorenzo Carcaterra's controversial book, it also starred box–office heavyweights Brad Pitt, Dustin Hoffman, and Robert De-Niro, among others. The story focused on the plight of four boys who cause an accidental death during a prank and are sentenced to do time at a juvenile home; while there, they endure serial rape by the guards. The four are later reunited at a trial when two of the men, as adults, kill one of their tormentors. When the book by Lorenzo Carcaterra came out, it was billed as nonfiction, but later, journalists later dug into archives and expressed doubt as to the authenticity of the tale. In any case, Driver played the only female among the high–profile cast, boosting her name even more. She also pulled off a New York accent.

For her next part, Driver played a radio disk jockey from the Detroit area in the dark comedy *Grosse Pointe Blank,* 1997, perfectly executing the smooth, even tone of an American broadcaster. In it, she plays a woman who reunites with her high school flame just before their ten–year reunion. John Cusack costars as the boyfriend who stood her up at the prom a decade prior in order to take a job as a trained hit man. Critics found this effort to be much more enjoyable than *Sleepers,* and it went far in showcasing Driver's ability at playing a romantic lead.

Indeed, Driver's believability as the sweet girlfriend came in handy for her next project, *Good Will Hunting,* written by and costarring friends Ben Affleck and Matt Damon. The film focused on a gifted young man (Damon) who must decide whether to leave the comfort zone of his loyal band of lower–income friends and pursue higher education. His life is complicated when he falls for a British student. Driver actually got to use her own voice for this role. The picture was highly acclaimed and led to a host of award nominations; Driver was nominated for an Academy Award and others, and took home a 1999 London Critics Circle Award for the performance.

During and after the making of *Good Will Hunting,* Driver was romantically involved with costar Damon off–screen as well. However, they soon split up, as everyone witnessed when they arrived separately at the Academy Awards. In addition, when Damon and Affleck won an Oscar for best screenplay, the camera caught a stunned expression on Driver's face. As she explained to Martha Frankel in *Cosmopolitan,* "I was feeling about a thousand different things…. It's very strange to have your joy inextricably linked with your sadness, but that's the way it went down."

Though much was made of the brief affair, the bigger issue was that thanks to the popularity of *Good Will Hunting,* Driver was transformed into a full–fledged star. "I went from being the girl next door to being a siren in a red dress on the cover of *People* magazine," Driver related to *In Style* 's Leslie Marshall. "Nobody was more surprised than I." However, celebrity has its down side, as Driver soon discovered. She noted to Frankel, "I used to just walk out of the house looking like crap and nobody would notice. But now? Forget about it. There are photographers everywhere, and they always seem to get you when you're at your worst. I'm more careful now."

Branching into a new genre altogether, Driver was then cast opposite Christian Slater in the action–packed *Hard Rain,* 1998, which concerns a failed bank robbery that happens as an Indiana town is being flooded. "By the time the movie was finished," Driver related to Louis B. Hobson in the *London Free Press,* "I felt like a prune. I haven't been near a pool since and I think it will be years before I can swim in anything but the ocean." After that, in another about–face, she appeared in the artsy work *The Governess,* 1998, in which she plays a Jewish woman in the 1840s who assumes a new identity and goes to work for a family on a remote Scottish island. In 1999, Driver again played a historical role in a version of Oscar Wilde's 1895 novel *An Ideal Husband.* Also that year, continuing to sidestep typecasting, she ventured into voice–overs as well, providing the voice of Jane in the animated film *Tarzan,* and the voice of Brooke Shields in *South Park: Bigger, Longer and Uncut.*

After her breakup with Damon, Driver was linked to various entertainment figures, but by fall of 1999, she and actor Josh Brolin (son of James Brolin, who is married to singer Barbra Streisand) announced their engagement. In addition to her successful love life, Driver's career was in full gear in 1998, she formed a production company, Two Drivers, with her sister, Kate (she also has an older half–sister and two younger half–brothers). That year, they backed their first project, *At Sachem Farm,* in which Driver also starred. Well before this time she had made the move to Los Angeles, where she told Barnes, "I live in the canyons and I love that. I love the mountains, I love the ocean, I love the sunshine and riding my bike." When Chris Petrikin in GQ asked if her lifestyle had changed since relocating, she replied, "Well, someone comes to my house and gives me a massage now and again. Oh, and I say 'dude' a lot." Although it looked like Driver was in the American movie business to stay, she remarked to Ivan Waterman in the *Independent,* "I will never be an 'insider' in Hollywood. Culturally, I will always be 7,000 miles away."

Sources

Periodicals

Cosmopolitan, August 1998, p. 192.
Entertainment Weekly, March 24, 1995, p. 44; April 24, 1998, p. 13.
GQ, January 1998, p. 142.
Independent, April 10, 1998, p. 4.
In Style, October 15, 1998, p. 84.
Interview, January 1996, p. 60.
Irish America, April 30, 1995.
London Free Press (Ontario, Canada), February 10, 1998, p. C5.
People, December 25, 1995, p. 131; November 18, 1996, p. 104.
St. Louis Post–Dispatch, April 13, 1997, p. 3D.

Seventeen, May 1995, p. 96.

Star Tribune (Minneapolis, MN), April 10, 1995, p. 3E.

USA Weekend, January 4, 1998, p. 27.

Vogue, September 1996, p. 420.

Online

"Minnie Driver," Internet Movie Database web site, http://us.imdb.com (October 4, 1999).

"Minnie Driver," Mr. Showbiz web site, http://mrshowbiz.go.com (October 4, 1999).

Tim Duncan

Basketball player

Born Timothy Theodore Duncan, April 25, 1976, in St. Croix, Virgin Islands; son of William (a mason) and Ione (a midwife) Duncan. *Education:* Wake Forest University, bachelor's degree in psychology, 1997.

Addresses: *Office*—c/o San Antonio Spurs, 100 Montana St., San Antonio, TX 78203.

Career

Wake Forest University college player, 1993–97; National Basketball Association (NBA) number one draft pick, 1997; San Antonio Spurs, center, 1997—.

Awards: National Collegiate Athletic Association (NCAA) defensive player of the year, 1994– 95, 1995–96, 1996–97; Atlantic Coast Conference (ACC) player of the year, 1995–96; John R. Wooden and James A. Naismith Awards, Consensus Best Player in College Basketball, 1997; NBA rookie of the month each month of his rookie season, 1997–98; NBA Schick rookie of the year and *Sporting News* rookie of the year, 1997–98; NBA Finals most valuable player award, 1999.

Sidelights

Tim Duncan, forward for the San Antonio Spurs, has become a standout in the league in his first two years in professional basketball. A throwback to the old–school style of play, he does not trash talk, yell, or throw elbows on rebounds, preferring to let his talent speak for itself. His size seven feet tall and 248 pounds makes him a viable force on the court, but Duncan is renowned for his well–rounded bank of skills: dribbling, defending, passing, shooting, scoring, and rebounding. In addition, he is considered to have sharp mental skills in the game, despite his uncanny knack for showing no emotion, often to the point of appearing distracted. Duncan's stoicism during play is legendary. Fans during his college days even nicknamed him "Spock" after the emotionless *Star Trek* character, but opponents soon learned that this belies a fierce competitiveness. Perhaps some of this can be attributed to his degree in psychology, which he completed even though multimillion dollar offers from the NBA were pouring in. The soft– spoken player racked up numerous achievements during his college years and in his rookie season in the NBA, but managed to remain gracious, deflecting much of the credit to teammates and coaches. In 1998 he helped lead the Spurs to the playoffs, and in 1999 he took them to their first–ever finals, not to mention championship.

Duncan was born on April 25, 1976, in St. Croix, Virgin Islands. His father, William, was a mason, and his mother, Ione, a midwife. She encouraged Duncan and his two older sisters to become swimmers and even changed her hours to the night shift so that she could attend all of their races. Duncan's sister Tricia competed in the 1988 Olympics in the 100– and 200–meter backstroke, and it was expected that Duncan would compete in the 1992 games. At age 13, he was one of the top U.S. swimmers in the 400–meter freestyle and holds records in the Virgin Islands for the 50–meter and 100–meter freestyle events. However, Hurricane Hugo blew through the Virgin Islands in 1989 and ruined the pool where Duncan trained. It was around this time that he took up basketball.

Then, in a shattering blow, Duncan's mother died of breast cancer the day before he turned 14, and he lost all interest in swimming. His sister, Tricia, told Tim Crothers in *Sports Illustrated*, "The hurricane broke Tim's routine by taking away our pool. Then when Mom passed, he lost his motivation." But he continued to play basketball, and when his sister Cheryl and her husband, Ricky Lowery, returned to St. Croix after Duncan's mother died, he trained with his brother–in–law, who had played college basketball at Capital University in Ohio. Duncan had always been tall, standing six feet in ninth grade, but he grew an extra eight inches in high school and began playing hoops for St. Dunstan's Episcopal High.

Although the local newspaper was starting to print enthusiastic reviews of Duncan's court skills, only a few colleges were checking him out, including Wake Forest, Providence, Hartford, and Delaware State. Wake Forest coach Dave Odom heard from former player Chris King that Duncan showed promise in guarding Alonzo Mourning during an NBA rookie tour, so Odom went to meet him. Duncan seemed withdrawn, watching television as the coach pitched his school. Odom finally asked him to turn off the set, thinking that Duncan was not listening, but soon discovered he had heard every word. Duncan later told Crothers, "I was listening, but the 49ers were on. It was the fourth quarter."

The Wake Forest Demon Deacons did not expect much from Duncan his first year. He was almost benched until another player was declared ineligible, so he was needed at center. His first game was at the University of Alaska at Anchorage—marking the first time this tropical island resident had ever seen snow—and he took no shots and scored zero points. His game geared up in no time, though, and by the season's end, in 51 games, he had set the school's record for blocked shots. The next year, he showed more offensive power, averaging 16.8 points per game and 12.5 rebounds per game, called a "double–double" because both statistics were in the double digits. Only one other player that year, Joe Smith, boasted a double–double.

Throughout his years at Wake Forest, Duncan earned a reputation as being expressionless, fair, and driven on the court. He did not engage in loud outbursts on the court, nor did he play dirty in order to build his impressive statistics. Even when other players tried to provoke him, Duncan refused to engage in verbal fights or to get wrapped up in off–court drama. For example, another player, Greg Newton of Duke University, once publicly stated that the way to prevail over Duncan was to play physical, because Duncan could not compete in that manner. When reporters egged on Duncan with this news, he replied, "Peace be to Greg Newton," according to Darryl Howerton in *Sport*. Although Duncan's calm demeanor prompted some critics to accuse him of not being tough enough, he trained diligently—never missing a practice even when his coach begged him to rest up for games—and proved to be an intense competitor.

Owing much to Duncan's prowess, Wake Forest became an NCAA contender each year he was on the court and, as a sophomore, he led them to their first Atlantic Coast Conference (ACC) championship since 1962. In his junior year, they won again. His freshman year he helped take them to the second round of the NCAA tournament; the next year they were in the final 16. His junior year, they entered the Midwest Regional final, and his senior year, they made it to the second round again. During his time in college, Duncan averaged 3.98 rejections per game the third–best in NCAA history, behind David Robinson and Shaquille O'Neal. In his senior year, he scored 20.8 points per game and averaged 14.7 rebounds, the best record in the country, and was named the 1997 College Player of the Year. In addition, he was crowned the NCAA Defensive Player of the Year an unprecedented three years running, in 1995, 1996, and 1997.

The NBA showed a keen interest in Duncan during his college years, and he was expected to become the number one draft pick for 1996. During the 1995–96 season, the media latched onto the 19–year–old phenomenon with the intriguing background and touted him as the next big thing. However, much to the delight of Wake Forest as well as his father, Duncan decided to finish his bachelor's degree in psychology. "I made a promise to my mother to finish school," he explained to David Higdon in *Boys' Life*, and he also noted in interviews that he did not consider himself ready for the pros. The NBA's interest in him did not wane, though, and Duncan used the extra time to become just the tenth player in NCAA Division I history to score 2,000 points and nab 1,500 rebounds in his college playing days.

Duncan never led Wake Forest to a spot in the Final Four, but when the 1997 draft rolled around, he was the top pick and signed a three–year deal with the San Antonio Spurs worth more than $10 million. The team was in need of a powerful player to work well with center David Robinson, and Duncan filled that gap. In his first few months on the court, Duncan was already proving that he was going to live up to the hype that preceded him. As Frank Clancy observed in the *Sporting News*, "He appears entirely comfortable with his back to the basket and on the high post, where he often initiates much of the team's offense. He can shoot from outside and drive with either hand. He passes and sees the court well. He's strong enough to hold his ground against most power forwards." The only complaints that some sportswriters noted were Duncan's turnovers and his less–than–stellar free–throw performance, which dropped from 75 percent as a freshman at Wake Forest to 64 percent as a senior, and then to 48 percent with San Antonio. Nevertheless, his outstanding footwork, on top of his other diverse pool of skills, earned Duncan rookie of the month honors every month of his first year in the pros, just the third player (besides Ralph Samson, 1983–84, and David Robinson, 1989–90) to have achieved this.

By the end of his rookie year in 1998, Duncan had racked up one of the best first–season records in NBA history. He led the NBA that year with 57 double–doubles and helped the Spurs achieve the best single–season turnaround in NBA history, taking them from 20 victories in 1996–97 to 56 in 1997–98. Duncan was ranked third in the league that year with 11 rebounds per game, fourth with a .529 field–goal percentage, sixth with 2.51 blocked shots per game, and twelfth with 21.1 points per game. In all of those categories, he was the top rookie, and in 34 Spurs games, he was the top scorer. Not surprisingly, Duncan was voted the *Sporting News* rookie of the year, winning 68 votes in a nearly unanimous decision. Four others received one vote each. He was also named NBA Schick rookie of the year as well, getting 113 of 116 votes, and became a unanimous selection to the 1997–98 Schick All–Rookie First Team. In addition, he was chosen as just the ninth rookie ever named to the Schick All–NBA First Team.

Unfortunately, Duncan was injured during the 1997–98 playoffs and the Spurs lost their series to the Utah Jazz. The next year, a dispute led to a player lockout and an abbreviated season, but it did not break Duncan's concentration. When he returned to the court, he helped lead the Spurs to a jaw–dropping four–game sweep of the Los Angeles Lakers, led by powerhouse Shaquille O'Neal, to win the Western Conference Semifinals. His performance was outstanding throughout the series, as he scored game–highs in several meetings with the Lakers

and with the New York Knicks in the finals. The Spurs rounded out 1999 as the champions, taking games 1, 2, 4, and 5 to prevail over the Knicks. Although Duncan had another top–notch season as the only player in the league to finish in the top ten in scoring (sixth), rebounding (fifth), blocked shots (seventh), and field goal percentage (tenth), he finished third in the race for regular season most valuable player awards. It was no surprise, however, when he was named the NBA Finals most valuable player. His playoff numbers were impressive, as he averaged 27.4 points, 14.0 rebounds and 2.20 blocks per game.

Duncan is single but has a steady girlfriend who "helps me cope with the everyday rigors of being an NBA player," as he noted in *Sport*. In that same article, which he penned, psychology major Duncan gave many insights into the workings of his mind, something he was not known to do with interviewers. He mentioned that "I've got a million things going on in my head at all times," and added, "If you ever see me and think I'm being standoffish, please forgive me…. [I]n those moments, I'm doing nothing but thinking." He also revealed that in order to handle pressure, he uses humor. He also noted that despite his fancy footwork on the court, he is a terrible dancer. Overall, Duncan noted, "If I were to psychoanalyze myself, I'd have to say I'm a clown cleverly disguised as a regular person. I enjoy jokes, smiling and making people smile."

Sources

Books

Contemporary Black Biography, volume 20, Gale Research, 1998.

Periodicals

Boys' Life, January 1998, p. 18.
Jet, July 14, 1997, p. 46.
Knight–Ridder/Tribune News Service, March 23, 1995; November 27, 1995; March 7, 1996.
Newsweek, May 17, 1999, p. 75.
Sport, December 1995, p. 12; July 1997, p. 34; May 1999, p. 34.
Sporting News, March 10, 1997, p. 12; March 31, 1997, p. 24; December 15, 1997, p. 52; May 18, 1998, p. 13; June 14, 1999, p. 38.
Sports Illustrated, November 27, 1995, p. 78; February 17, 1997; April 13, 1998, p. 22; May 31, 1999, p. 48; July 7, 1999, pp. 62, 77.

Online

"Tim Duncan player file," NBA web site, http://
www.nba.com/finals99 (September 24, 1999).

"Duncan Named MVP," NBA web site, http://
www.nba.com/finals99 (September 27, 1999).

David Duval

Golfer

Born David Robert Duval, November 9, 1971, in Jacksonville, FL; son of Robert "Bob" Duval (a golfer) and Diane (a secretary) Duval. *Education:* Attended Georgia Institute of Technology.

Addresses: *Home*—Ponte Vedra Beach, FL, and Sun Valley, ID. *Office*—c/o Professional Golfers Association (PGA) of America, Box 109601, 100 Avenue of Champions, Palm Beach Gardens, FL 33410.

Career

Professional golfer, 1993 . Member, Walker Cup team, 1991; President's Cup team, 1996.

Awards: U.S. Junior Amateur title, 1989; American Junior Golf Association player of the year, 1989; Collegiate Player of the Year, 1993; Dave Williams award, 1993; Nike Wichita Open, 1993, Nike Tour Championship, 1993, Jasper award, Jacksonville, FL, 1996; Michelob Championship at Kingsmill, 1997; Walt Disney World/Oldsmobile Classic, 1997; The Tour Championship, 1997; Tucson Chrysler Classic, 1998; Shell Houston Open, 1998; NEC World Series of Golf, 1998; Michelob Championship at Kingsmill, 1998; Mercedes Championship, 1999; Bob Hope Chrysler Classic, 1999; The Players Championship, 1999; BellSouth Classic, 1999.

Sidelights

In 1999, David Duval surpassed Tiger Woods to become the top-ranked golfer in the world. Though he later dropped again to second place, his powerful swing and string of victories had sealed his place as a top contender. He is a popular figure, especially with younger spectators, but early in his career Duval developed a reputation for being brusque and aloof. His lack of emotion on the course earned him the nickname "Rock," and he is known to be blunt, though some interviewers have also praised that kind of directness, which is rare in professional sports. Trying to counter his public image, Duval noted in a *Golf Digest* interview with Bob Verdi, "I'm a nice person. A lot of people have me pegged as the guy behind the sunglasses who once wore a goatee. The rebel, the robot." He added, "The people who don't know me, they interpret my shyness as arrogance." Despite Duval's stellar record, he has never won a major tournament the Masters, the U.S. Open, the British Open, or the PGA Championship and many are eager to see if he will eventually achieve this.

Duval was born on November 9, 1971, in Jacksonville, Florida, to Robert "Bob" and Diane Duval. He was raised in a family with a long tradition of golf. His grandfather, Henry "Hap" Duval, was a PGA member throughout his lifetime, and his father, now a PGA Senior Tour player, was formerly a resident golf pro at the Timuquana Country Club in Jacksonville. His mother worked as a secretary.

When Duval was nine, the family found out that his brother, Brent, who was 12, had a disease called aplastic anemia. It caused his bone marrow to stop producing white blood cells. With a bone–marrow transplant from a sibling who was a good match, his brother would have a 50–50 chance of surviving. Duval's marrow ended up being a better match than that of their younger sister, Deirdre, so he underwent a painful procedure to extract it from his bones. His brother began to recover, but soon died from an infection, leaving Duval to wonder if he had contributed to his death somehow. A year later, his father left the family. Though he would return by the time Duval was in high school to try to work things out, his parents divorced in 1996. His father later remarried. All of this contributed to Duval becoming a serious and subdued child.

To help cope with things, Duval began to immerse himself in golf. Instead of going to the mall or hanging out with his few friends, he spent all his time at the Timuquana Country Club on the greens. Golf "lends itself to solitude," he observed to Tom Cunneff in *People*. "You can practice some and play a round, and it takes up a big chunk of a day. It's all-consuming." When he was 13, he began to beat older men, some of whom had won city and state championships. He began playing for money and saved up about $1,000. Then, at a driving contest at the club, he outshot even the biggest players by 40 yards.

The night Duval graduated from high school, while others were out celebrating, he got on a flight to Texas for a tournament. That summer, in 1989, he won four prestigious junior events, and captured the U.S. Junior Amateur title. He then enrolled at Georgia Institute of Technology (Georgia Tech), and for four years straight, received NCAA Division I first-team All-American honors. He was only the third person after Phil Mickelson and Gary Hallberg to accomplish this. As a sophomore in 1991, playing in his second NCAA tournament, he finished second. However, Duval's mind was not on collegiate events. According to Gary Smith in *Sports Illustrated*, he later remarked, "College was just another stop on my journey . Everything I did was preparing for the next level. I was majoring in golf."

According to Smith's portrait of Duval, he was unpopular with his teammates. He was often surly with them and others, and once called them a "bunch of hacks" in the *New York Times*, according to the *Golf Digest* interview with Verdi. Behind his back, the team made fun of his weight. Still withdrawn, he rarely dated. However, his coach, Puggy Blackmon, stood by him and tried to initiate counseling sessions for the team to help Duval. When that did not seem to work, Blackmon settled for keeping his star player separate from other team members. Duval admitted in *Golf Digest*, "My personality problem probably hurt my reputation in college, but I was young and immature . Sometimes we forget that a lot of athletes are kids who have had limited interaction with the real world."

In 1993, Duval was named Collegiate Player of the Year and won the Dave Williams award. However, eager to start his career, he ended up leaving Georgia Tech that year, a little more than a quarter shy of graduation. But failing to earn his PGA card, he was relegated to playing on the Nike Tour, a less rigorous series of events than the PGA Tour. That year, 1993, he won the Nike Wichita Open and the Nike Tour Championship, but since he did not make it into the top ten money earners, he was not allowed to move up to the PGA. In 1994, though, he nailed 15 top-ten finishes, and landed in eighth place.

In Duval's first season on the PGA Tour, 1995, he finished fourteenth, then sixth, then second in his first three events, establishing him as a force to watch. However, he was still pegged as standoffish, due in large part to the wraparound sunglasses and hat he always wore onto the course. Eventually, people found out that the eyewear was a protective measure against the harsh sunlight and allergens that bothered him on the greens. But he was also seen as arrogant due to his aloof manner on the course. Whereas many players show outward excitement at making a good shot or nailing a putt, Duval became known for his restraint.

Throughout 1995, Duval posted eight top-ten finishes and managed to place second in three tournaments the AT&T Pebble Beach National Pro-Am, the Bob Hope Chrysler Classic, and the Memorial Tournament. He set a rookie earnings record of $881,438 and finished eleventh on the PGA money list. The next year, he finished in tenth place with nearly $1 million in earnings. However, a win continued to elude him. The press dubbed him "Sultan of Second," according to Smith in *Sports Illustrated*, who also noted that headlines like "BRIDESMAID AGAIN" would blare after his near misses.

In the meantime, Duval reconciled with his father, and even caddied for him in his first season on the 1996 Senior PGA Tour. He also urged his mother to enter an alcohol treatment program, and he began to expand his series of friends. In addition, he found a serious girlfriend, and he lost 40 pounds through diet and exercise, adding muscle and gaining flexibility. But he was still winless after 86 PGA events, and was outshined by Tiger Woods, who turned professional in August of 1996 and landed six victories in his first 11 months on the PGA Tour.

Finally, in 1997, Duval experienced his first PGA Tour victory, at the Michelob Championship at Kingsmill in Williamsburg, Virginia. A week later, he won the Disney World– Oldsmobile Classic, and two weeks after that, he won the Tour Championship, the last event of the season. This made him the first PGA player to win his first three victories consecutively. And only Woods, with four victories, won more events than Duval in 1997. Duval closed out the season as the second–top money earner next to Woods, with $1.8 million.

The next year, 1998, Duval led the Tour with four victories, at the Tucson Classic, the Shell Houston Open, the NEC World Series of Golf, and the Michelob Championship. In addition, he was in the lead at the Masters until Mark O'Meara sank a stunning 20–foot putt on the final hole. By the season's end, Duval had broken the PGA's single–season earnings record, with $2.59 million, putting him in first place (Woods earned $1.84 million). Also that year he won the Vardon Trophy, given to the player with the lowest strokes–per–round average on the PGA Tour.

Duvall kept up his streak in 1999, winning the season's first event, the Mercedes Championship, and the second, the Bob Hope Chrysler Classic. In the latter, he landed a one– stroke victory over Steve Pate and became only the third player in history to shoot 59 in a PGA Tour event. He went on to clinch The Players Championship and the BellSouth Classic, making him the first player since Johnny Miller in 1974 to win four events before the Masters. In addition, his win at The Players Championship fell on the same day as his dad's victory at the Emerald Coast Classic, making them the first father–son pair to win PGA Tour and Senior Tour events on the same day.

In 1999, Duval earned $2 million in the shortest time of any PGA player, and he became the first to ever surpass the $3 million mark. He thus reached the number one ranking without having won a major event, although he slipped back behind Woods that year after coming in tenth at the PGA Championship. In addition, Duval hit a small slump in 1999, tying for sixth at the Masters and then tying for 64th at the Shell Houston Open. He even failed to make the cut at the Compaq Classic, and tied for 62nd at the British Open.

By the year's end, Woods had earned a Tour record of $6,616,585 nearly $3 million more than Duval. Promoters capitalized on their respectful rivalry, staging a special event in August of 1999 in a rare face–off exhibition at the Sherwood Country Club in Thousand Oaks, California. Even more unusual, the match, called the "Showdown at Sherwood," was broadcast on prime–time television. Though

Woods won the contest, both players agreed that the event was a good way to rally interest in their sport. Some criticized the staged event as being phony, but Duval pointed out that $200,000 of each winner's purse was donated to charity.

Once he began to see success, Duval's personality began to soften. He began to remove his sunglasses after leaving the course and even sometimes gave them to young fans. Though he remained stoic on the greens, he would later oblige dozens of admirers with autographs. In addition, it was reported that he gave generously to charity, though he was reluctant to discuss it. Duval also once sent an autographed cap to a dying fan who was later buried with the token, and also, through the Make–a–Wish Foundation, he spent a day with a boy suffering from a rare blood disorder and gave him a putter and a driver.

Duval stands six feet tall and weighs 180 pounds, and had endorsement contracts with Titleist golf balls, Tommy Hilfiger apparel, Oakley sunglasses and the Charles Schwab financial firm. He is single but has a longtime girlfriend, former pharmacist Julie McArthur. He has a 6,000–square foot home in Ponte Vedra Beach, Florida, and a summer home in Sun Valley, Idaho, because he enjoys being in the mountains. Duval's hobbies include reading, fly fishing, skiing, snowboarding, surfing, and baseball. To Verdi in *Golf Digest*, he noted, "What really matters is the freedom and time I've got. I'm not fascinated by toys. It's all about time. Quality time. I enjoy my time playing golf, but I also enjoy my time not playing golf. What's the use in practicing so hard and grinding it out if you can't appreciate the time away from it?"

Sources

Periodicals

Golf, March 1998, p. 126; October 1998, p. 36; May 1999, p. 30.
Golf Digest, January 1999; October 1999, p. 45; September 1999, p. 182.
Newsweek, February 22, 1999, p. 44.
New York Times, October 31, 1997, p. C6; November 3, 1997, p. C6.
People, April 5, 1999, p. 175.
Sports Illustrated, November 10, 1997, p. 46; September 7, 1998, p. G4; October 26, 1998, p. G16; January 18, 1999, p. 4; February 1, 1999, pp. 38, G2; April 5, 1999, p. 58; April 12, 1999, p. 66; June 28, 1999, p. G6; August 30, 1999, p. G4; December 6, 1999, p. G4.
Time, April 12, 1999, p. 85.

Online

"David Duval," PGA Tour and Golfweb web site,
  http://www.golfweb.com (April 25, 2000).

Atom Egoyan

AP/Wide World Photos

Filmmaker

Born July 19, 1960, in Cairo, Egypt; son of Joseph (an operator of a furniture store) and Shushan (an operator of a furniture store; maiden name, Devletian) Yeghoyan (name later changed to Egoyan); married Arsinee Khanjian (an actress); children: Arshile (son). *Education:* University of Toronto, B.A., international relations, 1982.

Addresses: *Office*—Ego Film Arts, 80 Nicaragua St., Toronto, Ontario M5V 1C5, Canada.

Career

Director, producer, film editor, screenwriter, and actor. Ego Film Arts, Toronto, Ontario, director. Classical guitarist. Jury member, Cannes International Film Festival, 1996. Director of television series, including *Yo–Yo Ma Inspired by Bach,* 1997; television episodes, including *Alfred Hitchcock Presents,* 1985; *The Twilight Zone,* 1985; and *Friday the 13th,* 1987; and television movies, including *In This Corner,* 1980; *Looking for Nothing,* 1988; and *Gross Misconduct,* 1993.

Director and writer or cowriter of films, including *Howard in Particular* (short), 1979; *After Grad with Dad,* 1980; *Peep Show,* 1981; *Open House,* 1982; *Next of Kin,* 1984; *Men: A Passion Playground,* 1985; *Family Viewing,* 1987; *Speaking Parts,* 1989; *Montreal vu par* (segment *"En passant"*), 1991; *The Adjuster,* 1991; *Calendar,* 1993; *Exotica,* 1994; *A Portrait of Arshile,* 1995; *The Sweet Hereafter,* 1997; *Bach Cello Suite #4: Sarabande,* 1997; and *Felicia's Journey,* 1999.

Producer of films, including *Next of Kin,* 1984; *Family Viewing,* 1987; *Speaking Parts,* 1989; *Calendar,* 1993; *Exotica,* 1994; *Curtis's Charm* (executive), 1995; *A Portrait of Arshile,* 1995; *The Sweet Hereafter,* 1997; and *Jack & Jill* (executive), 1998.

Actor in films, including *Knock! Knock!,* 1985; *Calendar,* 1993; *Camilla,* 1994; *A Portrait of Arshile,* 1995; *The Stupids,* 1996; and *Vinyl,* 1997.

Awards: Gold Ducat Award, Mannheim International Filmweek, 1984, for *Next of Kin;* Toronto International Film Festival Award for best Canadian feature film, 1987, and Berlin International Film Festival honorable mention, 1988, both for *Family Viewing;* , Toronto International Film Festival Award for best Canadian feature film and Special Jury Prize, Moscow Film Festival, both 1991, for *The Adjuster;* Golden Gate Award, San Francisco Film Festival, 1992, for *Gross Misconduct;* best film award, new cinema category, International Jury for Art Cinema, 1993, for *Calendar;* Genie Awards for best picture, best director, and best writer, Cannes International Film Festival International Critics Award, and Toronto International Film Festival Award for best Canadian feature film, all 1994, for *Exotica;* Cannes Film Festival Grand Jury Prize and International Critics Award, Genie Awards for best director and best motion picture, Society of Texas Film Critics Award, Toronto International Film Festival Award for best Canadian feature film, and Valladolid International Film Festival Golden Spike and Youth Jury Awards, all 1997, and Independent Spirit Award for best foreign film and Writers Guild of Canada Top Ten Award, 1998, all for *The Sweet Hereafter;* named Chevalier of Ordre des artes et des lettres, France, 1997; Sao Paolo International Film Festival special jury award, 1997, for *Yo–Yo Ma Inspired by Bach;* Genie Award for best screenplay adaptation, 1999, for*Felicia's Journey;* grants from Canada Council, Ontario Arts Council, and Ontario Film Development Corp. Has also won awards as a playwright.

Sidelights

Filmmaker Atom Egoyan gained a following with critics and cinema buffs in the 1980s with his atmospheric, haunting, darkly humorous and intellectual works dealing with alienation, loss, and the search for identity. With efforts such as *Family Viewing* and *Speaking Parts,* he deftly explores the issue of human bonding and how media such as video and film can serve to deepen an individual's detachment. Though he is still not exactly mainstream, Egoyan's works became better known after the release of his breakthrough film, *Exotica,* an intricate investigation of several characters and subplots surrounding a strip club. David Edelstein in *Vogue* wrote that until then, the filmmaker "hadn't generated much enthusiasm in the non–egghead segment of the filmgoing public. Formally brilliant, they're also glacial, rigorously detached, and populated by characters so repressed that they seem only tangentially human." Subsequently, the filmmaker's name got its biggest boost to date with his release of 1997's *The Sweet Hereafter,* adapted from a book by Russell Banks. After that, he was also regaled in 1999 for *Felicia's Journey.*

Egoyan ("eh–GOY–en") was born on July 19, 1960, in Cairo, Egypt, the oldest of two children of Joseph and Shushan (Devletian) Yeghoyan, who changed their surname to Egoyan to make it easier to pronounce. They named his younger sister Eve, which led to a barrage of jokes on the theme of Atom (which sounds like "Adam") and Eve. She became an experimental concert pianist. Their parents were Armenian refugees and aspiring artists who operated a thriving furniture store in Cairo; they gave their son his unconventional name in honor of the onset of nuclear energy in Egypt.

When Egoyan was three, the family relocated to Victoria, British Columbia, Canada, where they opened another furniture business. His mother once had a painting accepted by the National Gallery of Armenia, and his father attended the Chicago Art Institute at age 16, but staged his last major show when Egoyan was ten. "They gave him the whole second floor of the provincial museum in Victoria, and his show was just images of dead birds," the filmmaker related to Johnson. "The year before, our house was full of dead birds—it did not go over well.... He would pose them around the house and paint them." Egoyan added, "I think I had a very early exposure to a very excessive mentality."

Assimilating into his new country, Egoyan enrolled in hockey school and soon refused to speak Armenian. Later, though, in college he joined an Armenian campus group and began to take private Armenian language courses, eventually becoming conversational. Meanwhile, Egoyan showed an early interest in the arts, learning classic guitar—which he still plays—and beginning to write plays at age 13. Some of his influences included Harold Pinter, Samuel Beckett, and Eugene Ionesco.

At age 18, Egoyan headed east and enrolled at Trinity College of the University of Toronto, where he earned a bachelor of arts in international relations in 1982. In addition to writing film reviews for the student newspaper, he joined the Trinity College Dramatic Society right away and began to direct his own works, which were not the most well–liked of campus productions. "I was trying to prove that I had something to express," Egoyan told Patricia Pearson in *Saturday Night,* "but at the same time I never wanted to bend to what was popular." Still, he pressed on, starting to create short films and submitting them to festivals. His first project, the 14–minute *Howard in Particular,* was financed by a small grant and equipment from the Hart House Film Board and the University of Toronto. It was about an old man who is retiring from a fruit cocktail factory when its line becomes automated. In Egoyan's senior year, he created a 30–minute short, *Open House,* about a young man who tries to express his love for his father. This aired in the early 1980s on the Canadian Broadcasting Corporation (CBC) as part of its *Canadian Reflections* series.

In the meantime, Egoyan worked in Toronto with the Tarragon Theatre, where he studied playwrighting. After *Open House* was aired, he was given $37,000 in grants from the Ontario Arts Council and the Canada Council, allowing him to shoot his first feature. Egoyan thus put together *Next of Kin,* about a bored young man who pretends to be the long–lost son of an Armenian couple. This established what would become recurring themes in his work: alienation, loss, and identity. The film was accepted for showing at Toronto's Festival of Festivals in 1984, then won the Gold Ducat Award at the Mannheim film festival in Germany the same year. In addition, Egoyan was nominated for a Genie Award—Canada's version of the Oscar—as best director.

While planning *Next of Kin,* which was released in 1984, Egoyan cast actor Arsinee Khanjian, an Armenian who immigrated to Canada from Lebanon at age 17. Though she was married at the time to an Armenian dental student who also had a part in the film, they began a romantic relationship. Her marriage broke up, and the two later married. She has appeared in all of Egoyan's films, and serves as his artistic muse. They have a son, Arshile, who was born in 1993.

Despite *Next of Kin'* s exposure in Toronto and Mannheim and the fact that it found favor among critics, it did not transform Egoyan into an overnight sensation. For a time after its release, he worked as a porter at University of Toronto's Massey College for $5 an hour. However, he soon landed work directing a 1985 television movie titled *In This Corner,* about an Irish–Canadian boxer who gets involved with an Irish Republican Army gunman. After that, he was hired as a freelance director on episodes of *Alfred Hitchcock Presents, The Twilight Zone,* and other American television series, as well as some Canadian programs.

In 1987, with financial help from the Ontario Film Development Corporation, Egoyan made his second feature film, *Family Viewing.* This unsettling drama involves a man who has split with his Armenian wife and tires to erase his past by taping over old home videos with scenes of him and his new lover engaging in sexual acts. Meanwhile, the man's mistress repeatedly propositions the son. The son, in turn, moves in with a woman who works as a telephone sex operator, who counts his father as one of her clients. Attempting to find some stability in his life, he begins visiting his maternal grandmother in a nursing home, where she has been placed by the father, and devises a plan to restore some semblance of order to his family.

Family Viewing gained praise at film festivals worldwide and won an award for best Canadian feature film at the Toronto Film Festival in 1987. Even more astounding, at the Festival of New Cinema in Montreal, legendary director Wim Wenders who was accepting an award for *Wings of Desire* offered his prize money to Egoyan, boosting his reputation even more. However, as Egoyan pointed out to Pearson, "The great myth was that he loved my film so much that he wanted to world to embrace me, but actually he hadn't seen the film. What he really wanted to embrace was the notion that a young film maker needed money more than he did."

Subsequently, Egoyan was able to make *Speaking Parts,* 1989, which continues to explore notions of voyeurism and deception. It is set in a hotel, a venue that Egoyan became familiar with as a teenager when he worked in housekeeping at a hotel in Victoria. The film involves a chambermaid who is obsessed with a coworker, an actor who has had bit parts in some films. She rents and replays his movies nightly. Meanwhile, the actor tries to impress a screenwriter staying at the hotel, and manages to win a part in her upcoming film after seducing her. This enigmatic film moves at a deliberately slow pace and offers a purposely stilted acting style, prompting viewers to remain conscious of the fact that they were watching a film, not a slice of reality, as Hollywood products attempt to do. When *Speaking Parts* first aired at the Cannes International Film Festival in 1989, the third reel burst into flames and the audience had to wait 40 minutes to see the rest. The delay did not water down the critics' praise, however. Though the film was inevitably compared to Steven Soderbergh's *sex, lies, and videotape,* which took the Golden Palm that year at Cannes, some critics found it surpassed the prize winner.

Egoyan was inspired to do his next project, *The Adjuster,* after a fire destroyed his parents' home and store on New Year's Eve in 1989. The story focuses on an alienated insurance adjuster who gets emotionally involved in his clients' lives. His wife, meanwhile, works as a government film censor and often tapes portions of the pornographic films she is assigned to watch. This dark comedy won a Toronto Film Festival Award and a Special Jury Prize at the Moscow Film Festival in 1991. Afterward, Egoyan embarked on a low–budget project resembling a home movie called *Calendar,* in which he also stars as a photographer who takes shots of Armenian churches for calendars. While overseas, his wife abandons him for a tour guide. This intimate effort, with a clever combination of unscripted moments and a postmodern sensibility, was made with help from a German television network, ZDF. It gained a small following among art–house circles and attracted applause from critics.

Just before Egoyan's wife became pregnant with their son, he started making *Exotica,* the tale of a grief–stricken father who has lost a young daughter and frequents a striptease club where he talks to the performers. The plot is complex, also weaving in a character who smuggles exotic pets and a love triangle involving the dancer, the club disc jockey, and the club owner. By the time shooting began on the film, his wife was seven months pregnant. "It was such a perverse film for a new parent to have made," Egoyan remarked to Brian D. Johnson in *Maclean's*. "But it wasn't conceived that way." As it turned out, *Exotica* won the International Critics Prize and was voted best foreign film at Cannes in 1994, in addition to reaping Genies for best picture, best director, and best writer along with another Toronto Film Festival Award. It also became his first widespread commercial success.

In 1997, Egoyan won even more acclaim for *The Sweet Hereafter*, about a group of grief–stricken people in a small Canadian town who try to rebuild their lives after a traumatic school bus accident as an attorney investigates. It was the first time Egoyan directed a feature film script that he did not also write, but it was nevertheless stamped with his trademark hypnotic style. However, the film at the same time branched away from the director's earlier coldness to delve into the emotion of the characters; Owen Glieberman in *Entertainment Weekly* described it as a "metaphysical soap opera." Indeed, Egoyan himself told Brian Johnson in *Maclean's*, "What makes this film such a huge step forward is that for the first time you can identify with the characters. You're not outside them. In all my other films, the characters have been fragments of aspects of my personality. They were people looking for their own identity through rituals or gestures. But they were just shells." *The Sweet Hereafter* reaped a total of eight Genie Awards, including for best picture and best director, and won the grand prize and International Critics Award at Cannes, among other honors at various festivals. It was also nominated for Academy Awards for writing and directing.

Egoyan's next endeavor, *Felicia's Journey*, 1999, was also an adaptation of a novel, this one by William Trevor, who won the Whitbread Prize for it. It concerns a pregnant, destitute Irish girl who ventures to England to locate the boyfriend who left her. Instead, she meets up with a sweet older man who is actually a psychotic killer of homeless girls. This was Egoyan's only film to be shot entirely outside of Canada (he had gone to Armenia for a few scenes in *Calendar*). He wanted to revise the script to move the story into his country, but the author objected. For *Felicia's Journey*, Egoyan won a Genie for screenplay adaptation and was nominated for a Golden Palm at Cannes.

In addition to his major feature films, Egoyan directed the television movie *Gross Misconduct*, 1993, a biographical movie about troubled hockey player Brian Spencer, and the series *Yo–Yo Ma Inspired by Bach*, 1997, featuring the famous cellist. In addition, he has dabbled in opera as well, although reaction to his work in this genre has not always been as positive as for his films. In addition to directing the Canadian Opera Company's production of *Salome* in 1996 and the world premiere of *Dr. Ox's Experiment* for the National Opera in London, England, he also wrote and directed his own opera, *Elsewhereless*, in Toronto and Ottawa in 1998. He developed that project from a play he originally wrote during his days with the Tarragon Theatre. Known for being a conscientious businessman, sticking to budgets and schedules, Egoyan is also considered an honestly nice person with whom to work.

Sources

Books

Contemporary Theatre, Film and Television, volume 15, Gale Research, 1996.

Periodicals

Canadian Forum, December 1991, p. 15; June 1993, p. 25.
Entertainment Weekly, March 24, 1995, p. 47; May 30, 1997, p. 51.
Film Comment, January 1998, p. 32.
Interview, March 1995, p. 58.
Maclean's, October 3, 1994, p. 44; September 22, 1997, p. 13; April 6, 1998, p. 61; September 8, 1997, p. 60; September 13, 1999, p. 54.
New York Times, October 4, 1999, p. B9.
Performing Arts & Entertainment in Canada, Summer 1998, p. 6.
Saturday Night, April 1998, p. 67.
Variety, December 22, 1997, p. 20.

Online

"Atom Egoyan," *Contemporary Authors Online*, Gale Group web site, http://www.galenet.com (December 1, 1999).
"Atom Egoyan," Internet Movie Database web site, http://us.imdb.com (February 9, 2000).

Omar Epps

Actor

Born Omar Hashim Epps, May 16, 1973, in Brooklyn, NY; son of a school principal; children: daughter, Aiyanna.

Addresses: *Publicist*—Leslie Sloan, Baker Winokur Ryder Public Relations, 250 West 57th St. £1610, New York, NY 10107.

Career

Actor. Television appearances include episodes of *ER*, 1996–97; and movies *Daybreak*, 1993; *Deadly Voyage*, 1996; and *First–Time Felon*, 1997. Film appearances include *Juice*, 1992; *The Program*, 1993; *Major League II*, 1994; *Higher Learning*, 1995; *Don't Be a Menace to South Central While Drinking Your Juice in the Hood*, 1996; *Scream 2*, 1997; *Breakfast of Champions*, 1999; *The Mod Squad*, 1999; *The Wood*, 1999; *In Too Deep*, 1999; and *Love & Basketball*, 2000.

Sidelights

Though he is not yet an A–list star like Will Smith or Denzel Washington, Omar Epps is a recognized talent who seems poised to break through to bigger projects anytime. Despite limited opportunities for black actors in Hollywood, he has managed to maintain steady work since his debut in 1992's *Juice*, a gritty tale of urban life. After that, he carried John Singleton's *Higher Learning*, 1995, and was notable in two made–for–television dramas, *Deadly Voyage*, 1996, and *First–Time Felon*, 1997. After a disastrous turn in the much– maligned *The Mod Squad*, 1999, he began to attract positive attention in 2000 for his first turn as a romantic leading man in *Love & Basketball*.

Epps was born on May 16, 1973, in Brooklyn, New York. His mother, an elementary school principal, raised him and his sister, Aisha, on her own. Epps said of his mother, "She always encouraged me to challenge myself, to believe, to follow my heart," as Liz Braun reported in the *Toronto Sun*. Epps penned short stories and poems as a child, he then began writing short screenplays at age ten. "Writing was my first love," he explained to Jack Garner of the *Gannett News Service*. "Acting was an extension of my poetry. I fell in love with acting from the first time I was on stage with my poetry."

Epps went on to attend New York's prestigious High School of the Performing Arts. Show business is nothing new to his family; all of his aunts are singers and his grandfather played upright bass for Sarah Vaughan. Shortly after graduating, Epps landed the part of an ambitious young DJ in Ernest Dickerson's *Juice*, 1992, a bleak tale of life in Harlem for four teenage boys. It costarred late rapper Tupac Shakur.

In 1993, Epps appeared in the television movie *Daybreak* and the film *The Program*, a football drama in which he played a an attractive high–school running back. Despite mixed reviews, Epps received praise for his role. The next year he followed up with another sports film, the baseball comedy *Major League II*. It was considered an overall dud. In 1995, he starred in John Singleton's *Higher Learning*, about the challenges facing students of color at universities. In it, he played a track champion attending school on a scholarship who feels he is being exploited. After this heavy–handed melodrama, Epps returned to comedy again in the 1996 spoof *Don't Be a Menace to South Central While Drinking Your Juice in the Hood*.

By 1996, Epps, at just 23 years old, was featured in *People* magazine's "Young & Hot: 30 Under 30" issue. In addition to his small string of starring roles, he also joined the cast of the popular television hospital drama *ER* for a season in 1996–97 playing eager resident Dennis Gant. Also, he had directed music videos for rap artists Heather B. and Special Ed.

In 1996 Epps made the HBO television movie *Deadly Voyage*, based on the true story of Kingsley Ofosu, a Ghanaian who hides out on a ship with six others in order to immigrate to the United States. All of his fellow stowaways were executed by the crew, but Ofosu managed to escape when the ship docked in France. "I really did relate to this role because it's the story of struggle," Epps told Tonya Pendleton of the *Knight–Ridder/Tribune News Service*. "Kingsley is the voice of the voiceless. It's about young men that love their wives and children but don't have any opportunity, whether they're in Africa or in the ghetto. Over here, we sell drugs. Over there, they stow away because they think it's all opportunity here." The next year, Epps was acclaimed for his role in another HBO movie, *First–Time Felon*, the tale of Chicago gang member Greg Yance, who is sent to a boot–camp–style facility after his conviction on drug charges. Also in 1997, Epps was cast in a small role in the teen horror film *Scream 2*.

The year 1999 would prove to be a banner year for Epps, as he showed up on screen in four films. In addition to a supporting role in *Breakfast of Champions*, an adaptation of the Kurt Vonnegut novel, he also snagged the coveted role of Lincoln "Linc" Hayes in an updated screen version of the groovy 1970s cop show *The Mod Squad*, about three troublesome teens who are offered the option of working undercover for the police department to clear their names. Linc was clearly the ringleader. Director Scott Silver noted in the *Los Angeles Sentinel*, "This was a role that nearly every black actor in Hollywood wanted to play. We saw everybody. Omar was the second to last actor that we saw. He came in, read two lines, and I stopped him and told him he had the part. Omar is cool. No one else could play Linc but him." Claire Dances and Giovanni Ribisi costarred as Linc's hip cohorts, Julie Barnes and Pete Cochrane.

Despite the original show's success and the continuing 1970s nostalgia fad permeating pop culture, *The Mod Squad* flopped. Epps later remarked in *Time* that even he fell asleep during the screening, and immediately said, "This movie in gonna bomb!" He fared slightly better with *The Wood*, a coming–of–age sentimental comedy in which a group of friends reminisce about the past as they try to sober up an AWOL groom and get him to the altar on his wedding day. Though the picture only opened nationwide on 1,100 screens and received lukewarm notices, it was applauded for being a portrayal of middle–class black American lives instead of the stereotypical "gangs and guns" picture. Also in 1999 Epps had a role as an undercover cop in the drama *In Too Deep*, also starring LL Cool J and Pam Grier.

In 2000, Epps was hoping to break through to the top echelon of Hollywood with the sports romance *Love & Basketball*, made by Spike Lee's production company. In it, he played a would–be professional basketball player who falls in love with the tomboy next door, whose talent on the court rivals his and who also wants to turn pro. Epps's real–life girlfriend, Sanaa Lathan, was cast as his costar, though they kept their relationship a secret for the first few weeks of the shoot. They initially met on the set of *The Wood*, and they have a daughter, Aiyanna.

When he is not acting, Epps writes scripts, and hopes to become a filmmaker, telling Pendleton, "I'm not going to be an actor–for–hire forever." In addition, he enjoys making rap music with his group, Wolf Pack. Nothing if not ambitious, Epps also hopes to run his own multimedia company, and he also told Nekesa Mumbi Moody in the *Washington Times*, "Watch, I'm going to be the first black president of the United States. If [Ronald] Reagan can do it, I know I can."

Sources

Books

Contemporary Black Biography, volume 23, Gale Group, 1999.

Periodicals

Arizona Republic, April 20, 2000, The Rep, p. 23.
Calgary Sun, April 18, 2000, p. 49.
Dallas Morning News, August 28, 1999, p. 5C.
Edmonton Sun, July 16, 1999, p. WE25.
Gannett News Service, April 19, 2000.
Jet, May 8, 2000, p. 60.

Knight–Ridder/Tribune News Service, June 13, 1996.
Los Angeles Sentinel, March 31, 1999, p. B4.
Newsday, August 24, 1999, p. B3.
People, November 18, 1996, p. 100.
Time, April 24, 2000, p. 73.
Toronto Sun, March 21, 1999, p. S3.
Washington Times, April 2, 1999, p. C16.

Online

"Omar Epps," Internet Movie Database web site, http://us.imdb.com (July 4, 2000).

Nancy Evans

Internet executive

Born April 12, 1950, in Fairfield, CT; married Seymour Wishman; children: Samantha. *Education:* Skidmore College, B.A. in English literature, 1972, Columbia University, M.A. in literature, 1974.

Addresses: *Home*—New York, NY. *Office*—iVillage.com, 212 Fifth Ave., New York, NY 10010.

Career

Harper's Weekly, associate editor, 1974–76; freelance journalist, 1976–83, contributed to periodicals including Family Circle, Harvard Business Review, Ms., and New York Times Book Review; First Edition, PBS, host, 1983–85; Book–of–the–Month Club, editor, 1985–87; Doubleday publishers, 1987–91; Family Life, editor in chief, 1991–95; iVillage:The Women's Network, cofounder, president, and editor in chief, 1995—, co–chairperson of the board, 1998—.

Awards: Women in Communications Matrix Award for Excellence in Book Publishing, 1989.

Sidelights

As cofounder and president of iVillage.com: The Women's Network, Nancy Evans is in charge of one of the first web sites to specifically gear itself to female online users. However, as its name implies, iVillage is more than just a simple site: It is a network of more than 15 channels, each devoted to areas of interest such as work, personal finance, health, travel, and even pets. Its motto is "Solutions for your life." A former publishing executive, Evans is responsible for the editorial content of iVillage, whether online, in print, or on television, and she is known for her strict attention to quality. Her efforts have helped make iVillage one of the most popular sites on the web.

Evans was born on April 12, 1950, in Philadelphia, and grew up in Fairfield, Connecticut. She received her bachelor of arts in English literature from Skidmore College in 1972 and obtained a master of arts degree in seventeenth–century literature at Columbia University in 1974. That same year took a job as an associate editor at *Harper's Weekly,* a reader–penned national newspaper. After two years on board, she left to forge a career as a freelance writer, contributing to publications such as the *New York Times Book Review, Ms., Harvard Business Review,* and *Family Circle.* In 1978, she cowrote (with Judith Applebaum) *How to Get Happily Published,* a how–to guide on breaking into the writing field that has been in print since its release, and later also cowrote a children's book, *Goodbye, House,* which was reissued in 1999.

From 1983 to 1985 Evans served as the host of the weekly public television show *First Edition,* which was devoted to books and included author interviews; in this capacity she was able to talk to Norman Mailer, Toni Morrison, John Updike, and others. The show was underwritten by the Book–of–the–Month Club, and thanks to that close association, Evans was named editor in chief of the Book–of–the–Month Club in 1985, even though she had scant direct experience in the publishing field. There, she launched the Children's Book–of–the–Month Club. Her performance was so impressive that Alberto Vitale, CEO of the Bantam Doubleday Dell Publishing Group, named her as the youngest–ever president and publisher of Doubleday in January of 1987. In 1989 she received the Women in Communications Matrix Award for Excellence in Book Publishing.

When Evans began heading up Doubleday, the company was ailing. Due to competition, it had lost its position in the marketplace that it had held for years. In 1986, the German publishing group Bertelsmann purchased Doubleday, and committed more money to boost it along. Evans was also instrumental in the turnaround and led it back into prominence. During her time there the firm published 22 best–sellers, and Evans was viewed as being a marketing whiz. However, Doubleday began losing money again and she resigned in 1990.

The next year, along with *Rolling Stone* publisher Jann Wenner, Evans launched a monthly magazine for parents called *Family Life* and served as its editor in chief. She envisioned it to be a kind of mass–media roundtable focusing on lifestyle topics such as family vacations and fashions for kids instead of nuts–and–bolts issues like child safety. Although the market was jam–packed with other parenting magazines, *Family Life* sold well. Evans gained a reputation for high editorial standards, though she was also notorious for being difficult to deal with. She was let go when Wenner sold the magazine to Hachette Filipacchi in 1995.

In the spring of 1995 Evans heard from a friend, Candice Carpenter, who called to ask her to team up with America Online (AOL) to start up an Internet magazine that would help teach newcomers how to use the web. Carpenter had gone online earlier that year for the first time and thought that the web was badly organized, though she was intrigued by the way that people with similar interests used the technology to relate to one another. When she and Evans teamed up along with entrepreneur Robert Levitan, they came up with the idea for a web site where people could discuss family, careers, and health, since they figured there is always keen interest in those topics.

By the fall of 1995, Evans and her partners had rented office space and dubbed their venture iVillage. But after continuing to watch the web grow, they decided that content–based chat sites were not doing well. After realizing that 85 percent of visitors to their site were women, they transformed it into iVillage: The Women's Network. Subsequently, traffic increased from nine million users in June of 1996 to 41 million a year later. The site originally conceived of making money by selling advertising as well as products, but soon realized it was just too early for e–commerce, which would not take off until a couple years later.

However, they did have success with advertisers. Instead of selling simple banner ads, they signed site "sponsors"—Toyota, Nissan, M–G–M, Polaroid, and Starbucks—and gave them a larger role in content in exchange for large commitments of money. Levitan, though, was primarily responsible for lining up the sponsors, and felt he was underappreciated in the firm, according to a *New Yorker* piece by Erik Larson, so he eventually quit. A handful of other executive staffers in their twenties and thirties were also asked to leave so that Evans and Carpenter could bring on more experienced talent, and they both set about to become mentors to the younger employees who remained so that they would grow into seasoned managers.

Though iVillage, like most web sites, has not made any revenues to date and has actually lost about $40 million a year since its inception, it has continued to find investors. Thanks to private financing and an initial public offering in March of 1999, which raised millions, it has stayed afloat. While Carpenter serves as the site's CEO, she and Evans are both co–chairpersons of the board, and Evans is known for creating the content on iVillage. By keeping close tabs on what people are discussing, she tailors the information to her users.

Evans also served for eight years as a contributing editor to *Glamour,* where she wrote a monthly book review column and oversaw book serialization. She now writes a column for *Redbook* called "One Problem, 20 Solutions," and also frequently gives speeches on female entrepreneurship and women's issues. A member of the board of Women in Communications, she lives in New York City with her husband, Seymour Wishman, and daughter, Samantha.

Sources

Periodicals

Fast Company, September 1998, p. 93.
New Yorker, October 11, 1999, p. 76.

Online

"Tech Women Who Inspire Us: Nancy Evans," Girl Geeks web site, http://www.girlgeeks.com July 7, 2000).

"iVillage," Hoover's Online, http://www.hoovers.com (July 7, 2000).

"Nancy Evans, iVillage Cofounder and Editor–in–Chief," iVillage.com: The Women's Network, July 7, 2000.

Garth Fagan

Archive Photos

Choreographer

Born May 3, 1940, in Kingston, Jamaica; son of S. W. Fagan and Louise I. (Walker) Fagan; married and divorced; two children. *Education:* Wayne State University, Detroit, MI, B.A. in psychology, 1968; University of Rochester, NY, D.F.A. 1986.

Addresses: *Office*—Garth Fagan Dance, 50 Chestnut Plaza, Rochester, NY 14604–2318.

Career

Director of Detroit's All–City Dance Company, and principal soloist and choreographer for Detroit Contemporary Company and Dance Theatre of Detroit, 1960s; Educational Opportunities Center, Rochester, NY, teacher, 1970s; Garth Fagan Dance, Rochester, founder, president, artistic director, choreographer, 1973 ; choreographer for Dance Theatre of Harlem, 1986, American Music Theatre Festival, Philadelphia, PA, 1986; New York Shakespeare Festival, 1988, the Jamison Project, New York, 1988; Alvin Ailey American Dance Theatre, 1993; Jose Limon Company, 1994, and *The Lion King* Broadway musical, 1997. State University of New York (SUNY) at Brockport, assistant professor, then associate professor, 1970–85, professor, 1985–86, Distinguished University Professor, 1986—.

Awards: Recipient of Arts and Culture Award, Rochester Black Communicators, 1983; Choreography Fellowship, National Endowment for the Arts, 1983; Distinguished Professor's Award, SUNY, 1986; New York State Governor's Arts Award, 1986; Monarch Award, National Council for Culture and Art,

1987; Guggenheim Fellow, Guggenheim Foundation, 1988; New York Dance and Performance "Bessie" Award, 1990; *Dance Magazine* award, 1990; Program Role Model Award, Learning through Art Guggenheim Museum program, 1992; Lillian Fairchild Award for meritorious production, 1993; Fulbright 50th Anniversary distinguished Fellow Award, 1996; Institute of Art, Jamaica, Gold Mulgrave Medal, 1998; Astaire Award, Drama Desk Award, Outer Critics Circle Award, and Tony Award for best choreography, all 1998, for *The Lion King*. Also awarded the Wayne State University Arts Achievement Award and numerous honorary doctorates.

Sidelights

Choreographer Garth Fagan has been lauded for developing a new kind of dance that draws inspiration from diverse sources. His eclectic style, dubbed the Fagan technique for lack of any other term to possibly describe it, melds elements of ballet, modern dance, and postmodern dance, in addition to pulling from Caribbean, African, and Afro–Brazilian movements. The music that sets the backdrop for the dancers can range from Vivaldi to Miles Davis to John Cage. Fagan's dancers are capable of jumping into the splits without bending their knees, turning in midair, and other feats that help constitute the unique visuals in a performance. Although the company is obviously a collaboration, Fagan allows plenty of room for individuals to express their personalities, which adds a fresh component to the world of dance. The company is highly regarded and has amassed numerous awards, and all of the accomplishments are more astounding considering that when Fagan began working with the dancers, none of them had any experience. His 1991 masterpiece *Griot New York* was perhaps their most impressive showcase. In 1998, Fagan reaped a number of honors, including a Tony Award, for his work choreographing the 1997 Broadway musical *The Lion King.*

Fagan was born on May 3, 1940, in Kingston, Jamaica, the son of S. W. Fagan and Louise I. (Walker) Fagan. His mother's family lived comfortably off profits from their banana plantation, and his father, who was educated at Oxford, served as Jamaica's chief education officer. He did not encourage his son's love of dance, which stemmed from an early interest in gymnastics. As Fagan recalled to William Harris in the *New York Times,* "He was very demanding and believed dance was a waste of time." Nevertheless, while in high school, Fagan joined the Jamaican National Dance Company, headed by Ivy Baxter. She had noticed him in a school production and invited him to join the group. They toured throughout Latin American and even appeared at the inauguration of Cuban leader Fidel Castro. In addition to Baxter, Fagan's major influences include Lavinia Williams and Pearl Primus.

In 1960 Fagan began attending Wayne State University in Detroit, Michigan, in order to get "the American and Motown experience," as he remarked to Valerie Gladstone in *Dance Magazine.* He earned a bachelor's degree in psychology and also did graduate work in the subject, although he continued to study dance, going to New York City during the summers to hone his craft with the likes of Martha Graham, Jose Limon, Alvin Ailey, and Mary Hinkson. He also worked with various dance companies in the Detroit area, including serving as director of Detroit's All–City Dance Company and as principal soloist and choreographer for Detroit Contemporary Company and Dance Theatre of Detroit.

After a back injury, though, in 1970 Fagan accepted a position teaching dance at the State University of New York (SUNY) at Brockport, outside of Rochester. He figured it would be a temporary one–year stint, but as it happened, he stayed for the long haul, and now holds the title of Distinguished University Professor, a rare honor at the school. While teaching at SUNY, part of Fagan's job required him to work at the Educational Opportunities Center in downtown Rochester, which helped prepare disadvantaged students for college. This experience inspired him to begin a mainly black dance troupe starting from scratch with members who had no previous training. He devised the plan in order to give opportunities to black dancers, whose options were often limited (as the company grew, it became more multicultural). Associates were pessimistic. "People asked me why I wanted to start with the bottom of the bucket," he recalled to Eric Taub in the *New York Times.* "I said, 'It's the bottom of the bucket now, but wait.'" Parodying his critics, Fagan named his troupe "The Bottom of the Bucket BUT Dance Theatre."

There was a method to Fagan's madness. He explained that by dealing with novices, he would not have to train them to lose any bad habits they may have picked up. "I wanted to mold them myself," he noted to Taub. In addition, following the lead of Katherine Dunham, Fagan insisted that his dancers become well–versed in all of the arts, including painting, sculpture, film, music, and architecture. He also taught them to move "from the inside out," as he told Taub, without using mirrors or barres, although he added that the company could not afford them anyway.

The first ten years Fagan's company was together, they were basically in training. He acknowledged that it takes about a decade to create a good dancer. Members lived by the idiom, "Discipline is freedom," according to David Vaughan in *Dance Magazine,* practicing diligently in order to execute their exotic movements. They are required to attend two–hour classes twice a day, and no talking is allowed. "The concentration is palpable yet utterly calm," described Vaughan. Fagan insisted that his dancers have full motion in any direction and at any speed, even into the air, without visibly preparing. But there are no pretensions among the troupe. "My dancers are wonderful because they do virtuosic stuff, but they never give you that show–off 'Look what I can do,'" Fagan commented to Francis Mason in *Ballet Review.* "They can do it but they don't praise themselves about it, you know."

Fagan created an energetic style based on a mosaic of rhythms and movements, including the speed and placement of ballet, the dynamics and sense of weight in American modern dance, the unorthodox characteristics of postmodern dance, and the floor work and torso flexibility taken from African styles. Pieces can be set to classical music, including Puccini, Brahms, and Dvorak, or more often, jazz composers such as Thelonious Monk, Miles Davis, Duke Ellington, and Keith Jarrett. Many reviewers have tried to encapsulate the essence of the works, but most have settled on referring to the style as simply the Fagan technique.

Another characteristic of Fagan's work is that it is multifaceted, allowing audiences to see a work numerous times and notice different nuances. Fagan remarked to Harris in the *New York Times*, "We go back to the opera or listen to that symphony several times. Why not give the same kind of analysis and inquisitiveness to contemporary work?" Indeed, as Vaughan commented in *Dance Magazine*, "Fagan's work is often called accessible, and so it is, on an immediate physical, even visceral, level. But he never condescends to his audiences. Every work has its secrets—in structure and subtext—which may become manifest only after repeated viewings." However, Harris did note that some critics have faulted Fagan's works for "being old–fashioned and accompanied by jarring music."

By 1981, Fagan felt his company's progress deserved recognition, so he revised the name to just the Bucket Dance Theater. Later it was changed again, to Garth Fagan Dance. Throughout the 1980s, the group's star began to rise as the dance world began to applaud their achievements. In 1983, the National Endowment for the Arts bestowed Fagan with a three–year choreography fellowship, and in 1985, the National Choreography Project gave him a grant to produce his first ballet, for the Dance Theatre of Harlem. Also in 1985, Fagan was named a Distinguished University Professor at SUNY, a special honor and the first time the title had gone to anyone in the dance department. The next year, Fagan received the New York State Governor's Arts Award and a Guggenheim Fellowship, and in 1990, *Dance Magazine* bestowed him with an award for his achievements in dance. Several local corporations have lent financial support to Fagan's efforts, including Eastman Kodak, Bausch & Lomb, and Xerox.

By the late 1970s and early 1980s, Garth Fagan Dance was becoming well–known for groundbreaking shows such as *Oatka Trail*, 1979, an adagio for three men set to Dvorak's Cello Concerto. As Joan Ross Acocella put it in *Dance Magazine*, the hopping and figure–eight movements "[make] you think of young children with their mothers, the endless escaping and returning. It also makes you think that Fagan has a sense of humor and a certain humility." Other major works in the 1980s included *Of Light, Night, & Melanin*, 1981; *Postscript Posthumous: Ellington*, 1983; *Never Top 40 (Juke Box)*, 1985; and *Traipsing*

through the May, 1987. In addition, although Fagan works mainly with his own company, he choreographed for the Dance Theatre of Harlem in 1986, creating his first work en pointe, *Footprints Dressed in Red*, and choreographed a solo for Judith Jamison, Scene Seen, in 1988. His later outside works include *Jukebox for Alvin*, 1993, for the Alvin Ailey American Dance Theatre, and *Never No Lament* for the Jose Limon Company, 1994.

Despite the impressive performances and many accolades, Fagan did not break through to the mainstream until the *Griot New York* performance opened in 1991. Considered his best work, it was a collaboration with composer and jazz trumpeter Wynton Marsalis, who created the score for a septet, and sculptor Martin Puryear, who designed the costumes and props. In African, a "griot" is a storyteller who passes down oral history through poetry, music, and dance, and in *Griot New York*, Fagan and his colleagues tell the tale of New York City as a celebration of multiculturalism. It was a perfect match: the combination of Fagan's mix of styles with a text about a range of cultures. "I get impatient with people who think they have to negate one culture to support another," Fagan stated to Peter M. Nichols in the *New York Times*. "My perspective is to find the good in each and praise it." The show toured during 1993 and also appeared on *The Tonight Show*; it was also seen on PBS in 1995 as part of the *Great Performances—Dance in America* series.

In 1997 Fagan entered a new realm when he choreographed a Broadway musical, *The Lion King*. He had never seen the animated film when asked to work on the play. "I had to borrow my grandson's video," he told Hilary Ostlere for the *New York Times*. Fagan's background in African and Caribbean rhythms made him a good fit, and also, he had experience with large stage productions from his role in Duke Ellington's street opera *Queenie Pie* and others. In addition, director Julie Taymor was seeking a new perspective and image. Fagan managed to make his distinctive technique shine through while not allowing it to overpower the show. As a result, reviewers praised *The Lion King* as audiences created a sold–out theater night after night, making it one of the year's biggest hits.

At the 1998 Tony Awards, *The Lion King* swept six categories, including best musical and best choreographer. Also that year for the work, Fagan reaped an Astaire Award, Drama Desk Award, and Outer Critics Circle Award. Despite his success on Broadway, Fagan eagerly returned to his company immediately afterward. "I'm extraordinarily proud of *The*

Lion King," he stated to Gladstone in *Dance Magazine,* "but what I really love is concert dance, where I have a clear canvas and can show off my beautiful dancers unencumbered." In 1999, he premiered *Two Pieces of One: Green* and was one of a group of choreographers contributing to a salute to Duke Ellington for the New York City Ballet's spring season.

Fagan's troupe has became one of the premier national companies, touring 27 weeks of the year, and has also ventured to Africa, Asia, Brazil, Germany, Italy, the Netherlands, New Zealand, the Near and Middle East, Switzerland, the West Indies, and more. In the earlier years, the dancers supported themselves with day jobs, from plowing snow to substitute teaching, but as they grew in prominence, they began receiving salaries. Though they do not tour year–round, they are paid 52 weeks of the year and receive medical benefits, something that is highly unusual in the world of dance. Fagan helps pay their salaries with his earnings from his professorship at SUNY, and such support has helped build loyalty throughout the close–knit company.

Selected works

From Before, 1978.
Oatka Trail, 1979.
Of Light, Night, & Melanin, 1981.
Touring Jubilee 1924 (Professional), 1982.
Postscript Posthumous: Ellington, 1983.
Sojourn, 1984.
Never Top 40 (Juke Box), 1985.
Queenie Pie, 1986.
Footprints Dressed in Red (for Dance Theatre of Harlem), 1986.
Traipsing through the May, 1987.
Time after Before Place, 1988.
Scene Seen (solo for Judith Jamison), 1988.
Telling a Story, 1989.
Until, By, & If, 1990.
Griot New York, 1991.
Moth Dreams, 1992.
Draft & Shadows, 1993.

Jukebox for Alvin (for Alvin Ailey American Dance Theatre), 1993.
Postcards: Pressures and Possibilities, 1994.
Never No Lament (for the Jose Limon Company), 1994.
Earth Eagle First Circle, 1995.
Postcards: Pressures and Possibilities, 1995.
Mix 25, 1996.
Nkanyit, 1997.
The Lion King, 1997.
Two Pieces of One: Green, 1999.

Sources

Books

Contemporary Black Biography, volume 18, Gale Research, 1998.
International Dictionary of Modern Dance, St. James Press, 1998.

Periodicals

about time, December 30, 1995.
Ballet Review, spring 1995, p. 18.
Dance Magazine, March 1986, p. 56; November 1990, p. 40; February 1995, p. 84; March 1995, p. 91; November 1998, p. 44; March 1999, p. 107; June 1999, p. 74.
Newsday, September 20, 1992, p. 13.
New York Amsterdam News, June 17, 1998, p. 23; January 5, 1999, p. 24.
New York Times, July 1, 1984, sec. 2, p. 16; December 1, 1991, sec. 2, p. 22; December 6, 1991, p. C3; September 20, 1992, sec. 2, p. 2; October 19, 1997, sec. 2, p. 29; February 1, 1998, sec. 2, p. 40.
Record (Bergen County, NJ), April 26, 1996, p. 11.

Online

Garth Fagan Dance web site, http://www.loopside.com/fagan (October 6, 1999).

Ruth Fertel

Corbis Corporation

Business executive and entrepreneur

Born in 1927 in New Orleans, LA; daughter of an insurance salesman and kindergarten teacher; married and divorced; children: Jerry and Randy. *Education:* Louisiana State University, chemistry degree.

Addresses: *Office*—3321 Hessmer Ave., Metairie, LA 70002.

Career

McNeese Junior College, Lake Charles, LA, instructor, c. 1946; custom drapery seamstress, c. late 1950s; Tulane University School of Medicine, lab technician, c. 1961– 65; owner of Chris Steak House (later renamed Ruth's Chris Steak House), 1965—.

Awards: Restaurateur of the Year, Louisiana Cattleman's Association, 1984; Business Leadership Award, *Restaurant Business* Magazine, 1989; Business Hall of Fame—Junior Achievement of New Orleans, 1989; Woman of the Year, Roundtable of Women, 1990; Business Role Model, Young Leadership Council, 1990; Restaurateur of the Year, Louisiana Restaurant Association, 1990; Entrepreneur of the Year, Retailing, Southern Region, 1992; Golden Chain Award (first female recipient), *Nation's Restaurant News*, 1992; Woman of Achievement, National Association of Woman Business owners, Chicago Chapter, 1993; named one of Top 50 entrepreneurs among women business owners nationwide, National Foundation for Women Business Owners, 1993; Horatio Alger Award, 1995; The

Golden Plate Award, International Association of Foodservice Equipment Manufacturers, 1995; The Beef Backers Award, The Beef Industry Council, 1995; Executive of the Year, *Restaurants and Institutions*, 1997.

Sidelights

Ruth Fertel, founder of the tongue–tying Ruth's Chris Steak House, has created a conglomerate of upscale eateries despite having no experience in restaurants before plunging into the business in 1965. Starting with one small joint, she has expanded her empire to 70 locations and sales of $250 million a year, earned by moving more than 12,000 steaks per day in the compnay's various franchises. The corporation's trademarked slogan, "The Home of Serious Steaks," describes Ruth Chris's giant portions (12 to 22 ounces) and sumptuous flavor. Fertel's steak house has become one of the best–loved institutions in the nation according to various polls, most likely due to the tender, juicy cuts of corn–fed beef that are cooked in her specially designed super–hot ovens. Side dishes such as sweet garlic mashed potatoes and creamed spinach are also favorites, as are desserts such as New Orleans bread pudding with whisky sauce and pecan pie with chocolate cream.

Although the level of cuisine at Ruth's Chris requires a higher price, the atmosphere is laid–back, with no dress code and an unpretentious serving staff. Another key element in Fertel's success has been her adherence to the Golden Rule, treating others—both customers and employees—as she would like to be treated. Her attention to customer service and her respectful relationship with her employees, in addition to her financial success, has led to her status as a role model.

Fertel was born in New Orleans, Louisiana, in 1927, and grew up in the bayou country near the Mississippi River, the daughter of an insurance salesman and kindergarten teacher. A tomboy as a child, she enjoyed climbing trees and hunting and fishing, following in the footsteps of her uncle and grandfather, who often returned from trips with ducks and other game birds. The family also fished shrimp and oysters from the bayou. These delicacies led to her appreciation of fine cuisine, as she would savor the tasty Creole dishes that her great–grandmother would serve up.

At the age of 19, Fertel earned a degree in chemistry from Louisiana State University. Briefly, she taught at McNeese Junior College in Lake Charles, Louisiana, before putting her career on hold in order to wed and have children. Her marriage ended 11 years later, though, and she began to make custom drapes to help support herself and her two sons. In 1961, she found work as a lab technician at Tulane University's medical school, but the wages were low. Fearful that she would not be able to send her teen–age sons, Jerry and Randy, to college, Fertel began to scour the classified ads, searching for a way to start up her own business.

Among the opportunities listed in the newspaper was an ad for a small restaurant for sale called the Chris Steak House. Despite a complete lack of experience in the field and warnings from her lawyer, Fertel mortgaged her house for a business loan. "It was a case of blind ambition, but I thought I could run a steakhouse," she remarked to Patricia B. Dailey in *Restaurants & Institutions*. "And at least it sounded more interesting that running a bar." She admitted being somewhat behind on the basics of business skills at that point, recalling to Joyce Smith in the *Kansas City Star*, "I was so naïve I told them I just needed $18,000 to buy the restaurant. The bank convinced me to take $4,000 more for food and supplies."

Immediately, Fertel embarked on a crash course in the food service industry. Chris Matulich, the original owner of Chris Steak House since opening it in 1927, abruptly left town, abandoning his promise to train her in the business. Thankfully, his employees stayed on and taught Fertel the basics, such as cutting meat, mixing drinks, and cooking steaks. Long days stretched into longer weeks, but in her first six months, Fertel made double her annual salary as a lab technician.

Incidentally, it was part of the deal that Fertel could keep the original name of the eatery as long as it stayed in the same location. In 1976, after the building burned down and she was forced to move, Fertel was required to change the name, which had become integral to the business. She thus added the "Ruth's" in front of the logo in order to keep some consistency, and though it is difficult to pronounce, it has proven to be memorable due to its uniqueness. In addition, it helped deter people from calling her Chris. The new location had another added benefit as well: Because it was bigger, it accommodated more people, and would–be customers who had been dismayed by long waits were now able to get seated quickly, thus boosting business.

In another hardship that Fertel managed to transform into a boon, a few months after taking over the business, Hurricane Betsy swept through the area. "We had no electricity for a week," she explained to Gayle Sato Stodder in *Entrepreneur*, "and I had a cooler full of steaks that would only last three or four days." Facing massive spoilage, she grilled up the inventory and distributed it for free to residents and disaster workers in a nearby area that was hit hard by the storm. Not only was she pegged as a good Samaritan, Fertel built up more loyal clientele, since many of the recipients later returned as paying customers.

In 1976, Fertel began her big rise. That year, she licensed her first franchise. Her decision to open more branches was driven by a customer who moved to Baton Rouge and complained that the 90–mile trek was too difficult. He ended up purchasing the first franchise, and since then, Fertel has seen numerous franchise owners become millionaires. Though Fertel knew nothing about licensing, she figured she would just choose good people, and it worked. In addition, from her early days working alongside her wait staff, she has cultivated a reputation for fairness to workers, paying them a good wage and treating them with respect. As a result, her staff has a low turnover; Dailey in *Restaurants & Institutions* noted, "20–year tenures are hardly uncommon." This allows an excellent level of customer service to flourish—guests can often expect servers to know their specific preferences when they walk in the door, from how they like their drinks mixed to how they want their steaks cooked.

Of course, clientele have to be impressed with the food as well, and by purchasing only the best cuts of beef and cooking them to exacting standards, Fertel's business boomed. Though Ruth's Chris also offers mega–meals featuring three–pound lobsters and other seafood, it remains more famous for its turf than its surf. In addition, the Creole–tinged menu allows for slight variations at its many locations, but customers can expect the key offerings to remain stable. In addition to buying premium ingredients, Fertel developed a specially built broiler to cook meat at 1700 to 1800 degrees Fahrenheit. The custom ovens helped her lock in the juices to keep the high–quality boneless beef cuts delectable, but Fertel also insists that each portion be topped with butter to make them extra mouth–watering. "The butter melts and mixes with the juice from the steak," she noted to Dailey. "Can you imagine anything tasting better?"

Apparently, there are enough people out there who cannot fathom a superior culinary experience. Fertel's empire continues to expand, with 70 locations spread throughout the United States, Puerto Rico, Canada, Mexico, Taiwan, and Hong Kong, with plans to eventually sustain anywhere from 100 to 150 stores. In 1997, Fertel was doubly honored when the prestigious *Robb Report* named her steak house the nation's best restaurant and *Restaurants & Institutions* magazine named her executive of the year. For a time, Fertel remained in place as the firm's chief executive officer but handed over the presidency, but by the late 1990s she was back in place as both, and still personally oversees the opening of each franchise. She is also a much–requested public speaker. In her time off, Fertel enjoys preparing Creole meals for friends and family, reading, spending time with her grandchildren, and traveling to Mexico.

Sources

Periodicals

Atlanta Journal & Constitution, July 30, 1999, p. Q1.
Entrepreneur, September 1997, p. 104.
Fortune, July 6, 1998, p. 34.
Kansas City Star, March 8, 1997, p. B1.
Los Angeles Times Magazine, June 29, 1997, p. 26.
New Orleans City Business, March 24, 1997, p. 22.
Newsday, June 21, 1995, p. A37.
People, October 20, 1997, p. 157.
Restaurant Business, May 1, 1989, p. 154.
Restaurants & Institutions, July 1, 1997; May 15, 1998.
Smoke Affair, Spring 1998.
Washington Times, October 22, 1998, p. M6.

Online

Ruth's Chris Steak House web site, http://www.ruthschris.com (December 28, 1999).

Other

Additional information for this profile was obtained from Ruth's Chris Steak House press materials, December 28, 1999.

Helen Fielding

Author

Born c. 1959, in England; daughter of a mill manager and a homemaker. *Education:* Oxford University, graduated, 1979.

Addresses: *Home*—London, England, and Los Angeles, CA. *Office*—c/o *Independent,*—1 Canada Sq., Canary Wharf, London E14 5DL, England.

Career

BBC–TV, London, England, producer, 1979–89; freelance writer, 1989—; London Independent, columnist, 1995—.

Awards: British Book Award, 1997, for *Bridget Jones's Diary.*

Sidelights

In the summer of 1998, British author Helen Fielding invaded America with her witty novel *Bridget Jones's Diary.* About a kooky, thirtyish, unmarried career woman, the book captured the attention of women who could easily identify with the heroine's daily trials, such as trying to quit smoking, cut down on drinking, and lose weight while fending off inquiries about why she is not married. Bridget Jones tackles all of this while managing to be an expert at droll social commentary, in addition to remaining quirky and lovable. After staying on top of the best– seller charts in England for six months, *Bridget Jones's Diary* was released in more than 30 countries, staying on best–seller lists in the United

States for several months as well. Fielding in 2000 released a sequel, *Bridget Jones: The Edge of Reason.* In addition, a film based on the first book was filmed in 2000 starring Renee Zellwegger as Jones and Colin Firth as love interest Mark Darcy.

Fielding admitted that she borrowed the plot for *Bridget Jones's Diary* from Jane Austen's *Pride and Prejudice,* observing, "I thought that it had been very well market– researched over a number of centuries," according to Andrew Essex in *Entertainment Weekly.* Of course, the updated character appealed to modern women battling high expectations. "I think it's sort of a relief for women," Fielding noted to Patti Thorn in the Denver *Rocky Mountain News.* "Everyone thinks they're supposed to be so perfect in so many areas: go to the gym at 5, then rush to the supermarket, then go to the board meeting, then rush home and fix dinner for 12 people. Women say it's a relief. Instead of stressing out about their imperfections, they can laugh at them."

Fielding was born about 1959 in England and raised in Yorkshire. She is the second of four children of a mill manager and a homemaker. Her father died in 1984 in an auto accident. She graduated from Oxford University in 1979, where she studied English, and while there had a relationship with Richard Curtis, the screenwriter of *Four Weddings and a Funeral.* Beyond that, Fielding has kept much of her personal life very private.

Out of college, Fielding worked for BBC–TV as a producer for a decade, then turned to writing. Her first work was a collaboration with her ex–boyfriend, Curtis, and Simon Bell. Released in 1987, *Who's Had Who: In Association with Berks' Rogerage: An Historical Rogister Containing Official Lay Lines of History from the Beginning of Time to the Present Day.* This spoofed a famous genealogical volume outlining Great Britain's nobility, and the words "rogerage" and "rogister" are plays on the British slang term "to roger," referring to sex.

Fielding's first novel, the satirical *Cause Celeb,* came out in 1994. It involves Rosie Richardson, an administrator of an international food charity who travels to Africa to work for famine relief in order to avoid the fallout from an unhappy love affair with a television host. The author uses flashbacks to recall her bad relationship while she is also relating her current attraction to a young doctor also employed with the relief agency. The two of them return to England to recruit celebrities, including Rosie's former lover, to publicize a possible impending famine in Africa. Though some critics enjoyed the book's wry wit and its pokes at public personalities, others found the humor to be in conflict with the more serious subject matter.

The year after *Cause Celeb* came out, the London *Independent* newspaper asked Fielding to pen a column for them based on one of the characters in her book in order to appeal to young, single, female readers. She began to detail the life of Bridget Jones, an over–thirty woman who discusses her life and concerns with a zany sense of humor and a sharp eye for social commentary. This led to a book deal.

Fielding became a national icon in England with her second novel, *Bridget Jones's Diary.* Structured as stream–of–consciousness journal entries, it chronicles a neurotic Londoner who diligently records the number of cigarettes, alcoholic drinks, and calories she has consumed each day. Jones spends her time smoking and relating details of her disastrous love life—including an ill–fated affair with her boss—with girlfriends over numerous glasses of Chardonnay. This is all in addition to deflecting snarky comments about her ticking biological clock and her parents' constant queries about her marital prospects.

Though many chastised Jones as being a feminist's nightmare, she obviously hit a common note with many other women in similar circumstances. As Carla Power wrote in *Newsweek,* "When Fielding went on book–signing tours, female fans would accost her, claiming, 'I am Bridget Jones!'" Many compared Jones to another neurotic single female character, American television's popular *Ally McBeal.*

Elizabeth Glieck wrote in the *New York Times,* "People will be passing around copies of *Bridget Jones's Diary* for a reason: it captures neatly the way modern women teeter between 'I am woman' independence and a pathetic girlie desire to be all things to all men." Indeed, Fielding quipped in *People,* "Women today are bombarded with so many messages, like we should have Naomi Campbell's body and Madeline Albright's career. Here's someone saying, 'I can't be all these things!' but trying anyway."

Thanks to the success of *Bridget Jones's Diary,* Fielding became a millionaire. The book gave rise to the term "singletons" to describe unmarried women, and "Bridget Jones" entered the popular lexicon to characterize certain kinds of erratic or hedonistic behavior typical of the heroine. Many asked if Fielding based the character on herself. In response, she commented in *People,* "I don't drink, I don't smoke and am a virgin...;yeah, right!"

In addition, Fielding received the 1997 British Book Award for her effort. After this blockbuster, she set to work on a screenplay of her novel, which began production in 2000 by Working Title Films, the same company that put out *Four Weddings and a Funeral.* Also, in early 2000 Fielding published a sequel, *Bridget Jones: The Edge of Reason.* In this second collection of journal entries, Fielding picks up where her first left off, with Jones in a relationship with dashing attorney Mark Darcy. Some critics were cool to the continuation, believing that Jones' appeal was wearing thin. As Veronica Chambers commented in *Newsweek,* "Like a relationship in its sixth month, *The Edge of Reason* challenges our affection." However, Carla Power wrote of the sequel in *Newsweek International,* "Life is full of guilty pleasures, and reading Bridget Jones' diary is one of them."

Fielding keeps an apartment in London's trendy Notting Hill Gate neighborhood and also lives in Los Angeles.

Sources

Periodicals

Daily Telegraph, June 6, 1998; April 13, 2000.
Dallas Morning News, April 16, 2000, p. 9J.
Entertainment Weekly, December 25, 1998, p. 44; March 3, 2000, p. 65.
Harper's Bazaar, July 1998, p. 62.
Newsweek, May 4, 1998, p. 82; March 6, 2000, p. 69.
Newsweek International, November 29, 1999, p. 101.
New York Times, May 31, 1998; February 27, 2000.

People, June 22, 1998, p. 199.
Publishers Weekly, May 13, 2000, p. 22.
Rocky Mountain News, July 12, 1998, p. 1E.
USA Today, May 28, 1998, p. 5D.

Online

"Helen Fielding," *Contemporary Authors Online,*
http://www.galenet.com (June 6, 2000).

Carleton S. Fiorina

Business executive

Born Cara Carleton S. Sneed, September 6, 1954; daughter of Joseph (a federal judge) and Madeline (a painter) Sneed; married and divorced; married Frank Fiorina (a business executive), 1985; children: two stepdaughters. *Education:* Stanford University, B.A. in medieval history and philosophy, 1976; University of Maryland, M.B.A. in marketing, 1980; Massachusetts Institute of Technology, M.S.; briefly attended the University of California law school.

Addresses: *Office*—Hewlett–Packard, 3000 Hanover St., Palo Alto, CA 94304.

Career

Worked as an English teacher in Bologna, Italy; AT&T, Washington, DC, began as account executive, 1980; joined Network Systems division; Lucent Technologies, various executive positions, became president of global service providers division; named president and CEO of Hewlett–Packard, 1999. Board member, Kellogg Co., Merck & Co.; member of U.S. China Board of Trade.

Awards: *Fortune* magazine, named the most powerful woman in business, 1998, 1999.

Sidelights

When Carleton S. "Carly" Fiorina landed the job of president and chief executive officer with computer firm Hewlett–Packard in mid–1999, it

Corbis-Bettmann

stirred much more attention than such corporate announcements normally do. Fiorina herself seemed irked at the coverage. "My gender is interesting, but it is not the story here," she told Karl Taro Greenfeld in *Time*. But she was wrong: It was exactly the story, because male CEOs are named all the time with no such fanfare. As the first woman to take the lead at a Fortune 100 company, and one of just three in the top 500, Fiorina was an exception. Although she remarked to reporters that "the accomplishments of women across the industry demonstrate that there is not a glass ceiling," according to a *New York Times* editorial, the statistics seemed to refute this, since roughly 11 percent of senior executives at Fortune 500 companies in 1998 were women. However, Fiorina's appointment was widely viewed as a positive step in opening doors for women in business, especially since no one could refute the fact that she was chosen for her expertise.

Born Cara Carleton S. Sneed in 1954, Fiorina's unique name has an unusual history: All of the men in her father's family named Carleton died during the Civil War, so in remembrance, all descendants name one family member either Carleton (for sons) or Cara Carleton (for daughters). Fiorina's father, Joseph, is a former law professor and deputy attorney general and serves as a federal appeals judge in

San Francisco, and her mother, Madeline, who is deceased, was an abstract painter who instilled in her daughter "a great zest for life," as Fiorina mentioned to Steve Lohr in the *New York Times*. She credits her parents with being very encouraging, but it could have been difficult for her to excel since she attended five different high schools due to the family's frequent moves. Nevertheless, she was accepted to Stanford University and obtained a bachelor's degree in medieval history and philosophy. Coincidentally, she even worked as a secretary at Hewlett–Packard during the summer before her sophomore year.

After getting her undergraduate degree in 1976, Fiorina enrolled in law school at the University of California, figuring that she would follow in her father's footsteps. The forward–thinker soon realized that she "disliked ... the emphasis on precedent, the singular emphasis on what had gone before," as she explained to Lohr. Fiorina decided after one semester that the field was not for her, but found it difficult to break the news to her dad. Nevertheless, she pursued her own path and, for a while after college, worked a number of jobs, including as an English teacher in Bologna, Italy. In addition, she earned a master's degree in business administration from the University of Maryland in 1980.

That year, Fiorina landed a position at the communications giant AT&T as an account executive, but, at the time, declined to participate in the savings plan there because she could not imagine herself staying a full two years to take advantage of it. She started off in their long–distance phone service business working out of the Washington, D.C. office and handling government accounts and soon built a reputation for her performance. As Elise Ackerman wrote in *U.S. News & World Report*, "Those who know Fiorina say she is the consummate corporate cheerleader." Pegged as management material, she was sent to the Sloan School of the Massachusetts Institute of Technology in 1988, where she received a master of science degree.

At MIT, Fiorina met the head of AT&T's Network Systems group, a low–profile manufacturing division that was considered stagnant. Though some considered it a bad career move, Fiorina thrived in the male–dominated area and shook up some of the conventions. In the early 1990s, she prodded them to think on an international scale, long before others had adopted a global focus. By the mid–1990s, AT&T decided to branch into three separate companies, adding Lucent Technologies and computer maker NCR. Lucent became a leader in cell–phone networking equipment and digital–switching systems that are integral to running the Internet.

In one of her most important accomplishments, Fiorina was chosen to manage Lucent's IPO, or initial public offering of stock, which became one of the largest and most successful IPOs in the nation's history–a $3 billion offering. After that, stock increased roughly tenfold in price by 1999. In addition to overseeing the spinoff, rapidly growing the business, increasing its market share, and developing Lucent's image with a snazzy marketing campaign (she even helped design its red–swirl logo), she was named president of Lucent Technologies global service provider business, its core division, in 1998. *Fortune* that year named Fiorina the most powerful woman in business, and she would soon nab the honor for a second consecutive year.

In July of 1999, the Hewlett–Packard computer company announced that Fiorina would be taking over as president and CEO for Lew Platt. This made Fiorina the highest–ranking woman in the Fortune 500, overseeing a $47 billion business and the world's second–largest computer manufacturer after IBM. It was also noteworthy because she was chosen to head up a major high–technology firm in Silicon Valley, traditionally a mostly male domain. However, Hewlett–Packard, like Lucent, was known for its good track record in promoting women and boasted three women on its seven–member board (the addition of Fiorina made four). In addition, the other main candidate for the CEO job was also female—Ann Livermore, a company insider as an executive and board member.

Progressive as they may be in their internal policies, Hewlett–Packard, the grandfather of technology firms with a 60–year history in Silicon Valley, has been criticized for being too old–fashioned and slow to meet market demands, and its earnings, though high, were lagging. Platt thus sought out someone with a proven history in building large businesses. With her background in the technological firm of Lucent and her reputation for taking businesses into new territory, Fiorina was seen as a beacon to help Hewlett–Packard branch into the Internet. Though the company built a strong brand name with everything from its workhorse inkjet printers to heart monitoring equipment, most analysts agree that the future lies online, which is where competitors IBM and Sun Microsystems have concentrated efforts. Beyond that, Fiorina is known for her ability to sell her product, mainly due to her strategy of maintaining smooth customer relations. She is also famous for her charismatic personality that commands loyalty, an important quality in a leader. Colleagues have recalled her sending balloons and flowers to reward them for doing a great job, although she reportedly has no patience with underachievers.

Fiorina was married and divorced soon after college, and later married Frank Fiorina in 1985. At the time, his daughters from a previous marriage were 8 and 12, and Fiorina told Lohr in the *New York Times*, "I regard them as my own daughters." Frank Fiorina was an executive with AT&T as well, rising to the post of chief information officer of the corporate business unit, but he took early retirement in 1998 at age 49 to help his wife concentrate on her career, and also so that he would not have any professional commitments that would conflict with spending time with her. He now keeps busy as a house husband and volunteer firefighter, and the two of them enjoy boating in their spare time.

Sources

Periodicals

Business Week, August 2, 1999, p. 76.
Christian Science Monitor, August 4, 1999, p. 2.
Dallas Morning News, July 20, 1999, p. 1D; July 25, 1999, p. 5J.
Fortune, October 12, 1998, p. 76.
Newsday, July 20, 1999, p. A35.
Newsweek, August 2, 1999, p. 56.
New York Times, July 21, 1999, p. A22; July 23, 1999, p. C1.
Star Tribune (Minneapolis, MN), July 20, 1999, p. 1D.
Time, August 2, 1999, p. 72.
U.S. News & World Report, August 2, 1999, p. 44,

Online

"Executive Biographies: Carleton (Carly) S. Fiorina," Hewlett–Packard web site, http://www.hp.com (September 30, 1999).

Brendan Fraser

Actor

Born Brendan James Fraser, December 3, 1967, in Indianapolis, IN; son of Peter (a Canadian tourism official) and Carol (a sales counselor) Fraser; married Afton Smith (an actor), September 27, 1998. *Education:* Cornish College of the Arts, Seattle, WA, B.F.A.

Addresses: *Home*—Los Angeles, CA. *Agent*—William Morris Agency, 151 El Camino Dr., Beverly Hills, CA 90212.

Career

Laughing Horse Summer Theater in Ellensburg, WA, member of summer stock company; appeared in productions of *A Midsummer Night's Dream, Arms and the Man, Romeo and Juliet, Waiting for Godot,* and *Moonchildren.* Television appearances include series *Duckman* (voice–over for animation), 1994; and *Fallen Angels,* 1995; movies *Child of Darkness, Child of Light,* 1991; *Guilty Until Proven Innocent,* 1991; and *The Twilight of the Golds,* 1997; and special *Mummies: The Real Story* (narrator), 1999. Film appearances include *Dogfight,* 1991; *School Ties,* 1992; *Encino Man,* 1992; *Twenty Bucks,* 1993; *Son in Law,* 1993; *Younger and Younger,* 1993; *With Honors,* 1994; *In the Army Now,* 1994; *Airheads,* 1994; *The Scout,* 1994; *The Passion of Darkly Noon,* 1995; *Now and Then,* 1995; *Kids in the Hall: Brain Candy,* 1996; *Mrs. Winterbourne,* 1996; *Glory Daze,* 1996; *George of the Jungle,* 1997; *Still Breathing,* 1998; *Gods and Monsters,* 1998; *Blast from the Past,* 1999; *The Mummy,* 1999; and *Dudley Do–Right,* 1999.

Awards: Seattle International Film Festival, Golden Space Needle award for best actor for *Still Breathing,* 1997.

Archive Photos

Sidelights

"I love diversity," actor Brendan Fraser related to Stephen Schaefer in *USA Today.* "If there is a through–line to my characters, it's that they're fish out of water. I love to act roles that allow me to make discoveries as if for the first time." Indeed, his film parts have run the gamut from silly to serious, and most cast him as an outsider or newcomer to either a place or time. This is a characteristic that he seems perfectly suited for, given that during his upbringing, he pulled up roots every couple of years or so due to his father's work and was thus perennially the new kid on the block. However, Fraser is no greenhorn in Hollywood anymore. In virtually all of his pictures, even the flops, he in usually singled out as a bright spot, not only due to his brawny good looks, but also because of his skill at transforming himself completely into his roles. From the goofy fun of *Encino Man, George of the Jungle,* and *Dudley Do–Right* to the more complex *School Ties, The Scout,* and *Gods and Monsters,* Fraser's range has shown few, if any, boundaries.

Fraser was born in Indianapolis, Indiana, on December 3, 1967, to Peter and Carol Fraser and is a dual Canadian–American citizen. His father is a retired Canadian Tourism Commission official and his mother is a sales counselor. As a child, Fraser and his three older brothers, Kevin, Sean, and Regan, moved about every two or three years due to their father's job, living in cities around Canada, the United States, and Europe. Some stops included Amsterdam, London, Ottawa, Cincinnati, and Detroit. He mentioned to Cindy Pearlman in *Seventeen*, "In London, I was 12 or 13, and I would go off on my own and see plays. The stage just fascinated me. I couldn't get enough."

When he was 14, Fraser and his family were in Seattle, Washington, and he began working with the Laughing Horse Summer Theater in Ellensburg, Washington, appearing in repertory classics such as *Waiting for Godot* and *A Midsummer Night's Dream*. After that, he attended high school at Upper Canada College Preparatory School in Toronto, where he was an average student in all but his theater courses, then moved back to Seattle to study drama at the Cornish College of the Arts, where he received his bachelor's degree in fine arts. Soon, he was landing parts with the local Intiman Theater and planned to pursue a master of fine arts at Southern Methodist University in Dallas, Texas.

However, before he made it to graduate school, Fraser landed a one–line role in a Hollywood film. That movie never hit the theaters, but he managed to make a good impression and continued to go on auditions. Unlike most would–be actors, Fraser never waited tables or parked cars; he went straight to the screen. He soon snagged a role playing "Sailor No. 1" in the Vietnam–era drama *Dogfight*, 1991, with River Phoenix and Lili Taylor, which was filmed in Seattle. Through this project, he met a casting agent who sent him to read for another role and introduced him to more contacts. Fraser then made two television movies that year and soon won the major role of Link in *Encino Man*, 1992, about a pair of high schoolers who thaw out a caveman (Fraser) and introduce him to the wonders of the modern era. Even though *Encino Man* was roundly panned, it established Fraser's place as a new Hollywood hunk, and he soon mailed a note to Southern Methodist University letting them know he would not be enrolling.

After *Encino Man*, Fraser really turned heads as the lead in the 1992 picture *School Ties*, one of Ben Affleck and Matt Damon's early movies. He actually filmed this picture before *Encino Man*, but it came out later in the year. In it, he played David Green, a Jewish boy who conceals his ethnicity from fellow students at a prep school in the 1950s. Next he reprised the character of Link in the Pauley Shore

duds *Son in Law*, 1993, and *In the Army Now*, 1994. He continued to run the gamut of roles, playing another preppy part in *With Honors*, 1994. In that project, his character is a Harvard student who befriends a homeless man. That same year, he also played one of the three rocker dudes who try to commandeer a radio station in *Airheads*.

Although Fraser's roles in *Encino Man* and *Airheads* led to many offers that he described as "'Hey dude, let's party!' stuff," he was outstanding in a more challenging role in *The Scout*, costarring Albert Brooks, as an eccentric baseball player and his mentor. For this film, at the age of 25, he commanded a reported $1.5 million salary. Unlike his character, however, Fraser had little aptitude for baseball in real life, as fans soon discovered: "I was asked to pitch the opening pitch of a Mariners game," he told Rebecca Ascher–Walsh in *Entertainment Weekly*, "and it was miserable. I pitched the worst slider you've ever seen." Off the field and back on camera, Fraser was impressive once again in *The Passion of Darkly Noon*, playing an orphan who tries to balance his religious beliefs with his lust for a woman (Ashley Judd). This allowed him to display his range even further. His next project, *Mrs. Winterbourne*, in which Fraser played a set of twins, fared poorly with critics and audiences, but he was singled out for praise. A reviewer for the *New Republic* noted that in the film, Fraser "suggests Robert Montgomery, the debonair charmer and skillful light comedian of the '30s and '40s. Montgomery later tried his hand at darker roles, as Fraser may, too, but in the lighter ones Montgomery could always rely on our chuckling along with him, and Fraser has much the same gift."

Fraser's next big project was anything but dark, however, as he tackled the dim yet lovable title character in *George of the Jungle*, based on the animated cartoon from the 1960s. "I've always been a fan of Tarzan films," Fraser remarked to Jeanne Wolf in the Minneapolis *Star Tribune*. "I've seen what I think must be the original that was made in 1918. It was *Tarzan the Ape Man*, starring Elmo Lincoln, who was rather potbellied but still one of my favorites." Unlike Lincoln, Fraser buffed up for the part, which required wearing a loincloth throughout. He had to go on a diet and spent six months working out. "I guess George's jungle had a Stair–Master in it," he mentioned to Chuck Arnold in *People*. Though this built Fraser's image as a sex symbol, the film was geared toward kids.

Continuing to avoid typecasting, Fraser also played a gay opera director in a 1997 cable movie, the acclaimed *The Twilight of the Golds*, and was also cast as the romantic lead in *Still Breathing*, for which he earned a best actor award at the 1997 Seattle International Film Festival. In 1998, he showed up in the highly lauded *Gods and Monsters*, opposite respected British Shakespearean actor Ian McKellen. The film is a fictionalized account of the last days of real–life Hollywood director James Whale, the creative force behind 1931's classic horror film *Frankenstein*, as well as *Bride of Frankenstein* and *The Invisible Man*. McKellen as Whale befriends Fraser as Clay Boone, a coarse–mannered lawn care contractor whose sensitive side is revealed. The film draws obvious parallels between the misunderstood Frankenstein monster and Fraser's character. Both McKellen and Fraser were roundly applauded for their work, as was Lynn Redgrave, who played Whale's dowdy housekeeper.

After the critical hit of *Gods and Monsters*, in early 1999 Fraser appeared in *Blast from the Past*, in which he emerges in the 1990s after dwelling in a bomb shelter with his odd parents since 1962. Many reviewers drew parallels between this role and his early *Encino Man*, which also cast him as a newcomer to the modern age. For his "gee–whiz" attitude, Fraser modeled his performance on the style of Dick Van Dyke, with his clean–cut, old– fashioned sensibility but his unselfconscious ability for physical comedy as well. Later that year, he had a smash hit with *The Mummy*, starring as part of a team of archaeologists that unearth a malevolent ancient Egyptian body.

Although many critics were not appreciative of *The Mummy*, others dubbed Fraser the next Harrison Ford due to his swashbuckling leading man antics, and audiences made it one of the year's blockbusters. For this project, Fraser endured 130–degree heat while filming in Morocco, but as he mentioned to Jim Slotek in the *Toronto Sun*, he was ready for "a straight–ahead action picture" and "relished the adventure of it all, being in the Sahara Desert." He was also excited about the film because, as he told Liz Smith in *Newsday*, it is "true to the original [Boris] Karloff version. It's a 'monster' movie, yes, but also it is a love story." *The Mummy* drew $44.6 million in its first weekend, the most ever for a non–summer opener, thus lifting Fraser's profile in the industry. Subsequently, his salary was boosted to an estimated $10 million per film. Also in 1999, Fraser landed another real–life cartoon role as the lead in *Dudley Do–Right* an appropriate part, considering that his great–great– grandfather was a Royal Canadian Mounted Policeman in the late nineteenth century.

Fraser is a stocky six feet, three inches tall with dark brown hair. Most interviews note his unassuming, polite manner, almost to the point of shyness. He met fellow actor Afton Smith at Winona Ryder's Fourth of July barbecue in 1993, and they married on September 27, 1998, after a romantic yet bungled proposal on the Seine in Paris. Too shy to come ask her outright, he popped the question in a creative way: He secretly pinned a note that read, "Will you marry me, Afton?" inside his jacket and then set a Polaroid camera on the edge of the bridge with a time to capture a picture of the two of them as he flashed open his coat. Once the image developed, though, the sign was too small to read. Afton asked if it was a price tag, and opened Fraser's coat to check, at which time she saw the sign. "I was such a clumsy clodhopper I dropped something," he related to Jan Stuart in *Newsday*. "I figured [since] I was already on bended knee I might as well say the words and come out with the ring . She wept. I wept." Fraser and his wife have a contemporary home in Los Angeles, and he remains an avid snapshot taker with his collection of vintage Polaroids.

Sources

Books

Contemporary Theatre, Film and Television, volume 16, Gale Research, 1997.

Periodicals

Calgary Sun, May 6, 1999, p. 45.
Cosmopolitan, June 1994, p. 86; April 1998, p. 206.
Dallas Morning News, May 8, 1999, p. 5C.
Entertainment Weekly, October 7, 1994, p. 50; August 22, 1997, p. 19.
Independent, December 12, 1997, p. 10.
Interview, August 1994, p. 108.
Jerusalem Post, June 9, 1999, p. 11.
Mademoiselle, July 1994, p. 66.
New Republic, May 13, 1996, p. 28.
Newsday, February 28, 1994, p. B3; November 12, 1998, p. B6; February 7, 1999, p. D4; March 1, 1999, p. A13.
Ottawa Sun, August 22, 1999, p. S3.
People, August 11, 1997, p. 146; May 31, 1999, p. 69; July 5, 1999, p. 115.
Premiere, June 1994, p. 60.
Seventeen, August 1994, p. 153.
Star Tribune (Minneapolis, MN), July 18, 1997, p. 12E.
Toronto Star, February 12, 1999; May 10, 1999.
Toronto Sun, May 8, 1999, p. 24.
TV Guide, May 1, 1999, p. 7.
USA Today, February 11, 1999, p. 10D.

Online

"Brendan Fraser," Internet Movie Database web site, http://us.imdb.com (September 28, 1999).

"Brendan Fraser," Mr. Showbiz web site, http://mrshowbiz.go.com (September 28, 1999).

Lucian Freud

Artist

Born Lucian Michael Freud, December 8, 1922, in Berlin, Germany; immigrated to England, 1932, became naturalized citizen, 1939; son of Ernst (an architect) and Lucie (Brasch) Freud; married Kathleen Garman Epstein, 1948 (dissolved, 1952); married Caroline Maureen Blackwood (dissolved, 1957); several children, including daughters Bella, Esther, and Ib.

Addresses: *Office*—c/o Acquavella Galleries Inc.,18 East 49th St., New York, NY 10021.

Career

Painter. Slade School of Art, instructor, 1948–58; Norwich School of Art, visiting assistant, 1964–65. British Merchant Navy, 1941. Individual exhibits include Lefevre Gallery, London (with Julian Trevelyan and Felix Kelly), 1944; London Gallery, (with John Craxton), 1947; Hanover Gallery, London (with Roger Vieillard), 1950; London Gallery, 1951; Hanover Gallery, London (with Martin Gray), 1952; Hanover Gallery, London, 1954; *Biennale,* Venice, Italy, 1954; Hanover Gallery, London, 1956; Marlborough Fine Art, London, 1958, 1963, 1968; Gray Art Gallery, Hartlepool, County Durham, 1972; Anthony d'Offay Gallery, London, 1972; Hayward Gallery, London (toured the U.K.), 1974; Anthony d'Offay Gallery, London, 1974; Tate Gallery, London (with Francis Bacon), 1977; Anthony d'Offay Gallery, London, 1978, 1982; Hayward Gallery (retrospective), London, 1988; Metropolitan Museum of Art (retrospective), New York, 1993; Tel Aviv Museum, 1996; Gallery of Modern Art, Edinburgh, 1997; Tate Gallery, London, 1998; Acquavella Gallery, New York, 2000.

The Gamma Liaison Network.

Group exhibitions include *Recent Paintings,* Lefevre Gallery, London, 1946; *La Jeune en Grand Bretagne,* Galerie Ren[0082] Drouin, Paris, 1948; *21 Modern British Painters,* Vancouver Art Gallery, 1951; *British Painting 1952-1977,* Royal Academy of Arts, London, 1977; *8 Figurative Painters,* Yale Center for British Art, New Haven, CT, 1981; *Aspects of British Art Today,* Metropolitan Art Museum, Tokyo, 1982 (toured Japan); *A School of London,* Louisiana Museum, Humlebaek, Denmark, 1987 (traveled to Venice and Dusseldorf); *The British Picture,* L.A. Louver Gallery, Venice, California, 1988; *Encounters—New Art from Old,* National Gallery, London, 2000.

Works are held in the collections of the Tate Gallery, London; the Arts Council of Great Britain, London; Walker Art Gallery, Liverpool; The Museum of Modern Art, New York; and Beaverbrook Foundation, Fredericton, New Brunswick, Canada.

Awards: Companion of Honour; Order of Merit, 1993.

Sidelights

While history is full of artists who were poverty–stricken and unappreciated their entire lives only to become legendary after their deaths, there are also those who have gained a solid reputation and made a tidy profit off of their art while alive. One such contemporary artist is Lucian Freud, a German–born figurative painter who has lived and worked in England most of his life. The familiar name is no coincidence; his grandfather was renowned German psychoanalyst Sigmund Freud. The artist had his first exhibition in 1944, and has gained acclaim ever since, though he did not make waves in the United States until the late 1980s. In 1998, Freud's work *Large Interior, W11 (After Watteau)* brought in 3.5 million British pounds, or more than $2 million in 1998 exchange rates, the largest sum ever paid for a British painting. Later that year, he also set the European record for a piece of contemporary art, as *Naked Portrait with Reflection* sold for 2.8 million British pounds (roughly $1.7 million in 1998 exchange rates).

The bulk of Freud's body of work consists of nude figures (though he prefers the term "naked), painted in a realistic yet gloomy style using subdued colors often tans, browns, and ivories usually laid on thickly. Most works, until the early 1990s, were very small. Though his portraits tend to accentuate what many would call flaws varicose veins, sores, cellulite, and the like Freud does not try to make his subject unappealing; he merely paints what is there. As he noted to John Richardson in *Vanity Fair*, "I paint people not because of what they are like, not exactly in spite of what they are like, but how they happen to be…. I don't want to have a type any more than I want to have habits."

Freud was born on December 8, 1922, in Berlin, Germany, the second of three sons of Ernst, an architect and the younger son of Sigmund Freud, and Lucie (Brasch) Freud. He and his two siblings, Stephen and Clement, all bore the middle names of the three archangels, Gabriel, Michael, and Raphael. Viewing the rise of the Nazis and Jewish persecution, his family relocated to London in 1933, where he received a spotty education at Dartington Hall, a progressive public school, and at Bryanston in Dorset. At Dartington, he admittedly tended goats in lieu of going to class, and explained to John Spurling in the *Independent on Sunday*, "I was very solitary. I hardly spoke English. I was considered rather bad–tempered, of which I was rather proud."

While at Bryanston, Freud in 1937 completed his only known sculpture, that of a three– legged sandstone horse with a neolithic feel. Thanks to that piece, the following year he was admitted to London's Central School of Arts and Crafts, and then attended the East Anglican School of Painting and Drawing on and off from 1939 to 1942. There,

he studied with Cedric Morris, who had a major influence of Freud's work. He took time off in 1941 to sail with the British Merchant Navy.

Given Freud's background, some observers have been able to read in his early portraits the influences of German artists of the 1920s such as Otto Dix and George Grosz, and of the "Neue Sachlichkeit" (New Objectivity). However, Robert Hughes suggested in *Time*, "Actually the basis was much earlier: Albrecht Durer, whose fixedly staring, ultra-detailed watercolors set Freud's first standards about the inspection of faces and bodies." In addition, Richard Ingleby wrote in the *Independent*, "Other, less specific influences creep in from time to time, more a matter of mood than anything defined—the spirit of Ingres, or of early Flemish art—a kind of fine–edged precision that comes in about 1943 as he started to draw and paint with increasing clarity."

Around 1958, Freud began using stiffer brushes made out of hog hair instead of sable, and this coarser effect "forced broader and more pictorially solid shapes into the paint with which he depicted flesh, helping him compose the body's structure in terms of twisting and displacement," according to Hughes in *Time*. Though many of Freud's works are nude portraits, he is also fond of using dogs in his pictures, and his body of work includes studies of plants or views of a backyard. He never paints from photographs or from initial sketches, as many artists do, preferring to work directly with the model from start to finish.

In addition, Freud himself never uses the term "nude" to describe his works, favoring "naked" instead. Critics have noted that this is apt, since his portraits do indeed lay bare the subject, paying attention to every detail, flattering or (more often) not. But he has also been accused of misogyny, since oftentimes his perspective is from a high angle looking down on the model, who is often splayed in an odd fashion and lit using bright, 200–watt electric bulbs.

In addition, many of Freud's subjects had not previously posed in the nude, creating an awkwardness that shows through in the person's demeanor. Thus, some have criticized his "nakeds" as being perhaps more harsh on his sitters than they could have been with different poses, natural lighting, or more experienced models. But Freud told Richardson in *Vanity Fair*, "I don't use professional models because they have been stared at so much that they have grown another skin. When they take their clothes off, they are not naked; their skin has become another form of clothing."

It should be noted that a great number of Freud's models have been his family members or close acquaintances, and have consented freely to the arrangement. In addition, they are allowed to choose their own poses, which is a great necessity when some of them must endure 80 or more sittings. But often the most comfortable positions are not those that translate gracefully to the canvas. Many of the models' slack positions made them appear sleeping or perhaps even dead. In addition, the artist has painted males in the same direct fashion, with legs spread and genitals lolling. Freud himself once remarked, according to Hughes in *Time*, "I think the idea of misogyny is a stimulant to feminists, and it's rather like anti–Semites looking for Jewish noses everywhere."

Not surprisingly given his approach and technique, Freud's nudes do not bring to mind the pink, plump freshness of bodies in many paintings from antiquity. In addition, they do not use metaphor even when the canvas is occupied by other objects, such as, say, a rat or a plate of eggs. But the pictures do not just hang emptily, either: as Martin Gayford cited in the *Sunday Telegraph*, Freud considers putting together a painting different from casting a play in that "the people themselves are the drama." He chooses subjects who intrigue him personally.

Though Freud had not stormed the international art world, he had developed of a cult following for his small, dour portraits and sprawling nudes, and became well–respected in England and Europe. From the 1940s to the 1980s he enjoyed several individual and group exhibitions in London, Paris, Tokyo, and Denmark. Finally, when a British Council retrospective toured to the Hirshhorn Museum in Washington, D.C. in 1988, Hughes of *Time* magazine wrote a catalog introduction that labeled Freud "the greatest living realist painter." This had a major impact on Freud's career, and he started gaining more attention in America.

Just as Freud's star began to rise in the international art world, he began to work with much bigger canvases. Throughout his career, the bulk of Freud's work had been done on a small scale. Sanford Schwartz observed in the *New Republic*, "Freud began as a miniaturist of sorts, and one of his real accomplishments over the years was keeping his appreciation for the tiniest detail even as he was mastering the art of oil painting with brushy brushes. His small, tightly cropped pictures are among his best." As his canvases grew to several feet on a side, he branched out from painting his extended family and friends to recruit larger models, including shaven and pierced performance artist Leigh Bowery, and the bountiful Sue Tilley, known as "Big Sue."

In May of 1998, Freud's *Large Interior, W11 (After Watteau)* became the most expensive British painting sold at auction at Sotheby's New York when it brought in more than $2 million. This shattered the record set by David Hockney in 1989. However, Freud did not see any of this money, since he had sold it outright to his former dealer, James Kirkman, in 1983, for less than 100,000 pounds. Making matters worse, Freud and Kirkman had been together 20 years but had a falling out in 1992. Still, Lucinda Bredin wrote in the *Sunday Telegraph*, "At first glance, the case seems to confirm the ancient stereotype of an artist, distracted by the Promethean struggle of making a masterpiece, being ripped off by an opportunistic businessman, who buys when the work is cheap and sells when the artist has gained a reputation. But most in the business wish Kirkman well, adding that Freud usually preferred to sell works to dealers, rather than place them on consignment." Also, in December of 1998, Freud's *Naked Portrait with Reflection*, painted in 1980, reached new heights for a piece of contemporary art by a living European artist when it sold for about $1.7 million.

Despite Freud's erratic schedule he often likes to paint in the wee hours and his tendency to not paint flattering pictures of his models, he was approached to do a portrait of the Queen of England. The concept was not unthinkable, as she had bestowed upon him the two highest civilian orders, the Companion of Honour and the Order of Merit. Negotiations between the Queen's most trusted confidant, Sir Robert Fellowes, and Freud (one of Fellowes's personal friends), continued for six years before the artist finally agreed in 1999 to paint Her Majesty. However, he insisted that she travel to his west London studio for sittings.

Although Freud is often asked to paint famous people, with few exceptions he tends to stay with subjects whom he knows well. He has caused controversy by rejecting suggestions that he paint notable names including the Pope, Princess Diana, and composer Andrew Lloyd– Webber's wife Madeline. In fact, Jo Knowsley reported in the *Sunday Telegraph* that Freud once complained he had been "threatened with the offer of free tickets to [Webber's] shows." But in 1998, he surprised even close friends when he agreed to paint Mick Jagger's wife Jerry Hall, who was heavily pregnant at the time. The nude portrait, *Eight Months Gone*, which measures just four by six inches, appeared in an exhibit at London's Tate Gallery which opened in June of 1998. Later, Freud also painted Hall breast–feeding her new son, Gabriel.

Freud's cluttered studio is located in a home in Holland Park, a residential area of London just west of Notting Hill Gate, and he also owns an elegant eighteenth–century town house. He is known to be prickly toward the media, and litigious when it comes to reports about him. However, Richardson in *Vanity Fair* noted that he is "remarkably considerate" toward his models, who often find themselves opening up and confiding in him.

Though Freud vehemently guards his personal history, it is known that he was married twice. First, in 1948 he wed Kathleen "Kitty" Garman Epstein, the daughter of sculptor Jacob Epstein, but the marriage dissolved in 1952. Later he married Caroline Maureen Blackwood, but the union broke up in 1957. He has several children by a number of women, including daughters Bella, a designer; Esther, a novelist; and Ib, who has modeled for him. Freud spends most of his time in his studio, rarely quitting before midnight, and thus has little social life. He sometimes indulges in betting on horse races.

Sources

Books

Contemporary Artists, fourth edition, St. James Press, 1996.

Periodicals

Daily Telegraph, September 4, 1999, p. 2; January 22, 2000, p. 2; April 13, 2000.
Independent, April 8, 1997, p. 5.
Independent on Sunday, December 13, 1998, p. 26.
Jerusalem Post, November 29, 1996, p. 26.
New Republic, February 14, 1994, p. 31.
Newsweek, June 8, 1998, p. 62.
Sunday Telegraph, March 8, 1998; November 15, 1998, p. 8; February 21, 1999.
Time, December 27, 1993, p. 74.
Vanity Fair, May 2000, p. 204.

Ann Fudge

Business executive

Born Ann Marie Brown, April 23, 1951, in Washington, D.C., daughter of Malcolm R. Brown (a U.S. Postal Service administrator) and Bettye (a manager at the National Security Agency; maiden name, Lewis) Brown; married Richard E. Fudge, Sr. (a consultant); children: Richard Jr., Kevin. *Education:* Simmons College, B.A. (with honors), 1973; Harvard Business School, M.B.A., 1977.

Addresses: *Home*—Westport, CT. *Office*—Kraft Foods, Inc., 555 S. Broadway, Tarrytown, NY 10591.

Career

General Electric Co., Bridgeport, CT, personnel executive, 1973–75; General Mills Corp., Minneapolis, MN, marketing assistant, 1977–78, assistant product manager, 1978–80, product manager, 1980–83, marketing director, 1983–86; Kraft General Foods, White Plains, NY, associate director of strategic planning, 1986–89, vice president for marketing and development in the Dinners and Enhancers division, 1989–91, general manager of same division, 1991–93, executive vice president, 1993 , president of Maxwell House Coffee division, 1994 .

Awards: COGME fellow, 1975–76; Young Women's Christian Association (YMCA) Leadership Award, 1979; named one of "21 Women of Power and Influence" by *Black Enterprise,* 1991; named one of the most powerful women in business by *Fortune,* 1998, 1999.

Sidelights

One of the most influential corporate executives in the United States is Ann M. Fudge, executive vice president of Kraft Foods, Inc. North America's largest food company and president of their Coffee and Cereals division. "To get to her perch, the 44–year–old had to crash through not merely the glass ceiling that stymies white women but an all–but–insurmountable 'concrete wall' that researchers say blocks blacks and other minorities from companies' upper echelons," wrote Judith H. Dobrzynski in the *New York Times.* Throughout the years, Fudge has proven herself time and again with successful campaigns that have freshened up old brands and made them healthy sellers. She is humble about her reputation as a marketing wiz, though, preferring to bestow much of the credit on her colleagues. Her theory is to "give your team the basic direction and let them run with the ball," Fudge explained in *Black Enterprise.* Indeed, Michael A. Miles, former chief executive of Philip Morris (Kraft's parent company) told Dobrzynski, "She's a low–key and confident manager who gets the most out of the people who work for her."

Fudge was born on April 23, 1951, in Washington, D.C. to Malcolm R. and Bettye (Lewis) Brown. Her father worked as U.S. Postal Service administrator, while her mother was a manager at the National Security Agency. They taught their daughter the value of a good education, and sent her to Roman Catholic schools all the way through the twelfth grade. She would later give credit to the nuns for challenging her scholastically. In high school, Fudge held a position on the Teen Board of a local department store, where she advised buyers on current fashions. This led to a trip to New York to visit fashion magazines.

After high school, Fudge attended Simmons College, a respected women's school in Boston, Massachusetts. She married Richard E. Fudge during her sophomore year and had her first son, Rich Jr., before she graduated. Fudge and her husband scheduled classes at different times so they could care for the baby, and when that was not possible, she paid for babysitters by giving them food. Fudge graduated with honors in 1973 and had another son, Kevin, soon afterward.

Out of college, Fudge landed a job as a personnel executive at General Electric in Bridgeport, Connecticut. After two years there, she enrolled at the Harvard University Graduate School of Business and earned her master's degree in business administration in 1977. Subsequently, she was hired as a marketing assistant at General Mills in Minneapolis, Minnesota, the sixth–largest food producer in the United States. By 1978, Fudge had been promoted to assistant product manager, and then rose to product manager in 1980, responsible for four brands simultaneously. Then, from 1983 to 1986, she served as a marketing director, becoming the first woman and the first African American to earn that title at General Mills. While on the job at General Mills, one of her proudest accomplishments was helping to develop and introduce the Honey Nut Cheerios brand, which became one of the nation's best–selling cereals.

In 1986, Fudge was poised to become a general manager at General Mills when she decided to take another job offer in order to be closer to her ill mother. She was hired at General Foods in White Plains, New York, as a director of strategic planning. The firm, a division of Philip Morris, Inc., is the country's largest manufacturer of consumables. In 1989 she moved up to vice president for marketing and development in the $600 million Dinners and Enhancers division, then in 1991 was promoted to general manager of that division.

In this position, Fudge oversaw brands such as Stove Top Stuffing Mix, Minute Rice, Log Cabin Syrup, and Good Seasons salad dressing. Such products at the time were facing stiff competition from cheaper store–label brands, but through slick ad campaigns, repackaging, and promotions like recipe clubs, Fudge managed to achieve double–digit sales and earnings for her division when the rest of the

corporation saw only a one percent revenue increase in 1991. Fudge also used innovative techniques such as offering coupons to kids that they could use to send in for products like Frisbees. She used this strategy in her successful "Wacky Warehouse" campaign to revitalize the sagging Kool–Aid powdered drink mix.

In addition, Fudge had a hit as head of the marketing team that came up with the "Why Fry?" campaign for Shake N' Bake, a breaded coating for meat. The product had not been the focus of television ads for several years, but after the new campaign, complete with commercials, coupons, print ads and some new flavors, sales were boosted into the double digits. The focus of the ads on healthier eating tied in with the nation's increasing attention to dietary concerns.

General Foods merged with Kraft Foods in 1994, and Fudge was named executive vice president as well as president of Maxwell House Coffee, one of the corporation's top divisions. It included the brands Maxwell House, Sanka, Brim, Gevalia, and Yuban. Maxwell House was second in the market with 24.6 percent of the share, running just behind Folger's which held 27.6 percent. Therefore, one of Fudge's first orders of business was to try to overtake the competition. However, she landed her new post at a time when store coffee brands were being increasingly edged out of the market by new specialty blends from firms like Starbucks. Acknowledging this, Fudge immediately left for Seattle to prowl around the city's coffee scene, sipping different brews and questioning the proprietors.

As a result, Fudge decided to offer a line of flavored Maxwell House coffees like French Vanilla and Irish Cream in order to target younger java drinkers. Part of her plan centered on offering a "coffeehouse" image but with the low price of Maxwell House and the convenience of buying it in the supermarket. She revived the "good to the last drop" slogan as a means of introducing a "retro–chic" image, and managed to double the division's earnings. In September of 1997 she was promoted to president of the new Coffee and Cereals division, which accounted for $2.7 billion of Kraft's $16.8 billion sales revenue. In both 1998 and 1999, *Fortune* magazine named her one of the 50 most powerful women in business.

In addition to her responsibilities at Kraft, Fudge sits on the board of directors of the Federal Reserve Bank of New York, General Electric, Liz Claiborne, Inc., AlliedSignal, and Catalyst. She has also served as vice president and president of the Executive Leadership Council, a nonprofit group of black corporate managers and directors. She and her husband live in Westport, Connecticut. Balancing work and family was not an easy road for Fudge, but she has succeeded. She told Dobrzynski in the *New York Times* that when her sons were young she would lay out clothes for them days in advance, and on Sundays she would cook meals for the following few days. "And my husband helped," she noted.

Sources

Books

Contemporary Black Biography, volume 11, Gale Research, 1996.

Periodicals

Advertising Age, February 3, 1997, p. S2.

Black Enterprise, August 1991, p. 52; February 1993, p. 94; June 1994, p. 63; August 1994, p. 68; August 1997, p. 64.

Fortune, October 12, 1998, p. 83; October 25, 1999, p. 103.

New York Times, May 11, 1995, p. D1.

Online

"Kraft Foods, Inc.," Hoover's Online web site, http://www.hoovers.com (March 17, 2000).

Sonia Gandhi

AP/Wide World Photos

Politician

Born Sonia Maino, December 9, 1947, in Turin, Italy; daughter of Stefano (a construction company owner) and Paolo Maino; married Rajiv Gandhi (a pilot and politician); children: son, Rahul, and daughter, Priyanka.

Addresses: *Home*—10 Janpath St., New Delhi, India.

Career

Leader of India's Congress party, 1998—; representative in Indian parliament, 1999—.

Sidelights

Running mainly on the basis of her famous name, Sonia Gandhi, a homemaker who never held political office in her life, was elected head of India's Congress party in 1998 and won a seat in parliament the next year. Although she was not even a natural–born Indian—a fact that caused great criticism among opponents and some citizens—she managed to capture the admiration of the masses thanks to her ties to the nation's prominent Nehru–Gandhi family, who ruled during three generations. As the wife of Rajiv Gandhi, she was the daughter–in–law to Indian Prime Minister Indira Gandhi, who held office from 1966 to 1977 and again from 1980 until her assassination in 1984. Indira Gandhi herself was the daughter of Jawaharlal Nehru, the first prime minister of India. After Gandhi's husband Rajiv, who also served as prime minister of India from 1984 to 1989, was assassinated after leaving office, Gandhi grieved for years. Eventually, seeing that the Congress party was deteriorating, she stepped in to provide a cult of personality that would boost the party's popularity, albeit temporarily.

Gandhi was born on December 9, 1947, in Turin, Italy, to Stefano and Paolo Maino. Raised as a Catholic in the town of Orbassano, near Turin, she was eight months old when India became independent from Great Britain. Her father, who owned a medium–sized construction firm, fought in World War II supporting Italian fascist leader Benito Mussolini. He later named his three daughters after Russian women who assisted his escape from a Russian prisoner–of–war camp. He named his dog Stalin.

At 18, Gandhi's father sent her to Cambridge, England. Some sources say she learned English at a foreign language school there; others say she attended Cambridge University. In any event, she would eventually become fluent in six languages. While in school, she lodged with a family whose cooking she despised, so Gandhi began frequenting a nearby Greek restaurant. There, in 1965, she met Rajiv Gandhi, an engineering student at Cambridge University who later left school and became a commercial airline pilot. She later wrote that it was love at first sight.

However, Gandhi was too intimidated to meet her boyfriend's mother, the esteemed Indira Gandhi, daughter of India's first prime minister, Jawaharlal Nehru. The second time Indira Gandhi visited London, however, Gandhi agreed to visit her, and immediately liked her. Gandhi's own parents, though, opposed the romance, even though Rajiv Gandhi worked long hours in construction to earn money to visit his sweetheart after her return to Italy. Eventually his persistence paid off, and the two were married in 1968 in New Delhi, India. They would have two children: a son, Rahul, and daughter, Priyanka.

Initially, Gandhi and her husband kept company with a chic social crowd, frequenting discotheques and wearing hip Western apparel. Once Indira Gandhi took over as prime minister, however, Gandhi and her husband moved in with her in the official residence, and she assumed the expected role of obedient and loyal daughter–in–law. She began wearing saris and speaking Hindi, albeit with an accent, and took to calling her mother–in–law "Mummy." They traveled together frequently, and for several years, Gandhi kept things running smoothly at the official residence, hosting foreign dignitaries and handling state events. At the same time, she kept family affairs private and limited her socializing to a select group of friends.

Despite Gandhi's close ties to her mother–in–law, her husband stayed out of politics. He was satisfied with his job at India Airlines, while his brother Sanjay was expected to take over as his mother's political heir. Meanwhile, throughout the 1970s, Indira Gandhi's popularity swelled and dipped. In 1971 she was hailed for a military success in East Pakistan which resulted in the creation of the state of Bangladesh. However, from 1975 to 1977 she declared a state of emergency and verged on becoming a dictator, jailing tens of thousands of suspected political opponents and cracking down on the media. At this point, Sonia and Rajiv Gandhi considered leaving for Italy.

Gandhi and her husband stayed in the country, though, and in 1980, Sanjay was killed while attempting an airplane stunt over New Delhi. His brusque wife, Maneka, whom Indira Gandhi had never liked, was eventually asked to leave the family home. Rajiv became the heir apparent, much to his wife's chagrin, who feared that opponents would threaten him with violence. Nevertheless, he ran for a seat in India's parliament in 1981 and won. But while Gandhi was vehemently against her husband entering politics, she dutifully supported his ambitions. Attuned to the fact that she was being

criticized as a "foreigner" while remaining so close to the top tier of India's power elite, she became a naturalized citizen in 1983.

Gandhi's life changed immensely on October 31, 1984, when Indira Gandhi was shot to death by two of her Sikh bodyguards on the grounds of her home in New Delhi. They were acting in retaliation for a political decision earlier that year in June: Military Sikhs requesting more autonomy had stockpiled weapons and holed up in the Golden Temple in Amritsar, and Indira Gandhi had sent troops to storm them. When Sonia Gandhi heard the shots, she ran out to the garden wearing a simple housecoat and cradled her mother–in–law as she lay dying. Rajiv Gandhi was sworn in as prime minister that very night.

While her husband ruled the country, Gandhi worked even harder to prove she was no outsider. After a two–year course in art restoration at the National Gallery of Modern Art in New Delhi, she worked diligently with a team of others to restore Indian landscapes painted by English artists. In addition, she edited letters sent between Indira Gandhi and her father, Nehru, which were published in two volumes, *Freedom's Daughter* in 1989 and *Two Alone, Two Together* in 1992. But scandal soon plagued Rajiv Gandhi's government, particularly a bribery deal in which a Swedish arms company paid off Indian officials in order to secure a lucrative contract to supply guns to the military. Rajiv Gandhi was voted out of office in 1989.

In 1991, Gandhi's husband ran again for a seat in parliament. On May 21 that year, as he was campaigning in Sriperumbudur, in the southern state of Tamil Nadu, a suicide bomber struck, killing him and about 28 others. The assassin, a woman probably in her twenties, triggered a belt of explosives as she draped a garland around his neck. It was determined that she was a Sri Lankan woman thought to be a member of the nationalist separatist group the Tamil Tigers. Although they denied responsibility, officials suspected they were behind the plot in retaliation for Rajiv Gandhi's move to provide Indian troops in the conflict between the Sri Lankan government and the guerilla Tamil Tigers.

Immediately after her husband's death, the Congress Party asked Gandhi to lead them, but she declined. She subsequently spent seven years in relative seclusion at her home in New Delhi, continuing her hobby of restoring artworks to help her deal with her grief. However, in 1992, she published a book, *Rajiv,* uncharacteristically detailing her personal life with her husband, and in 1994 wrote *Rajiv's World,* which revealed even more. In addition, Gandhi established trust funds all over the globe in order to preserve her husband's legacy, and became outspoken in accusing the state of Tamil Nadu of providing haven for the Tamil Tigers and not ensuring enough security for her husband's visit.

Throughout this period, there were whispers that Gandhi would return to politics. Many figured she could rescue the Congress party from its steady decline, which had suffered from corruption and defections to other parties. It had gotten to the point where it was a minor player as campaigning geared up for 1998 parliament elections. Meanwhile, the Hindu nationalist Bharatiya Janata Party (BJP) was gaining strength. Knowing that the Congress party was in dire straits, Gandhi joined their ranks in 1997 and began actively campaigning for the party, though not for a seat herself, in 1998. Though some were concerned that she effectively had no political experience, even her opponents gave her credit for giving her first speech in Sriperumbudur, where her husband had been killed, saying it was both courageous and a tactically wise political move.

Once she stepped into the spotlight, Gandhi's political enemies in the BJP tried to turn voters against her because of her Italian heritage. L. Ganesan, a BJP leader, related to Kenneth J. Cooper in the *Washington Post,* "Our slogan here is 'Be Indian, Buy Indian, Elect an Indian P.M. [Prime Minister].'" One prominent Hindu nationalist, Balasaheb Thackeray, proposed that a constitutional amendment be passed that would prohibit naturalized citizens from becoming prime minister or president, as is the case in the United States. Thackeray also pranced around dressed in saris and speaking in broken Hindi in order to mock Gandhi.

However, most citizens seemed to believe that Gandhi's foreign–born status was a non–issue. The bulk subscribed to the Indian custom that once a woman marries, she is part of her husband's family, regardless of her background. Gandhi helped play this up by her frequent use of the term "bahu," meaning a devoted daughter–in–law who serves her husband's family. Also, Indians seemed to grasp onto Gandhi for nostalgic reasons, and also identified with her suffering as a grieving widow, which she also underscored in her speeches. Throughout the campaign, she made 140 stops, appearing before massive crowds each time, despite her lack of oratory skills. When addressing audiences, a somber–faced Gandhi spoke in heavily accented Hindi, the national language, in a shaking and monotonous voice, and worked from speeches written partly by her daughter in the Roman alphabet instead of the Hindi alphabet.

Once the campaigns ended, John F. Burns wrote in the *New York Times,* "There were few in India who doubted that Mrs. Gandhi had turned the election upside down," explaining that the BJP did not seem to have a stronghold as it once did. Burns added, "She has emerged as a credible though still reluctant candidate for Prime Minister." Ironically, she was on the front page of newspapers almost daily and managed to build up her own and her party's popularity without giving a single interview to the media during the campaign.

When all the votes were in, the Congress party had made headway in the parliament, gaining 28 seats to bring their total to 166 out of the 545–member body—not a bad showing. Meanwhile, the United Front coalition won 96 seats. The Congress party had joined with them in the past to form two coalition governments. The BJP and its allies took 251 seats, which was a good share, but not a majority in parliament. They thus formed a coalition government with 17 other parties, and BJP leader Atal Behari Vajpayee took office as prime minister in March of 1998. In 1996, he had served as prime minister for only 13 days because the BJP could not form a coalition government, and this new government was shaky as well, managing to hold together only until April of 1999.

In the meantime, Gandhi, despite never having held office, managed to gain control of the Congress party from Sitaram Kesri after the 1998 campaign. Then, in local elections in November of 1998, her party won back three of the four states they had previously lost to the BJP, including the key New Delhi capital city. The victories were seen as testimony to the Congress party's renewal. After the BJP coalition government collapsed, due in large part to Gandhi's dealings, no party could display a clear majority, so elections—India's third in a span of three years—were scheduled in the fall of 1999. Despite her title as party chair, however, Gandhi never actually committed to running for prime minister.

Then, in May, three regional Congress party chiefs joined the chorus that questioned Gandhi's right to rule, given her foreign roots. She promptly resigned, but within a week, all three party bosses were ousted from their posts and other leaders begged her to return. Gandhi agreed to come back in early June, but it was still not clear whether she would run for the seat of prime minister, remaining enigmatic about the possibility. As it turned out, Gandhi did run for two parliamentary positions, including the one in which her husband sat, in Uttar Pradesh, the northern state with 160 million occupants. (Indian candidates are allowed to run for two seats simultaneously and can keep either one if they win both.) By this time, her accent was much improved, and Gandhi indeed snagged both posts, deciding to retain the one in Amethi, the district her husband had represented. However, the Congress party saw its poorest results ever, capturing only 112 seats.

The BJP rose to power again, and Vajpayee took his oath of office as prime minister once again in October of 1999, thus defusing the question of whether or not Gandhi would decide to take the post if her party gained control of the government. Though many did not foresee a time when Gandhi would ever assume leadership of the country, pundits suggested that the Gandhi family name would live on in politics through her daughter, Priyanka. She had accompanied her mother throughout numerous campaign stops and appeared to have an obvious interest in politics, thus appearing to seal her fate as the next in line in the legacy.

Sources

Periodicals

Business Week, February 22, 1999, p. 58.
Economist, December 5, 1998, p. 51; April 24, 1999, p. 37.
Maclean's, March 2, 1998, p. 28; May 31, 1999, p. 38; June 7, 1999, p. 53.
New Yorker, March 15, 1998, p. 36.
New York Times, May 23, 1991, p. A1; September 24, 1991, p. A1; September 2, 1992, p. A4; February 27, 1998, p. A1; April 22, 1999, p. A3; September 19, 1999, sec. 1, p. 14; October 2, 1999, p. A1.
Time, June 3, 1991, p. 8.
Time International, March 2, 1998, p. 28; December 14, 1998, p. 14; May 10, 1999, p. 17.
Washington Post, January 31, 1998, p. A15.
World Press Review, July 1999, p. 13.

Online

"Gandhi to Keep Parliamentary Seat," *AP Online,* October 19, 1999, obtained from Electric Library web site, http://www.elibrary.com (January 27, 2000).
"Indian Parliament Convenes," *AP Online,* October 20, 1999, obtained from Electric Library web site, http://www.elibrary.com (January 27, 2000).

Sue Grafton

AP/Wide World Photos

Author

Born April 24, 1940, in Louisville, KY; daughter of Cornelius Warren and Vivian Boisseau (Harnsberger) Grafton; married and divorced twice; married Steven F. Humphrey, October 1, 1978; children: (from first marriage) Leslie, (from second marriage) Jay, Jamie. *Education:* University of Louisville, B.A. in English, 1961.

Addresses: *Home*—Montecito, CA and Louisville, KY. *Agent*—Molly Friedrich, The Aaron Priest Agency, 122 West 42nd Street, No. 3902, New York, NY 10168.

Career

Screenwriter, lecturer, and novelist. Has also worked in the medical field as an admissions clerk, cashier, and clinical/medical secretary. Story editor, with Stephen F. Humphrey, *Seven Brides for Seven Brothers* (television series), 1982–83. Speaker at numerous conferences, including Midwest Writers Conference, Southwest Writers Conference, and Smithsonian Campus on the Mall. Member: International Association of Crime Writers, Writers Guild of America (West), Mystery Writers of America, Private Eye Writers of America (president, 1989–90).

Awards: Christopher Award, 1979, for *Walking through the Fire;* Mysterious Stranger Award, Cloak and Clue Society, 1982–83, for *"A" Is for Alibi;* Shamus Award, best hardcover private eye novel, Private Eye Writers of America, and Anthony Award, both 1986, both for *"B" Is for Burglar;* Macavity Award, best short story, and Anthony Award, both

1986, both for "The Parker Shotgun;" Anthony Award, 1987, for *"C" Is for Corpse* ; Doubleday Mystery Guild Award, 1989, for *"E" Is for Evidence;* American Mystery Award, best short story, 1990, for "A Poison That Leaves No Trace;" Falcon Award, best mystery novel, Maltese Falcon Society of Japan, and Doubleday Mystery Guild Award, both 1990, both for *"F" Is for Fugitive;* Doubleday Mystery Guild Award, Shamus Award, and Anthony Award, all 1991, all for *"G" Is for Gumshoe;* Doubleday Mystery Guild Award, and American Mystery Award, both 1992, both for *"H" Is for Homicide;* Doubleday Mystery Guild Award, 1993, for *"I" Is for Innocent,* and 1994, for *"J" Is for Judgment;* Shamus Award, 1994, and Doubleday Mystery Guild Award, 1995, both for *"K" Is for Killer.*

Sidelights

To fans of detective novels, author Sue Grafton is virtually synonymous with the character of Kinsey Millhone, a spunky, sharp–tongued, former police officer who is the heroine of an alphabetically titled series of mysteries. Starting with *"A" Is for Alibi* and running through volumes *like "C" Is for Corpse, "H" Is for Homicide,* and *"O" Is for Outlaw,* Grafton has crafted an iconoclastic yet believable female private detective who is in the same league as

Sara Paretsky's V. I. Warshawski. Offering heart–thumping suspense without the graphic violence of crime writers such as Elmore Leonard or Robert B. Parkers, Grafton's works not only weave page–turning plots, but also tend to blend a more human element into the tales. Published in 28 countries and 26 languages, the series has steadily grown in popularity while continuing to attract critical raves. As Andrea Chambers summed up in *People*, "To male readers, who make up about a third of Grafton's audience, Kinsey is tough yet unthreatening. To women she's sassy and down–to–earth." Of her heroine, Grafton told Susan Goodman in *Modern Maturity*, "Kinsey is a stripped–down version of me. She's who I would've been had I not married young and had children. She'll always be thinner and younger and braver, the lucky so–and–so. Her biography is different but our sensibilities are identical."

Grafton was born on April 24, 1940, in Louisville, Kentucky, the youngest of two daughters of Cornelius Warren "Chip" Grafton and Vivian Boisseau (Harnsberger) Grafton. Her father was an attorney and writer who published three mysteries and a novel as C. W. Grafton, and her mother was a high school chemistry teacher. They first met in China when their parents were missionaries, and later met again when they both returned to the United States for college. Although her parents (now deceased) were alcoholics, Grafton credits this with helping to mold her creative spirit. "As peculiar as my upbringing was," she told Anita Manning in *USA Today*, "I also considered it a gift. I had this great freedom because there was all this benign neglect going on."

In addition, Grafton has noted that her parents passed to her an intense love of reading, telling Jane Nicholls and Bonnie Bell in *People*, ""We had a revolving rack in the house where my parents would keep paperbacks under labels: dirty, dull or good. They were freethinkers and allowed us to read anything we wanted." She began reading adult crime novels while her friends were still engrossed with Nancy Drew mysteries. She would devour the works of Mickey Spillane, Dashiell Hammett, Raymond Chandler, and Ross Macdonald, and have in-depth conversations with her father about the skill of writing. However, Grafton was not nearly as inspired with her schoolwork. Though she got above-average grades, she was driven by her fright of poor performance rather than a devotion to schoolwork.

In junior high and high school, Grafton began to pen articles for the student newspapers, and also tried her hand at poetry. By age 18, she began to craft short stories and develop ideas for books. Though she received her bachelor of arts degree in English from the University of Louisville, she also took an extension course in creative writing through the University of California at Los Angeles. It was taught by Robert Kirsh, then the book editor for the *Los Angeles Times*, who encouraged her to write a novel.

Meanwhile, Grafton was married during her sophomore year and had a daughter, Leslie, the next year. Not long after her graduation in 1961, she divorced and soon married again. She and her second husband moved to California and had two children, a son, Jay, and a daughter, Jamie. For a few years she held various jobs, including doing secretarial and clerical work at hospitals or physicians' offices, and also worked as a secretary for Danny Thomas Productions in Hollywood. On her off hours, she continued to write, finishing four book–length manuscripts before seeing publication.

Grafton's first work, *Keziah Dane,* came out in 1967. It concerns a Depression–era widow and matriarch who valiantly tries to keep her family together. Reviewers saw potential in this work, but did not express the same sentiments upon release of her next work, *The Lolly–Madonna War,* 1969. Neither critics nor Grafton herself were pleased with this tale about a pair of feuding Appalachian families, but film studio Metro–Goldwyn–Mayer nonetheless bought the rights and asked Grafton, along with Rodney Carr–Smith, to write the script. The movie came out in 1973 starring Rod Steiger and Jeff Bridges.

After this, Grafton dabbled further in screenwriting, sending some work on spec to the producers of the television sitcom *Rhoda*. Though her own scripts were rejected, she was hired on contract to write the episode "With Friends Like These," which aired in the spring of 1975. For the next few years, she continued writing for television and also began adapting novels written by others for television movies, including *Walking through the Fire,* which won a Christopher Award in 1979, and a couple of Agatha Christie mysteries. Grafton and writer Steven F. Humphrey were married in 1978 and began collaborating on writing television movies, but she became increasingly disillusioned with the job. She remarked to Enid Nemy in the *New York Times*, "I didn't want to sit in a room with a 26–year–old network executive 'making my work better,' telling me what I should do—a kid whose only writing had been term papers…. The business of group writing was making me crazy."

In the meantime, Grafton reached out to mystery writing in order to satisfy her desire for a solo project. She chose mysteries partly because of her father's work in the genre, and also in order to spotlight her skill at plot development. Some of the feedback she got working in Hollywood mentioned that she was strong on characters but weak on plot, so as she explained to Goodman in *Modern Maturity,* "In mystery novels, plot is paramount. I thought, I'm going to write a mystery and make you eat your words. And I did just that."

Though Grafton knew nothing about the life of private detectives at the outset, she immersed herself in research, collecting information on forensics, anatomy, toxicology, crime of all kinds, and even poisonous plants. In addition, she learned to shoot a handgun, pick locks, and dust for fingerprints. Grafton decided to create a female protagonist first of all, because she felt she would better identify with a woman character, and also because part of the impetus for the story came out of custody battles with her second husband. She told Goodman that she "used to lie in bed just thinking of how much nicer it would be if he were a dead person instead of a live one." Eventually she came up with a murder plot involving poison and created a work of fiction that also served as a catharsis for her feelings toward her ex-husband.

In 1982, Grafton published her first mystery, *"A" Is for Alibi.* It set up the formula of basing each work on a letter of the alphabet, a plan she devised partly because her father had used sequential lines from a nursery rhyme for two of his titles, *The Rat Began to Gnaw the Rope* and *The Rope Began to Hang the Butcher.* Also, she admitted to Andrea Chambers in *People,* "It seemed like a catchy way of keeping readers." Grafton's debut book also introduced her now long-running central character, Kinsey Millhone, a gritty, self-reliant, twice-divorced and childless contemporary heroine who gorges on junk food yet jogs regularly, drives a beat-up Volkswagen, and lives in a converted garage in Santa Teresa, a fictional town based on Santa Barbara, California. In addition, she has a sharp wit, keen eye for detail, and a foul mouth. Displaying few stereotypical feminine behaviors, Millhone pays no attention to her appearance and eschews makeup, and has been known to cut her own hair with nail scissors.

Reviewers warmed to Grafton's first mystery, which won the Mysterious Stranger Award from the Cloak and Clue Society, 1982–83. The story revolved around the detective Millhone's assignment to help a woman prove her innocence in the murder of her husband. Subsequently, Grafton grappled with writer's block before publishing *"B" Is for Burglar* three years later, in 1985. Her second novel was even more impressive, earning the Shamus Award for best hardcover private eye novel from the Private Eye Writers of America, as well as the Anthony Award, both in 1986. This concerns Millhone's attempts to locate a wealthy widow who may have been murdered.

Since that second effort, Grafton has faithfully churned out another installment almost every year, ranging from *"C" Is for Corpse* to *"O" Is for Outlaw.* Critical reception has continued to be positive throughout the series, as Grafton has ensured that her characters remain fresh and her tales gripping. She manages to avoid becoming repetitious by revealing Millhone's flaws as well as her good qualities, thus making her more realistic, and by including topical references in her works. Despite the spiraling popularity of her books, though, Grafton has vowed time and again never to sell her detective books to the entertainment industry to create films or programs out of them. "Kinsey Millhone was my tiny pickax whereby I got out of prison," the author noted to Jonathan Bing in *Publishers Weekly,* referring to her exodus from Hollywood. "And I would be a fool to sell her back to them."

The bulk of Grafton's works have made it onto the best-seller lists, with several of them honored with Shamus And Anthony awards as well Doubleday as Mystery Guild awards. Some have criticized her for not using her heroine as more of a feminist platform, but the author stated to Manning in *USA Today,* "I am not interested in being politically correct," adding, "I take a lot of flack for that." Though Millhone has an occasional boyfriend, Grafton has insisted the character will never get remarried or have kids, let alone get a cat, because she does not want to write the scenes that would go along with such baggage in her character's life. In January of 2000, it was announced that Grafton, who had published with Henry Holt & Company since her series began, was moving to Putnam to follow her longtime editor, Marian Wood.

Though she and her husband have lived for several years in Montecito, just outside of Santa Barbara, Grafton in 1993 also purchased a 10-room English Tudor home in Louisville, Kentucky, where they live four months of the year. Her husband, who has a doctorate of philosophy, sometimes teaches at the University of California at Santa Barbara, and also functions as his wife's business manager. Grafton told Goodman in *Modern Maturity* that she and her husband "are not fashionable people," meaning they do not socialize frequently. For years, she rose early to jog three miles, then returned home to "read the Metro section to see what that day's absurd homicides are," as she told Goodman. However, a bone spur in her heel ended her running habit, so she took up swimming instead. Grafton writes from 9 a.m. to 3:30 p.m., breaking for lunch, then afterward exercises again. She eats dinner at 6 p.m. and is asleep by 7:30 or 8 p.m. Of course, many people wonder what Grafton will do once she gets to the letter Z, which is scheduled to come out around 2015. "I've always said that I'd switch to numbers," she told Marlene Cimons in *Runner's World*. "But I think I'll be entitled to a rest."

Selected works

Keziah Dane, Macmillan, 1967.
The Lolly–Madonna War, Owen, 1969.

Novels; Kinsey Millhone Series

"A" Is for Alibi, Holt, 1982.
"B" Is for Burglar, Holt, 1985.
"C" Is for Corpse, Holt, 1986.
"D" Is for Deadbeat, Holt, 1987.
"E" Is for Evidence, Holt, 1988.
"F" Is for Fugitive, Holt, 1989.
"G" Is for Gumshoe, Holt, 1990.
"H" Is for Homicide, Holt, 1991.
"I" Is for Innocent, Holt, 1992.
"J" Is for Judgment, Holt, 1993.
"K" Is for Killer, Holt, 1994.
"L" Is for Lawless, Holt, 1995.
"M" Is for Malice, Holt, 1996.
"N" Is for Noose, Holt, 1998.
"O" Is for Outlaw, Holt, 1999.

Short Stories

Kinsey and Me, Bench Press, 1992.

Screenplay

Lolly–Madonna XXX, with Rodney Carr–Smith, 1973.

Television Scripts

"With Friends Like These" (*Rhoda* series), 1975; *Walking through the Fire*, from the book by Laurel Lee, 1979; *Sex and the Single Parent*, from the book by Jane Adams, 1979; *Nurse*, from the book by Peggy Anderson, 1980; *Mark, I Love You*, from the book by Hal Painter, 1980; *Seven Brides for Seven Brothers, I Love You, Molly McGraw*, and *A House Divided*, with Steven Humphrey (*Seven Brides for Seven Brothers* series), 1982–83; *A Caribbean Mystery*, with Humphrey, from the novel by Agatha Christie, 1983; *A Killer in the Family*, with Humphrey and Robert Aller, 1983; *Sparkling Cyanide*, with Humphrey and Robert Malcolm Young, from the novel by Agatha Christie, 1983; *Love on the Run*, with Humphrey, 1985; *Tonight's the Night*, with Humphrey, 1987.

Sources

Books

Artists and Authors for Young Adults, volume 11, Gale Research, 1993.
Contemporary Popular Writers, St. James Press, 1997.
Contemporary Southern Writers, St. James Press, 1999.

Periodicals

Modern Maturity, July/August 1995, p. 74.
Newsday, August 18, 1994, p. B3; September 24, 1995, p. 32.
New York Times, August 4, 1994, p. C1.
People, July 10, 1989, p. 81; October 30, 1995, p. 115.
Publishers Weekly, April 20, 1998, p. 40; January 3, 2000, p. 22.
Redbook, April 1986, p. 68.
Runner's World, June 1992, p. 37.
USA Today, July 2, 1992, p. 4D.

Online

Sue Grafton web site, http://www.suegrafton.com (February 8, 2000).

Heather Graham

Actor and model.

Born January 9, 1970, in Milwaukee, WI; daughter of an FBI agent and a teacher/poet. *Education:* Attended the University of California at Los Angeles.

Addresses: *Agent*—Creative Artists Agency, 9830 Wilshire Blvd., Beverly Hills, CA 902112.

Career

Actor and model. Television appearances include episodes of *Fallen Angels*, 1995; and *The Outer Limits*, 1996; series *Twin Peaks*, 1991; special "O Pioneers!," *Hallmark Hall of Fame*, 1992; and movie *Student Exchange*, 1987. Film appearances include *License to Drive*, 1987; *Twins*, 1988; *Drugstore Cowboy*, 1989; *I Love You to Death*, 1990; *Shout*, 1991; *Guilty as Charged*, 1991; *Twin Peaks: Fire Walk with Me*, 1992; *Diggstown*, 1992; *Six Degrees of Separation*, 1993; *Even Cowgirls Get the Blues*, 1993; *The Ballad of Little Jo*, 1993; *Mrs. Parker and the Vicious Circle*, 1994; *Don't Do It*, 1995; *Terrified*, 1995; *Let It Be Me*, 1995; *Desert Winds*, 1995; *Swingers*, 1996; *Entertaining Angels: The Dorothy Day Story*, 1996; *Boogie Nights*, 1997; *Two Girls and a Guy*, 1997; *Nowhere*, 1997; *Scream 2*, 1997; *Lost in Space*, 1998; *Kiss & Tell*, 1999; *Austin Powers: The Spy Who Shagged Me*, 1999; *Bowfinger*, 1999.

Awards: MTV Movie Award, best breakthrough performance, 1998, for *Boogie Nights;* ShoWest Convention star of tomorrow, 1999.

Sidelights

Heather Graham took moviegoers by storm in the summer of 1999 playing the unabashedly sensual sidekick in the Mike Myers blockbuster *Austin Powers: The Spy Who Shagged Me*. Though she turned on the sex appeal full tilt in that romp, in her long list of supporting roles, Graham was known for exuding a naïve appeal that tempered the often corrupted characters that she has played, from drug addicts to porn stars. Her sweet looks, framed by blonde locks and clear blue eyes, belie a mysterious underside that managed to crop up in several of her parts. As the pill–popping Nadine in *Drugstore Cowboy* or the troubled Rollergirl in *Boogie Nights*, Graham has revealed that her range goes far beyond just showing up and looking pretty. Despite appearing in a bevy of well–known pictures, Graham was not catapulted into leading lady status until making the loopy *Austin Powers* sequel.

Graham was born on January 9, 1970, in Milwaukee, Wisconsin. Her father is a retired F.B.I. agent, and her mother, who was a schoolteacher, writes children's books. Graham and her younger sister, Aimee Graham, who is also an actor, moved often throughout childhood for her father's job, and spent some time in school in Virginia when he was learning anti–terrorist tactics at the FBI headquarters there. When Graham was in junior high, the family moved to the Los Angeles suburb of Agoura Hills. The atmosphere in Graham's family was old–fashioned and strictly Catholic; as she recalled to Jamie Diamond in *Mademoiselle,* "I went to church all the time and learned that sex was bad and dirty. I think Catholicism was detrimental to me."

In grade school, Graham began acting, and landed her first paid role, in a television commercial, in high school. Her classmates at Agoura High School named her "most talented" her senior year, and she was often traveling into Los Angeles for auditions. Her father disapproved at first, but when she began earning money at it, hawking products like Ivory soap and Mountain Dew soda, he relaxed. However, things changed when Graham started to land more adult roles. "My parents encouraged my acting ambitions as long as they thought it was just a fad," Graham related to Louis B. Hobson in the *Calgary Sun,* "but when I went professional and some of my roles conflicted with their Catholic beliefs, we parted ways." She noted in the 1999 interview with Diamond, "It's been four or five years since I've talked to them. I don't know if they've seen any of my movies." However, Stephanie Mansfield in *USA Weekend* reported that Graham's parents said that they did attend many of her earlier film premieres and that they only became estranged when she landed a racy part in *Boogie Nights,* a film loosely based on the porn industry in the 1970s.

Moving out at age 18, Graham immersed herself in Hollywood. She got her own apartment, began therapy sessions, and worked a string of odd jobs, including ushering at the Hollywood Bowl, in between acting. She had appeared in a small part in the 1987 television movie *Student Exchange,* but her big–screen debut was as the love interest in *License to Drive,* 1988, with Corey Haim and Corey Feldman. When she landed her first major role at age 18 in *Drugstore Cowboy,* Graham remarked to Christine Spines in *Premiere,* "I thought, Oh my God, I'm gonna be huge!" Directed by Gus Van Sant and co-starring Matt Dillon and Kelly Lynch, the film was about a quartet of drug addicts who wander from town to town robbing pharmacies in order to get their fix. The widely praised film was an art–house hit.

Around this time, Graham started taking classes at the University of California at Los Angeles as an English major, because she felt confident that she could balance college with her rising career. She left after two years, though, to concentrate on acting. A small role in 1990's *I Love You to Death,* was a good move, as was a regular role as a nun, Annie Blackburn, on the quirky David Lynch series *Twin Peaks* in 1991, but then Graham's resume enters a low period. The much–ignored musical *Shout,* 1991, did nothing to raise her profile, and though she reprised her role in *Twin Peaks: Fire Walk with Me,* 1992, the film was panned by critics.

However, in 1992, Graham's career took an upswing when she appeared in *Diggstown,* then in supporting roles in the independent efforts *Six Degrees of Separation,* 1993, with Will Smith as a charming con artist, and *Mrs. Parker and the Vicious Circle,* 1994, starring Jennifer Jason Leigh as cynical author Dorothy Parker. In addition, Graham had a minor part in another artsy Van Sant film, *Even Cowgirls Get the Blues,* in 1993. Tiny roles in a few more forgettable pictures came her way over the next couple of years, then Graham began to enter a new realm in 1996 in Jon Favreau's surprise hit, *Swingers.* In it, Favreau and Vince Vaughan star as two would–be Hollywood lounge hipsters looking to meet women, and Graham fits the bill as the dreamy Lorraine, who helps pull Favreau's character out of his doldrums.

In 1997, Graham had a small appearance in the teen horror hit *Scream 2,* then saw her breakthrough role that same year portraying a cherub–faced porn queen who will take off everything but her roller skates in the 1970s–era *Boogie Nights.* As Rollergirl, she got to fully demonstrate her capacity for transcending her angelic looks when her rage erupts in one particularly wrenching scene where she uses her skates as a weapon. This role, which required nudity and intense sexual situations, seriously tested her feelings of guilt and fear stemming from her religious upbringing. As she remarked to Spines in *Premiere,* "I was a little scared being naked. But it was kind of freeing. I just felt like I didn't have to live by the rules of Catholicism if I wanted to express myself artistically, and I'm not going to hell." Later that year, Graham showcased her seductive powers once again with her performance in *Two Girls and a Guy,* in which she plays a woman who discovers that her boyfriend (Robert Downey, Jr.) is a two–timer; she and the other woman (Natasha Wagner) then join forces to put him on the spot.

After a stint as Dr. Judy Robinson in the underwhelming *Lost in Space,* 1998, Graham came into her own with the 1999 smash *Austin Powers: The Spy Who Shagged Me.* This was the sequel to the 1997

Mike Myers spoof *Austin Powers: International Man of Mystery*, about a British spy who travels from the 1960s into the 1990s to thwart the villainous Dr. Evil. In the follow–up, set back in the 1960s, Graham storms the screen as Felicity Shagwell, a groovy secret agent whose hip huggers and sexual bravura impress Powers, who then falls hard for his partner. The picture was an immediate success, earning $57.2 million in its first weekend, a record for a sequel. That same year, 1999, Graham also showed up in the comedy *Bowfinger*, starring Steve Martin and Eddie Murphy, portraying a hopeful starlet who sleeps her way to the top in Hollywood.

Graham has been linked romantically in the past to other actors, particularly Kyle McLachlan and James Woods (with whom she costarred in *Diggstown*), but by the late 1990s, had entered a serious relationship with actor/director Edward Burns. They share the same birthday, and he is also Irish Catholic. Though they are both in the entertainment industry, they actually met at a bar in Los Angeles and exchanged numbers. They moved in together in November of 1998 and live in the Hollywood Hills. In addition to acting, Graham has a modeling contract with Emanuel Ungaro.

Sources

Books

Contemporary Theatre, Film and Television, volume 20, Gale Research, 1999.

Periodicals

Calgary Sun, May 30, 1999, p. 46.
Dallas Morning News, June 11, 1999, p. 4C.
Mademoiselle, July 1999, p. 60.
Newsday, June 17, 1999, p. B2.
New York Times, June 14, 1999, p. E1.
Ottawa Sun, August 20, 1999, p. 27.
Premiere, July 1999, p. 74.
Star Tribune (Minneapolis, MN), August 18, 1999, p. 5E.
Toronto Sun, June 24, 1999, p. 88.

Online

"Heather Graham," Internet Movie Database web site, http://us.imdb.com (October 8, 1999).
"Heather Graham," Mr. Showbiz web site, http://mrshowbiz.go.com (October 8, 1999).
"Celebs," USA Weekend online, August 8, 1999, http://www.usaweekend.com (September 8, 1999).

Kevin Garnett

Basketball player

Born Kevin Maurice Garnett, May 19, 1976, in Mauldin, SC; son of Shirley Irby (a hair stylist) and O'Lewis McCullough.

Addresses: *Home*—Minnetonka, MN. *Office*—c/o Minnesota Timberwolves, 600 First Ave. N., Minneapolis, MN 55403.

Career

Professional basketball player, 1995 . Drafted fifth overall by the Minnesota Timberwolves, 1995 National Basketball Association (NBA) Entry Draft.

Awards: Mr. Basketball for state of South Carolina, 1994; McDonald's All–America Game most outstanding player, 1995; Mr. Basketball for state of Illinois, 1995; named to *Parade* magazine All–America First Team, 1995; *USA Today* national high school player of the year, 1995; voted to NBA All–Rookie second team, 1996; named to NBA All–Star team, 1997, 1998, 2000.

Sidelights

One of the most outstanding players in the National Basketball Association (NBA), Kevin Garnett has proven wrong the naysayers who predicted that his young age would be a liability in his career. As one of only four American players up to that time to go directly from high school to the pros (the others were Moses Malone, Darryl Dawkins, and Bill Willoughby), he withstood a barrage of criticism for foregoing his higher education, as well as predictions that his lack of experience could lead to his downfall. On the contrary, Garnett became the star player on the Minnesota Timberwolves, the team that chose him fifth overall in the 1995 entry draft, and he helped land them in the playoffs four years in a row. Meanwhile, in 1998, he demanded and received the league's heftiest long–term contract, which helped provoke owners to renegotiate a deal for player salaries. Since his time with Minnesota, Garnett's game has steadily improved, and he has been the major factor in bettering the team's record and boosting their chances of eventual playoff success.

Garnett was born on May 19, 1976, in Greenville, South Carolina, and he has an older sister, Sonya, and younger sister, Ashley. His father and mother, O'Lewis McCullough and Shirley Garnett, never married, and when Garnett was very young, his father left the family. Then, when he was just five, his mother, a hair stylist, married Ernest Irby, and the family moved to the Greenville suburb of Mauldin when he was in the sixth grade. His mother felt it was a safe area and a good place to raise kids, but Garnett found the sleepy community of fast–food shops, strip malls, and car dealers to be a bore, and found refuge on the basketball court.

Though his mother and stepfather thought he should concentrate more on schoolwork and less on basketball, Garnett tried out for his high school team, the Mauldin Mavericks, when he was a freshman. He was the team's most valuable player by the end of his junior year, when the team posted a record of 22–7 for the season. Also that year, he became the first non–senior to be named Mr. Basketball by the state of South Carolina, with a per game average of 27 points, 17 rebounds, and 7 blocks.

Just as recruiters began to poke around, however, Garnett fell into trouble as his junior year was winding down. That May, he was arrested after a white student from another team was beaten by a group of blacks in the hallway. Reports indicated that the white player may have used racial slurs in addressing the others, but others said there was no provocation. Though Garnett insisted he was an innocent bystander, he was arrested and charged with second–degree lynching. However, since he was a first–time offender, he was able to take part in a pretrial intervention program, and his record was later expunged.

Meanwhile, Garnett had enrolled in a summer basketball camp and met the coaches at Farragut Academy in Chicago. They recruited him to play his senior year there for the Farragut Admirals, and his mother approved the plan. She and Garnett both felt that Mauldin school administrators had treated him unfairly during the earlier incident, and he wanted to play for a school where he would get more recognition for his hoop skills. But going from a laid–back Southern town to the inner city was "total hell gangs, guns, crime," as Garnett told Curry Kirkpatrick in *Newsweek*. "I had to deal with a gang leader named Seven–Gun Marcello. No fun."

Still, Garnett kept focused on the court and kept out of trouble. During his senior year, in 1995, the Admirals posted a record of 28–2 and made it to the Class AA state quarterfinals. He averaged 25.2 points, 17.9 rebounds, 6.7 assists, and 6.5 blocked shots per game, and was named Mr. Basketball by the state of Illinois, *USA Today*'s national high school player of the year, and a member of the *Parade* magazine All–America First Team. Also in 1995, he was named the most outstanding player of the McDonald's All–America Game. College recruiters from the Big Ten campuses began to hover.

While Garnett's scores on the court were impressive, his studies continued to suffer. Though he managed to raised his grade point average in 13 core classes to a 3.8, he did not post a high enough score on the SAT or ACT standardized exams to qualify for a Division I scholarship, despite repeated attempts. "Man, I wanted to go to college," Garnett told Greg Guss in *Sport*. "I went to class. I took the ACT classes. I wanted to have options." At that point, though, Garnett's choices were limited to two: either sit out the first year while proving himself academically, or join the pros.

Garnett thus decided to become the first high school player in 20 years to go straight to the professional league out of high school. He had impressed all 13 lottery teams, plus others who attended uninvited, when he displayed his skills at an audition in Chicago. Many believed he was the most talented player in the draft that year. However, even before the draft pick, observers voiced concerns that such a young man would become overwhelmed by the fame, wealth, and pressure of being in the NBA. They wondered if he could emotionally handle his responsibility on the court and the kind of mental stress that opposing players might deliver. Still others questioned whether he was NBA material physically. Since he only held 220 pounds on his six foot, eleven inch–tall frame, many figured his physique was still developing.

Though team officials also considered Garnett's age and maturity an issue, they also knew that on the other hand, his youth meant he had more years to pour into a career. On June 28, 1995, only about a month after his senior prom and nineteenth birthday, Garnett was drafted fifth overall by the Minnesota Timberwolves. They offered him an unprecedented three–year, $5.6 million contract the maximum allowed to a rookie NBA player. On the day of the draft, he found out he had posted a qualifying score on his SAT.

When Garnett joined the Timberwolves, the team had never won 30 games out of an 82– game season, and for four years they had lost at least 60 games, which was an unprecedented loss record in the NBA. They also had never made the playoffs. However, as Garnett related to Kirkpatrick, "I figured this was a place that wanted me, *needed* me, to make an impact." He was put in the position of small forward, where faster, shorter veteran players tended to isolate him on the floor. But he quickly displayed his worth when center Christian Laettner, the team's star player, sat out with an injury.

In addition, when Laettner harshly criticized Garnett in public, he showed a distinct maturity by addressing his teammate privately in order to work things out. After that, the Timberwolves traded Laettner to the Atlanta Hawks, and made Garnett their starter. Subsequently, the team also fired their coach, Bill Blair, when he did not give their new prodigy enough court time. By the end of his rookie year, Garnett had started in the last 42 games of the season, averaging 14 points, 8.4 rebounds, and two blocked shots per game during that time. For the year, he averaged 10.4 points and 6.3 rebounds per game, and led all rookies with 1.64 blocks per game. He also made the 1995–96 All–Rookie Second Team.

In addition to playing more and improving his game throughout the season, Garnett did not fall into any of the traps predicted for him. He bought a house and some luxury vehicles, but smartly, hired advisers to assist him with his money. And there were no instances of unruly behavior; he spent much of his time on the road in hotel rooms playing video games with his childhood pal, Jaime "Bug" Peters. In addition, thanks to his enthusiasm for the game and his pleasant personality, he became one of the league's most popular players. As he commented to Guss in *Sport*, "I know people were watching me. I know people wanted me to fall. But you've got to want to get better, and that's what really keeps me going. I want to get better every game I play. I want to show the world. I want to beat the odds." Following his lead, Kobe Bryant and others also made the leap straight to the NBA, though the concerns remained about players foregoing their education and needing to gain maturity before that step.

In his second season with Minnesota, Garnett got even better. He was named to the NBA All–Star Team that year, and was already considered the team's leader according to coach Flip Saunders, as Mike Lupica reported in *Esquire*. However, Garnett managed to have words of warning for any other upstarts who thought they could make the transition to the pros from high school. "I found out fast," he mentioned to Lupica, "you better be ready to act like a grown–up in this league." When Lupica asked what the biggest difference was in his second year of playing, Garnett answered, "I think it has a lot to do with being more comfortable. And I feel like I'm starting to get respect. All I ever heard from the first day was, 'This is a man's league, kid.' The only way you can get them to treat you like a man is to play like a man."

Though the Timberwolves saw their best season ever in 1996–97 and made it to the playoffs, they were shut out in a sweep by the Houston Rockets in the first round. Before the start of next year, the Timberwolves began to renegotiate Garnett's contract, since all NBA players are eligible to become a free agent after their third season. But when Minnesota owner Glen Taylor divulged to the media that Garnett had declined a six–year, $103.5 million offer, it looked as if the team might lose him. A couple weeks later, though, he accepted a six–year, $125 million contract with the Timberwolves, making him the second–highest player in the NBA after Chicago Bulls starter Michael Jordan. In addition, the deal was the richest long–term contract in American sports history, surpassing even Shaquille O'Neal's seven–year, $120 million contract with the Los Angeles Lakers.

During the 1997–98 season, Garnett's numbers improved again, as he averaged 18.5 points and 9.6 rebounds. He was named to the All–Star team once more, and again the team went to the playoffs, though they were knocked out in the first round by the Seattle SuperSonics. However, the team boasted its best record to date with 45 wins, 37 losses, and made the playoff series last longer than anyone had predicted.

The next season, 1998–99, was delayed for three months and two days due to a player lockout by owners. As Leigh Montville wrote in *Sports Illustrated*, Garnett "was the final reason for the lockout. He signed a contract for so much money that the people in charge scared themselves into action. 'Where will this end?' they asked. They risked the future of the league, shut down operations. Because of him. He is the kid who broke the NBA bank." Subsequently, the league, which was in its second year of a six–year labor agreement, exercised an option to reopen the agreement, and they managed to negotiate a salary cap on players signed after that point. During that abbreviated season, which did not feature an All–Star game, Garnett increased his statistics again, to average 20.8 points and 10.4 rebounds per game. Nevertheless, for the third time in a row, the Timberwolves were bounced from the playoffs as the top–ranked San Antonio Spurs, with their star player Tim Duncan, beat them 3–1 in the series.

Reaching new heights in his career, in February of 2000 Garnett started at forward in the NBA All–Star game, ahead of more prominent players such as Duncan and Karl Malone. He scored 24 points and 10 rebounds in the contest. By that point, the Timberwolves were one of the best teams in the league. Continuing his ascent, Garnett's averages increased that year to 22.9 points per game, the tenth best in the NBA, and 11.8 rebounds, the fourth–best record. By the end of the regular season, the Timberwolves had once again clinched a playoff spot.

Garnett, who grew an inch during his early NBA days, now stands seven feet tall. He owns a home in Minnetonka, a suburb of Minneapolis, also home to successful black music producers Jimmy Jam and Terry Lewis, who became his mentors. His hobbies include playing pool, air hockey, and video games. In addition, he owns 14 acres in the woods so that he and his friends can ride go–karts and all–terrain vehicles without disturbing the neighbors. In 1996, Garnett made his acting debut in the HBO movie *Rebound: The Story of Earl "The Goat" Maningault*, playing basketball legend Wilt Chamberlain, and he is also a spokesperson for Nike.

Sources

Books

Contemporary Black Biography, volume 14, Gale Research, 1997.

Periodicals

Esquire, March 1997, p. 54.

Jet, January 29, 1996, p. 51; September 1, 1997, p. 48; October 20, 1997, p. 46.

Newsweek, December 4, 1995, p. 72; February 14, 2000, p. 56.

Sport, November 1996, p. 50; January 2000, p. 32; March 2000, p. 32.

Sporting News, March 4, 1996, p. 26; April 8, 1996, p. 46.

Sports Illustrated, June 26, 1995, p. 64; March 11, 1996, p. 61; January 20, 1997, p. 70; May 12, 1997, p. 99; August 25, 1997, p. 17; May 3, 1999, p. 38.

Washington Post, June 27, 1995, p. C3.

Online

"Kevin Garnett," NBA web site, http://www.nba.com (April 20, 2000).

Gunter Grass

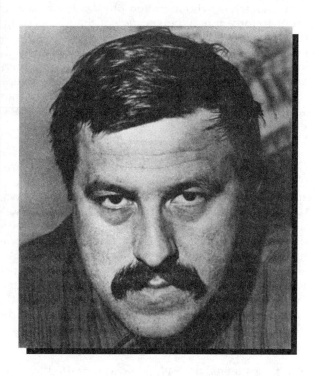

Author

Born Gunter Wilhelm Grass, October 16, 1927, in the Free City of Danzig (now Gdansk, Poland); married Anna Schwarz, 1954 (marriage ended); married Utte Grunert, 1979; children: (first marriage) Franz, Raoul, Laura, Bruno. *Education:* Attended Kunstakademie, Duesseldorf, Germany; attended Berlin Academy of Fine Arts, 1953–55.

Addresses: *Home*—Glockengiesserstrasse 21, 23552, Lubeck, Germany; Behlendorf, Germany. *Office*—Niedstrasse 13, Berlin–Grunewald 41, Germany.

Career

Novelist, poet, playwright, graphic artist, and sculptor. Former farm laborer in the Rhineland; worked in potash mine near Hildesheim, Germany; black marketeer; apprentice stonecutter during the late 1940s, chiseling tombstones for firms in Duesseldorf, Germany; worked as a drummer and washboard accompanist with a jazz band. Speechwriter for Willy Brandt during his candidacy for the election of Bundeskanzler in West Germany. Visited the United States in 1964 and 1965, giving lectures and readings at Harvard University, Yale University, Smith College, Kenyon College, and at Goethe House and Poetry Center of YMCA and YWCA, New York City; writer in residence at Columbia University, 1966. Has exhibited his drawings, lithographs, and sculptures.

Awards: Lyrikpreis, Sueddeutscher Rundfunk, 1955; prize from Gruppe 47, 1958; Bremen Literary Award, 1959; literary prize from the Association of German Critics, 1960; *Die Blechtrommel* (*The Tin Drum*) was selected by a French jury as the best foreign–language book of 1962; a plaster bust of Grass was placed in the Regensburger Ruhmestempel Walhalla, 1963; Georg Buechner Prize, 1965; Fontaine Prize, 1968; Theodor Heuss Preis, 1969; Berliner Fontane Preis, 1969; *Local Anaesthetic* was selected as one of 1970's ten best books by *Time,* 1970; Carl von Ossiersky Medal, 1977; Premio Internazionale Mondello, Palermo, 1977; International Literatur Award, 1978; *The Flounder* was selected as one of 1978's best books of fiction by *Time,* 1979; Alexander–Majokowski Medal, 1979; Antonio Feltrinelli Award, 1982; awarded distinguished service medal from the Federal Republic of Germany (declined by Grass), 1980; Nobel Prize in literature, Swedish Academy, 1999.

Sidelights

Gunter Grass cemented his reputation as one of the most important postwar German authors with *The Tin Drum,* which addresses the dark page in German history of Nazi leader Adolf Hitler's rise. While this book focused on the years before World War II, Grass later penned two others which became the Danzig Trilogy; the second centering on the war years and the last volume dealing with the postwar era. All of the three are set in Danzig, the writer's childhood home, and use mythic or folk-loric characters who are often physically unusual in order to force a new perspective of the events of the time. Thanks to these and other politically outspo-ken works, the left–leaning Grass was once widely known as the conscience of Germany's postwar gen-eration. A prolific writer, he has created several plays and works of poetry in addition to more than 45 books. In 1999, he was honored with the Nobel Prize in literature.

On October 16, 1927, Grass was born in the Free City of Danzig (now Gdansk, Poland), a German-speaking port on the Baltic. His father, Willy, was German, and his mother, Helena (Knoff) Grass, was descended from the Kashubians, a Slavic people distinct from the Poles. They owned a neighbor-hood grocery store and enjoyed a middle–class lif-estyle; his father also held a minor government post. Raised in a climate that saw the rise of the totalitar-ian Nazi state under Adolf Hitler, Grass joined the Hitler youth and was inundated with the party ide-ology.

Still in his teens, in 1944 Grass was drafted to serve as an auxiliary in the Luftwaffe, the German air force. A year later, after serving on the front lines, he was wounded in Cottbus. After his hospitaliza-tion, he landed in an American prisoner–of–war camp in Bavaria. Later, he was forced to view the notorious Dachau concentration camp. By age 18, he was discharged from the service, bitter about his lost childhood, the near–total destruction of his hometown caused by the war, and the nationalistic German leadership that had spurred the disastrous situation.

After leaving the military in the spring of 1946, Grass worked as a farm hand and in a potash mine, and eventually reunited with his parents and sister, who were living as refugees in terrible conditions in West Germany. He briefly went back to school in Gottingen, but became disillusioned with the les-sons and became an apprentice stonemason, engrav-ing tombstones for a cemetery in Dusseldorf. In 1949, he entered the Dusseldorf Academy of Art and began to study painting and sculpture. At night, he earned money playing drums for a jazz band. Also around this time, he started to write creatively.

In 1953 Grass moved to Berlin and enrolled at the Academy of Art there seeking a new instructor, but continued to write as well. In 1954, he married Anna Schwarz, a ballet student, and in 1955, she sent some of his work in to a poetry contest sponsored by a Stuttgart radio station. He won third prize. Subsequently, he was invited to join Gruppe 47 (Group 47), a casual assemblage of German experi-mental writers. He published his first book of surre-alist and satiric poems and drawings, *Die Vorzuge der Windhuhner* (*The Advantages of Windfowl*) in 1956, and also wrote several plays and ballet librettos in the mid–1950s as well.

Grass moved to Paris in 1956 and began to work on his novel *Die Blechtrommel* (*The Tin Drum*). By 1958, he won first prize from Gruppe 47 for two chapters of the work, which was published in 1959. *The Tin Drum* is narrated by a mischievous dwarf named Oskar Matzerath who willed himself to stop grow-ing at age three to protest the stunted morality of the time. Through his eyes, the reader is exposed to a recollection of the war and postwar years in Ger-many, complete with rich symbolism. His drum-ming and his messiah complex conjures Hitler and his tub–thumping oratory; that his voice can shatter glass is a nod to the infamous Kristallnacht, in which troops destroyed Jewish storefronts.

The Tin Drum, translated into more than 20 lan-guages, sealed Grass's reputation as an international literary figure and led to a long list of awards from around the globe. It became an immediate best-seller in the United States. Despite all of the posi-tive reception, however, many alleged that the work was obscene and blasphemous. In one instance, the City of Bremen, awarded Grass a literary prize but the Social Democratic municipal senate blocked it due to concern that the city might be perceived as having given official sanction to a literary anarchist or pornographer. In 1979, *The Tin Drum* was adapted for a film directed by Volker Schlondorff and won the Golden Palm Award at Cannes and an Acad-emy Award for best foreign film in 1980.

While still in Paris, Grass wrote a ballet, *Funf Koche* (*Five Cooks*), which was produced in 1959 in Aix-les–Bains and in Bonn; a radio play, *Zweiundreizig Zahne* (*Thirty–two Teeth*), which was broadcast in 1959 by South German Radio; and two one–act plays. He also penned more poems, which appeared in 1960 in the volume *Gleisdreieck* (*Three Rail Junc-tion*), the name of a bleak railway station between East and West Berlin. He also started another large novel that expanded on his efforts to address his nation's tarnished past. It would be published in 1963 as *Hundejahre* (translated into English as *Dog Years,* 1965). Before that, however, Grass took one episode from this book to create a separate novella of almost two hundred pages, which helped him clarify his ideas for the longer work.

This novella was published *Katz und Maus* (*Cat and Mouse*), in 1961. It is the second in what became known as the "Danzig Trilogy," due to the setting.

Dog Years would round out the series. *Cat and Mouse* takes place during the war years and concerns a man with an incredibly large Adam's apple, signifying his probable status as a nonconformist. Despite his achievements as a war hero, he never gains full acceptance in society. The third volume, *Dog Years*, is a complex exploration of the postwar years and contains a love–hate relationship between a Jew and a non–Jew. It features three narrators, making it a more challenging work for the reader than *The Tin Drum*. Grass told H. F. Peters in the *Saturday Review*, "I wanted the period to be seen through the eyes of three generations."

Once Grass was renowned for his novels, he began to stage his plays, some of which were written before his books. One, *The Plebians Rehearse an Uprising*, staged in New York City in 1966, was intensely controversial. As Keith Botsford summed up in the *New York Times Magazine*, "In it, the only all–German postwar national cultural hero, Bertolt Brecht, who died in 1956, is mercilessly examined and cross–examined for intellectual and political courage and honesty and, in the opinion of many, found sorely wanting."

In the 1960s, Grass was an avid supporter of Berlin's Governing Mayor Willy Brandt and the Social Democratic party. As he noted to Botsford in the *New York Times Magazine*, "We are all affected by politics. Why shouldn't we all take part?" He campaigned actively and condemned the re–emergence of reactionary organizations in his country, and he parlayed his political concerns into his later writings. In *Local Anesthetic*, published in Germany in 1969 and the next year in America, he attacked the slogans of the radical left. Set in Berlin, this was his first work to take place in a location other than Danzig. *From the Diary of a Snail*, published in 1972 and translated the following year, is a fictional account of his participation in the Brandt campaign and one of his most autobiographical efforts. Later, in the 1990s, Grass left the Social Democratic party, critical of its curbs on immigration and its environmental policies. He also opposed Chancellor Gerhard Schroeder's efforts to make the party more pro–business.

The Flounder, which came out in Germany in 1977 and the United States in 1978, was one of Grass's most humorous novels. Dealing with women's rights, it is based on the Grimm's fairy tale "The Fisherman and His Wife." Some reviewers found much of the work objectionable, perceiving it to be anti–feminist. Grass, however, explained to Gwen Kinkead, "I'm against the kind of feminism which tries to change women to react like men, to come to power and use power like men. We have had enough stupid men. And now we have stupid women using power the way stupid men have for centuries."

In 1987, Grass published the English version of *The Rat*, which focused on environmental and nuclear threats. After that, he came out with *Show Your Tongue*, 1989, which was spawned by the author's travels to various poverty–stricken areas of the Third World. In *Two States—One Nation?*, 1990, Grass, through personal essays, expresses his disagreement on joining East and West Germany, believing that if given the power, it would pose a dangerous nationalistic threat to the world once again. *The Call of the Toad*, 1992, deals with a couple who become more and more greedy as their cemetery–plot business thrives, symbolizing the German grasp for wealth after the nation was reunified. Another novel, *A Far Field*, 1995, also concerns his fear of a reunified Germany, and prompted a vehement backlash from both literary and political arenas. However, it made it on to Germany's best–seller lists.

On September 30, 1999, Grass was on his way to the dentist when he received word that he had won the Nobel Prize for literature. The Swedish Academy cited him as their choice because "his frolicsome black fables portray the forgotten face of history," as Ursula Sautter reported in *Time International*. Grass later commented, according to Roger Cohen of the *New York Times*, "It's a great joy for me, not just for myself but for all German literature, which is honored with me." Cohen noted, "It was an uncharacteristically patriotic remark from a man who was bitterly critical of German unification in 1990." The event marked the fifth year in a row that a European had won the prize, but only the third time ever that it was bestowed upon a German (Thomas Mann and Heinrich Boll were the others). Grass donated his nearly $1 million in Nobel Prize money to the foundation for Sinti and Roma (as many gypsies prefer to be called) that he established.

Subsequently, Grass in late 1999 released *My Century: A Novel of Stories*, which Cohen described as "a running commentary on his times." Made up of 100 monologues, one for each year of the century, the tales are told from the perspectives of various characters—including Grass himself. With these voices of a flapper, a soldier, an informer, and others, the effort "becomes the literary equivalent of a choral symphony," according to a review in *Publishers Weekly*. However, Daniel Johnson of the *Sunday Telegraph* suggested that the book "may baffle someone who knows nothing of German culture," and added, "even a German readership would have benefited from notes." On the other hand, Merle Rubin in the *Christian Science Monitor* remarked, "Readers unfamiliar with modern German politics, society, and culture may come across references they don't immediately recognize, but the problem is not insurmountable."

Grass and his first wife had four children together: twins Franz and Raoul, a daughter Laura, and a son, Bruno. They divorced, and he married Utte Grunert in 1979, who has two sons, Malte and Hans, from a previous marriage. The couple live in Lubeck, in northern Germany. Grass has remained an avid sculptor throughout the years, as well as a graphic artist who has illustrated many of his own works.

Selected writings

Die Vorzuege der Windhuehner (poems, prose, and drawings; title means "The Advantages of Windfowl"), Luchterhand, 1956, third edition, 1967.

(Author of text) *O Susanna: Ein Jazzbilderbuch: Blues, Balladen, Spirituals, Jazz*, Kiepenheuer & Witsch, 1959.

Die Blechtrommel (novel), Luchterhand, 1959, translation by Ralph Manheim published *as The Tin Drum*, Vintage Books, 1962.

Gleisdreieck (poems and drawings; title means "Rail Triangle"), Luchterhand, 1960.

Katz und Maus (novella), Luchterhand, 1961, translation by Manheim published *as Cat and Mouse*, Harcourt, 1963.

Hundejahre (novel), Luchterhand, 1963, translation by Manheim published as

Dog Years, Harcourt, 1965.

Rede ueber das Selbstverstaendliche (speech), Luchterhand, 1965.

(Illustrator) *Ingeborg Buchmann, Ein Ortfuer Zufaelle*, Wagenbach, 1965.

Dich singe ich, Demokratie, Luchterhand, 1965.

Funf Wahlreden (speeches; contains "Was ist des Deutschen Vaterland?," "Loblied auf Willy," "Es steht zur Wahl," "Ich klage an," and "Des Kaisers neue Kleider"), Nuewied (Berlin), 1965.

Selected Poems (in German and English; includes poems from *Die Vorzuege der Windhuehner* and *Gleisdreieck*), translations by Michael Hamburger and Christopher Middleton, Harcourt, 1966, published as *Poems of Gunter Grass*, Penguin, 1969.

Ausgefragt (poems and drawings; title means "Questioned") Luchterhand, 1967.

Der Fall Axel C. Springer am Beispiel Arnold Zweig: Eine Rede, ihr Anlass, und die Folgen, Voltaire Verlag, 1967.

New Poems (includes poems from *Ausgefragt*), translation by Hamburger, Harcourt, 1968.

Ueber das Selbstverstaendliche: Reden, Aufsaetze, offene Briefe, Kommentare (title means "On the Self–Evident," Luchterhand, 1968, revised and supplemented edition published as

Ueber das Selbstverstaendliche: Politische Schriften, Deutscher Taschenbuch–Verlag 1969.

Briefe ueber die Grenze: Versuch eines Ost–West–Dialogs by Gunter Grass and Pavel Kohout (letters), C. Wegner, 1968.

Ueber meinen Lehrer Doeblin und andere Vortraege (title means "About My Teacher Doeblin and Other Lectures"), Literarisches Collequium Berlin, 1968.

Gunter Grass: Ausgewaehlte Texte, Abbildungen, Faksimiles, Bio–Bibliographie, edited by Theodor Wieser, Luchterhand, 1968, also published as Portraet und Poesie, 1968.

Kunst oder Pornographie?, J. F. Lehmann, 1969.

Speak Out: Speeches, Open Letters, Commentarie s (includes selections from *Ueber das Selbstverstaendliche: Reden, Aufsaetze, offene Briefe Kommentare*), translated by Manheim, Harcourt, 1969.

Oertlich betaeubt (novel), Luchterhand, 1969, translation by Manheim published as

Local Anaesthetic, Harcourt, 1970.

Die Schweinekopfsuelze, Merlin Verlag, 1969.

Originalgraphik (poem with illustrations), limited edition, Argelander, 1970.

Gesammelte Gedichte ("Collected Poems"), introduction by H. Vormweg, Luchterhand, 1971.

Dokumente zur politischen Wirkung, edited by Heinz Ludwig Arnold and Franz Josef Goertz, Richard Boorherg, 1971.

Aus dem Tagebuch einer Schnecke, Luchterhand, 1972, translation by Manheim published as *From the Diary of a Snail*, Harcourt, 1973.

Mariazuehren Hommageamarie Inmarypraise, Bruckmann, 1973, bilingual edition with translation by Middleton published as *Inmarypraise*, Harcourt, 1974.

Liebe geprueft (poems), [Bremen], 1974.

Der Buerger und seine Stimme (title means "The Citizen and His Voice"), Luchterhand, 1974.

Gunter Grass Materialienbuch, edited by Rolf Geissler, Luchterhand, 1976.

Der Butt, Luchterhand, 1977, translation by Manheim published as *The Flounder*, Harcourt, 1978.

Denkzettel (title means "Note for Thought"), Luchterhand, 1978.

In the Egg and Other Poems (contains poems from *Selected Poems and New Poems*), translated by Hamburger and Middleton, Secker & Warburg, 1978.

Das Treffen in Telgte, Luchterhand, 1978, translation by Manheim published *as The Meeting at Telgte*, Harcourt, 1981.

Werkverzeichnis der Radierungen (catalogue), A. Dreher, 1979. (With Volker Schlondorff) *Die Blechtrommel als Film,* Zweitausendeins, 1979. (Contributor) *Danzig 1939: Treasures of a Destroyed Community,* Wayne State University Press, 1980.

Aufsaetze zur Literatur, 1957–1979 (title means "Essays on Literature, 1957–1979"), Luchterhand, 1980.

Danziger Trilogie (title means "Danzig Trilogy;" contains *Die Blechtrommel, Katz und Maus,* and *Hundejahre*), Luchterhand, 1980.

Kopfgeburten; oder Die Deutschen sterben aus, Luchterhand, 1980, translation by Manheim published as *Headbirths; or, The Germans Are Dying Out,* Secker & Warburg, 1982.

Zeichnen and Schreiben: Das bildnerische Werk des Schriftstellers Gunter Grass, Luchterhand, 1982, translation published as *Graphics and Writing,* Harcourt, 1983.

Kinderlied (poems and etchings; originally published in *Gesammelte Gedichte*), Lord John, 1982.

Zeichnungen und Texte, 1954–1977, Luchterhand, 1982, translation by Hamburger and Walter Arndt published as *Drawings and Words, 1954–1977,* Harcourt, 1983.

Ach, Butt!: Dein Maerchen geht boese aus, Luchterhand, 1983.

Radierungen und Texte, 1972–1982, Luchterhand, 1984, translation by Hamburger and others published as *Etchings and Words, 1972–1982,* Harcourt, 1985.

Widerstand lernen: Politische Gegenreden, 1980–1983 (title means "Learning Resistance: Political Countertalk"), Luchterhand, 1984.

On Writing and Politics: 1967–1983 (essays), translated by Manheim, Harcourt, 1985.

Geschenkt Freiheit, Akademie der Kuenste, 1985.

Die Raettin, Luchterhand, 1986, translation by Manheim published as *The Rat,* Harcourt, 1987.

Werkausgabe, ten volumes, edited by Volker Neuhaus, Luchterhand, 1987.

Die Gedichte 1955–1986, Luchterhand, 1988.

Zunge Zeigen, Luchterhand, 1988, translation by John E. Wood published as

Show Your Tongue, Harcourt, 1989.

Deutscher Lastenausgleich: Wider das dumpfe Einheitsgebot; Reden und Gesprache, Texte zur Zeit, Aufbau, 1990.

Ein Schnappchen namens DDR: Letzte Reden vorm Glockengelaut, Luchterhand, 1990.

Skizzenbuch, Steidl, 1990.

Schreiben nach Auschwitz, Luchterhand, 1990.

Totes Holz, illustrated by Grass, Gottingen, 1990.

Two States—One Nation?, Harcourt, 1990.

Ukenrufe: Eine Erzahlung, Gottingen, 1992.

The Call of the Toad, translation by Manheim, Harcourt, 1992.

Unkenrufe (title means "Toad Croaks"), Gottingen, 1992.

In Kupfer, auf Stein: Das grafische Werk, edited by G. Fritze Margull, Steidl, 1994.

Cat and Mouse and Other Writings, Continuum (New York City), 1994.

Ein Weites Feld, Steidl, 1995.

(With Kenzaburo Oe) *Gestern, vor 50 Jahren: ein Deutsch–Japanischer Briefwechsel,* Steidl, 1995.

Die Deutschen und Ihre Dichter, Deutscher Taschenbuch Verlag, 1995.

Novemberland: Selected Poems, 1956–1993, Harcourt Brace (New York City), 1996.

Aesthetik Des Engagements, P. Lang, 1996.

Rede uber den Standort, Steidl, 1997.

My Century: A Novel of Stories, translated by Michael Henry Heim, Harcourt Brace (New York City), 1999.

Plays

Die boesen Koeche: Ein Drama in fuenf Akten (first produced in West Berlin in 1961; translation by A. Leslie Willson produced as *The Wicked Cooks* on Broadway at Orpheum Theatre, January 23, 1967), Luchterhand, 1982.

Hochwasser: Ein Stueck in zwei Akten (two acts), Suhrkamp, 1963, fourth edition, 1968.

Onkel, Onkel (four acts; title means "Mister, Mister"), Wagenbach 1965.

Die Plebejer proben den Aufstand: Ein deutsches Trauerspiel (first produced in West Berlin at Schiller Theatre, January 15, 1966), Luchterhand, 1966, translation by Manheim published as *The Plebeians Rehearse the Uprising: A German Tragedy* (produced in Cambridge, MA, at the Harvard Dramatic Club, 1967), Harcourt, 1966.

The World of Gunter Grass, adapted by Dennis Rosa, produced off–Broadway at Pocket Theatre, April 26, 1966.

Hochwasser [and] *Noch zehn Minuten bis Buffalo* (title of second play means "Only Ten Minutes to Buffalo"), edited by Wilson, Appleton, 1967.

Four Plays (includes *The Flood* [produced in New York at Project III Ensemble Theater, June, 1986], *Onkel, Onkel,* [cited in some sources as "Mister, Mister"], *Only Ten Minutes to Buffalo,* and *The Wicked Cooks*), Harcourt, 1967.

Davor: Ein Stuck in dreizehn Szenen, first produced in West Berlin at Schiller Theatre, February 16, 1969, translation by Wilson and Manheim produced as *Uptight in Washington, DC,* at Kreeger Theatre, March 22, 1972, published as *Davor: Ein Stuck in dreizehn Szenen,* Harcourt, 1973 translation published as *Max: A Play,* Harcourt, 1972.

Theaterspiele (includes *Hochwasser, Onkel, Onkel, Die Plebejer proben den Aufstand,* and *Davor;* first produced in West Berlin at the German Opera, 1970), Luchterhand, 1970.

Other plays include *Beritten hin und zurueck* (title means "Rocking Back and Forth"), *Goldmaeulchen*, 1964, and *Zweiunddreizig Zaehne*.

Media Adaptations

Die Blechtrommel (*The Tin Drum*) was filmed and released by New World Pictures, April, 1980 and won several awards, including the Golden Palm Award from the Cannes Film Festival and an Academy Award for best foreign picture from the Academy of Motion Picture Arts and Sciences, both 1980.

Sources

Books

Dictionary of Literary Biography, Volume 75: Contemporary German Fiction Writers, edited by Wolfgang D. Elfe and James Hardin, Gale Research, 1988.

Dictionary of Literary Biography, Volume 124: Twentieth–Century German Dramatists, edited by Wolfgang D. Elfe and James Hardin, Gale Research, 1992.

Encyclopedia of World Biography, second edition, Gale Research, 1998.

Periodicals

Christian Science Monitor, November 24, 1999, p. 17.

Economist, September 2, 1995, p. 43; October 25, 1997, p. 57.

Independent, October 1, 1999, p. 7.

New Republic, December 23, 1978, p. 25.

New York Times, October 1, 1999, p. A13.

New York Times Magazine, May 8, 1966, p. 28.

Publishers Weekly, June 16, 1989, p. 54; November 15, 1999, p. 57.

Saturday Review, May 29, 1965, p. 25.

Sunday Telegraph, December 19, 1999, p. 17.

Time International, October 11, 1999, p. 28.

Online

"Gunter Grass," *Contemporary Authors Online*, Gale Group web site, http://www.glaenet.com (December 1, 1999).

Michael Graves

AP/Wide World Photos

Architect and designer

Born July 9, 1934, in Indianapolis, IN; son of Thomas Browning Graves (a livestock broker) and Erma Sanderson (a nurse; maiden name, Lowe) Graves; married and divorced twice; two children from first marriage; two stepchildren from second marriage. *Education:* University of Cincinnati (Ohio), B.S. in architecture, 1958; Harvard University, Cambridge, MA, M.Arch., 1959; attended American Academy, Rome, 1960–62.

Addresses: *Office*—341 Nassau St., Princeton, NJ 08540.

Career

Worked in the design office of George Nelson, New York, early 1960s; founder–principal,Michael Graves Architect architectural and design firm, Princeton, New Jersey, 1964 ; founder of Graves Design Studio Store, Princeton, marketing Graves Design furniture, furnishings, and artifacts; furniture, furnishing, and lighting designs for Atelier International, Kron, Dunbar, Arkitektura, Baldinger, Alessi, The Markuse Corporation, Steuben, Moller, Gilbert International, Belvedere Studio, Vorwerk, Tajima, Target, and others. Lecturer, 1962–63, assistant professor, 1963–67, associate professor, 1967–72, and Schirmer Professor of Architecture, 1972 , Princeton University, New Jersey; visiting fellow, Institute for Architecture and Urban Studies, New York, 1971–72; visiting professor, University of Texas, Austin, 1973–74, University of Houston, Texas, 1974, 1978, New School for Social Research, New York, 1975, and University of California at Los Angeles, 1977; architect–in–residence, American Academy, Rome, 1979. *Member:* American Academy and Institute of Arts and Letters.

Exhibitions include *40 Under 40,* Architectural League, New York, NY, 1966; *Architecture of Museums,* Museum of Modern Art, New York, NY, 1968; *Five Architects,* Princeton University, NJ, 1974 (traveled to Austin, Texas); *The New York Five,* Art Net, London, 1975; *Michael Graves: Projects 1967-76,* Columbia University, New York, 1976; *Beyond the Modern Movement,* Harvard University, Cambridge, MA, 1977; *Trends in Contemporary Architecture,* New Gallery of Contemporary Art, Cleveland, Ohio, 1978; *Ornament in the Twentieth Century,* Cooper-Hewitt Museum, New York, 1978; *Michael Graves: Progetti 1977-81,* Rome, 1981; *Design Since 1945,* Philadelphia Museum of Art, 1983; and *Intuition and the Block Print,* John Nichols Printmakers and Publishers, New York, 1984.

Works include Urban County Nature and Science Museum, Mountainside, NJ, 1967; N.E.S.T. rehabilitation housing, Trenton, New Jersey, 1967-71; Three murals in Transammonia Inc. offices, New York, 1974; Mural in the School of Architecture, University of Texas, Austin, 1974; Abrahams Dance Studio, Princeton, NJ, 1977; Mural in the John Witherspoon School, Princeton, NJ, 1978; Newark (NJ) Museum Children's Museum, 1978; furniture showrooms and office in New York and Cleveland, for E.F. Hauserman Corporation, 1978; The Portland Building, Portland, OR, 1980; Humana Building, Louisville, KY,

1982; San Juan Capistrano (CA) Regional Library, 1983; Riverbend Music Center, Cincinnati, OH, 1983; Diane Von Furstenberg boutique, Fifth Avenue, New York, 1984; Clos Pegase Winery and Residence, Napa Valley, CA, 1984; Columbus Circle Redevelopment, New York, 1985; Whitney Museum of American Art, New York, 1985; The Disney Company corporate headquarters, Burbank, CA, 1986; Historical Center for Industry and Labor, Youngstown, OH, 1986; Walt Disney World Dolphin and World Swan hotels, Florida, 1987; Yokohama Portside District Condominium Tower, Yokohama, Japan, 1987; 10 Peachtree Plaza office building, Atlanta, GA, 1988; Hotel New York, for Euro Disneyland, France, 1989; Indianapolis Art Center, Indianapolis, Indiana, 1990; Fukuoka Hotel and Office project, Fukuoka, Japan, 1990; Birth of Democracy exhibition, National Archives, Washington, D.C., 1991; Rome Reborn exhibition, Library of Congress, Washington, D.C., 1992; Pittsburgh Cultural Trust, Theater, and Office Building, Pittsburgh, PA, 1992; Federal Courthouse, Trenton, NJ, 1992; Taiwan Pre-History Museum, Taipei, Taiwan, 1993; International Finance Corporation headquarters, Washington, D.C., 1993; Bayou Place Theater, Houston, TX, 1993; Saint Martin's College Library, Lacey, WA, 1994; and Delaware River Port Authority office building, Camden, NJ, 1994. Awards: Arnold W. Brunner Fellowship, 1960; Prix de Rome, American Academy, Rome, 1960; New Jersey Society of Architects Awards, 1967, 1973, 1974, 1975 (2), 1976 (2), 1977, 1978 (4), 1980 (4), 1981 (2), 1982, 1983 (3), 1984, 1985 (2), 1987 (6), 1988, 1989 (2), 1990 (3), 1991 (6), 1992 (3), 1994 (3), and Special Recognition Honor Award, 1982; Progressive Architecture Design Awards, 1970, 1976, 1977, 1978, 1979, 1980 (3), 1983, 1988, 1989 (2), and Furniture Design Awards, 1982, 1983; American Institute of Architects National Honor Awards, 1975, 1979, 1982, 1983, 1985, 1987 (2), 1990, 1992; Arnold W. Brunner Memorial Prize in Architecture, American Academy of Arts and Letters, 1980; Resources Council Commendations, 1980, 1982; Institute of Business Designers Awards, 1982 (2), 1990; Indiana Arts Award, 1983; Euster Award, Miami, Florida, 1983; Honored Artist, Young Women of the Arts, Atlanta, Georgia, 1985; Henry Hering Memorial Medal, Portland, Oregon, 1986; Gold Plate Award, American Academy of Achievement, 1986; I.D. (International Design) Awards, Consumer Products, 1989, 1990, and Furniture, honorable mention, 1989; Award of Excellence in Graphic Design, American Federation of Arts, 1990; New Jersey Business and Industry Association Award, 1990; Downtown New Jersey Excellence Award for Downtown Development, 1990; Walt Whitman Creative Arts Award, New Jersey, 1991. Honorary doctorates from University of Cincinnati, 1982, Boston University, 1984, Savannah College of Art, 1986, Rhode Island School of Design, 1990, New Jersey Institute of Technology, 1991, and Rutgers University, 1994; fellow, Society for the Arts, Religion and Culture.

Sidelights

Architect Michael Graves has been a central figure in the evolution of postmodern design since the mid–1970s. Although he dislikes being labeled a postmodernist, Graves's works are most easily categorized by the term. As Carter Wiseman noted in the *Saturday Review*, "Indeed, his designs are so eclectic and so personal, that he seems to elude all easy labels. His designs embody an intriguing blend of history and fantasy infused with what can only be called a sense of the eternal." Wiseman also recognized that Graves's designs recall ancient Greece and Egypt, as well as a Baroque style. As with much public architecture, Graves's creations have been both highly praised and severely criticized. In any event, according to Paul Goldberger in the *New York Times Magazine*, "Graves…is the most truly original voice that American architecture has produced in some time…. His work is dazzling to look at, and yet it deals in issues more profound than simply the decoration of construction."

Though he started out in the modernist camp in the 1960s, Graves has veered away from such a spartan feel in order to incorporate a variety of classical elements. Thus, he has created more vibrant spaces that also are more inhabitable while keeping in mind that he is developing buildings that must fit into a contemporary environment. He has also been involved in creating home products for high–end resellers. Despite his influence on current designs and his long list of accolades, few outside of Graves's field were aware of his works until the late 1990s, when he signed on to design an extensive line of home products for Target stores. Now, although he still may not be a household name, millions of shoppers can pick out his distinctive work from the other hum–drum objects that usually sit on shelves at the lower–priced retail chains. From charming retro–look toasters and blenders to picture frames, patio sets, clocks, and more, Graves has made style affordable.

Graves was born on July 9, 1934, in Indianapolis, Indiana. His father, Thomas Browning Graves, was a livestock broker who never finished high school, and his mother, Erma Sanderson (Lowe) Graves, received training as a nurse. Since he was young, Graves aspired to be an artist, and loved to draw and paint. Though it is still a hobby of his, Graves's parents urged him to pursue a more practical field, so he ended up in architecture.

After receiving his bachelor of science degree from the University of Cincinnati in Ohio in 1958, Graves went on to get a master's degree in architecture from Harvard University the following year. Subsequently, he was awarded a Prix de Rome and a Brunner fellowship and studied at the American Academy in Rome from 1960 to 1962. While there, he was heavily influenced by Renaissance architecture. Returning to the United States, Graves worked for a short time in New York for a designer, but yearned for a more academic environment and began to seeking teaching positions. In 1962, he joined the Princeton University faculty because they made him the best offer—a salary of $8,000 a year. He has taught there ever since, in addition to acting as a visiting professor at other universities.

Initially, Graves immersed himself in teaching, taking only small local commissions out of his small office staffed by students. Even back then, he believed in a concept of total design—he even created apparel for his wife. Before long, Graves was recognized as part of a group of young architects, known as the New York Five, whose work, mainly residential, owed much to Swiss architect Le Corbusier, known for his abstract geometric designs. In 1972, Graves and the others, Peter Eisenman, John Hejduk, Charles Gwathmey, and Richard Meier, collaborated on a book to showcase their efforts, titled *Five Architects*. This drew attention to their modernist style and generated much critical discussion throughout the profession.

Later, Graves would stray from the thesis of creating sparse forms and austere spaces, thus altering his relationships with the other four. "The language of modernism was simply not rich enough to say everything I wanted to say," Graves explained to Paul Goldberger in the *New York Times Magazine*. "I love [Italian baroque architect Francesco] Borromini and want to get some of the feeling of the richness of that architecture into my work, but if you have to paint it white and make it flat, what's the point?" Graves enjoyed using colors, collages, and Cubist spatial effects, revealing his underlying interest in painting and further separating him from the tenets of modernism. Examples of this include the Benacerraf House addition (Princeton, New Jersey, 1969) and the Snyderman House (Fort Wayne, Indiana, 1972–77).

Moving even further away from modernism, by the mid–1970s Graves began using figurative metaphors in his buildings; he incorporated designs that resembled the human body. For example, a wall could be divided into three distinct parts, representing a head, body, and feet. By taking into account the fact that humans would inhabit the spaces he created, Graves became a more poetic designer. This approach won him a stellar reputation in his field, casting him as one of the profession's most influential members, even though he was respected mainly for his theoretical concepts. By 1982, he had only produced a total of four standing buildings, most of them minor: a small museum in New Jersey and three houses, in addition to several additions and interiors.

By this time, though, Graves began to line up larger projects. His first substantial work to showcase his postmodern pastiche was the $22.4 million, 15–story Public Office Building built in Portland, Oregon in 1980. At the time, his selection caused debate in the field, since he had never tackled such a major project. He had won a competition to be awarded the commission, and subsequently, some vocal Modernists demanded a second competition be held. Graves won that one as well, but the controversy was not over. Reaction was wildly mixed after the work was completed: Goldberger reported that Wolf Von Eckardt in *Time* "produced one of the most violent denunciations of an American building ever written by an architecture critic," although many others, including Goldberger himself, applauded the Portland building. The structure blended well with the city's older buildings and park, yet offered several distinctive accents, such as a richly colored fa[0087]ade in shades of terra cotta, ivory, and blue, as well as elements of Art Deco. Graves was cited for his attention to style as well as energy efficiency and cost–effectiveness.

Then, in the fall of 1981, Graves won the prestigious commission for an extension to the Whitney Museum of American Art in New York City. If he thought the earlier reaction to his Portland building was antagonistic, the backlash to this project was even more shocking—even I.M. Pei, himself a controversial figure, particularly for his glass pyramids on the grounds of the Louvre museum in Paris, signed a petition against Graves for the work. The previous year, Graves had declined to criticize Pei's pyramids, commenting, according to Calvin Tomkins in the *New Yorker*, "Architects don't do that sort of thing."

Other projects by Graves include the 27–story Humana Medical Corporation Headquarters in Louisville, Kentucky, which successfully incorporated the skyscraper into the downtown's assortment of lower buildings. In addition, he created a public library in San Juan Capistrano, California, in 1983, displaying influence from the Spanish mission style. Throughout the 1980s and 1990s, he continued to develop large–scale buildings, including the Disney Company headquarters in Burbank, California; a winery and residence in Napa Valley for Clos Pegase; the Indianapolis Art Center; a federal courthouse in Trenton, New Jersey; a museum in Taiwan; and various hotels and office space.

In addition to his revolutionary architecture, Graves has made his name in housewares as well. By the rarly 1980s, shunning any demarcations regarding his profession, Graves had branched into designing textiles for the Sunar Furniture and Fabric company, as well as creating four stunning showrooms. Soon, he was also designing furniture, rugs, dinnerware, jewelry, watches, and various home products, including clocks, pepper mills, ashtrays, and more. But perhaps his most famous item in that genre up to that point was his tea kettle for the Alessi company in Italy in 1985, complete with a chirping bird whistle—more than a million of the items have been sold at a price of $150 each. After that, Graves also created a Mickey Mouse tea kettle for Moller International.

Vaulting into the mainstream, in the late 1990s Graves made a deal with the discount retailer Target to design a line of home products. Graves made it clear that he would be innately involved in the project, responsible not just for adding his name to items, but also for overseeing the actual designs. His relationship with the store began when Target donated $6 million for the restoration of the Washington Monument in Washington, D.C., and asked Graves to provide a stylistic scaffolding. Pleased with his work, a vice president then approached the designer to see if he could offer advice on making Target products more appealing. The partnership of a renowned architect and a mass–market chain store, however, caused some consternation. "People asked me, 'Why are you doing this?'" Graves related to Paul Goldberger in the *New Yorker*. "I tell them, 'If I design a library in Denver, that's for the masses, so why not this sort of stuff?"

Indeed, Graves's talents shone through in the Target line. The sleek geometry and whimsical touches on the products did not detract from, and often added to, the functionality. His creations ranged from a $3.99 "Hipper Flipper" spatula to a $499 hardwood patio table and chairs, and in a clever word play, the white, rounded toaster with the yellow knobs and blue handle was even dubbed the "Toast Modern." The Graves line, offering fashion at an afford-able price, was a boon for the retailer, who has been successful in reaching a younger, higher–income market with its hip marketing campaigns and its efforts to stock stylish goods. Many of the customers even pronounce the store name as "tar–ZHAY" as a tongue–in–cheek reference to its placement as the most upscale of discounters. "Mr. and Mrs. America are a lot more sophisticated than we give them credit for," Graves remarked to Connie Nelson in the Minneapolis *Star Tribune*. After hitting the shelves in February of 1999, Graves's designs became popular items, prompting Target to ask him to continue expanding the line. Also, Graves finally got some respect from his peers as well for the endeavor when his toaster won a silver medal at the 1999 Industrial Design Excellence Awards.

Incidentally, Graves was one of the new breed of architects that Tom Wolfe took to task in his condemnation of the state of contemporary design in his 1981 book, *From Bauhaus to Our House*. He particularly cited Graves for rehashing the past instead of coming up with something entirely original. However, many others disagreed, and Graves throughout his career has amassed a long list of honors for his many creations, including several awards from the American Institute of Architects and the New Jersey Society of Architects.

Sources

Books

Contemporary Designers, third edition, St. James Press, 1997.
Encyclopedia of World Biography, second edition, Gale Research, 1998.

Periodicals

Art in America, September 1980, p. 99.
Christian Science Monitor, February 24, 1999, p. 11.
Dallas Morning News, January 29, 1999, p. 1G.
Fortune, May 24, 1999, p. 169.
Newsday, February 25, 1999, p. B14.
New Yorker, February 17, 1986, p. 58; February 1, 1999, p. 23.
New York Times Magazine, October 10, 1982, p. 42.
Saturday Review, March 1982, p. 41.
Star Tribune (Minneapolis, MN), January 17, 1999, p. 4F; March 4, 1999, p. 6.
Time, August 30, 1999, p. 41.

Mia Hamm

Soccer player

Born Muriel Margret Hamm, March 17, 1972, in Selma, AL; daughter of an Bill (an Air Force colonel) and Stephanie (a ballet dancer) Hamm; married Christian Corry (a U.S. Marine), 1995. *Education:* University of North Carolina, degree in political science, 1994.

Addresses: *Office*—c/o Nike, Inc., Soccer Division, 1 Bowerman Dr., Beaverton, OR 97005–6453.

Career

Member of U.S. women's national soccer team, forward, 1995—. Also played for University of North Carolina, 1990–94. Spokesmodel for Nike, AT&T, Pert shampoo, Power Bars, and Mattel.

Awards: Won World Cup with U.S. women's national soccer team, 1991, 1999; Missouri Athletic Club Award and Hermann Award, 1992, 1993; women's college player of the year, 1992; U.S. Soccer Athlete of the Year, 1994, 1995, 1996; U.S. Soccer Female Athlete of the Year, 1994, 1995, 1996, 1997, 1998; won Olympic gold medal with U.S. team, 1996; won U.S. Women's Cup with U.S. women's national team, 1999.

Sidelights

Soccer player Mia Hamm has scored more goals during her career than any other player, male or female, in the history of the sport. This five–foot–five, 125–pound speed demon has run her opponents ragged as she has helped lead her college team, the U.S. national team, and the U.S. Olympic team to victories. Hamm became the first player to receive the U.S. Soccer athlete of the year award three times, in 1994, 1995, and 1996, and only the second player ever to receive the U.S. Soccer female athlete of the year award two years in a row, in 1994 and 1995. Even more astounding, she clinched the award again every year thereafter until 1998 as well. In the summer of 1999, Hamm once again proved to be an integral part of the national team, as she led the women to triumph over China for the World Cup.

In an age where soccer as well as women's sports are becoming popular for the first time, Hamm has ridden the wave to become a pioneer as well as an icon. Though soccer is one of the most closely followed sports worldwide, it only caught on in the United States beginning in the 1980s, when more young people began to play. In addition, the establishment of more professional female sports organizations, such as the Women's National Basketball Association, has started to wipe away the stigma of female athletes; they were previously perceived to be too "masculine." Salary–wise, they have a long way to go in order to catch up to their male counterparts, but the culture of female athletes is growing, which portends a brighter future. Female fans proudly wear Hamm's number 9 jersey and pull their hair back in ponytails, clamoring after her for autographs and high–fives, and the record–setting crowds are a good sign that people are more accepting of women's sports. Though the humble player is, by all accounts, uncomfortable with her status as a role model, Hamm noted to Jere Longman in the New York Times, "It's very important for young girls to have female athletes they can identify with."

Muriel Margret "Mia" Hamm was born on March 17, 1972, in Selma, Alabama, and moved frequently throughout her childhood because her father, Bill, was a colonel in the Air Force. The family, which includes her three sisters and two brothers, lived on bases in Texas, California, Virginia, and Florence, Italy. When Hamm was five, her parents adopted her brother Garrett, eight years old at the time, who was very athletic and a big influence on Hamm. "When he'd go play pickup football or baseball, I was always right behind him," she told Longman. "He always picked me for his teams." Her mother, Stephanie, a former ballerina, tried to steer her into dancing at a young age, but Hamm would have no part of it, preferring to play soccer instead. It was one of her father's passions: He would take the family to games in Italy, and back in the United States, he coached and refereed his children's teams.

Hamm got her start at age five on the soccer field in a co–ed pee–wee league in Wichita Falls, Texas. "Our team record wasn't very good, but I managed to score a lot of goals," as she remarked in a People article. But she did not limit herself to one sport. On boys' teams, Hamm played baseball as a short-stop and pitcher, basketball as a point guard, and even football in seventh grade as a wide receiver and cornerback. "I was fast and could catch the ball," she explained to Kevin Sherrington of the Dallas Morning News. "My friends wanted me to play." She also put in time as a quarterback but did not enjoy it as much, although overall, she liked the sport. "I had a great time at it," she noted to Sherrington.

Hamm had her share of physical contact even in soccer, as the only girl in the boys' league. Her male opponents became angry when she scored and would then play rough and shove her down. Eventually she learned how to quickly get out of the way of a collision. Hamm was so talented at the sport due to her quick thinking as well as her dedication to practice she would usually be on the empty field by 8 a.m. most mornings during the summer, trying to nail every shot possible. Coach Lou Pearce at Notre Dame High School in Wichita Falls was impressed and suggested she try out for something bigger.

By the time she was 14, Hamm was playing on an Olympic development team for John Cossaboon (even though women's soccer was not even declared an Olympic event at this time). He, in turn, called his friend Anson Dorrance, who was coaching the national team. He went to see her play and remarked in People, "I'd never seen speed like that in the women's game. She had unlimited potential." In 1987, at age 15 years, 140 days, Hamm joined the team as the youngest member ever, male or female, and made her first appearance on August 3, 1987. She scored her first goal with the team on July 25, 1990, versus Norway. After her sophomore year of high school, Hamm moved to Burke, Virginia, where she was high school All–American. Then she enrolled at the University of North Carolina, where Dorrance was coaching. There, she earned a degree in political science in 1994, but in the meantime, she was ripping up the field as well.

Known as a soccer powerhouse, North Carolina cemented their reputation with Hamm on their side as she helped lead them to National Collegiate Athletic Association (NCAA) victories each of her four years there. She was a three–time All–American and set all–time conference records with 103 goals, 72 assists, and 278 points; her college number, 19, was retired in 1994. Hamm also became a star on the U.S. team that won the women's world championship in 1991, even though she was still the youngest player. During that game, she started five of six matches and scored two goals. In 1992 and 1993, she received the Missouri Athletic Club Award and Hermann Award and was named women's college player of the year, leading the NCAA with 32 goals and 33 assists.

In her senior year at North Carolina, Hamm found out that the Olympics had declared women's soccer a full–medal sport for the first time, to be included on the roster at the 1996 games in Atlanta, Georgia. She was ecstatic, now that she could follow in the footsteps of a couple of her heroes, gymnast Mary Lou Retton and track star Jackie Joyner–Kersee. "You hear all the cliches, that it's a dream come true," she remarked to Mike Spence of the Knight–Ridder/Tribune News Service. "Well, it is for myself and for every girl growing up who plays any sport." Not only did Hamm make it to the 1996 Olympics, she helped lead the team to the gold medal, pushing past China 2–1.

By this time, Hamm was considered the best player in women's soccer and became flooded with endorsement offers. Though shy by nature and reluctant to be made into such a public persona, she became convinced that her high profile would ultimately be a positive influence among young girls. She has made commercials for AT&T, Pert shampoo, Power Bars, and Nike, the latter of which even named a building in her honor at its headquarters in Oregon. In addition, Hamm helped market a special edition soccer Barbie doll for Mattel. But perhaps her most popular ad was the humorous spot for Gatorade in which she outperforms Michael Jordan in a number of sports from soccer and basketball to fencing and judo while the background music plays "Anything you can do, I can do better." In addition, after the Olympics, Hamm appeared on *Late Night with David Letterman* and in 1997, was the only female athlete to be named one of the 50 most beautiful people in the world by *People* magazine.

Women's soccer reached a new level during July of 1999 when much of the United States got wrapped up in following the Women's World Cup championships. After 120 minutes of scoreless play, including two nail–biting overtime periods, the game came down to a single penalty kick. Brandi Chastain finally kicked in a goal to squeak past China, 1–0. The event captured the attention of the nation and allowed everyone to rally around a winner. As Rick Reilly pointed out in *Sports Illustrated,* "Look at what our American men's international teams have done lately. Ryder Cup: humiliated. Presidents Cup: humiliated. USA Hockey: dead humiliated. World Cup: dead last." Not only was the team adored for their athletic prowess, they were admired for their well–roundedness as well. All team members had a college degree or were full–time students, and many were married with children as well.

Though the victory stirred much optimistic discussion about the future of women in sports, it also led to a flurry of debate about the sexuality of the female players. Many were critical that Chastain, immediately following her game–winning kick, tore her jersey over her head in a show of excitement. Though she was wearing a fully–covering sports bra top, she was the target of some who felt she was too immodest. Following that, she showed up in a men's magazine, Gear, covered by nothing but a soccer ball. Hamm managed to avoid much of the controversy, though the entire team did become a favorite of talk show host David Letterman, who repeatedly referred to them as "Babe City." Despite this side issue, the fact remained that the event had apparently gone far in promoting the idea of female sports: The final game between the U.S. and China was a sold–out event, drawing 90,185 fans, a record for a women's sporting event.

The year 1999 also marked an important personal milestone for Hamm. That year, she surpassed Elisabetta Vignotto of Italy, now retired, who had held the record of 106 for most goals scored in women's soccer. Also that year, the team went on to yet another championship. That October, they followed up their huge summer celebration by reigning at the U.S. Women's Cup tournament in Louisville, Kentucky, with a 4–2 win over Brazil. A 5–0 showdown against South Korea just a few days prior in Columbus, Ohio, had marked the team's twenty–third victory of the year, surpassing its year–old record for wins in a calendar year. In addition, another game in the series, in a 6–0 shutout against Finland, 36,405 people showed up to watch—the largest ever soccer crowd in Kansas City. This was a far cry from the old days before the Olympics, when the team would regularly play before just 5,000 or perhaps 10,000 spectators. Though Hamm had displayed a lackluster performance in some games earlier in the year, it appeared she was back on track by the year's end. By the time the 1999 U.S. Women's Cup contest was over, Hamm's goals had reached 114 and, undoubtedly, were bound to grow. At this point, she held the record for the most goals ever scored by a man or woman in all of soccer.

Hamm is married to Christian Corry, who is an officer in the U.S. Marine Corps, but they see each other infrequently due to her hectic travel schedule. In addition to her soccer games and product endorsements, Hamm keeps busy with the Mia Hamm Foundation, a nonprofit entity that she set up to raise funds to research bone marrow diseases and to assist young female athletes. Corporate partners Nike, Mattel, and Gatorade pitch in with special events as well. Much of Hamm's inspiration for the organization came from her brother, Garrett, who contracted a rare blood disease, aplastic anemia, in 1975 and died in 1997 at age 28. She has also written a book, *Go for the Goal,* 1999, which is ostensibly an autobiography but contains mainly self– help information and details on soccer.

Sources

Periodicals

Dallas Morning News, July 30, 1996, p. 20B.
Entertainment Weekly, July 16, 1999, p. 10.
Knight–Ridder/Tribune News Service, May 16, 1996; August 1, 1996; May 8, 1997.
Newsweek, July 19, 1999, p. 46.
New York Times, June 11, 1999, p. A1; June 20, 1999, sec. 1, p. 25; June 27, 1999, sec. 1, p. 21; July 11, 1999, sec. 1, p. 19.
New York Times Upfront, September 6, 1999, p. 32.
People, November 1, 1993, p. 63; May 12, 1997, p. 90.
Seventeen, June 1994, p. 42.

Sports Illustrated, July 5, 1999, p. 100.
U.S. News & World Report, June 21, 1999, p. 13.

Online

"U.S., Brazil win cup openers," ESPN web site, October 7, 1999, http://espn.go.com (October 12, 1999).

"Lilly, Hamm key U.S. rout of Finland," ESPN web site, October 8, 1999, http://espn.go.com (October 12, 1999).

"Hosts go 3–0 to capture U.S. Women's Cup," ESPN web site, October 10, 1999, http://espn.go.com (October 12, 1999).

"Mia Hamm," Women's Soccer World web site, http://www.womensoccer.com (October 11, 1999).

Tom Hanks

Actor

AP/Wide World Photos

Born July 9, 1956, in Concord, CA; son of Amos Hanks (a chef) and Janet Turner (a hospital worker); married Samantha Lewes (an actor and producer), 1978 (divorced, 1985); married Rita Wilson (an actor and producer), April, 1988; children: (first marriage) Colin and Elizabeth; (second marriage) Chester and Truman. *Education:* Attended Chabot College and California State University at Sacramento.

Addresses: *Home*—Pacific Palisades, CA. *Agent*—PMK, 955 S. Carillo Dr., Ste. 200, Los Angeles, CA 90048.

Career

Great Lakes Theater Festival, Lakewood, OH, intern, crew member, and actor, 1976–78; associate technical director at a community theater in Sacramento, CA, late 1970s. Television appearances include series *Bosom Buddies,* 1980–82; miniseries *From the Earth to the Moon,* 1998; movies *Mazes and Monsters,* 1982; and *I Am Your Child,* 1997; and episodes of *Taxi,* 1982; *Happy Days,* 1982; *Family Ties,* 1983–84; *Tales from the Crypt,* 1992; *Fallen Angels,* 1993; *The Naked Truth,* 1995; *Ruby Meets Wax,* 1997; and *Famous Families,* 1998; in addition to various specials, awards presentations, and talk shows.

Film appearances include *He Knows You're Alone,* 1980; *Splash,* 1984; *Bachelor Party,* 1984; *Volunteers,* 1985; *The Man with One Red Shoe,* 1985; *Nothing in Common,* 1986; *The Money Pit,* 1986; *Every Time We Say Goodbye,* 1986; *Dragnet,* 1987; *Punchline,* 1988; *Big,* 1988; *The 'burbs,* 1989; *Turner & Hooch,* 1989; *Joe Versus the Volcano,* 1990; *The Bonfire of the Vanities,* 1990; *Radio Flyer,* 1992; *A League of Their Own,* 1992; *Philadelphia,* 1993; *Sleepless in Seattle,* 1993; *Forrest Gump,* 1994; *Apollo 13,* 1995; *The Celluloid Closet,* 1995; *Toy Story* (voice), 1995; *That Thing You Do!,* 1996; *Saving Private Ryan,* 1998; *You've Got Mail,* 1998; *Toy Story 2,* 1999; and *The Green Mile,* 1999.

Other television work includes director of episodes of *Tales from the Crypt,* 1989, *Fallen Angels,* 1993; and *A League of Their Own,* 1993; cowriter of segments 6, 7, 11, and 12 of *From the Earth to the Moon,* 1998; and director of segment 1 of *From the Earth to the Moon,* 1998. Other film work includes director and cowriter of *The Thing You Do!,* 1996.

Awards: Cleveland Critics Circle Award for *Two Gentleman of Verona,* 1978; Los Angeles Film Critics Award for best actor, 1988, for *Big* and *Punchline;* Academy of Science Fiction, Horror and Fantasy Films, Saturn Award for best actor, and Golden Globe Award for best actor, both 1989, for *Big;* Academy Award, Berlin International Film Festival Silver Berlin Bear Award, and Golden Globe Award for best actor, all 1993, for *Philadelphia;* Academy Award for best actor, 1994, and Golden Globe and Screen Actors Guild awards for best actor, 1995, all for *For-*

rest Gump; Hasty Pudding Theatricals Man of the Year Award, 1995; Columbus International Film & Video Festival President's Award, 1998, for episode "Can We Do This?" from *From the Earth to the Moon;* Emmy Award for outstanding miniseries (shared with others), 1998, for *From the Earth to the Moon;* Blockbuster Entertainment Award for favorite actor in a drama, 1999, for *Saving Private Ryan;* and U.S. Navy Distinguished Public Service Award, 1999.

Sidelights

With his boyish looks, "gee–whiz" persona, and his repertoire of good–guy characters, Tom Hanks is one of the best–liked actors in the entertainment business. Though he started out playing the wise–cracking pal and made a string of forgettable pictures, his skills soon shone through and he began landing more substantial roles. Before long, he had racked up shelves full of awards, including back–to–back Oscars in 1994 and 1995 for *Philadelphia* and *Forrest Gump.* Hanks, whose talent recalls screen legends of a previous time, has been likened to Jack Lemmon, Cary Grant, and Henry Fonda, but he is most commonly compared to Jimmy Stewart. Like Stewart, he is the superstar who can convincingly play the Everyman. He is witty yet approachable, sensitive but not sexual, moral but not overbearing, and appeals to both men and women. Kurt Anderson summed up in the *New Yorker,* "Hanks has created human–sized heroes whom jaded contemporary audiences can accept and embrace not in spite of the characters' flaws and contradictions but because of them."

Hanks was born on July 9, 1956, in Concord, California, near Oakland. His parents separated by the time he was five, and he and his older siblings, Larry and Sandra, went to live with their father, Amos, while his younger brother, Jim, remained with their mother, who worked in a hospital. The family moved frequently because their father, a chef, pursued new jobs about every six months. "The good thing is that my childhood trained me for the nomadic lifestyle of an actor," Hanks remarked to David Wild in *Vogue.* "And I think all the new social positions I was put in as a kid helped spur the whole wisecracking thing." However, he also noted, "When it comes time to settle down and do all the stuff that you have to in order to start a family and be a responsible human being on this planet, it probably made things a little harder."

Though his parents reunited and remarried "any number of times," as Hanks told Susan Orlean in *Rolling Stone,* they gradually drifted apart permanently. His father one day packed up his kids and moved to Reno, where he married a woman with eight children. They later divorced, and when Hanks was ten, his father married again, to Frances Wong. At Skyline High School in Oakland, under his cover of being the class clown, Hanks was incredibly shy. However, in addition to being named "male class cutup" his senior year, he participated on the track team and played soccer in addition to joining a church youth group with some friends. Also in high school, Hanks caught the acting bug when he saw a friend of his playing the lead character in *Dracula* . After that, he signed up for drama class and began acting, telling Ingrid Sischy in *Interview* that he "had more fun than I could possibly imagine. It was an incredible group of people, some of whom are still my friends."

After graduating in 1974, Hanks began attending Chabot College in Hayward, California, and working as a hotel bellman. He allowed himself to take a drama course each quarter as a "treat," as he told Sischy, and remained an avid theater fan, attending plays while his friends went skiing or to sporting events. Finally, a friend urged him to get more involved with acting, and Hanks tried out for a part in *Our Town.* He won the part of George. After a year at community college, he transferred to California State University at Sacramento in 1976, telling Sischy that it was "the only institute of higher education that I could get into where you could do plays."

While at Cal State, Hanks met Vincent Dowling, who led the Great Lakes Theater Festival in Cleveland, Ohio. Dowling guest directed the actor in a campus production of Anton Chekov's *The Cherry Orchard* and subsequently recruited him to join his company, so Hanks left school to start his career. Beginning as an intern, Hanks learned everything from lighting to stage managing. His first professional role came there in 1977, when he played Grumio in *The Taming of the Shrew.* During this time, Hanks won a Cleveland Critics Circle Award for his turn as Proteus in *Two Gentleman of Verona,* one of his rare appearances as the bad guy.

After three years in Cleveland, where he became a big fan of the Indians baseball team, Hanks set out for New York City in 1978, where he acted for the Riverside Shakespeare Company and went through the typical grueling rounds of auditions for film and television roles. In 1980, he made his film debut in a slasher movie called *He Knows You're Alone,* and also that year landed a role on a television sitcom pilot called *Bosom Buddies,* which ended up running until 1982. In that show, he and Peter Scolari costarred as two men who dress as women in order to reside in an affordable women–only apartment hotel. Meanwhile, Hanks began showing up in guest spots on programs like *Happy Days, Family Ties,* and *Taxi* as well.

While working on *Happy Days,* Hanks impressed actor–turned–director Ron Howard, who asked him to try out for a supporting role in the film *Splash,* about a mermaid (Daryl Hannah) who falls in love with a human. Hanks ended up instead sailing into the lead role as Allen Bauer, the sea creature's love interest. The project proved to be a big breakthrough for both Hanks and Hannah, as the film tore up the box–office charts, earning more than $100 million.

Although Hanks seemed poised for stardom at this point, several of his following films throughout the mid–1980s were mediocre. *Bachelor Party, Volunteers, The Man with One Red Shoe,* and *Nothing in Common* were all rather unmemorable. However, he began to branch out from strictly comedies with 1986's *Nothing in Common,* about a man's relationship with his father (played by Jackie Gleason). This gave a glimpse into the actor's range, but subsequently, Hanks returned to comedy starring with Shelly Long in *The Money Pit,* about a pair of naïve home–buyers who unknowingly purchase a dilapidated mansion. He then appeared in 1987 with Dan Aykroyd in *Dragnet,* a dismal take on the old cop show.

In 1988, Hanks shared the screen with Sally Field in the comedy/dram *Punchline,* about an opportunistic would–be stand–up comedian. Though the project was not a hit, the role further showed that his talent extended into more than just wiseacre characters. Also that year, he developed his persona as an adorable comic genius with his turn in Penny Marshall's *Big,* playing a 13–year–old boy trapped in the body of a 35–year–old man. This romp endeared him to fans and critics alike, and earned him his first Academy Award nomination. Bill Zehme in *Rolling Stone* concluded, "Hanks's performance in *Big* transcends the film's premise . He is vulnerable. He is uncoordinated. He plays puberty as through his body hair sprouted yesterday. It is his finest work to date."

Although Hanks entered the realm of full–blown stardom after *Big,* he went on to make a string of critical duds from the late 1980s to early 1990s, including *The 'burbs, Turner & Hooch, Joe Versus the Volcano,* and *The Bonfire of the Vanities.* But in 1992 he rebounded as he worked with director Marshall again on the hit *A League of Their Own,* about the first female professional baseball league. Hanks was praised for his bittersweet role as the team's recovering alcoholic manager. The next year, he teamed with Meg Ryan in Nora Ephron's *Sleepless in Seattle.* That project, too, showcased Hanks's multifaceted

ability, as he portrayed a sad widower who manages to eventually find a new beginning after revealing his feelings on a radio talk show.

Also in 1993 Hanks managed to break his funny–man mold completely in a role as a gay attorney suffering from AIDS in *Philadelphia.* In this story, he is dismissed from his firm and loses his health insurance, forcing him to hire a lawyer of his own (Denzel Washington) to help him take legal action against the company. The film was highly praised for being the first Hollywood production to seriously address the subject of AIDS, and Hanks was acclaimed for his non–stereotypical performance as well as the fact that he was the first major star to play an AIDS victim. However, Hanks commented to Wild in *Vogue,* "I don't think of it as an especially brave move. I think of it as a great role that's an honor and a responsibility to play." He won his first Academy Award for his role as Andrew Beckett in *Philadelphia.*

On a roll, Hanks's next work, 1994's *Forrest Gump,* was one of the biggest hits of the year. In it, he played a simple man whose common sense and faith in the goodness of people gets him far; he once again paired up with Field in this project as the character's practical yet optimistic mother. Based on the Winston Groom novel, the film placed Gump as a somewhat naïve observer in a post–World War II American sociohistorical context, leading to a unique method of backhanded commentary. Hanks nabbed his second consecutive Academy Award for best actor the role, and the film overall took six Oscars. The film also spurred the fad of people repeating Gump's plodding catchphrases "Stupid is as stupid does" and "Life is like a box of chocolates; you never know what you're gonna get."

Following this, Hanks in 1995 starred with Kevin Bacon and Bill Paxton in *Apollo 13,* the retelling of the harrowing real–life experience of three astronauts whose mission to the moon went awry in 1970. Directed by Howard, the feature was a popular and critical success, and tied in well with Hanks's own interest on the topic. An avid space buff, Hanks mentioned to Jeff Gordinier in *Entertainment Weekly,* "I could name all the crews of Apollo 7 through 12." Gordinier added, "Not true. Actually, Hanks can name the crews of Apollo 7 through 17, with a few Gemini flights thrown in for good measure. He know the commanders, the missions, the glitches."

After this spate of runaway successes, Hanks managed to wow audiences even when he was not on screen. In *Toy Story,* 1995, the first film created in its entirety using computer animation, he stole the show as the lovable cowboy doll Woody, who serves as the benevolent kingpin of all his master's toys. His world is threatened when the child who owns him gets a new favorite for his birthday, the seemingly high–tech Buzz Lightyear spaceman. Ostensibly a children's film, many adults found it to be entertaining as well. Following this, Hanks made his first foray into film directing with *That Thing You Do!*, 1996, which followed the ups and downs of a fictional 1960s pop band. He also cowrote some of the music featured within, and also played a minor role in it as well. Previously, Hanks had done some directing in television, too, including working on an episode of *A League of Their Own* after it was made into a series. However, *That Thing You Do!* got mixed reviews and did not set off fireworks at the box office, causing critics to wonder if his "hot" streak was over.

Subsequently, Hanks was drawn back to the topic of space when he produced and appeared in the highly regarded HBO miniseries *From the Earth to the Moon*, 1998, which won an Emmy Award for outstanding miniseries. That same year, he laid to rest any thoughts that his film career had already peaked when he played Captain John H. Miller in 1998's highly regarded World War II epic *Saving Private Ryan*. This earned him another Oscar nomination and various awards, including the U.S. Navy's highest civilian honor, a Distinguished Public Service Award.

After *Saving Private Ryan*, Hanks veered back into comedy with another Ephron picture, *You've Got Mail*, also released in 1998. In this, he meets up with Ryan again in what was dubbed as a *Sleepless in Seattle* for the information age; it concerns Hanks and Ryan as business rivals who are unaware that they have begun an online romance. The movie was based on a Jimmy Stewart movie, *Shop around the Corner*, in which the two lead actors—in an era before computers—become pen pals. The next year, Hanks reprised his role as Woody in *Toy Story 2*, which was hailed by some as being even better than the original—a rare feat in the business.

Also in 1999, Hanks showed his serious again as a benevolent Depression–era prison guard in *The Green Mile*. Assigned to protect a hulking black man convicted of raping and murdering two young girls, Hanks's character, Paul Edgecomb, finds out his charge can perform miracles. Though some critics denounced the work as too sentimental and overly long, many were impressed, especially with Hanks. The *New York Times'* s Janet Maslin commented, "Tom Hanks, who is so unaffectedly good that it has become redundant to say so, helps ease the film into its just–folks storytelling mode." Almost as soon as the film was released, there was a murmur that Hanks could see yet another Oscar nomination.

In 1978, Hanks married actor–producer Samantha Lewes, and they have two children, Colin and Elizabeth. The marriage ended in 1985, but Hanks continued to have a close relationship with the children. In 1988 he married Rita Wilson, also an actor and producer with whom he costarred in *Volunteers*. They have two children, Chester and Truman, and live in the Pacific Palisades, California. Almost every article on the actor makes mention of the fact that he is a genuinely nice person. As Hanks quipped to Wild in *Vogue*, "With me, it's always the same story: I'm an average guy, down–to–earth, kinda quirky, blah blah blah. Please destroy that myth." This appeal has done nothing to tarnish his reputation as one of the entertainment industry's most unpretentious and likable performers.

Sources

Books

Contemporary Theatre, Film and Television, volume 12, Gale Research, 1994.

Periodicals

Entertainment Weekly, June 23, 1995, p. 14; December 29, 1995, p. 44; Fall 1996 Special Issue, p. 94; December 18, 1998, p. 24; December 25, 1998, p. 18; December 10, 1999, p. 73.

GQ, June 1995, p. 160.

Interview, March 1994, p. 112.

Maclean's, October 14, 1996, p. 90.

New Yorker, December 7, 1998, p. 104.

New York Times, December 10, 1999, p. B25.

New York Times Magazine, November 16, 1997, p. 124.

People, April 9, 1984; December 26, 1988, p. 100; February 12, 1996, p. 167; December 9, 1996, p. 34; August 3, 1998, p. 80; November 29, 1999, p. 90.

Rolling Stone, September 25, 1986, p. 43; June 30, 1988, p. 38.

Time, October 7, 1996, p. 92; December 21, 1998, p. 70; December 13, 1999, p. 97.

Vanity Fair, June 1994, p. 98.

Vogue, July 1993, p. 148.

Online

"Tom Hanks," Internet Movie Database web site, http://us.imdb.com (February 1, 2000).

"Tom Hanks," Mr. Showbiz web site, http://mrshowbiz.go.com (February 1, 2000).

Orrin G. Hatch

U.S. Senator

Born Orrin Grant Hatch, March 22, 1934, in Pitts-burgh, PA; son of Jesse (a metal lather) and Helen (Kamm) Hatch; married Elaine Hansen; children: Brent, Scott, Marcia, Kimberly, Alysa, Jesse. *Education:* Brigham Young University, B.S. in history and philosophy, 1959; University of Pittsburgh, J.D., 1962.

Addresses: *Office*—131 Russell Senate Office Bldg., Washington, DC 20510.

Career

Thomson, Rhodes & Grigsby law firm, Pitts-burgh, PA, attorney, 1962–69; Hatch & Plumb law firm, founder and attorney, Salt Lake City, 1969–76; U.S. Senator, Republican from Utah, 1976 ; campaigned for 2000 presidential nomination.

Sidelights

Known as a staunch conservative and a strong ally of President Ronald Reagan in the 1980s, United States Senator Orrin Hatch has wielded considerable influence on many issues facing the nation since his election in 1976. One of the more active politicians in the Senate, he has chaired the Labor and Human Resources Committee and the Judiciary Committee, and has served on the Finance Committee, the Committee on Indian Affairs, and the Select Committee on Intelligence, among others, in addition to numerous subcommittees. His conservative stances on abortion, busing, and prayer in the schools, as well as on fiscal matters, have earned him respect among right–wing supporters and derision from many on the left. However, he has also angered right–wing colleagues and delighted liberals with his efforts to expand day care programs and offer health insurance to poor children. In 1999, Hatch began to make a move for the 2000 presidential nomination amid a crowded field including Republicans George W. Bush, the governor of Texas, and fellow Senator John McCain of Arizona. By January of 2000, though, he had bowed out of the race and instead decided to pursue yet another term serving Utah in the U.S. Senate. In addition to his political career, Hatch is a prolific songwriter who has written hundreds of tunes, mostly faith–based or patriotic.

Hatch was born in Pittsburgh, Pennsylvania, on March 22, 1934, the son of Jesse Hatch, a metal lather, and Helen (Kamm) Hatch. His family was so poor that their home had no indoor plumbing. Though his father had only been educated through the ninth grade and his mother through the eighth, Hatch received a full education, including music lessons, upon his mother's insistence. He played piano for six months when he was young, then played violin throughout high school, becoming concert master of his high school orchestra as well as the all–state orchestra. He was also athletic, enjoying basketball and boxing.

After graduating in 1955 from Pittsburgh's Baldwin High School, Hatch, a Mormon, went on to Brigham Young University in Provo, Utah. He paid for his tuition with odd jobs, working as a janitor and jewelry salesperson. He also worked summers in construction and later continued to espouse the belief that youth should "learn the dignity of manual labor," as he noted in *U.S. News & World Report.* His father taught him the metal lathing trade, and for ten years, he was a journeyman in the AFL–CIO.

While in college, Hatch married Elaine Hansen, with whom he raised six children: Brent, Scott, Marcia, Kimberly, Alysa, and Jesse. "At law school, they said they wouldn't let me in school if I tried to hold a job as well. But I had to work. We had three kids when I graduated," Hatch recalled to Stephen Goode in *Insight on the News.* He thus found work in a law office and as an all–night desk attendant in a female dormitory. "I was the only young man they'd trust to do that," he explained to Goode.

After earning his bachelor of science degree in 1959, Hatch won a full scholarship to the University of Pittsburgh law school, where he obtained his degree with honors in 1962. That same year, he was admitted to the bar in Pennsylvania and began working for the Pittsburgh firm of Thomson, Rhodes & Grigsby. In 1969, he relocated to Salt Lake City and opened his own firm, Hatch & Plumb. Many of his cases involved representing corporations that were battling federal regulations. Still, he remained a liberal Democrat who admired small entrepreneurs far more than big corporate interests.

However, in 1960, Hatch became dismayed with the Democratic platform, believing that it would be economically harmful, and began to lean to the right. By 1976, on the last day for filing, he decided to run for a seat in the U.S. Senate. Although he had no political experience and had never run for an office, Ronald Reagan endorsed his bid, which boosted his profile. In the primary vote, Hatch beat bureaucrat Jack W. Carlson to land on the Republican ticket. Subsequently, he ran in the general election against incumbent Frank E. Moss, who had occupied the Senate seat for three terms, since 1958. But Moss, a labor supporter who opposed right–to–work laws, had been on shaky ground in the conservative state, and Hatch pounced on his opponents' liberal record. He countered Moss with his positions against abortion and gun control and for free enterprise, capital punishment, and a balanced federal budget.

In November of 1976, Hatch won the election with about 55 percent of the vote over Moss, who captured roughly 45 percent. This upset marked the largest margin of support for a Republican in a Utah race for the U.S. Senate since 1926. By spring of 1978, he was already getting media attention for a filibuster a political tactic involving a prolonged speech that is meant to kill efforts at passing certain legislation. Pairing up with Senator Richard Lugar of Indiana, Hatch led the filibuster to prevent a bill that would have made it easier for unions to organize employees and to negotiate collective bargaining agreements. For five weeks, sometimes 20 hours a day, he displayed his oratory, leading colleagues to bestow the nickname "Borin' Orrin." Though he had been a union member himself as a metal lather, he believed that union leadership no longer represented workers' needs, and also, he thought that more unions would lead to greater inflation, a grave concern in the atmosphere of the late 1970s. The Labor Law Reform Bill was eventually returned to committee and died.

In other areas as well, Hatch established himself as a strong conservative. He opposed many of the social welfare programs that Democratic President Jimmy Carter proposed, stating that they were too costly or inefficient. One of his main causes during his early years involved fighting to retain the Electoral College, which sends delegates from the states to vote for president instead of determining the winner by popular vote. When a Democratic senator introduced a Constitutional amendment to abolish the Electoral College, Hatch, along with Republican Senators Strom Thurmond of South Carolina and Jesse Helms of North Carolina, fought against it. The Senate voted on the issue in July of 1979 and failed to muster the two–thirds majority needed to pass an amendment to the Constitution, thus leaving the Electoral College in place.

When Reagan became president in 1980, Republicans took control of the Senate, and Hatch vaulted to the forefront as part of the new majority. He became chairman of the Labor and Human Resources Committee in 1981, a powerful body responsible for areas such as health, education, welfare, and labor, and headed it until 1986. In this position, he restructured his approach from relying on filibusters and other one–sided tactics to serve his particular constituents to focusing on compromise in order to take into account a broader range of needs by various committee members. During his tenure, he began meeting with labor leaders, and expressed concern over the high unemployment rate for African Americans, even though he opposed affirmative action.

In addition, though Hatch was against the eventually failed Equal Rights Amendment for women and laws barring gender bias in education, he convened hearings concerning allegations that women were facing discrimination in salary and other areas of employment. He also introduced a resolution to designate an official "Women's History Week." However, some criticized these measures as political posturing to balance out his negative image among feminists. Hatch was especially vilified among many women for vehemently supporting Reagan's nomination of Clarence Thomas to the Supreme Court, in light of the 1991 Senate confirmation hearings in which Anita Hill accused Thomas of ongoing sexual harassment.

Hatch was also at the center of the controversial national debate on abortion, which went far in estranging many liberals and civil rights supporters. As an abortion foe, he was instrumental in giving the states more power to restrict, though not prohibit, abortion, and in making the government cease to pay for abortions for poor women. Not surprisingly, Hatch was aligned with President Reagan on an array of issues, especially in regards to beefing up national security. He was an ardent supporter of the strategic defense system. Hatch occasionally interjected his own views, though. For example, he was more likely to offer federal support for educational issues, slashing less from the National Science Foundation's budget than Reagan desired, and refusing to cut subsidies to universities for research training.

Seeming contrary his other views, Hatch has long been an advocate of federal support to families, blazing the trail for laws that expand day care and pay for children's' nutrition programs. In addition, he has championed "hate–crime" legislation to protect the rights of homosexuals. Hatch also led efforts for bipartisan compromise on laws to allow family leave for parents. Throughout his career, he raised eyebrows for his frequent collaborations with Senator Ted Kennedy of Massachusetts, making a visible "odd couple" match. Hatch, the right–wing, strait–laced Mormon, seemed an odd ally of Kennedy, a hard–drinking, unabashed Roman Catholic liberal. However, the two together in 1997 supported a bill that would use higher taxes on tobacco to pay for health insurance for low–income children. Hatch also angered conservatives when he pushed through one of President Bill Clinton's federal judicial nominees.

A few of the other biggest landmarks in Hatch's career include his fight to achieve a balanced federal budget, his dedication to anti–crime measures, and efforts to protect individual property rights. Some of the legislation Hatch counts among his biggest achievements are the Religious Freedom Restoration Act; the Dietary Supplement Health and Education Act, which supports new labeling guidelines and manufacturing regulations; the Americans with Disabilities Act, which helps people with disabilities participate more actively in society; and two bills on AIDS, including one to help babies born with the virus.

On July 1, 1999, Hatch threw his hat in the ring for the Republican nomination for the presidential elections scheduled for November of 2000. However, even then, he announced to the press, "I believe in miracles—and it will take one to elect me," as Jay Nordlinger reported in the *National Review*. Indeed, there had been a legacy of other prominent and respected senators who had failed to gain the public's support in presidential campaigns, including Richard Lugar in 1996, Howard Baker of Tennessee in 1980, and Henry Jackson of Washington in 1976. Throughout the early race, Hatch trailed at or near the end of the list of contenders in most polls, and found it difficult to get media attention, which was lavished on the more likely candidates such as Bush and McCain. On January 26, 2000, he withdrew his bid for the Republican nomination and threw his support behind Bush, deciding instead to focus instead on winning another term in the Senate in 2000.

Hatch, who is active in the Church of Jesus Christ of the Latter–day Saints, is proud of his commitment to his family, which includes 19 grandchildren. In his spare time, he loves to attend sporting events, especially enjoying the Utah Jazz and Utah Starzz basketball teams as well as college events at Brigham Young, Utah State, the University of Utah, and Weber State. But one of his most intense hobbies is songwriting. He has written lyrics for hundreds of tunes, mostly hymns and patriotic and gospel songs, including two included on the 1998 album *Many Different Roads*, recorded by fellow Mormon Gladys Knight. Hatch was inspired to write the title song for *Many Different Roads* based on his admiration for Mother Theresa and Princess Diana. He has also produced or coproduced seven CDs, and as his official U.S. Senate web page states, "His music focuses on family, faith and love."

Sources

Periodicals

Christian Science Monitor, January 21, 2000, p. 1.
Chronicle of Higher Education, October 14, 1981, p. 13.
Congressional Quarterly Weekly Report, July 12, 1997, p. 1627.

Economist, August 29, 1998, p. 34.

Insight on the News, February 24, 1997, p. 16.

National Review, August 9, 1999, p. 18.

New Republic, November 15, 1976, p. 12; June 28, 1980, p. 9.

People, November 16, 1998, p. 11.

Time, April 21, 1997, p. 78; August 31, 1998, p. 39.

U.S. News & World Report, February 7, 1977, p. 25; August 28, 1978, p. 29.

Washington Post, August 16, 1999, p. C1.

Online

Orrin Grant Hatch web page, U.S. Senate web site, http://www.senate.gov/[]hatch (February 7, 2000).

Jeff Hawkins and Donna Dubinsky

Entrepreneurs

Jeff Hawkins born c. 1957; married; children: two daughters. *Education:* Cornell University, B.S. in electrical engineering, 1979.

Donna Dubinsky born c. 1956; children: one daughter. *Education:* Yale University, B.A., Harvard University, M.B.A.

Addresses: *Office*—Handspring, Inc., 189 Bernardo Ave., Mountain View, CA 94043.

Career

Hawkins: Intel, 1979–81; GRiD Systems, 1981–86, and vice president of research,1988–91; cofounded Palm Computing, 1992; cofounded Handspring, 1998.

Dubinsky: Apple Computer, 1981-87, began as customer support liaison, became senior manager; Claris Corp., vice president for international sales, 1987-91; cofounded Palm Computing, 1992; cofounded Handspring, 1998; also serves as a director of Intuit Corp.

Sidelights

Inventor Jeff Hawkins and business executive Donna Dubinsky together forged one of the biggest successes of the information age with one of the smallest devices, the hand–held Palm Pilot. Designed as a portable complement to a personal computer, it boasted a few simple but effective functions, like a calendar, address book, and memo pad. It also used handwriting– recognition software so that users could jot down items on it just as they would in a notebook. Business customers found the item to be a godsend, and many were so enamored with the Pilot that a kind of cult rose up around it, bolstered by devoted fans. Though Hawkins and Dubinsky founded Palm Computing as an independent firm, they found a happy coexistence with a parent company, U.S. Robotics, who bought them out but allowed them a great deal of autonomy. After 3Com purchased U.S. Robotics, though, the pair left and founded a new venture, Handspring. In the fall of 1999, it appeared they had a new success on their hands with the Visor, a pumped–up competitor to the Palm Pilot that promised to move hand–held computing into the next generation.

Hawkins was born around 1957, the son of an engineer who exposed him to a variety of ideas. His father once invented an air–cushion seagoing vessel that was inflated by vacuum– cleaner motors and was large enough to carry a 50–piece orchestra. As a teenager in 1974, Hawkins and two of his friends sailed the ship down the Hudson River while playing kettle drums. During the ride, however, the wind kicked up and slammed it into a railroad bridge, halting commuter traffic coming and going from Manhattan for a whole day.

After receiving a bachelor's degree in electrical engineering from Cornell University in 1979, Hawkins found a job at Intel, starting at the Oregon location and later moving to Boston. After three years, he wanted to move up, but the company felt he was too inexperienced, so he moved to GRiD Systems, a small Silicon Valley firm that set out to pioneer portable computers. Hawkins, however, was inspired to design a computer that would react to human impulses. When he was not writing code at his job, he would spend most of his free time researching the learning processes of the brain and trying to "map out" how people think. "My wife thought I was nuts," he recalled to Pat Dillon in *Fast Company*. "She suggested that I align myself with a university."

Enrolling at the University of California at Berkeley, Hawkins spent three years in the biophysics department studying intelligence. However, none of his professors would back up his theories, so he left in 1988 without earning his doctorate. Nevertheless, his studies into neural networks in the brain would become the genesis for his future endeavors. After investigating how the human brain learns patterns, he applied his knowledge to computers, and came up with a software program that recognizes handwriting. He patented his "PalmPrint" program and licensed it to GRiD, his former employer. In addition, he was hired back as vice president of research in 1988 and placed in charge of developing hardware and software for computers that would use pens rather than keyboards.

GRiD was bought out by Tandy, the parent company of Radio Shack, a year and a half after Hawkins returned. Though his team eventually released GRiDPad, the world's first pen- based computer, it was not sleek or fast. Other companies like IBM, NCR, and Apple stepped up efforts on "personal digital assistants," or PDAs, as they were termed. GRiD, meanwhile, was mainly concerned with providing these portable devices for corporate clients like railroad inspectors and oil–rig workers. Hawkins, frustrated by their lack of desire to reach out, decided to form his own business. In January 1992, with no capital and no product, he founded Palm Computing. Eventually he found financing, but he still needed a plan and a good product. Enter Donna Dubinsky.

Dubinsky was born around 1956 and grew up in an industrial port city in southwest Michigan, the daughter of a scrap–metal dealer. Despite attending woefully inadequate schools, she was accepted at Yale University. After graduating, she worked at a bank and enrolled in business school at Harvard University. While taking classes, she discovered the new Apple II computer and longed to work for the company that sold it.

After obtaining her master's degree in business administration, Dubinsky in 1981 started with Apple as a customer service liaison. Though her rank was low, she correctly assumed that the company would grow, and she would eventually move up. Though she would attain the rank of senior manager, some internal changes made her unhappy, so Dubinsky left in 1987 to become vice president for international sales for the software firm Claris. When Apple took over the company, though, she left, and spent a year in Paris.

Eventually, Dubinsky called her former boss at Claris and asked for assistance in locating a position. She was interested in being president of a small company and helping it grow. He put her in touch with Hawkins, and they immediately clicked. She joined forces with him in June of 1992, and they set out to define their plan and build a product. They came up with the Zoomer PDA, a misguided effort which featured no–frills handwriting–recognition software and a puny keyboard. In addition, it was dreadfully slow and too expensive, at $700. Thankfully, Apple's Newton showed up on the market in August of 1993—two months before Zoomer—and was extensively ridiculed, thus deflecting attention from the Zoomer and similar flops by other firms.

After completing some important market research, which showed that customers were mainly business users who wanted a hand–held device to complement a personal computer, not replace it, Hawking and Dubinsky retooled their strategy. Hawkins came up with Graffiti, a new handwriting–recognition program, and scaled down the device to fit into a pocket. It featured a calendar, memo pad, address book, and "to–do" list function. By August of 1994, they had a working concept for the invention, code–named Touchdown, but needed money to push the new product. After several disappointing meetings with companies interested only in taking over their intellectual property, Dubinsky made arrangements with U.S. Robotics, a modem manufacturer out of Illinois looking for a connection in Silicon Valley.

Though Hawkins and Dubinsky were looking only for an investor, U.S. Robotics offered to purchase Palm Computing and make it a division of their firm while allowing them a great degree of independence. The entrepreneurs accepted the offer, and six months later, Touchdown was renamed Palm Pilot. First released in April of 1996, it became one of the hottest–selling items on the market. It soon attracted a devout fan base of users. Programmers were soon writing new software to run on the Palm operating system, and the machines sold two million units by June of 1997. That month, 3Com acquired U.S. Robotics, and Hawkins and Dubinsky lobbied for them to spin off Palm Computing into its own publicly traded company, with no luck. By July of 1998, they announced they were leaving to found a new firm.

By late 1998, the word was out that the new company was named Handspring. Though Hawkins and Dubinsky initially remained secretive about their next product, they suggested they were moving into the consumer market and trying to reach younger users. By September of 1999, their new gadget, the Visor, went on sale through their web site. It used a licensed version of the Palm operating system and was designed to go head–to–head in the marketplace with the Palm Pilot, but with a substantially lower price for the basic model in order to appeal to the consumer and education markets. Following in the footsteps of Apple, which unveiled its appealing iMac line of computers earlier in 1998, the Visor came in various color options.

The Visor also introduced an innovation called Springboard, an expansion slot that would allow the device to play music or games, access remote e–mail, and even act like a digital camera or pager. By 2000, a module was expected to be offered that would convert it to a cellular phone. Perhaps not coincidentally, around the same time the Visor was released, 3Com announced plans to let Palm Computing go public. From the outset, the Visor seemed poised to make a serious dent in the Palm Pilot's 80

percent market share of hand–held computers; Handspring was overrun with orders from the moment they went on sale. Unfortunately for Hawkins and Dubinsky, however, their firm was not equipped to deal with the onslaught, and massive ordering and customer service problems arose which angered customers. The two founders sent personal e–mail replies to numerous irate buyers.

For all his success in the business world, Hawkins's first love remains brain research. As he told Charles C. Mann in *Technology Review*, "I plan to use the money that I am making to fund research on the human brain." In their spare time, Hawkins enjoys sailing and Dubinsky is a hiking enthusiast.

Sources

Periodicals

Economist, September 18, 1999, p. 68.
Fast Company, June 1998, p. 97.
Forbes, July 5, 1999, p. 122.
Fortune, January 11, 1999, p. 152; August 16, 1999, p. 142; November 22, 1999, p. S374.
InfoWorld, October 26, 1998, p. 5.
Newsweek, September 20, 1999, p. 73; September 27, 1999, p. 44.
PC Magazine, January 5, 1999, p. 10.
Technology Review, July/August 1999, p. 76.
USA Today, December 9, 1998, p. 3B; September 14, 1999, p. 91B.
US News & World Report, November 22, 1999, p. 78.

Online

Handspring web site, http://www.handspring.com (December 27, 1999).

William Least Heat–Moon

AP/Wide World Photos

Author

Born William Lewis Trogdon, August 27, 1939, in Kansas City, MO; son of Ralph G. (a lawyer) and Maurine (a homemaker; maiden name, Davis) Trogdon; married, 1967, wife's name, Lezlie (divorced, 1978); married Linda Keown (a teacher). *Education:* University of Missouri at Columbia, B.A. in literature, 1961, M.A., 1962, Ph.D., 1973, B.A. in photojournalism, 1978.

Addresses: *Office*—222 Berkeley St., Boston, MA 02116. *Agent*—Lois Wallace, 177 E. 70th St., New York, NY 10021.

Career

Stephens College, Columbia, MO, teacher of English, 1965–68, 1972, 1978; writer. Lecturer at University of Missouri School of Journalism, 1984–87. Contributor to magazines and periodicals, including *Atlantic Monthly, Esquire, Time,* and *New York Times Book Review. Military service:* U.S. Navy, served on USS Lake Champlain, 1964–65; became personnelman third class.

Awards: *Blue Highways: A Journey into America* was named a notable book of 1983 by the *New York Times* and one of the five best nonfiction books of 1983 by *Time;* Christopher Award, 1984, and Books–Across–the–Sea Award, 1984, both *for Blue Highways: A Journey into America; PrairyErth (a deep map)* was selected as the best work of nonfiction by the American Library Association, was named one of the year's four best books about the West by Mountains and Plains Booksellers Association, 1991, and was named a notable book of 1991 by the *New York Times.*

Sidelights

Author William Least Heat–Moon has earned high praise for his books that delve into the American consciousness, painting portraits of the landscapes and people who make up the nation. He has been compared to such great writers as Henry David Thoreau, Jack Kerouac, Alexis de Tocqueville, Mark Twain, John Steinbeck, and Herman Melville. His first work, 1982's *Blue Highways: A Journey into America,* explores the bulk of the country as the author winds his way through 13,000 miles of back roads, meeting individuals who live in the less–traveled areas of the country. Next, in *PrairyErth (a deep map),* 1991, Heat Moon focused his attention on a single rural county. His third effort, *River–Horse: The Logbook of a Boat Across America,* published in 1999, details yet another cross–country excursion, this time in a small motorboat on the nation's rivers. All of these works are illustrated by photographs that the author took along the way.

Heat–Moon's unique name comes from his Native American heritage, though it is not a given tribal name. His father, who is part Osage Indian, adopted the name Heat Moon based on Sioux tribal lore, according to Samuel Baker in *Publishers Weekly,* and called his eldest son Little Heat Moon. Thus, he dubbed his younger son Least Heat Moon to represent his place in the lineage. The family did not use their Indian names publicly, but after finishing his first book, the author felt compelled to revise it so that it would not carry a totally "Anglo point of view," as Heat–Moon put it in a *People* interview with William Plummer. The writer later added the hyphen to prevent anyone from calling him simply "Mr. Moon," reported Baker.

Born William Lewis Trogdon on August 27, 1939, in Kansas City, Missouri, Heat–Moon is the son of Ralph G. and Maurine (Davis) Trogdon. His father, an attorney, and mother, a homemaker, raised him and his older brother in Kansas City. He attended the University of Missouri at Columbia, collecting four degrees in all: a bachelor of arts in literature in 1961, a master of arts in 1962, a doctorate in 1973, and a bachelor of arts in photojournalism in 1978. Meanwhile, Heat–Moon did a stint in the U.S. Navy on the U.S.S. Lake Champlain in 1964–65, becoming a personnelman third class. It was then he discovered the book *Travels with Charley* by John Steinbeck, which would greatly influence his later creations. "I read it in 1962 when it came out," Heat–Moon noted to Baker, adding, "I said to myself, 'One of these days I want to take a trip around the country.'" He was also inspired by William Faulkner.

After leaving the military, Heat–Moon began teaching English at Stephens College in Columbia, Missouri, working there from 1965 to 1968, and again in 1972 and 1978. Subsequently, he lectured at the University of Missouri School of Journalism from 1984 to 1987. This standard resume, however, masks Heat–Moon's remarkable foray into literature. Coming to a crossroads in his life, he decided to take a journey. He had lost his teaching job, and his ten-year marriage to his wife, Lezlie, was dissolving. "Running away" from his troubles, as he noted to Plummer, on March 20, 1978 he set out with $450 cash in a Ford Econoline van—which he referred to as "Ghost Dancer"—equipped with a stove and a sleeping bag.

Heat–Moon detailed to Baker, "One belief that I'd long held was that human beings need to pay attention to who we were when we were about 10 years old, because we're well enough formed by then to have certain elemental passions that never leave us. I went back and asked, 'What did I want to do when I was 10, 11, 12? The answer was that I wanted to be a writer, or a photojournalist combining pictures and words." He was having no success thus far with this career, in addition to his other problems, and that was when he began to drive, musing that perhaps he would collect some stories and pictures along the way that would help finance his trip.

Heading east from his apartment in Columbia, Heat–Moon made a goal to follow back roads, which are generally drawn in blue lines on highway maps, and to investigate towns with odd names. His plan would take him through Intercourse, Pennsylvania; Scratch Ankle, Alabama; Humptulips, Washington; and Nameless, Tennessee; among other places. As Heat– Moon wrote in the final product, *Blue Highways: A Journey into America*, "I was going to stay on the three million miles of bent and narrow rural American two–lane, the roads to Podunk and Toonerville. Into the sticks, the boondocks, the burgs, the backwater, jerkwaters, the wide–spots–in–the–road, the don't–blink–or–you'll–miss–it towns. Into those places where you say, 'My God! What if you lived here!'"

Heat–Moon's van took him through Kentucky to the eastern seaboard and through the South, then to the Southwest, up through Nevada and the Pacific Northwest. He drove across the far north of the nation, through Montana, North Dakota, and Minnesota, then all the way to the coast of Maine. Along the way, Heat–Moon discovered a cast of characters in those remote locales by meeting and talking to people in hopes that "they might say something that would be a tonic for my misery, my lack of insight," as he told Plummer in *People*. After running across several welcoming souls, he began to record his experiences more extensively, taking notes and jotting down conversations. It soon became apparent to him that he would collect enough information for a full book.

Finally returning home, it took Heat–Moon four years to finish writing the book, and then he had to try to find a publisher. He quit his day job as a courthouse clerk in order to take a night job at a newspaper loading dock so that he could devote more daytime hours to pushing his book. He finally got the attention of Peter Davison, an editor at Atlantic Monthly Press with whom he continued to work even after Davison moved to Houghton Mifflin. Heat–Moon had decided to make his submission to Davison because he had handled a book that had a similar feel to *Blue Highways*; it was *Beautiful Swimmers* by William Warner, about blue crabs.

Many critics hailed *Blue Highways* for being an important addition to the American "road novel" genre. Don Shewey in the *Village Voice* wrote, "Unless you're planning to weather a Rocky Mountain snowstorm in the back of a pickup, or spend a night on Tangier Island, Maryland, talking to a wise old schoolmarm, *Blue Highways* works as vicarious adventure of the first order." However, other critics denounced various qualities. Shewey admitted that "the writing sometimes gets corny and precious," and Robert McDowell in the *Hudson Review* complained, "Heat Moon's sometimes defective sensibility manifests itself in snap judgments he makes of the people he meets along the way. If they are laid back, helpful, chatty, he is bound to wax poetic and philosophical about the mysterious bonds between us. If, however, they are truculent, grinding axes that are not sympathetic with Heat Moon's own, then they are haughtily dismissed as drones of the evil moneyed class. They deserve fast food, leisure suits, and plywood suburban tracts." And although Jim Crace in the *Times Literary Supplement* criticized the book as being "over–encrusted with folksy hostility toward the twentieth century, always equating changes with ruin" he conceded that the author "has a sharp eye for the paradoxes of American modernity." *Blue Highways* stayed on the *New York Times* best–seller list for 42 weeks.

Next, in 1991, Heat–Moon released *PrairyErth (a deep map)*, which narrowed his topic from an entire nation down to one specific region, the grasslands of Chase County, Kansas. Though the work deals with the history and people of this particular area, the author extrapolates larger ideas that can apply to America as a whole. Heat–Moon spent eight years doing research for the book, digging through libraries and courthouse and examining minutiae like arrowheads and fenceposts. He gathered data from— among others—a feminist rancher, coyote hunters, and Kaw Indians, whose tribe was displaced by white settlers. He also includes the stories of early settlers, for example, by including a 200–item list of the contents of a covered wagon.

Because *PrairyErth* has no real plot and no central characters besides a relatively anonymous narrator, it poses a challenge for readers. However, Heat–Moon explained that the structure was similar to the way that Native Americans tell stories, in a wandering, seemingly random manner, but revolving around a central theme. This way, the listener is given more responsibility for combining the elements to derive a meaning. Some felt the book was stronger for letting information about the region and its people stand on its own. This work, too, became a best–seller, staying on the charts for more than three months.

For Heat–Moon's next project, he widened his scope once again, as the subtitle of the work suggests. *River–Horse: A Voyage Across America* is basically a journal of his excursion through the United States on its many waterways, experiencing the land much as early navigators did. The author set out to journey 5,222 miles, crossing the continent in about 100 days starting on April 20, 1995. That day, he launched his 22–foot motorboat, which he dubbed Nikawa (meaning River–Horse in Osage), in New York Harbor, armed with twin outboard engines and scant provisions. The timetable adds a sense of urgency to the book, as Heat–Moon explains that he needs to make it through the Upper Missouri by late spring to avoid the rise in water level caused by snow melting off the Rocky Mountains.

The adversities Heat–Moon encounters along the way in his spartan craft add drama to the narrative. For example, he does not manage to complete his trip on time and faces frightening waters in the flooded Missouri; there are also times of trouble with motor mishaps. In addition to the tales of danger, Heat–Moon muses about moments of natural beauty, and also infuses humor, folklore, history, geography, and ecology into his prose. He also comments on pollution and the environmental effects of river management. He also draws frequently upon the material of other writers, quoting pertinent passages at length, and uses the construction of a composite "copilot," Pilotis, to represent the assortment of shipmates who rode with him during some legs of his voyage.

As in Heat–Moon's earlier books, the most gripping passages in *River–Horse* often come when he records human encounters, which help illustrate the nuances of a particular geographic location. In a review for *Business Week*, John Pearson calls these profiles "sharply etched, revealing, quirky," but laments that the nature of the journey, with its one–night stopovers in many instances, prevents Heat–Moon from penning more revealing portraits, as he did in his earlier efforts. Some critics also grumbled about slow spots in the narrative, and Malcolm Jones in *Newsweek* called in "a contrived journey and a contrived book." Still, Ted Leventhal in *Booklist* summed up, "There is a timeless quality to Heat–Moon's stories, all remarkably spellbinding and enchanting."

Heat–Moon, whose full beard is now white and close–trimmed, continues to make his home in Columbia, where he owns a house on an old tobacco farm. In addition to his individual works, he has contributed to other books and to periodicals such as *Atlantic Monthly, Esquire, Time,* and *New York Times Book Review*. In 1993, the author bequeathed one–third of his estate, valued at $400,000 plus several manuscripts and other materials, to the University of Missouri libraries to establish the William Trogdon Libraries Endowment. It was believed to be the largest gift ever made to that university library system.

Selected writings

(And photographer) *Blue Highways: A Journey into America,* Little, Brown, 1982.

(Contributor and author of introduction) *The Red Couch: A Portrait of America,* photography by Kevin Clarke and Horst Wackerbarth, Alfred Van der Marck, 1984.

(And creator of maps and petroglyphs) *PrairyErth (a deep map),* Houghton, 1991.

(Contributor) *Three Essays,* Nature Conservancy, 1993.

This Land is Your Land: Across America by Air, photographs by Marilyn Bridges, Aperture, 1997.

River–Horse: A Voyage Across America, Houghton/ Peter Davison, 1999.

Sources

Books

Authors & Artists for Young Adults, volume 9, Gale Research, 1992.

Contemporary Literary Criticism, volume 29, Gale Research, 1984.

Periodicals

Booklist, August 1999, p. 1980.
Business Week, November 29, 1999, p. 20.
Entertainment Weekly, November 29, 1991, p. 58.
Library Journal, October 1, 1999, p. 124.
Newsday, October 31, 1999, p. B9.
Newsweek, November 15, 1999, p. 79.
People, February 28, 1983, p. 18; April 18, 1983, p. 72.
Publishers Weekly, August 16, 1991, p. 40; August 23, 1999, p. 30; September 20, 1999, p. 55; November 22, 1999, p. 16.
St. Louis Post–Dispatch, March 28, 1993, p. 5D.
Time, November 15, 1999, p. 113.

Online

"William (Lewis) Trogdon," Contemporary Authors Online, Gale Group web site, http:// www.galenet.com (December 3, 1999).

Faith Hill

Singer and songwriter

Born Audrey Faith Perry Hill, September 21, 1967, in Jackson, MS; daughter of Pat (a factory worker) and Edna (a bank employee) Perry; married Dan Hill, c. 1987 (a songwriter; divorced, c. 1991); married Narvel Blackstock (a manager; divorced); married Tim McGraw (a country singer), October, 1996. *Education:* Attended one semester at Hinds Junior College, Raymond, MS.

Addresses: *Record company*—Warner/Reprise, 20 Music Square East, Nashville, TN 37203–4326.

Career

Began singing professionally, 1983; worked in Nashville as a T–shirt vendor, in mail–order for Reba McEntire, and as a receptionist for singer Gary Morris, 1980s; signed with Warner Bros., 1993; released debut album *Take Me as I Am,* 1993; toured with Reba McEntire, Brooks & Dunn, Alan Jackson, and George Strait, 1994–95; launched Faith Hill Literacy Project, 1996.

Awards: Academy of Country Music award for favorite new female, 1994, top vocal event, song of the year, single of the year, and top country video, 1998, for "It's Your Love," top female vocalist, 1999, vocal event of the year, 1999, for "Just to Hear You Say that You Love Me," and single of the year and video of the year, 1999, for "This Kiss;" *Billboard* magazine award for top female country artist, 1994; Country Music Association awards for top female vocal event, 1997, for "It's Your Love," video of the year, 1998, for "This Kiss," and video of the year,

1999, for "Just to Hear You Say that You Love Me;" *Performance* magazine award for best female country artist, 1994; and TNN/Music City News awards for star of tomorrow, 1995, female vocalist of the year, 1999, vocal collaboration of the year, 1999, for "Just to Hear You Say that You Love Me," and video of the year and single of year, 1999, for "This Kiss."

Sidelights

With her impressive soprano, engaging charm, and a streak of independence running through her hit songs, Faith Hill quickly developed into a "Young Country" superstar seemingly overnight. When her debut, *Take Me as I Am,* hit the stores in 1993, she became an immediate sensation, with hit after hit on the charts. The next two releases, *It Matters to Me and Faith,* both kept pace, with ten of her first 12 singles from her first three albums reaching the top five. Some of her most popular tunes include "Wild One," an upbeat version of "Piece of My Heart," "Take Me As I Am," the pop–oriented "Let's Go to Vegas," "This Kiss," and "Just to Hear You Say that You Love Me." Many of Hill's tunes venture into territory like women's rights and domestic violence, adding a strong component to her repertoire of more romantic offerings. A staple at country music awards ceremonies, Hill became part of a show business power couple in 1996 when she married fellow country artist Tim McGraw.

Hill was born Audrey Faith Perry on September 21, 1967, in Jackson, Mississippi, and she and her two older brothers were raised in nearby Star by adoptive parents Pat and Edna Perry. Her father worked for the Presto Manufacturing Company plant in Jackson, retiring after 37 years, and her mother is a retired bank employee. In 1990 Hill began looking for her biological parents, succeeding a few years later. She described in *People* "the awe of seeing someone that you actually came from," adding that "it fills something." She has never revealed her birth parents' identities, citing privacy reasons.

Hill discovered her love of music while singing in church as a child. Raised as a Baptist, Hill remains a highly spiritual person. Her first public performance came at age 10 at a women's club luncheon, and a few years later she learned to play guitar. As a teenager, she was inspired by the voices of country singers like Patsy Cline, Emmylou Harris, and her later role model, Reba McEntire. By age 16, Hill had started her own country band; one of her early appearances was at the Tobacco Spit competition in Raleigh, Mississippi. "It was so gross," she related to Peter Castro in *People*. "They had to clean the stage off with a towel before we played."

Eventually Hill worked her way up to county fairs and rodeos, and after graduating from McLaurin Attendance Center high school in 1986, spent a year at community college before heading for Nashville. Her father helped her move; as Hill recalled to Joanna Powell in *Good Housekeeping*, "I can still see his face to this day, sitting with empty boxes all around him. He had tears in his eyes, and he just waved good–bye and said, 'Take care. I love you. We are behind you one hundred percent." Success did not come immediately. Hill earned a living for six years in a variety of jobs, starting with selling T–shirts at Fanfare, a country music festival. For a time, she also was in charge of mail–order in the merchandising department for Reba McEntire.

Although Hill did not give up on her goal of becoming a singer, in the meantime, she began a day job as a receptionist for a publishing company owned by singer–songwriter Gary Morris. That experience taught her a lot about the business aspect of country music. "I was very, very young and naive," she told Bob Millard in *Country Music*. "I was very green, but I was thrust into learning real quick." Subsequently, Hill found another office position at McEntire's Starstruck Entertainment, a talent management firm. During this time, she was also filling in as a backup singer on demos around town, and also auditioned to become a backup singer for McEntire, but the slot went to Paula Kaye Evans, who was killed in 1991 in a plane crash, along with most of McEntire's touring entourage.

Hill's breakthrough came during a gig singing harmony with Gary Burr at the Bluebird Cafe, a favorite Nashville bar. A Warner/Reprise talent scout was in the audience that night and signed her to the label. The singer's debut album, *Take Me as I Am,* was released in 1993 and would reach triple platinum sales. The first single off of the CD, "Wild One," rose to number one on the *Billboard* chart and stayed their for four weeks, marking the first time a female country singer stayed at number one for a month with a debut single since Connie Smith in 1964 with "Once a Day." The next single, an uptempo version of Janis Joplin's classic bluesy number "Piece of My Heart," defied predictions and also climbed to the top spot.

Thanks to the popularity of her first effort, Hill embarked on a busy concert tour in 1994, opening for the likes of McEntire, Alan Jackson, and Brooks & Dunn. Unfortunately, the pace took its toll, and she underwent surgery to remove an enlarged blood vessel from a vocal chord that winter. By then she was a standout as a hot new presence, and won several honors for 1994, including best female country artist awards from *Billboard* and *Performance* magazines, the favorite new female award from the Academy of Country Music, and other nominations from the Country Music Association and Academy of Country Music.

The next summer, 1995, Hill was back on the charts with *It Matters to Me,* which hit double platinum twice as fast as her debut. That year, she continued her exhaustive tour schedule, opening for Alan Jackson and George Strait. Her third album, *Faith,* went platinum in only six weeks, and she has also shown up on other projects, including a Tammy Wynette tribute album, a children's album, and several film soundtracks. In the meantime, she amassed an impressive collection of awards, including the TNN/Music City News Star of Tomorrow Award, 1995, and female vocalist of the year award, 1999; song of the year for "It's Your Love," 1998, the top female vocalist award, 1999, from the Academy of Country Music; and many more.

When Hill began a joint tour with Tim McGraw titled Spontaneous Combustion in the spring of 1996, the gossip mill began to churn. After extensive rumors swirled, they married on October 6, 1996, in Rayville, Alabama, making them the reigning first couple of country. He proposed to her one day before playing a concert, and when he returned to his trailer, she had written "YES" on the mirror. The couple has two daughters, Gracie, born in 1997, and Maggie, born the following year. They live just outside of Nashville but travel frequently for tours. Hill's surname comes from her first marriage, to songwriter Dan Hill in the later 1980s. She was 20 years old and it only lasted four years. Later she was married for a time to her former manager, Narvel Blackstock, and they also divorced. She was also engaged to marry her producer, Scott Hendricks, in the mid–1990s.

One of Hill's biggest projects besides her recording career is the Faith Hill Family Literacy Project, a subject that hits close to home. Hill's father, one of 14 children, had to leave school in the fourth grade in order to work on the family farm, and never learned to read or write. "He's a very intelligent man," she remarked in a *People* article. "I guess he recognizes things easily and has a good memory." On May 1, 1996, with the cooperation of Warner Bros. and Time Warner, she launched the organization, which aims to raise awareness of adult illiteracy. One in five people, according to some estimates, are functionally illiterate.

In addition to everything else, Hill keeps busy endorsing Cover Girl cosmetics she is part of the new wave of country stars who eschew gaudy makeup and rhinestone bell–bottoms in exchange for a fresh–faced appearance and sleek Richard Tyler pantsuits and gowns. She has also made guest appearances on the television series *Touched by an Angel* and *Promised Land*. Despite her high profile and full schedule, Hill is vocal about her priority: family. She does not tour without taking her children along, and she and her husband never spend more than a few days apart at any given time, even with

their hectic performance schedules. As she remarked in *People*, "[Success] would be meaningless without anyone to share it with. Family will be there after everything's gone and I'm too old or tired to do this anymore."

Selected discography

Take Me As I Am, Warner, 1993.
It Matters to Me, Warner, 1995.
Faith, Warner, 1998.

Has also contributed to several film soundtracks, including *Prince of Egypt, Mr. Wrong, Message in a Bottle,* and *Practical Magic;* and other collections, including *Women & Songs 2 and Lost Voices.*

Sources

Books

Contemporary Musicians, volume 18, Gale Research, 1997.

Periodicals

Country Music, July/August 1994.
Entertainment Weekly, September 8, 1995, p. 80; October 25,1 996, p.18.
Good Housekeeping, May 1999, p. 28.
People, September 11, 1995, p. 23; April 20, 1998, p. 41; July 12, 1999, p. 95.
Time, June 28, 1999, p. 69.

Online

Faith Hill Official Web Site, http://www.faithhill.com (October 1, 1999).

bell hooks

Author

Born Gloria Jean Watkins, September 25, 1952, in Hopkinsville, KY; daughter of Veodis (a janitor) and Rosa Bell (a domestic worker; maiden name, Oldham) Watkins. *Education:* Stanford University, B.A. in English, 1973; University of Wisconsin, M.A. in English, 1976; University of California at Santa Cruz, Ph.D. in English, 1983.

Addresses: *Office*—222 Elm St., Oberlin, OH; or c/o Henry Holt and Company, 115 West 18th St., New York, NY 10011; or South End Press, 7 Brookline Street £1, Cambridge, MA 02139–4146.

Career

Worked as a telephone operator, 1973–74; lecturer at University of Southern California, 1976–79, University of California at Riverside, 1978, Occidental College, 1980, San Francisco State University, 1981, and University of California at Santa Cruz, 1981–84; Yale University, assistant professor of African American studies and English literature, beginning 1985; Oberlin College, associate professor of American literature and women's studies, beginning 1988; City College of New York, distinguished professor of English and teacher of courses in black studies, 1993—. Columnist for *Paper* magazine; contributor to various periodicals.

Awards: Before Columbus Foundation's American Book Award, 1991, for *Yearning: Race, Gender and Cultural Politics;* Lila Wallace Reader's Digest Fund Writer's Award, 1994.

Pinderhughes Photography, Inc.

Sidelights

Author bell hooks offers integral contributions to the dialogue of sexism and racism in modern American society with her books that bridge the academic and the popular. Often using her own personal accounts in her social criticism, her theoretical works have become respected in departments of African American studies, women's studies, and film and culture studies at universities across the nation. Some of her best–known works address her view that racism is prevalent in the feminist movement. She also often voices her concern that a white patriarchal media perpetuates negative images of blacks in the popular culture. In 1999, she broke away from her typical offerings in order to write a children's book, and in early 2000 she issued a work about love. Unconventionally, hooks lowercases the first letters of her first and last name because, as she explained to Rebecca Caroll in *Elle,* "The lowercase is about ego: What's in a name? It is the substance in my books, not who is writing them, that is important. And it is a way to remind myself that I am not my ideas in any kind of fixed and absolute way. My ideas are always changing, and so am I."

Born Gloria Jean Watkins on September 25, 1952, in Hopkinsville, Kentucky, hooks grew up in that small, segregated community with five sisters—Sarah, Theresa, Valeria, Gwenda, and Angela—and a brother, Kenneth. Her father, Veodis, worked as a janitor for the U.S. Postal Service, and her mother, Rosa Bell (Oldham) Watkins, was a domestic employee for white families. Hooks considers growing up in a household of strong women to be one of her primary influences. In order to pay homage to the female legacy, she changed her name to that of her great–grandmother. As she wrote in *Talking Back: Thinking Feminist, Thinking Black,* "I was a young girl buying bubble gum at the corner store when I first really heard the name bell hooks. I had just talked back to a grown person. Even now I can recall the surprised look, the mocking tones that informed me I must be kin to bell hooks—a sharp–tongued woman, a woman who spoke her mind, a woman who was not afraid to talk back. I claimed this legacy of defiance, of will, of courage, affirming my link to female ancestors who were bold and daring in their speech."

As a child, hooks was consumed by reading, her favorites including Emily Dickinson, Walt Whitman, Langston Hughes, William Wordsworth, Gwendolyn Brooks, and Elizabeth Barrett Browning. Sometimes when the power went out and there was no television to watch, her family would gather around as she recited her favorite poems from memory. In addition to verse, hooks was drawn to music, singing in the church choir and listening to jazz on soul radio programs.

Though hooks has recalled in various essays and books the strong female bonds of her upbringing, she is not oblivious to the patriarchy that gripped her young existence. In the essay "Black Is a Woman's Color," for example, she recounted one time when her father pulled out a gun during a fight with her mother, and she wrote of her shock at her mother's compliance. Hooks was also upset when she learned about the racism and sexism that pervaded America's political and social history. However, many of her black schoolteachers went far in instilling her and other students with a strong sense of self–esteem. She attended Booker T. Washington elementary and Crispus Attucks High School, both named after prominent African Americans.

Though at one time hooks harbored a dream of becoming an architect, she knew from a young age that she wanted to be a writer. After graduating from high school, she attended Stanford University on scholarships and loans, although she found it difficult to leave her community. She had never been on a plane before, not to mention a city bus or elevator. In addition, she became aware of class divisions at this time; for instance, she did not know how to eat lobster because she had never had it before. On top of this, she discovered that college was not exactly what she expected. As hooks related to Ingrid Sischy in *Interview,* "I left the South looking for a world that would embrace me as an intellectual," adding, "I had been taught that the essence of being an intellectual was open–mindedness." But she found that it was a "myth," as she told Sischy, because there was a "conservatizing function" to educational institutions.

Still, hooks managed to find some outlets for her voice, as the campus was teeming with the fledgling feminist movement. However, as she wrote in *Ain't I a Woman,* "It was in one of my first Women's Studies classes, taught by Tillie Olsen, that I noticed the complete absence of material by or any discussion about black women. I began to feel estranged and alienated from the huge group of white women who were celebrating the power of 'sisterhood.'" She also noticed a lack of material about African American women at her campus library. At 19, hooks thus began writing her own books about black women. Her coworkers at the telephone company in Berkeley, where she worked in 1973 and 1974, encouraged her. After several years and numerous revisions, she published *Ain't I a Woman: Black Women and Feminism* in 1981, her first book of theory. She had previously released a book of poetry, *And There We Wept,* in 1978.

Meanwhile, hooks received a bachelor of arts in English from Stanford in 1973 and went on to obtain a master's degree in English from the University of Wisconsin in 1976. After her first theory work was published, she then pursued a doctorate in English from the University of California at Santa Cruz, finishing in 1983 with a dissertation titled "Toni Morrison's Fiction: Keeping a Hold on Life." The next year, she released her second academic work, *Feminist Theory: From Margin to Center,* thus starting up her association with the South End Press cooperative, which would go on to publish all of her works until 1995. Until coming in contact with them, she had trouble finding a publisher because of her subject matter. There were books on feminism, and others on racism, but she was a pioneer in combining the topics and interpreting their intersections.

In *Ain't I a Woman,* hooks explains how racism pervades mainstream feminism and chides white women for ignoring blacks, while discussing how black women can find their place in feminism anyway. The title came from a famous speech given by feminist abolitionist activist Sojourner Truth. Using a feminist perspective, hooks chronicles the history of black women in America, from the slavery era through the 1970s, and posits the theory that African American women were more strongly feminist in the nineteenth century than the twentieth. The work got a chilly reception, as many critics questioned her methods of analysis and some of her assertions, such as her opinion that slavery was worse for women than for men.

However, Dorothy Randall–Tsuruta in the *Black Scholar* (excerpted in *Contemporary Literary Criticism*) gave hooks some credit, noting, "The excellent thing about Hooks' book is that it pinpoints annoyances over which many black American women daily sigh, yet repress, in an attempt to get through the work day without flying off the handle." Indeed, hooks later wrote in *Talking Back*, "When Ain't I a Woman was first published I would get dozens of letters a week, where, say, a Black woman from a small town, out in the middle of nowhere, would tell me that she read my book at the public library and it transformed her life."

Hooks's next volume, *Feminist Theory from Margin to Center,* continues to explore how feminist theory often addresses issues pertinent to mainstream white women (the "center" of the title) and rarely investigates the experiences of men or women "at the margin." The book especially targeted the feminist works of Betty Friedan, author of *The Feminist Mystique,* which concentrated mainly on disenfranchised suburban homemakers.

Beginning in 1989, hooks began to churn out volumes at a furious pace. That year, she issued *Talking Back: Thinking Feminist, Thinking Black,* which began to incorporate more of her personal experiences into her essays. The next year, she won the Before Columbus Foundation's American Book Award for *Yearning: Race, Gender, and Cultural Politics.* This effort firmly established her as an important contributor to feminist film and popular culture studies. She built upon this reputation with 1992's *Black Looks: Race and Representation,* which further criticized the image of black portrayed in the media and literature. Her pieces on Spike Lee and Madonna were especially influential. Meanwhile, she teamed up with activist and scholar Cornel West in a series of conversations for *Breaking Bread: Insurgent Black Intellectual Life,* 1991.

In 1995, hooks branched away from the progressive South End Press to sign a three–book contract with a large mainstream publisher, Henry Holt. However, she did not cut ties with South End, and further remained loyal to the independent press by re-

leasing a book of essays about contemporary art, *Art on My Mind,* with The New Press in July of 1995. It included some previously published pieces, such as one on street artist Jean–Michel Basquiat and another about the Whitney Museum's "Black Male" exhibit, as well as 13 new pieces that include discussions with artists such as Carrie Mae Weens and Alison Saar.

Of hooks's works for Holt, the first, *Killing Rage: Ending Racism,* came out in 1995, and is a collection of essays with the theme of effecting social change from a starting point of mental well–being. She explained to Carl Posey in *Essence,* "There can be no revolution if we are not well on a personal level. Revolutions made by people who are not well tend to result ultimately in chaos, or worse, in the reproduction of the very patterns and systems of domination that are being challenged." Though the book called for change even more urgently than her previous works, it also contained a greater deal of optimism regarding society's ability to reach the goals of eradicating racism and sexism.

In 1996, hooks shared with readers a personal account of her upbringing in *Bone Black: Memories of Girlhood.* She followed up with *Wounds of Passion: A Writing Life,* an account of her young adulthood from her teen years into her mid–thirties, as she was beginning to gain extensive attention as a writer. After that, she completed her memoir trilogy with *Remembered Rapture: The Writer at Work,* which chronicles her rise in status and gives insights about being an author. Then, in 1999, hooks surprisingly came out with a children's book called *Happy to Be Nappy,* which celebrated the numerous types and styles of hair. It came out on the heels of a controversy about author Carolivia Herron's similarly titled work, *Nappy Hair,* but hooks agreed with parents who objected to that volume, telling Liza Featherstone in *Newsday* that *Nappy Hair* was a "very negative book." Early in 2000, hooks released *All About Love,* a kind of self–help book that she told Featherstone was her "ultimate mass–culture book."

During graduate school and thereafter, hooks lectured at various universities before becoming an assistant professor of African American studies and English literature at Yale University. In 1988, she accepted a post as associate professor of American literature and women's studies at Oberlin College, where her courses were extremely popular. For the 1993–94 academic year, hooks took a leave of absence to teach at the City College of New York, then signed on there permanently in 1995 as a distinguished professor of English. She told Sischy in *Interview,* "After working for years at private institutions, it is really exciting for me to teach at an institution with an incredibly diverse student body." Hooks also contributes frequently to many periodicals, and is a desired speaker on the lecture circuit.

Despite hooks's fiery tone in her theory writings, leading readers to believe that she is perhaps angry and volatile, the author in real life is said to be agreeable and warm. She is single, lives in New York City, and is a practicing Buddhist. In addition to her favorite hobby, reading, hooks enjoys art as well as fashion, telling Caroll in *Elle*, "I am totally into shoes. People are constantly calling me Imelda Marcos II. I love Bruno Magli, Robert Clergerie." She then summed up to Caroll, "I'm passionate about leading my life with a certain quality of elegance and grace. But the ruling passion of my life is being a seeker after truth and the divine. That tempers everything else."

Selected writings

And There We Wept (poems), Golemics, 1978.

Ain't I a Woman: Black Women and Feminism, South End Press, 1981.

Feminist Theory: From Margin to Center, South End Press, 1984.

Talking Back: Thinking Feminist, Thinking Black, South End Press, 1989.

Yearning: Race, Gender and Cultural Politics, South End Press, 1990. (With Cornel West) *Breaking Bread: Insurgent Black Intellectual Life*, South End Press, 1991.

Black Looks: Race and Representation, South End Press, 1992.

A Woman's Mourning Song, Harlem River Press, 1992.

Sisters of the Yam: Black Women and Self–Recovery, South End Press, 1993.

Outlaw Culture: Resisting Representations, Routledge, 1994.

Teaching to Transgress: Education as the Practice of Freedom, Routledge, 1994.

Art on My Mind, The New Press, 1995.

Killing Rage: Ending Racism, Holt, 1995.

Bone Black: Memories of Girlhood, Holt, 1996.

Wounds of Passion: A Writing Life, Holt, 1997.

Remembered Rapture: The Writer at Work, Holt, 1999.

Reel to Real: Race, Sex and Class at the Movies, Routledge, 1996.

Happy to Be Nappy (children's book), illustrated by Chris Raschka, Hyperion/Jump at the Sun, 1999.

All About Love: New Visions, William Morrow, 2000.

Sources

Books

Contemporary Literary Criticism, volume 94, Gale Research.

Encyclopedia of World Biography, second edition, Gale Research, 1998.

Notable Black American Women, Book 2, Gale Research, 1996.

Periodicals

Elle, December 1994, p. 78.

Emerge, March 1997, p. 74.

Esssence, May 1995, p. 187.

Interview, October 1995, p. 122.

Newsday, January 31, 1999, p. B11.

New York Times, November 13, 1997.

New York Times Book Review, January 30, 2000, p. 21.

Publishers Weekly, March 27, 1995, p. 24; July 19, 1999, p. 194.

Hou Hsiao-hsien

AP/Wide World Photos

Film director

Born April 8, 1947 (some sources say September 8, 1947 or 1946), in Meixian, Kuangtung (Canton) province; son of a schoolteacher. *Education:* Attended the film program of the Taiwan National Academy of the Arts, 1969–72.

Addresses: *Office*—c/o Motion Picture Development Foundation, 2 Tien–tsin St., Taipei, Taiwan.

Career

Electronic calculator salesman, 1972–73; script boy, then assistant director, from 1974, scriptwriter, from 1975; director, 1979—.

Directing credits include *Jiushi liuliu de ta (Cute Girl*), 1980; *Feng er ti ta cai (Cheerful Wind*), 1981; *Zai na hepan qingcao qing (The Green, Green Grass of Home*), 1983; *Fengkuei-lai-te jen (The Boys From Fengkuei*), 1983; *Erzi de Dawan'ou (The Sandwich Man;* one episode of omnibus film), 1983; *Dongdong de jiaqi (A Summer at Grandpa's*), 1984; *Tong nien wang shi (A Time to Live and a Time to Die*), 1985; *Lianlian fengchen (Dust in the Wind),* 1986; *Niluohe (Daughter of the Nile*), 1987; *Beiqing chengshi (A City of Sadness*), 1989; *Hsimeng jensheng (The Puppetmaster*), 1993; *Haonan haonu (Good Men, Good Women*), 1995; *Nanguo zaijan, nanguo (Goodbye South, Goodbye*), 1996; and *Hai shang hua (Flowers of Shanghai*), 1998.

Producer or executive producer, *Hsiao pi te ku shih (Growing Up*), 1983; *Da hong deng long gao gao gua (Raise the Red Lantern*), 1992; *Shaolin Ye, An La! (Dust of Angels*), 1992; *Duo-Sang (A Borrowed Life*), 1994; *Qunian dongtian (Heartbreak Island*), 1995; and *Borderline,* 1999. Has also acted in *Qingmei Zhuma (Taipei Story*), 1985; and *Lao niang gou sao (Soul*), 1986; and appeared as himself in *Meiyou taiyang de rizi (Sunless Days*), 1990; *Gender in Chinese Cinema,* 1996; and *HHH: A Portrait of Hou Hsiao-Hsien,* 1997.

Awards: Nantes Festival of Three Continents, best film, 1984, for *The Boys from Fengkuei;* Asian–Pacific Film Festival best director award, 1985, for *A Summer at Grandpa's;* Golden Horse Award (Taiwan) for best director, and Venice Film Festival, Golden Lion award (grand prize), both 1989, for *A City of Sadness;* Berlin Film Festival, international critics' prize, 1986, for *A Time to Live and a Time to Die;* Cannes Film Festival, jury prize, and FIPRESCI Award, Istanbul International Film Festival, both 1993, for *The Puppetmaster;* Singapore International Film Festival, Silver Screen Award, 1996, for *Good Men, Good Women.*

Sidelights

In the *New York Times,* Phillip Lopate asked, "Could it be that one of today's most important film artists the critic J. Hoberman calls him 'the world's greatest active narrative filmmaker'—is a Taiwanese director virtually unknown here?" He continued by stating that despite the fact that he is generally overlooked in America, Hou Hsiao–hsien is "a star of the international circuit." Much of the reason why Hou is not recognized in the United States is because his films, for one, are more cerebral than audiences tend to like, and also possess static visual effects, as opposed to the quick–cut action often seen in contemporary cinema. He is known for his extended scenes shot from a distance with one camera trained on the action. As Lopate noted, "American scriptwriters are taught to make one point per scene and move on. With Mr. Hou, you feel your way into a scene, sorting as you go the characters' relationships and objectives."

Hou's works often focus on everyday Taiwanese citizens and their struggles, and require some knowledge about the nation's history. Also, sometimes the filmmaker's products are not shipped overseas because Hou's producers demand excessive profits in order to release his works abroad. In 1999, though, WinStar Cinema collected seven of his works for a U.S. tour, and planned to release them all later on video and DVD.

Born on September 8, 1947, Hou Hsiao–hsien (pronounced "ho shau–shen") is the son of a schoolteacher who moved his family from the Canton province in mainland China to Taiwan in 1948 for a job, but later found himself unable to return to the mainland after the communist Revolution. Hou was raised in Hualien, in southern Taiwan, also called the Republic of China. He "had a wild youth," according to Lopate, associating with gang members who often met violent deaths. "My father died when I was 13, my mother when I was 17, so I felt pressure at home," Hou related to Joan Dupont in the *International Herald Tribune*. "Outside, I got arrested for fighting and gambling; my brother and sister thought I was lost forever. Then I woke up one day and said, 'Enough.'"

After his required military service, Hou decided to enter show business, considering a career as a pop singer, actor, or perhaps filmmaker. This led him to attend the film program at the Taiwan National Academy of the Arts from 1969 to 1972. Afterward, he sold calculators for a brief spell before landing a job as a script boy in 1974, working his way up to assistant director. In 1975 he also began trying his hand as a scriptwriter. Hou directed his first film, *Cute Girl*, in 1979, followed by *Cheerful Wind* and *The Green, Green Grass of Home*. As the titles imply, these were "very lightweight comedies and love stories," as Hou told David Sterritt in the *Christian Science Monitor*, and they were all commercially very popular. But by the third film, he was starting to attract critical attention as well; as he noted to Sterritt, "I started thinking I could really make some *good* films. So I started to become my own boss."

Hou's fourth effort, *The Sandwich Man*, 1983, was actually an omnibus project with other progressive filmmakers, including Edward Yang, director of 1985's *Taipei Story*, in which Hou played the lead role. This group of radicals, known as the New Taiwanese Cinema, were compared to the French New Wave, shunning the popular, airy comedies and concentrating instead on socially pertinent themes. This was the first project in which he started to use long shots and long takes, which helped when shooting scenes using ordinary people instead of professional actors. The distance allows them to relax and focus on their characters. As it happened, these long shots also allowed the viewer to become involved with the characters while preventing the film from becoming too sentimental. This practice would become one of the hallmarks of Hou's filmmaking.

In 1983, Hou made *The Boys from Fengkuei*, about three poor teenagers who flee their backwater lives in search of opportunities in the city, only to encounter con men and disappointments. This picture was named best film at the Nantes Festival of Three Continents in 1984. After this, *A Summer at Grandpa's* also dealt with the pros and cons of city life versus country life, centering on a brother and sister who are sent to live with their rural grandfather when their mother is hospitalized.

The next year, 1985, Hou released *A Time to Live and a Time to Die*, a semiautobiographical tale of his childhood that is considered his first masterpiece. The film comments on the political situation of Taiwan and China at the time, as it also considers the effect that politics had on families. Hou followed this with *Dust in the Wind*, 1986, which is similar to *The Boys of Fengkui* in that it concerns two teenagers who leave their village for work in Taipei. However, the style of this work, which uses dream sequences and a jumpy editing style, is more impressionistic than his earlier efforts. The next year, Hou made *Daughter of the Nile*, which also concerns contemporary city life. Both of these received critical applause, but fared poorly at the box office. Finding himself deeply in debt, the director was forced to mortgage his home and borrow money from friends and family to continue his career.

In 1989, though, Hou's fortunes turned around with *A City of Sadness*. This family epic is set in the period from 1945 to 1949, when the Japanese surrendered Taiwan to China at the end of World War II and Chiang Kai–shek established his Nationalist government on the island in 1949. At the heart of the tale are four sons of a middle–class family who all fail to adapt to the new political and social climate in some way. One of the most startling aspects of this project was Hou's recreation of a 1947 event involving widespread protests and a subsequent massacre of civilians by Nationalist forces. Due to the right–wing political climate in Taiwan, filmmakers for years felt they could not address this subject. The film broke box office records in Taiwan, with half of the population viewing it, according to estimates. *A City of Sadness* won a Golden Lion Award (the grand prize) at the 1990 Venice Film Festival, the first time that a Chinese film was so honored there, and also won a Golden Horse award for best director in Taiwan.

Hou's next two films would combine with *A City of Sadness* to create a trilogy. *The Puppetmaster*, 1993, features an aging actor who played a grandfather in Hou's previous three films. In it, his life from the turn of the century to 1945 is dramatized as the director explores various political and historical nuances of Taiwan and the Japanese occupation. This film won the Jury Prize at the 1993 Cannes Film Festival and the FIPRESCI Award at the Istanbul International Film Festival. Hou's next effort, *Good Men, Good Women*, also delves into Taiwan's past and explores the optimism of an older generation contrasted with the malaise of the young. He followed this with *Goodbye South, Goodbye*, about the corruption of Taiwanese society. In 1998, for the first time, Hou set a film not in Taiwan, but in Shanghai in various brothels at the turn of the twentieth century. Lopate called this period drama, *Flowers of Shanghai*, "one of the cinematic highpoints of the 90s, by a master who keeps growing."

In addition to directing, Hou has executive produced a number of pictures, including the acclaimed *Raise the Red Lantern*, 1991; *A Borrowed Life*, 1994; and *Heartbreak Island*, 1995. In addition to acting in *Taipei Story*, he also had a role in *Soul*, 1986. In 1997, Hou appeared as himself in the film *HHH: A Portrait of Hou Hsiao–hsien*.

Sources

Books

International Dictionary of Films and Filmmakers, Volume 2: Directors, St. James Press, 1996.

Periodicals

Christian Science Monitor, November 16, 1989, p. 10.
Film Comment, November 1993, p. 56.
International Herald Tribune, December 5, 1998.
New York Times, October 10, 1999, p. AR13.
Time International, July 5, 1999, p. 48.
Variety, February 17, 1992, p. 62.

Online

"Hsiao–hsien Hou," Internet Movie Database web site, http://us.imdb.com (January 11, 2000).

Enrique Iglesias

Singer and songwriter

Born May 8, 1975, in Madrid, Spain; son of Julio Iglesias (a singer) and Isabel Preysler (a journalist). *Education:* Attended University of Miami.

Addresses: *Home*—Miami, FL.

Career

Singer and songwriter. Released debut album, *Enrique Iglesias*, Fonovisa, 1995.

Awards: Grammy Award for best Latin pop performance, 1997.

Sidelights

Helping to usher in the popularity of Latino music, Enrique Iglesias has become a leader in a pack of artists including Ricky Martin and others whose romantic ballads as well as lively salsa and dance rhythms have sold millions even before any of their English–language albums have hit the stores. "It had gotten to the point in the Latino music market where it wasn't cool for the young kids to listen to it," Iglesias outlined to Richard Harrington in *Newsday*. "We had a lot of great singers, but they were in their 40s and 50s. Suddenly you start getting a bunch of young Latino singers, and then the young listeners started getting into it." Indeed, one of the older generation of singers includes Iglesias's father, Julio Iglesias, known particularly for his sensual image and classic 1984 duet with

Willie Nelson, "To All the Girls I've Loved Before." Though Iglesias respects his father immensely, he has taken great pains to distinguish himself, and made a point of breaking into the business without any help from his dad. Even though Iglesias eschewed the "Latin lover" stereotype that his father perpetuated, he was nevertheless dubbed the sexiest man in the world by the Spanish–language edition of *People* in 1998.

Iglesias was born on May 8, 1975, in Madrid, Spain. His father, the famous Latino crooner, is ranked as the leading Hispanic entertainer in the United States, based on earnings, and his mother, Isabel Preysler, is a journalist and well–known actor in Madrid. His parents divorced in 1979 after eight years of marriage. Five years after that, Preysler became concerned that her sons, Enrique and Julio Jose, and daughter, Chabeli, were in danger of being kidnapped after the same fate befell their grandfather, so she sent them to Miami to live with their dad. Iglesias's father, however, being a celebrity performer, was gone frequently, so the children were raised mainly by a nanny, Elvira Olivares, to whom Iglesias later dedicated his first album. Iglesias has not expressed disappointment over being away from his parents, but his mother later doubted her decision: "It broke my heart to send them away, but we had to for security reasons," she explained to

Peter Castro in *People*. If I had known that their father wasn't around, it might have been different."

Although Iglesias wished to become a singer ever since he was a child, he kept his passion from his parents because he was concerned that they would not encourage him. "If I'd heard anything negative," Iglesias remarked in *USA Weekend*, "I wouldn't have been able to stand it." In addition, he commented to John Lannert in *Billboard*, "Maybe I never told my dad because he was not a big influence. He was a huge influence as a singer, but I never listened to his music." Instead, he has noted, his inspiration came from the likes of Foreigner, Journey, Dire Straits, John Mellencamp, Bryan Ferry, Bill Joel, and Fleetwood Mac.

While in his teens, Iglesias began writing songs and holding jam sessions with Mario Martinelli and Roberto Morales, two more established performers known for their gigs in restaurants around Miami's Little Havana. His early songs were disappointing. At first, he admitted to Harrington in *Newsday*, "I used to cry about how bad they sounded." All the while he confided his dream only in Olivares. He later enrolled at the University of Miami to study business administration, but ended up leaving as a sophomore because it detracted from his time pursuing music.

Soon, Iglesias was ready for his debut. He had been playing music for only about four years, but had made a tape by 1994 and called Fernan Martinez, his father's manager for nine years, for a favor. Martinez recalled to Harrington, "My first reaction was: He's in trouble! I thought it was something with a girl, he was so mysterious and secretive! I had no clue." As it happened, Iglesias just wanted Martinez to hear him perform, and they met at Morales's studio, where the manager was impressed, especially by Iglesias's Spanish–language material. Before long, he had cut a demo tape in Canada (in order to keep the secret from his parents) and Martinez began shopping it around to labels. Iglesias continued to refuse to ride on his father's coattails and made Martinez bill him as Enrique Martinez, a no–name would–be singer from Colombia. However, major labels known for their Latino artists such as Sony, EMI, and PolyGram showed no interest in the husky–sounding baritone

Finally, Guillermo Santiso, president and CEO of Fonovisa Records, called and said he was impressed by the sound as well as by the singer's photograph, although he was kept in the dark about Enrique's real identity. After Iglesias revealed that he was the son of Julio, Santiso signed him to a three–album deal worth $1 million, but he then needed a large promotional budget from Fonovisa's parent company, Televisa. Santiso went to the higher–ups at Televisa and won major backing to market the young talent.

Still, the record company decided to keep Iglesias's background under cover so that he would be accepted on his own merits. During the initial radio campaign to promote his self–titled debut release, he was identified only as "Enrique." Once the single "Si Tu Te Vas" (translated as "If You Go") came out in mid–1995, he embarked on hundreds of interviews at radio and television stations and the song went soaring to number one on the *Billboard's* Latin track chart. However, once word got out about his parents, interviewers began to introduce him as the son of Julio Iglesias, which irritated him. On several occasions, he walked out of studios if he was not introduced as Enrique Iglesias, and because of that, "A lot of people think me and my father don't get along," Iglesias remarked to Harrington. "Of course we get along...I'd kill for my father."

However, Iglesias's father, who holds a law degree from Cambridge University, initially was not happy when he learned his son had forsaken school for show business, but later stated that he was very proud. In fact, he heard about his son's career not from Iglesias himself, but from a music industry insider at a party. But the ball was already rolling, and soon Iglesias was the world's best–selling Latin artist at the time, moving 13 million copies of his three Spanish– language releases. His first self–titled effort and its follow–up, *Vivir* (*Living*), 1997, each sold six million copies, and he won a Grammy Award in 1997 for best Latin pop performance.

In 1998 Iglesias released his third work, *Cosas del Amor* (*Things of Love*). He had 12 hit singles in three years, and one of those, his single "Bailamos" ("We Dance"), which was heard on the soundtrack of the film *Wild Wild West*, reached number one in 16 countries. Iglesias was the only artist at that point in the year to top the Hot 100, Dance/Club Play, Hot Latin Tracks, and Latin 50 Album charts simultaneously. His first English–language album was scheduled for release in late 1999 by Interscope/UMG, according to his official web site.

Selected discography

Enrique Iglesias, Fonovisa, 1995.
Vivir, Fonovisa, 1997.
Cosas del Amor, Fonovisa, 1998.

Sources

Periodicals

Billboard, July 19, 1997, p. 1.
Dallas Morning News, January 29, 1997, p. 25A; December 5, 1997, p. 65.
Gannett News Service, January 12, 1996.
Newsday, March 15, 1999, p. B6.

People, April 22, 1996, p. 144l May 11, 1998, p. 141.
Time, November 6, 1995, p. 89.
USA Weekend, June 1, 1997, p. 22.
Variety, December 8, 1997, p. 68.

Online

Enrique Iglesias official web site, http://www.enriqueig.com (October 4, 1999).

Juli Inkster

Golfer

Born Juli Simpson, June 24, 1960, in Santa Cruz, CA; married Brian Inkster (a golf coach), July, 1980; children: two daughters; Hayley Carole, Cori Simpson. *Education:* San Jose State University, B.A. in physical education, 1982.

Addresses: *Home*—Los Altos, CA. *Office*—c/o Ladies Professional Golf Association, 100 International Golf Dr., Daytona Beach, FL 32124–1092.

Career

Amateur golfer, 1978–83; professional golfer, 1983—. Member of World Cup teams, 1980, 1982; U.S. Curtis Cup team, 1982; and U.S. Solheim Cup team, 1992, 1998.

Awards: Won three consecutive amateur titles, 1980–82; *Golf Digest* number–one ranked amateur, 1981, 1982; named California's amateur of the year, 1981; named Bay Area athlete of the year, 1982; Broderick Award, 1982; named LPGA rookie of the year, 1984; major tour victories include Nabisco Dinah Shore and du Maurier Classic, 1984; Nabisco Dinah Shore, 1989; and U.S. Women's Open and McDonald's LPGA Championship, 1999; other victories include SAFECO Classic, 1983; Lady Keystone Open, 1985; Women's Kemper Open, McDonald's Championship, Lady Keystone Open, and Atlantic City Classic, all 1986; Crestar Classic, Atlantic City Classic, and SAFECO Classic, 1988; Crestar Classic, 1989; LPGA Bay State Classic, 1991; JAL Big Apple Classic, 1992; Samsung World Championship of Women's Golf, 1997, 1998; Welch's/Circle K Championship, Longs Drug Challenge, and SAFECO Classic, 1999; named to LPGA Hall of Fame, 1999; named Sportswoman of the Year by the Women's Sports Foundation, 1999.

Sidelights

With 22 career victories, including five major wins, Juli Inkster is one of the top players of the Ladies Professional Golf Association (LPGA). As a rookie in 1984, she won two of the major events in women's golf, Nabisco Dinah Shore and du Maurier Classic, and is only the fifth LPGA player to have earned more than $5 million in her career. However, as James Deacon expressed in *Maclean's*, "As much as colleagues admire her ability, they say they are more impressed by Inkster the person. She is proud but modest, upbeat and supportive of others, and she is widely admired for remaining competitive while raising two daughters."

Some of the years were rough when Inkster's daughters were young; she wondered if she was doing the right thing by continuing to work and travel with two little girls. "I didn't like being a mediocre player," she confessed to Clifton Brown in the *New York Times*. "I was just going through the motions, hauling my kids around and not accomplishing much." Her doubt was reflected in her game. After deciding that she could devote herself to the game and be a good mother as well, she came back with a vengeance. By 1999, she became only the fourth woman to accomplish the "grand slam" of modern women's golf, winning the other two major events, the U.S. Women's Open and the McDonald's LPGA Championship. Also that year, Inkster was named to the LPGA Hall of Fame.

Inkster was born Juli Simpson on June 24, 1960, in Santa Cruz, California. The youngest of four children, she has two older brothers, Danny and Mike, and was raised in a home near the fourteenth hole at the Pasatiempo Golf Club. Growing up with male siblings, she began to enjoy sports at an early age, joining the basketball, track, and softball teams in high school. Her father once played briefly for the Cincinnati Reds baseball team.

Though she was always athletic, she did not take up golfing until age 15. As she told Sara Reeder in *Women's Sports & Fitness*, "A friend and I began together, because we'd figured out that that's where the boys were. But then I got really gung–ho about it." When she was 16, she began taking golf lessons at the Pasatiempo Golf Club from Brian Inkster, and they married when she was 20, just before her junior year in college.

On a golf scholarship, Inkster attended San Jose State University also her husband's alma mater in 1979, where she was a collegiate All–American all four years in school before graduating in 1982 with a bachelor of arts degree in physical education. All the while, she was making waves as an amateur golfer. She qualified for the U.S. Women's Open as an amateur in 1978, just after turning 18 and only two years after taking up the sport. She finished second–low amateur in 1978 at the U.S. Women's Open, just ten strokes behind Hollis Stacy. Two weeks after getting married, in 1980, she won her first U.S. amateur title. Her husband once quipped to Douglas S. Looney in *Sports Illustrated*, "She was nothing until she became an Inkster."

Golf watchers knew that Inkster was one to watch after she nailed her second consecutive U.S. amateur title, only the ninth player ever to do so. But they really took notice when in 1982, she did it again, making her only the fifth player and the first since Virginia Van Wie in 1934 to win it three years in a row. But as Bob Ottum wrote in *Sports Illustrated*, "What's more impressive, or at least considerably more fun, is that Inkster beat the challengers

in a dozen different ways. She destroyed them with her long game, featuring high, arcing drives powered by what she calls her Free Arm Swing . She also demoralized them with her short game, crisp approaches and a variety of calculated curlicue putts."

Inkster learned her signature swing from her husband, who modeled his approach after golf coach Leslie King, who emphasized powering the stroke with the arms as opposed to the lower body. Explaining to Ottum, Inkster related that American players "*insist* that you have to generate power with the swing of your hips. But not the Old Leslie King. With him, it's all arms first." In addition to winning the three amateur championships, Inkster was a member of the 1980 and 1982 Women's World Cup teams and a player on the winning Curtis Cup team in 1982. In addition, she won a bevy of amateur awards, including being ranked the number–one amateur in *Golf Digest* in 1981 and 1982, and being named California's 1981 amateur of the year.

In 1983, Inkster joined the LPGA and began competing on a regular basis in 1984, winning the fifth event she entered, the SAFECO Classic. Also that year, she captured both the Nabisco Dinah Shore and the du Maurier Classic, becoming the first rookie ever to win two major championships in one season. In a sudden–death playoff at the Nabisco Dinah Shore, she beat Pat Bradley, who had 11 years' experience on the pro tour. "That turned my career around right there," she later told Gordon S. White in the *New York Times*. Her husband added, "That was when she realized she could be one of the best out there." That year, Inkster was named LPGA rookie of the year.

The next year was disappointing for Inkster as she fell from being ranked sixth to number 19 and saw only one victory, at the Lady Keystone Open. Subsequently, she traveled to London to pay a visit to King for first–hand lessons. She soon saw another successful season in 1986 when she captured four events: the Women's Kemper Open, the McDonald's Championship, the Lady Keystone Open, and the Atlantic City Classic. During that season, she twice posted her career–low score of 64, and earned $285,293 in LPGA winnings for the year, almost tripling her previous year's LPGA earnings of $99,651.

In 1987, Inkster's rank fell from number three to number 14, but she pulled back up to number ten by 1988, with victories at the Crestar Classic, Atlantic City Classic, and SAFECO Classic. She also won the Crestar Classic in 1989, but sank back in the ranks that season to number 14. That year, Looney wrote in *Sports Illustrated*, "The book on her has been that she is at the very top in talent, but that inconsistent play has kept her out of sentences containing names like [Nancy] Lopez, [Jan] Stephenson, and [Betsy] King." Then, in February of 1990 Inkster gave birth to a daughter, Hayley Carole, and though she was back on the course by the time her baby was seven weeks old, she had trouble devoting her attention to the game. As she commented to John Goldstein in *Golf*, "My attitude on the golf course was horrible...; my confidence was down. I was trying to do too many things and do them all perfectly. When I was brought up, my mom was always home. I was having guilty feelings, wondering if it was all right to leave Hayley to play golf."

As a result, Inkster's rank slipped to number 73 in 1990, as she managed only three top ten finishes for the year, none better than fifth place. Her LPGA earnings sank to $54,251. However, she soon realized that unlike other working mothers, she was privileged enough to have half the year off, and a shorter workday when she was on the job. After 27 months without a win, she captured the 1991 Bay State Classic. By 1992, she was back in form, reaching a number seven ranking as she took the JAL Big Apple Classic and finished seventh in earnings for the year with a total purse of $392,063. She also posted her lowest scoring average to that point, 71.43. She was nevertheless disappointed over losing the Nabisco Dinah Shore and the U.S. Women's Open, but found that having other priorities—her daughter—helped her put things in perspective. "When I walk off the 18th green and sign my scorecard," she told Goldstein, "I don't take it with me. Before, if I played badly, I would mope all night long."

Inkster had her second child, daughter Cori Simpson, in 1994, and thus played a limited season of 16 events. The other years around this time were among the worst of her career, as she was ranked 47 in 1993 and 49 in 1994, but she managed to pull back up to 33 in 1995, then 21 in 1996. In the meantime, she struggled with a decision of whether to continue playing or not. "I was kind of straddling the fence," she recalled to John Garriety in *Sports Illustrated*. "Do I quit? Do I play? Do I quit? And if I'm going to do this, I've got to start working on my game."

After seeing no victories for five years, Inkster recommitted herself to the game and began working with renowned coach Mike McGetrick. In 1997, she landed the Samsung World Championship of Golf in a sudden–death playoff against Kelly Robbins

and Helen Alfredsson. Inkster repeated that win in 1998. Both years she was ranked number six, and posted her best averages, with 70.64 in 1997—her career best—and 70.78 in 1998. The 1997 Samsung win boosted her yearly LPGA earnings to over half a million dollars. Also that that year, she posted ten top–ten finishes, including second place at the Oldsmobile Classic, third at the ShopRite LPGA Classic, and ties for third at both the Longs Drug Challenge and the Corestates Betsy King Classic.

By 1999, Inkster was red–hot. She went into June's U.S. Women's Open in West Point, Mississippi, as the third top money–winner of the tour, with eight top–ten finishes and two victories, at the Welch's/Circle K Championship and Longs Drug Challenge. Throughout the tournament, she had only four bogeys, leaving her at 16–under–272, breaking the previous U.S. Women's Open record for lowest score relative to par of under 10, set by Allison Nicholas of England in 1997. She also tied Annika Sorenstam's 1996 record for low score. Inkster picked up a winner's check for $315,000 for the event after taking a five–shot victory over Sherri Turner.

In a back–to–back display, Inkster in July captured the McDonald's LPGA Championship. It was her fourth victory of the year, adding to her wins at the Welch's/Circle K Championship and Longs Drug Challenge. In addition, it marked her completion of the women's grand slam of golf, composed of her victories at the McDonald's LPGA Championship and U.S. Women's Open in 1999 added to her earlier wins as a rookie at the Nabisco Dinah Shore and du Maurier Classic. Inkster finished the McDonald's LPGA Championship at 16 under par, just shy of Betsy King's tournament record, and surpassed $4 million in career earnings, only one of nine players up to that time to do so.

Meanwhile, observers had been watching Inkster for some time to see if she would make it into the Hall of Fame. Members need 27 points for automatic inclusion, and she was getting close, having earned a point for each nonmajor event and two points for each major. After losing the du Maurier Classic in the summer of 1999, which would have put her over the line, she captured the SAFECO Classic in September to put her right at 27, making her the 17th player to be inducted. Additionally, she was named sportswoman of the year by the Women's Sports Foundation for the individual category (soccer star Mia Hamm earned honors in the team division).

An admitted sports nut, Inkster enjoys basketball, skiing, and Ping–Pong in addition to golf. She is also an avid spectator. A resident of Los Altos, California, about 40 miles southeast of San Francisco, her favorite teams include the San Francisco 49ers, Giants, and Warriors, and the San Jose Sharks. Her family also attends women's professional basketball games. As for balancing her duties as a mother and a celebrity golfer, Inkster remarked in a *Golf Digest* interview, "When I'm home, I'm a normal person. Up at 6:30 to get the kids ready for school." However, her daughters also tour with her regularly, going along to as many as 20 events each year. When asked if she ever had "any bad experiences being a woman jock," she replied, "Might have lost a few dates in school. Guys didn't like going out with someone who could beat them in hoops."

Sources

Periodicals

Golf, June 1993, p. 110; August 1999, p. LPGA–6.
Golf Digest, February 1999.

Maclean's, August 2, 1999, p. 46.
New York Times, May 18, 1984; July 7, 1986; September 27, 1999, p. D10; September 29, 1999, p. D2; October 19, 1999, p. D6.
Sports Illustrated, August 30, 1982, p. 56; April 10, 1989, p. 34; June 14, 1999, p. G6; July 5, 1999, p. G5.
Star Tribune (Minneapolis, MN), p. 11C.
Washington Post, June 7, 1999, p. D1.
Women's Sports & Fitness, September 1986, p. 30.

Online

"Juli Inkster," GolfWeb web site, http://www.golfweb.com (January 14, 2000).
"Player Biographies: Juli Inkster," LPGA Tour web site, http://www.lpga.com (January 14, 2000).

Thomas Penfield Jackson

U.S. District Court Judge

Born 1937; son of Thomas Searing Jackson; married and divorced twice; married; wife's name, Pat (a school administrator); children: three daughters. *Education:* Dartmouth University, graduated, 1958; Harvard Law School, graduated, 1964.

Addresses: *Home*—Washington, DC. *Office*—United States District Court for the District of Columbia, 333 Constitution Ave., N.W., Washington, D.C. 20001.

Career

Practiced law with Jackson & Campbell, Washington, DC; appointed to United States District Court for the District of Columbia, 1982. *Military service*— U.S. Navy, late 1950s–early 1960s.

Sidelights

U.S. District Court Judge Thomas Penfield Jackson might not be a household name, but the defendant in his biggest case to date is: Microsoft. In the U.S. government's antitrust case against computer giant, Jackson sat on the bench as both sides outlined their positions. With a case of this magnitude, it is not surprising that the press tried to find out what makes Jackson tick in hopes of getting an advance idea of how he might rule. Some qualities they discovered include his tendency to root for the underdog and reputation for being open–minded. He also has a history for being "a middle–of–the–road jurist who typically shies away from drastic penalties," as Paul Davidson reported in *USA Today*.

By late 1999, Jackson offered his "findings of fact," which were not a ruling but a simply a preliminary verdict indicating which side he tended to agree with. In a blow to Microsoft, his proclamation outlined that the firm was a monopoly, signaling continued troubles for the software vendor known best for its flagship product, the Windows operating system.

Jackson was born in 1937, the son of Thomas Searing Jackson, a prominent lawyer in Washington, D.C. with his own firm, Jackson & Campbell. Growing up in Kensington, Maryland, a Washington suburb, he won a choir scholarship to St. Alban's preparatory school thanks to his vocal ability. The school revoked it, however, when Jackson's voice changed, so he transferred to a top–notch public high school in Montgomery County, Maryland. There, he edited the student newspaper and played football.

After high school, Jackson attended Dartmouth University, and would remain involved with the institution long after graduating in 1958; he ran the alumni association in Washington for many years. Subsequently, he served three years in the U.S. Navy and was stationed most of the time aboard a destroyer in the Mediterranean. When he returned, he went to Harvard Law School, and after graduating in 1964, began his career in his father's firm. There, he mainly represented clients in medical malpractice and insurance cases. His powerful baritone voice and formal presence in the courtroom impressed juries.

In the meantime, Jackson was becoming more politically involved in his community. Though Montgomery County was heavily Democratic, this made it easier for him to shine as a Republican. In 1972, he served as an attorney to President Richard Nixon's reelection committee, and managed to avoid having his record marred by the Watergate scandal that resulted in the president's resignation.

By 1980, Jackson was in the running to be appointed to a seat on the District of Columbia Superior Court or the U.S. Court of Appeals for the District of Columbia Circuit. He was overlooked, however; some say because of his membership in a whites–only country club, which could have been a detriment if he sat on the bench in that mostly–black district. However, in 1982, President Ronald Reagan appointed him to the U.S. District Court for the District of Columbia, a more prestigious post. In that capacity, he has ruled in several high–profile cases.

In 1988, for instance, Jackson presided over the trial of Michael Deaver, a former aide to Reagan, in a case that investigated whether he had lied under oath about improperly lobbying White House associates. He was convicted, and Jackson fined him $100,000 for perjury. Then, Jackson was on the bench for the notorious 1990 trial of popular Washington, D.C. mayor Marion Barry, who was thereafter etched in the minds of much of the public as a figure in a grainy video image smoking a pipe containing crack cocaine in a hotel room. The racially charged case ended with Barry being jailed for possession of cocaine.

Also, Jackson was the judge who ordered Senator Bob Packwood to hand over his diaries to a Senate Ethics Committee after he was accused of sexual misconduct in incidents ranging from 1969 to 1990. Then, Jackson ruled for the automaker General Motors after the government tried to sue them, alleging they manufactured defective brakes. In that ongoing, highly technical case, Jackson determined that the consumer complaints were anecdotal. In 1997, he struck down the presidential line–item veto, which expanded the president's ability to remove specific items from spending bills, on the grounds that it was unconstitutional.

The government's case against Microsoft, though, would be the biggest assignment of Jackson's career to that point. The Federal Trade Commission in 1990 began to look into complaints that Microsoft held a monopoly on operating systems for personal computers with its nearly universal Windows software. The company in 1994 signed a consent decree stating that it would give computer manufacturers more leeway to install competitor's software. By 1997, the Justice Department filed suit, saying Microsoft violated the consent decree due to its actions regarding Internet browser software. Jackson in 1997 issued a preliminary injunction to prevent Microsoft from making it mandatory that computer makers carry their Explorer Internet browser, though an appeals court later struck down that ruling. The next year, the Justice Department and 20 states, plus the District of Columbia, filed antitrust suits against Microsoft, though one state later dropped out.

On October 19, 1998, the antitrust trial against Microsoft opened in Washington's Federal District Court. Jackson heard arguments, many of them concerning the fact that Microsoft integrated its Internet browser with its operating system, thus causing an unfair playing field, especially for rival browser manufacturer Netscape. Though a not a complete technophobe—Jackson was known to surf the web on occasion—he was not entirely familiar with the ins and outs of the complex realm of computers and the Internet. Thus, he often asked for detailed explanations, but not so much as to bog down the trial. As a result, he was praised for his diligence and skill in absorbing highly technical data. Testimony finally ended on June 24, 1999, and Jackson issued a preliminary decision, though not a final verdict, early that November. Though he had been known to write out opinions in longhand, when he sent his 207–page findings of fact to both sides in the Microsoft case, they received the document via e–mail.

As Jonathan Cassell summed up in *Electronic News,* "Judge Thomas Penfield Jackson's finding that Microsoft has used its power to harm other firms that could compete with it was a surprise to few. Perhaps the only surprise was the vehemence expressed in Judge Jackson's finding. Such findings are usually more circumspect in their language, with the stronger words coming later when the actual decision is rendered." A *Newsweek* writer questioned Jackson's harsh words, suggesting that his decision involved "conjecture about how the computer marketplace will evolve over the next few years." Still, competitors like Netscape hailed Jackson's findings. The next step, then, would be to search for some kind of solution, which could involve any number of options, from breaking up Microsoft into smaller units (the most drastic move) to finding some sort of settlement agreement with the company. Shortly after Jackson's findings were issued, Microsoft founder Bill Gates in January of 2000 announced he was stepping down as the firm's chief executive officer, giving the reins to longtime executive Steve Ballmer, though Gates would retain the position of chairman.

Jackson has been married three times; his wife, Pat, is a school administrator in Washington, D.C. They live in a luxury high–rise building in Washington, D.C., but he takes the subway to work. Jackson has two daughters and two granddaughters. He enjoys reading, especially historical biographies; attending Shakespearean theater; watching football (particularly the Washington Redskins); and sailing on the Chesapeake Bay.

Sources

Business Week, December 21, 1998, p. 84.

Computerworld, June 14, 1999, p. 14.

Congressional Quarterly Weekly Report, April 12, 1997, p. 833.

Electronic News, November 15, 1999, p. 8.

InfoWorld, November 15, 1999, p. 28.

Newsweek, November 15, 1999, p. 55; November 22, 1999, p. 68.

New York Times, November 6, 1999, p. A1.

PC Magazine, January 4, 2000, p. 32.

USA Today, March 22, 1999, p. 8B.

Wall Street Journal, November 8, 1999, p. A3; December 2, 1999, p. B1.

Gish Jen

Author

Born August 12, 1955, in New York, NY; daughter of a civil engineering professor and a schoolteacher; married David O'Connor; children: Paloma, Luke. *Education:* Harvard University, B.A., 1977; attended Stanford University, 1979–80; University of Iowa, M.F.A., 1983.

Addresses: *Home*—Cambridge, MA. *Agent*—Maxine Groffsky Literary Agency, 2 Fifth Ave., New York, NY 10011.

Career

Author. MacDowell Colony, New Hampshire, resident, 1985 and 1987; Radcliffe Bunting Institute and James A. Michener Foundation/Copernicus Society, fellow, 1986; Massachusetts Artists Foundation and National Endowment of the Arts fellow, 1988; Tufts University, lecturer in fiction writing, 1986; University of Massachusetts, visiting writer, 190–91. Contributor to periodicals, including *Atlantic Monthly, Iowa Review, New Yorker, Southern Review,* and *Yale Review,* as well as in anthologies, such as *Best American Short Stories of 1988,* Houghton, 1988; *New Worlds of Literature,* Norton, 1989; and *Home to Stay: Asian American Women's Fiction,* Greenfield Review Press, 1990.

Awards: Henfield Foundation Transatlantic Review Award, 1983; Katherine Anne Porter contest prize, 1987, for *Nimrod;* Boston MBTA Urbanarts Project prize, 1988.

Photograph by Jerry Bauer

Sidelights

Since her debut novel, *Typical American,* in 1991, Gish Jen's wry, multilayered fiction has explored culture clashes, relationships, social issues and more. She followed up her widely praised initial work with yet another engaging novel, *Mona in the Promised Land,* 1996, which involves the same family as in Jen's first book, then in 1999 came out with another lauded collection titled *Who's Irish?.* Although comparisons inevitably have been drawn between Jen and other Asian–American women writers such as Amy Tan, she provides a unique voice and fresh tales: Whereas Tan's work often spans centuries, and the characters look back at their history to find answers, Jen's rely on the future to find their identity. As Dottie Enrico put it in USA Today in a review of *Who's Irish?* , Jen "does a masterly job recounting the lives of the '1.5' generation of Asians born in the USA of immigrant parents who struggle to find their places in a land of Ford Explorers, country clubs and toothy ex–football heroes." In addition, Hilary Roxe in *Time International* commented that Jen "tackles immigrant life in the United States with irreverent aplomb." However, the author recoils from being labeled as simply a chronicler of immigrant tales. "I refuse to be marginalized. I refuse to be an ambassador," she stated to Martha McPhee in *Harper's Bazaar*. "It is more complicated than that."

Lillian Jen was born on August 12, 1955, in the Queens Borough of New York City. She was the second of five children, and her parents were immigrants from Shanghai, China. Jen later adopted the nickname "Gish" because she admired the actor Lillian Gish, and figured she needed a pen name because she was going to become a writer. Although her father was a professor of civil engineering and her mother a teacher, Jen was the only one in her family who showed an interest in reading for pleasure. When she was young, the family moved from Yonkers to the more upscale Scarsdale, New York, where the school library was much more well–stocked than her small Catholic school. Jen related to Terry Hong in *Notable Asian Americans*, "I felt like a kid in a chocolate factory. I must have read every book. I read indiscriminately, whether it was Albert Camus or Walter Farley. They all made me say, 'wow.'"

In school, Jen excelled in math and science, and even through her parents were proud of her, there was very little encouragement for girls to go into technical fields, so she felt pressured to change her interest to English. She did start off at Harvard University in 1972 as a pre–med major, but during her junior year she took a writing course taught by Robert Fitzgerald, a noted translator, and ended up getting her degree in literature in 1977. Still, though, she was skeptical that she could build a career out of writing, and her parents goaded her to enter a more practical field.

After graduating, with help from Fitzgerald, Jen found work at Doubleday publishers, where she enjoyed the literary atmosphere but felt that she was stuck in a nether–region between business and practicality. "I wasn't writing, nor was I making a living," she explained to Wendy Smith in *Publishers Weekly*. Deciding to follow the more–traveled path, she followed three of her siblings and enrolled in business school (another sibling attended medical school). She was accepted at Harvard but chose Stanford instead because she knew it also offered a quality writing program. Confused, she read novels voraciously and took writing courses in addition to her business studies. By her second year, she overslept every day for the first week of classes and realized that she was not going to finish her business degree.

Although Jen knew she wanted to be a writer, her family was unsupportive, and when she left graduate school, her parents refused to speak to her for more than a year. Even after she became successful, she noted to Smith, "I think my family would be more relieved than dismayed if I were to stop writing." With no means of support, Jen went to China and taught English. She recalled to Hong, "Not only was it a discovery of my roots, it was also the first time that I really felt I was contributing to something larger than myself…. I couldn't have written *Typical American* without that trip."

After teaching for a year overseas, Jen returned and enrolled at the University of Iowa where she entered the Writer's Workshop, obtaining her master of fine arts degree in 1983. There, teachers Bharati Mukherjee and James Alan McPherson were her biggest mentors. Afterward, she went back to San Francisco and married David O'Connor, whom she met at Stanford. He worked in computer software at Apple in Silicon Valley, and although Jen was happy that he was making a good living, she felt out of place among the technical professionals.

Jen soon grew weary of being what she termed a "dutiful wife," according to Hong, making beds each day and fixing dinner each night, and soon found that her husband totally supported her ambitions. They moved to Cambridge, Massachusetts, in 1985, where he had landed a job with the Massachusetts Institute of Technology. However, they had purchased a house in need of renovation, and Jen concentrated on that instead of on her writing for a while. Eventually, she attended a writer's colony in New Hampshire and wrote a story, "The Water Faucet Vision." But back in Cambridge, Jen applied for a job with the Harvard University Press, thinking she would go back into publishing because her career as a writer had not taken off.

Although the job never materialized, Jen soon received a year–long fellowship from the Bunting Institute at Radcliffe. In the midst of other goal–oriented women, Jen found that her motivation soared. The first week at the institute, she called herself a "would–be writer," as she recalled to Smith, and noted that, "everybody jumped on me. By the end of the week, not only was I identifying myself as a writer, but I was also saying, 'I'm writing a novel.'" In the meantime, before finishing her novel, Jen's short stories began to be published regularly in places like the *Atlantic Monthly, Iowa Review, New Yorker, Southern Review,* and *Yale Review,* as well as in anthologies.

Upon publication of *Typical American*, Jen was heralded for her unique style and wit, and most critics put her in the same league with regaled Asian–

American writers such as Amy Tan and Maxine Hong Kingston. The book examines the story on an immigrant family, the Changs, who struggle up from poverty only to fall prey to the dark side of the American dream, losing sight of their Chinese values. The novel was praised for its dark humor, its use of metaphor, pacing, and sentence structure. Though some reviewers harped about underdeveloped characters and a melodramatic ending, *Typical American* was overwhelmingly praised. In fact, Jen explained to Smith that the tale became gloomier as it went on partly because she suffered a miscarriage while writing the final section.

While writing the more somber part of *Typical American*, however, a new, more comical character arose and Jen began to develop a story that would become *Mona in the Promised Land*. After finishing her first novel, she began fleshing out *Mona*, all the while dealing with the pressures of being a first-time mother. From the time her son, Luke, was born until age five, she was exceptionally busy trying to raise him and write at the same time. "It was murder: I had to schedule time to take a shower," Jen remarked to Smith. "I did not go shopping, I did not do lunch, I didn't get any exercise." Jen also has a daughter, Paloma, born in the late 1990s.

Mona in the Promised Land extends the story of the Changs, this time through the eyes of the teenage daughter, who has decided to embrace Judaism. The work deals with transformations of many kinds, and deftly explores race, class, religion, politics, and sexuality in the process. A coming-of-age novel, in essence, Valerie Miner in the Nation described it as "a younger, upscale, East Coast version of *American Graffiti.*" *Publishers Weekly* reviewer called the book "wickedly and hilariously observant" and Jacqueline Carey in the *New York Times Book Review* claimed that it "has a wide-ranging exuberance that's unusual in what is still to its credit a realistic novel."

Jen's next effort was a collection of stories, titled *Who's Irish?* , published in 1999. Two were novella-length, including "Duncan in China," about a Chinese American man who does not find what he expects in contemporary China, and "House, House, Home," about a woman with marital problems. The tales involve Chinese characters, but as Dan Cryer pointed out in *Newsday*, "No matter what group we belong to, these stories suggest, we are individuals first and foremost. Being Chinese-American may or may not be as important to selfhood as being young, college-educated or female, or being an athlete, a birdwatcher or an engineer." *Who's Irish* also includes "The Water Faucet Vision," which Jen wrote at the MacDowell colony in New Hampshire, and two more tales about the Changs, in addition to other stories about assimilation, racism, family ties, and more.

Critics generally embraced Jen's stories with as much gusto as her novels, although some commented that her two novellas did not warrant their length. Also, their assessments differed in some respects. David Gates in *Newsweek*, for example, remarked that "Jen uses her ever-ready wit to provide ironic distance from genuinely dark places," but Cryer in *Newsday* mentioned that this collection, unlike her novels, includes virtually no humor. However, he did note that her other strengths—often touted by numerous other reviewers—are abundantly clear, including "depth of characterization, sentences that sing and signify, [and] a sure-handed grasp of our society's complexities." Jean Thompson in the *New York Times Book Review*, meanwhile, summed up, "Jen's gift is for comedy that resonates, and sadnesses that arise with perfect timing from absurdities."

Selected writings

Typical American (novel), Houghton, 1991.
Mona in the Promised Land (novel), Knopf, 1996.
Who's Irish? (collection), Knopf, 1999.

Sources

Books

Contemporary Literary Criticism, Volume 70: Yearbook 1991, Gale Research, 1992.
Notable Native Americans, Gale Research, 1995.

Periodicals

Booklist, April 15, 1996, p. 1421.
Entertainment Weekly, March 29, 1991, p. 50.
Harper's Bazaar, May 1996, p. 94.
Independent, May 14, 1998, p. 2.
Nation, June 17, 1996, p. 35.
Newsday, June 7, 1999, p. B9.
Newsweek, July 15, 1996, p. 56; June 7, 1999, p. 75.
New York Times Book Review, March 31, 1991, p. 9; June 9, 1996; June 27, 1999, p. 13.
Publishers Weekly, March 11, 1996, p. 40; April 26, 1999, p. 52; June 7, 1999, p. 59.
Time International, August 9, 1999, p. 48.
USA Today, June 24, 1999, p. 7D.

Online

"Gish Jen," *Contemporary Authors Online*, Gale
Group web site, http://www.galenet.com
(August 27, 1999).

Ha Jin

Author

B orn Xuefei Jin, February 21, 1956, in Liaoning, China; became U.S. citizen; son of Danlin (a military officer) and Yuanfen (a worker; maiden name, Zhao) Jin; married Lisah Bian (a math teacher), July 6, 1982; children: Wen. *Education:* Heilongjiang University, B.A., 1981; Shangdong University, M.A., 1984; Brandeis University, Ph.D., 1992.

Addresses: *Home*—Lawrenceville, GA. *Office*—Emory University, N 211 A Callaway Center, Creative Writing Program, Emory University, 537 Kilgo Cir., Atlanta, GA 30322. *Agent*—Christina Ward, P.O. Box 515, North Scituate, MA 02060.

Career

A uthor. Worked as a night watchman, busboy, and waiter, late 1980s–early 1990s. Emory University, Atlanta, GA, 1993 , began as assistant professor, became professor, 1998. *Military service:* Chinese People's Army, 1969–74.

Awards: Three Pushcart Prizes for fiction; *Kenyon Review* prize; Agni Best Fiction Prize; Ernest Hemingway Foundation/PEN Award for first fiction, 1997, for *Ocean of Words: Army Stories*; Flannery O'Connor Award for short fiction, 1997, for *Under the Red Flag*; National Book Award, 1999, and PEN/Faulkner Award for fiction, 2000, both for *Waiting*.

AP/Wide World Photos

Sidelights

I n 1999, Ha Jin won the prestigious National Book Award for his novel *Waiting*, which features spare prose and an undercurrent of humor that several have compared to the style of Anton Chekov. As with all of his fiction to that point, *Waiting* is set in China, where Jin spent his life until moving to the United States to attend graduate school in the mid–1980s. Much of his material has been culled from his observations of Chinese society during the Cultural Revolution. In 2000, Jin also picked up the PEN/Faulkner Award for fiction, the largest annual juried fiction prize in the United States, which bears a check for $15,000. This marked the first time ever that a novel won both this award and the National Book Award. In *Time*, Paul Gray observed, "Jin had the good luck to be born outside the U.S. and hence be protected from the homogenizing and potentially trivializing influences that afflict so many U.S.–born aspiring authors. Beginners are advised to 'write about what you know.' Ha Jin inherited a frame of reference broader than sex and MTV." However, Jin foresees the day soon ahead where he will abandon the topic of his homeland, because as he commented to Kristin Tillotson in the Minneapolis *Star Tribune*,

"The longer I am away, the less I know it." He also mentioned to Martha Baker in the *St. Louis Post–Dispatch* that there are "more significant stories to be told the stories of being an immigrant in America."

Xuefei ("shu–FAY") Jin was born in the Liaoning province of northeastern China on February 21, 1956, the son of Danlin and Yuanfen Jin. He later took the name "Ha" as a pen name for the sake of privacy, and also because it is easier for Americans to pronounce. As a boy, Jin aspired to become a military officer like his father. He remembered looking through books in the library when he was young, but in the mid–1960s, Chinese leader Mae Zedong began the Cultural Revolution, which scorned intellectual pursuits and initiated the closing of schools and universities. Jin thus grew up "basically illiterate," as he recalled to Tillotson. She had asked him which books had influenced him as a child, and he replied, "None. All the good ones were burned."

When he was ten, Jin became one of "the small Red Guards," as he explained to Mark Binelli in the *Atlanta Journal and Constitution*. "I wasn't old enough to travel around the country to disseminate the revolution. We just did propaganda on the streets one or two hours a day. You sang revolution songs. You shouted slogans." At age 14, Jin joined the military, where he was stationed in a small town about 20 miles from the Russian border. He started as an artilleryman and became a telegraph operator. There, he began to read, absorbing communist doctrine by Karl Marx, Vladmir Lenin, and others. Scant literature was available, and most of the works were sub–par anyway. He did manage to skim *Don Quixote* when a fellow soldier obtained a forbidden copy, but he had only one day to look through it.

After leaving the service, Jin worked as a telegrapher for the Harbin Railroad Company for a few years. During this time, universities were still closed, so he waited and hoped that institutions of higher education would open their doors again. Meanwhile, he began to learn English by listening to radio programs in the language, and started to educate himself on his own. He also started to compose poetry, though it was mainly Chinese army propaganda. "To write a poem that would praise this or that, that's how I started to write, but not seriously," he related to Liza Featherstone in *Newsday*.

Finally, in 1977, China's colleges reopened, and Jin earned a bachelor of arts degree at Heilongjiang University in Harbin, where he studied English. His focus was on American literature, including the works of William Faulkner, Robert Penn Warren, and Theodore Roethke, though he also cites Russian authors Chekov, Fyodor Dostoevsky, and Nikolai Gogol as influences. After graduating, Jin obtained a master's degree at Shangdong University in 1984, and the next year, left to study at Brandeis University in Waltham, Massachusetts. He received his doctoral degree there in 1992.

When he left for America, Jin never expected to stay. His parents remain in China, and his wife, Lisah Bian Jin, whom he married when he was 26, did not join him for a year and a half. Their son, Wen, who was six at the time, stayed in China with his grandparents for two more years after that. But when Wen arrived, Jin knew he would not return to his homeland. "When he came, one thing was very clear to me: He must be American," Jin stated to Binelli. "He has to stay in this country, get educated and get a job in this country." Then, in 1989, China saw the massacre of students by the army in Tiananmen Square, which sealed Jin's decision. He told Baker in the *St. Louis–Dispatch* that after the Tiananmen Square incident, "it would be impossible to write honestly in China." In 1990, he committed himself to writing and speaking only in English. "The process was excruciating like changing my blood," he remarked to Baker. "I was full of anxiety as if I were running a fever all the time." The family eventually all became U.S. citizens.

At Brandeis, Jin began to write poetry. He was first published after one of his professors, poet Frank Bidart, read a piece over the phone to the editor of the *Paris Review*. In 1990, his first collection of poems, *Between Silences*, was published by the University of Chicago Press. After getting his doctoral degree, Jin enrolled in Boston University's creative writing program, where he worked with poet and professor Leslie Epstein. "He taught me what good prose should be like," Jin stated to Stephen Martin in the *Chronicle of Higher Education*. "Not too fancy; not vulgar, either." In 1993, he was offered a position teaching English and creative writing at Atlanta's Emory University. His second poetry collection, *Facing Shadows*, was published in 1996.

Also in 1996, Jin saw publication of his first book of short stories, *Ocean of Words: Army Stories*, which he had completed even before starting work at Emory. It received a positive notice in *Publishers Weekly*, and Andy Solomon in the *New York Times Book Review* called the pieces "powerful in their unity of theme and rich in their diversity of styles." Jin drew upon his experiences in the military for the works, which were all set in the early 1970s on the Chinese–Russian border, the time and place of his own army career. The collection won the Ernest Hemingway Foundation/PEN Award for first fiction in 1997. That same year, Jin's second story collection, *Under the Red Flag*, about life during the Cultural Revolution, won the Flannery O'Connor Award for short fiction. One of the selections was chosen to appear in the *Best American Short Stories 1997*.

In early 1999, Jin published his first novel, *In the Pond*, which is mainly a comedy, although "the screwball plot turns out to have a chilly center," as Mei Chin described in the *New York Times Book Review*. Though Chin praised the work, *In the Pond* did not receive nearly as much attention as Jin's next novel, *Waiting*, which came out late in 1999. It spans the life of a Chinese doctor and military officer over the course of almost two decades, during which he attempts to free himself from an unwanted arranged marriage in order to pursue his love of an army nurse. Each summer, Lin Kong journeys from his military hospital to his native village to ask his wife for a divorce. But after she agrees, every year, she changes her mind in court. Despite the tragic circumstances, Jin injects humor into the work. Though some complained about the slow pace of *Waiting*, others applauded it as a revealing sketch of contemporary China. Jin, however, summed up to Jill Vejnoska of the *Atlanta Constitution*, "It's the love story. I think that's the reason it resonated for so many people."

Jin lives outside Atlanta, in Lawrenceville, Georgia, with his wife and son. Despite his successes, he does not envision becoming a full–time writer, telling Baker in the *St. Louis Post–Dispatch*, "I cannot imagine not teaching." Before becoming a professor, while getting his doctoral degree, he held a job waiting tables in a restaurant, but was demoted to busboy. He also worked as a night watchman in a factory. "I liked the night watchman's job best," Jin mentioned to Michael Skube in the *Atlanta Journal and Constitution*. "The factory was quiet and I could read. Every hour I would make rounds and check locks. I was good at it. If Emory decides it doesn't want me, I know I could do something else."

Selected writings

Between Silences (poems), University of Chicago Press, 1990.
Facing Shadows (poems), Hanging Loose Press, 1996.
Ocean of Words: Army Stories (fiction), Zoland Books, 1996.
Under the Red Flag (short stories), University of Georgia Press, 1997.
In the Pond (novel), Zoland Books, 1999.
Waiting (novel), Pantheon, 1999.

Sources

Periodicals

Atlanta Constitution, November 15, 1999, p. E1; April 4, 2000, p. D1.
Atlanta Journal and Constitution, November 23, 1997, p. K1.
Booklist, November 1, 1997, p. 454.
Chronicle of Higher Education, April 25, 1997, p. A8.
Library Journal, October 15, 1999, p. 105.
Newsday, November 28, 1999, p. B11.
New York Times Book Review, June 2, 1996; January 11, 1998, p. 14; January 31, 1999, p. 16; October 24, 1999, p. 9.
Publishers Weekly, February 26, 1996, p. 98; October 13, 1997, p. 58; October 12, 1998, p. 58; August 23, 1999, p. 42; November 1, 1999, p. 46.
St. Louis Post–Dispatch, December 6, 1999, p. D3; October 31, 1999, p. F12.
Star Tribune (Minneapolis, MN), November 14, 1999, p. 7F; January 24, 2000, p. 1E.
Time, December 1, 1997, p. 94; November 8, 1999, p. 144.
Washington Post, April 4, 2000, p. C1.

Online

"Ha Jin," *Contemporary Authors Online,* Gale Group web site, http://www.galenet.com (February 22, 2000).

Steve Jobs

Reuters/Archive Photos

Business entrepreneur

Born in 1955; son of Paul (a machinist) and Clara (an accountant) Jobs; married, 1991; wife's name, Laurene; children: (from previous relationship) Lisa; (from marriage) one son, one daughter. *Education:* Attended Reed College, Portland, OR.

Addresses: *Home*—Palo Alto, CA. *Office*—Apple Computer, 1 Infinite Loop, Cupertino, CA 95014; Pixar Animation Studios, 1001 W. Cutting Blvd., Richmond, CA 94804.

Career

Founded Apple Computer with Steve Wozniak, Palo Alto, CA, 1975; resigned from Apple, remaining chair of board of directors, 1985; founded NeXT Computer Company, 1985, sold it to Apple, 1996; bought Pixar Animation Studios, 1986; named interim CEO of Apple Computer, 1997.

Sidelights

Steve Jobs and his partner Steve Wozniak revolutionized the computer industry in the mid–1970s when they built and marketed the first Apple computers, designed specifically to be user–friendly desktop machines for the general public. "We started out to get a computer in the hands of everyday people, and we succeeded beyond our wildest dreams," Jobs remarked to Cathy Booth in *Time.* The company's fortunes then flagged as competitors flooded the market, so Apple developed the Macintosh in the mid–1980s, which set a new standard for ease of use. However, it did not boost profits because it did not catch on among businesses, other than eventually becoming the superior machine for graphic design and desktop publishing. As a result, Jobs was squeezed out of his position and founded a new computer company, NeXT, and later made another fortune with Pixar Animation Studios, which he bought from filmmaker George Lucas. His comeback was complete when he stepped in as a consultant once again at Apple and oversaw two new product lines, the iMac and iBook computers, which revitalized the company's image and sales.

Steven Paul Jobs was born in 1955 to unwed parents and soon adopted by Paul and Clara Jobs of Mountain View, California. Later in life, he tracked down his biological parents, who had another child, a daughter, whom they kept. For privacy reasons, Jobs declines to discuss them, but Steve Lohr in the *New York Times Magazine* revealed that Jobs's younger sister is novelist Mona Simpson, who once wrote a book about a Silicon Valley entrepreneur, and she and Jobs have a close relationship. Though he keeps in touch with his biological parents, Jobs is adamant that the parents who raised him are his real parents.

Early on, Jobs showed a proficiency in electronics and a thirst for education. In junior high, he groused that he was not learning anything at his school, so his parents moved to Los Altos instead. While in school, the headstrong Jobs once contacted William Hewlett, the head of the Hewlett–Packard computer firm, to ask for some parts he needed for a class project. Hewlett was so impressed that he offered Jobs a summer internship at his company. Always a tinkerer, in high school, Jobs earned money for college tuition by repairing old junk cars and selling them for a profit.

After graduating from Santa Clara's Homestead High School in 1972, Jobs went to Reed College in Portland, Oregon, but left after a year and a half. He went to work for Atari as a video game designer and saved enough money to pay for a journey to India in the summer of 1974. There, he embraced Eastern culture and religion, but fell ill with dysentery in the fall of that year and had to return home. Back in California, Jobs moved into a commune for a short time.

In 1975, Jobs began keeping company with a group calling themselves the Homebrew Computer Club. It was led by Steve Wozniak, whom Jobs knew from high school. At this time, computers were still too complicated for anyone but dedicated computer aficionados, and Wozniak was trying to engineer a small, simple system that average consumers could use in their homes in effect, the original desktop computer. Wozniak worked on building the machine in Jobs's parents' garage while Jobs lined up financing and grew his dream of marketing to the masses. The prototype that Wozniak executed was the original Apple computer. Their first customer was a local computer store owner, who immediately ordered 25 of the machines.

The first Apple went on sale in 1976 for $700, and the most striking feature was its circuit board. Designed by Wozniak, it could load and read programs from other sources. Instead of requiring users to type in commands in computer language, they could point and click on small picture icons, like a trash can and a file folder, thus putting computers within the reach of non–technical customers. By 1977, Jobs and Wozniak came out with the second generation of the machine, the Apple II, and Jobs began to urge programmers to design software for use on the machine. Before long, a bevy of applications were available, from business tools to video games. Soon, Jobs also linked laser printers to the machine, opening the door to desktop publishing.

Apple II sales were $2.7 million that first year, and in three years, growth had surged to $200 million in sales. Before long, Jobs and Wozniak (the "two

Steves," as they became known), both college dropouts, were multimillionaires before age 30. Two other cohorts, A. C. "Mike" Markkula, Jr., who became chairman, and president Michael Scott, shared the wealth as well. By the early 1980s, Wozniak, while remaining a shareholder, had left the firm and returned to Berkeley to finish college.

As of 1980, other competition had sprung up from IBM, Radio Shack, and Commodore. That year, the new Apple III was introduced, but it was plagued by technical problems and ineffective marketing. Apple ceased selling it for a time in order to rework it, but it never sold well. A new model, Lisa, was offered in 1983 for business people with few computer skills, but it could not compete with lower–priced machines from IBM. By this time, Apple had lost half of its market share to IBM.

Seeking to regain its prominence, Apple developed the Macintosh model in 1984 to be even more user–friendly, but Jobs made a fatal error by not installing a hard disk drive or offering a top–quality printer with it. Business buyers avoided it, and market share continued to dwindle, which set the stage for Jobs's forced departure. In a highly publicized blowout, the company's new CEO, John Sculley, whom Jobs handpicked for the post, made it clear that Apple did not want its founder to lead them anymore. "In my wildest imagination, I couldn't have come up with such a wild ending to all of this," he commented in a *Newsweek* interview. Jobs did, however, remain chair of the board of directors.

After leaving Apple, Jobs invested $7 million of his own money to start a new computer company, NeXT, which aimed to reach the educational market, mainly selling high–end machines and software to colleges. Working with a group of ex–Apple employees, he developed a faster microcomputer with excellent graphics and sound that went to market in 1989. However, the machine never caught on due to its black–and–white screen, and its inability to network or run common software. In addition, though it was slated to cost less than typical big–business workstations, Sun's SPARCstation and others quickly undercut NeXT's price of $9,995.

In addition to Jobs's failure to build a project that would see the same success as the Apple II, it was widely reported that he could be a difficult boss, known for micromanaging, berating underlings, and not listening to others. He even once vetoed a circuit board design because he did not like the way it looked, even though it would never be seen by anyone except technicians. By the 1990s, though, his attitude seemed to be maturing. "I trust people more," he explained to Lohr in the *New York Times Magazine*. And despite his authoritarian reputation, Jobs deserves credit for helping to transform the office dress code. Known for showing up in sandals, jeans and T–shirts to work, he was one of the first to introduce a casual workplace, which eventually began to change what much of America wore on the job.

Though NeXT was not becoming the powerhouse Jobs envisioned, in 1986 he purchased Pixar Animation Studios for $10 million from filmmaker George Lucas, known for his dazzling special effects in *Star Wars* and other movies. For several years, computers powerful enough to do the animation were too expensive, but as technology advanced, the prices came down, making the concept cost–effective. Jobs over the years invested another $40 to $50 million of his own funds in the project and by 1995, was seen as a pioneer once again when he released *Toy Story*, the first–ever full–length computer–animated film. The movie was a blockbuster and drove Pixar stock up, making Jobs's share worth $1 billion. He later had another hit with *A Bug's Life,* 1998, and by 1999, had begun working on a sequel to *Toy Story.*

In the meantime, Jobs was still running NeXT, and by 1993 it had scaled back to only offer customizable software for programmers, specifically those creating web sites, called NextStep. Jobs envisioned NextStep as "the operating system of the '90s," according to G. Pascal Zachary and Ken Yamada in the *Wall Street Journal,* but this never materialized. Instead, Microsoft Windows—which mimics the original Apple concept of pictorial icons as its basic design—kept its stronghold throughout the decade. Jobs decided to sell NeXT, and in December of 1996, Apple announced that it was buying the firm for more than $400 million, admitting that its internal efforts to develop an operating system had failed. In addition, Apple chair Gil Amelio also noted that Jobs would be brought back as a consultant to help the firm in their quest to provide a viable option to Windows. The company that once kicked him out now wanted him back in hopes that he could breathe new life into its sagging sales and increase their market share, now down to single digits as they were cast as the David against Microsoft's Goliath.

Although Jobs made it clear when he rejoined Apple that Pixar would remain his focus, he soon built up clout at his old firm. By July of 1997, Apple's board of directors asked Jobs to consider the post of CEO, but he declined. They then asked him to step in as chair, and again he turned them away, but did agree to increase his involvement with them. In August, he played a pivotal role in brokering a deal between Apple and its rival, Microsoft. The move stunned loyal "Mac" customers as well as many Windows fans, who felt betrayed by the partnership. John Markoff in the *New York Times* noted that the aficionados of each company were "divided into almost cult–like camps." When Jobs announced at a trade show that Microsoft would invest $150 million in Apple, many Macintosh devotees roundly booed him. The deal was not as unorthodox as it seemed, though: Microsoft, as the largest seller of software programs for Macintosh computers, could not afford to let that niche market wither away.

Before long, the business world was abuzz when it was officially announced in September of 1997 what had been suspected: Jobs was indeed rejoining Apple as an interim CEO. In this capacity, he came through for them. The partnership with Microsoft led to sales of new software titles, and a new processor, G3, was selling well as of early 1998. In addition, by May of that year, Jobs unveiled a new innovation as well: the iMac, a new kind of personal computer that invigorated the company and provided a vibrant new aesthetic in desktop systems.

With its rounded, brightly–colored monitors, the iMac system was popular with consumers new to the information superhighway. Though Jobs had been criticized in the past for his attention to style over substance, the look of the product was integral. It was initially available not in five colors, but "flavors," as Apple called them: blueberry, grape, lime, strawberry, and tangerine (Apple later added "graphite" as well). Unlike the typical system, available for years only in a dull beige or perhaps black, the iMac had a unique, fun appeal.

However, the iMac did have drawbacks, such as the fact that some of the most popular software could only run on Windows, and the machine was not equipped with a floppy disk drive. In addition, while similarly equipped machines were dropping well below the $1,000 mark, iMacs were initially offered at $1,299, but the price was later cut. Its ace–in–the–hole was that it was easy to get started. Unlike other personal computers, which required users to connect several wires and often came with little or no software, once plugged in, the iMac was running and Internet–ready in minutes. A success, the iMac nearly quadrupled Apple's retail market share to roughly 12 percent by the summer of 1999, and stock had doubled since Jobs's return to the company.

Subsequently, in a double–whammy, Jobs barreled into the portable market in the fall of 1999 with the iBook, a durable, affordable laptop computer aimed squarely at consumers instead of business users. Jobs was key to the project, dictating from the start that the it be rugged enough to throw in a backpack; thus, the outer shell was devised in an unusual clam–shell shape, and constructed out of polycarbonate plastic. One of its other major innovations was to offer a wireless high–speed Internet connection, dubbed an "AirPort," aimed mainly at users in classrooms. The iBook was so sought–after, stores were taking pre–orders in the summer of 1999 in advance of its debut. Though Jobs continued to resist returning to Apple on a permanent basis, his input had been key to their turnaround.

Despite his status as an icon of the Information Age, Jobs cherishes his privacy and does not reveal too much about his personal life. It has been reported that in his twenties, he had a daughter, Lisa, from a relationship with a woman he did not marry. Though he was not involved in raising her for several years, they reunited when she was seven, and she went to live with him when she was in her teens. Jobs later married Laurene, a graduate student whom he met around 1990 at Stanford's business school when he was there to give a speech. They have a son and daughter and live in an English–style country home in Palo Alto. The family are strict vegans—they eat no animal products and grow many of their own vegetables and herbs.

Sources

Books

Business Leader Profiles for Students, Gale Research, 1999.

Encyclopedia of World Biography, second edition, Gale Research, 1998.

Periodicals

Advertising Age, June 28, 1999, p. S38.

Business Week, January 27, 1986, p. 97; January 11, 1999, p. 63; August 2, 1999, p. 32.

Economist, August 16, 1997, p. 52.

Fortune, January 12, 1981, p. 68; October 9, 1989, p. 48; March 23, 1992, p. 114; September 18, 1995, p. 155.

Inc., May 18, 1999.

InfoWorld, September 22, 1997, p. 19.

Knight–Ridder/Tribune News Service, August 1, 1997.

Maclean's, January 13, 1997, p. 41.

Newsweek, September 30, 1985, p. 51; December 30, 1996, p. 78; May 18, 1998, p. 46; August 2, 1999, p. 50.

New Yorker, September 8, 1997, p. 34.

New York Times, November 30, 1995, p. A1; January 12, 1997, p. 14; August 7, 1997, p. A1.

New York Times Magazine, January 12, 1997, p. 14.

PC Magazine, December 16, 1997, p. 125; March 10, 1998, p. 9.

Rolling Stone, June 16, 1994, p. 73.

Time, February 15, 1982, p. 40; December 7, 1998, p. 205; August 18, 1997, p. 28; August 2, 1999, p. 66; October 18, 1999, pp.62–68.

U.S. News & World Report, December 11, 1995, p. 83.

Wall Street Journal, May 25, 1993, p. A1.

Angelina Jolie

Actor

Born Angelina Jolie Voigt, June 4, 1975, in Los Angeles, CA; daughter of Jon Voigt (an actor) and Marcheline Bertrand (an actor); married Jonny Lee Miller (an actor), c. 1995; divorced, c. 1997. *Education:* Attended New York University.

Addresses: *Agent*—William Morris Agency, 151 El Camino Dr., Beverly Hills, CA 90212.

Career

Actor. Television appearances include miniseries *True Women, 1997*; and *George Wallace, 1997*; and movie *Gia, 1998*. Film appearances include *Lookin' to Get Out, 1982; Cyborg 2: Glass Shadow, 1993; Without Evidence, 1995; Hackers, 1995; Mojave Moon, 1996; Foxfire, 1996; Love Is All There Is, 1996; Playing God, 1997; Hell's Kitchen, 1998; Playing by Heart, 1998; Pushing Tin, 1999; The Bone Collector, 1999;* and *Girl, Interrupted, 1999.*

Awards: Golden Globe Award for best supporting actress in a series, miniseries or motion picture, 1998, for *George Wallace*; National Board of Review award for breakthrough performance by an actress, 1998, for *Playing by Heart*; Los Angeles Outfest grand jury award for outstanding actress in a feature film, 1998, Golden Globe Award for best actress in a miniseries or motion picture made for television, 1999, and Screen Actors Guild award for outstanding performance by a female actor in a TV movie or miniseries, 1999, all for *Gia*; Broadcast Film Critics Association award and Golden Globe award for best supporting actress, 1999, for *Girl, Interrupted.*

Sidelights

In the late 1990s, Angelina Jolie became one of the most intriguing female actors to hit the screen, thanks to some meaty roles and an off–stage image of being dark and wild yet cerebral. Thanks to quirks like her knife collection and her assortment of tattoos, she has cultivated a reputation for being edgy, and she possesses a raw sexuality that she does not hesitate to discuss in interviews. However, Jolie also displays an innate maturity and a talent that has led her from playing everything from a drug–addled supermodel to a governor's wife. A large part of her appeal, undeniably, is her looks. Mim Udovitch in *Rolling Stone* noted, "Angelina is exceptionally beautiful, even among the professionally good–looking." And Andrew Essex observed in *Entertainment Weekly* that her naturally lush lips "are called 'bee– stung' so often you'd think she grew up farming honey." Although she is often noted for her beauty, Jolie's skill does not go unnoticed. Before turning 25, she had chalked up several Golden Globe awards, among others, and had jutted into the top tier of stardom, appearing with Denzel Washington in *The Bone Collector* and Winona Ryder in *Girl, Interrupted*, both in 1999. Several other projects were in the works as well, including a costarring role with Nicolas Cage.

Jolie was born on June 4, 1975, the daughter of American actor Jon Voigt and French actor Marcheline Bertrand. Though they divorced when their daughter was a year old and their son was only three, they continued to maintain a close relationship. Jolie noted to Louis B. Hobson in the *Calgary Sun*, "My mother was 20 when she married my dad. By the time she was 25, she was divorced with two small children. She was a promising actress who gave up her career to raise me and my brother." Of course, her father would go on to win acclaim for his role as Joe Buck, the would–be gigolo in 1969's *Midnight Cowboy*, and grab a best actor Oscar for 1978's *Coming Home*. Though Jolie told Hobson that she and her father have had their differences in the past, they are on good terms now and are even considering making a film together.

After her parents split up, Jolie and her brother were raised in and near New York City by their mother. (Both of them were given middle names that they could use as stage names later; her older brother, James Haven—whom she calls Jamie—is an aspiring director.) When Jolie was 11, the family returned to California, where she attended Beverly Hills High and admitted to Udovitch in *Rolling Stone*, she was "really into leather," adding, "I think I loved Michael Jackson or something. I used to wear the leather jackets with the zippers, or collars with studs on them, and I used to ask if I could go to school wearing studs."

Not surprisingly, given her parents' background, Jolie began studying acting as a child. However, she went through a stage where she strongly considered becoming a funeral director, telling Udovitch, "I'm very drawn to some things that are tradition, that are roots, and I think that may be why I focused on funerals." This feeling probably stemmed from her nomadic childhood, she noted, and might have been related to her feelings about her grandfather's death when she was about nine.

At age 12, though, Jolie went to the Lee Strasberg Institute and began performing, though she took time out for a while to have "some regular teen–age years, so that I had a little more to build on when I went back," as she commented to Elizabeth Snead in *USA Today*. At about age 15, she landed her first major role, playing a character that was originally written to be male: Mr. Wagner in the play *Room Service*. Her take on the part was to turn him into Frau Wagner, a German dominatrix.

By age 16, Jolie was firmly devoted to acting, and moved into her own apartment and began to study drama. When she went on auditions, she did not re-

veal her lineage so that she could prove herself on her own terms. Her first big role was starring in *Hackers*, 1995, a thriller about computer geeks. The next year, Jolie played an androgynous tough teenager in *Foxfire*, an adaptation of a Joyce Carol Oates novel. In 1997, she was hailed for her performance as Cornelia, the second wife of George Wallace (played by Gary Sinise) in the TNT miniseries about the four–term Alabama governor. For that, she won a Golden Globe Award for best supporting actress. Also in 1997 she steamed up the big screen with David Duchovny in *Playing God*.

Jolie's breakthrough role, though, was probably in the 1998 HBO movie *Gia*, based on the true story about lesbian, heroin–addict supermodel Gia Carangi, who died of AIDS at age 26. "I didn't know if I was strong enough to confront the parts of her story that were close to mine," Jolie told Ileane Rudolph in *TV Guide*, referring to her wild stage of drug experimentation in her teens. For the role, she did nude love scenes with another female actor, Elizabeth Mitchell. That was the easy part, though, as Jolie has openly expressed an attraction to women. What was more difficult was being made up to look like she was dying. She shaved her head, and the makeup artists would paint lesions on her skin to resemble Kaposi's sarcoma, a skin cancer common in AIDS patients. Her outstanding presence in *Gia* brought Jolie a Golden Globe Award, a Los Angeles Outfest grand jury award, and a Screen Actors Guild award.

After shooting *Gia*, Jolie was cast in the Rolling Stones video, "Anybody Seen My Baby," playing a bald stripper wearing five–inch heels and a corset. This was a tough assignment as well, telling Snead in *USA Today*, "Yeah, how much pressure is that? I can't dance at home." She added, though, that she managed to loosen up for the job. Also in 1998 she was cast as a gang member's girlfriend in the gritty crime picture *Hell's Kitchen* and costarred with Gillian Anderson in the romantic drama *Playing by Heart*, in which she played a brash young actor with a vulnerable underside. For the latter, she won a National Board of Review award for breakthrough performance. Meanwhile, she began studying film at New York University.

In 1999, Jolie appeared in the dark comedy *Pushing Tin*, playing the sultry wife of Billy Bob Thornton's character, an air traffic controller competing with a colleague (John Cusack) in the high–stress world of the New York–Newark airspace. Though the film was not critically well received, David Ansen praised the acting and remarked that that "Jolie almost steals the show as the tattooed, vodka–swilling, poignant Mary Bell." In addition, *Pushing Tin* was important personally for Jolie, who noted to Louis B. Hobson in the *Calgary Sun,* "It's probably the most fun I've had making a film…. I really understand the whole theme of the film which is dealing with your personal demons. It's what my whole life has been about. If I hadn't put a few of my demons behind me I don't think I'd have felt as secure and happy as I did working on *Pushing Tin. "*

That same year Jolie became a bona fide star when she was billed above the title, with Denzel Washington, in *The Bone Collector.* "I fell over laughing when I found that out," Jolie revealed to Bob Thompson in the *Toronto Sun,* adding, "I have never been above the title. I've never been in a big movie. So I'm excited." In this thriller about the search for a serial killer, she portrays a young cop, Amelia Donaghy, who does the leg work at gruesome crime scenes and communicates her findings to a bedridden forensics expert (Washington). Udovitch in *Rolling Stone* quoted the director, Phillip Noyce, as stating that several other A–list female actors were willing to do the film for less than their usual price, but they went with Jolie due to her blend of qualities: "The strength and the vulnerability, and also a fearlessness, both in the character she portrayed and—I realized when I met her—as an artist."

At the end of December, 1999, the film *Girl, Interrupted* opened in some cities, starring Jolie and Winona Ryder. The movie centers on a young woman (Ryder) who checks herself into a mental institution and finds she cannot get out, and the film came out just in time to be considered for that year's Academy Award ceremonies. Essex in *Entertainment Weekly* reported, "There are whispers that her Jack Nicholson–in–drag *Girl* role could nail her a Best Supporting Actress nomination." And in fact, Jolie indeed snagged the Broadcast Film Critics Association award and a Golden Globe Award for best supporting actress for the role.

At age 20, Jolie was married to actor Jonny Lee Miller, with whom she costarred in *Hackers,* although he is best known for his role as Sick Boy in *Trainspotting.* They filed for divorce 19 months later, though they remain close. On their wedding day, she wore black rubber pants and a white T–shirt with his name written on it in blood. She sports a number of tattoos, including a Chinese dragon, a cross, the letter "H," and a quote by Tennessee Wil-

liams: "A prayer for the wild at heart, kept in cages." In addition, across her stomach is tattooed in Latin, "What nourishes me also destroys me." Jolie remarked to Udovitch, "You know, people always say, 'Well, what if you regret having tattoos?' And there are just so many things to regret in life that if there's ever a day where I regret having a tattoo, I can certainly live with that."

Jolie's fascination with knives has become a staple of any profile of her; she has mentioned that it stems from an attraction to medieval history stemming from Renaissance fairs. She is also keenly interested in prisons and prison conditions, and makes no secret of her passion for eating red meat. Summing up herself to Udovitch in *Rolling Stone,* Jolie explained, "People do always think that because I have tattoos, I'm bad, or that there's something very dark about me, or that I think about death. And I'm probably the least morbid person. I've kind of discovered that if I think about death much more than some people have, it's because I love life more than those people." Elaborating to Essex in *Entertainment Weekly,* she stated, "I read things I've said and don't realize I'm being a 'bad' girl. I do like being sexual, I do collect knives, I do like tattoos. I like dark things. But there's a side of me that's soft. I love my family; I want to be a mother." She concluded, "Don't pin me down to one thing."

Sources

Periodicals

Arizona Republic, December 30, 1999, The Rep, p. 26.
Calgary Sun, April 18, 1999, p. 47.
Entertainment Weekly, November 5, 1999, p. 40.
Esquire, February 1998, p. 72.
Interview, June 1997, p. 76.
Los Angeles, November 1997, p. 46.
Newsweek, April 26, 1999, p. 69.
People, July 8, 1996, p. 89; May 11, 1998, p. 124.
Rolling Stone, August 19, 1999, p. 59.
Toronto Sun, April 11, 1999, p. S8.
TV Guide, January 31, 1998, p. 30.
USA Today, January 29, 1998, p. 3D.

Online

"Angelina Jolie," Internet Movie Database web site, http://us.imdb.com (January 5, 2000).

Daymond John

Entrepreneur

Born c. 1968 in Brooklyn, NY; son of Margot John (a flight attendant).

Addresses: *Office*—350 Fifth Ave., Ste. 6617, New York, NY 10118.

Career

Worked selling socks, running a delivery company, driving a gypsy cab, and waiting tables; began making hats and selling them, early 1990s; FUBU (For Us By Us) clothing company, founder and CEO, 1992—.

Sidelights

In 1992 Daymond John founded FUBU apparel the acronym stands for For Us, By Us and nurtured it throughout the decade to make it one of the hottest styles around in young, fashionable street wear, or urbanwear. Characterized by its bold designs and oversized style, urbanwear generally boasts the manufacturer's brand logo, and FUBU is one of the leaders in this genre, along with names like Karl Kani, Phat Farm, Mecca, Pelle Pelle, Enyce, and Ecko. The look has become highly prized not only by city dwellers, but also style–conscious suburbanites, and FUBU soon became the most mainstream hip–hop brand, selling alongside huge designers such as Tommy Hilfiger and Ralph Lauren. Though John started off as a humble hat peddler, his business soon ballooned to include shirts, jeans, bubble coats, aviator jackets, and shoes, in addition to a wide line of headgear. Much of his success is due to slick marketing. Once he persuaded rapper LL Cool J, a childhood friend from Queens, and other big–name starts to sport the gear, sales skyrocketed. Eventually, John's FUBU logo was seen on many top athletes as well, and his wares can be found in more than 500 retailers, from Macy's, Nordstrom, and all Federated and May department stores to Foot Locker and Footaction, and a host of outlets in Europe, Australia, and Japan.

John was born in Brooklyn, New York and raised in Hollis, Queens. He is the only child of Margot John, a flight attendant for American Airlines who also moonlighted to support the two of them. The philosophy in the John household was, as he noted in a *Sales & Marketing Management* article, "If you need, you earn." Early on, John showed a knack for business. In first grade, he sold pencils to other children, and later, he would salvage mirrors from the trash of a nearby factory and sell them. His first real sales job was selling socks at a booth in a local arena, and his first true foray into entrepreneurship was when he started up a delivery company after he graduated from high school. He also waited tables at a Red Lobster and drove a gypsy cab.

The impetus for John's foray into fashion came when he was searching for a "tie–top" hat. He thought that at $20, they were overpriced, and also poorly designed. "I said, 'For $20, I could make 20 of these a day,'" he related in a *People* article. He decided to make them himself, and asked his mother to teach him how to sew. He then began a grueling period where he would rise about 8 a.m. to buy fabric, make hats until 2 p.m., telephone stores or hit the streets with his wares until it was time to work the dinner shift at Red Lobster, then get home around midnight and continue sewing.

It was not long before John had turned a profit. He did what any good businessperson would do: He invested the money back into the operation, purchasing more fabric and expanding into other areas. And he got help from his mother, who refinanced her home for $100,000 and moved out so that John and his partners, Keith Perrin, Carl Brown, and J. Alexander Martin, could live there and transform it into a factory. The operation was officially underway in 1992, and they dubbed it FUBU—For Us, By Us. Originally the phrase indicated urban black empowerment, but as FUBU's appeal spread to a host of other demographics, including suburbanites of diverse backgrounds, the name has come to apply to the young generation it targets.

FUBU soon began making hip–hop–influenced T–shirts, sweatshirts, sweaters, and the ubiquitous baggy jeans, and also ventured into outerwear like hiking boots and coats in 1994, paring down the materials and slicing the prices so that they were affordable. John reasoned that much of the fashion out there "had a functionality that wasn't needed," as he explained to Robin Givhan in the *Washington Post*. You didn't need Gore–Tex for a ski jacket. You didn't need that on the street. People were paying $900 and we could do the same style for $300."

Though John's strategy sounded plausible, the styles were not exceptionally new the pieces were cut a bit roomier than usual, conforming to the current tastes, and much of the designs were borrowed from the athletic look, including hockey and baseball jerseys in fluorescent colors. The key to FUBU's success was when John convinced rap star LL Cool J, who grew up in his neighborhood, to wear the clothes in his music videos and in an advertisement in the *Source*, a popular hip–hop publication. Before long, John and his partners rang up $300,000 in sales at the MAGIC trade show in Las Vegas, even though they could not afford a booth the enterprising young men handed out fliers tempting patrons to visit their distant hotel, and it worked. Not long after that, Samsung America signed a distribution deal with FUBU. By the summer of 1997, Macy's had agreed to stock the apparel in its ten stores on the East Coast. "That was like cutting our own album and headlining above Michael Jackson at Wembley Stadium," John remarked in a *Time* article. FUBU also snagged an invaluable piece of publicity when LL Cool J showed up in a commercial for the Gap clothiers while wearing a FUBU cap.

Before long, FUBU spread to nearly all of the major department stores as well as mainstream retail outlets like Casual Male and Foot Locker. Some critics harped that prices were too steep, not only on FUBU's pieces but other black– and Latino–owned startup clothing companies as well. A FUBU sweatshirt, for example, runs about $80 and jeans around $75. However, the goods still cost less than Hilfiger or Nautica, and consumers seemed more willing to buy from someone who rose from their ranks. Indeed, sales jumped from $1 million in 1995 to $40 million in 1997 and $350 million in 1998, including $150 million from licensing deals.

By 1999, FUBU signed an unheard–of deal with the National Basketball Association to design trunks, jerseys, warm–up suits, and sweater vests for all 29 teams. With that deal estimated to boost revenues by perhaps $25 million, analysts suggested that FUBU's sales could hit a whopping $500 million by the end of 1999. FUBU has also branched into lines for women and children, and is marketing various accessories as well, including a backpack that has a compartment for a baseball cap. The firm has relocated its headquarters from John's mother's home in Queens—the first thing he did after finding success was pay off the mortgage—into a suite on the 66th floor of the Empire State building. With fans of the gear including celebrities like Mary J. Blige, the Fugees, Boyz II Men, Mariah Carey, and Sean "Puffy" Combs, not to mention a slew of professional athletes, the company's rise was inevitable.

Sources

Periodicals

Atlanta Journal and Constitution, August 9, 1998, p. M8.
Dallas Morning News, September 23, 1998, p. 1E.
Newsday, April 19, 1998, p. G1.
People, March 17, 1997, p. 62.
Sales & Marketing Management, October 1998, p. 128.
Star Tribune (Minneapolis, MN), July 4, 1999, p. 1D.
Time, January 19, 1998, p. 71.
Washington Post, August 19, 1999, p. c!.

Online

FUBU web site, http://www1.fubu.com (October 1, 1999).

Keyshawn Johnson

Football player

Born July 22, 1972; son of Vivien Jessie Johnson; married Shikiri Hightower, February 14, 1998; children: daughter, Maia; son, Keyshawn, Jr. *Education:* Attended West Los Angeles College, 1992–94; University of Southern California, history degree, 1996.

Addresses: *Office*—c/o Tampa Bay Buccaneers, One Buccaneer Pl., Tampa, FL 33607.

Career

First player selected in the NFL draft, 1996; New York Jets, wide receiver, 1996–2000; played in Pro Bowl, 1998; Tampa Bay Buccaneers, 2000—. Spokesperson for Adidas and Coca–Cola.

Awards: *The Sporting News,* first team All–American, and All–Pac 10 Conference first team selection, 1995; Pro Bowl most valuable player, 1999.

Sidelights

After a rough childhood on the streets of Los Angeles, Keyshawn Johnson overcame the odds to become the first draft pick of the 1996 National Football League season. He struggled through some setbacks, including spending two years at a junior college in his hometown instead of going straight to a top school, but he got back on track in time to land a scholarship to the University of Southern California (USC). A stellar career there led to the most lucrative contract ever, on average, for a rookie

football player. After helping bring the underdog team to the conference championships in 1999, the six–foot–three, 215–pound wide receiver wearing number 19 was traded to the Tampa Bay Buccaneers in 2000. Though he has been criticized for his head-strong nature, his charisma and enthusiasm has made him a popular player. And his drive has led him to accomplish more than many colleagues. As he told Darryl Howerton in *Sport,* "I've done lived the street life and now I'm living the professional life. I did every hustle there is to do. I went from ticket scalping, parking cars, selling drugs, to a college education, to a professional athlete, to a role model, to a real–estate developer and hopefully bigger things than that."

Johnson was born on July 22, 1972, and raised in the rough community of South Central Los Angeles, California, at a time when gang activity was ballooning. The youngest of six children, he never knew his father. His five siblings had a different father who left the family, and after that, his mother had Johnson by a different man. By age 12, Johnson's family was homeless and he was supporting the family by selling drugs and stolen property. As a teen, he twice spent time in juvenile detention centers, once for six months for scalping stolen football tickets and another time for violating probation.

However, Johnson also began to hang around the USC football practice field and eventually became a ball boy. He gradually became a fixture around the team, helping stuff envelopes in the office and carrying bags for the coaches. The USC campus became his second home.

At Dorsey High School in Los Angeles, Johnson began to play on the football team and became their star wide receiver. He also lettered in track. Even though his grades and SAT scores were poor, he was recruited by many of the top schools. As Johnson wrote in his autobiography, *Just Give Me the Damn Ball!: The Fast Times and Hard Knocks of an NFL Rookie*, "I thought I'd be able to talk my way into a four–year college . I thought if they wanted me badly enough, they'd get me into school. I tried every trick in the book to get into college without actually having to go through the system. It's how I had gotten by all my life."

Despite his promises that he would pull his grades up and pass the SATs on a subsequent try, Johnson did not deliver. As a result, he was forced to go to a junior college in 1992, and he settled on West Los Angeles College. He paid for tuition himself with money from his ticket scalping days. During his first year there, he got kicked off the team "for not having the 'proper attitude,'" as he admitted in his autobiography, and he decided to concentrate on amassing as many credits as possible so he could transfer to a four–year college the next fall and start playing.

Convinced he was going to be able to transfer after a year, Johnson began to scout universities However, NCAA rules required that he spend two years at the junior college, so he stayed another year at West L.A. and roomed with several other young men. Eventually, though, he moved in with a friend, Dave Darnell, and Darnell's mother in Inglewood in an area plagued by drugs and violence. There, in April of 1993, as Johnson emerged from a car after seeing a movie with friends, he was wounded in a drive–by shooting. The bullet pierced his leg but missed the bone. Thankfully, it did not do any lasting damage because Johnson was so muscular.

Of course, the incident nevertheless rattled Johnson, and it changed his attitude toward life. He ended up rooming with future Miami Dolphins player Sharmon Shah, who is now known by his Muslim name, Karim Abdul Jabbar. In the fall of 1993, Johnson played for the West L.A. College team and became a standout, catching 55 passes that year to become one of the top– ranked junior college play-

ers in the nation. "He came back strong, mature, focused, tremendous in a variety of ways," West L.A. coach Rob Hager remarked to Tim Layden in *Sports Illustrated*. The four–year schools came calling again.

In the fall of 1994, Johnson enrolled at USC, which gave him a scholarship. He played under coach John Robinson, who had been there when Johnson was just a ball boy. That year, he caught 66 passes for 1362 yards and scored nine touchdowns, including three in one game against Washington State. The Trojans' record that year was 8–3–1, and they made it to the Cotton Bowl. For the 1994–95 season, Johnson was a candidate for the Heisman Trophy.

In 1995, Johnson was featured on the cover of *Sports Illustrated* college football issue when the magazine picked USC to emerge as the number one team that season. He led them to a win at the Rose Bowl in January of 1996, catching 12 passes for 216 yards and a score.

Then, he graduated that May with a degree in history. He rounded out his career at USC breaking the school and Pac–10 records for receptions in a season (102 in 1995) and a school record for 100 yard games in a season—nine in 1994. In addition, Johnson ranked second on USC's career reception list with 176 and receiving yards list with 2,940. He also ranked fourth for career touchdown receptions with 19. In 1995, he was a unanimous All–America and All–Pac10 Conference First Team Selection.

Meanwhile, in the spring of 1996 the New York Jets snapped up Johnson as the first pick in the first round of the NFL draft. A dismal organization, they posted a 3–13 record in 1995. Thomas Hackett wrote in *New York*, "'Covering the Jets has been like covering a disease,' *New York Times* writer Gerald Eskenazi said to me. 'Maybe now they've discovered a cure.' Even the team's management admits it's been a pathetic run, not just in terms of losing games but also in terms of creating any kind of personality for the team."

Thus, as a fresh college graduate, Johnson entered multimillion dollar negotiations and began filming Adidas commercials. After bitter haggling, he landed a contract that paid $15 million over six years, the highest average salary ever for a rookie, with a $6.5 million signing bonus and a possible $2 million in incentives. "I was the No. 1 pick and I should be paid like the No. 1 pick," Johnson reasoned in his autobiography. "Not the sixth pick."

With his history and his salary, many had high expectations of Johnson in New York. Craig Ellenport wrote in *Sport*, "Keyshawn Johnson doesn't lack for confidence, and he carries that swagger both on and off the field, which is what makes him such a perfect fit for the Big Apple. He should have no trouble winning a starting job on an anemic Jets offense, and he should have an even easier time winning fans in the city that never sleeps."

In his rookie year, Johnson played in 14 games, starting in 12, and had eight touchdown receptions and 844 yards in receptions. These were not the sparkling numbers people had hoped for. He also dropped many easy passes, and the Jets won only one of 16 games that season. When the season wound down, Johnson published his autobiography, which focused on his relatively disappointing rookie season and criticized some of his teammates, especially fellow wideout Wayne Chrebet, whom he called a "team mascot." This led to a long–running feud with Chrebet as well as bristling relations among Johnson and other teammates.

Jeff Pearlman in *Sports Illustrated* called Johnson's autobiography "a bitter, self– aggrandizing book" and other critics were also unimpressed. The Jets and the NFL were reportedly not amused, either. The book's title reflected Johnson's opinion that his performance was underwhelming because he did not get a hold of the ball enough.

In 1997, Bill Parcells took over as coach from the unpopular Rich Kotite and the team spent the season rebuilding. Then, in the 1998–99 season Johnson's performance improved drastically, thanks to diligent work watching tapes and working extra hours to hone his catching technique. He finished sixth in the league in receptions, with 83, and tenth in receiving yards, with 1,131. The New York Jets that year made it to the conference championship game, though they lost to the Denver Broncos, 23–10. Also in 1999 Johnson played in the Pro Bowl and was named most valuable player.

In a stunning move, in April of 2000 the Jets traded Johnson to the Tampa Bay Buccaneers. He signed an eight–year, $56 million contract with the new team with a $13 million signing bonus, and the Jets in return got Tampa Bay's two top draft picks to give them an unprecedented four first–round selections. When the Jets refused to renegotiate Johnson's previous contract, which still had two seasons left on it, the new coach, Al Groh, compared Johnson's request for a salary increase to a child asking his father for more allowance. This did not set well with Johnson, who told Josh Elliot in *Sports Illustrated*, "I knew then that I couldn't play for the guy." He also remarked that he believed the team was planning to rebuild again and wanted him out all along.

Unlike many young athletes who squander their fortune, Johnson has a mind for business. He owns an elegant Southern–cuisine restaurant in Beverly Hills called Reign where he meets and greets notables such as director Forest Whitaker and U.S. Labor Secretary Alexis Herman. In addition, he runs a commercial real–estate firm that invests heavily in South Central Los Angeles, such as a 26–acre shopping center with big–name retailers like Home Depot so that residents do not have to drive miles for basic necessities. Though Johnson clearly considers the project a business, he is proud of the community involvement: "It's a good investment," he told Jeff MacGregor in *Sports Illustrated*. "And why wouldn't I want to do something like this in the place where I was born and raised?"

Johnson met his wife, the former Shikiri Hightower, at a party at USC and they married on Valentine's Day, 1998. They have a daughter, Maia, and son, Keyshawn, Jr. ("Kiki"). Shikiri Johnson, who has a degree in journalism, runs her husband's educational foundation, which gives out 20 scholarships each year. Johnson has other charities as well under the umbrella of Keyshawn Inc., including Key's Kids, a community outreach program for underprivileged children. He has also met several times with President Bill Clinton on national panels talking about the role of race in athletics.

Though he gives generously to his former neighborhood, as of late 1999 Johnson was custom building a mansion in Calabasas in the San Fernando Valley. As he noted to Darryl Howerton in *Sport*, "This is my first house. You know how most athletes go out and buy themselves a house as soon as they get some money? Well, I bought my mom her house, but I waited four years to build my own. It's a matter of economics. You want to set your foundation and make sure you set yourself up right."

Sources

Books

Johnson, Keyshawn, and Shelley Smith, *Just Give Me the Damn Ball!: The Fast Times and Hard Knocks of an NFL Rookie*, Warner Books, 1997.

Periodicals

Black Enterprise, November 1999, p. 32.
Newsweek, September 13, 1999, p. 60.
New York, May 13, 1996, p. 40.
New York Times, April 13, 2000, p. D1.
St. Louis Post–Dispatch, January 14, 1999, p. D3.
Sport, October 1996, p. 49; September 1999, p. 38.

Sporting News, July 12, 1999, p. 54.

Sports Illustrated, August 28, 1995, pp. 40, 140; April 21, 1997, p. 22; November 8, 1999, p. 48; April 24, 2000, p. 48.

Online

"Keyshawn Johnson," National Football League (NFL) web site, http://www.nfl.com (July 21, 2000).

Michael Johnson

Reuters/Archive Photos

Track and field athlete

Born Michael Duane Johnson, September 13, 1967, in Dallas, TX; son of Paul (a truck driver) and Ruby (an elementary school teacher) Johnson; married; wife's name, Kerry. *Education:* Baylor University, B.A. in accounting and marketing, 1990.

Addresses: *Home*—Dallas, TX, and Waco, TX. *Office*—MDJ Holdings, Ltd., 17130 Dallas Parkway, Dallas, TX 75248. Career

Track and field athlete. Turned professional in 1990; member of 1992 and 1996 U.S. Olympic teams.

Awards: Won 1989 National Collegiate Athletic Association (NCAA) 200–meter indoor championship; gold medal at world championships in 200–meter sprint, 1991, 1995; gold medal at world championships in 400–meter sprint, 1993, 1995, 1997, 1999; gold medal at world championships in 4X400–meter relay, 1997, 1998, 1999; *Track & Field News* male athlete of the year, 1990; won gold medal as part of 1992 American Olympic 4x400 relay team; U.S. national champion, 1992; named U.S. track athlete of the year, 1993, 1994; named U.S. Olympic Committee's Sportsman of the Year, 1993, 1995, 1996; won gold medals in 200–meter and 400–meter sprints, 1996 Olympics; Amateur Athletic Union's James E. Sullivan Memorial Award, 1996; *Sport* magazine Get Smart Player of the Year, 1996; International Amateur Athletics Federation (IAAF) Legend Athlete of the Year, 1996; holds world record in 200–meter and 400–meter sprint and record for most gold medals at world championships (nine).

Sidelights

Track star Michael Johnson, who has been nicknamed "Superman" for his startling speed, became an American hero at the 1996 Summer Olympics when he won gold medals for the 200– meter and 400–meter sprint, making him the first male athlete to win both of those events in the same year. In addition, his 19.32 time in the 200 set a world record. Then, in the summer of 1999, Johnson became a double world–record holder when he dashed past the previous record of 43.29 in the 400 to set a new time of 43.18. Shortly thereafter, Johnson also won a gold at the world championships in the 4X400 relay, bringing his total to nine and thus passing Carl Lewis's previous record of eight world championship gold medals. He accomplished this in the wake of several injuries, which gave him even more ambition to defend his Olympic titles at the games in 2000.

Michael Duane Johnson was born on September 13, 1967, in Dallas, Texas. His father, Paul, a truck driver, and his mother, Ruby, a former elementary school teacher, raised him and his four older siblings (brother Paul Jr., and sisters Deidre, Regina, and Cheryl) in the middle–class neighborhood of

Oak Cliffs in southwest Dallas. He enjoyed a rather typical childhood, but his parents placed a particular emphasis on education—even in the summers, his mother would tutor her children each morning. As a result, Johnson attended classes for the gifted throughout elementary and junior high school, and after that, he applied and was accepted to Skyline High School in east Dallas, widely regarded as the finest school in the city. His brother and three sisters did well academically as well; all of them graduated from the University of North Texas (formerly North Texas State University).

When Johnson was 11, he began to pursue running in earnest, and his parents tolerated his hobby as long as his studies did not suffer. In fact, Johnson, who ran in black horn–rimmed glasses, told Merrell Noden in *Sports Illustrated*, "I loved track, but at the time, it was a way to get to a better college. I wasn't as concerned with track as with education." His coach, Joel Ezar, also remarked to Noden, "He didn't look like an athlete he looked like a Rhodes scholar. In one race, he caught a crosswind and his glasses blew off. It looked like he might stop to pick them up." Ezar also described Johnson as a "nerdy kid" to Steve Wulf in *Time*. Johnson begged to differ, telling Wulf, "Coach Ezar always makes too much of that nerd stuff. The truth is that looking nice was the style then. I like my clothes, always have."

Planning to become an architect, Johnson did not run during his first two years of high school so that he could concentrate on classes. He joined the track team as a junior and finished third in the 200–meter for his school district, the year in which Roy Martin set the high school record of 20.13 seconds in that event. As a senior, Johnson won the district title, but was beaten at the state championship by Derrick Florence, who went on to capture the world junior title for the 100–meter.

After high school, where Johnson's best time in the 200–meter was 21.30, Baylor University coach Clyde Hart recruited him, but did not expect great performances. Instead, Hart felt the athlete's well–rounded nature, with his solid background, good grades, and mature outlook, would make him a good role model on the relay teams. "I didn't see him as a Southwest Conference champion, much less a national champion," Hart remarked to Wulf. As a college freshman, however, Johnson turned heads when he clocked 20.49 in his second race and came in a respectable second place, barely losing to Floyd Heard, the world's best in the 200–meter the previous year. In addition, Johnson ran the 400–meter for the first time in college, posting a time of 46.29 seconds.

In spring of 1988, Johnson ran the 200 in 20.09 and beat world champion Calvin Smith at the Drake Relays. He was also preparing for that year's Summer Olympics when he was plagued by a bad injury: a stress fracture in his left shin. This caused him to come in last in the 400–meter at the Olympic trials, so he bowed out of the 200. The next year, Johnson bruised his right quadriceps, which prevented him from competing at the NCAA championships. After that, he began to concentrate more on the 400–meter event, an unusual decision in the world of track. Most runners either focus solely on the 400, or they combine the 100 and 200, because the differing length of the events require a separate set of skills. Sheer speed is necessary in the 100 and 200, where more strength and strategy is required for the 400.

Graduating from Baylor with a bachelor's degree in accounting and marketing in 1990, Johnson turned professional and began to compete in Europe and Asia, where track and field is much more popular than in the United States. He won 47 straight races, 31 in the 200 and 16 in the 400 in 1990, and became the first man to achieve the top ranking in the world for both the 200 and 400 in a career, much less in the same year. In 1990, he was named male athlete of the year by *Track & Field News*. In 1991, Johnson was again the world champion in the 200 with a time of 20.01, and some commented that he may have been able to break Pietro Mennea's world record of 19.72 if it had not been for a strong head wind. Later that year at the International Amateur Athletics Federation (IAAF) Finals in Barcelona, Spain, he came even closer with a time of 19.88, the fastest of the year.

Coming off such victories, Johnson held high hopes for both the 200 and 400 in the 1992 Summer Olympics in Barcelona, Spain, but again ran into some bad luck, as he fell ill with food poisoning two weeks before the games and failed to qualify. However, he managed to help lead the 4X400–meter relay team to a gold medal, and also that year, he was the United States national champion. The next year, 1993, he once again took the world championship in the 400, and was named the U.S. track athlete of the year in 1993 and 1994.

As of 1995, Johnson was earning about $1 million annually for appearances and endorsements, in spite of his obscurity in his home country. That year, he began attracting more attention in the press as he broke the world indoor record for the 400 with a time of 44.97 in February, then a month later broke it again with a time of 44.63. He also won titles in both the 200 and 400 at the U.S. national championships, and at this point, had not lost a 400–meter race in six years. Soon afterward, he chalked up his first double world championship in the 200 and 400 in Goteborg, Sweden, the first man in 100 years to win both events, with times of 19.79 and 43.39. This feat made Johnson yearn for another try at the pair of events in the 1996 Olympics, and he even persuaded the Olympic Committee to reschedule the 200 and 400 on different days in order to allow him to compete in both. Some criticized his lofty ambitions. In a Newsweek interview with Mark Starr, Olympic runner Tommie Smith, who won a gold medal at the 1968 games, noted, "I'd sure rather win one gold than two bronze." In addition, fellow athlete Carl Lewis accused Johnson of lacking charisma and thus not generating any excitement about the U.S. track team, but he did not seem fazed by the remarks.

In fact, as Johnson headed into the 1996 Summer Olympics, his profile was on the rise. He began appearing in commercials for Nike, Coca-Cola, and Bausch & Lomb, and hosted a weekly radio show in Dallas. Interviews proliferated, as he became one of the focal points of the upcoming games. Johnson did not disappoint the American fans. First, he broke Mennea's world record for the 200 in the semifinals of the Olympic trials with a time of 19.66. Then, wearing gold-colored shoes, he won the gold medal in the 400 on July 29, 1996, setting an Olympic record of 43.49 seconds, followed three days later by a gold in the 200 at 19.32 seconds, breaking his own earlier world record. "I thought I could do it in 19.5," Johnson commented to Kenny Moore in *Sports Illustrated.* "But not this, not 19.3. I'd have lost a lot of money betting that I wouldn't get to 19.3." Only one other person, a woman, Valerie Brisco-Hooks, had won the gold in the 200 and 400, at the 1984 Olympics, but Johnson became the first man to do so.

The race was especially remarkable considering that throughout his career, Johnson had shattered all preconceptions about how to sprint. It was long believed that a leaning posture, long strides, and high knee lifts were best for speed, but Johnson broke the mold by running in an erect position and taking shorter, more rapid strides, while not lifting off the ground very far. Many noticed that this style was similar to that of Jesse Owens, a black Olympic hero at the 1936 games in Berlin who stole the gold in the 100, 200, and 400-meter relay as well as the long jump in front of Adolf Hitler, the German leader who believed in "Aryan supremacy." In addition, Johnson's win, not to mention his time, in the 200 were even more startling because he actually stumbled at one point early in the race, but managed to regain his composure in order to beat Namibia's Frankie Fredericks by four meters, the largest margin in an Olympic 200-meter sprint since Owens had defeated Mack Robinson 20.7 to 21.1.

After his big victories, Johnson wrote a motivational book, *Slaying the Dragon,* and toured to promote it late in 1996. Also, the U.S. Olympic Committee named him Sportsman of the Year for 1996, an honor he also won in 1993 and 1995. Additionally, in 1996 the IAAF named him Legend Athlete of the Year, *Sport* magazine named him their Get Smart Player of the Year, the Amateur Athletic Union gave him their 67th Annual James E. Sullivan Memorial Award, and the Associated Press voted his Olympic performance the top story of the year. Johnson also snagged a new contract with Nike worth an estimated $12 million over six years, about $1 million more than Nike contributes to the entire USA Track & Field federation.

In 1997, a cloud was cast over Johnson regarding a privately organized 150-meter race at the SkyDome in Toronto against Canada's Donovan Bailey, the 100-meter world record holder and Olympic gold medalist, ostensibly to determine who was the "world's fastest man." In a shock to many, especially bettors who favored Johnson three to one, the 200-meter record holder did not even finish the race. After Bailey blew past him just ten strides into the race, Johnson grabbed his left thigh halfway through the run and walked to the finish line. Bailey posted a time of 14.99 and called his opponent a "coward," a *Jet* article reported, and journalists nagged him to see if he had purposely thrown the race. Johnson explained that he had suffered an intense cramp, and later it was revealed that he tore his quadriceps muscle.

After recuperating from the muscle tear, Johnson suffered problems with his right hamstring and other troubles associated with a skeletal imbalance that caused his spine to misalign. Despite continuing leg injuries, he stayed in training. At the world championships in August of 1999, Johnson made headlines again when he broke the world's record for the 400-meter sprint. At the Estadio Olimpico in Seville, Spain, coach Clyde Hart clocked Johnson at 43.18, beating Butch Reynolds's time of 43.29 set 11 years prior, the longest-standing track record at that time. Three weeks before turning 32, Johnson was a double world record holder. As he explained to Christopher Clarey in the *New York Times,* "Since 1996, I've always felt I'm lucky and fortunate and never would complain, but I've always wanted this world record, and now everything is totally complete. But I'm still feeling motivated to go to Sydney next year and defend both Olympic titles." Also in 1999 Johnson anchored the 4X400 relay team, leading them to their third consecutive title. They broke the world record for that event three times with Johnson on the team; it stands at 2:54:20 minutes, set at the 1998 Goodwill Games. The relay victory was his ninth world championship gold medal, thus surpassing Carl Lewis's record by one.

The six–foot, one–inch tall, 175–pound Johnson is married; his wife's name is Kerry. He keeps homes in Dallas and Waco, Texas, and enjoys music and horseback riding. Though some reports paint him as a bit cocky, many others marvel at his modesty. By all accounts, however, he is well–organized and practical. As Gary Smith wrote in *Sports Illustrated,* "Everyone, to be honest, could use a friend like him. When Michael's friends have major decisions to make on the purchase of a house, the starting of a business, the choice of a spouse they call him. He alerts them to every conceivable pitfall, unadorns them of every emotional bias, slices through every pie in the sky as if it's lemon meringue. 'I'm the ultimate realist,' he says."

Sources

Books

Contemporary Black Biography, volume 13, Gale Research, 1996.

Periodicals

Christian Science Monitor, September 3, 1999, p. 12.
GQ, June 1996, p. 168.
Jet, March 27, 1995, p. 46; January 29, 1996, p. 50; August 26, 1996, p. 52; January 13, 1997, p. 48; January 20, 1997, p. 57; June 16, 1997, p. 51; April 7, 1997, p. 48.
Newsweek, August 31, 1995, p. 58; August 12, 1996, p. 18; September 6, 1999, p. 74.
New York Times, March 5, 1995, sec. 8, p. 1; August 27, 1999, p. C17; August 30, 1999, p. D2.
People, December 16, 1996, p. 37.
Runner's World, July 1995, p. 38; August 1997, p. 58.
Sport, May 1997, p. 40.
Sports Illustrated, May 20, 1991, p. 46; July 22, 1996, p. 72; August 12, 1996, p. 26; June 9, 1997, pp. 20, 48.
Sports Illustrated for Kids, August 1, 1999, p. 38.
Texas Monthly, September 1996, p. 124.
Time, Summer 1996 (special issue), p. 54; February 17, 1997, p. 93.

Robert L. Johnson

Photo courtesy Black Entertainment Television (BET)

Business executive

Born Robert Louis Johnson, April 6, 1946, in Hickory, MS; son of Edna Johnson (a factory worker); married Sheila Crump, January 19, 1969; children: daughter, Paige; son, Brett. *Education:* University of Illinois, B.A. in history, 1968; Princeton University, M.A. in public affairs, 1972.

Addresses: *Home*—Washington, DC. *Office*—One BET Plaza, 1900 W Place NE, Washington, DC 20018–1211.

Career

Corporation for Public Broadcasting, public affairs officer, early 1970s; Urban League, Washington, DC, director of communications, early 1970s; press aide to Washington, DC, city council member Sterling Tucker, early 1970s; press secretary for Walter E. Fauntroy, Congressional delegate from Washington, 1973–76; National Cable Television Association, vice president of governmental relations, 1976–79; Black Entertainment Television (BET), founder, president, chief executive officer, and principal shareholder, 1979—, changed company name to BET Holdings, Inc., 1993. Board of directors, US Airways, Hilton Hotels, General Mills, Gerald Stevens, United Negro College Fund, National Cable Television Association (NCTA)'s Academy of Cable Programming, and American Film Institute; board of governors, Rock and Roll Hall of Fame.

Awards: National Cable Television Association (NCTA) Presidential Award, 1982; National Association for the Advancement of Colored People (NAACP) Image Award, 1982; Capitol Press Club Pioneer Award, 1984; Washington, DC, Chamber of Commerce Business of the Year Award, 1985; Turner Broadcasting Executive Leadership Council Award, 1993; *Cablevision Magazine,* 20/20 Vision Award, 1995; *Broadcasting and Cable Magazine,* Hall of Fame Award, 1997; National Women's Political Caucus, Good Guys Award, 1998; Princeton University, Distinguished Alumni Award, 1998.

Sidelights

Robert L. Johnson is the founder of BET Holdings, Inc., formerly called Black Entertainment Television. As the originator of a cable network geared specifically toward African Americans, he is a pioneer in the black community and in telecommunications. These are merely pleasant byproducts of a solid business plan, however. "The idea for BET was not conceived out of idealism," Johnson explained to Caroline Waxler in *Forbes,* "but as a business opportunity that had been ignored." From meager beginnings using just $15,000 of his own money, Johnson's venture has mushroomed into a media conglomerate featuring several cable channels, a film production company, a publishing firm, and stakes in assorted black magazines. Its flagship channel, BET, reaches 56.7 million subscribers. BET

Holdings also has interests in other businesses ranging from merchandising to restaurants to financial services. As of 2000, Johnson was reaching for the sky again—literally this time—with a plan to open up his own airline.

Johnson was born on April 8, 1946, in the rural town of Hickory, Mississippi, the ninth child of ten children. His family moved to the industrial farming town of Freeport, Illinois, where his parents both worked at factories. "With 10 children it was kind of rough," his mother, Edna, told Marcia Slacum Greene in the *Washington Post*, "but we always had food to eat and clothes to go around." Still, Johnson contributed as well, working odd jobs such as delivering newspapers, mowing lawns, and cleaning up at the fair. He also worked briefly at a battery factory.

Growing up in Freeport, which was only ten percent black, Johnson had few role models besides his teachers and ministers, but he always aspired to something greater. "Bob didn't want to do common labor. He wanted to be his own boss," his mother told Greene. In high school, Johnson played sports. Although he was not a star, he developed a craving for competition that would come through later in his business career.

When he was young, Johnson aspired to be a fighter pilot—an idea he gleaned from reading comic books and from seeing his brother join the U.S. Air Force. However, he was not accepted because his vision was not twenty–twenty, so he concentrated on becoming an ambassador. Johnson graduated from high school with honors in history and was granted an academic scholarship to the University of Illinois. He received his bachelor of arts in history in 1968. Although he did not have the usual set of qualifications for acceptance to Princeton University, he was admitted to their Woodrow Wilson School of Public and International Affairs through a program designed to attract minorities to careers in international relations. He obtained a master of arts in 1972, graduating sixth in his class.

After college, Johnson decided against a career overseas, partly because he did not agree with the United States' involvement in Vietnam. Instead, through a Princeton contact who connected him with other influential people, he landed a job as a public affairs officer at the Corporation for Public Broadcasting. Johnson then moved to the Washington, DC, office of the Urban League as director of communications, then worked as a press aide to Sterling Tucker, a Washington, DC, city council member, from 1973 to 1976. He also campaigned for Marion Barry in his first bid for mayor of Washington, DC.

Throughout this time, Johnson developed important business and political connections. As he related to Greene, "The one thing I learned quickly in this town was that there are two types of power: actual power and derivative power. As Walter's press aide, I would get my calls returned not because I was Bob Johnson but because I worked for Walter. People thought it was good to get to know me, and I knew when I could trade my access to Walter for other things."

In 1976 Johnson was hired as vice president of governmental relations for the National Cable Television Association (NCTA), a trade organization representing 1,500 cable television companies. In that capacity, he came across a businessman who wanted to propose a cable television channel targeted toward elderly Americans. Johnson borrowed the plan and replaced the word "elderly" with "black" in order to develop his idea of a channel geared toward black viewers, complete with shows featuring black characters, thought, and philosophy.

Subsequently, Johnson convinced his boss at NCTA, Tom Wheeler, to give him a consulting contract worth $15,000 so that he could quit his job and start up his business. Using that money as collateral, he was able to borrow $15,000 for start–up costs. Then, Johnson got a loan for $230,000 from John C. Malone, head of Tele–Communications Inc. (TCI), one of the nation's largest builders and operators of cable systems. In addition, Malone and TCI paid Johnson $180,000 for a 20 percent share in the network.

On January 25, 1980, Johnson began broadcasting Black Entertainment Television from the basement of his home from 11 p.m. to 2 a.m. each Friday night. The first program aired was *A Visit to the Chief's Son*, a feature film set in Kenya with a an all–black cast. Once the financing was in place and the network was on the air, Johnson went to Hollywood to look for programming to fill his network. However, even though blacks watched more television than whites on average 70 hours per week as compared to 48 there were few shows featuring black characters in main roles and virtually none aimed directly at blacks.

To keep a lid on costs while attracting an audience, Johnson stuck to mainly showing low– budget films from the 1940s and 1950s as well as blaxploitation films from the 1970s. Sometimes he would also broadcast major films such as 1972's *Lady Sings the Blues,* in which Diana Ross depicted jazz legend Billie Holiday. In 1982, BET started showing music videos, which record companies provided for free. As of the mid–1990s, music videos would continue to make up about 60 percent of the programming. Eventually the channel began to air black–oriented talk shows, college sports featuring black players, and reruns of black sitcoms like *Benson*, which the network purchased for some tens of thousands of dollars an episode—a fraction of the $1 million or more networks pay for original shows.

In 1982 Johnson brought Taft Broadcasting Company on board as investor, which contributed $1 million in exchange for a 20 percent stake in BET. Two years later, the cable company Home Box Office (HBO) put up $600,000, and a week later, BET began using HBO's satellite to stay on the air 24 hours a day. By this point, Johnson still held a 62 percent share in the firm.

Like most companies in the business, BET lost money for several years. Realizing this, Johnson expected to see red, and when he brought in revenues he reinvested in the venture. In its seventh year, BET began to turn a profit, making $500,000 on revenues of $11 million. Despite its success, however, by 1989 it was still the smallest and least carried of all the cable networks, reaching 23 million homes in 1300 markets. In addition, its per subscriber fees of 2.5 cents, set by the NCTA, were much lower than the industry standard.

Meanwhile, with an investment of $100,000 from his own pocket, Johnson had started up a local cable service, District Cablevision Incorporated, in 1984. Observers claimed that he most likely won the bid to provide service for the Washington, D.C. area thanks to his connections to the mayor's office. However, the cable service was owned 75 percent by TCI, and thus faced legal challenges from competitors who filed suit to prevent a monopoly. This brought on subsequent legal woes, but DCI was able to start wiring homes in the area in 1988.

The next year, BET continued to grow, opening a $10 million production facility in Washington, D.C. for creating original programming. Nine new shows aired in 1989, and five more followed the next season. More money was coming in for such projects thanks to a successful lobbying effort that saw the NCTA raise BET's subscriber fees to five cents per subscriber, with an annual increase of a penny each year until 1994.

As of 1990, Johnson was starting to envision the future for BET. He told Benilde Little in *Essence*, "When I see BET, I don't see a cable network. I see

a Black media conglomerate. I want to be a communications giant." On October 30, 1991, Johnson made an initial public offering (IPO) of stock for BET Holdings, Inc., which he established as BET's parent company. This made BET the first black–controlled firm to be listed on the New York Stock Exchange (NYSE). Trading opened at $17 a share and closed that day at $23.50 a share, making BET worth $475 million. Johnson made $6.4 million in that one day.

However, in early 1992 cable systems operators realized that BET had far fewer subscribers than it had claimed during the IPO, and the stock plunged. Though Johnson cleared up the discrepancy, investors remained wary for some time. Still, he managed to fund new business growth thanks to continued earnings from the cable network.

Over the years, BET expanded its lineup to include several cable channels, including BET Gospel, BET on Jazz, BET Action Pay–Per–View, and the joint venture BET Movies/Starz!3. The latter was the first black–controlled movie premium channel. BET also branched into publishing with stakes in *Emerge, Heart & Soul,* and *BET Weekend,* which is the country's third–largest black publication with 1.3 million readers. (Another magazine, *Young Sisters and Brothers,* was shut down in 1996.)

In addition, the company started up Arabesque Books, the only line of romance novels written by and for African Americans. On top of this, BET acquired an interest in restaurants around Washington, D.C. and a nightclub at Disney World, and in the late 1990s Johnson laid plans to build the BET SoundStage Casino in Las Vegas. By obtaining a gaming license, in 1997 he became the first black to win approval by the state of Nevada as a director of a major public corporation. By the next year, he was entering talks with the Ghanian minister of commerce to try to license the BET cable channel in West Africa.

Also in 1998, Johnson introduced the production companies BET Pictures II for feature films and Arabesque Films for made–for–television movies. Again, he saw an opportunity: while blacks make up 12 percent of the population of the United States, they account for 25 percent of moviegoers. This is probably why films featuring black casts generally make a profit, while the average Hollywood film loses money.

Despite the apparent success of BET Holdings, Johnson realized its stock price was not doing well. In fact, none of BET's holdings outside of its core business had turned a profit by 1998, leaving investors and analysts with the opinion that he had overly diversified. Johnson thus took the company private again that year, buying back all the stock at $63 a share. Later, however, Liberty Media would buy 35 percent of the firm, leaving Johnson with a 65 percent stake.

In 2000 Johnson handed over day–to–day control of BET to Debra Lee, BET's president and chief operating officer, so he could concentrate on yet another business: an airline. When United Airlines proposed an acquisition of US Airways, part of the $11.6 billion deal would mean that United would have to sell the bulk of its operations in Washington, D.C. Johnson, meanwhile, had served on the board of US Airways for a couple of years, and that, along with his many other connections, put him in prime position to land the business, which he planned to call DC Air.

If the deal were approved by the U.S. Justice Department, it would make Johnson the only African American currently—and one of a very few ever—to own a commercial airline. Congress began hearings on the proposed merger in June of 2000. Even though Johnson had no experience in the airline industry, he remarked in *Jet*, "I know how to create value. I have no doubt in my mind that I can find the talent to run a very successful airline like I found the talent to run a successful cable programming business."

Johnson and his wife, Sheila, have a daughter, Paige, and a son, Brett. They live in an upscale neighborhood in Washington, D.C., and also have an expansive estate in Middleburg, Virginia. If Johnson were to write his epitaph, reported Brian Sharp of the *Gannett News Service*, it would read: "This guy made his mark and, in so doing, he created a lot of opportunity for black people that they would not have had otherwise."

Sources

Books

Contemporary Black Biography, Gale Research, 1992.
Notable Black American Men, Gale Research, 1988.

Periodicals

Essence, November 1990, p. 48.
Forbes, April 22, 1996, p. 98.
Fortune, November 9, 1998, p. 167.
Gannett News Service, June 16, 2000.
Jet, May 19, 1997, p. 36; June 12, 2000, p. 36.
Newsweek, April 1, 1996, p. 71; April 13, 1998, p. 44.
New York Times, May 29, 2000, p. A9.
Variety, August 3, 1998, p. 26.
Washington Post, August 5, 1985, p. C1.

Online

BET web site, http://www.betnetworks.com (August 2, 2000).
"BET Holdings II, Inc.," Hoover's Online, http://www.hoovers.com (August 2, 2000).

Spike Jonze

Universal (Courtesy Kobal)

Director, actor, and writer

Born Adam Spiegel, c. 1969, in St. Louis, MO (one source says Rockville, MD); married Sofia Coppola, June 26, 1999.

Addresses: *Office*—c/o Satellite Films, 941 N. Mansfield Ave., Los Angeles, CA 90038.

Career

Director, actor, and writer. Worked at a dirt–bike store in Rockville, MD, in junior high and high school; *Freestylin'* magazine, Torrance, CA, staff writer, late 1980s; photographer for *Freestylin'*, *Trans World Skateboarding*, *BMX Action*, and *Homeboy* magazines, c. late 1980s–early 1990s; began directing videos, c. early 1990s; directed first professional video, "100%," for Sonic Youth, 1992; has also directed videos for the Beastie Boys, Bjork, the Breeders, Fatboy Slim, Ween, and Weezer; director of commercials for Lee Jeans, Levi's, Wrangler, among others. Editor of *Dirt* magazine, 1991.

Film appearances include *Mi Vida Loca*, 1993; *The Game*, 1997; *Three Kings*, 1999; and *Being John Malkovich*, 1999. Director of *Being John Malkovich*, 1999. Cinematographer, *Free Tibet*, 1998.

Awards: Broadcast Film Critics Association Award for breakthrough artist, 2000, for directing *Being John Malkovich* and role in *Three Kings*; New York Film Critics Circle Award for best first film, Venice Film Festival FIPRESCI Award, and Online Film Critics Society Award for best debut, all 1999, for *Being John Malkovich*; Deauville Film Festival critics award and grand special prize, Florida Film Critics Circle Award, 2000, for *Being John Malkovich*.

Sidelights

Known for his offbeat music and commercial videos, director Spike Jonze plunged into the mainstream sort of in 1999 with his first feature film, *Being John Malkovich*. Though the sleeper hit nabbed the director an Oscar nomination, it was not typical Hollywood fare. It stars John Cusack as a puppeteer, Craig Schwartz, who discovers a portal into the mind of actor John Malkovich, who good–naturedly spoofs himself in the eccentric picture. Craig stumbles across a portal behind a filing cabinet in the office building where he works on the 7 1/2th floor. It is appropriately only half as tall as other floors, causing workers to walk in a perennially stooped position. Craig and a coworker, played by Catherine Keener, end up selling "rides" into John Malkovich's brain, which last 15 minutes, until the thrill–seeker is unceremoniously dumped from the sky into a ditch next to the New Jersey Turnpike. A purposely de–glamorized Cameron Diaz plays Craig's wife, who gets involved in a strange love triangle with Keener's character and Malkovich. All this adds up to the perfect project for Jonze, whose oddball wit and unconventional way of looking at the world helped make the project a success.

Born around 1969, Jonze's real name is Adam Spiegel. Beyond that, much of Jonze's life is a mystery, being that he provides differing accounts of his past and is known to assume various alter egos. As Ethan Smith noted in *New York*, "He avoids interviews, cancels press conferences, and routinely fabricates information about his past. In a recent British television profile, he presented himself as a Corvette–driving loudmouth dressed in a tank top and a do–rag."

Various sources, though, claim that Jonze and his older sister grew up in Bethesda, Maryland. Smith reported that Jonze's parents divorced when he was young, and his mother, Sandy Granzow, works in communications for the World Bank. His father, Arthur Spiegel III, runs an international health–care consulting firm. Though Jonze denies it, several sources say that he is an heir to the $3 billion–a–year Spiegel mail order catalog fortune. Karen Schoemer in *Newsweek*, however, noted that "he's only distantly related."

Ever since he was young, Jonze was an avid skateboarder and loved freestyle bike riding. In junior high and high school, he worked at a dirt–bike shop. The owner there, Jay Metzler, told Smith in *New York*, "For all intents and purposes, the kid kind of raised himself. He was basically a ward of the Rockville BMX store." It was there he earned the nickname Spike, because he would often arrive at work unshowered with his hair sticking up. The shop was legendary among bike enthusiasts and often received visits from out–of–town professional cyclists. Jonze enjoyed picking them up at the airport in a chauffeur uniform as a joke.

In high school, Jonze took up photography and started submitting work and writing letters to the Torrance, California–based *Freestylin'* magazine, a periodical devoted to the BMX culture. They offered him a job as a staff writer, so the day after his high school finals, he left for the West Coast. For two years, he and friend Mark Lewman lived in a townhouse on the same block as the magazine's offices and rode their skateboards to work each day. Eventually, Jonze began taking photographs for *Trans World Skateboarding*, *BMX Action*, and *Homeboy*, as well as for *Freestylin'*.

After the BMX craze died down and *Freestylin'* closed up shop, Jonze and Lewman were hired in 1991 to run *Dirt*, a magazine for teenage boys that

was the counterpart to *Sassy*. It only survived a few issues, but in the meantime, Jonze's reputation for photography and videos was growing. His first video project, *Video Days*, was a 20–minute hand-held tape of a skateboarding team performing tricks. But he differentiated his work with a couple of aspects: First, he skated alongside the team for some of the shots, providing some unique angles. Also, he introduced a wacky sense of humor, mainly by setting the visuals to the Jackson Five song "I Want You Back" instead of using the typical thrash–punk or speed–metal soundtrack.

Before long, *Video Days* was legendary around the Southern California music and skate scene. After the band Sonic Youth caught sight of it, they hired him to codirect their "100%" video, along with Tamra Davis, wife of Mike D of the Beastie Boys. Subsequently, director Peter Care hired Jonze as a cameraman, and helped him land a job directing for Satellite Films, owned by Polygram. Soon, he was shooting videos for cutting–edge groups like Weezer, Ween, and the Breeders. In the 1994 Weezer video "Buddy Holly," he used computer imaging to place the band into an episode of the television sitcom *Happy Days*.

Also in 1994, Jonze created the noteworthy "Sabotage" video for the Beastie Boys. It was shot as a hilarious takeoff on corny 1970s cop shows and featured the rap trio in fake mustaches, Afro wigs, aviator sunglasses, and sleazy polyester outfits. In 1995, his video for Bjork's "It's Oh So Quiet" recalled Busby Berkley's over–the–top choreography. Subsequently, Jonze began to branch out into commercials, heading up the somewhat surreal Lee Jeans spots featuring the doll Buddy Lee. He also directed a Levi's ad inspired by emergency–room drama shows; it includes a team of doctors singing Soft Cell's "Tainted Love" as an EKG monitor keeps time.

Jonze really began to make his name, though, with the video "Praise You" for British deejay Fatboy Slim. Codirected with Roman Coppola, now his brother–in–law, the video won an MTV Video Award for best direction and breakthrough video. However, when Jonze took the stage to accept the award, he arrived in character as Richard Koufey, the head of the fictional Torrance Community Dance Group. (Koufey is the bearded, rhythmless character Jonze played in the video.) He proceeded to perform with his "community dancers" on the show, even amusing the audience with a dance solo and a cartwheel.

Meanwhile, Jonze was yearning to break into feature films, but his first hoped–for project, an adaptation of the children's book *Harold and the Purple*

Crayon, ran into several behind–the–scenes road-blocks. He ended up in front of the camera in 1999 as he snagged a role in *Three Kings,* costarring George Clooney, Mark Wahlberg, and Ice Cube. In it, he plays Conrad Big, a racist Gulf War soldier who is plotting with his fellow soldiers to steal millions from Iraqi leader Saddam Hussein. This was a much higher profile job than his earlier forays into acting, which included minor roles in Allison Anders' *Mi Vida Loca,* 1993, and David Fincher's *The Game,* 1997. It also allowed him to do some stunt work, which was a long– held dream for him.

Later in 1999, Jonze scored his biggest coup to date as director of the off–the–wall *Being John Malkovich,* produced by Michael Stipe of the band R.E.M.. This film, written by Charlie Kaufman, is a surrealist romp hitting on themes of gender, identity, and love. The project earned Jonze an Academy Award nomination in 2000 for best director, thus boosting his reputation even further. In addition he was honored with various awards for *Being John Malkovich* from the New York Film Critics Circle Award, the Venice Film Festival, the Online Film Critics Society, the Deauville Film Festival, and the Florida Film Critics Circle Award. He also received a Broadcast Film Critics Association Award for breakthrough artist for his work on *Being John Malkovich* as well as his role in *Three Kings.*

Jonze met Sofia Coppola, daughter of director Francis Ford Coppola, while shooting the video for the Sonic Youth song "100%." Singer Kim Gordon told Schoemer in *Newsweek,* "They'd hang out together, but it was almost like the he's–too–nice syndrome. I was like, 'Show her your dark side!' We'd go to Thrifty's and try to find sunglasses for him." Jonze and Coppola were friends for years before they finally became involved. On June 26, 1999, Jonze wed Coppola at her father's Napa Valley vineyard. Tom Waits played music at the ceremony.

Sources

Periodicals

Daily Telegraph, November 2, 1999, p. 26.
Entertainment Weekly, March 17, 1995, p. 33; November 5, 1999, p. 49; December 24, 1999, p. 46.
Harper's Bazaar, November 1999, p. 146.
Interview, October 1999, p. 210.
Newsweek, October 18, 1999, p. 74; November 1, 1999, p. 85.
New York, October 25, 1999, p. 44.
Ottawa Sun, November 12, 1999, p. 47.
People, July 19, 1999, p. 79.
Variety, September 6, 1999, p. 61.

Online

"Spike Jonze," Internet Movie Database web site, http://us.imdb.com (March 23, 2000).
"Spike Jonze," Mr. Showbiz web site, http://mrshowbiz.go.com (March 23, 2000).

Andrea Jung

Business executive

AP/Wide World Photos

Born in Toronto, Canada; married Michael Gould (a business executive). *Education:* Princeton University, B.A.

Addresses: *Office*—Avon Products, Inc., 1345 Avenue of the Americas, New York, NY 10105–0196.

Career

Executive for Bloomingdale's and I. Magnin stores; Neiman Marcus, executive vice president in charge of merchandising for women's apparel, cosmetics, and accessories; Avon Products, Inc., consultant, 1993, president of product marketing group for U.S. operations, 1994–97, president, 1998–99, chief executive officer, 1999—.

Awards: *Brandweek* marketer of the year, health and beauty category, 1996.

Sidelights

In 1997, Avon Products, Inc. was looking for a new chief executive officer, and many suspected that a woman would finally take over for the first time at the distinctly female- oriented firm. Marketing mainly toward women, with 98 percent of its sales and 42 percent of its managers female, not to mention 27 percent of its officers at the time, it seemed likely that the company would be ready to choose a woman to take the reins, especially since there were a few top executives in line, including Andrea Jung. When it passed them over in 1997 to tap a man as the next CEO, many were incensed, and two female executives soon quit. Jung hung on, though, and by 1999, stepped into the role when Charles Perrin left the post a year earlier than planned. This made her the second woman that year to rise to CEO of a *Fortune* 500 firm, and the highest–ranking minority woman at any major public company in the United States. In addition, she was only one of four total female CEOs in that group of companies. A marketing talent, Jung gave Avon's image and product lines a makeover, and managed to reposition the brand as updated and classy, yet not exceptionally glamorous or over–priced.

Jung was born in Toronto, Canada, the daughter of Chinese immigrants. She graduated magna cum laude from Princeton University, worked for Bloomingdale's and I. Magnin department stores. Rising through the ranks to become and executive, she later joined Neiman–Marcus retailers as executive vice president in charge of merchandising for women's apparel, cosmetics, and accessories. In 1993, Jung became a consultant to Avon. "When I came to Avon, it was perceived as an outdated, old–fashioned beauty company," she told Diane Seo in the *Los Angeles Times.* "We had great products, but women were saying, 'This is my grandmother's makeup brand.'" Jung is generally credited with revamping that notion.

In January of 1994, Jung joined Avon as president of product marketing for their U.S. operations. Immediately, she recognized the importance of the brand, complete with the image of the Avon Lady as a cultural icon. However, that beacon of door–to–door cosmetics was sadly outdated; remembered, as Sean Mehegan described in *Brandweek,* as "that matronly figure from the 1960s with the beehive 'do who showed up at one's doorstep hawking rouge and lipstick." The "ding–dong" doorbell sound and the words "Avon calling!," which were used in previous ad campaigns, were forever linked with legions of women carting samples to their house–bound neighbors. However, with more and more women in the work force and not in the home during the day, this picture was incorrect. Sales associates and customers most often were working women who conducted their Avon transactions in the office.

Jung seized the opportunity to embrace the brand's reputation while updating the product lines and introducing more contemporary marketing efforts. In 1994, she spearheaded the successful Avon Apparel line, and ditched about 30 to 40 percent of the old fragrance offerings to come up with better ones, such as Far Away, Millennia, and Natori. The new, more upscale bottles came with a higher price tag as well, but customers responded favorably— Avon's U.S. fragrance sales rose eight percent in 1995, roughly three times the industry average for sales gains in that area. Cosmetic costs were increased as well, but remained lower than competitors, and were accompanied by slicker packaging and catalogs. Sales continued to grow. The firm also became an innovator with products like Anew, the first alpha hydroxy acid skin cream on the market, designed to conceal wrinkles, and Jung set out to capitalize on those kinds of successes by pushing related skin–care items.

In addition to focusing on the products themselves, Jung came up with a better pitch for them as well. She launched the "Just Another Avon Lady" campaign in the winter of 1995, which aimed to redefine the products as well as the sales force. The campaign also included Olympic athletes Jackie Joyner–Kersee and Becky Dyroen–Lancer, and was related with Avon's numerous marketing efforts during the 1996 Olympic Games in Atlanta, Georgia. The company was the official fragrance and cosmetics sponsor of the games, and also sponsored The Olympic Woman, a multimedia exhibition in Atlanta spotlighting women athletes. "We believe it was more than just an Olympic sponsorship," Jung explained to Mehegan in *Brandweek.* "We were sponsors of women in the Olympics…. We understand women and women's causes, and we went out on a grass roots effort to teach women and communicate winning in sports as part of self–esteem." The next year, 1997, Jung launched the "Dare to Change Your Mind about Avon" ad campaign.

By 1997, when Avon's CEO was planning to step down, many observers were certain that after 111 years in the business, Avon was ready to tap a woman to lead the company. *Fortune* magazine ran an article titled, "If Women Ran the World, It Would Look a Lot Like Avon," in which Betsy Morris stated, "Unlike the vast majority of FORTUNE 500 companies, Avon has no glass ceiling." Morris pointed out several impressive statistics, including the fact that more than 40 percent of managers worldwide were women, half of the eight top officers were women, and four of 11 board members were women. The consensus was that Jung had a good shot at being the next CEO of Avon, in addition to about two or three other inside women at the top.

However, in December of 1997, Avon announced that it had chosen an outsider for the CEO slot. Charles Perrin, formerly the CEO of Duracell, was brought on board as vice chairman and chief operating officer, and was named to succeed Preston in May of 1999. The move outraged women's groups, and shortly afterward, two of the other women who were in the running for the job resigned. According to Del Jones in *USA Today,* an Avon spokesman noted that the firm was seeking someone with prior CEO experience. This would by default narrow the field of candidates for women to reach the top at Avon, though, because at the time, there were only two other women CEOs in the *Fortune* 500—Jill Barad of Mattel and Marion Sandler of Golden West Financial—and just seven in the *Fortune* 1,000.

Staying with the company, Jung soon received a promotion to president of Avon by the beginning of 1998, which kept her on track for the future possibility of the CEO rank. In addition, Preston told *Fortune* that Perrin was only expected to fill Avon's CEO position for five to eight years, which inherently pointed to Jung as his successor. "I'm celebrating," she noted at that point to Anne Faircloth in *Fortune.* Before long, it became apparent that Perrin, who had no direct marketing or cosmetics experience, was not the best choice for the job. Sales began to lag, and in November of 1999, Perrin announced that he was retiring, more than a year before his contract was set to expire. Jung was immediately tapped as CEO of the $5.2 billion company, which is based in New York City.

Jung is married to Michael Gould, the CEO of Bloomingdale's department stores, making them a double–CEO family. A working mother, she also sits on the board of General Electric. Unlike Carleton S. Fiorina, who took over at Hewlett–Packard earlier in the year and downplayed her rare status as a female CEO of a high–powered corporation, Jung embraced it. "I'm proud of my heritage and certainly my gender," she related to Dana Canedy in the *New York Times.* "I think it's a privilege being a minority woman leading a *Fortune* 250 company."

Sources

Advertising Age, February 3, 1997, p. S12.
Brandweek, November 13, 1995, p. 22; October 7, 1996, p. 98.

Business Week, March 16, 1998, p. 57.
Forbes, January 11, 1999, p. 184; December 2, 1996, p. 135.
Fortune, July 21, 1997, p. 74; January 12, 1998, p. 36..
Los Angeles Times, January 8, 1998, p. D4.
Newsday, November 5, 1999, p. A6; November 12, 1999, p. A71..
New York Times, November 5, 1999, p. C1.
USA Today, December 12, 1997, p. 2B.

Pauline Kael

Film critic and author

Born June 19, 1919, in Petaluma, CA; daughter of Isaac Paul (a farmer) and Judith (Friedman) Kael; married and divorced three times; third husband's name, Edward Landberg; children: (with James Broughton, a filmmaker) Gina James. *Education:* University of California, Berkeley, graduated 1940.

Addresses: *Home*—Massachusetts. *Contact*—c/o NAL Dutton, 375 Hudson St., New York, NY 10014–3657.

Career

Employed at temporary jobs and worked as a seamstress, cook, textbook author, and other positions, 1940s; freelance writer, 1953—; Berkeley Cinema Guild and Studio, Berkeley, CA, manager, 1955–60; KPFA public radio, Berkeley, CA, reviewer, 1960s; film critic in New York City for *Life* magazine, 1965, *McCall's* magazine, 1965– 66, *New Republic,* 1966–67, and the *New Yorker,* 1968–79, 1980–91. Also worked as staff writer for *Partisan Review, Vogue,* and *Harper's.* Executive consultant on film projects for Paramount Pictures Corp., 1979–80. Lecturer on films to colleges and universities. Contributor to periodicals, including *Film Quarterly, Massachusetts Review, Sight and Sound, Modern Writing, Second Coming, Movie Goer, New York Times Book Review,* and others.

Awards: Guggenheim fellowship, 1964; Long Island University Department of Journalism's George Polk Memorial Award for Criticism, 1970; National Institute of Arts and Letters Award, 1970; National Book Award, 1974, for *Deeper into Movies;* Front Page Awards, Newswomen's Club of New York, 1974, for best magazine column, and 1983, for distinguished journalism; Independent Feature Project's Gotham Award in recognition of contributions to American film culture, 1995; National Book Critics Circle's Ivan Sandorof lifetime achievement award (joint recipient with Lawrence Ferlinghetti), 2000. **Sidelights**

Film critic Pauline Kael was in her forties before she began making a living as a writer, but once she broke into the mainstream press, she became the grande dame of reviews. Her opinions and observations were penned in plain language without the haughty academic tone of those that came before her, and frequently included autobiographical comments pertaining to her ex–husbands or life experiences, which was previously unheard of. She also became notorious for her stinging insults and jabs; she disliked a great many pictures. However, Kael vehemently loved good films, and her tastes ran the gamut from high–concept art films to kitschy Hollywood fare, as long as it showed originality and zest.

As Susan Goodman wrote of Kael in *Modern Maturity,* "Unlike most critics, she used herself as an instrument, analyzing her own reactions to orchestrate a deeper understanding of film. Fortunately, this instrument had rich tone and resonance. Kael could position a movie properly within film history, link it with other arts, and nestle it firmly into cultural context." Goodman also noted that the critic was "perceived as someone who could literally make or break a movie." In 2000, the National Book Critics Circle honored Kael and Lawrence Ferlinghetti, poet and founder of San Francisco's City Lights Books, as joint winners of the Ivan Sandorof lifetime achievement award.

Kael was born on June 19, 1919, in Petaluma, California, a town north of San Francisco in Sonoma County. She was the youngest of five children of Polish–born Isaac Paul Kael and Judith (Friedman) Kael. Her dad worked as a prosperous farmer, but, as Kael related in *People*, "It wasn't people's idea of a farm. My parents were theatergoers, and all five of us were given music lessons." However, the Great Depression of 1929 wiped out their finances, so the family moved to San Francisco, where Kael's father opened a grocery store chain.

In 1936 Kael graduated from Girls High School, then enrolled at the University of California at Berkeley, where she majored in philosophy. However, she had always been an avid reader and filmgoer since childhood, and in college she honed her passion for the arts and literature. She also joined the varsity debating team, where she displayed her acerbic tongue. After graduating in 1940, Kael took up with a group of bohemians and engaged in writing plays, film scripts, and literary essays. Meanwhile, she held a variety of day jobs, but was often let go due to her headstrong ways.

After having a daughter, Gina James, in the late 1940s with experimental filmmaker James Broughton, Kael worked mostly at home as a seamstress, cook, textbook author, and other jobs she disliked. She once complained in *People* that she was held back in her career due to men: "It's very difficult to be married to somebody and write books. When you're married, you can't read in bed, you can't write at all hours, you can't chase around. I wasted a lot of years being unhappy because I couldn't do the things I wanted to do." However, she noted that having her daughter was a positive element in her life.

In 1953, Kael's first film review was published in *City Lights* magazine out of San Francisco. The editor heard her arguing with a friend in a coffee shop about the Charlie Chaplin movie *Limelight* and asked both of them to write a piece voicing their opinions. Kael's friend never turned anything in, but her scathing article was published. After that, she sold several more film reviews and soon landed a weekly program of her own on KPFA public radio out of Berkeley. In addition, Kael's work began to appear in *Film Culture, Sight and Sound, Partisan Review,* and others, and she began to write regular reviews for *Film Quarterly.*

Meanwhile, Kael was married and divorced three times, including her third time to Edward Landberg, who owned an art cinema. When she was working at KPFA, he asked her to manage his theater, which evolved into a two–screen house, the Berkeley Cinema Guild Theatres. It was the prototype for twin movie theaters that gradually caught on around the nation, then expanded into the multiplexes of today. Kael ran the entire operation, from cleaning the seats to writing the outrageous and clever program notes, which firmly entrenched her as a popular film writer in the Bay Area.

Although Kael contributed to several film anthologies during the 1950s and by the 1960s was a frequent lecturer at California universities, she still was not supporting herself via her writing. Finally, a New York editor saw her work in *Partisan Review* and offered her a book contract. Her first collection of reviews, *I Lost It at the Movies*, came out in 1965. Some critics were upset at the down–to–earth wording and personal commentary, since film criticism to that point had been highly academic. But many other praised the volume, and it led to a string of well–paying assignments. Kael moved to New York City and began writing for *Life* and *Vogue*; she then joined *McCall's* as their resident critic in 1966.

Moara publication. "She blasted 'The Sound of Music' as 'the sugarcoated lie that people seem to want to eat,'" according to a *Newsweek* article, and readers bombarded the magazine with complaints. Five months into her contract, *McCall's* paid her for the year and let her go. As Kael commented in *Newsweek*, "From the beginning I thought I was the wrong person for their readers, but they were willing to take the risk. I had realized that I would sock the ladies right between the ears, but what the hell is the point of writing, if you're writing banality."

Subsequently, Kael found a more receptive audience at the *New Republic* in 1967, then jumped to the *New Yorker* in January of 1968. She wrote a weekly column for half the year in the fall and winter, while author Penelope Gilliatt took over for the other six months. Later that year, a writer for *Time* commented, "Though she is now considered one of the country's top movie critics, Miss Kael still feels ill at ease in the East and lacks rapport with fellow intellectuals in Manhattan. Not that she always makes things easy for them. She is even racier in her talk than in her writing, and does not hesitate to correct someone's erroneous ideas about a movie."

Indeed, Kael has always had strong opinions, many of them negative. In fact, the *McCall's* editor claimed in *Newsweek* that he did not fire her for *The Sound of Music* review, but because her reviews overall were "more and more uniformly unfavorable." But she did not dismiss Hollywood fare outright in favor of obscure art films. In addition, when Hal Espen in the *New Yorker* asked her, "Which do you like more, to pan or to praise?," she replied, "Panning can be fun—you roll up your sleeves and head into the Augean stable. But it's also showoffy and cheap—it isn't sustaining. If you really like something, writing becomes humble and stirring . Writing about it intensifies your own pleasure."

Many of Kael's opinions drew outrage from readers, especially when she slammed movies that were applauded for their message rather than for their artistic merit. For instance, she was criticized for her harsh words about the 1988 film *Rain Man*, starring Dustin Hoffman, because many thought that it went far in bringing awareness and sensitivity to the disease of autism. However, as she commented to Espen in the *New Yorker*, "I got very angry fan mail from people who felt that I didn't appreciate the real–life seriousness of autism, because I didn't appreciate the movie. The press, in general, publicizes what the director says he's doing, and afterward the reviewers tend to review his intentions rather than what's on the screen." She added, "If you can't make fun of bad movies on serious subjects what's the point?"

Whether in a positive or negative reaction, Kael was known for her tart language. A *Newsweek* article reprinted some notable excerpts, including comments like "Costner has feathers in his hair and feathers in his head" (in a review of *Dances with Wolves*); speaking of Julie Christie in *Shampoo,* she wrote, "she is the sexiest woman in films right now. In this role she's a gorgeous, whory–lipped little beast, a dirty sprite." She also turned heads for her breezy style, complete with rhetorical questions, a liberal use of superlatives, and a smattering of slang terms like "bummer" and concocted words such as "sleazo."

Unsurprisingly, Kael was not hesitant to go against the grain and support a film she liked even if all other critics dismissed it. She told Goodman, "Most

movies I cared about didn't get good reviews. *Bonnie and Clyde, Mean Streets,* even *The Godfather* initially did not get good press. Now critics refer to them as classics and don't say what their original opinion was." In addition, Kael noted that her goal as a critic was more than just to give her opinion; she wanted to discern what the movies meant on a deeper level. Her dissections were not always applauded, though. According to a *Newsweek* article, Richard Gilman in a *Village Voice* review of her book *Reeling* shot down her writing as "an amalgam of idiosyncratic opinion, star–gazing, myth–mongering, politics, [and] social punditry."

In addition to holding sway over audiences, Kael was given credit for ushering in a new generation of critics as well. According to David Handelman in *Esquire*, publications would call on her advice in their hiring choices. Janet Maslin moved up from the *Boston Phoenix* to *Newsweek* on Kael's recommendation, and when Maslin moved to the *New York Times*, Kael put in a word for David Ansen to step in at *Newsweek*.

In 1979, Kael was recruited to serve as an executive consultant on films for Paramount Pictures. She left the *New Yorker* for a five–month stretch and developed a few scripts that never saw production, but also during her time there she encouraged the studio to film *The Elephant Man*. Deciding that Hollywood was not a good fit and that she missed writing, she returned to the *New Yorker* in 1980.

Kael has admitted that her abrasiveness has at times alienated her associates in the industry. Criticism of Warren Beatty's *Reds,* Paul Schrader's *Hardcore,* and Woody Allen's *Stardust Memories,* for example, brought their friendships to a halt. As Kael noted in *People,* "Sometimes the people whose movies I've panned the hardest have been the ones I've been closest to. It did really hurt me to write about *Stardust Memories* because I like Woody a lot and we were really good friends for 10 years. That was very painful, but I hated the movie. I have so much pride about what I say that I just wouldn't fudge it."

In 1991, after suffering from Parkinson's disease since the early 1980s, Kael retired from the *New Yorker.* For many years she has lived in a Victorian house on four–and–a–half acres in the Berkshires, and had commuted in to New York City every other week to spend a few days in a hotel and see films.

Throughout her career, Kael released several collections of her published reviews, most of which featured romantic or sexually connotative titles such as

Going Steady, 1970; *Deeper into Movies*, 1973; *When the Lights Go Down*, 1980; and *Movie Love: Complete Reviews 1988–1991*, 1991. Her final work was *For Keeps: 30 Years at the Movies*, 1994. In 1974 Kael won a National Book Award for *Deeper into Movies*, in addition to the George Polk Memorial Award for Criticism and the National Institute of Arts and Letters Award, both 1970, and Front Page Awards from the Newswomen's Club of New York in 1974 and 1980.

To Goodman in *Modern Maturity*, Kael revealed that her favorite era in films was the 1970s, thanks to pictures such as *McCabe & Mrs. Miller*, *M*A*S*H*, *Taxi Driver*, *The Godfather*, and others. Some of her favorite actors are Marlon Brando, Sean Connery, Nicolas Cage, and John Travolta, and her favorite female actors include Michelle Pfeiffer, Anjelica Huston, Sigourney Weaver, and Diane Keaton. And, in a 1998 *Newsweek* interview, answering the question, "What's the greatest movie you've ever seen?," Kael remarked, "Some years I might have answered D. W. Griffith's *Intolerance*. Some days I might have said W. C. Fields in *Million Dollar Legs*. Right now I think I'd say [Dimitri] Kirsanoff's *Menilmontant*, a short French film from 1926. It has a lyricism Chaplin could only dream of."

When *Modern Maturity* interviewer Susan Goodman asked Kael, "Do you think your criticism has changed movies or affected filmmaking?," Kael responded, "I'd rather not say. If I say yes, I'm an egotist, and if I say no, I've wasted my life. Although I've been told I've influenced some people to become directors. Unfortunately, most of them are lousy."

Selected works

I Lost It at the Movies: Film Writings, 1954–1965, Atlantic Monthly Press, 1965.
Kiss Kiss Bang Bang, Atlantic Monthly Press, 1968.
Going Steady: Film Writings, 1968–1969, Little, Brown,1970.
"*Raising Kane*," *The Citizen Kane Book*, Limelight Editions, 1971.
Deeper into Movies, Little, Brown, 1973.

Reeling, Little, Brown, 1976.
5,001 Nights at the Movies, Holt,1982.
When the Lights Go Down, Owl Books, 1983.
Taking It All In, W. Abrahams Books, 1984.
State of the Art, W. Abrahams Books, 1985.
Spitting Images, W. Abrahams Books, 1985.
Pauline Kael on Jonathan Demme: A Selection of Reviews Accompanying the Retrospective Jonathan Demme, an American Director, Walker Art Center, 1988.
Hooked, Dutton (New York City), 1989.
Movie Love: Complete Reviews, 1988–1991, Dutton, 1991.
For Keeps: 30 Years at the Movies (includes selections from *Kiss Kiss Bang Bang*, *I Lost It at the Movies*, *Movie Love*, *Reeling*, and "*Raising Kane*"), Dutton, 1994.
Conversations with Pauline Kael, edited by Will Brantley, University Press of Mississippi, 1996.

Sources

Books

Contemporary Theatre, Film and Television, volume 20, Gale Research, 1998.

Periodicals

Esquire, November 1985, p. 242.
Modern Maturity, March–April 1998, p. 48.
Newsweek, May 30, 1966, p. 80; June 21, 1976, p. 76; March 18, 1991, p. 59; Summer 1998 special issue, p. 93.
New Yorker, March 21, 1994, p. 132.
People, April 18, 1983, p. 50.
Premiere, October 1995, p. 66.
Publishers Weekly, March 6, 2000, p. 22.
Time, July 12, 1968, p. 38.

Online

"Pauline Kael," *Contemporary Authors Online*, Gale Group web site, http://www.galenet.com (June 6, 2000).

Bernice King

Clergywoman and activist

Born Bernice Albertine King, March 28, 1963; daughter of Martin Luther King, Jr. (an activist) and Coretta (an activist and singer; maiden name, Scott) King. *Education:* Spelman College, B.A. in psychology, 1985; Emory University, J.D. and M.Div., 1990.

Addresses: *Office*—c/o Martin Luther King, Jr. Center for Nonviolent Social Change, 449 Auburn Ave. NE, Atlanta, GA 30312.

Career

Intern with City Attorney's Office, Atlanta, GA; student chaplain at the Georgia Retardation Center and at Georgia Baptist Hospital, 1985–90; first public speech, St. Sabina Church, Chicago, 1983; first sermon, Ebenezer Baptist Church, Atlanta, 1988; ordained Baptist minister, 1990; Ebenezer Baptist Church, Atlanta, GA, assistant minister, 1990–93; Greater Rising Star Baptist Church, Atlanta, began as associate minister, became assistant minister, 1994—; has worked as a law clerk in Georgia's Fulton County juvenile court system. Cofounder, Active Ministers Engaged in Nurturing (AMEN). Chair, national advisory committee, National King Week College and University Student Conference on Kingian Nonviolence.

Sidelights

The youngest child of civil rights pioneer Reverend Martin Luther King, Jr., Bernice King is the only one of his four children to enter the ministry.

As her father before her, she has used the pulpit not only to address spiritual issues, but also to work actively for the betterment of communities, speaking out for social and political causes. Not surprisingly, many people have positively commented that King's oratory style and mannerisms mimic her father's, but she has also proven herself on her own terms as well. Though she started out preaching at the same church where her father and grandfather gave sermons in Atlanta, Georgia—the Ebenezer Baptist Church—she soon looked for a new avenue that was not synonymous with her family name and joined Atlanta's Greater Rising Sun Baptist Church instead. Also, King has taken her father's messages on racial harmony and updated them; she believes it is time for social change to come not from broad legislation, but from reaching out on an individual level to promote understanding and tolerance.

King, who is nicknamed "Bunny," was born on March 28, 1963, the daughter of Martin Luther King, Jr. and Coretta Scott King. When King was just five years old in 1968, her father was assassinated in Memphis by a sniper (later, a drifter named James Earl Ray was convicted of the killing). Afterward, many people were moved by a Pulitzer Prize–winning photograph that showed her, sad–eyed, in her mother's arms at her father's funeral. As she noted in an *Ebony* article, "I never really knew my father, and the biggest problem that I have had in growing up is missing that fatherly love. Sometimes I go by the crypt [where Dr. King was laid to rest] and talk with him. Sometimes I even cry." She only remembers being with her father on a couple of occasions, because she was so young when he was killed.

Despite her famous name, King told Pearl Cleage in *Essence* that she had "a very normal upbringing, in spite of what people might think. I went to a public high school. I only remember a couple of times when we had to have protection. Once in 1977, when James Earl Ray escaped from jail, we had to have bodyguards following us everywhere we went, and it was very strange." But King's mother did ensure that her children recognized their father's legacy, and indeed, they all became involved in furthering his message in some way. King's eldest sister, Yolanda, is a director, producer, and actor who played Rosa Parks in a television movie about her father's life, and also played the daughter of Medgar Evers in the film *Ghosts of Mississippi.* Her brother Martin III is leader of the Southern Christian Leadership Conference, and her closest sibling, Dexter, runs the Martin Luther King, Jr. Center for Nonviolent Social Change in Atlanta.

Though she was always more reserved than her siblings, King showed a passion for social issues. "I definitely feel a special responsibility to contribute something worthwhile," she remarked to Cleage in *Essence,* "primarily because from one to whom much is given, much is expected." However, she added that her mother never tried to push any of her children onto a certain path, instead allowing them to make their own decisions.

King had times, though, when it was difficult to deal with the loss of her father. When she was 16 at a church youth retreat, she watched a documentary on the civil rights movement and became so upset about her father's death that she contemplated leaving the church. She admitted in an *Ebony* article, "Sometimes there are things in life that cause us to push away from God. For me it was my father's death, the way the death impacted on me; it caused me to say, 'Forget God; forget the church." She even noted in *Ebony,* "I came close to committing suicide," and felt "undeserving."

However, King never actually stopped attending services, and added in *Ebony,* "A year later, I get this spiritual tugging, an inner voice telling me that I was going to start preaching." The call came to her in a dream in which her father appeared. Explaining to Audrey Edwards in the *Ladies Home Journal,* she remarked, "I think God uses the very thing that pushed you away to bring you back. What was revealed to me was that in order to reconcile with God, I had to do what my father did to understand why he had to suffer and sacrifice and die."

King initially grappled with the decision to enter the ministry. She recalled to Nancy Stetson in *Christianity Today,* "I felt I needed to finish growing up. I felt I was not worthy to be a minister—my perception was that ministers were flawless people." She also had other career goals, having set her sights on becoming the first black woman on the U.S. Supreme Court. In addition, she toyed with the idea of becoming a television anchor. By the time she was in college, she decided to major in psychology with the eventual goal of approaching theology studies from that vantage point. While in college in 1983, King gave her first major speech at Chicago's St. Sabina Church in front of an audience of about 2,000. Later that year she also addressed the United Nations General Assembly in New York on the subject of apartheid.

In 1984, King's grandfather, Martin Luther King, Sr., who had served as pastor of Atlanta's Ebenezer Baptist Church for 44 years, died. Then, the day before she turned 25 in March of 1988, King began to carry the torch, giving her first sermon at Ebenezer to an overflow crowd about a week before the twentieth anniversary of her father' death. Mayor of Atlanta Andrew Young was on hand for the event, as were all of her siblings and her mother. Though she was sure to be compared to her father and grandfather, King indicated she felt no pressure, telling Cleage, "Maybe because I grew up in the church, it felt kind of like home to me. It felt like getting up in your own house and saying whatever it is you need to say." Afterward, many complimented her on her oration.

After earning a bachelor of arts from Spelman College in 1985, King entered Emory University in a dual–degree program, finishing a law degree and a master of divinity degree simultaneously in June of 1990. As part of her education, she served as a student chaplain at the Georgia Retardation Center and Georgia Baptist Hospital and also interned for the Atlanta City Attorney's office. In addition, she became politically involved. During her college years, she was arrested twice during anti–apartheid protests, in 1985 and 1986. Shortly after graduating, King fervently denounced the United States' involvement in the Persian Gulf War.

In addition, King has continued her father's mission of working for equal treatment of African Americans, and spoke at many public events celebrating Martin Luther King Day, which was first observed as a national holiday in January of 1986. She is also a much-requested speaker at schools, churches, colleges, and youth centers, and helped found an organization called Active Ministers Engaged in Nurturing (AMEN), which is devoted to counseling juvenile delinquents.

However, King eventually left the Ebenezer Baptist Church to join the ministry at Atlanta's Greater Rising Star Baptist Church instead, because she felt it would "provide an opportunity for my personal growth and participation," as she stated in *Ebony*. She was also buoyed by the church's various community programs, including substance abuse help and afterschool child care services. By 1994, she was an associate minister in charge of the singles ministry there, although she continued to be a member of Ebenezer's parish and a member of their Martin Luther King Sr. choir. In 1995 King became a senior pastor at Greater Rising Star, in charge of the youth and women's ministry, preaching about a dozen times a year there. She also travels frequently as a guest minister to churches around the nation.

In 1996, King published a collection 17 public addresses she had given in a book titled *Hard Questions, Heart Answers: Sermons and Speeches*. Even in print form, reviewers favorably compared her style to her father's. "People often make comparisons between my way of speaking and my father's," she expressed in a *Jet* article. "They say that I sound like him; that I remind them of him; that many of my words resonate with the same passion as his."

However, King's message differs from his in that she approaches race relations from a more personal standpoint, as opposed to a greater social one. As she remarked to Edwards in *Ladies Home Journal*, "We need to start confronting the issue of race straight on. There needs to be a dialogue between ministries. You come to my church, I come to yours. Understanding removes the tension and fear." She also noted to Kim Hubbard in *People*, "The civil rights movement addressed the legal side, but you can't legislate beliefs. Blacks and whites have got to figure out how to connect genuinely to each other's experiences if we're going to coexist."

In addition, King has been outspoken about addressing the issue of sexism, particularly in churches. Then, at an appearance on Long Island just before Martin Luther King Day in January of 2000, she also warned the crowd of the dangers of materialism in modern society. According to Olivia Winslow in *Newsday*, King commented, "These things are destroying the foundation and fiber of American society, arrogance and elitism, materialism and greed, and selfishness."

Incidentally, neither King nor any of her siblings have married to date. Reporters have often quizzed her about this, and she once told Cleage that men might be intimidated by her, both because she is a professional woman and because of her name. She also believes that some men might be put off because she is a preacher. However, she has expressed at various times her desire to marry and have a family. King lives in a suburb of Atlanta and in her spare time, she enjoys bowling, tennis, and listening to music.

Sources

Books

Contemporary Black Biography, volume 4, Gale Research, 1993.

Periodicals

Booklist, December 15, 1996, p. 694.
Christianity Today, June 16, 1997, p. 34.
Ebony, October 1983, p. 160; January 1987, p. 34; January 1995, p. 30.
Essence, January 1989, p. 69.
Jet, June 11, 1990, p. 10; April 11, 1988, p. 6; January 19, 1998, p. 9.
Ladies Home Journal, January 1998, p. 60.
Miami Times, January 20, 1994.
Newsday, January 15, 2000, p. A16.
New York Times, January 20, 1994.
People, January 27, 1997, p. 76.
Publishers Weekly, November 11, 1996, p. 69.

Kevin Kline

Archive Photos

Actor

Born Kevin Delaney Kline, October 24, 1947, in St. Louis, MO; son of Robert Joseph (a toy and record store owner and singer) and Peggy (Kirk) Kline; married Phoebe Cates (an actress), 1989; children: Owen, Greta. *Education:* Indiana University, B.A., speech and theatre, 1970; Juilliard Center, studied with Harold Guskin, diploma, 1972.

Addresses: *Home*—New York City. *Agent*—William Morris Agency, 151 El Camino Dr., Beverly Hills, CA 90212.

Career

Actor. Acting Company, New York City, founding member, 1972–76, artistic associate, 1987–88. Stage appearances include *Henry VI, Part I*, 1970; *Henry VI, Part II*, 1970; *Richard III*, 1970; *The Hostage*, 1972; *The Lower Depths*, 1972; *The School for Scandal*, 1972; *Women Beware Women*, 1972; *The Beggar's Opera*, 1973; *Measure for Measure*, 1973; *Scapin*, 1973; *The Three Sisters*, 1973; *Edward II*, 1975; *The Robber Bridegroom*, 1975; *Beware the Jubjub Bird*, 1976; *Dance on a Country Grave*, 1977; *Nest of Vipers*, 1977; *Playing with Fire*, 1977; *The Promise*, 1977; *The Robber Bridegroom*, 1977; *On the Twentieth Century*, 1978; *Loose Ends*, 1979; *The Pirates of Penzance*, 1980–81; *Holiday*, 1980–81; *Richard III*, 1983; *Isn't It Romantic?*, 1984; *Henry V*, 1984; *Arms and the Man*, 1985; *Hamlet*, 1986; *Much Ado about Nothing*, 1988; *Hamlet* (also director), 1990; *Measure for Measure*, 1993.

Television appearances include series *Search for Tomorrow*, 1976-77; specials *Hamlet* on *Great Performances*, 1990; and various awards shows; and episodes of *Cheers*, 1990; and *Sesame Street*. Film appearances include *Sophie's Choice*, 1982; *The Pirates of Penzance*, 1983; *He Makes Me Feel like Dancin'*, 1983; *The Big Chill*, 1983; *Silverado*, 1985; *Violets are Blue*, 1986; *Cry Freedom*, 1987; *A Fish Called Wanda*, 1988; *January Man*, 1989; *I Love You to Death*, 1990; *Grand Canyon*, 1991; *Soapdish*, 1991; *Consenting Adults*, 1992; *Chaplin*, 1992; *The Nutcracker* (narrator), 1993; *Dave*, 1993; *Princess Caraboo*, 1994; *French Kiss*, 1995; *Shakespeare's Children*, 1996; *The Hunchback of Notre Dame* (voice-over), 1996; *Looking for Richard*, 1996; *In & Out*, 1997; *The Ice Storm*, 1997; *Fierce Creatures*, 1997; *Wild Wild West*, 1999; and *A Midsummer Night's Dream*, 1999.

Awards: Drama Desk Award and Antoinette Perry (Tony) Award for best supporting or featured actor in a musical, 1978, for *On the Twentieth Century*; Drama Desk Award, *Village Voice* Obie Award, and Tony Award, all for best actor in a musical, 1980, for *The Pirates of Penzance*; Obie Award for sustained excellence, 1986; Academy Award for best supporting actor, 1989, for *A Fish Called Wanda*; William Shakespeare Award for Classical Theatre, Shakespeare Theatre at the Folger, 1989.

Sidelights

Kevin Kline is an incredibly well–rounded actor whose range spans serious Shakespearean works and thought–provoking dramas as well as light–handed Hollywood fare in which he usually manages to rise above lackluster scripts. Often associated with rollicking comedies like *A Fish Called Wanda*, 1988, or spoofs like *Dave*, 1993, Kline is also capable of multifaceted characters, as witnessed in *Sophie's Choice*, 1982, and *The Ice Storm*, 1997. In addition, he is a Broadway veteran with many years' experience starring in classical works, though his first big breakthrough happened when he took physical comedy to new levels in the smash hit *Pirates of Penzance*, which opened in 1981. Kline was particularly praised for playing a high school teacher who is "outed" as a homosexual on national television in the entertaining *In & Out*, 1997. In 1999, he costarred with Will Smith in *Wild Wild West*.

Kline was born on October 24, 1947, in St. Louis, Missouri, the son of Robert Joseph Kline and Peggy (Kirk) Kline. His dad owned a record store, and later a toy store, in St. Louis, and was also an opera fan and amateur singer and pianist who instilled in his son a love of music. Though his father was of German–Jewish heritage, he was not religious, so Kline was raised a Catholic, his Irish mother's faith. When he was young, Kline began to act in plays at his small Roman Catholic preparatory school, St. Louis Priory, which was taught by a British order of Benedictine monks. In addition, he loved to ham it up in home movies, as his sister, Kate Kline May, told William A. Henry III in *Time*, noting that her brother "had this way of waiting for his moment and just taking over." He also played piano, and went on to major in music at the University of Indiana, intending to do composing and conducting.

While in college, Kline took an acting class and immediately changed his course. He switched his major to drama and started an acting company that put on shows in a coffee house, including improvisational works, plays, and a weekly satirical revue they called "The Living Newspaper." Graduating from Indiana in 1970 with a bachelor of arts, Kline was just in time to enter the first class of the new drama department at Juilliard School at Lincoln Center, the prestigious music conservatory. His instructor was John Houseman.

The program at Juilliard was, in Kline's words, "a very cushy introduction to the acting profession," according to Leslie Bennetts in the *New York Times*. Instead of landing in New York with a full load of ambition but no prospects, as most struggling actors, the Juilliard students had a head start. As Kline noted to Dudley Clendinen in the *New York Times*, "I was very lucky to be in Juilliard because it was a wonderful kind of showcase where agents would come and see the shows we were doing in school. We didn't have to go to them. They came to us." In addition, Kline had begun his professional career in 1970 with the New York Shakespeare Festival.

In 1972, using his first graduating class, which included Kline and William Hurt, Houseman formed the Juilliard Acting Company, later called simply The Acting Company. For many years, this repertory group toured various cities across the United States performing in classic and contemporary works. It was steady employment—about 47 weeks a year—for the actors. Throughout this time, Kline took the lead in plays such as *The School for Scandal*, 1972; *The Beggar's Opera*, 1973; *Three Sisters*, 1973; and *The Robber Bridegroom*, 1975. Kline noted to Robert Berkvist in the *New York Times*, "It was wonderful training, because you stretch yourself and build your confidence as an actor. Repertory keeps you on your toes. Finally, though, I decided to see if I could make it on my own." In addition, the hectic pace and extensive travel took its toll. "When I got to the point where I'd see the bus and I could feel my body knot up, I knew it was time to go," Kline recalled to Bennetts.

Returning to New York in 1976 to "pay some dues," as he told Bennetts, Kline landed gigs in television commercials for the Dean Witter investment firm and Thom McAn shoes, and reluctantly took a recurring part on the soap opera *Search for Tomorrow*. However, this supporting role only required his attention one or two days a week, so in the meantime, he continued to work on the stage off–Broadway and off–off–Broadway. When auditions came up for the Broadway musical *On the Twentieth Century*, he tried out for the part of Bruce Granit, a dim–witted, second–rate movie star. Accustomed to portraying the lead in theater productions, he thought the supporting part may have been below his standards, but went anyway, not to mention showed up in costume for the part. "I thought it was tacky to rely on being dressed for the role, rather than on our acting. But nobody knew my work," Kline explained to Berkvist. As it turned out, Kline was not only cast as Granit in *On the Twentieth Century*, he virtually stole the show. Berkvist remarked that he "regularly bring[s] down the house with his athletic antics" and compared Kline to the swashbuckling Errol Flynn. For his work, Kline won a Drama Desk Award and the 1978 Tony Award for best supporting actor in a musical.

In 1979, Kline continued to make his name on Broadway in *Loose Ends*, a love story about a former hippie trying to save his marriage. Playing the lead character, Paul, his reviews were again outstanding. Then, in 1981, Kline was offered the lead in the high–energy Gilbert and Sullivan operetta *The Pirates of Penzance* with Linda Ronstadt, after Raul Julia declined the part. Julia had suggested Kline, who had been his understudy in *The Threepenny Opera* in 1978. Kline was skeptical at the outset, because he thought "it sounded pretty silly," as he commented to Joe Klein in New York. After listening to the tape of the music, he told Klein, "Yes, it was silly, but so wonderfully silly, so completely ridiculous." Eventually he concluded that the Pirate King should be played "as an Errol Flynn who misses."

As it turned out, Kline's physical comedy in *The Pirates of Penzance* had audiences and critics roaring with laughter and raving with accolades. He played the part as an earnest and valiant bumbler; it opened at the Delacorte Theatre in Central Park as part of the New York Shakespeare Festival and later moved to the Uris (now Gershwin) Theatre and then the Minskoff Theatre. As Klein reported, "Rex Reed described Kline as 'half Errol Flynn and half Gene Kelly,' and 'one of the contemporary treasures of our theater.' Frank Rich, in the *New York Times*, said Kline possessed 'extraordinary gifts,' including 'the best qualities of Ben Turpin, Errol Flynn, Chevy Chase, and Alfred Drake.'" This performance earned Kline another Tony Award, as well as a Drama Desk Award and *Village Voice* Obie Award for best actor in a musical in 1980.

Kline made the leap into film in 1982 costarring as Meryl Streep's schizophrenic lover in *Sophie's Choice,* a major assignment for a Hollywood newcomer, even if he was considered a veteran on Broadway. Though he was just coming off of *Pirates* and had staked a positive reputation for reinventing Broadway comedy, the complex part of Nathan Landau, the brilliant yet troubled companion of an Auschwitz survivor, required a new set of tools. Chosen over such heavyweights as Robert DeNiro, Dustin Hoffman, and Al Pacino, Kline did not disappoint. Following that, he appeared in the archetypal 1980s yuppie movie *The Big Chill*, 1983, about a group of now–mature college friends who reunite at a funeral after one of the old gang has committed suicide.

After a few more films, including 1985's *Silverado,* Kline once again had audiences rolling in the aisles with *A Fish Called Wanda*, 1988, in which he again displayed a manic physical presence in his role as a dimwitted hit man. This farce about a batch of double–crossing diamond thieves costarred John

Cleese, Jamie Lee Curtis, and Michael Palin. Kline won the 1989 Academy Award for best supporting actor for this work, which became something of a cult classic. Subsequently, he made a string of projects that were not as successful at the box office. In 1990, he starred as a philandering pizzeria proprietor whose wife and mother–in–law would like to see him bake his last pie in *I Love You to Death.* After this, he appeared in *Grand Canyon* and *Soapdish,* 1991, then in *Consenting Adults,* 1992. He also portrayed old–time actor Douglas Fairbanks in 1992's *Chaplin.*

In 1993, Kline had another hit with *Dave,* in which he played a sitting U.S. president and his lookalike who steps into the job when the nation's leader falls into a coma. He followed this with *French Kiss,* 1995, starring as a French crook who seduces an American woman, played by Meg Ryan. Kline then triumphed in the 1997 film *In & Out* as a high school teacher who is surprised when a former student, now a famous movie star, on a televised awards show reveals that his influential instructor is also gay. Kline's character, who is engaged to be married to his longtime girlfriend in just a few days, insists a mistake has been made.

In & Out was inspired by a real–life incident in which Tom Hanks, who played a gay attorney with AIDS in Philadelphia, thanked a former gay drama teacher in his Academy Award acceptance speech. In fact, Hanks had first asked his permission from the instructor, who was retired and thus had no job security issues, as Kline's character in the fictionalized version. The movie was hailed for its light humor, avoidance of stereotypes, and sensitivity to gay issues, and did very well at the box office, earning $15 million in its first weekend. It also drew a flurry of publicity due to the fact that Kline and Tom Selleck, playing a gay reporter, engage in a screen kiss in the film. Also in 1997, Kline was acclaimed for his role in director Ang Lee's *The Ice Storm,* a dark exploration of a changing society in the Watergate era, as exemplified by two troubled upper–middle–class families. He also had a turn with the Will Smith in *Wild Wild West,* 1999, in which his character first appears undercover dressed as a dance hall girl, while also appearing that same year in a film version of *A Midsummer Night's Dream.*

In between making movies, Kline continued to work in theater, appearing in several productions of the New York Shakespeare Festival throughout the 1980s and 1990s. He has starred in *Richard III, Henry V, Hamlet, Much Ado about Nothing,* and *Measure for Measure,* among others. The actor is six feet tall, with dark wavy hair, blue eyes, and a trademark moustache. He married fellow actor Phoebe Cates in 1989 and the couple lives in New York City with their children, Owen and Greta. Among his colleagues, Kline is admired for his wealth of talent, and even more so for his humble nature regarding it. Ross Wetzsteon wrote in *Rolling Stone*, "Everyone,*everyone*, who meets Kevin Kline agrees he's not just polite, cooperative, unassuming, debonair, charming, talented and handsome, he has a fabulous sense of humor as well. Those who know him a little better add 'well adjusted,' 'unspoiled' and 'modest.'"

Sources

Books

Contemporary Theatre, Film and Television, volume 17, Gale Research, 1997.
International Dictionary of Films and Filmmakers, Volume 3: Actors and Actresses, St. James Press, 1996.

Periodicals

Daily Telegraph, February 11, 1998, p. 19.
Entertainment Weekly, October 3, 1997, p. 18.
Independent on Sunday, January 25, 1998, p. 14.
London Free Press (Ontario, Canada), July 2, 1999, p. C1.
New York, January 19, 1981, p. 27; May 10, 1993, p. 38; September 8, 1997, p. 54.
New York Times, June 23, 1978; January 1, 1981, sec. 2, p. 1; December 12, 1982, sec. 2, p. 1; July 1, 1984, sec. 2, p. 1;
People, June 12, 1995, p. 138.
Rolling Stone, December 8, 1983, p. 14.
Star Tribune (Minneapolis, MN), October 2, 1997, p. 12E.
Time, March 24, 1986, p. 78; September 22, 1997, p. 88.

Online

"Kevin Kline," Internet Movie Database web site, http://us.imdb.com (October 25, 1999).
"Kevin Kline," Mr. Showbiz web site, http://mrshowbiz.go.com (October 25, 1999).

Tim Koogle

Internet executive

Born July 5, 1951, in Alexandria, VA; son of a firefighter/machinist; married and divorced.

Addresses: *Office*—Yahoo!, 3420 Central Expressway, Santa Clara, CA 95953.

Career

Worked as a mechanic, 1970s; owned business making controllers for electronics manufacturers, 1978– c. early 1980s; Motorola electronics firm, worked in management, 1983–92; Intermec manufacturing firm, hired as chief engineer, became president of company, 1992–95; Yahoo! Internet portal, president and CEO, 1995–99, also chairman, 1999—.

Sidelights

Tim Koogle, chief executive officer of the Yahoo! web portal, once told Saul Hansell in the *New York Times,* "I just love speed. And I love well–built, highly engineered machines." Though the former engineer used to build and race cars, most of Koogle's drive is now channeled into creating a quick, high–performance Internet search engine. As head of the popular Internet portal service, Koogle is in charge of one of the rare web companies that turn a profit. Yahoo! has about 3,800 advertisers who post "banner" ads that bring in most of the site's revenue, an idea Koogle spearheaded that is common practice today.

With its irreverent image and youthful staff (the average Yahoo! employee is 29), the graying and somewhat conservative Koogle is decidedly more low–

key. He refused to spray–paint his hair with the company's yellow and purple logo for a photo shoot, and has never tattooed the Yahoo! logo on his rear end, as has at least one other executive. However, Koogle is known for being willing to take risks, a quality that was essential when he decided to leave his stable job to join the staff of six at the tiny startup in the earlier days of the web.

Yahoo! began as a search engine in 1994 when Stanford University engineering students Jerry Yang and David Filo created a guide to assist fellow researchers in retrieving information from the Internet. Initially it was simply a list of their favorite sites, but as it grew they created categories for the listings. They developed software to help them locate and label material in order to categorize it, and the site became a useful database, grouped by umbrella categories such as "Business & Economy," "Education," and "Science," then getting more specific (such as "Astronomy," "Ecology," and "Physics." Soon it was one of the best–known brands on the web.

Though other search engines came into existence, Yahoo! continued to grow, adding elements such as free e–mail, chat rooms, news, auctions, and business services. By 1998 they were the most–visited site on the web, with some 40 million users logging on each month. Though they later lost their lead to American Online (AOL), in May of 2000 they were still the second–most visited Internet site with 48.3 million visitors per month as opposed to AOL's 59.8 million, according to Steve Rosenbush in *Business Week*. Koogle once asserted to Andrew Cave in the *Daily Telegraph*, "We are trying to build Yahoo! into the only place anyone would have to go to find or get connected to anything or anybody."

Koogle was born on July 5, 1951, in Alexandria, Virginia. His father (now deceased, as well as his mother) was a fire fighter and Navy machinist who taught him a strong work ethic early on. "He said nobody owes you anything, so go out and earn what you want," Koogle related to Hansell in the *New York Times*. Starting at the age of seven, he earned cash doing gardening and delivering newspapers. As a teen, he fixed machines at McDonald's and helped his father repair cars. He has an older brother, Grayson.

In 1973, Koogle graduated at the top of his class from the University of Virginia's School of Engineering and Applied Science with a bachelor's degree in mechanical engineering. He worked his way through school rebuilding race cars and restoring antique cars, and also won a full scholarship for graduate studies at Stanford University. There, in 1975 he obtained his master of science and in 1977 he earned a doctorate degree. In addition to rebuilding engines, as a graduate student Koogle started up his own industrial design business making controllers for electronics manufacturers. He later sold the operation to Motorola. By the time he earned his doctorate he had saved enough money to buy a house.

Koogle in 1983 went to work for Motorola, an electronics corporation specializing in communications equipment. He worked there for nine years in management in its operations and venture–capital groups. During this time he was responsible for deciding whether to sink millions of dollars into business plans, thus learning all about risk–taking. However, Koogle never felt comfortable in his marble–floored office in an imposing tower. "I never could stand it," he commented to Linda Himelstein in *Business Week*. He left in 1992 to take a job as chief engineer at Intermec, a Seattle–based subsidiary of the Raytheon corporation making automated data collection and data communications products such as bar code machines. He was soon promoted to president of the ailing company, and in that post more than doubled the firm's sales to $370 million. Also during that time he served as vice president of Intermec and Raytheon's parent company, Western Atlas, which boasted annual revenues of $2 billion.

In 1995 Yahoo! sent a headhunter to Koogle, and he took the proposition to become their president and CEO. Though many would balk at leaving an established company to head up a fledgling business in an uncharted field, he was excited. "I like building stuff," he remarked to Cave in the *Daily Telegraph*. "This looked great. It was going back full circle to my roots in Silicon Valley and start–ups . It looked like fun; joining something with a clean slate, six people, no business plan, the ability to craft a brand new enterprise in the face of a market which was probably going to be all about a major shift going on in the world." He added, "I have always had a lot higher tolerance for what most people would consider risk." In 1999 he was made chairman of Yahoo!

Soon after he took over at Yahoo!, Koogle pioneered the idea of making money by signing companies to post banner advertisements directly on the site's pages, instead of charging users, which other sites were doing at the time. As it turned out, his plan became the standard way of business. Also, Koogle broadened Yahoo! from being a search site into being a "portal," offering services such as free e–mail accounts, chat rooms, online auctions, and areas focusing on real estate, finance, health, and more. To use many of these services, web surfers need to register demographic information with Yahoo!, which the site then provides to businesses.

More notably, Koogle decided that Yahoo! would retain its independence, making it the "Switzerland" of the web, while other sites teamed up with bigger corporations or signed exclusive agreements with advertisers. For example, the Excite search engine was sold to the At Home Corporation, owned largely by AT&T and cable firms, and competitor Infoseek was acquired by the Walt Disney Company. But these deals caused various problems for the parent companies. And, as Koogle mentioned to Kara Swisher in the *Wall Street Journal*, "When an Internet–based company combines with one that is purely one kind of access or one provider of content, the offering for user is a little bit more narrow. That may be totally viable, but it's not what has made us successful."

Instead, Koogle chose to do the buying, rather than allowing his company to be put on the auction block. Yahoo! purchased Geocities in 1999, a web service that hosts a vast number of home pages, and then bought broadcast.com, an Internet audio and video service. In addition, Yahoo! teamed with Kmart to provide a free Internet service provider called Bluelight.com. It also began making money by charging retailers a fee for sales generated via its web site, which allows Yahoo! to collect a commission on sales without the cost of stocking warehouses or paying customer service employees. However, after a deal in early 2000 in which AOL announced plans to by Time Warner Inc., many wondered if the iconoclastic portal would be able to keep its pace. Steve Rosenbush wrote in May of 2000 in *Business Week*, "The tremendous scope of Time Warner's assets seems likely to widen the gap. Most important right now, Koogle has to catch up in e–commerce."

Thanks to Koogle's leadership, Yahoo! began to turn a profit in September of 1997, which is unusual considering the bulk of Internet ventures, including behemoth operations such as Amazon.com, had yet to operate in the black as of mid–2000. Koogle noted to Hansell in the *New York Times* in 1999, "I still have conversations with people asking, 'Why do you bother with profits?' But I've had enough experience to know at a gut level that if you don't build a company from the start to be profitable, you're never going to be able to get profitable later." The company went public in 1996, earning about 90 percent of its revenue from ad sales at the time of its initial public offering (IPO). Their 1999 sales reaches $588.6 million, according to Hoover's Online, with a net income of $61.1 million. By this time, the firm boasted almost 2,000 employees, a far cry from the handful on board just five years earlier.

Koogle, who is known casually as "T.K.," is worth a reported half a billion dollars thanks to stock ownership in Yahoo!. He is divorced and has no children, and has homes in Saratoga, California, and on Lake Washington in Seattle, near the home of Microsoft founder Bill Gates. Though he is not nearly as zany as Yahoo! cofounders Yang and Filo, he does have his quirks. In addition to driving fast cars (his Mercedes can reach 170 miles per hour), in his spare time he enjoys playing guitar, and collects vintage models such as a 1972 Stratocaster, a Beatles Rickenbacker, and an acoustic D–41 Martin.

In fact, before Koogle's fast–paced career with Yahoo!, he played in various rock bands, and continues to have the image of "an aging rock–and–roller," according to Hansell, who described him as sporting "black jeans, a denim shirt and a mane of gray hair." Another reporter, Umberto Tosi of *Forbes*, described him as having a "GQ look, which runs to hand– painted Italian ties or black turtlenecks." As a further testament to Koogle's artistic bent, his circle of friends includes a group of glass blowers outside of Venice, Italy. In addition, as Yahoo! marketing head Karen Edwards told Hansell, Koogle "is not one of those ego–C.E.O.'s who try to micromanage everything. He is easy to talk to, but it always seems like he's pondering life's true meaning."

Sources

Periodicals

Business Week, September 7, 1998, p. 67; September 27, 1999, p. EB 26; May 15, 2000, p. EB26.
Daily Telegraph, July 17, 1999, p. 33.
Forbes, October 7, 1996, p. S80.
Fortune, June 7, 1999, p. 76.
New York Times, August 23, 1999, p. C1.
Wall Street Journal, January 12, 2000, p. B1.

Online

Yahoo! company capsule, Hoover's Online web site, http://www.hoovers.com (July 6, 2000).

Michael Kors

Fashion designer

Born Karl Anderson, Jr., August 9, 1959, in Merrick, Long Island, NY; son of Karl and Joan Anderson (a model; later changed name to Kors); adopted by Bill Kors and changed name to Michael Kors. *Education:* Attended Fashion Institute of Technology, New York, 1977.

Addresses: *Office*—Michael Kors Inc., 550 Seventh Ave., New York, NY 10018– 3203.

Career

Lothar's boutique, New York, sales assistant 1977–78, then designer and display director, 1978–80; established own women's sportswear label, 1981; also designer for Lyle & Scott, 1989; under auspices of Italian firm Compagnia Internazionale Abbigliamento, introduced lower–priced "Kors" line and menswear collection, 1990; designer, womenswear collection for Erreuno J, from 1990; discontinued lower–priced line and reorganized Michael Kors Inc., 1993; designer of ICB collection for Onward Kashiyama, 1995–97; restarted Kors line, 1996; LVMH Moet Hennessy Louis Vuitton, Paris, France, artistic director of Celine line, 1997—.

Awards: Dupont American Original Award, 1980; Council of Fashion Designers of America womenswear designer of the year, 1999.

Sidelights

Designer Michael Kors appeals to women with his spare yet fashionable designs that bridge practicality and style. He has often been compared to Calvin Klein for his clean–lined American look, but does not want anyone to get the wrong impression. "When I think 'minimalist' I think pretentious," Kors expressed to Anne–Marie Schiro in the *New York Times.* "I think of a room so minimal you're afraid to sit in it." In fact, though his designs can be described as simple or refined, they are never without personality, some kind of added element that makes his clothing stand out while remaining tasteful. "I like to kick things—to take what you accept and kick it with color, texture proportions," he once remarked to Nina Darnton in *Newsweek.*

Through the years, Kors has attracted a customer base that includes author Gloria Steinem, journalist Barbara Walters, and actors Julia Roberts, Demi Moore, Claire Danes, Anjelica Huston, and Bebe Neuwirth, among many others. One of the main reasons Kors has continued to woo such a loyal following season after season is his reliance on customer feedback. While other designers may try to dictate what tastes women should have, Kors has always made a point to reach out to his clients and seek comments. He then uses that information in creating future lines. "I listen to what the women love, what they hate, what they can't find anywhere," he told Nina Darnton in *Newsweek.* "Then I know what to do."

Kors was born Karl Anderson, Jr., on August 9, 1959, in Merrick, Long Island, New York, next to Jones Beach. His Swedish father, Karl Anderson, was a college student, and his Jewish mother, Joan, was a model for Revlon. As a toddler, Kors also began to model, appearing in commercials for Charmin toilet paper and Lucky Charms cereal. However, when he entered first grade, his mother made him stop modeling because he enjoyed it more than going to school. She retired then herself, and later opened her own textile–design firm.

When Kors was very young, his parents divorced, and when he was five, his mother married Bill Kors, the owner of a chain of gas stations. His mother's new husband then adopted him. At the time, his mother suggested since he was getting a new last name, he could also choose a new first name if he wished. She suggested Michael or David, so he took Michael as his first name and David as his middle name. Kors's mother later divorced her second husband as well.

Although Kors took acting lessons in New York until he was 14, he harbored an eye for fashion. His mother had exposed him to design with her background in modeling, and she also purchased a great many outfits for her son. "I'm an only child," Kors explained to Michael Gross in *New York*. "I became the kid who *lived* to shop." As a teen, in order to help fund his insatiable appetite for fashion, he began to earn money working in telephone sales, doing caricatures for children's birthday parties, and buying tennis clothes for a local pro shop.

Meanwhile, Kors had been sketching outfits for years, and at age 15, began designing jeans and shirts. He told Elizabeth Sporkin in *People*, "I figured I'd have better luck as a designer. Besides, an out–of–work actor usually waits tables, but an out–of–work designer can work in a store." He had a friend whose father was involved in the fashion business, and he showed him some sketches and landed some freelance work.

At 17, Kors attended New York's Fashion Institute of Technology for two semesters. During that time, he recalled to Dodie Kazanjian in *Vogue*, "I wore tight white silk shirts that laced up the front and platform shoes. And I actually lay down on the floor to get into a pair of French jeans." He also noted to Karl Plewka in *Interview*, "It was at the height of disco madness in the late '70s, so I think perhaps Studio 54 was more important to me that college. In fact, back in high school, I went to Studio 54 instead of going to the prom."

Getting antsy to make his own way, Kors dropped out of school and took a job at Lothar's, a boutique that made tie–dyed French jeans famous. It was frequented by celebrities such as Cher, Farrah Fawcett, Diana Ross, Barbara Streisand, Jacqueline Kennedy Onassis, and Goldie Hawn. "It was certainly more exciting than going to a draping class," he commented to Plewka. Here, he honed his one–on–one customer relations skills, and continued to put these to use when he began putting on his own trunk shows, which is when designers make personal appearances at stores and display their collections.

In 1979 Lothar's asked Kors to do some designs to round out their collection, and his output was so impressive that they stopped importing clothing from Paris. Then, Dawn Mello, president of Bergdorf Goodman, saw his designs and gave him money to produce his first collection. "I didn't have a showroom," he remarked to Plewka. "I had people selling in my apartment, clothes all over my bed. This was in 1981; I didn't even know what a trunk show was."

However, Kors became a favorite of the trunk–show circuit, having an uncanny knack for remembering customers' names and tastes in clothes. Also on these trips, he began to pay keen attention to preferences so that he could use that information in future designs. "You'd be amazed at the difference between what you think people are going to want and what they actually end up buying," Kors revealed to Rachel Urquhart in *Vogue*. "It can be a little scary if you've guessed wrong." He also noted to Schiro in the *New York Times*, "I love doing trunk shows. It shows me who the customer is and what she wants." In fact, a large reason for the designer's success is because of his personal attention and his habit of listening to his customers.

Starting out, Kors already had a good idea of what would work. He gravitated toward clean shapes and contemporary lines, thinking that it would make it easier for women to dress. "It was also a form of protest," Kors told Bernadine Morris in the *New York Times Magazine*. "I grew up in the '60s and '70s when clothes were trendy and people rushed out to buy the newest style…. People don't have time for disposable clothes anymore. They just want to get dressed in the morning and get on with their lives. Besides, clothes are so expensive, nobody can afford to buy crazy outfits they only wear once." Kazanjian in *Vogue* approved, noting, "Everything is an improved version of a classic."

Kors's lines feature mix–and–match separates with accessories such as belts and scarves tailored to coordinate. The color scheme is mainly neutrals—gray, black, khaki, navy, and white—with a splash of color to accessorize. He also believes in certain basic pieces, such as a white shirt, turtleneck, and strapless black dress, which he includes in nearly every collection. Unlike many designers, who adhere to the idea that there must only be one skirt length each season, he offers skirts and pants in different lengths and cuts.

By the early 1990s, although Kors had been in business for over a decade, he began to be hailed as a popular "new" designer and was touted as the next Calvin Klein. "I'm the most established new name in town," he joked to Sporkin in a 1991 *People* article. In 1990, sales from Kors's womenswear collection topped $8 million, and also that year he signed a deal with Italian firm Compagnia Internazionale Abbigliamento to create a lower–priced sportswear line called Kors. At half the price of his designer pieces, the clothes started hitting stores in January of 1991.

The Kors collection was a success, reaching at least 150 stores, as compared to his higher– end line, which was sold in about 80. And because the prices were lower, he moved more pieces: while he might sell 15 of any given item from his signature collection, he ordered a minimum amount of 3,000 for each piece in his lower–priced line. This saved him money in manufacturing. Thanks to this success, Kors branched out to take more chances with his signature line, adding more adornments such as lacy bodysuits and shiny beads. He also launched a high–profile advertising campaign featuring supermodel Christy Turlington, and embarked on a menswear line as well.

Despite this rise, though, the Italian firm with whom Kors was working cut back their business in the United States and discontinued the lower–priced Kors line. This, and the fact that many smaller boutiques were going out of business around the same time, sent him into Chapter 11 bankruptcy in 1993. By the end of the year, though, he had reached an agreement with his creditors and was able to pull himself out of trouble. In 1995, Kors entered an agreement to create the lower–priced ICB collection for Onward Kashiyama, and by 1996 they provided financing so he could restart his own moderately-priced line as well.

Then, in 1997, Kors ended his association with ICB and became the artistic director of the upscale but somewhat conservative Celine line owned by LVMH Moet Hennessy Louis Vuitton. The company's chair, Bernard Arnault, chose him to breathe new life into the brand. Kors himself stated to Melissa Biggs Bradley in *Town & Country,* "Celine was always about wearable clothes. It always stood for quality and luxury, but there was a sense that Celine had become too classic. My goal was to keep the clothes wearable, but add a sense of fashion and fantasy."

Kors's appointment caused a stir among Parisians because he was one of a string of non– French designers to head up a prestigious French fashion house: Marc Jacobs, from America, works for Louis Vuitton; Alexander McQueen, from Britain, heads Givenchy; John Galliano, also British, runs Christian Dior; another Brit, Paul McCartney's daughter Stella, leads Chloe; and German Karl Lagerfeld is in charge of Chanel. In addition, some in America were also reluctant to loan talent to overseas fashion houses, and wondered if Kors would devote too much time to Celine and neglect his own line. Others were skeptical that he could rejuvenate the staid Celine designs. Surprising everyone all the way around, he managed to churn out must–have lines in his first two seasons with Celine while releasing his own impressive works simultaneously. In 1999, LVMH purchased a one–third stake in his firm, allowing him to explore the idea of expanding his line and opening his own boutique.

Still, heading into 2000, Kors did not have the name recognition of Klein or Tommy Hilfiger. Saks Fifth Avenue president Rose Marie Bravo commented to Frank DeCaro in *Newsweek,* "He hasn't exploited his name with licenses [for sheets, underwear, perfume] as aggressively as he could have." But he was gaining steam. Sue Patneaude, Nordstrom's vice president for designer apparel, told Anne–Marie Schiro in the *New York Times* in 1999, "Nordstrom kind of dabbled with Kors over the years, but we became vitally interested in the Michael Kors line this year and will carry Celine this fall for the first time. He seems to have matured and become very focused. All the talent he's been trying to harness all these years has come together. He's all of a sudden ended up from and center. It's cosmic."

Also in 1999, the Council of Fashion Designers of America named Kors the womenswear designer of the year. The award, fashion's version of the Oscar, had eluded Kors for so many years that he was considered the "Susan Lucci" of fashion, referring to the popular daytime drama actor who was passed up for an Emmy Award 19 times before snagging it in 1999.

Kors lives in a one–bedroom apartment in Greenwich Village. As for his personal style, he has always preferred simple, comfortable clothing, just as he designs for others. His wardrobe staples are jeans and sweatshirts. Kors once told Annemarie Iverson in *Harper's Bazaar,* "If I can genuinely make a woman look better and feel better, then I'm doing my job."

Sources

Books

Contemporary Fashion, St. James Press, 1995.

Periodicals

Harper's Bazaar, March 1997, p. 370.
Interview, December 1998, p. 116.

Newsweek, December 3, 1990, p. 62; July 29, 1996, p. 79.

New York, August 30, 1999, p. 118.

New York Times, July 13, 1993, p. B8; November 9, 1993, p. B11;November 25, 1997, p. B7; April 6, 1999, p. B9.

New York Times Magazine, August 24, 1986, p. 142.

People, April 8, 1991, p. 69; August 9, 1999, p. 73.

Town & Country, August 1999, p. 83.

Vogue, June 1989, p. 60; May 1990, p. 314; August 1999, p. 224.

Anna Kournikova

AP/Wide World Photos

Tennis player

Born June 7, 1981, in Moscow, Russia; daughter of Sergei (a former wrestling champion and government employee) and Alla Kournikova.

Addresses: *Office*—c/o Women's Tennis Association, 13 First St. NE, St. Petersburg, FL 33701.

Career

Tennis player; turned professional, 1995. Member of Russian Federation Cup team, 1996; member of Russian Olympic team, 1996.

Awards: International Tennis Federation World Junior champion, European Championships 18 and Under singles champion, Italian Open Juniors winner, and Orange Bowl 18 and Under singles champion, all 1995; Most Impressive Newcomer, Corel Women's Tennis Association Tour, 1996; Grand Slam doubles title (with Martina Hingis), Australian Open, 1999.

Sidelights

Although she had not won a singles championship as of spring of 2000, Russian tennis player Anna Kournikova had long been one of the most-watched women on the court. Fans were enamored of her blonde, tanned good looks, of which she was well aware. By the time she was 16, she was posing for magazines like *Details, Rolling Stone, Sports Illustrated*, and *Seventeen*, even though she had yet to break through to the top ten of women's tennis players. Often criticized for cultivating her image more than her game, Kournikova eventually began to steamroll top-ranked opponents like Martina Hingis and Monica Seles, though a title continued to elude her. By spring of 2000, she was ranked ninth, although her personal life and her appearance continued to make news just as much or more than her professional achievements.

Kournikova was born on June 7, 1981, in Moscow, Russia. She is the daughter of Sergei, a former Greco–Roman wrestling champion who works in the Russian physical culture ministry, and Alla Kournikova, a former 400–meter runner. When she was five, Kournikova began playing tennis, and her parents noticed her talent right away. They signed her up with coach Viktor Rubanov, and she played at Moscow's Spartak Club, home base of player Andrei Chesnokov. At age eight, she was competing in junior clinics, and by nine, she was competing in the juniors.

Through the grapevine, agent Paul Theofanous heard about Kournikova by the time she was ten. By that time, Italian apparel maker Ellesse was already outfitting the prodigy in high– end tennis wear. Theofanous had his reservations due to her young age, but after seeing her in action and hearing more about her, agreed to sign her to the International Management Group (IMG), an agency known for handling big–name athletes. They quickly negotiated her multimillion–dollar deals with Adidas apparel and Yonex racquets.

After becoming the youngest client in the history of IMG, Kournikova and her mother moved to Bradenton, Florida. Her mother noted to Robin Finn in the *New York Times*, "[The decision] was something that was difficult for us, and there have been some sacrifices, but believe me, we are not dying here in the U.S. Life is not all that bad compared to back home." Kournikova joined Nick Bolletieri's prestigious tennis academy in February of 1992 and made her debut on the junior circuit in April of that year. After winning her first event, she was the top seed in the under–14 age group.

Almost immediately, Kournikova was being measured against two other budding stars, Venus and Serena Williams, also living and training in Florida. But Kournikova often stole the spotlight due to her appearance. In a 1993 *Tennis* article, Curry Kirkpatrick called her a "knockout looker." However, Kirkpatrick also focused on her tendency to act spoiled and pushy. He related that at one tournament where a five–star restaurant catered the team meal, she insisted on ordering from the menu instead. She also got a reputation for being bossy, once pushing her coach, Bolletieri, out of the way to take cuts in line for a jump–rope machine. Bolletieri remarked to Kirkpatrick, "I'm telling you, this little girl is so assertive, it's frightening."

Indeed, Kournikova was driven. She told Kirkpatrick, "I am anxious to turn pro soon as possible even though Nick says to slow down." That year, she saw victory at the European Championships and the Italian Open Juniors, and was the Orange Bowl 18 and Under singles champion. In addition, she became the International Tennis Federation Junior World Champion in 1995. At age 14, in October of 1995, Kournikova made her pro debut. By the end of 1996, she had improved 224 spots in the ranking, edging up to number 57. Also that year, she made it to the fourth round of the U.S. Open by defeating Barbara Paulus, ranked 14, and became the youngest player ever to win a Federation Cup match, as she helped Russia defeat Sweden. In addition, she played for Russia in the 1996 Olympics.

In 1997, in only her fourth Grand Slam tournament, Kournikova made it to the semifinals at Wimbledon, though she lost 6–3, 6–2 to Martina Hingis the eventual winner after defeating tenth–seeded Anke Huber and fifth–seeded Iva Majoli. Understandably, many had high hopes for Kournikova at the U.S. Open, but she was defeated by Irina Spirlea in the second round. By the summer of 1997, though, she had improved her ranking to 26th. Still, she was unhappy about a Women's Tennis Association (WTA) rule that limited her to 16 tournaments a year until age 16. Hingis, on the other hand, who turned pro at age 14 in 1994, had been grandfathered in.

By 1997, Kournikova was gaining attention as well for her romance with hockey star Sergei Federov of the Detroit Red Wings. A former Red Army player who defected to the U.S., he was 27 and she 16 when they began to date, although they staunchly insisted they were simply good friends. As she explained to Michael Silver in *Sports Illustrated*, "In Russia there is no word for boyfriend. You're either married or you're friends. Maybe people want to see Sergei as my boyfriend, but he's just a good friend of mine a very good friend. Our families are close. We came from the same background, and we have a lot in common."

Still, with her older boyfriend and her sultry image, Kournikova was fast becoming a sex symbol. Despite the fact that she had not even reached the finals of a singles championship, by 1998, she was one of the most high–profile players on the circuit. In addition to her looks, her attitude remained one of her most outstanding qualities as well; the headline on Silver's *Sports Illustrated* article read simply, "Anna–tude." In it, Silver wrote that Kournikova compared herself to a menu, telling him that male fans "can look, but they can't afford it." She also remarked that commentators pronouncing her name "ANH–ya" were incorrect, noting, "No, it's AH–na. That's just people trying to be cool and pretend they know Russian. As if!"

However, in 1998 Kournikova began to show the kind of real power that many thought could take her to the top. At the Lipton Championships that March, she beat four top ten players Monica Seles, Conchita Martinez, Lindsay Davenport, and Arantxa Sanchez Vicario in an onslaught that was unprecedented for a 24th–ranked player. She had a new coach by then, Pavel Slozil, who worked with Steffi Graf from 1986 to 1991. He observed to Carter Coleman in *Women's Sports and Fitness*, "Anna's still improving, but she's more focused, more confident. Beating four great tennis players in one week is confirmation that she's not just a one–day player."

Though Kournikova eventually lost the Lipton Championships to Venus Williams, she scored another coup in June, the day before her seventeenth birthday, as she conquered the world's number–one player, Martina Hingis, in the quarterfinals at the German Open. This marked the first time Hingis had lost to a younger opponent. After that, Kournikova beat fifth– ranked Arantxa Sanchez Vicario in the third round, thus boosting her rank to number 13.

By this point, Kournikova had still not even cracked the top ten, yet she was one of the biggest celebrity tennis players thanks to her image as the "Russian Lolita." She furthered this reputation when she posed for a *Rolling Stone* photo shoot wearing high heels and a red miniskirt that showed off her underwear. In addition, she was widely quoted after bragging about the lack of fat on her posterior. However, in 1998, Kournikova left the IMG agency to sign with Advantage International, which promised to downplay her racy persona and place emphasis on her skills on the court. By the end of 1999, she had stated, "I'm still a virgin," according to a *Newsweek* article.

Finally in 1999, Kournikova nabbed her first Grand Slam win, albeit a doubles title. She and Hingis beat out top–ranked Lindsay Davenport and number–one ranked doubles player Natasha Zvereva 7–5, 6–3. Late in the year, though, she was sidelined due to a foot injury. But she was back on the court in February of 2000 at the State Farm Tennis Classic in Scottsdale, Arizona. Still, her youthful attractiveness was her main draw. Pedro Gomez wrote in the *Arizona Republic*, "Tennis may be her game, but sex appeal is her strength. The simple truth is that Kournikova attracts a crowd, mostly men." Though she still had not cinched a title and only took home prize money worth $748,000 in 1999, Kournikova by spring of 2000 was the highest earner in tennis off the court due to her lucrative contracts, raking in several million annually from Yonex, Adidas, and Berlei lingerie, for whom she began promoting sports bras.

Kournikova, who is five feet, eight inches tall, lives in Miami. In early 2000 she signed on with Athlete-Direct, a manager of web sites for professional sports players, and subsequently posted a trove of personal data for fans on this official site. AthleteDirect had noticed that there were 18,000 web pages in existence devoted to her, according to Peter Newcomb in *Forbes*, and asked her to become one of its flagship featured athletes in return for stock. Kournikova told Newcomb, "I saw what was out there, and most of it was inaccurate or outdated or worse. With my own official site I have control over the content." On this site, fans can look up her career history, her biography, and learn about her hobbies, which include reading, dancing, watching television, and listening to music.

Sources

Periodicals

Arizona Republic, February 29, 2000, p. C1; March 1, 2000, p. C1.
Forbes, March 20, 2000, p. 171.
Newsweek, November 29, 1999, p. 110.
New York Times, April 23, 1992.
Sport, October 1997, p. 30.
Sports Illustrated, March 30, 1998, p. 56; September 14, 1998, p. 90.
Tennis, August 1993, p. 46; May 1999, p. 66.
Time, September 8, 1997, p. 87.
Women's Sports and Fitness, June 1998, p. 98.

Online

"Anna Kournikova," AthleteDirect web site, http://www.athletedirect.com (March 30, 2000).
"Anna Kournikova," ESPN web site, http://espn.go.com (March 30, 2000).

Jude Law

Actor

Born December 29, 1971 (one source says 1972), in London, England; married Sadie Frost (an actor), 1997; children: Rafferty; Findlay (stepson).

Addresses: *Home*—London, England. *Agent*—Creative Artists Agency, 9830 Wilshire Blvd., Beverly Hills, CA 90212.

Career

Actor; partner in production company, Natural Nylon. Stage appearances include *Indiscretions*, New York City, 1995; and productions in Britain and Europe of *Pygmalion, Ions,* and *Les Parents Terribles*. Television appearances include series *The Casebook of Sherlock Holmes*, 1990; and *Families*, 1990; and movie *The Marshal*, 1994. Film appearances include *Shopping*, 1994; *I Love You, I Love You Not*, 1996; *Wilde*, 1997; *Gattaca*, 1997; *Bent*, 1997; *Midnight in the Garden of Good and Evil*, 1997; *Music from Another Room*, 1998; *Final Cut*, 1998; *The Wisdom of Crocodiles*, 1998; *Love, Honour and Obey*, 1999; *eXistenZ*, 1999; and *The Talented Mr. Ripley*, 1999.

Awards: Theatre World Award, 1995, for *Indiscretions*; London Film Critics Award, 1997, for *Wilde*.

Sidelights

British actor Jude Law made great strides in his career in 1999 with his role as Dickie Greenleaf in *The Talented Mr. Ripley*. Though he had headlined in numerous movies up to that point, including

Sam Emerson (Courtesy Kobal)

David Cronenberg's futuristic *eXistenZ* earlier that year, Law won the most acclaim for his part as a pampered society scion expatriate. The role did nothing to deter his snowballing reputation as a sex symbol. With his chiseled features and tanned physique, Law perfectly captured the free–spirited nature of the spoiled but likable layabout. The effort earned Law an Oscar nomination in 2000 for best supporting actor.

Law was born on December 29, 1971 or 1972 (sources vary), in London, England. His parents, Peter and Maggie Law, are retired teachers living in France. According to one source, they named him after the Beatles's song "Hey Jude;" but a *People* article claimed that they named him after the hero of Thomas Hardy's Victorian novel *Jude the Obscure*. Law got his start in acting at about age 12 or 13 when he began touring with the National Youth Musical Theater. Incidentally, an administrator mistakenly thought he was a girl and placed him in a female dormitory until the group's founder, Jeremy James, realized the error. "He didn't complain too loudly," James noted in a *People* article. Law spent the next several years with the troupe. During his time with the National Youth Music Theater, he emerged as a leader. One of his most prominent roles was playing the title character in *Joseph and the Amazing Technicolor Dreamcoat*.

In his teens, Law dropped out of school to pursue acting full–time. He aspired to study drama eventually, but as luck would have it, he kept on landing good roles and working steadily. His first major gig was a recurring role on the British soap opera *Families* in 1990. After that, he became well–respected around Europe for his stage work, appearing in Italy in *Pygmalion*, in London in Euripides's *Ions*, and in the role of Michael in Jean Cocteau's *Les Parents Terribles*. In 1995, the latter play opened on Broadway as *Indiscretions*, and Law was the only original cast member to travel with the show. In New York, he costarred with Kathleen Turner and Roger Rees as the "terrible parents," and for his role, he earned a Theatre World award and a Tony nomination. He also grabbed attention for a scene in which he appeared nude in a bathtub.

Meanwhile, Law landed his first film role as Billy in the 1994 British film *Shopping,* a teen action thriller. On the set, Law met costar Sadie Frost, and the two started to fall in love right away. They had a son, Rafferty, in 1996, and married in 1997. "We did it all in the completely wrong order!," Law proclaimed to Stephen Schaefer in *USA Today.* The family also includes Frost's son, Finley, whom she had in about 1990 with her previous husband, Gary Kemp, of the 1980s band Spandau Ballet.

After his Broadway success, Law returned to film with 1996's *I Love You, I Love You Not,* a coming–of–age romance starring Claire Danes. The next year, he attracted more praise in *Wilde,* starring Vanessa Redgrave and Stephen Fry, as he played the Irish author's young lover, Bosie. "I really liked Bosie because he was the blond bimbo," Law remarked to Judy Gerstel in the *Toronto Star,* "but I also felt it was important that the character be understood, that his dark side and explosions had a reason, and that the audience cared about him and understood him as a sad, weak, kind of mutilated young man." His approach was obviously a success, as he won a London Film Critics Award for the project. Also in 1997, Law played the small but pivotal role of a gay hustler in *Midnight in the Garden of Good and Evil.*

However, Law's biggest role in 1997 was in the science–fiction thriller *Gattaca,* starring Uma Thurman and Ethan Hawke. In it, he plays a former Olympic athlete who ends up embittered and paralyzed after he attempts suicide. Following that, he landed the lead in the 1998 romance, *Music from Another Room,* and also that year worked again with his wife in the British drama *Final Cut.* In addition, 1998 saw him in the lead in the vampire thriller *The Wisdom of Crocodiles.*

Still, Law was far from famous when director David Cronenberg cast him in the 1999 science fiction film *eXistenZ.* Also starring Jennifer Jason Leigh as the designer of a virtual reality game that goes awry, the picture featured Law as a marketing trainee who is swept up into a high–stakes adventure. "It deals with huge human obsessions, such as technology and genetics, and asks: What if we were to go this far?," Law noted in an interview with Dan Yakir reprinted in the *Arizona Republic.* "I also see it as a satire on our reliance on new realities virtual realities and sensory realities whether they're drugs or erotic literature or games or any of those things." He also commented, "It was a challenge to tap into the existentialist manifesto of the piece I read Kierkegaard, Dostoyevsky, Camus."

Although *eXistenZ* increased Law's stature in Hollywood, it would be overshadowed by his next effort, 1999's *The Talented Mr. Ripley.* Based on the 1955 novel by Patricia Highsmith, the thriller cast Law as Dickie Greenleaf, a pampered slacker living off his millionaire father's allowance in a seaside Italian village with his equally well–to–do girlfriend (played by Gwyneth Paltrow). Their upper–crust life of jazz clubs, sailing, and skiing is punctured by the presence of Tom Ripley (Matt Damon), who was sent by Dickie's father to persuade him to return to New York so he can prepare to take over the family business. Things go awry when Tom begins to develop an attraction to Dickie. For the part, Law took saxophone and sailing lessons in order to be more convincing.

Back during his time with the National Youth Music Theater, Law had befriended Ewan McGregor, later of *Trainspotting* and *Phantom Menace* fame. Later, he met another friend who was also in *Trainspotting*, Johnny Lee Miller, at an audition around 1990. In 1995, Law, along with his wife and friends McGregor and Miller, formed a London– based production company, Natural Nylon.

Law and his wife and children have a home in the artsy Primrose Hill neighborhood of London. They and their children often socialize with McGregor, his wife, Eva Mavrakis, and their daughter. A devoted dad, Law's contracts specify time off for his children's school activities, and he and his wife stagger their filmmaking schedules so they are not both on a shoot and away from the kids at the same time. "Your children don't care who you're working with, who your director is," he noted to Schaefer in *USA Today.* "They're interested in playing football in the park and having dinner, and that's real life . Having said that, I love working in films and the theater."

Sources

Periodicals

Arizona Republic, April 22, 1999, The Rep, p. 26.
Entertainment Weekly, June 25, 1999, p. 26.

Los Angeles Magazine, May 1998, p. 88.
People, January 24, 2000, p. 73.
Star Tribune (Minneapolis, MN), October 31, 1997, p. 13E.
Toronto Star, June 5, 1998.
USA Today, October 30, 1997, p. 6D.
Variety, December 13, 1999, p. 105; January 3, 2000, p. 57.

Online

"Jude Law," Internet Movie Database web site, http://us.imdb.com (March 23, 2000).

"Jude Law," Mr. Showbiz web site, http://mrshowbiz.go.com (March 23, 2000).

John leCarre

Author

Born David John Moore Cornwell, October 19, 1931, in Poole, Dorset, England; son of Ronald Thomas Archibald Cornwell and Olive (Glassy) Cornwell; married Alison Ann Veronica Sharp, November 27, 1954 (divorced, 1971); married Valerie Jane Eustace (a book editor), 1972; children: (first marriage) Simon, Stephen, Timothy; (second marriage) Nicholas. Education: Attended Bern University, Switzerland, 1948-49; Lincoln College, Oxford, B.A. (with honors), 1956.

Addresses: *Home*—Cornwall, England. *Agent*—Bruce Hunter, David Higham Ltd., 5–8 Lower John St., Golden Sq., London W1R 4HA, England.

Career

Author. Millfield Junior School, Galstonbury, Somerset, England, teacher, 1954–55; Eton College, Buckinghamshire, England, tutor, 1956–58; freelance illustrator, late 1950s; British Foreign Office, second secretary in Bonn, West Germany (now Germany), 1961–63, consul in Hamburg, West Germany (now Germany),1963–64; full-time novelist, 1964—. Also contributor to periodicals, including *Saturday Evening Post. Military service:* British Army, intelligence corps, beginning 1948.

Awards: Gold Dagger, Crime Writers Association, 1963, Somerset Maugham Award, 1964, and Edgar Allan Poe Award, Mystery Writers of America, 1965, all for *The Spy Who Came in from the Cold;* James Tait Black Memorial Prize, 1977, and Gold Dagger, 1978, both for *The Honourable Schoolboy;* Gold Dagger,

1980; honorary fellow, Lincoln College, Oxford, 1984; Grand Master Award, Mystery Writers of America, 1986; Malparte prize, 1987; Diamond Dagger, Crime Writers Association, 1988; various honorary doctorates.

Sidelights

A master of spy fiction, John le Carre is known for his classic contributions to the genre which include *The Spy Who Came In from the Cold* and *Tinker, Tailor, Soldier, Spy.* Most of his works have centered on Cold War–era espionage, rife with double agents and international intrigue. However, unlike Ian Fleming's flashy hero, James Bond, one of le Carre's main characters, George Smiley—though extraordinary at his career—was a rumpled, bespectacled cuckold. This was just one of the elements that made le Carre's novels realistic, a facet that was often praised. Though the author insisted for years that his stories were fabricated from sheer imagination and that no real spies would ever mistake them for being authentic, by the 1990s, le Carre began to reveal the truth: that he had, indeed, served in British intelligence in some capacity or other from the late 1940s to the early 1960s. Although the demise of the Cold War led some to wonder where he would find subject material, le Carre has persevered, likely because his works concern deeper emotional issues as well as finely–tuned plots. Into the late 1990s, his new books continued to climb the best–seller charts.

John le Carre (pronounced "lay ka–RAY") is a pseudonym of David John Moore Cornwell. He was born in Poole, England, the son of Ronald Thomas Archibald Cornwell and Olive (Glassy) Cornwell. Le Carre's father dropped out of school at age 14 and lived comfortably by investing in businesses, and enjoyed lavish tastes such as owning race-horses. He also ran for office on the Liberal ticket once. However, his ventures were often failures and sometimes fell outside the boundaries of the law, and he was convicted of insurance fraud and sent to prison when le Carre was a child. Subsequently, when le Carre was five, his mother left the family and began living with one of her husband's business colleagues. He did not see her again until he was 21, and his parents ended up getting divorced. His mother would remarry and divorce twice, and le Carre and his older brother Tony—two years his senior—went to live with their grandparents. Their grandfather was a builder and a lay preacher who also served as mayor of Poole.

Due to the unconventional circumstances of his family life, le Carre told Stefan Kanfer in *Time*, "I wondered if my father was some great spy who went off and did nationally vital things." Since his mother was totally separated from her sons and his father was often away, le Carre and his brother would eavesdrop intently for news about their parents, since their grandparents would not discuss the issue openly. It soon became obvious that le Carre, with no other authority figure to depend on, was becoming attached to his brother, so their father sent them to boarding schools 30 miles apart to teach them to be more independent. Nevertheless, the two would often ride their bikes and meet halfway to spend Sundays together. This sense of separation would later be reflected in his fictional characters.

After spending two years at the Sherbourne boys' school, le Carre refused to go back. His father then shipped him off to relatives in Switzerland, where at age 16, he enrolled at the University of Berne. There, he avidly studied German literature and became rather fluent, but he remained lonely. Subsequently, he joined the British army intelligence corps in 1948, and thanks to his language proficiency, was stationed in Vienna. There, he was exposed to war veterans and their many tales. At this time he became a spy for the M.I.5, the British counterpart of the CIA, though he denied it for years after becoming a celebrity author.

When his military stint was over, le Carre followed his father's wishes and went to law school. His brother, Tony, attended Cambridge, but the day after being called to the bar, he left for the United States and later attained a prominent position at a Manhattan advertising agency. Le Carre enrolled at Lincoln College of Oxford University and earned a degree in modern languages in 1956. In 1954 he married Alison Ann Veronica Sharp, whose father was a highly decorated field marshal in the Royal Air Force. Le Carre then worked as a teacher at Millfield Junior School in Glastonbury, Somerset, for a year before returning to Oxford to finish his studies. Throughout this time, he was still employed, secretly, as a British spy. One of his assignments, in fact, involved joining far–left groups on campus at Oxford in order to glean information about them.

After graduating, le Carre left the spy business and took a job as assistant master at Eton College in 1956, but found the experience stifling, so he quit in 1958 and tried his hand at being a freelance illustrator. He was lured back into espionage, and that same year, began working for M.I.5 out of the London headquarters. In 1960 he was transferred to the foreign service, the M.I.6, and worked as second secretary at the British Embassy in Bonn, Switzerland from 1961 to 1963, then was promoted to political consul in Hamburg, Germany, where he spent two years in 1963 and 1964.

During the time that he lived in the Buckinghamshire village of Great Missenden and worked for the M.I.5 in London, le Carre began writing fiction on the commuter train. His first novel, *Call for the Dead*, was released in 1961 and republished in 1964 as *The Deadly Affair*. This effort introduced George Smiley, a brilliant spy who was featured in many of le Carre's subsequent works. This short, stout, unassuming, and nearsighted middle–aged spy, with his ill–fitting suits and nagging wife, is a stark contrast to the dashing James Bond character in Ian Fleming's novels. And, with his degree from Oxford and interest in German literature, he is also somewhat of an alter ego to le Carre. Due to his secret job duties, the author had to publish under a pseudonym. The author chose the name "le Carre," which means "the square" in French, because he remembered seeing it on a shop window in London, although later efforts to locate the business were futile. He admitted to Kanfer, "Perhaps it's a lie I've come to believe." Some journalists have speculated that it was an ironic word play; "square" being slang for someone hopelessly unfashionable.

In *Call for the Dead*, Smiley, who has served with British intelligence for more than three decades, is in charge of investigating the death of a foreign officer. It is suspected that he committed suicide, but Smiley quickly discovers the man has been murdered. Though more of a detective novel than a an espionage tale, le Carre's first book established some common themes that he would include in future writings; namely, as Joan DelFattore summed up in the *Dictionary of Literary Biography*, "the tension between man and his institutions, the sacrifice of truth to expediency, and the loss of humanity in the drive for efficiency." In 1967 the book was adapted as the film *The Deadly Affair*, directed by Sidney Lumier.

Still working for the British embassy and M.I.6, le Carre penned his second novel, *A Murder of Quality*, 1962, which continued to focus on Smiley and again featured an investigation of a murder. Both of his books so far received positive attention, but sold only fairly well. It was his 1963 best–seller, *The Spy Who Came In from the Cold*, that sealed his reputation and allowed him to quit his day job. It is le Carre's first work to branch into actual espionage, but Smiley only appears as a minor character. The key figure is Alec Leamas, a former head of British intelligence in East Germany who wishes to retire but is convinced to take one final assignment. This job leads to a multitude of double– and triple–crossings as the plot unfolds, which creates confusing situations that are an integral part of the psychological complexity of the novel. *The Spy Who Came In from the Cold* was enthusiastically received; fellow spy writer Graham Greene, for one, called it "The best spy novel I have ever read," according to Kanfer. It has sold more than 20 million copies over the years, and received a Gold Dagger award from the Crime Writers Association in 1963, the Somerset Maugham Award in 1964, and the Edgar Allan Poe Award from the Mystery Writers of America in 1965.

The Spy Who Came In from the Cold was particularly praised for its realism. To achieve this, le Carre generously sprinkled his text with slang terms from the spy underworld, such as "mole," a double agent; "babysitter," a bodyguard; and "circus," the London headquarters of the British Secret Service. Some of the words were truly borrowed from the profession—for example, the KGB did actually use "mole"—but many others were invented by le Carre. In addition to introducing new terms to the popular lexicon, *The Spy* also began a public dialogue about the morality, or lack thereof, surrounding the Cold War. The clinical tone of the work provided an appropriate setting for the characters' lack of scruples.

Over the next few years le Carre released the titles *The Looking Glass War*, 1965; *A Small Town in Germany*, 1968; and *The Naïve and Sentimental Lover*,

1968; all of which sold very well, but did not meet the success of *The Spy*. In addition, the books continued to veer from the spy genre into mainstream fiction; *The Naïve and Sentimental Lover* was not even an espionage thriller—it was a psychological romance. However, le Carre's next novel, *Tinker, Tailor, Soldier, Spy*, swung back toward his original genre and again features George Smiley as the protagonist, pitted against a Soviet spy master named Karla. The plot revolves around suspicions that a British agent is actually a "mole" for Russia, and was inspired by a real–life incident that came to a head in 1963, in which a senior member of British intelligence defected to Moscow after several years of being a double agent. Critics were generally quite positive, and the work enjoyed further popularity when it was made into a miniseries on the BBC starring Sir Alec Guinness. Le Carre parlayed this into a trilogy composed of two more installments, *The Honourable Schoolboy*, 1977, and *Smiley's People*, 1980.

In 1983 le Carre abandoned his Cold War setting and tackled a different confrontation, the conflict between Israel and Palestine in *The Little Drummer Girl*. Some applauded his knack for viewing the situation from both angles, but others derided the work as being too far in favor of the Palestine Liberation Organization (PLO). His following work, *A Perfect Spy*, 1986, was an autobiographical novel delving into his troubled past with his father and was hailed as being one of his best works. Subsequently, le Carre released a string of stories dealing with the breakup of the former Soviet Union and the decline of the Cold War, including one set in Panama featuring a half–Jewish, half–Catholic main character. This sparked an unusual combat. When a writer for the *New York Times Book Review* labeled this 1996 work, *The Tailor of Panama*, "anti–Jewish," le Carre defended himself in the Guardian. In turn, writer Salman Rushdie wrote a letter to the *Guardian*, noting that le Carre had earlier sided with those who, for religious reasons, denounced his book *The Satanic Verses*, a work that caused his exile from Iran. Le Carre argued that Rushdie misrepresented his position, and a venomous public letter–writing feud between the two was sparked.

In 1999, le Carre published *Secret & Secret*, released in the United States as *Single & Single*. Some critics were lukewarm, but most were receptive. For instance, Dan Cryer in *Newsday*, while remarking that "the subtle texturing of the prose, the ability to summon up diverse settings, the psychological acuity, the ear for dialogue are impressive," he also commented that it "is anything but a barely disguised screenplay" and indicated that it lacked le Carre's "customary finesse." However, Timothy Garton Ash in the *New Yorker* observed, "This is powerful, evocative writing. And it goes straight to le Carre's greatest theme: betrayal." He noted that *Single & Single,* though it technically contains no spies, is highly representative of le Carre's body of work due to this main thread, as well as the fact that it is a story of father and son. *Single & Single* soon became a best–seller, proving that le Carre did not need a shady political underworld in order to display his knack for gripping fiction—a simple family relationship contained all the intrigue needed to keep readers enthralled.

In 1971 le Carre and his wife, with whom he had three sons, Simon, Stephen, and Timothy, divorced. The next year he married Valerie Jane Eustace, who was a book editor at his publishing house, and they are still together, living in Cornwall, England. They also had a son, Nicholas. Le Carre never reconciled his relationship with his father, whom he consistently painted as a consummate con man. After the author had become a millionaire, his father, who died in the mid–1970s, would often approach him for handouts. Le Carre noted that his father even calculated how much he spent on his son's education—avoiding the fact that many of the debts were never, in fact, paid—and tacked on how much interest he might have earned had he invested the sum in order to develop what he figured was owed to him. "I would pass him the odd couple of grand," he related to Joseph Lelyveld in the *New York Times Magazine,* "but nothing of the dimensions which he felt he was owed." His father also managed to use his son's name to his advantage, to impress women, wrangle free dinners, or stay at luxury hotels. On the other hand, Le Carre supported his mother financially until her death in 1989.

Selected writings; novels

Call for the Dead, Gollancz, 1960, published as *The Deadly Affair,* Penguin, 1966.
A Murder of Quality, Gollancz, 1962, Walker, 1963.
The Spy Who Came in from the Cold, Gollancz, 1963, Coward, 1964.
The Incongruous Spy: Two Novels of Suspense (contains *Call for the Dead* and *A Murder of Quality*), Walker, 1964.
The Looking Glass War, Coward, 1965.
A Small Town in Germany , Coward, 1968.
The Naive and Sentimental Lover, Knopf, 1971.
Tinker, Tailor, Soldier, Spy, Knopf, 1974.
The Honourable Schoolboy, Knopf, 1977.
Smiley's People, Knopf, 1980.
The Quest for Karla (contains *Tinker, Tailor, Soldier, Spy; The Honourable Schoolboy;* and *Smiley's People*), Knopf, 1982.
The Little Drummer Girl, Knopf, 1983.

A Perfect Spy, Knopf, 1986.
The Russia House, Knopf, 1989.
The Secret Pilgrim, Knopf, 1991.
The Night Manager, Knopf, 1993.
Our Game, Knopf, 1995.
John Le Carre: Three Complete Novels (includes *Tinker, Tailor, Soldier, Spy; Honourable Schoolboy;* and *Smiley's People*), Wings, 1995.
The Tailor of Panama, Knopf, 1996.
Single & Single, Scribner, 1999.

Media Adaptations: *The Spy Who Came in from the Cold* was filmed Paramount in 1965; *Call for the Dead* was filmed as *The Deadly Affair* by Columbia in 1967; *The Looking Glass War* was filmed by Columbia in 1970; *Tinker, Tailor, Soldier, Spy* was filmed for television by the BBC in 1980; *The Little Drummer Girl* was filmed by Warner Brothers; *A Perfect Spy* was a seven-hour BBC-TV series and was shown on public television's *Masterpiece Theatre* in the United States; a film version of *The Russia House,* written by Tom Stoppard, directed by Fred Schepisi, and starring Sean Connery and Michelle Pfeiffer, was released in 1990.

Sources

Books

Contemporary Novelists, sixth edition, St. James Press, 1996.
Dictionary of Literary Biography, volume 87: "British Mystery and Thriller Writers since 1940," First Series, Gale Research, 1989.

Periodicals

Entertainment Weekly, July 9, 1993, p. 42.
Harper's Magazine, February 1998, p. 18.
Life, February 28, 1964, p. 39.
Maclean's, April 5, 1999, p. 54.
Newsday, November 10, 1996, p. C37; March 1, 1999, p. B10.
New Statesman, February 5, 1999, p. 18.
New Yorker, March 15, 1999, p. 36.
New York Times, January 6, 1980; March 13, 1983;
New York Times Magazine, September 8, 1974, p. 55; March 16, 1986.
People, September 13, 1993, p. 63.
Sunday Telegraph, November 23, 1997, p. 22.
Time, October 3, 1977, p. 58; July 5, 1993, p. 32.
Toronto Star, March 24, 1999.
U.S. News & World Report, June 19, 1989, p. 59.

Online

David (John Moore) Cornwell, *Contemporary Authors Online*, Gale Group web site, http://galenet.gale.com (October 13, 1999)

Lee Teng–hui

Reuters/Archive Photos

President of the Republic of China (Taiwan)

Born January 15, 1923, in Sanchih, Taiwan; son of a landlord and farmer; married Teng Wen–fui (some sources say Teng Wen–hui), 1946; children: one son, Hsien–wen (deceased), two daughters, An–na and An–ni. *Education:* Attended Kyoto Imperial University; National Taiwan University, B.S. in agricultural economics, 1948; Iowa State University, M.A. in agricultural economics, 1953; Cornell University, Ph.D. in agricultural economics, 1968.

Addresses: *Office*—Office of the President, Chiehshou Hall, 122 Chungking South Rd., Sec. 1, Taipei, China.

Career

National Taiwan University (NTU), instructor, 1948–52, beginning again 1953; Taiwan Provincial Cooperative Bank, research fellow, 1948–57; National Chengchi University, lecturer, beginning 1953; also employed with the Provincial Department of Agriculture and Forestry, c. 1950s; United States–Republic of China Joint Commission on Rural Reconstruction (JCRR), 1957–72, began as specialist, served as head of Rural Economy Division, 1970–72; minister without portfolio in cabinet of Premier Chiang Ching–kuo, 1972–78; mayor of Taipei, 1978–81; governor of Taiwan Province, 1981–84; vice president of Republic of China (Taiwan) under Chiang Ching–kuo, 1984–88, president of Taiwan, 1988—.

Sidelights

Lee Teng–hui (pronounced lee tung WHAY) became president of the Republic of China, also known as Taiwan, in 1988, marking the first time a native–born Taiwanese had become leader of the land, even though 90 percent of the population is Taiwanese. Having received his higher education in the United States, Lee was a highly respected agricultural economist who worked his way up through the government with his contributions to modernization and the increasing economic success of his country. After serving as a cabinet member under Chiang Ching–huo and as mayor of Taipei, he assumed the vice presidency in 1984 and later became president upon Chiang's death. Subsequently, he provoked the wrath of the mainland, the People's Republic of China, for what they saw as his move toward independence. Lee's drive to democratize the island of Taiwan was considered a bold move and provoked China to threaten military strikes. In 1999, once again, Lee raised the ire of China by declaring that Taiwan should operate on a "state–to–state" basis with the mainland, spurring more warnings from China and a flurry of international commentary on Taiwan's future.

Taiwan and China have experienced strained relations since 1949, when the Kuomingtang (KMT), or

Nationalist regime, led by Chiang Kai–shek, was driven from mainland China by the Communists, led by Mao Tse–tung. The KMT and about two million people affiliated with them fled to Taiwan. Subsequently, both the Communists on the mainland in Beijing and the KMT claimed to be the legitimate government of China. The political tension has led to military action at times, but the nation has tried to retain a shaky alliance between the two parts. The KMT, plagued by charges of corruption and the legacy of martial law under Chiang Kai–shek, lost its grip in the United Nations as the governmental seat of China in 1971. Though the United States abandoned their support as well in the late 1970s and officially began to recognize Beijing as its diplomatic peer, Taiwan has continued to enjoy strong economic ties to America.

Lee was born on January 15, 1923, in Sanchih, Taiwan, a small rural village near the Taipei suburb of Tamsui. His father was a landlord who owned a rice and tea farm, and his grandfather was an educated village leader during the Japanese occupation of Taiwan from 1895 to 1945. During this time, few Chinese students were allowed to receive an education, but Lee went through grade school and a Christian middle school, and was one of only four Chinese students in his otherwise Japanese class in high school. Because he had to prove himself among all the Japanese students, he worked diligently and graduated with honors. Thus, he was fortunate enough to attend the prestigious Kyoto Imperial University, although his studies were interrupted by World War II.

After the end of the war, in 1946 Lee returned to Taipei and finished his bachelor of science degree in agricultural economics at National Taiwan University (NTU) in 1948. He stayed at the school as an instructor for four years, then in 1952 went to the United States on a scholarship from Iowa State University in Ames to study agricultural economics. He received a master's degree in 1953 then returned to Taiwan, where he resumed his career as a lecturer and researcher at NTU and National Chengchi University. He also took a position with the Provincial Department of Agriculture and Forestry.

From 1948 to 1957, Lee was also a research fellow at the Taiwan Provincial Cooperative Bank, and in 1957 he joined the United States–Republic of China Joint Commission on Rural Reconstruction (JCRR). He worked his way up from specialist to head of the Rural Economy Division in 1970, serving in that post until 1972. The JCRR modernized agriculture in Taiwan and helped usher in a prosperous era of economic growth. In the meantime, Lee had returned to the United States and earned a doctorate in agricultural economics from Cornell University in 1968.

In 1972, Lee's true political career began when Premier Chiang Ching–kuo appointed him as a minister without portfolio in the cabinet, the youngest person ever to hold such a position. The two had met a year earlier when Chiang was vice–premier and Lee presented an agricultural report to him. Chiang would thereafter serve as Lee's mentor. As a minister, Lee's chief responsibility was to oversee Taiwan's agricultural economy. In the 1970s, he was involved with the government's "Ten Major Construction Projects," and was integral in developing his nation's petrochemical industry. He also helped draft the Act for Agricultural Development and established farmer's associations, irrigation systems, mechanization efforts, and rural health networks. In addition, from 1972 to 1978, Lee helped create a five–year job training program for workers to adapt to Taiwan's increasingly industrialized economy.

Lee was appointed mayor of Taipei in 1978, an important stepping stone to higher levels of politics in Taiwan. Civic advancements surged under his leadership. He authorized major public works such as new freeways, a new sewage system, and the Feitsui Dam, which alleviated water shortages. He also automated city offices and streamlined management, and encouraged participation in local government. In addition, in 1979 he started an annual music festival. In 1981 Lee became governor of the Taiwan Province, a post considered a step removed from the president and premier. In this capacity, he continued to enact agricultural and economic reforms, including promoting rice–crop substitution, better irrigation, and improved produce marketing for farmers, as well as introducing regional planning techniques.

In 1984, the National Assembly elected Lee vice president of the Republic of China under Chiang's leadership. His victory was part of an effort to install more native Taiwanese in politics. In his four years as vice president he became Chiang's close adviser, and as Chiang's health started to decline, Lee was widely viewed as the natural successor. Indeed, when Chiang died of a heart attack in January of 1988 after a decade in power, Lee assumed the presidency, becoming the first ever president of the Republic of China to have been born there, and also the first to hold a doctoral degree. He came to power in the wake of Chiang's efforts to promote democracy: Chiang had allowed an opposition party, the Democratic Progressive Party (PDP), to participate in government; allowed Taiwanese to visit relatives on the mainland; and ended the decades–long martial law.

Many of the old guard, including Madame Chiang Kai–shek and the military establishment, worried that Lee would continue such reforms and thus tried to block his ascension. Meanwhile, the island natives rallied for more freedoms. Lee continued to loosen the political system to allow more native Taiwanese a role in government and administration, thus securing himself a broader support base. Running unopposed, Lee was reelected president of Taiwan in 1990, again amid protest from the established power elite. They had reason for concern: The next year, he revoked the seats of the Chinese officials who had held seats in the National Assembly since 1948 and held free elections. The opposition, the PDP, which called for Taiwan's independence, made a good showing, but the KMT retained their majority.

In an even broader move toward democracy, Lee in 1992 suggested direct presidential elections. In the past, the National Assembly were the only ones to cast votes. The measure was passed in 1994 and the assembly scheduled popular elections in 1996, when Lee's six–year term would end. For his efforts in opening up elections, Lee was nominated for a 1996 Nobel Peace Prize. As the March vote neared, China warned they would flex military might if Taiwan made any more strides toward independence. In what mainland China later admitted was a tactic to influence voters not to support Lee, China began conducting a series of noisy and intimidating military maneuvers off the coast of Taiwan in March. Fearing actual military action, the United States sent two aircraft carriers to the region. Residents were not bullied, however. In fact, China's plan appeared to backfire: Polls indicated that after the military exercises, for the first time ever, more Taiwanese supported independence than a formal reunification, though the overwhelming majority still preferred their current situation of having a tenuous connection to the mainland.

Expected to coast to an easy win in 1996, Lee fulfilled predictions, capturing 54 percent of the vote in a field of four candidates. It was the first time in 4,000 years of Chinese civilization that a leader was popularly elected. Beijing power brokers, unsurprisingly, were unhappy with the outcome, even though Lee had never openly wavered from the official stance that Taiwan was part of China. However, they suspected he was in favor of freedom, as evidenced by his unapproved visit to the United States in 1995 to speak at his alma mater, Cornell. China was especially infuriated because they took it as a sign that Americans were beginning to accept Taiwan as an independent nation, on a diplomatic level.

Lee argued that he was seeking only respect for his country, but in an interview with Maynard Parker in *Newsweek* shortly after his election, he revealed that in his inauguration speech, he would "declare that freedom and democracy are the most important things for the Republic of China on Taiwan and how to defend that freedom and democracy." He also declared Taiwan "a sovereign state" in the actual address, according to Caspar W. Weinberger in *Forbes.* Though Lee also commented frequently about reunification with the mainland, most observers doubted his sincerity, especially when he announced in early 1997 that he wanted to dismantle Taiwan's provincial style of government, which was a direct attack on the idea of reunification. Many were skeptical that he favored reunification due to the fact that his small nation's economic situation was so bright, particularly compared to Communist China's: On the mainland, per capita income stood at $2,000 annually, whereas on Taiwan, it was between $20,000 and $30,000, according to Lee in a 1998 *Time International* interview.

In July of 1999, Lee caused an uproar with an overt gesture toward Taiwanese independence. In a speech, according to an *Economist* article, he stated that instead of China–Taiwan relations being conducted on a "one–China" basis, as they had since 1991 when Taiwan gave up its claim to the mainland, they should be considered on a "special state–to–state" basis. This stopped just short of indicating that Lee felt that Taiwan should be considered an independent nation, but China interpreted the connotation.

Immediately, international commentary began to erupt, with columnists and writers trying to gauge Lee's intent and the reason for his timing, especially since about 70 percent of Taiwan favors keeping the status quo. Whatever the reason for his move, China's response was swift and harsh. According to the *Economist* article, Chinese defense minister Chi Haotian responded, "The Chinese People's Liberation Army is ready at any time to safeguard the territorial integrity of China and smash any attempt to separate the country." Within a week, China also, perhaps not coincidentally, announced that it had developed a neutron bomb, and they soon began flying warplanes over the Taiwan Strait, presumably in yet another attempt at intimidating voters from casting ballot for Lee's successor. The next presidential election was scheduled for the following year, 2000, but Lee had announced his intent to step down.

Lee is a prolific reader who enjoys philosophy, literature, and history; he is especially fond of Immanuel Kant and Confucian humanism. He is also a devout Presbyterian and has claimed that when he retires, he would not mind doing missionary work. He was married in 1949 to Tseng Wen–fui (some sources cite her name as Tseng Wen–hui). They have two daughters, An–na and An–ni, and also had a son, Hsien–wen, who died from cancer in 1983. Lee and his wife, who is also a native of Taiwan, are music lovers and avid golfers.

Sources

Books

Current Leaders of Nations, Gale Research, 1998.
Encyclopedia of World Biography, second edition, Gale
Research, 1998.

Periodicals

Business Week, July 26, 1999, p. 26.
Economist, May 25, 1996, p. 36; January 25, 1997, p.
35; July 17, 1999, p. 35; August 21, 1999, p. 31.

Forbes, July 15, 1996, p. 33.
Maclean's, February 19, 1996, p. 33; March 25, 1996,
p. 24.
National Review, August 9, 1999, p. 24.
Newsweek, April 1, 1996, p. 34; May 20, 1996, p. 38;
December 30, 1996, p. 46.
New York Times, January 15, 1988, p. A6.
People, April 8, 1996, p. 69.
Time, June 5, 1995, p. 34; February 12, 1996, p. 46;
April 1, 1996, p. 45; June 22, 1998, p. 41; July 26,
1999, p. 62; August 23, 1999, p. 20.
Time International, June 22, 1998, p. 27; July 26, 1999,
p. 14.
U.S. News & World Report, July 26, 1999, p. 36.

Lennox Lewis

AP/Wide World Photos

Boxer

Born September 2, 1965, in East London, England; son of Violet (a factory worker).

Addresses: *Home*—London, Canada, and Jamaica. *Office*—c/o International Boxing Hall of Fame Museum, P.O. Box 425, Canastota, NY 13032.

Career

Awards: World Juniors boxing title, 1983; all–Canadian super heavyweight title, 1984–88; won North American amateur title, 1987; Olympic boxing super heavyweight gold medal, 1988; turned pro, 1989; European heavyweight champion, 1990; British heavyweight champion, 1991; Commonwealth heavyweight champion, 1992; World Boxing Federation (WBC) heavyweight champion, 1993–94, 1997—, also claimed World Boxing Association (WBA) and International Boxing Federation (IBF) titles to become undisputed champion, 1999; named member of the Order of the British Empire, 1998.

Sidelights

In late 1999, boxer Lennox Lewis captured titles from all three boxing organizations to become the undisputed heavyweight world champion. He held the World Boxing Federation (WBC) title in 1993 and 1994 and then successfully defended it again beginning in 1997. He then stole the World Boxing Association (WBA) and International Boxing Federation (IBF) belts from Evander Holyfield in 1999. Before defeating Holyfield, his skills were often called into question, even though he held the WBC crown. Because Lewis was often paired with easy opponents and never met up with any of the top fighters like Mike Tyson, Riddick Bowe, or Evander Holyfield, he was not respected as a true champion. Many said he did not possess enough of a "killer instinct" to be successful in the ring. Some, however, pointed out that he was pegged as being soft because of his reserved personality, and others noted that oftentimes, champions simply refused to fight him, or other boxers' promoters could not strike a rich enough deal and thus declined a match. However, after a decisive bout in 1998 against a tough competitor, Andrew Golota, observers began to raise their opinion of him, becoming eager to see if he would hold his own in the ring with Holyfield. Their first match in March of 1999 was declared a draw, and after controversy erupted, they met again that November when Lewis was declared the winner.

Lewis was born on September 2, 1965, and raised in London's working–class East End. His father left the family when he was young. His mother, Violet, a Jamaican immigrant, relocated to Canada with Lewis when he was nine, then sent him back to London to live with his aunt the next year. Two years later, when he was 12 and starting to cause trouble, he reunited with his mother, who was earning decent money by then working in a Styrofoam factory.

His brother, Dennis, told William Nack in *Sports Illustrated* that if Lewis had not escaped their rough London neighborhood, "He'd be in prison today or worse. He was a rogue. He'd jump on my friends and have a go. Picked fights a lot as a kid." Dennis Lewis stayed in London and now runs a restaurant and bar there.

Settling with his mother in Kitchener, Ontario, about 60 miles west of Toronto, Lewis underwent a change for the better, channeling his energy into year–round sports. Though he excelled at Cameron Heights Collegiate High School in football, basketball, volleyball, and track, friends recall that Lewis would go from practicing whatever sport was in season straight to the gym to train for boxing. His first year in Canada, he visited Arnie Boehm's gym in the headquarters of the Kitchener police force and was immediately drawn to the sport, undeterred even after he took his first punch and his eyes watered. "Most kids would say, 'That's enough for me,'" Boehme related to Nack. "Lennox stayed in there."

Eventually Lewis gave up his other pursuits—his varsity fullback position, his slot as power forward on the basketball court, and the shot put—to concentrate on boxing. He became so muscular and skilled in the ring that Boehme found it hard to find competitors his age to match him. At age 15 and 175 pounds, he entered the Ontario intermediate championships for 17–and 18–year olds, but narrowly lost 3–2 to Donovan Ruddock, then age 17. Working his way up through the amateur ranks, he met up with opponents like a young Mike Tyson. "A rough kid, but a really sweet guy, I thought," Lewis commented to Nack.

At the 1983 world juniors in the Dominican Republic, Lewis won the title and went on to capture the first of five straight all–Canadian super heavyweight titles. In addition, he represented Canada at the 1984 Olympic Games in Los Angeles, California, but lost a quarterfinal bout to Tyrell Biggs of the United States. In 1988, Lewis showed up again at the Olympics in Seoul, South Korea, where he took the super heavyweight gold over a battered Riddick Bowe. The referee had ended the match in the second round after two standing–eight counts; after the fight, Bowe looked at Lewis and said, "See you in the pros," reported Nack. That bout marked his final win as an amateur; his overall Canadian amateur record would stand at 75–7.

Subsequently, Lewis joined up with manager Frank Maloney, who rounded financial up backing from investors and convinced the fighter to return to England to make his name as a professional. After signing with Maloney in April of 1989, Lewis hired former U.S. Marine John Davenport as his trainer. He kicked off his professional career by knocking out Al Malcolm in the second round in a London match. Over the next couple of years, Lewis honed his talents, becoming the European champion in October of 1990 after beating Jean Chanet in the sixth round. At this point, some dubbed him the "great Brit hope."

After losing a ten–round match to former football player Levi Billups in February of 1992, Lewis replaced Davenport with trainer Pepe Correa, who had previously worked with Sugar Ray Leonard. In October that year, Lewis met up with Ruddock again, who had by now developed a reputation as a formidable competitor. Fans were thus taken aback when Lewis sent him to the mat in the first round with a powerful right, then knocked him out the next round. This put Lewis in the running for the WBC heavyweight title, which his former Olympic opponent Bowe held at the time. Many were eager to see them contend in the ring, but Bowe declined to defend his WBC title against Lewis, and in a theatrical gesture, literally threw his title belt in a trash can. Therefore, after just 22 pro matches, Lewis by default became the WBC heavyweight champion in 1993, the first British fighter in the twentieth century to do so.

After winning by default, Lewis signed a contract with an American promotion company, Main Events, to fight in several high–profile, high–stakes bouts. In May of 1993, he fought Tony Tucker in Las Vegas, Nevada, winning $9 million while defending his title. This made him the first British heavyweight to win a title in the ring since 1897. Still, fans were not convinced that his record to that point without a doubt defined him as the champ; as Pat Putnam wrote in *Sports Illustrated*, "Clearly he has some talent, but he needs more work."

In October of 1993 Lewis defended his title again, this time against Frank Bruno. It marked the first time during the century that two British subjects fought for the heavyweight championship. However, the bout did little to increase anyone's opinion of Lewis's skill. Though admired among Brits (his trunks in the match were stitched with the boast, "THE REAL BRIT," according to Putnam), Bruno was not a top contender. Viewers were thus greatly surprised when he delivered a powerful jab that bloodied the titleholder's face, and Lewis hit back with little force. As Putnam observed, "The few attacks that Lewis was able to muster seemed spurred by anger, as if he'd been goaded by a bully until he could take no more." Though it appeared that Bruno was ahead after six rounds, the judges did not agree, and Lewis finally won by knockout in the seventh round.

In his third shot at defending his title, Lewis met up with American boxer Phil Jackson, as commentators again complained that he outmatched his opponent. He won that fight—and a guaranteed $4 million—with a technical knockout in the eighth round after the referee halted the action. Though the bout lifted his record to 25–0 with 21 knockouts, Daryl Bell of the *Philadelphia Tribune* groused, "What the people don't need or want to see is another championship bout with Lewis going against a relatively hopeless opponent such as Jackson."

After that, Lewis was paired in September of 1994 against Oliver McCall at London's Wembley Stadium. Ira Berkow in the *New York Times* noted, "McCall is a top–ranked contender, though he will be a decided underdog against the hard–punching Lewis." Thus, it was all the more startling when McCall knocked out the previously undefeated Lewis in the second round. Maloney, Lewis's manager, later claimed he intended to file a protest with the WBC for a rematch, claiming that the referee, Lupe Garcia, had stopped the fight prematurely by counting too quickly. "He landed a great right punch," Lennox admitted in an Associated Press article in *Newsday*. "I tried to get up too fast. I was a little wobbly. But I was really surprised at the referee's decision to stop the fight so early." Garcia defended his decision, however, and his result was upheld.

Lewis subsequently broke with his trainer, Correa, and hired Emmanuel Steward, who worked previously with McCall. He then worked on improving his jabs and combinations, and throughout 1995 won matches against Lionel Butler, Justin Fortune, and Tommy Morrison. He also saw a victory in the ring with Ray Mercer in May of 1996, but Jamie Dettmer in *Insight on the News* called the bout "a near–disastrous performance" and remarked, "The judges saved Lewis." Still, the boxer sought out tougher competitors. He was eager to fight Mike Tyson, but declined an offer of $10 million, holding out for more. Later in 1996, Tyson's promoters could not reach a deal with Lewis's handlers, and Tyson was forced to give up his WBC title because of it.

In February of 1997, Lewis instead fought McCall once again for the WBC championship. The odd spectacle ended when "McCall essentially stopped fighting in the middle of the third round and began reacting as if in a daze," according to Greg Logan in *Newsday*. The referee halted the fight in the fifth round when McCall continued to refuse to defend himself; he then started crying and fled the ring. Media accounts pointed out that McCall had been suffering from drug and alcohol addiction, and that promoter Dino Duva had previously pleaded with McCall's promoter, Don King, to call off the fight. Following that, Lewis retained his title after a match in July of 1997 against Nigeria's Henry Akinwande. In yet another strange chapter in Lewis's career, Akinwande was disqualified in the fifth round due to excessive holding.

When Lewis met up against Polish boxer Andrew Golota in October of 1997, many were expecting another strange match. Golota earned the nickname of the "Foul Pole" for his reputation as a dirty fighter, and the bout was coming on the heels of the infamous episode of June of 1997, in which Tyson bit off part of Evander Holyfield's ear. However, Lewis managed to swiftly knock out Golota in the first round. Up until then, despite his previous WBC title, "Lewis was…considered a fringe player, mostly because he had never engaged any of the marquee fighters of the day," according to Richard Hoffer in *Sports Illustrated*. After the Golota fight, Hoffer added, "It was reasonable to consider Lewis among the elite, a contender for a unified title." In his next fight, Lewis defeated Shannon Briggs in the fifth round in Atlantic City in March of 1998.

By the close of 1998, promoters announced that Lewis would meet up with WBA and IBF titleholder Holyfield on March 13, 1999 at New York's Madison Square Garden. It was the biggest boxing event there since Muhammad Ali had met Joe Frazier in 1971, and Lewis stood to earn at least $9.5 million, while Holyfield was promised $20 million. The winner would thus hold title belts from all three separate boxing organizations, becoming the first undisputed champion since Riddick Bowe in 1992. However, when all was said and done, Lewis and Holyfield's much–awaited clash ended in a draw, causing Hoffer in *Sports Illustrated* to moan that the fight "was as definitive a disappointment as is possible to deliver." Though the fighters seemed to deliver their all, it was the decision this time that was highly controversial: Many were certain that Lewis was the winner, and the outrage was so great that all three boxing authorities ordered a rematch within six months. Boxing legend Ali, meanwhile, publicly called the fight "the biggest fix in fight history," as a *Jet* article reported. The two fighters agreed on terms for a rematch and were guaranteed a purse of $15 million each.

That November, Lewis met Holyfield again, this time in Las Vegas. Going into it, Lewis was favored due to his earlier performance in New York. Also,

Lewis was three years younger, at 34, and bigger, standing six feet, five inches tall and 242 pounds to Holyfield's six feet, two inches and 212 pounds. Though the 12–round fight was not one of the more exciting moments in sports history, it did result in an undisputed heavyweight champion after receiving a unanimous decision for Lewis from the three judges. However, in yet another unconventional twist, the International Boxing Federation initially refused to give him the belt, saying that his promoters did not pay a $300,000 sanctioning fee. Lawyers soon worked out a deal and Lewis thus reigned as the undisputed champion, bringing that title to Britain for the first time in over 100 years.

A multifaceted personality, Lewis enjoys a wide range of interests outside of boxing. His official web site states that in addition to other sports such as basketball, football, tennis and swimming, he also owns a horse, Friendly Warning, and likes to play chess. He also plays video games and enjoys "walking on Jamaican beaches with his mother, Violet." The site goes on, "Violet is not only very pleasant company, supportive and loving, but also, according to Lennox, the greatest cook in the whole world." Some of his "favorites," as the web site lists, include not only eating his "Mum's West Indian cooking," but also rum raisin and chocolate ice cream. He also lists Bob Marley as his favorite singer, not surprising for someone who also wears his hair in dreadlocks.

Using money he has earned boxing, Lewis in 1995 established a private school in east London for disadvantaged children called Lennox Lewis College. The people Lewis most admires, including his boxing idol, Muhammed Ali, are apartheid activist and former South African president Nelson Mandela, and civil rights activists Malcolm X and Dr. Martin Luther King, Jr. He keeps homes in Canada and Jamaica as well as London, and was named a member of the Order of the British Empire in 1998.

Sources

Periodicals

Independent, October 8, 1994; February 10, 1997, p. S15.

Insight on the News, June 3, 1996, p. 37.

Jet, October 14, 1996, p. 46; July 28, 1997, p. 56; March 29, 1999, p. 51; April 5, 1999, p. 53; April 12, 1999, p. 48.

Knight–Ridder/Tribune News Service, December 1, 1998; March 15, 1999.

Maclean's, November 29, 1999, p. 80.

Newsday, September 25, 1994, p. 3.

New York Times, September 3, 1994, sec. 1, p. 27; October 1, 1997, p. C5; November 9, 1999, p. A27; November 13, 1999, p. B17; November 15, 1999, p. D1; November 16, 1999, p. C31.

Philadelphia Tribune, May 10, 1994.

Sports Illustrated, October 28, 1991, p. 102; February 1, 1993, p. 38; May 17, 1993, p. 58; October 11, 1993, p. 36; October 13, 1997, p. 68; March 22, 1999, p. 60; November 15, 1999, p. 54; November 22, 1999, p. 60.

Sunday Telegraph, February 21, 1999.

Online

Lennox Lewis official web site, http://www.lennox–lewis.com (January 20, 2000).

Bai Ling

AP/Wide World Photos

Actor

Born October 10, 1970, in the People's Republic of China; became U.S. citizen, c. 1998; daughter of a music professor and a literature professor.

Addresses: *Agent*—Agency for the Performing Arts, 888 7th Ave., £602, New York, NY 10106; 9200 Sunset Blvd. £900, Los Angeles, CA 90069.

Career

Performer in entertainment division of People's Liberation Army, People's Republic of China, c. 1984–87; stage and film actor in People's Republic of China, late 1980s; actor in the U.S., 1994 . Television appearances include movie *Dead Weekend*, 1995; and series *Angel*, 2000 . Film appearances include *Hu guang* (*Arc Light*), 1988; *The Crow*, 1994; *Dead Funny*, 1994; *Nixon*, 1995; *Red Corner*, 1997; *Row Your Boat*, 1998; *Somewhere in the City*, 1998; *Wild Wild West*, 1999; and *Anna and the King*, 1999.

Awards: Golden Apple award for female discovery of the year, and National Board of Review award for breakthrough performance for *Red Corner*, both 1997.

Sidelights

Chinese actor Bai Ling became a major star in her native country before leaving in the early 1990s to attend college and try to build her career in the United States. After a few minor roles, she made waves in 1997 with the thriller *Red Corner*, starring Richard Gere. In it, her character, Shen Yuelin, is a child of China's Cultural Revolution, like Bai herself. And like Shen, Bai takes a stance that could have dire consequences in order to state her beliefs. She knew that just making the film itself could lead to her permanent exile from her homeland, where she spent half of each year and was very connected to her family. But spurred by her refusal to be cowed, she went ahead with it. "It's like my character says, 'I do not wish to be silent anymore,'" Bai told Julia Szabo in *Newsday*. After the film's release, China declared Bai a traitor, banned her from entering the country, and made life difficult for her parents at their jobs. She continued to work in the United States, and in 1999, she caused a stir when she cut off her waist– length locks to appear in *Anna and the King*.

Bai Ling, which means "white spirit" in Mandarin Chinese, was born toward the end of the Cultural Revolution, which cracked down on intellectuals and sent many to "re–education" camps in rural areas. Her parents, both professors, were thus targets, so they sent Bai to live with her grandmother in the Szechwan province. Her father is now a professor of music; her mother, a former actor and dancer, teaches literature in Japan. Bai later reunited with her parents, but by then, she recalled to Szabo in *Newsweek*, she was "extremely shy and quiet. I lived more inside of myself and I was afraid of a lot of things, so another part of me needed to come out and be expressed." After watching a film for the first time, she retreated to her room and pretended to be the female actor she saw on screen. That was her only preparation for drama.

At age 14, Bai joined the People's Liberation Army as a member of the performing troupe and traveled to Tibet. For three years, she entertained troops with singing, dancing, and acting in musicals. "The altitude is so high in the Himalayas that it is very difficult to sing," she explained to Mal Vincent in the *Virginian–Pilot*, reprinted in the *St. Louis Post–Dispatch*. "We needed oxygen tanks." When Bai tried to keep a diary during that time, she found she was not free to express herself as she chose. A superior told her he needed to see it. After that, she began to use code names for the people she was writing about, but eventually became disillusioned at the repression, and stopped writing.

Another blow came when Bai, who had aspired to major in literature and become a journalist, was rejected by the University of Shanghai. Eventually, though, she became a professional actor, appearing in several plays and films, and reaching celebrity status in her nation. However, in 1989, when the army fired at student protestors and drove tanks over them in Tiananmen Square, she was in the thick of the demonstrators. She recalled to Yahlin Chang in *Newsweek*, "I saw a lot of people die. You know, we did not believe they were going to shoot. When the army came, we lay on the ground. When the gunshots stopped, we got up but a lot of people next to me could not. Afterwards, it rained for a whole month. The sky was mourning."

Following this melee, Bai left her country and began attending New York University's film school and waiting tables. She knew no English at the time. Before long, she was cast as the lead in Terence Malick's esteemed play *Sansho the Bailiff*, produced at the Brooklyn Academy of Music. In 1994, she landed a villainous role in *The Crow*, then showed up as a Chinese interpreter in 1995's *Nixon*. Bai also appeared in 1998 with Sandra Bernhard in *Somewhere in the City* as Lu Lu, a timid immigrant who gets a radical makeover.

The breakthrough picture for Bai, however, was 1997's *Red Corner*, costarring Richard Gere. In it, she plays Shen Yuelin, a court–appointed attorney who risks her freedom in order to defend an American, Jack Moore (Gere), accused of murder in Beijing. Jack, who is trying to arrange a business deal with the Chinese government on a satellite project, awakes to find he is covered in blood, and a beautiful woman is found dead in his hotel room. The film eventually delves into messages about Chinese nationalism and bureaucracy, and gives a rare glimpse into what was billed as an authentic representation of the Chinese justice system. In the film, it is revealed that the courts there have a 99 percent conviction rate, despite the fact that the average trial is less than four hours long. In addition, anyone found guilty of a capital offense is shot within a week, and the family receives a bill for the bullet. "If anything, the system is more strict than pictured," Bai revealed to Vincent. However, she explained to Chang, "This is not an anti–China movie. We're criticizing the judicial system because we want to make things better."

In 1997, Bai won a Golden Apple award for female discovery of the year and a National Board of Review award for breakthrough performance. But Bai knew that doing *Red Corner* might carry serious ramifications for her. Gere, a well–known activist on behalf of the liberation of Tibet, was already one of the most scorned names in China, and was blacklisted in the country. Also, the director of *Seven Years in Tibet*, Jean–Jacques Annaud, and its star, Brad Pitt, were both barred from visiting Tibet. In addition, the film's release coincided with a visit to America by Chinese leader Jiang Zemin. Bai told Maximillian Potter in *Premiere*, "I just pray. I hope nothing happens. I'm aware of the gravity."

Bai was, however, condemned by the Chinese government and prohibited from returning. After this, she ended up gaining American citizenship. In 1999, she went on to appear as the sultry Miss East in *Wild Wild West* with Will Smith and Kevin Kline, but she began to attract major attention later as Tuptim in *Anna and the King*. For the role, she shaved off all of her hair, which was more than three feet long. It had never been cut, besides a slight trim each year. Bai hoped they could create the illusion by using a bald cap, but she had too much hair to fit into it. "I debated for three months and the day they cut it, it felt like surgery," she told Louis B. Hobson in the *Calgary Sun*.

Anna and the King concerns a widowed British schoolteacher during the 1860s who travels to Siam to tutor the offspring of King Mongkut. In it, Jodie Foster plays Anna while Chow Yun–fat portrays King Mongkut. Bai plays a concubine who abandons the palace in order to be with her true love, a monk. Her hair was shorn because her character goes into hiding in the monastery. Although she cried the entire day that she got her hair cut, she was later happy with the new look. As she commented to Emily Dougherty in *Harper's Bazaar*, "I'm dressing more modern. It's helped me say goodbye to my old life, hello future."

After *Anna and the King*, Bai had a guest role beginning in early 2000 on the WB network series *Angel*, playing Jhiera, a leather–wrapped princess from another dimension. "It was supercool," she remarked to Shawna Malcolm in *TV Guide*. "She drives trucks, kicks ass and tries to seduce Angel." Afterward, she signed a contract to play the same character on a recurring basis. Bai is dating singer Chris Isaak and is reportedly writing a book in English about her time with the army in Tibet.

Sources

Periodicals

Asiaweek, April 10, 1998, p. 35.

Calgary Sun, December 20, 1999, p. 45.

Harper's Bazaar, December 1999, p. 142.

New Republic, November 24, 1997, p. 30.

Newsday, October 30, 1997, p. B3.

Newsweek, November 10, 1997, p. 78.

People, November 10, 1997, p. 23; November 17, 1997, p. 220; May 11, 1998, p. 129.

Premiere, November 1997, p. 96.

St. Louis Post–Dispatch, November 5, 1997, p. E3.

Time International, July 5, 1999, p. 48.

Toronto Sun, January 7, 2000, p. 47.

TV Guide, February 5, 2000, p. 5.

USA Today, October 31, 1997, p. 1D; December 3, 1999, p. 1E.

Variety, August 4, 1997, p. 35; November 3, 1997, p. 98; December 6, 1999, p. 83.

Online

"Ling, Bai," Internet Movie Database web site, http://us.imdb.com (March 23, 2000).

Lucy Liu

Actor

Born December 2, 1968, in Queens, NY; daughter of an engineer/watch vendor and biochemist/salesperson. *Education:* University of Michigan, degree in Asian studies.

Addresses: *Office*—c/o Ally McBeal, Manhattan Beach Studios, 1600 Rosencrans Ave., Bldg. 4A, 3rd Fl., Manhattan Beach, CA 90266.

Career

Worked as a secretary, an aerobics instructor, and a hostess at a rib joint; began acting professionally, early 1990s; television appearances include episodes of *Beverly Hills, 90210,* 1991; *L.A. Law,* 1993; *Coach,* 1994; *Home Improvement,* 1995; *Hercules: The Legendary Journey,* 1995; *ER,* 1995; *The X–Files,* 1996; *Nash Bridges,* 1996; *Jonny Quest: The New Adventures,* 1997; and *NYPD Blue,* 1997; series *Pearl,* 1996–97; and *Ally McBeal,* 1998—; and movie *Riot,* 1997.

Film appearances include *Bang,* 1995; *Jerry Maguire,* 1996; *Guy,* 1996; *Gridlock'd,* 1997; *City of Industry,* 1997; *Flypaper,* 1997; *Love Kills,* 1998; *Payback,* 1999; *True Crime,* 1999; *The Mating Habits of the Earthbound Human,* 1999; *Play It to the Bone,* 1999; *Molly,* 1999; *Shanghai Noon,* 2000; and *Charlie's Angels,* 2000.

Sidelights

After a series of minor film roles, Lucy Liu burst onto the television screen in 1998 as the litigious Ling Woo on the popular prime–time series

Ally McBeal. She won legions of fans playing the icy–cold attorney that people love to hate; in fact, the *Wizard of Oz'* s Wicked Witch of the West theme begins to play whenever she enters a room. Though the part has been criticized for perpetuating the Asian "dragon lady" stereotype, it grew to become more multifaceted by showing occasional glimpses of raw emotion. The *Ally McBeal* gig catapulted Liu from being a minor walk–on or supporting player to a top star working alongside the likes of Mel Gibson and Jackie Chan. Then, in 2000 she was slated to appear with Drew Barrymore and Cameron Diaz as one of a trio of female crime fighters in a film version of the 1970s television series *Charlies' Angels.*

Liu was born on December 2, 1968, in the Queens borough on New York City. The daughter of Chinese immigrants, she was raised in an Italian neighborhood. Her father was an engineer in China and her mother was a biochemist, but they met in New York, where they were both limited by the language barrier. Her father turned to selling watches in Atlantic City, New Jersey, and her mother worked at Macy's, among other employment. "My mom had so many jobs," Liu told Mike Hughes for the *Gannett News Service.* "I was pretty much a latchkey kid. Just come home from school and watch television."

Both Liu and her sister did not speak English until they enrolled in school. Though she went through a period where she wanted to be more American, she later embraced it and studied Asian languages and cultures at the University of Michigan in addition to art. Still an avid artist and photographer, she has exhibited mixed–media collages in solo shows in SoHo and California. As a senior in college, Liu began to act, winning the lead in a production of *Alice in Wonderland*. Afterward, as she pursued her career in New York theater, she worked as a secretary, an aerobics instructor, and a hostess at a rib joint. During this time she landed a gig in a production of *M. Butterfly*, and has continued to act on stage with the Met Theater Development Ensemble in Los Angeles.

Liu's Hollywood acting career began with minor parts on series such as *L.A. Law, NYPD Blue, Coach,* and *Beverly Hills, 90210* (playing Courtney, the waitress as the Peach Pit). She also played the recurring guest character Mei–Sun Leow, a woman with a child who has AIDS, on *ER* in 1995, and had a spot on *The X–Files* in 1996. Meanwhile, she made her film debut in 1995's *Bang* as a prostitute, and also had a supporting role as an extremely logical student on the short–lived 1996–97 sitcom *Pearl*, starring Rhea Perlman. She also had small roles in the blockbuster 1996 film *Jerry McGuire* and some other lesser–known projects.

In 1998, Liu's career took an upswing when she sashayed onto the set of the hit television series *Ally McBeal*, a quirky series about an East Coast law firm. At first, she auditioned for the part of cut-throat attorney Nelle Porter and was immediately disillusioned. Liu was the only woman of color at the try–out and assumed that as was often the case, she would be overlooked for a typical blonde actor. The part went to Portia de Rossi, but a few days later the show's producer, David Kelley, called Liu back with a role he wrote especially for her.

Liu first appeared on the September 21, 1998, episode in what was meant to be a guest spot, but over-whelming fan reaction led to a regular role. "I guess [Kelley] saw, you know, some kind of energy that I could bring to the Ally McBeal cast to cause a little conflict, a little trouble," Liu commented to Claire Bickley in the *Toronto Sun*. Indeed, Liu's character of Ling Woo ended up suing a Howard Stern–type radio host for perpetuating sexual harassment and filed a case against a plastic surgeon's nurse for claiming her breasts were the work of the doctor when in fact they were unaltered. She even thought about suing the law firm's own Fish (Greg Germann), with whom she embarked on a tentative romantic relationship, when his former girlfriend appeared nude in front of her. Adding to her aggressive demeanor, she yelled at a man in wheel-chair to watch where he was going. In later episodes, though, Ling was revealed to have breakthroughs of feeling.

Meanwhile, Liu was showing no sympathy on the set of the 1999 Mel Gibson film *Payback,* in which she plays a merciless dominatrix hooker. She followed up that same year with roles in *True Crime* with Clint Eastwood, *Molly* with Elizabeth Shue, *The Mating Habits of Earthbound Humans,* and *Play It to the Bone*. Also that year she was named one of "the 50 most beautiful people in the world" by *People* magazine.

Then, in 2000, Liu starred opposite action star Jackie Chan in *Shanghai Noon,* a new twist on Westerns. In it, Chan's character, Chon Wang, is a bumbling Imperial Guard to the Chinese emperor who volunteers to rescue the kidnapped Princess Pei Pei (Liu), who has been taken away to the Wild West. Also, Liu was slated to appear in an updated *Charlie's Angels,* which was due out in late 2000 despite several script rewrites and reports that shooting was postponed for a day after she and costar Bill Murray got into a heated argument on the set.

In addition to creating art, Liu enjoys skiing, rock climbing, horseback riding, and martial arts (she even knows knife and stick fighting). She also plays the accordion. "I somehow think (my dad) was very influenced by the Osmond family He really wanted us to play musical instruments," she remarked to Hughes. She began on the violin, but failing miserably, switched to accordion. As it happens, her Ally McBeal costar, Germann, also plays accordion—they even share the same instructor—and the two of them often jam together between takes on the set.

Sources

Periodicals

Gannett News Service, February 2, 1999.
Newsweek, November 30, 1998, p. 80.
People, May 10, 1999, p. 121.
Playboy, August 1999, p. 119.
Rolling Stone, March 4, 1999, p. 97.
Toronto Sun, February 8, 1999, p. 44.
TV Guide, November 14, 1998, p. 3.
Washington Post, April 25, 1999, p. Y7.

Online

"Lucy Liu," Internet Movie Database web site, http://us.imdb.com (July 7, 2000).
"Butchered *Angels* Script Grows Hellish," Mr. Showbiz web site, April 25, 2000, http://mrshowbiz.go.com (July 7, 2000).

Cheech Marin

Actor, comedian, and screenwriter

Born Richard Anthony Marin, July 13, 1946, in Los Angeles, CA; son of Oscar (a police officer) and Elsa (a secretary; maiden name, Meza) Marin; married Rikki Morley (a homemaker and actor), November 1, 1975 (divorced) married Patti Heid (a computer artist), 1984; children: (from first marriage) Carmine, (from second marriage) Joe, Jasmine. Education: California State University, Northridge, B.A. in English.

Addresses: *Home*—San Francisco, CA. *Agent*—Creative Artists Agency, 9830 Wilshire Blvd., Beverly Hills, CA 90212. Career

Joined improvisational theater group City Works, and comedy team Cheech and Chong with Tommy Chong; performed in clubs and concert halls throughout the United States and Canada. Has released several comedy albums, children's albums, and a children's book.

Television appearances include movies *Get out of My Room*, 1985; *The Cisco Kid*, 1994; and *The Courtyard*, 1995; series *The Golden Palace*, 1992; *Santo Bugito* (voice-over for animation), 1995; and *Nash Bridges*, 1996; specials *Get Out of My Room*, 1985; *Charlie Barnett Terms of Enrollment*, 1986; *Mother Goose Rock 'n' Rhyme*, 1990; *La Pastorella*, 1991; and *Latino Laugh Festival*, 1997; and episodes of *The Tracey Ullman Show*, 1987; *Married...with Children*, 1987; *Dream On*, 1990; and *Tracey Takes On...*, 1996. Film appearances include *Up in Smoke*, 1978; *Cheech and Chong's Next Movie*, 1980; *Cheech and Chong's Nice Dreams*, 1981; *Things Are Tough All Over*, 1982; *It Came from Hollywood*, 1982; *Still Smokin'*, 1983; *Yellowbeard*, 1983; *Group Madness*, 1983; *Cheech and Chong's The Corsican Brothers*, 1984; *After Hours*, 1985; *Echo Park*, 1986; *Born in East L.A.*, 1987; *Fatal Beauty*, 1987; *Oliver & Company* (voice-over for animation), 1988; *Ghostbusters II*, 1989; *Rude Awakening*, 1989; *Troop Beverly Hills*, 1989; *Far Out Man*, 1990; *The Shrimp on the Barbie*, 1990, *FernGully: The Last Rainforest* (voice-over for animation), 1993; *The Lion King* (voice-over for animation), 1994; *Ring of the Musketeers*, 1994; *A Million to Juan*, 1994; *The Magic of the Golden Bear: Goldy III*, 1994; *Charlie's Ghost Story*, 1994; *Mr. Payback: An Interactive Movie*, 1995; *Desperado*, 1995; *From Dusk Till Dawn*, 1996; *The Great White Hype*, 1996; *Tin Cup*, 1996; and *Paulie*, 1998.

Director of films, including *Born in East L.A.*, 1987. Director of television specials, including *Get Out of My Room*, 1985. Producer of six episodes of a comedy series for Fox Television starring Latino comedy team Culture Clash, 1991; narrator for audio books, including *The Milagro Beanfield War* by John Nichols. Writing credits include films *Up in Smoke*, 1978; *Cheech & Chong's Next Movie*, 1980; *Cheech & Chong's Nice Dreams*, 1981; *Things are Tough All Over*, 1982; *Still Smokin'*, 1983; *Cheech & Chong's The Corsican Brothers*, 1984; and *Born in East L.A.*, 1987.

Awards: Grammy Award (with Tommy Chong), 1973, for *Los Cochinos.*

Sidelights

Though he made his name as half of the doped–out comedy duo of Cheech and Chong in the 1970s, Cheech Marin cleaned up his image and has found success playing a variety of sidekick roles since his split with Tommy Chong in the mid–1980s. The pair became icons with their run of comedy albums and movies based on their drug–loving hippie characters, but Marin grew tired of the shtick and wanted to grow creatively. His first project after the demise of Cheech and Chong was the popular film *Born in East L.A.,* which he wrote, directed, and starred in. It provided belly laughs as it gently tackled Hispanic stereotypes and the issue of illegal immigration. Subsequently, Marin found a string of small roles in other films and television series, until finally landing a breakthrough part in 1996's *Tin Cup,* starring Kevin Costner, Don Johnson, and Rene Russo. This led to a costarring gig with Johnson on the highly–rated *Nash Bridges,* in which he lends a dose of comedy, albeit different than his earlier brand, to the police drama. In addition, he continues to pursue his own projects on the side, such as the well–received 1992 children's album, *My Name is Cheech, The School Bus Driver.*

Marin was born on July 13, 1946, in Los Angeles, California, to Oscar and Elza (Meza) Marin. His mother is a secretary and his father is a retired police officer. Marin got his nickname, "Cheech," from a Mexican snack food called chicharron, which are deep–fried pork skins. As a third–generation Mexican American, Marin did not learn Spanish as a child—his parents spoke Spanish when they were children, but began speaking English when they went to school, and raised Marin in an English–speaking home as well, although he learned some Spanish later. He affects the thick Latino accent that audiences are used to strictly for entertainment value. Growing up, Marin's sense of humor was influenced by popular sitcoms of the day, such as *I Love Lucy, The Red Skelton Show,* and *The Danny Thomas Show.*

Marin and his three sisters were raised in the mostly black area of South Central Los Angeles until his family moved to the predominantly white San Fernando Valley when he was ten. A straight–A student in school, he worked his way through college as a janitor and a dishwasher and earned a bachelor of arts degree in English from California State University at Northridge, with hopes of becoming a writer. After graduating, Marin moved to Canada to avoid being drafted into the Vietnam War during the late 1960s. In Vancouver, British Columbia, in 1969, he joined a topless improvisational theater group called City Works. It was "as close to Nirvana as I'll get in this lifetime," Marin related in *GQ.* "I stayed up all night and smoked hash with naked women."

At City Works, Marin met Tommy Chong, the club owner who also ran the troupe, and when the group disbanded in 1970, Marin and Chong, professionally dubbed "Cheech and Chong," formed a rock/comedy act and began touring the United States (Marin evaded military service at this point by receiving a 4–F classification due to a ski injury). Their music eventually fizzled out to make more room for the humor, and Cheech and Chong's unique style of comedy caught on like wildfire, especially among young audiences. They lampooned the culture of sex, drugs, and rock–and–roll, parodying hippies and pot smokers in specific, and adding a dash of potty humor as well. Their several comedy albums, including *Los Cochinos,* 1973, which won a Grammy Award for best comedy album, were staples in many record collections among high schoolers and college students.

Thanks to the success of their recordings, Marin and Chong landed a deal for a feature film, released in 1978. In *Up in Smoke,* they continued to portray two forgetful, hapless buffoons whose pursuit of a good high leads them into a series of misadventures. Though it was produced on a low budget, it was highest–grossing film of the year and became a cult favorite, even though critical reaction was mixed. Subsequently, the pair teamed up for the aptly title *Cheech and Chong's Next Movie,* 1980, which also featured Marin's first wife, Rikki Morley. After that, they played a couple of ice cream vendors who also deal drugs in 1981's *Nice Dreams,* and then acted in dual roles in 1982's *Things are Tough All Over,* as wealthy Middle Easterners and as their usual characters. This film began to veer away from the depiction of heavy drug use, as in their earlier films, but they were back as drug culture icons in *Still Smokin',* 1983, which combined rock concert footage and a plot involving the Amsterdam Film Festival. They also appeared together in *Yellowbeard,* 1983, and in Martin Scorsese's *After Hours,* 1985, as incompetent thieves. In 1984, *Cheech and Chong's The Corsican Brothers* adapted the short story by Alexandre Dumas into a comedy, but it would be their final film collaboration.

By the mid–1980s, Marin and Chong's creative differences split them up. Marin had grown weary of the Cheech and Chong characters and wanted to explore new directions, whereas Chong wanted to keep doing their usual act. Marin soon wrote, directed, and starred in the film *Born in East L.A.*, a farce depicting a United States citizen of third–generation Mexican descent who is inadvertently deported to Mexico after an illegal immigrant raid. Marin explained in a *Cineaste* interview that it was based on a true story that he read in the newspaper. He related, "At first I wrote a song, a sort of takeoff on Bruce Springsteen's "Born in the U.S.A." We made a video of that which was a big success, so then I decided to make the movie." The film details the character's time in Tijuana working in a variety of odd jobs—including orange seller, mariachi musician, tattoo artist, and fake passport dealer—to get a smuggler to return him to the United States.

Although *Born in East L.A.* got mixed reviews, it did well at the box office and won prizes for script and art direction, as well as third prize in the feature film competition at the Ninth International Festival of New Latin American Cinema in Havana, Cuba, in December of 1987. While the work was obviously humorous, it also contained a great deal of underlying social commentary as well. Marin included several characters from outside of Mexico, in order to demonstrate that illegal immigrants come from scores of nations around the world. Also, as Marin explained in *Cineaste,* "What I wanted to say in the larger context with the film was not just that Mexicans or Puerto Ricans or Cubans or other Latinos are coming to the U.S., but also that we're already here, that we have *been* here since before the beginning of the country." He later added, "One of my aims is to make people realize that Latino culture is part of American culture, just as much as English or Irish or Italian culture."

After that film, Marin began taking acting parts in a variety of films, usually in the capacity of a sidekick. However, he has not seemed to mind, telling Robert Dominguez of the *New York Daily News* (reprinted in the *Dallas Morning News*), "My point of view is, the sidekick really is the star. He gets all the bets lines, he gets the funny stuff and every once in a while he gets the girl. It's a much cooler place." His many appearances include roles in *The Shrimp on the Barbie,* 1990, *Desperado,* 1995, and *Tin Cup,* 1996, as Kevin Costner's caddie. After this job, Marin told Scott Moore of the *Washington Post* (reprinted in the *St. Louis Post–Dispatch*), "I feel I've finally cracked through. *Tin Cup* is really the culmination of having Hollywood accept me in a big–budget movie with big stars and a big A–list director and carrying a huge role." Marin also provided voice–overs in the animated films *FernGully: The Last Rainforest,* 1992, and *The Lion King,* 1994.

In addition to Marin's film work, he had small roles on the cable television movies *The Cisco Kid,* 1994, with Jimmy Smits, in which he portrayed Pancho without the foolishness, and *The Courtyard,* 1995. He also landed the part of Chuy, a hotel chef, on *The Golden Girls* spinoff *The Golden Palace,* for the 1992–93 season, and did the voice of Lencho Fleabondigas on *Santo Bugito,* 1995, an animated series set in Texas that expertly avoided Hispanic stereotyping. Marin also reached out to children with his educational, humorous, and toe–tapping album *My Name is Cheech, the School Bus Driver,* 1992, and subsequently taped a spot on *Sesame Street.* In addition, he was the grand prize winner on celebrity *Jeopardy!* in 1992. During the game show taping, he remarked in a *Premiere* interview, it was "the most nervous I've ever been. I mean you can really look like a dummy. I was sweatin' like a dog."

After shooting the film *Tin Cup,* costar and longtime friend Don Johnson offered Marin a role in his new television drama series, *Nash Bridges* , in which he plays a San Francisco cop—ironic, considering the many years he spent trying to outwit or outrun the law in his drug films. For Marin, it was an homage to his father, the veteran cop who served 30 years with the Los Angeles Police Department. For the show, Marin shaved his trademark moustache. *Nash Bridges* was the highest–rated new drama in 1996 and stood out because it offered a unique addition to the genre: humor.

Though many fans throughout the years hoped for a Cheech and Chong reunion, it does not seem to be in the cards. While Marin's acting career rolled along, Chong continued to try to perform stand–up alone, with little success. The pair met in 1995 to discuss a possible tour, but still could not overcome their creative differences. However, in 1997 for May ratings sweeps, Chong made a guest appearance on *Nash Bridges.* In the same episode, Philip Michael Thomas, who costarred with Johnson in the quintessentially 1980s hit *Miami Vice,* showed up as well. Subsequently, Marin and Chong have managed to "maintain a wary friendship," as Kyle Smith and Paula Yoo put it in *People.* Marin continued to resist suggestions of a reunion, telling them, "When you quit, it's over. I have too much respect for what we did then."

Marin married Rikki Morley in 1975, and they had a daughter, Carmine. They split up in the 1980s, about the same he and Chong were on the skids, and Marin married computer artist Patti Heid in 1984. They had a son, Joe, and a daughter, Jasmine.

Marin sometimes has uncomfortable moments as a father, given his past. He mentioned to Smith and Yoo in *People* that he was bowled over when his daughter asked him when was the first time he smoked marijuana. "There is no right answer," he noted. "You want to raise your kids with an open mind, but not so open their brains fall out." Once he began working on *Nash Bridges,* which shoots in San Francisco, Marin and his family moved from their home in Malibu to a six–bedroom townhouse in the Pacific Heights district of San Francisco. He is an avid collector of Chicano art and enjoys golf.

Selected discography

Cheech and Chong, Ode, 1972.
Big Bambu, Warner Bros., 1972.
Los Cochinos, Warner Bros., 1973.
Wedding Album, Warner Bros., 1974.
Sleeping Beauty, Warner Bros., 1976.
Up in Smoke, Warner Bros., 1978.
Greatest Hit, Warner Bros., 1981.
Get out of My Room, MCA, 1985.
Let's Make a New Dope Deal, Warner Bros., 1991.

Solo recordings

"Born in East L.A." (single), MCA, 1985.
My Name is Cheech, the School Bus Driver (children's album), Ode to Kids, 1992.

Sources

Books

Contemporary Theatre, Film and Television, volume 13, Gale Research, 1995.
Dictionary of Hispanic Biography, Gale Research, 1996.

Periodicals

Cineaste, volume 16, number 3, 1988, p. 34.
Dallas Morning News, April 22, 1998, p. 2C.
Entertainment Weekly, February 4, 1994, p. 44; August 16, 1996, p. 45.
GQ, January 1990, p. 28.
Hispanic, September 1996, p. 12.
Knight–Ridder/Tribune News Service, August 8, 1996.
Newsday, January 31, 1993, Kidsday, p. 1.
People, December 23, 1996, p. 57; April 27, 1998, p. 125.
Premiere, March 1996, p. 46.
St. Louis Post–Dispatch, December 26, 1995, p. 8D.
Star Tribune (Minneapolis, MN), December 9, 1995, p. 8E.
USA Today, August 16, 1996, p. 4D; April 24, 1997, p. 3D.

Online

"Cheech Marin," *Contemporary Authors Online,* Gale Group web site, http://www.galenet.com (August 26, 1999).
"Cheech Marin," Internet Movie Database web site, http://us.imdb.com (September 21, 1999).

Susan Marshall

© *Lois Greenfield, 1988.*

Choreographer

Born in 1958 in Hershey, PA; daughter of a behavioral scientist and a feminist writer; married Christopher Renino (a novelist); children: Nicholas. *Education:* Attended Juilliard School, New York City, 1976–78.

Addresses: *Office*—Susan Marshall & Company, Dance Continuum Inc., Box 707 Cooper Station, New York, NY 10276–0707.

Career

Choreographer; founded the Susan Marshall & Company dance troupe, c. 1982.

Awards: New York Foundation for the Arts fellowship, 1985; New York Dance and Performance Award ("Bessie") for outstanding achievement in choreography, 1985, 1996; National Endowment for the Arts fellowships, 1986–91; Brandeis University Creative Arts Award, 1988; National Corporate Fund for Dance's American Choreographer Award, 1988; *Dance Magazine* Award, 1995; MacArthur Foundation grant recipient, 2000.

Sidelights

Choreographer Susan Marshall explores a multitude of human emotion and interaction by using the physical presence of her dances to symbolize complicated emotional states. While many of her contemporaries, such as Mark Morris, and predecessors, such as Merce Cunningham, focused solely on the abstract motion of bodies, Marshall adds a subtext of personal interaction. Though her first goal is to create a dance, she recognizes that the work is connected with the people performing it. As she stated to Otis Stuart in *Dance Magazine*, "I'm not able to separate dance from what I feel is its inherent impact on a human level. The movement is very much about men and women as men and women. It's not about dancers, and so it's about individuals. That's where the subject matter lies, so that subtext becomes a structuring element, a throughline to hang the whole thing onto." Marshall has won an assortment of awards, including honors from *Dance Magazine* and two Bessie awards, and in 2000 received a MacArthur "genius" grant.

Born in 1958 in Hershey, Pennsylvania, Marshall grew up partly in Florida before returning to Pennsylvania. Her father, a behavioral scientist, and mother, a feminist writer, had a major influence on her life and work. They were both active in the civil rights movement, and her mother also cofounded the Pennsylvania chapter of the National Organization for Women. They encouraged her love of gymnastics and dance, and she also studied ballet as a child. However, modern dance intrigued her more, and in high school, she began choreographing unconventional dances using gymnasts, artists, and wrestlers.

Marshall studied at the Pennsylvania Governor's School for the Arts and with teachers in New York, and went on to attend New York City's Juilliard School, spending two years in the undergraduate modern dance program from 1976 to 1978. By the early 1980s she founded the Susan Marshall & Company dancers. For most of its existence, the troupe has included eight members. In 1983 and 1984 the troupe began to stage works in small venues around New York, with positive critical response.

Early on in her career, Marshall's trademarks became evident. Her 1984 piece, *Arms*, for example, exhibited her attention to structure and precise movement as well as her theme of human relationships and their multilayered, complex emotions. As Stuart described it in *Dance Magazine*, "Two dancers begin standing side by side in a spotlight, and their subsequent involvement is defined by the paths of their arms as they lace over, under, around, and through their partners' One slip, and somebody gets hurt." Despite Marshall's attention to subtext, though, Stuart noted that her pieces are never dogmatic. As she told Stuart, "I don't feel that art and politics are really compatible. I'm sure that everything shaping someone will go into that person's work, but I am not drawn to work that has a fixed message because the work will get subjugated to the message."

Another signature element of Marshall's work is her use of everyday motions to signify multiple possibilities in human interaction. For instance, in 1984's *Arms*, she uses various arm gestures to represent dramatic moments in her characters' lives. In other works she uses repeated motions—such as embraces—with subtle variations, in order to symbolize various levels of meaning in relationships.

In 1985 Marshall began the first of three seasons at the Dance Theater Workshop's Bessie Schonberg Theater, and she won her first "Bessie," or New York Dance and Performance Award, that same year. Subsequently, the company toured the United States and Europe, and Marshall was commissioned to create works for ballets in Dallas, Boston, and Frankfurt, Germany, as well as the modern dance division of the Paris ballet, the GRCOP.

Marshall's first full-evening work, *Interior with Seven Figures*, opened in November of 1990 at the Brooklyn Academy of Music (BAM) Next Wave Festival. The accompanying music was commissioned from Luis Resto. Its minimalist structure conveyed the desperate existence of a nuclear family in which the line between nurturing and conflict is blurred.

Marshall returned to BAM in 1990 with *Contenders*, which featured four couples engaged in motion from various athletic activities, from running and swimming to wrestling and tennis. The piece addresses the issue of competition with others and against one's self and then moves into the conflict that arises between lovers.

Tobi Tobias wrote of *Contenders* in *New York*, "As with all of Marshall's work, its greatest beauty lies in the transmuting of realistic movement into a semiabstract form—Marshall has an uncanny gift for this—which is very much in tune with contemporary taste." However, he also noted that though he appreciated the work's formal excellence, "It's the product of an obsessive; there's no air in it." He suggested that it lacked spontaneity and wit. Meanwhile, Joan Acocella in *Art in America* remarked, "Sports are…the perfect metaphor for something…that is critical to Marshall's work, and that is the sheer toil of the body, its heaviness and vulnerability." She added, "You can almost feel [the dancers] against you, straining, breathing." However, she later complained about the sports metaphor being a cliche.

Marshall introduced two new works, *Spectators at an Event* and *Fields of View* at the BAM Next Wave Festival in late 1994. Richard B. Woodward of the *New York Times* commented, "A mournful, icy wind seems to blow across the stage in both pieces, which can be seen as Ms. Marshall's meditations on AIDS. Arthur Armijo, one of the mainstays of her troupe, died of the illness last year." Another inspiration for the *Spectators* was the photographs of Weegee, who took shots of mayhem and violence in New York City during the 1940s and 1950s. Rather than focusing on the victims in the pictures, though, Marshall drew from the faces of onlookers. As she noted to Woodward, "There's so much to be said about people watching. Why are we so morbidly drawn to tragedy?" To further layer the piece, Marshall drew non–dancers from various communities where she performed the work to be onstage observers, thus watching as they were being watched by the general audience. Adding to this, she also used video projections of Weegee photographs. *Fields of View*, meanwhile, addressed loss on a more personal level. Like many of Marshall's works, it was set to the music of Phillip Glass.

In another collaboration with Glass, Marshall in 1996 directed his opera *Les Enfants Terribles: Children of the Game*, based on the novel *Les Enfants Terribles* by Jean Cocteau. It was the third in a trilogy based on the works of Cocteau, and the dance–opera melange was Marshall's second time as director. She had also written and directed a conventional stage play, *Walter's Finest Hours,* which was performed off–Broadway in 1993. It was about an elderly man coming to terms with a stroke. For *Les Enfants Terribles,* Marshall won her second Bessie Award.

Late in 1998, in her fifth appearance at BAM's Next Wave Festival in a decade, Marshall introduced *The Most Dangerous Room in the House* in late 1998. The crux of the work is a woman's recurring fear that her child will die from some domestic threat such as choking, falling, or drowning. Inspiration for the work came from a study on hazards in the bathroom. "It also hints at the unsettling notion that the home, the place we're supposed to feel most secure, might not be such a safe haven after all," Marshall related to Christopher Reardon in the *New York Times.* She created the work while pregnant with her son. Adding to the atmosphere was a minimalist score by David Lang, performed by the Bang On a Can All–Star Band.

In December of 1999, Marshall's *The Descent Beckons* premiered at New York's Joyce Theater, marking yet another step in her examination of human social themes. For this work, she used 75 blow–up dolls with which her dancers interacted in order to convey a variety of moods, ranging from frolicking to violent. Sylvaine Gold in *Newsday* wrote, "Your first thought is that Marshall is having fun with the conventions of dance the lifting, the partnering, the tossing about of women . But the imagery becomes more and more grim as the sound of thunder riddles the score and murder becomes an ever–present motif." Marshall herself commented to Kevin Giordano in *Dance Magazine,* "The work deals with groups, what drives them. That's a mysterious thing. What is the role of the individual in relation to the group, and how much are our individual choices products of the group?"

Marshall is married to novelist Christopher Renino, and they have a son, Nicholas. They have homes in Duchess County, New York, and the Upper West Side of Manhattan. In 2000 she was named one of 25 recipients of a MacArthur "genius" grant, which provides fellowships each year to people of achievement as "seed money or venture capital for intellectual, social, and artistic endeavors," according to Jany Scott in the *New York Times,* quoting the foundation. In 2000, the fellowship was raised to a flat $500,000 for all recipients, as opposed to past years, when amounts varied from $200,000 to $375,000 depending on the age of the recipient. Upon winning the grant, Marshall remarked, according to Scott, "In one sense it feels like I just want to reflect on my work, like I have mental breathing room that I don't normally have the luxury of. Then it's this

other feeling, as though someone has just thrown down the gauntlet. And it's a great feeling. It's just lovely that something is expected of you."

Selected works

Fault Line, The Yard, Martha's Vineyard, 1982.
Trio in Four Parts, Emanu–El Midtown YM–YWHA, New York, 1983.
Ward, CODANCECO, New York, 1983.
Routine and Variations, Performance Space 122, New York, 1984.
Arms, Performance Space 122, New York, 1984.
Kin, Brooklyn Anchorage, New York, 1985.
Opening Gambits, Dance Theatre Workshop, New York, 1985.
Common Run, CODANCECO, New York, 1985.
Arena, Dance Theatre Workshop, New York, 1986.
Gifts, for Le Groupe de Recherche Choreographique de l'Opera de Paris, 1986.
The Refrain, Dallas Ballet, 1986.
Overture, Boston Ballet, 1987.
The Aerialist, Dance Theatre Workshop, New York, 1987.
Kiss, Dance Theatre Workshop, New York, 1987.
Companion Pieces, Dance Theatre Workshop, New York, 1987.
Interior with Seven Figures, for BAM, New York, 1988.
In Medias Res, for Frankfurt Ballet, Frankfurt, Germany, 1989.
Figures In Opposition, Dancing in the Streets, New York, 1989.
Contenders, BAM, New York, 1990.
Articles of Faith, World Financial Center, New York, 1990.
Standing Duet, The Kitchen, New York, 1992.
Untitled (Detail), Ohio State University, Wexner Center, 1992.
Entr'Acte I, Serious Fun, Lincoln Center, New York, 1993.
Entr'Acte II, Serious Fun, Lincoln Center, New York, 1993.
Walter's Finest Hour, for Downtown Art Company, New York, 1993.
Solo, Ballet Hispanico, New York, 1993.
Fields of View, University of Texas (Austin) and Brooklyn Academy of Music (BAM), New York, 1994.
Spectators at an Event, University of Texas & BAM, New York, 1994.
Private Worlds in Public View, Whitney Museum at Philip Morris, 1994.
Central Figure, Lyon Opera Ballet, 1994.
Lines from Memory, Montreal Danse, 1995.
Les Enfants Terribles (music by Philip Glass), (commission), Zug, Switzerland, 1996.

Run Toward the Noise (music by David Lang, performed by Bang On a Can All–Star Band; text Christopher Renino), Dartmouth College, 1998.

The Most Dangerous Room in the House, BAM, New York, 1998.

The Descent Beckons, Joyce Theater, New York, 1999.

Sources

Books

International Dictionary of Modern Dance, St. James Press, 1998.

Periodicals

Art in America, February 1991, p. 57.

Dance Magazine, December 1988, p. 36; April 1995, p. 40; March 1999, p. 102; December 1999, p. 36.

Newsday, December 16, 1999, p. B9.

New York, December 17, 1990, p. 80.

New York Times, November 20, 1996, p. C21; December 13, 1998, sec. 2, p. 10; June 14, 2000, p. A24.

Star Tribune (Minneapolis, MN), February 4, 1995, p.1E.

Judith Martin

Author and columnist

Born Judith Sylvia Perlman, September 13, 1938, in Washington, DC; daughter of Jacob (an economist) and Helen (a teacher; maiden name, Aronson) Perlman; married Robert Martin (a scientist), January 30, 1960; children: Nicholas Ivor, Jacobina Helen. *Education:* Wellesley College, B.A., 1959.

Addresses: *Home*—1651 Harvard St. NW, Washington, DC 20009. *Office*—c/o *Vanity Fair,*—350 Madison Ave., New York, NY 10017.

Career

Washington Post, Washington, DC, reporter, beginning 1960; *Vanity Fair,* New York, NY, critic–at–large. Author of "Miss Manners," a weekly newspaper column distributed by United Features Syndicate, 1978 , and of several books on the topic of manners. Faculty member at George Washington University, 1978. President of board of trustees of Georgetown Day School.

Sidelights

In the words of Judith Martin, better known to her "gentle readers" as Miss Manners, "Etiquette is a little social contract we make that we will restrain some of our more provocative impulses in return for living more of less harmoniously in a community," as she told Hara Estroff Marano in *Psychology Today.* Martin continued, "The fact is that civilization requires some training in restraint so that we can get along." Far from concentrating solely on what Marano labeled "teacup formalities," such as proper utensil usage, Martin has made it her life's work to dispense advice on the entire range of human behavior in order to hopefully eradicate rudeness. Though many people believe that rules of etiquette serve to inhibit people, Martin feels the opposite is true: She thinks that people need to have guidelines on how to act properly in order to be free to reap full enjoyment from living in a society with others.

Martin's pseudonym stems from a Victorian English folkloric figure called Lady Manners. When children would consume their food too quickly, adults would urge them to leave a small amount on the plate for "Lady Manners." And not only does she write in a somewhat formal Victorian tone, she has assumed a similar image as well, dressing in high–collar blouses with a brooch at the neck, and wearing her hair in an upswept chignon. Still, Martin's acerbic wit regularly peeks through in her answers to inquiring readers, making her anything but a stuffy bore. Her column appears in 200 newspapers around the world. All of the letters to her are real, although some are edited, and she has published several books that compile letters and responses from her columns. Her works have touched on subjects such as etiquette in the workplace and how to politely deal with modern technology, and her 1999 effort, *Miss Manners' Guide to Domestic Tranquility: The Authoritative Manual for Every Civilized Household, However Harried,* delves into making the home a more peaceful and civil place to be.

Martin was born Judith Perlman on September 13, 1938, in Washington, D.C. Her father, Jacob, worked as a economist for the United Nations, and moved his family to the Philippines when she and her brother were young. Martin recalled in *Time*, "My father sat us down and said, 'Children, we have to tell you something. We have reached the crucial point when the servants outnumber us 2 to 1. It takes a while to get used to this kind of life. It takes about two minutes. And it takes the rest of your life to get unused to it.'" In this upbringing, Martin learned the ropes regarding entertaining dignitaries, but even as a youth she showed an unusual proclivity for tastefulness and decorum.

Eventually Martin attended Wellesley College, where in 1959 she earned a bachelor of arts degree in English, though some of her book jackets claim she majored in gracious living. While there, her parents urged her to find a summer job, so she applied at the *Washington Post*. Though she aspired to be a writer, she was not keen on being employed at that point in time, and hoped that they would reject her application because she had no experience. Instead, they gave her a job as a copy girl.

After graduation, Martin was hired as a *Post* reporter for the Washington social scene, covering White House parties with Lyndon B. Johnson, among other duties. Later she also became a feature writer and a critic, reviewing films, plays, and books. She never did any hard news reporting. While she was working as a social reporter, Martin was not allowed in to the wedding reception of President Richard Nixon's daughter Julie, but she managed to sneak in anyway posing as a friend of one of the bridesmaids. Later, she was the only reporter prohibited from covering Tricia Nixon's wedding after writing that the president's daughter dressed "like an ice–cream cone," according to Rust Hills in *Esquire*.

In 1972 Martin published *The Name on the White House Floor and Other Anxieties of Our Times*, a collection of her newspaper columns that discussed her life, her experiences as a reporter, and personal observations. Some of these writings included a glimpse into her pet peeves. But Martin's fascination with etiquette mainly grew out of her hobby of reading books dealing with the history of manners. In 1978, she asked her editor at the *Washington Post* if she could pen her own column on etiquette, and received a grudging approval. "Editors all thought etiquette was dead," Martin told Otto Friedrich in *Time*. "Even the word was a joke. I thought I was just writing for a bunch of old cranks like myself, but then I started getting floods of mail from young people who were supposed to think etiquette was stupid and ludicrous, and they were all writing me and asking me questions."

The same year Martin began writing her column, it was picked up for syndication by United Features Syndicate, running three times a week. Her columns would eventually be collected in several books on the topic of manners, her first being *Miss Manners' Guide to Excruciatingly Correct Behavior*, 1981. She thus became a fixture on the book–tour circuit and a regular on talk shows. She gave up her job at the *Post* in 1985 and became a regular critic for *Vanity Fair* magazine in addition to writing her column.

Martin believes that her writings struck a chord with baby boomers who were raised in the 1960s amid a rapidly changing social structure. As she remarked to Hilary DeVries in the *Christian Science Monitor*, children then "were told that etiquette is outdated and you just do whatever you feel like. Well, these people have grown up and discover that it's not true, and they're at a terrible handicap." She noted that people without manners are at a disadvantage in situations ranging from job interviews to romances. Her advice thus deals with far more than the notion of which fork to use (when in doubt, start with the one farthest out and work in). In many instances, Martin even shows a sly sense of humor in her responses to her "Gentle Readers," as she addresses them.

Martin's second book on manners, *Miss Manners' Guide to Rearing Perfect Children*, 1984, introduced her distinct opinions on how etiquette fits in with child rearing. She told Susan Goodman in *Modern Maturity*, "Most parents are not teaching their children the manners they need–from 13–year–old single mothers on crack to corporate executives who feel the limited time with their children should be pleasant so they don't ask them to do anything." Unlike many permissive parents who believe that teaching children manners stifles creativity, she believes that "the chief tools of child–rearing are nagging and example," as DeVries quoted out of her book.

Another of Martin's volumes is 1995's *Miss Manners on Painfully Proper Weddings*. It concerns everything from menu planning to videotaping, and points out faux pas like adding "and guest" on invitations. In 1996, she kept up with the times with *Miss Manners Rescues Civilization: From Sexual Harassment, Frivolous Lawsuits, Dissing and Other Lapses in Civility*. This volume spanned modern issues as serious as date rape and racism to minor troubles such as how vegetarians should thank their bosses who give out a turkey each year on Thanksgiving. A *Publishers Weekly* reviewer commented, "More than a book on etiquette, this is both entertaining and serious social commentary."

In this work, Martin theorizes that the decline of manners has made it difficult on all levels of society because their disuse has ushered in an era of legal action and even violence. Whereas etiquette once used cold stares and raised eyebrows to extract better behavior, now there are laws to prevent, say, smokers from infringing on nonsmokers' rights. And she feels that this change has caused undue government interference in private lives and a dearth of frivolous court cases. Martin even boils down "road rage" freeway shootings and killings due to one individual perceiving that someone else "dissing" him or her. Her belief is that a rude gesture should never be answered by another one, be it a gunshot or a put–down, telling Mary Vespa in *People* that the proper reply to a rude person is "with the icy stare or weak smile." She continued, "Facile expressions are wonderful ways of politely conveying that you cannot believe that this person has just behaved a certain way."

Miss Manners Rescues Civilization also devotes special attention to manners in the workplace, an issue that has been confused by what Martin deems "that phony 'we're all one happy family' idea," according to Tim Carvell in *Fortune*. Her thrust in this section deals with the fact that if employees do not treat each other cordially, then they are probably not treating customers very well, either, which is bad for business.

Continuing to address up–to–the minute concepts in etiquette, Martin wrote *Miss Manners Basic Training: Communication* in 1996. In this, she keeps up with technology by issuing her edicts on devices such as caller ID, fax machines, beepers, cellular phones, and the Internet. For example, Martin believes that call waiting is "the rudest thing on Earth," as she stated to Goodman, "because it effectively says, 'Last come, first served.'" She also dislikes cutesy messages on answering services and sending e–mails for important topics such as birth announcements. Not one to dismiss technology outright, however, she thinks screening calls is fine, and believes that e–mail is an excellent means of quick communication. She also applauds the growing trend of "netiquette," an informal set of rules which guides online behavior. Some of these suggestions on how to incorporate innovations into polite society were also examined in *Miss Manners' Guide for the Turn–of–the–Millennium*, 1989.

Though Martin might have strong opinions on how to treat one another, she does not forge moral judgments. For example, according to Friedrich, when someone asked her how to address a homosexual couple, she replied that the person should say,

"How do you do? How do you do?" In all cases, a practical approach seems to reign, with her view being that "Good manners are not just for the very rich," as she explained to Friedrich. "Good manners are for everyone. Good manners are free." She eschews the use of etiquette as a means of being pretentious or divisive, which negates its intent.

Martin sees no conflict between feminism and her ideas on etiquette. In fact, she has always considered herself a feminist and feels that her attention to respecting one another is an integral part of feminism. However, she did point out to Sandy M. Fernandez in *Ms.*, "Feminists made clear there were a lot of etiquette rules that needed to be adjusted and changed, and there were." For instance, she noted that it is not all right for men to stand up when a woman enters a board room, because it meant they were recognizing her as a female and not for her professional status. In addition, she remarked, "Another very common misconception about politeness is that it is martyrdom; that you have to let everybody else do whatever they want. People say to me, 'Doesn't etiquette all boil down to making other people feel comfortable?' No. There are times when you are going to have to upset people."

Although Martin does her best to advise on manners for modern times and nontraditional situations, such as divorced families or homosexual unions, she remains stumped on one subject: unmarried partners. "I've never found a satisfactory name for the other person in an unmarried couple," she admitted to Goodman in *Modern Maturity*. "'Sweetheart' or 'lover' invites people to peek into your intimate side. 'Companion' is not really right. 'Significant other' is ridiculous . My only rule is: Make it simple and nothing that vividly describes the personal side of the relationship."

In addition to her books on etiquette, Martin penned a novel, *Gilbert: A Comedy of Errors*, in 1982. It concerns a young con man who wheedles his way up the hierarchy of politics until he becomes an aide to the president. Martin began pondering the idea when she was a college student, and gleaned more material for it during her years as a reporter hobnobbing with the Washington elite. The work earned several favorable reviews. Other books by Martin include *Miss Manners' Basic Training: Eating*, 1997; *Miss Manners' Basic Training: The Right Thing to Say*, 1998; and *Miss Manners: A Citizen's Guide to Civility*, 1999.

Also in 1999 Martin published *Miss Manners' Guide to Domestic Tranquility: The Authoritative Manual for Every Civilized Household, However Harried* . In this, she dispenses advice on topics from recycling and laundry to parties and babysitters, and bemoans the rise of materialism and commercialism and their affect on families. That same year, Akadine Press printed a new edition of the formerly out–of–print *Common Courtesy: In Which Miss Manners Solves the Problems that Baffled Mr. Jefferson*, regarding Thomas Jefferson's attempt to do away with courtesy titles in hopes of a more egalitarian system.

Martin married Robert Martin, a scientist with the National Institutes of Health, on January 30, 1960, and they have two children, Nicholas Ivor and Jacobina Helen. Both children attended Harvard University. Martin keeps a home and a separate house as an office in Washington, D.C.

Selected writings

The Name on the White House Floor, Coward, 1972.

Miss Manners' Guide to Excruciatingly Correct Behavior, illustrated by Gloria Kamen, Atheneum, 1982.

Gilbert: A Comedy of Manners, Atheneum, 1982.

Common Courtesy: In Which Miss Manners Solves the Problems that Baffled Mr. Jefferson, Atheneum, 1985, reissued, Akadine Press, 1999.

Miss Manners' Guide to Rearing Perfect Children, illustrated by Gloria Kamen, Atheneum, 1984.

Style and Substance: A Comedy of Manners, Atheneum, 1986.

Miss Manners' Guide for the Turn–of–the–Millennium, illustrated by Gloria Kamen, Pharos Books, 1989.

Miss Manners on Painfully Proper Weddings, Crown Publishers, 1995.

Miss Manners Rescues Civilization: From Sexual Harassment, Frivolous Lawsuits, Dissing, and Other Lapses in Civility, illustrations by Daniel Mark Duffy, Crown Publishers, 1996.

Miss Manners' Basic Training: Eating, Crown, 1997.

Miss Manners' Basic Training: Communication, Crown, 1997.

Miss Manners' Basic Training: The Right Thing to Say, Crown, 1998.

Miss Manners: A Citizen's Guide to Civility, illustrations by Daniel Mark Duffy, 1999.

Miss Manners' Guide to Domestic Tranquility: The Authoritative Manual for Every Civilized Household, However Harried, Crown, 1999.

Sources

Periodicals

Booklist, January 1, 1996, p. 760; November 15, 1996, p. 547; February 15, 1998, p. 947; July 1999, p. 1891.

Christian Science Monitor, July 7, 1981, p. 18; November 8, 1984, p. 31.

Entertainment Weekly, August 22, 1997, p. 128.

Esquire, June 1989, p. 194.

Fortune, September 9, 1996, p. 44.

Insight on the News, August 5, 1996, p. 32; December 6, 1999, p. 27.

Library Journal, August 1999, p. 104.

Modern Maturity, March–April 1996, p. 56.

Ms., March/April 1997, p. 50.

Newsweek, September 1, 1997, p. 14.

People, August 9, 1982, p. 38; July 8, 1996, p. 27; November 8, 1999, p. 109.

Psychology Today, March–April 1998, p. 26.

Publishers Weekly, April 22, 1996, p. 51; November 18, 1996, p. 55.

Reason, April 1997, p. 61.

Southern Living, November 1997, p. 130.

Time, November 5, 1984, p. 62; January 13, 1997, p. 76.

Whole Earth, Fall 1998, p. 48; Winter 1998, p. 23; Spring 1999, p. 112.

Online

"Judith (Sylvia) Martin," *Contemporary Authors Online*, Gale Group web site, http://www.galenet.com (March 20, 2000).

Walter Matthau

AP/Wide World Photos

Actor

Born Walter Matthau (some sources say Matthow), October 1, 1920, in New York, NY; son of Milton (an electrician and process server) and Rose (a sewing machine operator; maiden name, Berolsky) Matthow; married Grace Geraldine Johnson, 1948 (divorced, 1958); married Carol Grace Marcus Saroyan, August 21, 1959; children: (first marriage) David, Jenny; (second marriage) Charles. *Education:* Attended Columbia University and Oxford University; studied acting with Erwin Piscator at the Dramatic Workshop, New School for Social Research, 1946–47, and with Raiken Ben–Ari.

Addresses: *Office*—The Matthau Company, 10100 Santa Monica Blvd., Ste. 2200, Los Angeles, CA 90067. *Agent*—Ernst and Young, 1999 Avenue of the Stars, No. 2100, Los Angeles, CA 90067.

Career

Actor and director. Worked as a file clerk, boxing instructor, basketball coach, and radio operator. *Military service:* U.S. Army Air Forces, 1942–45; served in Europe; became staff sergeant; received six battle stars. Stage appearances include *Ten Nights in a Bar Room*, Erie, PA, 1946; (off–Broadway debut) *The Aristocrats*, New York City, 1946; *The Flies*, New York City 1947; (Broadway debut) *Anne of the Thousand Days*, New York City, 1948; *The Liar*, New York City, 1950; *Season in the Sun*, New York City, 1951; *Twilight Walk*, New York City, 1951; *Fancy Meeting You Again*, New York City, 1952; *One Bright Day*, New York City, 1952; *In Any Language*, New York City, 1952; *The Grey–Eyed People*, 1952; *The Ladies of the Corridor*, New York City, 1953; *Three Men on a Horse*, 1953; *The Burning Glass*, New York City, 1954; *The Wisteria Trees*, New York City, 1955; *Guys and Dolls*, New York City, 1955; *Will Success Spoil Rock Hunter?*, New York City, 1955; *Maiden Voyage*, Philadelphia, PA, 1957; *Once More with Feeling*, New York City, 1958; *Once There Was a Russian*, New York City, 1961; *A Shot in the Dark*, New York City, 1961; *My Mother, My Father, and Me*, New York City, 1963; *The Odd Couple*, New York City, 1965; *Juno and the Paycock*, Los Angeles, 1974.

Television appearances include episodes of *Studio One, Philco Television Playhouse, Schlitz Playhouse of Stars, Kraft Television Theatre, The Armstrong Circle Theatre, Danger, The Campbell Television Soundstage, Plymouth Playhouse, Suspense, Goodyear Playhouse, The United States Steel Hour, The Motorola Television Hour, Center Stage, Robert Montgomery Presents Your Lucky Strike Theatre, Justice, The Alcoa Hour, Climax,* and *Alfred Hitchcock Presents,* throughout 1950s; *Play of the Week, Route 66, Target: The Corrupters, Westinghouse Theatre, General Electric Theatre, DuPont Show of the Month, Naked City, Eleventh Hour, The Bob Hope Chrysler Theatre, The Rogues, D. Kildare, Profiles in Courage, Hollywood Television Theatre,* and *Insight,* throughout 1960s; series *Tallahassee 7000,* 1961; and various specials and awards shows.

Film appearances include *The Kentuckian*, 1955; *The Indian Fighter*, 1955; *Bigger than Life*, 1956; *A Face in the Crowd*, 1957; *Ride a Crooked Trail*, 1958; *Onionhead*, 1958; *King Creole*, 1958; *Voice in the Mirror*, 1958; *Gangster Story*, 1960; *Strangers When We Meet*, 1960; *Who's Got the Action?*, 1962; *Lonely Are the Brave*, 1992; *Island of Love*, 1963; *Charade*, 1963; *Fail-Safe*, 1964, *Ensign Pulver*, 1964; *Goodbye Charlie*, 1964; *Mirage*, 1965; *The Fortune Cookie*, 1966; *A Guide for the Married Man*, 1967; *The Odd Couple*, 1968; *The Secret Life of an American Wife*, 1968; *Candy*, 1968; *Hello Dolly!*, 1969; *Cactus Flower*, 1969; *Kotch*, 1971; *A New Leaf*, 1971; *Plaza Suite*, 1971; *Pete 'n' Tillie*, 1972; *The Laughing Policeman*, 1973; *Charley Varrick*, 1973; *The Taking of Pelham One Two Three*, 1974; *The Front Page*, 1974; *Earthquake*, 1974; *The Sunshine Boys*, 1975; *The Gentleman Tramp*, 1975; *The Bad News Bears*, 1976; *Casey's Shadow*, 1978; *California Suite*, 1978; *House Calls*, 1978; *Hopscotch*, 1980; *Little Miss Marker*, 1980; *First Monday in October*, 1981; *Buddy Buddy*, 1981; *I Ought to Be in Pictures*, 1982; *The Survivors*, 1983; *Movers and Shakers*, 1985; *Pirates*, 1986; *Il Piccolo diavolo (The Little Devil)*, 1988; *The Couch Trip*, 1988; *JFK*, 1991; *Grumpy Old Men*, 1993; *Dennis the Menace*, 1993; *I.Q.*, 1994; *The Grass Harp*, 1995; *Grumpier Old Men*, 1995; *I'm Not Rappaport*, 1996; *Out to Sea*, 1997; *The Life and Times of Hank Greenberg*, 1998; *The Odd Couple II*, 1998; *The Marriage Fool*, 1998; and *Hanging Up*, 2000.

Awards: New York Drama Critics Award, 1951, for *Twilight Walk*; New York Drama Critics Award, both 1959, both for *Once More with Feeling*; Antoinette Perry (Tony) Award, best supporting or featured actor in a play, 1962, for *A Shot in the Dark*; Film Daily Award, 1962, for *Lonely Are the Brave*; Tony Award, best actor in a play, and New York Drama Critics Award, both 1965, both for *The Odd Couple*; Academy Award, best supporting actor, 1966, for *The Fortune Cookie*; British Academy of Film and Television Arts Award, best actor, 1973, for *Pete 'n' Tillie* and *Charley Varrick*; Golden Globe Award, best actor in a musical or comedy film, 1976, for *The Sunshine Boys*; ShoWest Convention, Lifetime Achievement Award, 1993; American Comedy Awards, Lifetime Achievement Award in Comedy, 1997.

Sidelights

Actor Walter Matthau has been an unmistakable presence in American theater, film, and television for over half a century. With his droopy-dog features, bulbous nose, and overall frumpy image, he was an unlikely candidate to become a Hollywood star. But he used this to his advantage in creating some of the most memorable humorous characters in entertainment. After becoming an award-winning stage actor on Broadway, Matthau parlayed his talents into television and film, reaching a then-career high in 1965 for his unforgettable role as grouchy slob extraordinaire Oscar Madison in *The Odd Couple*. Thereafter, he became known for his hilariously persnickety roles, as well as for being just as much of an acerbic cut-up in real life. Much later, in the 1990s, Matthau was admired by a new generation who found him irresistible as one of the pair of *Grumpy Old Men*, along with longtime foil Jack Lemmon. Approaching and into his eighties, he continued to keep audiences laughing as he landed parts in comedies such as 1998's *The Odd Couple II* and 2000's *Hanging Up*.

Matthau was born on October 1, 1920, in New York City. His father, Milton Matthau (some sources spell the surname Matthow), was a Russian-Jewish immigrant from Kiev, Ukraine, and his mother, the former Rose Berolsky, was a Lithuanian-born Jew. His father held various jobs, working for a time as an electrician and serving subpoenas for a law firm, but he left his wife when Matthau was three and his brother, Henry, was five. Their mother raised them by working as a sewing machine operator in the city's garment district sweatshops. Matthau found out when he was 15 that his father died in Bellvue Hospital.

Due to these circumstances, Matthau grew up in poverty, living in cold-water tenement apartments on the Lower East Side in a Ukrainian pocket of the city. The family was continually evicted because of nonpayment of rent. Amid this harsh upbringing, Matthau began reading Shakespeare at age seven and daydreamed of becoming a famous writer and actor. He began to act in school plays and recite poetry at assemblies, which attracted regular beatings by schoolyard bullies. He responded by pumping iron, and in high school, he excelled at sports, reportedly earning letters in track, basketball, and soccer, among others.

However, as Thomas Meehan pointed out in a later *New York Times Magazine* piece, much information about Matthau's background should be taken with a dose of skepticism due to the actor's tendency for exaggeration and tale-spinning. In fact, as Meehan noted, "Bored with repeating the story of his life over and over again to interviewers, Matthau has on more than one occasion told newspapermen and magazine writers that his father was a defrocked Russian Orthodox priest who'd had to flee for his life from the Czarist Kiev in 1906 because he'd been preaching sermons in support of Pope Pius X. And this story, told by Matthau to interviewers with an absolutely straight face, has appeared several times as the God's truth in such usually accurate publications as *Time* and *Current Biography*. " Indeed, periodicals for years recounted this misinformation, and also inaccurately reported that his original surname was Matuschanskayasky, or some variant thereof.

Meehan went on to report that Matthau got the acting bug about age 11, when he got a job selling soft drinks at a Yiddish theater. After only a couple months, he landed a small part in a musical comedy called "The Dishwasher," earning 50 cents for each performance while continuing to sell concessions during intermissions. At Seward Park High School, he starred in several student plays. But Matthau's career did not take off right away. After graduating in 1939, he worked a series of low–level jobs, including scrubbing floors and hauling cement bags. He applied to the Works Progress Administration (WPA), a government job–creating program to spur the economy during the 1930s and 1940s, hoping to get into its Federal Theater Project. But Matthau was rejected for lack of experience, and ended up taking a position with the WPA as a basketball coach instead.

From 1942 to 1945, Matthau served in the Army Air Force during World War II. He worked as a radio operator and gunner in combat missions over Europe and earned six battle stars, and was discharged with the rank of staff sergeant. Afterward, he enrolled in the New School's Dramatic Workshop, because, as he remarked in *Time*, it was "the easiest thing to do on the G.I. Bill." In addition, he noted, the school was located near Madison Square Garden, and "I didn't want to miss too many events." Matthau is a devoted sports buff and an admitted gambler, preferring to bet on sporting events and at the racetrack rather than play casino–style games. However, he has also been known to roll a few craps or play high–stakes poker.

Matthau spent three years at the Dramatic Workshop, studying alongside other future celebrities such as Rod Steiger and Tony Curtis. During the summers, he performed with repertory companies, appearing in his debut in *Ten Nights in a Bar Room* at the Erie County playhouse in Pennsylvania in 1946. But when he began to try out for professional theater roles, he found that his basset–hound looks shut him out of leading men parts, and his youth prevented him from being right for character roles. In addition, his ungraceful stoop–shouldered, ambling gait was a far cry from the usual rod–straight posture of successful actors.

Nevertheless, Matthau ended up in the off–Broadway production of *The Aristocrats* in 1946 and then snagged a Broadway part in 1948 as an understudy

for various roles in *Anne of the Thousand Days*. He wound up on stage at various times playing an octogenarian British bishop. After that, he appeared as a singing and dancing Venetian guard in 1950's *The Liar* and then in 1951 understudied and appeared as a foreign correspondent in *Season in the Sun*. Also in 1951 he won a New York Drama Critics Award for his role as detective Sam Dundee in *Twilight Walk*.

A string of other stage parts followed, and by this time, Matthau was starting to show up on episodes of television series as well. His first job was on the CBS show *Studio One* in 1950, and then he acted in a series of programs such as *Philco Television Playhouse*, *Kraft Television Theatre*, *The Goodyear Playhouse*, and *Alfred Hitchcock Presents* in the 1950s. His film debut came as a villain in 1955 in *The Kentuckian*, starring Burt Lancaster. Also that year he appeared in another western, *The Indian Fighter*, starring Kirk Douglas. Mainly a character actor, Matthau in his early film roles fit the bill for such characters as a writer in *A Face in the Crowd*, 1957; a racketeer in *Slaughter on Tenth Avenue*, 1957; a doctor in *Voice in the Mirror*, 1957; and a menacing crime boss who torments Elvis Presley's character in *King Creole*, 1958.

By the 1960s, Matthau was gaining acclaim for performances such as his portrayal of a sarcastic sheriff in *Lonely Are the Brave*, 1962; and a cynical government scientist in *Fail Safe*, 1964. He was still making waves on Broadway, winning a Tony Award for best supporting or featured actor in 1962 for his portrayal of a haughty French aristocrat in *A Shot in the Dark*. His career spiked in 1965 when he accepted the role of Oscar Madison in Neil Simon's Broadway play *The Odd Couple*. According to a *Time* article, the famous playwright noticed the actor at a cocktail party and approached him to say, "You're gonna be in my next play." Matthau responded, "Who are you?" At the time, this was a brash question. Although he had been in 21 films, 21 Broadway plays, and 158 television shows, Matthau was still not a household name.

Nevertheless, Simon hired Matthau for his first lead role ever, playing tough–talking, unkempt sportswriter Oscar Madison, who ends up living with an uptight neatnik, Felix Unger. He won a Tony Award for best actor and a New York Drama Critics Award for the part. The actor carried over this role to the film version, where he was paired with Jack Lemmon as the clean freak. He had first teamed up with Lemmon earlier in 1966's *The Fortune Cookie*, in which Matthau won a best supporting actor Oscar for playing a shady, fast–talking attorney who convinces his brother–in–law (Lemmon) to fake an injury for a lawsuit. The two exhibited a screen chemistry that would serve them well throughout upcoming decades. In *The Odd Couple*, Matthau was perfectly cast as the cigar–chomping, beer–swilling, poker–playing roommate whose messy habits perturb the finicky Felix.

Shortly after this success, Matthau was paired with Barbra Streisand in the 1969 film version of the musical *Hello, Dolly!* He told C. Robert Jennings in *Esquire* that he was "nervous and embarrassed" about having to dance, and it became public knowledge that the two quarreled on the set. By the early 1970s, Matthau was established as a bona fide movie star, despite his saggy jowls and perennially slouched posture. Nevertheless, he once remarked to Sherry Sonnett in the *New York Times*, "If I thought I was a Hollywood actor, I'd kill myself. A Hollywood actor is an actor who can't act, a robot. A New York actor is intelligent; he understands what he's saying, he thinks."

In the early 1970s, Matthau continued to draw praise, winning a British Academy of Film and Television Arts Award for best actor for the efforts *Pete 'n' Tillie*, 1972, and *Charley Varrick*, 1973. He then won a Golden Globe Award for best actor in a musical or comedy film in 1976 for the bittersweet 1975 comedy *The Sunshine Boys*, in which he costarred with George Burns. They played retired vaudeville partners who continued to feud long after retirement. Neil Simon wrote the screenplay for the work, which had seen an earlier incarnation on the stage. Another of Matthau's most memorable roles was the ornery, disheveled Little League coach in *The Bad News Bears*, 1976. He also had a supporting part in Simon's 1978 film *California Suite*, and also that year starred as the doctor in *House Calls*.

In 1993, Matthau's career hit another high when he and Lemmon teamed again in *Grumpy Old Men*. This rollicking comedy concerns two cranky retirees who have competed against each other in everything from fishing to romance for the past 50 years. When a new woman moves into the neighborhood, their rivalry reaches a boiling point. After this blockbuster, they saw another hit in 1995 with *Grumpier Old Men*, in a rare case of the sequel being as funny as the original. Then, in 1998, Matthau and Lemmon reprised their roles from decades past when they starred in Neil Simon's *The Odd Couple II*. In this flash– forward, the former roommates are reluctantly reunited when Oscar's son and Felix's daughter plan to get married. Meanwhile, Matthau also showed up as the crotchety Mr. Wilson in 1993's *Dennis the Menace* and as Albert Einstein in 1994's

I.Q., and paired up again with Lemmon in 1997's *Out to Sea*. Then, in 2000, Matthau shared the screen with Diane Keaton, Meg Ryan, and Lisa Kudrow in *Hanging Up*, about three busy sisters whose father is on his deathbed.

Matthau was married to Grace Geraldine Johnson in 1948, and they divorced in 1958. They had two children, David and Jenny. While still married, he met actor Carol Grace Marcus Saroyan, who was Jayne Mansfield's understudy on Broadway. She, too, was married at the time, to novelist and playwright Charles Saroyan, and had two children together, Aram and Lucy. After their divorces, they married on August 21, 1959, and together had a son, Charles. Matthau and his son, now a director, are seemingly inseparable; they worked together on the 1995 picture *The Grass Harp*.

In 1966 Matthau suffered a heart attack and subsequently cut down on his three–pack–a– day habit and his gambling, and began jogging 10 miles a day on the beach near his home in the Pacific Palisades. He later had open–heart surgery in May of 1977. A notorious joker off screen as well as on, Matthau once played a gag on film executives and the star of *Hopscotch*, a movie he was doing. Brian Garfield, the author of the book *Hopscotch*, recalled to Maurice Zolotow in *Reader's Digest* that the actor entered the meeting and declared, "My doctor only gave me six months to live." As the group sat in shock, he added, "And when he found out I couldn't pay the bill he gave me another six months."

Sources

Books

Contemporary Theatre, Film and Television, volume 14, Gale Research, 1995.
International Dictionary of Films and Filmmakers, Volume 3: Actors and Actresses, St. James Press, 1996.

Periodicals

Entertainment Weekly, February 25, 2000, p. 55.
Esquire, December 1968, p. 192.
Ladies Home Journal, June 1977, p. 40.
McCall's, February 1986, p. 48.
Newsweek, May 19, 1975, p. 89; February 21, 2000, p. 57.
New Yorker, May 31, 1993, p. 130; November 25, 1996, p. 126.
New York Times Magazine, October 18, 1953, p. 65; July 4, 1971; April 21, 1974.

People, September 23, 1996, p. 20.

Readers Digest, January 1981, p. 119; April 1997, p. 142.

Redbook, January 1969, p. 68.

Saturday Evening Post, March 1979, p. 60.

Time, March 26, 1965, p. 52; May 24, 1971, p. 86; February 28, 2000, p. 94.

TV Guide, March 3, 1990, p. 35.

Vanity Fair, April 1997, p. 384.

Online

"Walter Matthau," Internet Movie Database web site, http://us.imdb.com (May 4, 2000).

Tim McGraw

Singer

Born Samuel Timothy Smith, May 1, 1966, in Jacksonville, FL; son of Tug McGraw (a baseball player) and Betty Trimble; married Faith Hill (a singer), October 6, 1996; children: Gracie, Maggie. *Education:* Attended Northeast Louisiana University, 1986–89.

Addresses: *Home*—Nashville, TN. *Agent*—Creative Artists Agency, 9830 Wilshire Blvd., Beverly Hills, CA 90212.

Career

Began performing in clubs in Nashville, TN, 1989; signed with Curb Records, 1990; released debut album, *Tim McGraw*, 1993; released first number one single, "Indian Outlaw," 1994; has appeared on numerous television specials and talk shows.

Awards: Academy of Country Music top new male vocalist award and album of the year award for *Not a Moment Too Soon*, *Billboard* top new country artist award and top new country album award for *Not a Moment Too Soon*, Blockbuster Entertainment Award for favorite CD for *Not a Moment Too Soon*, Country Music Television (CMT) male video artist of the year award, and Country Radio Music Award for best new country artist, and TNN/Music City News Songwriter Awards, best song, for "Don't Take the Girl," all 1994; American Music Award for favorite new country artist, Country Music Association SRO award for new touring artist, Country Dance Music Award for best dance album for *Not a Moment Too Soon*, and TNN/Music City News Star of Tomorrow

Award, all 1995; Country Music Association SRO Award for best tour package, for Spontaneous Combustion Tour, 1996; *Billboard* magazine single of the year award, Billboard Monitor single of the year, *Radio & Records* single of the year, Gavin single of the year, and CMT vocal event award, all for "It's Your Love," and CMT male artist of the year, video of the year, and top video of all time awards, all 1997; Academy of Country Music Awards single of the year, song of the year, video of the year, and top vocal event, for "It's Your Love," *Billboard* country single of the year for "Just to See You Smile," Country Music Association album of the year award, *Radio & Records* country radio readers poll award for best album, both for *Everywhere*, and Country Radio Music Award for best male artist, all 1998; Academy of Country Music Awards male vocalist of the year and vocal event of the year (with Faith Hill) for "Just to Hear You Say that You Love Me," Country Music Association Awards for male vocalist of the year and album of the year as artist and producer, for *A Place in the Sun*, *Radio & Records* country radio readers poll award for best male vocalist and best album, for *Everywhere*, and TNN/Music City News awards for male artist of the year, and song of the year and vocal collaboration of the year (with Faith Hill) for "Just to Hear You Say that You Love Me," all 1999; Academy of Country Music Award for best male vocalist, 2000.

Sidelights

One of the most popular "Young Country" stars to emerge in the 1990s, Tim McGraw quickly began to top charts and pack arenas after the release of his second album in 1994. With his high-pitched, rather growly voice, McGraw became known for his ability to stir up a range of emotions with everything from jumping dance tunes to heartfelt ballads. As he remarked to David Zimmerman in USA Today, "There's a lot of people who can pick up a guitar and sing you a great song, but there's very few people that can tell you how they feel. That's the main purpose of acting or doing an opera or painting or anything. It's to tell somebody how you feel and more importantly, tell them how they feel." His strong appeal has led to millions upon millions of album sales, and a healthy list of awards from the likes of the Academy of Country Music, Billboard, the Country Music Association, Country Music Television, and more. Though some critics wondered after his first hit the controversial "Indian Outlaw" if he was going to be a one-hit wonder and fade into oblivion, McGraw has continued to score hits. In 1999, he released A Place in the Sun and toured with George Strait and then the Dixie Chicks. McGraw is married to another celebrated country star, Faith Hill.

McGraw was born Samuel Timothy Smith in Jacksonville, Florida, the son of Betty Smith (now Betty Trimble) and Tug McGraw. However, McGraw grew up thinking that his mother's husband, Horace Smith, a trucker, was his father. The couple divorced when McGraw was nine, and after that, he and his mother were often forced to relocate around Richland Parish. One time after moving, McGraw, then 11, opened a box that contained his birth certificate, which had his father's name scribbled out but listed the occupation as "baseball player." His mother eventually divulged that she had a brief summer romance with Tug McGraw, who was a minor league pitcher at the time. He quickly left her, though, and she married Smith when her son was seven months old.

Tug McGraw went on to make his name with the New York Mets and Philadelphia Phillies. By the early 1970s, he was the highest-paid and most popular relief pitcher in professional baseball. McGraw met him once at a game in Houston, but his biological father showed little interest in maintaining a close relationship. The baseball star had married and had two other children by then, though he and his wife divorced in 1988. McGraw was initially angry at his father for not supporting him, but later forgave him, telling Steve Dougherty and Meg Grant in People, "He was 22 and immature when it happened." Ironically, McGraw had his father's baseball card taped to his bedroom wall even before he knew he was his father.

Though he was raised in Start, Louisiana, a tiny town in Richland Parish, McGraw spent a good deal of time on the road in the cab of Smith's 18-wheeler. In the truck, he would sing along to country artists like Charley Pride, Johnny Paycheck, and George Jones. "By the time I was six," McGraw related to Christopher John Farley in Time, "I felt as if I knew the words to every album Merle Haggard ever recorded." He also sang spirituals in church, and belted show tunes in elementary school plays. Though he played Little League as a boy, McGraw had given up his dreams of becoming a pro ball player like his dad by the time he went to college. When he was a senior at Monroe Christian High School, he met up again with Tug McGraw, who agreed to pay for his higher education. McGraw graduated as salutatorian in 1985. Shortly after that he changed his surname to match that of his biological father, though he continues to consider his stepfather, Smith, as his true dad.

As a freshman at Northeast Louisiana State University, McGraw took pre-law courses after seeing the film And Justice for All, starring Al Pacino. But he ended up enjoying parties more than classes, and became more interested in music. He ended up buying a guitar at a pawn shop, and within a year, he was singing in clubs around Monroe, Louisiana. Soon, he decided to quit school and try his luck in Nashville. His father told him to finish school first, but McGraw reminded him that he had quit college for baseball. Besides, as McGraw noted to Dave McKenna in the Washington Post, "The only thing I learned in college was how to float a keg, and I didn't figure that was going to get me too far. So even though it was kind of scary, I wasn't giving up much. I thought I could make it." His dad continued to support him while he tried to rev up a career.

Landing in Music City in May of 1989, McGraw had little experience in performing and no contacts. But the industry was ripe for smooth, handsome male vocalists, and he managed to line up gigs in Printers Alley clubs. Within a year and a half, he cinched a contract with Curb Records. His first self-titled album came out in April of 1993, but sank into oblivion. To drum up attention, the label sent McGraw on the road with his band, the Dance Hall Doctors, and his live act went over big. With power ballads and party hits like Steve Miller's "The Joker" he found his audience.

In February of 1994, McGraw released the infectious single "Indian Outlaw," and it quickly raced up the country charts and became a radio hit. However, it also earned him unwanted status as a novelty act, and attracted a bitter backlash from many who found it offensive to Native Americans. The lyrics included lines like "I'm an Indian outlaw / Half–Cherokee, half–Choctaw / My baby she's a Chippewa," and lines like "You can find me in my wigwam / I'll be beatin' on my tom–tom." But McGraw stated he meant no harm, and simply used the tribal names and other words for their rhyming qualities. In addition, the outcry surprised him since he had been closing his stage show with the tune for four years. However, Cherokee Nation leader Wilma Mankiller sent a letter to stations claiming the song exhibited "crass exploitative commercialism at the expense of Indians," and expressed that it "promotes bigotry," according to a *Billboard* article by Peter Cronin. As a result, some radio stations in Arizona, Nevada, Oklahoma, and Minnesota started refusing to play it. On the other hand, the Eastern Band of Cherokee Indians based in North Carolina wrote to McGraw's management company in support of the song.

Shortly after this brouhaha, McGraw's second album was released. *Not a Moment Too Soon* became the number one country hit in its first week on the charts. Also, three more singles off the effort topped the charts in addition to "Indian Outlaw." The album and the number one single "Don't Take the Girl," a melodramatic ballad, racked up awards from the likes of the Academy of Country Music and Country Music Television. McGraw was also named best new country artist by *Billboard* and others. *Not a Moment Too Soon* hugged the top spot on the country album chart for 26 consecutive weeks and sold about eight million copies over the next few years. Immediately, McGraw was catapulted from playing honky–tonks to embarking on a major headlining tour.

The next year, in September of 1995, McGraw released *All I Want*. Though it was an attempt to show more serious musicianship, the first single released was the jaunty "I Like It, I Love It." As he explained to Deborah Evans Price in *Billboard*, "It was a cool, fun, back– to–school song. It doesn't really say a lot. We put it out because it's a fun sing–along song, and it will call attention to some of the meat songs on the album that I really want people to hear." The song stayed at number one for five weeks and the album sold three million copies, but McGraw was largely passed over at the 1996 awards ceremonies.

Still, 1996 saw the successful Spontaneous Combustion tour, which featured country singer Faith Hill as the opening act. By the end of the tour, McGraw's personal life was sizzling as well, and he asked Hill, who has a laundry list of country music awards herself, to marry him. They were on tour at the time in Montana, and he popped the question in his dressing room, which was housed in a trailer. He related to Jeremy Helligar and Lorna Grisby in *People,* "She said, 'I can't believe you're asking me to marry you in a trailer house,' and I said, 'Well, we're country singers, what do you expect?'" She later accepted the proposal by writing "yes" on the mirror in his trailer while he was on stage, and they married on October 6, 1996. Their daughter Gracie was born in 1997, and another daughter, Maggie, was born the following year.

In the meantime, McGraw began to diversify in order to have options in case his popularity bottomed out. He formed production and management companies, and he and Byron Gallimoer coproduced Joe Dee Messina's debut album, which contained the hit "Heads Carolina, Tails California." McGraw need not have worried. In June of 1997, he spawned another winner with *Everywhere*, which rose to the top of the charts and included three number–one singles, including "It's Your Love," which he sang with Hill. In addition, that song made the crossover to hit the top ten on the pop chart as well. *Everywhere* reflected a new stability in his life as a married man and father, and attracted the biggest onslaught of awards to that point. Among other honors, in 1997 "It's Your Love" was named *Billboard* magazine single of the year award, *Radio & Records* single of the year, and Country Music Television deemed him male artist of the year, in addition to bestowing upon McGraw video of the year and top video of all time awards. Also, in 1998 he won awards from the Academy of Country Music for single of the year, song of the year, video of the year, and top vocal event, all for "It's Your Love," as well as winning *Billboard'*s country single of the year for "Just to See You Smile."

In 1999, McGraw's hot streak continued after the release of *A Place in the Sun* that May. It debuted at the top of *Billboard'*s album chart and spawned a number one country chart hit, "Please Remember Me." The awards continued to pile up as McGraw won Academy of Country Music Awards for male vocalist of the year and vocal event of the year (with Faith Hill) for "Just to Hear You Say that You Love Me," and Country Music Association Awards for male vocalist of the year and album of the year as artist and producer, for *A Place in the Sun,* among others. In addition, for the second year in a row, a *Radio & Records* country radio readers poll award voted *Everywhere* the best album. He also collected several other nominations for *A Place in the Sun* from awards ceremonies to be held in 2000. To top it off,

People magazine named him the "sexiest country star" that year in their annual issue devoted to dreamboats. Adding to his cache of honors, in 2000, McGraw won an Academy of Country Music Award for male vocalist of the year.

McGraw lives in a six–bedroom home on 200 acres just outside of Nashville. As he explained to Zimmerman in *USA Today,* "It's the most relaxing place in the world. We have bonfires all the time on the Back Forty and hang out on tailgates and pick guitars and have a few beers." He and his wife are away on tour frequently, but Hill never leaves without the children. "I love my wife more than anything in the world," McGraw remarked in another *People* article. "But boy, when she had our babies, it quadrupled. There's just something about the connection."

Selected discography

Tim McGraw, Curb, 1993.
Not a Moment Too Soon, Curb, 1994.
All I Want, 1995.
Everywhere, Curb, 1997.
A Place in the Sun, Curb, 1999.

Sources

Books

Contemporary Musicians, volume 17, Gale Research, 1996.

Periodicals

Billboard, March 19, 1994, p. 38; August 19, 1995, p. 6.
Country Music, July–August 1995, p. 16; January–February 1996, p. 18.
Entertainment Weekly, November 10, 1995, p. 30; October 25, 1996, p. 18; June 13, 1997, p. 66.
People, April 25, 1994, p. 65; July 7, 1997, p. 25; April 27, 1998, p. 85; July 12, 1999, p. 95; November 15, 1999, p. 106.
St. Louis Post–Dispatch, August 5, 1999, p. 19.
Time, June 28, 1999, p. 69.
USA Today, February 24, 1997, p. 1D.
Washington Post, May 15, 1999, p. C1.

Online

Tim McGraw Official Web Site, http://www.timmcgraw.com (April 7, 2000).

Megawati Sukarnoputri

Indonesian politician

Born in 1947; daughter of Sukarno (president of Indonesian) and Fatmawati; married and divorced twice; married Taufiq Kiemas (a business owner); children: two sons, one daughter. *Education:* Attended Padjadjaran University, Bandung, Indonesia; studied agriculture and psychology.

Addresses: *Home*—Jakarta, Indonesia.

Career

Indonesian politician. Homemaker and wife, late 1960s–1979; florist, 1979–87; member of Indonesian parliament, 1987–97; chair of Indonesian Democratic Party (PDI), 1993–97; vice president of Indonesia, 1999—.

Sidelights

In 1999, Megawati Sukarnoputri became vice president of Indonesia, the world's fourth–most–populous nation, after a tumultuous time in that country's political affairs. First, in 1998, Indonesians rioted and looted as they demanded new leadership. President Suharto had pilfered money from state coffers, placing him among the wealthiest people in the world. Suharto had originally risen to leadership in the late 1960s after Megawati's father, Sukarno, the first leader of independent Indonesia, was forced out. During this time, Suharto maintained a tight grip on the power structure with his ruling party, Golkar, and the citizenry did not rebel, because he helped pull his nation out of poverty with oil sales. When the economy flagged in the

Archive Photos

1980s and the Asian crisis hit in the 1990s, though, his days were numbered. After Suharto resigned, he named a successor, Bacharuddin Jusuf Habibie, who had been a close ally for over three decades. Amid further protests, Habibie agreed to hold open, multiparty elections in 1999.

Meanwhile, in the late 1980s and early 1990s, Megawati had risen to become leader of the opposition party, the Indonesian Democratic Party (PDI). Her popularity, in addition to the financial situation, helped destabilized the Suharto regime. Entering politics in middle age, she was often described as "matronly," and many outside observers questioned her ability to become a world leader, especially because up until her election to parliament in 1987, her occupation had been as a homemaker and mother. Her lack of outspokenness on issues and her quiet nature were sometimes read as serenity, but others saw these qualities as signs of being uneducated, unprepared, and uninteresting. By the mid–1990s, however, Megawati had garnered a great deal of support, enough to worry Suharto that her party could pose a serious threat to his control. He banished her from politics, but after his downfall, she rose again and became the front–runner for the presidency. Though the office ended up going to a rival party leader after a startling vote in the national assembly, parliament voted her in as vice president in October of 1999.

Megawati Sukarnoputri (pronounced meg–ah–WAH–tee soo–kar–no–POO–tree) was born in 1947, the second of five children of Sukarno, the founder of independent Indonesia, and his first wife, Fatmawati. (He had three other children by three more wives.) "Sukarnoputri," literally translated, means "daughter of Sukarno," but many Indonesians, including her, use only their first name. Sukarno led the drive to secure independence from the Netherlands and became Indonesia's first president under home rule in 1949. As such, Megawati grew up in the posh Merdeka Palace until her father's downfall. As the nation is composed of more than 13,000 islands, maintaining centralized control was difficult, so Sukarno imposed martial law. In addition, the period of his leadership was marred by famines, out–of–control inflation, and a near–economic collapse. Following a coup attempt in 1965, Sukarno became even more unpopular, and the stage was set for his rival, General Suharto, to take power in 1967. Suharto remained a heroic figure for his historical contributions, however, and there are still many signs of respect for him in the country.

Despite his political prominence, Sukarno left little wealth when he died in 1970. Megawati lived modestly throughout her life, adding to her image as a champion of the poor. Although she attended college, studying agriculture and psychology, she left without graduating after the coup attempt; a friend told Mark McDonald of the *Knight–Ridder Tribune News Service*, "No children of Sukarno were allowed to go to university. They had no money, no education, no jobs. The family was so poor then." Megawati settled into a middle–class lifestyle of marriage and children. She married an Indonesian Air Force pilot in the late 1960s and had two sons; she was pregnant with their daughter when her husband's plane crashed. She later married again, but was divorced quickly, and the relationship has remained a mystery.

Megawati's third husband, Taufiq Kiemas, owns and operates several gas stations in Jakarta, where they have a nice but not ostentatious home in a well–guarded area of the city. He ran for parliament from southern Sumatra, and encouraged his wife to become involved in politics as well. Though she and her siblings vowed not to seek office while Suharto was alive, Megawati's oldest brother, Guntur, a photographer, and younger brother, Guruh, a choreographer, both held seats in parliament briefly. Also, sisters Guruh and Rachmawati ran for parlia-

ment in 1999. Nevertheless, Megawati's brother Guntur told McDonald, "We are not cut out for politics. It's Mega who has staying power.... She has guts."

Still, nothing in Megawati's background exemplified her readiness for the political arena. In 1979 she opened a flower shop with three friends, selling arrangements to upscale hotels and donating the proceeds to a foundation for poor children. Besides that, her background was as a homemaker. With encouragement from her husband, though, she won a seat in parliament at age 40, in 1987, joining the original Indonesian Democratic Party (PDI), a collaboration between nationalist and Christian parties. Though she was often criticized for her lack of participation, she was named leader of PDI in 1993.

While Megawati at that point denied any interest in challenging Suharto's power structure, many in her country as well as international observers saw her as having the potential to shake up the regime. Suharto only allowed two opposition parties to exist the PDI and the Muslim–based United Development Party (PPP)—in order to give a slight nod toward democracy so as to appease the masses, and even then, they were forbidden from campaigning outside towns. Under Megawati, though, the PDI began to show an unprecedented growth in support after she spoke out against nepotism and the growing schism between the working class and ultra–wealthy. Thus, the Suharto government orchestrated a coup within her party in June of 1996 that placed a former Golkar member, Sujadi, in her place.

That same month, a demonstration in favor of Megawati ended in violence as protestors chanting "Mega! Mega! Mega!" clashed with government troops. Many PDI regional offices continued to support Megawati, but the government cracked down on them, too, forcing out her supporters at PDI headquarters in Jakarta in July of 1996 which caused more riots. Four people were killed, and the government reported that 171 were arrested, though Megawati claimed the number was closer to 250. Meanwhile, she denounced the violence, and through it all, she staunchly insisted she had no intentions of challenging Suharto's leadership. Some predicted that since his five–year term in office would be up in 1998, and because his health seemed to be taking a bad turn after the unexpected death of his wife in 1996, Megawati would try to assume the presidency. However, she was only eligible to run as chair of one of the three major parties, and by deposing her, the government ended her chances as a possible candidate. Despite her vocal statements against the goal of seeking the country's highest office, she did go to court to seek reinstatement in her position as PDI chair, and she was becoming an icon for those dissatisfied with the current system.

Still, others figured that even if Suharto stepped down, he would find a way to transfer power to his family or a strong nationalist from the military. Democracy was still just an empty concept in a land where gatherings of more than five people for the purpose of discussing political issues were banned, and where the press was highly censored. Others mused that Megawati might not be able to muster enough support from the fledgling middle class even if running for president did become viable. Yet many Indonesians began comparing her to the Philippines' Corazon Aquino, who led the "People Power" effort to force out Ferdinand Marcos, as well as Aung San Suu Kyi of Burma and Benazir Bhutto of Pakistan. Suharto continued to crack down on her, harassing her and her supporters, and left her name off the list of parliamentary candidates up for election in 1997.

When Megawati tried to get back on the election list by offering her name, as well as names of supporters, on a separate "Megawati slate," she was denied. Undaunted, she expected that popular protest would help her return to parliament, but if not, she recognized that she was still a rallying point for those calling for a change. As she noted to Keith B. Richburg in the *Washington Post*, "In our culture, there is not only a formal leader. There is also an informal leader. Sometimes the informal leader can be more powerful than the formal leader. You can see how my father, even though he has already passed away, in spirit still lives inside the Indonesian people."

In May of 1997, the Golkar captured the majority of votes, Suharto was reelected, and Megawati was excluded from elections. This only served to strengthen her position, and by 1998, she was calling for the president to step down. Further rioting, looting, and deadly violence by restless citizens that year led Golkar to vote Suharto out of office. After he resigned in May of 1998, his political ally, Habibie, who had been vice president for just ten weeks, took the office of president but promised free elections in 1999. Subsequently, Megawati formed a new branch of the PDI called the PDI–P, or Indonesian Democratic Party for Struggle.

In June of 1999, elections were held for the Indonesian legislators, and candidates for president were in place. They included Megawati, who was un-

doubtedly popular yet widely criticized for her soft–spoken manner that was interpreted variously as being dull, unmotivated, or uninformed on issues; Habibie, who was trying to distance himself from his predecessor, Suharto; Amien Rais of the National Mandate Party (PAN), a charismatic supporter of student protests; and Abdurrahman Wahid, also known as Gus Dur, a driving force in the National Awakening Party (PKB) and the leader of the largest Muslim group in Indonesia.

Despite Megawati's high profile, her bid for the presidency came under fire because of her gender. In the largest Islamic nation in the world 90 percent of Indonesia's 200 million inhabitants are Muslim her opponents began to play up the idea that as a woman, she should not be elected. Although Islamic law does not prohibit a woman from leading the country, and religion is not seen as having nearly as much clout as politics in the nation, some were trying to stir public sentiment against the concept. And, although Megawati herself was a practicing Muslim, some were suspicious of how much of an adherent she was due to her wide support from non–Muslims. Other criticisms included her three marriages and her lack of a formal degree.

In the June elections, the PDI–P party garnered 153 of the 462 seats up for grabs (out of a total of 700), a good deal more than Golkar's 120 positions. Megawati thus seemed assured of the presidency. However, an electoral college, mainly from the House of Representatives, votes in the president, and Megawati needed a coalition to ensure her seat. From June to October, though, she seemed unwilling to forge integral ties with rival parties. A former cabinet minister, Sarwono Kusumaatmadja, told Seth Mydans of the *New York Times* that if Megawati lost the election, "the country [would] be thrown into total chaos total civil chaos." By this time, she not only had the backing of the poor, but also the elite classes, who saw her as being good for the business climate. And as Mydans reported in another *New York Times* article, "Many people have made their voices heard in continuing mass rallies and in outbursts of violence."

Hours before the assembly vote was scheduled in October of 1999, the Golkar party humiliated Habibie by replacing him as a presidential candidate with party chair, Akbar Tanjung, the speaker of the parliament. This change did not make a difference, though. In a surprise shift in support, the assembly voted in Wahid, the Muslim leader respected for his teachings on tolerance and self–respect. The vote was 373 for Wahid, 313 for Megawati, and five abstentions. As predicted, there were outbursts of violence, but not nearly as bad as anyone expected.

Megawati appeared on television holding Wahid's hand, and she commented, according to Mydans, "For the unity of the nation I call on the people of Indonesia to accept the results of the election."

Though some supporters wept and others rioted after Megawati's defeat, the next day, parliament voted her in to the post of vice president. This was an important gesture and helped bring stability to the troubled nation. With Megawati as vice president, Mydans indicated that her party may be more willing to work with Wahid. He also noted, "Their cooperation may be enhanced by the fact that the President is in poor health, and should he die, Ms. Megawati may yet have the chance to take over the presidency before his five–year term is up."

Sources

Business Week, June 21, 1999, p. 52.

Dallas Morning News, September 8, 1996, p. 28A.

Economist, April 8, 1995, p. 35; June 29, 1996, p. 15; June 29, 1996, p. 31; August 3, 1996, p. 21; September 21, 1996, p. 39; October 17, 1998, p. 48; June 26, 1999, p. 47.

Knight–Ridder/Tribune News Service, June 7, 1999; June 17, 1999.

Maclean's, August 19, 1996, p. 30.

Newsweek, August 26, 1996, p. 41.

New York Times, August 4, 1996, sec. 1, p. 3; June 20, 1999, sec. 1, p. 3; September 27, 1999, p. A6; October 6, 1999, p. A10; October 15, 1999, p. A14; October 18, 1999, p. A8; October 19, 1999, p. A3; October 20, 1999, p. A1; October 21, 1999, p. A1; October 22, 1999, p. A1; October 23, 1999, p. A8.

Time International, August 12, 1996, p. 14; August 12, 1996, p. 12; October 12, 1998, p. 24; June 7, 1999, p. 41; July 26, 1999, p. 17.

Vogue, April 1998, p. 246.

Washington Post, September 20, 1996, p. A25.

Bebe Miller

Choreographer and dancer

Born September 20, 1950, in New York, NY; daughter of a ship steward and schoolteacher. *Education:* Earlham College, Richmond, IN, B.A. in fine arts, 1971; Ohio State University, M.A. in dance, 1975.

Addresses: *Office*—Bebe Miller Company, 54 W. 21st St., Ste. 502, New York, NY 10010.

Career

Studied dance with Ruth Grauert, Murray Louis, Fran Reid, Phyllis Lamhut, and Nina Wiener, 1976 to 1982; performed with Dana Reitz in New York and Europe, 1983; first independent choreography, 1978; founder and artistic director, Bebe Miller Company, 1985; has taught at the University of Illinois at Champaign/Urbana, UCLA, New York University, Mt. Holyoke College, Movement Research in New York City, Sarah Lawrence College, University of Minnesota, Mills College, Middlebury College, Virginia Commonwealth University, Texas Women's University, Cal Arts and Stanford University, with residencies at Ohio State University in Columbus, Portland State University in Oregon, Bates Dance Festival, SUNY/Purchase, NYU, and the Colorado Dance Festival. International teaching included The Dance Factory in Johannesburg, 1994; Thamesdown Dance in Swindon, England; T Junction in Vienna, Austria, 1995; and Lasica Associates in Melbourne, Australia, 1995.

Awards: Creative Artists Public Service Fellowship, 1984; National Foundation for the Arts Choreographer's Fellowship, 1984, 1991; National Endowment for the Arts Choreographer's fellowships, 1985–88; New York Dance and Performance Award (Bessie) for Choreography, 1986, 1987; American Choreographer Award, 1988; Guggenheim Fellowship, 1988; Outstanding Young Alumna, Earlham College, 1988; Dewar's Young Artists Recognition Award, 1990; National Dance Residency Program, 1996.

Sidelights

Modern dance choreographer Bebe Miller is renowned for her innovative, eclectic performances, with their corkscrewing, energetic movements and complex themes. Borrowing talents from writers, set and lighting designers, and visual artists, her pieces exude a theatrical mood, which she feels accentuates the stories she tells through dance. Despite the visual clues, though, her messages are often ambiguous, a quality for which she strives. And oftentimes, Miller has been questioned for not devoting more of her art to specific ideas about race, being that she is a black woman working in a mainly white field. She related to Jean Battey Lewis in the *Washington Times,* however, that she avoids making blanket statements with her work. "I think if you approach questions like [racial issues] intellectually you're trying to solve problems and show solutions," she offered. "But I've been searching for movement metaphors and leaving their meanings open."

Miller was born September 20, 1950, in Brooklyn, New York City, and raised in a public housing project in Red Hook along the waterfront there. Her father was a ship steward and her mother taught elementary school. As a child, Miller's mother took her to concerts at Carnegie Hall and Town Hall, and signed her up for dance lessons at the Henry Street Playhouse when she was four. She also sent her kids—including Miller's twin brother and older sister—to camp in Maine. "The woods, the music lessons, and dance lessons were formative experiences," Miller remarked to Kevin Giordano in *Dance Magazine.* "But it was sort of alienating for a kid in Brooklyn." However, she also commented to Jean Battey Lewis in the *Washington Times,* "The idea of creative expression was something I was lucky enough to grow up with."

Initially, Miller's mother had started going to the Henry Street Settlement community center for exercise classes to help her arthritis, and she took her children along with her. There, Miller studied modern dance with Murray Louis, who later founded the prestigious Nikolais and Louis Dance Theater on New York's Lower East Side, along with Alwin Nikolais. However, Louis did not start with traditional dance elements, but rather instilled a sense of creativity and improvisation in his students. Later, at age 13, Miller took a few months of classical ballet training at Carnegie Hall, but remarked to Elizabeth Zimmer in *Dance Magazine,* "All those little bunheads and me from the projects. I was intimidated, so I stopped."

Miller went on to attend Earlham College in Richmond, Indiana, where she received a bachelor of fine arts degree in 1971. Though she admitted to Zimmer that she "wasn't very good" at art, she continued to study piano and dance at college. After graduating, she returned to New York and found work waiting tables. She resumed dance classes with Louis, as well as studying with Nikolais. Meanwhile, Miller was living with her boyfriend, renting a loft for $350 a month. "The kind of economic commitment you have to have now is totally different from what it was ten or fifteen years ago," she related to Zimmer in the 1989 article.

In the early 1970s, after choreographing and performing with small modern dance groups in New York, Miller won a fellowship to attend Ohio State University. There, she studied with Nina Wiener, who had studied with Alvin Ailey, worked with the renowned Twyla Tharp Dance Company, and was the resident choreographer at Ohio State. Miller earned a master's degree in dance in 1975, and later danced professionally with Nina Wiener and Dancers for six years. Later, she also studied with choreographer Dana Reitz.

In the meantime, Miller was staging her own solo and small group performances in the late 1970s and early 1980s around New York City. She created her first piece, *Tune,* in 1978. In the early 1980s, she left Wiener's company, and around 1985 formed her own group. At the time, she was one of the few black choreographers in New York, but she preferred to downplay her race. Eventually, she realized that people were inevitably going to comment on her color, but she continued to resist focusing on racial issues, instead hoping to show that she could be a black female choreographer who could deal with a wide range of subjects.

In 1981, Miller staged a set of works at New York City's Bessie Schonberg Theater, including *Tune, Square Business* and *Jammin',* which were reviewed in the *New York Times.* These dances featured performance set to music by David Bowie, Brian Eno, Van Morrison, and Sweet Honey in the Rock. Subsequently, Miller set her pieces to original compositions; 1982's *Vespers* was accompanied by music from Linda Gibbs, and 1983's *Story Beach* and *Gotham* were set to works by Hearn Gadboia. Also that year, she staged *Guardian Angels,* set to Gregorian chants.

One of Miller's most acclaimed performances came in 1986. *Two* was created in collaboration with award–winning choreographer Ralph Lemon, and set to music by Christopher Hyams–Hart. The duet explored the shifts in relationships by variously moving together and pulling away during the dance. Jennifer Dunning in the *New York Times* commented, "Ms. Miller and Mr. Lemon know how to move and how to charge the stage space with turbid electricity." Some of Miller's other praised efforts included *Trapped in Queens,* 1984, which captured an urban mood, and *Spending Time Doing Things,* 1985, a solo choreographed to the Duke Ellington tune "In My Solitude." The latter led to an array of fellowships, and Miller was soon asked to stage new works around the city and the country.

Then, in 1987, the Alvin Ailey Repertory Ensemble and other companies commissioned a set of new works by Miller. These were performed in Amsterdam, the Netherlands. That same year, she choreographed *Habit of Attraction,* which premiered in 1989 at the Womanworks festival—an event held in New York City to spotlight female modern dance choreographers—along with *Thick Sleep* (1989). *Habit of Attraction,* according to Anna Kisselgoff in the *New York Times,* "describes the uneven course of male–female relationships," and though she noted that it "suffers from too even a pace," she summed up, "The hard, no–nonsense idiom, shorn of flourishes, has a welcome if artificial–looking clarity."

Also in 1989, Miller choreographed *Allies,* generally considered to be the nadir of her career. It was also the most expensive dance performance to that point, costing $80,000 to stage. Performed at the Next Wave Festival at the Brooklyn Academy of Music (BAM), which also helped commission the work, this 35–minute piece featured a score by noted experimental composer Fred Frith and scenery by photographer Robert Flynt, who shot photos of dancers underwater and used a projection technique to create an ethereal atmosphere. The theme concerned telling friends from enemies and understanding that the same human being might be one person's ally and another's nemesis. In the piece, dancers warily split off into groups, then at times some dancers would pull others away, or hang onto one of their fellow dancers without a clear notion of whether they were being held voluntarily or against their will.

Also at the Next Wave Festival, Miller performed the solo effort, *Rain*, "in which she portrayed a woman weighted down by a host of cares, yet refusing to be totally crushed by them," as Jack Anderson described in the *New York Times*. In it, wearing a red velvet dress, she ran in place fast, then slowing, as if running out of energy; she then crawled to a mat of grass and rested her head on it. Some critics viewed this piece as a personal statement by Miller on a range of topics, from the environment to African liberation, since the colors black, red, and green figured prominently.

In the meantime, Miller was hatching an idea to put together a project based on the music of legendary guitarist Jimi Hendrix. She was inspired by the sense of social activism of the 1960s and wanted to bring that to the current era in order to address contemporary issues. Her company performed *The Hendrix Project*, which also included music by folk artist Bob Dylan, in 1991 in Los Angeles and San Francisco as part of a program titled *Black Choreographers Moving Towards the 21st Century*. Later it was staged in New York and Europe. Critics noted the political overtones of the piece, which used Hendrix's controversial guitar solo rendition of "The Star Spangled Banner."

Writing for the *New York Times*, Jack Anderson wished that Miller would have put forth more commentary on the subjects she raised, concluding that "*The Hendrix Project* deserves to be intellectually as well as emotionally stirring." Other critics, however, praised the energy and movement in the piece. Miller would later use Hendrix's music in other performances; namely, 1992's *Paisley Sky* and 1994's *Arena*, which also featured works by Led Zeppelin and Bill Frisell.

In 1992, the Phoenix Dance Company in Leeds, England, a mainly black troupe, commissioned a work from Miller. Some predicted that she would use this opportunity to firmly address her racial roots, but instead, she drew upon folk dances from Greece. *Spartan Reels* continued on the theme of gender that was prominent in her earlier pieces, but this time displayed a more conventional approach, with the women wearing dressing and taking small steps, and the men performing more bold movements. After that, in 1994 she created a work called *Tiny Sisters in the Enormous Land*, which she based on a true story of British twin sisters who communicated solely with each other.

After a trip to Africa in 1994–95, Miller was inspired to do works that had more of a connection to her heritage, though she created two entirely different kinds of pieces. *Blessed*, set to gospel music by The Cafe of the Gate of Salvation, was a celebration of humanity, whereas Yard Dance, featuring music by James Brown, tackled apartheid. As Miller explained to Kevin Giordano in *Dance Magazine*, the visit to Africa made a distinct impression on her. "I was seeing myself as a black woman in an African country and seeing that I wasn't African. As an African American there are certain ways that I disown the culture here, but I definitely can't own Africa. Seeing it dispelled my myths of what I could and should be."

Later, Miller teamed up with jazz clarinetist Don Byron, BAM's artistic director of jazz, on 1998's *Going to the Wall*. This piece deals with racial differences and how blatantly they exist, whether or not people always acknowledge that fact. By posing direct questions about race and other characteristics, she confronts the fact that people do indeed make judgments based on appearance, but it also has to do with recognizing that though people are different from each other, they still share a great deal. The work, which was accented by her ethnically diverse troupe, also featured music by hip–hop groups Nonchalant and The Fugees. The next year she premiered a new solo, *Rhythm Studies*. In a review for *Dance Magazine*, Joseph Carmen surmised that with this work, Miller "may be creating a new genre of dance: black urban flamenco."

Miller, who holds an arts workshop each year in Maine, lives in Brooklyn, moving back there after spending two decades in Manhattan. She makes annual visits to Cape Town and Johannesburg, South Africa, to work with dance groups there, and has also taught in Austria, Australia, and England, in addition to various American universities. Her works have been performed by repertory companies across the United States, Europe, and South Africa.

Selected works

Tune (music by Van Morrison), New York, 1978.

Square Business (music by M,), New York, 1981.

Task/Force (music by David Bowie, Brian Eno), New York, 1981.

Jammin' (music by reggae, Sweet Honey in the Rock), New York, 1981.

Task Force (solo), New York, 1981.

Vespers (original music by Linda Gibbs), New York, 1982.

Story Beach (original music by Hearn Gadboia), New York, 1983.

Gotham (original music by Hearn Gadboia), New York, 1983.

Guardian Angels (music by Gregorian Chants), commissioned by CoDance Co, Pace University, New York, 1983.

Trapped in Queens (original music by Scott Killian, Jonathan Kane), New York, 1984.

Reet City (music by Hearn Gadbois), Brooklyn, 1984.

Spending Time Doing Things (music by Duke Ellington), New York, 1985.

Gypsy Pie (original music by Mike Vargas), New York, 1985.

No Evidence (original music by Lenny Pickett), Seattle, 1985.

A Haven for Restless Angels of Mercy (original music by Saqqara Dogs and George Sempepos), New York, 1986.

Working Order (original music by Hearn Gadbois, Jonathan Kane; text by Holly Anderson, other music by Bach), Boston, 1986.

Heart, Heart (music by Ladysmith Black Mombazo; text John Cheever), New York, 1986.

Two (collaboration with Ralph Lemon; original music by Christopher Hyams–Hart), New York, 1986.

Walt's (original music by Scott Killian), commissioned by CoDanceCo, New York, 1986.

The Habit of Attraction (original music by Christopher Hyams–Hart), Richmond, 1987.

This Room Has No Windows and I Can't Find You Anywhere (original music by Christopher Hyams–Hart), commissioned by Zenon Dance Company, Minneapolis, 1987.

Butte (music by Bach), commissioned by Creach/Koester, New York, 1987.

Simple Tales (original music by Christopher Hyams–Hart, Jay Bolotin; text by Holly Anderson), New York, 1988.

Cracklin' Blue (music by Patsy Cline), commissioned by Alvin Ailey Repertory Ensemble, New York, 1988.

Thick Sleep (original music by Lenny Picket), Philadelphia, 1989.

Allies (music by Fred Frith), Keene, New Hampshire, 1989.

Rain (original music by Hearn Gadbois, other music by Heitor Villa–Lobos), Brooklyn, 1989.

Vital Boulevard of Love (music by Lou Reed), commissioned by Concert Dance Company, Boston, 1989.

The Hidden Boy: Incidents from a Stressed Memory (music by Jay Bolotin), Louisville, 1990.

The Hendrix Project (music by Jimi Hendrix Experience), Minneapolis, 1991.

Sanctuary (music by Marianne Faithfull, Gospel at Colonus, traditional), commissioned by Zenon Dance Company, Minneapolis, 1991.

Spartan Reels (music by Jonathan Kane, George Sampapos), commissioned by Phoenix Dance Company, Leeds, England, 1992.

Paisley Sky (music by Jimi Hendrix Experience) commissioned by Boston Ballet, 1992.

Nothing Can Happen Only Once (original music by Christian Marclay; text by Ain Gordon), Columbus, OH, 1993.

Things I Have Not Forgotten (music by Fred Frith), commissioned by Dayton Contemporary Dance Company, 1993.

Cantos Gordos (original music by Don Byron), New York, 1994.

Daughter (music by Robin Holcomb), commissioned by Pennsylvania Dance Theatre, State College, PA, 1994.

Heaven + Earth (solo; music by Ellen Fullman), New York, 1994.

Heaven + Earth (music by The Five Blind Boys), Gabriel Faure, New York, 1994.

A Certain Depth of Heart, Also Love (music by Robert Schumann, Led Zeppelin, The Pogues, Bill Frisell, Verdi), commissioned by Oregon Ballet Theatre, Portland.

Arena (music by Led Zeppelin, Bill Frisell, Jimi Hendrix Experience), commissioned by PACT Dance Company, Johannesburg, 1994.

Tiny Sisters in the Enormous Land (original music by Robin Holcomb, text by Holly Anderson, video Kit Fitzgerald), Lewiston, ME, 1995.

Blessed (music by Cafe of the Gate of Salvation), New York, 1996.

Yard Dance (music by Vusi Mahlassala, James Brown), New York, 1996.

Voyages Plein d'Espoir (music by Richard Strauss, Cafe of the Gate of Salvation, Fred Frith, Bob Dylan), commissioned by Groupe Experimental Danse Compagnie, Fort de France, Martinique, 1997.

Roses in a Righteous Garden (music by Cafe of the Gate of Salvation, Jim Morrison, the Holmes Brothers), commissioned by Oregon Ballet Theatre, Portland, 1997.

Going to the Wall (music by Don Byron, The Fugees, and Nonchalant), 1998.

Rhythm Studies, New York, 1999.

Sources

Books

Contemporary Black Biography, volume 3, Gale Research, 1992.

International Dictionary of Modern Dance, St. James Press, 1998.

Periodicals

Columbian, June 10, 1999.

Dance Magazine, December 1989, p. 34; May 1999, p. 52; August 1999, p. 79.

Newsday, May 13, 1999, p. B9.

New York Times, December 2, 1981, p. C23; December 22, 1986, p. C14; January 22, 1989, sec. 1, p. 47; November 30, 1989, p. C20; May 26, 1991, sec. 1, p. 60.

Washington Times, November 1, 1998, p. D2.

Moby

Musician, performer, and producer

Born Richard Melville Hall, September 11, 1965, in New York, NY. *Education:* Attended University of Connecticut.

Addresses: *Home*—New York City. *Office*—c/o Elektra Records, 75 Rockefeller Plaza, New York, NY 10019; 345 North Maple Dr., Ste. 123, Beverly Hills, CA 90210.

Career

Club deejay, c. late 1980s–early 1990s; began releasing singles on Instinct, 1989; signed with Elektra Records and released EP, *Move,* 1993; released debut album, *Everything Is Wrong,* 1995. Also creator of music for film soundtracks. Has done remixes for artists such as Aerosmith, Brian Eno, Michael Jackson, Metallica, Red Hot Chili Peppers, Smashing Pumpkins, and Soundgarden; has produced for Ozzy Osbourne. Toured with Lollapalooza festival, 1993.

Sidelights

Moby is perhaps the most well–known name in the subculture of music and style known as techno. This fast–paced electronic dance music is mainly heard at nightclubs, parties, and especially "raves," generally described as giant, marathon dance parties. While raves are notorious for rampant drug use, Moby is substance–free and Christian, although he admits a weakness for chasing members of the opposite sex. He steers clear of alcohol, drugs, and tobacco, and is also a vegan,

someone who does not consume any meat or animal products, including dairy or eggs. Despite the contradictions inherent between this lifestyle and that of hedonistic ravers, Moby is arguably the leader of the techno genre, though he did take a detour in 1997 with a heavy metal album, *Animal Rights.* But in 1999 he went back to his roots with Play, which once again showcased techno, though it was an eclectic melange that reached beyond sheer dance music.

Moby was born Richard Melville Hall on September 11, 1965, in New York City and raised in the suburb of Darien, Connecticut. His singular nickname, which he has had since he was a baby, is based on the novel *Moby Dick,* written by his great–great–great uncle, Herman Melville. Moby's father, chemistry professor James Melville, died in a car accident after driving drunk when his son was two. His mother, Elizabeth, who became a doctor's aide, then worked as a secretary by day and played keyboards in a band at night. Moby lived during the week at the spacious home of his well–to–do grandparents, who belonged to the country club and played golf, but spent weekends with his unconventional mother at her apartment. His grandparents also taught Sunday school, but Moby's childhood was not particularly religious. He told Chris Norris in *New York* that he was raised "sort of Presbyterian."

Discovering music and drugs at a young age, Moby played the guitar in elementary school and was smoking pot and listening to Led Zeppelin at around age ten. His tastes switched to the Clash and Sex Pistols by age 14, and at that stage, he quit using drugs and alcohol and began a "straight–edged" hardcore punk band, so called because the members were devoted to staying straight, or sober. The Vatican Commandos, as they were called, performed at high–profile Manhattan punk clubs like CBGBs and Great Gildersleeves. However, when he went off to the University of Connecticut, he fell into drinking again, attending parties and playing in bands in addition to studying religion and philosophy. Some of his other musical collaborations included the Pork Guys, Shopwell, and Peanuts.

In college, Moby began spinning records at the campus radio station, most of it "New Wave alternative stuff of early '80s—New Order, Big Country and the Clash," he told Roger Catlin of the Minneapolis *Star Tribune*. He dropped out after just eight months and began hanging out in clubs in New York City, where he learned to love dance music. "I just realized how powerful and celebratory dance music was," he recalled to Norris. "I love that real anthemic quality. Just big piano breaks, screaming diva vocals, and real high energy." He began working as a DJ for a club in Port Chester, New York, and then moved to venues in New York City, including the club Mars. By 1987, under a variety of stage names like Voodoo Child, Barracuda, and Mindstorm, Moby was spinning for big names like Cher, Run–D.M.C., and Big Daddy Kane and started recording his own club mixes on the Instinct label in 1989.

In the meantime, just about the time Moby left college, he became a born–again Christian. Though he does not belong to any specific church and has been known to sharply criticize religious conservatives, he is open about the fact that he lives his life trying to live by the principles taught by Jesus Christ. He does admit that he has trouble at times, especially when it comes to resisting sex, as well as in his efforts to be humble, unselfish, and nonjudgmental, but says that he puts in a sincere effort. "I try to live up to his teachings but fail all the time," he told Lorraine Ali in *Rolling Stone*. In addition to living according to Christian principles, which includes reciting the Lord's Prayer daily, Moby is a vegan, meaning he consumes no animal products, and he does not drink alcohol, smoke cigarettes, or bleach his clothes (citing that bleach harms the water supply).

When Moby remixed the theme song from the popular David Lynch television series Twin Peaks with a thumping beat to create the track "Go," he became a major name not only among the ranks of deejays but also on the charts. The song reached the top ten in Britain in 1991, and Moby continued to churn out club singles for Instinct, like subsequent hits "Next Is the E" and "Thousand." He also compiled a number of singles on *Moby*, 1992, and experimented with a minimalist sound on *Ambient*, 1993. Also in 1993, Moby signed a five–record deal with Elektra and released the EP *Move*, appealing to many fans who were not previously fond of dance music.

Right after the release of *Move*, Moby toured with the Lollapalooza festival concert headlined by the Red Hot Chili Peppers. He fit in with the rollicking tour, because unlike some deejays who somberly stand at the turntables, Moby's stage antics are bombastic. This exposure helped reveal Moby to a much more mainstream audience and made him virtually the only techno deejay at the time known outside the clubs to a widespread audience. The next year, 1994, Neil Strauss wrote in *Rolling Stone*, "A year ago, the name Moby and the word *techno* were practically synonymous." However, Strauss went on to say that some techno fans began to think of Moby as a "traitor," due to his lifestyle, not to mention the fact that he had worked on a remix for pop star Michael Jackson.

In 1995, Moby released his debut album, *Everything Is Wrong*, deriving the title from his philosophy of the world. "I think 500 years from now, people are going to wonder what was going on now," Moby related to Strauss. "They'll see this race of people that smoked cigarettes and drove cars and fought wars and persecuted people for their beliefs and sexual orientation, and none of it accomplished anything…. Everything is absolutely 100 percent wrong, and how do we change it is the question." For the album's liner notes, Moby wrote two essays about what he believes is wrong with the world and ticked off 67 statistics concerning topics such as the plight of the rain forests and the destruction of trees to make disposable diapers.

Everything Is Wrong cut across several musical genres, from jazz to classical piano to hard rock to disco grooves, but as Ali noted in *Rolling Stone*, "Amazingly, these transitions aren't jerky or abrupt; rather, the music evolves naturally from one style to the next." The album soon became a critical favorite but some techno purists rejected it as a "sell–out." He explained that the change came because he moved in a different direction from the rest of the dance community. "Lately I've been bored to death with techno," he remarked to Ali. "It all sounds the same to me." He also noted to Catlin in the *Star Tri-*

bune, "In the rave community,…the enthusiasm is more for the drugs and the clothes than for the celebratory aspects of it. It just seems very unhealthy."

Moby's discontent with dance music came to a head with *Animal Rights,* 1997, in which he gave up his synth sound in favor of a hard rock style. Much of the content revealed his early punk influences and featured his screaming voice and wailing guitar riffs. This effort was not warmly received, but did not slow down his career. In the meantime, Moby was busy working on other artists' projects, remixing "1979" for Smashing Pumpkins, "Falling in Love (Is Hard on the Knees)" for Aerosmith, "Until It Sleeps" for Metallica, and "Dusty" for Soundgarden; he also produced "Walk on Water" for Ozzy Osbourne. In addressing the fact that his religious beliefs seem to run counter to the kind of company he keeps, Moby explained in a *New York* interview, "Well, if I were Satan, I wouldn't spend my time with guys who wear black leather and listen to metal. I would spend my time with *CEOs!*"

Subsequently, Moby began getting calls to mix music for film soundtracks. In 1997, he came out with the album *I Like to Score,* a collection of 12 pieces that he originally created for movies and television (thus the title, a pun on the word "score," which refers to making music for such media). It included an energetic re–mix of the "James Bond Theme," as well as his early hit "Go" in addition to "First Cool Hive" from the horror flick *Scream* and a cover of Joy Division's "New Dawn Fades" from the film *Heat.* After this, he began to indicate that he was regaining his enthusiasm for techno. "Overall, the scene feels healthier to me, and I certainly like the music more than I did two or three years ago," Moby noted to Michael Mehle in the *Rocky Mountain News.*

In the summer of 1999, Moby issued *Play,* an effort that harkened back to his techno roots while displaying an even more fervent eclecticism that intrigued and delighted many critics. In addition to the drum machines and hip–hop beats, much of the structure is developed from old blues and gospel music. Moby sampled, or excerpted, a 1943 version of the gospel classic "Run On for a Long Time," featuring slide guitar and a haunting piano. He also used samples from Alan Lomax's field recordings of African American folk music from the early twentieth century, not to mention the Bessie Jones blues tune "Honey."

Play seemed to indicate a shift from Moby's earlier works in that it did not contain any overt references to his thoughts on subjects like the environment,

politics, veganism, and the like. He commented to David Proffitt in the *Arizona Republic,* "With *Play,* I wanted to make a record that was very personal but also that people could bring into their lives and fall in love with." He also remarked to Vickie Gilmer of the Minneapolis *Star Tribune,* "The songs I used are human and there's this quality of striving to them. They're beautiful songs, and the lyrics are interesting. But it's me singing, too." He noted that it was a pet peeve of his that people think his electronic music consists solely of samples.

Moby, who is five feet, eight inches tall and sports a shaved head, lives in Manhattan's East Village where he keeps a stash of equipment including keyboards, mixers, samplers, recording equipment, and more. Keeping with his conviction about not harming living creatures, Moby refuses to even kill cockroaches or mosquitoes, living with a bevy of bugs in his studio.

Selected discography

"Mobility," Instinct, 1990.
"Go," Instinct, 1991.
"Voodoo Child," Instinct, 1991.
(Contributor) *Instinct Dance: A Collection of Dance Music from Instinct Records,* 1991.
Moby, Instinct, 1992.
The Story So Far, 1993.
Ambient, Instinct, 1993.
Early Underground, Instinct, 1993.
Move (EP), Elektra, 1994.
Everything Is Wrong, Elektra, 1994.
Rare: The Collected B–Sides 1989–1993, Instinct, 1996.
Animal Rights, Elektra, 1997.
I Like to Score, Elektra, 1997.
Play, Elektra, 1999.
Also contributor to film soundtracks.

Sources

Books

Contemporary Musicians, volume 17, Gale Research, 1996.

Periodicals

Arizona Republic, August 12, 1999, p. 32.
Entertainment Weekly, February 21, 1997, p. 125.
Interview, March 1996, p. 92.
Newsday, May 25, 1995, p. B9.
Newsweek, June 14, 1999, p. 69.

New York, March 27, 1995, p. 48; March 17, 1997, p. 48.

New York Times, July 31, 1999, p. B17.

People, November 1, 1993, p. 82; March 10, 1997, p. 24; August 23, 1999, p. 45.

Rocky Mountain News, November 23, 1997, p. 18D.

Rolling Stone, November 17, 1994, p. 102; March 23, 1995, p. 125; May 4, 1995, p. 58; October 30, 1997, p. 68; June 24, 1999, p. 64.

St. Louis Post–Dispatch, September 6, 1999, p. E2.

Star Tribune (Minneapolis, MN), June 4, 1995, p. 3F; August 20, 1999, p. 3E.

Time, August 17, 1992, p. 60.

Online

Moby web page, Elektra Records web site, http://www.elektra.com/ambient_club/moby (October 19, 1999).

"Moby," *Rolling Stone* web site, http://rollingstone.tunes.com (October 24, 1999).

Yoshiro Mori

Japanese prime minister

Born on July 14, 1937, in Neagari, Ishikawa Prefecture, Japan; son of Shigeki (a mayor) and Kaoru Mori; married Chieko Mori, 1961; children: son, Yuki; daughter, Yoko. *Education:* Waseda University School of Commerce, Japan, graduated, 1960.

Addresses: *Office*—Liberal Democratic Party, 1–11–23 Nagata–cho Chiyoda, Tokyo, 100, Japan.

Career

Sankei Shimbun newspapers, Tokyo, Japan, reporter for the *Japan Industrial Journal*, 1960–62; secretary to a member of the House of Representatives from Ehime Prefecture, beginning 1962; House of Representatives, Tokyo, member from Ishikawa Prefecture District, 1969–96, member from Ishikawa Prefecture District 2, 1996—, chair of standing committee on finance, 1981–82; chair of standing committee on rules and administration, 1991; Prime Minister's Office, Miki Cabinet, deputy director general, Tokyo, 1975–76; Fukuda Cabinet, deputy chief cabinet secretary, 1977–78; Liberal Democratic Party (LDP), Tokyo, deputy secretary–general, 1978–79, and director of educational division of Policy Research Council, 1978–81; Nakasone Cabinet, minister of education, 1983–84; LDP, acting chair of Policy Research Council, 1986, acting chair of general counsel, 1986–87, chair of special committee on educational reform for Policy Research Council, 1984–87, chair of National Organization committee, 1987–88, and chair of research committee on educational systems for Policy Research Council, 1989–91; LDP, chair of Policy Research Council, 1991–92; Miyazawa Cabinet, minister of international trade and indus-

try, 1992–93; LDP, secretary–general, 1993–95; Murayama Cabinet, minister of construction, 1995–96; LDP, chair of general counsel, 1996–98, secretary–general, 1998—; elected prime minister of Japan, May, 2000, re–elected, July, 2000. Sidelights

When Japanese prime minister Keizo Obuchi died in May of 2000, the majority Liberal Democratic Party (LDP) chose longtime political insider Yoshiro Mori to take the reins as acting leader. "Many commentators," according to Howard W. French in the *New York Times*, "said that by choosing Mr. Mori, a burly raspy–voiced politician not known for his personal popularity or campaigning skills, the party was taking a huge risk in the national elections." But when parliament held a vote in June, Mori hung onto his seat, despite his verbal gaffes that drew criticism in preceding months. "Like most of Japan's past prime ministers," wrote Doug Struck in the *Washington Post*, "his election by parliament today is the payoff for faithful party service and good relations with his fellow politicians, with little regard for attributes of leadership or questions of policy." However, Mori was also known for being a good conciliator and for looking closely after the interests of his constituents. He took over at a shaky time in Japanese politics, when his party was facing challenges from newly emboldened and vigorous opposition on top of the fact that the country was trying to pull out of a decade–long economic recession.

Mori was born on July 14, 1937, in Neagari, a small town in the Ishikawa Prefecture of Japan. Soon after he was born, his father, Shigeki, went off to serve during World War II in the Pacific Ocean and did not return to Japan until 1946. Mori's mother, Kaoru, had died the previous year from an illness. Afterward, he was raised by his mother's younger sister, Akiko. Politics has a long history in Mori's family; his grandfather and then his father both served as mayor of Neagari for much of their lives.

While attending Waseda University, Mori joined the debate society, which was a fertile training field for may of Japan's political leaders. There, he met Noboru Takeshita and Keizo Obuchi, who went on to become Japanese prime ministers. After graduating in 1960, Mori became a reporter for the *Japan Industrial Journal*, a business publication that was put out by the *Sankei Shimbun*, a major newspaper in Japan. During this time, he met influential business leaders such as Soichiro Honda.

Kicking off his career in politics, in 1962 Mori left the newspaper to become a secretary to a member of the House of Representatives, or lower house of the Japanese Diet (parliament), for the Ehime Prefecture. He himself was elected to the House of Representatives from the Ishikawa Prefecture district in 1969, running a grass–roots campaign without backing of any major party on a platform of "youth, action, power," according to Struck in the *Washington Post*. Subsequently, the LDP invited him to join. On the official Ministry of Foreign Affairs of Japan web site, a biography of Mori noted that he "came under the tutelage of the noble– minded former Prime Minister Takeo Fukuda, who preached simplicity and humbleness."

Thus began a steady rise for Mori throughout the party ranks. From 1978 to 1979 he was the party's deputy secretary–general, and also served as director of educational division of the party's Policy Research Council from 1978 to 1981. In 1986 he was named acting chair of the Policy Research Council as well as acting chair of the general counsel, serving in the latter post until 1987. Also, from 1984 to 1987 Mori was the chair of the special committee on educational reform for Policy Research Council. From 1987 to 1988 he was chair of the National Organization committee, then from 1989 to 1991 he served as chair of the research committee on the Policy Research Council's educational systems. Mori chaired the Policy Research Council from 1991 to 1992, served as secretary–general from 1993 to 1995, and rose to chair of the general counsel from 1996 to 1998. In 1998, he again became secretary–general of the party, the number two post, under Prime Minister Keizo Obuchi.

Meanwhile, Mori held a number of top–level posts in many governments. He served in the Prime Minister's Office during the Miki Cabinet as deputy director general from 1975 to 1976, and in the Fukuda Cabinet as deputy chief cabinet secretary from 1977 to 1978. For the Nakasone Cabinet, Mori held the post of minister of education from 1983 to 1984. During the Miyazawa Cabinet, he was minister of international trade and industry from 1992 to 1993 and for the Murayama Cabinet, he served as minister of construction from 1995 to 1996.

In April of 2000, after just 21 months in power, Prime Minister Obuchi suffered a cerebral hemorrhage which left him comatose. This sudden turn was shrouded in mystery, as Chief Cabinet Secretary Mikio Aoki initially reported that Obuchi had been hospitalized for exhaustion and had left the hospital to return home for rest. After a few days of conflicting and erroneous reports, the Japanese government announced that Obuchi was unconscious and breathing with aid from a respirator. Mori was appointed prime minister by the party, and Obuchi died after six weeks in a coma.

After assuming the post of prime minister, Mori and his past were scrutinized. His reputation for being indecisive and overly cautious raised a red flag, and his lack of experience in foreign policy and finance were also concerns. In addition, many brought up the fact that he was implicated in a scandal in 1988 in which in several politicians bought low–cost stocks from a favor–seeking business contact before the shares were made public. Though prosecutors said there was no evidence to indict Mori and 13 others, the affair led to the resignation of Prime Minister Takeshita in 1989. Later, in 1992, Mori was also criticized for accepting unsavory donations from a trucking company.

On the other hand, Mori was known to be an excellent coordinator, which is a key element in Japanese politics. Some also pointed to his dedication to the needs of the common person and his self–sacrificing manner, exemplified by the fact that he sometimes foregoes food and rest in order to dedicate himself to his job. "His favorite saying," according to Struck in the *Washington Post*, "translates roughly to 'give yourself to the people.'"

When Mori became prime minister, he faced a number of serious issues. In addition to combating the Japanese recession that had plagued his country for about ten years and the accompanying skyrocketing unemployment rates, he would also be plagued with fighting ongoing corruption and a stagnant bureaucracy in the nation. In his first speech, Mori basically pledged to continue the types of economic reforms that Obuchi had instigated, which had staved off a more serious depression that would have affected the world's economy. However, he was criticized for not introducing any new plans.

Upon Mori's election, the LDP alliance partner, the Liberal Party, abandoned the coalition. But the new prime minister formed a three–party coalition of the LDP, the New Komeito–Reformers' Network, and the New Conservative Party, proving his ability as a shrewd back–room negotiator. However, Mori was also notorious for making incendiary public statements. In May, he attracted harsh criticism for his remark to a Shinto religious group of lawmakers that "Japan is a divine nation with the emperor at its core, and we want the people to recognize this," according to Howard W. French in the New York Times. French reported that many thought the statement "alarmingly echoed Japan's militaristic past," which helped move the world into World War II.

Though Mori tried to smooth over the situation by claiming that he was simply trying to urge Japan's youth to adopt spiritual values, the fact that he did not retract the words exacerbated the situation. He also committed another error in early June by referring to the nation as a "kokutai," a pre–World War II term that connotes nationalism and emperor worship. However, some observers noted that his wording may have been a carefully calculated move to appeal to more conservative rural voters, whose unswerving support of the LDP have given it a nearly uninterrupted hold on power for four decades.

Around the same time as this flap, Mori announced that elections would be held on June 25, 2000, for seats in the House of Representatives. Though his popularity declined to 19 percent in May, polls showed that voters were reluctant to abandon the long–running ruling party. In the general elections, the LDP lost 38 seats and its outright majority, but retained its grip on power with the three–party coalition. That July, the LDP re–elected Mori to continue as prime minister.

At five feet, eight inches tall and 215 pounds, Mori has a commanding physical presence. While in college, he met fellow student Chieko Maki. They married in 1961 and have a son, Yuki, a daughter, Yoko, and a granddaughter. As a child, Mori enjoyed baseball, but he eventually became more fond of rugby and has continued to play avidly throughout his life. He also enjoys golf.

Sources

Periodicals

Business Week, April 17, 2000, p. 163.

Christian Science Monitor, June 6, 2000, p. 6.

Economist, June 3, 2000, p. 43.

New York Times, April 5, 2000, p. A1; April 8, 2000, p. A5; May 26, 2000, p. A3; May 31, 2000, p. A12.

Time, April 17, 2000, p. 61.

Time International, April 17, 2000, p. 20; June 26, 2000, p. 26.

U.S. News & World Report, April 17, 2000, p. 34.

Wall Street Journal, April 5, 2000, p. A18; April 6, 2000, p. A17; May 19, 2000, p. A14; June 2, 2000, p. A12; June 5, 2000, p. A21.

Washington Post, April 5, 2000, p. A15; June 26, 2000, p. A11.

Washington Times, July 5, 2000, p. A11.

Online

"Profile of Prime Minister Yoshiro Mori," Ministry of Foreign Affairs of Japan web site, http://www.mofa.go.jp (July 15, 2000).

Pervez Musharraf

Leader of Pakistan

Born Pervez Musharraf Nish–I–Imtiaz, August 11, 1943, in New Delhi, India; son of Syed Musharraf (a diplomat); married; wife's name, Sehba; children: son, Bilal; daughter, Ayla. *Education:* Attended Pakistan Military Academy, 1961–64.

Addresses: *Office*—Islamabad, Pakistan.

Career

Joined Pakistani army, 1964, served in Special Services Group, 1971, also commanded infantry division and strike corps, became lieutenant general, promoted to general and army chief, 1998, staged coup and took over as leader of Pakistan, 1999. Also taught on faculty at Command and Staff College, Quetta, Pakistan, and at the National Defense College.

Sidelights

In October of 1999, General Pervez Musharraf, chief of the Pakistani army, took over his nation in a bloodless coup. As of that year, Pakistan had been under military rule for 25 of its 52 years as an independent state. Though a democratically elected government was currently in place, Musharraf's move did not seem to worry citizens, who remained calm throughout the transition and even appeared to welcome the new situation. Weary of the corruption and cronyism of the recent leadership, they seemed to believe a forceful military presence would help pave the way for new elections. No organized protests took place, and an alliance of 19 political parties who opposed former Prime Minister Nawaz Sharif praised Musharraf as they held out hope that he would "clean house" and restore true democracy. Although he was seen on television wearing camouflage fatigues and brandishing a weapon, Robert Marquand in the *Christian Science Monitor* wrote, "His friends describe Musharraf as a liberal in a conservative army who advanced by his intelligence, courage, and independence. In meetings with often surprised senior diplomats here, Musharraf has been described as 'broad–minded,' 'serious,' 'moderate,' and 'a patriot.'"

Musharraf was born on August 11, 1943, in Delhi, India, the middle of three sons of Syed Musharraf–ud–Din, a civil servant in British–ruled India who later worked in the Foreign Ministry for Pakistan. His mother, a homemaker, also served the International Labour Organization, retiring in 1987. Days before the nation was divided into India and Pakistan in 1947, Musharraf relocated with his parents and three brothers to Pakistan, growing up in the port city of Karachi. He attended a Roman Catholic high school for boys in Turkey, moving there in 1949 for his father's job. He is said to count Turkish leader Mustafa Kemal Ataturk as one of his heroes. Even though no one in his family had joined the army, he decided when he was young to become a soldier.

An average student, Musharraf pursued football, cricket, and body building as a teen, and attended St. Patrick's High School in Karachi after moving back from Turkey. He went on to attend Forman Christian College in Lahore, then studied at the Pakistan Military Academy beginning in 1961. He joined an elite artillery regiment of the Pakistan army in 1964. The next year, during the 16–day war with India, he fought Indian troops in the Punjab province and earned a medal for bravery. When Pakistan fought India again in 1971 over land that became Bangladesh, Musharraf served in the Special Services Group, an elite commando unit. Other assignments included commanding a strike corps and an infantry division, and he has also taught at war schools.

One of Musharraf's most important postings came in 1995 as a lieutenant general, when he became a commander in Mangla in Pakistani Punjab, a key military area near the Indian border. In 1998, after General Jehangir Karamat resigned, he was appointed army chief. Musharraf, who spent most of his career in field duty, did not seem to be interested in politics. Karamat, on the other hand, had been forced out because he suggested that the military be given more input in making national policy.

Meanwhile, military coups appeared to a thing of the past in Pakistan. Although it had been ruled by military dictators for most of its history, the nation had been civilian–run since 1985, and headed by elected leaders since 1988 upon the election of Benazir Bhutto. After several stormy years in which Bhutto and Sharif battled for control, Sharif's party won by a landslide in1997 elections, but Pakistanis were becoming increasingly fed up with his rule. They were dismayed with the a deteriorating economy and a rise in violent crime, not to mention the rampant cronyism that led to a government full of Sharif's hand–picked appointees. There was also widespread corruption, where bribery and tax cheating was business as usual. In addition, Sharif was unpopular for his handling of a crisis in Kashmir in 1999.

According to Musharraf, although he lacked confidence in Sharif's ability to govern, he got along with him and tried to figure out ways to help improve Sharif's performance. However, Musharraf told Barry Bearak in the *New York Times* that Sharif began a "whispering campaign" among top army leaders in order to divide the officer corps, and that is when the two began to have a split. On October 12, 1999, Sharif fired Musharraf as he was on a commercial flight returning from Sri Lanka. No official explanation was given for the dismissal. The plane, carrying 198 people, was not allowed to land in Karachi and ordered to leave Pakistan. However, as Musharraf told Bearak, military officers intervened and allowed the flight to set down with seven minutes of fuel remaining.

Hours later, the army staged a nonviolent coup and took control of the government. Taking over as the country's leader, Musharraf pledged to get rid of corruption, improve the shabby economy, and lead the nation to democracy. He later painted the coup as being a spontaneous response from his fellow military officers who supported him after his dismissal. However, others have alleged that perhaps Sharif was trying to quash a coup that he suspected was coming. In any event, most Pakistanis seemed relieved at Musharraf's takeover. According to Gwynne Dyer in the Minneapolis *Star Tribune*, 75 percent of Pakistan's 135 million in a snap Gallup poll supported the coup.

Afterward, Musharraf promptly arrested Sharif and charged him with treason, hijacking, and conspiracy to commit murder, charges that could bring the death penalty. In November he appeared before an "anti–terrorist court," as article in the *Economist* described it, and one of his brothers that month was arrested on corruption charges. Other relatives of Sharif were charged with defaulting on loans. However, Sharif's courtroom was stocked with government intelligence officers, and in January, the judge in charge of Sharif's trial quit the bench. According to Bearak, he stated, "I cannot provide a fair trial in these circumstances. Is it an open, free, fair and impartial trial when intelligence people sit in my room in plainclothes?" He then sent the case back to the lower court that had initially sent it to him.

A number of nations opposed Musharraf's power grab and demanded that democracy be restored immediately. Also, in January of 2000, the administration of President Bill Clinton announced that Pakistan was at risk of being placed on a list of nations supporting terrorism, thus jeopardizing any financial support from America. It was reported that the administration believed that the Pakistani military supported a terrorist group that hijacked an Indian jetliner in December of 1999. Meanwhile, India remained on alert, being that the two nations nearly declared full–out war in the summer of 1999, after both testing nuclear devices in 1998.

Musharraf's official web site reveals that he married his wife, Sehba, on December 28, 1968, and they have a son, Bilal and a daughter, Ayla, both of whom are married. He also has a granddaughter,

Mariam. An avid outdoorsman, he enjoys playing squash, badminton, and golf, as well as sailing and canoeing. Musharraf has relatives living in the United States, including a brother in Chicago, Naved Musharraf, who is an anesthesiologist and a naturalized American citizen.

Sources

Periodicals

Business Week, October 25, 1999, p. 64.
Christian Science Monitor, October 21, 1999, p. 7; November 17, 1999, p. 1.
Economist, November 27, 1999, p. 35.
New Republic, November 1, 1999, p. 11.
New York Times, October 13, 1999, pp. A1, A12; October 24, 1999, sec. 1, p. 8; October 26, 1999, p. A12; November 11, 1999, p. A5; November 18, 1999, p. A8; November 21, 1999, sec. 1, p. 10; January 13, 2000, p. A12; January 25, 2000, p. A1; January 28, 2000, p. A8.
Star Tribune (Minneapolis, MN), January 23, 2000, p. 17A.
Time, December 6, 1999, p. 66.
U.S. News & World Report, October 25, 1999, p. 38.
Washington Post, January 26, 2000, p. A2.

Online

"Army chief: Pakistan coup launched as 'last report,'" CNN web site, October 13, 1999, http://cnn.com (October 14, 1999).
"Chief Executive of Pakistan General Pervez Musharraf," Islamic Republic of Pakistan official web site, http://pak.gov.pk (January 28, 2000).

Edward Norton

The Kobal Collection

Actor

Born August 18, 1969, in Boston, MA; son of Edward Sr. (an attorney) and Robin (a teacher; later worked for a civic trust) Norton. *Education:* Yale University, B.A. in history, 1991.

Addresses: *Office*—c/o Banner Entertainment, 8000 Sunset Blvd., 3rd Floor, Los Angeles, CA 90046.

Career

Actor. Stage appearances include *Waiting for Lefty,* New York City, 1992; *Fragments,* New York City, 1994; and *Bible Burlesque,* New York City, 1994; also appeared in *Lovers, Italian American Reconciliation,* and *Bring Me Smiles.* Film appearances include *Primal Fear,* 1996; *Everyone Says I Love You,* 1996; *The People vs. Larry Flynt,* 1996; *Out of the Past* (voice), 1998; *Rounders,* 1998; *American History X,* 1998; *Fight Club,* 1999; and *Keeping the Faith,* 2000.

Awards: Los Angeles Film Critics Association, best supporting actor award, 1996, and Chicago Film Critics Association, most promising actor award, 1997, both for *Everyone Says I Love You, The People vs. Larry Flynt,* and *Primal Fear;* National Board of Review Award for best supporting actor, and Southeastern Film Critics Association Award for best supporting actor, both 1996, and Golden Globe award for best supporting actor in a motion picture, 1997, all for *Primal Fear;* Golden Satellite Award for best actor in a drama, 1999, for *American History X;* Southeastern Film Critics Association Award for best actor, 1999, for *American History X* and *Rounders.*

Sidelights

A newcomer to Hollywood when he was cast in 1996's *Primal Fear,* Edward Norton soon took the town by storm. In his debut, he won an integral supporting role in a film anchored by Richard Gere, and before shooting even began, he was considered a hot property. After it came out, the young actor won several major award nominations for the role, thus boosting his profile even more. Compared to a young Dustin Hoffman, Norton was not a favorite of casting directors due to his connections in the movie business (he had none) or his good looks (Ray Mark Rinaldi in the *St. Louis Post–Dispatch* called him "conspicuously average looking"). Instead, Norton was chosen for that first role due to his uncanny ability to act better than the 2,100 or so hopefuls he beat out at casting calls, and continued to be in demand for his raw talent. In only his second feature film, he was tapped by none other than Woody Allen, and in his third venture, he landed a juicy part in the Milos Forman film *The People vs. Larry Flynt.* After these three projects, all released in 1996, Norton won kudos for his gritty portrayal of a white supremacist in *American History X,* 1998, then stunned critics and audiences opposite Brad Pitt in the complex, controversial *Fight Club,* 1999. With a variety of awards and two Academy Award nominations under his belt, Norton then felt it was time to branch out into directing.

Norton was born on August 18, 1969, in Boston, Massachusetts, and raised in Columbia, Maryland. The eldest child of Edward Norton Sr., a federal prosecutor with a penchant for environmental activism, and Robin Norton, a teacher who later worked for a civic trust, he has two siblings, James and Molly. Norton's grandfather, James Rouse, developed Boston's Faneuil Hall marketplace and Baltimore's Harbor Place. He also designed the planned community where Norton grew up, but instead of being an antiseptic, homogeneous upbringing, the area actually contained a vibrant mix of cultures and income levels.

Despite his lack of family connections to the entertainment business, Norton was always drawn to acting, appearing in plays from the age of five. Throughout grade school, he was involved in drama, but distanced himself from acting in high school because it was not considered cool. However, at age 16, his class went to see Ian McKellen's one–man show, *Acting Shakespeare*, in Washington, D.C., and the experience sparked Norton's interest again. He began taking drama classes and continued to perform while in college. Despite his acting ambitions, he started out as an astronomy major at Yale University, but finding physics too difficult, he ended up getting a history degree in 1991. Subsequently, he spent a summer in Osaka, Japan, working for a low–income housing foundation started up by his grandfather, and learned to speak the language fluently.

After graduating, Norton lived the typical life of the struggling actor in New York City, working odd jobs while trying to land parts. He waited tables, proofread for a court–reporting service, and worked at a temp agency. Once, he auditioned for the New York Shakespeare Festival, where casting director Georgianne Walken, wife of actor Christopher Walken, informed Norton that he should consider quitting acting. As he recalled to Peter Biskind in *Vanity Fair*, "Those moments can be very important, because if they make you doubt yourself, you oughta get out." Instead, Norton was angered by her assessment and inspired to prove her wrong.

After playing several parts in off–off–Broadway productions, Norton impressed the legendary Edward Albee in a 1994 audition. He was cast in the world premiere of the playwright's *Fragments*, then joined New York's Signature Theatre Company. In the meantime, he was trying to win parts in Hollywood as well, trying out for roles in films like *Hackers, With Honors,* and *Up Close & Personal.* Eventually, he got his break with the Richard Gere vehicle *Primal Fear* playing Aaron Stampler, an Appalachian choir boy with an apparently spotless reputation who is accused of killing a Chicago archbishop.

The studio's first choice for the part in *Primal Fear* was an up–and–coming Leonardo DiCaprio, but he declined the project. Subsequently, casting agents auditioned more than 2,100 possible actors from London to Texas, but they could not find anyone with the right stuff, not even Matt Damon, who auditioned for the part but was turned down. The character had to possess both a believable innocence and a streak of psychopathic menace. Gere and the director, Gregory Hoblit, were thinking of abandoning the film when they got a call from a casting director who had seen Norton at an open casting call in New York City. There, he stayed in character before and after the audition, and led the casting director to believe he was actually from Kentucky. "I don't think I lied," he explained to Biskind. "But I think I said I had family from eastern Kentucky. Maybe I augmented a little bit." He also noted to David Handelman in *Vogue*, "I knew the accent because my grandparents were from that area. But I certainly don't have it, so I prepared by watching *Coal Miner's Daughter.*"

After performing just the screen test for *Primal Fear*, released in 1996, Norton's reputation in the business bloomed, even before the critical raves, his Golden Globe and National Board of Review awards, and a nomination for a supporting actor Oscar for the part. Within weeks, he was offered meaty parts in Woody Allen's *Everyone Says I Love You* and Milos Forman's *The People vs. Larry Flynt*, which both also came out in 1996. The former, in which Norton plays a lovestruck lawyer, is an homage to classic musicals where the dialogue is parlayed into song and dance, which none of the actors even knew was required until a couple weeks before the shoot. Allen wanted to keep it secret so that they would not take voice lessons. "He wanted it to be as if these characters were just singing to themselves," Norton revealed to Handelman. He also revealed that Drew Barrymore's voice was dubbed, telling him, "There is a difference between unprofessional and tone–deaf."

In *The People vs. Larry Flynt*, Norton had a major supporting part in the biographical film as Alan Isaacman, the lawyer and friend of *Hustler* magazine publisher Larry Flynt. During and after this project, he was romantically linked with costar Courtney Love, though he adamantly denied this, saying they were just friends. Unfortunately, just as Norton's star was on the rise, he met with two personal tragedies: In 1996, his grandfather, the prominent developer, died, and the next year, his mother died after an operation to remove a brain tumor. In the meantime, in 1997 he appeared with Matt Damon in *Rounders,* winning a Southeastern Film Critics Association award for best actor for the role, in addition to several other regional awards for *Everyone Says I Love You.*

The part in *Rounders* was a break away from the attorney characters of Norton's previous two films. In this picture, he played Lester "Worm" Murphy, an ex–con card shark. During filming, he learned the nuances of poker and managed to get good enough to take on the film's financial backers, Harvey and Bob Weinstein, in a real–life game. As Harvey Weinstein related to Biskind, "Norton, I think, took $1,300, and Matt [Damon] won $800 or $900. That's Edward—he's a total Method actor. You give him two months and he becomes an expert in whatever. He wiped us out."

In the meantime, Norton had also landed a starring role in *American History X,* a project that became embroiled in controversy when he and the studio clashed with British director Tony Kaye over his final edit of the movie. Norton was asked to assist with a new version of the film, while Kaye worked on a new cut as well. The director ended up publicly charging Norton with stealing the film from him, and said some unflattering things about him to the media. Eventually, the studio took over the editing and combined some of each cut to deliver the product to theaters. Norton subsequently received critical acclaim for his role in *American History X,* as Derek Vinyard, the violent neo–Nazi skinhead, for which he added 25 pounds of muscle to his thin frame and displayed a swastika on his chest. Though it was only his sixth film, he received his second Oscar nomination, this time for best actor.

Norton's next project, 1999's *Fight Club,* cast him alongside Hollywood heavyweight Brad Pitt in what would become one of the most controversial movies of the year. In it, he plays a disaffected yuppie who feels alienated from society and its consumerism. He befriends an anarchistic waiter and soap salesman, and together they form a kind of support group called the Fight Club, where men congregate to deal with their tormented psyches by lashing out at one another with their bare fists. Though it was created as a dark comedy with undercurrents of commentary on the pitfalls of modern American society, many critics called it irresponsible due to the graphic violence, sexual content, and terrorist incidents. The timing of the film had a lot to do with the outrage as well, coming in the wake of several mass shootings at schools nationwide, and in the midst of a widespread public and political debate on violence in entertainment. David Ansen in *Newsweek* remarked, "*Fight Club* is the most incendiary movie to come out of Hollywood in a long time."

As it turned out, though, many critics were receptive to *Fight Club* as well, holding similar views to Norton, who explained in *Entertainment Weekly,* "This movie examines violence and the roots of frustration that are causing people to reach out for such radical solutions. And that's exactly the sort of discussion we should be having about our culture. Because a culture that doesn't examine its violence is a culture in denial, which is much more dangerous." In *Newsweek,* feminist author Susan Faludi, in fact, called *Fight Club* a "consciousness–raising buddy movie," doing for men what 1991's *Thelma & Louise* did for women. The film, incidentally, was created from an apocalyptic novel by first–time author Chuck Palahniuk and directed by David Fincher, who also did *The Game* and the also–controversial, intensely violent *Seven.* Though he could count the number of films he had made on his fingers, Norton made the leap into directing with his next project, due out in 2000, a romantic comedy he also cowrote and stars in titled *Keeping the Faith.*

Unlike most celebrities whose lives are open to scrutiny in the press, Norton is known for being a very private person and shying away from revealing any personal information. As he explained to Graham Fuller in *Interview,* "I feel that the value of things in your personal life gets somehow diminished by the sharing of them randomly, arbitrarily, with everybody . It cheapens things. When your own complicated, nuanced experience is communicated in the media, its complexity is inevitably reduced to a very convenient, oversimplified, usually hyperbolized positive or negative experience.... It's just...it's maddening."

Sources

Books

Contemporary Theatre, Film and Television, volume 19, Gale Research, 1998.

Periodicals

Entertainment Weekly, March 1, 1999, p. 26; October 15, 1999, p. 24.
Interview, January 1997, p. 82.
Newsweek, September 6, 1999, p. 66; October 18, 1999, p. 77; October 25, 1999, p. 89.

People, November 18, 1996, p. 73.

Premiere, August 1999, p. 68.

Star Tribune (Minneapolis, MN), April 28, 1996, p. 9F; January 16, 1999, p. 31.

Vanity Fair, August 1999, p. 128.

Vogue, January 1997, p. 80.

Online

"Edward Norton," Internet Movie Database web site, http://us.imdb.com (January 11, 2000).

"Edward Norton," Mr. Showbiz web site, http://mrshowbiz.go.com (January 11, 2000).

Trevor Nunn

Theater director

Born Trevor Robert Nunn, January 14, 1940, in Ipswich, Suffolk, England; son of Robert Alexander Nunn (a cabinetmaker) and Dorothy May (Piper) Nunn; married actor Janet Suzman, 1969 (divorced); married Sharon Lee Hill, 1986 (divorced); married actor Imogen Stubbs, 1994. *Education:* Downing College, University of Cambridge, B.A., 1962.

Addresses: *Office*—Royal National Theatre, Upper Ground South Bank, Cambridge Circus, London SE1 9PX, England.

Career

Director, producer, and writer. Belgrade Theatre, Coventry, England, began as trainee director, became producer, 1962–64; Royal Shakespeare Company, associate director, 1964–68, artistic director, 1968–78, chief executive, 1968–86, joint artistic director, 1978–86, associate director, director emeritus, and advisory director, 1986—; Royal National Theatre, London, England, artistic director, 1997—.

Director of stage plays, including *The Caucasian Chalk Circle*, Belgrade Theatre, Coventry, England, 1962-65; *A View from the Bridge*, Belgrade Theatre, 1962-65; *Peer Gynt*, Belgrade Theatre, between 1962-68; *The Thwarting of Baron Bolligrew* (juvenile), Royal Shakespeare Company, (RSC), Aldwych Theatre, London, 1965; *The Revenger's Tragedy*, RSC, Royal Shakespeare Theatre, Stratford-upon-Avon, England, 1965, revived at Aldwych Theatre, 1969; (also appeared as actor) *Tango*, RSC, Aldwych Theatre, 1966;

The Taming of the Shrew, RSC, Royal Shakespeare Theatre, 1967, then Aldwych Theatre, then toured England; *The Relapse*, RSC, Aldwych Theatre, 1967-68; *King Lear*, RSC, Royal Shakespeare Theatre, 1968; *The Winter's Tale*, RSC, Royal Shakespeare Theatre, 1969; *Coriolanus*, RSC, Royal Shakespeare Theatre, 1972, then Aldwych Theatre, 1973; *Julius Caesar*, RSC, Royal Shakespeare Theatre, 1972, then Aldwych Theatre, 1973; *Antony and Cleopatra*, RSC, Royal Shakespeare Theatre, 1972, then Aldwych Theatre, 1973; *Titus Andronicus*, RSC, Royal Shakespeare Theatre, 1972, then Aldwych Theatre, 1973; *Macbeth*, RSC, Royal Shakespeare Theatre, 1974; (artistic director) *Richard II*, RSC, Brooklyn Academy of Music, Brooklyn, NY, 1974; *Hedda Gabler*, RSC, Aldwych Theatre, 1975; (artistic director) *Summerfolk*, RSC, Brooklyn Academy of Music, 1975; (artistic director) *Sherlock Holmes*, RSC, Broadhurst Theatre, 1975; (artistic director) *Henry V*, RSC, Brooklyn Academy Opera House, Brooklyn, 1976; *Romeo and Juliet*, RSC, Royal Shakespeare Theatre, 1976; (with others) *The Winter's Tale*, RSC, Royal Shakespeare Theatre, 1976;(with others) *King Lear*, RSC, Royal Shakespeare Theatre, 1976; *Macbeth*, RSC, Royal Shakespeare Theatre, 1976, then Young Vic Theatre, London, 1978; *As You Like It*, RSC, Royal Shakespeare Theatre, 1977; *The Alchemist*, RSC, The Other Place Theatre, Stratford-upon-Avon, 1977, then Aldwych Theatre, 1978; *Every Good Boy Deserves Favour*, RSC,

Festival Hall, London, 1977, then Mermaid Theatre, London, 1978; *Three Sisters*, The Other Place Theatre, 1978, then regional tour, later Warehouse Theatre, London, 1979; (with John Caird) *The Life and Adventures of Nicholas Nickleby*, RSC, Aldwych Theatre, 1980, then Plymouth Theatre, New York, 1981; *Henry IV*, RSC, Barbican Theatre, London, 1982; *All's Well That End's Well*, RSC, Barbican Theatre, 1982, then Stratford-upon-Avon, 1982, then Martin Beck Theatre, New York City, 1983; (with Caird) *Peter Pan*, RSC, Barbican Theatre, 1982, revived, 1984-85; (artistic director with Terry Hands) *Much Ado about Nothing*, RSC, Gershwin Theatre, 1984; (with Caird) *The Life and Adventures of Nicholas Nickleby*, Broadhurst Theatre, New York City, 1986; *The Fair Maid of the West* (adapted from plays by Thomas Middleton), RSC, Swan Theatre, Stratford-upon-Avon, 1986, then Mermaid Theatre, 1987; *Othello*, RSC, The Other Place Theatre, 1989, then Young Vic Theatre, 1989; *Timon of Athens* , Young Vic Theatre, 1991; *Measure for Measure*, RSC, Other Place Theatre, 1991, then Young Vic Theatre, 1992; *Heartbreak House*, Royal Haymarket Theatre, London, 1992; *Arcadia*, Royal National Theatre, London, England, 1993, then Vivian Beaumont Theatre, New York City, 1995; *An Enemy of the People*, Olivier Theatre, London, England, 1996; *Not About Nightingales*, Cottesloe Theatre, London, England, 1996, then New York City, 1999; *Mutabilitie*, Cottesloe Theatre, 1997; *Betrayal*, Royal National Theatre, 1998.

Director of musicals, including *The Comedy of Errors* (adapted from play by William Shakespeare), RSC, Royal Shakespeare Theatre, 1976; *Starlight Express*, Apollo Victoria Theatre, London, 1984, then Gershwin Theatre, New York City, 1987; *Cats*, New London Theatre, London, 1981, then Winter Garden Theatre, 1982; (adapted from novel by Victor Hugo, with Caird) *Les Miserables*, RSC, Barbican Theatre, 1985, then Broadway Theatre, New York City, 1987; *Chess*, Prince Edward Theatre, London, 1986, then Imperial Theatre, New York City, 1988; *The Baker's Wife*, Phoenix Theatre, London, 1989; *Aspects of Love*, Prince of Wales Theatre, London, 1989, then Broadhurst Theatre, 1990; *The Blue Angel*, RSC, The Other Place Theatre, 1991, then Globe Theatre, 1992; *Sunset Boulevard*, Adelphi Theatre, London, England, 1993, then Minskoff Theatre, New York City, 1994-95; *Oklahoma!*, Royal National Theatre, 1997; also director of Sydney, Australia, production of *Cats*.

Director of operas, including *Idomenco*, Festival Opera Theatre, 1982; and *Katya Kabanova*, 1994. Director of films, including *Hedda*, 1975; *Lady Jane*, 1985; and *Twelfth Night; or, What You Will* (also known as *Twelfth Night*), 1996. Director of television specials, including *The Comedy of Errors*, 1976; *Every Good Boy Deserves Favour*, 1978; *Macbeth*, 1978; *Three Sisters*, 1978; *Shakespeare Workshops Word of Mouth*, 1979; (with John Caird) *The Life and Adventures of Nicholas Nickleby* (also known as Nicholas Nickleby), 1982; *The Great Hamlets*, 1983; *The Comedy of Errors* (also known as *Shakespeare Festival: The Comedy of Errors*), 1990; *Othello*, 1990; *Porgy and Bess* (also known as *The Gershwins' Porgy and Bess*), 1993; and "Les Miserables in Concert," *Great Performances*, 1996.

Writer of lyrics for *The Comedy of Errors*, Royal Shakespeare Company, Royal Shakespeare Theatre, then Aldwych Theater, both 1976; and additional lyrics (with Richard Stilgoe), for *Cats* (based on the poetry collection *Old Possum's Book of Practical Cats* by T. S. Eliot), New London Theatre, 1981, then Winter Garden Theatre, New York City, beginning in 1982. Also writer of screenplays, including *The Comedy of Errors* (based on the play by William Shakespeare), Royal Shakespeare Company, Royal Shakespeare Theatre, then Aldwych Theatre, both 1976; (with John Caird) *Les Miserables* (based on the novel by Victor Hugo), Royal Shakespeare Company, Barbican Theatre, 1985, then Broadway Theatre, 1987-90; *The Fair Maid of the West* (based on plays by Thomas Middleton), Royal Shakespeare Company, Swan Theatre, 1986, then Mermaid Theatre, 1987; (with John Caird) *Peter Pan, or, the Boy Who Would Not Grow Up: A Fantasy in Five Acts* (based on the book by J. M. Barrie), 1998, published by Dramatists Play Service (New York City), 1993.

Also writer of screenplays *Hedda* (based on the play *Hedda Gabler* by Henrik Ibsen), 1975; and *Twelfth Night; or, What You Will* (based on the play by William Shakespeare; also known as *Twelfth Night*), 1996; and television specials *Shakespeare Workshops Word of Mouth*, 1979; *The Comedy of Errors* (based on the play by William Shakespeare; also known as *Shakespeare Festival: The Comedy of Errors*), 1990; and *Porgy and Bess* (also known as *The Gershwins' Porgy and Bess*), 1993.

Awards: London Theatre Critics Award, 1966, 1969; *Plays and Players* Award for best director, 1969, for *The Revenger's Tragedy* and *The Winter's Tale;* Ivor Novello Award for best British musical, 1976; Society of Film and Television Arts, 1976; Sydney Edwards Award, 1977–78; named a commander of the Order of the British Empire, 1978; *Evening Standard* Award and Sydney Edwards Award, both for best director, 1979, for *Once in a Lifetime;* New Standard Drama Award, 1980; *Evening Standard* Award (with John Caird), Olivier Award for best director (with Caird), Society of West End Theatre Award, and Sydney Edwards Award, all 1980, for *Nicholas Nickleby; Drama* Award, 1982; New York Drama Critics Circle Award, 1982; Tony Award for best director of a dramatic play (with Caird), 1982, for *The Life and Adventures of Nicholas Nickleby*; New York Drama Critics Circle Award, 1982; Society of West End Theatre Award, 1982; Drama Desk Award for best director, 1983, for *All's Well that Ends Well*; Tony Award for best director of a musical, 1983, for *Cats*; Tony Award (with Caird) for best director of a musical, 1987, for *Les Miserables*; *Evening Standard* Award for best director, for *Timon of Athens*.

Sidelights

Theater director Trevor Nunn is respected for his distinguished career first with England's Royal Shakespeare Company (RSC) and then with its Royal National Theatre. At the RSC, he packed houses with contemporary tellings of the works of the Bard, which shocked some traditionalists but delighted millions of others, making the company a wild success at its locations around Britain and on tours throughout Europe, Japan, North America, and Australia. Nunn also became a sensation for directing award–winning productions of the musicals *Cats* and *Les Miserables*. In 1997, he moved to London's Royal National Theatre as artistic director, which he aimed to make more appealing to a wide audience from all walks of life.

Nunn was born on January 14, 1940, in Ipswich, Suffolk, England, the son of Robert Alexander Nunn (a cabinetmaker) and Dorothy May (Piper) Nunn. At age five, Nunn had decided he would go into show business, and he was definitely enticed into a career in the theater at age eight after seeing a production of *Robin Hood* in his hometown. The only other family member with connections to the entertainment world was a second cousin who was a magician and ventriloquist. While still a boy, Nunn once snagged a small role in a local production. As he got older, he sang and joined a rock band, and began to dabble in directing with a school revue in which he performed an act dressed in drag.

Despite his working–class roots, Nunn managed to gain acceptance into an academic preparatory school based on his stellar test scores. After graduating from Northgate Grammar School in Ipswich, he became a school teacher and founded a theater group. His first effort was directing a five–hour version of *Hamlet*. From 1959 to 1962, Nunn attended Downing College of Cambridge University, where he studied English literature with noted scholar F. R. Leavis. Also in college, he stayed busy acting and directing with the Amateur Dramatic Club, the Marlowe Society, and the Footlights Club, and he also served as president of the University Actors.

After receiving his bachelor's degree with honors from Cambridge in 1962, Nunn took a job with the Belgrade Theatre in Coventry, England, as a trainee director. At first, his assignments were slim, but he eventually mounted several productions, mostly formulaic comedies or big hits fresh from London. By 1963, he was named resident producer and placed in charge of ten productions, a load that caused him great stress. At age 25, he joined the Royal Shakespeare Company after an invitation from director Peter Hall, who had seen Nunn's work at the Belgrade. His first job was to direct a musical based on the British General Strike of 1926. Unfortunately for Nunn, it was never performed in front of an audience.

Nunn soon had a hit in 1965 with *The Thwarting of Baron Bolligrew*, a children's play at London's Aldwych Theatre. He went on to seal his reputation that same year with *The Revenger's Tragedy*, a Jacobean drama by Cyril Tourneur. Though the production was not a financial success, its 1969 revival at the Aldwych led to an award for best director from the London Theatre Critics. In addition, his 1967 staging of *The Taming of the Shrew* was widely praised as well.

Just three years into his tenure at the RSC, Hall approached the young Nunn to take over as artistic director of the company. After some persuading, he accepted the job the next year, thus becoming, at age 28, the youngest ever director of a major British theater organization. In that position, Nunn first attracted applause with a creative 1969 staging of *The Winter's Tale*, in which Judi Dench played both Queen Hermione and her daughter, Perdita. Soon, the director was winning acclaim for making the RSC the most renowned company in the western world, thanks to his numerous Shakespearean productions. One of his biggest triumphs came in 1972 with his "Roman Season," which chronicled the rise and fall of the Roman empire with *Coriolanus, Julius Caesar, Antony and Cleopatra*, and *Titus Andronicus*. His 1976 staging of *Macbeth* was also a tour de force, as was 1980's *Nicholas Nickleby*, which brought him and codirector John Caird a slew of honors, including a 1982 Tony Award.

However, Nunn is perhaps best known for his elaborate productions of the Andrew Lloyd Webber musical *Cats*, which started at RSC in 1981, and *Les Miserables*, which began there in 1985. Though some criticized his decision to stage such commercial ventures at the RSC, Nunn told Jack Kroll in *Newsweek*, "Now that government subsidies are dwindling, I can't take an attitude of intellectual snobbery toward a show that's going to help us survive and do Shakespeare." And in fact, the director wrote additional lyrics for *Cats* and also penned the stage play of *Les Miserables* —based on the novel by Victor

Hugo—with director John Caird. Eventually, Nunn's participation with the RSC dwindled; by 1986, he held the posts of associate director, director emeritus, and advisory director.

In October of 1997, Nunn started a new post, this time as artistic director of Britain's prestigious National Theater. Chosen from a pool of about 50 candidates, he accepted the job in March. Many observers, including Nunn, had figured that the post would go to a younger candidate such as Sam Mendes, Stephen Daldry, or Nicholas Hytner. "It was only when the approaches didn't or wouldn't go away that I became attracted to what is essentially a new idea," Nunn told Matt Wolf in *Variety*. His salary was set at between $130,000 and $135,00 a year, which would come on top of the estimated $20 million annual income he reaped from royalties, mainly due to his lyrics to the song "Memory" from *Cats*.

Subsequently, Nunn began his first season at the National with a revival of the musical *Oklahoma!*; *Private Lives*, a new comedy by director Deborah Warner, with whom he worked at RSC; and an obscure Tennessee Williams play titled *Not About Nightingales*. He also staged a new version of *Peter Pan* directed by his colleague Caird and starring Ian McKellen, and several others ranging from bawdy comedies to political period pieces. Nunn's approach, as he noted in a *Time International* interview, was to build a repertoire by "concentrating on diversity," adding. "A National Theatre has to be a broad church, there need to be particular chapels in that church where very specialized things can go on, but there also have to be things that unify, that bring people from every background into the building." He also noted, however, his intention to continue producing the works of Shakespeare.

Nunn wears a full beard and is five feet, eleven inches tall. He was married in 1969 to actor Janet Suzman, and after a divorce, was married to Sharon Lee Hill in 1986. They, too, divorced, and he wed actor Imogen Stubbs in 1994. Nunn's contract with the National Theatre was scheduled to last through 2002. In 1999, *Not About Nightingales* opened in New York. Nunn has also directed televised versions of various works of Shakespeare, as well as the films *Hedda*, 1975; *Lady Jane*, 1985; and *Twelfth Night; or, What You Will*, 1996.

Sources

Books

International Dictionary of Theatre, Volume 3: Actors, Directors, and Designers, St. James Press, 1996.
Contemporary Theatre, Film, and Television, volume 21, Gale Group, 1999.

Periodicals

Independent, March 6, 1998, p. 1.
Independent on Sunday, February 28, 1999, p. 1.
Newsweek, February 10, 1986, p. 71.
Time International, April 20, 1998, pp. 54, 56.
Variety, March 11, 1996, p. 51; June 16, 1997, p. 39; June 8, 1998, p. 75.

Joyce Carol Oates

Author

Born June 16, 1938, in Lockport, NY; daughter of Frederic James (a tool and die designer) and Caroline (Bush) Oates; married Raymond Joseph Smith, January 23, 1961. *Education:* Syracuse University, B.A. in English, 1960; University of Wisconsin, M.A. in English, 1961.

Addresses: *Office*—Department of Creative Writing, Princeton University, Princeton, NJ 08544. *Agent*—John Hawkins, 71 West 23rd St., New York, NY 10010; (for plays) Peter Franklin, c/oWilliam Morris Agency, 1350 Avenue of the Americas, New York, NY 10019.

Career

Writer. University of Detroit, Detroit, MI, instructor, c. 1961–65, assistant professor, 1965–67; University of Windsor, Windsor, Ontario, Canada, member of English department faculty, 1967–78; Princeton University, Princeton, NJ, writer–in–residence, 1978–81, professor, 1987—, Roger S. Berlind Distinguished Professor.

Awards: Mademoiselle college fiction award, 1959, for "In the Old World"; National Endowment for the Arts grants, 1966, 1968; Guggenheim fellowship, 1967; O. Henry Award, 1967, for "In the Region of Ice," and 1973, for "The Dead," and 1983, for ""My Warszawa"; Rosenthal Award, National Institute of Arts and Letters, 1968, for *A Garden of Earthly Delights;* National Book Award, 1970, for *them;* O. Henry Special Award for Continuing Achievement, 1970 and 1986; Lotos Club Award of Merit, 1975;

Pushcart Prize, 1976; *Unholy Loves* was selected by the American Library Association as a notable book of 1979; St. Louis Literary Award, 1988; Rhea Award for the short story "Dungannon Foundation," 1990; Alan Swallow Award for fiction, 1990; cowinner, Heidemann Award for one–act plays, 1990; Bobst Award for Lifetime Achievement in Fiction, 1990; Bram Stoker Lifetime Achievement Award for horror fiction, 1994; Bram Stoker Award for Horror, Horror Writers of America, and Fisk Fiction Prize, both 1996, both for *Zombie.*

Sidelights

One of the most prolific and respected contemporary American authors, Joyce Carol Oates is admired for her haunting tales of the dark underside of society. Her talent for suspense and for finding the terrifying within the ordinary are trademarks that she carries over various genres, including short stories, novels, plays, and poetry. Most of Oates's works are not graphically violent, although they often contain disturbing subject matter. Instead, they are psychological and social, exploring the moral state of the post–World War II United States, and are thus generally labeled as "gothic" writings. Though many critics have complained that someone with her staggering output could not be a high–

quality writer, she has amassed numerous awards and been on the short list for the Nobel Prize in literature several times. Despite her rapid–fire publication schedule, Oates keeps a low profile, so when her authorized biography came out in 1998, fans were offered an extensive peek into her life and the many inspirations for her tales. Also in 1998, Oates surprisingly found something new to try: She wrote a book for children, with a happy ending at that. In 1999, she published her 29th novel, *Broke Heart Blues*. The author also publishes under the pseudonym Rosamond Smith.

Oates was born on June 16, 1938, in Lockport, New York, to Frederic James and Caroline (Bush) Oates. Her father made a comfortable working–class living as a tool and die designer, and her family included a brother, Frederic Jr. and sister, Lynn Ann. Her early education was gained in a one–room schoolhouse in rural Erie County, on which she based the fictional Eden County, the setting of many of her later tales. From a young age, Oates displayed a talent for storytelling. Before she could write, at age three and four, she drew picture books. Later, her works would run as many as 200 hand–written pages long, and she designed the covers herself. By age 12, she was using a typewriter, and in her teens, she was introduced to short stories in her literature class, which she immediately knew she had been creating for years.

At age 15, Oates submitted her first manuscript, a 250–page novel about a rehabilitated drug addict, but publishers rejected for being too bleak for the youth market. An excellent student her whole life, she went on to earn a New York State Regents scholarship and enrolled at Syracuse University to study literature. In 1959, Oates shared first prize in *Mademoiselle's* college fiction contest for her story "In the Old World." Soon, another story was published in the literary journal *Epoch*. In 1960 Oates learned she was the class valedictorian, and thus was obligated to give a speech, a frightening prospect due to her introverted nature. As Greg Johnson related in *Invisible Writer*, his biography of her, Oates asked if she could get out of the appearance somehow, but was told only in case of rain. Syracuse's commencements had never been rained out in the history of the institution, and as the ceremony began that day, the sun was shining. As the graduates began filing onto the field, a drizzle started, and the audience was dismissed. Oates was exceedingly pleased.

Afterward, Oates went to the University of Wisconsin, which offered her a generous fellowship, and received her master of arts in English in 1961. There,

she was disappointed with the academic environment. As Johnson wrote, "Joyce discovered that most of the graduate faculty in English were extreme conservatives who discouraged students from studying either American literature or creative writing—the two fields in which she was most interested." Instead, she slogged through courses taught in Old English and dull seminars on British literature from the sixteenth century. One professor even derided her for writing a paper on Franz Kafka, because he had never read the author and did not consider him an important figure. Oates, meanwhile, idolized Kafka, noting in a *Newsweek* article, "In college, I was Franz Kafka for a while." Some of her other influences include Fyodor Dostoyevsky, William Faulkner, Sigmund Freud, Thomas Mann, Herman Melville, and Friedrich Nietzsche. Though her studies in Madison did not intrigue her, they consumed all of her time, and she did not write fiction at all during her year there.

However, some good came out of Wisconsin, as it was there that Oates met Raymond Joseph Smith, who was getting his doctorate in English, and they married on January 23, 1961, a date they chose because they had met on October 23 and got engaged on November 23. Subsequently, they moved to Beaumont, Texas, where Smith had accepted a position as an assistant professor at Lamar State College of Technology. Both Oates and her husband were immediately disillusioned with the small–town atmosphere and pervasive racism, and she was further frustrated when the teaching job promised to her at Lamar did not pan out. She thus began doctoral work in English at Rice University in 1962, taking a bus some 70 miles west to Houston for her classes. After a few weeks of this commute, she stumbled upon one of her own works in the anthology *Best American Short Stories*.

Subsequently, Oates quit school in order to devote herself to writing professionally. Her first collection of stories, *By the North Gate*, was published in 1963, and held all the elements for which she would become known: random violence, the seedy underside of seemingly normal people, descents into madness, and the like. After her book was accepted, Oates and her husband left Texas. The previous winter, they had both received offers to teach at universities in Detroit, Michigan, so she started her academic career at the University of Detroit, a Catholic institution, in 1962. As the intense social turmoil escalated in Detroit, including rioting and a spike in the crime rate, Oates and her husband began teaching at the University of Windsor in Ontario, Canada. He began there in 1964 and she in 1967, and they moved to Windsor in 1968. They founded the *Ontario Review* during their time there; she left in 1977 and to become a writer–in–residence at Princeton University in New Jersey. Since 1987, she has held the title of professor there. However, much of her writing was shaped by her experiences in Detroit. Johnson related that Oates once noted, "Detroit, my 'great' subject, made me the person I am, consequently the writer I am for better or worse."

In the meantime, Oates published her first novel, *With Shuddering Fall,* in 1964. This was a violent tale, concerning a destructive romance between a teenage girl and a 30–year–old stock car racer. The plot contains incidents of rape, miscarriage, suicide, a race riot, and a car crash. The book was generally was well–received. The next year, Oates ventured into playwrighting with *The Sweet Enemy,* which opened in February of 1965 at the Actors Playhouse in Greenwich Village. This was her first real taste of critical barbs, and the play closed after only a few performances. She followed this with another volume of stories, *Upon the Sweeping Flood and Other Stories,* in 1966, and won her first National Endowment for the Arts grant that year as well. Another would follow in 1968, and in 1967, she reaped a Guggenheim fellowship, as well as an O. Henry Award for the story "In the Region of Ice."

Also in 1967 Oates penned what would be the first in a trilogy, *A Garden of Earthly Delights,* about a the daughter of a migrant worker who marries a wealthy man, gaining security and financial comfort for her and her illegitimate son. However, the character lapses into a meaningless existence of shallow materialism, and her son ends up killing his stepfather. Reviews were mixed but more positive than not, and sales were brisk; Oates was pleased that *A Garden of Earthly Delights* received a good deal of attention and was taken seriously. Her next novel, *Expensive People,* also published in 1967, continues with an economic theme, investigating an 18–year–old obese genius who is spiritually bankrupt due to his suburban affluence. The final volume in the trilogy, *them,* traces three generations of a Detroit family, from the Depression to the riots of 1967 (during which, in real life, Oates and her husband were out of town on an extended vacation). The work won the National Book Award for fiction; the other two were also nominated.

During this time, Oates continued to contribute short stories to periodicals; they were also compiled in a number of books. One of her most renowned is "Where Are You Going, Where Have You Been?," first published in 1966, about a teenage girl who gets a rude awakening when she takes a ride with an older man. Oates's first poetry collection, *Women in Love and Other Poems,* came out in 1968, and she

would publish several more volumes over the next couple of decades. In 1970, another play, *Sunday Dinner,* was produced off–Broadway, but she did not take up playwrighting again in earnest for a couple more decades, when several were published and produced from 1990 to 1995. In addition to creating novels at a rapid–fire pace, she also kept a hand in academic works as well. Oates composed a critical study of D. H. Lawrence in 1973, and she also helped edit or compile various literary collections, including *Best American Short Stories of 1979, Oxford Book of American Short Stories,* 1992, and others. She also penned a book–length philosophical essay titled *On Boxing,* 1987, which led to an appearance on television as a commentator on the sport.

In the 1980s, Oates began to write Gothic–style novels with her works *Bellefleur, A Bloodsmoor Romance,* and *Mysteries of Winterthurn,* which displayed elements of parody, though they take the genre quite seriously. Such books contained stock elements of Gothics including ghosts, haunted houses, and enigmatic deaths, but deal with real issues such as crimes again women, children, and the poor. She would return to the themes of race and violence in *Because It Is Bitter, and Because It Is My Heart,* 1990, and again examined economic conditions and their effect on the upper–middle class in *American Appetites.* Other works include *Zombie,* a horror novel which centers on a serial killer, and *We Were the Mulvaneys,* 1996, about a family that is marred after the rape of the daughter. Throughout her career, Oates has been honored with several literary prizes, including the O. Henry Special Award for Continuing Achievement in 1970 and 1986, the Pushcart Prize in 1976, the Alan Swallow Award for fiction, 1990; the Bobst Award for Lifetime Achievement in Fiction, 1990; the Bram Stoker Lifetime Achievement Award for horror fiction, 1994; and the Bram Stoker Award for Horror, Horror Writers of America, and Fisk Fiction Prize, both in 1996, for *Zombie.*

In 1998, Oates ventured into one of the few genres of literature she had not yet touched when she penned *Come Meet Muffin!,* about an eccentric stray cat who is adopted into a family. Though the tale, about the fear of getting lost, flirts with Oates's dark style, all ends well when Muffin finds his way home. In 1999, Oates saw publication of her 29th novel, *Broke Heart Blues.* D. T. Max in the *New York Times Book Review* wrote, "It's about how lonely, unhappy people mythologize their adolescence" and called it "funny and playful, written with focused energy."

Oates, a quiet woman, is renowned among her colleagues for her intelligence and wit. Though slender, she has battled anorexia, an ailment that also has affected a number of her fictional characters. A devout reader, she and her husband shun popular culture; they rarely catch a television program and only occasionally view art films. A good deal of personal information of this type was revealed in 1998 in the authorized biography by Johnson, who had earlier written two critical studies of Oates's works. He painted an in–depth portrait of her personal life intertwined with her professional accomplishments while pointing out the institutionalized sexism that did not keep the writer from excelling. Though many other books about Oates had been published, this was the first to use the author's personal journals and letters and to encompass her entire life, rather than to focus on certain time periods or genres.

Sources

Books

Encyclopedia of World Biography, second edition, Gale Research, 1998. Johnson, Greg, *Invisible Writer: A Biography of Joyce Carol Oates*, Dutton, 1998.

Periodicals

Arizona Republic, July 5, 1998, p. E15.
Commonweal, December 5, 1969, p. 307.
Newsday, July 28, 1998, p. B2.
Newsweek, March 23, 1970, p. 108.
New York Times, March 19, 1989.
New York Times Book Review, August 8, 1999, p. 26.
Rocky Mountain News, April 26, 1998, p. 3E.
St. Louis Post–Dispatch, April 26, 1998, p. D5.
Saturday Review, October 26, 1968, p. 33.
Time, October 10, 1969, p. 108.

Online

"Joyce Carol Oates," *Contemporary Authors Online*, Gale Group web site, http://www.galenet.com (August 27, 1999).

Olusegun Obasanjo

President of Nigeria

Name pronounced "oh–loo–SHEH–gun oh–bah–SAN–jo;" born Matthew Olusegun Aremu Okikiolakan Onaopemipo Obasanjo, March 5, 1937 (some sources cite May 5, 1937, or March 6, 1935), in Abeokuta, Nigeria; son of Obasanjo Bankole (a farmer) and Bernice Ashabi; married Oluremi Akinlawon (some sources give her name as Oluremi Akinbwon or Oluyemi Akinlaja; a nutritionist; divorced); married Stella Ajike Abede; children: two sons; four daughters. *Education:* Abeokuta Baptist High School; Mons Officers' Cadet School, Aldershot, England; Royal College of Military Engineering, Chatham, England; School of Survey, Newbury, England; British Royal Engineers' Young Officers School, Shrivenham, England; Indian Defence Staff College; Indian Army School of Engineering; Royal College of Defence Studies, London.

Addresses: *Office*—c/o P.O. Box 2286, Abeokuta, Ogun State, Nigeria.

Career

Enlisted in the Nigerian Army, 1958; served in 5th Battalion, Kaduna and the Cameroons, 1958–59; second lieutenant, 1959; lieutenant, 1960; captain and commander of Nigerian Army's Engineering Unit, 1963; major and commander of Field Engineering Unit, 1965; lieutenant–colonel, 1967; commander of Ibadan Garrison, 1967–69; colonel, 1969; commander of 3rd Marine Commando Division, 1969–70; accepted Biafran surrender ending Nigerian Civil War, 1970; federal commissioner for Works and Housing, 1975; led coup to overthrow head of state Yakubu Gowon, 1975; head of state and commander in chief of the Nigerian Armed Forces, 1976–79; founder, Obasanjo Farms Nigeria Ltd. in Otta, Ogun State, 1979 ; elected president of Nigeria, 1999. Founder and chair, African Leadership Forum; board member, Ford Foundation, International Negotiations Network. Author of *A March of Progress: Collected Speeches,* 1979; *My Command: An Account of the Nigerian Civil War,* 1980; *Africa in Perspective: Myths and Realities,* 1987; *Africa Embattled,* 1988; *Constitution for National Integration and Development,* 1989; *Not My Will,* 1990; and many articles for periodicals, including *Foreign Policy, Foreign Affairs, Review of International Affairs,* and *New Perspectives Quarterly.*

Sidelights

When Olusegun Obasanjo was elected president of Nigeria in 1999, he had come a long way from the days in the 1970s when he rose to power through a military coup. Even then, though, after ruling from 1976 to 1979, he became the first Nigerian dictator to relinquish his post voluntarily. Thereafter, he owned a farm, set up a think tank for African issues, and became a respected figure in international politics. Meanwhile, other military juntas managed to grab control in Nigeria, and Obasanjo, along with dozens of others, was eventually imprisoned when dictator Sani Abacha cracked down on those who opposed his rule. When Obasanjo took office for a second time in 1999, he found support through a democratic vote, but he rose to power at a time when serious problems in his country would prove to be a formidable challenge for any leader. Outsiders watched to see if he could preserve the democracy and restore some order to Africa's largest country, home to 120 million.

Obasanjo's date of birth was reported as March 5, 1937, according to Norimitsu Onishi in the *New York Times,* but other sources list it as May 5, 1937, or March 6, 1935. He was born and raised in Abeokuta in southwest Nigeria, about 60 miles north of Lagos in the center of Yorubaland. The area is now known as Ogun State, but was then part of the nation's western province, which is predominantly populated by members of the Yoruba tribe, one of the three main groups in the country. Within a year of Obasanjo's birth, two other future famous Nigerians would be born in Abeokuta as well: Moshood K. O. Abiola, a political leader and business mogul, and Fela Anikulapo–Kuti, who created Afro–beat music.

Although Obasanjo's given name was Matthew Olusegun Fajinmi Aremu Obasanjo, he dropped the Matthew in high school when many Nigerians began to resist Western influences. The first child of Obasanjo Bankole and Bernice Ashabi, Obasanjo had one half–sister, Oluwola Adunni. His father had taken a second wife, Aduke, and both women had several children, but no others survived infancy.

Raised as a Christian, Obasanjo attended Baptist Boys' High School in Abeokuta starting in 1952. His father, previously a successful farmer, had suffered financial hardships and left the family just before his son began high school. Obasanjo passed the London General Certificate of Education exam, then worked at the United African Company in a clerical position for a short spell. Subsequently, he spent about a year teaching religion and science at African Church Modern School in Ibadan. Though he wished to attend college, he could not afford it, so he joined the army in 1958.

During his two decades with the Nigerian army, Obasanjo rose through the ranks. At the Regular Officers' Special Training School in Teshie, Ghana, he became a cadet. He also received training in Britain at Chatham's Royal College of Military Engineering and at the School of Survey in Newbury. In addition, Obasanjo won student awards at the British Royal Engineers' young Officers School in Shrivenham, and also studied at the Indian Defence Staff College and the Indian Army School of Engineering.

From 1958 to 1959, Obasanjo served in the 5th Battalion in Kaduna and the Cameroons, and was commissioned second lieutenant in 1959. In 1960, the year that Nigeria gained formal independence from Great Britain, he became a lieutenant and served seven months with the United Nations peacekeeping force in the Congo. In 1963, he began commanding the Nigerian Army Field Engineering Squadron, the only engineering unit of the army, and was also promoted to captain that year. Obasanjo was promoted to major in 1965, to lieutenant–colonel in 1967, and to colonel in 1969.

Meanwhile, after Nigeria claimed its independence in 1960, the nation suffered a period of turmoil. In 1966, there were two violent military coups, which sparked ethnic tension. Subsequently, the Eastern Region, populated mostly by Christian Ibos, seceded from the Northern and Western regions and declared itself the Republic of Biafra. A three–year civil war ensued, and during this period Obasanjo served as the commander of the 3rd marine commando division, winning various key battles. The war ended in 1970 as the Ibo forces surrendered.

After the war, Obasanjo once again headed the army engineers, and was promoted to brigadier–general in 1972. At that point, he attended an advanced training course at the Royal College of Defence Studies in London for two years, returning to Nigeria in 1974. In January of 1975, Nigerian leader Yakuba Gowon appointed him federal commissioner for works and housing. That July, however, General Murtala Muhammed and Obasanjo led a bloodless coup, after which Muhammed took over as head of state and named Obasanjo chief of staff of the Nigerian army.

In February of 1976, Muhammed was assassinated, and Obasanjo assumed leadership of Nigeria, becoming the first Yoruban to do so. He was also named commander in chief of the armed forces as a lieutenant general. Right away, he pledged to honor Muhammed's promise to hold democratic elections. While he was in office, Obasanjo challenged British colonialism in Africa and adopted a new constitution in 1978 which guaranteed some basic human rights. Also that year he lifted the state of emergency and a ban on political parties. His move toward reforms earned him praise from many.

However, Obasanjo was also criticized for some of his harsh actions as dictator. Crackdowns on journalists as well as students protesting tuition hikes made for a repressive atmosphere. In an infamous incident, Obasanjo's soldiers in 1977 burned down musician Fela's home in Lagos and threw his 77–year–old mother out of a second–story window. She eventually died from the injuries. Fela, an outspoken critic of the military rule, later wrote a song called "Coffin for Head of State," which tells of how he tried to present Obasanjo with his mother's coffin and takes a jab at the ruler's "big fat stomach."

In 1979, Nigeria held elections, and Obasanjo was defeated by Shehu Shagari. Thereafter, he became the only military ruler in the nation's history to voluntarily step down. This enraged fellow Yorubans. They felt betrayed because Obasanjo, after a tight vote, declared that Shagari, a Hausa–Fulani member, had won the election. Retiring from the armed forces, he subsequently started a farming company, raising chickens and pigs, and growing bananas. He also began to serve on numerous advisory committees regarding the future of Africa, and acted as a mediator in international affairs concerning other African nations. He also served on the board of the Ford Foundation and in 1988 founded and became chair of the African Leadership Forum, in addition to serving on former President Jimmy Carter's International Negotiations Network, an organization holding the goal of peaceful resolution of international conflicts. By the late 1980s, some thought Obasanjo would be a candidate for secretary general of the United Nations.

In the meantime, Nigeria was plagued by corruption from the newly elected government, and in 1983, a group of generals led yet another coup, installing Muhammadu Buhari as leader. In two years, yet another coup led to a new head of state, General Ibrahim Babangida, who once again promised democratic elections. Finally, in 1993 elections, Moshood Abiola seemed to have won the popular vote, but Babangida refused to honor the results. After massive protests, Babangida resigned and Ernest Shonekan took his place.

Despite a cutoff of aid from the European Union, the military government in Nigeria refused to let go of its power. In 1993, General Sani Abacha became head of state in yet another coup, and accused Abiola of treason and Obasanjo of plotting a coup. They were both jailed for life, along with some 40 others, some of whom were given death sentences for charges that were never revealed. After an international outcry, Abacha reduced the sentences, but Obasanjo spent three years in prison.

Abacha died suddenly in 1998; the cause was not determined. Taking his place, General Abdulsalami Abubakbar immediately stated his intentions to re-store a democracy once again. He released Obasanjo and several other prisoners, though Abiola died in jail on July 7, 1998. Elections were scheduled for February of 1999, and by November of 1998, Obasanjo declared that he would be in the running. He became the candidate for the People's Democratic Party, facing Chief Olu Falae, who opposed him on a coalition of the Alliance for Democracy and the All People's Party.

On March 1, 1999, Obasanjo was declared the president of Nigeria with 62.8 percent of the popular vote, and he took office on May 29. Although Falae, who received 37.2 percent, disputed the numbers and alleged fraud, international observers reported that both parties had actually engaged in tactics like ballot stuffing and misreporting of figures. Some critics also contended that the military rigged the elections. Obasanjo admitted that abuses happened on both sides, but asked Falae to accept defeat in order to keep the peace. Other nations breathed a sigh of relief when violence was kept to a bare minimum, and collectively seemed to accept the results and hope for the best.

When Obasanjo assumed leadership for the second time, he inherited a dismal set of problems. For three decades, the nation had suffered under a kleptocracy, in which the military outright stole resources and wealth from the people. The corrupt government for years did not invest, leaving it dependent on its rich oil deposits. Even worse, although oil accounts for 90 percent of exports and 75 percent of government revenue, Abacha let two of the refineries become run–down. This caused fuel shortages, forcing Nigeria to purchase foreign oil and driving prices way up. Lines for gas stretched for miles. Abacha, incidentally, had invested in the foreign oil suppliers.

In addition to the economic problems, various ethnic groups like the Ogoni and Ijaw began lobbying for more autonomy as well as more money from oil sales and compensation for damage to the environment caused by spills. To get their way, they threatened to continue engaging in terrorist activities like kidnapping and vandalism. Also, social problems such as drug use, crime, and AIDS were rampant. On a more basic level, electricity and telephones worked sporadically, and education and health care services had collapsed. Agriculture, once a mainstay in the nation's economy, had plunged so far that Nigeria became a major food importer. Though it was once one of the richest of African nations, as of 1999, more than half of the residents were living on less than a dollar per day.

However, Obasanjo vowed to make a difference. He set about writing a new constitution, and agreed to privatize and deregulate business, thus taking it out of the government's hands and setting up a free market economy. He vowed to make agriculture a priority, followed by education. Before long, the gas shortage was eased, and more importantly, almost as soon as he took office, Obasanjo purged the military and police forces of 93 top officers who held political posts. He also cancelled government contracts that had been given to the military regime that ruled after Abacha's death. This showed his commitment to a renewal and seemed to display that he was not an army stooge, as some previously surmised. He also established a panel to investigate corruption and human–rights abuses under Abacha, and Nigeria was able to freeze more than $2 billion of Abacha's family's Swiss bank accounts.

Obasanjo was married to Oluremi Akinlawon (some sources give her name as Oluremi Akinbwon or Oluyemi Akinlaja), a nutritionist, and they had five children together. They divorced, and Obasanjo married Stella Ajike Abede, with whom he has at least one child. A Christian since childhood, Obasanjo often publicly refers to his faith, and is a staunch advocate of religious freedom. In his spare time, Obasanjo plays table tennis and squash, and he is the author of various books on African politics and the military, in addition to an autobiography.

Sources

Books

Contemporary Black Biography, volume 22, Gale Group, 1999.
Current Leaders of Nations, Gale Group, 1999.

Periodicals

Africa News Service, February 17, 1999.
Christianity Today, April 26, 1999, p. 21.
Economist, May 22, 1999, p. 50.
Jet, March 15, 1999, p. 54.
Maclean's, March 15, 1999, p. 29.
New Republic, March 22, 1999, p. 9.
Newsweek, June 7, 1999, p. 55.
New York Times, February 8, 1976; July 15, 1998, p. A1; March 2, 1999, pp. A1, A10; October 29, 1999, p. A18; November 23, 1999, p. A1.
Time, August 7, 1995, p. 39.
Time International, March 15, 1999, p. 24.
U.S. News & World Report, November 1, 1999, p. 48.
World Press Review, August 1999, p. 20.

Bernadette Peters

Actor, singer, and dancer

Born Bernadette Lazzara, February 28, 1948, in Queens, NY; daughter of Peter (a truck driver) and Marguerite (a homemaker; maiden name, Maltese) Lazzara; married Michael Wittenberg (an investment adviser), July 20, 1996. *Education:* Attended Quintano's School for Young Professionals, New York City; studied acting with David Le Grant, tap dancing with Oliver McCool III, and singing with Jim Gregory.

Addresses: *Home*—New York City. *Agent*—Jeff Hunter, William Morris Agency, 1325 Avenue of the Americas, New York, NY 10019.

Career

Actor, singer, and dancer. Stage appearances (all in New York City, unless otherwise noted) include *The Most Happy Fella,* 1959; *The Penny Friend,* 1966–67; *The Girl in the Freudian Slip,* 1967; *Johnny No–Trump,* 1967; *Curley McDimple,* 1967–68; *George M!,* 1968; *Dames at Sea,* 1968–69; *La Strada,* 1969; *Nevertheless They Laugh,* 1971; *On the Town,* 1971–72; *Tartuffe,* Philadelphia, PA, 1972–73; *Mack and Mabel,* 1974; *Sally and Marsha,* 1982; *Sunday in the Park with George,* 1983, 1984–85; *Song and Dance,* 1985–86; *Into the Woods,* 1987–89; *Goodbye Girl,* 1993; and *Annie Get Your Gun,* 1999. Also toured with *Gypsy,* 1961–62, and *W.C.,* 1971, and appeared in *This Is Google,* 1962; and *Riverwind,* 1966.

Television appearances include episodes of *McCloud,* 1971, 1976; *Maude,* 1972, 1975; *All in the Family,* 1971, 1975, *Love, American Style,* 1973; *McCoy,* 1976; *Satur-*

day *Night Live,* 1981; and *The Closer,* 1998; series *The Carol Burnett Show,* 1970s and 1991; *The Muppet Show,* 1977; and *Animaniacs* (voice-over for animation), 1993; miniseries *The Martian Chronicles,* 1980; and *The Odyssey,* 1997; and movies *Paradise Lost,* 1974; *The Islander,* 1978; *Sleeping Beauty,* 1983; *An American Portrait,* 1984; *Sunday in the Park with George* (on *Great Performances*), 1986; *Into the Woods* (on *American Playhouse*), 1990; *The Last Best Year,* 1990; *The Last Mile,* 1992; *Beauty and the Beast: Enchanted Christmas* (voice-over for animation), 1997; *Cinderella,* 1997; *What the Deaf Man Heard,* 1997; and *Holiday in your Heart,* 1997; also numerous specials and awards programs.

Film appearances include *Ace Eli and Rodger of the Skies,* 1973; *The Longest Yard,* 1974; *Silent Movie,* 1976; *Vigilante Force, 1976; W.C. Fields and Me,* 1976; *The Jerk,* 1979; *Heartbeeps,* 1981; *Pennies from Heaven,* 1981; *Tulips,* 1981; *Annie,* 1982; *Slaves of New York,* 1989; *Pink Cadillac,* 1989; *Alice,* 1990; *Impromptu,* 1991; *Anastasia* (voice-over for animation), 1997; and *Snow Days,* 1999.

Awards: Drama Desk Award for outstanding performance, 1968, for *Dames at Sea;* Theatre World Award, 1968, for *George M!;* Best of Las Vegas Award, 1980; Golden Globe Award for best film actress in a musical/comedy, 1981, for *Pennies from Heaven*; Antoinette Perry ("Tony") Award for best actress in a musical, and Drama Desk Award for best actress in a musical, both 1986, for *Song and Dance*; Distinguished Performance Award, Drama League of New York, 1986; Hasty Pudding Woman of the Year Award, 1987; "Mr. Abbott" awards Dinner, President's Award, 1995; Drama Desk Award for outstanding actress, Outer Critics Circle Award for outstanding actress in a musical, and Tony Award for best actress in a musical, all 1999, for *Annie Get Your Gun*; Sarah Siddons Actress of the Year Award; youngest person inducted into the Theatre Hall of Fame.

Sidelights

With her cherubic face, saucer–like eyes, full, pouty lips, and springy mass of curly red hair, Bernadette Peters is one of the most recognizable actors on stage and screen. Her energetic performances add zest and vitality to virtually all of the projects in which she appears, from children's shows to zany movies to her best–known vehicles, Broadway musicals. Peters got her start as a child actor on television shows and in plays, and by the late 1960s, had begun raking in theater awards and nominations for several productions. In the 1970s, she ventured into television and film, earning accolades for her work on *The Muppet Show* and standing out as a comic force in films like *Silent Movie* and *The Jerk*. Returning to the stage in the early 1980s, she became a standard in Stephen Sondheim musicals, but earned her first Tony for the Andrew Lloyd Weber production *Song and Dance*. In 1999, she was the darling of Broadway when she amassed three important awards, including another Tony, for her work in the musical *Annie Get Your Gun*.

Peters was born Bernadette Lazzara on February 28, 1948, in the Queens borough of New York City and grew up in the Ozone Park area. She was the youngest child of Peter and Marguerite Lazzara. Her father, Peter, drove a bread truck, and her mother was a homemaker, but had a keen interest in show business and urged her daughter to perform. By age three–and–a–half, Peters was taking singing and tap dancing lessons, and soon began making appearances on television. She started out on *The Horn & Hardart Children's Hour* and also appeared on *The Juvenile Jury* and *Name That Tune*. At age ten, her Italian American surname was changed to prevent her from being typecast; her father's first name became the source of her stage name.

Even before she was in her teens, Peters was landing roles in stage productions such as *This is Google*, directed by the legendary Otto Preminger, as well as *The Most Happy Fella* and *The Penny Friend*. At age 13, she was cast as Baby June in a touring company of *Gypsy*. During her high school years, she backed off from her career temporarily and attended private school, Quintano's School for Young Professionals in Manhattan, graduating in 1966. In the meantime, she studied acting with David Le Grant, tap dancing with Oliver McCool III, and singing with Jim Gregory.

After graduation, Peters performed in some off-Broadway shows, then landed her Broadway debut in 1967 in *Johnny No-Trump*. The following year, she garnered acclaim when she starred with Joel Gray in the musical *George M!* For the role of Josie Cohan, she earned a Theatre World Award. Also in 1968, she brought in a Drama Desk Award for the humorous off-Broadway hit *Dames at Sea*, in which she played Ruby. Some subsequent plays, including an adaptation of Federico Fellini's *La Strada*, were not well-reviewed, but Peters was often singled out for praise. For example, reception was mixed regarding a 1971 revival of *On the Town* and 1974's *Mack and Mabel*, but Peters was nominated for Tony Awards for both.

By the early 1970s, Peters began trying her hand in Hollywood, but although she was a star on the stage, she was relegated mainly to supporting parts in film. Her screen debut came in the obscure 1973 movie *Ace Eli and Rodger of the Skies*, then she played a secretary in the football film *The Longest Yard*, 1974, starring Burt Reynolds. Later, she demonstrated her comedic talent in the Mel Brooks slapstick spoof *Silent Movie*, 1976, and the romp *The Jerk*, 1979, written by and starring Steve Martin. Although *The Jerk* was widely panned by critics for its lowbrow humor, Peters received kinder notices for her role as the cosmetologist girlfriend of Navin Johnson (Martin), a goofball who becomes wealthy off of a simple invention. Martin was romantically involved with Peters off–screen during this time as well and had written the part specifically for her.

Peters and Martin teamed up again in 1981's *Pennies from Heaven*, an unusual musical about a schoolteacher during the Depression who is seduced, then dumped, by an out–of–work salesman (Martin); she subsequently has an abortion and becomes a prostitute. Attempting to deal with her bleak situation, she imagines herself in a series of fanciful musical numbers. Based on a successful British television miniseries, *Pennies from Heaven* received mixed reviews, but Peters was hailed for her role as the teacher and won a 1981 Golden Globe. She also starred that year in the dismal *Heartbeeps*, about a lovestruck robot who falls for another android (played by Andy Kaufman). Afterward, in 1982 she worked with Carol Burnett in a film version of Annie. She was also cast as the lead character in the movie version of the Tama Janowitz novel *Slaves of New York,* as a New York bohemian who develops self–confidence upon finding success at making and selling quirky hats. In 1990, Peters played the Muse in the Woody Allen film *Alice,* starring Mia Farrow, and the next year, worked with Hugh Grant, Judy Davis, and Mandy Patinkin in *Impromptu,* a romantic comedy about composer Frederic Chopin.

In addition to making films, Peters was busy during the 1970s with television appearances. She was nominated for an Emmy Award for her work on the lovable children's variety program *The Muppet Show,* and was also a regular on *The Carol Burnett Show.* In 1976 she took a part in the series *All's Fair,* about a liberal photographer in love with a conservative journalist; though the series was critically liked, it did not catch on with audiences and was canceled after one season. Peters has also made a number of television movies, including *David,* 1988, and *The Last Best Year,* 1990, with Mary Tyler Moore. In addition Peters provides the voice of Rita the Cat on Steven Spielberg's popular cartoon program *The Animaniacs.* She also starred in Terrence McNally's *The Last Mile,* 1992, for the *Great Performances* series on PBS, and played the stepmother in *Cinderella,* 1997, one of the highest–rated television movies of that year.

After being away from the theater for nearly ten years, Peters returned to Broadway in 1982. Moving completely into new territory, she portrayed a frumpy homemaker from South Dakota in *Sally and Marsha,* and critics applauded her performance for showing a new depth. She carried this over to the Stephen Sondheim production *Sunday in the Park with George* (which won a Pulitzer Prize), playing the mistress and model of pointillist painter George Seurat. This brought her a third Tony Award nomination. Peters was also nominated for a Drama Desk award for her role as the Witch in Sondheim's *Into the Woods,* 1987. Finally in 1986, Peters nabbed her first Tony Award, as well as her second Drama Desk Award, for her sparkling performance in Andrew Lloyd Webber's hit musical *Song and Dance.* Also in 1986, she was honored with the Drama League of New York's Distinguished Performance Award. Peters also received the Hasty Pudding Woman of the Year Award in 1987 and has a star on the Hollywood Walk of Fame. She was also the youngest person to be inducted into the Theater Hall of Fame.

In the early 1990s, Peters took a hiatus from Broadway for a few years to concentrate on recording albums and giving concerts. Her first self–titled solo release came out in 1980 and featured a conglomeration of cover tunes by a range of artists such as Elvis Presley, Marvin Hamlisch, and Fats Waller. The next year, she released another disc, *Now Playing.* In 1996, Peters was nominated for a Grammy Award for the best–selling *I'll Be Your Baby Tonight,* which is a cornucopia of popular songs from composers including John Lennon, Paul McCartney, Lyle Lovett, Hank William, Sam Cooke, and Billy Joel. Of course, it also contains many Broadway classics by Leonard Bernstein, Rogers and Hammerstein, and others.

When Peters puts an album together, she chooses a surprising mix of material based on whether she feels a connection to the songs. As she noted to Jon Bream in the *Minneapolis Star Tribune,* "The connection can be from anywhere. It can be from something spiritual or something uplifting or something dramatic, funny, just a witty song." In April of 1996, Peters performed at the White House for President Bill Clinton, and also sang and provided a voice–over for the animated film *Anastasia,* 1997. Her fourth solo work, *Live at Carnegie Hall,* came out in 1999. Peters's voice can also be heard on cast recordings of various musicals, including *Dames at Sea, Mack and Mabel,* and *Sunday in the Park with George.*

In 1999, Peters had a blowout year starring in a revival of the 1946 Irving Berlin hit *Annie Get Your Gun,* which first opened for a pre–Broadway run on December 29, 1998, at the Kennedy Center in Washington, D.C. In a role made famous by the big–boned, booming–voiced Ethel Merman as the bawdy Wild West sharpshooter Annie Oakley, many were skeptical that the petite, squeaky–voiced Peters could pull it off. After all, the number "There's No Business like Show Business" was a signature Merman tune throughout her career. Peters, in fact, had doubts as well. Not only was she reluctant to do a revival, she was also initially concerned about some of the politically incorrect references to women and American Indians. However, her fears were put to rest when she discovered that the writer was committed to doing a revision of the original.

As a result of the script changes, the character of Annie is more self–directed, and her lover, Frank Butler (played by former *Dukes of Hazzard* star Tom Wopat), is more sensitive. Though she still purposely misses her shots to make her man feel better, it is Annie's own choice, and Frank's response helps even the balance of power in the relationship. As Pacheco observed in *Newsday,* "Loving compromise, not female sacrifice, is what finally unites the two." This updated text was imbued with irony to make it more palatable, and in the eyes of most fans and critics, it worked. Though some reviewers found fault with nuances, such as the stereotypical Indian dialogue or the contradictions in Annie's pseudo–feminist character, most considered the show a success and were especially please with Peters's talent. For *Annie Get Your Gun*, she won a Drama Desk Award and Outer Critics Circle Award as well as her second Tony for best actress in a musical, and the play itself earned a 1999 Tony Award for best revival of a musical.

On July 20, 1996, Peters married for the first time, to investment advisor Michael Wittenberg. The ceremony was performed at the home of Mary Tyler Moore in Millbrook, New York. They met serendipitously, as she recalled to David Patrick Stearns in *USA Today:* "I was just standing in front of my (apartment) building waiting for somebody and he walked by. He was wearing a tuxedo and I was all dressed up and he said, 'Well, are you ready to go?'" The two reside in New York City. Peters considers herself a "late bloomer" in both her love life and her career, as she remarked to Patrick Pacheco in *Newsday*, adding, "I guess I've been blooming all along, but I think I'm really just beginning to get it right. When I'm considering a role I'm looking for what I may learn from it, and I've still got a lot to learn."

Sources

Books

Contemporary Musicians, volume 7, Gale Research, 1992.

Contemporary Theatre, Film and Television, volume 10, Gale Research, 1993.

Periodicals

Atlanta Journal and Constitution, October 16, 1998, p. 1; March 5, 1999, p. F2.
Columbian, July 2, 1999.
Dallas Morning News, March 6, 1999, p. 41A.
Entertainment Weekly, August 9, 1996, p. 12.
In Style, June 1999, p. 218.
Newsday, February 28, 1999, p. D10; March 5, 1999, p. B2.
People, March 29, 1982, p. 70.
St. Louis Post–Dispatch, July 2, 1998, p. 21.
Star Tribune (Minneapolis, MN), June 22, 1996, p. 1E.
Time, March 15, 1999, p. 86.
USA Today, January 28, 1999, p. 3D.
USA Today Magazine, May 1999, p. 81.
Variety, March 8, 1999, p. 72.

Online

Bernadette Peters Official Web site, http://www.bernadettepeters.com (October 14, 1999).
"Bernadette Peters," Internet Movie Database web site, http://us.imdb.com (October 13, 1999).

Regis Philbin

AP/Wide World Photos

Television show host

Born Regis Francis Xavier Philbin, August 25, 1933 (some sources say 1934), in New York, NY; son of Frank (a personnel director) and Florence Philbin; married Catherine Faylan, 1957 (divorced, 1968); married Joy Senese (a television show host), March 1, 1970; children: (first marriage) Amy Ferguson, Danny; (second marriage) Jennifer, Joanna. *Education:* University of Notre Dame, B.A. in sociology, 1953.

Addresses: *Office*—c/o WABC–TV, 7 Lincoln Sq., New York, NY 10023. *Agent*—William Morris Agency, 151 El Camino Dr., Beverly Hills, CA 90212.

Career

Television show host and actor. NBC–TV, page for *The Tonight Show,* 1956; KCOP–TV, Los Angeles, CA, began as a stagehand and courier, became news and sports writer, 1950s; KSON radio, San Diego, CA, news reporter, late 1950s; KFMB–TV, San Diego, CA, features reporter, 1959; KOGO–TV, San Diego, features reporter and news anchor, 1960–64; *The Joey Bishop Show,* announcer and side-kick, 1967–69; KHJ–TV, Los Angeles, talk show host, 1969–73; *A.M. Los Angeles,* KABC–TV, host, 1975–81; *The Morning Show,* WABC, cohost, 1982–87; *Regis Philbin's Health Styles,* Lifetime, 1980s; *Live with Regis and Kathie Lee,* syndicated, 1988—; *Who Wants to Be a Millionaire,* ABC, host, 1999—. Performed as a night club comedian; released album, *It's Time for Regis,* Mercury, 1968. National Rehabilitation Week, honorary chairperson, 1996; Paralympics, Atlanta, GA, honorary chairperson, 1996. *Military service* U.S. Navy, c. 1953–55.

Other television appearances include episodes of *The Big Valley,* 1968; *Get Smart,* 1968; *CHiPs,* 1978; *Super Dave,* 1987; *Long Ago and Far Away* (voice), 1989; *Family Edition,* 1992; *Mad about You,* 1993; *The Larry Sanders Show,* 1994; *Seinfeld,* 1994; *Madman of the People, Women of the House,* 19965; *Hope and Gloria,* 1995; *The Fresh Prince of Bel-Air,* 1995; *Biography,* 1996; *Life's Work,* 1996; *Spin City,* 1997; *Second Noah,* 1997; *Soul Man,* 1997; *Caroline in the City,* 1997; *Diagnosis Murder,* 1998; *Style and Substance,* 1998; and various episodes of *Late Night with David Letterman;* and movies *Mad Bull,* 1977; *SST-Death Flight,* 1977; *Mirror, Mirror,* 1979; *For the Love of It,* 1980; *California Girls,* 1985; and *Perry Mason: The Case of the Telltale Talk Show Host,* 1993.

Film appearances include *Everything You Always Wanted to Know about Sex (But Were Afraid to Ask),* 1972; *The Bad News Bears Go to Japan,* 1978; *Sextette,* 1978; *The Man Who Loved Women,* 1983; *Malibu Express,* 1985; *Funny about Love,* 1990; *Night and the City,* 1992; *A Bronx Tale,* 1993; and *Open Season,* 1996.

Sidelights

Television personality Regis Philbin rose to fame in the 1990s as the enthusiastic cohost of the wildly popular talk show host *Live with Regis and*

Kathie Lee. Together with Kathie Lee Gifford, he brought an odd but infectious mix of personal chat and celebrity interviews to the screen. With his trademark blend of excitability, aggravation, and indignation that seeps out profusely as he makes mundane discussions with Gifford appear like significant world events, he became fodder for both sincere imitation and satire alike, and fans ranged from college students to celebrities. Madonna called and asked to be a guest. He repeatedly showed up on David Letterman's late–night talk show to help out with gags. Dana Carvey imitated him on *Saturday Night Live.* In addition, Philbin has made cameos in several television shows and films often playing himself and like many other famous names, he expanded his fame to sell his own exercise video, a best–selling autobiography, and cook books. Then, on the cusp of 2000, he took on yet another project, hosting a new game show for ABC called *Who Wants to Be a Millionaire?* which promised riches if contestants could answer a series of trivia questions. The program seemed to hit a nerve with audiences across the nation, sweeping the ratings and spawning a spate of copycat shows on other networks.

Philbin was born on August 25, 1933 (though some sources say 1934) in New York City. He is the eldest son of Frank Philbin, a director of personnel, and Florence Philbin, the daughter of Italian immigrants. Philbin got his unusual first name from Regis High School, a Jesuit institution in Manhattan where his part–Irish father attended classes for a couple of years. Growing up in the Bronx in a home owned by his great–aunt, he and his family shared quarters with his Italian grandmother and uncle.

Raised in a strict Catholic family, Philbin attended Our Lady of Solace Grammar School and Cardinal Hayes High School. He went on to Indiana's Notre Dame University, where he earned a bachelor of arts degree in sociology in 1953. Subsequently, he served in the U.S. Navy for two years. All the while, Philbin dreamed of being a broadcaster like his idol, Jack Parr, so upon his discharge, he drove to Hollywood in search of work. There, he managed to meet with the program director of KCOP–TV in Los Angeles, who told the completely inexperienced Philbin that he would keep him in mind if anything opened up.

Returning to New York, Philbin's uncle, a CBS radio press agent, helped him get a job as a page at NBC, where he worked for *The Tonight Show,* then hosted by Steve Allen. He had dismissed the possibility of hearing from KCOP when they sent a telegram asking him for his phone number, which he had forgotten to include on his resume. They offered him a job as a stagehand and courier, and before long, he was back on the West Coast. At the time, virtually everything on television other than movies was broadcast live, including the commercials, and the pace was frenetic. Philbin eventually worked his way up to newswriter, although he still had to perform his duties driving the film–delivery truck for the station as well.

Soon, Philbin was helping to pull together the daily 15–minute sports show on KCOP. One day, when the sportscaster could not make it to the station after a drinking binge, Philbin was asked to sit in for him. It was his first appearance on camera. When he had to return to his behind–the–scenes drudge work, though, he became surly and was asked to quit. A few months later, however, the station manager who fired him called and told him about a position open at a radio station in San Diego.

Moving south to San Diego, Philbin worked at KSON radio, which broadcast out of the U.S. Grant Hotel. There, he continued to hone his writing talents and developed a following for his offbeat style. Before long, KFMB–TV hired him away, and he continued to do quirky features on the nightly eleven o'clock news. After a year there, cross–town rival station KOGO–TV in 1960 offered him a job doing features at 6 p.m. and a news anchor position at 11 p.m., with a promise of eventually hosting his own talk show. In 1961 KOGO began producing *The Regis Philbin Show* for its late–night lineup, which was syndicated nationally as *That Regis Philbin Show.* Later Philbin also hosted the program on KTTV in Los Angeles.

In 1967, Philbin landed a job as the announcer and sidekick on *The Joey Bishop Show* on ABC, which competed with *The Tonight Show* hosted by Johnny Carson on NBC. Despite this high–profile job, he was unhappy, because he was often made the butt of on–air jokes. In addition, in July of 1968 he heard that the network was planning to fire him because they thought he might be the reason for the show's poor ratings. He aired his concerns to Bishop, who suggested Philbin tell his issues to viewers in order to gain sympathy. On the air during a live performance one night, as he noted to Larry Eisenberg in *Good Housekeeping,* "I explained to Joey that I didn't want to come between him and success and I walked off." Letters from fans immediately poured in to show support, and Philbin remained on the show until Bishop quit in 1969.

One night on Bishop's show, the guest was crooner Bing Crosby, one of Philbin's longtime idols. Bishop was planning to ask him to sing "Pennies from

Heaven" to Philbin as a favor, but the words came out wrong, and he told Crosby that Philbin, an amateur vocalist, would like to sing the tune to him instead. Subsequently, Philbin belted the song, and the next day, Mercury Records offered him a deal. In 1968, he released the album, *It's Time for Regis!*, which was later reissued on compact disc.

After Bishop's show went off the air, Philbin worked for KHJ–TV in Los Angeles, where he hosted various local talk shows from 1969 to 1973. After that, he worked at several jobs around the country, including hosting shows in St. Louis, Missouri, and Denver, Colorado. He also filled in for several months on the program *A.M. Chicago*, hoping to land a permanent position, but it fell through. He later became the host of *A.M. Los Angeles* from 1975 to 1981, working first with Sarah Purcell and then Cindy Garvey. He left after lining up a job hosting a show for NBC, but the deal fell apart and he returned to New York City, where he again teamed with Garvey on *The Morning Show*, which was sagging in the ratings. After Philbin's entry, though, the show's popularity picked up, and then became more successful when cohost Ann Abernathy came on board after Garvey left. When Kathie Lee Gifford joined the show in June of 1985, ratings soared even more.

Meanwhile, Philbin had also been doing a show for the Lifetime cable channel called *Regis Philbin's Health Styles*, which focused on health and beauty, and would occasionally bring in celebrity fitness personalities like Jack LaLanne or wrestler Hulk Hogan. The show aired from 1982 to 1987 and was eventually transformed into more of a celebrity talk show. Eventually, this was parlayed into a syndication deal in 1988 for *The Morning Show*, and its title was changed to *Live with Regis & Kathie Lee*. The opening 17 minutes of the show is devoted to Host Chat, which Bill Zehme in *Esquire* noted "has been regarded as perhaps television's truest sheer human comedy." The two share personal anecdotes, during which time Philbin often regales viewers with stories of him being put upon in some way or another, after which he expresses his pseudo–mock outrage at the event. Gifford, meanwhile, would usually respond with, "Oh, Reege!" She, in turn, was known for her tendency to reveal intensely personal details of her life, and would frequently spin yarns about her son, Cody, after his birth.

By 1990, *Regis & Kathie Lee* was a runaway hit, nipping at the heels of established morning shows like *Donahue*, within two months knocking it out of the top– rated daytime spot for the first time in 14 years. By 1996 it was reaping the highest ratings on televi-

sion between 9 a.m. and 3 p.m. As opposed to other daytime programs that often featured salacious or inflammatory topics, Philbin and Gifford stuck to traditional subjects like cooking tips and friendly celebrity interviews. Much of the appeal was based on the hosts' good–natured ribbing of each other and by the spontaneity that live television offers. As Eisenberg related in *Good Housekeeping*, "While Regis is never at a loss for words, his comments are occasionally derailed by a habit of mixing up names and dates. The job then falls to Kathie Lee to correct him on the air, like a teacher talking to the class nerd." According to Philbin in his book, *I'm Only One Man*, the chemistry between him and Gifford is authentic; they are close friends both on and off camera.

Among the many other segments on *Regis & Kathie Lee*, Philbin often asks trivia questions to advertise the next day's guest. So perhaps it was no surprise when in 1999 he was hired to host a new prime–time show on ABC called *Who Wants to Be a Millionaire*, featuring contestants facing a series of questions with multiple–choice answers in hopes of winning $1 million. The show was a sensation in England for a year before being imported to the United States, and worked its magic for ABC as well, rescuing it from the ratings basement and causing a huge buzz in the entertainment business.

After it became a surprise hit during a limited two–week run in August and November of 1999, the network decided to air *Who Wants to Be a Millionaire* three times a week starting in January of 2000. The questions, as Dan Snierson reported in *Entertainment Weekly*, "ranged from annoyingly easy (What is your power source if you use solar energy?) to ridiculously arcane (Which English king did William Shakespeare refer to as Bolingbroke?)." Subsequently, other networks quickly responded by coming out with big–money quiz shows of their own. Philbin signed a five–year contract to host *Who Wants to Be a Millionaire?* and told a *People* reporter that although his contract with *Live with Regis and Kathie Lee* was up in August of 2001, he was not sure if that would spell the end of that stint or not.

Philbin has been married twice, first in 1957 to actor Catherine (Kay) Faylan; they were divorced in 1968. From that marriage, he has a daughter, Amy Ferguson, who is a musician, and a son, Danny, a political scientist who was born with no muscles in his legs and some missing vertebrae. He eventually had to have both legs surgically removed, and at one point was hospitalized for an entire year. Despite his disability, he finished college and interned in Washington, D.C., and Philbin remarked to Zehme in *Esquire*, "He's my hero in life." Though he has never publicly discussed his son on his television shows, Philbin has always been very close to him, despite reports to the contrary in gossip tabloids.

On March 1, 1970, Philbin married Joy Senese, a television show host, and they have two daughters, Jennifer and Joanna. They met when Senese was working as Bishop's assistant. Sometimes Philbin's wife fills in for Gifford on their show. In his spare time, Philbin works out diligently, and his gym partner is none other than supermodel Cindy Crawford. Though he is a household name and hobnobs with the elite, Philbin by all accounts remains down–to–earth and approachable. In fact, an excerpt from *I'm Only One Man* gives insight into his humble nature, as he wrote, "I'm a cab guy. Limousines just embarrass me. Like anybody else, when I see a limo on the street, I wonder who's riding in back. Whoever it is, I expect to be impressed. Whenever I've gotten talked into riding in a big sedan, I can't help but think I'm going to let people down by stepping out of it. They want Madonna to be in that car. Or Donald Trump. Or Kathie Lee! I don't want to be responsible for that kind of disappointment!"

Selected writings

(With Kathie Lee Gifford and Barbara Albright) *Cooking with Regis and Kathie Lee: Quick and Easy Recipes from America's Favorite Television Personalities*, Hyperion (New York City), 1993.

(With Gifford and Albright) *Entertaining with Regis and Kathie Lee: Year Round Holiday Recipes, Entertaining Tips, and Party Ideas*, Hyperion, 1994.

(With Bill Zehme) *I'm Only One Man* (autobiography), Hyperion, 1995.

Sources

Books

Contemporary Theatre, Film and Television, volume 21, Gale Group, 1999.

Philbin, Regis, with Bill Zehme, *I'm Only One Man!*, Hyperion, 1995.

Periodicals

Entertainment Weekly, September 3, 1999, p. 49; November 5, 1999, p. 25; December 24, 1999, p. 40.

Esquire, June 1994, p. 80.

Good Housekeeping, May 1992, p. 176.

Newsweek, September 1, 1969, p. 45.

New York Times, December 3, 1999, p. C1.

People, September 30, 1991, p. 34; December 6, 1993, p.154; November 22, 1999, p. 72.

TV Guide, August 19, 1995, p. 10.

Variety, October 14, 1996, p. S61.

Wall Street Journal, November 19, 1999, p. W17.

Joaquin Phoenix

Actor

Born October 28, 1974, in Puerto Rico; changed name to Leaf at age four, but changed it back, c. early 1990s; first name pronounced "wa–keen;" son of John Bottom and Arlyn (name later changed to Heart) Dunetz; family surname later changed to Phoenix.

Addresses: *Agent*—United Talent Agency, 9560 Wilshire Blvd., Ste. 500, Beverly Hills, CA 90212.

Career

Television appearances include episodes of *Seven Brides for Seven Brothers*, 1982; *Murder, She Wrote*, 1984; and *The Adventures of Superboy*, 1990; series *Morningstar/Eveningstar*, 1986; and movies *Backwards: The Riddle of Dyslexia*, 1984; *Kids Don't Tell*, 1985; and *Secret Witness*, 1988. Film appearances include *SpaceCamp*, 1986; *Russkies*, 1987; *Parenthood*, 1989; *Walking the Dog*, 1991; *To Die For*, 1995; *Inventing the Abbotts*, 1997; *U Turn*, 1997; *Return to Paradise*, 1998; *Clay Pigeons*, 1998; *8MM*, 1999; *Gladiator*, 2000; and *The Yards*, 2000.

Sidelights

After an itinerant childhood with unconventional parents, Joaquin Phoenix broke into acting at age eight when he was cast in guest role on the television series of *Seven Brides for Seven Brothers*, starring his brother, River. After this, although two of their sisters would also enter show business, River would become the star of the family. He went on to major roles in the films *Stand By Me* and *Dog-*

fight, while Joaquin made just a handful of films. But after River's death in 1993, Phoenix broke through in the quirky 1995 drama *To Die For*, which was, coincidentally, directed by Gus Van Sant, who had worked with River on one of both of their biggest projects, *My Own Private Idaho*, in 1991.

In 2000, in an unexpected choice of roles, Phoenix costarred with Russell Crowe in the blockbuster epic *Gladiator*. Phoenix was flabbergasted when asked to audition because he could not see himself playing a sandal–clad young emperor in a big–budget period epic after making his name in a string of edgy projects. After his screen test, though, it was apparent he could hold his own. Subsequently, Phoenix told Chris Nashawaty in *Entertainment Weekly*, "It's weird for the first time people in traffic call out to me for an autograph. I guess my other films have had smaller and more specific audiences."

Phoenix, whose first name is Spanish for "John," was born on October 28, 1974, in Puerto Rico. He changed his name to Leaf when he was four, but changed it back in the early 1990s. His parents, the former John Bottom and Arlyn Dunetz, were roaming hippies who met when Bottom picked up Dunetz hitchhiking. They joined a religious cult, the

Children of God, with whom they traveled around the West Coast and throughout Mexico, Puerto Rico, and South America. They used to send out their children, including Phoenix's older brother and sister, River and Rainbow (now known as Rain), and younger sisters, Summer and Liberty, onto the street to sing and perform. In the 1970s they changed the family's surname to Phoenix.

Probably as a result of this upbringing, Phoenix and three of his siblings became actors and entertainers. Eventually, his brother River became the family's main provider, as he began to win roles in commercials and on television series and then in major films. Phoenix's sister Rain costarred in *Even Cowgirls Get the Blues* and has toured as a backup singer for the Red Hot Chili Peppers. Both other sisters have appeared on television and in films as well, though Liberty made only one television movie—in 1986—and is no longer in the business.

After leaving the Children of God commune in 1977, the Phoenix family moved to Florida. Phoenix, who had been mostly home–tutored, attended high school there for a while but dropped out. Soon, the family headed to California to see if the kids could make a go of it in Hollywood. River landed a part in the series *Seven Brides for Seven Brothers,* and in 1982 Phoenix made his debut on the show as well. Phoenix remarked to Cindy Pearlman in *Seventeen,* "All I had to do was scream, 'No, no, don't fight! Not on Christmas!' It was heavy drama for me because I didn't think I could scream. I had never raised my voice. It wasn't allowed in our house."

After a few made–for–television movies, in 1986 Phoenix made his film debut in the science–fiction adventure *SpaceCamp.* Throughout the decade, he made just two more films, 1987's *Russkies* and 1989's *Parenthood,* in addition to the 1988 television movie *Secret Witness.* Phoenix then decided there were no decent scripts for actors his age and took a few years off, other than an appearance in 1991's *Walking the Dog,* a short film by Bonnie Palef. He and his father toured Mexico for a while during his hiatus.

Tragedy struck the Phoenix family on October 31, 1993, when River died of an overdose of heroin and cocaine at the Viper Room in Los Angeles. The media subsequently swarmed the family, and Phoenix, who was at his brother's side during his death, was harshly criticized afterward for remaining calm on the 911 emergency call. Of the aftermath, he told Lorraine Ali in *Premiere,* "They were heartless.... They had planes flying over our house, they said on the news where we live. We had reporters outside

our gate." He also related to Pearlman in *Seventeen,* "Can you imagine my mother seeing cover after magazine cover of my dead brother's face? It was a terrible thing that was made much more difficult by the frenzy."

After this upheaval, Phoenix returned to acting in 1995 with the Van Sant film *To Die For,* which was a career–making turn for both him and costar Nicole Kidman. The tale is based on a novel by Joyce Maynard that was inspired by the true story of a teaching assistant who convinced two youths to murder her husband. In it, Phoenix played Jimmy Emmett, an introverted and gullible teenage boy who is seduced by a beautiful television weathercaster, Suzanne Stone Maretto (Kidman), when she goes to his school to give a talk. She coerces him into killing her husband, then turns on him.

Following this, Phoenix starred in the romance *Inventing the Abbotts* with Liv Tyler in 1997, and that same year had a supporting role as a riled–up 19–year–old who believes his girlfriend is cheating on him in Oliver Stone's *U Turn.* Subsequently, he basically stopped eating temporarily to play a gaunt prisoner in 1998's *Return to Paradise,* a moral tale of two friends (Anne Heche and Vince Vaughn) who must decide whether to allow their friend to be executed for a drug crime that all three committed, or to turn themselves in and share jail time. That same year, Phoenix starred in the dark comedy *Clay Pigeons,* about a small–town affair that results in a suicide and murder.

In 1999, Phoenix dyed his hair and donned vinyl pants and tattoos for a role as a sex shop employee in *8MM* who assists an investigator (Nicholas Cage) trying to find out whether a "snuff film" is real or not. After this series of deep and quirky films, Phoenix surprised many, including himself, when he landed a part in director Ridley Scott's *Gladiator* as the paranoid, sadistic Commodus. For the part, Phoenix gained weight and acquired a pale complexion to illustrate the emperor's downward spiral into decadence. The film was a summer blockbuster in 2000. That year also saw the screening of the crime/mystery *The Yards* at Cannes, in which he starred with Mark Wahlberg and Charlize Theron.

Phoenix has been described as a "vulnerable ragamuffin" by Nashawaty in *Entertainment Weekly,* and other interviewers have noted his disheveled appearance and bitten fingernails. With heavy eyebrows and a scar above his lip, he has a brooding image. For a time, Phoenix had a very public relationship with actor Tyler, whom he met on the set of *Inventing the Abbotts,* but the two had split up by early 1999. He is a vegan (he eats no meat, fish, or dairy), but besides eating animal parts, he will do almost anything for a role. He even pierced his eyebrow for his part in *8MM*. Phoenix told Jeanne Fay in *Cosmopolitan*, "I hate acting acting—I try to be."

Sources

Periodicals

Cosmopolitan, November 1997, p. 217; February 1999, p. 206.
Entertainment Weekly, June 9, 2000, p. 40.
Interview, October 1995, p. 134.April 1997, p. 88.
People, September 7, 1998, p. 129.
Premiere, October 1995, p. 57; March 1997, p. 70
Seventeen, October 1997, p. 132..

Online

"Joaquin Phoenix," Internet Movie Database web site, http://us.imdb.com (July 11, 2000).
"Joaquin Phoenix," Mr. Showbiz web site, http://mrshowbiz.go.gom (July 11, 2000).

Natalie Portman

Actor

Born June 9, 1981, in Jerusalem, Israel; daughter of a doctor and an artist.

Addresses: *Agent*—International Creative Management, 8942 Wilshire Blvd., Beverly Hills, CA 90211.

Career

Actor. Stage appearances include *The Diary of Anne Frank*, 1997– 98. Film appearances include *The Professional*, 1994; *Developing*, 1995; *Heat*, 1995; *Beautiful Girls*, 1996; *Everyone Says I Love You*, 1996; *Mars Attacks!*, 1996; *Better Living through Circuitry*, 1999; *Star Wars: Episode I The Phantom Menace*, 1999; and *Anywhere but Here*, 1999.

Sidelights

While many movie stars might seem like overnight sensations, in reality, most of them toiled years to win attention from a major studio. Not so with Natalie Portman. With no drama training behind her, at age 11 she was cast as a co–star in the 1994 film *The Professional*, and from there on, she has shared the bill with the likes of Hollywood's A–list, from Robert DeNiro to Susan Sarandon. Along the way, she managed to catch the attention of producer George Lucas, who cast her as Queen Amidala in 1999's much–awaited fourth *Star Wars* installment, *The Phantom Menace*. When Portman agreed to do the film, it was one of three to which she committed over the course of ten years. Nevertheless, she has expressed reservations at making acting her lifelong career, telling Leslie Bennetts in

Vanity Fair, "There are so many things that interest me—I love math, science, literature, languages." By all accounts, Portman remained a grounded and intelligent young woman throughout her teen years as she became a celebrity, unfazed by fame and devoted to her principles. Even after her fame in *Phantom Menace,* she attended her public high school prom with a classmate, although she did get the benefit of borrowing a designer gown for the event. Portman, an honor student who reads French, Hebrew, and Japanese, enrolled at Harvard University in the fall of 2000.

Portman was born on June 9, 1981, in Jerusalem, Israel. Her Israeli father is a doctor specializing in infertility, and her American mother is an artist. She is an only child. When she was three, her family moved to the United States, to Washington, and when she was seven, they relocated to Connecticut. Two years later, they moved to Long Island, New York, where they stayed. At age four, Portman began taking dance lessons, and at age ten, a representative from the Revlon cosmetic company noticed her at a Long Island pizza parlor and asked if she would like to model. She precociously told him she "was way more into acting," as she recalled to Elizabeth Brous in *Seventeen.* Thanks to his connections, she was signed by the Wilhelmina Agency and began to go on auditions.

By the tender age of 11, Portman had sailed through a casting call for the film *The Professional*, directed by Luc Besson and released in 1994. She filmed it when she was 12. In it, Portman plays Mathilda, a young girl who is taken under the wing of an area hit man after her family is murdered by drug–running cops. Critics were immediately impressed with the newcomer, but expressed reservations at such a young girl appearing in such a violent and gruesome movie. Some also commented on her revealing clothing and the fact that she was attracted to the older man who became her mentor. However, Portman explained to Kristine McKenna in *USA Today*, "I understood what was going on, so it wasn't as if I was being used. This girl is at an age where she's just starting to learn about sexuality, but there's nothing disgusting in the way it's handled." Portman continued, "I felt it was important to maintain her innocence, and when I first read the script, there were a few scenes I felt went too far, so Luc took them out." For one thing, she refused to do a nude scene.

Still, after *The Professional*, Portman was offered the title role in a remake of *Lolita* by Adrian Lyne. Although she was assured that body doubles would be used for nude shots, she refused, telling McKenna, "I said people will still think it's me, so no thank you." Instead, she took the minor role of Lauren in Michael Mann's 1995 film, *Heat*, about a mastermind crook and an obsessed detective who is determined to rope him in. In this project, Portman, who plays a troubled teenager who attempts suicide, shares the screen with the likes of Robert De-Niro, Al Pacino, Val Kilmer, and Jon Voigt.

After *Heat*, Portman appeared in 1996's *Beautiful Girls*, starring Matt Dillon. For this project, she again portrayed a young girl with a crush on an older man; in this case, Timothy Hutton, who plays a character of about 30. The film is about a group of friends from high school who reunite and discuss their lives and their issues with relationships and careers. Or, as Portman explained to Ted Demme and Ingrid Sischy in *Interview*, "It's about these guys who have this fantasy of finding supermodels as girlfriends . Their girlfriends are real women and don't fulfill that plastic image. Which is not to say models are the problem— but their image is." After *Beautiful Girls*, Portman landed a part in Woody Allen's 1996 musical *Everyone Says I Love You*, and that same year appeared in the Tim Burton spoof *Mars Attacks!*

In 1997, director James Lapine cast Portman in the lead role of his Broadway production of *The Diary of Anne Frank*, which opened in December that year at the Music Box theater. It is based on Frank's *Diary of a Young Girl*, which she wrote while hiding from the Nazis during World War II. Though Portman is Jewish, as Frank was, she noted in *New York*, "My family isn't really religious at all. I believe in God and a lot of the Jewish laws, but some of it, especially the stuff about 'Thank God I'm not a woman,' makes me cringe." Still, her great–grandparents, great–uncle, and many other family members were Holocaust victims.

Portman first became interested in Frank's life at age 12 while shooting *The Professional* in Paris. During that time, she and her mother traveled to Amsterdam and visited the Anne Frank house, and upon her father's suggestion, she read a copy of Frank's diary. Portman wrote in *Seventeen*, "This is the most honest book I've ever read because it is a true diary. It made me feel as if someone understood me. Anne Frank wrote about things that every teenager goes through but doesn't really discuss openly." Portman added, "Her faith in humanity, even when she was starving and sick in the attic— all because she was Jewish—has had a huge influence on me . I decided to do this play because I am truly convinced that people need to be constantly reminded of compassion."

Returning to the screen in 1999, Portman snagged the desirable role of Queen Amidala in the summer blockbuster *Star Wars: Episode I—The Phantom Menace*. This "prequel" to the earlier *Star Wars* trilogy was much–awaited among fans, and sent Portman's profile to new heights. In it, she plays the young version of the queen who later marries Anakin Skywalker (later to become villain Darth Vader) and becomes the mother of twins Luke and Leia. Despite the popularity of the earlier films, though, the actor had never seen any of them until signing on to act in *Phantom Menace*. Portman remarked to Susan Wloszczyna in *USA Today*, "Most people are appalled by that. But it's not the type of movie I would normally go to see. And they came out when I was really young." Instead, she noted, one of her favorite films is *Dirty Dancing*, which she has seen "a hundred times," as she told Wloszczyna. "I love movies that don't take themselves too seriously," she commented to Frank DeCaro in *TV Guide*. Still, Portman was thrilled about her part in *Phantom Menace* as the only female in the cast, and a powerful one at that. She summed up her place in the movie to Jill Bernstein in *Premiere*: "What a cool role model to have—this girl who's fourteen and running a planet and doing well, you know?"

Later in 1999, Portman shared the screen as Susan Sarandon's daughter in Wayne Wang's *Anywhere but Here*. About a bored mom who decides to uproot her rebellious daughter and head for Beverly Hills, the picture is an adaptation of Mona Simpson's best–selling 1986 novel. Though the film got mixed reviews, Portman was singled out for praise and nominated for a Golden Globe award for her performance. During the shoot, Sarandon took Portman and her own kids to see the 1975 cult classic *The Rocky Horror Picture Show,* in which Sarandon stars as a stranded motorist who loses her inhibitions amid a freakish entourage in a remote castle.

Throughout Portman's rise to stardom, she maintained a relatively normal lifestyle, living on Long Island and getting all A's at the public Syosset High School there. She insisted that she not receive special treatment, and despite her work schedule, she remained committed to getting an education. During the staging of *Anne Frank,* she was also busy preparing for SATs and going to school full time— taking honors calculus, among other courses while performing eight times a week. Throughout the run of the play, "I didn't really sleep," Portman admitted to Bennetts in *Vanity Fair.* In the 1996 interview with McKenna, she noted that she had only missed two months of school in the previous three years. However, when Ted Demme and Ingrid Sischy in *Interview* asked her if she loved to study, Portman replied, "You make me sound like a nerd. I don't love studying. I hate studying. I like learning. Learning is beautiful."

As a senior, Portman was a semifinalist in the Intel Science Talent Search for her research paper, "A Simple Method to Demonstrate the Enzymatic Production of Hydrogen from Sugar." She was also involved in extracurriculars as a student, participating in the Japanese and French clubs as well as on the forensics team. In addition, she ran track and was a member of the National Honor Society. None of this information was revealed, though, until after Portman's role in *Phantom Menace,* which caused the media to pry deeper into her personal life. Throughout her teen years, she and her parents had diligently attended to their privacy. The name of her high school was held confidential, and in fact, Portman is not even her real surname; she took her grandmother's maiden name as her stage name when she began acting.

Portman's parents continue to fret about her celebrity status, and they maintained a say in her projects throughout her youth. Initially, they objected to her working on *Anywhere but Here* due to a sex scene, but agreed when the director rewrote it so that it was not explicit. Wang remarked to Bennetts, "Sometimes I think Natalie's parents were overpro-

tective, but if I look at it from their point of view, in this industry you almost need to overcompensate, and maybe that's good. If I had a daughter like Natalie, I would probably do exactly what her parents are doing."

However, Portman insisted to Bennetts that her parents are "not really strict; they just don't have anything to worry about." She later added, "They practice what they preach. My parents can say, 'Don't drink,' or 'Don't do drugs,' because they don't. There's an honesty I have with my parents that a lot of kids can't have. I'll hang out with my parents on a Friday night when my friends are going to a party I don't want to go to." Portman also stressed that her parents naturally instilled her strong work ethic and her love of learning by means of example and by setting high standards for her.

In addition to having a clean lifestyle free of drugs and alcohol, Portman has been a vegetarian since age eight, after she accompanied her dad to a medical conference on animal testing. "All I could think about was my dog, Noodles," she told Brous in *Seventeen.* "I never ate meat again." She cut fish out of her diet by age 11 as well, and swore off cheeses at 15, because many of them contain rennet, which is from animal stomachs. However, she remains a self–confessed chocolate addict.

Sources

Periodicals

Entertainment Weekly, June 28, 1996, p. 38.
Harper's Bazaar, November 1997, p. 224.
Interview, February 1995, p. 112; March 1996, p. 116.
Newsday, June 29, 1999, p. A5.
New York, September 8, 1997, p. 69.
People, November 18, 1996, p. 68.
Premiere, May 1999, p. 93.
Seventeen, November 1995, p. 142; January 1998, p. 71.
TV Guide, May 15, 1999, p. 20.
USA Today, February 14, 1996, p. B3; May 28, 1999, p. 8E.
Vanity Fair, May 1999, p. 148.
Variety, September 20, 1999, p. 81; January 3, 2000, p. 57.

Online

"Natalie Portman," Internet Movie Database web site, http://us.imdb.com (March 23, 2000).

Vladimir Putin

President of Russia

AP/Wide World Photos

Born Vladimir Vladimirovich Putin, October 1, 1952, in Leningrad (now St. Petersburg), Russia; son of Vladimir Spiridonovich Putin (a factory foreman); married; wife's name, Lyudmila (a former schoolteacher); children: daughters Katya, Maria. *Education:* Leningrad State University, law degree, 1975; Ph.D. in economics.

Addresses: *Office*—The Kremlin, Moscow, Russia.

Career

KGB agent, Leningrad, Soviet Union, 1975–85, Dresden, East Germany, 1985–90, Leningrad, 1990–91; external aide to mayor of St. Petersburg, Russia, early 1990s–1994; deputy mayor of St. Petersburg, 1994–97; deputy chief Kremlin administrator, 1997–98; director of the Federal Security Service (FSB), 1998–99; secretary of Security Council, 1999; appointed prime minister of Russia, 1999; named acting president of Russia, 1999–2000; elected president of Russia, 2000.

Sidelights

When Vladimir Putin was appointed prime minister of Russia in August of 1999, very little was known about his background, as exemplified by headlines such as "Putin the Great Unknown" (in the *Economist*) and "Russia's Mystery Man" (in *Newsweek*). Formerly an agent for the Soviet intelligence agency the KGB during the Cold War era, he lived undercover for a decade and a half. Putin then suddenly entered politics in the early 1990s and subsequently saw a meteoric rise. By August of 1999, ailing President Boris Yeltsin appointed him prime minister, and when Yeltsin stepped down that December, Putin became the acting president. Many were wary of his background in the KGB, which had a terrible reputation for human rights abuses, and were also concerned about his status as a relative newcomer to politics, but he won the popular election in March 2000 to retain his post as president.

Putin ("POO–teen") was born on October 1, 1952, in Leningrad (now St. Petersburg), Russia. He is an only child. His father, a decorated war veteran, was a foreman in a metal factory. He died in August of 1999, the week his son was appointed prime minister of Russia. Putin's mother, who did not work outside the home—which was atypical for women at the time—died a year and a half before that. Growing up in Leningrad, Putin lived with his parents in a communal apartment with two other families; it was not an unusual arrangement there. Though religion was not permitted in the Soviet Union, his mother secretly had him baptized as an Orthodox Christian as a baby, and he is a practicing member of the church who delivered a Christmas Eve speech in Moscow in 1999.

Though he was a small–built child and is still a short and slim man, Putin could hold his own in fights thanks to martial arts classes. By age 16 was a top–ranked expert at sambo, a Russian combination of judo and wrestling. He attended a prestigious high school, School 281, which only accepted students with near–perfect grades. The institution was the only one in Russia to stress chemistry, which was Putin's interest. However, he soon gravitated toward liberal arts and biology, and worked at the school radio station, where he played music by the Beatles and other Western rock bands. Though he attended parties, he was reportedly more mature than others his age, according to one of his fellow students quoted by Michael Wines in the *New York Times*. Fascinated with spy movies as a teen, he began aspiring to become a KGB agent.

Going on to Leningrad State University, Putin was the school's judo champion in 1974. He graduated from the law department with in 1975. Wines in the *New York Times* noted that Putin had graduated with honors, but a *Newsweek* article reported that his thesis adviser, Valery Musin, said he had received "good but not great grades," though he was a "meticulous" student. The *Newsweek* piece pointed out that his scholastic record had been removed from the university's archives. Later, he received a doctorate in economics as well.

Instead of entering the law field right out of school, Putin landed a job with the KGB, the only one in his class of 100 to be chosen. Though some reports stated that he joined the elite foreign intelligence arm, called the First Chief Directorate, the *Newsweek* article claimed that his first position was actually in a department called Service Number One in the agency's Leningrad office. This branch was responsible for recruiting foreigners in the country to serve KGB intelligence purposes. Another report by Wines in the *New York Times* stated that a German newspaper stated he "was a mid–level K.G.B. agent performing fairly routine duties."

Putin in the early 1980s met and married his wife, Lyudmila, a former teacher of French and English. After that, in 1984 he was selected to attend the prestigious Red Banner Institute of Intelligence, where he mastered German and also learned English in preparation for an international assignment, which he had coveted for some time. In 1985 the KGB sent him to Dresden, East Germany, where he lived undercover as Mr. Adamov, the director of the Soviet–German House of Friendship, a social and cultural club in Leipzig. According to Wines, he spoke so fluently that he could easily mimic regional dialects. Putin appeared to genuinely enjoy socializing with Germans, unlike many other KGB agents there, and respected the German trait of discipline.

What Putin did in East Germany has been a matter of some speculation. Wines wrote, "Officially—and perhaps actually— his task was to track the political leanings of East Germans and their contacts with the West." And John Lloyd stated in the *New York Times Magazine*, "His real task was to recruit agents to supply technical and economic information: he may have been involved in setting up a K.G.B. network to prepare for the collapse of East Germany." *Insight on the News* reporter J. Michael Waller, meanwhile, claimed that Putin oversaw the notorious Stasi secret police force during the 1980s.

Around the time Putin went to East Germany, Soviet leader Mikhail Gorbachev was beginning to introduce economic and social reforms. Putin was apparently a firm believer in the changes. In 1989 the Berlin Wall, which separated the Communist East Germany from the free West Germany, was torn down and the two began to unite. Though Putin supposedly had known that this was inevitable, he was disappointed that it occurred amid chaos and that the Soviet leadership had not managed it better.

Afterward, in 1990 Putin returned to Leningrad and took a job in the international affairs department at his alma mater, screening foreign students. However, that was a cover for his continuing intelligence work. Before long, one of his former university professors, Anatoly Sobchak, who had become the first mayor of St. Petersburg (the former Leningrad), asked him to join his administration. Just as the Soviet Union was beginning to be unraveled, Putin resigned from the KGB in 1991 at the rank of colonel in order to get involved in politics. He allegedly quit because he was excited to be part of the important changes going on in Russia at the time, or perhaps because many of his colleagues in the KGB were persecuted after the fall of the Berlin Wall. In any event, he became the mayor's external affairs aide, and in 1994 became deputy mayor. However, a *Newsweek* report suggested that he might have been an infiltrator there as well.

During his time in city government, Putin "excelled at unraveling the Goridan knots of Russian bureaucracy and building an infrastructure highways, telecommunications, hotels— to support foreign investment," according to Wines. Although St. Petersburg never grew to the financial powerhouse that many had hoped, its fortunes improved as many foreign investors such as Coca–Cola and Japanese electronics firm NEC moved in. Putin thus attracted the nickname "the gray cardinal" in response to his sphere of behind–the–scenes influence in addition to his low profile. He was investigated in the early

1990s for allegations of favoritism in granting import and export licenses, but the case was dismissed over lack of evidence.

In 1996, when Sobchak lost his mayoral campaign, Putin was offered a job with the victor, but declined out of loyalty. The next year, he was asked to join President Boris Yeltin's "inner circle" as deputy chief administrator of the Kremlin. He left the Kremlin in 1998 to become head of the Federal Security Service (FSB), the domestic intelligence arm and successor of the KGB, which had been dismantled. In March of 1999, he was named secretary of the Security Council, a body that advises the president on matters pertaining to foreign policy, national security, and military and law enforcement.

Then, in August of 1999, after Yeltsin had gone through five prime ministers in 17 months, he appointed Putin, who was originally dismissed by many observers as not a viable heir apparent to the ill president. For one thing, he had little political experience, and for another, his appearance and personality seemed bland. However, Putin increased his appeal among citizens for his role in vehemently pursuing the war in Chechnya. In addition to blaming various bombings in Moscow and elsewhere on Chechen terrorists, he also used harsh rhetoric in condemning his enemies. As Wines reported, this "established his image as a tough and no-nonsense leader at a time when Russians were seeking just such a person." Soon, Putin's popularity ratings were soaring at 50 percent in a nation where an approval rating of even 20 percent is considered a good showing.

In December of 1999, Russia held elections for the 450-seat Duma, the lower house of Russia's parliament. Putin's Unity party, formed just three months prior, came in a close second to the Communists in a stunning showing, and with allies, were expected to wield just about as much power. Though Putin was not a candidate on the ballot in this election, the candidates rode on his coattails as the obvious front-runner in the upcoming presidential race scheduled for June of 2000.

Then, on New Year's Eve in 1999, Yeltsin unexpectedly stepped down as president, naming Putin as acting president. The election was thus moved up to March 26 in accordance with the Russian Constitution. Many observers speculated that Yeltsin's move was calculated in order to ensure Putin's success, just in case public support for the war in Chechnya turned and caused his ratings to fall. It was rumored that Yeltsin also wanted to install Putin in order to escape any prosecution, since Putin had been a loyal follower and Yeltsin had long been accused of corruption and nepotism. Indeed, one of Putin's first actions as acting president was to grant Yeltsin immunity from any future criminal or administrative investigations. The decree also granted continued housing, salary, staffing, and benefits for Yeltsin and his family.

Immediately, Western news media and the United States government scrambled to create a profile of the new Russian leader. Due to Putin's secretive background as a KGB agent, information was scarce, and many articles focused on the fact that despite his popularity, few even in his own nation knew details of his background or where he stood on issues. Not to mention, his history as a spy caused many Westerners and some Russians as well to question whether he should be feared as a foe of democracy. In addition, Christian Caryl wrote in *U.S. News & World Report*, "Putin's watch at the FSB (from July 1998 until August 1999) coincided, in part, with a series of high-profile prosecutions of environmental activists accused of 'betraying state secrets' (actually publicizing the lackadaisical disposal of dangerous nuclear waste by the Russian military)."

In Putin's first speech as acting president, however, he promised, "Freedom of speech, freedom of conscience, freedom of the press, the right to private property these basic principles of a civilized society will be protected," according to a *Newsweek* report. In addition, Putin rid his cabinet of several of Yeltsin's cronies and relatives, including Yeltsin's daughter, who served as his chief adviser. However, an *Economist* article dismissed the changes as "cosmetic," saying, "other Kremlin insiders remain firmly in place." In addition, Putin raised eyebrows when, a couple of weeks later, he made a power-sharing pact with Communists in the Duma that effectively shut out most free-market democrats. Still, his popularity among Russians hovered at 50 percent or higher in the weeks leading up to the election.

On March 26, 2000, Russians elected Putin out of a field of 11 candidates, including Communist leader Gennady Zyuganov, who won 42 percent of the vote in a tight race in 1996 against Yeltsin. Putin won with 52.6 percent of the vote as compared to runner-up Zyuganov, who gathered 29.3 percent. After his election, Putin's first legislative initiative, in April of 2000, was to win approval of the Start II arms reduction treaty from the Duma. The deal, which was negotiated seven years earlier, involved decreasing both the Russian and American nuclear buildup by half. Putin's move on this issue was seen as both a positive step in his willingness to develop a positive relationship with the United States but also as a sign that he would resist American efforts on antimissile defenses. In addition to forging talks with the United States, one of Putin's earliest moves involved working with a team of economists to try to develop a plan to improve the country's economy. On May 7, 2000, Putin was officially sworn in as Russia's second president and its first in a free transfer of power in the nation's 1,100–year history.

Putin, a soft–spoken and stone–faced man, keeps his personal life very private. He and his wife have two daughters, Katya and Maria, who were both in their early teens when he became president. Putin has a black belt in judo and enjoys running. He does not smoke, and does not drink alcohol, or at least drinks so rarely that it appears that way. In early 2000, an American publishing company announced that in May it would release an English–language translation of his memoirs, *First Person*, which was banned from being published in Russia until after the March 26 presidential election.

Sources

Periodicals

Business Week, April 24, 2000, p. 151.
Economist, January 8, 2000, p. 19; January 15, 2000, p. 49.

Insight on the News, September 6, 1999, pp. 6, 18; January 31, 2000, p. 14; February 14, 2000, p. 20.
Maclean's, January 10, 2000, p. 25; January 17, 2000, p. 46.
Nation, April 17, 2000, p. 3.
Newsweek, January 10, 2000, p. 52; January 17, 2000, p. 30.
New Yorker, December 20, 1999, p. 33.
New York Times, January 1, 2000, p. A11; January 10, 2000, p. A8; January 17, 2000, p. A6; January 20, 2000, p. A12; February 20, 2000, p. A1; March 8, 2000, p. A5; March 20, 2000, p. C14; March 22, 2000, p. A1; March 24, 2000, p. A1; March 27, 2000, p. A1; March 28, 2000, p. A11; April 15, 2000, p. A1; May 8, 2000, p. A1.
New York Times Magazine, March 19, 2000, p. 62.
People, February 28, 2000, p. 125.
Time, December 31, 1999, p. 210; January 1, 2000, p. 90.
U.S. News & World Report, January 3, 2000, p. 26.
Wall Street Journal, December 20, 1999, p. A18; January 24, 2000, p. A26.

Online

"Newsmakers: Vladimir Putin," ABC News web site, http://www.abcnews.go.com (May 3, 2000).
"Vladimir Putin: Spy Turned Politician," BBC News Online web site, January 1, 2000, http://news.bbc.co.uk (May 3, 2000).

A. Barry Rand

Business executive

Born Addison Barry Rand, November 5, 1944, in Washington, DC; son of Addison Penrod (a postal clerk) and Helen Matthews (an elementary school principal) Rand; married and divorced; married, 1990; wife's name, Donna; children: Christopher (stepson) and Allison. *Education:* Attended Rutgers University; American University, B.S. in marketing, 1968; Stanford University, M.B.A., 1972, M.A. in management science, 1973.

Addresses: *Home*—Stamford, CT. *Office*—Avis Rent–a–Car World Headquarters, 900 Old Country Rd., Garden City, NY 11530.

Career

Corporate executive. Retail salesperson in department stores, c. middle to late 1960s; Xerox Corp., sales representative, 1968–70, regional sales representative, 1970–80, corporate director of major account marketing, 1980–81, vice president of major account marketing operations, 1981–82; vice president of field operations, 1983–84; vice president of eastern operations, 1984–85; corporate vice president, 1985–86; president of U.S. Marketing Group and senior vice president, 1986–92; executive vice president of operations, 1992–98; Avis Rent A Car, chief executive officer, 1999 . Director on the boards of Honeywell Inc., Abbott Laboratories, the College Retirement Equities Fund (CREF) and the U.S. Chamber of Commerce; serves on the board of overseers for the Rochester Philharmonic Orchestra, the board of directors for the Garth Fagan Dance Theatre, and the advisory council for the Stanford University Graduate School of Business.

Awards: Inducted into the National Sales Hall of Fame, 1993.

Sidelights

Late in 1999, A. Barry Rand became the third African American to become chief executive officer of a Fortune 500 company when he took the wheel at Avis Rent A Car. The world's second–largest car rental system with $4 billion in annual revenue, Avis brought in Rand because of his proven track record at boosting profits at Xerox. Rand had started his career at Xerox in sales, and in three decades he worked his way up to being a mere step away from the CEO post. Throughout his time there, he was known not only for his stellar performance and talent for persuasive speech, but also for his diligent work in creating networks for the advancement of blacks. In fact, Alfred Edmond, Jr. in a 1987 *Black Enterprise* article remarked, "The company has a history of 'enlightened' behavior when it comes to giving minorities and women serous opportunities to perform and advance."

However, when it came time for the CEO of Xerox to hand over leadership, the company brought in a white outsider instead of promoting Rand, so he resigned in search of a CEO post elsewhere. When his appointment was announced, Martin L. Edelman, chairman of the executive committee of the board at Avis, proclaimed in *Black Enterprise* that Rand's "successes in both the business–to–business and retail arenas fit perfectly with Avis, which is primarily a business–to–business operation and has a major consumer brand. Barry has shown that he can realize a company's potential to develop profitable revenue streams from outsourcing and information–based solutions, an essential component in Avis' strategy moving forward."

Rand was born on November 5, 1944, in Washington, D.C., the only child of Addison Penrod Rand and Helen Matthews Rand. His father worked as a postal clerk, while his mother was an elementary school principal. They lived in a cozy middle–class neighborhood of Washington, and his parents stressed education. They sent him to an integrated, private high school, where he served as class president and excelled as captain of the football, basketball, and baseball teams. His parents expected him to go to college and become a professional, and they encouraged their son to do his best in everything. If Rand received a B on his report card, his father would ask why. If he came in second at an athletic event, his father would ask why he was not first. "I thank him because he made me realize that settling for anything other than your maximum effort was not acceptable," Rand told Edmond in *Black Enterprise*. "Even if you were considered No. 1, if you looked in the mirror and said, 'I could have done better,' then it still wasn't acceptable."

After high school, Rand for two years attended Rutgers University, but never found his niche. His grades were average, and though he played on the football and basketball teams there, he found himself on the bench more often than not. Still, Rand would later credit his ability to work with diverse groups to his earlier experience with ethnically diverse sports teams. Returning to Washington, he transferred to American University, where he received his bachelor of science degree in marketing in 1968. Later, he went on to Stanford University, obtaining a master's degree in business in 1972 and a master of arts in management science in 1973.

Meanwhile, though, Rand worked in sales for local department stores. Shortly out of college, he worked his way into a private recruiting session for the Xerox Corporation being held in a Washington hotel room. He announced, according to Blair S. Walker in *USA Today*, "Everyone needs good salespeople. Therefore, you need me." Though the company at the time was interviewing for chemists, they hired him as their first black sales trainee in the Washington region. Rand was interested in working for Xerox due to their positive reputation on racial issues. In addition to their commitment to recruiting blacks, the company was instrumental in rebuilding the town of Rochester, New York the location of its headquarters after race riots there in 1964.

Putting in 14–hour days, Rand soared in his career with Xerox, and became the top sales representative in the area. By 1970, he was the third–best salesperson in the entire nation. He was soon promoted to sales manager and named one of the top five in his position in the country. In the meantime, affirmative action was bringing in more blacks to Xerox, and along with them, Rand formed networking groups to discuss career development and communication. In the 1960s and early 1970s, blacks were still a tiny part of the power structure, so the groups helped them form contacts with other blacks as well as those in powerful positions in the company.

In addition, in order to improve their performance, the black employee groups borrowed company video equipment in order to tape and critique themselves giving sales presentations. The networks "helped give us added confidence," Rand recalled to Jonathan P. Hicks in the *New York Times*. At the outset, the company was cool to receive the black support groups, but upper management eventually embraced the idea, which was copied by other firms. In particular, chairman David T. Kearns was helpful in supporting black issues. Kearns had been vital in resolving a walkout and class-action lawsuit by black employees in San Francisco in 1971, which led to the formation of a Minority Advisory Committee to combat racism and keep tabs on the progress of black employees. Rand was one of seven employees on the committee.

By 1980, Rand was promoted to corporate director of major account marketing. In that capacity, he was responsible for developing a new marketing program for *Fortune* 1,000 companies. He told Hicks in the *New York Times* that the job was "perhaps the toughest" at Xerox. Among other issues, the firm was facing competition from Japanese products at the time, which caused their market share to drop from 70 percent to 40 percent in about a decade. Rand knew he needed to come up with a new approach, despite resistance to change from others at Xerox. One of his successful efforts was the well–respected Leadership Through Quality program, which retrained employees and helped stave off the threat from competitors.

Thanks to Rand's efforts, he was promoted to vice president of major account marketing operations in 1981 and vice president of field operations in 1983.

After that, he became vice president of eastern operations in 1984, and moved up to corporate vice president in 1985. In 1986, he began to attract outside attention as a black business leader when he was promoted to president of the U.S. Marketing Group as well as senior vice president. This made him one of six executives who directly reported to the president, Paul Allaire, and put him in line to one day take over the firm, some observers noted.

As he assumed his new post, Rand was in charge of roughly 34,000 sales employees bringing in revenues of $4 billion at the then–$12.9 billion firm. When he stepped in, Rand told Edmond, "My first reaction was not 'I've really achieved something,' but 'There's a lot to do.'" Right away he cited one of his goals as being customer satisfaction, and he was also faced with the need to cut costs and increase productivity. Though one option was layoffs, Rand tried to come up with alternatives like job freezes, part–time arrangements, and early retirement. In addition, he moved people voluntarily from overstaffed to understaffed areas, even if it meant a change in their job position.

In addition to the bottom–line needs of the company, Rand recognized his status as a role model for other blacks, and felt his performance would affect whether decision–makers at Xerox and elsewhere would be more apt to promote blacks. Although this brought on intense pressure, it was nothing new to the very driven Rand. "I have always wanted to show that blacks can perform as well as or better than their counterparts," he commented to Hicks. "And I've always wanted to show that, in programs that provide affirmative action opportunities, you're not getting someone who is less qualified." As he took over the U.S. Marketing Group, about 50 percent of the force was women and/or minorities.

In 1992, Rand moved up yet again, this time to executive vice president of operations. The promotion came after a company reorganization which split its copying and printing operations into nine divisions. This made Rand a member of the corporate office in Stamford, Connecticut, with duties of managing $18 billion in revenue and 70,000 employees in more than 150 countries. He ranked, along with three others, just a notch below chairman and CEO Paul Allaire after the firm did away with the posts of president and chief operating officer (COO). Even so, he remarked to Walker in USA Today, "You would like to think that racism gets old, but it doesn't. It consistently resurfaces."

As Rand neared the top rung, many wondered if he would succeed Allaire as head of Xerox. However, in June of 1998, Xerox hired a white executive, G.

Richard Thoman, from IBM to groom him for the top position instead. "I had always wanted to be a CEO, and when it became obvious that it was not going to happen at Xerox, it was time to move on," Rand explained to Tom Incantalupo in Newsday. In January of 1999, Rand resigned, though he continued to maintain a relationship with the company in order to help with the transition, even keeping an office and staff in Stamford. Meanwhile, he embarked on a search for a new position, but he also took the time off to enjoy a good deal of leisure travel as well.

By the end of 1999, Rand had reached his goal of becoming a CEO as he joined the Avis Rent A Car company based in Garden City, New York. Avis had been without a leader ever since R. Craig Hoenshell left in December of 1998. They launched a CEO search in February of 1999 but called it off after its acquisition of PHH Vehicle Management Services, which doubled the firm's revenue to about $4.5 billion a year and introduced new kinds of businesses to their mix. Instead, Avis figured that they would continue having a three–part leadership structure with Robert Salerno, Kevin Sheehan, and Mark Miller each focused on a different area of the company. However, they soon changed their minds and interviewed Rand in July, but again suspended their search a few weeks later.

Eventually, Kenneth I. Chenault, president and COO of American Express, suggested Rand be considered for a spot on the board of directors of Cendant, which owns the Avis system and part of Avis Rent A Car. Stephen Holmes, Cendant's vice chairman, soon began to consider Rand for the CEO spot, and Avis renewed their search with him in mind. By the end of the year, Avis announced his appointment. Though Rand was drawn to Avis because its earnings were on the rise and its future looked promising, he knew that he had challenges ahead due to Avis's recent acquisitions. As he assumed leadership, he gave indication that he would try to transform the firm from a rental company into something more in order to maintain its growth. "We are in the process of transitioning from the rental car business to a full array of what we call automotive services and vehicle management solutions," he explained to Incantalupo. "And it's the transformation that is one of my challenges."

Back when Rand landed his first sales job at Xerox, he was married, but as he rose through the ranks his personal life took a plunge. According to Walker in USA Today, "He bluntly blames his lack of maturity then for the breakup, not his work." He later married again, and with his wife, Donna, he has a teenage stepson, Christopher, and a young daughter, Allison. Rand still enjoys playing basketball, though he has admitted a decline in his skills from his days as a high school standout.

Sources

Books

Contemporary Black Biography, volume 6, Gale Research, 1994.

Periodicals

Black Enterprise, August 1987, p. 58; May 1987, p. 17; February 1988, p. 110; May 1992, p. 24; January 2000, p. 19.

Business Week, November 22, 1999, p. 56.

Jet, November 29, 1999, p. 22.

Los Angeles Times, April 17, 1988, sec. 4, p. 1.

Newsday, January 29, 2000, p.C8.

New York Times, December 10, 1986, p. D2; May 22, 1987, p. D1; February 5, 1992, p. D4.

Sacramento Observer, December 16, 1998, p. G6.

USA Today, March 25, 1992, p. 1B.

Lee R. Raymond

CEO of ExxonMobil

Born August 13, 1938, in Watertown, SD; son of a railroad conductor; married Charlene; children: triplet sons. *Education:* University of Wisconsin, bachelor's degree in chemical engineering, 1960; University of Minnesota, Ph.D. in chemical engineering, 1963.

Addresses: *Office*—Exxon Corp., 5959 Las Colinas Blvd., Irving, TX 75039.

Career

Exxon Corp., Tulsa, OK, production research engineer, 1963–72, Exxon, New York City, manager of planning at the international division 1972–75, Lago Oil & Transport Company (an Exxon refinery on the island of Aruba), vice president and then president and director, 1975–79, Exxon Nuclear Company, 1979–81, Exxon Enterprises, New York City, 1981– 83, Esso Inter–American, Inc. (a subsidiary of Exxon), Coral Gables, FL, 1983–84, senior vice president and board member, 1984–87, Exxon, president, 1987–93, chair and chief executive officer, 1993–98; ExxonMobil, president, chair, and CEO, 1998 . Board of directors, J.P. Morgan & Co., Inc., Morgan Guaranty Trust Company of New York, the JASON Foundation for Education, United Negro College Fund, and Business Council for International Understanding, Inc. (also trustee); director and member, Committee on Nomination of the American Petroleum Institute; member, Advisory Board of Project Shelter Pro–Am, College Board's National Task Force on Minority High Achievement, National Advisory Council of the American Society for Engineering Education, and Golden Plate

Awards Council of the American Academy of Achievement; member, The Business Council, The Business Roundtable (also on Roundtable's Policy Committee and Taxations Task Force), Dallas Committee on Foreign Relations, American Council on Germany, Council on Foreign Relations, Emergency Committee for American Trade, Singapore–U.S. Business Council, National Academy of Engineering, National Petroleum Council and its Product Supply Committee, Trilateral Commission, Dallas Citizens Council, and University of Wisconsin Foundation. Partner emeritus, New York City Partnership. Trustee, Southern Methodist University, Wisconsin Alumni Research Foundation.

Sidelights

When Exxon merged with Mobil in 1998, Lee Raymond became chair and chief executive officer (CEO) of the world's largest oil firm. Exxon-Mobil the fourth–largest corporation on the *Fortune* 500 list, behind General Motors, Ford, and Wal–Mart in 1999 posted sales of more than $160 billion. The merger was historic in that it brought together two companies that were previously one of the 34 that were split off from Standard Oil Company after a federal court ruled in 1911 that it violated anti-trust laws. John D. Rockefeller had built the oil empire, which accounted for 90 percent of the oil business in the United States. The deal joined together the two largest of these spinoffs, which together had made up half of Standard Oil. It was the biggest corporate merger in America's history, joining together the nation's number one and two oil firms. Raymond, who had been with Exxon since 1963, signed the deal along with Mobil's CEO, Lucio A. Noto.

Raymond was born on August 13, 1938, in Watertown, South Dakota, the son of a railroad engineer. He obtained a bachelor's degree in chemical engineering from the University of Wisconsin in 1960, then earned a doctorate in the same field from the University of Minnesota in 1963. That same year, he took a job at Exxon in Tulsa, Oklahoma, as a production research engineer. Over the next ten years, he also worked for the firm in Latin America and the Caribbean. In addition, he managed the Creole Petroleum Corporation, an Exxon affiliate in Venezuela which was later nationalized by the government there.

From 1972 to 1975, Raymond worked for Exxon in New York City as manager of planning at the international division. After that, until 1979 he served as vice president and then president and director of Lago Oil & Transport Company, an Exxon refinery on the island of Aruba in the Caribbean. Before Raymond took over, the firm was losing $10 million a month, but by the time he left it was earning $25 million a month.

In 1979, Raymond became president of Exxon Nuclear Company, which was falling on hard times due to a downturn in the nuclear energy business. There, he became known for his cost–cutting techniques, as he initiated layoffs and plant closings. By lowering expenses, he ended up transforming the money–losing venture into an asset. Raymond returned to New York City in 1981 to assume the position of executive vice president of Exxon Enterprises, one of the firm's subsidiaries. The sprawling area included everything from a computer chip manufacturer to a solar energy company. Raymond decided to shut down the whole effort to stop any further losses, and was praised for this move.

Subsequently, Raymond was named president and director of Esso Inter–America Inc., where he oversaw Exxon operations in Central and South America and the Caribbean. The next year he became senior vice president and a member of the Exxon board of directors. In 1987, Raymond became president of Exxon when Lawrence Rawl moved up to take over as chair and CEO. In this capacity, he continued his strategy of cost–cutting and job eliminations.

One of the most significant moments of Raymond's career came in 1989, when the Exxon Valdez oil tanker crashed into a charted reef off the coast of Alaska and spilled 11 million gallons of crude oil into Prince William Sound. This accident was one of the worst environmental disasters in American history. In the wake of the spill, Raymond oversaw the $2.1 billion cleanup and helped settle the $900 million civil suit brought by Alaska and the U.S. government. Though he kept his composure, Raymond was criticized for how the company handled public relations throughout the ordeal.

In 1993, Raymond was named chair and CEO of Exxon when Rawl retired. He was one of the youngest CEOs in the company's history. Later into the 1990s, after a period where Exxon slowed its research in looking for new oil, the company stepped up exploration efforts around the globe. Thanks in great part to Raymond's leadership, they had smartly waited out the boom during the 1980s when other firms spent large sums on looking for reserves that did not pan out. Instead, Exxon bought back 27 percent of its common shares, allowing its share to rise while the others lost billions. In this "relentless pursuit of efficiency," as Raymond dubbed it, according to Toni Mack in *Forbes*, Exxon also cut operating costs by $1.3 billion and sliced staffing from 101,000 to 79,000.

When Raymond decided to start investing again in exploration, he did so slowly and systematically. By 1997, the company–the second–largest oil firm in the world, next to Royal Dutch/Shell–began to develop new fields in places like Africa, Indonesia, and Russia, in projects that would have been rejected a decade prior. The reason Raymond agreed to the projects at that point was that drilling technology had improved to the point that made it more cost–feasible. In addition, Raymond kept busy managing its often troubled refineries, and began to look toward ideas for retaining a competitive edge with its 31,369 gas stations, especially after BP and Mobil became more streamlined after merging European marketing and refining operations in 1996. In April of 1997, Richard Teitelbaum wrote in *Fortune*, "Other big oil companies are rumored to be in discussion to link their U.S. retail operations as well. Where does this leave Exxon? It too may eventually need to partner up."

In fact, Raymond soon laid plans for just that. Not only did he look into teaming up, he chose one of Exxon's biggest competitors, Mobil, the world's fourth–largest oil company. He first discussed the possibility of a merger with Noto, Mobil's CEO, in June of 1998, after the two met to talk about combining refining operations in Japan. On December 1, 1998, the two signed the merger agreement, making ExxonMobil the largest oil firm in the world. Exxon paid $80 billion in the deal, which analysts considered "fairly high but reasonable," according to Allen R. Myerson in the *New York Times*. Under Raymond as president, chair, and CEO of the new corporation, Noto became vice chair.

Right away, observers noted that the federal government would probably make ExxonMobil divest some of its business to keep from running afoul of antitrust regulations. As it happened, the company won regulatory approval after agreeing to sell off 2,432 gas stations, a refinery in California, and several marketing and refinery operations in Europe. Headquarters for ExxonMobil remained at Exxon's offices in Irving, Texas, while refining and marketing operations were based out of Fairfax, Virginia. The new firm boasted a combined total of about 48,500 service stations and 122,700 employees.

However, at the end of 1999, ExxonMobil announced massive layoffs of 16,000, or about 13 percent of its work force. This was much more than was expected: The year before, when they announced the merger, they anticipated job cuts of 9,000. But this also meant that ExxonMobil would exceed its original expectations for cost savings. Initially, the companies predicted the venture would save them $2.8 billion a year thanks to cost reductions in office operations, purchases of supplies and services, and their negotiating power, in addition to job cuts. But the additional layoffs helped add another $1 billion to their savings, which pleased investors. Many were also impressed when ExxonMobil announced it would raise production by four percent in 2000, twice what some analysts expected.

Raymond, a heavy–set man with a booming voice, is on the board of a variety of firms and agencies, including J.P. Morgan & Co., Inc., Morgan Guaranty Trust Company of New York, the JASON Foundation for Education, the United Negro College Fund, and the Business Council for International Understanding, Inc. He is also a member of The Business Council, The Business Roundtable, the Dallas Committee on Foreign Relations, the American Council on Germany, the Council on Foreign Relations, the Emergency Committee for American Trade, and the Singapore–U.S. Business Council, among others. He is known professionally as being intelligent to an uncanny extreme, able to recite arcane statistics about his business on demand. But according to Teitelbaum in *Fortune*, colleagues say this can be intimidating, and he can come across as arrogant. In fact, Allen R. Myerson wrote in the *New York Times*, "He seldom hesitates to let reporters, analysts or aides know when he thinks what they are asking or doing is just plain dumb." Raymond seemed to agree with these assessments, remarking to Teitelbaum, "I'm not known to suffer fools gladly."

Teitelbaum also noted that Raymond's personal life is generally off limits. He has no hobbies and no close associates, but the absence of a circle of friends in the company has been welcomed by some for making for less of a clubby atmosphere. And although it is known that his wife's name is Charlene and he is the father of triplets, he keeps his family out of the limelight. When Teitelbaum mentioned the scarcity of data in the public realm about Raymond, he replied, "That's terrific. I'm pleased to hear that."

Sources

Periodicals

Financial Times, December 16, 1999; February 15, 2000.
Forbes, April 21, 1997, p. 42.
Fortune, April 28, 1997, p. 134.
New York Times, December 2, 1998, pp. A1, C1, C3; December 4, 1998, p. C1; December 16, 1999, p. C1.
USA Today, December 2, 1998, p. 1B.
Vital Speeches, July 1, 1996, p. 564.
Wall Street Journal, August 28, 1986, p. 2.

Online

"Lee R. Raymond," ExxonMobil Executive Profiles, http://www.exxonmobil.com (April 16, 2000).

Trent Reznor

Musician and composer

Photograph by Ken Settle

Born Michael Trent Reznor, May 17, 1965; son of Mike (an interior designer and amateur musician) and Nancy (a homemaker) Reznor. *Education:* Attended Allegheny college; studied computer engineering.

Addresses: *Office*—c/o Nothing Records, 2337 West 11th St., Ste. 7, Cleveland, OH 44113; or Interscope Records, 10900 Wilshire Blvd., Ste. 1230, Los Angeles, CA 90024. *Manager*—c/o Formula Public Relations, 225 Lafayette St., Ste. 603, New York, NY 100112.

Career

Began playing with bands in Mercer, PA, Erie, PA, and Cleveland, OH, c. 1980s; worked at Right Track recording studios, Cleveland, c. late 1980s; signed contract with TVT, c. 1989; released debut album, *Pretty Hate Machine*, 1989. Toured with Lollapalooza festival, 1991; appeared at Woodstock '94, 1994.

Awards

(As Nine Inch Nails) Grammy Award for best metal performance, 1992, for "Wish," and 1995, for "Happiness in Slavery."

Sidelights

Rock idol Trent Reznor, who records under the name Nine Inch Nails, struck a chord among discontented youth in the 1990s with his morose yet ferocious industrial sounds and gothic, enigmatic presence. As Steve Dougherty wrote in *People*, "Like Alice Cooper and Ozzy Osbourne before him, [he] has built his name on theatrics and nihilism. Nearly all of Reznor's lyrics are unprintable, and his videos, with their frightful scenes of dismemberment and sadomasochism, have been censored or banned by MTV." Like the generations before Nine Inch Nails, young audiences clung to the despair–laden messages and the raucous music and drove it into the mainstream. Before long, Reznor was a rock star, selling out strings of concert dates and hitting the *Billboard* charts with his intriguing mix of violence, misanthropy, agonizing soul–searching, and throbbing beats, all tinged with just the slightest holdout of hope. He became the poster boy for misery, attracting legions of similarly angst–ridden fans. Toni Ruberto of the *Gannett News Service* remarked, "Reznor can be considered the first sex symbol of industrial music."

Reznor was born on May 17, 1965, to Mike and Nancy Reznor. He has one younger sister, Tera. His father, an interior designer and amateur bluegrass musician, and his mother, Nancy, a homemaker, divorced when he was five. Subsequently, Reznor's grandparents raised him in the small town of Mercer, Pennsylvania, in the midst of Amish country. As a youngster, they insisted he take piano lessons, but he put his own creative spin on the pieces even as a child. By the time he was an adolescent, Reznor realized the power of expressing himself through music, and would take up saxophone and tuba as well. In his teens, he joined his first band, the Innocence, which played mostly cover songs by artists like the Fixx and Journey. Classmates and teachers from his days at Mercer Area Junior and Senior High Schools recall him as "clean–cut, handsome and popular," according to Dougherty.

After graduating from high school in 1983, Reznor moved to Erie, Pennsylvania, and studied computer engineering at Allegheny College. He also played in a new wave band called Urge. After about a year, he relocated to Cleveland, Ohio, where he worked odd jobs while singing and playing keyboards in bands. Eventually he got a job cleaning toilets for $100 a month at a recording studio, where he worked his way up to MIDI programmer. On his own time, he also worked on completing a one–man demo tape on which he did nearly all of the songwriting, producing, and performing. He dubbed the project Nine Inch Nails. In the meantime, he kept busy playing live with a variety of bands such as Exotic Birds, Slam Bamboo, and Lucky Pierre. He also had a stint as a hard rock band member in a scene in the 1987 film *Light of Day*, starring Michael J. Fox and Joan Jett.

Thanks to Reznor's demo tape, he landed a contract with Tee Vee Toons (TVT) Records in New York City. Though the label was known mostly for releasing compilations of television show theme songs, the owner, Steve Gottlieb, signed Nine Inch Nails and released *Pretty Hate Machine* in 1989. The effort was an original blend of industrial and pop, featuring dark lyrics and screaming vocals over infectious beats. Reznor wrote and coproduced the entire project, sang all vocals, and also played all the instruments. The first two singles off this effort, "Head like a Hole" and "Down in It," became major dance club hits, eventually booming on college and alternative radio as well.

Most of the lyrics on *Pretty Hate Machine* were culled from Reznor's personal journals and concerned topics like nihilism, religious doubt, sex, identity crises, and other despairing topics. However, they struck a chord with a disaffected young audience, and stayed on the *Billboard* charts for more than two years. Reznor told Edna Gunderson in *USA Today*, "It seemed abstract to me that all these secret, intimate feelings would be in a store for people to buy and hear." After this release, Reznor collected a few musicians to accompany him during live performances and toured as Nine Inch Nails, opening for other gloom–rock bands like The Jesus and Mary Chain

and Peter Murphy. The band was also a big draw at the first Lollapalooza festival in 1991, which traveled the United States, and it opened for Guns n' Roses on a European tour. The much–publicized and extremely popular Lollapalooza shows boosted Nine Inch Nails' name—the band sold more T–shirts than any other at the shows—and pushed sales of its debut album to over a million copies.

During his three years on the road, Reznor became embattled with TVT Records trying to get released from his contract. He complained that Gottlieb was trying to push him toward making more commercially accessible works, and accused him of not paying him what was due in royalties. He took TVT to court to try to disconnect himself from the firm, and continued to tour in order to cover his legal bills. The Interscope label finally managed to negotiate a deal whereby they would release Nine Inch Nails works in conjunction with TVT, and they also gave Reznor and his manager, John Malm, their own label, which they called Nothing. Some of the bands they signed included Pop Will Eat Itself and Marilyn Manson.

In 1992, after recording under assumed names due to legal reasons, Reznor put out an EP titled *Broken*, which bore the stamp of all three labels and earned him his first Grammy Award. "Wish" was honored as best metal performance in 1992 and also reached the top ten. That same year he also released the limited–edition EP *Fixed*, a collection of songs from Broken which were reinterpreted by other artists from bands such as Foetus and Coil. In the meantime, Reznor's videos were getting attention for their graphic and shocking nature. MTV refused to run the video for "Sin," off of his first album, because it showed genital piercing and gay men smearing blood on each other. Later, the FBI investigated footage from the video for "Down in It," suspecting that a shot of a half–naked man being thrown off of a building was an excerpt from an actual "snuff" film, a movie that captures someone truly being killed. When the FBI eventually discovered that the man was none other than Reznor, the embarrassing publicity for them only enhanced the profile of Nine Inch Nails.

After releasing *Broken*, Reznor moved to Los Angeles to start work on his next album. He took up quarters in the mansion where actress Sharon Tate and others were murdered by Charles Manson's followers in 1969. After Reznor moved out, the home was torn down. There, he set up a recording facility called Le Pig studios and created *The Downward Spiral*, 1994, which featured the guitar work of Adrian Belew. Like his earlier works, it had a depressing, angry edge, and lots of profanity, dealing with issues like self–loathing, sexual obsession, and suicide. It entered the *Billboard* charts at number two; Reznor told Gunderson that it was "the most uncommercial record that's ever been in the top 50." Elements on the work ranged from computerized cacophony to pained vocals and human screaming. In *Newsday,* Tony Fletcher wrote, "*The Downward Spiral* is suitably furious, a brutal exorcism of Reznor's demons that will only serve to further his figurehead status among outcasts of the Lollapalooza generation."

Also in 1994, Nine Inch Nails appeared in front of about 350,000 mud–soaked fans at a revival of the famous Woodstock music festival, where they stole the show. They also played 83 sold–out concerts in 71 cities on the Self-Destruct tour to promote *The Downward Spiral,* while Christian groups picketed outside asserting that Reznor was in cahoots with Satan. Reznor released a re–mix album in 1995 titled *Further Down the Spiral* and also toured with David Bowie. In addition, while at his Tate mansion studio, Reznor recorded the Tori Amos song "Past the Mission" and also produced the soundtrack for the Oliver Stone film *Natural Born Killers.* That project featured two Nine Inch Nails tracks, "Something I Can Never Have" and "Burn," and mixed snippets of dialogue in with the music to more strictly bind the songs to the text of the film.

Nine Inch Nails won a second Grammy award for best metal performance in 1996 for "Happiness in Slavery," a live track off of the Woodstock '94 album. The next year, Reznor produced the soundtrack of the David Lynch film *Lost Highway,* also contributing two solo songs and a Nine Inch Nails tune. He shared the album with David Bowie, the Smashing Pumpkins, and shock rock group Marilyn Manson, whom he greatly helped to promote, although he later became estranged from them. Also in 1997, *Time* magazine named Reznor one of the 25 most influential Americans, calling him "the anti–Bon Jovi" and noting, "Reznor wields the muscular power of Industrial rock not with frat–boy swagger but with a brooding, self– deprecating intelligence."

However, 1997 marked the year Reznor's grandmother died, and he thus retreated from the public eye. He went to Big Sur, California, to try writing songs, but the grip of writer's block overtook him. Feeling intense pressure to come out with the next big thing, he ended up shutting himself in a big new home in New Orleans, Louisiana, watching the bleak film *Taxi Driver* again and again. Finally he saw a therapist, who told him he was mildly de-

pressed. Reznor related to David E. Thigpen in *Time* that after the sessions, he was "not repaired but enlightened. I'm aware of my fragility now, which is a better thing. I'm not afraid to admit it." This finally inspired the theme for his next work.

Meanwhile, five years went by before Reznor released his next album, which he recorded in a converted funeral home near his New Orleans mansion. Much anticipated, the double–CD set *The Fragile* came out in 1999, and critics immediately embraced it. The project evolved to become moodier and even more introspective, but without the earlier head–banging, adrenaline–rush blasts. Again, Belew contributed guitar work, and six of the tracks were purely instrumental. The pieces featured sounds ranging from cello, violin, and piano to ukulele, with Reznor himself doing most of the musicianship as well as singing.

Some critics, and Reznor himself, acknowledged that the new album, while still melancholy, contained a great deal more optimism. But it was also sprinkled with a dash of the old anger, as heard in "Star****ers, Inc.," a bitter blow to those he considers fake rock stars. The tune mixed in clips from Carly Simon's "You're So Vain" and the Kiss number "Shout It Out Loud," and was undeniably catchy, earning a nomination for a Grammy in 2000 for best metal performance. "The Fragile" was also nominated that year for best alternative performance.

Will Hermes in *Entertainment Weekly* described *The Fragile* as an "art– rock epic" and added that it is "a visceral concept piece that revolved loosely around betrayal and its aftermath." The only minor gripe he had was that "by the second CD, the suicidal impulses and pleading/bleeding rhyme schemes can feel exhausting." Rob Sheffield in *Rolling Stone* compared the effort to Pink Floyd's acclaimed set *The Wall,* and commented, "The stun–volume guitar riffs, intricate synth squeals and interlocking drum–machine patterns flow together as a two–hour bubble bath in the sewer of Trent's soul." Other reviewers were similarly smitten with Reznor's accomplishment. Thigpen in *Time* noted, "*The Fragile* has very little fat on it, and in the age of the Backstreet Boys, it courageously dares to not pander to radio."

Looking toward the future, Reznor in 1999 put out the word that he was looking for a female singer for Nine Inch Nails, and told Anthony Bozza in *Rolling Stone* that he was planning to step back from the project on a certain level. "I want to do everything I do for Nine Inch Nails and produce it, but not sing," he explained to Bozza. In addition, he is planning to do more film scoring, telling Bozza, "It sounds kind of jive, but I like the idea of getting deeper into music, minus the constraints of pop music and being an icon."

Selected discography

Pretty Hate Machine, TVT, 1989.
Broken (EP), Nothing/TVT/Interscope, 1992.
The Downward Spiral, Nothing/TVT/Interscope, 1994.
Further Down the Spiral (remixes), Nothing/Interscope, 1995.
The Fragile (2–CD set), 1999.

Sources

Books

Contemporary Musicians, volume 13, Gale Research, 1994.

Periodicals

Entertainment Weekly, January 22, 1999, p. 65; September 24, 1999, p. 142.
Gannett News Service, December 2, 1994.
Newsday, March 6, 1994, p. 15.
New York Times Upfront, November 1, 1999, p. 29.
People, February 6, 1995, p. 105.
Rolling Stone, February 22, 1990, p. 30; October 14, 1999, pp. 58, 120.
Time, April 21, 1997, p. 40; September 27, 1999, p. 92.
USA Today, August 29, 1994, p. 1.
Washington Post, September 29, 1999, p. C1.

Online

Grammy Awards web site, http://www.grammy.com (January 21, 2000).
"Trent Reznor," Mr. Showbiz web site, http://mrshowbiz.go.com (January 21, 2000).
"Nine Inch Nails," Rolling Stone web site, http://www.rolllingstone.com (January 21, 2000).

Faith Ringgold

Photo courtesy of Faith Ringgold

Artist, writer, and activist

Born Faith Willie Jones, October 8, 1930, in New York, NY; daughter of Andrew Louis, Sr. (a sanitation worker) and Willi Edell (a dressmaker and designer; maiden name, Posey); Jones; married Robert Earl Wallace (a musician), 1950 (marriage annulled, 1956); married Burdette Ringgold (an auto worker), 1962; children (from first marriage) Barbara, Michele. *Education:* City College of the City University of New York, B.S. in art, 1955, M.A. in art, 1959.

Addresses: *Home*—La Jolla CA, and Englewood, NJ. *Agent*—Marie Brown Associates, Room 902, 625 Broadway, New York, NY 10012.

Career

Painter, mixed media sculptor, performance artist, and writer. Professor of art, University of California, San Diego, 1985 . Art teacher in public schools, New York City, 1955–73. First gallery show, 1966, as part of "Art of the American Negro." Began making paintings framed in cloth (tankas), 1972; began creating soft sculptures, costumes, and masks, 1970s, and used these in masked performance pieces. Produced first painted quilt, 1980, created first story quilt, 1983. Performances include appearances at various colleges, universities, and museums, including Purdue University, 1977, University of Massachusetts, 1980, Rutgers University, 1981, Occidental College, 1984, Long Island University, 1986, Baltimore Museum of Art, 1988, De Pauw University, 1989, and Washington and Lee University, 1991. Visiting lecturer and artist at art centers, universities, and museums, including Mills College,

1987, Museum of Modern Art, 1988, University of West Florida, 1989, San Diego Museum, 1990, Museum of African American Art, 1991, and Atlantic Center for the Arts, 1992. Began writing books for children, 1991.

Exhibitions include shows at museums and numerous galleries around the U.S., Europe, Asia, South America, and Africa. Artwork has been featured in many one-person shows, including shows at the Spectrum Gallery, New York City, 1967, 1970, and the Bernice Steinbaum Gallery, 1987, 1989, 1992. Artwork is held in many public and private collections, including Boston Museum of Fine Art, Chase Manhattan Bank Collection, Clark Museum, Guggenheim Museum, High Museum, Metropolitan Museum of Art, Museum of Modern Art, Newark Museum, Philip Morris Collection, and Studio Museum in Harlem. Her work was also featured in *Faith Ringgold: A 25 Year Survey,* a nationally touring retrospective exhibition, curated by the Fine Arts Museum of Long Island, 1990-93. Ringgold was also featured in *Faith Ringgold: The Last Story Quilt,* a video by Linda Freeman that won the 1992 Cine Gold Eagle Award.

Awards: Creative Artists Public Service Award from the New York State Council on the Arts, 1971; American Association of University Women Award for travel to Africa, 1976; National Endowment for the Arts award for sculpture, 1978, and for painting, 1989; John Simon Guggenheim Memorial Foundation fellowship, 1987, for painting; New York Foundation for the Arts Award, 1988, for painting; Henry Clews Foundation Award, 1990, for painting in the south of France; Coretta Scott King Illustrator Award and Caldecott Honor Book Award, both 1992, both for *Tar Beach*; Jane Addams Children's Book Award, 1993, for *Aunt Harriet's Underground Railroad in the Sky*.

Sidelights

From her early paintings on race issues to her mixed media sculpture, story quilts, and children's books, Faith Ringgold for four decades has been producing works that deal with the lives and experiences of contemporary black Americans. In addition to creating art and writing books that reflect what she stands for, she has also throughout her career remained an activist for African American and feminist causes. Ringgold has also aimed to share her beliefs on battling racism and sexism with her teaching and speaking careers. Her paintings, quilts, and other artworks hang in the Guggenheim Museum, the Metropolitan Museum of Art, and other museums, as well as in the collections of Oprah Winfrey, Bill Cosby, and Maya Angelou. In 1999 and 2000, she published four new works for children, including *The Invisible Princess* and *If a Bus Could Talk: The Story of Rosa Parks*.

Ringgold was born on October 8, 1930, in New York City to Andrew Louis Jones, Sr. and Willi Edell (Posey) Jones. Though she grew up in Harlem during the Great Depression, her father had steady employment as a sanitation worker for the city. Ringgold has a brother, Andrew Jr., six years older than her, and a sister, Barbara, three years her elder. Being the youngest, she spent a lot of time as a child with her mother, who took her to museums and to see stage shows, which usually featured a comedian, a dance act, two bands, a newsreel, and a movie. Though they never had time to stay for the film because they had to pick up her siblings from school, Ringgold and her mother caught all the big jazz artists and singers like Count Basie, Cab Calloway, Louis Armstrong, Duke Ellington, Lena Horne, Billie Holiday, and more. In addition, Ringgold was often sick with asthma as a youngster, so she stayed home quite a bit and learned to draw and sew.

Though Ringgold has often recalled a very happy childhood, her parents separated when she was two or three. However, her father remained close to the family, visiting often to see the children or provide money. Eventually, though, Ringgold's mother found work at a factory making army jackets, and soon decided to become a fashion designer. As a successful dressmaker, she made a good living and moved the family to the affluent Sugar Hill neighborhood in 1940. Many black celebrities, including Marian Anderson, Harry Belafonte, Willie Mays, Sarah Vaughn, and Dinah Washington, had homes there. Ringgold's parents officially divorced in 1942.

Since she was a child, Ringgold knew that she would attend college. She was not terribly fond of school, as she wrote in her memoir, *We Flew over the Bridge*, mostly due to the fact that she never had a black teacher in all her years growing up, and most of her white teachers were racist. She also disliked the cliquish atmosphere and the cruelty of other children. However, she noted, "I knew that I wanted to communicate ideas and thereby make a contribution to society; and to do that would require a college education."

After graduating from George Washington High School in Washington Heights in 1948, Ringgold enrolled at the City College of the City University of New York. Discovering that women, at the time, were not allowed to major in liberal arts, she signed up in the School of Education instead, majoring in art and minoring in education. In her junior year of college, on November 1, 1950, she eloped with her high school sweetheart, Earl Warren. In 1951, after finding that her husband, a jazz musician, was taking drugs, she moved out into a rooming house on campus. However, she soon realized that she was pregnant. In January of 1952, she gave birth to a girl, Michele, and in December of that year, she had another daughter, Barbara.

With her husband still involved with drugs, Ringgold left him in 1954 and was granted an annulment based on his drug addiction in 1956. Ten years later, he died of a heroin overdose. Meanwhile, she graduated from City College in 1955 and began teaching art in a junior high school in Harlem that fall. She would later earn a master's degree in art in 1959 from City College, and continued to teach in the New York City public schools until 1973. In addition, Ringgold forged a close friendship with one of her ex–husband's friends, Burdette "Birdie" Ringgold, after her divorce, and the two married in 1962. He worked for General Motors for 36 years, retiring in 1992.

Throughout her years of teaching, Ringgold learned as much from her students as they learned from her. She had studied all of the great European artists in college, and traveled through Europe in the 1960s studying art. But as a teacher, she began to be able to express herself without constraints. Becoming inspired by her students as well as by African art forms, she found her own style, blending her European training with her appreciation of African designs. In this way, she created a uniquely African American art form.

In addition, Ringgold was maturing as an artist at the same time that American society was in the throes of a great many changes in the 1960s. She called her style "super–realism," explaining in her memoir, "The idea was to make a statement in my art about the Civil Rights Movement and what was happening to black people in America at that time, and to make it super–real." Her first works were heavily populated by looming figures featuring large heads and hands, and dealt specifically and obviously with racial issues. She found her voice with help from the writings of activist–authors such as James Baldwin and Amiri Baraka (then called Leroi Jones). Baraka included some of her work in his Black Arts Theater show in Harlem in 1966.

Ringgold's first official gallery exhibit came in the fall of 1966 at the "Art of the American Negro" show sponsored by the Harlem Cultural Council. Romare Bearden curated it. That same year, she was invited to join the Spectrum Gallery on West 57th Street, the only black member there. Her first one–person show, "American People," opened there in December of 1967. By then, Ringgold had incorporated works such as *The Flag Is Bleeding* and *Die,* which were violent yet ironic, and *U.S. Postage Stamp Commemorating the Advent of Black Power,* which prominently features the saying "Black Power," but also contains the hidden message "White Power." The exhibit received notice in periodicals such as *Art News* and *Arts Magazine.*

Though she was gaining recognition, Ringgold was upset at the lack of representation of black artists at large museums. She thus became one of the first to organize a protest against a major institution when she demonstrated against the Whitney Museum of American Art in 1968. Subsequently, she spent the better part of the years 1968 through 1970 protesting the absence of black artists at the Museum of Modern Art in New York City. Despite her best efforts, she wrote in *We Flew over the Bridge,* "And today, some twenty–five years later, nothing much has changed at the Modern except which white man gets the next show."

Meanwhile, in the 1960s Ringgold was working on a technique she called "black light," incorporating the use of darker colors juxtaposed with each other and elements of cubism to show nuances in the palette that compose African Americans' hair and skin. These were displayed in her second show at Spectrum, *American Black,* in January of 1970. Later that year, Ringgold was arrested in Greenwich Village on the charge of desecrating the Stars and Stripes at the People's Flag Show, which argued against laws dictating the use of the American flag in artworks. The action surprised her, since she had been painting the flag in her pieces since 1964. In court the next year, she was found guilty and paid a $100 fine.

It was also in 1970 that Ringgold developed a feminist perspective. As she recounted in her memoir, "Trying to get the black man a place in the white art establishment left me no time to consider women's rights. I had thought that my rights came with the black man's. But I was mistaken. Now what was I to do?" She later answered, "I got involved with the women's movement." Her artworks began to reveal a distinctly feminist slant. However, as Lucy R. Lippard wrote in *Ms.,* "Both as a feminist and a black activist, Ringgold has been isolated from other black women artists; she has been ostracized for speaking out against black male domination at a time when black solidarity seemed more important than women's rights." To be fair, Ringgold commented to Lippard, "There is racism in the Women's movement and black women should be attacking it."

In 1971, Ringgold produced her much–reproduced *United States of Attica,* dedicated to the inmates who died at the Attica prison in upstate New York while staging a demonstration against despicable conditions. She also installed a mural, *For the Women's House,* at the Women's House of Detention on Riker's Island. In addition, she began producing her first cloth–framed paintings in the 1970s, inspired by viewing such works from Nepal and Tibet at the Rijksmuseum in Amsterdam. Later she discovered these were called "tankas." She started showing them in her Slave Rape Series, in which she placed herself in the context of her ancestors' experiences. Also in that decade, she began to do soft rubber sculptures based on African mask art. This evolved into full–body sculptures, some of which were of famous blacks such as civil rights leader Martin Luther King, Jr., basketball star Wilt Chamberlain, and politician Adam Clayton Powell, Jr.

By 1980, Ringgold began collaborating with her mother on quilts. They completed one, *Echoes of Harlem,* before her mother's death in 1981. She did another one, *Mother's Quilt,* in 1983, then came up with the idea for her first story quilt, *Who's Afraid of*

Aunt Jemima?, in 1984. These quilts are a blend of written text, fabric, and painting, combined to tell a story. In many of them, Ringgold expresses her political and social views. *Aunt Jemima* concerns the responsibilities, and thus the power, of black "supermoms." Other of Ringgold's story quilts include *Slave Rape Story*, about a young girl on a Southern plantation; *Street Story Quilt*, about modern urban America; and *Flag Story Quilt*, about a disabled Vietnam veteran. She even did a coat quilt to commemorate her weight loss of more than 100 pounds. Also in the 1980s, Ringgold put on performance pieces that incorporated elaborate African–inspired masks and costumes.

In the 1990s, Ringgold began to write and illustrate children's books. Her first, *Tar Beach*, 1991, is adapted from one of her five *Women on a Bridge* story quilts. She had wanted to publish books since 1987, but were told there would be no market for "art books." An editor at Crown, however, recognized the potential for young readers. Centering on eight– year–old Cassie Louise Lightfoot, *Tar Beach* tells the tale of how she escapes from her poverty–stricken life through her dreams and imagination. In it, Cassie believes that by flying over the George Washington Bridge, she can claim it as her own. This gave rise to the title of Ringgold's autobiography, *We Flew Over the Bridge*, published in 1995.

Ringgold published her next work, *Aunt Harriet's Underground Railroad in the Sky*, in 1993. It deals with Harriet Tubman's underground railroad which helped slaves escape, but puts contemporary children in the context of the nineteenth century as it was happening. For *Tar Beach*, Ringgold received the Coretta Scott King Illustrator Award and Caldecott Honor Book Award in 1992, and the next year, she was honored with the Jane Addams Children's Book Award for *Aunt Harriet's Underground Railroad in the Sky*. She went on to pen other works for children, including *Dinner at Aunt Connie's House*, 1993 and *Bonjour, Lonnie*, 1996. In 2000, she published two board books, *Counting to Tar Beach* and *Cassie's Colorful Day*.

In addition to her artworks and books, Ringgold is an educator who taught at the college level at various institutions after leaving the New York public schools. She also did several artist–in–residencies and conducted seminars and workshops. In 1985, she took a post as a full professor at the University of California at San Diego, and continues to appear as a speaker around the country. Both of her daughters are teachers as well. Ringgold has homes in both La Jolla, California, just outside of San Diego, and in Englewood, New Jersey.

Selected works

(Contributor) Amiri Baraka and Amina Baraka, editors, *Confirmation: An Anthology of African American Women*, Morrow, 1983.
Faith Ringgold: A 25 Year Survey (exhibition catalog), Fine Arts Museum of Long Island, 1990.
Tar Beach (for children), Crown, 1991.
Aunt Harriet's Underground Railroad in the Sky (for children), Crown, 1993.
Dinner at Aunt Connie's House (for children), Hyperion, 1993.
My Dream of Martin Luther King (for children), Crown, 1995.
(With Linda Freeman and Nancy Roucher) *Talking to Faith Ringgold*, Crown, 1995.
We Flew Over the Bridge: The Memoirs of Faith Ringgold, Little, Brown, 1995.
Bonjour, Lonnie, Hyperion (for children), 1996.
If a Bus Could Talk: The Story of Rosa Parks (for children), Simon & Schuster, 1999.
The Invisible Princess (for children), Crown Publishers, 1999.
Counting to Tar Beach (for children), Crown, 2000.
Cassie's Colorful Day (for children), Crown, 2000.
Also contributor of articles, essays, and short stories to periodicals, including *Artpaper, Heresies: A Feminist Publication on Art and Politics, Women's Art Journal, Women's Artists News, Feminist Art Journal, Arts Magazine*, and *Art Gallery Guide*.

Sources

Books

Authors and Artists for Young Adults, volume 19, Gale Research, 1997.
Contemporary Black Biography, volume 4, Gale Research, 1993.
Encyclopedia of World Biography, second edition, Gale Research, 1998.
Ringgold, Faith, *We Flew Over the Bridge: The Memoirs of Faith Ringgold*, Little, Brown, 1995.
St. James Guide to Children's Writers, fifth edition, St. James Press, 1999.

Periodicals

Art in America, March 1996, p. 101.
Essence, May 1990, p. 78.
Modern Maturity, March–April 2000, p. 42.
Ms., July 1976, p. 34.
Publishers Weekly, February 15, 1991, p. 61; January 10, 2000, p. 70.
Record (Bergen County, NJ), April 11, 1999, p. 101.
St. Louis Post–Dispatch, March 31, 1994, p. 1G.

Dennis Ritchie and Kenneth Thompson

Computer scientists

Dennis M. Ritchie born September 9, 1941, son of Alistair (an engineer) and Jean (a homemaker; maiden name, McGee) Ritchie. *Education:* Harvard University, B.S. in physics, 1963; graduate work in applied mathematics.

Kenneth Randall Thompson born February 4, 1943, in New Orleans, LA; son of Lewis Elwood (a Navy pilot) and Anna Hazel (Lane) Thompson; married July 2, 1967; wife's name, Bonnie; children: son, Corey. *Education:* University of California at Berkeley, B.S. in electrical engineering, 1965, M.S. in electrical engineering, 1966.

Addresses: *Office—*—c/o Lucent Technologies, 700 Mountain Ave., Murray Hill, NJ 07974.

Career

Ritchie: Bell Laboratories, New Jersey, 1967 , began working with Computer Science Research Department, late 1960s, head of the Computing Techniques Research Department, 1990—, became manager, early 1990s. Helped develop Unix operating system; developed C programming language.

Thompson: General Dynamics, San Diego, CA, work study employment, 1963 and 1964; Bell Laboratories, New Jersey, Computer Science Research Department, 1966; later with Computing Techniques Research Department. Developed Unix operating system. Also instructor at University of California at Berkeley and University of Sydney in Australia. Developed chess program and chess-playing computer.

Awards: (Both Ritchie and Thompson) Association of Computing Machinery (ACM) award for the outstanding paper of 1974 in systems and languages; Institute of Electrical and Electronics Engineers (IEEE), Emmanuel Piore Award, 1982; Bell Laboratories fellow, 1983; ACM, Turing Award and Software Systems Award for developing and implementing the UNIX operating system, both 1983; IEEE, Hamming Medal, 1990; National Medal of Technology for developing the UNIX system and C programming language, 1998.

Sidelights

Dennis Ritchie and Kenneth Thompson are computer scientists who created the Unix operating system, a popular program for running computers. Throughout the years, Unix has gained a strong following in big business as well as well as in scientific and technical fields. It holds an important place in the rise of computers because the C programming language was developed concurrently with it. The efficiency of the C language made it popular among programmers, and served as the basis for future generations of languages like Java and C++, which remain the common languages for creating software applications and Internet programs. Thompson created the Unix system in the late 1960s, while Ritchie wrote the original C programming language. The longevity of Unix and C is awe–inspiring in an industry known for the short life span for many products, and its portability to an array of hardware systems is one of its biggest assets. Though many companies have altered Unix to only work on certain systems, in theory, it is an "open" system, able to run on many different kinds of computers with little modification.

Dennis M. Ritchie was born September 9, 1941, in Bronxville, New York, and grew up in New Jersey. His father, Alistair, worked for Bell Laboratories as a switching systems engineer, and his mother, Jean McGee Ritchie, was a homemaker. Ritchie earned a bachelor of science degree from Harvard University in 1963 and then spent five years pursuing a doctorate in applied mathematics. During this time, his interest began to lean toward computers, and even though his studies were mostly rooted in theory, he became involved in actual applications of his studies on the side.

While in graduate school, Ritchie got involved with Multics, an early operating system, and worked part–time for Project MAC, a computer time–sharing project at the Massachusetts Institute of Technology (MIT). Ritchie completed a thesis on subrecursive hierarchies of functions, which was "sort of the mathematics of computations, the theory of what machines can possibly do," as he explained it, according to Robert Slater in *Portraits of Silicon*. However, he did not get his doctoral degree because, as he related to Slater, "I was so bored, I never turned [the thesis] in." Following in his father's footsteps, he got a job at Bell Laboratories in 1968, working in the Computing Science Research Center.

Kenneth Randall Thompson was born on February 4, 1943, in New Orleans, Louisiana, the son of Lewis Elwood and Anna Hazel (Lane) Thompson. His father was a fighter pilot for the U.S. Navy, which required Thompson to move frequently as he growing up, living in San Diego, Seattle, San Francisco, Indianapolis, and Kingsville, Texas. As a youth, he loved using ham radios and often hung around a radio shop in Kingsville that serviced radios used by oil rig workers. The town at the time had no telephones, so radio was the main means of communication. Thompson at times would visit the oil rigs with the radio shop employees and scale the rigs to retrieve the radios in need of repair.

In 1960 Thompson began attending the University of California at Berkeley and graduated in 1965 with a bachelor of science degree in electrical engineering. The next year he received his master's degree there in electrical engineering, but it was a field he never entered. Instead, Thompson began writing code at a computer center in 1962 and troubleshooting when anyone had problems with programs. In 1963 and 1964, he worked for General Dynamics in San Diego on a work–study program for two half–year stretches. Thus, computer code became his passion instead of electronic devices. As he explained in *Portraits in Silicon,* "I used to be an avid hacker in an electrical sense, building things. And ever since computers, I find it very similar. Computing is an addiction. Electronics is a similar addiction but not as clean. Much dirtier. Things burn out." He got a job at the Computing Science Research Center at Bell Laboratories in 1966, and was married on July 2, 1967. He and his wife, Bonnie, have a son, Corey.

Soon after Ritchie and Thompson started at Bell Labs, the company started to phase out the Multics operating system, which replaced the old batch programming that used punch cards in a mainframe computer. Once programmers wrote code on the cards, they had no more contact with the system until they saw a printout an hour or so after the cards were fed into the machine. This made programming difficult and time–consuming. A multi–user operating system would allow several programmers to work on a system at the same time, and the computer would be able to process various sets of information at once. Bell had entered the Multics project in conjunction with General Electric and MIT, but felt it was too costly and not viable in the near future, so they withdrew their support. Disappointed with being set back to the punch card days, Ritchie and Thompson in 1969 asked the firm if they could design a new system. Given their underwhelming experience with Multics, Bell rejected Thompson's proposals for equipment.

Despite the lack of support from Bell, Thompson managed to salvage an old computer, a PDP–7 made by Digital Equipment Corporation, which featured a nice graphic display and fast disk drive but limited processing and storage ability. He and Ritchie decided the first order of business was to create file system that could efficiently store data. Thompson wrote the program, while Ritchie's main early contribution was to suggest that external devices like tape drives and terminals be linked to the file system with file names similar to the other items. After a couple of years, however, their ideas grew too complex for the PDP–7, so they approached Bell Labs again for a more advanced PDP–11 computer. Knowing that the firm probably would not agree to their plans only to develop an operating system, they couched their request in the offer of building a word processing system for office tasks. Though Bell was skeptical at first, they approved the project in May of 1970.

That year, Ritchie and Thompson continued to fine–tune their operating system, which they called Unix, a play on the word Multics. One of the main advantages of their system was that it could run with few modifications on a variety of computer systems. Other operating systems are developed to run on computers built a certain way with a certain kind of processor or amount of memory, for instance but Unix was relatively adaptable to many different systems. By the end of 1971, Ritchie and Thompson tested Unix with their first real–world users: three typists in the patent department at Bell Labs. The area soon embraced the system, although some credit must be given to the PDP–11. Still, other areas began to catch on to the system as well, and Unix became so useful within Bell's business, they officially unveiled it at a computing symposium at IBM in 1973. In 1975, they began licensing it to universities as a way to attract engineers; incidentally, in 1976, Bill Gates obtained the first Unix license not given to a university.

Improving on Unix, Ritchie created the new programming language of C, building on Thompson's earlier B language. It combined elements of high–level and low–level languages. High–level languages are closer to English and easier to learn, whereas low–level languages are more specific to machines and are more difficult. This hybrid meant that although C was not for beginners, it was more flexible, allowing programmers to copy preexisting blocks of code to their own systems in order to write new programs without starting from scratch. Though C was set up originally to ensure that Unix would remain portable to a variety of systems, it has gone far beyond its intended use, becoming one of the most widely used languages for a bevy of applications from hand–held systems to supercomputers. It was the basis for its well–known descendant, C++, written by Bjarne Stroustrup.

Though Unix was mainly favored in scientific and technical communities, it began to gain a larger following in industry as time went on. In 1988, AT&T, which owned Bell Labs at that point, licensed its millionth copy of Unix. However, Unix experienced difficulties later in its lifetime because it lacked any kind of a standard, since many of the licensers modified and repackaged it. Whereas a universal set of standards was applied to the C language in 1983, Unix alterations were not governed by any kind of guidelines to ensure that it would remain portable. Thus, a given version of Unix, created by a certain firm, may only be compatible on a specific kind of system, sold by that firm. In addition, Unix eventually faced stiff competition from Microsoft NT. In the meantime, AT&T was broken up into smaller companies, and Bell Labs became part of Lucent Technologies, while the AT&T spinoff Unix System Laboratories was sold to Novell Inc. Ritchie and Thompson are still employed at Bell Labs, working together in a computer research area of the company.

Together, Ritchie and Thompson have amassed several awards for their contributions to the growth of computers. They have received the Association of Computing Machinery (ACM) award for the outstanding paper of 1974 in systems and languages; the Institute of Electrical and Electronics Engineers (IEEE) Emmanuel Piore Award in 1982; the 1983 ACM Turing Award and Software Systems Award for developing and implementing the UNIX operating system; and the IEEE Hamming Medal, 1990. In addition, they were both named Bell Laboratories fellows in 1983. Perhaps their most impressive achievement, though, was the 1998 National Medal of Technology for developing the UNIX system and C programming language, bestowed by President Bill Clinton in April of 1999.

Though Thompson had broken away from the Unix project in 1978, for years Ritchie continued to work on subsequent editions. They both ended up moving on to other projects within Bell Labs, a company known for its commitment to research and for giving a good deal of intellectual freedom to its employees. Ritchie's and Thompson's later accomplishments include developing the Plan 9 operating system, announced in 1995, and the Inferno operating system, released in April of 1996. Thompson has also taken sabbaticals from Bell to teach computing at the University of California at Berkeley and the University of Sydney in Australia. In addition to designing three–time American champion chess software, Thompson also built a chess–playing computer called Belle. Ritchie, the prototypical computer type, puts in long hours in his cluttered office, and is a town council member in Carlstadt, New Jersey, according to his personal page on the Bell Labs web site.

Sources

Books

Notable Twentieth–Century Scientists, Gale Research, 1995.
Slater, Robert, *Portraits in Silicon,* MIT Press, 1987.

Periodicals

New York Times, October 3, 1993, sec. 3, p. 7.

Online

"Dennis M. Ritchie," Bell Labs web site, http://cm.bell–labs.com (October 17, 1999).

Fred Rogers

Television show host

Born Fred McFeely Rogers, March 20, 1928, in Latrobe, PA; son of James Hill (a brick manufacturer) and Nancy (McFeely) Rogers; married Sara Joanne Byrd (a concert pianist), July 9, 1952; children: James Byrd, John Frederick. *Education:* Attended Dartmouth College, 1946; Rollins College, Mus.B., 1951; Pittsburgh Theological Seminary, M.Div., 1962; University of Pittsburgh, 1964–67, graduate work in child development.

Addresses: *Office*—Family Communications, Inc., 4802 Fifth Ave., Pittsburgh, PA 15213.

Career

National Broadcasting Company (NBC), Inc., New York, NY, assistant producer of Voice of Firestone and NBC Opera Theatre, network floor director of shows, including Your Lucky Strike Hit Parade and Kate Smith Hour, 1951–53; WQED (television station), Pittsburgh, PA, executive producer and children's programming developer for National Education Television, 1953–62, producer, writer, composer and puppeteer of Children's Corner, 1954–61; Canadian Broadcasting Corp., Toronto, Ontario, producer and host of Misterogers, 1962–64; Public Broadcasting Service, Pittsburgh, executive producer and host of Misterogers' Neighborhood (later Mister Rogers' Neighborhood), 1965– 75 and 1978—. Adjutant professor, University of Pittsburgh, Graduate School of Library and Information Sciences, 1976; president, Family Communications, Inc., Pittsburgh; director of Latrobe Die Casting Co. and Vulcan, Inc.; chairman of child development and mass media forum for the White House Con-

ference on Children; member of board of directors of McFeely–Rogers Foundation and Children's Hospital (Pittsburgh).

Awards: Sylvania Award, 1955, for *Children's Corner;* George Foster Peabody Radio and Television Award from University of Georgia, 1969, for *Mister Rogers' Neighborhood; Saturday Review* television award, 1970, for *Mister Rogers' Neighborhood;* Ralph Lowell Medal from the Corporation for Public Broadcasting, 1975, for extraordinary contributions to public television; Christopher Award, 1984; star on Hollywood Walk of Fame, 1998; Emmy Lifetime Achievement Award, 1998; National Educational Television Award for excellence in children's programming; three Daytime Emmy Awards; several honorary degrees.

Sidelights

The greeting "It's a beautiful day in the neighborhood" has become more than just a pleasant sentiment. This line, now entrenched in popular culture, is synonymous with Fred Rogers, the host of the children's show *Mister Rogers Neighborhood.* For more than three decades, Rogers has reached out to kids with his program, teaching the values of self–worth and respecting others while also addressing children's fears with his gentle, reassuring manner. Each show begins with Rogers arriving home, changing from a sport coat into his relaxed cardigan, and removing his shoes while singing his trademark song, "Won't You Be My Neighbor." He has been admired by generations of children and parents for its emotionally healthy themes in the midst of years of television lineups dominated by vacuous and often violent cartoons and action shows. Rogers writes the show's songs and scripts, and also provides the voices of most of the puppets. As of the spring of 2000, more than 870 episodes of the show had aired, and it is the longest–running show on the Public Broadcasting System (PBS).

Fred McFeely Rogers was born on March 20, 1928, in Latrobe, Pennsylvania, an industrial town on the western side of the state about an hour from Pittsburgh. His parents, James Hill Rogers and Nancy McFeely Rogers, named him after his maternal grandfather, Fred McFeely. His father was the president of the McFeely brick company, one of the largest firms in town.

Growing up, Rogers told Glenn Collins in the *New York Times*, "I know I was expected to be perfect." He spent a lot of time alone because he was an only child until the age of 11, when his parents adopted a girl, Elaine. Until then, he mainly immersed himself in the piano and also took comfort in his imagination, playing with puppets to help ease his fears after hearing frightening news stories, for instance. Once his sister joined the family, Rogers was the only one who could calm her exuberance. Later, on his show, he named the feisty puppet Lady Elaine Fairchild after her.

As a boy, Rogers admired his pastors and always aspired to join the ministry. After spending a year at Dartmouth in 1946, he transferred to the small Rollins College in Winter Park, Florida, where he earned a music degree in 1951. He planned to enter the seminary after graduation. However, while Rogers was in school, his parents bought a television when they first came out, and on a visit he watched it for the first time. What he saw was "people throwing pies at one another," he announced with displeasure to Tom Junod in *Esquire.* Rogers immediately felt he could use the medium to spread better ideas, and decided that instead of becoming a minister, he wanted to go into television.

Though Rogers's parents were disappointed, and even he himself was not sure how God had changed his calling to television, he went to New York City after graduation and began working in the business. At the National Broadcasting Company (NBC), he was employed as an assistant producer of *Voice of Firestone* and *NBC Opera Theatre* and a network floor director of shows such as *Your Lucky Strike Hit Parade* and *Kate Smith Hour* from 1951 to 1953. In 1952, he married Sara Joanne Byrd, a concert pianist whom he met in college. They had two sons, James Byrd and John Frederick.

Rogers gained a good reputation around the studios, but became homesick for Pennsylvania. Yearning to bring quality television to his home state, he left New York in 1953 and along with four friends, helped launch WQED, the first community–supported public television station in the country. There, he started up the show *Children's Corner.* The day before it was set to air, the producer, Dorothy Daniel, threw a party and gave everyone gifts. Rogers received a tiger puppet, and decided to incorporate it into the program. On the first day, Daniel Striped Tiger was a hit, and puppets became the focus of the show. He later introduced characters such as X the Owl and King Friday XIII.

Meanwhile, Rogers began to attend the Pittsburgh Theological Seminary on his lunch breaks beginning in the fall of 1954, hoping to eventually create a religious television program. He graduated in 1962 and was ordained as a Presbyterian minister. The day before he was set to get his diploma, though, the seminary told him they did not have the funding to help him produce his show. Two days later, however, he got a call from the Canadian Broadcasting Corporation out of Toronto asking him to host a 15–minute children's program.

Although Rogers and his wife were reluctant to leave Pittsburgh, he took the opportunity to work on the show, called *Misterogers.* It marked the first time he appeared in front of the camera instead of just as the voice of a puppet. However, he did not want to eliminate his puppet friends completely, so Rogers divided the time between talking to the camera and putting on the puppet shows, a time he called the Land of Make Believe.

After a couple years, Rogers longed to return home, so in 1964 he went back to Pittsburgh, taking the rights to *Misterogers* with him. By now, he knew what his calling was: In 1965, he began to develop and produce a 30–minute children's show called *Misterogers' Neighborhood,* "because he wanted the children to think of the program not as being about him, but about a place—where they could come and visit," according to Wendy Murray Zoba in *Chris-*

tianity Today. He later changed the show's title to *Mister Rogers' Neighborhood* because he felt that it would be less confusing for children.

For a couple of years, *Misterogers' Neighborhood* was distributed only through the Eastern Educational Network. But in 1967, the Sears–Roebuck Foundation provided funding to broadcast it across the country, and it premiered nationwide on PBS on February 19, 1968. In the meantime, while in the seminary Rogers had begun to work closely with Margaret McFarland, a prominent child psychologist who had cofounded the Arsenal Family and Children's Center with Erik Erikson and Benjamin Spock. He met with her weekly to discuss how his program's content would affect young viewers, and she remained an informal consultant to the show until her death in 1988.

While McFarland encouraged Rogers to express positive messages to children, he also shaped the show based on things he learned from his grandfather. Rogers related to Zoba, "We used to visit him in the country almost every Sunday. He was the kind of person who would say, 'You know, you've made this a special day by being here.'" He also taught Rogers to have a healthy self–image and appreciate people for their uniqueness, messages that Rogers made cornerstones of his show. He tells kids that he likes them just the way they are, and teaches them to care about their neighbors. And despite undertones of Christian teachings, Rogers rarely directly brings up God. Kenneth A. Briggs in the *New York Times* reported that to one letter–writer who asked why he was not more openly religious, Rogers replied, "I hope that the love communicated through our program is a witness of our own and is able to reach people who would not be able to hear a more overtly spiritual message."

Another basis of the show is Rogers' empathetic attention to childhood concerns. He once brought a barber on the set to prove that haircuts do not hurt, and also invited a doctor to give him an on–air shot to show that it is not terrifying. He also spent an entire program to explain to kids that they would not be sucked down a bathroom drain, using a song to illustrate his point. "Our goal is to confront children with what bothers them," Rogers once noted in *Newsweek*. "It is good to re–evoke their fears and teach them to deal with them. That's why children are held by the program…it deals with their inner dramas."

Indeed, *Mister Rogers Neighborhood* continues to hold appeal for the very young even as other television programs have attracted children with sappiness or even violence. "So many people think a kids' program is just a lot of clowns, balloons and that sort of thing," Rogers explained to Robert Berkvist in the *New York Times*, "but I think of it as a direct offering of care. 'Misterogers' is a caring man." In addition, Rogers early on railed against what he called the Saturday morning "cartoon ghetto," according to a *Newsweek* article. At a Senate hearing in May of 1969 to illustrate the need for more PBS funding, he stated, according to Berkvist, "It is no secret that commercial children's television has reached an all–time low. Unfortunately, for our children's sakes, this outlandish fare is being created by people who are obviously dipping into their own unresolved childhood fantasies and, without appropriate thought for their young audience are spewing unbelievable amounts of trash onto our children. At best, most of these programs are a waste of time; at worst, some of them encourage pathology."

In 1975, Rogers took a hiatus from the show to vacation in the Far East and retreat to his house on Nantucket. For three years, the program was seen in reruns, but the host returned in 1978 to shoot new episodes. Rogers himself has not made money off of his programs or his nonprofit production company, instead living off of money inherited from his family's prosperous business. He rarely watches television himself, and when he does, prefers the rare wholesome offering such as *The Waltons*.

In addition to hosting his show, Rogers has put out several recordings for children and in the 1970s began to write books for children that explored the kinds of tough and scary topics that he handled expertly on his show. He tackled a bevy of subjects in 1974's *Mister Rogers Talks about the New Baby, Moving, Fighting, Going to the Doctor, Going to School, Haircuts*, and also in 1975's *Tell Me Mister Rogers about Learning to Read, Sleeping Away from Home, Going to the Dentist, Thunder and Lightning, When Pets Die, Nobody Feels Perfect*. Then, beginning in the mid–1980s, Rogers focused on one problem at a time, penning a series of volumes featuring such titles such as *Going to the Potty, Going to the Doctor*, and *Going to Day Care*, and moving on to topics like *Adoption, Divorce, Stepfamilies*, and *Extraordinary Friends* (about children with disabilities), all dealing in a frank but caring way with the issues at hand. Many reviewers applauded the works for their helpfulness as well as their non–condescending tone.

By all accounts, Rogers's offscreen persona is no different than the one on television. He neither smokes, nor drinks, nor goes to bed late, and he is also a vegetarian. He rises early and swims a quarter–mile a day, which helps him keep his weight to exactly

143, which it has been since high school. His mother knitted all the cardigans he wore on his show until her death in 1981. Rogers has at times pondered his effect on television on the whole, since his show is an anomaly in the vast market of more slick, fast–paced programs that are arguably not as good for kids. He mentioned to Glenn Collins in the *New York Times*, "I wonder if ours is a still, small voice," but added, "I've realized there's an awful lot of pleasure in doing work that has value."

Selected writings

For children, except as noted

Mister Rogers' Songbook, illustrated by Steven Kellogg, piano arrangements by John Costa, Random House, 1970.

(Adaptor) *The Elves, the Shoemaker, and the Shoemaker's Wife: A Retold Tale*, illustrations by Richard Hefter, Small World Enterprises,1973.

The Matter of the Mittens, photographs by John Naso, edited by Susan Tyler Hitchcock, Small World Enterprises, 1973.

Mister Rogers Talks About the New Baby, Moving, Fighting, Going to the Doctor, Going to School, Haircuts, photographs by Myron Papiz, Platt, 1974.

Mister Rogers Tells the Story . . . Time to Be Friends, illustrations by Carl Cassler, Hallmark, 1974.

Tell Me Mister Rogers About Learning to Read, Sleeping Away From Home, Going to the Dentist, Thunder and Lightning, When Pets Die, Nobody Feels Perfect, photographs by Sheldon Secunda, Platt, 1975.

Mister Rogers' Neighborhood: The Costume Party, Western Publishing, 1976.

Many Ways to Say I Love You (for general readers), Judson, 1977.

(With Barry Head) *Mister Rogers Talks with Parents*, drawings by Jim Prokell, Berkley Books, 1983.

Going to Day Care, photographs by Jim Judkis, Putnam, 1985.

New Baby, photographs by Judkis, Putnam, 1987.

Going to the Doctor, photographs by Judkis, Putnam, 1986.

Going to the Potty, photographs by Judkis, Putnam, 1986.

(With Head) *Mister Rogers' Playbook: Insights and Activities for Parents and Children*, illustrations by Jamie Adams, Berkley Books, 1986.

If We Were All the Same, illustrated by Pat Sustendal, Random House, 1987.

Making Friends, photographs by Judkis, Putnam, 1987.

Moving, photographs by Judkis, Putnam, 1987.

(With Clare O'Brien) *Mister Rogers Talks with Families about Divorce*, Berkley Books, 1987.

A Trolley Visit to Make–Believe, illustrated by Sustendal, Random House, 1987.

Wishes Don't Make Things Come True, illustrated by Sustendal, Random House, 1987.

Going to the Hospital, photographs by Judkis, Putnam, 1988.

When a Pet Dies, photographs by Judkis, Putnam, 1987.

No One Can Ever Take Your Place: A Story from Mister Rogers' Neighborhood, illustrated by Sustendal, Random House, 1988.

When Monsters Seem Real: A Story from Mister Rogers' Neighborhood, illustrated by Sustendal, Random House, 1988.

Going on an Airplane, photographs by Judkis, Putnam, 1989.

Going to the Dentist, photographs by Judkis, Putnam, 1989.

Adoption, photographs by Judkis, Putnam, 1994.

You Are Special: Words of Wisdom from America's Most Beloved Neighbor, Viking, 1994.

Divorce, photographs by Judkis, Putnam, 1996.

Stepfamilies, photographs by Judkis, Putnam, 1997.

Friends with Special Needs, photographs by Judkis, Putnam, 1999.

Extraordinary Friends, photographs by Judkis, Putnam, 2000.

Also contributor of articles to periodicals, including *Parents' Magazine*, *Saturday Evening Post*, *Today's Health*, and *Redbook*.

Sources

Books

Contemporary Heroes and Heroines, Book III, edited by Terrie M. Rooney, Gale Research, 1998.

Contemporary Theatre, Film, and Television, volume 6, Gale Research, 1998.

Periodicals

Booklist, May 15, 1996, p. 1589; October 15, 1997, p. 410; January 1, 2000, p. 934.

Christianity Today, March 6, 2000, p. 38.

Esquire, November 1998, p. 132.

Horn Book, March 2000, p. 216.

Mothering, May/June 2000, p. 96.

Newsweek, May 12, 1969, p. 97.

New York Times, November 16, 1969, sec. 2, p. 21; May 8, 1975; June 20, 1983.

People, May 15, 1978, p. 89; February 2, 1998, p. 17.

Publishers Weekly, May 27, 1996, p. 77.

Online

"Fred McFeely Rogers," *Contemporary Authors Online*, Gale Group web site, http://www.galenet.com (June 6, 2000).

Ileana Ros-Lehtinen

U.S. Representative

Born Ileana Ros, July 15, 1952, in Havana, Cuba; daughter of Enrique Emilio (an accountant) and Amanda Adato Ros; married Dexter Lehtinen (a U.S. attorney); children: Amanda, Patricia; stepchildren Katherine, Douglas. *Education:* Miami–Dade Community College, A.A., 1972; Florida International University, B.A. in English, 1975, M.S. in educational leadership, 1986; University of Miami, doctoral studies in educational administration.

Addresses: *Home*—Miami, FL. *Office*—2160 Rayburn House Office Bldg., Washington, DC 20515–0918; 9210 SW 72nd Street, Suite 100, Miami, FL 33173.

Career

Worked as an educator; founded Eastern Academy, a private elementary school in Florida; Florida House of Representatives, 1983–87; Florida state senate, 1987–89; U.S. House of Representatives, 18th district, 1989—. Member of international relations committee (also chair of subcommittee on international economic policy and trade and vice–chair of subcommittee on the Western Hemisphere), and government reform and oversight committee.

Sidelights

Cuban–American politician Ileana Ros–Lehtinen has established herself as a role model for Hispanics and a firm defender of democracy. The first Cuban–born woman to hold a seat in the Florida legislature, she served as a Republican representa-

AP/Wide World Photos

tive and then senator there before capturing a seat in the U.S. House of Representatives in 1989. This made her the first Cuban American, not to mention the first Hispanic female, to make it to the U.S. Congress. Several terms later, she remains a visible opponent of Cuban dictator Fidel Castro and a champion of Hispanic causes and tax reform.

Ros–Lehtinen (pronounced "ross–LAY–ti–nin") , known as Lily to friends and family, was born Ileana Ros on July 15, 1952, in Cuba's capital city of Havana. She is the daughter of Enrique Emilio Ros, a certified public accountant, and Amanda Adato Ros. When she was seven years old, she and her family fled their country after Fidel Castro's communist revolution established his dictatorship. In 1961, an invasion at Cuba's Bay of Pigs failed to topple Castro, and Ros–Lehtinen's father realized that returning home was becoming less likely. He thus decided to raise his children as Americans and taught them to be patriotic about their new country.

In 1972, Ros–Lehtinen earned an associate of arts degree from Miami–Dade County Community College, then obtained a bachelor of arts degree from Florida International University in Miami in 1975. In 1986, she finished a master of science degree in educational leadership and later took doctoral studies courses as well. Meanwhile, Ros–Lehtinen began a career in education, then founded the Eastern Academy, a private elementary school in southern Florida.

Encouraged by her father to enter politics, Ros–Lehtinen ran for a seat in the Florida legislature and was elected in 1982. She served there until 1986, then landed a seat in the state senate, holding that post until 1989. In the state legislature, Ros–Lehtinen started out as a global– thinking politician, more concerned with greater issues than with her specific constituent base, but as time went on, she was faulted for taking the opposite approach, and becoming too narrowly attached to the needs of her district. One of her main achievements in state politics was the creation of the Florida Pre–Paid College Tuition Program.

When Florida political powerhouse Claude Pepper died in May of 1989, Ros–Lehtinen resigned from the state senate to run in a special election to fill the longtime representative's seat from the eighteenth district. Other candidates in the primary vote were four Republicans, including Carlos Perez, and seven Democrats, including Rosario Kennedy and Jo Ann Pepper, the late congressman's niece. Going into the August 3 primary, Laura Parker in the *Washington Post* wrote, "Ros–Lehtinen is expected to easily win Tuesday's four–way Republican primary." In addition, Kennedy was seen as the Democratic front–runner, which would have put two Hispanic females on the ballot.

However, it turned out that Gerald Richman emerged as the Democratic candidate, and a divisive battle ensued. Lee Atwater, chair of the Republican party, in June noted that his main goal was to see a Cuban American take Pepper's former seat, since Hispanics constituted close to half of the district. Richman, a Jewish attorney and former president of the Florida Bar Association, replied by stating, "This is an American seat," according to a *Time* article. Many voters were thus offended at Atwater's indication that Hispanics were not true Americans. The duration of the race was marred by racial tensions and accusations of bigotry on both sides. John Ellis "Jeb" Bush, who later won election as Florida's governor, managed Ros–Lehtinen's campaign, and his father, President George Bush, that August made a stop in Miami to personally endorse her.

As it turned out, Ros–Lehtinen won the seat with 53 percent of the vote, causing Hispanics to rejoice. As Jeffrey Schmalz reported in the *New York Times*, her victory "is being viewed by many here as a turn-

ing point in the ethnic balance of power in the Miami area." It was also a key election for Republicans, since the seat had been held by a Democrat for 26 years, although the local party officials complained that the National Republican Congressional Committee in Washington, D.C. was exercising too much control over the race, from advertising to hiring staff.

The vote was split mainly among racial lines, with 88 percent of non–Hispanic whites and 96 percent of blacks voting for Richman. But as Schmalz noted, the black population of the area, small to begin with, accounted for only 12 percent of the ballots cast, so their numbers were negligible in deciding the outcome. Ros–Lehtinen's election was also a victory for opponents of abortion: a Roman Catholic, she made it clear that she was only in favor of abortion if a woman's life was in danger.

When elections came around again in 1990, Ros–Lehtinen won 60 percent of the vote and was later reelected several times. During her tenure, she has spoken out vehemently against Castro's rule. This was exemplified by a column she wrote for the *Christian Science Monitor* in which she condemned Cuba's hosting of the 1991 Pan American Games, a series of contests similar to the Olympics in that they promote international goodwill through free and fair competition. "Why Havana, capital of the only communist country in the Western Hemisphere, was selected to host these games is a mystery," she concluded.

In addition to her staunch anti–communist sentiment and her anti–abortion stance Ros– Lehtinen is conservative on many other issues, including advocating the death penalty for those convicted of organizing drug rings, and favoring a constitutional amendment to ban flag burning. However, she has been fighting for federal funds to clean up the Miami River, and sponsored an act that would give tax credits to employers who offer child care. In other tax–related matters, she helped propose various acts that would allow parents to save for their children's college tuition by deferring taxes, and supported an act that would phase out inheritance taxes. In addition, she is an original cosponsor of the Marriage Tax Elimination Act of 1999 that aimed to get rid of the "penalty" caused when two people marry and are then pushed into a higher tax bracket.

Ros–Lehtinen also continues to be outspoken in her defense of democracy and her opposition to Castro, and has criticized what she sees as President Bill

Clinton's softening in Cuban relations. She also remains a supporter of immigration and bilingual education. A member of the international relations committee, Ros–Lehtinen also chairs that body's subcommittee on international economic policy and trade, and is vice–chair of the subcommittee on the Western Hemisphere. In that capacity, she voted against the North American Free Trade Agreement. Ros– Lehtinen also serves on the Government Reform Committee.

While involved in state politics, Ros–Lehtinen met Dexter Lehtinen, who was also serving in the state legislature. They later married and have two daughters, Amanda and Patricia, and Ros–Lehtinen also became the stepmother to his two children, Katherine and Douglas. Her husband, formerly a U.S. attorney for the southern district of Florida, later entered private practice. They live in Miami.

Sources

Books

Encyclopedia of World Biography, second edition, Gale Research, 1998.

Periodicals

Christian Science Monitor, August 9, 1991, p. 18.
Insight on the News, February 22, 1999, p. 21.
National Review, November 24, 1989, p. 39.
New York Times, August 31, 1989, p. A16.
Time, September 11, 1989, p. 31.
Washington Post, July 30, 1989, p. A3; August 17, 1989, p. A4.

Online

Ileana Ros–Lehtinen web site, http://www.house.gove/ros–lehtinen (December 29, 1999).

J. K. Rowling

AP/Wide World Photos

Author

Born Joanne Rowling, c. 1965 in Chipping Sod-bury, England; daughter of Peter (an aircraft factory manager) and Ann (a lab technician); married and divorced; children: Jessica. *Education:* Attended Exeter University.

Addresses: *Home*—Edinburgh, Scotland. *Office*—c/o Scholastic, Inc., 555 Broadway, New York, NY 10012.

Career

Worked as a secretary for Amnesty International and the Manchester chamber of commerce; teacher of English as a foreign language, Portugal, c. 1990–94; French teacher, Edinburgh, Scotland, c. mid–1990s; author of *Harry Potter* series, 1996—.

Awards: Scottish Arts Council Grant, 1996; Children's Book of the Year, British Book Awards, and Gold Winner, Smarties Book Prize, both 1997, Birmingham Cable Children's Book Award, the Young Telegraph Paperback of the Year, Sheffield Children's Book Award, and short–listed for *The Guardian* Fiction Award and the Carnegie Medal, all for *Harry Potter and the Philosopher's Stone;* Gold Winner, Smarties Book Prize, 1998, and shortlist, Whitbread Children's Book of the Year Award, both for *Harry Potter and the Chamber of Secrets;* Anne Spencer Lindbergh Prize in Children's Literature, 1997–98, and ABBY Award, American Booksellers Association, 1999, both for *Harry Potter and the Sorcerer's Stone.*

Sidelights

It is rare for a children's book writer to attract a following in the millions, and even more unusual when those readers include a great many adults as well. British author J. K. Rowling, creator of the *Harry Potter* series of books for young readers, has overcome the odds to become a literary sensation, landing squarely at number one on various best–seller charts with her first three published efforts in a row. Critics favorably compare Rowling to classic children's authors such as Roald Dahl, C. S. Lewis, and J.R.R. Tolkein, thanks to the fantasy present in the books. However, Rowling's works offer a sub-stantial amount of humor and satire, thus appealing to fans of all ages, and are a hit among boys as well as girls. The *Harry Potter* series is about a young boy who discovers he has a magical legacy and must attend a special school for witches and wiz-ards; along the way, he travels a path to self–dis-covery. The books trace Harry's adventures from age 11 onward and detail his battles with evil–doers as well as more common issues like excelling in sports. As of September of 1999, just one year after Rowling's book hit the stores in the United States, the series had sold close to 2 million copies in Brit-ain, 5 million in the U.S., and numerous more copies throughout 130 nations around the globe, printed in over two dozen languages.

Joanne Rowling (pronounced "rolling") was born around 1965 in Chipping Sodbury, England. Her father, Peter, is a retired aircraft factory manager, and her mother, Ann (now deceased) was a lab technician. Rowling and her sister Di, almost two years her junior, grew up partly in Yate, just outside Bristol, and then moved to Winterbourne, on the other side of Bristol. Since she was a child, Rowling had a penchant for storytelling, and many of her early tales involved rabbits, since she and her sister desperately wanted one as a pet. Her first written effort concerned a rabbit named Rabbit who contracted the measles and received visits from friends, including a large bee named Miss Bee.

When Rowling was nine, the family moved again to Tutshill near Chepstow in the Forest of Dean, near the border of England and Wales, in a country setting that "had always been my parents' dream, both being Londoners," as Rowling remarked on the Harry Potter web page. She and her sister enjoyed playing in the fields, although Rowling disliked her new school because it was small. She initially did not get along well with her teacher, but she was eventually promoted from the "stupid" row, as she noted in the web site, to a better seat, but at a cost the teacher made her swap positions with her best friend.

After grammar school, Rowling attended Wyedean Comprehensive, where her favorite subject was English. Still an avid story–spinner, the she would entertain her bookish friends at lunchtime with tales involving the group's various fictional heroic deeds. Rowling continued to write as a teenager, but never showed her work to anyone, with the exception of some humorous tales she shared with friends. Also, she began wearing contact lenses and started to come out of her shell, and was named Head Girl of her school during her final year.

Although Rowling knew early on that she wanted to become a writer, her parents urged her to study French so that she could become a bilingual secretary, so she studied at Exeter University. She worked for a time for the human rights organization Amnesty International and then at the Manchester chamber of commerce. However, she found she was "the worst secretary ever," according to the Harry Potter web site, because she was not only extremely disorganized, she was always too busy dreaming up new stories. She would jot down ideas in the margins when she was supposed to be taking the minutes of a meeting, and type up tales on the computer when no one was around. It was on the train from London to Manchester when she first developed the idea for Harry Potter.

In 1990, Rowling's mother died at age 45 of multiple sclerosis, and then Rowling soon lost her job in Manchester. Around this time, she was burglarized as well. She subsequently went to Portugal in September of that year to teach English as a foreign language. She enjoyed this work, and since her hours were in the afternoon and evening, she could spend the earlier part of the day immersed in writing. While abroad, she married a Portuguese journalist and they had a daughter, Jessica, in 1993, but the marriage soon dissolved. At that point, Rowling decided to move to Edinburgh, Scotland, to be near her younger sister.

In Edinburgh, Rowling went on public assistance because she could not afford child care, and the state would not help subsidize her. During her time on welfare, she wrote her first *Harry Potter* book longhand while sitting in a coffee shop with her baby girl in a stroller by her side, in order to be able to work in a more comfortable setting, since her damp apartment had no heat. She eventually landed a job as a French teacher, but before starting her position, she vowed she would finish the novel she had been polishing, about a boy who attends wizard school. She typed it up and landed an agent she found in a writers' directory, who shopped it to several publishers who deemed it too lengthy for children's fiction (the first in the *Harry Potter* series ran 320 pages).

A year after finishing the book, Bloomsbury Press bought her manuscript, *Harry Potter and the Philosopher's Stone*, for $4,000 in 1995. Rowling was published under her initials, J.K., so that the book would appeal to both boys and girls, because boys often avoid anything they regard as being too female–oriented. Before long, the title was a sensation among adults as well as the children's audience for which it was intended, and by 1998, Bloomsbury released it with a new cover design to appeal to the older crowd. "I didn't write with a target audience in mind," Rowling explained to Sue Corbett of the *Knight–Ridder/Tribune News Service*. "I think if it is a good book, anyone will read it."

Rowling and Harry Potter became an overnight sensation in literary circles. The book focuses on an orphan boy who lives with his mean–spirited aunt and uncle, the Dursleys, and their obnoxious son, Dudley, who torments Harry. At age 11, Harry finds out that his parents, a witch and wizard, had been killed in an attack by the evil sorcerer Lord Voldemort, and that he himself is legendary in witch circles for having survived the ordeal. The battle left a distinctive lightning–shaped scar on his forehead. In addition, he is being summoned to attend the Hogwarts School of Witch and Wizardry, where his classroom supplies include a magic wand and a messenger owl. Between the fantasy elements of the coming–of–age tale, Rowling cleverly and comically skewers the English boarding school experience, complete with eccentric teachers, student rivalry, and an emphasis on sporting events.

Before long, Rowling was a transatlantic star. The work immediately garnered high praise in Britain and led to several awards, including a British Book Award and a Smarties Book Prize in 1997, among others. Then the American publisher Scholastic in 1998 bought the rights at an auction for more than $100,000—the highest amount ever for a first–time writer's children's book—and released the work in September of 1998 under the title *Harry Potter and the Sorcerer's Stone*, which was the first Scholastic hardcover ever to show up on the *New York Times* best–seller list, even though the company was well–known for marketing other wildly successful youth titles: They had also published the runaway hit children's series *Goosebumps* by R.L. Stine and the *Baby–sitter's Club* books by Ann M. Martin. In addition, Scholastic signed Rowling to a seven–book contact, and after months of secret negotiations, Warner Brothers bought the rights to *Harry Potter* for a live action film and merchandising rights in a seven–figure deal.

When the second installment, *Harry Potter and the Chamber of Secrets,* was released in England in the summer of 1998, it debuted at the top of both the children's and adult's best seller lists, soaring past John Grisham and Tom Clancy. In this segment, after a summer back with the Dursleys, Harry returns to his second year at the Hogwarts School, where mysterious events—even for a magic school—necessitate further investigation by Harry and his sidekicks, Ron and Hermione. This title immediately opened at number one on numerous adult fiction best–seller lists in the United States. Soon, Rowling's third installment, *Harry Potter and the Prisoner of Azkaban,* was published in Britain, and three weeks later, in September of 1999, hit the stores and the charts in America as well. In this effort, Sirius Black, a murderous henchman of Voldemont—the nemesis of Harry's parents—is out to get Harry. To protect him, an intimidating security force has been posted around the school grounds. As in the first two novels, a series of odd questions pops up to keep the reader turning the pages as Harry figures out the answers while overcoming evil forces.

Although a few critics by this point were starting to note that the series was becoming formulaic, it did not seem to matter much. Amanda Craig in the *New Statesman* declared, "There is comfort in formulas as good as this one, and the inventiveness, the jokes, the characterisation and suspense are as enthralling as ever." Audiences agreed: In Britain, *Harry Potter and the Prisoner of Azkaban* overtook Thomas Harris's *Hannibal,* about the cannibalistic serial killer made infamous in *Silence of the Lambs,* as the fastest–selling novel ever in the United Kingdom. *Hannibal* had sold 58,000 copies in five days, but *Harry Potter* blew past it with 68,000 copies moved in three days. In fact, Bloomsbury did not begin sales of the book until 3:45 p.m., so as to prevent children from skipping school in order to buy it.

After its release in the United States, *Harry Potter and the Prisoner of Azkaban* jumped to number one on the *New York Times* fiction best–seller list, while the other two Harry Potter books remained in positions number two and three as well. By this time, Warner Brothers had optioned Rowling's second book as well, and corporations were already chomping to get licenses from them for Harry Potter merchandise. *Time* magazine even featured Rowling on its cover, the first time it ever spotlighted a children's author this way. As for the future of her hero, Rowling indicated that the plots would take a darker turn, and that Harry, progressing through his teens, would deal with hormonal influences just like any other adolescent male.

The widespread popularity of Rowling's books opened up a troubling question for publishers. In the United States, Scholastic was originally not set to release *Harry Potter and the Chamber of Secrets* until September of 1999, but eager American customers could not stand the anticipation, and began ordering the British edition through online booksellers. A few enterprising bookstores did the same, offering the title on their shelves. This problem had arisen in the past, but usually, it was a matter of a small number of British buyers getting a hold of American titles before they were available overseas. The issue of a large number of Americans desiring a British book before its U.S. unveiling was vexing for Scholastic, who contacted the vendors and ordered them to cease and desist selling of the book. However, as far as online sales were concerned, Scholastic had to abide by a law that allowed one export copy per customer for personal use. As a result, the company lost perhaps tens of thousands of orders, and as a result, Scholastic moved up its release date of *Harry Potter and the Chamber of Secrets* to June of 1999. Subsequently, Scholastic planned to release the American editions simultaneously with Bloomsbury.

Selected writings

Harry Potter and the Philosopher's Stone, Bloomsbury, 1997, published in the U.S. as *Harry Potter and the Sorcerer's Stone,* Scholastic/Levine, 1998.

Harry Potter and the Chamber of Secrets, Bloomsbury, 1998, Scholastic/Levine, 1999.

Harry Potter and the Prisoner of Azkaban, Bloomsbury, 1999, Scholastic/Levine, 1999.

Sources

Books

Something about the Author, volume 109, Gale Group, 1999.

Periodicals

Arizona Republic, August 15, 1999, p. E17.

Booklist, September 15, 1998, p. 230; May 15, 1999, p. 1690.

Business Week, August 9, 1999, p. 54.

Entertainment Weekly, July 9, 1999, p. 70.

Horn Book, January 1999, p. 71; July 1999, p. 472.

Independent on Sunday, October 18, 1998, p. 7.

Knight–Ridder/Tribune News Service, June 9, 1999.

Newsday, August 15, 1999, p. B9.

New Statesman, July 12, 1999, p. 47.

Newsweek, December 7, 1998, p. 77; August 23, 1999, p. 58.

People, July 12, 1999, p. 85.

Publisher's Weekly, July 20, 1998, p. 220; May 31, 1999, p. 94; July 19, 1999, p. 195.

Time, February 15, 1999, p. 33; April 12, 1999, p. 86; July 26, 1999, p. 72; September 20, 1999, p. 66.

USA Today, September 20, 1999, p. 1D.

Variety, July 19, 1999, p. 13.

Online

"Harry Potter's web site," OKUKBooks web site, http://www.okukbooks.com (October 5, 1999).

Keri Russell

Actor

Born Keri Lynn Russell, March 23, 1976, in Fountain Valley, CA; daughter of David (an automobile company executive) and Stephanie Russell.

Addresses: Home Los Angeles, CA. *Agent*—The Gersh Agency, P.O. Box 5617, Beverly Hills, CA 90210.

Career

Television appearances include series *The All New Mickey Mouse Club*, 1991–93; *Emerald Cove*, 1993; *Daddy's Girls*, 1994; *Malibu Shores*, 1996; *Roar*, 1997; and *Felicity*, 1998 ; movies *The Babysitter's Seduction*, 1995; and *When Innocence Is Lost*, 1997; special *MMC In Concert*, 1993; and episodes of *Boy Meets World*, 1993; *Married With Children*, 1995; *7th Heaven*, 1997; and *Star Search*. Film appearances include *Honey, I Blew Up the Kid*, 1992; *Eight Days a Week*, 1997; and *Dead Man's Curve*, 1998.

Awards: Golden Globe award for best performance by an actress in a TV series–drama, 1999, for *Felicity*.

Sidelights

As the likable title character on the television series *Felicity*, Keri Russell plays a coming–of–age college student dealing with big life issues and her emerging sexuality. However uneventful this may sound, critics were giddy months ahead of the show's fall 1998 premiere, impressed with the mix of comedy and drama and the attention to making Russell as natural and realistic as possible. Many trumpeted it as the best new program of the season, and most gave high marks to the actor for her wit and charm. The show marked her big break into the limelight after a string of short–lived series, a few television movies, and a couple of low–profile films. Suddenly, Russell found herself on magazine covers and in high demand for interviews, though she seemed, much like her character, to remain grounded through all of the attention.

Keri Lynn Russell was born on March 23, 1976, in Fountain Valley, California, to David and Stephanie Russell. Her father, an executive for the Nissan car company, and her mother, a homemaker, provided a typical suburban upbringing. When she was a year old, the family, which includes her older brother Todd and younger sister Julie, moved to Mesa, Arizona, where they lived until Russell was 13. As a youth, she enjoyed sports especially softball and also took lessons in ballet, jazz dance, and other styles. She joined the Mesa Stars Dance and Drill team, which toured the country and led to a number of dance scholarships. When she was 14 or 15, she was training in a dance studio when a photographer doing a shoot there asked her to pose for him. She ended up putting together a portfolio and eventually landed an appearance on *Star Search*.

In the meantime, just before she began high school, Russell moved to Denver, Colorado, where she attended Highlands Ranch High. However, her portfolio and the *Star Search* gig had caught the attention of talent scouts for Disney, who cast her on the *All New Mickey Mouse Club* in 1991. At 15, she began working on the series in Orlando, Florida, a stint that lasted three years and "paid nothing," as she recalled to Jamie Diamond in *Mademoiselle*, conceding, "Well, you get more than if you worked at Starbucks." This led to a spot as the babysitter in the 1992 film *Honey, I Blew Up the Kid*. Meanwhile, when she was 16, Russell's family moved again, to Texas, due to her father's job. "There I was again, at a new school in the middle of the year, with no friends," she noted to Diamond. "It was probably the only time I rebelled. I'd stay out until three in the morning with my boyfriend."

At age 17, Russell moved to California to pursue her acting career. She started off in a couple of short–lived series, 1993's *Emerald Cove* and 1994's *Daddy's Girls,* then appeared in the television movie *The Babysitter's Seduction* in 1995. Moving up, in 1996 she snagged a lead role in the Aaron Spelling prime–time drama series *Malibu Shores,* but it suffered the same fate as her earlier efforts. After a couple more television movies, *The Lottery,* 1996, and *When Innocence Is Lost,* 1997, Russell appeared in the low– budget, fluffy teen sex comedy *Eight Days a Week,* in 1997, and the dark comedy *Dead Man's Curve,* 1998, about a pair of college students who kill their roommate.

After one more try at a television series, appearing in the pilot for the unsuccessful *Roar,* 1997, Russell was understandably gun–shy about auditioning for another, but she liked the premise of *Felicity.* The show is about a college student, Felicity Porter, who ditches her plans for Stanford to follow a boy she likes who enrolls at a college in New York City. However, once she gets there, the would–be romance falls through, and the spotlight shines on Felicity as a wholesome young woman finding her way on the road to adulthood. Initially, the creators of the program were seeking a down–to–earth, average–looking actor to star in the series, and thought Russell was simply too beautiful for the part. However, her attitude and sense of humor bowled them over right away.

Although several writers immediately dubbed *Felicity* "Ally McBeal Goes to College," after the successful show starring Calista Flockhart as a young attorney, the idea for the program was sold to the WB network even before *Ally McBeal* got its start on Fox. In addition, while the character of Ally McBeal has often been criticized for her unrealistic apparel, like miniskirts in the courtroom, and her cartoonish behavior, Felicity dresses and acts like an average college student, which is part of what drew Russell to the concept. "There's a lack of real girls on TV right now," she commented to Chuck Barney in the *St. Louis Post–Dispatch,* adding, "I love the fact that my character doesn't wear makeup. I love that she puts her hair back, that she wears big baggy sweaters and Converse tennis shoes. I want a chance to be a positive influencev on girls." Even though she has never attended college herself, Russell told Jefferson Graham In *USA Today,* "To me, a university is being out of your comfort zone. I was in Ireland this summer . That's what college is about finding yourself."

Felicity received an awe–inspiring amount of positive critical attention for a new program, even in advance of its premiere in the fall of 1998. Some chided the series for being too serious, tackling issues like date rape, but most were impressed with the show's realism. *Variety'* s Ray Richmond summed up, "Through the radiant Russell, the show astutely transmits the conflicting blend of giddy anticipation and neurotic dread that defines the early college experience." While the audience numbers did not quite live up to the hype, ranking a mere 99th in the ratings according to an *Entertainment Weekly* piece in December of 1998, the program managed to appeal to a very desired demographic. Of all prime–time network series that season, *Felicity* reaped the highest number of viewers age 18 to 34 in households earning $75,000 or more. Russell herself is pleased with the audience she pulls in as well, remarking in *Entertainment Weekly,* "The teenage girls that come to me are smart and cool exactly the kind of girls I want to be watching. And they don't go [affects high–pitched squeal], 'Omigod! Keri!! Omigod!' They're more like, 'Hey, aren't you on *Felicity*? I really like that show.'" In 1999, Russell won a Golden Globe award for her debut season of the series and at the start of the 1999 season caused a flurry of press when she showed up with her trademark long, flowing locks cut short.

The five–foot, three–inch Russell has green eyes and curly hair, and claims she is "definitely not a makeup person," according to an article in *People* proclaiming her one of the 50 most beautiful people in the world for 1999. She lives in the Pacific Palisades suburb of Los Angeles with fellow former Mouseketeer Tony Lucca, now an aspiring musician, and her cat, Nala, and claims she avoids the Hollywood party scene: "My life is so boring; I'm in bed by ten–thirty every night," she told Sarah

Goldsmith in *Seventeen*. Her main hobby is photography, and she manages to combine this interest with her acting career by taking her camera with her when she shoots on location in various places.

Sources

Periodicals

Arizona Republic, August 11, 1998, p. D1; September 29, 1998, p. D1.
Atlanta Constitution, September 29, 1998, p. D4.
Dallas Morning News, June 13, 1998, p. 8C; September 27, 1998, p. 3.
Entertainment Weekly, September 4, 1998, p. 36; October 2, 1998, p. 56; December 11, 1998, p. 22; December 25, 1998, p. 22; September 10, 1999, p. 114; October 15, 1999, p. 59.
In Style, August 1999, p. 226.
Mademoiselle, May 1999, p. 120.
Newsday, September 29, 1998, p. B3.

People, September 28, 1998, p. 29; December 28, 1998, p. 114; May 10, 1999, p. 180.
Rocky Mountain News, August 23, 1998, p. 4; January 24, 1999, p. 6D.
Seventeen, October 1998, p. 94.
St. Louis Post–Dispatch, September 29, 1998, p. D1.
Star Tribune (Minneapolis, MN), October 25, 1998, p. 1F; October 29, 1998, p. 10E.
Toronto Star, June 13, 1999.
TV Guide, November 7, 1998, p. 10.
USA Today, September 29, 1998, p. 3D.
Variety, January 20, 1997, p. 46; February 2, 1998, p. 34; September 28, 1998, p. 86.

Online

"Keri Russell," Internet Movie Database web site, http://us.imdb.com (October 25, 1999).

"Keri Russell," Mr. Showbiz web site, http://mrshowbiz.go.com (October 25, 1999).

Rene Russo

Actor

Born February 17, 1954, in Burbank, CA; daughter of Nino (a sculptor) and Shirley (a factory worker and bartender) Russo; married and divorced; married Danny Gilroy (a screenwriter), c. 1992; children: Rose.

Addresses: *Agent*—Progressive Artists Agency, 440 S. Beverly Dr., Ste. 216, Beverly Hills, CA 90212.

Career

Model, actor. Signed with Ford Modeling Agency, c. 1971, appeared on cover of *Vogue, Cosmopolitan,* and others; began acting, 1987. Television appearances include series *Sable,* 1987. Film appearances include *Major League,* 1989; *Mr. Destiny,* 1990; *One Good Cop,* 1991; *Freejack,* 1992; *Lethal Weapon 3,* 1992; *In the Line of Fire,* 1993; *Major League II,* 1994; *Outbreak,* 1995; *Get Shorty,* 1995; *Tin Cup,* 1996; *Ransom,* 1996; *Buddy,* 1997; *Lethal Weapon 4,* 1998; and *The Thomas Crown Affair,* 1999.

Awards: Blockbuster Entertainment Award for favorite supporting actress, 1999, for *Lethal Weapon 4.*

Sidelights

Rene Russo is a sought–after actor not only for her graceful carriage, charm, and flawless looks, but also because she can deliver a good swift kick or block a punch if needed. She cornered the market on playing spunky girlfriend characters in action films once she showed up as Mel Gibson's

Corbis Corporation

match in *Lethal Weapon 3* and *4,* Clint Eastwood's Secret Service colleague and love interest in *In the Line of Fire,* and the wise B–movie star in *Get Shorty.* However, Russo was more than merely an attractive accessory for the big male stars; she added a new dimension to fast–paced, shoot–'em–up films with her brainy and fiery characters who could fire off a wry one–liner as easily as a round of ammunition. As Michael Walker put it in the *Los Angeles Times,* she "established a solid reputation playing strong, accomplished women handy with their wits, fists, and often enough, automatic weapons."

Russo brought a maturity to the big screen as a romantic lead, a category dominated by younger female stars. She did not appear in her first film until her mid–30s, and much was made in the press of her age, especially as she edged over 40. Although many male box–office bigwigs like Eastwood can carry a film well into their senior years, women have a harder time in Hollywood. But for Russo, breaking into acting was a better option than being relegated to low– paying modeling work once her long and glamorous career of being a top cover girl fizzled out. The career move has paid off with excellent notices about not only her ability to brighten a scene with her appearance, but also for her natural, likable presence.

Russo was born on February 17, 1954, in Burbank, California, to Nino and Shirley Russo. Her father, a sculptor, left the family when she was two, and her mother supported Russo and her younger sister Toni by working two jobs, in a factory by day and as a bartender at night. Russo would also earn money babysitting afterschool for the numerous single mothers in the area, which she described as "welfare row," according to Luaine Lee in a *Knight–Ridder/Tribune News Service* article. When she was ten, she was diagnosed with scoliosis (curvature of the spine) and spent her early teen years in a body cast to help correct it. She admitted that she wore a bra over top of the cast and stuffed it with tissue paper to approximate a level of physical development. The experience of being in a cast caused her self–esteem to suffer greatly. "You know, I got that cast off, and in a way I didn't really get it off for a long, long, time," she mused to Michael Walker in the *Los Angeles Times.*

Around the time she entered Burroughs High School, Russo shed her body cast, but she still considered herself gawky and unattractive. Other kids would call her the "Jolly Green Giant" because she was so tall and thin. Actor and director Ron Howard, who was one of her classmates, told Jill Gerston in the *New York Times* that Russo was "something of a rebel and pretty much an outsider," adding that "whenever guys would evaluate the girls and her name came up, there would be a pause, because no one could figure her out. She had this sense of mystery even then."

Finding it difficult to concentrate on schoolwork, Russo dropped out during the tenth grade and worked at various low–paying jobs for a while including at a movie theater concession stand and at an eyeglass factory. When she was 17, she was discovered while standing outside of a Rolling Stones concert at the Los Angeles Forum. Agent John Crosby, who worked for International Creative Management at the time, noticed her face and her long, flowing hair, and literally stopped his car in the middle of the street to give her his card. "I thought she was the most beautiful girl I'd seen in my life," he told Walker. "Fortunately, my wife agreed with me."

In a few weeks, Russo was on her way to New York City to for a shoot with renowned photographer Richard Avedon. "I was scared to death," she remarked to Jeff Giles in *Newsweek.* "I walked into his studio and burst into tears." Though she was soon one of the top models at the Ford agency, her picture beaming out from the cover of *Cosmopolitan* and *Vogue,* she was still haunted by insecurity.

Russo longed to have the looks of colleague Cheryl Tiegs or Christie Brinkley instead. Avedon, who became something of a father figure to her, suggested she get counseling.

Once Russo became a cover model, her father called and wanted a reunion with her. It did not go well. As she told Giles, "Here's a man who leaves you for 17 years, meets you because you're on the cover of *Vogue,* and then tells you you're ignorant. What kind of person is that?" She withdrew even more. Though she made enough money to buy herself and her mother each a home, she recognized that she was not happy. While other models tried to soothe their problems through substance abuse, Russo told Walker, "My drug was sleep. I would just do my job and go home." She went through a series of bad relationships and even a brief, unsuccessful marriage when she was 29. Her father died in 1997.

Though she reined as a top model for about a dozen years, Russo knew that her days were numbered, because she had long heard of women whose careers were over by the time they were 30. Indeed, once Russo reached that mark, she noticed that good work was drying up. Before long, she was modeling maternity wear for catalogs. One day while standing on the beach wearing a pillow on her stomach to approximate a pregnant figure, Russo had a revelation: She decided to quit modeling, and looked toward religion. She took theology classes and embraced Christianity, finding particular meaning in the writings of British author C.S. Lewis.

After a few years, Russo made up her mind to try acting, figuring that if it was not the right path, she would not be indebted to continue with it. In 1987 she landed a role as a literary agent on the short–lived television series *Sable,* then saw her film debut in the 1989 film *Major League,* about a misfit baseball team. After that, she landed parts in *Mr. Destiny,* 1990, a comedy starring James Belushi and Linda Hamilton; *One Good Cop,* 1991, costarring as the wife of Michael Keaton's character; and *Freejack,* 1992, a science fiction action flick with Mick Jagger and Emilio Estevez.

Russo's breakthrough role came in 1992 when she appeared in the blockbuster *Lethal Weapon 3* with Mel Gibson and Danny Glover. This sequel to the first two successful cop– buddy action flicks cast her as Gibson's love interest. As the sassy police officer Lorna Cole, Russo was the perfect match for Gibson's prickly Martin Riggs. She took kickboxing lessons to prepare for the rough–and–tumble part and even performed some of the stunts herself. Critics were warm to the addition of her part and impressed with her ability to shine on screen alongside Gibson and Glover. The cast teamed up again in 1998 for *Lethal Weapon 4,* when Russo and Gibson's characters take their relationship to another level when Cole finds out she is pregnant. Though some critics by this time were getting weary of the formula, the film stormed the box office once again, reaping $50 million in its opening weekend to become the top draw.

In the meantime, Russo's career had seen several other high points as well. After *Lethal Weapon 3,* she was billed with two other big names, Clint Eastwood and John Malkovich, for 1993's *In the Line of Fire,* about a pair of Secret Service agents who are protecting the president of the United States. In that, she steamed up the screen as Eastwood's lover. Afterward, she and Dustin Hoffman played a couple of virologists in *Outbreak* who work on containing a lethal virus while their marriage is on the rocks. This suspense–packed drama soared to the top of the box office charts.

Continuing her streak of performing strong, savvy characters, Russo was highly regarded for her part as a blonde, bosomy B–movie actor with street smarts in 1995's *Get Shorty,* an adaptation of an Elmore Leonard novel concerning a loan shark (John Travolta) who goes to Hollywood seeking a debtor. For that part, she had to wear a Wonderbra to accentuate her bustline. As she told Kim Cunningham in *People,* "My motto was, 'Have pads, will travel!'" Subsequently, she played a therapist romanced by Kevin Costner in the golf comedy *Tin Cup,* 1996. Also in 1996, Russo met up again with Gibson in the suspense–driven *Ransom,* about a wealthy couple whose son is kidnapped.

In Russo's first true headlining film in which she did not play a wife or girlfriend, she paired up instead with a gorilla. Starring in the 1997 quirky comedy *Buddy,* she portrayed wealthy Brooklynite Gertrude Lintz, who was known in the 1920s and 1930s for raising exotic animals. Buddy was one of her primate companions. Russo also shared the screen with a menagerie of creatures from horses to wild birds. This project, however, was one of her rare flops. The next year she sizzled with Pierce Brosnan in *Thomas Crown Affair,* for which she had to do sexually charged and nude scenes. Russo mentioned to Griffin that disrobing on camera "was not something I did lightly. I prayed about it, and I thought about it." Eventually, though, she went ahead. "I don't know where in the Bible it says 'Don't be nude in a motion picture.' In some of the most beautiful paintings in the Vatican, people are in the nude."

Among her peers, Russo has a good reputation for being easy to work with; she lacks vanity and displays an even temperament. Jill Gerston in the *New York Times* observed, "As Hollywood stars go, Ms. Russo is pretty low maintenance no shrieking for script revisions, flattering camera angles or bottles of Évian with which to shampoo her honey blond hair. Perhaps that's one reason she's in such demand on high–testosterone movie sets dominated by powerful male egos." In addition, Russo has eschewed plastic surgery, telling Nancy Griffin in the *Los Angeles Magazine* that she thinks women who have cosmetic surgery "look strange" and not any younger. She also commented that she is "sick to death of beauty campaigns that say 'Defy your age.'...I'd like to be able to say, 'Don't defy your age.'"

In 1992 Russo married screenwriter Danny Gilroy, whom she met when he worked on the script for *Freejack.* They live in Brentwood, California, with their daughter, Rose, who was born in 1994. Becoming a mother opened many painful scars for Russo, who told Bernard Weinraub in *Redbook,* "I didn't want to have kids. I didn't have a happy childhood." When she was pregnant, however, she saw a counselor who explained that her ambivalent feelings about motherhood stemmed from her own unpleasant background.

Subsequently, Russo commented to Weinraub that her daughter is "the best thing that's ever happened to me, obviously." She also remarked that her husband, who is a morning person while she is not, helps immensely with child rearing, and also remarked to Weinraub that she is grateful to her daughter for helping her understand more about life and about herself. Summing up to him, Russo revealed, "I've had so much in terms of worldly wealth, whether it's fame, a career, a husband, a child, money.... [A]nd all I can say is at the end of the day, money and fame don't bring you happiness. I was on 50 covers and I was not happy. And that was a blessing for me because it forced me to look in other places for it."

Sources

Periodicals

Entertainment Weekly, June 28, 1996, p. 41; June 13, 1997, p. 19.
Harper's Bazaar, September 1991, p. 76.
Knight–Ridder/Tribune News Service, October 16, 1995.
Los Angeles Magazine, August 1999, p. 134.
Los Angeles Times, March 5, 1995, Calendar, p. 5.
Newsweek, March 27, 1995, p. 64.
New York Times, June 7, 1992, sec. 2, p. 14; August 11, 1996, sec. 2, p. 9.

People, March 27, 1995, p. 108; October 16, 1995, p. 180; November 4, 1996, p. 142; September 13, 1999, p. 104.

Redbook, August 1998, p. 94.

Time, August 9, 1999, p. 67.

Vanity Fair, January 1992, p. 116.

Online

"Rene Russo," Internet Movie Database web site, http://us.imdb.com (January 19, 2000).

"Rene Russo," Mr. Showbiz web site, http://mrshowbiz.go.com (January 19, 2000).

Sonia Rykiel

Designer

Born Sonia Flis in Paris, France, May 25, 1930; married Sam Rykiel, 1953; children: Nathalie, Jean–Philippe.

Addresses: *Office*—175 Boulevard Saint–Germain, 75006 Paris, France.

Career

Free–lance designer for Laura boutique, Paris, 1962; opened first Paris boutique, 1968; opened household linens boutique, Paris, 1975; opened Sonia Rykiel Enfant boutique, Paris, 1987; introduced cosmetics line in Japan, 1987; introduced Inscription Rykiel collection, designed by Nathalie Rykiel, 1989; opened new flagship boutique, Paris, 1990; introduced menswear line, Rykiel Homme, 1990; opened second Inscription Rykiel boutique, Paris, 1990; opened Rykiel Homme boutique, Paris, 1992; launched footwear collection, 1992; introduced Sonia Rykiel fragrance, 1993; introduced Le Parfum, 1994. Also columnist for *Femme,* from 1983, and author of books. Exhibitions include*Woman of the Year 2000,* Forum des Halles, Paris, 1979; *Tables en Fetes,* International entre of Tableware, Paris, 1979; *Sonia Rykiel, 20 Ans de Mode* (retrospective), Galeries Lafayette, Paris, 1987; Seibo Shibuya department store, Tokyo, 1987; retrospective, the Orangerie, Palais du Luxembourg, 1993.

Awards: French Ministry of Culture Croix des Arts et des Lettres, 1983; named Chevalier de la Legion d'Honneur, 1985; Fashion Oscar, Paris, 1985; New York Fashion Group Award, 1986; Officier de l'Ordre de Arts et des Lettres, 1993; Chicago Historical Society's Award for Design Excellence, 1994.

Sidelights

"Style is something that is yours," fashion designer Sonia Rykiel once told Jean Bond Rafferty in *Town & Country.* "It comes from the bottom of your soul, from the bottom of your heart." She added, "Not everyone has it." But of course Rykiel has it, in abundance. Though she never studied design, this Parisian has been one of the darlings of the fashion world since she started creating clothes in the early 1960s. Her slim–fitting "poor boy" sweater transformed the modern silhouette, and subsequent generations of clingy knit and jersey creations earned her the nickname "the Queen of Knitwear." Her styles epitomize Parisian fashion; Tamsin Blanchard in the *Independent on Sunday* proclaimed, "The Sonia Rykiel woman is as French as the Ralph Lauren woman is all–American." Summing up Rykiel in the *Sunday Telegraph,* Hilary Alexander wrote, "If you had to think of a face that embodied all the qualities of Left Bank chic, designer Sonia Rykiel's is the one that would probably come to mind. She is a flame–haired, fairytale Goth; her hair appearing as a wild extension of the fox–fur collar on her habitual black garb; her bone structure part–bird, part–vixen, part–siren."

Rykiel was born Sonia Flis in Paris, France, on May 25, 1930, to a Russian mother and a Romanian father. Her father was an industrialist, and fashion was not emphasized in her upbringing. "The only clothes I liked were old clothes, always the same ones," she told Charlotte Aillaud in *Architectural Digest*. "My mother got so exasperated she would throw them out. So one day to get back at her, I marched out into the garden without a stitch on." A rough–and–tumble tomboy, she grew up climbing trees, riding bikes, and finding places to hide around the large home where her family spent their summers.

When Rykiel was young, she told Aillaud, "I really didn't envisage working, but I did think of becoming an actress or a writer until I decided to be a sculptor." Her parents, though, felt that such a profession was unsuitable, so they redirected her artistic aspirations. They contacted a friend who owned a Paris shop and helped her land a job decorating windows there. As Rykiel told Aillaud, "One day I happened to arrange some colorful scarves that I liked, and an elderly gentleman stopped to admire them. He came in, bought them all and asked to pay his compliments to me in person. His name was Henri Matisse."

Despite this strong start, Rykiel was in her thirties before she began designing. She married Sam Rykiel around 1953, the owner of a women's clothing boutique called Laura on the avenue de General Leclerc in Paris. In the 1950s she had her daughter, Nathalie, and then in the early 1960s, when she was pregnant with her son, Jean–Philippe, she decided to create her own maternity apparel. As she told Rafferty in *Town & Country*, "I wanted to have ten children. I only had two, so I started to do clothes, just to play, for a joke. It was just for me." Rykiel's first designs, rather than camouflaging her pregnancy, accentuated it with oversized but form–fitting knits in order to show off her delight in carrying a child. "My mother–in–law was scandalized, but my friends asked how they could find one like it," she recalled to Linda Bird Francke and Seth S. Goldschlager in *Newsweek*.

From there, Rykiel met a woman who made sweaters and explained to her the kind of design she wanted: a small, slim–fitting pullover with high armpits. Thus was born her famous "poor–boy" sweater, which went through seven revisions at the Italian knitters before she was satisfied. Rykiel began selling it in 1962 at Laura, where an *Elle* reporter immediately noticed it and was highly impressed. The next month, it was featured on the magazine's cover, and soon became the rage in Paris and then the United States.

Before long, Rykiel added dresses, skirts, and suits to her repertoire, and gained a following among wealthy, thin women who adored the chic, skinny

designs. The long, soft lines provided a clean look that managed to be both timeless and modern. Though her palette included basic colors like black, gray, navy, and beige, Rykiel was also applauded for introducing innovative colors in striped patterns, such as grayed seafoam green and grayed teal. Her clients also liked that she used fabrics such as knits, crepes, and jersey, which drape over the body elegantly and move with the natural contours of the figure. In addition, the designer began to create complementary pieces that could be layered, allowing women to mix and match.

In 1968, Rykiel opened her own shop on the rue de Grenelle on Paris's Left Bank, the year that student uprisings rocked Paris. She and her husband divorced around the same time, but Rykiel wanted to continue working together with him. Though their business relationship did not pan out, she told Bernadine Morris in the *New York Times*, "But he spends a lot of time with my son today. They build things together. He is very good with him."

Rykiel was soon credited with transforming the sweater the way Coco Chanel reinvented the suit. No longer were knits considered simply conservative and boring, suited only for golf cardigans or bland twinsets. They became haute couture, sought after by style–conscious women worldwide. Not long after Rykiel opened her first shop, Henri Bendel in New York City became the first retailer in the United States to carry her designs. Her clothes became popular in Asia and Australia as well, and over the next six years, 40 stores began selling her creations. Her designs would eventually be distributed by large department stores such as Bergdorf Goodman, Neiman Marcus, Saks Fifth Avenue, and Bloomingdales, as well as various specialty stores.

By the early 1970s, Rykiel debuted a line of cosmetics, and in 1975, she unveiled her household linens line. Also in the 1970s she began to incorporate written words on her designs; sweaters and dresses might display words like "MODE," "MOI," or "FETE," or even English words and phrases such as "ARTIST," "BLACK TIE" or "BLACK IS THE BEST." Overall, though, the most common inscriptions read simply "Sonia Rykiel" or "Rykiel."

Throughout the decade of the 1970s, Rykiel became more daring in her designs. She introduced darker and bolder hues like red and other primary colors, and was one of the pioneers of the "deconstructed" look. This featured elements like exposed seams and unfinished hems, and eschewed buttons, padding, and linings. The idea was to allow women freedom of movement. In her 1979 book, *Et Je La Voudrais Nue* (*And I Would Like Her Naked*), Rykiel wrote, "I affirmed that the other side of the garment, that which touches the skin, the wrong side, was much more beautiful because it was emphasized by the seams (now visible) like the beams of a house or the columns of a cathedral. It gave it symbolic value."

In 1976, Rykiel caused a ruckus in the fashion world with her "fanny wrappers," which were modeled at her boutique in Paris. These items foot–wide tubes or sashes covering the hips snugly caused one photographer to put down his camera, stating that he was "too overwhelmed by the sensuality of it all to continue," as Francke described in *Newsweek*. By this time, Rykiel counted among her devotees Lauren Bacall, Jacqueline Onassis, and Catherine Deneuve.

Branching out into new territory in the 1980s, Rykiel introduced a children's store, Sonia Rykiel Enfant boutique, in Paris in 1987. Three years later she expanded into apparel for men, debuting Rykiel Homme in Paris. That same year, a new flagship boutique opened in Paris as well, moving the shop on to the boulevard St.–Germain. She then launched a footwear collection in 1992, and Sonia Rykiel fragrance in 1993. An additional fragrance, Le Parfum, came out in France in 1994 and was later carried in America; it comes in a bottle shaped like a sweater. Another one of her mainstays is outerwear; she produces numerous coats in fine woolens and in fake fur.

In 1994, Rykiel appeared in the Robert Altman film *Pret–a–Porter* (*Ready–to–Wear*), about the fashion industry. The humorous film was studded with real–life designers, but in addition, Rykiel provided the inspiration for the character of Simone Lowenthal, played by Anouk Aimee. In 1998, Rykiel celebrated the thirtieth anniversary of the opening of her shop, which posted earnings in 1997 of 450 million francs, or about $75 million at the time. As she approached 70, critics continued to have high praise for her designs. Rebecca Lowthorpe in a 1999 *Independent* review of her autumn/winter 2000 collection stated, "Although her hallmark style hasn't changed, her gift is to update it every season, so it is always fresh and of the moment."

In 1983, Rykiel was honored with the French Ministry of Culture Croix des Arts et des Lettres. Two years later, she was named Chevalier de la Legion d'Honneur in addition to receiving a French "Fashion Oscar" in Paris. In 1986, she won an award from the New York Fashion Group, and in 1993 she was named an Officier de l'Ordre de Arts et des Lettres. The following year, she won the Chicago Historical Society's Award for Design Excellence. Rykiel's exhibits include retrospectives at the Galeries Lafayette, Paris, in 1987, and at the Orangerie, Palais du Luxembourg, in 1993.

In spite of her longstanding success, Rykiel admitted to Aillaud, "As a slave to the Slavic temperament, I work in doubt and anguish. Nothing I do is ever good enough. Every day for 12 years I wanted to quit. Now, if I did, it would be to write." In addition to *Et Je La Voudrais Nue*, she has also penned a children's book titled *Tatiana Acacia*, and another volume, *Celebration*, 1988, is a look back on the two decades since she opened her first boutique. She is also the author of *Rykiel*, 1985; *La collection*, 1989; *Collection Terminee, Collection Interminable*, 1993; and *Les levres rouges: roman* , 1996. Since 1983, she has also written a column for the French magazine *Femme*.

Though Rykiel's work took up a great deal of her time as her children were growing up, she told Morris in the *New York Times*, "Nathalie is very strong and clever. She takes care of my son." Jean–Philippe, a musician, has been blind since he was a baby. Rykiel's daughter became involved with the business, and in 1989 designed the Inscription Rykiel collection. Rykiel's son–in–law, Simon Burnstein, serves as the company's vice president, and one of Rykiel's sisters assists with accessories. In addition, Burnstein's mother, Joan, is also a fashion maven, as the owner of Browns in London.

A five–feet, five–inch–tall redhead, Rykiel wears her hair in longs bangs over her thin, pale face. In addition to her love of fashion, Rykiel admits a weakness for chocolate, and she dotes on her three granddaughters. She frequently spends time socializing with her sisters and friends over big meals. Inspiration, for Rykiel, comes from all avenues of life. "The creator," as she explained to Rafferty in *Town & Country*, "is someone who can't listen to music, read a book, look at a painting or a color, a woman or a man, with impunity. Each thing she sees, hears or lives through is to be stolen and used. There is always part of you that is saying, 'What will I do with that?'"

Selected writings

Et Je la Voudrais Nue (*And I Would Like Her Naked*), Paris, 1979, Tokyo, 1981.
Rykiel, Paris, 1985.

Celebrations, Paris, 1988.
La collection, Paris, 1989, Tokyo, 1989
Collection Terminee, Collection Interminable, Paris, 1993.
Tatiana Acacia, Paris, 1993.
Les levres rouges: roman, B. Grasset (Paris), 1996.

Sources

Books

Contemporary Designers, third edition, St. James Press, 1997.
Contemporary Fashion, St. James Press, 1995.

Periodicals

Architectural Digest, September 1988, p. 196; October 1994, p. 272.
Independent, March 12, 1999, p. 9.
Independent on Sunday, December 28, 1997, p. 34.
International Herald Tribune, April 28, 1998.
Newsweek, January 12, 1976, p. 49.
New York Times, December 1, 1973, p. 28.
St. Louis Post–Dispatch, April 6, 1995, p. 7.
Sunday Telegraph, March 22, 1998, p. 7.
Town & Country, December 1994, p. 178.

William Safire

Columnist and author

Born William Safir, December 17, 1929, in New York City; name legally changed to Safire; son of Oliver C. (a manufacturer) and Ida (Panish) Safir; married Helene Belmar Julius (a jewelry designer), December 16, 1962; children: Mark Lindsey, Annabel Victoria. *Education:* Attended Syracuse University, 1947–49.

Addresses: *Home*—Chevy Chase, MD. *Office New York Times,*—1627 Eye St. NW, Washington, DC 20006. *Agent*—Morton Janklow, 598 Madison Ave., New York, NY 10036.

Career

New York Herald–Tribune Syndicate, reporter, 1949–51; WNBC radio and WNBT–TV, correspondent in Europe and Middle East, 1951; WNBC, New York City, radio–TV producer, 1954–55; Tex McCrary, Inc. public relations firm, vice president, 1955–60; Safire Public Relations, Inc., New York City, president, 1961–68; The White House, Washington, DC, speechwriter and special assistant to the President, 1968–73; *New York Times*, Washington, DC, author of political column "Essay," 1973 , and "On Language" column in *New York Times Magazine*, 1979. Also contributor to *Harvard Business Review, Cosmopolitan, Playboy, Esquire, Reader's Digest, Redbook,* and *Collier's.* Member of Pulitzer Prize Board, 1995. *Military service:* U.S. Army, 1952–54.

Awards: Pulitzer Prize for distinguished commentary, 1978, for articles on Bert Lance.

Sidelights

Longtime *New York Times* columnist William Safire is renowned for his keen wit, critical mind, and prolific puns in his editorial page "Essay," which is syndicated in 300 publications. In addition, his weekly *New York Times Magazine* piece, "On Language," has established him as a reigning wordsmith. This column explores both written and oral trends, and often delves into the historical origin of words and phrases. Also from this pulpit, he is fond of lobbing "gotchas" at those who misuse words. Many of Safire's musings on language stem from his monitoring of the political scene, but they also mix in social observations as well. Throughout his columns, Safire sprinkles alliterative puns as well as newly coined words ("neologisms"). For example, he has written about "'pressycophants,' those involved in 'trendustry,' 'journafiction,' and the 'anomie–too' set," as well as the "Spock–marked generation,' couples who 'neither marry nor kick the cohabit,' [and] 'the President's populism and the First Lady's momulism,'" according to Victor Navasky quoting Safire in *Esquire*

Though now one of the most respected journalists in the nation, Safire (known to colleagues as "Bill") caused controversy when he started at the *Times* due to his background as a public relations executive and as a speechwriter for President Richard Nixon. Many of his associates also disliked his right–leaning views. Safire described himself to Victor Gold in the *Washingtonian* as a "libertarian conservative," explaining, "I'm not a Libertarian–party type, but one who believes in the idea of the less government the better; in the use of government exclusively for national defense and those matters that state and local governments can't handle." In addition to his opinion pieces and musings on language for the *Times,* Safire has written several books on political communication and language, as well as some novels.

Safire was born William Safir on December 17, 1929, the youngest of three sons of Oliver C. and Ida (Panish) Safire. He changed the spelling of his surname later, after a stint in the army, because he grew weary of others mispronouncing it as "safer" or "saffer." Though he was born in New York City, Safire at the age of six months moved with his family to Bristol, Virginia, where his father owned a thread–making factory. However, the Depression ruined the business and it closed in 1933. The next year, when Safire was a toddler and his brothers, Leonard and Marshall, were in their teens, his father died of lung cancer. His mother later relocated the family to California and back to New York City twice. His father's small annuity barely kept the family afloat.

As a teenager, Safire attended the prestigious Bronx High School of Science. There, he worked for the student newspaper, and upon graduation, won a Regents scholarship to Syracuse University. He supplemented his stipend by waiting tables. As a freshman in college, he wrote a radio show called *Say Hello* featuring fellow student Dick Clark as an announcer. Eager to start his career, Safire dropped out of school after his sophomore year in 1949 in order to parlay his summer job into permanent employment. He had started working as a copy boy for Tex McCrary, an early media mogul who wrote a celebrity column for the *New York Herald Tribune* and hosted a radio show and a television show. Working with him, Safire was able to interview notables such as Mae West and Lucky Luciano.

In 1951, Safire worked as a correspondent for WNBC radio and WNBT–TV (later to become WNBC–TV) in Europe and the Middle East. The next year, he became intrigued with politics when he organized the Eisenhower for President rally at Madison Square Gardens. Also that year, he joined the army and went to Europe, where he was a reporter for the American Forces Network. After his discharge in 1954, he returned to NBC and teamed up again with McCrary and his wife, Jinx Falkenburg, and produced the *Tex and Jinx* radio and television shows.

When McCrary started up his own public relations firm in 1955, Safire was made a junior partner and given the title of vice president. The company represented businesses including Lionel Trains, Republic Aviation, the Franklin National Bank, and the "Levittown" housing developments in New Jersey and Pennsylvania. Working on the latter, Safire was able to urge the National Association for the Advancement of Colored People to drop a lawsuit against the project when he promised there would be an open housing policy. In addition, while with McCrary's agency, Safire hired future television personality Barbara Walters to work at the firm as well.

In 1959, Safire was the brains behind the famous "kitchen debate" held between Vice President Richard Nixon and Soviet Premier Nikita Krushchev. At the time, Safire was representing a household products firm at the American Exhibition in Moscow. He managed to steer the two politicians into a display featuring a typical American house, where they debated capitalism versus Communism. Using a camera tossed to him by an Associated Press photographer, Safire snapped the famous shot of the encounter. In 1960, Safire acted as chief of special projects for Richard Nixon in his unsuccessful presidential bid against John F. Kennedy.

Shortly before the Tex McCrary agency closed, Safire resigned in 1960 and started up his own firm, Safire Public Relations, Inc., in New York City in January of 1961. Also in the early 1960s he also worked on other Republican political campaigns in New York City and in the state. He also supervised public relations for New York Governor Nelson Rockefeller when he ran for president in 1964. Meanwhile, Safire's first book, *The Relations Explosion,* came out in 1963, followed the next year by *Plunging into Politics,* cowritten with Marshall Loeb. The latter provided advice to candidates on how to run campaigns, from staffing to financing. One of his best–known works, *The New Language of Politics,* came out in 1968 and was regarded as a clever dictionary of political language. It was later reissued as *Safire's Political Dictionary: The New Language of Politics,* 1978, and in 1993 a revised edition was published as *Safire's New Political Dictionary: The Definitive Guide to the New Language of Politics.*

In the mid–1960s, Safire became a volunteer speechwriter for Nixon in preparation for the 1968 elections. He thus became one of the cadre of speechwriters that included Patrick Buchanan, Raymond K. Price, Jr., and others who were dubbed Nixon's "word factory" by William H. Honan in a 1969 *New York Times Magazine* piece. Honan noted that Safire was the "resident pro for zingers and snappers (as punchlines are known in the trade)." Safire also assisted Buchanan with Nixon's syndicated newspaper column.

When Nixon moved into the White House, Safire sold his agency and joined the presidential staff as an assistant. There, he represented Republican party moderates and gave statements on the economy and the Vietnam War. While working for Vice President Spiro Agnew in 1970, Safire coined a memorable phrase for him which labeled the news media as "nattering nabobs of negativism."

During Nixon's successful reelection campaign in 1972, Safire began writing opinion articles for the *Washington Post.* They were part of an ongoing debate with Frank Mankiewicz, the campaign manager for Nixon's opponent, Senator George McGovern. Following the election, the *Post* offered Safire a position, but he ended up accepting another offer, from *New York Times* publisher Arthur "Punch" Sultzberger. At the *Times,* Safire provided a twice–weekly right–leaning viewpoint that countered the left–of–center sentiments of fellow columnists.

Safire's debut in the field of journalism was greeted with hostility, not only due to his politics but also because those in the news media generally regard former public relations people as inferior. But he aroused even more criticism for his support of Nixon throughout the Watergate scandal, which broke just after he penned his first column. However, Safire later admitted his error in backing Nixon when he learned that during his time at the White House, his conversations had been secretly taped.

Safire eventually published a memoir of his time as a Nixon speechwriter; *Before the Fall* came out in 1975. Though he had harsh words for Nixon's defensive stance with the media, much of the work tried to humanize the former president and painted a generally positive view of the administration, despite some criticisms of Henry Kissinger. Some reviewers derided the work for being too soft on Nixon, whereas others felt it gave better insight into the shamed leader.

In time, Safire earned respect for his sharp mind and his expert word play. In 1978 he won a Pulitzer prize for commentary about President Jimmy Carter's budget director, Burt Lance, whom he ac-

cused of shady financial dealings. Later, though, after Lance was acquitted following a jury trial, the two men became friends. Also in the 1970s, Safire criticized Agnew for anti–Semitism, though most of his jabs were aimed at Democrats.

Safire's first novel, *Full Disclosure,* was published in 1977 and became a best–seller, earning the author an estimated $1 million. It deals with a president in danger of being removed from office after he is blinded in a freak accident during a tryst with a woman on the White House press corps. Then, in 1979, Safire began to write the "On Language" column in the *New York Times Magazine,* which earned him recognition as a definitive source on language usage. Several collections of his opinion and language columns have been published in book form.

In addition, Safire turned his pen again to fiction writing, creating the dense historical novel *Freedom* in 1987. It is about the White House years from 1861 to 1863, starting with Abraham Lincoln issuing the Emancipation Proclamation and examining his role during the early years of the Civil War. In the work, Safire creates an image of the president as a person plagued by depression and suffering from normal human shortcomings, as opposed to the vision that is often conjured of a revered martyr. Though many reviewers applauded the book, some felt the author overlooked the role of blacks. Safire worked on *Freedom* for seven years and turned in a triple–spaced project that ran 3,300 pages. Because it was too large to fit into a binding, he cut out a section so that it would only run 1,152 pages.

In 1992, Safire composed an ambitious nonfiction work titled *The First Dissident: The Book of Job in Today's Politics.* It looks at the Biblical figure Job as a voice that challenged authority the highest authority, in fact. Shortly after its publication, Safire commented to Marjorie Williams in *Vanity Fair,* "I identify with dissidents rather than governors, with challenge to authority rather than authority. And, sure, the power of being on the op–ed page of *The New York Times* confers authority, but the way I try to use it is to goad and to criticize and to go against the grain."

In 1995, Safire published another novel, *Sleeper Spy,* a U.S.–Soviet espionage thriller, and in 2000 tried fiction again with *Scandalmonger.* This work centers on a journalist who exposes the sexual affairs of two American presidents. However, the story is based on a real newspaper reporter, James T. Callender (1758–1803), who wrote about the dalliances of Alexander Hamilton and Thomas Jefferson. Callender was reviled throughout history for tarnishing the reputations of two of the country's most popular leaders, and Safire set out to create a more sympathetic profile in addition to delving into the issue of a free press. Though the book is fiction, Safire provided a bibliography and footnotes to support the true history within.

Scandalmonger debuted at number 14 on the *Publishers Weekly* best–seller list. Safire subsequently made several appearances on radio and television shows to discuss the parallels between the book's content and current–day media and politics. However, Safire explained to Ron Charles in the *Christian Science Monitor*, "I didn't go into this book saying, 'OK, I'm going to write a book about the previous scandals that will illustrate the current ones.'" As it happened, he noted, he first became interested in muckraker William Cobbett, and decided later to focus on Cobbett's archrival, Callender.

Safire married British–born Helene Belmar Julius, a former model and pianist who became a jewelry designer, on December 16, 1962. They have two grown children, Mark Lindsey and Annabel Victoria. Safire and his wife reside in the tony Kenwood area of Chevy Chase, Maryland, a suburb of Washington, D.C., in a 20–room Georgian home they bought in 1969. Unsurprisingly, he is an avid book collector. He and his wife are known for being entertaining hosts, and Safire has a reputation for being a steadfastly loyal friend to those who are close to him.

Selected writings

The Relations Explosion, Macmillan,1963.
(With M. Loeb) *Plunging into Politics*, McKay.1964.
The New Language of Politics, Random House, 1968, 3rd edition published as
Safire's Political Dictionary: The New Language of Politics, 1978, revised and enlarged edition published as *Safire's New Political Dictionary: The Definitive Guide to the New Language of Politics*, 1993.
Before the Fall, Doubleday, 1975, published as *Before the Fall: An Inside View of the Pre– Watergate White House*, Da Capo Press (New York City), 1988.
Full Disclosure (novel; Literary Guild selection), Doubleday, 1977, limited edition with illustrations by George Jones, Franklin Library, 1977.
On Language (collection of weekly columns), Times Books,1980.
Safire's Washington, Times Books, 1980.
What's the Good Word?, Times Books, 1982.
(Compiler with brother, Leonard Safir) *Good Advice*, Times Books, 1982.

I Stand Corrected: More on Language (collection of weekly columns), Times Books, 1984.
Take My Word for It: More on Language (collection of weekly columns), Times Books, 1986.
Freedom (novel; Book–of–the–Month Club main selection), Doubleday, 1987.
You Could Look It Up: More on Language, Times Books, 1988.
Fumblerules: A Light–Hearted Guide to Grammar and Good Usage, Doubleday, 1990.
Words of Wisdom, Fireside Books (St. Louis), 1990.
Language Maven Strikes Again (collection of weekly columns), Holt, 1990.
Coming to Terms (collection of weekly columns), Doubleday, 1991.
The First Dissident: The Book of Job in Today's Politics (nonfiction), Random House, 1992.
(Compiler and author of introduction) *Lend Me Your Ears: Great Speeches in History*, Norton (New York City), 1992.
(Compiler with L. Safir) *Good Advice on Writing: Writers Past and Present on How to Write Well*, Simon & Schuster,1992.
Quoth the Maven (collection of weekly columns), Random House, 1993.
In Love with Norma Loquendi (collection of weekly columns), Random House, 1994.
Sleeper Spy (novel), Random House, 1995.
Watching My Language (collection of weekly columns), Random House, 1996.
Spread the Word, Times Books, 1999.
Scandalmonger, Simon & Schuster, 2000.

Sources

Books

Encyclopedia of World Biography, second edition, Gale Research, 1998

Periodicals

Christian Science Monitor, January 20, 2000, p. 17.
Columbia Journalism Review, January 1, 2000, p. 77.
Esquire, January 1978, p. 38; January 1982, p. 44.
Library Journal, January 1, 2000, p. 162.
Newsweek, February 12, 1973, p. 46; January 27, 1975, p. 59; March 3, 1975, p. 71; April 23, 1979, p. 87.
New York Times, January 31, 1973, p. 38; September 4, 1995; September 17, 1995; February 6, 2000.
New York Times Magazine, January 19, 1969, p. 20.
Publishers Weekly, June 30, 1997, p. 59; December 20, 1999, p. 53; February 14, 2000, p. 85.
Time, February 12, 1973, p. 38; August 6, 1973, p. 44; August 20, 1973, p. 21; October 3, 1977, p. 101; February 12, 1990, p. 62.

Vanity Fair, November 1992, p. 148.
Washingtonian, August 1991, p. 66.

Online

"William Safire," *Contemporary Authors Online*, Gale Group web site, http://www.galenet.com (February 22, 2000).

Buffy Sainte–Marie

Singer, songwriter, artist, and activist

Corbis-Bettman

Born February 20, 1941 (some sources say 1942 or 1943), on Piapot Reserve in Craven, Saskatchewan, Canada; adopted daughter of Albert C. (a mechanic) and Winifred (a proofreader; maiden name, Kendrick) Sainte–Marie; married Dewain Kamaikalani Bugbee, September 16, 1967 (divorced, 1972); married Sheldon Peters Wolfchild (an actor), 1975; children: (second marriage) Dakota Wolfchild Starblanket. *Education:* University of Massachusetts, B.A., 1963; Ph.D. in fine arts.

Addresses: *Home*—Kauai, Hawaii. *Office*—c/o Institute of American Indian Arts, P.O. Box 20007, Santa Fe, NM 87504.

Career

Began performing in coffeehouses, early 1960s; performed at clubs, concerts, and festivals, 1963 ; recording artist, 1964 ; digital artist. Founder and president of Gypsy Boy Music, Inc., and Caleb Music, Inc.; founder of Nihewan Foundation for Native American Education, Native North American Women's Association, and Creative Native, Inc.; member of advisory council of Upward Bound program. Actor in television programs, including *The Virginian, Then Came Bronson,* and *Sesame Street.* Associate editor of *Native Voice,* Vancouver, British Columbia. Lecturer on Native American culture and history. Composer of over three hundred songs. Contributor of articles to magazines and periodicals on Native American history and culture. Member, American Federation of Television and Radio Artists; American Federation of Musicians; American Society of Composers, Authors, and Publishers.

Awards: *Billboard* award, 1965; Premio Roma Award (Italy) performance at Sistina Theatre; outstanding artist of the year award from National Association of FM Broadcasters, 1975; Academy Award for best song, 1982, for "Up Where We Belong," from film *An Officer and a Gentleman;* named best international artist of the year, France, 1993, Juno Hall of Fame Award, Canada, 1995; Award for Lifetime Musical Achievement, First Americans in the Arts, 1996; inducted into Juno Hall of Fame, 1999.

Sidelights

Best known for her protest anthems during the 1960s, Buffy Sainte–Marie throughout the years has remained an active force in Native American causes while expanding her art to encompass digital creations in addition to singing and songwriting. As a member of the Native American Cree tribe, she has used her fame to increase awareness of, and lend support to, Indian issues. Also, she has appeared on television and movies in roles that seek to crush stereotypes, and she works to improve the lives of those on reservations with her support for scholarships and other educational programs. In addition to creating electronic paintings on her Macintosh computer, Sainte–Marie who has degrees in philosophy, teaching, and fine art devotes a great deal of her time to the Cradleboard Teaching Project, which uses technology to nurture Native American culture and foster a better understanding of it among non–Indians. "Before (Christopher) Columbus arrived we have a vague notion of Indian people as hunters and gatherers, wanderers living off the land and it's just not true," Sainte–Marie explained to Tanya Talaga in the *Toronto Star*. "We have very little representation in the mainstream, on TV, on the writing end of movies. We are continually misperceived by people who deserve to know who we really are."

Beverly Sainte–Marie, nicknamed Buffy as a child, was born on the Piapot Reserve in the Qu'Appelle Valley, Saskatchewan, Canada, on a Cree reservation in the early 1940s. As an infant, she was orphaned and was soon adopted by Albert C. Sainte–Marie, a mechanic, and Winifred (Kendrick) Sainte–Marie, a proofreader, who raised her in Wakefield, Massachusetts, north of Boston. They were part Micmac Indian and had lost a baby daughter about the same age. Sainte–Marie spent her summers in Sebago Lake, Maine, on the ocean, where she began to write songs. She had learned piano as a child and also composed poetry; she set her words to music after teaching herself to play guitar in her teens. As she once noted in a *Time* article, she devised her own finger patterns and "32 different tunings, which account for the strange flavor of my music." Also in her teens, she found out about her Cree background and met some of her relatives for the first time.

A dual citizen of Canada and the United States, Sainte–Marie obtained a government loan and enrolled at the University of Massachusetts. There, she obtained a bachelor's degree in Oriental philosophy and elementary education in 1963 and was named one of the top ten graduating seniors that year. She also later earned a doctorate in fine arts. While in college, Sainte–Marie began performing at coffeehouses and local clubs, and became a popular singer, drawing large crowds with her original love songs and protest tunes as well as covers of folk and jazz standards, though she concentrated mainly on her own compositions.

Shortly after graduating, Sainte–Marie did a stint at an open mic night at the Gaslight Cafe in Greenwich Village, then a hotbed for the rising folk music scene. She immediately caught the attention of record companies and landed a recording contract with Vanguard, which released her first full–length album, *It's My Way,* in 1964. By now Sainte–Marie had left behind her plans to become a teacher and was instead appearing regularly at clubs around Manhattan such as the Bitter End and Gerde's Folk City, as well as the Gaslight Cafe. However, a serious bout with bronchial pneumonia in 1963 almost left her without a voice. Later, professional voice lessons and vocal exercises helped preserve her talent, but during the time of her illness, she became addicted to codeine, an experience recounted in her song "Cod'ine."

Although Sainte–Marie would become best known for her activist pieces, what was unusual was that while most other acts focused on the controversial Vietnam War going on at the time Sainte–Marie chose to address a more personal topic: the treatment of Indians by the United States government. She did have one big antiwar hit with "The Universal Soldier," included on her first release; a *Life* magazine writer noted that it was "almost the battle hymn of the draft card burners." However, most of her pieces focused on Indian affairs, bringing the topic of mistreatment and murder of Native Americans by the government to the general public, as well as environmentalism. Another of her classics, also on her first album, is "Now That the Buffalo's Gone," which addressed the near–extinction of the buffalo, in addition to the plight of Native Americans. In addition, Sainte–Marie developed a singing style that incorporated traditional repetitive Indian sounds while mixing in a rich vibrato, and she also used the mouth bow, a Native American instrument that added a distinct flair. Her versatile alto voice can come across as sultry, angry, happy, humorous, uplifting, and much more.

By the mid–1960s, Sainte–Marie had reached icon status and had graduated from the intimate club scene into the big arenas, including a date at New York's Carnegie Hall. She toured internationally and also began to show up on television roles, where she often made a stance for Indian rights and sought to dispel stereotypes. For one episode of *The Virginian*, she demanded that all Indian characters be portrayed by Indians, and she assisted with the script, which was applauded for its realism. She was also a regular guest on the children's program *Sesame Street* for several years and joined the cast from 1976 to 1981.

In addition, Sainte–Marie frequently visited reservations and lobbied the government regarding various Native American issues. She argued for better job training and scholarship money, as well as better textbooks that were not racially biased. "Do you know how much despair there is among our people?" Sainte–Marie asked Mary Smith in *McCall's*. "The government breaks our hearts with their boarding schools where they teach that *Columbus* discovered America!" She also donated generously to the Indian struggle at Alcatraz, a major battle in the Native American rights movement, and to the Save the Children Federation, which assisted Indian children. Sainte–Marie set up the Nihewan Foundation to provide Indian scholarships as well and is involved with Creative Native, an organization devoted to bringing Indian art and culture to depressed Native American areas. She also has served as a member of the advisory council of Upward Bound and as associate editor of *Native Voice,* a publication out of Vancouver, British Columbia, Canada.

Sainte–Marie moved to Hawaii in the 1960s and married surfing instructor Dewain Kamaikalani Bugbee, whose ancestry included Hawaiian, Indian, and European heritage, but they divorced in 1972. She later married Sheldon Peters Wolfchild, an actor, in 1975, and they had one son, Dakota Starblanket. Despite her popularity, none of Sainte–Marie's records were hits until the early 1970s, when she made her mark on the charts with the singles "She Used to Wanna Be a Ballerina" and "Mister Can't You See." However, many of the songs she wrote became hits for other performers, including the love song "Until It's Time for You to Go," recorded by Elvis Presley. Some other entertainers who have performed her work include Barbra Streisand, Neil Diamond, Janis Joplin, Tracy Chapman, and the Indigo Girls. In the late 1970s Sainte–Marie decided to take a hiatus from recording to raise her son, who often appeared with her on *Sesame Street.* During her time on that show, she continued to educate people about Native Americans while dispelling myths.

Those who do not remember her vehement activist tunes from the 1960s may recall the 1982 duet "Up Where We Belong," sung by Joe Cocker and Jennifer Warnes and cowritten by Sainte–Marie, Jack Nitzsche, and Will Jennings. It received a 1983 Academy Award for best song, as well as a British Academy Award and Golden Globe, when it was used in the film *An Officer and a Gentleman.* Her compositions have also been heard in the films *The Strawberry Statement,* 1970; *Soldier Blue,* 1970; *Spirit of the Wind,* 1979; and *Stripper,* 1985. In addition, Sainte–Marie has appeared in the film *Broken Rainbow,* 1985, about the Hopi–Navajo land dispute, and the television movie *The Broken Chain,* 1993. She also provided a voice–over for the television movie *Son of the Morning Star,* 1991, and has also been spotted in commercials for Ben & Jerry's ice cream.

Sainte–Marie has remained dedicated to Indian issues, continuing to speak and play music at schools and reservations and to perform live internationally, often to lend publicity to causes. One issue that she supports is to free Leonard Peltier, an activist for the Native American rights group American Indian Movement (AIM) who was sentenced to two life sentences in prison for a shooting in which two FBI agents were killed. Many believe Peltier is a political prisoner who was unjustly jailed. In addition, Sainte–Marie contributes articles to publications such as *Akwesasne Notes* and also penned a children's book, *Nokomis and the Magic Hat,* published in 1986. She is also an adjunct professor at several institutions, where she lectures on an assortment of topics, including Indian women's issues, film scoring, songwriting, and electronic music. At the Institute for American Indian Arts in Santa Fe, New Mexico, she is an artist in residence teaching digital art.

Widely appreciated for her electronic paintings, Sainte–Marie considers the computer her canvas, and uses a stylist (digital pen) with a pressure–sensitive Wacom tablet instead of a mouse to create her images. The stylist can be told to replicate a piece of chalk, a brush, a pen, and more, and the computer can be set to approximate a bumpy or smooth canvas, or to work with virtual "paint" that is a thicker or thinner consistency. Sainte–Marie uses a Macintosh computer and mainly Photoshop software for her paintings, which she then prints out at a digital lab. They range from two to seven feet in height, and have been exhibited both in real–world galleries and online. She believes that the new technical era has led to much greater opportunities for artists. "It used to be that Mr. Man and his brother and his cousin owned everything the publishing houses, the recording companies, the political scene," Sainte–Marie remarked to Ophira Edut in *Ms.* "In order to do something as an artist, or as an outsider, you had to go stand in that line until you got the stamp of approval. Technology is changing that."

In addition to her digital art, Sainte–Marie is heavily involved with the Cradleboard Project, an educational initiative that began when her son was in fifth grade. When his teachers asked her to get involved with the Indian studies curriculum, Sainte–Marie was shocked that the materials had not changed much over the years. To remedy the misinformation that students were getting about Native Americans, she assisted in finding better books, videos, and computer materials as well as writing lesson plans. In addition, the program uses technology by linking classrooms via the Internet in order to share information between Indian and non–Indian students using e–mail and live chat, which really gave the effort a boost. Cradleboard receives funding from Kellogg's.

After her long break from recording, Sainte–Marie issued a comeback album, *Coincidence and Likely Stories,* by EMI in Canada in 1992, but it was largely overlooked in the United States. It was created at her home in Hawaii using a Macintosh computer to record and was sent via modem to the coproducer in London. Another record, *Up Where We Belong,* 1996, featured re–recordings of many of her favorites along with a couple of new songs. It was issued in Canada and overseas in 1996, but not immediately in the United States. Though she has never re-captured the widespread fame in the United States that she had during her heyday, Sainte–Marie remains a heroine in Canada. Miles Morrisseau of *Aboriginal Voices* magazine noted in *People,* "She's like our Elvis. You can go on reserves and hear 5–year–old girls singing her songs."

Selected discography

It's My Way, Vanguard, 1964.
Many a Mile, Vanguard, 1965.
Little Wheel Spin & Spin, Vanguard, 1966.
Fire and Fleet and Candlelight, Vanguard, 1967.
I'm Gonna Be a Country Girl Again, Vanguard, 1968.
Illuminations, Vanguard, 1970.
She Used to Want to Be a Ballerina, Vanguard, 1971.
The Best of Buffy Sainte–Marie, Volume 1, Vanguard, 1970.
The Best of Buffy Sainte–Marie, Volume 2, Vanguard, 1971.
Native Northamerican Child, Vanguard, 1973.
Moonshot, Vanguard, 1973.
Quiet Places, Vanguard, 1973.
Buffy, MCA, 1974.
Changing Woman, MCA, 1975.
Sweet America, ABC, 1976.
Coincidence and Likely Stories, Ensign (EMI), 1992.
Up Where We Belong, EMI, 1996.

Sources

Books

Contemporary Musicians, volume 11, Gale Research, 1994.
Contemporary Theatre, Film, and Television, volume 16, Gale Research, 1997.
Notable Native Americans, Gale Research, 1995.

Periodicals

Life, December 10, 1965, p. 53.
McCall's, March 1971, p. 45.
Ms., August/September 1999, p. 86.
People, June 17, 1996, p. 132.
Saskatchewan Sage, April 1, 1998, p. 7.
Time, December 10, 1965, p. 62; March 28, 1977, p. 66.
Toronto Star, February 19, 1999.

Online

"Beverly Sainte–Marie," *Contemporary Authors Online,* Gale Group web site, http://galenet.gale.com (August 27, 1999).
"Buffy Sainte–Marie," Internet Movie Database web site, http://us.imdb.com (September 21, 1999).
Buffy Sainte–Marie web site, http://www.aloha.net/[]bsm (September 19, 1999).
Buffy Sainte–Marie biography, Vanguard Records web site, http://www.vanguardrecords.com/buffy (September 21, 1999).

Loretta Sanchez

Evan Agostin/Liason Agency

U.S. Congresswoman

Born January 7, 1960, in Lynwood, CA; daughter of Ignacio Sandoval Sanchez (a machinist) and Maria Socorro Sanchez (a secretary; maiden name, Macias); married Stephen Simmons Brixey III (a securities trader). *Education:* Chapman University, Orange, CA, B.S. in economics, 1982; American University, Washington, DC, MBA in finance, 1984.

Addresses: *Office*—529 Longworth Building; Washington, DC 20515; 12397 Lewis Street, Ste. 101; Garden Grove, CA 92840–4695.

Career

Orange County Transportation Authority, Santa Ana, CA, special projects manager, 1984–87; Fieldman, Rolapp & Associates, Irvine, CA, assistant vice president, 1987– 90; Booz, Allen & Hamilton, Los Angeles, CA, associate, 1990–93; Amiga Associates, Inc. consulting firm, Los Angeles, CA, president and principal owner, 1993–96; U.S. House of Representatives, member from California, District, 46, 1996, co–chair of Democratic National Committee, 1999 . Member of Educational Opportunities Committee, House Committee on Education and the Workforce, Postsecondary Education Subcommittee, House National Security Committee, Oversight and Investigations Committee, Welfare and Recreation Subcommittee, House Armed Services Committee, and Special Oversight Panel on Morale. Member of Hispanic Caucus, Blue Dog Democrats, New Democratic Coalition, Congressional Human Rights Caucus, Women's Congressional Caucus, Older Americans Caucus, Law Enforcement Caucus, Congressional Sportsman's Caucus, National Society of Hispanic MBAs (past president), Los Amigos of Orange County, Rotary Club of Anaheim, and Anaheim Assistance League.

Sidelights

In a stunning upset in 1996, Loretta Sanchez defeated a nine–time incumbent for a House of Representatives seat from her district in Orange County, California. With no political experience, this financial analyst received backing from major national educational and abortion rights groups as well as Hispanics, who all wanted to oust her opponent, Robert K. Dornan, due to his conservative views. After the election, she was catapulted into the spotlight as Dornan alleged that her slim victory was due to voter fraud. However, Sanchez prevailed and went on to win re–election in 1998 by a much wider margin. Though Sanchez holds many liberal views, including supporting abortion rights and gay rights, she is a fiscal conservative who tries to find common ground with the Republican party. Upon invitation from President Bill Clinton and Vice President Al Gore, she became co–chair of the Democratic National Committee in March of 1999 during just her second term in office.

Sanchez, one of seven children of Mexican immigrants, was born on January 7, 1960, in Lynwood,

California. Her father, Ignacio Sandoval Sanchez, a machinist, and her mother, Maria Socorro (Macias) Sanchez, a secretary, met each other while working in a manufacturing plant in Los Angeles. Her mother helped organize a union at the plant. Since they spoke only Spanish in the home, Sanchez learned English in a Head Start program for disadvantaged children. The family moved to Anaheim in 1965, where some neighbors sold their homes and left rather than live near a Hispanic family.

Along with her siblings, who are now all professionals, Sanchez was an excellent student. She gives credit to her parents for her success. Her mother volunteered at her children's school, and her father demanded that the children study hard and adhere to strict codes of behavior so that they would not face the same discrimination he had when he arrived in the United States. Still, Sanchez noted that racism persisted, telling Jim Lewis in *Harper's Bazaar,* "When I was growing up, Mexicans could only swim in the pool on Friday nights, because Saturday morning they changed the water. Since then, the city's gone from being mostly white to being half Latino. And the yet power structure hasn't changed: In 1988, they dressed people up to look like INS [Immigration and Naturalization Service] agents and sent them to the polls to discourage new immigrants from voting."

In 1982 Sanchez graduated from Orange, California's Chapman University with a bachelor of science degree in economics and was also voted student of the year. She went on to obtain a master's degree in business administration, specializing in finance, from American University in Washington, D.C. Afterward, she worked from 1984 to 1987 for the Orange County Transportation Authority as a special projects manager, where her first major success was in raising money to install emergency call boxes on the highways. Subsequently, she held a career as a financial analyst, mainly in areas of municipal and public finance. From 1987 to 1990 she was employed with Fieldman, Rolapp & Associates, in Irvine, California, as an assistant vice president, then with Booz, Allen & Hamilton in Los Angeles from 1990 to 1993 as an associate. She was president of Amiga Advisors, Inc. in Los Angeles from 1993 to 1996.

Meanwhile, throughout the 1980s and 1990s Sanchez was active in community affairs, though mainly behind-the scenes. She got involved with planning and financing for schools, libraries, and police stations, and helped raise funds for school programs and scholarships. She was not extremely political until the elections of 1992. Until then, she and her

husband, Stephen Simmons Brixey, a securities trader, lived an upper-middle-class lifestyle and were members of the Republican party due to their fiscal conservatism. But she became disturbed by what she considered attacks on immigrants and women by the Republicans, and felt that the party's social stances against issues like abortion and gay rights were out of step with hers.

After switching her affiliation to Democrat, Sanchez ran for a seat on the Anaheim City Council in 1994, campaigning under her married name, Loretta Sanchez Brixey. As a relative unknown, she came in eighth in a field of 16 candidates. Later, in 1996, she decided to take on a much bigger challenge: opposing nine-term incumbent Robert Dornan for his seat in the U.S. House of Representatives from California's 46th District. Dornan not only endorsed right-wing social views, he was known for making outrageous and often incendiary statements to air his positions, earning him the nickname "The Mouth of the House." He frequently made negative comments about homosexuals, especially those with AIDS, and according to Francis X. Clines in the Minneapolis *Star Tribune,* he once called President Clinton "a sleazeball who can't keep his pants on." Dornan was also characterized as "B-1 Bob" for his staunch advocacy of military spending, especially for the B-1 bomber, and he was a fervent supporter of gun rights. In addition, he was not known to be especially sympathetic to the needs of his Hispanic constituents, which made up about one-third of his district. However, since only about a third of the eligible population cast votes, and because his largely Catholic constituency supported many of his conservative views, Dornan continued to win re-election.

When Sanchez decided to run against Dornan, the Democratic party initially backed a different candidate in the primary. After she won, local Democratic leaders "took their time getting behind her," according to Lewis in *Harper's Bazaar,* and he claimed that the National Organization for Women "was just about as reluctant." Dornan, who was $200,000 in debt after squandering funds on a failed 1996 presidential bid to begin with, figured that Sanchez was hardly a contender, and ended up pouring less money into his House campaign than usual. However, Hispanic forces soon rallied behind Sanchez. She wound up outspending him $760,328 to $589,447.

Although Sanchez ran under her maiden name rather than her married name in this race, she concentrated on a platform of basic concerns like education, jobs, and Social Security, rather than hotbed issues like immigration. Still, Dornan attacked her as a "Hispanic pretender," as she remarked to Clines, who said that Dornan denounced her as "a carpetbagger in her hometown." Clines also quoted the congressman as calling her "a Catholic for abortion and sodomy rights." In November of 1996, she won the seat in a surprise upset by a narrow margin of about a thousand votes.

However, the race was not exactly over. Dornan called for a recount, and alleged voter fraud. He maintained that Sanchez gained votes from Hispanic non–citizens signed up on voter rolls the previous year by a Hispanic community group; he alleged that some were even illegal immigrants. Investigations by the House of Representatives, the state of California, and the Orange County district attorney dismissed the election fraud charges. The House found that although 784 of the votes were illegally cast, this was still 231 shy of Sanchez's victory. Meanwhile, though, Dornan, apparently optimistic that he would resume his seat, continued to show up on the House floor at times during votes. Afterward, a poll showed that Dornan's approval rating among Hispanic voters had plunged to just 27 percent. In addition, Vietnamese voters were displeased, because they, too, had been investigated amid the alleged fraud charges.

In November of 1998, Dornan challenged Sanchez to reclaim his seat, but she won with 57 percent of the vote. In her time in office, Sanchez focused on education, crime reduction, economic development, and senior citizens' issues. Proud of the fact that she became the first member of Congress to have benefited from the "Head Start" program, she is committed to continuing to provide opportunities for disadvantaged children. In her district, she was involved in 14 major federal grant projects that reaped $25 million in federal monies to agencies in Orange County. She has served on several committees and subcommittees, including the House Committee on Education and the Workforce and the House Armed Services Committee. She commutes from Washington to her home in Orange County each weekend.

Sources

Books

Notable Hispanic American Women, Book 2, Gale Research, 1998.

Periodicals

Congressional Quarterly Weekly Report, January 4, 1997, p. 52.
Harper's Bazaar, April 1997, p. 207.
Hispanic, October 1998, p. 48; November 1999, p. 35.
New Republic, October 27, 1997, p. 13.
Roll Call, February 5, 1998.
Star Tribune (Minneapolis, MN), December 19, 1996, p. 29A.
Working Woman, May 1999, p. 24.

Online

Loretta Sanchez web site, http://www.house.gov/sanchez (March 16, 2000).
"California's Sanchez becomes national symbol," Reuters news service, January 21, 1998, obtained from Electric Library web site, http://www.elibrary.com (March 16, 2000).

Carlos Santana

Photograph by Ken Settle

Musician

Born July 20, 1947, in Autlan de Navarro, Mexico; son of Jose (a traditional violinist) and Josefina Santana; adapted religious name Devadip (means "the light of the lamp of the Supreme"), 1973; married Deborah Sara King, 1973; children: Salvador, Stella, Angelica.

Addresses: *Home*—San Rafael, CA. *Publicist*—Jensen Communications, Inc., 230 East Union Street, Pasadena, CA 91101.

Career

Began performing in 1961 in Tijuana, Mexico; lead guitarist of group Santana (founded as Santana Blues Band in San Francisco, CA), 1966 ; recording artist with Columbia/ CBS, 1969–1991; recording artist with Polydor, 1991—; founded Guts and Grace record label, 1994; appeared at Fillmore West, 1968, Woodstock Music and Arts Festival, 1969, Altamont Festival, 1969, California Jam II, 1978, LiveAid, 1985, first Amnesty International concert tour, 1986, Woodstock '94, 1994; has recorded and performed with: Mike Bloomfield, Al Kooper, Mahavishnu John McLaughlin, Jose Feliciano, Miles Davis, Flora Purim, Herbie Hancock, Buddy Miles, John Coltrane, Turiya Alice Coltrane, Wayne Shorter, Aretha Franklin, Babatunde Olatunji, John Lee Hooker, Eric Clapton, Buddy Guy, Blues Traveler, Lauryn Hill, Wyclef Jean, Dave Matthews, Rob Thompson, and Eric Clapton.

Awards: For music: *Playboy* All–Star Jazz and Pop Poll, record of the year, for *Abraxas*, 1972; Latin New York Music Awards, Latin rock band of the year,

1975; Bay Area Music Award (Bammy Award) for best guitarist, 1976, 1977, 1980, 1981, 1994, 1995; Bammy Award for best album, 1977, for *Moonflower*; Bammy Award for best group, 1980; *Playboy* Reader Music Poll, number one pop/rock guitarist, 1983, 1984, 1995; pop/rock guitarist, 1984; Grammy Award for best rock instrumental performance for *Blues for Salvador*, 1988; Bammy Award for musician of the year, 1978, 1988, 1993; *Billboard* Century Award for distinguished creative achievement, 1996; received star on Hollywood Rock Walk of Fame, 1996; inducted into Bay Area Music Awards Walk of Fame, 1997; Chicano Lifetime Achievement Award, 1997; Nosotros' Golden Eagle Legend in Music Award, 1997; inducted into the Rock & Roll Hall of Fame, 1998; National Council of La Raza, Alma Award, 1999; Grammy Awards for record of the year, song of the year, and pop collaboration with vocals for "Smooth," album of the year and rock album for *Supernatural* , pop instrumental performance for "El Farol," rock performance by a duo or group with vocal for "Put Your Lights On", and rock instrumental performance for "The Calling," all 2000.

Other

Awards: Commendation for achievement and support in California from Governor George Deukmejian, 1986; National Hispanic Heritage Week, outstanding leadership award, 1986; Comite Mexicano Civico Patriotico of San Francisco Commendation, 1987; Board of Supervisors of the City and County of San Francisco certificate of honor, 1987; Consulate General of Mexico in San Francisco award, 1987; San Francisco declared June 6, 1987 "Santana Day;" California State Latino Legislative Caucus Resolution honoring Carlos Santana, 1991; National Society of Fund Raising Executives, Golden Gate chapter, outstanding philanthropist award, 1994; Hispanic Congressional Caucus, Medallion of Excellence Award for community service, 1999.

Sidelights

In the late 1960s, when acid rock reigned and the British Invasion was still raging, Carlos Santana and his band introduced the music scene to a new Latin–based rock sound featuring an Afro–Cuban beat. This would effectively usher in the concept of "world music" years before the description would catch up with the style. After soaring in popularity and becoming one of the biggest acts of the day, the group went through various personnel changes, but they continued to make music together even as Santana, finding new spiritual and musical paths, began to record jazz fusion on his own with many other top names. Though his rock records continued to sell vigorously, he would not have a radio hit after 1982.

Then, in 1999, Santana became one of the most often–heard performers on the airwaves. He had teamed up with some of the hottest young acts of the day, including Lauryn Hill, Dave Matthews, and Everlast, along with the legendary Eric Clapton, to produce a work that harkened back to his early Latin sounds, but with a contemporary slant. With an irresistible hook and his trademark low, cool vocals, the single "Smooth" began racing up the charts, and the album, Supernatural, sold more than six million units. The project overall won a phenomenal total of 8 Grammy Awards, tying Michael Jackson's 1983 record for most Grammys won on a single night. Some wondered if his comeback could be attributed to the sudden boom in Latin music beginning in the late 1990s that spawned such names as Ricky Martin, Enrique Iglesias, Jennifer Lopez, and others. Santana, however, credits a force more high–minded than a fad or marketing appeal. "It's not really chance or luck," he remarked to Jeff Gordinier in Entertainment Weekly. "It's something more paranormal like divine synchronicity. My intention was to spread a spiritual virus."

Santana was born to Jose and Josefina Santana on July 20, 1947, in Autlan de Navarro, a small village in the state of Jalisco, Mexico. His father, a tradi-

tional violinist who played mariachi music, exposed him to the basics of music theory when he was five years old and tried to teach him violin. "My father's a musician, his father was a musician, my great–grandfather was a musician," he told James Schaffer in Down Beat. Santana added, "Dad…taught me the violin for almost seven years, and I could never get anything out of it. I always sounded like Jack Benny no matter how hard I tried. Only Jack Benny could really play, but I sounded like Jack Benny when he was fooling around."

More interested in rock and roll than the mariachi sounds anyway, Santana began to learn the guitar at age eight, imitating the style of greats such as B.B. King, John Lee Hooker, and T–Bone Walker. However, he still credits his father with teaching him to appreciate music in general. After the family of 12 moved to the border town of Tijuana in 1955, he began playing in nightclubs along the strip there when he was just 11 years old.

Around the early 1960s, Santana's family moved to San Francisco, California, but he soon ran away to return to Tijuana and play the circuit again. His older brother came to retrieve him, though, and he ended up in San Francisco with the rest of his family, where he went to Mission High School and learned English. There he also discovered a thriving cultural scene with a diversity of musical styles, including jazz, blues, international folk music, classical salsa by the likes of Tito Puente and Eddie Palmieri.

While working full–time as a dishwasher in a restaurant, Santana continued to play music, performing on the street for change in the evenings and jamming with others to try to get a band together. With mentoring from Jerry Garcia of the successful hippie group the Grateful Dead, he quit his job. Joining with bassist David Brown and keyboard player Gregg Rolie, he formed the Santana Blues Band, eventually abbreviating the name to simply Santana.

In the thriving scene of the San Francisco area in the 1960s, new bands were sprouting up all the time, so it was not easy to get noticed. For three years, Santana played small clubs around town, particularly in the Mission District, a predominantly Hispanic area. Before long, though, promoter Bill Graham noticed their unique sound and began to book them at his Fillmore West and Winterland clubs. Blending an Afro–Cuban beat with a fast–tempo rock and blues base and low–key vocals, Santana created the new style of Latin Rock.

Although they were approached by several record companies in the late 1960s, the band declined a contract. Therefore, when they played for half a million people at the legendary rock music festival Woodstock in 1969, they did not even have an album out. There, they performed a piece titled "Soul Sacrifice," written specifically for the event. On stage, Santana noted in a *Rolling Stone* article marking the occasion's twentieth anniversary, "I was struggling to keep myself grounded, because I had taken some strong psychedelics right before I went onstage." By now Santana included drummer Mike Shrieve and percussionists Jose Chepito Areas and Mike Carrabello. After getting a warm reception at Woodstock, they were booked on the popular *Ed Sullivan Show,* then signed to Columbia Records by the end of the year. The effort, *Santana,* stayed on the *Billboard* charts for two years, eventually selling more than four million copies. It spawned the hits "Evil Ways" and "Jingo."

The next year, 1970, Santana continued to ride a wave of success, releasing its second hit album, *Abraxas.* This featured the classic rock staples "Oye Como Va" (written by Tito Puente) and "Black Magic Woman" (penned by Peter Green), and went platinum in sales. In 1971, the group had a gold album with *Santana III,* and in 1972 it saw platinum again with *Caravanserai.* Meanwhile, Santana became more fond of jazz, and recorded his first effort without the rest of the band in 1972, pairing up with Buddy Miles. The band also began to experience a shift in members, as musicians came and went from the group. Guitarist Neal Schon had joined in 1971 and later left, along with original member Rolie, to form Journey. Eventually, Santana was the only initial member who remained.

After the much–publicized drug–related deaths of several prominent musicians in the late 1960s and early 1970s, including Jimi Hendrix, Janis Joplin, and Jim Morrison, Santana began to reassess his lifestyle. He had skyrocketed to fame in a short time, like the others, and found himself indulging in the familiar trappings of a rock star, including excesses of drugs and casual sex. Finding a religious path, he became a devoted follower of Sri Chimnoy, a spiritual guru and proponent of meditation. In August of 1973, he changed his name to Devadip (meaning "the light of the lamp of the Supreme") Carlos Santana. In April of that year, he had married Deborah Sara King, founder of a health food shop in San Francisco and daughter of a guitarist known for his work with blues singer Billie Holiday. The couple has three children, Salvador, Stella, and Angelica.

Through his association with Sri Chimnoy, Santana got to know guitarist Mahavishnu John McLaughlin. Together, they created a spiritual jazz–fusion album, *Love, Devotion, and Surrender,* released in 1973, which reached gold record status. Throughout the 1970s, Santana would release four more albums with spiritual themes, recording without his band but in collaboration with others such as Ron Carter, Herbie Hancock, and Wayne Shorter. He once admitted to Lee Underwood in a 1981 *Down Beat* interview that he "felt insecure" when he began to venture into jazz, since he did not read music and was treading in unfamiliar territory. However, he eventually gained self–confidence through experience, and told Underwood, "I still do not read music, but I know how to compose and make melodies come alive. Every time I see Wayne Shorter, Joe Zawinul or Herbie Hancock, they say, 'Hey, Melody Man!' I have learned how to improvise, and have also learned you do not have to be superfast or supercomplex in order to improvise well."

By the mid–1970s, Santana began to drift back toward his Latin rock sound. Promoter Graham took over as his manager in 1975, and he began to record again with the group, even though Santana himself found more meaning in his spiritual efforts. Despite the fact that from 1969 to 1981, all of the group's works would hit either gold or platinum, they did not hit the top ten until 1976's *Amigos.* After that, CBS records re–signed Santana to a seven–album contract.

During the 1980s, Santana and the band recorded less frequently, only putting out five albums throughout the decade. However, they toured prolifically, selling out stadiums and appearing at high–profile events like LiveAid, the US Festival, and on the first Amnesty International concert tour. He also helped organize the "Blues for Salvador" concert in Oakland, California, in 1988, which benefited children in El Salvador. That year, he won a Grammy Award for best rock instrumental performance for "Blues for Salvador." 1988 was especially active as he toured with saxophonist Wayne Shorter and also embarked on a tour with the original Santana band members Rolie, Areas, and Shrieve who had not played together since the early 1970s. In addition, in 1988 he released a 30–song retrospective album which featured previous hits as well as unreleased studio tracks, live cuts, and sound checks.

Back in 1982, Santana discontinued his association with Sri Chimnoy, and he and his wife converted to Christianity in the early 1990s. In 1992, ending his lengthy association with Columbia, Santana signed a deal with Polydor Records which included forming his own label, called Guts & Grace. John Swenson in *Rolling Stone* called Santana's first effort for this label, *Milagro,* "one of the finest sessions he's done," and added, "The album reaffirms Santana's position as the standard–bearer for fusion music." In 1993, he toured with folk icon Bob Dylan, and in 1996, he toured with guitar great Jeff Beck. Though Santana still sold seats, he noticed that radio stations no longer played any of his music besides his early hits, and the media was not paying him much attention. He received a star on the Hollywood Rock Walk of Fame in 1996, but it would take him until 1998 to be inducted in to the Rock and Roll Hall of Fame.

Therefore, by the late 1990s, Santana was looking for a comeback. He explained to Andy Ellis in *Guitar Player* that in his meditation and dreams, he had received instructions telling him the following: "We want you to hook up with people at junior high schools, high schools, and universities. We're going to get you back into radio airplay." He felt his music could have a positive effect on youth of the day. Along with producer Clive Davis, who had first signed him to his contract at Columbia in the 1960s, Santana devised a plan. He told David Wild in *Rolling Stone*, "I didn't want Santana to sound like a Seventies jukebox. I wanted to be relevant today or as Wayne Shorter would say, 'Completely new, totally familiar.'"

Though many acts were not interested in working with someone they perceived to be old and washed–up, Santana, working with his band, managed to assemble a collection of some of the biggest talents in the industry, including Lauryn Hill, Wyclef Jean, Eagle Eye Cherry, Dave Matthews, Rob Thompson of Matchbox 20, Everlast, and the Dust Brothers, producers for Beck and the Beastie Boys. Even Eric Clapton made an appearance. The result was 1999's *Supernatural,* which reached number one on the *Billboard* album chart and generated a number–one single, "Smooth." *Supernatural* also became one of the most critically acclaimed CDs of the year and sold six million copies by the turn of 2000. The title, Santana told an *Entertainment Weekly* interviewer, "deals with the paranormal relationship between Lauryn Hill, Eric Clapton, and myself. Most of my collaborators said, 'I knew I was going to work with you because you were in my dreams.'" Surprisingly, *Supernatural* got nearly all of its airplay on pop and rock radio, with little support from Latino stations, despite the fact that five of the tracks are in Spanish.

In February 2000, Santana won a whopping total of 8 Grammy Awards, including record of the year, for "Smooth," and album of the year and best rock album, for *Supernatural.* He also won an American Music Award that year for best album. For Santana,

it is not about the recognition as much as it is touching people with his art. "I want my music to clue my listeners into something beyond the song itself," he once related to Dan Ouellette in *Down Beat.* "For example, this guy who had considered suicide wrote me a letter. He had seen the video of John Lee Hooker performing 'The Healer' and it inspired him to seek another way of dealing with his problems. Now that's more important to me than how many Grammys I get or how much money I could make selling Pepsi."

Selected discography

(With Buddy Miles) *Carlos Santana & Buddy Miles! Live!,* Columbia, 1972.
(With Mahavishnu John McLaughlin) *Love, Devotion, Surrender,* Columbia, 1973.
(With John Coltrane) *Illuminations,* Columbia, 1974.
Oneness, Silver Dreams–Golden Reality, Columbia, 1979.
Swing of Delight, Columbia, 1980.
Havana Moon, Columbia, 1983.
Blues for Salvador, Columbia, 1987.
Spirits Dancing in the Flesh, CBS Records, 1990.

With the Santana band

Santana, Columbia, 1969.
Abraxas, Columbia, 1970.
Santana III, Columbia, 1971.
Caravanserai, Columbia, 1972.
Welcome, Columbia, 1973.
Greatest Hits, Columbia, 1974.
Borboletta, Columbia, 1974.
Lotus, Columbia, 1975.
Amigos, Columbia, 1976.
Festival, Columbia, 1976.
Moonflower, CBS, 1977.
Inner Secrets, Columbia, 1978.
Marathon, Columbia, 1979.
Zebop, Columbia, 1981.
Shango, Columbia, 1982.
Beyond Appearances, Columbia, 1985.
Freedom, Columbia, 1987.
Viva Santana!, Columbia, 1988.
The Sound of Carlos Santana, Pair, 1989.
Milagro, Polygram Records, 1992.
Sacred Fire, Polydor, 1993.
Brothers, Polygram Records, 1994.
Dance of the Rainbow Serpent, Columbia, 1995.
Live at the Fillmore 1968, Sony, 1997.
Best of Santana, Columbia, 1998.
(Also with others) *Supernatural,* Arista, 1999.

Sources

Books

Contemporary Musicians, volume 19, Gale Research, 1997.

Dictionary of Hispanic Biography, Gale Research, 1996.

Periodicals

Arizona Republic, January 18, 2000, p. A10.

Down Beat, January 1981, p. 13; February 1988, p. 16; August 1991, p. 28.

Entertainment Weekly, September 10, 1999, p. 151; December 24, 1999, p. 36.

Guitar Player, January 1993, p. 58; January 1996, p. 61; August 1999, p. 74.

Hispanic, October 1992, p. 80; March 1996, p. 18.

Latin Beat, September 1999, p. 20.

Newsweek, February 14, 2000, p. 66.

New York Times, January 5, 2000, p. B5.

Rolling Stone, February 21, 1980, p. 26; September 22, 1988, p. 27; August 24, 1989, p. 65; September 3, 1992, p. 68; December 9, 1993, p. 24; October 28, 1993, p. 30; August 19, 1999, p. 47.

Star Tribune (Minneapolis, MN), February 8, 2000.

Online

Santana official web site, http://www.santana.com (February 14, 2000).

Barry Scheck

Attorney and educator

Born September 19, 1949, in Queens, NY; son of George (a tap dancer, television host, and manager) and Eleanor Scheck; married; wife's name, Dorothy (a social worker); two children. *Education:* Yale University, B.S., 1971; University of California at Berkeley, J.D., 1974.

Addresses: *Office*—c/o Benjamin Cardozo School of Law, Brookdale Center, 55 Fifth Ave., New York, NY 10003.

Career

Legal Aid Society, Bronx, NY, 1974–79; Yeshiva University, Benjamin M. Cardozo School of Law, instructor, 1977—, founder of Innocence Project, 1991—. Coauthor, with Peter Neufeld and Jim Dwyer, of *Actual Innocence: Five Days to Execution and Other Dispatches from the Wrongly Convicted*, Doubleday, 2000. Also teacher and organizer of trial advocacy programs for public defender's offices, bar associations, and firms; and commissioner on New York's Forensic Science Review Board.

Sidelights

Criminal defense attorney Barry Scheck has handled a number of high–profile cases in his career, and is perhaps most often connected with the trial of O.J. Simpson, who was accused and acquitted of double murder in 1994. Since then, Scheck, a professor at the Benjamin N. Cardozo School of Law at Yeshiva University, has been recruited to serve on other defense teams due to his work in the field of DNA testing, including working on the case of nanny Louise Woodward, accused of killing the infant she was caring for, and immigrant Abner Louima, who was victimized in a New York City police station.

At Yeshiva University, Scheck cofounded the Innocence Project, a clinical program through which dozens of men have been cleared of crimes and thus released from prison or even spared the death penalty. He and two coauthors related details of some of these cases in the book*Actual Innocence: Five Days to Execution and Other Dispatches from the Wrongly Convicted*, published in 2000. DNA tests can be performed on any bodily fluid, including blood or saliva, and provides a genetic "fingerprint" of that person. However, the Federal Bureau of Investigation did not routinely perform DNA tests until 1989, so an untold number of prisoners may not be guilty. "If we are going to acknowledge that the system is so imperfect that innocent people are convicted," Scheck stated to T.J. English in *New York*, "it is inevitable to conclude that innocent people will be executed. It is the most powerful argument against the death penalty that I know of."

Scheck was born on September 19, 1949, in Queens, New York, to George and Eleanor Scheck. His father had been a tap dancer and operated a children's performance school for a time. In the 1950s, he started up *Star Time*, a children's televised talent show. Scheck yearned to perform as well, but his father steered him away. "He hated the rapacious nature of show business," Scheck told Paul Schwartzman in *Playboy*. "He didn't want me to get into it unless I had a license to practice law. He said the only people who survived show business were the lawyers."

While hosting *Star Time*, the elder Scheck discovered singer Connie Francis, and became her manager. He later also handled singer Bobby Darin and jazz pianist Hazel Scott. This made the family well–off, and by the mid–1950s, they moved from their Queens apartment to a three–bedroom home on Long Island.

Tragedy struck the family, though, when Scheck was 11 years old. On the eve of Thanksgiving, the house burned down, killing his younger sister, seven–year–old Marilyn. Afterward, his mother suffered bouts of serious anger and depression, and sometimes took it out on her son. "Because of all that," Scheck commented to Schwartzman, "I learned to deal with damaged people."

The family later moved to the Upper East Side of New York, where Scheck finished up at a public junior high school before attending a private boys' school, Horace Mann. There, he became keenly interested in politics, and often vocally criticized the administration of President Lyndon B. Johnson. As editor of the school paper, he made waves by interviewing lawyer F. Lee Bailey, who gained notoriety by representing clients such as the Boston Strangler, Albert DeSalvo. Later, he would work hand–n–hand with Bailey on the Simpson trial.

In 1967, Scheck enrolled at Yale University and continued to be a leading campus activist. He threw away his Vietnam War draft card and called for an end to all student draft deferments, which allowed young men in college to avoid service. He claimed that if this happened, then economically privileged families—who were not as affected by the war because they could send their sons to school—would put so much pressure on the government that they would find a way to end the war. Scheck also joined the "Dump Johnson" movement and campaigned for Robert F. Kennedy.

After receiving his bachelor of science degree in 1971, Scheck graduated from the University of California at Berkeley law school in 1974, despite the fact that he longed to write screenplays or a novel.

However, he decided to practice law on his own terms, and thus waved off corporate law in favor of public interest law. "I always saw the money as a trap," he told Schwartzman. "I wanted to remain true to a set of social values."

Once he obtained his law degree, Scheck returned to New York City and found work at the Bronx Legal Aid Society, where he mainly represented indigent clients. In one of his early cases, he helped defend some Irish men accused of filtering weapons to the Irish Republican Army. Though some people considered the men terrorists, Scheck saw them as freedom fighters, and insisted they were being denied their civil liberties. The men were acquitted.

In 1979 Scheck left Legal Aid and joined the faculty at Yeshiva University's Benjamin Cardozo School of Law in New York. There, he began a criminal law clinic, and students began to compete to work on his real–life cases outside of the classroom. In his earliest major case, Scheck defended a woman named Hedda Nussbaum, who was accused of negligent homicide. She and her lover, Joel Steinberg, had together adopted a baby girl, Lisa Steinberg, who died at age six after being physically and psychologically abused. Nussbaum was charged with allowing the abuse to continue, but Scheck argued that his client was similarly abused by Steinberg. She suffered from a broken nose, broken ribs, split lips, and a gangrenous leg. "Speaking with her was like talking to a torture victim," Scheck related to Schwartzman. He convinced prosecutors to drop charges against Nussbaum, and she later testified against Steinberg, who was sent to prison for murder.

Meanwhile, when previously working at the Legal Aid Society, Scheck met lawyer Peter Neufeld, and the two joined forces to try cases together. Neufeld had left Legal Aid to become a sole practitioner and to teach at Fordham University, and together Scheck and Neufeld began pioneering work using DNA evidence in criminal cases, which began to emerge in the mid– 1980s. Scheck and Neufeld were not easily swayed by expert testimony claiming that DNA tests could prove guilt beyond a reasonable doubt. They delved into the technology, reading all of the literature, attending seminars, consulting scientists, and visiting laboratories. They came to discover that while a DNA test can give evidence of a highly probable match, it cannot conclusively prove a match.

Scheck and Neufeld first used their knowledge in the courtroom in 1988, when they represented building superintendent Joseph Castro, who was accused of murdering a 28–year–old pregnant woman and her two–year–old daughter. In that case, blood on the man's watch matched the blood of the victims, implicating him in the crime. Scheck and Neufeld protested the admissibility of DNA testing in proving their client's guilt. One expert, the director of a DNA testing lab, stated that there was a one in 189,200,000 chance of having a random match. The judge thus decided that no DNA evidence would be allowed in the murder trial of the superintendent, but the man ended up pleading guilty anyway and was sentenced to prison.

In doing their research, Scheck and Neufeld realized that although DNA testing cannot conclusively prove a match, it can indeed rule when two samples are definitely not the same. They reasoned, then, that the tests would be more important in exonerating suspects than in convicting them. This led Scheck to found the Innocence Project at Cardozo Law School in 1991. This program takes on cases of prisoners who insist they have been wrongly convicted, and uses DNA testing to try to help clear them. It is funded primarily by the law school and also obtains money from private foundations such as George Soros's Open Society Institute. Prisoners' families also contribute $5000 to $8000 for the DNA testing. Law students staff the office.

The Innocence Project rejects about one–fourth of cases outright, because there is no testable evidence, or because additional evidence would not affect the conviction anyway. But for the hundreds of others it has accepted, it has had a great impact. Through the efforts of Scheck and Neufeld, dozens of prisoners, including many on death row, have been released due to their efforts. But despite these errors in the criminal justice system, Scheck and Neufeld found that it is often difficult to overturn convictions due to time limits on introducing new evidence, or because evidence is lost or was never gathered in the first place.

Due to his work, Scheck became a regular on the talk–show circuit, where he spread the word about innocent people in prison. In addition, he helped convince New York State to form a Forensic Regulatory Commission to ensure that forensic laboratories meet certain standards. He also became a member of that commission. But Scheck would make his name not for his work with unknown, indigent defendants or obscure procedural rules; he would become a household name for his involvement on one of the most famous trials in recent American history.

In June of 1994, Scheck and Neufeld were called upon to help defend former professional football star–turned–actor O.J. Simpson, who was accused of killing his ex–wife, Nicole Brown Simpson, and her friend Ronald Goldman. The Los Angeles–based trial was one of the major events of the decade, capturing the public consciousness. Simpson's attorneys were dubbed the "Dream Team," because it included high–powered names such as F. Lee Bailey, Johnnie Cochran, and Robert Shapiro. They asked Scheck and Neufeld to act as consultants, but the pair became enmeshed in the daily activities of the case and spent months involved with it.

Some people criticized Scheck and Neufeld for their work on the Simpson case, because they were previously known for standing up for those who were undoubtedly wrongly accused, and many firmly believed that despite the verdict, Simpson was guilty. Others questioned why Scheck, who had so sensitively defended domestic abuse victim Nussbaum, would join the side of Simpson, who had previously pleaded no contest to spousal abuse. Scheck, however, explained the situation by saying it was an opportunity to showcase the merits of DNA testing in front of a nationwide audience.

During the trial, Scheck became a vivid player as he thoroughly cross–examined prosecution witnesses regarding location and collection of evidence, and also as he explained DNA testing to the jury. He was especially diligent in cross–examining chief police evidence collector Dennis Fung. Thanks to Scheck's input regarding the science of the case, the jury—in a move that stirred emotions and polarized a great many based on race—acquitted Simpson of both murders.

After the Simpson trial, Scheck continued teaching and working with the Innocence Project, but he soon went back to work on media–saturated cases. In February of 1997 he acted as an unpaid consultant on matters of DNA and crime–scene analysis for the case of JonBenet Ramsey, a young Colorado girl found dead in the basement of her own home. The case went unsolved. Later that same year, Scheck joined the defense team of Louise Woodward, a British au pair charged with killing an eight–month–old baby in her care in Connecticut. The child had suffered head trauma and had been violently shaken. Woodward was convicted of second–degree murder and faced life in prison, but after vehement protests in the U.S. as well as Britain, a judge reduced her sentence and she was released.

Also, in September of 1997, Scheck joined Neufeld and Cochran to represent Abner Louima, a Haitian immigrant who accused the New York City police department of sodomizing him the previous month with a broomstick at the 70th Precinct station house in Brooklyn. In December of 1999, former police officer Justin Volpe was convicted of the crime and sentenced to 30 years in prison. Three other officers were also convicted of covering up the incident.

In early 2000, Scheck, along with Neufeld and Pulitzer Prize–winning columnist Jim Dwyer, published the book *Actual Innocence: Five Days to Execution, and Other Dispatches from the Wrongly Convicted.* The book chronicles the fates of 64 people—ten in detail—who were sent to death row for crimes they did not commit. When a *Publishers Weekly* interviewer asked him if these cases did not make it "easy to become disheartened about our system of justice," Scheck replied, "I think it's an optimistic book, because for every problem we identify, we also identify simple reforms that anyone of good will, or any political persuasion, can get behind."

Scheck met his wife, Dorothy, a social worker, while both were college students hitchhiking around Europe. He proposed at a Grateful Dead concert in 1974. They have two children. Scheck and his family often vacation together with Neufeld and his family.

Sources

Esquire, April 1993, p. 83.
Library Journal, February 15, 2000, p. 181.
Newsday, June 28, 2000, p. A3.
New York, January 2, 1995, p. 38.
New York Times, August 5, 1994, p. A20; April 6, 1995, p. B8; April 17, 1995, p. A14; September 29, 1995, p. A1;
Playboy, August 1998, p. 80.
Publishers Weekly, January 10, 2000, p. 52.
Time, September 13, 1999, p. 26.

Juergen Schrempp

Business executive

Born September 15, 1944, in Freiburg, Germany; son of a university admissions director; married; wife's name, Renate; children: two sons. *Education:* Degree in engineering.

Addresses: *Office*—c/o DaimlerChrysler Corp., Epplestrasse 225, D–70546 Stuttgart, Germany; or 1000 Chrysler Dr., Auburn Hills, MI 48326.

Career

Daimler automobile company, Freiburg, Germany, apprentice mechanic, c. late 1950s, returned in 1967 and worked mostly in sales, then worked in customer service in South Africa, 1974–82, worked in Cleveland at Euclid truck unit, 1982–84, became vice–president of Mercedes–Benz South Africa, 1984, and president and CEO, 1985, then worked in truck division in Stuttgart, 1987, president of Deutsche Aerospace (later renamed Daimler–Benz Aerospace), 1989–95, chairman and CEO of Daimler–Benz, 1995–98, co–CEO of DaimlerChrysler (with Robert J. Eaton), 1998—.

Sidelights

Juergen Schrempp became chief executive officer in 1995 of Daimler–Benz, Germany's beloved manufacturer of the respected Mercedes–Benz sedans as well as fleets of trucks and other heavy equipment. There, he made his name with American–style cost–cutting practices, slashing jobs, cutting out management layers, and making hard–driving deals with unions in order to restore the

Archive Photos

firm to profitability. He also got rid of several money–losing ventures outside of its core business of automaking. After rescuing Daimler–Benz from disaster, he looked toward expanding the company by taking over some other car firm—not a surprising action in most cases, but the target in this instance was an automaker much larger than Daimler. On November 16, 1998, Daimler–Benz merged with the number three car company in the United States to become DaimlerChrysler, the world's fifth–largest automaker. Once the acquisition went through, observers waited to see whether the two companies would experience culture clash or find success by lending a hand in each others' weaker areas.

Schrempp's image as an aggressive dealmaker and a heartless hatchet man led to stern criticism from fellow Germans. However, after his successes at Daimler, he was also hailed for those very qualities. Personally, Schrempp "comes across as a macho, take–charge guy," described Karen Lowry Miller in *Business Week*. "But he is also a subtle man in many ways. He listens carefully to others before taking action. His close friends include artists, photographers, and mountain climbers, as well as other powerful executives." Though he has a reputation for heeding only the bottom line, he has at times shown keen attention to social causes, and told Miller, "Many people think emotions are not needed in business. I think emotions, what I call the stomach and the heart, are the decisive factors at the end of the day."

Schrempp was born on September 15, 1944, in Freiburg, Germany, home to the University of Freiburg. His father worked as an admissions director there, but did not earn enough to pay for his three sons' education and urged Schrempp to learn a trade. By 15, he had become distracted from school with his hobbies of skiing and dancing, so he dropped out and became an apprentice mechanic at the Daimler-Benz automobile company.

When he was 20, Schrempp met a 19-year-old woman named Renate, who became his wife a year later. They enjoyed listening to jazz in the basement clubs of Freiburg, and Schrempp eventually borrowed $25 from his father for a trumpet and learned to play without reading music. He later returned to school and got an engineering degree, earning money for tuition by playing in a wedding band and at jazz clubs. Returning to Daimler in 1967, he worked mainly in sales in Freiburg, then transferred to the company's South African unit in 1974, where he learned to speak English.

From 1974 to 1982, Schrempp worked in customer service, throwing lavish parties to help promote truck fleets. However, even as he was selling wares to prominent residents, he would openly express his views against the apartheid system. "I had to make a decision whether I was a businessman looking at the bottom line or whether I had a social responsibility," he told Rachel Konrad of the *Knight-Ridder/Tribune News Service*. "I decided the latter." He added, "When you run a big company, you are considered a capitalist, but there is something else in life. You should give the world something back." Later, South African President Nelson Mandela made him an honorary consul general to the nation.

From 1982 to 1984, Schrempp was reassigned to Cleveland, Ohio, where he sold off Euclid, a troubled heavy-truck subsidiary. Afterward, he wound up in South Africa for two more years, where he was promoted to vice-president of Mercedes-Benz South Africa in 1984, then president and CEO the following year. Schrempp moved to Stuttgart in 1987 and two years later was named head of Deutsche Aerospace, later renamed Daimler-Benz Aerospace (DASA). Throughout the 1980s, Daimler-Benz expanded rapidly, investing in industries including railways, military aircraft, and commercial jets, and Schrempp's duties involved combining all of these units into one division.

By the time he was serving with DASA, Schrempp was on the Daimler-Benz management board with other top executives and his career seemed to be on the fast track to the top. However, in 1993 he acquired 51 percent of Fokker, a money-losing Dutch airplane builder. The deal was criticized to begin with due to Fokker's financial troubles, and additionally, the timing of the deal was miserable. Airline deregulation in the United States spurred price wars among aircraft firms, causing profits to suffer; also, a recession was beginning to plague Europe. The firm lost a great deal of money for Daimler-Benz, and these woes contributed greatly to Daimler-Benz's huge losses of $3 billion in 1995 (some reports said they lost as much as $4 billion). By 1996, Schrempp halted support to Fokker, and the company eventually filed for bankruptcy

Regardless of Schrempp's missteps, he took over Daimler-Benz as chairman on May 24, 1995, from Edvard Reuter. In addition to the Fokker debacle, many of the financial troubles at the firm were due to Reuter's decision to expand into a wide range of industries, from the aerospace concerns and railways to software and consumer electronics. Schrempp immediately vowed to undo these moves and concentrate on only the most profitable areas, insisting on meeting a 12 percent profit target for all operations. To do this, he cut jobs and reorganized the company to combine all the units under more direct control. Schrempp's hard-nosed tactics were common in the United States, but shocking in Germany, where his actions were called "Uber leichen gehen," which means "to walk over dead people," according to Alex Taylor III in *Fortune*.

Back when he was head of DASA, Schrempp began to attract his reputation for cutbacks, eliminating 40,000 jobs there during the 1990s and moving about $1 billion in production work to suppliers in Asia. This drew comparisons to American business executive Jack Welch, who slashed about 300,000 jobs at General Electric, earning him the nickname "Neutron Jack" for his ability, like a neutron bomb, to get rid of people while leaving buildings standing. Schrempp was soon dubbed "Neutron Juergen" for his similar practices, and he would further this image as head of Daimler-Benz, cutting the work force by 40,000 from 1991 to 1995 and selling or shutting down 12 money-losing businesses. He also convinced local union members to cut costs, otherwise he would move even more production out of Germany.

However, investors were happy with Schrempp's tactics, as he managed a dramatic turnaround with the cutbacks. Profits increased at Daimler-Benz 78 percent from 1996 to 1997, to roughly $2.4 billion. The new chairman focused on successful areas such as car and truck production, in addition to the more successful aerospace operations, and sold off the electronics division and a stake in a French software services company. However, one person was not so thrilled: After two years of clashing with Schrempp, Helmut Werner, CEO of the Mercedes–Benz division, was forced out so that Schrempp could keep a closer eye on that core business.

By the end of 1997, Daimler–Benz had a whole new image in international business. As Taylor wrote in *Fortune*, "Long viewed as stodgy and arrogant, Daimler is now seen as progressive and fast–moving." At that year's auto show in Frankfurt, the firm unveiled a wider line of new vehicles than any other carmaker, including its first economy car to compete with the Fiat and Renault subcompacts popular in Europe. Daimler also that year added a sport–utility vehicle, built at its plant in Alabama, and announced that it was researching alternative–fuel vehicles, such as one powered by liquid methanol. And once the company began to turn around, Schrempp directed his goal of social responsibility toward his fellow Germans, training more apprentices at Daimler in hopes that young workers could put their education to use at other firms.

Meanwhile, with his attention centered on Daimler's auto business, Schrempp began to consider a joint venture with some other carmaker, possibly in Lain America or Asia. However, after meeting with Robert J. Eaton, CEO of Chrysler, at the Detroit Auto Show in January of 1998, he set his sights on the third–largest car company in America. After months of secret talks, although Daimler–Benz was the fifteenth–largest carmaker in the world and Chrysler was the sixth–largest, Daimler acquired Chrysler in the largest industrial takeover ever. The company, renamed DaimlerChrysler, had $131 billion in combined revenues in 1997 and would become the fifth–largest auto manufacturer on the globe, behind General Motors (GM), Ford, Toyota, and Volkswagen. In the meantime, Alex Trotman, CEO of Ford, stepped in to thwart the plans and suggest a joint venture, but in the end, the Ford family did not want to relinquish their 40 percent stake.

The merger seemed to be an odd fit on the surface. Though Chrysler ran the gamut from budget wheels like the Dodge Neon to more pricey sport utilities like the popular Jeep Cherokee, overall they appealed to middle class consumers. Daimler, meanwhile, was synonymous with the prestigious Mercedes Benz luxury sedans, and also offered well–built heavy trucks. However, both Schrempp and

Eaton viewed this lack of overlap as a boon. Daimler would help Chrysler pump up international sales and Chrysler could assist Mercedes in marketing their wares in North America. In addition, the two firms could merge research and development, thus saving costs. Eaton and Schrempp planned to run the new corporation side–by–side as co–CEOS, though the headquarters would remain in Germany and Eaton announced he would step down by 2001. The deal in effect made obsolete the term "Big 3," which for years had referred to America's three largest automakers—GM, Ford, and Chrysler.

However, outsiders watched to see if the deal would be as much of a benefit to both firms as they expected. Miller in *Business Week* pointed out that Chrysler had worked hard to forge a more agile environment in which product development cycles were fast and smooth, whereas Daimler–Benz, despite their improvements, still grappled with a middle–management hierarchy that could slow down decisions. Before long, four top American executives had fled the company, including Thomas T. Stallkamp, president of the firm's U.S. operations, indicating troubles at the top. By late in 1999, stock had dropped 35 percent, and reports surfaced that employee morale at the former Chrysler corporation was dismal. But some Germans, too, were disappointed with aspects of the merger; for instance, many were unhappy that English became the official company language.

In his spare time, Schrempp, who has two sons, enjoys going on safaris in Africa, mountaineering, and driving fast cars. Though it was once reported that he was arrested during a run–in with Italian police after a late–night drinking excursion with two others, John Templeton in *Business Week* noted that this was untrue: He had been picked up for an identity check and had been drinking, but the episode was just an embarrassment, not a legal issue. A chain smoker with a penchant for Cuban cigars and Marlboro cigarettes, Schrempp nevertheless keeps in shape and relaxes by working out at home on a treadmill, stationary bike, or stair machine. He lives in a contemporary home filled with art works outside Stuttgart in a woodsy area, and also owns a vacation home in Capetown and owns a game reserve near Kruger National Park in South Africa with two friends.

Sources

Business Week, August 21, 1995, p. 38; February 5, 1996, p. 56; November 4, 1996, p. 64; February 3, 1997, p. 52; February 10, 1997, p. 52; November 16, 1998, p. 82; January 11, 1999, p. 60; October 4, 1999, p. 34.

Detroit Free Press, November 11, 1999.

Economist, March 16, 1992, p. 72; July 29, 1995, pp. 5, 48; May 20, 1995, p. 62; January 25, 1997, p. 7.

Forbes, April 22, 1996, p. 165; January 11, 1999, p. 65.

Fortune, November 10, 1997, p. 144; June 8, 1998, p. 138; January 11, 1999, p. 92.

Knight–Ridder/Tribune News Service, May 29, 1998.

Time, May 18, 1998, p. 66.

U.S. News & World Report, October 4, 1999, p. 14.

Andres Serrano

Corbis Corporation

Artist and photographer

Born August 15, 1950, in New York, NY; son of Andres (a merchant marine) and Eulalia (a factory worker; maiden name, Negual) Serrano; married Julie Ault (an artist); children: daughter, Miranda. *Education:* Attended Brooklyn Museum Art School.

Addresses: *Home*—Brooklyn, NY. *Office*—c/o Paula Cooper Inc., 534 W. 21st St., New York, NY 10011–2812.

Career

Artist and photographer, 1979—. Work has appeared at numerous galleries and museums in the U.S. and Europe. Selected individual exhibitions include Leonard Perlson Gallery, New York, 1985; *The Unknown Christ,* Museum of Contemporary Hispanic Art, New York, 1986; Greenberg/Wilson Gallery, New York, 1988; Stux Gallery, New York, 1988, 1989, 1990; The Seibu Museum of Art, Tokyo, 1990, 1991; Gallery Hibbel, Tokyo, 1990; BlumHelman Gallery, Santa Monica, California, 1990; Saatchi Gallery, London, 1991; Gallery Via 8, Tokyo, 1991; *Nomads,* Denver Museum, Colorado, 1991; *KKK Portraits,* University of Colorado at Boulder, 1991; Galleri Susanne Ottesen, Copenhagen, 1991; Galleri Riis, Oslo, 1991; Institute of Contemporary Art, Amsterdam, 1992; *The Morgue,* Yvon Lambert Gallery, Paris (traveled to La T[0088]te d'Obsidienne, Fort Napoleon, La Seyne–sur–Mer; Palais du Tau, Rheims; Grand Hornu, Mons, France; Paula Cooper Gallery, New York), 1992; *Selected Works: 1986–1992* (retrospective), Feigen Gallery, Chicago, 1993; *The Church Series,* Paula Cooper Gallery, New York, 1994; *Budapest,* Paula Cooper Gallery, New York, 1994; *A History of Sex,* Paula Cooper Gallery, 1997.

Awards: National Endowment for the Arts grant, 1986; New York Foundation for the Arts grant, 1987; Louis Comfort Tiffany Foundation grant, 1989; Cintas Foundation grant, 1989; New York State Council on the Arts grant, 1990.

Sidelights

Artist Andres Serrano caused a stir in the art world and beyond in 1989 with a controversial photograph that featured a crucifix submerged in a jar of his own urine. Along with the homoerotic photographs of Robert Mapplethorpe, this piece, titled *Piss Christ,* was targeted by critics who found it to be a poor use of taxpayer funds, since the artists had received grants from the National Endowment of the Arts (NEA). Senator Jesse Helms, in particular, led a movement to prevent grants from being given for artworks deemed indecent. According to Heather Vogell in *Newsday,* he wrote that Serrano was "not an artist. He is a jerk. And he is taunting the American people."

Though the controversy eventually simmered down, it riled up enough sentiment to cause the NEA's budget to be severely curtailed. Then, another uproar came over a decade later with an exhibit at the Brooklyn Museum of Art over another artwork,

Chris Ofili's *The Holy Virgin*. The painting of the Virgin Mary splattered with dung caused New York Mayor Rudolph Giuliani to denounce it as "sick stuff," reported Vogell, and cut off a city subsidy to the museum. While The *Holy Virgin* was on display, a vandal got behind the Plexiglass covering it and flung white paint on it. The incidents recalled comparisons to the furor surrounding the Serrano piece, which meanwhile hung undisturbed at the Whitney Museum in New York, though it was attacked with a hammer in 1997 at an exhibit in Melbourne, Australia. and his exhibit was subsequently canceled.

For all the uproar, Serrano's pieces are usually technically stunning and many times aesthetically beautiful, though the subject matter often provokes feelings of disgust or wrath. Most of the pieces are shot on Cibachrome, a high–quality film usually used in click advertisements. Serrano once told Lucy R. Lippard in *Art in America* that his art is influenced by "unresolved feelings about my own Catholic upbringing which help me redefine and personalize my relationship with God. For me, art is a moral and spiritual obligation that cuts across all manner of pretense and speaks directly to the soul."

Serrano was born on August 15, 1950, the son of Andres and Eulalia (Negual) Serrano. His father, a merchant marine, was often away from home, and his mother, a factory worker who did not speak English, was frequently hospitalized for mental illness. He was raised in an Italian area of Brooklyn by his mother and grandmother and has a varied ethnic heritage—his great–grandfather was Chinese, his mother, from Haiti, is of African and Caribbean heritage, and his father was born in the Honduras but is white.

Serrano's home did not contain fine art, but it was filled with Catholic iconography such pictures of Jesus and the Madonna—although no crucifixes. Each Sunday until he was 13 he attended a local Catholic church, and the imagery left a strong impression. Serrano wanted to become an artist from a tender age, and as soon as he could begin riding the subway alone at age 12, he began to frequent New York's Metropolitan Museum of Art. "Actually, my first interest was in art history rather than in drawing or painting," he remarked to Lippard in *Art in America*. "I became fascinated with the lives of painters. My religious imagery owes a lot to Renaissance art."

At age 15, Serrano dropped out of school, but at age 17, began attending the Brooklyn Museum Art School, where he studied with African American painter Calvin Douglas and also sculpted. However, he felt he was subpar at those art forms, so he borrowed his girlfriend's camera and began to experiment with photography. After two years, Serrano left school again to pursue his career on his own. He got sidetracked working various jobs, including as an assistant art director at an advertising agency, and abandoned his art for a decade. He also became mired in drug abuse for seven years in the 1970s and into the early 1980s, but managed to quit altogether when he decided he wanted to get his career back on track. Initially, Serrano returned to photography with color landscapes, but then turned to taking pictures of raw meat. The surrealistic quality of the works recalled those of Luis Bunuel and Salvador Dali. He started producing these tableau photographs in 1983, which featured elaborate backdrops and props. Serrano's first show came in 1984 in "Artists Call Against U.S. Intervention in Central America." The pieces in this exhibit showed his interest in religious themes, such as the pagan Anti–Christian, in which a woman bows her head against a wooden pole with a deer's head mounted on it. Other works of this time include The Passion, showing Christ's head mounted over a lamb's carcass to literally display the metaphor of the sacrificial lamb; and The Rabble, a crucifix surrounded by chicken claws. By using religious iconography, Serrano aimed to make viewers uneasy with what are typically spiritually reassuring images.

Moving on, Serrano in late 1986 began to use bodily fluids in his works, telling Charles Hagen in *ARTNews*, "I'd used a lot of blood in my imagery, and so I thought I should focus in on it. I felt I could paint with fluids—they automatically had content built in." He began using milk, water, blood, semen, and urine. The inclusion of such substances, according to Amei Wallach in *Newsday*, "were at once human, religious and dangerous in the age of AIDS, particularly when juxtaposed with Christian imagery." The first in Serrano's "Bodily Fluids" series was a diptych with one side made of a rectangle of blood and the other a rectangle of milk. Serrano told Hagen that it refers to artist Piet Mondrian, known for his minimalist color– block paintings.

Of course, the most notorious in Serrano's series was *Piss Christ*. The work attracted little notice until its display at the Southeast Center of Contemporary Art in North Carolina. There, it caught the attention of Senator Helms, who was livid that federal funds had been used to support the creation of such a piece. On the Senate floor, he tore up an exhibition catalog and stomped on it while denouncing the artist. Right–wing and Christian groups joined his crusade to end funding for so–called offensive art.

Instead of drawing a mass public outcry against certain artists, though, the issue polarized free–speech and art–world advocates against the others, and created a swirl of publicity for targeted artists such as Serrano. He became a regular on the lecture circuit, and his works began to fetch $5,000 to $8,000 at galleries. Serrano's photographs were entered into collections at the Brooklyn Museum of Art and the High Museum in Atlanta, Georgia, along with the Museum of Contemporary Art in Nimes, France. Though the publicity certainly boosted Serrano's career, he remarked in *Independent on Sunday*, "I think I also helped [Helms] get re–elected. We were partners in crime sometimes you have to shake hands with the devil."

Serrano continued to produce photographs using fluids, including *White Christ*, a crucifix submerged in milk and water, as well as *Blood Cross*, a tubular crucifix filled with blood. In 1989, he created a series titled "Ejaculate in Trajectory," featuring pictures of semen sprays against dark backgrounds. Some of the works "are appropriately explosive," wrote Lippard; "others describe graceful arcs, and one is so serenely monumental it resembles Brancusi's *Bird in Space.*" She added, "These works, too, once the process is comprehended, set in motion a series of puns about conception, about art and creativity, photography and reproduction." Serrano's pictures using soiled menstrual pads were decidedly less successful. Lippard observed, "When he showed them in a photo workshop there was the inevitable disgusted mutter in the audience; piss and sperm are one thing, but *women's* bodily functions are apparently less noble."

Moving into new territory, Serrano in the early 1990s showed a series at the Stux gallery featuring outsiders one group consisted of hooded Ku Klux Klan members, the other of homeless people. The idea was spurred by the artist's earlier interest in portraits. He told Hagen in *ARTNews*, "I got to thinking, What could be more unusual than a portrait in a mask? And the Klan naturally came to mind." Through contacts in Atlanta, he managed to contact a retired imperial wizard of the white supremacist group and thus get in touch with other members. The resulting works continue his exploration of quasi–religious themes. As he cited to Eleanor Heartney in Art *in America*, "I saw the Klan in those robes and wanted to show how they see themselves as religious figures."

The other set of shots featuring the homeless, "Nomads," was inspired by photographs of Native Americans taken by Edward S. Curtis in the early twentieth century. In Serrano's eyes, street people are similar to a vanishing tribe. The artist paid his subjects ten dollars to take their pictures at a makeshift studio in the subway. Then, in 1991, Serrano introduced his "Church" series, which included shots of actual Catholic churches in addition to portraits of Catholic priests and nuns in Italy, France, and Spain. He later examined death in his 1992 series "The Morgue," in which he took close–up shots of corpses.

In 1994, the formerly maligned Serrano became a mentor to a group of inner–city high school students developing an anti–drug poster. As part of a team of three artists, including painter Alison McGoran and public art specialist Adam Simon, he worked with Jersey City's Public School 9 to develop the poster, which became a billboard that was put up statewide. Despite this leadership role, Serrano remarked, "I never like to see myself as any sort of authority figure. I'm one of them…. In a way, I certainly distrust authority as much as they do," as Laurence Chollet reported in the Bergen County, New Jersey *Record*. The students earned about $5 an hour for their time, thanks to grants from organizations to combat substance abuse and others.

In 1995, Serrano's retrospective opened at the New Museum of Contemporary Art in New York's SoHo district. As it had throughout his career, critical reaction to the show ranged from applause and fascination regarding certain works to dismissal of others. Some of his photographs, such as the "Bodily Fluids" pieces, were considered successful for the plethora of reactions in viewers and for the mischievous wit and puns that they sometimes revealed. However, at times reviewers have found his work lacking in depth; as Amei Wallach commented in *Newsday* of his portraits, "The second time you see these photographs, you walk past. You've done that. Not enough subtext, too much style." And, as Paul Elie noted of one picture in *Commonwealth*, "'Heaven and Hell' (1984), which depicts a bishop figure indifferently looking away from a nude, mutilated woman, is sheer agitprop."

Later into the 1990s, Serrano tackled another volatile topic with his show *A History of Sex*. Again, it sparked protest when religious groups in the Netherlands objected to the use of one of the photographs to publicize his retrospective. It was a shot of a woman urinating into a man's mouth. Other pieces in the collection were also disturbing, though many simply featured May–December couples juxtaposed without contact. The show received some negative reviews, including one in *ARTNews* that deemed the shots "boring." After this exhibit, Serrano expressed his intention to begin doing commercial work, and in 2000 was a runner–up for an Alfred Eisenstaedt award for his illustration accompanying a *New York Times Magazine* article about the fourteenth century mystic, Saint Catherine of Siena.

Serrano is six feet, two inches tall and soft–spoken. He married Julie Ault, also an artist, but throughout the years their marriage dissolved, though they remained friends. Serrano has a daughter, Miranda, from a relationship he had while in his early twenties. The woman left him when their daughter was an infant and he subsequently had no contact with Miranda until she was 18, when she located him at one of his openings. Serrano lives in Brooklyn in an apartment decorated with plush red and brown velvets, stained glass windows, and a wall of crucifixes. It is also filled with animal skulls, stuffed boar, bear, and deer heads, and brains in glass jars. He explained to Wallach in *Newsday*, "I like the idea of living either in a museum or church, where you don't expect people to live."

Sources

Books

Contemporary Black Biography, volume 3, Gale Research, 1992.

Contemporary Photographers, third edition, St. James Press, 1996.

Periodicals

Art in America, April 1990, p. 238; February 1997, p. 32.
ARTNews, September 1991, p. 61; June 1997, p. 126.
Commonweal, June 2, 1995, p. 18.
Independent on Sunday, May 24, 1998, p. 16.
Life, April 15, 2000, p. 112.
Newsday, January 22, 1995, p. 16; January 22, 2000, p. B6.
Record (Bergen County, NJ), August 11, 1994, p. C9.

William Shaw

Minister

Born c. 1934; son of Henderson and Effie Shaw; married, c. 1958; wife's name, Camellia; children: Timothy. *Education:* Bishop College, bachelor's degree in philosophy and religion, 1953; attended Union Theological Seminary; Colgate Rochester Divinity School, doctor of divinity degree, 1975.

Addresses: *Office*—c/o White Rock Baptist Church, 5240 Chestnut Street, Philadelphia, PA 19139.

Career

White Rock Baptist Church, Philadelphia, PA, minister, 1955, pastor, 1956. National Baptist Convention USA, elected president, 1999.

Sidelights

In September of 1999 Reverend William Shaw became head of the largest black church group in the United States when he was elected president of the National Baptist Convention USA Inc. With 43 years of experience behind him as pastor of Philadelphia's White Rock Baptist Church, Shaw beat out ten other candidates who were hoping for the post. The group was in need of a strong leader after a scandal sent the previous president to jail for five–and–a–half years, rocking its foundation. Many of the contenders subsequently called for limits on the president's power, especially in regards to financial matters.

Shaw was born about 1934 to Henderson and Effie Shaw and grew up in Marshall, Texas. Though his parents had not completed elementary school, they

were avid readers and encouraged their six children to get an education. As far back he can recall, Shaw wanted to be a minister, and he delivered his first sermon at New Bethel Baptist Church age 11. The next year, he was named valedictorian of his elementary school. From then on, his fate was sealed, and he was ordained to Gospel Ministry at 17.

Meanwhile, Shaw graduated from high school early, at age 16, as valedictorian once again. Afterward, he earned a degree in religion and philosophy, summa cum laude, from Bishop College at age 19. Subsequently he was accepted to Union Theological Seminary in New York, but needed to raise $1,300 before he could enroll. Shaw moved in with his brother in Philadelphia and found work; meanwhile, he began his affiliation with White Rock Baptist Church. Thanks to his savings and an $800 scholarship, Shaw was able to go off to graduate school, but he continued to maintain ties to White Rock.

When Shaw was in his second year of graduate school, White Rock burned down and its pastor fell ill, so the church asked him to give sermons, even though he was still a student. He faithfully made the trek each week from New York to Philadelphia, and when the pastor died in 1956, the church named Shaw then just 22 as pastor. He helped find the church a new home and oversaw its expansion while continuing to build the congregation. Charles Whitaker wrote in *Ebony*, "Dr. Shaw's pastoral manner in gentle and democratic. Though he retains a certain veto power of day–to–day decisions, White Rock is not run like his personal fiefdom." Indeed, Shaw told him, "Much of the responsibility for the caring and functioning fall in the hands of laypersons and the very capable core of clergy who assist me."

As pastor of White Rock, Shaw became a member of the National Baptist Convention USA, a coalition which began in 1880. According to their own figures, the National Baptist Convention USA represents about 30,000 churches and as many as 8.5 million members, though some say the numbers are inflated. One person who claimed that the group only counts about one million members was the prosecutor in the highly publicized trial of the convention's former president, Henry J. Lyons. In the scandal, Lyons, a minister from St. Petersburg, Florida who took the post in 1994, came under state and federal investigation in 1997 for bilking money from the group as well as other organizations and companies. Shaw who placed third in the 1994 election and several others tried to oust him at that time, with no luck.

Finally, Lyons resigned after he was convicted in February of 1999 of racketeering and grand theft. He had kept nearly $250,000 from the Anti–Defamation League of B'Nai B'rith earmarked for rebuilding black churches that had been burned down in the South, and he swindled $4 million from companies who had donated money in hopes of doing business with church members. Lyons used these funds to live lavishly, and his deeds were discovered after his wife set fire to a $700,000 home he had purchased with Bernice Edwards, the public relations director for the National Baptist Convention USA. Lyons's wife had found the deed to the home and suspected that her husband was having an affair with Edwards.

In September of 1999, at the convention's annual meeting in Tampa, Florida, 60,000 church members gathered to elect a new president. Eleven people, all men, vied for the presidency, with Shaw running on a platform of "VISA: vision, integrity, structure, and accountability," as an article in the *Christian Century* related. W. Franklyn Richardson of Grace Baptist Church in Mount Vernon, New York, who had been the runner–up to Lyons in 1994, was generally expected to win. But Shaw came out on top with 3,694 votes to Richardson's 3,451. The upset startled many, and several of those supporting Richardson walked out after the results were heard, charging that they thought the vote was rigged. But others thought that Shaw would be the right one to lead the church into a new era and redirect attention away from Lyons's misdeeds.

After his election, Shaw hired an outside firm to conduct an audit on the convention's financial status, and he called a halt to all nonessential spending. He also pledged to enact internal reforms that would pare down the president's powers, especially in money matters. A couple of ways to do this, as he proposed, would be to cut the number of presidential appointees to the board of directors, and to limit the president's term to two years. In addition, Shaw noted that he wanted to see an accurate count of the convention's membership. He was inaugurated in January of 2000.

A stately and reserved man, Shaw is perennially dressed in a conservative, dark suit and tie, except for on occasion when he is relaxing at home. He married his wife, Camellia, around 1958, and they have a son, Timothy, and a granddaughter, Brittany. Shaw has few hobbies, preferring instead to concentrate on his ministry. He received a doctor of divinity degree in 1975 from Colgate Rochester Divinity School at Crozer Theological Seminary in Rochester, New York.

Sources

Atlanta Constitution, September 10, 1999, p. A3.
Christian Century, September 22, 1999, p. 890.
Christianity Today, October 25, 1999, p. 13.
Ebony, February 2000, p. 154.
Jet, September 27, 1999, p. 7; December 13, 1999, p. 8.
Tampa Tribune, September 11, 1999, p. 12.
USA Today, September 10, 1999.
Washington Times, September 10, 1999, p. A3.

Vijay Singh

Golfer

Born February 22, 1963, in Lautoka, Fiji; son of an airplane technician/golf teacher; married Ardena Seth; children: son, Qass Seth.

Addresses: *Home*—Ponte Vedra Beach, FL. *Office*—c/o South Florida PGA, 10804 West Sample Road, Coral Springs, FL 33065–2632.

Career

Professional golfer, 1982—. Member of Presidents Cup team, 1994, 1996, 1998.

Awards: PGA Tour Rookie of the Year, 1993; won PGA European Tour Scandinavian Masters, 1994; Phoenix Open Buick Classic, 1995; Memorial Tournament and Buick Open, 1997; PGA Championship and Sprint International, 1998; Honda Classic, 1999; and Masters Tournament, 2000.

Sidelights

After a steady rise throughout the 1990s, golfer Vijay Singh captured a win at the Masters Tournament in 2000. Up to that point, he had posted several Professional Golfers Association (PGA) tournament wins, but had never won a major until the PGA Championship in 1998. For much of his career, he was often called "golf's hardest worker," according to John Garrity in Sports *Illustrated.* In addition, Mick Elliott of the *Tampa Tribune* noted that Singh is "the game's ultimate practice machine," spending the bulk of his time on the greens or hitting balls at

the range. The PGA win catapulted him into the top level of players, and the Masters victory cemented his position as a golf great, thus giving credence to his first name, which means "victory" in Hindi.

Singh was born on February 22, 1963, in Lautoka, on the South Pacific island nation of Fiji. His parents are Indian, and his father, an airplane technician, also gave golf lessons. Ever since he was a child, Singh wanted to be a professional golfer, and he would upset his father by skipping school to hit the greens. While growing up, he admired Tom Weiskopf, whose swing he emulated early on.

At age 16, Singh left Fiji to pursue his golf dreams. "There was nothing going on in Fiji for me," he told Robinson Holloway in *Golf.* "You could get a job, but you could hardly make a living out of it. I just wanted to play golf, and the only way to do that was to get out." His parents and siblings all subsequently relocated to Australia and Great Britain as well. Though Singh would become the biggest sports star to come out of Fiji, he has only returned to his native country a handful of times since leaving.

Joining the Australian Tour, Singh found that even as the best young player in Fiji, he was not prepared for the level of competition. Though he continued to improve, he could not land a sponsor. In addition, his name was marred by an incident on the Asian tour in which officials suspended him for improving his score by a stroke in order to make the cut for a tournament. Though Singh has denied cheating, calling it a misunderstanding, *Sports Illustrated* writer John Garrity insisted, "There is nothing alleged or unsubstantiated about the fact that the Southeast Asia Golf Federation suspended Singh indefinitely for altering his scorecard in the second round of the '85 Indonesian Open in Jakarta. It's also a fact that Singh was banned from playing the Australian PGA circuit—not for cheating but for failing to pay off loans and long–distance phone bills."

Exiled from professional golf, Singh gave lessons for a couple of years at a golf club on the island of Borneo, two–and–a–half hours by dirt road from civilization, teaching swings to oil riggers and lumberjacks. However, Garrity pointed out that Singh at the time of the offense was very young and driven, and since then he has never had any brushes with officials over rules. Singh then joined the Safari Tour in Africa in 1988, and joined the European Tour the next year, at age 26. He won the Volvo Open as a rookie.

In June of 1992, Jack Nicklaus invited Singh to the Memorial Tournament, where he finished an impressive seventh. The next week, he placed thirteenth at the Federal Express St. Jude Classic, and in August premiered at the Buick Open and PGA Championship. He took in a total of $70,680 for the year.

In 1993, Singh' earnings increased drastically, to more than $657,000 for 14 events. He won the Buick Classic that year over Mark Wiebe and placed second at the Nestle Invitational, and came in fourth at the PGA Championship. That year he was named PGA Tour Rookie of the Year. In 1994, Singh suffered back and neck problems and saw earnings cut in half. He placed second at the Nestle Classic and Northern Telecom Open, but made the top ten in just one other event.

However, in 1995, Singh came back to win the Phoenix Open and the Buick Classic, and had top ten showings in several other tournaments, including tenth place at the U.S. Open. But he was cut from the Masters and PGA Championship, as well as a few others. Still, his earnings for the year topped out at just over $1 million.

During the next season, 1996, Singh saw a hot streak in June and July, winning top–ten finishes at the U.S. Open and PGA Championship. The rest of the year, he landed in the top ten seven other times, but also posted many other lower finishes as well. His official winnings sunk to about $855,000. In 1997, though, Singh captured the number one spot at the Memorial Tournament and the Buick Open, and watched his earnings top the $1 million mark again.

By this point, however, Singh was still not ranked in the top echelon of golfers. Even with the other PGA wins, seven European event victories, and top finishes in 11 other international tournaments, he still had never won a major PGA tournament. That changed on August 16, 1998, when he captured the PGA Championship at Sahalee Country Club outside of Seattle, Washington, fending off a pack of competitors with major wins under their belts. The following weekend, he also won the Sprint International. That season, his winnings exceeded $2,200,000.

In 1999, Singh reiterated his place as one of the PGA's top players with his victory at the Honda Classic in Coral Springs, Florida, in March, as well as several other high finishes. He was ranked third in the All–Around category that year and took home almost the same amount of money as the prior season. The win was the eighth in his PGA career and his fifth in less than two years. Nevertheless, he was still overshadowed by high–profile players Tiger Woods and David Duval. Some observers say this is because he is not nearly as close with the media as the others. Tim Cowlishaw wrote in the *Dallas Morning News*, "He is generally polite but not all that forthcoming in interviews." Cowlishaw suggested that Singh's aloofness may be due to the media's continued focus on the 1985 incident in which he doctored his score, and wrote, "Perhaps it's time to leave Singh's past in the past. His present is intriguing enough."

Indeed, Singh grabbed the limelight in April of 2000 with his second major victory, this time at the Masters Tournament. At the outset, Elliott reported in the *Tampa Tribune,* Singh noticed on his golf bag a note from his son reading, "Dad, trust your swing." By the final round, he led Duval by three shots and had a four–swing advantage over Ernie Els. Though Duval closed the gap to one, Singh held on for the win. Alan Shipnuck wrote in *Sports Illustrated* that not only did Singh lead the others in regulation and exhibit "peerless ball striking, but more impressive was a series of recovery shots and clutch putts that trumped David Duval in a nerve–jangling showdown that lasted much of the final round." Later, in August of that year, Singh placed eighth at the U.S. Open, giving him three top–ten finishes in the last five U.S. Opens, three more than Woods.

Though Woods and Duval continued to get the lion's share of attention, after the Masters win many were amazed that Singh—always known as a reserved, lone wolf—was surrounded by a cadre of devoted family and friends. The media was also surprised to learn that he is known to those close to him as a relentless joker who loves James Bond films and Fleetwood Mac. The rangy, six–foot–two–inch Singh in 1985 married Ardena Seth, who had been one of his golf students. Their son, Qass Seth, was born in 1990, and the family has homes in Ponte Vedra Beach, Florida, and London, England. Singh dotes on his six German shepherds, and his hobbies include cricket, rugby, soccer, and the billiards game snooker. He claims that he literally owns a thousand putters.

Sources

Periodicals

Golf, September 1993, p. 51;
Sports Illustrated, August 24, 1998, p. 32; March 22, 1999, p. 13; April 17, 2000, p. 32; May 1, 2000, p. G20; May 22, 2000, p. G24.
Tampa Tribune, April 10, 2000, Sports, p. 1.
Wall Street Journal, April 11, 2000, p. A24.

Online

"Vijay Singh," PGA Tour web site, http://www.golfweb.com (August 9, 2000).

Kevin Smith

Director, producer, screenwriter, and actor

Born August 2, 1970; son of Donald (a postal clerk) and Grace Smith; married Jennifer Schwalbach (a journalist); children: daughter, Harley Quinn. *Education:* Attended Vancouver Film School.

Addresses: *Office*—View Askew Productions, 69 Broad St., Red Bank, NJ 07701.

Career

Worked at Quick Stop, Leonardo, NJ, c. early 1990s; filmmaker, 1993—; also author of comic books *Bluntman and Chronic* and some issues of *Daredevil* and *Green Arrow*. Writer, director, and producer of *Mae Day: The Crumbling of a Documentary*, 1992; and *Clerks*, 1994; writer and director of *Mallrats*, 1995; *Chasing Amy*, 1997; and *Dogma*, 1999; producer of *Drawing Flies*, 1996; and *A Better Place*, 1997; executive producer of *Vulgar*, 1998; *Big Helium Dog*, 1999; and *Clerks: The Animated Series* (television series), 2000; and co–executive producer of *Good Will Hunting*, 1997.

Film appearances include *Mae Day: The Crumbling of a Documentary*, 1992; *Clerks*, 1994; *Mallrats*, 1995; *Drawing Flies*, 1996; *Chasing Amy*, 1997; *Vulgar*, 1998; *Dogma*, 1999; and *Scream 3*, 2000.

Awards: Cannes Film Festival, Young Cinema Award, Deauville Film Festival Audience Award, and Sundance Film Festival Filmmaker's Trophy, all 1994, for *Clerks*; Independent Spirit Award for best screenplay, 1998, for *Chasing Amy*.

Corbis Corporation

Sidelights

When independent films began to have their heyday during the 1990s, Kevin Smith was at the forefront of the movement with *Clerks*, his witty depiction of disaffected youth working in the service industry. He was immediately hailed as one of the preeminent voices of Generation X for his mix of gritty, hilarious banter and personal musings. "I like to write stuff that you don't usually see on the screen," Smith stated to Benjamin Svetkey in *Entertainment Weekly*. "The conversations you have with your friends the frank sexual discussions—you never see that." Subsequently, his works have grown more sophisticated in their content while remaining sharply funny. After concentrating mainly on relationship issues in his first few endeavors, Smith in 1999 caused waves with *Dogma*, which turns its attention to religion. Though some condemned the picture as heretical even before it was made, Smith has avidly defended it as an affirmation of faith. That is not to say, however, that it has shied away from scatological and sexually–oriented humor, which remains a cornerstone of Smith's works and has helped ensured his success.

Smith was born on August 2, 1970, in Red Bank, New Jersey, and raised in nearby Highlands. He is the youngest of three children of Donald, a retired postal clerk, and Grace Smith. His father used to yank Smith out of school sometimes to go catch a matinee. "Thank God he did that," Smith remarked to Chris Smith in *New York*. "His tastes are awful, though. My dad's the kind of dude that liked *Navy SEALS.*"

Though Smith had dreamed of making his own film ever since he saw *Jaws* at age five, he did not immediately enter the career track to directing. After attending Henry Hudson Regional High School, where he daydreamed of writing for the television show *Saturday Night Live*, he enrolled in a writing program at New York City's New School for Social Research. By age 20, he had dropped out and had broken up with his girlfriend, and seemed destined solely for jobs in delis and convenience stores.

Inspiration came to Smith on his twenty–first birthday, when he and a friend went to a theater in Greenwich Village to see Richard Linklater's *Slacker*. It is a meandering film that follows around several quirky, mostly college–age layabouts, and was shot on a budget of $23,000. "I was always a big movie fan," Smith related to Kenneth M. Chanko in the *New York Times*. "I was a 'Star Wars' generation kid. But here was a movie, 'Slacker,' that had no plot, no car chases, no villain and no three acts, and yet it was really engaging because of the dialogue. And dialogue was the thing I did best." Smith was also intrigued by *Slackers* because it was set wholly in the director's hometown of Austin, Texas, which led Smith to believe he could shoot a relevant film about his environs, too.

Lured by a newspaper ad, Smith set out for film school in Vancouver, British Columbia. There, he met Scott Mosier, and the two agreed that the school was not for them. Smith did end up making one project, however—*Mae Day: The Crumbling of a Documentary*, which outlined his ordeal of a film falling through when the subject decided not to cooperate. Four months into the program—halfway through—Smith dropped out and returned to Leonardo to work at the Quick Stop. Soon, figuring that the daily human drama of selling lottery tickets and beer would make a fascinating tale, he also began working on a script based on his experiences behind the counter.

Smith finished the script for *Clerks* in 30 days and asked the Quick Stop's owners, Saral and Tralochan Thapar, if he could film on location in the store and video–rental shop. They agreed, and Smith then recruited his friend Mosier, who had graduated from the Vancouver Film School by then, as coproducer. Another film school cohort, David Klein, served as its cinematographer.

Smith raised funds by maxing out several credit cards and selling his prized comic book collection. His parents chipped in as well, and Smith also ironically got lucky when two of his cars were totaled in a storm and flood, reaping him $3,000 from the Federal Emergency Management Agency. Mosier also went into debt to finance the project. In addition, Smith signed up for a cooking class at the New School for Social Research in order to obtain a student I.D. card so he could get a discount on film stock. He immediately dropped the course once he bought his supplies.

Using a collection of friends and would–be actors from the community theater, Smith and Mosier filmed *Clerks* over the course of 21 nights at the Quick Stop in between shifts. They would shoot from 10:30 p.m. to 6 a.m., then Smith would open the store at 6 a.m., work until 11 a.m., and go home and sleep until 4 p.m. He returned to the store from 4 p.m. until the store closed at 10:30. Many a time, Mosier would fill in at the register while Smith edited film. The two of them also appeared in the picture, with Smith playing the aptly named Silent Bob and Mosier as dope–smoking Willam.

Like *Slacker*, *Clerks* is a free–form extended dialogue regarding the lives of aimless twentysomethings, but *Clerks* focuses on two main characters, Dante, a mild– mannered Quick Stop clerk who has to put up with annoying customers and bothersome friends, and Randal, a philosopher–clerk at the adjacent video store. The patrons provide an endless parade of amusements, until a dirty old man meets his end in the store's bathroom while aroused. In between dealing with this incident and doing their jobs, Dante and Randal pontificate on free will and other existential questions.

The finished version of *Clerks* had its premiere in 1993 at the Angelika Theater. Only about a dozen people, mostly friends and family of Smith, attended. Mosier noted to Smith in *New York*, "Kevin was devastated. I had to talk him down from the ledge, basically." In addition, Smith told Chanko, "After seeing the movie, my mother said, 'You spent $27,000 on this piece of trash?" However, a positive review ran in the *Village Voice*, and a scout from the Sundance Film Festival caught the opening and pushed for its inclusion. *Clerks* ended up snagging the Filmmaker's Trophy at Sundance in 1994 and the Young Cinema Award at the Cannes Film Festival in France that year as well.

Before long, Harvey Weinstein of Miramax picked up *Clerks* for $250,000 and it ended up earning $2.8 million. Smith used the funds to pay his actors and pay off his credit cards, then he purchased a Dodge Neon and a condo. He also bought back his comic books. The film initially received an NC–17 rating, the first ever to garner the industry's most restrictive rating strictly for foul language. After protests by some other directors and attorney Alan Dershowitz, the Motion Picture Association of America relented and nudged it down to an R rating. Meanwhile, Smith also directed the video for Soul Asylum's "Can't Even Tell," which appears on the soundtrack to *Clerks*.

After this early blast of success, Smith signed with the Creative Artists Agency and he and Mosier went to Hollywood to sniff out their next project. There, they were offered several abominable films. "What's really funny," Smith commented to Smith in *New York*, "is that these studio guys start off going, 'Clerks is such a really good film; it's really intelligent, it's well–written—,'" and Mosier added, "'So here, do something dumb.'" One of the possibilities they heard about was a comedy called *Beer Money*, about two young men working at a fast food restaurant called the Taco Pup who stumble across an alien who has crashed in the woods. They plan to sell him to a television show so that they can have beer money to last the rest of their lives, but when the alien heals, they befriend him instead.

Getting past the initial round of stinkers, Smith finally signed with Universal to direct 1995's *Mallrats*, which he envisioned as an updated John Hughes–type teen comedy. It features a couple of adolescents who loiter in the mall and try to get back with their girlfriends after being dumped; they embark on rollicking adventures as they try to elude security staff. In it, Smith appears again as Silent Bob, this time with Jason Mewes as his talkative colleague. *Mallrats* was generally dismissed by critics and ignored at the box office. Its budget was $6.1 million but it grossed less than *Clerks*.

Rebounding from his sophomore slump, Smith in 1997 released *Chasing Amy*, shot on a budget of just $250,000. In it, Holden (played by Ben Affleck) and his friend Banky (Jason Lee) are coauthors of a popular comic book. Holden meets Alyssa (Joey Lauren Adams, who was Smith's girlfriend for about two years at the time), who also creates comics, and he falls for her even though she is a lesbian. The film delves into an array of gender stereotypes while spinning a tale of love found and lost. Once Holden finally does woo Alyssa, he then finds out about a heterosexual incident in her past that he cannot accept. As Smith told Svetkey in *Entertainment Weekly*, "The lesbian angle is a red herring. It's really a movie about a guy who fancies himself a liberal but is forced to face his conservatism."

As with Smith's previous films, *Chasing Amy* is overall a comedy, despite the heavier themes that emerged. Critics were much kinder to this third effort, and it reaped more than $12 million. Although it still contained coarse language, many reviewers applauded the script. Svetkey called it "Smith's most maturely written, deftly lensed film so far," and Mark J. Huisman in the *Advocate* noted, "Chasing Amy eschews political correctness to explore sexual identity with more thoughtfulness that we've seen before, at least from a filmmaker who happens to be a 26–year–old straight guy." However, Huisman did complain that "The introduction of Alyssa's lesbianism is a hackneyed, amateurish moment, played for laughs at the woman's expense." Several critics, though, applauded the honest depiction of a flawed modern romance; Richard Schickel in *Time* noted approvingly, "If you loved Sleepless in Seattle, you'll just hate [Chasing Amy]."

Incidentally, the comic book that Smith featured in *Chasing Amy*, titled *Bluntman and Chronic*, was a real creation of his and was published by Oni Press. Following the success of the film, Marvel Comics hired Smith as a writer to help them relaunch their floundering *Daredevil* series, and D.C. Comics contracted him to write their relaunch of *Green Arrow*. In addition, Smith was hired to pen the script for a *Superman* film, but director Tim Burton later decided not to use it.

Moving on, Smith tackled a much larger subject with 1999's *Dogma*, which stirred controversy due to its religious themes. In this black comedy, two angels who have been exiled from heaven (Affleck and Matt Damon) plot to get back in, even though they might destroy the world in the process. An abortion clinic staffer (Linda Fiorentino), who is a distant relative of Jesus Christ, is recruited to stop them. Salma Hayek plays a stripper who doubles as a celestial muse, Chris Rock is a militant 13th apostle, and God appears in the form of Alanis Morrissette. Jay and Silent Bob also reappear as unwitting prophets.

Even before its release, *Dogma* caused an uproar because of its content, which included such elements as a discussion about the sex life of Joseph and Mary and a giant monster made of excrement. The Catholic League for Religious and Civil Rights protested the production even before filming began. Smith, however, revealed that the film grew out of a crisis of faith but helped him get back in touch with it. He was raised Catholic and was even an altar boy for several years, and continued going to Mass as an adult. However, he told to Bruce Kirkland in the *Toronto Sun*, "I was sick of going to church and not feeling any inspiration of any sort. At church, I had to say: 'Wait a minute! If this is a celebration of our faith, why does it feel like a funeral dirge?' Nobody seems to have much passion for what s going on in there." And, as Smith commented to Stephan Talty in *Playboy,* "To me *Dogma* is a reverent script. It's pro–faith, pro–God. It looks at what we built around religion." Later, various reviewers also concluded the picture was pro–faith.

Because of the controversy brimming around *Dogma,* Disney, the parent company of Miramax, decided not to release it. Subsequently, Miramax cochairs Bob and Harvey Weinstein contributed $12 million of their own money to find a distributor. Lions Gate eventually picked it up, and critics overall embraced *Dogma,* appreciating the thoughtful messages despite nitpicking at a few items. Subsequently, Smith and Mosier, who work out of their New Jersey–based View Askew offices, embarked on creating an animated series for ABC based on *Clerks.*

Despite his livelihood, Smith decided against moving to Hollywood after his relationship with Adams soured in June of 1997. Instead, he keeps a home in Red Bank, New Jersey, where he has a house full of *Star Wars* memorabilia and comics. Smith also owns a comic book store in Red Bank, and often works behind the counter. He is married to Jennifer Schwalbach, a former *USA Today* writer, and in 1999 they had a daughter, Harley Quinn.

Sources

Periodicals

Advertising Age, October 19, 1998, p. 24.
Advocate, April 1, 1997, p. 71.
Entertainment Weekly, April 11, 1997, p. 25; November 12, 1999, p. 47.
Esquire, March 2000, p. 217.
Film Comment, November 1999, p. 60.
Interview, April 1997, p. 42; October 1999, p. 180.
Maclean's, November 15, 1999, p. 16.
New Republic, May 5, 1997, p. 24.
New Statesman, November 14, 1997, p. 49.
Newsweek, April 7, 1997, p. 73.
New York, October 24, 1994, p. 50.
New York Times, October 16, 1994, sec. 2, p. 20.
People, December 12, 1994, p. 156.
Playboy, December 1998, p. 150.
Saturday Night, September 1996, p. 110.
Time, April 7, 1997, p. 76; November 15, 1999, p. 103.
Toronto Sun, September 7, 1999, p. 32.
Variety, February 23, 1998, p. A14; November 22, 1999, p. 17.
Washington Post, November 7, 1994, p. D1.

Online

"Kevin Smith," Internet Movie Database web site, http://us.imdb.com (August 28, 2000).

Suzanne Somers

Actor, singer, and entrepreneur

Born October 16, 1946, in San Bruno, CA; daughter of Frank and Marion (Turner) Mahoney; married Bruce Somers, 1963 (divorced, c. 1965); married Alan Hamel (a manager); children: (first marriage) Bruce; stepson, Stephen; stepdaughter, Leslie. *Education:* Attended San Francisco College for Women; trained for the stage with Charles Conrad.

Addresses: *Home*—Malibu, CA. *Agent*—The Chasin Agency, 190 N. Canon Dr., Ste. 201, Beverly Hills, CA 90210.

Career

Actor, singer, and entrepreneur. Began modeling, c. mid–1960s; nightclub performer, beginning 1980. Author of memoirs and books on diet and fitness. Television appearances include series *Three's Company*, 1977–81; *Goodbye, Charlie*, 1985; *She's the Sheriff*, 1987–89, *Step by Step*, 1991–98; *The Suzanne Somers Show*, 1994; and *Candid Camera*, 1998; movies *Sky Heist*, 1975; *It Happened at Lakewood Manor*, 1977; *Zuna Beach*, 1978; *Happily Ever After*, 1978; *Rich Men, Single Women*, 1990; *Keeping Secrets* (also co–executive producer), 1991; *Exclusive* (also co–executive producer), 1992; *Seduced by Evil*, 1994; *Devil's Food*, 1996; *Love–Struck*, 1997; and *No Laughing Matter*, 1998; miniseries *Hollywood Wives*, 1985; and episodes of *Ben Casey*, 1963; *Lassie*, 1965; *Rockford Files*, 1974; *Starsky and Hutch*, 1975, 1976; *One Day at a Time*, 1976; *The Love Boat*, 1977; *Six Million Dollar Man*, 1977; *Billy*, 1979; *The Ropers*, 1979; *On Stage America*, 1984; *The Late Show*, 1986; *Public People, Private Lives*, 1988; *Studio 59*, 1991; *Lotsa Luck*, and *Mantrap*, and various appearances on talk shows, including *The*

Tonight Show, The Today Show, Good Morning America, The Phil Donahue Show, Sally Jesse Raphael, and others. Film appearances include *American Graffiti*, 1973; *Magnum Force*, 1973; *Billy Jack Goes to Washington*, 1977; *Yesterday's Hero*, 1980; *Nothing Personal*, 1980; and *Serial Mom*, 1994. Has also appeared on the Home Shopping Network, on infomercials, and in various fitness videos.

Awards: People's Choice Award for favorite actress in a new series, 1977, for *Three's Company*, and 1991, for *Step by Step*; named Las Vegas entertainer of the year, 1986.

Sidelights

Suzanne Somers made her name as the bubbly, flaky–but–lovable character of Chrissy on the 1970s situation comedy series *Three's Company*, becoming one of the decade's best– known icons. However, a disagreement over her salary brought about her downfall, transforming her from an A–list star to a has–been almost overnight. Determined not to be defeated, Somers launched a career as a nightclub performer in Las Vegas before landing new opportunities in television. In the meantime, she and her husband forged a successful industry based on an unusual exercise item which grew to become one of the biggest fads of the 1990s: the ThighMaster. In addition, Somers used her business savvy to promote a line of jewelry on the Home Shopping Network. She also reaped a generous contract worth high in the seven figures for her memoirs and a series of diet and fitness books.

Somers was born on October 16, 1946, in San Bruno, California, the daughter of Francis ("Frank") and Marion Elizabeth (Turner) Mahoney. She has an older sister, Maureen, an older brother, Danny, and a younger brother, Michael. Somers's father was the youngest in a family of 13 children and dreamed of becoming a professional athlete before taking a job at a brewery and moonlighting at a liquor store to support his family. Her mother worked odd jobs at a wool company and dog food factory before she was married, then paid her tuition to secretarial school on the assembly line at Kraft. She eventually got a job with the Social Security Board of San Francisco, and later went back to work as a secretary when her children were older so that she could afford their tuition to parochial school. As Somers recalled in her book *Keeping Secrets,* her father was an alcoholic, and though her childhood seemed pleasant on the surface a nice house, family vacations, picnics, baseball games her dad's drinking lent an undercurrent of fear and violence to their lives. He humiliated his wife and children by insulting them, although he met all his financial obligations and also coached the varsity baseball team at the Catholic high school.

Somers attended Mercy High School, where her studies were affected by her father's all–night rages. She had trouble doing her homework due to the environment at home, and fell asleep in class. However, she won the lead in the school musical, Gilbert and Sullivan's *H.M.S. Pinafore,* and noted in *Keeping Secrets,* "Thank God for music. It was the only thing keeping me in school. I got A's in music." However, at age 14 she was expelled from school for writing sexually suggestive notes to a boy, even though they were all fantasy and she never sent them. She then transferred to Capuchino High School in San Bruno. There, she continued to act in school plays, her first being *Guys and Dolls,* and graduated in 1964.

After high school, Somers attended Lone Mountain College, also known as San Francisco College for Women, a half an hour from home. While there, she became pregnant and got married on April 15, 1965, to Bruce Somers, her high school sweetheart. They lived in San Francisco while her husband worked in construction and finished college. Somers, meanwhile, worked as an Avon salesperson until she had her son, Bruce Jr., in November of 1965. Afterward, she began classes at a modeling school, and found work as a nurse's aide while her husband attended law school, although he later dropped out to pursue a doctorate in sociology and eventually became a child psychologist. Unsatisfied with her marriage and her life, Somers ended up having an affair with a former teacher, who then told her husband. The marriage survived for a while, though, and later, the couple moved to a new housing development outside the city. Somers wrote in *Keeping Secrets,* "Here I was in this nondescript tract home development, married to a man with whom I felt frigid, being invited to the block coffee klatch. Is this all there is? I thought. Is this the prison to which I've condemned myself at age nineteen?"

Eventually Somers got her modeling career going. Her first assignment was to lie in traction at an American Medical Association convention, although she later appeared in advertisements. However, she was not pulling in enough money, so she took a job as a cocktail waitress. She an her husband divorced after about two years of marriage, and she began living in a small apartment in Sausalito as she raised her young son on her own. Her economic situation bottomed out and eventually she was arrested for writing bad checks.

However, Somers was starting to scrape up more modeling work, and had made a few small appearances in television shows and films. Her first breakthrough role was in a tiny part as the beautiful blonde in a convertible in the 1973 George Lucas film *American Graffiti,* and that same year, she appeared in *Magnum Force,* a Clint Eastwood movie. Both were box office hits, and the *American Graffiti* role, despite being small, won her a legion of admirers and a positive reception in Hollywood. Meanwhile, in 1968 she began an affair with Alan Hamel, a former talk show host and manager, who was married when they began seeing each other. Their relationship endured, though, and he divorced his wife and married Somers in 1977. He has two children, Stephen and Leslie, from his first marriage.

Though Somers also published a book of poetry in 1973, *Touch Me Again,* her acting work received much more attention than her literary talents. She landed a guest appearance on *The Tonight Show* with Johnny Carson after the release of *American Graffiti,* and eventually moved to Los Angeles to concentrate on her career. In April of 1977, she auditioned for the situation comedy *Three's Company,* about two women who share an apartment with a male roommate who must pretend that he is homosexual in order for the landlord to consent to the unusual living arrangement. Somers played Chrissy Snow, the stereotypical ditzy, busty blonde, and became one of the biggest icons of the 1970s, on par with Farrah Fawcett, star of the series *Charlie's Angels.*

Three's Company was goofy and formulaic virtually every plot dealt with some kind of misunderstanding that led to hilarious high jinks but it was a smash hit. It costarred Jack Ritter as Jack Tripper and Joyce DeWitt as Janet Wood, the two roommates. The top–rated series was so big, it landed Somers on the cover of 55 magazines in one year; the news magazine show *60 Minutes* also profiled her. For her role, she won a People's Choice Award for favorite actress in a new series, and was nominated for a Golden Globe in 1979. She also signed a deal to appear in feature films, and made *Yesterday's Hero* in 1979 and *Nothing Personal*, with Donald Sutherland, in 1980.

In the meantime, Somers had hired Fawcett's publicist, Jay Bernstein, to work his magic on her as well. However, he had persuaded Fawcett to leave her series after a year for bigger opportunities, and many at the ABC network held a grudge against him for it. Therefore, a lot of doors at ABC remained closed to Somers. In 1980, her husband took over managing her, and helped her forge a new image as a nightclub entertainer in Las Vegas. Somers wanted to gear up a singing career, so Hamel arranged a deal for her to appear at the MGM Grand Hotel eight weeks a year for two years, and after working on the set of *Three's Company* each day, she would rehearse her act until the wee hours of the morning. When she was on hiatus from the television series, Somers also toured various clubs across America, and also performed for U.S. navy troops aboard the U.S.S. Ranger along with Gladys Knight and the Pips and Marie Osmond.

Back on the set of her series, as Somers related in her book *After the Fall*, her relationship with her costars, Ritter and DeWitt, was deteriorating. After five seasons on *Three's Company*, when her contract was up for renegotiation, Somers asked for a raise so that she would be paid as much as Ritter. "I guess I was ahead of my time because I wanted the same money as the man," she explained to Walt Belcher of the *Tampa Tribune*. "But when I stood up for my rights, I was booted off the show and blacklisted for a decade." After she was written out of the script, Somers was cast in the media as the "greedy" star, even though the networks were making millions from her hit show. The ratings plunged after her departure and the series ended in 1984.

Weary of playing the "dumb blonde," Somers tried to land more substantial roles, but found that she had been branded a troublemaker and could not find work. In 1984, she managed to snare a high–profile turn in the musical *The Moulin Rouge*, being produced at the Las Vegas Hilton, and transformed it from a flop to a sell–out success. She was named Las Vegas entertainer of the year in 1986. By 1987, she was asked to star in a new television series, *She's the Sheriff*, about a woman who takes over as the town law officer after her husband's death. It was canceled after two seasons, and in addition, work began taking a toll on Somers, who had dropped to 92 pounds.

Taking some time off from acting, Somers wrote *Keeping Secrets*, an autobiography that deals explicitly with her father's alcoholism and its effect on her entire family. Published in 1988, it reached number one on the *New York Times* best–seller list. Subsequently, she and her family made a heart–wrenching appearance on the *Phil Donahue Show*, and Somers ended up speaking on a bevy of other talk shows as well, including *Sally Jesse Raphael, Good Morning America*, and *The Tonight Show*. She also began giving lectures at hospitals, universities, and corporations, speaking of her experiences and of forgiveness. As she wrote in her next book, *After the Fall*, "During these times, I realized the tremendous opportunity I had been given on *Three's Company*. The pettiness of my departure seemed insignificant compared with the platform I had been given as a result of the exposure and fame I had won during my years on the show. Chrissy had made me lovable and trusted. That is who my audiences thought they would meet. Instead, they met the real me; and to my good fortune, they were not disappointed." Later, she published *Wednesday's Children*, a book of interviews with people of abusive families.

Also around this time, Somers was seeking a way to keep her career going without the strain of making constant appearances. When her husband came in contact with a man trying to market a piece of exercise equipment that had been in existence for 20 years, Somers was doubtful, thinking that Jane Fonda already had the fitness market cornered. She agreed to meet with the man, though, and he showed her what he called the V–Toner, for working out the upper body, shoulders, and biceps. Somers asked if it would work on inner thighs, and he said yes. She and her husband renamed it the Thigh-Master, and asked for part ownership in the company. Somers used her picture on the product's box, and starred in infomercials touting its benefits.

In no time, the ThighMaster went from being an obscure toning device to a piece of popular culture. *Saturday Night Live* began satirizing the ThighMaster; television show hosts made frequent references to it; and it showed up in a number of popular films including *Heat, Forever Young*, and *The Nutty Professor*. Even then–President George Bush made a joke out of it in a speech. Soon, "ThighMaster" became an entry in the dictionary, and was used in a Trivial Pursuit game question. The product was selling in the millions as well. Eventually, Somers and her husband bought out the other half of the company, now called Body Solutions. She also branched out to sell a line of jewelry on the Home Shopping Network, becoming one of the early celebrities to get involved with home shopping enterprises.

In the meantime, Somers continued to appear in Las Vegas. Then, in 1991 she began costarring with Patrick Duffy in a new sitcom called *Step by Step*, an updated version of *The Brady Bunch,* about a couple who each has three children from a previous marriage. Somers found the project to be a good fit, since she and her husband had gone through many challenges raising stepchildren. Some predicted the project would be short–lived, but in fact, *Step by Step* ran until 1998. For this role, Somers won another People's Choice Award for favorite actress in a new series. Also in 1991 she executive produced and starred in a television movie based on *Keeping Secrets.* As time went on, she landed roles in a number of television movies and a cameo in the 1994 John Waters feature *Serial Mom,* then in 1998 became the cohost of a new generation of the series *Candid Camera,* along with Peter Funt, son of the original *Candid Camera* founder, Alan Funt. She also starred in a 1998 television movie, *No Laughing Matter,* playing an alcoholic mother.

By this time, Somers's main focus seemed to be on her business franchises rather than her entertainment career. Before long, she began making workout videos and added the ButtMaster to her product line, though later she told Joel Stein in *Time* that "the ButtMaster got a raw deal. There were certain religious groups that picketed stores objecting to the name. We had to repackage it as the Lower Body Exerciser." Then, Somers in 1997 penned *Suzanne Somers' Eat Great, Lose Weight,* a book that "isn't a diet; it's how to change the way you eat so you can eat what you want and never put on a pound," as she told Craig Modderno in *TV Guide.* It included more than 100 of her favorite recipes.

The next year, 1998, Somers published another autobiography, *After the Fall,* detailing her rise to stardom on *Three's Company* and subsequent decline, as well as her drive to reinvent her career. After that, she concentrated once again on fitness videos and books, including *Suzanne Somers' Get Skinny on Fabulous Food* and *Suzanne Somers' 365 Ways to Change Your Life,* both released in 1999. *Get Skinny* asserts that weight can be lost or maintained depending on which foods are eaten in combination with each other. Even though Nanci Hellmich in *USA Today* reported that "nutrition scientists say there is no research to back her theories," the work hit number one on the *Publishers Weekly* best– seller chart.

In addition to her businesses, Somers founded the Suzanne Somers Institute for the Effects of Addiction on Families. Its goal is to set up outpatient centers in every major city in the United States for treating addicts and family members of addicts. Somers and her husband live in Malibu, California.

Selected writings

Touch Me (poems), Nash, 1973.
Keeping Secrets (autobiography), Warner Books, 1988.
Wednesday's Children: Adult Survivors of Abuse Speak Out, Putnam/HealingVision, 1992.
Suzanne Somers' Eat Great, Lose Weight, Crown, 1997.
After the Fall: How I Picked Myself Up, Dusted Myself Off, and Started All Over Again (autobiography), Crown, 1998.
Suzanne Somers' Get Skinny on Fabulous Food, Crown, 1999.
Suzanne Somers' 365 Ways to Change Your Life, Crown, 1999.

Sources

Books

Contemporary Theatre, Film and Television, volume 11, Gale Research, 1993. Somers, Suzanne, *Keeping Secrets,* Warner Books, 1988.
Somers, Suzanne, *After the Fall: How I Picked Myself Up, Dusted Myself Off, and Started All Over Again,* Crown, 1998.

Periodicals

Booklist, December 1, 1996, p. 636; May 15, 1999, p. 1655.
Entertainment Weekly, September 27, 1991, p. 50; May 22, 1992, p. 20.
Family Circle, April 23, 1996, p. 15.
Good Housekeeping, September 1996, p. 26.
Ladies Home Journal, May 1998, p. 92.
Newsday, September 27, 1994, p. B4.
People, November 11, 1991, p. 99; March 3, 1997, p. 42; May 25, 1998, p. 41.
Publishers Weekly, August 25, 1997, p. 22; May 24, 1999, p. 24.
St. Louis Post–Dispatch, April 1, 1998, p. E8.
Star Tribune (Minneapolis, MN), February 24, 1998, p. 1E.
Tampa Tribune, February 18, 1998, p. 4.
Time, August 9, 1999, p. 73.
TV Guide, January 27, 1996, p. 8.
USA Today, June 22, 1999, p. 8D.

Online

"Suzanne Somers," Internet Movie Database web site, http://us.imdb.com (November 1, 1999).

Britney Spears

Singer and actor

Born Britney Jean Spears, December 2, 1981, in Kentwood, LA; daughter of Jamie (a building contractor) and Lynn (a schoolteacher) Spears.

Addresses: *Home*—Kentwood, LA. *Agent*—c/o Elephant Walk Entertainment, 9200 Sunset Blvd., Ste. 430, Los Angeles, CA 90069.

Career

Singer, actor. Appeared in television commercials; stage appearances include *Ruthless*, 1991; television appearances include series *The Mickey Mouse Club*, 1993–94. Signed to Jive Records, 1997; released debut single, " Baby One More Time," 1998, and debut album of the same name, 1999; toured with Backstreet Boys, 1998; embarked on solo tour, June, 1999.

Awards: American Music Award, favorite new pop–rock artist, 1999.

Sidelights

With a combination of youthful wholesomeness and budding sexuality, Britney Spears has become a famous teen singing sensation whose music sales have reached epic proportions. Her signature hit, "Baby One More Time," was 1999's biggest seller by a solo artist, moving more than 11 million copies, and as of spring of 2000, sales had reached 18 million copies worldwide. Also, in 1999, the single and her debut album of the same title both reached number one, making her the youngest female performer ever to accomplish this dual feat. The ellipses in her song title stand for "Hit Me," which caused many to wonder at, and to object to, the lyrics. "It doesn't mean physically hit me," Spears explained to Steven Daly in *Rolling Stone.* "It means just give me a sign, basically. I think it's kind of funny that people would actually think that's what it meant." Spears also came under fire for her racy image, which many considered inappropriate for a teenage girl. Again, she deflected the concerns, exuding an innocent persona in interviews and promising that she would never become as risque as Madonna, even though she admires the performer and aspires to have a similarly long–running career.

Spears was born on December 2, 1981, in Kentwood, Louisiana, a tight–knit community of 2,600. Her father, Jamie, is a building contractor, and her mother, Lynn Spears, teaches second grade. Spears has an older brother, Bryan, and a younger sister, Jamie Lynn. Growing up in Kentwood, about an hour north of New Orleans, she showed a natural inclination toward entertaining. She began singing and dancing at age two, and made her debut at age five singing "What Child Is This" at her kindergarten graduation. Soon, she began taking gymnastics and dance lessons. She also attended Bela Karolyi's gymnastics training camp; later, her video for " Baby One More Time," features Spears herself doing a backflip. Meanwhile, her vocal ability stemmed from her love of singing along with radio hits by the likes of Madonna and Mariah Carey. Before long, she was performing at school and in talent shows.

At age eight, Spears attended an open audition for cast members for a new incarnation of *The Mickey Mouse Club* on the Disney channel, but was considered too young despite her bubbly presence. Weary of the talent show circuit, she began making television commercials and appearing in some off–Broadway plays. In one of them, 1991's *Ruthless,* she played an evil young girl. Spears and her mother and younger sister temporarily lived in New York City, where she studied at the prestigious Professional Performing Arts School for three summers. She was also a winner on *Star Search.*

Finally, at age 11, Spears landed a position on *The Mickey Mouse Club,* filmed in Orlando, Florida. For two seasons, from 1992 to 1993, she was a cast member. Other Mouseketeers at the time included Justin Timberlake and Joshua "JC" Chasez, who later became part of the heartthrob band N'Sync; singer Christina Aguilera; actor Keri Russell of *Felicity;* actor Ryan Gosling of *Young Hercules;* and Nita Booth, who was crowned Miss Virginia 1998.

After *The Mickey Mouse Club* was canceled in 1993, Spears returned home and attended the private Park Lane high school in McComb, Mississippi, near Kentwood. However, she soon grew restless to take the stage again. As she remarked in *People,* "I did the homecoming and prom thing, and I was totally bored." She went to prom with her older boyfriend, a senior, whom she dated for two years, but the relationship ended even before she became famous. At age 15, she auditioned to be part of an all–female singing group, but decided she would prefer the solo life instead.

Spears got her big chance in June of 1997, when her dad contacted entertainment attorney Larry Rudolph. He organized an audition for her at Jive Records. They signed her to a contract at age 15 and sent her to Sweden to work with writer–producer Max Martin, who helped create hits for the Backstreet Boys and Ace of Base. However, it was Spears herself who nixed Jive's suggestion of an animated superhero theme for her video and suggested instead a naughty schoolgirl motif. The cliched fetish was one that apparently has not lost its appeal, given the level of popularity that she achieved after its release.

In coming up with the idea for the video, Spears explained that the director had an idea loosely resembling a Power Rangers theme. However, she related Daly, "I said, This is not right. If you want me to reach four–year–olds, then OK, but if you want me to reach my age group ' So I had this idea where we're in school and bored out of our minds, and we have Catholic uniforms on. And I said, 'Why don't we have knee–highs and tie the shirts up to give it a little attitude?' so it won't be boring and cheesy." Ironically, though, the school–age singer was not a student at the time. Due to her hectic career, she had no time for a traditional education, but was taking correspondence courses.

In the summer of 1998, Spears kicked off a tour of 26 shopping malls before even releasing a single on the radio. Jive Records heavily backed up the promotion, setting up a web site and sending out hundreds of thousand of postcards. Teen magazines were also pushing her heavily, making her a celebrity even before her song first aired in October. Soon, Spears toured as the opening act for the Backstreet Boys until the beginning of 1999, and landed a Tommy Hilfiger modeling contract that was tied in to the tour.

By the end of 1998, Spears's single " Baby One More Time" reached the top of the charts, and in January of 1999, her album followed. Before long, she became a headliner as she became the idol of teenage girls and the heartthrob of teenage boys. She landed numerous appearances on television shows and in scores of magazines. In 1999, Spears won an American Music Award for best new pop–rock artist. She was also nominated for a 2000 Grammy for best new artist as well, but was beat out by her former fellow Mouseketeer, Aguilera.

Especially in light of the fact that she is a practicing Baptist, some criticized Spears for her vixen image. In addition to her sultry schoolgirl video, a 1999 *Rolling Stone* photo shoot featured unmistakably Lolita–like qualities. On the cover, she wore only underwear and clutched a Teletubbies figure. Inside, she was photographed in a bra and hot pants in her bedroom, surrounded by a doll collection; in another shot, she wore a tube top and hot pants with the word "BABY" spelled out on the back as she stood next to a little girls' bicycle. This spurred a boycott by the American Family Association out of Mississippi, and caused Nestle to pull out of backing her solo tour in the summer of 1999.

Spears, however, explained in *People,* "I'm not going to walk around in hot pants and a bra on the street, but when you're an artist, sometimes you play a part." She added, "I was becoming a young woman, and it's nice to feel sexy sometimes." And, as she commented to Annable Vered in *TV Guide*, "As long as I'm comfortable, I don't worry what other people think." Still, Spears has admitted that the attention can, at times, be off–putting. She noted in *People*, "When I just want to dance and there's a lot of drunk guys just standing there staring at me, it's like, 'Eeewwww!' I have to say the older [fans] are creepy. The 40–year–olds, people who are in your face too much."

Because Spears has been stalked by admirers who have tended to show up at her Kentwood home, she finally bought her parents a newer, larger, gated house on seven–and–a–half acres in her hometown to try to prevent such episodes in the future. She continues to live with her parents, and insists that her celebrity status carries little weight in regard to household chores. "I wash the dishes. I vacuum. I clean, make my bed. I do everything, man!" she exclaimed to Laudadio in *Teen Magazine*. She admitted, though, "I don't live a completely normal life because I'm not, you know, a typical teenager who goes to school every day. But I try to make it as normal as possible."

Even though her image is undeniably sexy, Spears continues to exude a fresh–faced naturalness, despite persistent rumors that she had breast implants. She has consistently denied the accusation, explaining to Vered in *TV Guide*, "When I first signed with the record label, we took a lot of photos, and those were pictures that got used. I weighed 105 pounds; I weigh 130 now. I went through a major growth spurt." Spears also has been an opponent of body piercing, telling Marisa Laudadio in *Teen Magazine*, "I don't want to pierce anything. I think it's outdated. Belly rings and all are, like, old." As for what is current, she noted to Laudadio, "I think just being pure and doing nothing to destroy your body is cool." However, in the typical spirit of teenage fickleness, she relented and had her famous belly button pierced by early 2000.

The five–feet, five–inch Spears has naturally brunette hair that she gets lightened. She admits to being a big fan of Ben Affleck and Brad Pitt, and she avoids what she calls "party movies" that appeal to young audiences, preferring adult fare such as *Titanic*, *Stepmom*, and *Steel Magnolias*. After one viewing of the animated television show *South Park*, she deemed it "sacrilegious," according to Daly in *Rolling Stone*. Though she scoffed at reports that she was dating N'Sync's Timberlake, the two were spotted together at several functions, according to Vered in *TV Guide*. By early 2000, she was also romantically linked to Britain's young Prince William, though Spears only admitted to sending a few e–mails back and forth.

Looking ahead, Spears may return to acting. Although her scheduled guest appearances on the series *Dawson's Creek* had to be canceled due to scheduling difficulties, she may be creating a pilot for her own show, though it will have to wait until her recording and touring pace lets up. Spears in 2000 was working on a new album, which was expected to include the first original song she wrote, and after that she has plans for a global tour. She has also received a slew of movie offers, and has signed deals worth $6 million with Clairol, Polaroid, and the Got Milk? advertising campaigns. In any event, Spears hopes to avoid the pitfalls of other quickly forgotten pop princesses like Tiffany and Debbie Gibson, hoping instead to smartly manage her career to ensure its long–term success, as did Madonna. As she stated to Daly in *Rolling Stone*, "I want to be big all over the world."

Sources

Periodicals

Entertainment Weekly, March 5, 1999, p. 20; September 17, 1999, Bonus section, p. 7; December 24, 1999, p. 28.
Forbes, March 20, 2000, p. 162.
Newsweek, March 1, 1999, p. 64.
People, February 1, 1999, p. 35; February 15, 1999, p. 71; May 10, 1999, p. 114; February 14, 2000, p. 98.
Rolling Stone, April 15, 1999, p. 60.
Teen Magazine, August 1999, p. 60.
Time, December 28, 1998, p. 186; March 1, 1999, p. 71.
TV Guide, May 8, 1999, p. 30; October 9, 1999, p. 28.
USA Today, February 23, 1999, p. 1D.

Online

Britney Spears official web site, http://www.britneyspears.com (April 3, 2000).
"Britney Spears," Mr. Showbiz web site, http://mrshowbiz.go.com (April 3, 2000).

Susan Stroman

AP/Wide World Photos

Choreographer

Daughter of Charles (a salesperson) and Frances Stroman; married Mike Ockrent (a director), December, 1995. *Education:* Graduated from University of Delaware.

Addresses: *Agen*—Flora Roberts, Inc., 157 West 57th Street, New York, NY 10019.

Career

Dancer until mid–1980s; choreographer, 1980—. Dancer, *Chicago,* 1977–78; *Whoopee,* 1979, *Richard III,* 1980, *Peter Pan,* 1983; and regional and stock theater. Assistant choreographer and assistant director, *Musical Chairs* (off–Broadway), 1980; co–conceiver, *Trading Places,* Equity Library Theatre Informals, 1983; director and co–conceiver, *Living Color* (off– Broadway), 1986.

Choreographer, *Broadway Babylon* (off-Broadway), 1984; *Sayonara,* 1987; *Flora, the Red Menace,* 1987; *Shenandoah,* 1988; *Slasher,* 1988; *Rhythm Ranch,* 1989; *Don Giovanni,* 1989; *A Little Night Music,* 1990; *The Roar of the Greasepaint-The Smell of the Crowd,* 1990; *Gypsy,* 1991; *And the World Goes 'Round,* 1991; *Liza Minnelli: Stepping Out at Radio City Music Hall,* 1991; *Crazy for You,* 1992; *110 in the Shade,* 1992; *Picnic,* 1993; *Show Boat,* 1994; *A Christmas Carol,* 1994; *Big,* 1996; *Steel Pier,* 1997; *Oklahoma!* (National Theater, London, England), 1998; *Contact: A Dance Play* (also director and coauthor), 1999-2000; and *The Music Man,* 2000.

Television work includes director, *An Evening with the Boston Pops A Tribute to Leonard Bernstein,* 1989; and choreographer and co-conceiver, *Sondheim—A Celebration at Carnegie Hall,* 1992.

Awards: Outer Critics Circle Award, 1991, for *And the World Goes 'Round;* Tony Award, Drama Desk Award, and Outer Critics Circle Award, 1992, and Laurence Olivier Award, 1993, all for *Crazy for You;* Tony Award, 1995, for *Show Boat;* Theater Development Fund, Astaire Award, 1995; Outer Critics Circle Award, 2000, for choreography for both *Contact* and *The Music Man;* Outer Critics Circle Award for best Broadway musical, 2000, for *Contact;* and Tony Award for choreography and for best new musical, 2000, for *Contact.*

Sidelights

Choreographer Susan Stroman, who has been hailed for her work in Broadway musicals, is famous for a style that recalls dance eras of old and for using a variety of props in her numbers. Though her steps are not intricate, they blend seamlessly into the projects. After her first big hit, *Crazy for You,* in the early 1990s, she attracted more acclaim for *Show Boat* and *Big.* In 2000, she was twice nominated for a Tony Award for choreography, for the 1999 efforts *Contact* and *The Music Man,* and won her third Tony for *Contact.*

A native of Wilmington, Delaware, Stroman once told Hilary Ostlere in *Dance Magazine,* "I always wanted to be a choreographer even when I was so little I hardly knew what the word meant." Though her father sold instruments and appliances by day, he was also a self–taught musician. Stroman recalled sitting under the grand piano as he pounded out show tunes, standards, and contemporary hits. "All our family—Mom, Dad, my brother and sister—have music in us, and when I listened to those tunes I visualized the music and saw people dancing," she noted to Ostlere.

Early on, Stroman's parents recognized her musical ability and her dancing talent. When she was five, they sent her to the Anna Marie Dance Studio in Wilmington, Delaware, and every Saturday they would encourage her by turning on *American Bandstand*. They also showed her old films featuring dancers Fred Astaire and Ginger Rogers, and this would influence her style later in her life. She remarked to Ostlere, "Astaire and Hermes Pan's way of incorporating props into their routines particularly impressed me."

Eventually, Stroman studied ballet at James Jamieson's Academy of the Dance, but her heart stayed with jazz and tap. In high school, she choreographed the halftime shows at football games. Stroman went on to major in theater at the University of Delaware while continuing to study dance at the Delaware Center for Tap and Jazz.

Though Stroman was determined to become a choreographer, she knew she could not break into the business in New York City without first getting work as a dancer in order to learn the city and the business. After graduating, she earned parts around the Wilmington area, then toured with the cast of *Chicago* in the late 1970s. Subsequently, Stroman landed small dancing roles in Broadway shows such as *Whoopee*, 1979, and began to work extensively in stock and regional theater.

In 1987, Stroman got her big break when director Scott Ellis hired her to choreograph an Off–Broadway revival of *Flora, the Red Menace*. It premiered at a tiny Greenwich Village venue that Stroman thought would not attract much attention, but it allowed her to become friends with John Kander and Fred Ebb, who wrote the play. She would later work with them again in 1991 on their successful Off–Broadway revue *And the World Goes 'Round*, which ran for over a year. Stroman won her first award, from the Outer Critics Circle, for that project. *Flora* also attracted to the audience producer Hal Prince and entertainer Liza Minnelli, who had been in the original. Later, when Minnelli needed a choreographer who could tap dance, she recruited Stroman for her show *Liza—Stepping Out at Radio City Music Hall.*

Meanwhile, in 1989 Prince hired Stroman to choreograph *Don Giovanni* for the New York City Opera. She then ventured into directing with the PBS special *An Evening with the Boston Pops—A Tribute to Leonard Bernstein*. In addition, she choreographed New York City Opera's *Little Night Music,* which was broadcast on PBS in 1990.

However, it was 1992 before critics began to hail Stroman began as the next big thing in the dance world. That year, she choreographed the smash Broadway hit *Crazy for You,* with dances based on those from George and Ira Gershwin's 1930 work *Girl Crazy*. Reaction was overwhelming, with some reviewers comparing Stroman to the likes of Bob Fosse, Tommy Tune, and even George Balanchine. For this work, Stroman won a Tony Award, Drama Desk Award, and Outer Critics Circle Award in 1992 and a Laurence Olivier Award in 1993. Then, in 1995, she won another Tony Award for choreography for the 1994 musical *Show Boat*.

Subsequently, Stroman in 1996 worked on the blockbuster *Big,* a stage adaptation of the popular 1988 film starring Tom Hanks. The work is about a 13–year–old boy who suddenly inhabits the body of a 30–year–old man and finds being a grownup is not as enchanting as he thought it would be. Though the tale did not initially lend itself to dance numbers, Stroman felt the numbers worked well after some rewriting.

For *Big,* Stroman made five trips to toy store FAO Schwartz to find props, and also scouted malls to help come up with dance moves. She eventually incorporated hip–hop, "signal" dancing including handshakes, finger snaps, and waves and other moves from the world of adolescents. Stroman was impressed with the turnout when the show called for auditions. "Eight hundred teenagers turned up!" she exclaimed to Ostlere in *Dance Magazine.* "They came from New Jersey, Philadelphia, New York, and Connecticut. And you know, it was exciting that so many teenagers are interested enough in theater to audition just on spec. If we don't introduce them to theater now, we'll never have a future Broadway. We need young audiences, too."

In 1997, Stroman teamed again with Kander and Ebb on *Steel Pier,* a musical about marathon dancing, then later that year also choreographed *A Christmas Carol* at Madison Square Gardens. The next year, she worked on an updated version of the workhorse musical *Oklahoma!* at London, England's National Theatre. Kate Kellaway wrote in the *New Statesman,* "Susan Stroman's choreography is tremendous, with cowboys flying through the air as if they were human lassos."

Stroman saw another outstanding season on Broadway in 1999 and 2000 with two projects, the original *Contact: A Dance Play* and a revival of the 1957 blockbuster *The Music Man*. As with *Oklahoma!*, she received permission from the respective estates in order to tinker with the dance arrangements in *The Music Man*. Jack Kroll raved in *Newsweek*, "Director–choreographer Susan Stroman's rousing revival does brilliant justice to this all–American classic."

For *Contact*, not only did Stroman handle the choreography and direction, but she was also listed, along with John Weidman, as its author, due to the fact that the dancing was such an integral part of the storylines. She and Weidman joined forces to come up with a creative new form in which three "short stories" are depicted primarily by dancers trained in acting. Stroman explained to Susan Reiter in *Newsday*, "All three [segments] deal with fantasy. And they all involve connecting."

The first segment, "Swinging," introduces a trio of dancers decked in eighteenth– century garb but moving to Rodgers and Hart's "My Heart Stood Still." The scene is based on a famous Jean–Honoré Fragonard painting, *The Swing*. The next episode, "Did You Move," is set in an Italian restaurant in 1954; in it, a homemaker uses her daydreams to escape subordination by her husband. The third piece, comprising the second act, is the longer "Contact," which tells the tale of a suicidal man who meets an exquisite woman in a yellow dress at a present–day swing club. The entire show was danced to prerecorded music rather than a new score. Terry Teachout wrote in *Time*, "All this may sound implausible on paper—how can you have a musical without singers?—but the results are magical."

Almost universally, critics were enthused about *Contact* because of its strong intermingling of dance and plot and due to its appealing characters. Stroman explained her involvement in the project to Reiter, stating, "In every show I do, the dance is always about carrying the show along. Since I'm a choreographer for the theater, my work is always about plot and character, developing dance to propel a story line. It just so happens that this time it's my story, one I've created with John Weidman."

Even before it officially opened, *Contact* sold out its run at the Mitzi Newhouse Theater thanks to word–of–mouth. It moved to Broadway's Vivian Beaumont Theater in March of 2000, and also that year, Stroman won her third Tony for choreography for the project. It also won a Tony for best new musical, despite some grumblings that it used canned music and did not have any singing. The lead actors, Boyd Gaines and Karen Ziemba, also took home Tonys for their performances. In addition, Stroman in 2000 picked up two more Outer Critics Circle Awards, for choreography for both *Contact* and *The Music Man*, and for best Broadway musical for *Contact*.

Stroman's success with *Contact* and *The Music Man* was even more remarkable considering the personal trauma she experienced around the time those shows opened. In December of 1995, she had married director Mike Ockert, whom she met while working on *Crazy for You*. He was later diagnosed with leukemia and died at age 53 in late 1999. To cope with the loss, Stroman kept busy with her career, choreographing the film *Center Stage*, about up–and–coming ballet dancers; collaborating with Mel Brooks on a stage version of his zany film *The Producers*; and creating new musicals of her own. "I truly believe in the power of musical theater," Stroman told Patrick Pacheco in *Newsday*. "Theater's never let me down yet."

Sources

Daily Telegraph, July 10, 1998.

Dance Magazine, May 1992, p. 36; April 1996, p. 63; December 1999, p. 64; February 2000, p. 64; August 2000, p. 37.

Harper's Bazaar, January 2000, p. 76.

Newsday, October 3, 1999, p. B2; March 30, 2000, p. B2; April 21, 2000, p. D11.

New Statesman, July 24, 1998, p. 41.

Newsweek, May 5, 1997, p. 70; May 8, 2000, p. 79.

New York, April 29, 1996, p. 36.

Time, October 18, 1999, p. 104.

Variety, December 22, 1997, p. 72; October 11, 1999, p. 162; October 18, 1999, p. 47; May 8, 2000, p. 206.

Hilary Swank

Actor

Born July 30, 1974, in Bellingham, WA; daughter of a military officer; married Chad Lowe (an actor), September 28, 1997.

Addresses: *Agent*—Kevin Huvane, Creative Artists Agency, 9830 Wilshire Blvd., Beverly Hills, CA 90212.

Career

Actor. Television appearances include episodes of *Growing Pains, Evening Shade,* and *Harry and the Hendersons* ; series *Camp Wilder,* 1992; *Leaving L.A.,* 1997; and *Beverly Hills, 90210,* 1997–98; and movies *Cries Unheard: The Donna Yaklich Story,* 1994; *Terror in the Family,* 1996; *Dying to Belong,* 1997; and *The Sleepwalker Killing,* 1997. Film appearances include *Buffy the Vampire Slayer,* 1992; *The Next Karate Kid,* 1994; *Sometimes They Come Back Again,* 1996; *Kounterfeit,* 1996; *The Way We Are,* 1997; *Heartwood,* 1998; and *Boys Don't Cry,* 1999.

Awards: Boston Society of Film Critics Award, Gijon International Film Festival Award, Los Angeles Film Critics Association Award, New York Film Critics Circle Award, Stockholm Film Festival Award, and Toronto Film Critics Association Award, all for best actress, and National Board of Review Award for breakthrough performance by an actress, all 1999, all for *Boys Don't Cry;* Academy Award, BSB Movie Brazil Award, Broadcast Film Critics Association Award, Chicago Film Critics Association Award, Dallas–Forth Worth Film Critics Association Award, Florida Film Critics Circle Award, Golden Globe Award, Golden Satellite Award, Independent Spirit Award, and Southeastern Film Critics Association Award, all for best actress, Las Vegas Film Critics Society Sierra Award for best actress and most promising actress, and ShoWest Award for female star of tomorrow, all 2000, all for *Boys Don't Cry.*

Sidelights

In 1999, female actor Hilary Swank went from being a virtual unknown to a celebrated award–winner with one poignant role. Cast as Brandon Teena in *Boys Don't Cry,* she portrayed a young Midwestern woman with a confused gender identity who had changed her name and began to pass for being male. The true story ended in tragedy after some of her male friends discovered her secret. She was raped and later killed, in 1993. Swank transformed herself as completely as possible for the part, and ended up stunning audiences and critics, who raved about her performance. For her effort, she won an armload of prizes for best actress in 1999 and 2000, including an Academy Award, Golden Globe, Golden Satellite Award, Los Angeles Film Critics Association Award, New York Film Critics Circle Award, and several others.

Swank was born on July 30, 1974, in Bellingham, Washington, a college town north of Seattle. She loved the outdoors, and enjoyed hiking, rafting, biking, and all kinds of sports. She once told Malissa Thompson in *Seventeen*, "I'm completely a tomboy. I know how to do everything play baseball, soccer, football, you name it. I can't stand it when girls act like they can't throw a ball or climb a tree or hike or something." In addition, she competed as a swimmer in the Junior Olympics and Washington State championships, and was ranked fifth in the state in gymnastics. Swank's early ambition was to become an astronaut. "Only I found out you had to get straight A's in science," she told Stephen Schaefer in *USA Today*. "I decided to act."

At a young age, Swank began to get involved in local theater and school plays, in addition to taking drama courses. One of her earliest roles, when she was in fifth grade, was playing Mowgli in a local production of *The Jungle Book*. Her mother decided to encourage her by moving to California. Swank's father, a military officer, and her mother separated when she was a teenager, and her older brother had also moved out, so it was just the two of them. In 1990, they found a $500 a month one–room flat in Los Angeles, and she began attending South Pasadena High School. Before long, she landed an agent.

Starting out, Swank landed guest parts in sitcoms like *Growing Pains, Evening Shade,* and *Harry and the Hendersons*. She snagged her first film role as the title character's best friend, Kimberly, in 1992's *Buffy the Vampire Slayer*. That same year, Swank landed a regular spot on the series *Camp Wilder*. In 1994, she had a major supporting role in the television movie *Cries Unheard: The Donna Yaklich Story,* starring Jaclyn Smith as a woman trapped in an abusive relationship.

Also in 1994, Swank started to increase her profile with a role as lonely orphan Julie Pierce in *The Next Karate Kid*. Competing against 500 others, she was one of seven finalists for the part. In the end, her predisposition toward athletics cinched her the job. She not only read lines, she also had to demonstrate spin–kicks and other moves in order to prove that she could handle the physical aspects required. After winning the audition, she spent five hours a day training with martial arts expert Pat Johnson in order to prepare for the part.

However, the film was a dud, and Swank's career did not soar right away. She toiled for a few years in low–budget films like the 1996 horror flick *Sometimes They Come Back Again,* and more television

movies. In 1997, she wound up on the popular prime–time drama series *Beverly Hills, 90210* as single mother Carly Reynolds. However, her character moved out of town after 16 episodes. Some of Swank's other projects included a small part on the short–lived ABC series *Leaving L.A.,* 1997, and a starring role in the television movie *The Sleepwalker Killing,* 1997. She also was a supporting cast member in the German–made *The Way We Are,* 1997, a comedy/drama heavy on sex scenes.

Swank's breakthrough role came in 1999's *Boys Don't Cry* playing Brandon Teena, a Nebraska teenager in a small blue–collar town who changes her name from Teena Brandon and begins dressing like a boy and passing for male. Swank went to the audition with her breasts taped down, a sock stuffed in her pants, and her hair hidden in a cowboy hat, wearing clothes she borrowed from her husband. The director, Kimberly Peirce, wanted someone relatively unknown for the part so that the character would be more true–to–life, and searched for three years to find the perfect actor. At an audition, she did not even recognize Swank in costume.

To gear up for the part of Brandon Teena, Swank began working out to lose body fat and accentuate her prominent jawline. In addition, she cut off her long brown hair, consciously began to speak in a deeper register, and practiced her Midwestern accent by listening to tapes that her cousin sent her from Iowa. She developed her masculine swagger and mannerisms from imitating her father.

However, Swank's most intensive preparations were mental. She read transcripts from Teena's murder trial, and for a month before the shoot, she lived in disguise, trying to pass as a man around Los Angeles. Director Peirce related to Dave Karger in *Entertainment Weekly* , "I said to her, 'Go pass for a boy for four weeks. And if people discover you, you better go back home and feel embarrassed. Feel terrified about what it means to be an imposter.'" Swank added to Karger, "I don't think I was really prepared for what I went through. There were people who couldn't figure out what I was. They didn't look me in the eye. I was treated poorly by people in stores, people that I had known as Hilary. I cried for two days straight."

For the six weeks of making the film, Swank continued to pass for male on the set and off. A few weeks into the shoot, she told Robert Abele in *Premiere*, "I felt I'd lost every inch of femininity." The more explicit scenes were extremely hard on her as well, especially since the film was generally shot in chronological order, which is a rare occurrence in the business. "Simulating the rape scene was a terrifying ordeal," she noted to Louis Hobson in the *Calgary Sun.* "The other actors were so understanding, but after a while your brain can't differentiate. Worse still was that bathroom scene where they force me to strip. I could just feel how humiliating and terrifying that must have been for Teena. It made me physically ill." Swank's honest depiction of Teena and the long list of awards that she racked up for it sent her into the upper echelon of Hollywood. Costar Chloe Sevigny, who played Teena's girlfriend, was also nominated for an Academy Award.

On September 28, 1997, Swank married actor Chad Lowe, younger brother of actor Rob Lowe. They met at a Hollywood Athletic Club party and fell in love at first sight, according to Lowe, and they later appeared together in the film *The Way We Are.* They wed after four years of being together. Their household includes two dogs, a cat, a parrot, and a bunny. During the time that she was living as a man before and during the making of *Boys Don't Cry,* Swank introduced herself to people as her "brother," James. Though other unknowns have been catapulted into fame by winning the Oscar, some, including Elizabeth Shue (*Leaving Las Vegas*), Pauline Collins (*Shirley Valentine*) and Mary McDonnell (*Passion Fish*), seemed to fizzle out. Swank is hoping to sidestep that pitfall, but she is not worrying inordinately about it. As she remarked in *Time,* "A lot of people in my position might be scared this moment will pass. But if you just have fun and enjoy it, you'll be doing the right thing. You hope you make good choices and things fall into place. If they don't, well, that's fate."

Sources

Periodicals

Calgary Sun, March 7, 2000, p. 32.
Dallas Morning News, October 23, 1999, p. 5C.
Edmonton Sun, February 18, 2000, p. WE4.
Entertainment Weekly, October 15, 1999, p. 50; October 29, 1999, p. 23; March 1, 2000, p. 36.
InStyle, February 1998, p. 203.
Newsweek, October 11, 1999, p. 85.
People, February 14, 2000, p. 53.
Premiere, November 1999, p. 46.
Seventeen, September 1994, p. 86.
Time, January 17, 2000, p. 88.
USA Today, October 22, 1999, p. 14E.
Variety, September 6, 1999, p. 61; January 3, 2000, p. 53; January 31, 2000, p. 8.

Online

"Hilary Swank," Internet Movie Database web site, http://us.imdb.com (April 18, 2000).
"Hilary Swank," Mr. Showbiz web site, http://mrshowbiz.go.com (March 23, 2000).

John J. Sweeney

Labor union leader

Born John Joseph Sweeney, May 5, 1934, in New York, NY; son of John (a bus driver) and Patricia (a domestic worker) Sweeney; married Maureen Power (a schoolteacher); children: John, Patricia. *Education:* Iona College, degree in economics, 1956.

Addresses: *Home*—Bethesda, MD. *Office*—AFL–CIO, 815 16th St. NW, Washington, DC 20006.

Career

Formerly employed as a grave digger, building porter, and IBM clerk; International Ladies Garment Workers Union (now Union of Needletrades, Industrial and Textile Employees–UNITE), researcher, 1956; Building Service Employees International Union (now Service Employees International Union SEIU), New York City Local 32B, contract director, 1960–76, assistant to the president and executive board member, 1972–80, vice president, 1973–76, president, 1976–81, national headquarters president, 1980–81; AFL–CIO, Washington, DC, vice president, 1981–95, president, 1995. Member, American Arbitration Association; Catholic Youth Organization; Citizen–Labor Energy Coalition; American Red Cross; Asian American Free Labor Institute; George Meany Labor Studies Center; Iona College; Federal Mediation and Conciliation Service; AFL–CIO Committee for Change; American Center for International Labor Solidarity. *Military service:* U.S. Army, 1943–46.

Awards: Workers Defense League of New York, David L. Clendenin Award, 1981; Eighth Annual John H. Fanning Conference on Labor–Management Relations, Quirk Award, 1983.

AP/Wide World Photos

Sidelights

John J. Sweeney is president of the American Federation of Labor and Congress of Industrial Organizations (AFL–CIO), a large and powerful collection of 68 labor unions. It represents about 13 million of the nation's 16.5 million unionized workers, including doctors, teachers, engineers, musicians, construction workers, miners, pilots, carpenters, bakers, and more. Sweeney has been a force in labor since his early career with the International Ladies Garment Workers Union, but spent most of his career with the Service Employees International Union, which grew to more than a million members under his leadership. The AFL–CIO and its unions are driving forces in the lives of unionized workers on subjects such as wages, safety, and protection from discrimination. They have also been influential in pushing for legislative changes that affect all employees, on topics ranging from health coverage and minimum wage to family and medical leave. Since it has much political impact, the AFL–CIO has an especially high profile in election years. Moving into the year 2000, the media watched closely to see who received backing from the federation and how much.

Sweeney was born in the Bronx borough of New York City on May 5, 1934, the son of Irish immigrants. His father, John J. Sweeney drove a city bus and belonged to the Transport Workers Union. His mother, Patricia, was a domestic worker. Sweeney and his siblings grew up in a strongly pro–union household, and as a child, he would often accompany his father to union meetings. There, he would hear speeches by the controversial union leader Michael J. Quill. He also accompanied his father on a successful strike to reduce transit employees' workweek from 48 to 40 hours, and from six days to five.

When Sweeney was 11, his family moved to Yonkers, New York. He attended the St. Barnabus parochial school and then graduated from Cardinal Hayes High School. Afterward, he attended another Catholic institution, Iona College, in nearby New Rochelle. In 1956, Sweeney graduated with a degree in economics "and an appetite for political action," as Lee Dembart reported in a *New York Times* profile. As a student, Sweeney worked as a grave digger and then a building porter to pay his tuition, and became a union member at that time.

After graduation, Sweeney landed a job as a clerk at IBM. Soon, though, he took a pay cut to two–thirds of what he was earning to join the International Ladies Garment Workers Union as a researcher in 1956. Eventually, he met Thomas R. Donahue, a union worker for what was then called the Building Service Employees International Union (BSEIU), which was chartered by the Americal Federation of Labor in 1921. It eventually expanded to include office workers, and during the Depression became the first union to organize public sector employees and those in the health care field. Donahue asked Sweeney to take the job of contract director for the union's local 32B in New York City.

Starting with the 32B in 1960, Sweeney began to climb the ladder. He later was promoted to assistant to the local's president, and the union was renamed the Service Employees International Union (SEIU) in 1968. In 1972 he was named an executive board member, and made a vice–president the following year. He was elected president of Local 32B in 1976, which then had 45,000 members. Three months after taking office, Sweeney made headlines when he ordered a surprise strike of maintenance workers at New York City buildings. For weeks, the unions had been negotiating with the New York Realty Advisory Board, but a day before the deadline, Sweeney called the strike. Both sides agreed that virtually no progress had been made in talks. After 17 days, the groups struck a deal to increase wages. Sweeney led another successful strike in 1979, two years after 32B merged with local 32J to form one of the AFL– CIO's largest locals.

In 1980, Sweeney was elected president of the SEIU, which then included about 625,000 members. He and his family then moved from New York to Washington, D.C., where the union's national headquarters were located, though he continued to serve as president of 32B until mid– 1981 as well. After Sweeney became president, the SEIU made several gains. First, it joined with 9 to 5, the National Association of Working Women, and together spearheaded an effort to unionize office workers. Then, in 1983, along with the United Food and Commercial Workers Union, the SEIU began to unionize workers at the nation's largest nursing home chain, Beverly Enterprises. Other organizing efforts included steps to unionize home health–care employees and maintenance workers.

In addition, the SEIU in 1986 began to push its "Work and Family Campaign," which eventually led to federal legislation on family and medical leave as well as employer–paid health insurance and an increase in the minimum wage. It has also made headway in safety concerns and protecting against sexual harassment and discrimination. The SEIU also began to argue for national health care reform back in the late 1980s, and initiated efforts to organize low–income workers in the South.

However, perhaps the most notable accomplishment of the SEIU under Sweeney was the union's swelling membership at a time when the percentage of American workers represented by unions was shrinking. During the 1980s, throughout the administrations of Presidents Ronald Reagan and George Bush, the climate was not agreeable for unions. This was epitomized by strike–breaking tactics such as those that Reagan used on air traffic controllers. But by Sweeney's fourth four–year term, in 1993, the SEIU had doubled in size to one million members, making it the first AFL–CIO affiliate in 20 years to reach that figure. About half of that was due to mergers with other unions, such as independent public employee unions and larger groups like the National Association of Government Employees.

Sweeney devoted a third of the SEIU budget to organizing efforts, as opposed to the usual five percent at most unions. By the mid–1990s the SEIU was the nation's third–largest labor union, after the International Brotherhood of Teamsters and the American Federation of State, County, and Municipal Employees (AFSCME). It included professions ranging from lawyers to police officers to geologists. In addition, Sweeney worked to diversify the union ranks. About half of the members in the mid–1990s were female, and 17 percent were African American. Also, the SEIU was the only labor group to include a gay rights caucus.

Despite some gains, unions continued to see hard times throughout the 1990s. As of 1996, only 11 percent of private workers were unionized, as opposed to the 1950s, during which about a third of all workers were organized. However, the AFL–CIO, the umbrella group of labor, had been doing little to address falling numbers and harsher conditions for workers, such as downsizing, skyrocketing health care costs, and a decline in real income. As a result, the union's low–profile leader since 1979, Lance Kirkland, was coming under fire.

In 1995, Sweeney suggested to Kirkland that he retire and allow his heir apparent, Donahue at that time the AFL–CIO's secretary treasurer to run for president of the union federation. However, Kirkland soon declared that he planned to run again, and Donahue subsequently announced his retirement, so Sweeney the entered the race. After that, Kirkland retracted his earlier decision and said that he would not seek another term and would retire in August of 1995. Donahue was then named interim president until the October, 1995 elections, and he also went back on his earlier statement and declared his candidacy.

Because Sweeney was involved with so many committees and had served as vice–president of the AFL–CIO's Public Employee Department since 1981, he easily obtained the backing of leaders of several of the larger unions. He won the election on October 25, 1995, by a vote of 7.3 million to 5.7 million, and took office that same day. His running mates were Richard Trumka, the president of the United Mine Workers union, who became secretary–treasurer, and Linda Chavez–Thompson, the executive vice–president of AFSCME, who became executive vice–president. This made her the first minority to enter the top leadership ranks of the AFL–CIO.

As during his reign at SEIU, Sweeney immediately directed efforts at adding numbers to the union, especially more women and minorities. This included $20 million to be spent on organizing drives, particularly in Southern states. In 1997, the AFL–CIO increased its numbers by 400,000. As usual, pushing for wage increases were also a high priority. As Sweeney noted in a speech, according to Robert T. Gray in *Nation's Business*, "America needs a raise. Profits are up, productivity is up, executive compensation is up, and the stock market is up; worker wages and health benefits and pensions are down." He also warned of corporate mergers that left thousands of employees in the lurch, and suggested that business and the government join together to provide job retraining.

In addition, just after his election, Sweeney emphasized the importance of mobilizing voters to cast ballot for union–friendly candidates. The AFL–CIO in 1996 sponsored a "Union Summer" youth activism drive in which college students were recruited to campaign for certain candidates as well as help organize workplaces. It also led a "Union Fall" devoted to purchasing advertising to support union–endorsed candidates. Though many have criticized political contributions by unions, especially since they almost universally go to Democrats, Jonathan Cohn pointed out in the *New Republic*, "Labor is no more partisan than other nominally independent groups such as the Christian Coalition and the National Rifle Association, and business still outspends labor by seven–to–one."

Still, the AFL–CIO is indeed a powerful lobby. In 1996 they spent $35 million on political activities, and were planning to spend "lots more" than that in 1998, as Sweeney told Jim McTague in *Barron's*. Then, in early 2000, as America was starting to gear up for the fall's elections, Sweeney announced that the AFL–CIO would spend about $40 million to elect candidates supporting workers, the highest amount ever. "This year we are conducting the broadest and most intensive program we have ever conducted," he told Steven Greenhouse in the *New York Times*. Sweeney also said that labor had mobilized 1,600 union officials and members to assist with the project four times as many as in 1998. He also noted that efforts would be spread over 35 states and focus on 71 "swing" Congressional districts (those that were more likely to be up for grabs by either party). Not to mention, a large part of the drive would be to put Vice President Al Gore into the White House, despite his support of a trade pact with China.

Also in early 2000, Greenhouse reported, "Union membership nationwide rose faster last year than at any time in the past two decades." He cited a Bureau of Labor Statistics statement that announced union membership had increased 265,000 to 16.5 million, which included 112,000 private sector workers. Labor leaders such as Sweeney asserted that their organizing efforts had begun to pay off, though he told Greenhouse, "These numbers show we've got this train rolling, and it's picking up speed, but we're not at our destination yet." Still, the overall percentage of unionized workers remained steady, at 13.9 percent in 1998 and 1999, due to a 2.7 million increase in the number of total jobs. That number was still up from previous years, but was a far cry from the earlier heyday of the unions. But many were optimistic that so much of the growth came from the private sector.

Sweeney has co–edited a study about labor issues and co–written two books on the topic, including *America Needs a Raise: Fighting for Economic Security and Social Justice*, 1996. He is married to Maureen Power, formerly a schoolteacher, and they live in Bethesda, Maryland. They have two children, John (a chef) and Patricia, who also works for the AFL–CIO. Sweeney's hobbies include golf and bowling, though he once told Dembart in the *New York Times*, "My golf score should be my bowling score, and my bowling score should be my golf score."

A soft–spoken man with a high–pitched voice, Sweeney has a low–key manner in the board room but has no problem hitting the streets on a picket line to support his fellow union members. He received the Workers Defense League of New York's David L. Clendenin Award in 1981, and at the Eighth Annual John H. Fanning Conference on Labor–Management Relations in 1983, he was presented with the Quirk Award. Commenting on the perception among many Democrats that unions are "just another special interest group," as Steven Greenhouse put it in the *New York Times*, Sweeney replied that it was unfair but added, "I don't get upset being referred to as a special interest. If representing American workers is a special interest, then I'm proud to represent that special interest."

Sources

Books

Profiles of American Labor Unions, second edition, Gale Research, 1998.

Periodicals

Barron's, December 15, 1997, p. 30.
Business Week, February 17, 1997, p. 56.
Challenge, January–February 1997, p. 127.
Fortune, September 28, 1998, p. 177.
Industry Week, July 5, 1993, p. 38.
National Catholic Reporter, January 12, 1996, p. 3.
Nation's Business, February 1996, pp. 16, 18.
New Republic, October 6, 1997, p. 21.
New York Times, May 4, 1976, p. 1; October 26, 1995, p. 1; February 16, 1996, p. A18; January 20, 2000, p. A10; February 16, 2000, p. A19; February 20, 2000, p. 25.
Publishers Weekly, June 3, 1996, p. 33.
U.S. News & World Report, April 1, 1996, p. 26..

Online

AFL–CIO web site, http://www.aflcio.org (May 2, 2000).

Richard Tafel

Log Cabin Republicans. Reprinted by permission.

Activist and minister

Born in 1962; son of Louis I. And Mary Agnes (Robb) Tafel. *Education:* East Stroudsburg University, B.A., 1984; Harvard University, M.Div., 1987.

Addresses: *Home*—1735 19th St. NW, Washington, DC 20009–1648. *Office*—Log Cabin Republicans, 1633 Q St. NW, Ste. 210, Washington, DC 20009–6351.

Career

Ordained minister, American Baptist Church, 1988; Memorial Church at Harvard University, Cambridge, MA, assistant to minister for special projects, 1987–91; Massachusetts Department of Public Health, Boston, director of adolescent health services, 1991– 93; Log Cabin Republicans, executive director, 1993—.

Sidelights

Richard L. Tafel is the executive director of the Log Cabin Republicans (LCR), a political group for gay and lesbian GOP supporters. Many consider these to be contrary positions because of the party's general lack of acceptance of homosexuals, a position influenced by the Republican Christian right wing. But Tafel sees no contradiction. As he remarked to Fred W. Lindecke in the *St. Louis Post–Dispatch*, "We are conservatives who pay our taxes, fix up our neighborhoods and pay for kids to go to schools. We come from families. Some people who talk about family values kick their kids out of the family. We're trying to bring families back together."

In addition, Tafel is a Baptist minister, and thus brings an intriguing combination of values to the party and to gay activism. This combination leaves him open to criticism from many sides, however, including from some homosexuals who consider him a detriment to their cause, and from some Republicans who would rather not be affiliated with gay groups. In fact, Tafel and his group made news in 1996 when Republican presidential candidate Bob Dole's campaign staff rejected a campaign contribution from the group. (However, Dole later accepted it.)

As elections approached in 2000, though, more candidates seemed to warm to the idea of gay supporters. Tafel noted to Katharine Q. Seelye in the *New York Times*, "The tone has totally changed.... It looks like Republicans for the first time are saying, 'This is a community I'm not going to alienate and maybe I want to reach out to it.' That's kind of a shocking revelation." In 1999 Tafel wrote a book detailing his struggle to gain the GOP's acceptance of gays called *Party Crasher: A Gay Republican Challenges Politics as Usual.*

Tafel was born in 1962 and raised in a suburb of Philadelphia. His grandfather and a great–uncle were both pastors and also both served as presidents of the Swedenborgian Church at different times. As a child, Tafel enjoyed attending Sunday school, and noted in his book that he had memorized the Bible by fourth grade. However, he did not enjoy actual church services, finding them boring, so he was relieved that his German soccer team practiced on Sundays.

To make up for the lag in Tafel's churchgoing, his father would engage him in theological discussions in the car on the way to practice. "These were much more valuable than any church service I ever attended," Tafel wrote in his book. "In all of his discussions, he would stress the Swedenborgian message, that earthly life is temporal and we must live life for the eternal. We should not be overly worried about life on earth, but much more concerned with our eternal life, which begins now."

As he entered puberty, Tafel began to acknowledge his homosexuality, and grew more and more concerned that this would end his lifelong dream of becoming a minister. However, as he wrote in his book, "More than once, I thought that it would be easier to be dead than to be a homosexual.... In the midst of that confusion and turmoil, I finally did hear the still, small voice of God. It told me the last thing I expected to hear; it said that He had created all things good, and that I was good, and that God loved me no matter what the world did or thought."

When Tafel was 23 he decided to tell his parents he was gay. His older brother, Jim, told Patrick J. Kiger in *GQ*, "It was tough for Mom and Dad." Also, as Tafel had feared, he alienated some of his childhood friends. But his family ended up being supportive. Meanwhile, Tafel enrolled at East Stroudsburg University in Pennsylvania, graduating with honors in 1984 with a bachelor of arts in philosophy. He then obtained his master of divinity degree from Harvard University in 1987 and was ordained a minister in the American Baptist Church that same year. While in college, Tafel became active in charity work, serving as a Big Brother, adopting a grandfather, organizing a canned food drive, and actively working with the campus ministry.

In 1988, Tafel was hired at Harvard University's Memorial Church as the assistant to the minister for special projects. The church's chaplain, Peter J. Gomes, in 1992 revealed his homosexuality. While at Harvard, Tafel was in charge of restoring the fiscal soundness of Memorial Church. He accomplished this with budget cuts and increased fund-raising. By the time he left in 1991, the church was one of the school's best-endowed non-academic facilities.

In the meantime, Tafel became active in politics when he managed a Boston-area congressional campaign in 1990 for his Harvard friend, Mike Duffy, who is also a gay Republican. Though Duffy lost by a slight margin, Tafel's efforts went far in drumming up Republican support from gays and lesbians which led to the election that year of Massachusetts Governor William Weld, a strong supporter of gay rights. In recognition of Tafel's efforts, Weld named him director of adolescent health services for the Massachusetts Department of Public Health. He served in this post until 1993.

Meanwhile, Tafel cofounded the Log Cabin Federation and became its first president. It drew its name from President Abraham Lincoln's campaign in which he referred to growing up in a log cabin; the name is meant to return the Republican party to its roots and also signifies the group's desire for fair treatment for homosexuals. The group began as an umbrella for a collection of gay and lesbian groups and served as a fundraising vehicle for Republican candidates in addition to running a nonpartisan educational foundation. Tafel soon began to appear on shows like *Nightline* to denounce the Republican party's reluctance to include gays.

The Log Cabin Federation evolved into the Log Cabin Republicans and opened offices in Washington, D.C. in 1993. That year, Tafel became the group's executive director. In this post, he drew fire from "Religious Right" Republicans who opposed his homosexuality and the involvement of gays and lesbians in the party. In addition, Tafel told Kiger in *GQ*, some gays derided him as a "Jew working for the Nazis," due to their belief that the Republicans were their foe because of their condemnation of gays. Democratic Massachusetts Congressman Barney Frank, one of the nation's most prominent gay legislators, was one such detractor, calling the LCR the "Uncle Tom's Cabin Club."

In addition, other gays and lesbians were dismayed that Tafel would support Republicans' fiscally conservative causes. However, Tafel's former boyfriend, Jarrett Barrios, told Kiger, "Rich is a very special person, a melange of somewhat contradictory characteristics. One likes to put Republicans in a box—they want to cut aid to the poor, don't care about social problems—but Rich defies that mold." In fact, Barrios noted that Tafel often spent Saturdays in Boston's inner city working with a Catholic youth group.

After the Bob Dole incident in 1996, the LCR was in the news again during presidential primaries in November of 1999, when Texas Governor George W.

Bush who became the GOP's nominee stated on the television show *Meet the Press* that he did not want to meet with the LCR because it "creates a huge political scene," as Christopher Lee reported in the *Dallas Morning News*. Later, in May of 2000, Bush also excluded the group from an invitation–only meeting with other gay Republicans at his headquarters. These incidents came after Tafel's comments in the *New York Times* that he felt the party was becoming more inclusive.

In 1999, Tafel wrote a book, *Party Crasher: A Gay Republican Challenges Politics as Usual*, which was divided into three sections: "Life," "Liberty," and "The Pursuit of Happiness." In it, he discusses why homosexuals have traditionally allied themselves with the Democratic party, and he promotes the libertarian ideals of "live and let live" and limited government. A *Publishers Weekly* reviewer commented that the book "is part memoir, part political analysis and part infomercial for the [LCR] itself." Toward the book's end, Tafel commented, "There will be periods of backlash and major setbacks for us, but we are riding a wave into the information society, which will only speed up our successes, to the day when our people will have to really think hard to remember when gays and lesbians weren't accepted as part of the fabric of our country."

Sources

Books

Tafel, Richard, *Party Crasher: A Gay Republican Challenges Politics as Usual*, Simon & Schuster, 1999.

Periodicals

Booklist, June 1, 1999, p. 1785.
Dallas Morning News, September 19, 1999, p. 10J; April 12, 2000, p. 8A.
Gannett News Service, February 16, 1999; April 29, 1999.
GQ, January 1994, p. 80.
Library Journal, June 15, 1999, p. 95.
New York Times, August 11, 1999, p. A1.
Publishers Weekly, May 3, 1999, p. 58.
St. Louis Post–Dispatch, March 24, 1996, p. 9C.

Lili Taylor

Corbis Corporation

Actor

Born February 20, 1967, in Glencoe, IL. *Education:* Attended DePaul University's Goodman School of Drama.

Addresses: *Home*—New York, NY. *Agent*—William Morris Agency, 151 El Camino Dr., Beverly Hills, CA 90212.

Career

Actor; has worked with Naked Angels and Machine Full in New York City. Stage appearances include *Brighton Beach Memoirs,* 1986–87; *What Did He See?,* 1988–89; *The Myth Project: A Festival of Competency,* 1989; *Aven'U Boys,* 1993; *Mud, The Love Talker,* and *Fun.* Also director, *Halcyon Days.* Television appearances include movie *Night of Courage,* 1987; miniseries *Family of Spies,* 1990; specials *Sensibility and Sense,* 1990; *Herself, Luck, Trust, and Ketchup: Robert Altman in Carver County,* 1994; and *Subway Stories: Tales from the Underground* (segment "The Listeners"), 1997; and episodes of *Mad About You,* 1997–98; and *The X–Files,* 1998.

Film appearances include *Mystic Pizza,* 1988; *She's Having a Baby,* 1988; *Say Anything,* 1989; *Born on the Fourth of July,* 1989; *Dogfight,* 1991; *Bright Angel,* 1991; *Watch It,* 1993; *Rudy,* 1993; *Household Saints,* 1993; *Arizona Dream,* 1993; *Short Cuts,* 1993; *Ready to Wear* (*Pret-a-Porter*), 1994; *Cold Fever,* 1994; *Touch Base,* 1994; *Mrs. Parker and the Vicious Circle,* 1994; *Four Rooms* (segment "The Missing Ingredient"), 1995; *The Addiction,* 1995; *Things I've Never Told You,* 1996; *Plain Pleasures,* 1996; *Illtown,* 1996; *I Shot Andy Warhol,* 1996; *Girls Town,* 1996; *Killer: A Journal of Murder,* 1996; *Letters Not About Love* (voice), 1997; *Kicked in the Head,* 1997; *Pecker,* 1998; *O.K. Garage,* 1998; *The Imposters,* 1998; and *The Haunting,* 1999.

Awards: Independent Feature Product (IFP) Award for best supporting actress, 1993, for *Household Saints;* Golden Globe Award (with others) for best ensemble, 1993, for *Short Cuts;* Sundance Film Festival Special Recognition Award for Acting, and Seattle International Film Festival Golden Space Needle Award for best actress, both 1996, for *I Shot Andy Warhol;* Thessaloniki International Film Festival jury prize for best actress, 1996, for *Things I Never Told You;* Blockbuster Entertainment Award for favorite supporting actress, 1997, for *Ransom.*

Sidelights

With her unconventional looks, feminist politics, and preference for off–beat projects, it is no surprise that actor Lili Taylor is not one of Hollywood's big headliners. However, among those who enjoy art films and pictures that take risks, she is a mainstay. Jack Mathews in *Newsday* once commented that Taylor was "becoming the Meryl Streep of independent film." And Mary Ann Marshall in

Ms. also observed, "No airy ingenue or blond bombshell, she's on a par with some of the most respected actors working—Jennifer Jason Leigh, Alfre Woodard, Judy Davis—actors whose beauty is consequential, not cosmetic." As Taylor herself explained to Christine Spines in *Premiere,* "I don't do lingerie. I don't play roles that diminish females or tell the same story about the whore with a heart of gold."

Instead, Taylor has carved out her place as the queen of the underground, throwing herself into parts like the complex Valerie Solanas, the would–be assassin in *I Shot Andy Warhol,* 1996, or the manipulative, condescending Manhattan art agent in John Waters's *Pecker,* 1998. But she also ventures into the occasional blockbuster, such as 1996's *Ransom,* starring Mel Gibson. "I do need a little bit of money," Taylor mentioned to Marshall. "Jesus, I live in New York." In 1999, she also appeared in the summer spooker *The Haunting.*

Taylor was born in the Chicago suburb of Glencoe, Illinois on February 20, 1967, the second youngest of six siblings to working–class parents. As a teenager, she was diagnosed as a manic–depressive, but eschewed drug treatment because she was concerned it would compromise her artistic tendencies; additionally, she was skeptical of the assessment. After graduating from New Trier High School, she enrolled at the Goodman School of Drama at DePaul University. According to Marshall, Taylor was kicked out after two weeks for "creative differences." The actor's online biography claimed that she left when the school refused to allow her to perform on a professional level while still a student.

In any event, Taylor dove into acting, starting out as Laurie in a production of *Brighton Beach Memoirs* at the New American Theater in Rockford, Illinois, in 1986. Later she became a member of the Naked Angels theater company in New York City, and appeared in *What Did He See?* with the New York Shakespeare Festival in 1988–89 and in a critically acclaimed starring performance as Wendy in *Aven'U Boys* in 1993. She also formed her own company, Machine Full, and began directing for that group, her debut being *Halcyon Days* at the Work House Theater. Meanwhile, with her film career in full gear, Taylor continued to work on the stage, taking a role in Scott Elliot's production of *Three Sisters* at the Roundabout Theatre in 1997. "Even if I become a huge movie star," she told Kevin Koffler in *Seventeen,* "I'll continue to do theater, because it grounds me."

After appearing in a television movie called *Night of Courage* in 1987, Taylor made her film debut in 1988's *Mystic Pizza* as a would–be bride who cannot

decide whether to tie the knot. She shared the screen in that picture with another newcomer, Julia Roberts, who took a decidedly different career path than Taylor, going on to become a Hollywood superstar. One reason their careers took different routes is that although Taylor's high cheekbones, full lips, and arched brows are attractive, her look is not the typical definition of beauty in the entertainment business, and she often foregoes makeup, even while shooting movies. "(Hollywood's) beauty standard is so strict," she remarked to Meredith Berkman in *Entertainment Weekly,* noting that a former agent suggested she have cosmetic surgery on her nose. This could be one reason she was cast in *Dogfight,* 1991, as the "ugly" girl in a demeaning contest to find the worst–looking date.

Taylor's turn in the independent film *Household Saints,* about three generations of Italian women, won her further acclaim, not to mention an Independent Feature Product (IFP) Award for best supporting actress in 1993. She then caught the attention of Robert Altman, who cast her in *Short Cuts.* That film ended up winning a 1993 Golden Globe award for best ensemble. Taylor worked with Altman again in 1994's *Ready to Wear,* also known as *Pret–a–Porter.* Some of her other earlier works included a supporting role in Oliver Stone's Vietnam–era *Born on the Fourth of July* and the romantic teen comedy *Say Anything,* both 1989. In *Say Anything,* she was wrenchingly funny as a lovelorn teen singer–songwriter whose repertoire consisted solely of tunes about the boy who broke her heart. Taylor was also memorable as the author Edna Ferber in 1994's *Mrs. Parker and the Vicious Circle,* starring Jennifer Jason Leigh as writer Dorothy Parker.

One of Taylor's premier roles came in 1996 when she starred in *I Shot Andy Warhol* as Valerie Solanas, one of Warhol's admirers who tried to become part of his clique at the Factory during its heyday in the 1960s. After being dumped from the group, Solanas shot and nearly killed Warhol in 1968. The film cast Taylor as Solanas, a prostitute turned feminist who founded, and was the sole member of, the Society for Cutting Up Men (SCUM), for which she wrote a manifesto that visualized a utopian future where men would no longer be needed for procreation. Taylor's multifaceted portrayal of Solanas as more than simply a psychotic drew raves and earned her awards at the Sundance Film Festival and the Seattle International Film Festival. Also in 1996, Taylor was applauded for playing an angry single mother in the feminist *Girls Town,* about three female teenagers coming to grips with their friend's suicide. She helped write the script.

In addition to these smaller–budget films, in 1996 Taylor ventured into the mainstream as a kidnapper in *Ransom,* directed by Ron Howard and starring

Mel Gibson as the worried father whose son is taken. For that role, she won a 1997 Blockbuster Entertainment Award for favorite supporting actress. Taylor then slipped back into cult territory when she signed on with famously edgy director John Waters for 1998's *Pecker*. In that film, she plays Rorey Wheeler, a Manhattan art–scene insider who "discovers" a talented teenage photographer in a gritty area of Baltimore and makes him a reluctant star by exploiting his work, which tends to feature candid shots of the lower–class friends and family who populate his environment. Her condescending attitude and manipulative powers backfire on her, however.

During the summer of 1999, mainstream cinema audiences could catch Taylor in *The Haunting*, costarring Catherine Zeta–Jones and Liam Neeson. This remake of a 1963 movie, which was based on a 1959 novel, was generally panned by critics, but struck gold at the box office, reaping $48.7 million in its opening week and setting a box–office earnings record for a DreamWorks picture. Though it appeared with this winner that Taylor was poised to break through to more major films, she expressed a desire to continue seeking good roles. However, as she commented to Jamie Painter in *Interview*, this was becoming more difficult even with art films, since their costs were increasing and their expected returns were thus greater: "When there's a bigger budget there's more of a formula, and the women fit into that formula in a very specific way. Usually a complicated woman is not part of it." Still, Taylor did not seem to be giving up; she noted to Spines in *Premier*, "I just want to keep doing honest work, and showing people as many women as I can."

Sources

Books

Contemporary Theatre, Film and Television, volume 17, Gale Research, 1997.

Periodicals

Entertainment Weekly, December 9, 1994, p. 47; November–December 1997 (Special Issue), p. 54.

Independent, November 21, 1996, p. 4.

Interview, January 1999, p. 44.

Knight–Ridder/Tribune News Service, May 16, 1996.

Ms., September/October 1996, p. 76.

Newsday, April 30, 1996, p. B9.

New York Times Magazine, November 16, 1997, p. 79.

Premiere, November 1996, p. 86.

Record (Bergen County, NJ), September 24, 1998, p. 1.

Seventeen, October 1990, p. 78.

Star Tribune (Minneapolis, MN), May 23, 1996, p. 7E.

Variety, August 2, 1999, p. 12.

Online

"Lili Taylor," Internet Movie Database web site, http://us.imdb.com (December 17, 1999).

Lili Taylor web site, http://www.lilitaylor.com (December 17, 1999).

George Tenet

AP/Wide World Photos

Director of the CIA

Born January 5, 1953, in Flushing, NY; son of John (a restaurant proprietor) and Evangelia (a homemaker) Tenet; married Stephanie Glakas; children: John Michael. *Education:* Georgetown University, B.S. in foreign service; Columbia University, master's degree in international affairs.

Addresses: *Office*—Central Intelligence Agency, Office of Public Affairs, Washington, DC 20505.

Career

American Hellenic Institute, research director, 1978–79; Solar Energy Industries Association, 1979–82; legislative assistant to Senator John Heinz, 1982–85; Senate Select Committee on Intelligence, staff member, 1985–89, staff director, 1989–93; member of President Bill Clinton's national security transition team, 1993, promoted to special assistant to the president, became senior director for intelligence programs at the National Security Council; Central Intelligence Agency (CIA), deputy director, 1995–96, director, 1996.

Sidelights

As Director of Central Intelligence for the United States since 1996, George J. Tenet heads not only the flagship Central Intelligence Agency (CIA), but also a network of about a dozen branches of intelligence. Before that, Tenet had served in numerous government posts relating to intelligence and national security, including the second in charge of the CIA, but he did not keep a high profile. According to Tim Weiner in the *New York Times*, "Until he was catapulted into the job of Deputy Director of Central Intelligence in 1995, Mr. Tenet had always been a staff man the devoted assistant who sits behind his mentor at a meeting, the man handing up a paper he has drafted for the President's signature, or whispering an idea to a Senate chairman." Assuming leadership of the CIA after a revolving–door period for that position, Tenet has vowed to remain in place until forcefully removed.

Tenet was born on January 5, 1953, in the Queens borough of New York City, the son of John and Evangelia Tenet. His parents were both born in Albania but forced to move to Greece by the communist government. They relocated to the United States in 1952, the year they married. The elder Tenet ran a restaurant, the 20th Century Diner, in Little Neck, New York, while his wife worked as a homemaker. Tenet and his fraternal twin brother, Bill, helped out in the business, and all three continued to work at the diner even after his father sold it in 1961 once he began to suffer heart ailments.

Growing up, Tenet spoke Greek at home and enjoyed homemade Greek foods like patsichio, a pasta and lamb meal which is one of his favorite dishes. He attended Benjamin Cardozo High School in Bayside, where he was known for both his grades and athletic prowess. His brother was more soft–spoken and introverted, and decided to become a cardiologist following his father's heart problems (the elder Tenet died in 1983), but Tenet was more boisterous.

In a *Newsday* article, Margaret Ramirez wrote that Tenet's mother "remembers him as being quite a lady's man, bringing home a different girlfriend every week." In addition to women, one of his main pursuits was watching television news, and from there he developed an interest in politics. His father discouraged him from working toward a career in the government, but as his mother told Ramirez, "George was strong. George said, 'I will decide.'"

Tenet went on to attend the Georgetown University School of Foreign Service in Washington, D.C., graduating in 1976, then went on to get a master's degree in international affairs from Columbia University in 1978. After that, he got a job as a research director with the American Hellenic Institute, an organization devoted to strengthening relations between the United States and Greece and Cyprus, and within the American Hellenic community. He left in 1979 and went to work for the Solar Energy Industries Association.

In 1982, Tenet began his career in government as a legislative assistant to Senator John Heinz, a Pennsylvania Republican. His job duties concerned issues like defense, energy, and foreign affairs. He changed jobs again in 1985, joining the staff of the Senate Select Committee on Intelligence, where he worked for about 14 months for Patrick Leahy, a Democrat from Vermont, who was serving as the committee's vice chairman. In this capacity, Tenet directed the committee's oversight of all arms control negotiations between the United States and the Soviet Union, and prepared a report on the topic for the Senate. He also quickly established himself as a respected and well–liked colleague.

In January of 1989, Tenet assumed the post of staff director of the committee, supervising 40 staff members and keeping an eye on the senators overseeing the CIA. And according to Tenet's biography on the CIA web site, during this time he also beefed up requirements for reports on covert actions, created a statutory Inspector General at the agency, and introduced legislation to reorganize U.S. intelligence. Also during his tenure, Tenet aided in guiding the committee through controversial confirmation hearings for Robert M. Gates, Jr., who was nominated in 1991 to become the new CIA director.

After President Bill Clinton took office in January of 1993, Tenet resigned from the Senate Intelligence Committee to join the national security transition team. He was soon promoted to special assistant to the president, and in a few more months, became senior director for intelligence programs at the National Security Council. There, he dealt with setting confidential intelligence priorities in a post–Cold War era, and also issued new directives to the Federal Bureau of Investigation (FBI) and the CIA for working in conjunction to catch spies.

In 1995, Deputy Defense Secretary John Deutch was appointed as director of the CIA, and that July, he chose Tenet as the agency's deputy director, or number two in charge. During this time, Tenet made progress in coordinating rocky relations between the CIA and the FBI as well as the Justice Department. He also began to run staff meetings when his boss was not available. Also at this time, he was overseeing the Directorate of Operations, or "house of spies," as Weiner called it, which was then reeling from the revelation that one of its agents, Aldrich H. Ames, had sold secrets to Moscow.

Deutch resigned from his post in December of 1996, and Tenet was named acting director of the CIA. Though Anthony Lake was originally nominated to fill the position, he withdrew after three days of confirmation hearings, weary of being questioned and investigated. Soon after, in March of 1997, President Clinton tapped Tenet as a permanent replacement, which led to public hearings for his confirmation. No one seemed to expect any major problems, since he had already been thoroughly checked out when he was assigned to serve as deputy director.

There were a few criticisms, however, of Tenet's leadership that some thought might emerge. First of all, a former State Department official accused him of leaking to the press the name of a CIA informant connected to two Guatemalan murders. The allegation came up on the television program *60 Minutes*, but Tenet denied it. Also, some alleged improper connections between the CIA and the Democratic National Committee, concerning writing a positive CIA report allowing a Democratic donor to attend White House events. Tenet also came under fire when the CIA revealed that as far back as 1984, they had obtained information that an Iraqi target in the Gulf War housed chemical weapons. He was also criticized for not doing more to raise morale at the agency. In addition to the Ames incident, the CIA was harshly reprimanded for its failure to predict India's nuclear weapon detonation in 1998, and were lambasted for not knowing in advance that the U.S. Embassies in Kenya and Tanzania were going to be bombed that same year.

Another issue that raised a red flag was the discovery that Tenet had not revealed on federal financial disclosure forms that he owned some telephone company stock and real estate in Greece. He explained, though, that he was unaware of the holdings which were inherited from his father until 1994, when his brother found the paperwork in a safe deposit box. Afterward, according to a White House spokesman in a *New York Times* report by Weiner, he revised his financial disclosure forms and recused himself from any issues that might concern those holdings. His nomination was thus put on hold until the completion of a Justice Department investigation, which eventually cleared him of any wrongdoing.

As expected, Tenet's nomination sailed through the Senate by a vote of 19–0, and he was confirmed on July 10, 1997. This made him the 18th director in the CIA's 50–year history, and the fifth in six years. In November of 1998, it looked like there might soon be yet another turnover, too, as Tenet threatened to resign if Israeli spy Jonathan Jay Pollard was released as part of a Middle East peace agreement. Israeli Prime Minister Binyamin Netanyahu was asking for Pollard's release as a condition of signing an agreement with Palestinian leader Yasser Arafat. However, Clinton refused to release Pollard, and Tenet remained on the job.

By early 1999, Tenet seemed firmly entrenched in his spot, telling Nurith C. Aizenman in the *New Republic,* "I love it here. It's the perfect job. They're going to have to blow me out of here." Aizenman praised Tenet's tenacity, commenting, "His obvious enthusiasm for the job has already given the agency a major morale boost." He also noted, though, that some claimed Tenet needed to be more hard–nosed about turning around the institution, which suffered from dramatic turnover of employees and a stifling bureaucracy, according to one source. In fact, some members of Congress had even begun to question the agency's purpose, since the Soviet Union's collapse erased one of its main reasons for being.

In another glitch on the CIA's record, in early 2000 reports surfaced that an investigation of its previous director, Deutch, had been impeded by top officials. In December of 1996, as he was leaving office, the CIA discovered Deutch was keeping a great deal of classified material on his home computer. However, the agency did not tell the Justice Department about it for more than a year. Though Deutch was not prosecuted, Tenet suspended the former director's security clearances indefinitely. Subsequently, Tenet maintained that no CIA officials had held up the internal investigation. He stated to James Risen in the *New York Times,* "The bottom line is that a complete investigation was done, decisive action was taken and steps have been implemented to improve our security process." Tenet also established a special panel within the CIA to review the actions of those officials connected with the Deutch case.

In his *New Republic* article, Aizenman noted that Tenet gives infrequent interviews and dislikes being quoted. But if he is tight–lipped to the media, he is warm and informal among colleagues. For example, he is known to call and thank people for a job well done. Aizenman reported, "He is passionate, a man who his staff says 'cares deeply about issues' and who gets emotional when delivering speeches honoring CIA officers who were killed in the line of duty. He is unpretentious, eschewing a limousine in favor of a Ford Explorer and often stopping his convoy at a McDonald's drive–in for lunch on the way to a briefing at the White House." In addition, he is an iconoclast, attending meetings with other officials such as Madeline Albright and Sandy Berger dressed in jeans and a black leather jacket bearing the CIA insignia. Though Tenet had some heart problems in previous years, he reportedly began a regimen of exercising, eating in moderation, and relaxing in order to combat the trouble. He is married to A. Stephanie Glakas–Tenet and they have a son, John Michael.

Sources

Periodicals

Congressional Quarterly Weekly Report, April 12, 1997, p. 857; July 12, 1997, p. 1644; May 10, 1997, p. 1086.
New Republic, March 22, 1999, p. 22.
Newsday, March 21, 1997, p. A7.
New York Times, March 20, 1997, p. A1; May 6, 1997, p. B10; May 8, 1997, p. D25; February 1, 2000, p. A1; February 2, 2000, p. A15.
Time, March 31, 1997, p. 38.
U.S. News & World Report, March 31, 1997, p. 16.
Washington Post, November 11, 1998, p. A4.

Online

"George Tenet," Central Intelligence Agency web site, http://www.cia.gov (April 13, 2000).

Felix Trinidad

Boxer

Born January 10, 1973, in Cupey Alto, Puerto Rico; son of Felix Trinidad, Sr. (a boxing trainer and manager); married; two children.

Addresses: *Office*—c/o Don King Productions, 501 Fairway Dr., Deerfield, Fl 33441.

Career

Professional boxer, 1990—.

Awards: International Boxing Federation (IBF) welterweight champion, 1993 ; World Boxing Council (WBC) welterweight champion, 1999—; World Boxing Association (WBA) super welterweight champion, 2000—.

Sidelights

With a record of 38 wins and 31 knockouts, Felix Trinidad has one of the best knockout percentages in the history of boxing. Yet it was still a shock when, in September of 1999, the International Boxing Federation (IBF) champion since 1993 defeated favorite Oscar De La Hoya in Las Vegas, Nevada. The much–anticipated match attracted witticisms about "The Odd Couple" of boxing, referring to the film of the same name in which the lead characters are also named Oscar and Felix. It also held great interest for spectators not only because De La Hoya held the World Boxing Council (WBC) welterweight title, but because he is Mexican and Trinidad is Puerto Rican, so it stirred nationalist pride.

In addition, De La Hoya is known as a more colorful and popular character in the boxing world, while Trinidad is more reserved. In the end, Trinidad won by decision after De La Hoya thought he had it neatly wrapped up. After that, in 2000 Trinidad also snagged the World Boxing Association (WBA) super welterweight title as well.

Trinidad, whose nickname is "Tito," was born on January 10, 1973, in Cupey Alto, Puerto Rico.Trinidad's trainer is his father, Felix Trinidad, Sr., who is known as Don Felix. He also trains several other boxers, and fought professionally himself in the 1970s, compiling a 19–6 record. When working together for an upcoming fight, Trinidad's blood relationship to his father is subordinated to his professional one. Unlike many other father–son boxing teams, the Trinidads seem to work extraordinarily well together. As Trinidad, Sr. told Greg Cote of the *Knight–Ridder/Tribune News Service*, "It has not always been a bed of roses! There were some difficult situations. But at the moment of truth, we both came to an understanding. My son is very cooperative. We have never had problems as far as the training aspect." Trinidad added to Cote, "We know what the common goal is here. It is for me to continue being the best fighter."

Around age 11 or 12, Trinidad began boxing. In just a few years, he captured five amateur Puerto Rican national championships, with his wins occurring in five different weight classes, as he increased from 100 pounds to 112 pounds, then 119 pounds, then 126 pounds, and finally, 132 pounds. In 1988, he tried out for the Puerto Rican boxing team, but failed to qualify. Upset at this turn of events, Trinidad's father arranged for him to turned professional on March 10, 1990, at the young age of 17. By then, he had an outstanding amateur record of 51–6 behind him, even though only 12 were by knockout.

Going pro, Trinidad decided to concentrate on becoming a knockout artist. Many surmised that this would not happen, but in his first ten fights, all victories, he had nine knockouts. "I started planting myself, with my feet more firmly on the ground, and the punches got stronger," he explained to William Nack in Sports Illustrated. Early on, he showed his tenacity in a fight against Jake Rodriguez in December of 1991. Though Trinidad hurt his right hand in the second round and then injured his left in the fourth round, he pushed through the pain to win the ten–round fight by unanimous decision.

On October 3, 1992, Trinidad was knocked down the first time in his professional career by Alberto Cortes of Argentina, who had already won 51 fights. After hitting the mat twice in the second round, Trinidad got back up and pummeled Cortes in the third round, and the referee ended the fight. Less than a year after that, Trinidad snagged his first IBF welterweight, beating two–time champion and current belt holder Maurice Blocker. Trinidad won by knockout in the second round.

Subsequently, Trinidad defeated challengers to keep his title. On August 6, 1993, he knocked the undefeated Luis Garcia to the mat four times in the first round before the match was ended. Next, against Antony Stephens on October 23, 1993, he was knocked down in the second round but came back to mat his opponent in the tenth. Then, in January of 1994 Trinidad won a unanimous decision against the aging Hector "Macho Man" Camacho.

After taking eight months off at the request of his father, Trinidad returned on September 17, 1994, to meet the undefeated Luis Ramon "Yory Boy" Campas, an intimidating fighter with a 56–0 record. The match occurred during the Mexican Independence Celebration. Campas floored Trinidad in the second round with a fast left, but he came back in the fourth to deliver a series of a dozen shots to the head, prompting the referee to halt the fight. On December 10, 1995, Trinidad faced Oba "Motor City" Carr in Monterrey, Mexico. Again, he fell in the second round, but came back to send his opponent to the mat twice in the eighth. As Carr got up, Trinidad landed another to his head, and the referee called a stop to the match.

On February 10, 1996, Trinidad's record improved to 28–0 with 24 knockouts when Rodney Moore surrendered in a match at the MGM Grand in Las Vegas, Nevada. After the fourth round, Moore's legs were shaking and his face was bloodied by Trinidad's relentless pursuit. He refused to emerge for the fifth round, thus giving Trinidad a technical knockout. Moore told Nack in Sports Illustrated that after Trinidad delivered a low hook to his hip in the fourth round, he thought his leg was broken.

Afterward, Trinidad on August 23, 1997 faced Troy Waters at Madison Square Garden. Waters, from Sydney, Australia, was the WBC's top contender in the junior–middleweight division and posted a record of 24–7. He went down in a first–round knockout. By this point, Trinidad's record was 32–0 with 28 knockouts, and he had gone up from 147 pounds to 154 pounds in order to attract more fighters.

As the new WBC top contender, Trinidad was scheduled to meet Terry Norris in a mandatory defense of Norris's WBC junior middleweight title. Timothy W. Smith wrote in the New York Times, "A match against Norris could be a defining moment in Trinidad's career." However, Norris lost his championship to Keith Mullings of Brooklyn, so Trinidad decided to keep his welterweight title and continue fighting at 147 pounds. In April of 1998, Trinidad posted an easy win against Mahenge Zulu.

Meanwhile, Trinidad was itching to fight charismatic WBC welterweight champ Oscar De La Hoya, stating that "everyone in the world" wanted to see the fight, according to Jack Curry in the New York Times. "I have no doubts about myself," Trinidad added. "I know that I'm the best pound for pound." His promoter, the colorful Don King, and his father goaded De La Hoya by calling him "Oscar De La Chicken," and Trinidad accused De La Hoya for some time of avoiding him in the ring.

But the match was slow in coming, and Trinidad became frustrated with King. Several months passed after the Zulu fight with no prospects for Trinidad, so he filed a lawsuit against King and his company in order to find new representation. In June of 1998 he signed with promotional firm Main Events, run by Don Duva. The case went to the U.S. Federal Court in August of 1998, where King's lawyers argued that Trinidad's contract, which technically expired in June of 1998, stipulated an automatic two–year extension if he were still champion. Trinidad's lawyers, though, insisted that the extension was only valid if the boxer had won an addition belt on top of the IBF title. A judge ruled in favor of King that November, and Trinidad was forced to sign a $49.9 million contract for three fights over four years.

Subsequently, King lined up a fight for Trinidad with Pernell "Sweet Pea" Whitaker, a 35-year-old fighter with six titles in four weight classes. He had lost the WBC welterweight championship to De La Hoya in 1997, and after that, became mired in controversy. He was suspended from the ring for a drunk-driving arrest and for failing a drug test, and later tested positive for cocaine twice, earning him the derogatory nickname "Snow Pea." By early 1999, though, he claimed he was just as much in shape as when he won the Olympic gold in 1984. On the other hand, Trinidad's weight was up to 156—exceeding the welterweight limit of 147—just two weeks before the fight with Whitaker. Trinidad shed the pounds just in time, and beat Whitaker in a 12-round decision at New York's Madison Square Gardens. He also broke his challenger's jaw. Three months later he knocked out Hugo Pineda in San Juan, Puerto Rico.

In the meantime, shortly after the Whitaker fight, King announced that Trinidad would finally meet De La Hoya at the Mandalay Bay resort in Las Vegas. For both men, both age 26, the fight would carry the largest paycheck of their careers, with each earning $20 million. Trinidad and his father vocally insisted the contest would be lopsided in his favor. Some observers agreed that Trinidad was a harder hitter, but noted that De La Hoya had fought tougher opponents than had Trinidad.

The fight itself was not the rout that Trinidad expected. De La Hoya, fast on his feet, circled out of Trinidad's range and jabbed him forcefully when he did come in for a punch, bloodying his opponent's nose in the second round and giving him a swollen and cut left eye after rounds five and six. At the conclusion, De La Hoya raised his gloves in a victory pose. "I thought I had the fight won easily," he later told the media, according to Frederick C. Klein in *the Wall Street Journal*. "I really believe I was giving him a boxing lesson."

Judges, however, disagreed with De La Hoya, and handed him his first-ever defeat. Trinidad walked away with the WBC title, adding it to his IBF belt.

One called the fight a match, one gave a win to Trinidad by one point, and the other approved Trinidad by two points. Though Klein wrote, "It wasn't the worst decision I've seen," he also pointed out that De La Hoya landed 263 hits to Trinidad's 166, and that he had a higher rate of connections, with 41 percent to Trinidad's 36 percent. Trinidad, though, had come back in the last few rounds.

Afterward, both fighters promised a rematch. However, the wait was on again as both fighters went on to other opponents. In March of 2000 in Las Vegas, Trinidad took away the WBA super welterweight title from David Reid, who had won the Olympic gold medal in 1996. After this match, Trinidad fought Mamadou Thiam from France, originally from Senegal, to retain his super welterweight title. Thiam retreated from the ring and surrendered in the third round, causing the referee to halt the fight.

Subsequently, it appeared that Trinidad and De La Hoya would not meet again after all, when De La Hoya refused to agree to fight at 151 pounds instead of 147. Instead, Trinidad began discussing the possibility of moving up a weight class to face Roy Jones Jr., the undisputed light-heavyweight champion. Tim Smith of the *Knight-Ridder/Tribune News Service* agreed with the move, writing, "Trinidad needs De La Hoya as much as Don King needs an appointment at the Hair Club for Men." He noted that Trinidad was holding his own in better and better matches, and that he did not need the rematch with De La Hoya for validation.

The five-foot, ten-inch tall Trinidad is married and has two children. When he is not in the ring, he "tends to his horses or putters around the house," according to Smith in the *New York Times*.

Sources

Hispanic, January–February 2000, p. 16.
Knight-Ridder/Tribune News Service, September 15, 1999; July 19, 2000; July 22, 2000; July 23, 2000.
New York Times, August 20, 1997, p. B15; August 25, 1997, p. C2; February 4, 1998, p. C4; March 31, 1998, p. C5; June 7, 2000, p. C29.
Sports Illustrated, February 19, 1996, p. 30; March 1, 1999, p. 78; September 27, 1999, p. 56; March 13, 2000, p. 52.
Wall Street Journal, September 20, 1999, p. A26.

Charlie Trotter

Chef

B orn c. 1960; son of an IBM manager and Dona–
Lee Trotter (a homemaker); married, 1991; wife's
name, Lynn; children: Dylan. *Education:* University
of Wisconsin, political science degree, early 1980s.

Addresses: *Office*—c/o Charlie Trotter's, 816 West
Armitage, Chicago, Illinois 60614.

Career

W orked at various restaurants, early– to mid–
1980s; opened own restaurant in Chicago, IL,
1987, opened second restaurant at MGM Grand casino, Las Vegas, 1995 (closed). Author of six cook-
books and host of PBS television show, *The Kitchen
Sessions with Charlie Trotter,* 1999—. Also gives cooking demonstrations and speeches and does consulting. James Beard Foundation, trustee, Kennedy–
King College Culinary Advisory Board.

Awards: Trotter: James Beard Foundation, named
best chef in Midwest, 1992, Who's Who in Food and
Beverage Award, 1996, Outstanding Chef Award,
1999; *Nation's Restaurant News,* named one of 50
Power Players, 2000.

Restaurant: *Restaurants and Institutions,* Fine Dining
Ivy Award, 1990; *Nation's Restaurant News,* "Fine
Dining Hall of Fame," 1991; AAA Five Diamonds
(highest rating), 1993—; James Beard Foundation,
outstanding wine service award, 1993; *Wine Spectator* Grand Award, 1993—; Relais & Chateaux, Relais
Gourmand, 1995—; Mobil Travel Guide Five Stars

Charlie Trotter's. Reprinted by permission.

(highest rating), 1996—; Traditions & Qualitie, Les
Grandes Tables Du Monde, 1998—; *Wine Spectator,*
named best restaurant in the world for wine and
food, 1998; James Beard Foundation, outstanding
restaurant award, 2000; *Wine Spectator,* named best
restaurant in the United States, and *The Kitchen Sessions with Charlie Trotter* named best national television cooking show, both 2000.

Sidelights

C harlie Trotter did not create one of the world's
finest restaurants by consensus. "It's a real
simple system that we run here," he explained to
Dennis Ray Wheaton in *Chicago* magazine. "It's my
way or the highway." By putting his perfectionist
touches on everything, his eponymous Chicago eatery has consistently received the highest ratings by
travel associations and reaped awards from gourmet publications and professional organizations. In
1998, the *Wine Spectator* dubbed Charlie Trotter's
the best restaurant in the world for wine and food,
and in 2000 called it the best restaurant in the
United States. The James Beard Foundation gave
Trotter the outstanding chef award in 1999 and the
outstanding restaurant award in 2000. "You have a
finite number of mouthfuls in your life," Trotter
told Michael Neill in *People.* "I want to make every
one count."

Trotter was born around 1960 and grew up in the Chicago suburb of Wilmette, Illinois. His father worked as an IBM executive before founding his own executive search firm, and his mother, Dona-Lee, was a homemaker. Trotter's father was also a part-time trumpeter in a Chicago sextet, and named his son after virtuoso sax player Charlie Parker.

Little in his background would suggest that Trotter would become a world-class chef. "I didn't give him his gift for cooking," his mother told Neill in *People.* "He says I did well- balanced meals. Coming from him, that's not a compliment." In high school, Trotter worked as a busboy at the Ground Round hamburger chain, but was far more interested in gymnastics and shooting home movies.

Enrolling at the University of Wisconsin in 1977, Trotter hoped to become a filmmaker, but later changed his major to political science. In college, he became interested in cuisine. One time, he came home for a visit and cooked up a poached salmon and spinach souffle. In his junior year, his roommate—a friend since childhood who also considered himself an amateur chef—challenged him to cook-off. Trotter recalled to Neill, "It turned into a bit of an elaborate competition multiple courses, bread-baking, searching out recipes in Julia Child [cookbooks]. That's when I got the bug to cook."

After graduating in the early 1980s, Trotter tried to stay on a typical job path, interviewing with insurance and brokerage firms. When nothing intrigued him, he decided to learn the restaurant business. Over the next four years or so, he spent time in Chicago, San Francisco, Florida, and did a six-month tour of Europe, "reading every cookbook I could get my hands on, working like a maniac, and eating out incessantly," as he noted in his biography on the Charlie Trotter's Restaurant web site.

When he returned to Chicago in 1987, his parents gave him financial support to open his own eatery. It is located on Armitage in the trendy Lincoln Park neighborhood of the city in a building that Trotter owns outright. In the Gallic tradition, he named the place after himself. Several of his staff have stayed with him since the start and have risen through the ranks from dishwasher to assistant sous-chef or from waiting tables to management. Trotter used to accept 200 guests per night but as of 1999 was down to 150, and was hoping to eventually decrease that to 120. The average bill per person is $155, not including tax and tip. He also opened a Charlie Trotter's at the MGM Grand casino in Las Vegas in 1995, but it later closed.

Initially, Charlie Trotter's offered a menu with several choices, which is the norm at most restaurants. But in about 1990 he began offering a "tasting menu," which serves only the choice of the chef. Jonathan Black in *Chicago* magazine wrote, "To those who grouse—'Suppose I'm not in the mood for oxtail ravioli?'—Charlie retorts, 'When you go to Orchestra Hall, do you request Mozart?'"

As of 2000, Trotter was featuring three tasting menus daily: a Grand Degustation multi- course menu with seafood, meats, vegetables, and grains; a meatless vegetable-only menu; and a Kitchen Table menu (in which guests dine at the special chef's table) with an assortment of 15 small courses of meats, seafood, vegetables, and grains. Some examples of his cuisine include rabbit loin with tiny fennel, wilted watercress, zucchini blossoms and sugar snap pea emulsion with preserved onion; or ragout of braised farro, tiny squash, Japanese eggplant, chanterelle mushrooms and vidalia onion-brown butter vinaigrette. For dessert, diners can choose from offerings such as lychee-lemongrass soup with vanilla sorbet and gooseberries or strawberry- ginger sorbet with machta tea emulsion and rhubarb soup. His eatery is also renowned for its superb wine list.

Although his recipes might seem extravagant for mainstream tastes, Trotter's philosophy is basic. He noted in a *U.S. News & World Report* interview that in choosing his ingredients, he has to have "'exquisite' food." He explained, "When I say exquisite, I don't mean expensive or exotic. I really mean the freshest, purest product. You can't improve upon the simplest things in the height of their season."

Beginning in 1994, amateur chefs could try their hand at Trotter's creations—or just gaze longingly at them—with the introduction of his first lavishly photographed self- titled cookbook. Over the next several years, he continued the series. *Charlie Trotter's Vegetables,* 1996, included such recipes as Arugula Noodles with Smoked Yellow Tomato Sauce, Black Olives, and Roasted Garlic Puree, which required gastronomes to smoke their own tomatoes over hickory chips lit by a propane torch. Another dish required hazelnuts from one specific farm in Oregon. After this came volumes on seafood and desserts, as well as *Gourmet Cooking for Dummies.*

In 1998 Trotter published *The Kitchen Sessions with Charlie Trotter,* a companion book to his 1999 PBS series by the same name. In *U.S. News & World Report,* he remarked, "The idea is to show people how involved a very intense restaurant kitchen is, and to translate that cuisine into home cooking by simplifying the steps and not using such pricey or hard–to–find ingredients." However, he added, "But I don't really see people in front of the TV with a pad jotting down the recipe and saying, 'Oh, I've got to make this tonight.' The show is meant to inspire, to get people excited about food."

From the early days, Charlie Trotter's was recognized for its quality. An *Esquire* writer applauded it as one of the best new restaurants of the year when it opened, and over time it collected a number of honors, including five stars—the highest rating—from the Mobil Travel Guide since 1996, and five diamonds, AAA's best rating, since 1993. In addition to his other James Beard Awards, the foundation named Trotter the best chef in the Midwest in 1992 and recognized the eatery for outstanding wine service in 1993. They also gave him the Who's Who in Food and Beverage Award in 1996 and recognized *The Kitchen Sessions with Charlie Trotter* as the best national television cooking show in 2000.

Trotter married his wife, Lynn, in the early 1990s, and they have a son, Dylan. She frequently hosts at his restaurant. "It's the only way I get to spend time with him," she told Neill in *People.* Trotter is in the restaurant virtually every night it is open, and on off nights, he puts on special events elsewhere. For example, he hosts dinners regularly at the James Beard House in New York City, and he also performs cooking demonstrations, gives speeches, and does consulting. He also does charity work for the Make–A–Wish Foundation, the Mercy Home for Boys and Girls, the American Cancer Society, and the Providence St. Mel High School. He is also a trustee of the James Beard Foundation and is on the Kennedy–King College Culinary Advisory Board.

Selected writings

Charlie Trotter's Cookbook, Ten Speed Press, 1994.
Charlie Trotter's Vegetables, Ten Speed Press, 1996.
Charlie Trotter's Seafood, Ten Speed Press, 1997.
Charlie Trotter's Desserts, Ten Speed Press, 1998.
Gourmet Cooking for Dummies, IDG Books Worldwide, 1997.
The Kitchen Sessions with Charlie Trotter, Ten Speed Press, 1999.

Sources

Periodicals

Booklist, October 13, 1997, p. 374; September 15, 1998, p. 182.
Chicago, December 1994, p. 133; September 1997, p. 108.
Esquire, March 1995, p. 53.
Library Journal, October 15, 1998, p. 92.
People, April 10, 1995, p. 123.
Publishers Weekly, June 3, 1996, p. 76; November 2, 1998, p. 77.
USA Today, January 15, 1999, p. 12D.
US News & World Report, January 11, 1999, p. 70.

Online

Charlie Trotter's Restaurant web site, http://www.charlietrotters.com (July 20, 2000).

Tina Turner

Singer and actor

Born Annie Mae Bullock, November 26, 1939, in Brownsville, TN; daughter of Floyd Richard (a farm overseer and church deacon) and Zelma Bullock; married Ike Turner (a singer and musician), 1958, divorced, 1978; children: (by Raymond Hill) Richard Craig; (by Turner) Ronald Renelle; two stepsons, Ike Jr. and Michael.

Addresses: *Home*—Nice, France; and Zurich, Switzerland. *Manager*—Roger Davies, 3575 Cahuenga Ave. W., Los Angeles, CA 90068. *Agent*—Triad, 10100 Santa Monica Blvd., 16th Floor, Los Angeles, CA 90067.

Career

Singer, 1956 , and actor. Performed with Ike Turner's Kings of Rhythm (name later changed to The Ike and Tina Turner Revue), 1956–76; solo performer, 1976 . Participated in relief concert Live Aid, 1984, and charity recording "We Are the World," for the USA for Africa relief effort, 1985. Television appearances include guest role on *Ally McBeal*, 2000; and numerous appearances on talk and variety shows. Film appearances include *The Big T.N.T. Show*, 1970; *Gimme Shelter*, 1970; *Taking Off*, 1971; *Tommy*, 1975; *Sgt. Pepper's Lonely Hearts Club Band*, 1978; *Sound of the City: London 1964–73*, 1981; *Mad Max Beyond Thunderdome*, 1985; *The Who's Tommy, The Amazing Journey*, 1993; *What's Love Got to Do with It*, 1993; *Last Action Hero*, 1993; *The History of Rock 'N' Roll, Vol. 1*, 1995. Author (with Kurt Loder) of autobiography, *I, Tina*, 1986.

Awards: Eight Grammy Awards, including for best R&B performance by a duo or group (with Ike Turner), 1971, for "Proud Mary," for best female

Photo by Ken Settle

rock vocal performance, 1984, for "Better Be Good to Me," for song of the year, record of the year, and best female pop vocal performance, 1984, for "What's Love Got to Do with It," 1984, and for best female rock vocal performance, 1985, for "One of the Living," 1986, for "Back Where You Started," and 1988, for "Tina Live in Europe;" American Music Awards for best female vocalist and best video performer, 1984; NAACP award for best actress, 1985, for *Mad Max Beyond Thunderdome*; inducted (with Ike Turner) into the Rock 'n' Roll Hall of Fame, 1991; *Essence* award, 1993.

Sidelights

With her wild wigs, shapely legs, and husky voice, Tina Turner has been an unmistakable presence in the international music scene since the 1960s, despite her ups and downs. She first made her name as part of the Ike and Tina Turner Revue with her husband and their backup band and singers. Though the group had no huge hits until 1971's "Proud Mary," they became a sensation in Europe and opened for the Rolling Stones during the British Invasion heyday. After a stormy marriage rife with extreme mental and physical abuse, however, Turner left her husband in 1976 and eventually rebuilt her career as a solo artist. She saw a major success in 1984 with the album *Private Dancer,* which re–established her image complete with fishnet stockings, stiletto heels, and a wild mane of hair to a new generation of fans. Continuing to record into her sixties, she was back in music news again in early 2000 with the release of her first album in four years.

Turner was born Annie Mae Bullock in Brownsville, Tennessee, on November 26, 1939, and grew up in nearby Nut Bush. Her father, Floyd Richard Bullock, worked as the resident overseer for a white–owned farm, and also served as a deacon at the Woodlawn Baptist Church. Her mother, Zelma, was of Native American and African American heritage. The family included another daughter, Alline, three years Turner's senior. As a child, Turner was a "brazen tomboy," as she remembered in her autobiography, *I, Tina.* When she was about three, her parents left the farm to seek work on the other side of the state. Though they reunited at times, Turner and her sister mainly were raised by their grandmothers.

While living with her parents for a time in Spring Hill, Tennessee, Turner joined the church choir. Though she recalled in her memoir that "I wasn't much of a one for church, to tell you the truth," she loved singing and dreamed of having a glamorous career far from a life of picking cotton on the farms. When she was about ten, her mother left home to live with an aunt in St. Louis, Missouri, and her father soon married again, but he and his new wife fought often–she even stabbed him–and they divorced after about a year.

When she was 13, Turner's dad moved to Detroit and left her and Alline with a cousin. Soon, Turner found work with a white man, Guy Tucker Henderson, who owned a Chevrolet dealership in Ripley, and his wife, Connie. She took care of their baby and helped with housework, and eventually moved in with them. She enjoyed their warmth and the fact that they displayed a stable and loving relationship. Turner attended Lauderdale High School and became a cheerleader, but later had to move back to Nut Bush, where she enrolled at Carver High School in Brownsville. There, she was a school leader, involved in basketball, track, and cheerleading, as well as being an organizer of parties, dances, and class trips. She also performed in talent shows. Meanwhile, she continued to commute to Ripley on weekends to work for the Hendersons.

In the mid–1950s, Turner moved to St. Louis to live with her mother and attend Sumner High School. However, her older sister, Alline, was already working as a barmaid in a jazz club, so Turner began to go see bands with her. It was then she first saw Ike Turner play at Club Manhattan with the Kings of Rhythm, the most popular local act of the day and one of the seminal groups of the burgeoning genre of rock music. Their 1951 single "Rocket 88" was a number–one R&B hit and has been called the first rock and roll record ever made. Recalling her first impression of him in *I, Tina,* she wrote, "I thought, 'God, I wonder why so many women like him? He sure is ugly.' But I kept listening and looking. I almost went into a trance just watching him."

Turner's sister was dating the group's drummer, who arranged for her to showcase her vocal talent for Ike Turner. She began singing regularly with the Kings of Rhythm in 1956 under the name Little Ann. After becoming pregnant by the band's saxophone player, Raymond Hill, Turner had her first son, Raymond Craig, in 1958. The family lived in Ike Turner's house for a while, but Craig eventually left. After that, she moved back home with her mother and supplemented her income by working as a nurse's assistant in a hospital. But soon, she moved back in with Ike Turner in East St. Louis and he gave her a pay increase. Turner related in her autobiography, "In the very beginning, Ike and I really were just like brother and sister . But we communicated through music."

Meanwhile, Ike was still living with his second wife, Lorraine, and the two had a son in 1959. He also had another child by another mistress, and he got Turner pregnant in January of 1960. They had a son, Ronald Renelle. Amid this personal turmoil, Turner cut the single, "A Fool in Love" in 1960 when the scheduled session singer failed to show up. The song became the duo's first crossover hit, reaching number 27 on the pop chart and number two on the R&B chart. It was released under the name the Ike and Tina Turner Revue, and the band thus changed its name.

Turner married Ike in Tijuana, Mexico, in 1962, even though he remained married to Lorraine until 1974. In the meantime, he began to beat Turner viciously, constantly giving her black eyes and cuts on her lips, face, and head. He also had relationships with women in the Ikettes their backup singers and dancers and others. But the stage act was going well; the group had appeared on *American Bandstand* and played nationally, in addition to charting with a few more singles. Sue Records resigned Ike Turner, which allowed him to buy a house in a mainly white area of Los Angeles.

In the 1960s, Ike and Tina Turner released the single "River Deep, Mountain High," which attracted no attention at the time in the United States, but would later be considered a classic. "That record never found a home," she explained in *I, Tina.* "It was too black for the pop stations, and too pop for the black stations." But it hit number three on the British pop charts in 1966. They were thus invited to tour Europe with the Rolling Stones, who were big aficionados of bluesy African American rock. Turner then became a major influence on the dancing style of front man Mick Jagger.

In 1969, the Ike and Tina Turner Revue toured the United States with the Rolling Stones, and started to gain a wider audience in America with appearances on television variety shows. They had another hit with a cover of Otis Redding's "I've Been Loving You Too Much" in 1969, and in 1970 released versions of the Beatles' "Come Together" and Sly and the Family Stone's "I Want to Take You Higher." Then, in 1971 they scored their first top ten hit in the United States with a remake of the Creedence Clearwater Revival tune "Proud Mary." Reaching number four on the pop chart their highest–charting record ever the cut sold a million copies. It came off their album *Working Together,* which peaked at number 25. This energetic interpretation became one of their signature hits, and won them a Grammy Award for best R&B performance by a duo or group in 1971.

Also in 1971, Ike and Tina Turner scored a gold record with *Live at Carnegie Hall.* Then, in 1973, they charted with Turner's own composition, "Nutbush City Limits." However, Ike's abuse and his reliance on cocaine was wearing down the singer, and their popularity was starting to wane. She began practicing Buddhism, which increased her self–esteem, and was further emboldened after landing an acting role, playing the Acid Queen in the 1975 film version of The Who's rock opera, *Tommy.* After that, she and Ike released their final charting single, "Baby Get It On," which only reached number 88.

Meanwhile, Turner also recorded two solo albums, *Let Me Touch Your Mind,* 1972; and *Tina Turns the Country On,* 1974. Though neither were hits, she was becoming closer to making a break from Ike. Finally, in 1976 she literally ran away from him, darting down an alley from a hotel before a scheduled concert with just 36 cents in her pocket. She had no money because Ike had kept tight control on the finances, so she stayed with friends, living on food stamps and earning her keep by cleaning their houses. Soon, Ike sent the four children their two sons and his two to live with Turner. The couple's divorce was final in 1978. That same year, Turner released another solo album, *Rough,* but it was a flop.

By now, Turner was about $500,000 in debt, mainly to the IRS and because of breaking appearance contracts after leaving Ike. Rebuilding her career from the bottom up, Turner got in touch with Australian Roger Davies, who became her manager. She toured again with the Rolling Stones, and after cutting an electronic–oriented version of "Ball of Confusion," she began to emerge again. Another cover, of the Al Green ballad "Let's Stay Together," became a dance hit in England and America. Upon release of her 1984 album, *Private Dancer,* for Capitol, she was re–established as a superstar. Turner won four Grammy Awards for the effort, including song of the year, record of the year, and best female pop vocal performance for "What's Love Got to Do with It," which was also her first number–one hit. She landed on the cover of *Rolling Stone* and in numerous other magazines, and on scores of television shows.

Also in 1984, Turner was asked to appear in the film *Mad Max Beyond Thunderdome,* portraying the ruler of a futuristic dystopia and costarring with Mel Gibson. The film was released in 1985, and she received an NAACP award for best actress for her role as Aunty Entity. Also, her soundtrack cut, "We Don't Need Another Hero (Thunderdome)," reached number two on the charts. She also appeared at the benefit concert Live Aid in 1984 and toured with Lionel Richie, and the following year, sang on the charity recording "We Are the World," for the USA for Africa relief effort. By March of 1985, "Private Dancer" reached the top ten, becoming along with "Be Good to Me" the third top ten hit from her album. Meanwhile, Ike Turner fell into obscurity, and had been arrested in 1981 for allegedly shooting a newspaper deliveryman in the ankle.

In 1986, Turner's next album on Capitol, *Break Every Rule,* reached number three on the charts and spawned the top two single "Typical Male." Also that year she penned her autobiography with journalist Kurt Loder, and the next year, she embarked on a wildly successful world tour which broke box office records in 13 nations. In 1989, Turner released another effort, *Foreign Affair,* which she helped produce and arrange, but it was a much bigger hit in Europe than in the United States.

After her 1987–88 tour, Turner claimed she would back off her live performances so that she could concentrate on her acting career. However, she vowed to quit touring time and again, and continued to take the stage anyway as her acting career never quite geared up. She signed a deal with Virgin Records in 1992, and the next year, was nominated for two Grammys for "I Don't Want to Fight," which was featured on the soundtrack to 1993's

What's Love Got to Do with It, a film based on her life starring Angela Bassett and Lawrence Fishburne. In 1995, she teamed with U2's Bono and the Edge on the theme for the James Bond movie *Goldeneye.*

Also in 1995, Turner started work on her first studio album in five years, and began a European tour the following year. She also put out a new album, *Wildest Dreams*, in 1996, and toured to promote it in 1997. Not surprisingly, the tour was sponsored by hosiery company Hanes, which featured Turner and her famous legs in their advertisements. In January of 2000, Turner performed at the Super Bowl halftime show, and in February released another album, *Twenty Four Seven.* It entered the charts at number 21, the highest of any album in her career.

Turner moved to Zurich, Switzerland, in the 1990s, and spends her time there and at her dream home in Nice, in the south of France on the Mediterranean, which took years to complete. She noted in *Jet* that she decided to live in Europe because her fan base is larger there, and she also has a boyfriend there. She has been romantically attached to Erwin Bach, a German EMI Records executive, since the late 1980s. As she edges past 60, Turner has retained her sultry good looks and toned figure, which she has attributed to a sensible diet and Buddhist chanting. As far back as when she was in her forties, some began to marvel about her stamina and presence at "her age," but Turner told Edna Gunderson in *Ebony,* "Age and color are things I don't think about. It can be a real obstacle to assume I can't have something because I'm a Black woman. Or to tell myself I'm too old for this or that. I guess I've broken some rules. I don't put limits on my life."

Selected discography

With Ike Turner

It's Gonna Work out Fine, Sue, 1961.
The Soul of Ike and Tina Turner, Sue, 1964.
The Ike and Tina Turner Show Vol. 1, Warner, 1965.
The Ike and Tina Turner Show, Warner,1965.
Greatest Hits, London, 1965.
Finger Poppin', Warner, 1966.
The Ike and Tina Turner Revue, Ember, 1966.
River Deep Mountain High, London, 1966.
Somebody Needs You (EP), Warner, 1967.
The Ike and Tina Turner Show Vol. 2, Warner, 1967.
Greatest Hits, Hallmark, 1968.
So Fine, London, 1969.
Outta Season, Liberty, 1969.
In Person, Minit, 1969.
Ike and Tina's Greatest Hits, Warner, 1969.

The Ike and Tina Turner Show, Valiant, 1970.
Come Together, Liberty, 1970.
The Hunter, Harvest, 1970.
Workin' Together (includes "Proud Mary"), Liberty, 1971.
The Fantastic Ike and Tina Turner, Sunset, 1971.
Her Man His Woman, Capitol, 1971.
Live in Paris, Liberty, 1971.
What You Hear Is What You Get, United Artists (UA), 1971.
'Nuff Said, UA, 1972.
Feel Good, UA,1972.
The Ike and Tina Turner Revue, New World, 1972.
16 Peaches, Mojo, 1973.
The World of Ike and Tina Turner, UA, 1973.
Nutbush City Limits, UA, 1973.
The Gospel According to Ike and Tina, UA, 1974.
Sweet Rhode Island Red, UA, 1974.
Souled From The Vaults, DJM, 1976.
Delila's Power, UA, 1977.
Airwaves, 1979.

Solo albums

Let Me Touch Your Mind, UA, 1972.
Tina Turns the Country On!, UA, 1974.
Acid Queen, UA, 1975.
Tina Turner Country, 1976.
Rough, UA, 1979.
Love Explosion, UA, 1979.
Sunset on Sunset, 1979.
Mini, Fantasy, 1984.
Private Dancer (includes "What's Love Got to Do with It?" and "Better Be Good to Me"), Capitol, 1984.
The Edge, Fantasy, 1985.
Mad Max Beyond Thunderdome (original soundtrack recording; includes "We Don't Need Another Hero" and "One of the Living"), Capitol, 1985.
Break Every Rule (includes "Back Where You Started"), Capitol, 1986.
(With others*) The Prince's Trust 10th Anniversary Birthday Party*, A&M, 1987.
The Ike and Tina Turner Sessions, Kent, 1987.
Tina Live in Europe, Capitol, 1988.
I Don't Wanna Lose You, Capitol, 1989.
Foreign Affair, Capitol, 1989.
(With others) *Days of Thunder* (soundtrack), DGC, 1990.
Tina Turner Goes Country, Laurie Records, 1990.
Simply the Best, Capitol, 1991.
What's Love Got to Do with It (movie soundtrack), Virgin, 1993.
(With others) *Black on White: Great R&B Covers of Rock Classics*, Rhino, 1993.
(With Ike Turner) *Sexy, Seductive, Provocative* (reissue of previously released material), Paula Records, 1993.

Tina Live Private Dancer Tour 1985, 1994.
Tina Turner: The Collected Recordings Sixties to Nineties, 1994.
Wildest Dreams, Virgin, 1996.
Twenty Four Seven, Virgin, 2000.

Has also performed duets with other artists, including David Bowie, Bryan Adams, Eric Clapton, and Rod Stewart.

Sources

Books

Contemporary Black Biography, volume 6, Gale Research, 1994.
Contemporary Musicians, volume 1, Gale Research, 1989.
Contemporary Theater, Film and Television, volume 14, Gale Research, 1995.
Encyclopedia of World Biography, second edition, Gale Research, 1998.
Notable Black American Women, Book 1, Gale Research, 1992.
Turner, Tina, with Kurt Loder, *I, Tina*, Morrow, 1986.

Periodicals

Ebony, May 1971, p. 88; June 1982, p. 66; May 1985, p. 76; November 1986, p. 31; January 1982, p. 102; July 1993, p. 110; September 1996, p. 38.
Entertainment Weekly, May 28, 1999, p. 34.
Essence, July 1993, p. 50; October 1996, p. 50.
GQ, June 1993, p. 180.
Harper's Bazaar, December 1996, p. 150.
Jet, March 17, 1997, p. 32.
Ladies Home Journal, April 1987, p. 34.
McCall's, August 1985, p. 16; November 1997, p. 52.
Newsweek, November 3, 1969, p. 92.
People, December 7, 1981, p. 100; July 15, 1985, p. 44; January 31, 2000, p. 35.
Rolling Stone, October 11, 1984, p. 18; October 23, 1986, p. 46.
Time, June 21, 1993, p. 64.
Vogue, May 1985, p. 318.

Online

"Tina Turner," Internet Movie Database web site, http://us.imdb.com (April 4, 2000).
Tina Turner official web site, http://www.tina-turner.com (April 4, 2000).

Abdurrahman Wahid

AP/Wide World Photos

President of Indonesia

Known as "Gus Dur;" born August 4, 1940, in Jombang, East Java, Indonesia. *Education:* Attended college in Cairo, Egypt; and Baghdad, Iraq.

Addresses: *Home*—South Jakarta, Indonesia.

Career

Head of Nahdlatul Ulama (Indonesian Islamic organization); President of Indonesia, 1999 .

Sidelights

On October 20, 1999, Abdurrahman Wahid was elected as president of Indonesia, the world's fourth most populous nation. As the fourth leader of the country since its independence from the Netherlands 54 years prior, he became the first freely elected leader in its history. Long one of the most popular figures in Indonesia, Wahid is better known as Gus Dur, meaning "older brother." However, his ascent was still a surprise, given that the front–runner for the presidential race was Megawati Sukarnoputri, the daughter of Sukarno, who was the first president of independent Indonesia. In his first political move after receiving the winning vote by the national assembly, Wahid named her his vice president, thus putting her in line as the heir apparent and quelling the bulk of controversy from her supporters. Though he is the nation's first cleric to become president, he made his name as a moderate Islamic leader known for extolling tolerance in this nation of 220 million which is rife with differences.

Not a great deal is known about the background of Abdurrahman Wahid (pronounced "ab– door– RAH–man wah–heed"). In fact, shortly before his election, a biography came out in Indonesia titled *Gus Dur: Who Are You?* It is known that he was born on August 4, 1940, in Jombang, East Java, Indonesia, and educated in Cairo, Egypt; and Baghdad, Iraq. He became a prominent religious scholar and was long one of the most influential people in his country. His grandfather had started Nahdlatul Ulama, a moderate Islamic organization, and his father had been revered as its leader as well. Wahid eventually took over the group, too, which counts about 20 million members and 40 million followers. The organization also runs traditional Islamic schools. As a religious leader, Wahid is thought to have supernatural powers, and some continue to believe that his grandfather can bless people from beyond the grave.

Wahid established himself as a unifying force in Indonesia, a country plagued by internal strife. Made up of 7,000 inhabited islands, religious and cultural differences abound; the nation counts 300 languages and dialects. And though government statistics claim that 87 percent of its people are Muslims, an *Economist* report noted that only 30 percent are actually practicing. In this mix, Wahid has been respected for his ongoing pleas for religious and cultural tolerance and cooperation, and is a staunch defender of the Christian and Chinese minorities. He also became a driving force in the small National Awakening Party (PKB).

Meanwhile, Megawati, after spending much of her life as a homemaker, decided to enter politics in the late 1980s. She rose to become leader of the Indonesian Democratic Party (PDI), which opposed the ruling Golkar. Indonesia had been under control of Golkar and leader Suharto since the late 1960s, when he forced Megawati's father, Sukarno, out of power. Since then, the nation had been lifted out of poverty thanks to growth in oil sales, but Suharto had also been harshly criticized for banning most opposition parties, for rampant nepotism under his rule, and for the growing divide between the very poor and the ultra–wealthy. Once the oil market declined and the Asian crisis hit in the 1990s, the country started to resist, and the two legal opposition parties that were allowed in order to somewhat appease the masses gained in popularity. One of these was the PDI.

In 1997 elections, Suharto did not let Megawati run for office, and the result was massive rioting, looting, and violence in the streets. Golkar forced Suharto to resign in 1998, and his vice president, Bacharuddin Jusuf Habibie, assumed office. However, he held elections again in June of 1999, and candidates included Habibie (who dropped out at the last minute), Megawati, Wahid, and Amien Rais, who supported student protests. Megawati's PDI party captured 462 out of 700 seats, far ahead of second–place Golkar, which had a stronghold on Indonesian politics until then. However, it was still not a clear majority, which meant that she would need to form a coalition. Wahid's party captured just 12 percent.

After Megawati showed no interest in forming a coalition, Wahid became concerned that she would end up dividing the government further. He decided to run against her and formed his own coalition. Once Wahid announced his candidacy, some questioned his ability to lead due to his health problems. Bedridden much of the time and nearly blind due to high blood pressure and circulatory problems, he also suffered two strokes in the years prior to his election. His failing eyesight requires him to have help maneuvering around his own home. However, he traveled to an eye clinic in Salt Lake City, Utah, in 1999, which he said helped restore some black–and–white vision. And according to Seth Mydans in the *New York Times*, after he declared his candidacy he told a local magazine, "Everything has been examined. Stomach, kidney,

blood, mental and memory assessment. Everything is good, excellent." Nevertheless, a *Newsweek* report stated that he suffers from kidney problems and diabetes, and cannot walk without assistance. In addition, many pointed out that he was known for making unusual and sometimes conflicting public statements, and thus questioned his mental capacity. Others, however, staunchly defended him as being sharp and wise.

In October of 1999, the national assembly elected Wahid president by a vote of 373 to 313, with 5 abstentions. After his win, about 10,000 of Megawati's supporters poured into the streets after the vote, charging security forces and setting fires, but there was only one reported fatality. Subsequently, in a savvy move, Wahid nominated Megawati as his vice president, which quieted the unrest. She was voted in the next day.

In one of Wahid's early decisions, he appointed a civilian as Defense Minister, thus wresting power away from the strong military, which historically had a large hand in Suharto's dictatorship. The rest of his cabinet was also quite diverse, creating what he called a "national unity cabinet," according to Mydans in the *New York Times*. It featured an array of political affiliations but shied away from anyone formerly connected to the corruption under Suharto. Wahid's efforts in this realm were applauded.

One of Wahid's most pressing concerns upon taking office was the economy. During Suharto's rein, corruption became rampant at all levels, and the economy suffered greatly. In his acceptance speech, Wahid promised economic reform but kept his talk brief, explaining, "the longer I speak, the more we will have to account for later." This was just one example of how he acquired his reputation for having a keen wit. Upon taking office, Wahid delegated a great deal of power to Megawati, thus further placating her supporters. He also allowed her close advisors to begin running the economy.

Soon, though, Wahid witnessed an uprising in violence on the remote Molucca islands, where Christian and Muslim fighting left 400 dead. And, he became embroiled in a flap over military leaders when investigators asked for a trial for some top army generals. They were accused of human rights violations in East Timor, which gained its independence around the same time as the elections. One of the generals implicated was Wiranto, the former army chief whom Wahid picked to be his political affairs minister. At first, Wahid indicated that he would ask for Wiranto to be exempted from the investigation, but later, after some confusing and seemingly contradictory statements, he asked for Wiranto's resignation along with three other top generals in his cabinet.

By spring of 2000, Wahid seemed to be making progress in his fledgling democracy. Civilian rule was being restored, and the economy was stronger. Interest rates, for instance, had fallen from 70 percent at their peak to 12 percent. In addition, a rise in oil prices was helping to bring in revenue. His next steps included boosting investors' confidence, which would involve bringing in foreign aid and selling off assets from failed banks. However, an *Economist* article noted that Wahid needed to do better in stamping out corruption.

A personable man, Wahid is renowned for his down–to–earth manner and his ability to put people at ease. "Meeting Abdurrahman Wahid at his modest South Jakarta home is like visiting a respected village elder," wrote Ron Moreau and Maggie Ford in *Newsweek*. "You always find a line of people waiting to see him: slick–suited businessmen, social activists, poor East Javanese farmers all come to unload their troubles and receive his blessing." He is said to enjoy Western literature and music, including Beethoven and Mozart, and he can speak English, Arabic, German, Indonesian, and Bhasa Indonesian, his country's official language.

Sources

Periodicals

Business Week, November 8, 1999, p. 43; February 14, 2000, p. 26.
Economist, October 23, 1999, pp. 17, 41; October 30, 1999, p. 43; January 8, 2000, p. 38; January 22, 2000, p. 40; February 12, 2000, pp. 4, 37; February 19, 2000, p. 42; March 25, 2000, p. 44.
Newsweek, November 1, 1999, p. 54.
New York Times, October 21, 1999, pp. A1, A8; October 27, 1999, p. A6; December 15, 1999, p. A14; December 27, 1999, p. A3; February 8, 2000, p. A14; February 14, 2000, p. A6; February 15, 2000, p. A8.
Time, November 1, 1999, p. 54.
Time International, November 1, 1999, p. 27.
U.S. News & World Report, November 1, 1999, p. 49.

Online

"Indonesian Parliament Chooses New President," *New York Times* web site, October 20, 1999, http://www.nytimes.com (October 23, 1999).

Kurt Warner

AP/Wide World Photos

Football player

Born Kurtis Warner, June 22, 1971, in Burlington, IA; son of Gene (a telephone company supervisor) and Sue (a clerk) Warner; married Brenda Meoni (a nurse), 1997; children: stepdaughter Jesse; stepson Zachary; son Kade. *Education:* Northern Iowa University, communications degree, 1994.

Addresses: *Office*—c/o St. Louis Rams, One Rams Way, St. Louis, MO 63045.

Career

Arena League football, quarterback for Iowa Barnstormers, 1995–97; signed with St. Louis Rams, 1997; NFL Europe, quarterback for Amsterdam Admirals, 1998; St. Louis Rams, began as third quarterback, 1998, became starting quarterback, 1999.

Awards: Gateway Conference offensive player of the year, 1994; *Sporting News* player of the year, 1999; NFL and Super Bowl most valuable player, 1999.

Sidelights

When Kurt Warner became a third–string quarterback for the St. Louis Rams of the National Football League (NFL) in 1998, no one would have predicted that by the end of the next season, he would be the hero of Super Bowl XXXIV. At six feet tall and 220 pounds, he was not exceptionally big,

nor was he particularly fast, and no one had ever heard of him. In addition, it seemed unlikely that the Rams would have made it to the Super Bowl coming off the heels of their dismal 1998 season, when they posted a 4–12 win–loss record. But after an injury sidelined their starting quarterback for 1999, Warner proved to be more than able to do the job.

Though Warner was a virtual unknown when he began as the Rams' starting quarterback, he had paid his dues for a few years in a minor league after not making the cut for the NFL following his one year in college ball. As he mentioned to Peter King in *Sports Illustrated*, "People think this season is the first time I touched a football; they don't realize I've been doing this for years just not on this level, because I never got the chance. Sure, I had my tough times, but you don't sit there and say, 'Wow, I was stocking groceries five years ago, and look at me now.' You don't think about it, and when you do achieve something, you know luck has nothing to do with it." In addition to his talents on the field, Warner is known as a dedicated family man and devout Christian.

Warner was born on June 22, 1971, in Burlington, Iowa. His father, Gene, works as a supervisor for a telephone company, and his mother, Sue, is a clerk for a plastic–bag manufacturer. They divorced when he was five. His mother raised him and his step-brother, Matt Post, in Cedar Rapids, Iowa, where Warner attended Cedar Rapids Regis High School. He lettered in football, basketball, and baseball. Though he had always played receiver on the football field, he changed positions as a high school freshman because the team needed a quarterback.

Despite his athleticism, Warner was not offered a Division I–A college scholarship offer. Instead, he enrolled at Northern Iowa University, a Division I–AA school, and was benched for three seasons. He finally started in his senior year in 1993, and was named Gateway offensive player of the year by the season's end. In 1994, he went to NFL training camp for the Green Bay Packers, where Brett Favre was the starter and Mark Burnell and Ty Detmer were competing for the number two and three positions.

After being cut from the Packers, Warner went back to Cedar Falls and worked at a 24–hour supermarket by night while continuing to work out and sharpen his skills on the football field by day. "That was obviously a very humbling experience," Warner remarked to Michael Silver in *Sports Illustrated.* "I was making $5.50 an hour and I was darn happy to get it. I'd tell the other guys at the store, 'I'll be playing football again someday,' and they'd look at me like I was some guy who just couldn't let go."

In 1995, Warner joined the Arena League and played for the Iowa Barnstormers, helping to take them to two Arena Bowl games in his three seasons there. During that time, he threw for 10,465 yards and 183 touchdowns, and still holds all of the Barnstormers' individual passing records. This caught the attention of Al Luginbill, coach of the Amsterdam Admirals in the NFL Europe League. He wanted to harness Warner's passing abilities, but could only get him if an NFL team offered him a contract, then assigned him to Amsterdam. Luginbill pitched his idea to at least ten NFL teams before the St. Louis Rams finally signed Warner on December 26, 1997. Subsequently, he played starting quarterback for all ten of the Amsterdam Admirals games, leading the league that year in yardage, completions, and touchdowns. Then, at the Rams' 1998 training camp, he beat out Will Furrer for the team's third quarterback position.

On December 27, 1998, Warner played in his first NFL contest, in the fourth quarter of the Rams' final game against San Francisco. It was the only action he saw that year, spending the season behind Tony Banks and Steve Bono. He completed four passes in 11 attempts for 39 yards in that performance. After the Rams lost twice as many games as they won that year under starter Banks, the team signed Trent Green, a $16.5 million free agent they nabbed from the Washington Redskins, and moved up Warner to the number two slot in the spring of 1999.

Green's year came to a halt in the preseason when he suffered a knee injury during an exhibition game on August 28, 1999, and the Rams thus called upon Warner to fit the bill. At the time, David Fleming in *Sports Illustrated* wrote, "Can he do the job?" Coach Dick Veremeil had faith that Warner would do well, but he admitted that did not expect him to be the team's savior. In fact, the Rams had listed Warner when they needed to make five players available in the expansion draft, but the Cleveland Browns had not selected him.

At the time he became the starting quarterback for the Rams, Warner was an unknown who was frequently confused with Curt Warner, a standout running back for Penn State and the Seattle Seahawks who had not played pro ball since his final year with the Los Angeles Rams in 1990. In fact, in 1998 Warner got a call from his agent's office asking if he would appear on a talk radio show devoted to discussing the 1983 Sugar Bowl. According to Silver in *Sports Illustrated,* he quipped, "Sure, I'd love to. I was 12 at the time, and I remember watching it on TV."

Just six weeks after Green's injury, Warner began to attract attention. As Silver wrote, "Highly drafted quarterbacks typically don't shine until their third season, if ever, but Warner, with all his minor league seasoning, burst onto the scene like an old pro. His accuracy is uncanny, and he shows poise, toughness and an aptitude for reading defenses in a hurry." Fifteen games into the season, he had thrown 475 passes, completing 313 for an outstanding record of 65.9 percent. "This is what I expected to do when I got a chance to play," Warner remarked to Phil Sheridan of the *Knight–Ridder/Tribune News Service.* "I expected to play well and I expected my team to win. And I expect to go a lot farther."

By the season's end, Warner had thrown for 41 touchdowns, joining Dan Marino to become the second quarterback ever to throw 40 in a season. He also threw for 4,353 yards in the regular season, leading the Rams to a 13–3 record for 1999 the most wins in the history of their franchise. He also closed the season with the best completion percentage in the NFL, at 65.1 percent, and posted nine 300–yard passing games, tying the record for most in season. He also boasted a 109.2 passer rating, the best in the NFL for the year and the fifth–highest single–season rating ever. In January of 2000, Warner was named player of the year by the *Sporting News*, and took his team to victory in the divisional playoffs as they trounced the Minnesota Vikings 49–37.

Then, on January 30, 2000, Warner and his team-mates squeaked through a tense game to beat the Tennessee Titans 23–16 and clinch the Super Bowl. With only 1 minute 54 seconds left in the game, Warner connected on a 73–yard pass to Isaac Bruce to break a 16–16 tie. Mike Freeman of the *New York Times* wrote that the play "will surely go down as one of the most spectacular in championship history." During the game, Warner set a Super Bowl record of 414 passing yards and won the game's most valuable player honors. He was also named the NFL's most valuable player for the season. The Rams' win was even more remarkable considering that coach Vermeil, the second–oldest in the league, had not coached for 14 years until getting hired by the Rams in 1997 after their first four choices did not pan out. A couple of days after the Super Bowl, Vermeil retired.

In addition to Warner's uphill battle to become an NFL player, let alone a star, he has had to deal with challenges in his personal life. In college in 1992 at a country music club, he had met nurse Brenda Meoni, a 25–year–old former Marine and a single mother of a daughter, Jesse, and son, Zachary ("Zach"), who suffered brain damage and became legally blind after his biological father dropped him on his head when he was a baby. Meoni's husband found it difficult to cope with the accident, and their marriage broke up shortly before the birth of their daughter. When Meoni met Warner, she assumed that he would shy away from the responsibility, but instead, he called her the next day, and they married in 1997. He adopted her children and they also have a son, Kade. In addition, Warner helped his wife through a difficult time when both of her parents were killed in a tornado that leveled their Mountain View, Arkansas home in 1996.

Warner attributes the positive events in his life to his strong Christian faith. He gives weekly Bible study classes in his home, and does not drink, smoke, or swear. In fact, after talks developed about giving him a raise to a multimillion dollar salary, he stated that any increase above what he earned in 1999 the league minimum for a second–year player, $245,000 would be donated to Camp Barnabus, a Christian retreat for special–needs children and their families in Purdy, Missouri. He also donated to charity his seven–figure sum for endorsing a breakfast cereal.

Sources

Periodicals

Arizona Republic, January 31, 2000, p. C1.
Knight–Ridder/Tribune News Service, December 30, 1999.
New York Times, January 31, 2000, p. D1.
People, January 17, 2000, p. 99.
Sporting News, January 31, 2000, p. 12; February 7, 2000, p. 71.
Sports Illustrated, September 13, 1999, p. 112; October 18, 1999, p. 58; February 9, 2000, p. 76.

Online

"Kurt Warner," NFL web site, http://www.nfl.com (April 24, 2000).
"Warner named MVP by Associated Press," NFL web site, http://nflcom/news (April 24, 2000).
"Once Upon a Time Five years after bagging groceries, Kurt Warner is living a dream," NFL Insider Spotlight on NFL web site, http://www.nfl.com (April 24, 2000).

Alonzo Washington

Comic book artist

Born Alonzo Lavert Washington, June 1, 1967, in Kansas City, MO; son of Millie C. Washington (a preschool teacher); married, March 24, 1993; wife's name, Dana D. (an HIV counselor); children: five sons, Antonio S. Davis, Akeem Alonzo, Kamaal Malik, Malcolm, Khalid; one daughter, Alona. *Education:* Attended Kansas City Community College and Pioneer Community College, Kansas City, MO.

Addresses: *Home*—Kansas City, MO. *Office*—Omega 7 Inc., P.O. Box 171046, Kansas City, KS 66117.

Career

AD HOC Group Against Crime, Kansas City, MO, gang and youth counselor and intervention specialist, 1990–92; Swope Parkway Health Center, outreach specialist and counselor, 1992–94; Omega 7 Comics Inc., president, publisher, writer, and designer, 1992 . Member of Black National Congress (president, 1990), Black United Front (honorary member, 1990), Association of African American Comic Book Publishers (president, 1994), New Democracy Movement (1995).

Awards: Black United Front (Kansas City chapter) Malcolm X Leadership Award, 1991; UB & UBS Communication Systems publisher of the year award, 1992; Mayor Emmanuel Cleaver II (Kansas City, MO) Certification of Appreciation, 1993; United Minority Media Association distinguished community service award, 1993; Kansas City Masterminds Alliance Golden Eagle community service award, 1994.

Sidelights

Alonzo Washington is the owner and president of Omega 7 comics, which produces a line of titles featuring black superheroes. One of the few artists creating African American comic books, he started with one prototype that he developed in order to help steer kids away from crime. "The comic books are part of the activism that I was involved with before I started the company," he noted in an interview with *Newsmakers.* Since then, the business has expanded to carry seven separate titles all of which Washington develops and writes featuring an extensive collection of characters. A comic aficionado since he was a small child, Washington had always been dismayed by the lack of positive black characters. Tired of seeing African Americans portrayed as ex–cons, villains, jokers, and sidekicks, he set out to establish a black superhero, but one who would deal with real events rather than make–believe scenarios. "With my product," he stated in *Black Enterprise,* "I knew I was going to break stereotypes and address social issues. I wanted to educate and enlighten African American youth."

Washington was born on June 1, 1967, in Kansas City, Missouri, to Millie C. Washington, a divorced mother who raised him on her own while working as a preschool teacher. As far back as he can recall, Washington has been an avid comic book fan. When he was young, he began to admire superheroes such as Superman, Batman, and Spiderman. However, there was an absence of black comic characters on the pages. "At the worst, they were sidekicks or stereotypes," Washington noted to Jack Mingo in the *Washington Post.* "At best, they were like Superman dipped in chocolate not really African American."

In school, Washington began to paint his action figures to look black and pressed on clay afros, and he began drawing his own black superheroes. By fifth grade, he was selling his drawings to other students for 25 cents. As he grew up, he developed an interest in fighting crime in real life as well. After graduating from Kansas City's Washington High School, he hosted a public television show that aimed to show positive role models to kids in order to steer them away from bad elements. He also became a community activist to oppose gangs and drugs and helped organize groups to mentor children, teach self–defense courses to women, paint over graffiti, and other efforts that demonstrated that not all news regarding African Americans was negative. Washington served as a youth counselor in Kansas City from 1990 to 1994 and has remained dedicated to anti–crime initiatives. He was involved with Quest for Peace, a push to address the gang situation in his city, and also helped organize a gang "summit" in order to persuade members to abandon their rivalry. Later, Washington would also become active in teaching children about how to avoid being abducted by drilling in them the "three R's" run, resist and report.

In the meantime, Washington combined his interest in comics with his social involvement in creating the Original Man comic book, which he gave to African American kids to improve their self–esteem. The concept was a hit around Kansas City, so by 1992, Washington began looking for publishers. None of the large comic publishers felt it would work, so he decided to do it himself. Promoting the idea on posters and flyers and by sending information to local bookstores, churches, and community organizations, Washington managed to line up about $1,000 worth of advance orders. He began churning out issues and eventually printed a first run of 5,000 copies.

The character had developed by now into Omega Man, a caped African American superhero who sports a black, red, and yellow bodysuit the colors of African liberation. In addition, he wears a braid down his back, a symbol of African royalty. In the comics, Omega Man travels back from the future where crime, drug abuse, and racism are a thing of the past, and he works to prevent ne'er–do–well time travelers from attempting to alter history in order to foil the utopia. Omega Man uses his powers of advanced intelligence and strength, not to mention his qualities of being bullet–proof and able to fly, to protect this ideal future. In his adventures, Omega Man addresses current events, such as the Million Man March and the murders of Nicole Brown and Ron Goldman. Omega Man, according to Washington in the *Newsmakers* interview, is "more than a comic book. It's dealing with social issues."

When the first printing of Omega Man sold out at $2 per copy, Washington invested in 10,000 more. Soon, Diamond Comics stepped in as a distributor, and Washington began developing new titles under the umbrella company name Omega 7. By 1999, according to Washington, his various books had sold more than a half a million copies collectively, making Omega 7 the largest African American–owned comic company in the nation. And, he has branched out to include black female heroes within his titles as well: His repertoire of titles includes Omega 7 (which features a diverse group of characters, including Original Woman and Dark Queen), Omega Man, Darkforce, Mighty Ace (also featuring the female character Lady Ace), Shadow Knight, Original Man, and Original Boy. And, in 1997, Omega 7 made news by becoming the first black–owned comic–book firm to market an action figure. It is sold directly by Omega 7 and hit the shelves at Toys R Us in Kansas City in January of 1997, available in both light and dark skin tones. By fall of 1999, Washington was expecting to release new editions of the Omega Man figure, as well as an action figure of Mighty Ace.

In 1999, after a number of school shootings had the nation enmeshed in a dialogue about youth and violence, Washington announced on his web site that he would be creating a special strip, available at no charge, to deal with such issues. The new strip was being launched with help from the Kansas City police department, which was planning to distribute trading cards featuring the Omega Man, Original Woman, and the Mighty Ace in conjunction with the effort. Washington's Omega 7 web site also noted that the company was asking for youth to write essays on violence in America, and the best were scheduled to run at a later date on the web site.

Washington was married on March 24, 1993, and his wife, Dana, is heavily involved with Omega 7, which is still based in his hometown of Kansas City. Dana Washington even dresses up as the superhero Original Woman to give anti–drug talks at schools. Washington's mother, Millie, is active in the business as well. Through mail–order, Omega 7 offers an extensive line of products such as hats, T–shirts, mugs, posters, watches, and trading cards, in addition to the comic books and action figures. Washington and his wife have six children five boys and a girl, the youngest all of whom are also involved with feedback in the business. "If I'm working and they won't stop looking over my shoulder or stop asking questions," he related to Mingo, "then I know I've come up with something good."

Sources

Books

Who's Who among African Americans, twelfth edition, Gale Group, 1999.

Periodicals

Black Enterprise, May 1997, p. 28; November 1998, p. 29.

Emerge, July/August 1998, p. 24.

People, April 14, 1997, p. 102.

Washington Post, July 13, 1998, p. D4.

Online

Creative Kansas City web site, http://www.creativekc.com (September 19, 1999).

Omega 7 web site, http://www.omega7.com (October 4, 1999).

Other

Newsmakers interview with Alonzo Washington, October 6, 1999.

Karrie Webb

Golfer

Born December 21, 1974, in Ayr, Queensland, Australia; daughter of Robert (construction company owner) and Evelyn (a restaurant owner) Webb.

Addresses: *Home*—Orlando, FL. *Office*—c/o LPGA, 100 International Golf Dr., Daytona Beach, FL 32124–1082.

Career

Professional golfer, 1994—.

Awards: Australian junior golf champion, 1991; won Weetabix Women's British Open, 1995; Women's Professional Golf (WPG) European Tour rookie of the year, 1995; won Ladies Professional Golf Association (LPGA) HealthSouth Inaugural, Sprint Titleholders Championship, SAFECO Classic, and ITT LPGA Tour Championship, 1996; named LPGA rookie of the year, 1996; won Weetabix Women's British Open, Susan G. Komen International, and SAFECO Classic, 1997; won Vare Trophy, 1997; won Australian Ladies Masters and City of Hope Myrtle Beach Classic, 1998; named LPGA player of the year, 1999; won LPGA Vare Trophy, 1999; won du Maurier Classic, The Office Depot, Australian Ladies Masters, Standard Register PING, Mercury Titleholders Championship, and the Wegmans Rochester International; won The Office Depot, Australian Women's Open, Australian Ladies Masters, Takefuji Classic, Nabisco Championship, and the U.S. Women's Open, 2000.

Sidelights

In 1996, Webb became the first Ladies' Professional Golf Association (LPGA) player to win $1 million in a single season, and the first–ever rookie, male or female, to pull in that amount. She was named rookie of the year in 1996 and went on to rival Annika Sorenstam as the tour's best player. In 1999, after posting 14 victories, she won her first major event at the du Maurier Classic in the midst of an outstanding season. With a total of six wins and some more broken records, Webb was named LPGA player of the year in 1999. By 2000, she had improved even more, and by then was attracting comparisons to male golf great Tiger Woods. As Webb commented in *USA Today*, "I have a gift, and that is to play golf. And I am not going to waste it . I really get caught up in the game. I work at getting better and better. I try to get as close to perfection as I can get."

Karrie (rhymes with "starry") Webb was born on December 21, 1974, in Ayr, Queensland, Australia, a town with a population of just under 9,000. Its biggest claim to fame until she came along was its sugarcane industry. Webb's parents, Robert and Evelyn Webb, own a construction firm and a fast–food business, and she has two younger sisters, Katie and Janelle. Growing up, she was a tomboy who participated on every boys' team possible. Webb began accompanying her parents to the nine–hole Ayr Golf Course as a toddler and could not wait to play, but the rules prohibited children under the age of age eight from playing. Not wasting time, her maternal grandmother bought her a set of clubs for her eighth birthday, and she began to make her way across the greens.

In 1986, as a Christmas/birthday gift, Webb's grandparents sent her to her first tournament, buying her a plane ticket to the Queensland Open to see her idol, Greg Norman. A Queensland native, he was at the time the world's top–ranked male player. At the event, Webb was one of hundreds of fans who lined up for his autograph. When she returned home, she was set on becoming a professional golfer. Webb gave up all other sports as well as playing the guitar and tap dancing in order to give full attention to her goal.

At the Ayr Golf Course, Webb started taking lessons with her future fiancé's uncle, Kevin Haller, who was also the greenskeeper. (Webb broke off the engagement with Todd Haller in 1996 so she could remain dedicated to her game.) "Karrie was very determined," Kevin Haller mentioned to Robinson Holloway in *Sports Illustrated*. "You didn't have to chase her down to practice; she'd be there before you. She was winning tournaments from the beginning, beating girls much older than she was." Haller has been Webb's coach ever since, even after an angioplasty operation caused him to have a stroke in the early 1990s and left him a paraplegic.

Before long, Webb was winning nearly every amateur tournament in her native country. She made the Australian junior team at age 16 and began traveling the globe for events. In 1991, she won the national junior championship. The prize for both the boy and girl winners was a week at Norman's home in Hobe Sound, Florida. He intended the trip to be like a golf boot camp. "They had to do everything I did, live the life of a professional for a week, to see if they had the dedication required," Norman told Holloway. "If I was up at dawn, they were up at dawn. If I lifted weights, they lifted weights. If I hit 400 balls, they hit 400 balls. Karrie was right there the whole way, whereas the boys couldn't keep up. She had the right attitude." Webb, meanwhile, did not recall the week with Norman as quite so rigorous, telling Holloway that they also went fishing and saw Universal Studios while on their visit.

After graduating from high school in Ayr, Webb won no offers to play college golf. She worked at her family's fast–food lunch stand flipping burgers and making sandwiches until 1993, then decided to give her all to golf. After about a year of amateur experience, she turned pro a month before her twentieth birthday. Her boyfriend, Haller, gave up his insurance career to become her caddie. They borrowed $5,000 from Webb's grandparents and embarked on the Women's Professional Golf (WPG) European Tour in 1995.

Webb had to face some challenges in her early career, such as dealing with a new language and currency each week while traveling through Europe.

"You can get ripped off if you don't think quickly enough," she remarked to Jim Burnett in *Golf Magazine*. A tournament in Austria marked the first time she ever saw snow. Beyond this, though, Webb had little trouble on the links. She made the cut every time and shined throughout the tour, winning the 1995 British Women's Open by six strokes. She also finished in the top ten in seven other tournaments and was the third–highest money winner on the tour. Webb was also named the tour's rookie of the year.

Subsequently, Webb was ready to move on to the LPGA Tour in the United States, which required her to compete at Q school to qualify. A few weeks prior, though, she had cracked a bone in her right forearm in a fall down some steps. After a doctor fit her with a special brace, she was able to hit balls again less than three weeks after the accident. Remarkably, she ended up finishing second at Q school.

As the youngest player on the 1996 LPGA Tour at age 21, Webb posted a strong start, finishing second in her first event, the Tournament of Champions, and winning her next, the HealthSouth Inaugural. She also finished second at her next event as well, and had top–ten showings in the next three. Later that year, she beat a number of strong players to win the Sprint Titleholders, one of the LPGA's most prestigious and lucrative events. By the season's end, Webb had also captured the SAFECO Classic and ITT LPGA Tour Championship as well, and had brought in more $1,002,000, thus earning more than any rookie in golf history. After finishing in the top five 12 times throughout the year, in December of 1996 she was named LPGA rookie of the year.

In 1997, Webb vied with Swedish player Annika Sorenstam at the top of the LPGA heap. Sorenstam, the 1995 LPGA player of the year, also won the Vare Trophy, which goes to the player with the lowest scoring average, in 1995 and 1996. However, Webb was soon on her heels. In 1997 she won her second consecutive Women's British Open with a final score of 269 (19 under par), smashing the previous record of 274 set by Jane Geddes in 1989. In the third round, she set a record with a nine-under-par-63 to take an eight-stroke lead and go into the final round 18 under par.

Also in 1997, Webb came out on top at the Susan G. Komen International and defended her title at the SAFECO Classic. Though she lost the LPGA Tour Championship to Sorenstam in Las Vegas, Nevada, she wrapped up the season with 21 top–ten finishes in her 25 events, and pulled in nearly $1 million. Though Sorenstam was again named player of the year, Webb took the Vare Trophy away from her, with an average score of 70.00 to Sorenstam's 70.04.

The next year, Webb posted 20 finishes in the top 20 and made her first hole–in–one at the ShopRite LPGA Classic during the third round. She also won twice, at the Australian Ladies Masters and the City of Hope Myrtle Beach Classic. She also tied for second place at the PageNet Tour Championship and finished third at the Oldsmobile Classic and Jamie Farr Kroger Classic. However, her earnings dropped to just over $700,000, and she still had not won a major event. Her ranking was fourth in 1998.

Webb rose to the top of the pack again in 1999, though, recording one of the most impressive seasons in LPGA history. Her earnings reached $1,591,959, breaking the single– season earnings record set by Sorenstam in 1998, and she became the fastest player in LPGA history to pass the $3 million and $4 million marks in career earnings. Also, up to that point, only she and Sorenstam had ever topped the $1 million mark for two separate seasons. During the year, Webb posted six wins and 22 top–ten finishes, and set a new record for LPGA single– season scoring average, with a 69.43, bumping Sorenstam's previous record of 69.99, set in 1998.

Perhaps most importantly, Webb finally won her first major tournament in 1999 with the du Maurier Classic, her fourth victory of the year. She also won The Office Depot, Australian Ladies Masters, Standard Register PING, Mercury Titleholders Championship, and the Wegmans Rochester International. Not to mention, at the Australian Ladies Open, Webb set an all–time record for lowest 72–hole score in relation to par with a 26–under–par (262) performance. Though she missed the cut twice, including at the LPGA Championship, Webb finished out of the top ten just once in the 23 events in which she competed. She also set a record for top–ten consecutive finishes, with 16.

Up until this point, although Webb was considered to have the best swing of any female player, she had been a bit weak on putting. In January of 1999, she started working with putter– maker Scotty Cameron, who used a high–speed camera to record her stroke. They discovered that she produced a truer roll with a crosshanded, or left–hand low, grip. In 1998, she was ranked forty–ninth for putting, but after the improvements, she was bumped up to sixteenth in 1999.

Webb swept the LPGA again in 2000, capturing her second major tournament in March at the Nabisco Championship, the women's equivalent of the Mas-

ters. She even scored a hole–in– one at the fifth hole, and won by a tournament–record 10 strokes with a 14–under 274 total. It was her fourth victory in her first five events she also captured The Office Depot, Australian Ladies Masters, and the Takefuji Classic. In addition, Webb won the Australian Women's Open, a non– LPGA event, that year.

By June, Webb had nine top ten finishes, and in late July, nabbed her third major tournament by beating Meg Mallon by five shots at the U.S. Women's Open. Reporters then started getting excited about the possibility of Webb earning a career "Grand Slam" if she could seal the McDonald's LPGA Championship in the future. Her earnings as of August, 2000, surpassed $1.5 million.

At five feet, six inches tall, Webb has blond hair and hazel eyes. She owns a home in Orlando, Florida, and enjoys reading, fishing, and basketball in her spare time. She is known as fiercely competitive, even off the course and with friends. Fellow golfer Juli Inkster once told Alan Shipnuck in *Sports Illustrated*, "Karrie doesn't just want to win, she wants to beat you. That's a different thing entirely." However, she added, "She goes about it in the right way. She's very gracious."

Sources

Periodicals

Golf Magazine, August 1996, p. 70.
New York Times, March 26, 2000, sec. 8, p. 7; March 27, 2000, p. D7; June 22, 2000, p. C28.
People, April 28, 1997, p. 68.
Sports Illustrated, March 25, 1996, p. G12; May 13, 1996, p. G8; May 12, 1997, p. 68; May 17, 1999, p. G15; August 9, 1999, p. G6; March 6, 2000, p. G15; March 13, 2000, p. 46; April 3, 2000, p. 99; July 31, 2000, p. G5.
USA Today, August 10, 2000, p. 3C.

Online

"2000 LPGA Tournament Results," CNN/Sports Illustrated web site, August 14, 2000, http://SportsIllustrated.cnnsi.com (August 15, 2000).
"Karrie Webb," LPGA Tour web site, http://www.lpga.com (August 15, 2000).

Wellington E. Webb

Mayor

AP/Wide World Photos

Born February 17, 1941, in Chicago, IL; son of
Wellington M. Webb (a railroad porter) and
Mardina Webb Devereaux; married Wilma J. Ger-
dine (a state representative); children: (first
marriage) Anthony, Allen; (second marriage;
stepchildren) Keith, Stephanie. *Education:* Colorado
State College at Greeley, B.A., 1964; University of
Northern Colorado at Greeley, M.A., 1971.

Addresses: *Office*—Office of the Mayor, 1437 Ban-
nock St., Denver, CO 80202.

Career

Teacher and counselor, early 1970s; Colorado
General Assembly, representative, 1973–77; Department of Health, Education and Welfare, Region
VIII, principal regional director, 1977–90; Colorado's
State Department of Regulatory Agencies, executive
director, 1980–87; city auditor of Denver, CO, 1987–
91; mayor of Denver, elected 1991, re–elected 1995,
re–elected 1999. Member, National League of Cities
advisory council, National Conference of Black
Mayors (president).

Sidelights

Although politics in Colorado was formerly a
bastion of the Ku Klux Klan in the 1920s, multiculturalism had set in by the 1980s and 1990s. In
1991, Wellington E. Webb, who is African American,
replaced Federico Pena, Denver's first Latino mayor,
who took office in 1983. Since then, Webb has gone
on to win re–election two more times, leading his

city into an era of booming prosperity. His popularity was such that in the 1999 campaign, two–thirds
of residents polled could not even name one of his
opponents. His win that year marked the first time
since 1979 that a Denver mayor won without a run–
off. To be fair, however, many potential candidates
decided not to run until after his third and legally,
his final term had expired.

Webb was born on February 17, 1941, in Chicago, Illinois, to Wellington M. Webb and Mardina Webb
Devereaux. He grew up on the city's South Side until age seven, when he moved to Denver to live with
his grandmother in the hopes that the new environment would help ease his asthma. The mountain air
did indeed improve his health, and he began to excel at sports, especially basketball. He went on to
Colorado State College at Greeley on a basketball
scholarship, and graduated in 1964 with a bachelor's
degree in education. He had always yearned for a
career in teaching, because he wanted to give back
to his community and act as a role model.

However, Webb failed to land a teaching position.
His grandmother, active in Democratic politics, contacted the mayor and set up a meeting, after which
Webb was offered a job. However, he turned it down
and returned to school, earning a master's degree

in sociology in 1971 from the University of Northern Colorado at Greeley. Meanwhile, he held various jobs in the social service system, including as a teacher for emotionally disturbed children and a counselor for welfare recipients.

In 1972, at age 31, Webb ran for a seat as state representative from his old neighborhood in northeast Denver. He won decisively, and served three terms until 1977. During that time, he forged a reputation for his strong stances, even if his views countered the Democratic party line. A strong supporter of welfare and health–related issues, he also helped write the state's first civil rights bill concerning the disabled. In 1975, he and State Senator Regis Groff protested Governor Richard D. Lamm's failure to appoint blacks to high state posts by staging a walkout at the governor's inauguration.

Additionally, in 1976 Webb was chosen as chairman of Colorado's campaign to elect Jimmy Carter to the presidency. The next year, Carter appointed him regional director of the U.S. Department of Health, Education, and Welfare for the area that included Colorado, Montana, Utah, Wyoming, and North and South Dakota. In this capacity, Webb managed a $3 billion budget and oversaw nearly 3,000 social service programs. During his leadership, he did much to improve the lives of Native Americans on reservations throughout the West.

When President Carter lost the election to Ronald Reagan in 1980, Colorado Governor Richard Lamm asked Webb to take the post of executive director of the State Department of Regulatory Agencies. Webb related in an *Ebony* article, "I told him, 'governor, I want to remind you I'm the one who helped organize a walkout on your inauguration.'" Webb took the job, though, making him the only African American in the governor's cabinet.

Meanwhile, Webb's second wife, Wilma J. (Gerdine) Webb, was elected to the state assembly in the late 1970s, making them a political power couple in the state. During her tenure, she passed legislation that her husband had introduced during his time in office: a bill that recognized Reverend Martin Luther King's birthday as a state holiday. However, Webb admitted in *Ebony* that working to get his wife re–elected to a second term may have hurt his campaign for mayor of Denver in 1983. "Getting into the race as late as I did really hurt my chances," he noted. He finished fourth on a slate of seven.

His initial run for office thwarted, Webb stayed with the governor's cabinet until 1987, when he was elected city auditor. In 1990 he announced another mayoral bid, this time challenging seven others. He trailed badly early in the race, and he lacked the kind of funding that some other contenders had behind them. To compensate, Webb hit the streets, walking more than 300 miles for weeks on end, never returning home or getting into a car. He spent his nights with city residents, sometimes bunking in homeless shelters or housing projects.

Although he lost 25 pounds in the process, Webb managed to boost his image and garner 57 percent of the vote. After the general election, the contest was down to him and District Attorney Norm Early, the only other African American on the ticket. Webb snagged 29 percent of ballots cast, compared to Early's 41 percent. Since Early did not attract more than 50 percent, a runoff was necessary. Still, this ensured that in 1991, Denver for the first time would put a black mayor in office.

During the runoff election, Webb continued his walking campaign. This and an early lag in the polls established him as the underdog, a positive factor in Denver politics. As a result, he victored over Early with 57 percent of the vote. At the time, the city of 467,000 was still predominantly white, counting blacks as 12 percent of its population and Hispanics as about 20 percent. Webb's election seemed to echo a national trend around that time in which several mostly white cities were electing black mayors. These included Kansas City, Missouri, and Seattle, Washington, as well as mid–size cities like Tallahassee, Florida; Rockford, Illinois; and Dayton, Ohio.

Being that Denver is the state capitol as well as the largest city in Colorado, Webb was undertaking a great deal of responsibility. He was under pressure not only due to his race but also because the city was just coming out of an economic recession. Vacancy in downtown buildings stood at 30 percent. To help ease the downturn, the previous mayor had spearheaded various costly endeavors, including a $2.1 billion expansive international airport which became the largest in the nation, a new convention center, a major league baseball park, and the $91 million renovation of the main library.

Although Webb at his inauguration hailed the civic efforts, the city's debt stood at $3 billion as he took over. Thus, his first speech promised a "back–to–basics" approach centering on issues like snow removal, crime prevention, and health care. "You've got to do the fundamentals before you can do the fancy stuff," he remarked, according to Alex Poinsett in *Ebony*. "That's not to say there won't be major initiatives like downtown revitalization. But I think we have to focus on the people who are already here. Are we giving them adequate police protection, adequate trash pickup?"

Right away, Denver's fortunes began to turn around under Webb. During his tenure, the technologically advanced airport and the baseball field became successful realities, and in 1992 *City and State Magazine* ranked Denver number two for sound fiscal management and health. Also, *Fortune* named Denver the second–best city in America in which to do business, and *Money* magazine cited it as the twelfth most livable city in the nation. In 1993, Webb announced that Denver General Hospital's eight–year, $30 million–plus deficit had been deleted. In addition, Webb won a reputation for running high–profile events well, such as his 1993 hosting of the Roman Catholic Church's World Youth Day, which saw half a million visitors, including President Bill Clinton and Pope John Paul II.

Meanwhile, however, Webb was criticized for the rise in crime, though he did manage to win praise for orchestrating the revitalization of downtown, bringing vacancy down to less than six percent. This helped slow the flight of residents from the inner city, but it was managed through a combination of public and private funding so that taxes would not increase. "My staff, as well as my kids, say I'm fiscally tight," he mentioned in *Ebony*. "But it works. These are difficult times for our cities. Nobody is coming to our rescue." Webb was also hailed for his attention to the rights of women and minorities, though some criticized the mayor for awarding several major airport and city contracts specifically to African Americans, Hispanics, Native Americans, and Asian Americans.

Still, Webb was in place as Colorado voters passed a state constitutional amendment that negated local laws against gay discrimination in 1992. Though Webb pointed out that Denver residents were not in favor of getting rid of the laws, the action led to steep losses in convention revenue due to boycotts. Webb was outspoken in his defense of civil rights for gays as well as any other marginalized group, and worked to draw attention to the diversity of his staff. But by 1993, the city suffered an estimated $30 million in losses from the boycotts.

In 1995 Webb ran for re–election against Mary De-Groot, a city council member who had accused him of doling out city contracts to friends and relatives. The primary race was close, with DeGroot collecting 42.8 percent of the vote to Webb's 42.7. How-ever, in the general election, Webb prevailed with 54 percent. Over the next few years, the mayor increased his national profile with appearances on various national television shows.

Upon his first election to office, Webb had pledged not to serve more than two terms, but in 1999 he decided to run again. (His tenure marked the last time Denver's mayor would be able to seek a third term: In 1994, a two–term limit was voted in for local officials, but his first term did not count.) In February of 1999, Webb outlined his platform to manage growth and traffic congestion, spur development in poor inner–city areas, increase the amount of affordable housing, and help the unemployed and low–income residents find decent–paying jobs.

After winning a third term, Webb devoted part of his time to spreading the word about the changing function of a big–city mayor. As he noted in *Emerge*, "It used to be that when you talked about cities and mayors, you thought about cities that were financially bankrupt, where crime was up, where people were leaving the cities. The mayor had his hand out with a tin cup in his hand, and that's not the case anymore. The mayors are the grunts of public service . Cities matter. Cities are booming. Mayors are running their cities like a private business with a public mission." He noted that under his leadership, the city had grown to more than half a million people, crime was down more than 12 percent, and many minorities that were previously jobless were employed.

Webb and his wife, both divorced parents when they met, shared the upbringing of his children, Anthony and Allen, and her children, Keith and Stephanie. He once remarked in *Ebony*, "We have never used the word 'step'" to describe each other's children." In 1996, *Newsweek* named Webb one of the top 25 mayors in the country. He serves on the National League of Cities advisory council and as president of the National Conference of Black Mayors.

Sources

Books

Contemporary Black Biography, volume 3, Gale Research, 1992.

Periodicals

Christian Science Monitor, June 5, 1991, p. 8.
Ebony, October 1978, p. 44; October 1984, p. 128; September 1991, p. 69; December 1993, p. 29.

Emerge, October 1999, p. 37.

Jet, May 24, 1999, p. 6.

La Voz de Colorado, November 20, 1996.

Nation's Cities Weekly, September 28, 1998, p. 1; November 29, 1999, p. 1.

New York Times, June 19, 1991, p. A22; June 20, 1991, p. A16.

Rocky Mountain News, February 10, 1999, p. 4A.

Washington Post, July 1, 1991, p. A5.

Harvey and Bob Weinstein

Corbis Corporation

Film industry executives

Harvey Weinstein born March 19, 1952; son of Max (a diamond cutter) and Miriam (a homemaker) Weinstein; married Eve Chilton, 1988. *Education:* Attended University of Buffalo.

Bob Weinstein born October 18, 1954; son of Max (a diamond cutter) and Miriam (a homemaker) Weinstein; married; wife's name, Vickie (divorced); two daughters. *Education:* Attended State University of New York at Fredonia.

Addresses: *Office*—Miramax Films, 375 Greenwich St., New York, NY 10013.

Career

Cofounders and cochairs of Miramax Films distribution company, 1979—, added film production company, 1989; began *Talk* magazine (joint venture with Hearst publishing), 1999; also began Miramax record label.

Awards: Independent Feature Project's Gotham Awards, Lifetime Achievement Award, 1997.

Sidelights

Harvey and Bob Weinstein of Miramax Films are known in the film industry as the brothers who raised art films from obscurity to mass appeal. Beginning in the late 1980s, they ushered in a golden era in independent film as they fervently supported projects that had small budgets and big ideas. To stir up interest in a previously overlooked genre, they used savvy marketing techniques and worked the media to the full extent so they did not have to shell out much on advertising budgets. For example, the *New York Times* published eight stories alone on *The Piano,* including one on the musical instruments used in the film. To promote other works, they have come up with imaginative twists, such as sending out screening invitations wrapped as subpoenas for a courtroom drama, or staging a runway show to introduce a movie about the fashion industry.

In addition to being respected for bringing thoughtful, intelligent films to the masses, though, the Weinsteins are infamous for their intense management style and for their competitive nature. "The word on Miramax is that the Weinstein brothers are passionate, relentless and sometimes ruthless in their search for, acquisition of and marketing of obscure films," wrote Betsey Sharkey in the *New York Times.* They are also notorious for being hard on their staff. Nevertheless, few argue that the Brothers Miramax, as they are often known, have changed the face of moviegoing.

Bob and Harvey Weinstein are the sons of Max and Miriam Weinstein. Harvey was born on March 19, 1952, and Bob was born on October 18, 1954. They were raised in Flushing, New York, an area of the Queens borough near Shea Stadium. Bob Weinstein related to Sharkey in the *New York Times,* "Every Saturday when we were growing up, Miriam would go have her hair done. On the way out, she'd say, 'Max, take the boys fishing or go play ball. Do something healthy.'" But he always took them to see a movie instead. Their company is named after the combination of their parents' names.

In addition to this early exposure to cinema, the Weinsteins' fate was sealed when they stumbled across the Francois Truffaut classic *The 400 Blows.* "We were young males with hormonal problems raging, and we thought this was going to be a sexy movie," Harvey Weinstein noted to Sharkey. Their disappointed friends hit the exits early, but the brothers stayed on and watched in awe. Subsequently, the Weinsteins became regulars at the local Mayfair Theater, viewing all sorts of foreign films.

Going on to college, Harvey attended the University of Buffalo and Bob enrolled at the State University of New York at Fredonia, though neither received a degree. Instead, they became sidetracked by business pursuits. Along with a friend, Harvey began to promote concerts on campus in the early 1970s, and even backed a Steven Stills show himself with a $2,500 loan. In 1978, the Harvey Weinstein purchased a run–down local movie theater, the Century, and asked Bob to help him run it. They used the venue for concerts, booking acts from the Grateful Dead to Billy Joel, and started showing film festivals to bring in patrons between concerts. "We'd show *Alice's Restaurant* at 7, *The Sting* at 9, and *Jimi Plays Berkeley* at midnight," Harvey related to Lisa Gubernick in *Forbes.* "Two thousand kids would show up and live at the theater on weekends."

In 1979, the Weinsteins made the transition from just showing films to actually distributing them. They headed to France's Cannes Film Festival that year looking for a movie and ended up purchasing *Goodbye, Emmanual,* a soft–core porn film. Thus, Miramax was born. They followed up with a few more unremarkable titles until finally getting their breakthrough in 1982 with *The Secret Policeman's Ball,* a concert film featuring Sting, Phil Collins, and Monty Python alumni. Then, in a move that would become so commonplace that it earned him the name "Harvey Scissorhands," the elder Weinstein re–cut the project to his liking, splicing together some of the original film with part of its sequel. The finished work, *The Secret Policeman's Other Ball,* became a hit at art–film houses upon its release, grossing $6 million.

Eschewing the glitz of Hollywood, the Weinsteins decided to remain in New York, setting up offices in Harvey's one–bedroom apartment in Manhattan.

For the first few years, they only released three or four films annually. They also briefly tried to break into production, and in 1986 cowrote, codirected, and coproduced the film *Playing for Keeps.* In 1987, they began to garner more attention with the Lizzie Borden picture *Working Girls,* about prostitution, and in 1988 attracted a swirl of media coverage after the release of Errol Morris's *The Thin Blue Line,* which helped free an innocent prisoner.

However, Miramax for the first few years remained small. At the time, independent film was still extremely fringe, with many financed by government grants and thus relegated to an amateurish quality. In addition, studios were unwilling to take chances on these low–budget projects because they often held scant mainstream appeal due to the subject matter and absence of famous–name actors, as well as the lack of slick visuals. Still, the Weinsteins managed to make money off of these small films, including *I've Heard the Mermaids Singing,* 1987, and *Pelle the Conqueror,* which won the Oscar for best foreign film in 1989.

Meanwhile, in 1988 Miramax got a boost when the British company of Midland Montague invested $5 million in the business and gave the Weinsteins a $25 million credit line. The next year, Miramax released ten films, including *Scandal,* which became the first indie hit of 1989. It surprised industry watchers that the story of a 1963 British sex scandal would draw so many viewers, but the film grossed more than $7 million at the box office. Harvey figured the tale would go over well simply because he himself had a personal interest in it: He had long admired Christine Keeler, the woman in the case, ever since he had seen a photograph of her posed nude in a black chair in *Life* magazine. Smartly, he marketed the movie using the film's star, Joanne Whaley–Kilmer, in that same pose on the poster, similarly intriguing moviegoers.

Also in 1989, Miramax put out *Cinema Paradiso, sex, lies, and videotape,* and *My Left Foot.* These works put the Weinsteins on the map when they earned a combined total of seven Academy Awards. Even more impressive, however, was the fact that all of their releases turned a profit. When they purchased the North American rights to Steven Soderbergh's *sex, lies, and videotape* for $1.1 million—not including video rights—observers clucked that it was extremely steep for an independent film. But the Weinsteins smelled a hit, not just because of the film's racy title, but also because of its literate script. It brought in $26 million in its first year. In addition, *My Left Foot,* about an artist with cerebral palsy, seemed destined for limited appeal based on the topic, but it became one of the most celebrated films of the year.

Subsequently, the Weinsteins had another huge success in 1992 with *The Crying Game,* which features an intriguing blend of subjects including Irish terrorists and an unusual homosexual love affair. It was one of the most successful art films ever released, with earnings of about $60 million, and it also captured six Academy Award nominations. The next year, *The Piano* won three Oscars in addition to the Palm d'Or, the top prize at Cannes. The ballooning success of Miramax projects stunned major studios, which believed that mass audiences would not accept edgy themes. However, as actor Sean Penn remarked to Lynn Hirschberg in *New York,* "I don't see the Miramax pictures as little uncommercial alternative art films. Don't forget that in 1975, when *Jaws* came out, *Taxi Driver* was also a hit. Miramax wants to make the kind of commercial films that were at one time called *Lenny* and *Taxi Driver.*"

Indeed, the big studios began to realize that there was a trend toward independent film and started to jump on the bandwagon. Sony bought Orion Classics in 1991 for putting out art films and renamed it Sony Classics. Universal then joined with PolyGram to acquire Gramercy Pictures. Meanwhile, Miramax was actively seeking a buyer that could infuse cash so they could step up their production efforts. Jeffrey Katzenberg at Disney ended up approaching the Weinsteins about a deal, and ended up buying Miramax for about $60 to $80 million. The agreement included $20 million worth of stock options, $25 million in operating capital, and a five-year employment contract.

Some observers believed this partnership to be an odd fit. Not only was Disney was known for G-rated family-oriented fare and children's animation, but the firm was also reputed to oversee projects very tightly. However, the deal with Miramax gave the Weinsteins complete artistic freedom on any film under $12 million, and the only stipulation was that no film could receive a harsher rating than R, meaning no one under 17 could be admitted without a parent or guardian.

This fine point became a bigger issue, though, when Miramax sued the Motion Picture Association of America's Ratings Board after they slapped Pedro Almodovar's *Tie Me Up! Tie Me Down!* with an X rating. Afterward, the board came up with a new rating, the NC–17, which was more restrictive than R because no one under 17 would be allowed into a film with this designation. It was meant for films that were not pornographic, but contained extremely adult content such as erotic scenes excessive violence. This led to further battles. Kevin

Smith's *Clerks,* about a couple of guys working at a convenience and video store, was the first to receive the NC–17 for its pervasive foul language. Miramax went to court again and got it downgraded to an R. And, Disney later refused to release the Martin Lawrence concert film *You So Crazy* because the board would not budge on the NC–17 rating, and it later refused to carry another of Smith's films, 1999's *Dogma,* because they were concerned that its religious content offended some Catholic groups.

In the meantime, after the Disney deal, Miramax invested heavily in production deals such as Quentin Tarantino's *Pulp Fiction,* Robert Altman's *Ready to Wear,* and others, leading some people to worry that the Weinsteins would overlook up-and-coming directors. But Miramax also continued to work with smaller and foreign films such as *Trainspotting* and *Il Postino,* and consistently rolled out works that attracted high critical acclaim as well as positive votes at the box office. In 1995, Miramax's seven films pulled in a combined 22 Academy Award nominations, more than any other distributor. In 1996, the company grossed $250 million, as much as all other independent distributors combined. Also that year Disney signed the Weinsteins to another five-year contract. In 1997, Miramax had another banner year, claiming 20 Oscar nominations—more than any major studio and the most ever for an independent film distributor—and winning 20 of them.

Not only do the Weinsteins have a knack for choosing the cream of the crop in pictures, they are also noted for picking up winning projects after major studios have passed on them. For instance, Castle Rock shelved *Good Will Hunting,* TriStar turned down the chance at *Pulp Fiction,* and Twentieth Century-Fox pulled out of *The English Patient* just before the shoot was set to begin. All of these became wildly successful, with *Pulp Fiction* becoming the first independent film to break the $100 million mark, and *The English Patient* went on to win the Academy Award for best picture. In 1999, another Miramax film, *Shakespeare in Love,* nabbed that coveted honor.

In addition to running Miramax, Bob Weinstein in 1993 founded Dimension Films, devoted to more mainstream genre pictures, which put out hits like *Scream* and other horror and comedy films that did well on video. Also, Miramax in 1999 helped launch *Talk* magazine, owning it jointly with Hearst Communications. Its start was plagued by criticism, but as of August of 2000 it was still in print. In addition, Miramax also began a record label and began financing Broadway plays. The brothers in 2000 signed another deal with Disney keeping them on board until 2007.

Harvey Weinstein is married to Eve Chilton, and Bob was married and divorced and has two daughters. The pair do not project the image of being cultivated art–film aficionados; their burly figures and gruff voices have earned them comparisons to longshoremen. The two work extremely closely together on all aspects of their business.

Sources

Books

Contemporary Theatre, Film and Television, volume 21, Gale Group, 1999.

Periodicals

Entertainment Weekly, Special Issue, November–December 1997, p. 34.

Film Comment, July–August 1989, p. 72.

Forbes, October 16, 1989, p. 109.

Fortune, October 18, 1993, p. 38; March 6, 2000, p. 169.

GQ, October 1995, p. 224.

Newsweek, February 28, 2000, p. 64.

New York, October 10, 1994, p. 48; April 6, 1998, p. 155.

New York Times, April 24, 1994, sec. 2, p. 1.

Time, February 24, 1997, p. 62; April 21, 1997, p. 40.

Variety, January 20, 1997, p. 7; May 12, 1997, p. 1; September 22, 1997, p. 4; August 31, 1998, p. 80; January 4, 1999, p. 1; August 9, 1999, p. 5; December 20, 1999, p. 1; May 8, 2000, p. 4.

Wall Street Journal, May 5, 2000, p. B8.

Meg Whitman

Business executive

Born in 1957 in Cold Spring Harbor, NY; daughter of a businessman and a homemaker; married Griffith R. Harsh IV; children: two sons. *Education:* Princeton University, economics degree, 1977; Harvard University, M.B.A., 1979.

Addresses: *Office*—eBay Inc., 2125 Hamilton Ave., San Jose, CA 95125.

Career

Proctor & Gamble, Cincinnati, OH, brand assistant, became brand manager, late 1970s; Bain & Co., San Francisco, CA, consultant, 1981–89; Walt Disney Co., senior vice president of marketing, 1989–92; Stride Rite Co., Lexington, MA, division president, 1992–95; Florists' Transworld Delivery (FTD), president and chief executive officer (CEO), 1995–97; Hasbro, Inc., general manager, 1997; eBay, San Jose, CA, CEO, 1998 .

Sidelights

As chief executive officer of the auction web site eBay, Meg Whitman is one of the biggest players in online commerce at the turn of the century. Overseeing what amounts to a gigantic global flea market with roughly 10 million registered users, she is head of one of the best–known sites on the web. Not to mention, Whitman has managed to make the site turn a profit a challenge for even the biggest "dot–coms." With $224.7 million in revenue in 1999, the company had a net income of $10.8 million, according to Hoover's Online. Contrast that

with Amazon.com, one of the first dot–coms to gain widespread brand recognition, which posted sales of $1.6 billion in 1999 but had yet to turn a profit. Though Amazon.com could become one of eBay's hardiest competitors, Whitman has so far kept the lead with a strong brand image, and she has also managed to tap into a new market by acquiring Butterfield & Butterfield auctioneers. So far, not only is eBay thriving, but Whitman has become one of the wealthiest Internet CEOs, worth more than $1 billion on paper, at least thanks to early investing.

Whitman was born in Cold Spring Harbor, on the north shore of Long Island, New York, in 1957. She is the youngest child of a businessman and an adventurous homemaker. When she was six, Whitman's mother packed her and her siblings into a camper along with a family friend with five children of her own, and took them on a three–month camping excursion through Canada to Alaska. When the kids got unruly, Whitman's mom made them get out and run ahead of the camper while she trailed them until they got tired. Occasionally, truckers would ask if anything was wrong. "We finally put a sign on the back of the camper that said, 'We're O.K.,'" Whitman related to Laura M. Holson in the *New York Times.*

In 1977, Whitman graduated from New Jersey's Princeton University with a degree in economics. She then obtained a master's degree in business administration from Harvard University in 1979. Out of school, she landed a job as a brand assistant with Proctor & Gamble in Cincinnati, Ohio, and worked her way up to brand manager. In 1981, Whitman moved to San Francisco when her husband, Griffith R. Harsh IV, a neurosurgeon, began a residency at the University of California. Whitman then found work as a consultant for Bain & Company, where she stayed for the next eight years.

Moving to the Walt Disney Company in 1989 as a senior vice president of marketing, Whitman helped the firm acquire *Discover* magazine. After her husband took a new position as co–director of the brain tumor program at Massachusetts General Hospital in Boston in 1992, she accepted a job as president of Stride Rite Shoes in Lexington, Massachusetts. This children's shoe manufacturer also produces Sperry topsiders and Keds sneakers. In 1995, she left that post to become CEO of Florists' Transworld Delivery (FTD), an alliance of commercial florists. There, she faced the challenge of transforming it to a privately held company. This met with much resistance from higher–ups, and in addition, the federation was facing new competition from Internet floral delivery services.

In 1997, Whitman changed jobs again to go to Hasbro, Inc., one of the largest toy and game manufacturers in America. She was hired as general manager of the Playskool division, the profitable umbrella under which many of the firm's best–known toys reside, including Mr. Potato Head and the Teletubbies. She would not stay there long, though. In November of 1997, a headhunter told Whitman about a job with an Internet start–up in Silicon Valley. Reluctant to uproot her husband and two sons, she turned down the suggestion. However, after visiting the offices of online auction site eBay in San Jose, she packed up and headed West in February of 1998. "There's no substitute in the land–based world for eBay," she remarked to Kathleen Melymuka in *Computerworld*. "I just had an overwhelming instinct that this thing was going to be huge."

The concept of eBay began in 1995. Pierre M. Omidyar's girlfriend, whom he later married, was smitten with Pez dispensers, which feature a cartoon head atop a stalk that holds a row of chalky candy tablets. When she expressed a desire to buy and trade with other enthusiasts, he founded the site to allow her to pursue her interest, not only buying from and selling to other Pez fans, but also

communicating with them. This led to eBay's reputation as not just a commerce site, but more of a community, where like–minded hobbyists and collectors could reach out to each other.

Soon, eBay became an auction enterprise linking buyers and sellers. It makes money by charging small listing fees (25 cents to $2) and taking a 6 percent commission 5 percent of which is gross profit, thanks to an automated system. To prevent scams, Omidyar set up a message boards whereby buyers and sellers could rate each other. Even though the company did no marketing from 1995 to 1998, the site grew by leaps and bounds, thanks to aficionados of everything from Beanie Babies plush toys to pinup calendars. But Omidyar knew he needed a proven leader if he was to take the company public.

Though Whitman had no in–depth technical experience, it was not considered a handicap. One of eBay's major investors, Robert Kagle, explained to Holson in the *New York Times*, "I was looking for a brand builder to help make eBay a household name." Thanks to making quick decisions and trusting her instincts, Whitman soon proved that she had the capability to move at a fast enough pace for e–commerce. She immediately set to work to improve the appearance of the site, including developing its mascot, an anthropomorphic apple. She also snagged Brian Swette, head of marketing at Pepsi, to join their efforts. In addition, she blocked off firearm and pornography items into age–restricted areas (the firm would later block firearm sales altogether, in addition to alcohol, drugs, tobacco, and organs for transplant). Thus, eBay was ready for its initial public offering (IPO) on September 24, 1998. From an initial price of $18, the shares had increased by the day's end to more than $47, a jump of 163 percent.

In less than two years as head of eBay, Whitman grew the customer base from 750,000 to about 10 million. She also took steps to guarantee the technical reliability of the site, which plagued it for some time. At one point the site was down for 22 hours, and she worked 100 hours a week for a month to fix the outages. "We put in cots, and I was just there," she noted to Melymuka in *Computerworld*. "I lived it." Subsequently, she hired Sun Microsystems to maintain the eBay network, and greatly strengthened eBay's in–house technology department as well.

In addition, Whitman made strides in combating fraud, granting customers free insurance through Lloyd's of London for purchases up to $200, minus a $25 deductible. Then, in April of 1999, she announced that eBay had purchased Butterfield & Butterfield Auctioneers a 134–year–old auction house in San Francisco for $260 million. With the average auction piece selling for about $47 on eBay, giving a commission of $3, this acquisition ensured the site's ability to move into higher–end transactions and boost its revenue further. Other acquisitions have included Kruse International, a collectible car house; Alando de AG, the largest online auction in Europe; and Billpoint Inc., a firm that allows person–to–person credit–card transactions.

Despite the fact that eBay fell short of its 1999 profit projections, netting only $10 million instead of $24 million, it was still ahead of the bulk of fledgling and not–so–fledgling dot–coms that were also worth a fortune in stock, but had no profits to show. Amazon.com, for example lost $720 million in 1999. However, facing competition from Amazon, Yahoo!, and about 1,000 other online entities who have entered the online auction business, Whitman was under pressure to not only keep up, but greatly expand eBay's presence. She appeared ready for the task as she told Melymuka in *Computerworld*, "I am a far better executive than I was, and I have a deep understanding of the technology challenges and what the options are."

Sources

Periodicals

Business Week, May 31, 1999, p. 128; September 27, 1999, p. EB32.
Computerworld, January 10, 2000, p. 48.
Fortune, July 5, 1999, p. 81; October 25, 1999, p. 94.
New York Times, May 10, 1999, p. C1.

Online

"Meg Whitman," eBay web site, http://pages.ebay.com/community/aboutebay/overview/management.html (March 28, 2000).
"eBay Inc.," Hoover's Online web site, http://www.hoovers.com (March 28, 2000).

Jeffrey Wigand

AP/Wide World Photos

Scientist, educator, and activist

Born c. 1943 in New York City; son of a mechanical engineer; married; wife's name, Linda (divorced); married Lucretia, 1986; children: (from first marriage) Gretchen; (from second marriage) Rachel, Nicole.

Addresses: *Office*—c/o Smoke Free Kids Inc., P.O. Box 13886, Charleston, SC 29422.

Career

Worked at Boehringer Mannheim Corp., New York, 1960s; held senior management positions with Pfizer and Union Carbide, 1970s–1980s; Ortho Diagnostic Systems (a division of Johnson & Johnson), director of marketing, 1980s; Technicon, senior vice president, 1980s; Biosonics, Fort Washington, PA, president, 1987; performed consulting work, 1988; Brown & Williamson tobacco company, vice president of research and development, 1988–93; duPont Manual High School, teacher, 1995–98; Smoke Free Kids, Inc. nonprofit organization, founder and director, c. 1998—. *Military service*—U.S. Air Force, early 1960s.

Sidelights

Jeffrey Wigand remarked to Marie Brenner in *Vanity Fair* "I have a very bad problem—saying what's on my mind. I don't take too much crap from anybody." This kind of outlook helped earn Wigand dismissal from his top executive post at Brown & Williamson tobacco company in 1993. But it also led him to become a whistle-blower, a corporate insider who revealed a number of secrets, including the fact that tobacco companies knew that nicotine was addictive. His story, aired on *60 Minutes,* was startling enough, but the behind–the–scenes ordeal was even more fascinating. CBS, the parent corporation of *60 Minutes,* ordered the show not to air the segment, and many believed it was because some top executives did not want to jeopardize a potential business deal. The entire tale became the basis of a hit 1999 film, *The Insider,* which was nominated for seven Academy Awards. His testimony had led to the companies providing $246 billion to the 50 states based on the reasoning that public tax dollars were used to subsidize medical treatment for countless people whose lives were affected by tobacco use and nicotine addiction.

Wigand was born around 1943 in New York City, the son of a mechanical engineer and the eldest of five siblings. He had a strict Catholic upbringing in the Bronx, and his father stressed independence. When the family moved to Pleasant Valley in upstate New York near Poughkeepsie, the sons helped build the new home.

Because he had always shown a talent for the sciences, Wigand aspired to study medicine. He enrolled at Dutchess Community College, where he ran track and worked as a nurse's aide at a local hospital. However, he abruptly left school and joined the air force in 1961. Wigand was sent to the air base of Misawa in Japan, where he managed an operating room. There, he became fluent in Japanese and began to study the martial arts while also volunteering as an English teacher at a Catholic orphanage. In 1963 he went to Vietnam briefly.

Returning to America, Wigand attended the State University of New York (SUNY) at Buffalo, where he obtained a bachelor's degree in chemistry and later received his master's degree in biochemistry after writing a thesis on vitamin B12. He also holds a doctorate in biochemistry from SUNY. After graduating, he landed a job with the German health–care firm of Boehringer Mannheim. By the early 1970s, he had moved on to Pfizer, then was recruited for a prestigious position at Union Carbide. He went to Japan to create a subsidiary to test medical equipment in clinical trials.

Meanwhile, in 1970 Wigand met a woman in a judo class, Linda, and they were soon married. Seven months later, she was diagnosed with multiple sclerosis. Although he searched vigorously for specialists to treat her, the condition worsened and he eventually withdrew. They had a daughter, Gretchen, in 1973. Linda Wigand returned to the United States from Japan, and the marriage fell apart. Wigand lost contact with his ex–wife, and in 1981 met a woman named Lucretia, whom he married in 1986.

Wigand in the meantime left Union Carbide to take a job at the Johnson & Johnson subsidiary of Ortho Diagnostic Systems as director of marketing, and then moved up to become a senior vice president at Technicon. However, all of the firm's senior management were dismissed one day, and he subsequently became president of Biosonics, a small company in Fort Washington, Pennsylvania, that produced medical equipment. He had a falling out with the owner, though, and then did consulting work on his own for a year. Afterward, Wigand sought the services of a headhunter, who asked if he would work for the Brown & Williamson tobacco firm in Louisville, Kentucky. He took the position of senior vice president of scientific research, which paid $300,000 a year and oversaw a staff of 243 and a budget of $243 million.

At Brown & Williamson, Wigand was in charge of developing a low–tar cigarette to compete with the Premier brand, produced by the rival R.J. Reynolds (RJR) company. From the outset, the idea of a man

with so many years in the health industry working for a tobacco firm seemed unusual, but Wigand explained to Brenner, "I thought I would have an opportunity to make a difference and work on a safer cigarette." However, he realized he would never be able to return to the health care industry. Wigand subsequently set to work on a safer, nontoxic and fire– retardant cigarette. He also started smoking.

Eventually, the safer–cigarette project was shelved and Wigand became increasingly vocal about the hazards in tobacco. Among other things, he was dismayed by the industry's marketing efforts toward youth, and he was concerned about additives in tobacco that were known carcinogens. Meanwhile, a new chief executive officer, Thomas Sandefur, took over Brown & Williamson in January of 1993, and the two had been at odds in the company for some time. Wigand was fired in March of 1993.

Subsequently, Wigand expected to land a decent position elsewhere in corporate management, but began to fret when nothing came up. He made a passing remark to a friend griping about his compensation package from Brown & Williamson, and the person repeated it to his former boss. Some months later, the company then called him in to tell him they were cutting off his medical benefits because he had breached his severance contract with the comment. This was an especially onerous threat, because Wigand has two daughters, Rachel and Nicole, and the eldest suffers from spina bifida, which requires expensive daily treatments. "If Brown & Williamson had just left me alone," Wigand told Brenner, "I probably would have gone away. I would have gotten a new job." In a court settlement, the firm ended up forcing him to sign an even more binding, lifelong confidentiality agreement directing him to never say anything about the corporation.

Meanwhile, producer Lowell Bergman at *60 Minutes* was seeking a tobacco scientist to help him dig through reams of papers that arrived on his doorstep one day from Philip Morris. They were in regards to the fire safety of cigarettes. He heard about Wigand from a contact and tried to reach him, but Wigand's wife continued to tell him Wigand was not home or did not want to speak with him. Finally, Bergman rang up Wigand at midnight and said, "If you are curious to meet me, I'll be sitting in the lobby at the Seelbach Hotel tomorrow at 11 a.m.," as Brenner reported. Wigand showed up, and the two men established what became an intense relationship.

Initially, Wigand was paid about $1,000 a day to decipher the fire–safety studies, which was a typical amount for a corporate consultant, and ended up making about $12,000 for the job. This made him even more angry at the industry, because he claims that Philip Morris—although they deny it—had developed a fire–safe cigarette as early as 1986 or 1987. After this, Wigand began to do more work for the government, advising the Food and Drug Administration on cigarette chemistry and how to ask tobacco companies for specific papers so that they were not inundated with reams of studies to slog through. He began to help locate evidence that the tobacco firms knew that nicotine was addictive, despite sworn testimony by the heads of several companies that refuted this. Wigand soon began to receive death threats, and he and his family were given FBI protection.

Meanwhile, Bergman knew that Wigand had more to say, but figured that he could not talk until his severance package was completed in March of 1995. Bergman did not know about Wigand's other contract preventing him from ever discussing Brown & Williamson. However, Bergman told Brenner, "The idea of somebody having a confidentiality agreement didn't even occur to me as a problem! That was my job, to get people to talk!" Wigand was reluctant not only because his medical benefits could get cut off, but because his wife was hesitant.

Finally, though, Wigand agreed to be taped, and he and Lucretia flew to New York in 1995, where he was interviewed by Mike Wallace. Wigand made several bold assertions, including stating that the tobacco firm chiefs had committed perjury when they stated under oath that nicotine was not addictive. Furthermore, he claimed that the companies produced cigarettes to be nicotine delivery devices, which would result in more sales. And he also indicated that Brown & Williamson continued to add cumarin to pipe tobacco even though they were aware the substance caused liver tumors in lab mice.

Subsequently, the legal department at CBS met with *60 Minutes* staff to discuss possible liability if they ran the interview, given Wigand's confidentiality agreement. The lawyers used the term "tortious interference," which involved one person persuading another to break a contract. The legal risks were deemed too steep, and CBS ordered *60 Minutes* to kill the piece. Soon, the internal CBS ordeal over shelving the interview was leaked to the *New York Times,* which broke the story on November 9, 1995. Many press commentators theorized that because CBS was in the midst of being sold to Westinghouse, the story and a possible costly lawsuit would halt the deal. Some pointed out that Eric Ober, president of CBS News, and Ellen Kaden, general counsel for CBS, both stood to profit handsomely from the merger. On the date that the Wigand interview was scheduled to run, *60 Minutes* instead aired a story about the tobacco companies withholding information from the public. Wallace went on the air to relate his unhappiness over the affair, but CBS News trimmed that segment as well.

After all this, the New York *Daily News* got a hold of the transcript of the Wigand interview and printed it. CBS then provided Wigand with an attorney in case of a breach–of– contract suit, and the next day, Brown & Williamson filed a compliant in Kentucky charging Wigand with breach of contract, theft, and fraud, and the court issued a temporary restraining order preventing him from discussing the company further. However, he was scheduled to give a deposition on November 29 in a Mississippi case against tobacco firms, and the judge there ordered him to do so, even though it meant Wigand could face arrest in Kentucky for breaking the restraining order.

While all this was raging, Brown & Williamson was working diligently on a "smear campaign" against Wigand. They hired investigators to dig up several negative items in his past, including a domestic violence call and his breakup with his first wife, which they characterized as abandonment. The stress of the entire ordeal with the tobacco industry damaged Wigand's relationship with his wife, and she finally asked for a divorce in January of 1996. Meanwhile, in 1995 Wigand took a job teaching science and Japanese at duPont Manual High School in Louisville, earning one–tenth of his previous salary. He taught for three years, winning the Sallie Mae First Class Teacher of the Year award in 1996.

Finally, after the *Wall Street Journal* ran an article about Wigand and his claims in February of 1996, CBS decided to allow *60 Minutes* to air the story as well. By then, filmmaker Michael Mann had taken note and figured the episode would make a good project. He based his movie on the lengthy *Vanity Fair* piece by Brenner that ran in May of 1996. Russell Crowe starred as Wigand, and Al Pacino was cast as Bergman. The film was highly acclaimed and nominated for several awards, including the Academy Award for best picture and best actor, for Crowe's performance. The Brown & Williamson suit against Wigand for breach of contract was later dropped as a condition of the historic settlement between the tobacco firms and the 50 states.

Wigand has received much recognition for his actions. He is also the founder of the nonprofit group Smoke–Free Kids, dedicated to reducing tobacco use among teenagers, and in that capacity he often travels to address groups. He was also appointed a special advisor to Canada's minister of health.

Sources

Periodicals

Columbia Journalism Review, January–February 1996, p. 39.
Entertainment Weekly, November 5, 1999, p. 46; November 12, 1999, p. 34.

National Catholic Reporter, December 3, 1999, p. 17.
New York Times, February 6, 1996, p. A17.
Reason, February 1996, p. 42.
Time, February 12, 1996, p. 54; March 11, 1996, p. 57; November 1, 1999, p. 92.
Vanity Fair, May 1996, p. 196.

Online

Jeffrey Wigand web site, http://www.jeffreywigand.com (August 29, 2000).

Anthony Williams

Mayor

Born Anthony Stephen Eggleton, July 28, 1951, in Los Angeles, CA; adopted by Lewis Williams III and Virginia Williams (both postal workers) and renamed Anthony Allen Williams; married Diane Simmons; children: Asatewa Foster. *Education:* Attended Santa Clara University; Yale University, B.A. in economics, 1983; Harvard University, law degree and graduate degree in public policy, 1987.

Addresses: *Home*—Washington, DC. *Office*—Office of the Mayor, 441 4th St. NW, Ste. 1100, Washington, DC 20001.

Career

Boston Redevelopment Authority, head of neighborhood housing and development, 1988–90; St. Louis Community Development Agency, executive director, 1990–91; deputy state comptroller of Connecticut, 1991–93; U.S. Department of Agriculture, chief financial officer, 1993–95; District of Columbia, chief financial officer, 1995–98; mayor of Washington, DC, 1999—. *Military service*— U.S. Air Force, 1971–74.

Awards: *Governing* magazine, named public official of the year, 1997.

Sidelights

Anthony Williams, mayor of Washington, D.C., made the unlikely move from "bean counter" to public official after a dark era in the city's history in which the federal government took over its operations. After years of mismanagement under former Mayor Marion Barry, who was reelected even after being jailed for drug charges, Congress began to oversee the city's finances under the auspices of an appointed chief financial officer (CFO) and a control board. Barry tapped Williams for the post, leading observers to wonder if the preppy bureaucrat would be able to get anything accomplished in the dog–eat–dog world of big–city politics.

In a stunning move, though, Williams not only created a surplus in the budget, he also shook up the very foundation of the city, and in doing so, ran counter to the desires of Barry. Then, he made a successful run for mayor after initially rejecting the idea of even becoming a candidate. "Williams has been labeled a 'Yale–talking geek' and seems more at ease with budget spreadsheets than bouncing babies," an *Economist* writer quipped. "But he knows that charm and charisma are not what the capital's voters are looking for. They just want the city functioning again."

Williams was born Anthony Stephen Eggleton on July 28, 1951, in Los Angeles, California, and placed with a foster family as an infant. His foster mother would proudly show off photographs of him at the U.S. Postal Service where she worked, but as he turned three years old and still would not speak, she decided to place him in a home for the mentally retarded. One of his foster mother's colleagues, Virginia Williams, could not bear to see this happen, so she tried in vain to find someone else to adopt the boy.

Finally, Virginia Williams told her husband, Lewis Williams III, also a postal worker, that she wanted to take the boy herself. At the time, they already had two children, and she was pregnant again. Despite her husband's initial reluctance, the Williams family added a new son and renamed him Anthony Allen Williams. Over time, Williams's parents would raise nine children.

Williams grew up in a black, working–class area just south of downtown Los Angeles. His mother worked days and his father nights so that someone would always be home with the children. His mother, who gave up a chance at an opera career to focus on her family, had performed off–camera in the films *Carmen Jones* and *Porgy and Bess*. She was also a community activist who once ran for the Los Angeles City Council. She rose to become a foreman at the Postal Service, and Williams's father worked his way up from a clerk to local superintendent of customer service. They were driven by the desire to give their family a good upbringing. In addition to giving the children piano or modeling lessons and taking them on cross–country camping trips, Williams's parents stressed education and sent all of the children to Catholic schools. As a result, all would graduate from college.

Soon after he was adopted, Williams came out of his shell and began to say "Mommy" and "Daddy." In no time, he started playing rough–and–tumble games with his siblings and showed a normal pattern of development. Though Williams received good grades, he would often daydream in school. After attending Holy Name of Jesus elementary, he went on to the nearly all–white Loyola High School, where he became a class leader and a well–liked class clown. He also impressed the nuns with his illustrations of Bible stories, and considered entering the priesthood until his father steered him away from it.

After high school, then, Williams had no clear path. He enrolled at Santa Clara University in 1969 and became enmeshed in student activities and protests during a hotbed time of anti– Vietnam war demonstrations. He even volunteered at an organization

that supported draft dodgers who had moved to Canada. However, after two years of attending college and collecting only about a year's worth of credits to show for it, Williams decided to join the Air Force to give his life some focus. This shocked his anti–war activist friends, but impressed his father, who had received a Bronze Star during World War II.

Though Williams volunteered for duty in Vietnam, he remained in the United States as an administrative aide. Hoping to become a pilot, Williams applied to the U.S. Air Force Academy, but because of his poor college record, he was required to attend the academy's preparatory school first. After a year, he was admitted to the academy, but then changed his mind and asked to be released as a conscientious objector, claiming that the service conflicted with his moral and religious views. "I wanted to make a statement," he told Michael A. Fletcher in the *Washington Post*. Williams collected 60 letters supporting his application for conscientious objector status, including one from his father, who was irate at the turn of events. It said that his son may have been affected by a head injury as a child that caused him to suffer ever since. "It was an ugly letter," Williams told Fletcher.

The Air Force gave Williams an honorable discharge in 1974. Subsequently, he counseled Vietnam veterans and gave clay sculpting and piano lessons to blind children. At some point he tried to launch a pest–control business that would use sterilized bugs instead of chemicals, but it never got going. Williams eventually went back to college, gaining admission to Yale University in 1975 after speaking just once with an admissions officer. His veteran's benefits helped pay the tuition, and he excelled in classes. In his spare time, he worked with youth programs. However, Williams took another detour in 1977 to start a business selling antique maps.

When his map endeavor failed and his parents rescued him financially, Williams returned to Yale in 1979 and began working as a banquet waiter and pizza deliveryman. The next year, he landed a seat on the New Haven Board of Aldermen, serving until 1983. While there, he stirred controversy when he sponsored a bill to cut off black organizations that were receiving money from the city to develop minority–owned firms. He felt they were not using the funds wisely.

Meanwhile, Williams got his bachelor's degree in economics from Yale in 1982. After that, he stayed on track and attended Harvard University, obtaining both a law degree and a graduate degree in public policy from Harvard's Kennedy School of Government in 1987. Afterward, a Harvard classmate, Chris Grace, hired Williams to head up the neighborhood housing and development for the Boston Redevelopment Authority. In that capacity, he managed a program to bring low–income housing developers into troubled areas.

Later, Grace moved to St. Louis to become the city's director of development, and he asked Williams to join him as the executive director of the city's Community Development Agency. In that post, Williams angered two contractors by refusing to pay them for work he found unsatisfactory. They retaliated by beating him up as they yelled, "Uncle Tom!" The incident sent him to the emergency room with a broken nose, and the men were later convicted of assault.

From 1991 to 1993, Williams worked as the deputy state comptroller of Connecticut. There, he vocally opposed the governor's questionable practice of delaying tax refunds in order to make up for budget shortfalls. Then, from 1993 to 1995, Williams served as the chief financial officer for the U.S. Department of Agriculture, where he got a healthy dose of complex budget management and wide–ranging bureaucracy. He oversaw 10,000 employees and managed a network of 29 agencies with a budget of $62.3 billion.

In the meantime, the city of Washington, D.C. was in a shambles. The mayor, Marion Barry, who was first elected in 1978, had been arrested and convicted of smoking crack, but after his release from prison, was reelected in 1994. During his early years he had made some significant improvements to the city, but in later years the infrastructure was crumbling. Jonathan Walters wrote in a 1997 *Governing* article, "For more than a decade, the district has been a monument to budgeting and management hijinks that would best be described as hilarious if their consequences weren't so serious notoriously lousy city services, dysfunctional departments and bottomless–pit budgets." By the mid–1990s, school roofs were falling in, AIDS plagued the residents while federal money targeting the disease was left unspent, and morgue officials announced that they lacked funds to refrigerate corpses. The mismanagement caused a domino effect, leading to social problems and the nation's highest crime rate.

This disarray was of particular embarrassment to the federal government, located in the center of the storm. In 1995, Congress stepped in and established a control board, transferring the city's fiscal responsibilities to a five–member congressional oversight committee. The mayor was allowed to appoint a chief financial officer to manage the city's finances, but had little to do with city management beyond that and tourism duties. The mayor could not dismiss the CFO, either—that would be the domain of the control board.

Barry chose Williams for the post, but the two began to have differences right away. Initially, many suggested the Ivy League Williams would have difficulty operating in the rough political waters of Washington, D.C. However, he surprised people when he held his ground against the mayor, using his post's independence to make integral changes. He imposed deep budget cuts and took Barry to task for not meeting the city's fiscal obligations. Barry was also irked that Williams would not allow him to decide which city contractors would receive payment first, and he was upset that Williams took issue with his projected 1996 budget deficit of $59 million, placing it closer to $200 million.

In addition to upsetting the mayor, Williams drew fire from unions for firing 300 employees of the bloated bureaucracy, labeling them incompetent. At the time the city carried 50,000 on the payroll, an enormous work force for a city of 550,000. He was later named as a defendant in lawsuits filed on behalf of dismissed workers. Williams also called for more accountability on the part of city employees. Some critics labeled him a puppet of the Republican–controlled Congress. Williams ignored the snipes, telling Rob Gurwitt in *Governing*, "We're not here to get along. We're here to ensure results."

By the end of 1997, the District of Columbia, expecting to see a budget deficit of $74 million, instead posted a surplus of $185.9 million. It also managed to produce a clean tax audit, once thought impossible due to the extent of the disorganization of files. Williams, meanwhile, began to hold community meetings—over 150 in all—in order to explain his policies in plain language to residents. The district was also back on track for regaining its self– government, and Williams was named "public official of the year" by *Governing* magazine in December of 1997.

It should have been no shock, then, when Williams was asked to run for mayor in the 1998 elections. However, in early 1998 he proclaimed that he would not seek the office and would not serve if elected, stating that his family did not agree with the idea and that he still had unfinished business as CFO. A grass–roots group convinced him to change his mind, and by May of that year he announced his candidacy. Williams won the Democratic primary over opponents' accusations that he took too much credit for the city's turnaround and protests that he was a "carpetbagger" since he had only been in the area three years. In the general election, he defeated Republican candidate Carol Schwartz.

Shortly after taking office, in January of 1999, Williams saw his first major controversy as mayor in an incident that heightened racial tension. A white aide, David Howard, remarked in a meeting that his department's funding levels were "niggardly"—a term of Scandinavian origin meaning "stingy" that has no relation to the similar–sounding racial epithet. Still, two other black staffers became offended, and the incident rocketed into a national debate. Many felt this was a litmus test to see whether Williams was sensitive enough to African American issues.

Howard apologized and resigned, and Williams accepted the resignation. However, this sparked an outcry from gay groups, who supported Howard as Williams' only homosexual nominee, as well as language mavens and others. Many lambasted Williams for accepting the resignation, claiming he was pandering to those who had long criticized him as not being "black enough" to run the district, which has a demographic makeup up of 63 percent African Americans. Howard eventually agreed to return to a city post.

In another bump in the road, Williams came under scrutiny for failing to report consulting fees worth $40,000. Though he contended that the work, performed for the Arthur Anderson accounting firm and the Nationsbank Corporation, did not pose a conflict of interest with his mayoral duties, he admitted that he should have disclosed the employment and noted that it was a mere oversight. He paid a fine of $500 for each violation for a total of $1000. In addition, Williams was rebuked for failing to appoint a full–time city administrator or fill several other management posts. He also got into a bitter dispute with the city council regarding a tax–cut proposal.

On the other hand, Williams worked diligently to keep his campaign promises. He introduced a rid–a–rat program to get rodents off the streets, he set up 50,000 new trash cans, and added 300 new police officers to the force, successfully making the city cleaner and safer. Though some bemoaned his lack of slick appeal, others saw his low–key image as a welcome change in the wake of the city's former problems. Perhaps most notably, Congress released its hold on the power structure during Williams's first month in office, restoring the district's independence.

Williams is a dapper man who sports bow ties in the Nation of Islam style, although he does not practice the religion. He married Diane Simmons and they have a daughter, Asatewa Foster. He lives in the Foggy Bottom area of Washington, D.C.

Sources

Books

Contemporary Black Biography, volume 21, Gale Group, 1999.

Periodicals

Economist, September 19, 1998, p. 37.
Governing, June 1997, p. 88; December 1997, p. 25.
Jet, October 5, 1998, p. 9; January 18, 1999, p. 4.
Knight–Ridder/Tribune News Service, January 29, 1999; February 3, 1999; July 7, 1999.
New York Times, June 14, 1999, p. A16; May 21, 2000, sec. 1, p. 14.
Time, September 14, 1998, p. 49.
Washington Post, May 31, 1998, p. A1; September 3, 1998, p. C1.

Ricky Williams

Football player

Born Errick Lynne Williams Jr., May 21, 1977, in San Diego, CA; son of Errick and Sandy Williams (a government purchasing agent); children: one daughter, Marley. *Education:* Attended University of Texas.

Addresses: *Office*—c/o Integrated Sports International, One Meadowlands Plaza, Ste. 1501; East Rutherford, NJ 07073.

Career

Philadelphia Phillies baseball team, chosen in eighth round of amateur draft pick and signed four–year contract, 1995; New Orleans Saints football team, chosen fifth overall in NFL draft pick and signed eight–year contract, 1999.

Awards: Doak Walker Award for top collegiate running back, 1997, 1998; Heisman Trophy, Walter Camp Football Foundation Award, Maxwell Award, and Associated Press college player of the year, 1998.

Sidelights

One of the most talented players in the history of college football, Ricky Williams has been a fan favorite for both his skill on the field and his nice–guy persona off of it. With a rare combination of size and speed, he emerged as one of the most formidable running backs in the National Collegiate Athletic Association (NCAA) during his time at the

AP/Wide World Photos

University of Texas. After his junior year, he decided to wave off the promise of millions that he could have made in the National Football League (NFL) in order to stay and play ball at Texas. He ended his college years with a spectacular season in which he broke the record for total rushing yards—in addition to numerous others—and scooped up the Heisman Trophy, among other honors. In addition to Williams's presence on the field, his dreadlocks and facial piercings made him an easily– recognized figure in the media. When he signed with the New Orleans Saints NFL team in 1999, coach Mike Ditka wore a dreadlock wig to welcome him aboard.

Williams was born Errick Lynne Williams Jr. on May 21, 1977, in San Diego, California, to Errick and Sandy Williams, a government purchasing agent. He has a twin sister, Cassandra (Cassie) and a sister, Nisey, six years younger. When he was five, his parents split up. Williams's mother related to Tim Layden in *Sports Illustrated* that she got a divorce because her son told her that his father was sexually abusing him. Though Williams's father denies this, he was convicted of a misdemeanor for annoying or molesting children and told Layden that he got a six–month suspended sentence and three years probation, and had to register as a sex offender. He later remarried and had four more children with his second wife. By high school, Williams reestablished a relationship with his father, though, and told Layden, "I don't remember anything . He's my dad. We get along O.K."

Williams's parents' divorce was final in September of 1983, and he reportedly harbored a great deal of anger after this. Layden noted that he lashed out at other children physically and underwent counseling to help him control his rage until he was in junior high school. However, Williams later told Fred Schruers in *Rolling Stone* that too much was made of his behavior problems: "I never had anger problems," he commented, adding, "It was just my mom saying that." Meanwhile, he was a gifted student who was placed in advanced courses thanks to his outstanding scores of standardized tests. But in junior high, his interest in schoolwork waned, until he began attending a different school after his family moved to a mostly white neighborhood. There, Williams found a challenging atmosphere where his studies thrived once again. By ninth grade, he was named the school's most improved student.

Despite Williams's academic talents, Kirk Bohls revealed in the *Sporting News,* he was an absent-minded kid who lost bicycles frequently by leaving them at playgrounds. He could also be mischievous, sniffing out his mother's hiding place for Christmas presents and then telling his sisters in advance of their gifts. He once managed to talk a neighbor boy into trading a prized baseball card for a worthless one; the deal was reversed when the child's father found out and threatened legal action.

When he was at Patrick Henry High School, Williams learned to redirect his fury into football. There, he befriended Chad Patmon, and the two became best friends. Also in high school, Williams developed his attachment to reggae music, which inspired him to twist his hair into dreadlocks like singer Bob Marley. Patmon would later become Williams's college roommate and teammate at the University of Texas.

In the meantime, Williams was so exceptional on the baseball diamond that the Philadelphia Phillies signed him during the eighth round of the 1995 amateur draft when he was a high school senior. The gig came with a $50,000 signing bonus, which he promptly spent on gifts for friends, family, and even strangers. Thereafter, Williams spent four summers playing in the outfield for Phillies minor league teams.

However, Williams was even more impressive on the football field. Throughout his four years on the high school team, he rushed for 4,129 yards and scored 55 touchdowns. Several colleges offered him football scholarships, and he finally chose the University of Texas at Austin, because he was ready to assert his independence and put some distance between himself and his close–knit family in San Diego. However, his mother soon followed, and both sisters enrolled at Texas as well. "I love my family," Williams told Richard Deutsch in *Sports Illustrated,* "but when I join an NFL team, my mother and sisters won't follow me." Still, his family came in handy during his college years: At times he would ask his sister to pose as his girlfriend because he hated to say no when women asked him out.

On the field at Texas, Williams rushed for 990 yards, setting a school record for a first– year player. This was even more amazing considering that he was playing fullback. At the end of the season, the team won the Southwest Conference title, and he was named Southwest Conference freshman of the year in 1995. His next year, Williams rushed for 1,272 yards and took the Longhorns to the championship in their new conference, the Big 12, which they joined at the outset of the 1996 season. By his junior year, Williams changed positions to tailback, giving him more chances to run with the ball. That season, he led the NCAA and set a school record with 1,893 rushing yards in addition to completing 25 rushing touchdowns and averaging 13.2 points per game. His achievements earned him the nickname "Little Earl," after Earl Campbell, the all–time leading rusher at Texas who won the 1977 Heisman Trophy.

In 1997, Williams received the Doak Walker Award for being the top college running back in the country. The honor was named after the legendary running back for Southern Methodist State who won the Heisman in 1948. Subsequently, Williams developed a friendship with the former football star, who was paralyzed in a skiing accident a few weeks after the two met. Also that year, Williams was in the running for the Heisman Trophy, but he may have lost votes because his team's record was a shoddy four wins, seven losses.

During his junior year, Williams was planning to enter the NFL draft, and would probably have been the number one pick, but he chose instead to stay in school. One of the reasons he chose to stay was new coach, Mack Brown, formerly of the University of North Carolina. "I just didn't want to go 4–7 again," he told Layden in *Sports Illustrated.* "After meeting with Coach Brown, I thought things might be O.K. This team needs discipline." Also, Williams had his sights set on breaking Tony Dorsett's all–time rushing record for total yardage in a college career set in 1976 during Dorsett's final year at the University of Pittsburgh and figured he had a chance at winning the Heisman.

Overall, though, Williams simply enjoyed playing college ball. As Bohls observed in the *Sporting News*, "Williams is that rare selfless individual who puts contentment over cash, devotion over dividends." Brown also suggested to Bohls in the *Sporting News*, "He's very goal–oriented. I think he wanted to leave with a better team. Four–and–seven really bothered him." Bohls noted that Williams most likely turned down a contract worth about $20 million to stay in college. His grades by this point were not outstanding—he was a mainly B and C student—but he expressed his desire to eventually finish his degree and possibly teach elementary school.

In Williams's final year with Texas, the Longhorns finished with a record of eight wins and three losses, a significant improvement over the previous year. During that time, he posted one of the most impressive seasons of any individual player in college football. He ended up rushing for 2,124 total yards, becoming only the eighth player in NCAA history to exceed 2,000 in a season. He also accomplished 27 rushing touchdowns. However, the most outstanding play of the year, and of Williams's entire season, was in the final game of the regular season against Texas A&M, who were ranked number two in the nation at the time. In that game, he surpassed Dorsett's college career rushing record of 6,082 yards when he broke several tackles and ran for a 60–yard touchdown. By the time the Longhorns won the game 26–24, Williams had rushed for 259 yards in the game and rounded out his college career with 1,003 carries.

By the end of the season, Williams had set the new college career rushing record at 6,279 yards and also had more total combined yards for rushing and receiving than any other player in NCAA Division I history, with 7,206. In addition, he set a record for rushing touchdowns (72) and career touchdowns (75), as well as the record for most points by a player other than a field– goal kicker (452). Overall, he broke or tied 21 NCAA records and 44 school records, averaged 136.5 rushing yards per game, and never missed a game throughout his four years on the team. To cap off the year, the Longhorns beat Mississippi State University 38–11 at the Cotton Bowl in January of 1999.

Subsequently, Williams became one of the most highly decorated players in all of college football. First of all, he reaped the prestigious Heisman Trophy, winning by the fourth–largest margin of votes in its history. In accepting the award, he displayed his humble nature by stating, according to Brian Carney in the *Washington Post*, "I owe the greatest amount of gratitude to my teammates. They say that this is an individual award, but in this case it is a team award." He also commented, according to a *Jet* article, "I want to thank my beautiful mother; she raised three kids alone." In addition, he dedicated the season to Walker, noting that 1998 was the fiftieth anniversary of his winning the Heisman. Also in 1998, Williams was named the Associated Press college player of the year, and also won the Walter Camp Football Foundation Award and the Maxwell Award.

In the 1999 NFL draft, the New Orleans Saints chose Williams as their first draft pick, fifth overall. They had traded away all their other picks in the 1999 draft and some of the 2000 draft as well—eight players total—in order to move up to fifth from twelfth so that they could sign him. In the meantime, Williams had fired his agent and became the first major football star to sign with No Limits Management, the representation company owned by rap artist and entrepreneur Master P, who also owns a record company. Offered three different salary and bonus packages by the Saints, Williams chose an eight–year deal that included the highest signing bonus, $8.84 million, and extra pay based on performance. If he did not play well, he would earn the league minimum of $175,000 the first year, increasing to $400,000 by the eighth.

Some asserted that Williams's representative was inexperienced and did not bargain well. Though his earnings would depend on performance, the contract called for him to rush at least 1,600 yards to improve on his base salary. Only 15 players—and just three rookies—had ever reached that goal. To collect the highest annual salary, $3 million, Williams would have to rush for 2,106 yards, a lofty mark that only one player had ever hit. As it turned out, his first season was a disappointment all around: He only made the minimum salary plus a $50,000 bonus for playing time, and the Saints amassed an embarrassing record of 3–13. However, Williams had been plagued with injuries throughout the year, and also insisted that he was not the only problem with the team's performance. Coach Ditka was fired following the season.

In addition to his signature dreadlocks, Williams sports piercings in his nose and tongue, and a tattoo of the cartoon character Mighty Mouse. His official NFL player biography notes that he is five feet, ten inches tall and 236 pounds. At ease around children, Williams often visits schools, and once attended a boy's birthday party even though he thought he might miss his flight to attend the Doak Walker Award ceremony. Williams is not married but has a daughter, Marley, by a former girlfriend. Despite his colorful appearance, he considers himself "quiet and shy," as he remarked in a *People* article that dubbed him the "sexiest athlete" of 1999.

Sources

Periodicals

Jet, December 14, 1998, p. 56; December 28, 1998, p. 53; May 31, 1999, p. 51.

New Orleans Magazine, July 1999, p. 57.

People, November 15, 1999, p. 98.

Rolling Stone, June 10, 1999, p. 92.

Sport, December 1998, p. 56; April 19, 1999, p. 51.

Sporting News, August 17, 1998, p. 68; November 2, 1998, p. 45.

Sports Illustrated, November 24, 1997, p. 100; May 18, 1998, p. 72; November 16, 1998, p. 42; July 19, 1999, p. 88.

Tampa Tribune, January 10, 2000, p. 9.

Washington Post, December 13, 1998, p. D10.

Online

National Football League web site, http://www.nfl.com (January 18, 2000).

Ricky Williams official fan web site, http://www.rickywilliams.com (January 18, 2000).

Other

Additional information was obtained from the NCAA office of Division I–A/I–AA football records, January 25, 2000.

CeCe Winans

Gospel singer

Born Priscilla Winans, October 8, 1964, in Detroit, MI; daughter of David (a minister, barber, and gospel singer) and Delores (a medical transcriptionist and gospel singer) Winans; married Alvin Love II (a sales account executive), June 23, 1984; children: Alvin III, Ashley.

Addresses: *Home*—Forest Hills, TN. *Record company*—Chordant Distribution Group, 101 Winners Circle, Nashville, TN 37201.

Career

Gospel singer. Began singing together with brothers BeBe and David as The Winans Part 2; launched career as duo with The PTL Singers on *The PTL Club* television show, Charlotte, NC, 1982–84; co–owned a salon, Detroit, MI, mid–1980s; signed with Sparrow Records, 1985, and released first album, *Introducing BeBe and CeCe Winans,* 1987; numerous television appearances, including *The Tonight Show, Live with Regis and Kathie Lee, Martin, Sesame Street,* and the 1994 Grammy Awards telecast; tours include Winans One Family World Tour, 1992; Young Messiah Tour, 1993; and 1994 tour featuring The Sounds of Blackness. Established solo recording and concert career, 1995; released debut solo album, *Alone In His Presence,* Sparrow, 1995; started own company, CW Wellspring Entertainment, and record label, Wellspring Gospel Records, 1999. Wrote autobiography, *On a Positive Note,* with Renita J. Weens, Pocket Books, 1999.

Awards: (With brother, BeBe Winans, except as noted) Gospel Music Association's Dove Award, new artists of the year, 1987, group of the year, 1990,

1992, contemporary album of the year, 1990, and (CeCe only) female vocalist of the year, 1996; Grammy Award for best female gospel soul vocal performance (CeCe only), for "For Always," 1987, best female gospel vocal performance (CeCe only), for "Don't Cry," 1989, and best contemporary soul gospel album, for *Different Lifestyles,* 1992; Stellar Award for best new gospel artist, 1988, best performance by group or duo, contemporary album of the year, contemporary song of the year, and best inspirational gospel performance, 1990; NAACP Image Award, best gospel artist, 1990, 1992; Soul Train Music Award for best gospel album of the year, for *Heaven,* 1990; Motor City Music Award, outstanding gospel recording, outstanding gospel soloist, duo or group, 1991; (CeCe only) Grammy Award for best contemporary soul gospel album for *Alone in His Presence,* 1995.

Sidelights

CeCe Winans rose to gospel fame as half of a duo that included her brother, BeBe. The pair got their start on Jim and Tammy Faye Bakker's religious program, *The PTL Club,* then launched a successful recording career. After winning a bevy of awards for her recordings with BeBe Winans, she issued her first solo album in 1995, and has continued to reap accolades on her own. Along the way, Winans has been credited with helping to popularize gospel, thus opening doors for other artists like The Sounds of Blackness and Kirk Franklin. Her 1998 effort, *Everlasting Love*, featured the talents of songwriters and producers such as Tony Rich, Keith Crouch, and Daryl Simmons, who have worked for top R&B names like Aretha Franklin, Tony Braxton, Brandy, and Boyz II Men; she has also collaborated with hip–hop's Lauryn Hill. In 1999, Winans started up her own record label and then issued another solo project, *Alabaster Box*, in addition to publishing an uplifting autobiography, *On a Positive Note*.

Priscilla (CeCe) Winans was born on October 8, 1964, in Detroit, Michigan, the daughter of David and Delores Winans. When she came along, she was the youngest and the only girl among seven older brothers David, Ronald, Marvin, Carvin, Michael, Daniel, and Benjamin but later her parents had two more girls, Angelique and Debbie. Her father worked as a barber and her mother as a medical transcriptionist, but they were also devout Pentecostalists who sang in gospel choirs.

In fact, Winans's parents had met each other when they were both members of the Lemon Gospel Chorus in 1950. They married in 1953, and would pass along their talent for music to their children. They raised their family in a three–bedroom, two–story brick home on the west side of Detroit, where Winans noted in her autobiography, *On a Positive Note*, they "worked hard to create a home environment in which love took priority over things. Discipline was second to love. Laughter ran a close third." And of course, music filled the home constantly, as all family members loved to sing.

In addition to gospel, all of the Winans children loved the Motown sounds growing up the Four Tops, the Supremes, Marvin Gaye, Stevie Wonder, the Temptations, and others and would secretly sing along with these artists, but never let their parents catch them for fear of being chastised for performing secular music. In the early 1970s, Winans's oldest brothers, David, Ronald, Carvin, and Marvin, began singing gospel together as the Testimonials, and by the early 1980s had changed their name to The Winans. Meanwhile, CeCe Winans began performing with her brothers Daniel, BeBe and Michael as The Winans Part II, appearing mainly at church and family events.

A self–described loner at Detroit's Mumford High School, Winans stood out because of her modest appearance long dresses; no nail polish or flashy jew-

elry and because she was forbidden to attend parties or movies. Despite being part of such a talented family, Winans was perhaps the most introverted of the bunch, and she never considered a music career beyond the usual teenage fantasies. As she noted in her book, "I lacked the confidence. I couldn't imagine myself as a singer, and I didn't believe I had what it took . Aspiring for a regular, nice, respectable, nine–to–five job was my safe dream." She ultimately wanted to become a court stenographer, and after high school, attended cosmetology school, thinking that she could pay for college by styling hair.

While Winans was learning cosmetology, in 1981 the family received a call from a family friend, Howard McCrary, who was a musical director on the religious television program *The PTL Club*, based in Charlotte, North Carolina, and hosted by evangelists Jim and Tammy Faye Bakker. ("PTL" has been cited as standing for "Praise the Lord" or "People that Love.") McCrary asked if CeCe and BeBe Winans would be interested in singing on the show, and they joined six other PTL Singers in 1982. The atmosphere was much different than in their experiences singing at church in Detroit. At *The PTL Club*, the audiences were mostly white, and it took a while for Winans to understand that their quiet, understated reaction to the singing did not mean they were not moved by the music.

Winans and her brother were occasionally paired up to sing together on *The PTL Club*, but when they began to perform "Lord, Lift Us Up," they became a regular duo, and people began referring to them as "the black Donny and Marie Osmond." Audiences frequently requested them to sing their hit, which Tammy Fay Bakker adapted from the song "Up Where We Belong," performed by Joe Cocker and Jennifer Warnes on the soundtrack for the film *An Officer and a Gentleman*. The Bakkers later divorced, Jim Bakker went to prison for bilking money from his church enterprise, and their ministry was closed down, but Winans noted in her book that she refused to say anything bad about her experience on *The PTL Club*.

During her time on the show, Winans was exposed to a much different lifestyle than she had growing up in Detroit. She admired the surroundings and warm feelings at Heritage USA, a posh Christian campground that housed the PTL ministries, but during her time there, she ventured into territory that was formerly forbidden she began wearing makeup on stage, and started to go to movies. Winans only went to clean shows, though; her first film was *Tootsie*. *The PTL Club* also introduced Winans and her brother to a vast audience, with the show as well as with an independent album released by PTL. They received incessant offers for bookings, and before long, producers were showing interest. However, as Winans wrote in her autobiography, "Eventually I grew restless at PTL. I began feeling disconnected to the flurry activities that went with the job. I began feeling that it was time to go."

In the spring of 1984, Winans left *The PTL Club* and moved back to Detroit. In the meantime, at age 18, she had met her future husband at a church bowling outing on one of her trips home to Detroit. A few months later, her brother, Ronald, came to visit her in Charlotte and brought the man, Alvin Love, a sales account executive 16 years Winans's senior, with him. After spending a weekend together, he asked her to marry him. She would not make a decision without consulting people she respected, so she asked the blessing of her whole family and her pastor before committing. Winans remarked to Joy Duckett Cain in *Essence*, "Certain people in my life had to be at peace with the situation. Thank God I had enough wisdom to know that." Her entire family was at their wedding on June 23, 1984.

Though Winans told Cain that it was initially difficult learning how to communicate well, she and her husband found it helpful to attend marriage conferences at their church, Born Again. "God's word and having Him at the center of our marriage is definitely the glue that keeps us together," she commented to Cain. Winans's husband became her personal manager also began writing songs for her. Before she started her recording career, though, Winans finished cosmetology school and got her beautician's license, then opened a shop in Detroit called CeCe's. As she explained in her book, "I hate starting things and not finishing them," and also, she wanted something to fall back on, just in case her singing career fizzled out. Eventually she had 14 stylists working for her.

In 1985, Winans and her brother signed with Sparrow Records, a Christian label that had no other black artists under contract at the time. They recorded a single, "I.O.U. Me," which BeBe Winans had written. It did well on the gospel charts. The first time she heard the song on the radio, she and her brother were riding in a car together in Detroit, and she was amazed to hear herself. The duo released their debut album, *Introducing BeBe and CeCe Winans,* in 1987, produced by Keith Thomas, with most of the songs penned by BeBe Winans. It included the hits "I.O.U. Me" and "For Always," which hit number one on Christian radio and also were best–sellers on the Inspirational and R&B

charts. Winans won a Grammy Award for best female soul gospel performance for the song "For Always," and she and her brother were named best new artists at the 1987 Dove Awards.

BeBe and CeCe Winans's next effort, *Heaven,* 1988, was an even bigger hit. It was the first gospel album to reach the top ten on *Billlboard'* s R&B charts and only the second (after Aretha Franklin's *Amazing Grace,* 1972) to achieve gold album status, meaning 100,000 copies sold. *Heaven* also featured vocals by Winans's good friend Whitney Houston on the hit "Hold Up the Light." The project led to a second Grammy for Winans for the song "Don't Cry" as well as an NAACP Image Award. Some complained that their next release, *Different Lifestyles,* 1991, sounded too pop–oriented, but many more enjoyed the slick new sound: It became the first gospel work to reach number one on the *Billboard* gospel and R&B charts. This brought the duo a 1991 Grammy for best contemporary soul gospel album and another Image Award, and featured background vocals by Houston. In turn, Winans sang on some of Houston's projects as well, including on the song "Count on Me," featured on the *Waiting to Exhale* soundtrack.

In addition to collaborating on a Christmas album, *First Christmas,* in 1993, BeBe and CeCe Winans spawned more crossover hit singles with 1994's *Relationships.* They developed a higher profile as well, appearing on television shows such as *Sesame Street, The 700 Club,* and *The Tonight Show,* and they even showed up on the situation comedy *Martin* after the script was revised to eliminate elements that the Winans found offensive. Winans has appeared on Broadway and several other television programs as well. While in Salt Lake City preparing for a guest role on the series *Touched by an Angel* , she got a call that her brother Ronald was in the hospital in serious condition with heart problems. The family rallied around him, and he managed to pull through, despite being clinically dead for close to four minutes on the operating table.

Meanwhile, BeBe Winans was trying his hand at producing works for others, and CeCe Winans soon decided to find her own path as well. Her other siblings had been churning out gold records and reaping Grammy Awards as well, and she decided to do her own project. The album, *Alone in His Presence,* came out in 1995. "Singing solos isn't anything new to me," Winans commented to Barry Cooper in the *New Pittsburgh Courier,* "But listening to the whole 10 songs and not hearing BeBe anywhere is different." However, BeBe Winans did produce a song and sang background on others, and more family members contributed vocals as well. One track featured the singer in a duet on with her mother on "Great Is Thy Faithfulness," Winans's favorite hymn. *Alone in His Presence* became a top five gospel hit and won the 1995 Grammy Award for best contemporary soul gospel album. The next year, she became the first black woman to win the Dove Award for female vocalist of the year.

Although a BeBe and CeCe Winans greatest hits album was issued in 1996, Winans has continued to focus on her solo career, though she insists that her hiatus from her brother is temporary. In 1998, the singer released *Everlasting Love,* which has a more mainstream pop–oriented sound and boasts influences from jazz, R&B, hip–hop, and Afro–Caribbean styles. It landed at number one on the gospel charts. Also that year Winans released a solo Christmas album, *His Gift.* Her fourth solo work, *Alabaster Box,* came out in 1999, recorded on her own label, Wellspring Gospel Records, and distributed by Chordant, a Christian division of EMI. Her label is an arm of a larger company that she and her husband set up called CW Wellspring Entertainment, based in Franklin, Tennessee.

As Winans told Deborah Evans Price in *Billboard,* discussing her previous recording labels, "Pioneer folded and I was out of my contract with Sparrow. I was trying to decide whether to sign with another company, and it was clear that it was time for me to do it now." On Wellspring, she plans not only to sign gospel artists, but also contemporary Christian music of various styles. "You might have a country sound. You might have hip–hop, contemporary, or traditional. I just want people that God has called to do this," she explained to Evans. That same year, 1999, Winans issued her autobiography, *On a Positive Note,* which a *Publishers Weekly* reviewer complimented as having "the feel of two friends conversing over tea about their lives." The singer also hosts her own hour–long show, *CeCe's Place,* on the family and interfaith cable channel Odyssey.

Winans and her family have a three–level, 20–room home in upscale Forest Hills, Tennessee, outside of Nashville, where her children, son Alvin Lemar III and daughter Ashley Rose, are home–schooled according to Family Christian Academy guidelines. The children enjoy performing as well, and have been in commercials and stage plays. Winans also supports two Ethiopian sisters through the World Vision hunger–relief organization, and in 1995, she founded Sharing the Vision, Inc., which sponsors youth programs such as Christian camps, mentoring, social activities, support groups, and other community services.

Selected discography

Introducing BeBe & CeCe Winans, 1987.
Heaven, 1988.
Different Lifestyles, 1991.
First Christmas, 1993.
Relationships, 1994.
Greatest Hits, 1996.

Solo albums

Alone In His Presence, Sparrow, 1995.
Everlasting Love, Pioneer Music, 1998.
His Gift (Christmas album), Pioneer Music, 1998.
Alabaster Box, EMI/Chordant, 1999.

Sources

Books

Contemporary Black Biography, volume 14, Gale Research, 1997.
Winans, CeCe and Renita J. Weens, *On a Positive Note,* Pocket Books, 1999.

Periodicals

Billboard, August 21, 1999, p. 6.
Essence, December 1992, p. 80; February 1996, p. 64; June 1999, p. 76.
Jet, October 9, 1995, p. 58.
New Pittsburgh Courier, August 30, 1995.
Newsday, November 17, 1994, p. B9.
People, January 15, 1996, p. 26.
Philadelphia Tribune, December 4, 1998, p. 6D.
Publishers Weekly, April 26, 1999, p. 74.
USA Today, April 7, 1998, p. 4D.

Online

The Recording Academy Grammy Awards web site, http://www.grammy.com (November 3, 1999).

Obituaries

Hafez Assad

Born October 6, 1930, in Qurdaha, Syria; died of heart failure, June 10, 2000, in Damascus, Syria. Syrian president. Hafez Assad, president of Syria from 1971 until his death in 2000, established himself as a ruthless leader and a pillar of Arab opposition to Israel. For years, the nation was a U.S. foe, derided for human rights abuses and terrorist activities. However, Western leaders begrudgingly conceded that Assad brought stability to what had been one of the most volatile countries since World War II. Nevertheless, Assad was a holdout in Mideast peace talks for years, refusing to make any deals with Israel except on his own terms.

Assad was born into a large family in the village of Qurdaha near the Mediterranean coast, in the Ansariya Mountains. Originally, his family name was Wahish, meaning "wild beast," but they changed it to Assad, which means "lion." His father, 'Ali Assad, lived with his two wives and numerous children in a two–room stone house in the poor village, which was made up of about 100 homes and no restaurants, stores, or mosques. Nevertheless, the area was a safe haven for his ethnic group, the Alawites, a minority Muslim sect often derided as heretical by the majority Sunni Muslims. Alawites, or Alawis, which make up about 12 percent of the Syrian population, were mostly centered near the coastal regions.

During Assad's youth, the Alawite district of Syria was administered by the French, who set up schools there in order to help recruit Alawite clans to help govern the Sunni Muslims in the typical divide–and–conquer method of colonialism. Assad was sent to these schools and later became the first in his family to pursue secondary education. He soon became enmeshed in political dialogue and joined the

Baath party, which was founded on the precepts of Arab unity, socialism, and freedom. In high school, he was head of the Union of Syrian Students and used his position to try to stir student protests nationwide against the government and non–Baath parties.

After completing high school at age 20 in 1951, Assad went to a military academy and joined the air force. He later rounded out his training in the Soviet Union and graduated as a lieutenant in 1955. Meanwhile, Syria had decided to join Egypt as part of the United Arab Republic, and when Assad returned from the Soviet Union in 1959, he was transferred with his squadron to Egypt. He and some fellow officers, disgruntled by the treatment of Syrians in the deal, secretly plotted to take over the Syrian Army and dismantle the union.

In 1963, Assad's group staged a series of coups and claimed control, thus breaking down the union. Subsequently, Syria remained in turmoil with various factions rising to power through the years. In the meantime, Assad was appointed commander of the air force in 1965 and became defense minister the following year under a regime led by General Salah Jadid. He was in this post during the Six–Day Arab–Israeli War in 1967 during which the Arabs lost the eastern part of Jerusalem, the Golan Heights, and the Sinai peninsula.

Assad rose to head of state following the Jordanian crisis of 1970 in which King Hussein quelled an armed Palestinian uprising. Syria sent tanks to support the guerillas but pulled out when Jordan sent air attacks, and Hussein remained on the throne. Afterward, Assad seized power from Jadid in November of 1970. He was elected president four months later.

Under Assad's control, Syria joined forces with Egypt to advance into the Golan Heights in October of 1973 in order to save face for the bitter 1967 defeat. However, a cease–fire was declared by the end of the month and it was clear the Arabs had been defeated again. Secretary of State Henry Kissinger tried to broker a peace deal at that time and was the first of a succession of Americans to be thwarted in their efforts by the stalwart Assad.

In addition to being seen as a blockade to peace progress in the Middle East, Assad was harshly criticized by human rights groups for ruling with an iron fist. Torture was rampant in prisons, political opposition was stifled, free speech was halted, and arrests and imprisonments without trials were widespread. The most infamous example of Assad's brutal regime came in the early 1980s, when his security forces leveled about a fourth of the city of Hama after a Sunni Muslim uprising, killing an estimated 10,000 residents. Assad was also known for installing fellow Alawites in government, practicing nepotism, and installing a feared and ubiquitous security force.

Another facet of Assad was his reputation as a savvy political strategist. He spearheaded an Islamic resistance movement in Lebanon that fought against Israeli troops for decades, even as he began working on a peace treaty with Israel. In addition, he wisely forged an alliance with the United States during the Gulf War in 1991 to oppose his arch–rival, Iraqi leader Saddam Hussein. This came at a time when his longtime funding from the Soviet Union was in danger due to the collapse of that regime. Afterward, he agreed to more peace dealings with the Israelis.

Throughout his rule, Assad withstood several coup attempts, including one by his brother, Rifaat, after Assad suffered a heart attack in 1983. Rifaat was then exiled to France until 1992. Assad married Anisse Makhluf, who came from a prominent Alawite clan, and they had four sons and a daughter. After years of poor health, including a battle with diabetes, Assad died at age 69 of a heart attack in Damascus.

After Assad's death the Syrian government embarked on a plan to install as president his eldest surviving son, Bashar, an ophthalmologist with virtually no political experience. He took over leadership that same month. Subsequently, the world began to try to determine what the future held for the peace negotiations in the Middle East. Assad is survived by his wife, a daughter, and three sons. Another son a military officer considered for years his father's heir apparent died in an automobile acci-

dent in 1994. **Sources:** *Chicago Tribune,* June 11, 2000; *Encyclopedia of World Biography,* second edition, Gale Research, 1998; *Newsmakers 1992,* Cumulation, Gale Research, 1992; *New York Times,* June 10, 2000; *Times* (London), June 12, 2000; *Washington Post,* June 11, 2000, p. A1.

Paul Bowles

Born Paul Frederick Bowles, December 30, 1910, in New York, NY; died of a heart attack, November 18, 1999, in Tangier, Morocco. Author and composer. Paul Bowles, known as the leading figure of the "Beat" movement, was perhaps most famous for his first novel, *The Sheltering Sky.* Published in 1949, the book attracted attention for its unconventionality, but also became a best–seller and "has since been praised as a masterpiece of existential literature," according to an article in *Contemporary Authors.* After this first work, Bowles shifted his attention away from composing music and began to concentrate on his literary ambitions. Like *The Sheltering Sky,* most of Bowles's subsequent novels, poems, and short stories deal with adventurers in exotic locations, which was similar to Bowles's own life. After traveling through Europe, Africa, India, Japan, Hong Kong, Singapore, South America, and Mexico, Bowles moved to Tangier, Morocco, where he lived until his death.

Despite Bowles's exotic lifestyle, he started out in a middle–class family in Jamaica, Queens, on Long Island, at a time when it was still marked by its pastoral setting. The only child of Claude Dietz Bowles, a dentist, and Rena (Winnewisser) Bowles, a poet, he learned to read at age three. He spent his upbringing in the suburbs, with summers at his paternal grandparents' home in Seneca Lake, New York, or his maternal grandparents' farm in western Massachusetts. However, he has characterized his childhood as less than idyllic. He was a lonely boy, and wrote unfavorable accounts of his relationship with his father.

As a youngster, Bowles attended the Model School, where he studied piano, including music theory and ear training. At age nine, he tried to compose an opera, and he avidly listened to music on the family phonograph. However, although his father was once an aspiring concert violinist, he forbade his son to play music while he was at home. Bowles went on to Jamaica High School, a public school in Queens, and became involved with the monthly literary magazine there. Around the time of his graduation in 1928, he published a surrealist poem in the prestigious Modernist magazine *transition* out of Paris.

After studying painting at the School of Design and Liberal Arts in Manhattan, Bowles went on to the University of Virginia in Charlottesville, following in the footsteps of author Edgar Allen Poe. During his first term, though, he abruptly set off for Paris to become a switchboard operator at the *Herald Tribune*, an English–language newspaper aimed at Americans living in Europe. There, he befriended luminaries such as Gertrude Stein, Jean Cocteau, and Andre Gide. His parents eventually persuaded him to return to the United States to finish his first year of college.

Subsequently, Bowles sought out composer Aaron Copland, who became his teacher and mentor. After traveling to Europe to follow Copland, who was going to Berlin, Bowles visited Stein and her companion Alice B. Toklas in Paris. Stein dismissed his poetry, but encouraged him to go to Tangier. Though he was initially disappointed with the destination, he would later thrive there, and moved there permanently in 1948.

In the meantime, Bowles returned to Berlin and continued to study under Copland. In Germany, he met up with British writers Christopher Isherwood and Stephen Spender. Isherwood would go on to write the story "I Am a Camera," which was adapted as the Broadway play *Cabaret* in the late 1960s. For his story, Isherwood named the lead character, Sally Bowles, after Paul Bowles.

During the 1930s Bowles worked with the Federal Theater Project in New York, which was part of the Works Progress Administration (WPA). This was a government–funded effort to employ hundreds of thousands of Americans in fields ranging from construction to the fine arts. At this time, Bowles began to pen music for plays as well as creating his own pieces, and he became a major name in theater in New York. His first big effort was the 1937 opera *Denmark Vesey*, followed by *The Wind Remains*, 1941. He also wrote ballets, including *Yankee Clipper*, 1937, and scored the music for Tennessee Williams's play *The Glass Menagerie*, 1945, in addition to composing music for documentaries.

In 1938 Bowles married writer Jane Sydney Auer, a day before her twenty–first birthday. She was ill with tuberculosis of the bone, and he cared for her until her death in 1973. Although both frequently had homosexual encounters, they would have some physical relationship at times, though their bond was mainly emotional. After marrying, Bowles began writing critical reviews for the *New York Herald Tribune* from 1942 to 1946. He then began translating (one of his efforts was Jean–Paul Sartre's play *No Exit*) and writing stories. Soon he was offered an advance on a novel from Doubleday, but when he submitted the manuscript for *The Sheltering Sky*, they rejected it, claiming it was not a novel. The work recounted the spiritual journey of a married couple from New York who trek across the Saharan Desert. New Directions ended up publishing it, and the book established Bowles as a leading figure of the Beat movement. Poets Allen Ginsberg and William Burroughs ended up traveling to Tangier to see him.

Bowles's next book, *Let It Come Down*, 1952, was set in Tangier and involves an American bank clerk who becomes involved in an underworld of corruption. In 1955, he published *The Spider's House*, about an American writer in Fez during a political upheaval. Some of his other works include *Up Above the World*, 1966; *Points in Time*, 1982, and various collections of poetry and short stories. He also continued to compose, creating operatic works based on the writings of Federico Garcia Lorca, as well as concertos. Also during his time in Morocco, Bowles collected and organized the music of the people of the Rif Mountains for the United States Library of Congress.

The Sheltering Sky was made into a film in 1990 narrated by Bowles, directed by Bernardo Bertolucci, and starring John Malkovich and Debra Winger. Despite mixed reviews and the author's disappointment in the adaptation, it created a resurgence in interest of his works. A documentary, *Paul Bowles: The Complete Outsider*, was released in 1994, and an anthology of his prose and photography, *Too Far from Home*, was published in 1995. Bowles was hospitalized in Tangier in early November, 1999, and died of a heart attack there on November 18 at age 88. He had no survivors. **Sources:** *Chicago Tribune*, November 19, 1999, sec. 2, p. 10; "Paul (Frederick) Bowles," *Contemporary Authors Online*, Gale Group web site, http://www.galenet.com (March 6, 2000); *Encyclopedia of World Biography*, second edition, Gale Research, 1998; *Los Angeles Times*, November 19, 1999, p. A 32; *New York Times*, November 19, 1999, p. B14; *Times* (London), November 19, 1999; *Washington Post*, November 19, 1999, p. B7.

Leo Castelli

Born Leo Krauss, September 4, 1907, in Trieste, Austro–Hungary; died August 21, 1999, in New York,

NY. Art dealer. New York art dealer Leo Castelli was not only a dapper and charming salesman with an eye for new talent, he was also highly influential in the art world, shaping movements and ushering in acceptance of often– controversial artists and their works. Thanks to his enthusiasm and business acumen, he was the first to demand prices in the millions of dollars for the products of living artists, and he was notable for refusing to represent established artists, or for that matter, anyone who he did not personally discover. In addition, he was instrumental in helping rising American artists to gain international recognition. Associated early in his art career with Abstract Impressionists, he was later a vanguard during the Pop Art era, as well as being involved in Minimalism, Conceptualism, and Neo–Expressionism. Some of his most famous associations were with Jasper Johns, Robert Rauschenberg, Andy Warhol, and Roy Lichtenstein.

Castelli was born Leo Krauss, the son of Ernest Krauss, a Hungarian banker, and Bianca Castelli, of the prominent Castelli family in Trieste, then part of the Austro– Hungarian empire. When Trieste became part of Italy in 1919, Castelli changed his named to Krauss–Castelli, but later dropped the Krauss. His father encouraged his education, and although Castelli was poor at math, he learned five languages, reading and writing fluently in Italian, English, French, German, and Greek. He also absorbed a deep knowledge of art history.

Bowing to pressure to enter a conventional profession, Castelli earned a law degree at the University of Milan in 1924 and worked for an insurance company in Trieste for a time. However, his schedule was free enough to allow him to become something of a playboy. In addition to socializing with women, he swam, played tennis, and became an avid mountain climber and skier, despite his small build. In 1932 he was transferred to Bucharest, Romania, and fell in love with Ileana Schapira, the daughter of one of the wealthiest families in Bucharest. They married in 1933 and soon purchased their first piece of art, a watercolor by Henri Matisse.

Castelli and his wife moved to Paris in 1937, where his father–in–law helped him land a job with a bank. There, the couple was introduced to many of the Surrealist artists including Salvador Dali, Max Ernst, and others. In 1939, Castelli opened a gallery on the Place Vendome with friend Rene Drouin, an architect and designer. Their only show, held that year, focused on surrealism. However, World War II soon broke out, and Castelli, being Jewish, headed for New York City in 1941.

After attending graduate art history courses at Columbia University, Castelli was drafted into the U.S. Army, where he worked in intelligence in Bucharest. This earned him American citizenship. After his discharge, Castelli's father–in–law established him in a sweater–manufacturing business. In the meantime, though, Castelli continued to collect art, and soon began to sell as well. By 1951, he helped finance the landmark "Ninth Street Show," a Abstract Expressionist exhibit, and was involved in promoting the up–and–coming New York School.

In 1957, Castelli and his wife opened a gallery in the living room of their townhouse on East 77th Street. The lively and wealthy Castelli easily made his name in the New York art world, and sought to represent fledgling artists whom he felt offered something new and different. In the late 1950s and early 1960s, he discovered Jasper Johns, Robert Rauschenberg, Frank Stella, and Cy Twombley, making Castelli's gallery, which moved to a commercial space in 1960, the hotspot for New York art. He and his wife divorced amicably that year as well, and she went on to found her own gallery, the Sonnabend, in Paris and the SoHo district of Manhattan. She and Castelli remained friends and teamed up throughout the years on various business ventures.

Into the 1960s, Castelli became identified with the emerging Pop artists, such as Andy Warhol, Roy Lichtenstein, Claes Oldenburg, and James Rosenquist. This movement included images like Warhol's paintings of Campbell's soup cans and sculptures of Brillo pad boxes, and Lichtenstein's large–format Benday dot paintings featuring takeoffs of comic strips. Pop Art was thus controversial for this assumption of lowbrow images, and attracted an unbelievable amount of popular press while also reaping severe criticism from many. Castelli, due to his large part in the rise of the movement, was chided for ushering in the death of Abstract Expressionism, but he deflected the accusations by stating that that era had already ended anyway.

Integral in spreading the word about American artists in Europe, Castelli was rewarded in 1964 when Rauschenberg became the first American to win the grand prize of the Venice Bienniale. Later, in 1988, Castelli donated a Rauschenberg worth roughly $10 million which he purchased for $1,200 in 1958 to the Museum of Modern Art in New York, at a time when such gifts were not tax–deductible. Other artists in Castelli's stable, to whom he referred as "friends" and never "clients," included Dan Flavin, Donald Judd, Ellsworth Kelly, Robert Morris, Kenneth Noland, Bruce Nauman, and Richard Serra. However, the most influential artist in his life was his friend Marcel Duchamp, as he told the *Los Angeles Times* in 1996.

When Castelli moved his gallery to 420 West Broadway in 1971, it marked the dawning of SoHo as the premier neighborhood for emerging artists in New York City. Later, he acquired a large space on Greene Street, where he showed big pieces. This ushered in the trend of galleries assuming gigantic spaces. Despite Castelli's lower profile in later years, he remained an active member of the art world, and by 1987, his gallery was moving $10 million worth of art annually. By the art boom of 1990, this number doubled, although revenue suffered somewhat in the 1990s when the art market experienced a global recession. In 1998, Castelli was honored with the Centennial Medal of Honor by New York's National Arts Club.

After Castelli's divorce from his first wife in 1960, he married Antoinette Fraissex du Bost in 1963. His second wife died in 1987, and in 1995, he married art critic Barbara Bertozzi, which set off a flurry of gossip in art circles. Fifty years his junior, Bertozzi was said to have cut off Castelli from his old acquaintances. Castelli died at age 91 his home in Manhattan on August 21, 1999, after a short illness. He is survived by his third wife; a daughter from his first marriage, Nina Sundell; and a son, Jean-Cristophe, from his second marriage. **Sources:** "Influential art dealer Leo Castelli dead at 91," *CNN Interactive* web site, August 23, 1999, http://cnn.com (August 24, 1999); *Chicago Tribune*, August 23, 1999; *Los Angeles Times*, August 24, 1999; *Newsweek*, September 6, 1999, p. 68; *New York Times*, August 23, 1999, p. A1; *Times* (London), August 24, 1999; *Washington Post*, August 24, 1999, p. B7.

Wilt Chamberlain

Born Wilton Norman Chamberlain, August 21, 1936, in Philadelphia, PA; died of a heart attack, October 12, 1999, in Los Angeles, CA. Basketball player. Basketball superstar Wilt Chamberlain, whose career spanned from 1959 to 1973, became a sports icon for his prowess on the court, setting countless records and becoming the only player to score 4,000 points in one season and 100 points in a single game. He played for the Philadelphia (later San Francisco) Warriors, the Philadelphia 76ers, and the Los Angeles Lakers, never fouling out of a game. His height of seven feet and one inch earned him the nickname "Wilt the Stilt," which he despised, preferring the name "The Big Dipper." Due to his influence, the game evolved, becoming a contest focused mainly on large, powerful, yet agile players who dominate the court near the net. In addition to his personal achievements, Chamberlain was known for his match-ups with Boston Celtics center Bill Russell.

Born in west Philadelphia, Chamberlain was named after the street on which he was born, Wilton. His father, William, worked as a porter at a publishing company, and his mother, Olivia, cleaned houses. Neither his parents nor any of his eight brothers and sisters were very tall. Chamberlain began to experience growth spurts at age 14, gaining four inches in one summer alone. By high school, he was six feet, eleven inches, and led Overbrook High to a 56-3 record over three seasons. He also excelled at track and field, running cross country and winning a conference title in the long jump.

After high school, Chamberlain attended the University of Kansas on a scholarship, where he was an outstanding player. As a sophomore, he led the Jayhawks to the National Collegiate Athletic Association (NCAA) championship but lost to North Carolina in triple overtime. At the time, college players could not play for the National Basketball Association (NBA) until their class had graduated, but nevertheless, the athlete left school a year early to tour with the Harlem Globetrotters in 1958-59, reaping $65,000 a year, the largest basketball contract up to that point. Though he subsequently joined the NBA, Chamberlain still toured with the Globetrotters during some summers.

In the meantime, the Philadelphia Warriors managed to snag Chamberlain under a territorial rule, initially meant for teams to be able to draft from regional colleges. However, when Chamberlain was still in high school, the Warriors managed to get the rule changed so they could exercise regional rights over high school players as well, and they agreed to sign the player later even if his college career was a dud. That did not happen, of course, and in his first game with Philadelphia Chamberlain scored 43 points and had 28 rebounds against the New York Knicks.

In his debut professional season, Chamberlain became the first player to be named rookie of the year as well as the NBA's most valuable player simultaneously. He went on to win a total of four most valuable player awards (the others were from 1966 through 1968) throughout his 1,045 regular-season and 160 playoff games. After starting his career with Philadelphia, Chamberlain stayed with the team through their move to San Francisco in 1962, then returned to Philadelphia to play for their fledgling team, the 76ers, two days after the 1965 All-Star Game.

With the 76ers, Chamberlain saw his first championship, in 1967, as his team beat Boston in five games. After a trade to the Los Angeles Lakers in 1968, he won another championship in 1972, beating the Knicks in five games. Those would be his only two championship rings, though he led his team to playoffs 13 times. Though much of his career, he was known for his on–court rivalry with Bill Russell of the Boston Celtics, whose team won 11 titles in 13 years, as opposed to Chamberlain's two. Outside the arena, though, the two were friends.

The record books are stocked with pages of Chamberlain's accomplishments, including highest scoring average in a season, with 50.4 in 1961–62, and the most rebounds for a career, at 23,924. He also racked up most points for a career at the time with 31,419, a record broken only by Kareem Abdul–Jabbar in 1984 (who played six more seasons than he did). In addition, Chamberlain nabbed 20 of the 30 best regular–season scoring records, and was the top rebounder in the league 11 of his 14 seasons. He holds the three top scoring games in the history of the NBA, and 15 of the top 20 performances. The only other player to have averaged more than 30 points a game over a career (a minimum of 400 games) is Michael Jordan. Chamberlain even led the league in assists during 1967–68, with 702. But the most awesome feat of all was probably Chamberlain's single–game record of 100 points, amassed on March 2, 1962, with the Philadelphia Warriors in Hershey, Pennsylvania against the New York Knicks. The final score was 169 to 147.

After retiring from basketball following the 1972–73 season, Chamberlain kept busy. He coached the now–defunct American Basketball Association's San Diego Conquistadors for a season, and took up tennis, volleyball, and racquetball; he also ran the Honolulu marathon. He also appeared in the 1984 film *Conan the Destroyer*, along with Arnold Schwarzenegger and Grace Jones. In 1978, Chamberlain was elected to the Naismith Memorial Basketball Hall of Fame, and in 1996–97 he was named to the NBA 50th Anniversary All–Time Team.

In 1991 Chamberlain published his autobiography, *View from Above,* which caused a flurry of controversy due to his revelation that he had sexual relations with 20,000 women throughout his lifetime. Many were critical of his promiscuity; others dismissed the statement as an irresponsible boast. After suffering from heart trouble in his later years, his health declined quickly over the last few weeks

of his life, and he died of a heart attack at his home in the Bel–Air section of Los Angeles at age 63. Chamberlain, who never married, is survived by his sisters Barbara Lewis, Margaret Lane, Selina Gross, and Yvonne Chamberlain, and two brothers, Wilbert and Oliver. **Sources:** *Chicago Tribune,* October 13, 1999; "Pride of Philadelphia: Chamberlain revered in hometown as its greatest athlete," CNNSI web site, http://cnnsi.com (October 12, 1999); *Detroit Free Press,* October 13, 1999; "Basketball's Chamberlain Dies at 83," *Los Angeles Times* web site, http://www.latimes.com (October 14, 1999); "Wilt Chamberlain," NBA web site, http://www.nba.com (October 13, 1999); *New York Times,* October 12, 1999; *USA Today,* October 12, 1999; October 13, 1999; *Washington Post,* October 13, 1999, p. A1.

Alex Comfort

Born February 10, 1920, in London, England; died March 26, 2000, in Oxfordshire, England. Author, physician, and biochemist. Though Alex Comfort could post numerous job titles on his resume, including poet, physician, gerontologist, philosopher, and activist, he was best known for his witty and engaging 1972 how–to book, *The Joy of Sex.* According to a *Washington Post* obituary, the London *Independent* in 1994 called Comfort "the grand old man of sex," and added, "In the Seventies, his name was synonymous with uninhibited hedonism and liberated sex." Indeed, his work coincided at a time when the birth control pill and changing mores allowed for burgeoning sexual freedoms, and before AIDS and other threats loomed on the horizon. *The Joy of Sex* eventually sold 12 million copies and was translated into two dozen languages. Though this will be his legacy, Comfort was also the author of dozens of other titles, including works of poetry and fiction, as well a highly–regarded textbook on aging.

Comfort was born to Alexander Charles and Daisy Elizabeth (Fenner) Comfort in the north London neighborhood of Palmer's Green. He admitted to being a rambunctious child; at age 14, he blew off four fingers of his left hand while making gunpowder. His mother, a former teacher, schooled him at home, and he enrolled at Trinity College of Cambridge University as a Robert Styring scholar. There, he studied medicine and trained for the field at London Hospital. He became a licensed doctor in 1944.

During World War II, Comfort was a conscientious objector and actively campaigned to stop the bombing of Germany. His pacifism gave way to anarchism, and he began writing political tracts. Also, from 1941 to 1945, he wrote four books of poetry, three novels, and two plays, most of them criticizing the patriotism rampant at wartime. Though some reviewers applauded his work, others considered it naive.

After the war, Comfort began a 25–year teaching career at London Hospital Medical College. In 1947, he earned a doctorate in biochemistry, and the next year he published a textbook, *First Year Physiological Technique*. He then became an honorary research associate in the zoology department at the University College of London in 1951, where he engaged in research on the coloring of snails. Comfort was also named head of the Medical Research Council's Group on Ageing. Out of this, he published *The Biology of Senescence*, a textbook that brought the topic of growing older into sharp focus and helped draw attention to the way society cares for seniors. Several editions were eventually published.

Though outwardly gentle, Comfort fervently held to his beliefs, and in the early 1960s was one of the group known as the "Committee of 1000," which were jailed for anti–nuclear demonstrations. During his month in prison, he taught Irish Republican songs to fellow activist Bertrand Russell.

Throughout his career, Comfort continued to produce fiction, poetry, literary criticism, and social histories. Early glimpses of his approach to sex can be witnessed in his 1961 book of verse *Haste to the Wedding*, which espouses that physical love should be pleasurable and uninhibited. He repeated this theme in the sociological 1963 work *Sex and Society*, and in 1967, gained notice with *The Anxiety Makers*. It details the way in which doctors in the Victorian era often sought to suppress natural body functions, sometimes by horrific methods. Also, in 1962, Comfort caused a stir in England by advocating that teenage boys should carry condoms.

The Joy of Sex, published in 1972, came about after someone told Comfort that London Hospital was not properly educating its students about sex. He spoke to the head of the psychiatry department and ended up agreeing to write a book on the topic, which he claimed only took him two weeks. A large appeal of the *Joy of Sex* was its clever, unthreatening approach to the topic. It followed the same format as a popular cookbook, *The Joy of Cooking*, with segments titled "Starters," "Main Courses," and "Sauces and Pickles." It also provided drawings illustrating positions, and included helpful tips like "Never fool around sexually with a vacuum cleaner."

According to Comfort, the content of *The Joy of Sex* was based on personal experience, reading, and talking to others. However, it was often suggested that part of his research came out of a longtime affair with Jane Henderson, a sociologist at the London School of Economics. After *The Joy of Sex* was released, Comfort and his wife of 29 years, Ruth Muriel Harris, divorced in 1973. He married Henderson that same year.

In the early 1970s, Comfort moved to the United States, where he lectured on psychiatry at Stanford University and later became a professor at the Neuropsychiatric Institute at the University of California at Berkeley. While in California, he lived for a while at the Sandstone experimental sexual community. In 1974, Comfort published *More Joy of Sex*, and in 1991, wrote another volume, *The New Joy of Sex*. The latter work was tempered by the threat of AIDS and other sexually transmitted diseases, and was updated to strongly urge condom use.

Throughout the 1990s, Comfort suffered a series of strokes and became confined to a wheelchair. He was living in a nursing home in England when he died at age 80. Comfort's second wife, Henderson, died in 1991. He is survived by a son from his first marriage, Nicholas Comfort, who is a political journalist, and three grandchildren. **Sources:** *Chicago Tribune*, March 29, 2000, sec. 2, p. 10; *Los Angeles Times*, March 29, 2000; *New York Times*, March 29, 2000, p. A29; *Times* (London), March 28, 2000; *Washington Post*, March 29, 2000, p. B7.

Pete Conrad

Born Charles P. Conrad Jr., June 2, 1930, in Philadelphia, PA; died from injuries sustained in a motorcycle accident, July 8, 1999, in Ojai, CA. Astronaut. Pete Conrad was a former Navy pilot and astronaut who became the third man to walk on the moon. An exuberant and fun–loving man who yelled "Whoopee!" when he first set foot on the moon, Conrad was a veteran who logged more than 1,100 hours in space during his four missions in 1965, 1966, 1969, and 1973, setting a record at that time. He also set an endurance record for his stint on Skylab 2, a permanent space station. The outgoing engineer's first love was of planes, and he also loved fast cars and motorcycles. Renowned as a practical joker, he was one of the more colorful characters in the elite corps of astronauts, a profession known for its strong personalities.

Conrad was born in the upscale Main Line suburbs of Philadelphia. His father was an investment broker who had served as a balloonist in World War I. Though officially named Charles P. Conrad Jr., he was always known as Pete because his mother liked the name. Growing up, Conrad built model airplanes and was enthralled with engines and aviation. As a teen, he worked part–time cleaning a machine shop in order to pay for flying lessons, and first flew solo at age 16.

Because Conrad spent so much time engrossed in his passion of flying, his studies suffered. He was sent to Darrow School in New Lebanon, New York, for his final two years in high school, and his grades improved drastically. Though he was built small at five feet, six inches tall and 135 pounds, the wiry and enthusiastic Conrad was voted captain of the football team. After graduating with honors in 1949, he studied aeronautical engineering at Princeton University and received his degree in 1953.

After college, Conrad joined the U.S. Navy in order to become a pilot. He attended the Navy Test Pilot School at Patuxent River, Maryland, and after graduating, served as a test pilot, then flight instructor and performance engineer. In 1959, he applied to enter NASA's Mercury space program but did not make the cut to become one of the first group of seven astronauts, even though he passed the physical and mental exams. In 1962, however, he was chosen for the second group of nine. On August 21, 1965, he and L. Gordon Cooper Jr. set a record for manned space travel on the Gemini 5 flight by staying in space eight days, the length of time it would take to fly a person to the moon and back. They had to overcome several mechanical problems and severe physical discomfort and were almost ordered back after just two days, but managed to stay aloft the planned amount of time.

On Conrad's next voyage into space, he commanded the three–day Gemini 11 flight on September 18, 1966. His subsequent journey, the Apollo 12 flight, lasted from November 14 to 24, 1969, and made him the third person to set foot on the moon, after Neil Armstrong and Edwin "Buzz" Aldrin, who landed on July 20, 1969. On that trip, Conrad and Alan Bean traversed the moon's surface, spending seven hours and 45 minutes collecting rocks, inspecting a research vehicle already there, and setting up a nuclear generating station to power future experiments. For his final mission, in May and June of 1973, Conrad became the first person to command a mission to the space station Skylab 2, where he walked in space several times in order to repair damage done to Skylab during its landing. There, in

addition to bringing his total time in space to 1,179 hours and 38 minutes, he also set a record at the time for endurance for staying in space 28 days. Conrad considered this accomplishment even more important than being one of the dozen (to date) people to have stood on the moon.

Highly decorated for his service to the space program and military, Conrad was honored with the Congressional Space Medal of honor, two NASA Distinguished Service Medals, two NASA Exceptional Service Medals, two Navy Distinguished Service Medals, and two Distinguished Flying Crosses. In addition, he was inducted into the Aviation Hall of Fame in 1980. After he retired from the service and NASA in 1973, Conrad worked for the American Television and Communications Corporation in Denver, Colorado, then for the McDonnell Douglas Corporation, the airplane manufacturer, beginning in 1976. He retired from there in 1996 and founded Universal Space Lines and various sister companies, all of which set out to mine the commercial possibilities of space.

Conrad met his first wife, Jane DuBose, while he was attending college. They had four sons and divorced in 1990. He subsequently married Nancy Fortner. At age 69, Conrad died after he crashed his 1996 Harley–Davidson motorcycle on a mountain road near Ojai, California. Though he did not appear to be badly hurt at first, it was found that he suffered massive internal bleeding; he died about five hours after the accident at Ojai Valley Community Hospital. He had been en route to Monterey, California, from his home in Huntington Beach, just south of Los Angeles, in order to attend a motorcycle event. He was obeying the speed limit and wearing a helmet. Conrad is survived by his wife and three sons, Peter, Thomas, and Andrew (a fourth son, Christopher, died of bone cancer in 1990). **Sources:** "Apollo 12 astronaut Pete Conrad killed in motorcycle accident," July 9, 1999, CNN Interactive web site, http://cnn.com (July 9, 1999); *Los Angeles Times*, July 9, 1999; *New York Times*, July 10, 1999, p. C15; *Times* (London), July 10, 1999; *Washington Post*, July 10, 1999, p. B6.

Quentin Crisp

Born Denis Pratt, December 25, 1908, in Sutton, Surrey, England; died November 21, 1999, in Manchester, England. Author and actor. With his sharp wit and flamboyant style, writer and actor Quentin Crisp became an eccentric gay icon after the publication of his autobiography, *The Naked Civil Servant,* in 1968. Admired for his unwavering devotion to being himself, no matter what the consequences, he sported silk blouses, upswept hair, painted fingernails, and lilac eyeshadow even in the face of hostile comments and physical torment from others during his many years in his native England. He once noted, according to a *New York Times* obituary, that people in London "stood with their faces six inches from mine and hissed, 'Who do you think you are?' What a stupid question. It must have been obvious that I didn't think I was anybody else." He found a much more tolerant atmosphere in New York's East Village, where he lived from the 1970s to his death.

Crisp was born in a suburb of London on Christmas Day, 1908. He was the youngest of four children of a lawyer and former nursery governess. As a child, he became fond of dressing in his mother's apparel and pretending to be a princess. His family withstood his antics well, but once he was thrust into mainstream society, he was taunted. Though his family was often in debt, they managed to send him to a boarding school, where he was unpopular and feared his classmates. Crisp compared his student years to being imprisoned. Later, he attended King's College and studied journalism for a short time, but soon dropped out.

Struggling with the need to find a job and his awareness of his homosexuality, Crisp soon fell in with a crowd of male prostitutes in London's West End. He modeled his appearance after their exaggerated style, with heavy make–up and flamboyant clothing. Later, his mother helped him find work first as a book illustrator, then in a series of clerical jobs with the government. Still, he did not give up his affinity for outrageous dress or his mingling in the gay underworld. He refused to moderate his dress or actions just to fit in.

Finally, at age 34, Crisp found a job that perfectly suited his temperament: He became a nude model for life drawing courses at art schools subsidized by the government, and continued this work for the next 35 years. This gave rise to the title of his autobiography, *The Naked Civil Servant.* Its publication marked what was thought to be the first time that an author so openly discussed his homosexual identity. The work not only provided a glimpse into his lifestyle and the perils it wrought, including violent attacks, but it also offered an intriguing overview of British society from the Depression era through the post–World War II recovery. In addition, *The Naked Civil Servant* established Crisp as a keen wit, and won him acclaim as a man who was dedicated to being true to himself in spite of the negative repercussions from the greater society.

In 1975, Crisp's autobiography was adapted for television starring John Hurt, and it received positive reviews. This led to Crisp staging a one–man show, *An Evening with Quentin Crisp,* in London's West End in 1978. Afterward, he took the production to the United States and performed it at Players Theatre in 1979, earning a special Drama Desk Award for unique theatrical experience. Meanwhile, realizing that New York was a haven for eccentrics, he decided to remain in America. Thus, at about age 70, he left his tiny Chelsea apartment and took up residence in Manhattan's East Village area. He immigrated to the United States his proudest achievement, he has said and legally his changed name.

After his move, Crisp continued to write, penning numerous articles, reviews, and opinion pieces as well as several books. They included *How to Have a Lifestyle,* 1979; *How to Become a Virgin,* 1984; and *Resident Alien: The New York Diaries,* 1997, which was a collection of his contributions to *New York Native,* a gay publication. He also has appeared in ads for Calvin Klein's CK1 fragrance and in the film *Philadelphia* as Oscar Wilde, with whom he was often compared. In addition, he played Queen Elizabeth I in the 1992 film *Orlando,* based on Virginia Woolf's novel about a gender–bending time traveler.

In spite of the fact that Crisp is considered to be an early gay activist, he was derided by some in the gay community for his belief that homosexuality was perhaps an illness, and for his refusal to be more active in gay issues and culture. As he once noted in a *Contemporary Authors* interview, "I think it is true that the gay people now seem to have deliberately separated themselves from the rest of the world. They *want* gay bars; they *want* gay clubs. They want to write gay books and gay plays. I just want to live in the world. So I feel the deliberate separation is not much help . What one wants is to creep out into the world. And I think this is more easily done, not by retreating, by any means, but by not threatening the world."

A regular on the party circuit, Crisp was noted for his outgoing nature. However, he was outspoken about the fact that he had never fallen in love. According to a *New York Times* obituary, he once stated, "I've spread my love horizontally, to cover the human race, instead of vertically, all in one place. It's threadbare, but it covers." Crisp died at age 90 in Manchester, England, the day before he was scheduled to open a new run of *An Evening with Quentin Crisp.* **Sources:** *Chicago Tribune,* November 22, 1999, sec. 2, p. 6; "Quentin Crisp," *Contemporary Authors Online,* Gale Group web site, http://www.galenet.com (March 10, 2000); *Gay & Lesbian Biography,* St. James Press, 1997; *Los Angeles Times,* November 22, 1999, p. A20; *New York Times,* November 22, 1999, p. A29; *Times* (London), November 22, 1999; *Washington Post,* November 22, 1999, p. B7.

Pham Van Dong

Born March 1, 1906, in Mo Duc, Quang Ngai, Vietnam; died in Hanoi, Vietnam, April 29, 2000. Prime minister. Pham Van Dong served as the prime minister of North Vietnam, then Vietnam, from 1955 to 1986. As one of the nation's most influential Communist leaders, he served under legendary leader Ho Chih Minh and later under Le Duan. He also played a large role in expelling the Americans at the end of the prolonged and controversial Vietnam War, and after that victory, saw the reunification of Vietnam under Communist rule. He also played a large role in the Geneva peace talks in 1954 after the defeat of the French at Dien Bien Phu.

Dong was born in a village in central Vietnam. His father, a Confucian scholar and member of the elite Mandarin class, was a court secretary to Emperor Duy Tan, who was deposed by the French in 1916 for being too nationalistic. As a youth, Dong attended upper–class French schools, including the National Academy in Hue, the old imperial capital of Vietnam. One of his fellow students was future South Vietnamese President Ngo Dinh Diem.

In 1925, Dong enrolled at Hanoi University to study law, and became known for organizing a student strike against the French. Subsequently, he was expelled and fled to Canton, China, where he joined Ho Chi Minh's Revolutionary Youth Association (Thanh Nien). With this Communist nationalist group, he studied Marxism as well as Leninist party organization techniques.

Soon after Dong returned to Vietnam in the last 1920s to organize Communist party chapters, the French arrested him and sent him to the deplored Poulo Condore prison island in the South China Sea. He was incarcerated for seven years, until a new French government in 1936 gave amnesty to political prisoners in colonial jails. The experience made Dong an even more fervent Communist, and while imprisoned, he met several men—including

Le Duan and Le Duc Tho—who would later join him in the party Politburo.

Upon Dong's release, he continued Communist activities in Hanoi. Three years later, after another failed uprising and at the start of World War II, he fled to China again and joined Ho at a guerilla camp. There, he recruited and trained forces to cross into northern Vietnam. In 1941, he became a founding member of the Viet Minh, a nationalist guerilla organization that was ostensibly formed to oppose French colonialism, and thus attracted a great many followers disgruntled with French rule. However, its true purpose was to give rise to Communism. The Viet Minh was also a forerunner of the Viet Cong, which would later fight the United States during the Vietnam War.

By 1945, Dong was a close colleague of Ho. In August of that year, the Viet Minh formed a provisional government, the Democratic Republic of Vietnam (DRV), with Ho as president and Dong as finance minister. Fighting then broke out with the French, sparking three decades of war. Dong and Ho went to Paris in July and August of 1946 to engage in peace talks, but the French refused to allow Vietnamese independence and the talks disintegrated. Subsequently, the battles began anew, with American troops joining the French and the Chinese Communists aiding the Viet Minh.

Meanwhile, Dong was named vice premier in 1951 and then acting foreign minister in 1954. The Viet Minh under General Giap then badly defeated the French at the battle at Dien Bien Phu that same year, ending France's colonial power. Later in 1954, Dong was sent to Geneva, Switzerland, to head the DRV delegation to the Geneva Conference that ended the Viet Minh war. But instead of giving full independence to all of Vietnam under the DRV, the nation was partitioned into the Communist North Vietnam and the pro–West, non–Communist South Vietnam.

In 1955, Dong was appointed chairman of the Viet Minh Council of Ministers in effect, prime minister. He would hold this position as the Communists battled for reunification, serving as the main spokesman for North Vietnam during its extended conflict with South Vietnam and the United States, which raged from the 1960s into the early 1970s. In this role, Dong established himself as a savvy behind–the–scenes operator.

Due to pressure from the Soviet Union, Dong signed a cease–fire agreement in 1973 that led to the withdrawal of American troops, but he resumed the war in 1974. In 1975, he approved the offensive that captured Saigon and ended the war. Subsequently, Vietnam was reunited, and Dong spearheaded the effort to do away with villages and introduce agricultural districts. This led to an exodus of South Vietnamese and a serious economic crisis. The Vietnamese invasion of Cambodia in the late 1970s and later clashes with China worsened their economic situation.

In the 1980s, Dong's health took a downturn. This, along with worsening economic conditions, prompted his resignation in December of 1986. Two other longtime party leaders, General Secretary Truong Chinh and Politburo member Le Duc Tho, also stepped down at that time. According to an obituary in the *Washington Post*, Dong once remarked, "Waging a war is simple, but running a country is very difficult."

Dong's personal life always remained a mystery. He married at age 40 to a woman who was 20. Various sources claim that she later either died or was confined to a mental institution. They reportedly had two children, a boy and girl. Dong died at age 94 at a hospital in Hanoi. **Sources:** *Encyclopedia of World Biography*, second edition, Gale Research, 1998; *Los Angeles Times*, May 3, 2000, p. B6; *New York Times*, May 2, 2000, p. C27; *Times* (London), May 3, 2000, p. 21; *Washington Post*, May 2, 2000, p. B7.

Douglas Fairbanks, Jr.

Born Douglas Elton Ulman Fairbanks, Jr., December 9, 1909, in New York, NY; died May 7, 2000, in New York, NY. Actor, producer, author, artist, and businessman. Though the dapper Douglas Fairbanks, Jr. never attained the superstar status of his silent film–era father, he nevertheless appeared in some 80 films, most made from the 1920s to the 1950s. A mainstay in the Hollywood social scene, Fairbanks also befriended the British royal family during the 1940s, during which time he also became a decorated war hero. As his acting career petered out, he turned to producing. In addition to his activities in the entertainment world, Fairbanks dabbled in art and also penned three autobiographies.

Fairbanks was born to Douglas and Anna Beth (Sully) Fairbanks. They divorced when he was nine, and his mother retained custody. His father married again, to Hollywood superstar and mogul Mary Pickford. Later, in Fairbanks's 1988 autobiography *The Salad Days*, Fairbanks recalled that he and his father were not close during his youth, but that they became good friends by the 1930s. Growing up in Manhattan and the Los Angeles area, Fairbanks was privately schooled, and he was tutored for two years while living in Paris and London. He also studied art in Paris, and much later in his life would often exhibit paintings and sculptures, though Hollywood remained his favorite milieu.

At age 13, Fairbanks began his acting career with a role in 1923's *Stephen Steps Out,* but the effort was a failure. In need of money because, he claimed, his mother had squandered her divorce settlement, he turned to earning money by writing titles for silent films, including some in which his father appeared. He also worked as a cameraman and prop mover, and began acting on stage in Los Angeles in 1927. In fact, he wrote in one of his autobiographies that from age 13 to 20, he was the major provider for a collection of people in his mother's family.

Fairbanks first attracted widespread attention at age 15 in his appearance in the 1925 melodrama *Stella Dallas.* Subsequently, he began to land better parts, acting in a Greta Garbo film, *A Woman of Affairs,* in 1928, and working that same year with director Frank Capra on *The Power of the Press.* Most of the time Fairbanks was relegated to supporting parts, though he was often a standout on screen even in the company of stars like Cary Grant and Ronald Colman. Some of his other memorable projects included *Little Caesar,* 1930; *The Dawn Patrol,* 1930; *The Narrow Corner,* 1933; *The Prisoner of Zenda,* 1937; and *Gunga Din,* 1939. Fairbanks also had a lead role in 1934's *Catherine the Great,* and starred with Ginger Rogers in 1938's *Having a Wonderful Time.* Also, he played twins in *The Corsican Brothers,* 1941, in which he engaged in a three–and–a–half minute sword-fight scene, which was shot in one take.

After posting a prolific resume of films throughout the 1920s and 1930s, Fairbanks became immersed in international affairs, an area which had long interested him. He helped organize a visit to the United States by King George VI and Queen Elizabeth in the late 1930s, and also around that time he served as a member of the British War Relief Association. In 1941 President Franklin D. Roosevelt appointed him as a special envoy to South America.

A U.S. Navy reservist, Fairbanks was called to active duty for five years staring in 1941, reaching the rank of commander. He trained forces and led commando units, seeing combat in Europe and the Mediterranean. In addition, he served under British Admiral Lord Louis Mountbatten, who then introduced Fairbanks to his nephew, Prince Philip, the husband of Queen Elizabeth II.

For his military endeavors, Fairbanks was rewarded with the Silver Star, Legion of Merit, the British Distinguished Service Cross, and the French Legion of Honor. After the war, he was a United Nations volunteer and also lent his famous name to a variety of human service efforts, including serving as chairman of the fundraising committee for CARE, a relief organization that sent food and other items to Europe. Fairbanks also received an honorary knighthood from King George VI in 1949.

Subsequently, Fairbanks only made a handful of films, then stayed behind the scenes on the big screen for 30 years until showing up again in 1981's *Ghost Story*. Meanwhile, he began cowriting and producing some of the films in which he appeared during the 1950s, and served as executive producer and host of the popular 1950s television anthology program, *Douglas Fairbanks Presents*. He also starred in roughly a quarter of the 117 half–hour episodes. Later in life, Fairbanks served as a chairman, director, or consultant on the boards of several companies, and also continued to act on stage sporadically. In addition, he invested in business ranging from real estate to ball point pen manufacturing. He was also quite proud of his contributions to magazines such as *Esquire, McCall's,* and *Vanity Fair.*

In 1929, amid a flurry of publicity, Fairbanks married acting legend Joan Crawford. The media attention was even more intense when they divorced 1933. He married again in 1939 to Mary Lee Epling Hartford, the former wife of A&P supermarket heir Huntington Hartford. They had homes in Manhattan; Palm Beach, Florida; and London, and had three daughters: Daphne, Victoria, and Melissa. When his wife died in 1988, Fairbanks married Vera Shelton, a merchandiser, who survives him. Fairbanks died at age 90 at Manhattan's Mount Sinai Medical Center. **Sources:** *Chicago Tribune,* May 8, 2000; *Los Angeles Times,* May 8, 2000; *New York Times,* May 8, 2000, p. A25; *Washington Post,* May 8, 2000, p. B6.

James Farmer

Born January 12, 1920, in Marshall, TX; died July 9, 1999, in Fredericksburg, VA. Civil rights activist. One of the founding members of the Congress of Racial Equality (CORE), James Farmer was the final survivor of the "Big Four" in the civil rights struggle that reached full steam in the 1950s and 1960s. The other leaders included Revered Martin Luther King, Jr., of the Southern Christian Leadership Conference (SCLC), assassinated in 1968; Whitney Young of the Urban League, who died in 1971; and Roy Wilkins of the National Association for the Advancement of Colored People (NAACP), who died in 1981. As the head of CORE, Farmer organized successful nonviolent tactics in effecting equal rights for blacks, including sit–ins and the Freedom Rides of 1961.

Farmer was the son of James Leonard Farmer Sr. and Pearl Marion (Houston) Farmer. The elder Farmer, the son of a slave, was an ordained minister and had earned a doctorate from Boston University. He was believed to be the first black man from Texas to receive a doctorate. A campus chaplain and professor of religion and philosophy, he worked at several small black Methodist colleges in the South. Farmer's mother held a teaching certificate as well.

Growing up in the rather sheltered world of academia especially since he was raised on black campuses Farmer rarely encountered racism as a child, although he once recalled an incident when he was very young that stuck with him. He was about three years old, and saw a white boy go into a drugstore to get a soft drink. Farmer wanted his mother to do the same, but she explained to him that they were not allowed into the store because they were black. As Farmer entered his teens, other forms of segregation began to affect him more directly. For example, he was confined to the balcony at the movie theater, and no longer associated with white childhood friends.

A precocious child, Farmer entered first grade at age four and began attending Wiley College in Texas at 14. He hoped to become a doctor and received a bachelor's degree in chemistry in 1938, but after discovering that he became sick at the sight of blood, he went on to study religion at Howard University, hoping to use the ministry as a way to become involved with the civil rights movement. Howard at the time boasted some of the best minds of the day, such as Ralphe Bunche in political science, Carter G. Woodson in history, and religion professor Howard Thurman, who was Farmer's mentor. Howard exposed Farmer to the ideas of Indian spiritual leader Mohandas Gandhi, who led the nonviolent protest movement for India's independence from Britain. Farmer was also influenced by V. F. Calverton, who introduced him to socialism.

As his studies progressed, Farmer began to have doubts about entering the ministry. He wrote his graduate thesis on religion and racism, and became disillusioned with the Methodist church, which was segregated by race. During World War II, he was a conscientious objector who worked as a race relations secretary for the Fellowship of Reconciliation, a pacifist group dedicated to social change.

In 1942 Farmer became a founding member of what was then called the Committee of Racial Equality (CORE) in Chicago after being refused service at a coffee shop. He subsequently organized the first sit–in with about 25 others, black and white, who refused to leave until the African American customers had received service. The group eventually gained national recognition, and Farmer was elected as chairperson, then an unpaid position. He devoted much of his attention to other posts, serving as a labor organizer for the Upholsterer's International Union and later for the State, County, and Municipal Employees Union. For a time, he acted as an elder statesman in CORE.

After the famous bus boycott in Montgomery, Alabama, in 1956, Farmer immersed himself in the civil rights struggle and joined the NAACP. However, that group was not known for its involvement in direct action, so CORE once again came to the forefront. In 1961, Farmer took a paid position as national director of CORE, and soon initiated the Freedom Rides, one of the most important campaigns of the civil rights movement. Although discrimination was illegal on interstate bus lines, many Southern states still had segregated waiting rooms and made blacks ride at the back of the bus. Farmer and a dozen others set out in 1961 to challenge these practices. Though there were few violent incidents at first, several riders in Alabama were beaten one paralyzed for life and at one point the bus was firebombed. Farmer had just left the group at that time because his father had died. He rejoined for the final leg of the Freedom Rides, though, and was arrested and imprisoned for 40 days. U.S. Attorney General Robert Kennedy ordered desegregation of buses, and the effort attracted untold numbers of new supporters, both black and white.

However, Farmer, like other civil rights leaders, remained in danger, receiving death threats as well as facing backlash from law enforcement. In one protest in 1963, Louisiana State Troopers threatened him with cattle prods, tear gas, and guns. With assistance from a local funeral director, he was driven out of the city in the back of a hearse. By the mid–1960s, Farmer realized that the civil rights movement was equally threatened by dissension within the ranks of the protestors themselves. Many militant members of the movement were growing dissatisfied with the nonviolent tactics, claiming they were not working fast enough. Also, a growing number of factions were competing for attention and support, thus dividing their power. Farmer resigned from CORE in 1965 to pursue other activities.

In the late 1960s, Farmer held a teaching position at Lincoln University, a black institution about 45 miles outside of Philadelphia. In 1968 he unsuccessfully ran for Congress in New York's twelfth district on the Liberal party ticket and was endorsed by the Republicans, despite the fact that he supported the Democratic candidate for president, Hubert Humphrey. Interestingly, he was defeated by a black female, Shirley Chisholm. In 1969 he accepted the post of assistant secretary in the Department of Health, Education and Welfare under President Richard Nixon, where he implemented affirmative action programs and saved the Head Start program. Dismayed with the bureaucracy and with many of the government's policies, though, he resigned in 1970.

Since 1984, Farmer lectured at Mary Washington College in Fredericksburg, Virginia, and wrote books on labor and race relations. He also penned an autobiography, *Lay Bare the Heart*, which was published in 1985. Bill Clinton awarded him the Presidential Medal of Freedom in January of 1998. Farmer was married briefly and divorced, and then married Lula A. Peterson in 1949. She died in 1977, and he lived alone near Fredericksburg, where he was in poor health for many years before his death in Fredericksburg at Mary Washington Hospital at age 79. He is survived by two daughters, Tami and Abbey. **Sources:** *Chicago Tribune*, July 10, 1999, sec. 1, p. 23; "Civil rights pioneer James Farmer dead at 79," CNN Interactive web site, July 9, 1999, http://cnn.com (July 13, 1999); *Contemporary Black Biography*, volume 2, Gale Research, 1992; *Encyclopedia of World Biography*, second edition, Gale Research, 1998; *Los Angeles Times*, July 10, 1999, p. A5; *New York Times*, July 10, 1999, p. A1; *Times* (London), July 12, 1999; *Washington Post*, July 10, 1999, p. A1; July 12, 1999, p. C1.

Allen Funt

Born September 16, 1914, in New York, NY; died September 5, 1999, in Pebble Beach, CA. Television show host. Allen Funt was synonymous with the television program *Candid Camera*, his creation that caught unknowing passersby "in the act of being themselves," as he put it. However, Funt's mischievousness was to credit for much of the hilarity. He would concoct outrageous situations for unsuspecting participants and used a hidden camera to record their antics and reactions. He would then emerge and sheepishly urge them, with his famous tag line, to "Smile! You're on *Candid Camera!*" Some of his famous stunts included a talking mailbox, a car that split in half while being driven, a guard posted at the Delaware border who informed drivers that the state was closed for the day, and a movie theater manager who insisted customers line up in alphabetical order. Another of his ploys was to post some kind of ridiculous official order and watch as people appeared baffled, then eventually complied with instructions. For example, he designated a sidewalk a "backward zone" where pedestrians had to traverse according to the rules. Though Funt had his share of critics who accused him of making his subjects appear foolish, the popular show ran from 1948 to 1967, as well as in reruns and later incarnations in the 1970s and 1990s.

Funt was born in Brooklyn, the son of Isidore and Paula Funt. His father was a Russian immigrant and diamond importer who moved to the United States the year before Funt was born. A bright child, Funt was allowed to skip some grades and graduated from high school at 15. Afterward, he earned a bachelor's degree in fine arts from Cornell University in 1934 while waiting tables to pay for school. Then, he continued his education at Columbia and Pratt Art Institute.

Funt's first job was with an advertising agency in the art department, but he became interested in radio and became a copywriter, devising gimmicks for programs. He began to create humorous shows that involved audience participation, a forerunner of his *Candid Camera* idea. One of his early programs, *The Funny Money Man,* involved paying a listener a small sum of money, such as 99 cents, for giving up something like the shirt off of his back. According to a *Los Angeles Times* obituary, Funt himself called it "the stupidest show on radio," but it was a great success.

During World War II, Funt put his radio experience to use in the Army Signal Corps recording messages from soldiers to their loved ones back home. However, Funt found that the men would become self–conscious when the tape was rolling, so he would turn it on early in order to capture a more spontaneous and realistic side. This sowed the seeds for the radio show *Candid Microphone,* which aired on ABC shortly after he returned from the military. However, Funt soon realized that his hidden microphones were not picking up especially funny or interesting material. Before long, he was inspired to try television, and would don disguises in order to fool unwitting victims. *Candid Microphone* was thus born on ABC in 1948 and became a top–rated show during its heyday on CBS in the 1960s.

As producer and host of *Candid Camera,* Funt eventually became so recognized that he had to leave the pranks to anonymous hired actors, though he would appear at the end of the gag to offer his good–natured line. As his son Peter Funt noted in a *People* obituary, "He was never really out to make people look bad. He was eternally grateful for the fact that people were such good sports." The appeal to audiences was obviously rooted in the reality of human behavior, and thus Candid Camera can be credited as the precursor of later popular shows like *America's Funniest Home Videos, Cops, World's Most Dangerous Animals,* and others. In addition, Funt's reels have been used in university courses studying psychology, sociology, and even business and medicine. Peter Funt noted, according to a *Los Angeles Times* obituary, "I once asked [my father] what he considered his proudest achievement. His answer: 'To be able to go almost anywhere in the world and have people say, 'Thanks, Allen. You made us smile.'"

Funt was married and divorced twice and had five children. In addition to his television work, he wrote three books, produced 40 shorts for Columbia Pictures, recorded seven albums, and made two films: *What Do You Say to A Naked Lady?,* 1970, and *Money Talks,* 1972. He spent his later years raising horses on his ranch in Big Sur, California, and continued to oversee specials and spinoffs. He managed a racy version of Candid Camera for adult cable television, and a newer *Candid Camera* hosted by Dom DeLuise aired for a short time in the early 1990s. Also, his son Peter along with Suzanne Somers began cohosting a new incarnation in September of 1999, with the first program debuting shortly after Funt's death. Funt was incapacitated after a 1993 stroke, and died at his home in Pebble Beach, California, at age 84. He is survived by his five children, Peter, Patricia, John, Juliette, and William, and four grandchildren. **Sources:** "Allen Funt," *Contemporary Authors Online,* Gale Group web site, http://www.galenet.com (September 10, 1999); *Contemporary Theatre, Film and Television,* volume 9, Gale Research, 1992; *Los Angeles Times,* September 7, 1999; *New York Times,* September 7, 1999, p. A17; *People,* September 20, 1999, p. 259; *USA Today,* September 7, 1999, p. 3D; *Washington Post,* September 7, 1999, p. B5.

John Gielgud

Born Arthur John Gielgud, April 14, 1904, in London, England; died May 21, 2000, in Buckinghamshire, England. Actor, director. Throughout a career that spanned eight decades, Sir John Gielgud epitomized the British stage actor, taking his place alongside Laurence Olivier and Ralph Richardson as one of the most highly regarded thespians of the twentieth century. In addition, he became respected for his directing talents. Though he was most famous for more than 500 performances of *Hamlet*, Gielgud also graced the stage as most of William Shakespeare's great characters, including Julius Caesar, Othello, Romeo, Mercutio, King Lear, Mark Antony, Macbeth, and Richard II. Gielgud was respected for his sensitive interpretations as well as for the clarity of his voice, and for his uncanny ability to continually breathe new life into well–known works. He was also a major instigator in reforming the style of Shakespearean theater to make it less affected.

Gielgud was one of four children of Frank and Kate (Terry–Lewis) Gielgud. His father was a stockbroker, and their surname was not Scottish, as many people assumed, but Lithuanian. Gielgud's maternal lineage boasted several famous actors and theatrical managers. His great aunt, Ellen Terry, was a leading lady of the British stage during the nineteenth century, as was his grandmother, Kate Terry. In addition, his father's grandparents had been top actors in Poland during the eighteenth century.

Though he was a mediocre student, Gielgud unsurprisingly was a standout in school productions. He initially expressed interest in becoming a set designer, but soon gravitated toward acting, against his parents' wishes that he study architecture. After deciding to concentrate on performing, Gielgud won a scholarship to Lady Benson's drama school. His professional debut came in at age 17 at London's Old Vic Theater in 1921, in an unpaid walk–on part as a French herald in Shakespeare's *Henry V*. He had one line. His first substantial role was as Trofimov in Anton Chekhov's *The Cherry Orchard*.

Later, Gielgud won a scholarship to the Royal Academy of Dramatic Art, where he studied for two years before plunging into his career in the mid–1920s. He played several roles, including his first Romeo at age 19, though he conceded it was not an impressive performance. However, the next year he was Noel Coward's understudy for the leading role in *The Vortex*, and he ended up on stage after the author left the cast. He would later credit Coward for teaching him his sense of timing. In 1926, he again understudied Coward in *The Constant Nymph*.

In 1928 Gielgud landed his first lead role in a farce called *Holding Out the Apple*. Though he felt this and two subsequent efforts were failures, he became poised at the edge of success, and that same year saw his Broadway debut in Alfred Neumann's *The Patriot*. After working for a while with J.B. Fagan's company in Oxford, Gielgud joined the acting company at the Old Vic in 1929. For two seasons, he starred in productions such as *Richard II* and *Macbeth* and his first *Hamlet*, which was highly acclaimed.

In addition to his Shakespearean roles, Gielgud was noted for work in modern plays. He won rave notices for playing an ultra–conservative school headmaster in Alan Bennett's 1968 satire *Forty Years On*. Other notable efforts included David Storey's *Home*, in which he played a man confined to a convalescent home, and in Harold Pinter's *No Man's Land*, in which he portrayed a down–on–his–luck poet. In both, he costarred with his peer, Richardson, who died in 1983.

Gielgud began directing as well in 1932 with *Richard of Bordeaux* at London's New Theatre. His directing heyday came in the 1950s, with critically applauded productions of Enid Bagnold's *The Chalk Garden*, 1956; Graham Greene's *The Complaisant Lover*, 1959, and Hugh Wheeler's *Big Fish, Little Fish*, the latter of which won a Tony Award for best direction for the 1960–61 season.

As an actor, Gielgud would return to Broadway time and again, playing *Hamlet* in 1936 and appearing in the lauded solo recital *The Ages of Man* in 1958 and 1963. His last New York performance was in *No Man's Land* in 1977, and his final stage role was as George Bernard Shaw's friend Sir Sydney Cockerell, in Hugh Whitemore's *The Best of Friends*, 1989. He also played that part on radio and television adaptations.

Gielgud additionally appeared in about 130 films and television movies and specials. In his film debut he was cast an opium addict in the 1924 silent movie *Who Is This Man?* He took breaks from his stage work throughout his career, appearing in several filmed versions of Shakespearean plays as well as popular films such as 1980's *The Elephant Man*, 1982's *Gandhi*, and the experimental 1991 Peter Greenaway movie *Prospero's Books*, the latter of which he considered his best part ever. In 1981, he won an Academy Award for best supporting actor for his role as the quintessential British butler in *Arthur*, starring Dudley Moore. He also won a British Academy Award for his part in 1974's *Murder on the Orient Express*. In addition, Gielgud had a minor part in Bob Guccione's controversial *Caligula*, 1980, and in the 1980s appeared in a series of humorous television commercials for Paul Masson wine. His last film appearance was playing Pope Paul IV in 1998's *Elizabeth*.

In addition to acting and directing, Gielgud was a producer as well as an author. His written works include two autobiographies, two collections of essays, and a book on acting technique. In 1953, Queen Elizabeth knighted Gielgud, and in December of 1996, she named him to the Order of Merit. He lived in London most of his life and in 1976 moved to an impressive carriage house in Buckinghamshire, west of London. There, he enjoyed tending his garden and reading. Gielgud reportedly often finished four books a week. He died at his home at the age of 96 and leaves no survivors. **Sources:** *Chicago Tribune*, May 23, 2000; *Encyclopedia of World Biography*, second edition, Gale Research, 1998; *Los Angeles Times* web site, http://latimes.com (May 22, 2000); *New York Times*, May 23, 2000; *Times* (London), May 23, 2000; *Washington Post*, May 23, 2000, p. B7.

Raisa Gorbachev

Born Raisa Maksimova Titorenky, January 5, 1932, in Rubtsovsk, Siberia, Russia; died of leukemia, September 20, 1999, in Munster, Germany. Former Soviet First Lady. Raisa Gorbachev introduced a new image of the wife of a Soviet Union leader in an era of rapid change in that nation. At a time when social and economic reforms raged under her husband's guidance, Gorbachev helped signify these new times with her intellectual persona and stylish appearance. Many in her native land felt she was too bold, but outsiders applauded her intelligence and modern appearance.

The oldest of three children of a railroad engineer, Gorbachev was born in Siberia in the former Soviet Union and grew up in various places around the nation, as her father's work required frequent relocating. Despite his stable job, the family was direly poor, and her mother encouraged Gorbachev to apply herself in school. An excellent student, she graduated with top honors and entered the University of Moscow, where she studied philosophy. During this time, in 1951 she met Mikhail Sergeyevich Gorbachev at a dance, and they married in 1953, the year that Soviet leader Joseph Stalin died. After graduating in 1954, she stayed in Moscow while her husband finished his law degree. The two of them had an extremely close relationship throughout their marriage.

In 1955, Gorbachev and her husband moved to Stavropol in southern Russia, near where he grew up, and there he began his career in politics. In 1970, he became First Secretary of the Communist Party for the province of Caucasus. Meanwhile, in the 1960s, Gorbachev had conducted extensive research on the peasant farmers in the area, and earned a Candidate's degree (equivalent to a doctorate) in sociology from the Lenin Pedagogical Institute in Moscow. Subsequently, she taught at the Stavropol Agricultural Institute, among other institutions. Her husband, in turn, used her research to initiate agricultural reforms, thereby gaining the attention of national leaders.

The couple returned to Moscow in 1978, where Mikhail Gorbachev joined the Kremlin, the seat of power in the Soviet Union, as a Central Committee secretary in charge of agriculture. Unlike many other wives of prominent politicians, Raisa Gorbachev was extremely cultured and intellectual, and thus did not tend to fit in easily. Keeping to herself, she took a teaching post at the University of Moscow. By 1985, when her husband became General Secretary of the Communist Party, she stepped down to become an unpaid member of her husband's staff and became a more public figure.

Once her husband became the Soviet leader, Gorbachev immediately captured the interest of the Western media. Charming, intelligent, outspoken, attractive, and stylish, she was a far cry from the stereotype of the plain and dowdy Communist woman. Abroad, she was almost as much of a cult of personality as her husband, and occupied a position analogous to the typical First Lady, joining her spouse on official visits, ceremonies, charity events, and the like. *Time* magazine named her one of the "world's ten most important women" in 1987.

At home, however, Gorbachev was less admired, perhaps because Soviet wives were expected to remain in the shadows. Her husband was open about the fact that he shared everything with her, including political discussions, and many Soviet men and women held the opinion that a wife should not exercise so much control over matters of state. In addition, Gorbachev's glamorous image caused resentment during a time of hardship among the average citizens. Rumors surfaced that she purchased her elegant outfits in Paris, when in reality her clothes were tailored by a shop in Moscow.

Also, when Gorbachev began meeting with Nancy Reagan, wife of President Ronald Reagan, the two clashed, and their lack of warm feelings were fodder for journalists as well as Reagan herself, who made a point of noting her dislike for Gorbachev in her memoirs. Reagan remarked that she was specifically put off by Gorbachev's tendency to talk for long stretches of time. In addition to meeting with other leaders' wives and accompanying her husband on official matters, Gorbachev became a board member of the Soviet Cultural Foundation, which preserved the nation's arts and culture.

Gorbachev's status was heightened by the fact that her husband was the driving force behind *glasnost,* a new openness in the Soviet Union, and *perestroika,* or social and economic reforms. These changes signaled the end of an era of tight government control and oppression. Censorship was eased, and exiled thinkers were allowed to return to the country. Religion was no longer banned. Democratic elections were held. Most notably and most symbolic of all, the Berlin Wall, which separated the western part of Germany from the eastern, Soviet–held section, was torn down. For these and other actions, Mikhail Gorbachev was awarded the Nobel Peace Prize in 1990.

However, with reforms came growing pains. The economy suffered greatly, and people became irate. Several former Soviet holdings declared independence and broke away. In August of 1991, a group of hard–line communists staged a coup and held Gorbachev and his family under house arrest at their seaside summer home in the Crimea. Though support for the hard–liners was scarce and the coup failed by August 21, Mikhail Gorbachev found it difficult to resume control. He resigned on December 25, 1991. Afterward, Raisa Gorbachev kept a much lower profile, most memorably coming out to accompany her husband on his 1996 campaign for president. He received less than one percent of the vote in that election.

After the coup, Gorbachev reportedly suffered a stroke and a nervous breakdown, and in 1993 she checked into a hospital in Virginia during a visit to the United States. In July of 1999, she was diagnosed with acute leukemia and was admitted to a clinic in Munster, Germany, where she underwent chemotherapy. After a couple of months, she died there of the disease at age 67, shortly before what would have been her 46th wedding anniversary. Gorbachev is survived by her husband; her daughter, Irina; and two granddaughters, Ksenia and Anastasia. **Sources:** *Encyclopedia of World Biography,* second edition, Gale Research, 1998; *Los Angeles Times,* September 21, 1999; *New York Times,* September 21, 1999; *Times* (London), September 20, 1999; *USA Today,* September 21, 1999; *Washington Post,* September 21, 1999, p. B5.

King Hassan II

Born Moulay Hassan ben Mohammed, July 9, 1929, in Rabat, Morocco; died of a heart attack, July 23, 1999, in Rabat, Morocco. King. In his 38 years on the throne, which made him the longest–serving monarch in the Arab world, King Hassan II of Morocco established himself as a peacemaker in the Middle East, despite the tumult that gripped his own nation throughout the years. Hassan acted as an intermediary among Arab nations while working to democratize and modernize his own country. He was the seventeenth leader in an Alawite dynasty stretching back 400 years, and his family claimed they were directly descended from the Prophet Mohammed.

Born in 1929, Hassan was the eldest of six children of Sultan Sidi Mohammed ben Youssef, who later became King Mohammed V. Hassan was named after his great– grandfather, who had been Sultan of Morocco from 1874 to 1897. At the time of Hassan's birth, most of Morocco was a French protectorate, with the exception of some Spanish areas and the city of Tangier, which was an international zone. As Hassan grew up, nationalism swelled as Moroccans sought to end colonial rule.

Hassan received a classical education in French and Arabic at the palace and the imperial college, then earned a law degree at the University of Bordeaux in France. In the meantime, he got involved with youth and sports clubs that included other nationalists. After college, Hassan served in the French Navy on the battleship Jeanne d'Arc. In 1953, hoping to defuse nationalist spirit and deprive Moroccans of a rallying symbol, the French forced the Sultan and Hassan into exile in Corsica and Madagascar.

Following rioting and guerilla warfare in Morocco, talks began in Paris, and the Sultan regained his title in 1955. The next year, Morocco gained its independence, the Sultan became King Mohammed V in 1957, and Hassan became Crown Prince. He worked with his father to uphold the power of the monarchy, serving as chief of staff of the armed forces, which he led to defeat rebel uprisings in the late 1950s. He also acted as regent when his father was out of the country, as well as holding the positions of deputy prime minister, defense minister, and head of the Moroccan delegation at the United Nations.

When Mohammed V died unexpectedly in 1961 following a minor operation, Hassan, who had been named prime minister in 1960, assumed leadership as premier, and became the head of the ministries of defense, interior, and agriculture. In 1962, he proposed the nation's first constitution, ensuring freedom of the press and of religion, and setting up a legislature with two elected chambers. Though it was ratified, the new parliament, elected in 1963, was sharply divided, and Hassan disbanded it in 1965 and declared a state of emergency. Meanwhile, the dismal economy prompted agitation and riots, as many opposition leaders were imprisoned or executed, and one of the most notable leaders, Mehdi Ben Barka, was abducted in Paris and never seen again. In addition to the political goings–on, Hassan was unpopular because fellow Moroccans considered him a playboy, an image spurred on by the Western press.

Hassan, who had renamed himself prime minister in 1965, retained control until 1970, when he lifted the state of emergency and enacted a new constitution. However, the opposition remained dissatisfied. In 1971, at Hassan's forty–second birthday gathering at his seaside palace, troops attempting a coup stormed in and opened fire, killing 100 of the king's prominent guests and wounding 125. The king hid in a bathroom and when he emerged after the firing subsided, he was face–to–face with the rebel leader. According to reports, Hassan looked him in the eye and recited the opening verse of the Koran, after which the leader knelt and kissed the king's hand, thus defusing the situation. Loyal forces ended up crushing the mutiny.

Roughly one year after this incident, Hassan's defense minister attempted to shoot down his royal plane. The plane was able to land safely, but only after Hassan used the radio to trick the attackers by claiming that the "tyrant" was dead. The rebels retreated and were later arrested and executed, and the defense minister allegedly committed suicide, though this was a matter of debate. His widow and six children spent 18 years in detention without a trial. Subsequently, Hassan kept keen personal control over the military.

Hassan was perhaps most noted for his role in relations in the Middle East. He helped arrange Egyptian President Anwar Sadat's historic trip to Jerusalem in 1977, and assisted with negotiations between France and Libya in Chad in 1984. In addition, he played a central mediator role in the ongoing meetings among various chiefs of state regarding peace in the region. In 1986, he met with Israeli prime minister Shimon Peres, a move that was heavily criticized by most other Arab leaders. He also welcomed Israeli Prime Minister Yitzhak Rabin in 1993,

making Morocco the only Arab nation other than Egypt to accept an official visit by an Israeli leader.

Hassan also worked to keep a lid on domestic discontent. In 1975, he united the country against a common enemy when he shrewdly organized 350,000 unarmed peasants to march into the Western Sahara in order to wrest it from Spain, which ended up handing over the region to Morocco and Mauritania. However, this spurred a long guerilla war with those in the area seeking independence. The dispute eventually reached the hands of the United Nations. Hassan also tried to placate both the peasant and elite classes by alternately enacting reforms that would benefit one or the other. As continuing poor economic conditions prompted sporadic rioting, though, Hassan at times used troops to keep control. Roughly 100 were killed in such a confrontation in 1984. Also, Hassan kept a tight rein on left–wing activities and Islamic fundamentalists alike, imprisoning many activists. However, by the 1990s, the economy was doing a little better, and Morocco's human rights record had reportedly improved.

Hassan had been in poor health for several years before his death from a heart attack at age 70. He had been admitted to a hospital in Rabat suffering from pneumonia on July 23, 1999, and died that same day. He is survived by his wife, Lalla Latifa, a commoner whose official designation is Mother of the Royal Children; sons Sidi Mohammed (the Crown Prince) and Moulay Rashid; and three daughters. **Sources:** *Encyclopedia of World Biography,* second edition, Gale Research, 1998; *New York Times,* July 24, 1999; *Times* (London), July 26, 1999; *Washington Post,* July 24, 1999, p. A13.

Screamin' Jay Hawkins

Born Jalacy J. Hawkins, July 18, 1929, in Cleveland, OH; died February 12, 2000, in Neuilly– sur–Seine, France. Singer, songwriter, and guitarist. Screamin' Jay Hawkins, a blues singer and guitarist known for pioneering macabre stage antics, made his name mainly on the strength of his trademark tune, "I Put a Spell on You." Featuring a tense vocal style marked by moaning, grunting, and screaming, the song never hit the charts, but it became a sensation for his untamed vocals and gave rise to his "wild warrior" image. Long before acts like Alice Cooper, Ozzy Osbourne, or Marilyn Manson, Hawkins captivated audiences with horror–show imagery. Wearing a black satin cape, he carried a cane topped by a flaming skull named Henry, among other bizarre props, including tarantulas, snakes, shrunken heads, and a crawling severed hand. To kick off his act, he emerged from a zebra–striped coffin. "I Put a Spell on You" was later covered by various artists such as Nina Simone, The Animals, and Creedence Clearwater Revival, and was used as a sample by rapper Notorious B.I.G. on "Kick in the Door" off his million–selling album *Life after Death*.

Details surrounding Hawkins's life are muddied because various versions of his history exist, even by his own accounts. He has noted that there were many children in his family some sources say seven by different fathers, and he claims his mother put him in an orphanage when he was an infant. Though Hawkins has claimed he was adopted by Blackfoot Native Americans, most sources say that he was raised in orphanages or foster homes.

At age four, Hawkins began to play the piano, and he soon displayed the talent for reading and writing music. He studied opera at the Ohio Conservatory of Music, and two of his role models were singers Paul Robeson and Enrico Caruso. In his teens, he won a Golden Gloves boxing championship in 1943, and later, after a stint in the service, he won a middleweight boxing championship in Alaska in 1949.

According to his own statements, Hawkins joined the U.S. Army in his teens. Accounts of this time vary, however. He has said that he fought in the Pacific, but it is more likely that he switched to the Army Air Force and entertained soldiers on the tenor saxophone, performing at home as well as in Germany, Japan, and Korea. Upon his discharge in 1952, he hoped for a career in opera.

Hawkins instead returned to jazz. To earn a living, he began working as a chauffeur and musician for bandleader Tiny Grimes. In the early 1950 he cut his first single, "Why Did You Waste My Time," backed by Grimes and his Rockin' Highlanders. However, what Hawkins really wanted to play was the danceable post–War blues. He tried recording a raw version of a tune he wrote called "Screamin' Blues," but it was never released because the chief of Atlantic Records, Ahmet Ertegun, thought his style was too rough around the edges. Hawkins refused to deliver a smooth, pop–oriented sound, and soon left Grimes's band to forge his own path. He found himself adrift, gigging with other acts including Fats Domino's band, but Domino fired Hawkins after he upstaged his boss by appearing onstage in a gold leopard–skin suit and turban.

Finally, Hawkins landed a solo appearance at Small's Paradise in Harlem, New York City. There, and at other venues around Atlantic City, New Jersey, Hawkins honed his image and developed his stage name. During this period, he penned his signature composition, "I Put a Spell on You," after a girlfriend broke up with him by waving goodbye while he was onstage with his band. According to David Segal in the *Washington Post*, Hawkins told the paper in 1990 that he thought, "She didn't know she's was messing with a witch doctor . I'll put a spell on her." He originally recorded the tune as a ballad on the Grand label, but the subdued version did not have an impact.

In 1955, Hawkins signed with Okeh Records, and producer Arnold Maxim decided he wanted a raunchier version of "I Put a Spell on You." He plied the singer and his band with liquor all night in order to extract a raucous cut of the tune. Ten days later, Hawkins was surprised when a courier delivered the single. He had been so drunk, he could not remember the recording session. Some radio stations claimed it sounded "cannibalistic" and banned it from the airwaves. Building on this publicity, Hawkins subsequently transformed his live act into a theatrical display of savagery. He stuck a bone through his nose, wore a loincloth, carried a spear and shield, and subsequently recorded songs like "Alligator Wine" and "Feast of the Mau–Mau." African American rights groups such as the National Association for the Advancement of Colored People were displeased with what they saw as buffoonery, but these antics drew the crowds.

In fact, Hawkins's act soon became more outrageous as disk jockey Alan Freed, known for his publicity stunts, convinced him to take the stage by rising up from a coffin. This became a staple of his show for years until the National Casket Company started to prohibit retailers from selling their wares for entertainment purposes. Later, Hawkins claimed he grew tired of the voodoo image, and he relocated to Hawaii, where he opened a bar. However, by the 1960s he had dusted off his bogeyman act and resumed playing, even as he insisted he wanted to be taken seriously as an opera singer.

During the 1980s, Hawkins opened for the Rolling Stones at Madison Square Garden. Also that decade, he gained a new following after independent director Jim Jarmusch used "I Put a Spell on You" as a major part of his film *Stranger than Paradise,* 1984. Hawkins was applauded for his acting role as a hotel desk clerk in Jarmusch's *Mystery Train,* 1989, and also appeared in the movies *American Hot Wax,* 1978, and *Harlem Nights,* 1991. In 1998, he received the Pioneer Award from the Rhythm–and–Blues Foundation.

Hawkins died of multiple organ failure in Neuilly–sur–Seine, a suburb of Paris, after emergency surgery to treat an aneurysm. A couple of years before his death, he married his ninth wife, a 29–year–old woman from Cameroon; he had also been married to a woman from Japan and a woman from Hawaii, and had numerous other relationships. By his own account, he estimated that he had some 57 children. After his death, friends set up a web site to try to locate the descendants who might not have known that the blues artist was their father, although it warned that they would reap no financial gain from the knowledge. According to a Reuters news wire report, friends said the search was not to find heirs, but for "closure" and to assemble everyone to honor their late father. **Sources:** *Contemporary Musicians*, volume 8, Gale Research, 1992; *Daily Telegraph*, February 22, 2000; *Los Angeles Times*, February 13, 2000; *New York Times*, February 14, 2000, p. A23; *Reuters* news wire service, March 3, 2000, obtained from Electric Library web site, http://www.elibrary.com (March 13, 2000); *Times* (London), February 17, 2000; *Washington Post*, February 13, 2000, p. C8; February 15, 2000, p. C1.

Joseph Heller

Born May 1, 1923, in Brooklyn, NY; died of a heart attack, December 12, 1999, in Long Island, NY. Author. Joseph Heller was the mind behind the satirical *Catch–22*, the 1961 novel about the absurdity of war that also stood as a metaphor for the madness present in everyday life and the common but frustrating bureaucracies that everyone faces. In the book, Captain John Yossarian, the lead bombardier and main character, wants to be relieved of flying bombing missions and thus pleads insanity. However, an Air Force doctor informs him, "There was only one catch ... and that was Catch–22." This rule, as Yossarian soon learns, stipulates that anyone rational enough to want to be grounded could not possibly be insane and therefore must return to duty. In addition to expounding on the inanities of war, Heller's novel delves into the evils of capitalism as well with the character of Milo Minderbinder. *Catch–22* began as a cult favorite but eventually found its place as a classic, and the title was absorbed into the popular lexicon as a synonym for any similar paradox. Heller went on to pen several other works, though none had the same impact as his first.

Heller was born and raised in the Coney Island area of Brooklyn, New York, the son of first–generation Russian–Jewish immigrants. His father, Isaac

Donald Heller, who drove a bakery truck, died after a botched operation when Heller was only five years old, so he was raised by his mother, Lena Heller, and his step–siblings from his father's first marriage. His half–sister Sylvia was seven years older, and his half–brother Lee was 14 years his senior. To help with expenses, his mother took in renters. Throughout his upbringing, Heller displayed a sharp wit and a penchant for practical jokes.

After graduating from Abraham Lincoln High School in 1941, Heller found a job with an insurance office, and would later draw upon this time for his 1974 novel *Something Happened*. He also worked briefly at the Norfolk Navy Yard in Virginia as a blacksmith's helper. In 1942, he joined the Army Air Corps, and flew 60 combat missions in Corsica as a wing bombardier. He left the military as a lieutenant and had earned an Air Medal and a Presidential Unit Citation. Despite this experience, most critics believe that *Catch 22* was only slightly based on his own war years.

After leaving the service in 1945, Heller took advantage of the G.I. Bill to go to college, attending the University of California, then transferring to New York University. He received a bachelor of arts degree in English in 1948, followed by a master's degree in literature from Columbia University the next year. He then attended Oxford University as a Fulbright Scholar for a year before becoming an English instructor at Pennsylvania State University from 1950 to 1952. Heller then became an advertising copywriter in New York City, working for *Time* from 1952 to 1956 and *Look* from 1956 to 1958 before serving as a promotion manager at *McCall's* from 1952 to 1961. In these offices, he found further material for *Something Happened*.

During his advertising days, Heller wrote short stories and scripts for film and television while simultaneously working on *Catch–22*. Some of his first published stories appeared in *Esquire* and *Atlantic* in 1947 and 1948. The first chapter of *Catch 22* was printed in *New World Writing* magazine in 1955 under the title *Catch–18,* but Heller had to change it because another writer, Leon Uris, had written a book called *Mila 18*. The full novel was published in 1961 after eight years in the making, and Heller quit his job to focus on writing. He supplemented his income by teaching at Yale University, the University of Pennsylvania, and the City University of New York.

Incidentally, *Catch–22* originally received mixed reviews, and many of the top critics found little to compliment. However, the novel became an underground hit thanks to word–of–mouth, and by the mid–1960s, *Newsweek* ran an article on the cult sensation. Timing played a large part as well: The work became a symbol to a legion of youth who resisted being drafted into the Vietnam War. Eventually, *Catch–22* sold more than 10 million copies in the United States alone, and was translated into several languages. It was adapted into a 1970 film by Mike Nichols as well.

Though none of Heller's other efforts reached the status of his first novel, he did not seem to be bothered by it. He went on to compose five more novels during his lifetime, including *Good as Gold,* 1979, a comic work which skewers the government, especially the White House; and *Closing Time,* 1994, which reintroduces several characters from *Catch–22* and deals with the illogical nature of civilian life. Another novel, *God Knows,* 1984, made some of the best–seller lists for a brief spell. A *New York Times* obituary described this book as "basically the story of King David told in the voice of Mel Brooks." Heller also composed a play based on *Catch–22* and another, *Clevinger's Trial,* based on chapter eight of *Catch–22,* as well as *We Bombed in New Haven,* an anti–war play which opened on Broadway in 1968. In addition, Heller cowrote screenplays for *Sex and the Single Girl,* 1964; *Casino Royale,* 1967; and *Dirty Dingus Magee,* 1970.

Heller was married in 1945 to Shirley Held, and they had a daughter, Erica Jill, and a son, Theodore Michael. They divorced in 1984, and during the breakup, Heller discovered he had contracted Guillain–Barre syndrome, a rare life–threatening disease of the peripheral nervous system. It caused partial paralysis, hospitalizing him for two months and leading to several months of rehabilitation. He chronicled his medical problems and difficult recovery in *No Laughing Matter,* 1986, with Speed Vogel, a friend who helped him during his illness.

In 1987 Heller married Valerie Humphries, a nurse who also assisted with his recovery. The author died of a heart attack at his home in Long Island, New York, at age 76. His agent reported that he had left a finished manuscript for a novel scheduled for publication in the fall of 2000. He is survived by his wife and children, as well as a sister, Sylvia Heller. **Sources:** *Chicago Tribune,* December 14, 1999; *Encyclopedia of World Biography,* second edition, Gale Research, 1998; *Los Angeles Times,* December 14, 1999; *New York Times,* December 14, 1999, p. A1; *Times* (London), December 14, 1999; *Washington Post,* December 14, 1999, p. A1.

Doug Henning

Born Douglas James Henning, May 3, 1947, in Fort Gary, Manitoba, Canada; died of cancer, February 7, 2000, in Los Angeles, CA. Magician. With his curly, shaggy mass of hair, bushy moustache, and talent for showmanship, Doug Henning sparked a renaissance in the world of magic in the 1970s. Instead of taking the stage in a top hat, cape, and magic wand, he started out in tie–dyed T–shirts to appeal to the hippie style of the times. By updating the image of magic, he made it appealing for a new generation after it had experienced a long decline. To help this transformation, he spiced up his tricks by adding music and comedy, and he gradually began to don form–fitting flashy jumpsuits. In addition to revamping the genre, Henning was a respected illusionist who performed Harry Houdini's "Water Torture Escape" before a live audience several times. This consisted of having his hands and feet shackled and being entombed in a steel canister underwater, from which he broke free in less than 60 seconds. Henning's public profile eventually faded as he devoted more time to transcendental meditation.

Henning, who grew up in Winnipeg, Manitoba, Canada, was the son of Clarke (a pilot) and Shirley (a homemaker) Henning. He became interested in magic at age six, when he saw a levitation act on television's *Ed Sullivan Show.* Subsequently, he asked for a magic kit, and by age 14, was performing at parties. He earned $15 a week levitating his sister. Henning attended McMaster College in Hamilton, Ontario, where he studied psychology but held fast to his goal of becoming a magician, moonlighting at Rotary Club events and similar functions. His senior thesis was on hypnosis.

Meanwhile, when Henning was 20, he applied for a $4,000 study grant from the Canadian government, arguing that magic and theater could be considered an art form. They complied, and he took a three–month course at Hollywood's Magic Castle, where he studied with veteran magicians. Afterward, he created a successful stage event, *Spellbound,* which ran in Toronto.

In May of 1974, Henning debuted *The Magic Show,* which ran for four–and–a–half years on Broadway and was nominated for a Tony Award. The show combined dance, rock, and magic into a musical entertainment extravaganza, and it made him a star. Meanwhile, he also performed regularly at casinos in Las Vegas and Lake Tahoe. Following the success of *The Magic Show* , he was nominated for five Tony Awards in the 1980s for the Broadway show *Merlin*.

In addition to his stage shows, Henning became one of the best–known magicians in the world thanks to his television specials. From 1975 to 1982, he annually staged the "Water Torture Escape" on each of his *Doug Henning's World of Magic* programs. The first such event, which ran without commercials, attracted an amazing 50 million viewers. He won one Emmy Award and several Emmy nominations for these specials.

Another one of Henning's major feats was "Metamorphosis," also an illusion borrowed from Houdini. In it, Henning's assistant was handcuffed and placed in a sack, which was put into a box and padlocked. Henning stood atop the chest and counted to three, after which the assistant suddenly appeared on top of the trunk while Henning was locked in the box in handcuffs. His illusions became more involved as time went on. On one 1980 show, it appeared that he was eaten alive by a shark. In stunts in *Merlin,* a flying horseman seemed to disappear into thin air, and Henning's costar, Chita Rivera, appeared to turn to stone.

In the mid–1980s, Henning retired from performing and sold some of his illusions to David Copperfield. Long a practitioner of transcendental meditation who also practiced yoga daily, he devoted himself to meditation. He announced in 1992 that he and spiritual adviser Maharishi Mahesh Yogi were planning to create a $1.5 billion theme park near Niagara Falls, Ontario, called Veda Land. They envisioned it as the first theme park devoted to spiritual enlightenment, and expected it to feature a levitating building and a journey into the molecular structure of a rose. Although a *New York Times* obituary of Henning reported, "The project's status is uncertain," a *People* obituary noted that Henning's associates hoped to open the park by 2005. Henning also made unsuccessful bids for political office in England in 1992 and Canada in the 1990s as a member of the maharishi's Natural Law party.

Though he was no longer much in the public eye, *Magic Magazine* reported in July of 1999 that Henning had been making impromptu appearances at magic stores around the United States to sign autographs and pose for pictures. Henning was briefly married to self–help author Barbara DeAngelis, then in 1981 met artist Debby Douillard at a school for transcendental meditation. They married that year and had an extremely close relationship but did not have any children. They lived in Los Angeles. Hen-

ning was diagnosed with liver cancer in September of 1999, but just one chemotherapy treatment made him so ill that he decided to end that treatment and begin fasting. His wife said that he regained strength after that, but he eventually died in February of 2000 at age 52. **Sources:** *Chicago Tribune,* February 9, 2000; *Los Angeles Times,* February 9, 2000; *People,* February 21, 2000, p. 115; *New York Times,* February 9, 2000, p. A23; *Washington Post,* February 9, 2000, p. B6.

Basil Cardinal Hume

Born George Haliburton Hume, March 2, 1923, in Newcastle upon Tyne, England; died of cancer, June 17, 1999, in London, England. Religious leader. Basil Cardinal Hume was head of the Roman Catholic Church in England and Wales for 23 years, establishing himself as an influential spiritual and moral leader even among many Protestants, who are in the majority there. Known to be modest, sympathetic, and humorous, Hume was noted for his nonjudgmental approach to sensitive issues like homosexuality, abortion, and birth control, while remaining an unwavering supporter of church positions on these topics. In addition, he spoke out on secular issues such as social welfare, race relations, housing problems, and peace in Northern Ireland. Hume also endeared himself to non– Catholics with his down–to–earth image as an avid sportsman. He enjoyed playing rugby and squash, and was an intense supporter of the Newcastle United soccer team.

Hume was the third child and first son of Sir William Errington Hume and Lady Marie Elisabeth (Tisseyre) Hume. His father, who was knighted, was a physician and heart specialist who had served as an army doctor in France, and his mother was the daughter of a senior French officer. Thanks to his mother's influence, Hume was raised speaking both English and French, and later learned German as well. Though his father was Scottish Protestant, Hume's mother, a devout Roman Catholic, had the biggest influence on his religious upbringing.

After attending Newcastle Preparatory School, and later Gilling Preparatory School from 1931 to 1934, Hume enrolled at Ampleforth College in North Yorkshire, considered the most prestigious boarding school for Catholics in England. Afterward, he entered the monastery there and was professed as a monk in September of 1942. He took the vows of priesthood in 1945 at Ampleforth, and took the name Basil, preferring to be called simply Father Basil throughout his life. From 1944 to 1947, he studied history at St. Benet's Hall, Oxford University, graduating with a master of arts. Hume then spent four years at the University of Fribourg and became ordained in 1950.

Subsequently, Hume took a position as an assistant priest in Ampleforth village and taught at the secondary school. He became housemaster of St. Bede's House and coach of the rugby team, and was soon promoted to head of the modern languages department in 1952. In addition, Hume taught dogmatic theology to monks in training. In 1957 his fellow monks elected him to represent them at the general chapter of the English Benedictine congregation, and the general chapter elected him Magister Scholarum of the congregation.

In 1963 Hume was elected Abbott of Ampleforth. In that capacity, he oversaw roughly 150 monks and became a respected leader for clergy of various faiths in the surrounding area. Though popular and intensely devoted in his spirituality, Hume was still relatively obscure when Pope Paul VI appointed him head of the British church in 1976. In this surprising move, he was chosen over all of the bishops in Britain and Wales to become the first Benedictine monk to take the position in 126 years. Though some were concerned that he was not experienced enough, the Church leaders in Rome had been seeking a charismatic person to renew interest in the faith in Britain, where Catholics are in the minority.

Hume indeed established himself as a strong and well-liked leader, expressing an empathy for many who struggle with the teachings of the faith, especially on subjects like the Church's opposition to abortion, birth control, and homosexuality. Many appreciated his personal sentiments in 1993 when he stated that gay people should "not develop a sense of guilt or think of themselves as unpleasing to God. On the contrary, they are precious to God," as a *New York Times* obituary related. On the other hand, Hume never strayed from his steadfast endorsement of church policy on the matter, and on other issues as well, such as the ordination of women to the priesthood. However, he was heavily involved in the early 1990s in helping the Church reach a compromise in allowing several hundred Anglican clergy many of whom were married become Catholic priests. Many non-Catholics, incidentally, respected Hume for his support of minorities and the poor, and for speaking out on political issues.

Queen Elizabeth II in June of 1999 bestowed on Hume the Order of Merit, one of the few awards that she hands out herself rather than relying on government recommendation. Hume died of cancer at age 76 in London. As a Roman Catholic priest, Hume was obviously never married and had no children. Though he respected the vow of celibacy, he once commented that it was normal to regret that he was never married. As a *Chicago Tribune* obituary reported, he told the BBC in 1992, "Deep down, we remain human, very human, and we have all the desires to love and be loved by one other person." **Sources:** *Chicago Tribune*, June 18, 1999, sec. 2, p. 11; "George Haliburton Hume," *Contemporary Authors*, Gale Literary Databases, http://www.galenet.com (June 22, 1999); *New York Times*, June 18, 1999, p. A33; *Times* (London) June 18, 1999.

Catfish Hunter

Born Jim Augustus Hunter, April 8, 1946, near Hertford, NC; died of Lou Gehrig's disease, September 9, 1999, in Hertford, NC. Baseball player. Legendary baseball pitcher Catfish Hunter enjoyed a phenomenal career, first with the Oakland Athletics and then the New York Yankees, winning 224 games and five World Series, earning a place in the baseball Hall of Fame in 1987. As the first big-contract free agent in the game, he was also known for opening the door to higher salaries for players. Hunter also pitched a perfect game during his career and was the recipient of a Cy Young award in 1974, and was regaled for performing under pressure. According to a CNNSI online report, his plaque at the Hall of Fame in Cooperstown, New York, reads, "The bigger the game, the better he pitched."

Hunter was born near Hertford, Connecticut, on a farm in Perquiman County. His father, Abbott, was a tenant farmer, and when Hunter and his three older brothers were not helping out with farm duties, they were avid baseball fans. The boys would tune in regularly to listen to Cleveland Indians games on the radio, and practiced pitching using potatoes or corncobs when they did not have baseballs. Thanks to his skill in pick-up games, Hunter became known as a talented pitcher around town when he was young. At Perquiman High School, he joined the baseball team, and as a junior in 1963, led them to the state Class AA title.

Scouts swarmed the stands to watch Hunter rack up a 13–1 record during his junior year. During his senior year, Hunter was injured when his brother's shotgun misfired, blowing off the little toe of his right foot and leaving pellets imbedded in the foot. Nevertheless, the Kansas City Athletics signed him for $50,000 and sent him to the Mayo Clinic for surgery.

After sitting out 1964 on the disabled list while his foot healed, Hunter started for the major leagues in 1965, bypassing the minors completely. According to a *New York Times* obituary, owner Charles O. Finley, famous for his promotional stunts, gave Hunter the colorful nickname "Catfish" and invented a story to go along with it. He related that when Hunter was young, he had run away from home, and later returned carrying two catfish. Hunter's mother was reportedly upset that anyone would believe that her son would run off. Friends and family called Hunter "Jimmy" throughout his life.

At age 19, Hunter won his first major league game, and in 1965 and 1966, he was named to the American League All–Star team, despite his team's lackluster performance. In 1968, Finley moved the A's to Oakland, California, and on May 8, Hunter pitched a perfect game against the Minnesota Twins, marking the American League's first regular–season perfect game since 1922 and only the seventh in modern baseball history at the time. The team's record began to sharply improve, and they ended up winning three consecutive World Series, from 1972 to 1974. Even though Hunter was a burly six feet tall and 190 pounds, he used precision control instead of raw power in his pitches.

In 1974, Hunter became baseball's first free agent after a contract dispute with Finley. An arbitrator ruled that Finley had negated Hunter's contract by breaching part of it, and on December 16, 1974, Hunter was able to offer his talents to the highest bidder. More than 20 teams extended deals, but the New York Yankees' George Steinbrenner won. He signed Hunter to a five–year, $3.75 million deal, then the largest contract in baseball, ushering in a new era for higher salaries. Part of this package included two $25,000 annuities to pay for college tuition for his son and daughter (another son had not been born yet). In his five seasons with the Yankees, Hunter won two more World Series rings, in 1977 and 1978. He retired at age 33 with a 224–166 record and a 3.26 earned–run average.

Hunter married his high school sweetheart, Helen Overton, on October 9, 1966, and they had three children, Todd, Kimberly, and Paul. They lived in the same house just outside of Hertford for more than 20 years, though they expanded their land from 100 acres to 1,000 acres over the years. After his retirement, Hunter farmed corn, peanuts, and soybeans full–time for ten years before leasing the land to a friend. He also enjoyed hunting and fishing, and kept deer hounds and bird dogs so that he could hunt quail, pheasant, rabbit, and deer. He was diagnosed with diabetes in 1978 but controlled it through diet, exercise, and insulin shots.

In the winter of 1998, while out hunting, Hunter noticed he was having trouble lifting his shotgun. He was tested for a tick bite, but the results were negative. His motor skills became worse, and doctors eventually diagnosed him with amyothropic lateral sclerosis, or ALS, commonly known as Lou Gehrig's disease, after another New York Yankee who died from the neurological disorder in 1941. His health deteriorated over the months and he was also hospitalized in August after falling and hitting his head on concrete steps outside of his home, after which he lost consciousness for several days. He died at his home in Hertford at age 53. Hunter is survived by his wife, three brothers, three sisters, three children, and a grandson, Taylor. **Sources:** "Jim Augustus Hunter," *Biography Resource Center Online,* Gale Group web site, http://galenet.gale.com (September 10, 1999); "Catfish Hunter dead," CNNSI web site, http://CNNSI.com (September 10, 1999); *Los Angeles Times,* September 10, 1999; *New York Times,* September 10, 1999; *USA Today,* September 10, 1999.

Madeline Kahn

Born September 29, 1942, in Boston, MA; died of ovarian cancer, December 3, 1999, in New York, NY. Actor. Best known for her string of hilarious films in the 1970s, including *Blazing Saddles, Young Frankenstein,* and *Paper Moon,* Madeline Kahn was one of entertainment's great funny women. Her image as the high–pitched, nasally redhead who often stole the show with her madcap antics did not give enough credit, however, to her expansive career, which included musicals, dramas, and Broadway hits. Nominated for several Academy Awards and Golden Globes, she won a Tony Award for her role as a flamboyant Jewish woman in 1993's *The Sister Rosensweig.*

Kahn was born in Boston and had a middle–class upbringing there and in New York City. Her mother, Paula Kahn, was an aspiring singer and actor, and her father, Bernard Wolfson, was a garment worker. At her mother's urging, Kahn went to Hofstra University on Long Island, New York, on a drama scholarship, where she then studied speech therapy. There, she participated in student productions as a classical singer, and also joined an opera workshop.

After graduating with a bachelor of arts in 1964, Kahn found work as a schoolteacher in Levittown, New York, but disliked the job. She decided to move into acting, and debuted as a chorus girl in a 1965 revival of *Kiss Me, Kate*, at the City Center Theater. During the late 1960s and early 1970s, she appeared in revues at Upstairs at the Downstairs, a New York City club, and appeared in the short film, *The Dove,* in 1968.

Kahn's career kicked into high gear with her first major film appearance in the 1972 comedy *What's Up, Doc?*, directed by Peter Bogdanovich. Initially, she was reluctant to get her big break in a picture alongside Barbra Streisand, but many critics thought Kahn stole the show. As Eunice Burns, the disgruntled fiancee to Ryan O'Neal's character, she talked with "a voice that sounds as if it had been filtered through a ceramic nose," as *New York Times* reviewer Vincent Canby memorably put it, according to a *Los Angeles Times* obituary. Indeed, one of Kahn's most distinctive features was her nasal-sounding speech, which she used to her comic advantage, although she never considered herself a particularly funny person. In her personal life, in fact, she was reported to be quite reserved.

In 1973 and 1974, Kahn was nominated back-to-back for Academy Awards for her roles in the comedies *Paper Moon* and *Blazing Saddles*. In *Paper Moon*, Kahn played an outrageous Depression-era stripper named Trixie Delight, and in Mel Brooks's *Blazing Saddles* she provided rollicking laughter as a would-be Marlene Dietrich-type diva stuck in a western saloon. She was also notable in the 1974 Brooks parody *Young Frankenstein*, playing the voluptuous fiancee of Dr. Frankenstein (played by Gene Wilder). She worked again with Brooks in 1977's *High Anxiety*. Despite this auspicious start, however, Kahn became relegated to mostly supporting parts. Some of her other films include *The Muppet Movie*, 1979; *History of the World, Part I*, 1981; *Yellowbeard*, 1983; *Clue*, 1985; and *Mixed Nuts*, 1994. She also provided voices for animated films, including *An American Tail*, 1986, and *A Bug's Life*, 1998.

Keeping her theater career rolling while also making movies, Kahn earned a 1974 Tony nomination and a Drama Desk Award for her turn as Chrissy in the musical *The Boom Boom Room*. She went on to act in other Manhattan productions such as *On the Twentieth Century*, 1978, and a revival of *Born Yesterday*, 1989, garnering Tony nominations for those, in addition to making her Tony Award–winning appearance as the kooky Gorgeous Teitelbaum in *The Sisters Rosensweig*.

In 1987, Kahn won an Emmy Award for her role in a 1987 *ABC Afterschool Special*, and she also starred in the series *Oh Madeline* (1983–84) and *Mr. President* (1987–88). Then in 1996, she took a role on the situation comedy *Cosby*, costarring as Phylicia Rashad's best friend and business partner, Pauline. Kahn was intrigued not only by the positive theme of racial harmony, but also by the appeal of a project that allowed some improvisation. In September of 1998, Kahn was diagnosed with ovarian cancer, and continued undergoing chemotherapy while continuing to work on *Cosby*. Her last film appearance, shot before she fell ill, was in an independent film titled *Judy Berlin,* scheduled for release in early 2000.

Kahn kept her illness private until stating in October of 1999, "It is my hope that I might raise awareness of this awful disease and hasten the day that an effective test can be discovered to give women a fighting chance to catch this cancer in its earliest stage," according to a *Los Angeles Times* obituary. The actor, who lived in a Park Avenue apartment lined with books, married attorney John Hansbury, her partner of ten years, in October of 1999. She died at age 57 at Mount Sinai Hospital in Manhattan, and is survived by her husband and her brother, Jeffrey Kahn. **Sources:** *Contemporary Theatre, Film and Television,* volume 15, Gale Research, 1996; *Entertainment Weekly,* December 17, 1999, p. 26; *Los Angeles Times,* December 4, 1999; *New York Times,* December 4, 1999, p. A16; *People,* December 20, 1999, p. 71; *Times* (London), December 7, 1999; *Washington Post,* December 4, 1999, p. B6.

DeForest Kelley

Born January 20, 1929, in Atlanta, GA; died June 11, 1999, in Woodland Hills, CA. Actor. DeForest Kelley was best known for playing the cranky country doctor aboard the starship U.S.S. Enterprise on the popular 1960s television show *Star Trek*. As Dr. Leonard McCoy, better known by "Trekkies" as "Bones McCoy," Kelley was one of the three most recognizable characters on the original program that captured the imaginations of viewers for decades. Along with William Shatner as Captain James Kirk and Leonard Nimoy as the logical Mr. Spock, he traversed the galaxy healing human and alien patients alike. However, when presented with tasks that exceeded his capabilities, McCoy was often known to respond in exasperation with what became one of his most famous lines: "Damn it, Jim, I'm just a country doctor!" His other trademark line was, "Jim, he's dead." Kelley was also a character actor in other series and several films, usually Westerns and cop dramas.

Born in Atlanta, Georgia, Kelley was the son of a Baptist minister and sang in the church choir and on local radio shows while growing up. Though he hoped to become a doctor like the uncle who helped deliver him, his family could not afford tuition. After graduating from high school, he traveled to Long Beach, California, for a visit and ended up staying a year. He returned to Georgia for a short time but decided to go back to the West Coast to pursue acting. Before making it big, he found work as an elevator operator and usher. He began performing with theater groups and on radio shows as well, and auditioned for roles in Hollywood. In 1941, he lost a part in the film *This Gun for Hire* to Alan Ladd.

During World War II, Kelley served in the Army Air Forces in New Mexico, but was transferred to Culver City in order to act in a Navy training film titled *Time to Kill*. A talent scout for Paramount noticed him and offered him a three–year contract to work in low– budget pictures. In his debut Hollywood role in 1947's film noir *Fear in the Night*, Kelley played a man who supposedly committed murder while hypnotized. Eventually, Kelley moved to New York and worked in the theater again while also landing roles on early television dramas like *Schlitz Playhouse of Stars*. In the mid–1950s, he went back to Hollywood, where his weathered appearance and slight Southern drawl was often put to use in small parts as farm hands, town folk, and bad guys. He was also sometimes cast as the heavy on police shows. Some of his credits include appearances on the television series *The Lone Ranger, Rawhide, Bat Masterson, Perry Mason, 77 Sunset Strip, and Route 66*. Outside of television, he held roles in some 30 films, including *Gunfight at the O.K. Corral,* 1957; *Gunfight at Comanche Creek,* 1964; and *Apache Uprising,* 1966, in addition to several *Star Trek* films.

Of course, Kelley was most famous for his character in the television series *Star Trek*, created by Gene Rodenberry. "Bones" McCoy was popular for providing down– home humanity and convincing arguments for following "gut" instincts, in contrast to Nimoy's Vulcan logic, which although rational, often did not apply in the emotional realm. *Star Trek* ran for only 79 episodes, from 1966 to 1969, and never was a ratings success in its day. However, it

became a sleeper hit as it lived on in reruns around the world for decades and spawned several films in which the actors reprised their characters. It also inspired spinoff television series such as *Star Trek: The Next Generation* and *Star Trek: Deep Space Nine,* an animated series, books, comics, toys, and other products, not to mention a entire subculture of fans known as "Trekkies," who hold conventions during which some dress up in costumes that are replicas of those from the various television shows. Kelley was said to enjoy his work on *Star Trek* and often made appearances at conventions, although he personally was not a science fiction fan and never watched the later *Star Trek* shows.

After retiring from entertainment, Kelley lived on a ranch in Sherman Oaks, California, where he indulged his hobbies of growing roses and collecting paintings. He met Carolyn Dowling in 1942 when they were both acting in the play *The Innocent Young Man,* a production of the Long Beach Theater Group, and they married in 1944. A few months before his death, Kelley had entered a convalescent home, the Motion Picture and Television Fund Hospital, in Woodland Hills, California. He died at age 79 with his wife, his only survivor, by his side. **Sources:** *Chicago Tribune,* June 13, 1999, sec. 4, p. 9; *Contemporary Theatre, Film, and Television,* volume 8, Gale Research, 1999; *Los Angeles Times,* June 12, 1999, p. B1; *New York Times,* June 12, 1999, p. A13; *Times* (London), June 14, 1999; *Washington Post,* June 12, 1999, p. B6.

Hedy Lamarr

Born Hedwig Eva Maria Kiesler, November 9, 1913 (some sources say 1914 or 1915), in Vienna, Austria; died January 19, 2000, in Casselberry, FL. Actor. One of Hollywood's most glamorous actors of the 1930s and 1940s, Hedy Lamarr was billed in her time as "the world's most beautiful woman," according to a *Washington Post* obituary. With her raven hair and exotic looks, she was often cast as a sultry temptress. Perhaps her most famous role was in the film *Samson and Delilah,* but she caused a sensation earlier in the 1933 Czech film *Ecstasy,* in which she appears nude. In addition to her acting skills, Lamarr was also the co–inventor of a frequency–shifting radio communication system that would later become integral in some data transmission devices, including some cellular phones and wireless computer links.

Lamarr was the only child of a prosperous banker and an aspiring concert pianist. As a child, she learned several languages and traveled extensively. In her teens, she was discovered by Austrian director Max Reinhardt, who personally tutored her. She began serving as a script secretary and acting in minor roles. When she was 19, she married Austrian arms dealer Fritz Mandl, who was becoming wealthy by selling weapons to the Nazis. He had contacted her parents and arranged to marry her, and she once remarked, "I was sort of his slave," according to Ludwig Siegele in the *World Press Review*.

Around the same time, in 1933 Lamarr created a stir in the film *Ecstasy,* appearing nude when a horse runs off with her clothing as she is swimming, and again in a lovemaking scene that was especially racy at the time. Mandl tried to purchase all copies of the film after its European release, but his efforts at hoarding failed. The movie debuted in America in 1934 but was prohibited in several areas for years. Though few people actually saw it, the film's reputation served to intensify interest in the young actor and would spur her later career, although she made no more movies for some time due to her husband's possessiveness. The picture eventually became a cult favorite and was appreciated as an early art film.

Tiring of her husband's control, Lamarr fled to Paris, then England, where she met a Hollywood talent scout. She signed a contract with MGM studios and sailed to America, where Louis B. Mayer changed her named from Hedwig Kiesler to Hedy Lamarr, recalling a 1920s screen siren he admired named Barbara La Marr. Lamarr was cast in the 1938 film *Algiers,* which catapulted her into stardom, though critics would thereafter compliment her beauty far more than her acting skills. She would go on to make films with Clark Gable, Spencer Tracy, Judy Garland, Lana Turner, and other luminaries, and reached the peak of her career with 1949's *Samson and Delilah,* directed by Cecil B. DeMille and costarring Victor Mature. Some of her other pictures included *Comrade X,* 1940; *Boom Town,* 1940; *Ziegfeld Girl,* 1941; *Tortilla Flat,* 1942; *Cooper Canyon,* 1950; and a comedy, *My Favorite Spy,* 1951. Her final efforts were *The Story of Mankind* and *The Female Animal,* both 1957. Lamarr became a U.S. citizen in 1953.

Earlier, during her marriage to Mandl, Lamarr dutifully served as his trophy wife, attending numerous dinner parties at his side. Throughout this period, she picked up reams of knowledge about weapons technology by listening to guests. She developed an idea on how to prevent an enemy from jamming a radio signal that was being used to steer torpedoes. Later, in Hollywood, she approached George An-

theil, a Parisian experimental composer, and explained her proposal, hoping that it would benefit the Allied forces. She asked if the signal could be made to shift, seemingly at random, through different frequencies. But she was perplexed as to how the receiver could be synchronized to simultaneously pick up the changing signal.

Antheil, however, was working on a similar solution in order to get 16 player pianos in his *Ballet Mecanique* to play together, and he had done so using punched tape. They combined their efforts and were awarded a patent in August of 1942, but the system would not be put to use until the Cuban missile crisis of 1962, when the military used the technology to prevent the Soviets from listening in to their communications. By the 1990s, the idea was brought to wireless telephone transmitters and used in order to serve a greater number of customers. In 1997, the Electric Frontier Foundation gave its Pioneer Award to Lamarr and Antheil, who had died in 1959. However, they never made any money from their invention.

After retiring from acting, Lamarr was twice arrested for shoplifting, in 1966 and 1991, but in both cases was acquitted. She denied all offers to appear on screen but did publish her autobiography, *Ecstasy and Me: My Life as a Woman,* in 1966. However, she later sued the publisher and ghostwriter, claiming that the book was "deliberately written as an obscene, shocking, scandalous, naughty, wanton, fleshy, sensual, lecherous, lustful and scarlet version" of her life, according to a *New York Times* obituary. She did not prevail in court. Lamarr moved to New York and took up painting, and in her later years lived in a quiet suburb of Orlando, Florida, were she was said to be legally blind and could not get around on her own.

In addition to Mandl, Lamarr was married and divorced five more times, to screenwriter George Markey, actor John Loder, nightclub proprietor Ernest Stauffer, oil mogul W. Howard Lee, and attorney Lewis W. Boies Jr. She adopted a son, James, now a retired police officer, with her second husband, Markey, and also had a son, Anthony Loder, and daughter, Denise, with her third husband. Loder is the owner of a phone store in Los Angeles. Lamarr died in her sleep at age 86; she is survived by all three of her children. **Sources:** *Chicago Tribune,* January 20, 2000;*New York Times,* January 20, 2000, p. A16;*People,* February 7, 2000, p. 107;*Times* (London), January 20, 2000;*Washington Post,* January 20, 2000, p. B5;*World Press Review,* July 1997, p. 34.

Tom Landry

Born Thomas Wade Landry, September 11, 1924, in Mission, TX; died February 12, 2000, in Irving, TX. Football coach. Legendary coach Tom Landry shaped the Dallas Cowboys into a powerhouse contender in the National Football League (NFL), leading them through their first 29 seasons and taking them to five Super Bowls, two of which were victories. Along the way, he helped build football into the nation's premier spectator sport while earning the Cowboys the nickname "America's Team." Respected as the force behind the team's success from 1960 into the 1980s, Landry is the third–winningest coach in NFL history, behind Don Shula and George Halas. However, he was known equally well for his stoic and dapper image. Perennially seen on the sidelines with folded arms and an emotionless expression, Landry dressed in a snappy ensemble of fedora hat, sport coat, and tie. He was also recognized for his dedication to his Christian faith.

Landry was the son of Ron Landry, a mechanic who also served as the fire chief and a Sunday school superintendent in Mission, Texas. At Mission High School, Landry was an all– regional fullback whose football team outscored their opponents 322–0 during his senior year. In addition, he was an all–A student, president of his class, and a member of the National Honor Society. Entering the University of Texas, he played for renowned coach Dana X. Bible during the 1942 season. Subsequently, he entered the Army Air Forces to serve in World War II, during which time he flew 30 B–17 combat missions over Europe and survived a crash landing.

In 1945 Landry was discharged as a first lieutenant. He returned to Texas, where he resumed playing fullback and some quarterback and defensive back for the Longhorns. During his junior year he made the all–Southwestern Conference second team, and in his senior year, he served as co–captain. In 1948, Texas won the Sugar Bowl, and in 1949 his team won the Orange Bowl.

After graduating with a business administration degree in 1949, Landry joined the ranks of professional football as a cornerback with the New York Yankees, which merged with the New York Giants of the National Football League after the 1949 season. Thereafter, he played for the Giants until 1955, making the All–Pro defensive team in 1954. Meanwhile, on the off seasons, he continued to take college courses, obtaining a degree in mechanical engineering from the University of Houston.

In 1954, Jim Lee Howell was named head coach of the Giants, and Landry became a player–coach under him for that season. He left the field as a player in 1955 to become the team's defensive coordinator from 1956 to 1959, joining the assistant coaching ranks alongside offensive coordinator Vince Lombardi, who later went on to fame coaching the Green Bay Packers. In terms of style, Lombardi tended to focus on fundamentals and physical power, whereas Landry was more innovative regarding strategy. During his time with the Giants, Landry developed his famous 4–3 defense, which became a basic play in professional football. It entailed using four down linemen and three linebackers. In Landry's four years as defensive coach, the Giants had a record of 33–14–1, with two Eastern Conference division titles and one NFL championship, in 1956.

Landry left New York in 1960 to take a job as head coach of the Dallas Cowboys expansion team. During his first season, their record was a dismal 0–11–1. By 1965, they finally posted an equal number of winning and losing games, and in 1966 and 1967 they won the Eastern Division title. Soon, Landry began to build the team up to become an institution, not only in Texas but in all of the country. The Cowboys eventually made it to the Super Bowl five times, winning in 1972 and 1978, and losing in 1971, 1976, and 1979. Overall, Landry posted a record of 250–162–6 in the regular season and 20–16 in the playoffs.

In addition to leading his team, Landry was at the forefront of the Cowboys at a time when they were pioneers in the sport. In addition to computerizing the annual draft of college players, they also stirred up a level of interest in football that made it the most–watched professional sport. Even their cheerleading squad enjoyed a new level of appreciation. Landry himself was also famous, appearing in a commercial for American Express. His stony–faced demeanor and crisp appearance was legendary. Though some detractors called him "plastic man" or "computer face" and criticized his aloofness, others expressed admiration for a man they saw as caring, warm, and devoutly religious. Still, a former Cowboys wide receiver, Pete Gent, wrote a novel, *North Dallas Forty*, loosely based on his time with the team which described an organization concerned solely with the bottom line and not with the welfare of the players. It was later made into a movie.

At the start of the early 1980s, the Cowboys began to fade. The owner sold them to a consortium, and they never seemed to regain strength. Landry's last season with the team was 1988, after which former college football player Jerry Jones purchased the team and fired Landry and longtime general manager Tex Schramm. Subsequently, Landry and his son became partners in an investment firm, and he also served as a goodwill ambassador for the Fellowship of Christian Athletes. He was elected to the Pro Football Hall of Fame in 1990, and was inducted into the Dallas Cowboys Ring of Honor in 1993.

In May of 1999, Landry began undergoing treatment for acute myelogenous leukemia, and died at Baylor University Medical Center in Texas the following February at age 75. He married Alicia Wiggs, whom he met in college, in 1949, and she survives him along with their children, Tom Landry, Jr. and Kitty Phillips. The couple also had another daughter, Lisa Childress, who died of liver cancer in 1995.
Sources: *Chicago Tribune*, February 13, 2000; *Los Angeles Times*, February 13, 2000; *New York Times*, February 14, 2000, p. A23; *Washington Post*, February 13, 2000, p. A1.

Jeff MacNelly

Born Jeffrey Kenneth MacNelly, September 17, 1947, in New York, NY; died June 8, 2000, in Baltimore, MD. Cartoonist. Jeff MacNelly was known for his sharp editorial cartoons as well as his daily comic strip, *Shoe*, which started up in 1977. It featured a group of disheveled anthropomorphic birds working at the newspaper the Treetops Tattler, anchored by their sneaker–clad, cigar–chomping editor, P. Martin Shoemaker. The strip ran in 1,000 papers around the globe, and his political cartoons were syndicated in 500 publications. Throughout his career, MacNelly managed to become a respected wry humorist despite the fact that he steered clear of mean–spirited humor—often a mainstay in political cartooning. Along with Garry Trudeau and Pat Oliphant, MacNelly was regarded as one of the finest political cartoonists in the United States. He won Pulitzer Prizes for editorial cartooning in 1972 and 1978 with the *Richmond News Leader* and in 1985 with the *Chicago Tribune*.

MacNelly was born in New York City, the son of Clarence Lamont MacNelly and Ruth Ellen (Fox) MacNelly, and grew up in Cedarhurst, an upper–class area of Long Island. His father worked as an advertising executive and then as publisher of the *Saturday Evening Post*, and after retiring, he was a professional portrait painter. MacNelly was highly influenced by his father and has said he owes his conservative streak to his dad's die–hard Republi-

canism. Nevertheless, he did not fail to lambaste both Republicans and Democrats in his later work.

MacNelly attended the prestigious Phillips Academy in Andover, Massachusetts, and then enrolled at the University of North Carolina when he could not gain admittance to Yale University. He had been drawing since he was young, and in college began to submit drawings to the campus newspaper, the *Daily Tar Heel*. But MacNelly failed several courses, including studio art, and dropped out in 1969 during his senior year to take a job as a political cartoonist for North Carolina's *Chapel Hill Weekly*. There, he earned $120 a week as he developed a keen ear for political humor and burnished his artistic skills. The editor of the newspaper, Jim Shumaker, who later became a professor at the University of North Carolina, became the model for the title character of MacNelly's comic strip.

After a year at the *Chapel Hill Weekly*, MacNelly landed a job at the *Richmond News Leader* in Virginia in 1970. He applied there because it was the hometown of his then–wife, Marguerite "Rita" Dewey Daniels, whom he married in 1969. Just 16 months after joining the Richmond paper, MacNelly at age 24 won his first Pulitzer Prize for editorial cartooning for his body of work for the prior year. One of the pieces in his portfolio at the time was a cartoon concerning President Richard Nixon's handling of the economy. In his next winning selection in 1978, he featured a cartoon showing the complex IRS form 1040 which asked a taxpayer how many talking chickens he owned and whether they play the oboe. MacNelly's last Pulitzer–awarded collection, culled from his work at the *Chicago Tribune*, included works on the 1984 presidential campaign.

Though MacNelly briefly stopped drawing editorial cartoons in 1981 to devote himself to *Shoe*, he returned in 1982 when he took the position with the *Chicago Tribune*. At the time, he noted, "When it comes to humor, there's no substitute for reality and politicians," according to a *Washington Post* obituary. Since 1987, MacNelly was based out of the paper's Washington, D.C. bureau. He lived and drew his cartoons in Rappahannock County, in the Blue Ridge Mountains of Virginia about a half an hour from the nation's capitol. He also had a winter home in Key West, Florida, where he enjoyed painting and sculpting. In addition to his Pulitzers, MacNelly twice received the Reuben Award, the top prize given by the National Cartoonists Society, as well as the 1991 Sigma Delta Chi National Award for editorial cartooning.

MacNelly's son, Jeffrey Jr., followed in his dad's footsteps. He assisted with his father's work and also held an editorial cartooning job with the *Aspen Times*. In 1996, he died after sustaining injuries in a rock–climbing accident, and afterward, MacNelly included his son's nickname, "Jake," in all of his editorial cartoons.

At six feet, five inches tall with a thick shock of white hair, MacNelly was often mistaken for television talk–show host Phil Donahue. Late in 1999, he began outpatient treatments for lymphoma at Baltimore's Johns Hopkins Hospital. Subsequently, he curtailed the output of his editorial cartoons, though he kept producing *Shoe* and illustrations for syndicated columns by humorist Dave Barry. In early June MacNelly was admitted for emergency surgery and died at the hospital about a week later at age 53. MacNelly was wed three times: first to Daniels; then to wife Scottie; and then to his wife, Susan. He is survived by his third wife and sons Danny and Matt. **Sources:** *Chicago Tribune,* June 8, 2000; "Jeff(rey) (Kenneth) MacNelly," *Contemporary Authors Online,* Gale Group web site, http://www.galenet.com (June 27, 2000); *Los Angeles Times,* June 9, 2000; *New York Times,* June 9, 2000; *Washington Post,* June 9, 2000, p. B6.

David Merrick

Born David Margulois, November 27, 1912, in St. Louis, MO; died April 25, 2000, in London, England. Producer. From the mid–1950s to about 1980, producer David Merrick was the bigwig of Broadway. Starting with his first hit, 1954's *Fanny,* and ending with *42nd Street,* which opened in 1980, he consistently cranked out profitable productions thanks to relentless hype, which led to his nickname, the "Abominable Showman." Though he won a legion of admirers for his drive and tactics, he also won scores of enemies. He was a notorious negotiator who would hire talent as cheaply as possible, and he had a reputation for arguments with talent and critics. He embellished this by consciously maintaining a sinister image, sporting a black handlebar moustache. However, Merrick was also highly regarded as a dedicated craftsman. Though he was feared for his frequent firings, he kept some of the same behind–the–scenes people on staff for their entire careers, giving jobs to their children after they retired. Merrick produced more than 80 plays and musicals and won six Tony Awards and two special Tonys for his efforts.

Born in St. Louis, Missouri, Merrick was the youngest of six children of Samuel and Celia Margulois.

His father, a salesman, was a poor provider, and he and his wife divorced when Merrick was young. Afterward, Merrick was raised by relatives and recounted his adolescence as "Dickensian," according to a *New York Times* obituary. In fact, the *New York Times* writer claimed, as an adult he refused to board any plane that was required to fly over St. Louis, out of fear that he would be forced to land in the detested city.

Merrick won a scholarship to Washington University in St. Louis. There, he won second prize in a playwriting contest that fellow student Tennessee Williams also entered, or so he claimed. After obtaining his bachelor's degree, he transferred to Missouri's St. Louis University to study law, which would prove valuable in his later career as he hammered out contract negotiations. In law school, he once won the part of Tubal in a student production of *The Merchant of Venice.*

After receiving his law degree, Merrick moved to New York City. One year later, in 1940, he went into the office of Broadway producer Herman Shumlin and invested $5,000 in the comedy *The Male Animal.* It became a hit and reaped him $20,000. He then changed his name to Merrick as an homage to eighteenth–century English actor David Garrick. Merrick did not serve in World War II during the 1940s due to ulcers, and in 1946 went to work for Shumlin as his general manager.

Merrick's first attempt at producing, with the minor 1949 comedy *Clutterbuck,* was a failure, but he kept it running for six moths with his marketing efforts: He would call various New York hotel bars and restaurants and ask them to page a "Mr. Clutterbuck." Subsequently, his promotions paid off for the 1954 musical *Fanny.* Initially the work attracted tepid reviews, but Merrick doggedly pushed his wares, slapping racy stickers on numerous men's rooms mirrors that read, "Have You Seen Fanny?" He also ran radio and television ads years before Broadway shows would do so regularly, and he enlisted a sculptor to create a life–sized nude statue of the show's belly dancer, Nejla Ates, and put it in Central Park. *Fanny* eventually broke even after 17 weeks and went on to run for two years.

In 1955, the year after *Fanny* debuted, Merrick saw another hit with Thornton Wilder's *The Matchmaker,* which he later adapted into the wildly popular 1964 musical *Hello, Dolly!* The latter effort created Carol Channing's signature role, as Dolly Levi. Throughout the 1960s, Merrick would produce six or more plays and musicals in an average season. In 1962 he produced the musical *I Can Get It for You Wholesale,* which helped launch Barbra Streisand's career, and he also produced two works by filmmaker Woody Allen: *Don't Drink the Water,* 1966; and *Play It Again, Sam,* 1969. In the twilight of his career in 1980, he produced the smash *42nd Street,* which was his longest–running show and one of the longest–running in Broadway history. It closed in 1989. Other successes included *Romanoff and Juliet,* 1957; *Jamaica,* 1957; *Gypsy,* 1958; and *Irma La Douce,* 1960.

Some of Merrick's other publicity stunts included the time he hired a woman to jump up from the audience onto the stage to slap an actor playing a misogynist character during a performance of *Look Back in Anger.* The tale circulated in newspapers for three weeks before Merrick admitted to staging the attack. In another celebrated incident, he looked up seven people in the phone book with the same names as prominent theater critics, and called to invite them to his musical, *Subways Are for Sleeping.* He also treated them to dinner and then plied enthusiastic endorsements out of them, which he ran in an ad in the New York *Herald Tribune* one time before editors nixed it. Still, the attempt created media attention around the globe. Merrick was also notorious for antagonizing talent and critics, all with the intent of creating a better show and drumming up good publicity.

In addition to glitzy shows, Merrick took on thoughtful works such as *The Entertainer,* which created Laurence Olivier's most highly respected postwar performance as Archie Rice. He also produced acclaimed dramas such as John Osborne's *Look Back in Anger,* Brian *Friels's Philadelphia, Here I Come!,* and Tom Stoppard's *Rosencrantz and Guildenstern Are Dead.* Merrick also put on two substantial Royal Shakespeare Company productions directed by Peter Brook: *Marat/Sade,* 1965, and *A Midsummer Night's Dream,* 1971. Merrick suffered a stroke in 1983 and was wheelchair– bound and rendered unable to speak except in a few words and grunts. Still, he continued to frequent the theater, though he disliked what he saw as the mass–produced nature of the shows.

Merrick was married several times. In the 1930s, he married Lenore Beck, a woman he met in college. Her small inheritance made it possible for them to relocate to New York City. Later he was married to Jeanne Gilbert, who did press relations for the Savoy Hotel in London; Etan Aronson; dancer Karen Prunczik; and again to Aronson. His second marriage to Aronson ended in 1999 after a decade of litigation. In November of that year, Merrick married Natalie Lloyd, his spokesman and live–in companion since 1989. He died in his sleep at St. George's rest home in London at age 87, and is survived by Lloyd as well as his children, Cecilia Ann Merrick, whom he had with Gilbert, and Marguerite Merrick, daughter of Etan Merrick. **Sources:** *Los Angeles Times,* April 27, 2000; *New York Times,* April 25, 2000; *Times* (London), April 27, 2000; *Washington Post,* April 27, 2000, p. B7.

Ashley Montagu

Born Israel Ehrenberg, June 28, 1905, in London, England; died of heart disease, November 26, 1999, in Princeton, NJ. Author, anthropologist. Ashley Montagu was an anthropologist who helped close the gap between the academic and the popular, with readable works that explained his theories and research. With books on topics including human aggression, infant nurturing, why people cry, the history of profanity, and the equality and even superiority, in his opinion of women to men, he stirred interest as well as controversy. Montagu became a public intellectual who appeared frequently on talk shows like *The Tonight Show with Johnny Carson* and in mainstream publications such as the *Washington Post* and *Ladies' Home Journal;* he was best known for his ideas on racial myths and gender issues. He also penned a volume on John Merrick, the disfigured Victorian man known as the "Elephant Man."

Montagu was born in the generally working–class East End of London. According to a *New York Times* obituary, his biographer, Susan Sperling, noted that Montagu had previously reported that he was the son of a stockbroker, but in fact, his father was a tailor. Both parents were Jewish; his father, Charles, was from Poland, and his mother, Mary, was Russian. Anthony Ramirez in the *New York Times* noted that Sperling did not know why Montagu changed his name from Israel Ehrenberg, except that it probably had to do with discrimination against Jews.

As a child, Montagu loved to browse at the used book shops in his neighborhood, and befuddled his parents by picking up copies of works by intense thinkers such as John Stuart Mills, Thomas Henry Huxley, and Friedrich Nietzsche. When he was 15, he won a literary contest and chose as his prize the book *Introduction to Social Psychology.* Even earlier, by age 10, he was engrossed in examining the variances between the accents of his Cockney neighbors and the university students who often rented quarters in his parents' home. This spawned Montagu's keen interest in the effect of an environment on a human, and this common thread would run through his future studies of behavior.

After attending the University of London from 1922 to 1925, where he studied physical anthropology, Montagu enrolled at Columbia University in about 1927 or 1928. He then studied ethnography and anthropology at the University of Florence in Italy in 1928 and 1929. Eventually he returned to Columbia in 1934 and earned his doctorate there in 1937, after learning under Franz Boaz, who also mentored Margaret Mead and Ruth Benedict. Montagu had decided to immigrate to the United States in 1927 after the British government in 1926 crushed a general labor strike, and he became a naturalized U.S. citizen in 1940. He once remarked, according to a *Los Angeles Times* obituary, "I was brought up as a stuffed shirt Englishman. I wasn't very human. What America did for me was humanize me, democratize me."

Montagu's debut book, published in 1937, was on the Aborigines of Australia, but his first major work, *Man's Most Dangerous Myth: The Fallacy of Race,* came out in 1942. This argued that characteristics based on race were a sociological, not biological, construct. In 1998 it entered its sixth edition. In 1949, Montagu was named to a United Nations task force and became the principal author of the "Statement on Race" that spelled out his ideas. He also wrote studies on such subjects as anatomy, heredity, love, marriage, sex, and even the history of swearing, using a combination of disciplines to aid him in his theories.

Perhaps Montagu's most famous work, however, was 1953's *The Natural Superiority of Women,* in which he put forth the opinion that women are biologically superior to men. It was also radical for its day for suggesting that women should receive equal compensation for jobs. However, though it seems the title alone would make it a hit among feminists, many women were angry with Montagu's views that women should stay home with children before entering the outside world of work. He expanded on his theories about women and nurturing in 1971's *Touching: The Human Significance of the Skin,* which encouraged parents to breast–feed babies and let them sleep in bed with them, concepts popular among many societies, but not in America at the time.

Throughout his career, Montagu was a frequent guest lecturer at various universities. From 1931 to 1938 he was on staff as an assistant professor of an-

thropology at New York University, and subsequently held a post at Hahnemann Medical College in Philadelphia from 1938 to 1949. He then became a professor and headed the anthropology department from 1949 to 1955 at Rutgers University in New Brunswick, New Jersey. After that, his teaching was generally on a visiting basis at institutions such as Harvard and Princeton universities. In addition, Montagu served as the director of the New Jersey Committee on Physical Growth and Development from 1951 to 1957, and as an advisory consultant to the Peace Research Institute in Washington, D.C. and the International Childbirth Education Association.

Montagu married Marjorie Peakes in 1931, and they had two daughters and a son. He suffered from heart disease and was hospitalized in March of 1999 while working on his memoirs, and he died that November at age 94. Montagu is survived by his wife; daughters Audrey Murphy and Barbara Johnstone; son Geoffrey Montagu; four grandchildren; and two great–grandchildren. **Sources:** *Chicago Tribune,* November 29, 1999; "Ashley Montagu," *Contemporary Authors,* Gale Group web site, http://wwww.galenet.com (December 17, 1999); *Los Angeles Times,* November 28, 1999; *New York Times,* November 29, 1999, p. A23; *Washington Post,* November 28, 1999, p. C6.

Clayton Moore

Born Jack Carlton Moore, September 14, 1914, in Chicago, IL; died of a heart attack, December 28, 1999, in West Hills, CA. Actor. The most well–known of several actors who have played the Lone Ranger, Clayton Moore starred on the popular television series of the same name from the late 1940s to the late 1950s, with the exception of one season, and also appeared in two Lone Ranger films. He personified the good–guy cowboy, riding along on his horse, Silver, with his faithful Indian friend Tonto by his side to help him fight for justice. In cultural terms, the program forever linked the strains of the "William Tell Overture" with the line, "Hi–yo, Silver, away!," indicating that the hero was off once again to battle evildoers. Besides playing the Lone Ranger, Moore appeared as various characters in dozens of feature films from the 1930s to the 1960s.

The son of a real–estate developer, Moore grew up on the north side of Chicago in the Edgewater neighborhood. He spent his Saturdays watching serial films and idolizing the cowboy heroes of the silver screen, and he always wanted to be a cowboy or a police officer when he grew up. Instead, he kicked off his career in entertainment with a trapeze act in 1934 at Chicago's Century of Progress exhibition, using skills in acrobatics and tumbling that he gained at the Illinois Athletic Club.

After an injury ended Moore's ability to perform circus tricks, he was employed as a model in Chicago and New York before going to Hollywood in 1937. There, he changed his name to Clayton Moore and began to land bit parts in westerns and cliffhanger serials such as *Dick Tracy Returns*, 1938, and *The Perils of Nyoka*, 1942. He eventually earned the nickname "King of the Serials" for acting in these multi–part films that kept audiences returning to theaters each week. During World War II, he took time out to serve three years in the Army Air Force

In 1949, Moore beat out 75 others to win the part of the Lone Ranger as the program made the transition from radio to television. The radio show's writer and a station executive had noticed the handsome, broad–shouldered actor in the serial *The Ghost of Zorro* and gave him the role, but wanted his voice to carry the same deep tone as that of his radio counterpart, Brace Beemer, who played the Lone Ranger over the airwaves from 1941 until the series ended in 1954. Moore thus practiced singing scales and imitating Beemer's voice in order to create the authoritative sound.

The Lone Ranger debuted on September 15, 1949, making it the first western created specifically for television. There had been other western programs, but they were excerpts from films. The first episode of *The Lone Ranger* set up the legend that had begun on the radio series. The hero, John Reid, is the sole survivor among six Texas Rangers ambushed by Butch Cavendish's gang. Reid's brother is one of the five who were killed, and Reid himself is left for dead. However, he is nursed to health by an Indian, Tonto (played by Jay Silverheels, a Canadian–born Mohawk Indian). Tonto dubs Reid "kemo sabe," meaning "trusty scout." Going undercover to avenge the deaths, Reid cuts a mask from his dead brother's vest and dons a white hat, the typical symbol of benevolence.

The Lone Ranger was the purest of all the good guys of the time. Parents enjoyed him as much as did youth, because he used perfect grammar, he did not drink or smoke, he was impeccably dressed and clean at all times, and he showed respect for others. In fact, it is believed that he never killed anyone

during the series, instead showing an incredible talent for marksmanship that allowed him to shoot the gun out of villains' hands. In addition, the program was applauded for making Tonto an equal, and for its scripts that dealt with addressing the rights of Indians threatened by outlaws.

Moore played the Lone Ranger in 169 episodes until June of 1957, when the series ended, with the exception of the season spanning from September, 1952 to September, 1953. That year, John Hart, an actor who had been the bad guy in some previous episodes, sported the mask instead. Meanwhile, Moore who claimed he had no idea why he was replaced during that time was relegated to secondary characters for the season. Moore also played the Lone Ranger in two Hollywood films, *The Lone Ranger*, 1956, and *The Lone Ranger and the Lost City of Gold*, 1958.

Though Moore had roles in a handful of other television shows after the series ended, he basically gave up acting in order to extend his career as the Lone Ranger off–screen. He made public appearances in costume for years, even showing up with Silverheels in a commercial for Jeno's Pizza Rolls. However, the Wrather Corporation, which had purchased the rights to the Lone Ranger in 1954, eventually asked him to stop using the image. In 1979, they decided to make a new Lone Ranger movie with a younger actor, Klinton Spilsbury, and obtained a restraining order that required Moore to unmask himself. In its place, he began wearing a pair of sunglasses shaped to resemble the mask.

However, after the 1981 movie, *The Legend of the Lone Ranger*, flopped at the box office, Moore embarked on a crusade to resume portraying the character. He stated his case at press conferences and on talk shows, and maintained that he collected 400,000 letters of support. Adding to his difficult time, Moore's costar Silverheels, who had long remained a friend, died in 1980. In 1984 the Wrather Corporation backed off, allowing Moore to resume posing as the famous character at events such as parades, shopping mall openings, rodeos, and county fairs. In 1996 he wrote an autobiography, *I Was That Masked Man*, but by then had retired from public life and even refused to give interviews.

Inducted into the National Cowboy Hall of Fame in Oklahoma City in 1990, Moore also saw his star placed on the Hollywood Walk of Fame in 1987. It is the only star to feature the name of both the actor and the character. Late in December of 1999, Moore suffered a heart attack at his home in Calabasas,

California, and later died in the emergency room of a hospital in West Hills, a suburb of Los Angeles. He was 85. Married for 43 years to the former Sally Allen, who died in 1986, he was later married another two or three times, depending on the source. He is survived by his fourth wife, Clarita (one source gives her name as Carlita) Petrone, and his daughter, Dawn Moore Gerrity. **Sources:** *Chicago Tribune,* December 29, 1999, sec. 2, p. 11; *Los Angeles Times,* December 29, 1999, p. A1; *New York Times,* December 29, 1999, p. B8; *Washington Post,* December 29, 1999, p. B5.

Akio Morita

Born January 26, 1921, in Nagoya, Japan; died of pneumonia, October 3, 1999, in Tokyo, Japan. Physicist, business executive. Physicist Akio Morita co-founded the Sony Corporation along with engineer Masaru Ibuka, ushering in a new era of personal electronics. The company first gained recognition for popularizing the transistor radio, and went on to introduce a high–quality color television set, the Sony Trinitron. It also came out with videotape recorders and players, video projection systems, and the revolutionary Sony Walkman and Sony Discman for playing music on the go. Morita started as a managing director of the company and became president in 1971, then chairman in 1976 when Ibuka entered the position of honorary chairman. Despite his background in physics, Morita had a reputation as a top–notch salesperson and was known more as the marketing whiz of the pair, while Ibuka was credited with much of the technical know–how. Both men, however, were known for encouraging a sense of fun and individuality in their company, which was rare in the Japanese corporate world, and for manufacturing quality products, countering Japan's longstanding reputation for shoddy workmanship.

Morita was born in Nagoya, an industrial city located in central Japan. His father was a well–to–do brewer of the alcoholic beverage sake, and the business had been in his family for 300 years. Since Morita was the eldest son, he was expected to assume leadership after his father. However, by junior high, his studies began to suffer due to his avid interest in electronics. He was captivated by his mother's hand–cranked Victrola phonograph, and was excited when a local merchant would get new records. Eventually, Morita built his own phonograph and radio.

In college at Osaka Imperial University, Morita studied physics, then enlisted in the navy toward the end of World War II, where he helped develop heat–seeking weapons. Not only did this allow him to avoid combat, it would also lead him to Ibuka, a civilian engineer for the navy who was 13 years his senior. Though Morita promised his father he would take over the brewery after his military stint, he went to Tokyo after reading in the newspaper that Ibuka had established an electronics business in a bombed–out warehouse there. The firm sold electronics components and kits that converted AM radios into short–wave receivers.

When Ibuka decided to incorporate his company, he asked Morita to enter the business. After getting the blessing of Morita's father, who later lent financial backing to the venture, they established the Tokyo Telecommunications Engineering Corporation on May 7, 1946. Their first major invention, around 1949 or 1950, was the reel–to–reel tape recorder, which weighed a whopping 75 pounds. Their next big project was the transistor radio, first produced in 1955. They licensed the transistor from Bell Laboratories in New Jersey, which did not see any pertinent use for the device outside of hearing aids. An American firm had used them to make portable radios a few month earlier, but had no luck selling them. Morita and Ibuka, however, marketed the product successfully and continued to improve it, making it even more compact.

In 1958, the company changed its name to Sony, from the Latin word "sonus," meaning sound. The firm began selling a transistor television set in 1960. However, the next big breakthrough came in 1968 when they manufactured the Sony Trinitron television set, which greatly improved the quality of color television. The company sold the first consumer video tape recorder in 1965, and introduced color video projection by 1971. In 1975, Sony began offering the Betamax video recorder and player, which gave rise to home video systems. Even though Betamax was eventually phased out in favor of the VHS format, Sony was integral in making the technology affordable and therefore exposing it to the mass market.

One of the Sony Corporation's most famous designs, the Walkman, came out in 1979, which allowed music fans to listen to tapes through a personal portable headset. Before that, no one conceived that a device capable of only playing, not recording, music would be successful. Soon, an array of companies had copied the idea, and the little gizmo with its tell–tale personal earphones became ubiquitous. Later, Sony would also introduce the Discman after compact discs became popular, a transition that they helped spearhead in conjunction with Philips. Though the original idea for the Walkman was credited to Ibuka, the Walkman and Discman were pioneered and became big sellers under Morita's leadership.

Eventually Sony would branch out from being just an electronics firm to become a leader in the overall entertainment business, purchasing two large film studios, Columbia and Tristar Pictures, and taking over CBS Music, ranking it among the top four music companies in the world. Sony would also break into the home computer market with its Vaio line of portable notebooks. Although they became popular, they would not capture nearly the market share of the bigger manufacturers and distributors. However, back in 1982, Sony had introduced the 3.5 inch floppy disk, which took over from the 5.25 as the industry standard.

Reaching the pinnacle of his career, Morita in 1993 was chosen to head Keidanren, an organization representing Japan's largest corporations. Unfortunately, on the day of his official appointment, he suffered a serious stroke while playing tennis, one of his favorite hobbies Subsequently, Morita gave up leadership at Sony and retired to Hawaii, where he underwent rehabilitation therapy. After his health continued to decline, he succumbed to pneumonia at age 78 in 1999. He is survived by his wife, Yoshiko; two sons, Hideo and Masao, and a daughter, Naoko Okada; brothers Kazuaki and Masaaki, and sister Kikuko Iwama. **Sources:** *Business Leader Profiles for Students*, Gale Research, 1999; *Chicago Tribune*, October 4, 1999; *Los Angeles Times*, October 4, 1999; *New York Times*, October 3, 1999, p. A28; *Times* (London), October 4, 1999; *Washington Post*, October 4, 1999, p. A1.

Julius Nyerere

Born Kambarage Nyerere, April 13, 1922 (some sources say March, 1922; or 1923), in Butiama, Tanganyika; died after suffering from leukemia and a stroke, in London, England, October 14, 1999. Tanzanian president. Julius K. Nyerere, the founding father of Tanzania, was integral in leading his nation peacefully to independence and was admired for his efforts in trying to unite a diverse population of 32 million representing 120 ethnic groups. He was applauded for his staunch opposition to racial bigotry and for his commitment to his people, eschewing personal wealth and assuming leadership out of a mission to improve life in his nation instead of out of any kind of authoritarian grab at

power. Though he became known as Africa's most original thinker for meshing Marxist thought and longstanding tribal customs into a new kind of socialism, his policies, especially his utopian rural agricultural system, were a failure. Still, the people of Tanzania benefited from Nyerere's guidance, particularly because they enjoyed political and social stability as well as an outstanding human rights record.

Nyerere was born in 1922 or 1923 in Tanganyika, a nation formerly known as German East Africa that came under British Rule after the 1920 Treaty of Versailles. He was the son of Burito Nyerere and one of his many wives, Mugaya, getting his first name, Kambarage, from that of a rain spirit, since it rained on the day of his birth. He would later take the name Julius at age 21 at his baptism after attending Christian schools. Nyerere's father, who would eventually have 22 wives and 26 surviving children, was one of various tribal chiefs of the Zanaki, a group of about 40,000 or 50,000 members. As a child, Nyerere helped tend goats and worked in the garden, and went bow–and–arrow hunting with his elders.

Although Nyerere's father was illiterate, he knew that an education would benefit his son, who had displayed a keen intellect early on. He sent Nyerere, then 12, to a boarding school in Musoma, about 30 miles from the tribal village, on the shores of Lake Victoria. Completing his studies in three years as opposed to the usual four, he then was admitted to the Tanganyika Government School at Tabora in 1937. He graduated in 1943 and then entered Makerere College, a teacher's school in Kampala, Uganda. There, he became known for his debating skills.

After graduating in 1945 with his degree in education, Nyerere taught history and biology at St. Mary's College in Tabora, a Roman Catholic high school. There, he met Maria Gabriel Magige of the Msinditi tribe, who had also converted to Catholicism, and they became engaged. In 1949, he won a scholarship to Edinburgh University, becoming the first person from Tanganyika to study at a British university. He obtained a master's degree in history and economics there in 1952. Returning to Tanganyika, Nyerere assumed the post of history master at St. Francis' College, Pugu, near the nation's capital of Dar es Salaam. He and Magige married in 1953.

Developing his sense of politics while in Scotland, Nyerere decided he would devote himself to

Tanganyika's independence. He had joined the Tanganyika African Association (TAA), founded by British officials as a forum for African ideas, while at Makerere College, and was elected secretary of the Tabora branch in 1952. The next year, he became president of the TAA. However, civil servants were not allowed to be members of the TAA, thus severely limiting its clout, since most educated Africans were government employees. So in 1954, Nyerere and other TAA leaders formed the Tanganyika African National Union (TANU), which called for racial harmony, social equality, and a peaceful revolution to ensure independence.

In the late 1950s, TANU became more politically powerful, thanks to vocal lobbying by Nyerere, and by 1960, the colony's British governor, Sir Richard Turnbull, asked him to help form a new government. Tanganyika became independent in 1961 and Nyerere became the nation's first prime minister. Independence was declared on December 9, 1961, and the next month, Nyerere resigned to devote himself to building his party. He was overwhelmingly elected the country's first president in 1962. After a Tanganyikan military mutiny and a revolution in Zanzibar in 1964, the two nations united, forming Tanzania, with Nyerere at the helm.

Under Nyerere, the quality of life drastically improved in Tanzania. Literacy rates soared from about 50 percent to 83 percent, and Swahili was accepted as the national language an impressive feat, considering dozens of tribal tongues had been in use. Nyerere insisted on protecting civil rights for all, and the life expectancy increased, probably because a great many doctors were trained and access to water was expanded. Most importantly, Tanzania remained one of the most stable nations, politically and socially, throughout a time when unrest was rampant in Africa. Also, in an era when some African leaders were siphoning great wealth off citizens, Nyerere lived modestly.

However, Nyerere's major fault would be his adherence to a policy of a socialist agricultural system as the backbone of the economy. People did not embrace the collective farms as he wished, despite his pleas, and the nation failed to evolve into the agrarian utopia he had imagined. His country remained direly poor, relying heavily on foreign handouts, with a per capita income of $200 in 1985. Still, Nyerere was greatly respected for his many positive qualities and for uniting the many peoples of his land. He was widely known as "Mwalimu," the Swahili term for teacher.

In 1985, after 24 years in office, the ruling party nominated Ali Hassan Mwinyi to succeed Nyerere,

and he stepped down that November, though in his semi-retirement he held the post of party chair until 1990. Nyerere was diagnosed with leukemia in 1998 and began treatment in September of 1999. The next month, about a week after suffering a major stroke, he died at age 77 in a London hospital. He is survived by his wife, five sons, and a daughter. **Sources:** *Chicago Tribune,* October 15, 1999; *Contemporary Heroes and Heroines, Book III,* Gale Research, 1998; *Encyclopedia of World Biography,* second edition, Gale Research, 1998; *New York Times,* October 15, 1999, p. C20; *Times* (London), October 15, 1999; *Washington Post,* October 15, 1999, p. B6.

Keizo Obuchi

Born June 25, 1937, in Nakanojo, Gumma prefecture, Japan; died of complications from a stroke, May 14, 2000, in Tokyo, Japan. Japanese prime minister. Career politician Keizo Obuchi served more than three decades in the Japanese legislature before rising to the post of prime minister. An unassertive man who admitted that he drew his opinions from those around him, he was characterized by one analyst as having "all the pizzazz of a cold pizza," a description that dogged him throughout his time as prime minister. Nevertheless, he was admired for his consensus-building capabilities, a strong point particularly among Japanese. In addition, he came to be considered the best person for the job of leading Japan when the nation suffered an economic recession and was in dire need of stable leadership. Obuchi was in power for less than two years when he died.

Obuchi was born in the mountainous Gumma prefecture to a middle-class family. His father, Kohei, managed a silk mill and was a member of parliament (known as the Diet). Obuchi's older brother became the mayor of Nakanojo, their hometown. Their father died when Obuchi was a 21-year-old college student, and he vowed to carry on the political legacy. After obtaining a degree in English literature from Waseda University in Tokyo in 1962, Obuchi set off on a nine-month worldwide backpacking trip to 38 countries. To finance the journey, he worked as a dishwasher, a television camera crew assistant, and an aikido instructor.

In a bold move, while on his travels, Obuchi delivered a note to the office of U.S. Attorney General Robert Kennedy to ask for a meeting. A few days later, Kennedy agreed to meet with the upstart, and encouraged him to pursue a career in politics. The next year, 1963, Obuchi ran as a member of the Liberal Democratic Party (LDP) and at age 26 won the seat previously held by his father. This made him the youngest person ever elected to Japan's parliament. He served 12 terms in the lower house of the Diet, of House of for a total of 38 years of service.

During his career in parliament, Obuchi held a low profile, but rose steadily through the ranks. He became a cabinet member in 1979 managing the Hokkaido and Okinawa Development Agency, and also that year became general director of the prime minister's office. In 1986 he was named chairman of the budget committee of the House of Representatives, and the following year was named chief cabinet secretary. In that position, he worked closely with Prime Minister Takeshita and dealt with public affairs such as coordinating Emperor Hirohito's funeral. Also as chief cabinet secretary, in 1989 he became more of a public figure when he introduced the start of the era of "Hesei" (Achievement of Universal Peace), which came after the era of "Showa" (Enlightened Peace) upon Hirohito's death and the accession of his son, Akihito.

In the early 1990s, the LDP appointed Obuchi as secretary general, a powerful post regarded as a rung on the way to the prime minister's seat. He became vice president in 1994, and was named minister for foreign affairs in 1997, a post he won due to his support of Ryutaro Hashimoto during the 1996 elections. As foreign minister, he pushed for Japan to join an international treaty to ban land mines, and he also facilitated warmer relations with Russia.

When the Japanese economy plunged into a recession in the late 1990s, voters responded by taking away the LDP's majority in the Upper House of parliament. Subsequently, Hashimoto resigned and the legislature voted in Obuchi as his successor, to the surprise of many. He was not regarded as a front-runner, and younger party members felt he was too old, staid, and bland, and they criticized him as not being financially savvy enough to run the economy.

However, Obuchi immediately hired former Prime Minister Kiichi Miyazawa to become finance minister, and soon announced plans for deep personal and corporate tax cuts, a dramatic increase in public works projects, and the distribution of shopping coupons, all in order to spur the economy. In addition, he authorized an effort to help banks get rid of heaps of bad debt, which plagued the nation. While this produced a huge fiscal deficit, many credited

Obuchi with staving off a global recession or depression, since Japan's woes would have had a domino effect on other nations.

Obuchi served as prime minister for only 21 months when he suffered a cerebral hemorrhage on April 2, 2000, and slipped into a coma. This occurred after several stressful days following a volcano eruption in northern Japan that required thousands to evacuate their homes. The circumstances surrounding his stroke caused international attention, as Chief Cabinet Secretary Mikio Aoki initially reported that Obuchi had been hospitalized for exhaustion and then went home to rest. On April 3 Aoki revealed that Obuchi had had a stroke, but did not say that he was unconscious, and in fact announced that Obuchi had named him acting premier—a claim Aoki later admitted was false.

The world finally received news of Obuchi's condition on April 3, when Aoki said that he was in a coma and breathing with aid from a respirator. His cabinet then resigned, and Yoshiro Mori succeeded him as prime minister. Obuchi was comatose for six weeks before his death at age 62 at a hospital in Tokyo. His survivors include his wife of 33 years, Chizuko; a son, Takeshi; and two daughters, Akiko and Yuko. **Sources:** *Chicago Tribune,* May 15, 2000; *Facts on File,* April 6, 2000, p. 221; *Los Angeles Times,* May 15, 2000; *Newsmakers 1999,* Issue 2, Gale Group, 19999; *New York Times,* May 15, 2000; *Times* (London), May 15, 2000; *Washington Post,* May 15, 2000, p. B6.

Cardinal John O'Connor

Born John Joseph O'Connor, January 15, 1920, in Philadelphia, PA; died of cardiopulmonary arrest, May 3, 2000, in New York, NY. Clergy. Roman Catholic Cardinal John O'Connor was regarded as the most prominent spokesman in the United States for the Vatican. He led the 2.37 members of the New York archdiocese the nation's richest and second-largest and was one of the church's most powerful and controversial representatives on moral and political matters. A staunch supporter of Pope John Paul II, he was often know as the Pope's "echo," and his tenure was stamped most notably with his outspoken view against abortion. Despite his strong personality and opinions, O'Connor was not a pulpit-thumper, but a soft-spoken man known for his intellect. Though at times he was criticized for off-the-cuff statements, he was remembered by many as a caring person. He was the nation's oldest active bishop until his death.

O'Connor was the fourth of five children born to Thomas and Dorothy O'Connor. His father restored antique furniture and worked as an interior painter specializing in applying gold leaf to decorative ceilings. Later in his life, O'Connor recalled in several columns for the archdiocesan weekly newspaper that his youth was shaped by his family's strong religious beliefs and by his father's support for labor unions, as well as by the financial hardships caused by the Great Depression.

As a child, O'Connor attended public and Catholic grade schools before enrolling at Philadelphia's West Catholic High School for Boys. He later noted that the Christian Brothers who ran the institution prompted his decision to enter the priesthood. While a teen, O'Connor worked as a vegetable vendor on the street and also fixed bicycles. He entered the St. Charles Borromeo Seminary at age 16, and became an ordained priest on December 15, 1945.

O'Connor started his career teaching at the Catholic St. James High School in Chester, Pennsylvania, and served as an assistant pastor at a Philadelphia church for seven years. He also taught adult education and hosted two weekly local radio programs. Later, he also developed educational programs while working with the Pennsylvania Association for Retarded Children. His work with developmentally disabled children would remain a lifelong interest, and he once expressed regret at not devoting his career to this area.

Straying from the usual career path for priests, O'Connor followed a call by the church for more clergy to enter the military during the Korean War. He would spend 27 years as a Navy chaplain. Throughout his career he served with troops on aircraft carriers and front lines, and was awarded the Legion of Merit. O'Connor detailed some of his experiences in the book *A Chaplain Looks at Vietnam*, which supported continued U.S. military presence there. Later, he recanted his position and said that he regretted its publication.

During his military career, O'Connor obtained master's degrees in advanced ethics and clinical psychology from the Catholic University of American and a doctorate in political science from Georgetown University. This was unusual, since most priests went on to further study in theology. By 1975 O'Connor was navy chief of chaplains in Washington, with a rank of rear admiral, and this job required travel to naval bases worldwide. He retired from the Navy in 1979, asking for a low–key assignment in a quiet parish.

Instead, O'Connor was made a bishop at the military vicariate, the unit serving U.S. armed forces around the globe. In this capacity, he made waves as a member of the national committee of bishops that drafted an influential pastoral letter concerning nuclear weapons and peace. O'Connor, the most hawkish of the five, argued against a total nuclear freeze and disarmament, fearing it would make the United States too vulnerable. In the end, the letter called for rejecting the use of nuclear weapons in almost all circumstances, and approved their possession only in conjunction with major steps toward disarmament.

The committee's meetings concluded in May of 1983, and subsequently, the Pope named O'Connor bishop of the rather obscure parish of Scranton, Pennsylvania. Some wondered if he was being banished to an outpost, or being groomed for bigger steps. The answer came on January 31, 1984, when he succeeded Terence Cardinal Cooke who had died four months earlier of leukemia as the eighth archbishop of New York. A year and a half later, O'Connor was boosted to cardinal.

During his tenure, O'Connor was admired by some and reviled by others for his firm support of church doctrine. Many, especially in a city known for its diversity and liberal slant, denounced his unyielding positions against abortion, contraception, homosexuality, and the ordination of women. But while he raised the ire of gays and feminists, he also drew accolades for his support of Jewish causes and his work to improve the lives of the homeless and poor. And while O'Connor opposed giving out needles to drug users or condoms to help diminish the spread of AIDS, he was sympathetic to the plight of AIDS victims. O'Connor was also criticized for making several incendiary public statements on issues such as homosexuality and abortion, though sometimes he was taken out of context or misquoted.

A dedicated priest, O'Connor preached every Sunday Mass at St. Patrick's, even if he had to fly in from Rome and back again just to deliver the sermon. He instilled much effort in keeping open inner–city Catholic schools, and was often uncomfortable with the lavish lifestyle afforded to priests, recognizing that the wealthy image of the church was detrimental to its survival. Though he often expressed humility and a self–deprecating sense of humor, O'Connor was adept at hobnobbing with New York's elite and with a great many Catholic politicians, though he offended some of them with his hard–line position on moral issues.

In August of 1999, O'Connor had surgery to remove a brain tumor. Subsequently, his health declined, and he was seen in public less frequently. In March of 2000, he was awarded the country's highest civilian honor, the Congressional Gold Medal. He died at his residence in Manhattan near St. Patrick's Cathedral from cardiopulmonary arrest, which his spokesman said was the result of complications from the cancer. O'Connor was 80 years old and is survived by his sisters, Dorothy Hamilton and Mary Theresa Ward; and a brother, Thomas J. O'Connor. **Sources:** *Los Angeles Times,* May 4, 2000; *Newsmakers 1990,* Issue 3, Gale Research, 1990; *New York Times,* May 4, 2000, p. A1; May 11, 2000, p. A2; *Times* (London), May 5, 2000; *Washington Post,* May 4, 2000, p. A1.

David Ogilvy

Born June 23, 1911, in West Horsley, England; died July 21, 1999, in Loire Valley, France. Advertising executive. Founder of Ogilvy & Mather, David Ogilvy changed the face of advertising during the 1950s and beyond with his memorable, stylistic branding of products like Hathaway shirts, Schweppes tonic water, and Rolls–Royce automobiles. The pipe–smoking, tweed–wearing Ogilvy wrote copy for these and many of his company's other most successful campaigns. One of his favorite adages, according to a *New York Times* obituary, was, "The consumer is not a moron. She is your wife. Try not to insult her intelligence." His concise, image–based campaigns replaced repetitious ads that lacked any hint of creativity, although he himself would later criticize those who were so concerned with style that they lost sight of their goal, which was to sell the product. Ogilvy & Mather now boasts more than 350 offices in 100 countries.

Ogilvy was the youngest child born to Francis Longley John Ogilvy and Dorothy (Fairfield) Ogilvy, sharing his birthday, June 23, with his father and grandfather. The Ogilvys were well–off when he was a child, but his father, a stockbroker, was financially ruined during World War I. Ogilvy's father even slashed his own throat in an unsuccessful suicide attempt when his own father refused to loan him money. After attending Fettes College in Edinburgh, Ogilvy won a scholarship to Christ Church College at Oxford University, where he studied history.

A dismal student, Ogilvy dropped out of Oxford in 1931. Later in his life, after he was an astounding success, he found it amusing that his I.Q. was on the low end of the normal range, at 96. After spending a year as an apprentice chef at the Hotel Majestic in Paris, where his first assignment was to prepare meals for clients' dogs, Ogilvy returned to Britain and became a door–to–door stove salesman. He did so well that his employer asked him to write a guide for fellow workers; later, *Forbes* magazine touted it as perhaps the best sales manual ever written, according to a London *Times* obituary.

In 1935 Ogilvy landed a job with the London advertising firm of Mather & Crowther, and was promoted to managing director after just two years there. In 1938, he took a sabbatical and traveled to the United States, where he began working with George Gallup, the famous poll–taker, at the Audience Research Institute in Princeton, New Jersey. He soon quit his job in England and stayed on with Gallup. This experience had a major influence on Ogilvy, who thus learned volumes about American tastes during the 400 public opinion surveys he helped conduct.

From 1942 to 1944, during World War II, Ogilvy served in British Intelligence in the United States, then became second secretary at the British Embassy in Washington, D.C. from 1944 to 1945. Afterward, he moved to Pennsylvania and farmed tobacco for a time. At age 37, with financial backing from his former employer, Mather & Crowther, Ogilvy set up his own advertising firm. Hewitt, Ogilvy, Benson & Mather, as it was known then, soon secured the account for Hathaway, a small apparel company out of Maine that wanted to promote a line of men's shirts. Ogilvy masterminded the simple campaign, "The Man in the Hathaway Shirt," which featured a model wearing the product as well as an eye patch, which lent it an air of sophistication and sent shirt sales soaring.

The eccentric "man in the eye patch" became one of the most effective examples of branding at a time when most advertisements were dreadfully dull and repetitive. Another of Ogilvy's memorable campaigns was for Schweppes tonic water, which featured Commander Edward Whitehead, an unmistakably British gentleman with a full beard. In fact, Whitehead (the surname was real) was the British director of Schweppes American operations, and Ogilvy convinced him that his interesting appearance would make for a distinctive ad. Also, Ogilvy devised the idea of the old–fashioned horse–drawn carriage to market mass–produced Pepperidge Farms baked goods. Again, these images were popular, and served to boost sales considerably. Ogilvy's firm also produced the distinctive line, "At 60 miles an hour the loudest noise in this new Rolls–Royce comes from the electric clock," which touted the quality of Rolls–Royce. His agency also handled accounts for Shell Oil, Guinness beer, and the tourism board of Puerto Rico.

In 1964 Ogilvy's agency merged with Mather & Crowther to become Ogilvy & Mather. He retired to France in 1973 to a 60–room medieval chateau, but continued to remain in close contact with the agency. He received so much mail, in fact, that the local post office was forced to expand, and the postmaster was given a raise. In 1989 the British holding company WPP bought Ogilvy & Mather, much to Ogilvy's consternation, but his fury was soothed when chief executive Martin Sorrell offered him the position of non–executive chairman, a title he held from 1988 to 1992. Ogilvy was the author of two books, *Confessions of an Advertising Man,* 1963, and an autobiography, *Blood, Brains, and Beer,* 1978.

Ogilvy supported a bevy of causes, including the World Wildlife Fund, the United Negro College Fund, the New York Philharmonic, and an antilittering campaign in New York City. After retiring, he devoted much of his time to gardening, and for his eightieth birthday, his advertising agency presented him with a hybrid rose named in his honor. In 1967 Ogilvy was made a Commander of the British Empire by Queen Elizabeth, and was named an officer in the Order of Arts and Letters by the French Government in 1990. However, he always lamented that he had never been knighted.

Ogilvy had suffered a decline in health for about a year before his death at age 88 at his home near Bonnes in the Loire Valley of France. His marriages to Melinda Street and Ann Cabot ended in divorce. He is survived by his third wife, Herta Lans, whom he married in 1973; a son, David, from his first marriage, and three stepgrandsons. **Sources:** *Chicago Tribune,* July 22, 1999, sec. 2, p. 8; *Encyclopedia of World Biography,* second edition, Gale Research, 1998; *Los Angeles Times,* July 22, 1999; *New York Times,* July 22, 1999, p. A1; *Times* (London), July 22, 1999, p. 27; *Washington Post,* July 23, 1999.

Walter Payton

Born Walter Jerry Payton, July 25, 1954, in Columbia, MS; died of cancer, November 1, 1999, in Barrington, IL. Football player. Football's all–time greatest rusher Walter Payton was admired not only for his speed and power during his 13 seasons on the professional field, but also for his pleasant disposition, which earned him the nickname "Sweetness." In addition to his rushing record, Payton set six

others, including most yards in a game, at 275, and most games with 100 or more yards rushing, with 77. His records stand for rushing attempts (3,838), and combined yards (21,803 rushing, receiving, and returning). Barry Sanders tied his record for most 1,000 yard seasons, at ten, and Marcus Allen and Emmitt Smith later broke Payton's record of 110 rushing touchdowns. A two–time NFL most valuable player, he was selected to the Pro Bowl nine times. Named to the Pro Football Hall of Fame in 1993, his first year of eligibility, Payton was also inducted into the College Football Hall of Fame in 1996.

The youngest of three children, Payton was the son of Peter, a factory worker, and Alyne Payton. The family included his brother Eddie and sister Pamela. Growing up, Payton's first big interest was playing the drums, and he performed with the marching band at the segregated Columbia High School. He would later join various jazz–rock groups. By ninth grade, he was an athlete as well, participating in the long jump with his school track team, but shied away from football, mainly because his brother excelled as a running back. Eddie Payton would go on to play for the Minnesota Vikings.

After his brother graduated, Payton took up an offer from the high school coach to try out for the team, but only on the stipulation that he could remain in the band as well. Not only did he continue to play drums, a hobby he enjoyed throughout his life, he also played basketball and baseball as well, and continued to long–jump for the track team. During his final two years in high school, which was desegregated in his junior year, he scored in every football game and made the all–state team.

Several colleges recruited Payton, but he decided to join his brother at Jackson State College (now Jackson State University), a historically black school. There, he was the nation's top collegiate scorer as a junior with 160 points, and he set a National Collegiate Athletic Association (NCAA) record with a career total of 464 points. He graduated with a bachelor's degree in communications after only three and a half years, then entered graduate school to work toward a master's degree in education for the deaf.

Deciding to go pro, Payton was chosen fourth overall in the National Football League (NFL) 1975 draft by the struggling Chicago Bears. They offered him a $126,000 signing bonus, which was a team record at that time. During his first year on the field, he led the league in kickoff returns, though he missed several games due to an ankle injury. Before long, though, his value to the team was obvious. On November 20, 1977, Payton saw his record–setting 275–yard rushing game against the Minnesota Vikings, and he led the Bears to their first winning season in ten years.

That season, at age 23, Payton became the youngest player up to that point to be voted the NFL's most valuable player, and was simultaneously named offensive player of the year. The next year, he was offered a three–year contract worth a total of $1,275.000, a spectacular sum at the time. After the 1983 season, Payton signed the richest NFL contract ever written, guaranteeing him $240,000 a year for life. At five feet, ten inches tall and 202 pounds, Payton was on the small side for a power running back, but made up for it with his aggressive strength and his uncanny speed, marked by an unusual stiff–legged, churning running style and an elusive stutter–step strategy.

Despite Payton's dedication, energy, and contributions to the Bears, success continued to elude the team. After Chicago got a new coach in Mike Ditka and added quarterback Jim McMahon, however, Payton played in his first conference championship game in 1984. That year he surpassed Jim Brown as football's all–time rusher. The next season, with a record of 15–1, the Bears stomped the New England Patriots 46–10 in Super Bowl XX, their first NFL victory since 1963. In that contest, Chicago often used Payton, who rushed 22 times for 61 yards, as a decoy.

By the time he retired in 1987, Payton rushed 16,726 yards. Some thought Barry Sanders would break this record, but he was 1,458 yards short when he retired from the Detroit Lions in July of 1999. Retirement for the energetic Payton did not mean a sedentary lifestyle. He founded Walter Payton, Inc. in the Chicago area, which invested in an array of opportunities from real estate to travel agencies. He also raced cars and boats and purchased a Indy–car racing team, and stepped in as a partner in about 20 different restaurants. On the board of directors with the Chicago Bears, Payton was also a visible public persona who reaped fees for endorsements and motivational speeches. He also raised money for charities.

On February 2, 1999, Payton announced that he was suffering from primary sclerosing cholangitis, a rare condition in which the bile ducts are blocked. He was put on a liver transplant waiting list, but his name was later removed when doctors discovered that he was also suffering from bile duct cancer that had spread throughout his body, a common complication of the liver disease. The public was not informed of the cancer until after his death at age 45 at his home in Barrington, Illinois. He is survived by his wife, Connie (Norwood) Payton; his son, Jarrett; his daughter, Brittney; and his mother, Alyne. **Sources:** *Chicago Tribune,* November 2, 1999; "Walter Payton dead at 45," November 1, 1999; CNNSI web site, http://cnnsi.com (November 2, 1999); "Walter Payton: A Tribute to Sweetness," November 2, 1999; CNNSI web site, http://cnnsi.com (November 2, 1999); "NFL's all–time rusher dies at 45," "Walter Payton career highlights," and "Watching Payton was pure Sweetness," November 1, 1999, ESPN web site, http://espn.go.com (November 2, 1999); *Los Angeles Times,* November 2, 1999, pp. A1, A25; *New York Times,* November 2, 1999; *USA Today,* November 1, 1999; November 2, 1999; *Washington Post,* November 2, 1999, p. D1.

Tito Puente

Born Ernest Anthony Puente Jr., April 20, 1923, in New York City; died June 1, 2000, from complications due to surgery, in New York City. Bandleader. Legendary musician and bandleader Tito Puente was one of the architects of Latin jazz, a sound that fused Afro–Caribbean rhythms and big band. He earned the nickname "El Rey" ("The King") in recognition of his importance to the genre. Incidentally, he did not care at all for the term "salsa," coined decades after his debut, and dismissed it as nothing more than something to eat. In his more than five decades of performing, Puente recorded more than 100 albums and toured indefatigably, appearing on stage 200 to 300 times a year. He also played himself in the 1992 film *The Mambo Kings.* The five–time Grammy Award winner was also known as the composer of the Carlos Santana hit "Oye Como Va."

Puente, the son of Puerto Rican immigrants, was born at New York's Harlem Hospital and grew up in a neighborhood known as Spanish Harlem, or the Barrio. His father worked at a razor blade factory. Puente had a younger sister and brother, but his brother died at age four from a fall from a fire escape. When he was a boy, Puente was small–built and was also named Ernest Jr., so his mother began calling him "Ernestito" (Little Ernest), which was shortened to Tito.

When he was young, Puente's mother recognized her son's talent and began paying for music lessons.

He learned piano at age seven, drums at ten, and then timbales—a rack–mounted set of percussion instruments which are integral in Latin music. By age 13, he was considered a prodigy, already having performed with local Latin bands at area events and hotels. Also as a teen, Puente joined Noro Morales and the Machito Orchestra—one of the first groups to fuse Latin rhythms and jazz—when that band's drummer was drafted into World War II. He later dropped out of Manhattan's Central Commercial High School.

At age 19, Puente was drafted as well, and served three years in the U.S. Navy, earning a presidential commendation for his valor in nine battles. Afterward, he returned to New York City and studied at the Juilliard School under the GI Bill from 1945 to 1947. During this time and later, Puente played with the bands of Jose Curbelo and Fernando Alvarez. In the late 1940s, he joined the Pupi Campo Orchestra and began to attract admiration for his outstanding arrangements.

In about 1947 or 1948, Puente formed his own group, called the Piccadilly Boys, which soon became known as the Tito Puente Orchestra. They gained a following at New York's Palladium, and began recording on New York's SMC (Spanish Music Center) label, then on Tico Records. A single from one of these early sessions, "Abaniquito," became the first crossover mambo hit. It established his trademark style, using percussive polyrhythms added to a mambo beat and vocal tag–lines.

Throughout the 1950s, mambo's popularity swelled, and Puente pounded out dance favorites like "Mambo la Roca," "Mambo Gallego," "Barbara-batiri," and "El Rey del Timbai." In 1956 he released *Puente Goes Jazz*, his first big band jazz album, and followed up with hits like *Dance Mania*, 1958, and *Top Percussion*, 1960. In the late 1950s he became the premier name during the "cha–cha–cha" fad.

During the 1960s, Puente teamed up with some of the biggest names in jazz, including bandleader Woody Herman, guitarist Barry Galbraith, trumpeters Doc Severinsen and Bernie Glow, trombonist Buddy Morrow, and drummer Jimmy Cobb, who played with Miles Davis. He also collaborated with Cuban musicians Celia Cruz and La Lupe. Fans could often find Puente at regular gigs at the Salsa Meets Jazz series at Manhattan's Village Gate nightclub.

In 1968, Puente hosted his own show, *The World of Tito Puente,* on Hispanic television. Though Carlos

Santana released a version of "Oye Como Va" in 1975, introducing the bandleader's sound to a new generation, that decade would be a slower time for Puente. By the 1980s and 1990s, though, his schedule was packed with projects with the likes of jazz musicians George Shearing, Dave Valentin, Phil Woods, Terry Gibbs, Hilton Ruiz, and others. In addition, his band often performed with symphonies.

Appearing in Puerto Rican parades, Puente was recognized as a symbol of Puerto Rican pride. He opened a 250–seat restaurant on City Island in 1995. Until the very end, the cherub–faced and effervescent Puente was a dedicated entertainer, the kind who insisted "the show must go on." He often joked around while on stage to the delight of his audience.

Puente married a longtime girlfriend, Mirta Sanchez, while he was on leave during the war. They had a son, Ronald, in 1947, but later divorced. During the 1950s he maintained a relationship with dancer Ida Carlini, with whom he had a son, Richard Anthony, in 1953, who also became a musician. Subsequently, Puente was in a 30–year relationship with Margaret Acenio, and they had a son, Tito Puente, Jr., a musician, and daughter, Audrey, a weather forecaster. Puente and Acenio married about four or five years before his death, according to a *New York Times* obituary, with their son and daughter serving as the best man and maid of honor.

In May of 2000, on tour in Puerto Rico, Puente was treated for heart trouble. He then underwent open heart surgery on May 31 at New York University Medical Center and died there that same night of complications at the age of 77. He is survived by his wife, sons, and daughter. **Sources:** *Encyclopedia of World Biography*, second edition, Gale Research, 1998; *Los Angeles Times,* June 2, 2000; *New York Times,* June 2, 2000; *Times* (London), June 3, 2000; *USA Today,* June 1, 2000; *Washington Post,* June 2, 2000, p. C1.

Mario Puzo

Born October 15, 1920, in New York, NY; died of apparent heart failure, July 2, 1999, in Long Island, NY. Author. Mario Puzo was best known as the writer of the Mafia drama *The Godfather*, which was adapted into a trilogy of gripping films. Published in 1969, the book became the best–selling novel of the 1970s. The first two films, *The Godfather* (1972) and *The Godfather: Part II* (1974), directed by Francis

Ford Coppola, became classics, although the third, *The Godfather: Part III* (1990), received mixed reviews. Coppola also cowrote the screenplays, and he and Puzo won Academy Awards for best screenplay for the first two installments. Puzo went on to write more screenplays and a handful of novels, some of which continued in the vein of organized crime.

Puzo was born in the Italian neighborhood of Hell's Kitchen on Manhattan's west side. He was the one of seven children of Antonio and Maria (Le Conti) Puzo, poor Italian immigrants from Naples. His father, who worked as a trackman for the New York Central Railroad, left the family when Puzo was 12. Growing up, Puzo scrupulously avoided the lure of street gangs, heeding his mother's advice to stay inside much of the time. In fact, his mother was the prototype for the character of the Godfather, as well as the main character, Lucia Santa, in *The Fortunate Pilgrim*. Puzo has emphatically denied ever having any personal contact with the mob growing up, although their presence was widely known in his neighborhood.

By the time he was in his teens, Puzo was composing stories and harboring dreams of being a writer. However, he left high school to work as a messenger for the same railroad that employed his father. During World War II, he served with the U.S. Army Air Forces in Germany as a public relations administrator. There, he met a German woman, Erika Lina Broske, and they married in 1946. Returning to New York, he attended college on the G.I. Bill and began writing short stories. His first published work, a story titled "The Last Christmas," appeared in *American Vanguard* in 1950. To support his family, he worked as a clerk in a government office. He and his wife had five children.

In the meantime, Puzo also started his first novel, *The Dark Arena*, published in 1955. Set in Germany, it was about an American soldier who returns to locate his former mistress. Though it was critically well–received, it did not sell well. Puzo in 1960 became an assistant editor of a group of men's magazines, for which he penned several action stories, most of them set during World War II. His next work, 1964's *The Fortunate Pilgrim*, was considered by some, including Puzo, to be his best. This autobiographical tale, according to a *New York Times* obituary, was called "a small classic" by a writer for the *New York Times Book Review*, but again, it was not a popular success.

However, Puzo's publisher was intrigued by a minor character in *The Fortunate Pilgrim* and suggested that the author develop him. Frustrated with failing to achieve commercial recognition for his prior efforts not to mention being in debt Puzo took the advice and set out to purposely write a blockbuster. He got an advance from Putnam and came out with *The Godfather* in 1969. It held the number one spot on the *New York Times* best–seller list for 67 weeks and sold 21 million copies around the globe. Loosely based on true stories about factional rivalry in the New York Mafia, the tale also explored the importance of family loyalty and the corruption of the American dream. Some criticized the work for glorifying gangsters, but Puzo insisted he that he actually abhorred violence. He noted that although he needed to allow readers sympathize with the characters in order to make the story gripping, he was surprised that so many readers adored the Godfather.

The Godfather was adapted for film and released in 1972 to immediate acclaim, and it achieved more enduring success than even the book. It reaped several honors in addition to Puzo and Coppola earning the Oscar for best screenplay, and its stars, including Marlon Brando, Al Pacino, and Robert DeNiro, James Caan, and Robert Duvall, were widely recognized as well. Brando as the patriarch, Don Vito Corleone, won an Academy Award for best actor, but refused to accept it. The movie, with its famous line "an offer he couldn't refuse" and its startling image of a decapitated horse head under the sheets, became a highly influential piece of cinema. However, the sequel, *The Godfather: Part II*, was released in 1974, and many felt it was superior to the first. The final leg of the trilogy, released in 1990, was not as well–received.

Puzo went on to publish four more novels. *Fools Die*, 1978, garnered mixed reviews but was a commercial success. It was an inside look at the high–stakes world of gambling, publishing, and filmmaking. His next, *The Sicilian*, 1984, returned to the topic of the mob and the Corleone family. This was made into a film in 1987, although it was plagued by production problems and was far inferior to the *Godfather* films. Then Puzo published *The Fourth K*, 1991, a political thriller about a distant Kennedy cousin who becomes president of the United States in the early twenty–first century. This was followed by *The Last Don: A Novel*, 1996, a best–seller that was made into a television miniseries the next year. When he died, Puzo had also finished another novel, *Omerta*, which was scheduled for publication in the summer of 2000. It reportedly was a continuation of the themes in *The Godfather*. In between completing novels, Puzo was heavily involved in writing screenplays for Hollywood as well. He cowrote *Earthquake*,

1974; *Superman,* 1978; *Superman II,* 1981; *The Cotton Club,* 1984; and *Christopher Columbus: The Discovery,* 1992.

Puzo was a heavy–set man who was known for his avid gambling habit. He also read voraciously and enjoyed playing tennis and eating Italian cuisine. Puzo's wife died in 1978, and he and his wife's former nurse, Carol Gino, subsequently became companions for the next two decades. Puzo, who underwent a quadruple bypass in the 1990s, died of heart failure at his home in Bay Shore, New York, on Long Island. He is survived by Gino; his children, Anthony, Dorothy, Eugene, Virginia McLaughlin, and Joseph; a sister, Evelyn Murphy; a brother, Anthony Cleri; and nine grandchildren. **Sources:** *Chicago Tribune,* July 3, 1999, sec. 1, p. 3; "Mario Puzo," *Contemporary Authors,* Gale Literary Databases, http://www.galenet.com (September 6, 1999); *Los Angeles Times,* July 3, 1999; *New York Times,* July 3, 1999, p. B7; *Times* (London), July 5, 1999; *Washington Post,* July 3, 1999.

Steve Reeves

Born January 21, 1926, in Glasgow, MT; died of complications from lymphoma, May 1, 2000, in Escondido, CA. Actor, bodybuilder. Steve Reeves used his physique as a champion bodybuilder to become a movie star in Europe and the United States, appearing in a series of mostly low–budget Italian–made features showcasing his rippling muscles during the 1950s and 1960s. After being named Mr. America at age 21 in 1947 and winning the Mr. Universe title three years later, he turned his sights to a film career. He made his name in the title role in 1957's *The Labors of Hercules,* which became a surprise hit in the United States when it was released in 1959. Though he was never critically acclaimed for his acting, Reeves made a total of 18 films and served as a prototype for future beefcake action heroes such as Arnold Schwarzenegger and Sylvester Stallone.

Born in Montana near the Canadian border, Reeves spent his youth riding horses on his uncle's ranch. His father, Lester, died in a farming accident when Reeves was a tot, and at age ten, he moved to Oakland, California, with his mother. He once remarked to the *Los Angeles Times* that he was prompted to begin working out with weights as a teen after he was beaten at arm–wrestling by a much smaller boy. When he learned that the rival was an avid weightlifter, he began taking lessons from him. "He used to charge me 50 cents a lesson," Reeves said in the

interview, according to a *Los Angeles Times* obituary. "Joe became a barber. I became Mr. Universe."

Reeves bought his own weight bench and once claimed he added 30 pounds of muscle in three months. Soon he caught the eye of Ed Yarick, the proprietor of a bodybuilding center. After high school, Reeves joined the army and served in World War II in the Philippines and later in Japan. Back home in 1946 he returned to his regular workouts at Yarick's gym, and that year, was named Mr. Pacific Coast. In 1947, he won the Mr. Western America competition, and was also crowned Mr. America. In 1948, he won the Mr. World title, and in 1950, he became Mr. Universe. He was six feet, one inch tall and weighed 215 pounds, and at his best, boasted a 51– inch chest, 18–inch bicep, and 29–inch waist.

Thanks to his physical presence, Reeves began to attract attention from Hollywood, and he stopped competing as a bodybuilder after winning Mr. Universe. But although he started appearing on television shows, many film studios initially thought he was too large even for the big screen. He once stated that he auditioned for director Cecil B. DeMille for the lead in *Samson and Delilah,* but when DeMille instructed him to lose 20 pounds of muscle, Reeves declined. The role went to Victor Mature instead.

In 1954, Reeves landed his first speaking role in the B–movie crime drama *Jail Bait,* directed by Ed Wood. Also that year he showed up in the musical satire *Athena,* starring Jane Powell. After a few years, though, Reeves had virtually given up on acting and was planning to return to a steady job with a gym when he was wired $10,000 and a round–trip ticket by Italian director Pietro Francisci, who cast him in his first *Hercules* film in 1957. He reprised the role two years later in *Hercules Unchained.*

Subsequently, Reeves became known for portraying superhuman feats on camera, such as throwing around columns of Roman temples and fighting with tigers, lions, and bulls. Though critics lambasted his acting skills, he became a top box office draw. Reeves appeared in his last film, a spaghetti western titled *A Long Ride from Hell,* in the late 1960s. For his first *Hercules* effort, he earned only $10,000, but eventually his salary increased to $250,000 a picture—not a paltry sum in his time. He invested the money in stocks, bonds, and real estate, allowing him to live comfortably when he retired from film.

Until his last days, Reeves lived a fit and active life. One neighbor told a *People* writer, "It was very common to see him 45 miles from home on a bicycle." After his film career, Reeves became a fitness guru and early practitioner of "power walking." He was also a vocal champion of drug–free bodybuilding, which he touted with his book, *Building the Classic Physique the Natural Way,* and through the Steve Reeves International Society web site.

Reeves married Aline Czarawicz in 1963, and the couple lived on a ranch near Escondido, California, where they raised horses. They had no children, and Reeves's wife died of a stroke in 1989. He was diagnosed with lymphoma just two months before his death at the Palomar Medical Center in Escondido from complications due to the disease. Reeves was 74 and left no immediate survivors. **Sources:** *Los Angeles Times,* May 4, 2000, p. A3; *New York Times,* May 5, 2000, p. A24; *People,* May 22, 2000, p. 166; Steve Reeves International Society web site, http://www.stevereeves.com (June 14, 2000); *Times* (London), May 5, 2000, p. 23; *Washington Post,* May 4, 2000, p. B7.

Maurice "Rocket" Richard

Born Joseph Henri Maurice Richard, August 4, 1921, in Montreal, Quebec, Canada; died of stomach cancer, May 27, 2000, in Montreal, Quebec, Canada. Hockey player. National Hockey League (NHL) Hall of Famer Maurice "Rocket" Richard was a star player on the Montreal Canadiens for during the 1940s and 1950s, and is considered one of the best hockey players of all time. He earned his nickname due to his speed and strength; despite his relatively small size (five feet, ten inches and 170 pounds), he terrorized opponents with his single–minded drive to win. When he retired in 1960, he boasted a record as having the most goals in a career, though this was bested by the Detroit Red Wings' Gordie Howe in 1963. Richard is also infamous for his role in a citywide riot sparked by his suspension in 1955 following his violent outbursts on the ice.

Richard was born in the Bordeaux section of Montreal, the son of a former semi–pro hockey player who worked as a machinist for the Canadian Pacific Railway. He skated on a homemade hockey rink behind his house as a child, and learned to wield a hockey stick not long after he learned to walk. While studying to become a machinist at the Montreal Technical School, he played for junior leagues in the area during the winters.

In 1940, while earning $40 a week as a machinist, Richard landed a spot on the Montreal Canadiens farm team, in the Senior Hockey League of Quebec. Though he suffered injuries in his first two seasons, he signed a free agent contract with the Canadiens for the 1942–43 season, scoring five goals and six assists during his first 16 games. But he broke his ankle after that, and attracted a reputation for being injury–prone. Nevertheless, coach Dick Irvin kept him on the roster.

During the 1943–44 season, Richard, who was left–handed but could shoot from either side, was put on the right wing of one of hockey's legendary trios. Known as the "Punch Line" for its uncanny ability to slap in goals, it included Elmer Lach at center and Hector "Toe" Blake on the left. That year, Richard racked up 32 goals and took Montreal to its first Stanley Cup in 13 years. The next year, he set a single–season record of 50 goals, a number he reached in 50 games. Eventually the record was surpassed, but the benchmark of 50 goals a season remains a remarkable feat that only elite players achieve.

Though Richard was small as far as hockey players go, he was fiesty, and other teams regularly assigned fight–prone players to guard him. He would strike back using his fists and stick, and led the league in penalty minutes one season. Known for his hot temper, he once attacked a referee in a hotel lobby the day after a game. However, Richard's most notorious tirade came in March of 1955, at a game in Boston when he brutally struck the Bruins' Hal Laycoe several times with his stick. When linesman Cliff Thompson intervened, Richard punched him.

Subsequently, NHL President Clarence Campbell suspended Richard for the final three games of the season and all of the playoffs. This stunned fans, who began verbally and physically attacking Campbell at the next game, against Detroit at the Montreal Forum arena on March 17, 1955. After the first period, with Detroit leading 4–1, he declared the game a forfeit, which enraged fans further. They threw bottles, rocks, and ice, and set off a smoke bomb, then poured into the street, where they broke windows and looted shops. Eventually, Richard made a plea over the radio for fans to restore the peace.

Though Richard remained on suspension for the rest of the playoffs and Detroit took the Stanley Cup that year, he would return to the ice to win the Cup for Montreal the next five seasons running, from 1956 to 1960—the only instance of a team accomplishing this. In addition, his brother Henri, a center known by the name the "Pocket Rocket," joined the team in 1955–56 to skate as Richard's linemate; he would later become a Hall of Famer as well.

During his 18 years with the Canadiens, Richard presided over eight Stanley Cup wins in all. Five seasons, he led the league in goal scoring, and in addition to setting a then–record of career goals, he wrapped up his career with an impressive 82 play-off goals. His record of six playoff overtime goals in one game stands as a record. Also, for 13 years, from 1947 to 1959, Richard played in the NHL All-Star Game. However, only once did he win the Hart Trophy as the league's most valuable player, in 1947.

After retiring from the ice in 1960, Richard worked in public relations for the Canadiens for many years, as well as for a brewery. In addition, he ran a home-based fishing supply business and wrote a popular Sunday column in *Le Journal de Montreal.* Just nine months after his retirement, he was named to the Hockey Hall of Fame, an honor usually reserved for players who have been retired at least five years. In 1972 Richard coached the World Hockey Association's Quebec Nordiques, but quit after two games. He later became a Canadiens representative at special events. In the 1998–99 season, the NHL introduced the Maurice Richard Trophy, awarded to the league's top goal–scorer.

Richard was diagnosed with cancer in 1998, but after treatment he resumed work as a team ambassador for the Canadiens. However, he was also suffering from Parkinson's disease and osteoarthritis, and was heavily medicated for his various ailments. At age 78, Richard died of abdominal cancer at a Montreal hospital. He and his wife, Lucille, who died in 1994, had seven children and 14 grandchildren. **Sources:** *Detroit Free Press,* June 1, 2000, p. 2D; *Encyclopedia of World Biography Supplement,* volume 19, Gale Group, 1999; "The Rocket lit up hockey," ESPN web site, http://espn.go.com (May 30, 2000); *Los Angeles Times,* May 28, 2000; *New York Times,* May 28, 2000, p. 34; *Washington Post,* May 28, 2000, p. C6.

Nathalie Sarraute

Born Nathalie Tcherniak, July 18, 1900, in Ivanovo–Voznessensk, Russia; died October 19, 1999, in Paris, France. Author. French writer Nathalie Sarraute was known as the leader of the "New Novel" movement that abandons traditional storytelling elements like plot and characters in favor of a psychologically–based exploration of thoughts and emotions.

Though her first work was published in 1939, she was not widely recognized until the 1950s and 1960s. She completed a total of 17 books, including ten novels. Sarraute's writings can be challenging for many readers, but they are intriguing in their re-assessment of common assumptions about literature and its relationship to life. Other authors grouped with the "New Novel" movement include Samuel Beckett and Claude Simon.

Sarraute was born in Ivanovo–Voznessensk, Russia, northeast of Moscow, in 1900. Her Russian–Jewish father, Elie, a chemist, and mother, Pauline, a writer who published under a male pseudonym, divorced when she was two. Subsequently, she went to live with her mother in Paris, who had married a man 11 years her junior. She continued to visit her father for two months each year, and then returned to St. Petersburg, Russia, with her mother in 1906. Her father then emigrated to France, where he lived in Paris with his second wife, Vera. In 1908, Sarraute decided to begin living with her father full–time. Later she would write a book titled *Childhood,* which examined the complexities of trying to maintain two families in two countries while speaking two languages.

After attending schools in Paris, Sarraute obtained a *licence de lettres* (the equivalent of a degree) in English literature at the Sorbonne in 1920. That year, she went to Oxford University, where she studied history. Leaving before completing her degree, at the request of her father, she then spent a year in college in Berlin before starting law school at the University of Paris in 1922. There she met fellow student Raymond Sarraute, and they married in 1925.

Though Sarraute practiced law from 1925 to 1939, her husband encouraged her writing career. She enjoyed reading Virginia Woolf, James Joyce, Franz Kafka, and Marcel Proust, and was also inspired to write thanks to the oral presentations required in the legal field. By 1932, she began to write, composing short pieces that have been described as either prose poems or experimental fiction. Sarraute finished the 24 works in 1927 and they were eventually published in 1939 as *Tropisms.* The title is a term concerning the involuntary movement of organisms as a reaction to external stimuli such as plants to sunlight but Sarraute incorporated it to mean the impulse a person feels before expressing it in word or action.

When Nazi German forces occupied France in 1940, Sarraute refused to wear the yellow star marking her as Jewish. She and her husband divorced so that his job would not be threatened, but they did not separate, and they later remarried in 1956. At one point, in danger of being recognized as a Jew, she went into hiding, posing as the governess of her own children. She finished her first novel in 1946, and published it in 1948. Prominent existentialist Jean–Paul Sartre wrote an introduction for *Portrait of a Man Unknown*, which he described as "an anti-novel that reads like a detective story," according to a *New York Times* obituary by Alan Riding.

By 1953, with the publication of her third book, *Martereau*, Sarraute was established as a pioneer "new novelist," and in 1956, her book of essays titled *The Age of Suspicion* was billed as "the first theoretical manifestation of the Nouveau Roman school," reported Riding. After this, another novel, *The Planetarium*, came out in 1959, followed by the acclaimed *The Golden Fruits* in 1963. Sarraute once called *The Golden Fruits* her most abstract work, and it was also her most successful, winning the International Prize for Literature in 1964. It centered on a literary discussion of a fictional book, also called *The Golden Fruits*, and allowed the author to take jabs at criticism while simultaneously raising important points.

In the 1960s, Sarraute ventured into drama as well, penning the radio play *The Silence* in 1964. She followed up with other radio scripts, including *The Lie*, and the famous actor–director Jean–Louis Barrault used these two works to open his new theater, the Petit Odeon, in 1967. In 1970 Sarraute began writing specifically for the stage, which required her to be more explicit in her dialogue. One of her novels, *Childhood*, 1983, which was an autobiographical account of her first 12 years, was also adapted as a one–act play and opened in New York starring Glenn Close in 1985.

Sarraute's last novel, *Here*, was released in 1995 in France and 1997 in the United States. In 1996, the prestigious Pleiade series published her complete works, a rare honor for an author to see in his or her lifetime. However, she went on to publish one more book, *Ouvrez*, in October of 1997, a book concerning the French language, and was even working on another project when she died at age 99 at her home in Paris, France. Her husband had died in 1985, and Sarraute is survived by three daughters: Claude, Anne, and Dominique. **Sources:** *Chicago Tribune*, October 24, 1999, sec. 4, p. 10; *Encyclopedia of World Biography*, second edition, Gale Research, 1998; *Los Angeles Times*, October 20, 1999, p. A24; *New York Times*, October 20, 1999, p. C25; *Times* (London), October 21, 1999.

Charles Schulz

Born Charles Monroe Schulz, November 26, 1922, in Minneapolis (some sources say St. Paul), MN; died of a heart attack, February 12, 2000, in Santa Rosa, CA. Cartoonist. Charles Schulz added an important chapter to popular culture with his enormously successful comic strip *Peanuts*. Featuring a group of children, it provided a novel take on "the funnies" due to its often tragic quality and for its attention to psychological and social issues. However, besides an occasional light–handed religious interjection, Schulz never used the strip to push his personal beliefs on readers. His strip centered on the perennial loser, Charlie Brown, and often dealt with the sadly humorous element in human foibles.

In addition to Charlie Brown, the strip included a cast of intriguing child characters, from Schroeder, the classical pianist, to Lucy, the bossy antagonist, to Linus, the blanket–toting philosopher. Of course, one of the favorites was Charlie Brown's precocious dog, Snoopy, whose ripe imagination led him to delusions of grandeur. *Peanuts* became the most widely syndicated comic strip in history, carried in roughly 2,600 newspapers and translated into 21 languages, reaching more than 355 million readers in 75 nations. Schulz drew and wrote each strip himself in an era when many comic artists hired staffs to assist with production and even draw for them. He never took suggestions from others, and his contract demanded that no one else could create new strips after his death.

Schulz was the son of Carl Schulz a barber, like Charlie Brown's father and Dena (Halverson) Schulz. When he was two days old, his uncle began calling him Sparky, after the horse Spark Plug in the comic strip Barney Google. The nickname stayed with him throughout his life. As a child, Schulz devoted his attention to copying his favorite cartoon characters, including Popeye, Mickey Mouse, and Krazy Kat. He once submitted drawings to St. Paul's Central High School yearbook, but they were rejected. He also failed several subjects in school. However, when he was 15, "Ripley's Believe It or Not!" accepted his drawing of a dog that ate razor blades, pins, and tacks. Nevertheless, Schulz would focus on his failings more than his successes in life, which would provide rich fodder for his later cartoons.

After seeing an ad asking, "Do you like to draw?," Schulz enrolled in a correspondence course with Art Instruction, Inc. in Minneapolis, but his education was cut short when he was drafted into the army during World War II. Just days after his mother died of cancer, he was shipped off to boot camp, and he later suggested this was the root of his distaste for travel. He served from 1943 to 1945 in Germany and France, leading a machine gun squad and becoming a staff sergeant in the 20th Armored Division.

Upon his discharge, Schulz worked odd jobs and submitted cartoons to a Catholic magazine called *Timeless Topix*, where he debuted some of his child characters. In the late 1940s, he began submitting the comic strip *L'il Folks* to the *St. Paul Pioneer Press*; it was the precursor to *Peanuts*. He also sometimes sold spot cartoons to the *Saturday Evening Post*. Meanwhile, Schulz got a job teaching at Art Instruction, where he had a friend named Charlie Brown and fell in love with a red–haired girl, Donna Johnson, who spurned his marriage proposal and wed a fire fighter.

Eventually, Schulz stopped providing *L'il Folks* to the *Pioneer Press* when they refused to move it from the women's section to a higher–profile location. He convinced the United Feature Syndicate in New York to accept the strip, but they insisted on changing the name to *Peanuts*, since his original title was too close to that of another comic, *L'il Abner*. Schulz hated the name from the start and never warmed to it, but it stuck. *Peanuts* debuted on October 2, 1950.

From the start, *Peanuts* opened a new chapter in comics for its focus on the insecurities that everyone faces in life. The main character, Charlie Brown, served as an Everyman in a newly complex age rife with anxieties. He was incessantly vexed by a kite–eating tree, a losing baseball team, and a little girl who pulled away the football each time he tried to kick it. His dog refused to obey, his friends ridiculed him, and his love for a little red–haired girl went unrequited. However, he never gave up hope.

The wild popularity of *Peanuts* led the characters into a world of new venues. In 1952, in an unprecedented move, several of Schulz's strips were collected in paperback format. In 1958, the first plastic Snoopy and Charlie Brown dolls were sold, and in 1960, Hallmark began marketing a line of Peanuts greeting cards. The characters were used in ads to sell Ford Falcon cars in 1957, and later appeared in commercials for the Metropolitan Life Insurance Company. The Peanuts gang later showed up in a Broadway play, award–winning television specials, and on a plethora of products ranging from toys and clothing to home furnishings. By 1999, the *Pea-*nuts characters could be seen on 20,000 new products a year. Schulz was worth an estimated $55 million at the time of his death.

Schulz received the Reuben Award, the highest honor in the world of cartooning, from the National Cartoonists Society in 1955 and 1964. At the International Pavilion of Humor in Montreal in 1978, his colleagues named him the International Cartoonist of the Year. The French government named him a commander of arts and letters in 1990. Posthumously, he received a lifetime achievement award at the National Cartoonists Society convention in May of 2000.

In addition to drawing Peanuts, Schulz enjoyed classical music, golf, ice skating, and ice hockey. He was married to Joyce Halverson in 1949 and divorced in 1972; they had five children. He met his second wife, Jeannie Forsythe, at the ice arena he built near his home, where they were both watching their daughters figure skate. They married in 1974.

In late 1999, Schulz was diagnosed with colon cancer and suffered a series of small strokes in November of that year during emergency abdominal surgery. Subsequently, he announced he would retire. On the night of February 12, just before the Sunday papers carrying his final strip hit the stands, Schulz died of a heart attack at his home in Santa Rosa, California, at age 77. He is survived by his wife; daughters Meredith, Amy, and Jill; and sons Craig and Monte. **Sources:** *Chicago Tribune*, February 14, 2000; *Los Angeles Times*, February 14, 2000; *Newsmakers 1998*, issue 1, Gale Research, 1998; *New York Times*, February 14, 2000, p. A1; *Times* (London), February 14, 2000; *Washington Post*, February 14, 2000, p. A1.

George C. Scott

Born George Campbell Scott, October 18, 1927, in Wise, VA; died of a ruptured abdominal aortic aneurysm, September 22, 1999, in Westlake Village, CA. Actor. George C. Scott, the intense, craggy–faced, raspy–voiced actor best known for his performance as the legendary general in the 1970 film *Patton*, often stole the show whether in a lead or supporting role. His capacity for convincing portrayals ran the gamut from villains to larger–than–life heros. An imposing presence, Scott was most notably connected with drama, but occasionally ventured into comedy as well; for example, he was uproarious as General Buck Turgidson in Stanley Kubrick's *Dr. Strangelove.* Scott was known to be of unpredictable temperament and attracted a reputation for being difficult to work with. He drank heavily and five times suffered a broken nose four in bar brawls and one in a mugging. An opponent of awards ceremonies due to their "childish and damaging unnatural competitiveness," according to a *New York Times* obituary, he declined to accept the Academy Award for best actor for his work in *Patton,* and also shunned nominations for other roles as well. Scott also refused a 1971 Emmy Award for his role in the televised Arthur Miller play*The Price.* The actor was also widely honored with nominations and awards for his stage work.

The grandson of an Appalachian coal miner, Scott was born in the mining town of Wise, Virginia, to George C. Scott and Helena Scott. When the Depression hit, his father moved the family to Detroit, Michigan, where he worked on the assembly line at the Buick automobile plant and later started a business. Scott's mother, an amateur poet, died when her son was eight, and afterward, his sister, Helen, helped raise him. Scott graduated from Redford High School in 1945 and joined the Marines, but World War II was winding down and he did not see combat. Instead, he worked at Arlington National Cemetery burying the dead as well as at a desk job. He once noted that he drank a lot during his military days.

After his discharge in 1949, Scott attended the University of Missouri School of Journalism, where he landed a role in a student production of *The Winslow Boy,* by Terence Rattigan, and became enamored of the footlights. He left college in 1950 to pursue acting full–time, appearing in more than 125 roles in stock theater in Toledo, Ohio; Ontario, Canada; and Washington, D.C. He also worked in Washington, D.C. in construction, then moved to New York City in 1956 where he moonlighted as a check–sorting machine operator at a bank while hunting for acting jobs during the day.

Scott's big break came in New York in 1957 when he landed the title role in *Richard III,* directed by Joseph Papp, followed by parts in *As You Like It* and *Children of Darkness* the next year. He won several awards for these works, including an Obie Award for best actor and a Drama Desk Award. His success was surprising, considering he was a newcomer with scant experience performing Shakespeare, let alone one of the most demanding roles in classical theater in *Richard III.* His Broadway debut came in 1958 in *Comes a Day,* in a disturbing role that required him to decapitate a bird each night on stage.

In 1959, Scott appeared in his first film, *The Hanging Tree,* in another malevolent role as a zealous drunk who rouses his fellow townspeople to hang a man. He followed this with an Oscar–nominated part as a prosecutor in Otto Preminger's *Anatomy of a Murder,* going head–to–head in the courtroom with Jimmy Stewart's character. This film marked his evolution into stardom. His career continued to blossom with a memorable role as a pool shark in *The Hustler,* 1961, and this was the first time he openly rejected the Oscar nomination.

Subsequently, Scott was hilarious in *Dr. Strangelove,* 1964; and then brilliant in a serious turn at a military role in his masterwork, *Patton,* 1970, for which he rejected the winning Academy Award. He was also nominated for an Oscar the next year for his turn as a doctor defeated by bureaucracy in *The Hospital* . He would also work extensively in television series, miniseries, and movies, winning his first Emmy nomination in 1962 for a role on the hospital drama *Ben Casey.*

Meanwhile, Scott kept busy in theater as well, appearing in *The Merchant of Venice,* 1962, and *Uncle Vanya,* 1974, among many others. He also starred in and directed *Death of a Salesman* in 1975. His final stage role was in 1996's Broadway revival of *Inherit the Wind,* about the Scopes trial regarding the teaching of evolution in schools, playing a character based on attorney Clarence Darrow. However, he fell ill during the run and missed many performances; it was later learned that he suffered an aortic aneurysm. After recovering, he appeared in a 1997 remake of *Twelve Angry Men* along with Jack Lemmon and Hume Cronyn, and a remake of *Gloria* in 1999. He also starred with Lemmon in a 1999 television version of *Inherit the Wind.*

Scott was married in the 1950s to actresses Carolyn Hughes and then to Patricia Reed, and had two daughters, Victoria and Devon, and a son, Matthew. He also had a child born out of wedlock while in college. In 1960, Scott married actress Colleen Dewhurst, whom he met when they worked together on the play *Children of Darkness*. They divorced in 1965 but remarried in 1967, then divorced again in 1972. They had two sons, Alexander and Campbell. Scott then married Trish Van Devere in 1972. After experiencing declining health, Scott died from a ruptured abdominal aortic aneurysm at age 71 in 1999. He is survived by his wife and six children. **Sources:** *Chicago Tribune,* September 24, 1999; *Contemporary Theatre, Film and Television,* volume 15, Gale Research, 1996; *New York Times,* September 23, 1999; September 24, 1999, p. C20; *USA Today,* September 23, 199;*Washington Post,* September 24, 1999, p. B5.

Hank Snow

Born Clarence Eugene Snow, May 9, 1914, in Brooklyn, Nova Scotia, Canada; died December 20, 1999, in Madison, TN. Country singer. Hank Snow's number–one 1950 hit song "I'm Movin' On" stayed at the top of the charts for 21 weeks and sold a million copies, establishing the expressive baritone as a country mainstay. The tune was recorded in 36 languages and recorded by more than 60 artists, including Elvis Presley, Emmylou Harris, and Ray Charles. About hopping a train to leave a wayward lover, it features the opening lines, "That big eight–wheeler rollin' round the track/Means your true lovin' daddy ain't coming back/I'm movin' on." Born in Canada, Snow moved to the United States in the mid–1940s, becoming a citizen in 1958. With his trademark flashy rhinestone cowboy suits, he was a staple of the Grand Ole Opry in Nashville, Tennessee, until the mid–1990s.

Snow was born in Brooklyn, a village near Liverpool in Nova Scotia, Canada. His parents divorced when he was eight, after which two of his three sisters were sent to an orphanage and he went to live with his grandmother. She physically abused him, so he ran away to reunite with his mother. After returning to his mother, however, his stepfather also beat him, and kicked him out of the house when Snow was just 12. These experiences would later provide fodder for moving tunes like "The Drunkard's Boy" and others. He revealed his troubled childhood in the 1970s, when he formed a foundation to prevent child abuse and neglect and began holding benefit concerts for the cause.

As a mere pre–teen, Snow went to work on fishing boats in the north Atlantic, where he found his talent for entertaining his fellow crew members with his singing, guitar, and harmonica. After nearly drowning during a shipwreck when he was 16, Snow gave up the fishing trade and decided to concentrate on a less risky occupation. Modeling himself after the yodeling country blues artist Jimmie Rodgers, he performed in local bars, where some dubbed him the Yodeling Ranger. Later, as his voice became deeper, he was nicknamed "The Singing Ranger."

In the 1930s, Snow landed a gig singing for a radio station in Halifax, Nova Scotia, on a weekly show called *Down on the Farm*. There, he was billed as Clarence Snow, the Cowboy Blue Yodeler. The station announcer there encouraged him to change his stage name to Hank because it sounded more country. Not long after his radio debut, Snow landed a contract with RCA Victor out of Montreal and recorded *Lonesome Blue Yodel* and *The Prisoned Cowboy*. Though he was a hit in Canada, these and subsequent releases were largely ignored elsewhere.

Electing to outfit himself in flamboyant Western wear, Snow took his act to the United States, where he appeared with a performing horse named Shawnee and tried to break into films. In 1949, he managed to reap a minor success with the hit song "Marriage Vow," but his big opportunity came when country legend Ernest Tubb helped him get into the Grand Ole Opry. Reception to his act was initially mediocre, though, and he was thinking of going back to Canada when success struck. His self–penned "I'm Movin' On" climbed the charts in 1950, cementing his career.

In 1954, Snow formed a booking company with Colonel Tom Parker, the future manager of Elvis Presley. Snow convinced the Grand Ole Opry to showcase Presley, and became something of a mentor to the young rising star. The two sometimes toured together. Subsequently, throughout the 1950s and 1960s, Snow enjoyed his heyday in country music, introducing boogie, rockabilly, Hawaiian music, and Latin sounds while remaining true to his traditional roots.

Although Snow may not be as familiar to younger country fans as performers such as Hank Williams Sr., Ernest Tubb, Roy Acuff, and others, he was a prolific artist who churned out roughly 140 albums and sold some 70 million records, including 85 songs that hit the country charts. Some of his other hits include "I've Been Everywhere," "(Now and Then, There's) A Fool Such as I," "Let Me Go Lover," and "Golden Rocket." He was particularly proud of his work entertaining U.S. troops overseas, singing for soldiers in Germany, Norway, England, Italy, Korea, Japan, and Vietnam. He released his autobiography, *The Hank Snow Story*, in 1994, and began to suffer respiratory illness in 1995. His last public performance was at the Grand Ole Opry in 1996.

Snow was elected to the Country Music Hall of Fame in 1979 and spent nearly 50 years as a member of the Grand Ole Opry radio cast. He was also signed to RCA Records for 45 years, holding the record for the longest time any musician has spent in a recording contract. In addition, according to a *Los Angeles Times* obituary, Snow was the oldest performer to have a number one hit, scoring the top spot at age 61 in 1974 with "Hello Love." In 1936

Snow was married to Minnie Blanch Aalders, and they had a son, Jimmie Rodgers Snow. Snow died of an apparent heart attack at his home, the Rainbow Ranch, in Madison, Tennessee, just outside of Nashville. He is survived by his wife; son; a sister, Marion Peach; and several grandchildren. **Sources:** *Chicago Tribune,* December 21, 1999; *Daily Telegraph,* December 22, 1999; *Los Angeles Times,* December 21, 1999; *New York Times,* December 21, 1999, p. C22; *USA Today,* December 20, 1999; *Washington Times,* December 21, 1999, p. A7.

Payne Stewart

Born January 30, 1957, in Springfield, MO; died October 35, 1999. Professional golfer. Payne Stewart was one of the most colorful golfers on the professional course, literally speaking. Known for his flashy manner of dress, he was easily recognizable in his brightly-colored knickers, argyle socks, Hogan caps, and custom-made alligator- or eel-skin golf shoes. As Rick Reilly put it in a *Sports Illustrated* obituary, comparing him to a legendary flamboyant entertainer, "It was like meeting Liberace's pro." Stewart was also known for his smooth swing, and was enjoying the best year of his career when he was killed at age 42 in an airplane mishap, probably when the jet lost cabin pressure and ran out of oxygen. At the time of his death, he was ranked eighth in the world with career winnings of more than $11 million.

Stewart began playing golf at age four, learning from his traveling furniture salesman father, William Lewis (Bill) Stewart, who had formerly been the Missouri State Amateur Champion and once made it to the 1955 U.S. Open. He also taught his son the value of good sportsmanship and passed along his love of showy apparel. The elder Stewart used to wear loud sport coats, telling his son to "wear something they'll remember," as Reilly reported. Stewart graduated from Southern Methodist University with a business degree in 1979 and immediately became a professional golfer. Failing to immediately obtain his US Tour player's card, though, he went off to Asia, where he won the Indonesian Open and the Indian Open in 1981.

In 1982, Stewart received his tour card and also that year won his first big U.S. event, the Miller High Life Quad Cities Open. It would be the only contest his father would see him win, because he died of cancer in 1985. In 1987, when Stewart won the Hertz Bay Hill Invitational, he donated the prize winnings

(more than $100,000) to a hospital in memory of his father. Also in 1982, Stewart captured the Coolangatta–Tweed Head Classic in Australia, and the next year he won the Walt Disney World Golf Classic.

In 1989, Stewart saw his first major tournament victory at the U.S. Professional Golfers' Association (PGA) Championship at Kemper Lakes outside of Chicago, Illinois, where he beat Mike Reid by one stroke. Following this, in 1991 he took the U.S. Open in Chaska, Minnesota, defeating Scott Simpson in an 18-hole playoff. Subsequently, Stewart entered a slump, seeing only one victory between 1991 and 1998.

At times, Stewart was taken to task for having a brusque manner, avoiding fans and reporters if he was not having a good day, but as his game improved, so did his personality. As time went on, he became known as one of the most personable, charming, and approachable players on tour. Much of Stewart's change in outlook, according to a *New York Times* obituary, stemmed from his recommitment to Christianity, which he embraced in 1998 thanks to his newfound devotion to his family, which included his wife and two children.

In addition to his rich personal life, Stewart's career had markedly improved just before his death. In June of 1999 he won his third major championship, the U.S. Open, and was ranked third on the list of top money earners on the tour, amassing more than $2 million. The victory at the Open signaled his place as one of golf's top contenders. In that event, he sank a 15-foot par putt on the final hole to defeat Phil Mickelson by one stroke. It marked the longest putt to decide Open on the final hole in the 99-year history of the contest. The prior year, he had lost the Open by one stroke to Lee Janzen at the Olympic Club in San Francisco.

Throughout Stewart's 19-year career, he won 18 tournaments worldwide and earned $11.7 million in tour purses, a figure he matched through endorsement deals and appearances. He made his home in Orlando, along with several of his golf colleagues, including Tiger Woods, one of his teammates in the U.S. victory at the 1999 Ryder Cup, an international competition held every two years. Stewart had also been on winning Ryder Cup teams in 1991 and 1993.

On October 25, 1999, Stewart and five others, including two of his agents, two pilots, and a golf course designer, set out in a chartered Learjet from Orlando, Florida, bound for Dallas, Texas. Somewhere along the line, all passengers died, and preliminary investigations concluded that they suffered from a lack of oxygen, most likely because the airplane lost cabin pressure. Once trouble was determined, military jets intercepted the flight and could not see any signs of life on board. The plane apparently flew on autopilot for more than four hours until crashing in a field of cows near Mina, South Dakota.

The National Transportation Safety Board was expected to continue research into the following year to verify the cause of death of the passengers and to examine the fragments of the aircraft, including the pressurization and oxygen systems. Stewart is survived by his Australian–born wife, Tracey; his children Chelsea and Aaron; his mother, Bee, and his sisters, Susan and Lora. **Sources:** *Chicago Tribune,* October 25, 1999; *Dallas Morning News,* November 24, 1999, p. 4A; *Los Angeles Times,* October 26, 1999; *Newsday,* October 29, 1999, p. A22; *New York Times,* October 26, 1999; *People,* November 8, 1999, p. 99; *Sport Illustrated,* November 1, 1999, p. 50; *Times* (London), October 26, 1999; *USA Today,* October 26, 1999; *Washington Post,* October 26, 1999, p. B5.

Derrick Thomas

Born January 1, 1967, in Miami, FL; died February 8, 2000, in Miami, FL. Football player. One of the most respected players in the National Football League (NFL), Kansas City Chiefs linebacker Derrick Thomas was admired for his athletic skills as well as his commitment to his community. Not only did he help turn around the team's fortunes with his terrifying presence against opposing quarterbacks, he also dedicated himself to charity work, earning the 1993 NFL Man of the Year award. On the field, Thomas held the record for most sacks in a single game, at seven, which he set against the Seattle Seahawks in 1990. He was also was ninth on the all–time NFL list for career sacks, with 126.5, and made nine Pro Bowl appearances. Thomas in 1992 was declared one of President George Bush's "1000 Points of Light" for setting up a reading program for disadvantaged children, as well as helping out communities and individuals in other ways.

Thomas was the son of Robert Thomas, an Air Force B–52 pilot whose plane was shot down in Vietnam on December 17, 1972, when his son was five. He had been returning from a mission called Operation Linebacker II. All other occupants of the plane parachuted to safety, and although Thomas's father parachuted out as well, he was never found. In 1980 he was declared legally dead. Thomas later made several trips to the Vietnam Memorial in Washington, D.C. to trace his father's name, and he delivered a moving speech there in 1993.

Growing up, Thomas was raised by his mother and grandmother, and although the family's needs were met by his father's Air Force compensation, at age 14, he was convicted of burglary and car theft and served a few months in a juvenile detention center. As an adult, he credited his stay as a success story of the justice system, and lobbied a subcommittee of the U.S. House of Representatives to increase funding for juvenile justice programs. Thomas went on to become a football all–American at the University of Alabama, setting a school record with 52 career sacks. Afterward, the Kansas City Chiefs drafted him as the fourth choice overall in 1989. The year before he joined the team, their record was 4–11–1, and they had made the playoffs just once in the previous 17 years. Thomas, under Coach Marty Schottenheimer, turned around their fortunes and made the Chiefs one of just three teams to win 100 games during the 1990s. With his size and speed, he was often able to steal the ball out of quarterbacks' hands, a move labeled the "Kansas City Strip."

Though his professional skills made him feared by opponents during games, Thomas was personable and had many friends. He held a reputation for enjoying the good life, socializing with celebrities like Michael Jordan and Chris Rock. However, Thomas was also known for his humanitarian efforts. In 1990 he founded the Third–and–Long Foundation, a reading program for low–income youth. Every Saturday when the Chiefs were in town he would read books to children at local libraries. In addition, he once organized a basketball fundraiser for a boy in Oklahoma with the HIV virus, and though he did not publicize it, he gave generously to various charitable organizations. In 1995 Thomas was honored with the Byron "Whizzer" White Humanitarian Award for service to team, community, and country.

On January 23, 2000, Thomas was critically injured in an automobile accident. En route to the Kansas City airport to travel to St. Louis for the NFC championship game, he was driving his Chevrolet Suburban on an icy highway when he lost control of the vehicle. It rolled over three times, throwing him and longtime friend Michael Tellis out of the side windows. Tellis died in the crash, but another passenger, the only one who was wearing a seat belt, had only minor injuries. Thomas suffered broken vertebrae and a bruised spine, and was paralyzed from the chest down. At Jackson Memorial Hospital in Miami, home of the world's largest spinal cord injury research center, doctors performed surgery, and Thomas soon showed signs of improvement. He aggressively sought rehabilitation, and was optimistic that he would eventually walk again.

However, a couple of weeks after the accident, as Thomas was being transferred from his bed to a wheelchair to be taken to physical therapy, he went into cardiorespiratory arrest and died. Doctors said that he suffered a massive blood clot that traveled through the lungs, not an uncommon complication after such a major trauma. Still, friends, colleagues, and hospital staffers were shocked. He had been up and around in a wheelchair, joking with staffers and visitors, and had even left the hospital the previous weekend. Thomas is survived by his mother, Edith Morgan, who was at his side when he died. **Sources:** *Chicago Tribune*, February 9, 2000; *Los Angeles Times*, February 9, 2000; *New York Times*, February 9, 2000; *USA Today*, February 9, 2000, p. 3C; *Washington Post*, February 9, 2000, p. D1.

Jacobo Timerman

Born January 6, 1923, in Bar, Ukraine; died of a heart attack, November 11, 1999, in Buenos Aires, Argentina. Journalist. Argentinean journalist Jacobo Timerman was the central figure in an international outcry regarding human rights in that nation. The prominent writer and publisher was held captive and tortured for a year and a half in the 1970s as leading humanitarians and groups around the world lobbied for his release. He subsequently wrote a book about the experience and the events leading up to it. *Prisoner Without a Name, Cell Without a Number* was translated into several languages and became a best–seller.

Timerman was born the son of Nathan and Eva Berman Timerman in Bar, Ukraine, then part of the Soviet Union. When he was five, the family fled the pogroms threatening Jews at the time, and relocated to Argentina. There, Timerman grew up in the 11th District of Buenos Aires, the hub of the Jewish community. His father, a clothing vendor, died when he was 12, and he and his brother Jose (Yoselle) worked in maintenance at their tenement building so that they and their mother could live rent–free in their one–room apartment. Timerman also held a job as a courier for a jeweler.

During the 1920s and 1930s, anti–Semitism began to grow in Argentina and elsewhere, as Adolf Hitler's Nazi party rose to power in Germany. Due to his mother's urgings, when Timerman was 14, he joined Avuca, a student group that studied Jewish culture and history. As a result, he became a strong supporter of the idea of a Jewish homeland. Also in his teens, Timerman was influenced by socially conscious authors such as Jack London, John Dos Passos, Upton Sinclair, and others. He also took up Socialist causes and joined the Youth League for Freedom during World War II, which was declared a Communist front and banned. However, Timerman insisted he was never a Communist. The league sided with the Allied forces when Argentina backed Germany.

In college, Timerman studied engineering at the National University of La Plata, but soon switched his major to journalism. He began writing for literary magazines in 1947 at a time when Argentina was filled with political turmoil surrounding the rise and then overthrow of Juan Domingo Peron. Subsequently, during the 1950s and 1960s, Timerman became a nationally– known journalist for the newspaper *La Razon.* He was also involved in radio, television, and magazine work.

Along with some associates, Timerman started up his own weekly news magazine, *Primera Plana* (which means "Front Page"). It was similar to the American publications *Time* and *Newsweek.* He sold it in 1969 and founded a different magazine, *Confirmado,* which he also later sold. In May of 1971 Timerman helped start up *La Opinion,* a popular and respected newspaper. Based along the same lines as the liberal *La Monde* out of Paris, *La Opinion* was embraced by left–leaning intellectuals and appreciated for its arts and culture coverage as well as its pro–Israel commentary. Young financier David Gravier purchased 45 percent of the paper in 1974, allowing Timerman to build a new printing plant and gear up a small publishing firm, Timerman Editores. He would later be criticized for this business relationship, as Gravier was accused of amassing fortunes from investing money obtained from guerilla activities, including kidnapping ransoms and bank robberies.

Known for his strong political opinions and harsh criticism of the Argentinean military government, Timerman would regularly publish lists of names of citizens who were missing and presumed to be illegally imprisoned. An estimated ten percent were Jewish. Due to his outspoken nature and, likely, his Jewish heritage, Timerman and his paper became a target of the government as well as forces on the right and the terrorist left. Reporters were harassed and sometimes kidnapped.

Timerman was finally arrested in April of 1977 by a cadre of armed civilians on orders from the army, who vaguely accused him of a Jewish plot. For more than a year, he was held captive, interrogated, given electrical shocks to his genitals, and frequently put in solitary confinement. He suffered through several mock executions. Afterward, he and his family were put under house arrest for 17 months. Meanwhile, international support for his release grew. Numerous dignitaries and institutions campaigned for his rights, including former Secretary of State Henry Kissinger, President Jimmy Carter, author Aleksandr Solzhenitsyn, Amnesty International, and the Vatican.

Although two Supreme Court decisions found Timerman innocent, in September of 1979, his Argentinean citizenship was revoked and he was exiled to Israel. He later left Israel after citing what he considered to be attacks on civil liberties there, and lived in Manhattan and Spain until 1983. That year, a democratic government came to power in Argentina and eventually restored his citizenship. Timerman in 1986 testified against his former captors and sued for compensation for the loss of his newspaper. The government reimbursed him $5 million, and he established homes in Buenos Aires and the resort of Punta del Este, Uruguay.

In 1981, the English translation of Timerman's best-selling book, *Prisoner Without a Name, Cell Without a Number,* was published, outlining his ordeal. It provoked much controversy for his opinion that prominent Argentinean Jews did not speak out enough against his persecution. Later, Timerman wrote three more works. *The Longest War: Israel in Lebanon,* 1982, criticizes Israel's invasion and occupation of Lebanon, while *Chile: Death in the South,* 1987, is a harsh diatribe on General Augusto Pinochet's dictatorship. His 1990 work, *Cuba: A Journey,* explores the Cuban revolution.

Shortly after his exile from Argentina, in 1979 Timerman received the David Ben–Gurion Award from the United Jewish Appeal and the Hubert H. Humphrey Freedom Prize from the Anti–Defamation League of B'Nai B'rith. The next year he was awarded the Golden Pen of Freedom from the International Federation of Newspaper Publishers. Timerman was married to pianist Risha (sometimes spelled Riche) Mindlin in 1950, and they had three sons, Daniel, Hector, and Javier. Timerman suffered two heart attacks in 1999, the second one fatal. His wife died in 1991, and he is survived by his sons and eight grandchildren. **Sources:** *Chicago Tribune,* November 12, 1999, sec. 2, p. 11; "Jacobo Timerman," *Contemporary Authors Online,* Gale Group web site, http://www.galenet.com (March 6, 2000); *Dictionary of Hispanic Biography,* Gale Research, 1996;

Encyclopedia of World Biography, second edition, Gale Research, 1998; *Los Angeles Times,* November 12, 1999, p. A30; *New York Times,* November 12, 1999, p. B11; *Washington Post,* November 12, 1999, p. B6.

Franjo Tudjman

Born May 14, 1922, in Veliko–Trgovisce, Croatia; died of stomach cancer, December 10, 1999, in Croatia. Croatian leader. Franjo Tudjman, president of Croatia from 1990 until his death in 1999, was one of the most influential people involved in the breakup of the six republics that formed the Yugoslav Federation. He was one of the key players in the war in the Balkans during the 1990s. After leading the Croatian movement for independence in 1991, Tudjman then found his nation engaged in a civil war between the Croats and the Serb minority; he was one of three to sign a peace accord in 1995. Despite accusations of corruption and human rights offenses, Tudjman was revered by many in his country for leading them to independence.

Tudjman was born on May 14, 1922, in Veliko–Trgovisce, Croatia, in the hills north of Zagreb in the Zagorje region. When he was seven, his mother died, and his father, Stjepan, later married again. The elder Tudjman was a landlord and the chief administrator for his village. He was also active in the Croatian Peasant Party, which sought land reform and an end to what they thought was Serb domination of the new state known as the Kingdom of Serbs, Croats, and Slovenes. This first Yugoslav nation was formed three–and–a–half years before Tudjman was born.

In 1941, Nazi Germany invaded Yugoslavia, and Tudjman and his two brothers joined their father as Communist Partisans under Josip Broz, known as Tito. The movement led a guerilla uprising against the Nazis and the Ustashe, the extreme nationalist Croatian army that killed at least half a million Serbs, Jews, and Gypsies in concentration camps, according to historians. Tudjman's youngest brother died in the struggle against these forces, but he emerged from the war as one of Tito's youngest and most promising generals. However, in 1946 his father and stepfather were found shot to death in what authorities called a double suicide. Later, in the 1980s, Tudjman would insist that the Communist party had killed them because of their Croatian nationalist views.

Meanwhile, in 1944, Tudjman was made a political commissar of the 32nd Partisan Division and became a trusted ally of Tito. He attended the Yugoslav High Military Academy in Belgrade after World War II, and in 1955 published *War Against War,* a book about guerilla warfare and the first of his several works on history. In 1960, at age 38, he became the youngest peacetime major general in Yugoslavia's history. The next year, however, propelled by his desire to write, he quit the army to devote himself to academic research in military and political history. With help from Tito and the Communist leadership, he landed a post as director of the Institute of the History of the Working Class Movement in Croatia. In addition, from 1963 to 1967 he served as an associate professor of history at the University of Zagreb. That school rejected his doctoral dissertation in 1964, but the next year, it was accepted at the less–prestigious university at Zadar.

Becoming increasingly nationalist in his ideas, Tudjman broke with Tito and was expelled from the Communist party. After attending Harvard University briefly on a fellowship, he was arrested in 1972 when Tito cracked down on nationalism after a short–lived upsurge. Sentenced to two years in prison, he was released after ten months thanks to an appeal from a prominent Croatian writer, Miroslav Krleza. Still, Tudjman continued to publish his heavily nationalist works. His most controversial book was 1989's *Impasses of Historical Reality* (also translated as *Wastelands of Historic Truth*) in which he concluded that less than 60,000 were killed in the Croatian death camp at Jasenovac. He also asserted that estimates of six million Jews being killed in the Holocaust were "emotional" and "exaggerated," according to a *Washington Post* obituary by Michael Dobbs. The work also perpetuated negative stereotypes of Jews, although later Tudjman issued an apology for his remarks.

Due to a strong increase in nationalism in neighboring Serbia, Tudjman in 1989 helped found the Croatian Democratic Union (known by its acronym, the HDZ party), a nationalist group calling for Croatian separatism. In February of 1990, the group elected him president, and that April, he won a seat in parliament in the country's first free elections. The parliament then elected him president, and he won a second term in 1992. Under Tudjman's leadership, the economy suffered and the United Nations accused his government of human rights abuses. Many Serbs, which made up about 12 percent of citizens, were dismissed from government jobs. Additionally, he greatly upset Western governments as well as Serbs when he commented, "Thank God my wife is not a Serb or a Jew" during the 1990 elections, according to Dobbs.

On June 25, 1991, Croatia declared its independence from Yugoslavia, becoming a sovereign state after 900 years of rule by others. Subsequently, a civil war ensued pitting the Serb minority against the Croats. Despite a truce in January of 1992, the fighting continued. Eventually, Croatia was successful in driving out ethnic Serbs from what Tudjman felt was Croatian territory, even though Croatia lost about a third of its land in the battles. In 1995, he signed a peace accord in Dayton, Ohio, along with Serbian leader Slobodan Milosevic and Alija Izetbegovic of the Bosnian Muslims.

Throughout his reign as president, Tudjman attracted reproach for his lavish lifestyle and his attachment to an elaborate manner of dress. Attired in a white dress uniform, very similar to Tito's, he appeared incessantly on state television. His vacations were spent on Tito's yacht and at his palace on the private Brioni Island. Despite evidence that he had a serious illness, Tudjman won reelection to another five–year term in June of 1997, capturing 61 percent of the popular vote. After suffering from stomach cancer for three years, however, he died at age 77 in a Croatian clinic. He is survived by his wife, Ankica; two sons, Miroslav and Stjepan; a daughter, Nevenka Kosutic; and three grandchildren. **Sources:** "Croatian President Tudjman dies at 77," December 11, 1999, CNN web site, http://cnn.com (December 13, 1999); *Current Leaders of Nations,* Gale Research, 1998; *Encyclopedia of World Biography,* second edition, Gale Research, 1998; *Los Angeles Times,* December 11, 1999; *New York Times,* December 11, 1999; *Washington Post,* December 11, 1999, p. A1.

Jim Varney

Born June 15, 1949, in Lexington, KY; died of lung cancer, February 10, 2000, in White House, TN. Actor. Jim Varney will forever be linked with the character of Ernest P. Worrell, known to television and movie fans for his nasally, run–together catch phrase, "KnowhutImean, Vern?" The rubber–faced actor gained recognition in commercials for playing the dimwitted Ernest, a hayseed who incessantly bombards his unseen neighbor, Vern, with rapid–fire, well–intentioned advice. His ads showcased the kind of physical humor that involved Ernest falling off of ladders, smashing his fingers in a window, or getting shocked by a television set. In one estimate, Varney figured he had appeared in about 3,000 ads. The actor parlayed the cult appeal of the regional commercials into a full–fledged Hollywood career, starring in a series of films featuring Ernest.

Varney was born in Lexington, Kentucky, and began acting at age eight in local theater. By age 16, he appeared professionally in a regional production of Shakespeare's *A Midsummer Night's Dream* as Puck. At 18, he left for New York City and found work off–Broadway and in dinner theater, appearing in plays like *Death of a Salesman* and *Guys and Dolls.* He also did stand–up comedy. In the 1970s he landed roles on television series such as *Fernwood 2–Night* and *Operation Petticoat.* He got his big break, though, in commercials.

In 1980, during an actors' strike, Varney returned to Kentucky and met with John Cherry, an executive at the Carden & Cherry Advertising Agency. Cherry was trying to concoct a television ad for an amusement park so dilapidated that he did not want to show it in the spot. He created a character who would portray a happy park patron, and hired Varney for the part. At first, viewers hated the silly, motor–mouth Ernest, but in a couple of weeks he began to catch on. Though Carden & Cherry assumed that Ernest would catch on mainly with Southern audiences, they found that his appeal spanned the nation and could be applied to a range of products. Eventually Varney appeared in ads for ice cream, Toyotas, gas stations, fast food, soft drinks, cereal, and furniture stores. The agency usually filmed him using a wide–angle lens in order to exaggerate his already comical expressions. The actor's standard apparel consisted of faded jeans, a denim vest, a T–shirt, and baseball cap. "It's a lovely outfit that can be worn gracefully six days a week," he once explained, according to a *Los Angeles Times* obituary.

Breaking into film, Varney's first big–screen role was in the 1986 spoof *Dr. Otto and the Riddle of the Gloom Beam,* playing Ernest and a host of other characters. He cowrote the script and financed the effort with Cherry, who directed the independently distributed picture. After that, they found backing for the next two Ernest films, *Ernest Goes to Camp,* 1987, and *Ernest Saves Christmas,* 1988. These two were picked up by Disney and made into box–office hits. *Camp* made $24 million on a budget for $3.5 million, and *Christmas* earned $28 million on a budget of $6 million.

After this beginning, Varney made three more films for Disney, and five other independent Ernest features for television and video. These included *Ernest Goes to Jail,* 1990; *Ernest Scared Stupid,* 1991; *Ernest Rides Again,* 1993; *Ernest Goes to School,* 1994; *Slam Dunk Ernest,* 1995; *Ernest Goes to Africa,* 1997; and *Ernest in the Army,* 1998. The Ernest character spawned tie–in products, such as *Ernest P. Worrell's Book of Knawledge,* a line of greeting cards, and a talking doll. Also, in 1988 Varney hosted the Saturday morning show, *Hey, Vern, It's Ernest,* for which he won an Emmy Award for outstanding performer in a children's series. However, it was canceled after one season due to low ratings. Meanwhile, Varney began to branch out from being only Ernest, landing the high–profile role of family patriarch Jed Clampett in the film version of *The Beverly Hillbillies,* 1993. He also provided the voice of Slinky Dog in the computer animation feature films *Toy Story,* 1996, and *Toy Story 2,* 1999.

In August of 1998, Varney learned he had lung cancer, and subsequently had two–thirds of his right lung removed. The cancer spread to his brain within months. The disease appeared to be in remission in 1999, and he was cast that year in the film *Daddy and Them,* starring Billy Bob Thornton. In February of the next year, at age 50, he died of cancer at his home in White House, Tennessee, about 20 miles north of Nashville. He was twice divorced. **Sources:** *Chicago Tribune,* February 11, 2000; *Contemporary Newsmakers,* 1985 Cumulation, Gale Research, 1986; *Contemporary Theatre, Film, and Television,* volume 11, Gale Research, 1993; *Entertainment Weekly,* April 13, 1990, p. 46; *Los Angeles Times,* February 11, 2000, p. A48; *New York Times,* February 11, 2000; *Washington Post,* February 11, 2000, p. B7.

2000 Nationality Index

This index lists all newsmakers alphabetically under their respective nationalities. Indexes in softbound issues allow access to the current year's entries; indexes in annual hardbound volumes are cumulative, covering the entire *Newsmakers* series.

Listee names are followed by a year and issue number; thus **1996**:4 indicates that an entry on that individual appears in both 1996, Issue 4 and the 1996 cumulation. For access to newsmakers appearing earlier than the current softbound issue, see the previous year's cumulation.

ALGERIAN
    Zeroual, Liamine **1996**:2

AMERICAN
    Abbey, Edward
        Obituary **1989**:3
    Abbott, George
        Obituary **1995**:3
    Abbott, Jim **1988**:3
    Abdul, Paula **1990**:3
    Abercrombie, Josephine **1987**:2
    Abernathy, Ralph
        Obituary **1990**:3
    Abraham, Spencer **1991**:4
    Abrams, Elliott **1987**:1
    Abramson, Lyn **1986**:3
    Abzug, Bella **1998**:2
    Achtenberg, Roberta **1993**:4
    Ackerman, Will **1987**:4
    Acuff, Roy
        Obituary **1993**:2
    Adair, Red **1987**:3
    Adams, Patch **1999**:2
    Adams, Scott **1996**:4
    Addams, Charles
        Obituary **1989**:1
    Affleck, Ben **1999**:1
    Agassi, Andre **1990**:2
    Agnew, Spiro Theodore
        Obituary **1997**:1
    Aguilera, Christina **2000**:4
    Aiello, Danny **1990**:4
    Aikman, Troy **1994**:2
    Ailes, Roger **1989**:3
    Ailey, Alvin **1989**:2
        Obituary **1990**:2
    Ainge, Danny **1987**:1
    Akers, John F. **1988**:3
    Akers, Michelle **1996**:1
    Akin, Phil
        Brief Entry **1987**:3
    Albee, Edward **1997**:1
    Albert, Marv **1994**:3
    Albert, Stephen **1986**:1
    Albom, Mitch **1999**:3
    Albright, Madeleine **1994**:3

Alda, Robert
    Obituary **1986**:3
Alexander, Jane **1994**:2
Alexander, Jason **1993**:3
Alexander, Lamar **1991**:2
Alexie, Sherman **1998**:4
Ali, Muhammad **1997**:2
Alioto, Joseph L.
    Obituary **1998**:3
Allaire, Paul **1995**:1
Allen, Bob **1992**:4
Allen, Debbie **1998**:2
Allen, Joan **1998**:1
Allen, John **1992**:1
Allen, Mel
    Obituary **1996**:4
Allen, Tim **1993**:1
Allen, Woody **1994**:1
Alley, Kirstie **1990**:3
Allred, Gloria **1985**:2
Alter, Hobie
    Brief Entry **1985**:1
Altman, Robert **1993**:2
Altman, Sidney **1997**:2
Alvarez, Aida **1999**:2
Ameche, Don
    Obituary **1994**:2
Amory, Cleveland
    Obituary **1999**:2
Amos, Tori **1995**:1
Amos, Wally **2000**:1
Amsterdam, Morey
    Obituary **1997**:1
Anastas, Robert
    Brief Entry **1985**:2
Ancier, Garth **1989**:1
Anderson, Gillian **1997**:1
Anderson, Harry **1988**:2
Anderson, Laurie **2000**:2
Anderson, Marion
    Obituary **1993**:4
Andreessen, Marc **1996**:2
Andrews, Maxene
    Obituary **1996**:2
Angelos, Peter **1995**:4
Angelou, Maya **1993**:4
Angier, Natalie **2000**:3

Aniston, Jennifer **2000**:3
Annenberg, Walter **1992**:3
Anthony, Marc **2000**:3
Antonini, Joseph **1991**:2
Applegate, Christina **2000**:4
Applewhite, Marshall Herff
    Obituary **1997**:3
Archer, Dennis **1994**:4
Arden, Eve
    Obituary **1991**:2
Aretsky, Ken **1988**:1
Arison, Ted **1990**:3
Arledge, Roone **1992**:2
Arlen, Harold
    Obituary **1986**:3
Arman **1993**:1
Armstrong, Henry
    Obituary **1989**:1
Armstrong, Lance **2000**:1
Arnaz, Desi
    Obituary **1987**:1
Arnold, Tom **1993**:2
Arquette, Rosanna **1985**:2
Arrau, Claudio
    Obituary **1992**:1
Arrested Development **1994**:2
Arthur, Jean
    Obituary **1992**:1
Ash, Mary Kay **1996**:1
Ashe, Arthur
    Obituary **1993**:3
Aspin, Les
    Obituary **1996**:1
Astaire, Fred
    Obituary **1987**:4
Astor, Mary
    Obituary **1988**:1
Atwater, Lee **1989**:4
    Obituary **1991**:4
Aurre, Laura
    Brief Entry **1986**:3
Autry, Gene
    Obituary **1999**:1
Avedon, Richard **1993**:4
Axthelm, Pete
    Obituary **1991**:3
Aykroyd, Dan **1989**:3 **1997**:3

Azinger, Paul **1995**:2
Babbitt, Bruce **1994**:1
Babilonia, Tai **1997**:2
Bacall, Lauren **1997**:3
Backus, Jim
  Obituary **1990**:1
Bacon, Kevin **1995**:3
Badu, Erykah **2000**:4
Baez, Joan **1998**:3
Bailey, F. Lee **1995**:4
Bailey, Pearl
  Obituary **1991**:1
Baird, Bill
  Brief Entry **1987**:2
Baiul, Oksana **1995**:3
Baker, Anita **1987**:4
Baker, James A. III **1991**:2
Baker, Kathy
  Brief Entry **1986**:1
Bakker, Robert T. **1991**:3
Baldessari, John **1991**:4
Baldrige, Malcolm
  Obituary **1988**:1
Baldwin, James
  Obituary **1988**:2
Ball, Edward **1999**:2
Ball, Lucille
  Obituary **1989**:3
Ballard, Robert D. **1998**:4
Ballmer, Steven **1997**:2
Banks, Dennis J. **1986**:4
Banks, Jeffrey **1998**:2
Banks, Tyra **1996**:3
Barad, Jill **1994**:2
Baraka, Amiri **2000**:3
Barber, Red
  Obituary **1993**:2
Barbera, Joseph **1988**:2
Barkin, Ellen **1987**:3
Barkley, Charles **1988**:2
Barksdale, James L. **1998**:2
Barnes, Ernie **1997**:4
Barney **1993**:4
Barr, Roseanne **1989**:1
Barrett, Craig R. **1999**:4
Barry, Dave **1991**:2
Barry, Lynda **1992**:1
Barry, Marion **1991**:1
Barrymore, Drew **1995**:3
Barshefsky, Charlene **2000**:4
Baryshnikov, Mikhail Nikolaevich
  1997:3
Basie, Count
  Obituary **1985**:1
Basinger, Kim **1987**:2
Bassett, Angela **1994**:4
Bateman, Justine **1988**:4
Bates, Kathy **1991**:4
Battle, Kathleen **1998**:1
Bauer, Eddie
  Obituary **1986**:3
Baumgartner, Bruce
  Brief Entry **1987**:3
Baxter, Anne
  Obituary **1986**:1
Bayley, Corrine
  Brief Entry **1986**:4
Beals, Vaughn **1988**:2
Bean, Alan L. **1986**:2
Beattie, Owen
  Brief Entry **1985**:2
Beatty, Warren **2000**:1

Beck **2000**:2
Beers, Charlotte **1999**:3
Begaye, Kelsey **1999**:3
Bell, Art **2000**:1
Bell, Ricky
  Obituary **1985**:1
Belle, Albert **1996**:4
Belushi, Jim **1986**:2
Belzer, Richard **1985**:3
Ben & Jerry **1991**:3
Benatar, Pat **1986**:1
Bening, Annette **1992**:1
Bennett, Joan
  Obituary **1991**:2
Bennett, Michael
  Obituary **1988**:1
Bennett, Tony **1994**:4
Bennett, William **1990**:1
Benoit, Joan **1986**:3
Benson, Ezra Taft
  Obituary **1994**:4
Bentsen, Lloyd **1993**:3
Bergalis, Kimberly
  Obituary **1992**:3
Bergen, Candice **1990**:1
Berger, Sandy **2000**:1
Berle, Peter A.A.
  Brief Entry **1987**:3
Berlin, Irving
  Obituary **1990**:1
Bernardi, Herschel
  Obituary **1986**:4
Bernardin, Cardinal Joseph **1997**:2
Bernhard, Sandra **1989**:4
Bernsen, Corbin **1990**:2
Bernstein, Leonard
  Obituary **1991**:1
Berresford, Susan V. **1998**:4
Berry, Halle **1996**:2
Bettelheim, Bruno
  Obituary **1990**:3
Bezos, Jeff **1998**:4
Bialik, Mayim **1993**:3
Bias, Len
  Obituary **1986**:3
Biden, Joe **1986**:3
Bieber, Owen **1986**:1
Biehl, Amy
  Obituary **1994**:1
Bigelow, Kathryn **1990**:4
Bikoff, James L.
  Brief Entry **1986**:2
Billington, James **1990**:3
Bird, Larry **1990**:3
Bishop, Andre **2000**:1
Bissell, Patrick
  Obituary **1988**:2
Bixby, Bill
  Obituary **1994**:2
Black, Cathleen **1998**:4
Blackmun, Harry A.
  Obituary **1999**:3
Blackstone, Harry Jr.
  Obituary **1997**:4
Blair, Bonnie **1992**:3
Blakey, Art
  Obituary **1991**:1
Blanc, Mel
  Obituary **1989**:4
Bledsoe, Drew **1995**:1
Blige, Mary J. **1995**:3
Bloch, Erich **1987**:4

Bloch, Henry **1988**:4
Bloch, Ivan **1986**:3
Bloodworth-Thomason, Linda
  1994 :1
Bloomberg, Michael **1997**:1
Blume, Judy **1998**:4
Bly, Robert **1992**:4
Bochco, Steven **1989**:1
Boggs, Wade **1989**:3
Bogosian, Eric **1990**:4
Boiardi, Hector
  Obituary **1985**:3
Boitano, Brian **1988**:3
Bolger, Ray
  Obituary **1987**:2
Bolton, Michael **1993**:2
Bombeck, Erma
  Obituary **1996**:4
Bonds, Barry **1993**:3
Bonet, Lisa **1989**:2
Bonilla, Bobby **1992**:2
Bon Jovi, Jon **1987**:4
Bono, Sonny **1992**:2
  Obituary **1998**:2
Boone, Mary **1985**:1
Booth, Shirley
  Obituary **1993**:2
Bopp, Thomas **1997**:3
Bose, Amar
  Brief Entry **1986**:4
Bosworth, Brian **1989**:1
Botstein, Leon **1985**:3
Bowe, Riddick **1993**:2
Bowles, Paul
  Obituary **2000**:3
Bowman, Scotty **1998**:4
Boxcar Willie
  Obituary **1999**:4
Boxer, Barbara **1995**:1
Boyer, Herbert Wayne **1985**:1
Boyington, Gregory Pappy
  Obituary **1988**:2
Boyle, Gertrude **1995**:3
Bradley, Bill **2000**:2
Bradley, Tom
  Obituary **1999**:1
Bradshaw, John **1992**:1
Brady, Sarah and James S. **1991**:4
Brandy **1996**:4
Braun, Carol Moseley **1993**:1
Bravo, Ellen **1998**:2
Braxton, Toni **1994**:3
Bremen, Barry **1987**:3
Brennan, Edward A. **1989**:1
Brennan, Robert E. **1988**:1
Brennan, William
  Obituary **1997**:4
Breyer, Stephen Gerald **1994**:4
  1997:2
Bridges, Llyod
  Obituary **1998**:3
Bristow, Lonnie **1996**:1
Brokaw, Tom **2000**:3
Bronfman, Edgar, Jr. **1994**:4
Brooks, Albert **1991**:4
Brooks, Diana D. **1990**:1
Brooks, Garth **1992**:1
Brooks, Gwendolyn **1998**:1
Brower, David **1990**:4
Brown, Edmund G., Sr.
  Obituary **1996**:3
Brown, James **1991**:4

Duke, Red
  Brief Entry **1987**:1
Duncan, Tim **2000**:1
Duncan, Todd
  Obituary **1998**:3
Dunlap, Albert J. **1997**:2
Dunne, Dominick **1997**:1
Dupri, Jermaine **1999**:1
Durocher, Leo
  Obituary **1992**:2
Durrell, Gerald
  Obituary **1995**:3
Duval, David **2000**:3
Duvall, Camille
  Brief Entry **1988**:1
Duvall, Robert **1999**:3
Dykstra, Lenny **1993**:4
Dylan, Bob **1998**:1
Eastwood, Clint **1993**:3
Eaton, Robert J. **1994**:2
Eazy-E
  Obituary **1995**:3
Ebert, Roger **1998**:3
Eckstine, Billy
  Obituary **1993**:4
Edelman, Marian Wright **1990**:4
Edmonds, Kenneth Babyface **1995**:3
Edwards, Bob **1993**:2
Edwards, Harry **1989**:4
Ehrlichman, John
  Obituary **1999**:3
Eilberg, Amy
  Brief Entry **1985**:3
Eisenman, Peter **1992**:4
Eisenstaedt, Alfred
  Obituary **1996**:1
Eisner, Michael **1989**:2
Elders, Joycelyn **1994**:1
Eldridge, Roy
  Obituary **1989**:3
Elfman, Jenna **1999**:4
Ellerbee, Linda **1993**:3
Ellis, Perry
  Obituary **1986**:3
Ellison, Ralph
  Obituary **1994**:4
Elway, John **1990**:3
Engelbreit, Mary **1994**:3
Engler, John **1996**:3
Englund, Richard
  Obituary **1991**:3
Engstrom, Elmer W.
  Obituary **1985**:2
Ephron, Henry
  Obituary **1993**:2
Ephron, Nora **1992**:3
Epps, Omar **2000**:4
Epstein, Jason **1991**:1
Ertegun, Ahmet **1986**:3
Ervin, Sam
  Obituary **1985**:2
Esiason, Boomer **1991**:1
Estefan, Gloria **1991**:4
Estes, Pete
  Obituary **1988**:3
Estevez, Emilio **1985**:4
Estrich, Susan **1989**:1
Etheridge, Melissa **1995**:4
Evans, Janet **1989**:1
Evans, Joni **1991**:4
Evans, Nancy **2000**:4
Evers-Williams, Myrlie **1995**:4

Ewing, Patrick **1985**:3
Factor, Max
  Obituary **1996**:4
Fagan, Garth **2000**:1
Fairbanks, Douglas, Jr.
  Obituary **2000**:4
Fairstein, Linda **1991**:1
Falkenberg, Nanette **1985**:2
Faludi, Susan **1992**:4
Farley, Chris
  Obituary **1998**:2
Farmer, James
  Obituary **2000**:1
Farrakhan, Louis **1990**:4
Farrell, Perry **1992**:2
Farrell, Suzanne **1996**:3
Farrow, Mia **1998**:3
Faubus, Orval
  Obituary **1995**:2
Faulkner, Shannon **1994**:4
Favre, Brett Lorenzo **1997**:2
Fawcett, Farrah **1998**:4
Fehr, Donald **1987**:2
Feinstein, Dianne **1993**:3
Feld, Eliot **1996**:1
Feld, Kenneth **1988**:2
Feldman, Sandra **1987**:3
Fell, Norman
  Obituary **1999**:2
Fender, Leo
  Obituary **1992**:1
Fenley, Molissa **1988**:3
Fenwick, Millicent H.
  Obituary **1993**:2
Fernandez, Joseph **1991**:3
Ferraro, Geraldine **1998**:3
Ferrell, Trevor
  Brief Entry **1985**:2
Fertel, Ruth **2000**:2
Fetchit, Stepin
  Obituary **1986**:1
Field, Sally **1995**:3
Fielder, Cecil **1993**:2
Fields, Debbi **1987**:3
Filo, David and Jerry Yang **1998**:3
Finley, Karen **1992**:4
Fiorina, Carleton S. **2000**:1
Fireman, Paul
  Brief Entry **1987**:2
Firestone, Roy **1988**:2
Fish, Hamilton
  Obituary **1991**:3
Fishburne, Laurence **1995**:3
Fisher, Carrie **1991**:1
Fisher, Mary **1994**:3
Fisher, Mel **1985**:4
Fitzgerald, A. Ernest **1986**:2
Fitzgerald, Ella
  Obituary **1996**:4
Flanders, Ed
  Obituary **1995**:3
Flatley, Michael **1997**:3
Fleming, Art
  Obituary **1995**:4
Flockhart, Calista **1998**:4
Flood, Curt
  Obituary **1997**:2
Florio, James J. **1991**:2
Flutie, Doug **1999**:2
Flynn, Ray **1989**:1
Flynt, Larry **1997**:3
Foley, Thomas S. **1990**:1

Folkman, Judah **1999**:1
Fomon, Robert M. **1985**:3
Fonda, Bridget **1995**:1
Foote, Shelby **1991**:2
Forbes, Malcolm S.
  Obituary **1990**:3
Forbes, Steve **1996**:2
Ford, Harrison **1990**:2
Ford, Henry II
  Obituary **1988**:1
Ford, Tennessee Ernie
  Obituary **1992**:2
Ford, Tom **1999**:3
Ford, William Clay, Jr. **1999**:1
Foreman, Dave **1990**:3
Forsythe, William **1993**:2
Foss, Joe **1990**:3
Fosse, Bob
  Obituary **1988**:1
Fossey, Dian
  Obituary **1986**:1
Foster, David **1988**:2
Foster, Jodie **1989**:2
Foster, Phil
  Obituary **1985**:3
Foster, Tabatha
  Obituary **1988**:3
Foster, Vincent
  Obituary **1994**:1
Fox, Matthew **1992**:2
Fox, Vivica **1999**:1
Foxworthy, Jeff **1996**:1
Foxx, Redd
  Obituary **1992**:2
France, Johnny
  Brief Entry **1987**:1
Franciscus, James
  Obituary **1992**:1
Frank, Barney **1989**:2
Frank, Robert **1995**:2
Franken, Al **1996**:3
Frankenthaler, Helen **1990**:1
Franklin, Aretha **1998**:3
Franklin, Melvin
  Obituary **1995**:3
Franz, Dennis **1995**:2
Fraser, Brendan **2000**:1
Freeh, Louis J. **1994**:2
Freeman, Cliff **1996**:1
Freeman, Morgan **1990**:4
Freleng, Friz
  Obituary **1995**:4
Friedan, Betty **1994**:2
Fudge, Ann **2000**:3
Fulbright, J. William
  Obituary **1995**:3
Fulghum, Robert **1996**:1
Funt, Allen
  Obituary **2000**:1
Furman, Rosemary
  Brief Entry **1986**:4
Futrell, Mary Hatwood **1986**:1
Futter, Ellen V. **1995**:1
Gabor, Eva
  Obituary **1996**:1
Gacy, John Wayne
  Obituary **1994**:4
Gaines, William M.
  Obituary **1993**:1
Gale, Robert Peter **1986**:4
Gallo, Robert **1991**:1
Galvin, John R. **1990**:1

Galvin, Martin
   Brief Entry **1985**:3
Garbo, Greta
   Obituary **1990**:3
Garcia, Andy **1999**:3
Garcia, Cristina **1997**:4
Garcia, Jerry **1988**:3
   Obituary **1996**:1
Garcia, Joe
   Brief Entry **1986**:4
'Gardner, Ava Lavinia
   Obituary **1990**:2
Gardner, Randy **1997**:2
Garnett, Kevin **2000**:3
Garofalo, Janeane **1996**:4
Garr, Teri **1988**:4
Garrison, Jim
   Obituary **1993**:2
Garson, Greer
   Obituary **1996**:4
Garzarelli, Elaine M. **1992**:3
Gates, Bill **1993**:3 **1987**:4
Gates, Robert M. **1992**:2
Gathers, Hank
   Obituary **1990**:3
Gault, Willie **1991**:2
Gebbie, Kristine **1994**:2
Geffen, David **1985**:3 **1997**:3
Gehry, Frank O. **1987**:1
Geisel, Theodor
   Obituary **1992**:2
Gellar, Sarah Michelle **1999**:3
Geller, Margaret Joan **1998**:2
Gephardt, Richard **1987**:3
Gerba, Charles **1999**:4
Gere, Richard **1994**:3
Gergen, David **1994**:1
Gerstner, Lou **1993**:4
Gertz, Alison
   Obituary **1993**:2
Gerulaitis, Vitas
   Obituary **1995**:1
Getz, Stan
   Obituary **1991**:4
Giamatti, A. Bartlett **1988**:4
   Obituary **1990**:1
Gibson, Kirk **1985**:2
Gibson, William Ford, III **1997**:2
Gifford, Kathie Lee **1992**:2
Gilbert, Walter **1988**:3
Gilford, Jack
   Obituary **1990**:4
Gill, Vince **1995**:2
Gillespie, Dizzy
   Obituary **1993**:2
Gillespie, Marcia **1999**:4
Gillett, George **1988**:1
Gingrich, Newt **1991**:1 **1997**:3
Ginsberg, Allen
   Obituary **1997**:3
Ginsburg, Ruth Bader **1993**:4
Gish, Lillian
   Obituary **1993**:4
Giuliani, Rudolph **1994**:2
Glaser, Elizabeth
   Obituary **1995**:2
Glass, David **1996**:1
Glass, Philip **1991**:4
Glasser, Ira **1989**:1
Gleason, Jackie
   Obituary **1987**:4
Glenn, John **1998**:3

Gless, Sharon **1989**:3
Glover, Danny **1998**:4
Glover, Savion **1997**:1
Gobel, George
   Obituary **1991**:4
Gober, Robert **1996**:3
Goetz, Bernhard Hugo **1985**:3
Goizueta, Roberto **1996**:1
   Obituary **1998**:1
Goldberg, Gary David **1989**:4
Goldberg, Leonard **1988**:4
Goldberg, Whoopi **1993**:3
Goldblum, Jeff **1988**:1 **1997**:3
Goldhaber, Fred
   Brief Entry **1986**:3
Goldwater, Barry
   Obituary **1998**:4
Gomez, Lefty
   Obituary **1989**:3
Gooden, Dwight **1985**:2
Gooding, Cuba, Jr. **1997**:3
Goodman, Benny
   Obituary **1986**:3
Goodman, John **1990**:3
Goody, Joan **1990**:2
Goody, Sam
   Obituary **1992**:1
Gordon, Dexter **1987**:1 **1990**:4
Gordon, Gale
   Obituary **1996**:1
Gordon, Jeff **1996**:1
Gore, Albert, Jr. **1993**:2
Gore, Albert, Sr.
   Obituary **1999**:2
Gore, Tipper **1985**:4
Goren, Charles H.
   Obituary **1991**:4
Gorman, Leon
   Brief Entry **1987**:1
Gossett, Louis, Jr. **1989**:3
Gould, Chester
   Obituary **1985**:2
Gould, Gordon **1987**:1
Grace, J. Peter **1990**:2
Grafton, Sue **2000**:2
Graham, Bill **1986**:4
   Obituary **1992**:2
Graham, Billy **1992**:1
Graham, Donald **1985**:4
Graham, Heather **2000**:1
Graham, Katharine Meyer **1997**:3
Graham, Martha
   Obituary **1991**:4
Gramm, Phil **1995**:2
Grammer, Kelsey **1995**:1
Granato, Cammi **1999**:3
Grange, Red
   Obituary **1991**:3
Grant, Amy **1985**:4
Grant, Cary
   Obituary **1987**:1
Grant, Charity
   Brief Entry **1985**:2
Grant, Rodney A. **1992**:1
Graves, Michael **2000**:1
Graves, Nancy **1989**:3
Gray, Hanna **1992**:4
Gray, John **1995**:3
Graziano, Rocky
   Obituary **1990**:4
Green, Richard R. **1988**:3

Greenberg, Hank
   Obituary **1986**:4
Green Day **1995**:4
Greenspan, Alan **1992**:2
Gregorian, Vartan **1990**:3
Gregory, Cynthia **1990**:2
Gregory, Dick **1990**:3
Grier, Pam **1998**:3
Griffey, Ken Jr. **1994**:1
Griffith, Melanie **1989**:2
Grisham, John **1994**:4
Grodin, Charles **1997**:3
Groening, Matt **1990**:4
Gross, Terry **1998**:3
Grove, Andrew S. **1995**:3
Grucci, Felix **1987**:1
Grusin, Dave
   Brief Entry **1987**:2
Guccione, Bob **1986**:1
Guccione, Bob, Jr. **1991**:4
Gumbel, Bryant **1990**:2
Gumbel, Greg **1996**:4
Gund, Agnes **1993**:2
Gunn, Hartford N., Jr.
   Obituary **1986**:2
Guyer, David
   Brief Entry **1988**:1
Gwynn, Tony **1995**:1
Haas, Robert D. **1986**:4
Hackman, Gene **1989**:3
Hackney, Sheldon **1995**:1
Hagelstein, Peter
   Brief Entry **1986**:3
Hagler, Marvelous Marvin **1985**:2
Hahn, Jessica **1989**:4
Hair, Jay D. **1994**:3
Ha Jin **2000**:3
Hakuta, Ken
   Brief Entry **1986**:1
Haldeman, H. R.
   Obituary **1994**:2
Hale, Alan **1997**:3
Hale, Clara
   Obituary **1993**:3
Haley, Alex
   Obituary **1992**:3
Hall, Anthony Michael **1986**:3
Hall, Arsenio **1990**:2
Halston
   Obituary **1990**:3
Hamilton, Margaret
   Obituary **1985**:3
Hamilton, Scott **1998**:2
Hamm, Mia **2000**:1
Hammer, Armand
   Obituary **1991**:3
Hammer, Jan **1987**:3
Hammer, M. C. **1991**:2
Hammond, E. Cuyler
   Obituary **1987**:1
Hammond, John
   Obituary **1988**:2
Hanauer, Chip **1986**:2
Hancock, Herbie **1985**:1
Hanks, Tom **1989**:2 **2000**:2
Hannah, Daryl **1987**:4
Hardaway, Anfernee **1996**:2
Haring, Keith
   Obituary **1990**:3
Harkes, John **1996**:4
Harmon, Mark **1987**:1

Harmon, Tom
  Obituary **1990**:3
Harriman, Pamela **1994**:4
Harriman, W. Averell
  Obituary **1986**:4
Harris, Barbara **1996**:3
Harris, Barbara **1989**:3
Harris, Emmylou **1991**:3
Harris, Patricia Roberts
  Obituary **1985**:2
Harry, Deborah **1990**:1
Hart, Mary
  Brief Entry **1988**:1
Hart, Mickey **1991**:2
Hartman, Phil **1996**:2
  Obituary **1998**:4
Harvard, Beverly **1995**:2
Harvey, Paul **1995**:3
Harwell, Ernie **1997**:3
Haseltine, William A. **1999**:2
Hassenfeld, Stephen **1987**:4
Hastert, Dennis **1999**:3
Hatch, Orin G. **2000**:2
Hatem, George
  Obituary **1989**:1
Hawke, Ethan **1995**:4
Hawkins, Jeff and Donna Dubinsky
  2000:2
Hawkins, Screamin' Jay
  Obituary **2000**:3
Hawn, Goldie Jeanne **1997**:2
Hayes, Helen
  Obituary **1993**:4
Hayes, Isaac **1998**:4
Hayes, Robert M. **1986**:3
Hayes, Woody
  Obituary **1987**:2
Hayworth, Rita
  Obituary **1987**:3
Headroom, Max **1986**:4
Healey, Jack **1990**:1
Healy, Bernadine **1993**:1
Healy, Timothy S. **1990**:2
Heard, J.C.
  Obituary **1989**:1
Heat-Moon, William Least **2000**:2
Heche, Anne **1999**:1
Heckerling, Amy **1987**:2
Heckert, Richard E.
  Brief Entry **1987**:3
Hefner, Christie **1985**:1
Heid, Bill
  Brief Entry **1987**:2
Heifetz, Jascha
  Obituary **1988**:2
Heinz, H.J.
  Obituary **1987**:2
Heinz, John
  Obituary **1991**:4
Heller, Joseph
  Obituary **2000**:2
Heller, Walter
  Obituary **1987**:4
Helms, Bobby
  Obituary **1997**:4
Helms, Jesse **1998**:1
Helmsley, Leona **1988**:1
Hemingway, Margaux
  Obituary **1997**:1
Henning, Doug
  Obituary **2000**:3
Hensel Twins **1996**:4

Henson, Brian **1992**:1
Henson, Jim **1989**:1
  Obituary **1990**:4
Hepburn, Katharine **1991**:2
Hernandez, Willie **1985**:1
Hershey, Barbara **1989**:1
Hershiser, Orel **1989**:2
Heston, Charlton **1999**:4
Hewitt, Jennifer Love **1999**:2
Highsmith, Patricia
  Obituary **1995**:3
Hilbert, Stephen C. **1997**:4
Hilfiger, Tommy **1993**:3
Hill, Anita **1994**:1
Hill, Faith **2000**:1
Hill, Grant **1995**:3
Hill, Lauryn **1999**:3
Hill, Lynn **1991**:2
Hillegass, Clifton Keith **1989**:4
Hills, Carla **1990**:3
Hines, Gregory **1992**:4
Hirschhorn, Joel
  Brief Entry **1986**:1
Hirt, Al
  Obituary **1999**:4
Hiss, Alger
  Obituary **1997**:2
Hoffa, Jim, Jr. **1999**:2
Hoffman, Abbie
  Obituary **1989**:3
Hoffs, Susanna **1988**:2
Hogan, Ben
  Obituary **1997**:4
Hogan, Hulk **1987**:3
Holbrooke, Richard **1996**:2
Holmes, John C.
  Obituary **1988**:3
Holtz, Lou **1986**:4
Holyfield, Evander **1991**:3
Hooker, John Lee **1998**:1
hooks, bell **2000**:2
Hootie and the Blowfish **1995**:4
Horne, Lena **1998**:4
Horner, Jack **1985**:2
Hornsby, Bruce **1989**:3
Horovitz, Adam **1988**:3
Horowitz, Paul **1988**:2
Horowitz, Vladimir
  Obituary **1990**:1
Horrigan, Edward, Jr. **1989**:1
Houseman, John
  Obituary **1989**:1
Houston, Cissy **1999**:3
Houston, Whitney **1986**:3
Howard, Desmond Kevin **1997**:2
Howard, Ron **1997**:2
Howser, Dick
  Obituary **1987**:4
Hubbard, Freddie **1988**:4
Hudson, Rock
  Obituary **1985**:4
Huerta, Dolores **1998**:1
Hughes, Cathy **1999**:1
Hughes, Mark **1985**:3
Huizenga, Wayne **1992**:1
Hull, Jane Dee **1999**:2
Hullinger, Charlotte
  Brief Entry **1985**:1
Hundt, Reed Eric **1997**:2
Hunt, Helen **1994**:4
Hunter, Catfish
  Obituary **2000**:1

Hunter, Holly **1989**:4
Hunter, Howard **1994**:4
Hunter, Madeline **1991**:2
Hurt, William **1986**:1
Huston, Anjelica **1989**:3
Huston, John
  Obituary **1988**:1
Hutton, Timothy **1986**:3
Hwang, David Henry **1999**:1
Hyatt, Joel **1985**:3
Hyde, Henry **1999**:1
Hynde, Chrissie **1991**:1
Iacocca, Lee **1993**:1
Ice Cube **1999**:2
Ice-T **1992**:3
Iglesias, Enrique **2000**:1
Ilitch, Mike **1993**:4
Imus, Don **1997**:1
Inatome, Rick **1985**:4
Indigo Girls **1994**:4
Ingersoll, Ralph II **1988**:2
Inkster, Juli **2000**:2
Inman, Bobby Ray **1985**:1
Ireland, Patricia **1992**:2
Irvin, Michael **1996**:3
Irwin, Bill **1988**:3
Irwin, James
  Obituary **1992**:1
Isaacson, Portia
  Brief Entry **1986**:1
Ito, Lance **1995**:3
Ives, Burl
  Obituary **1995**:4
Ivins, Molly **1993**:4
Jackson, Bo **1986**:3
Jackson, Cordell **1992**:4
Jackson, Janet **1990**:4
Jackson, Jesse **1996**:1
Jackson, Jesse, Jr. **1998**:3
Jackson, Michael **1996**:2
Jackson, Phil **1996**:3
Jackson, Samuel L. **1995**:4
Jackson, Thomas Penfield **2000**:2
Jacobs, Joe **1994**:1
Jacuzzi, Candido
  Obituary **1987**:1
Jahn, Helmut **1987**:3
James, Etta **1995**:2
Jamison, Judith **1990**:3
Janklow, Morton **1989**:3
Janzen, Daniel H. **1988**:4
Jarmusch, Jim **1998**:3
Jarrett, Keith **1992**:4
Jarvik, Robert K. **1985**:1
Jay, Ricky **1995**:1
Jemison, Mae C. **1993**:1
Jen, Gish **2000**:1
Jenkins, Sally **1997**:2
Jeter, Derek **1999**:4
Jewel **1999**:2
Jillian, Ann **1986**:4
Jobs, Steve **2000**:1
Joel, Billy **1994**:3
Joffrey, Robert
  Obituary **1988**:3
John, Daymond **2000**:1
Johnson, Betsey **1996**:2
Johnson, Don **1986**:1
Johnson, Earvin Magic **1988**:4
Johnson, Jimmy **1993**:3
Johnson, Kevin **1991**:1
Johnson, Keyshawn **2000**:4

McDormand, Frances **1997**:3
McDuffie, Robert **1990**:2
McElligott, Thomas J. **1987**:4
McEntire, Reba **1987**:3
McEntire, Reba **1994**:2
McFarlane, Todd **1999**:1
McFerrin, Bobby **1989**:1
McGillis, Kelly **1989**:3
McGowan, William **1985**:2
McGowan, William G.
    Obituary **1993**:1
McGraw, Tim **2000**:3
McGwire, Mark **1999**:1
McIntyre, Richard
    Brief Entry **1986**:2
McKee, Lonette **1996**:1
McKenna, Terence **1993**:3
McKinney, Cynthia A. **1997**:1
McKinney, Stewart B.
    Obituary **1987**:4
McMahon, Jim **1985**:4
McMahon, Vince, Jr. **1985**:4
McMillan, Terry **1993**:2
McMillen, Tom **1988**:4
McMurtry, James **1990**:2
McNamara, Robert S. **1995**:4
McNealy, Scott **1999**:4
McRae, Carmen
    Obituary **1995**:2
Meadows, Audrey
    Obituary **1996**:3
Mellinger, Frederick
    Obituary **1990**:4
Mello, Dawn **1992**:2
Mellon, Paul
    Obituary **1999**:3
Melman, Richard
    Brief Entry **1986**:1
Mengers, Sue **1985**:3
Menninger, Karl
    Obituary **1991**:1
Menuhin, Yehudi
    Obituary **1999**:3
Merchant, Natalie **1996**:3
Meredith, Burgess
    Obituary **1998**:1
Merrick, David
    Obituary **2000**:4
Merrill, James
    Obituary **1995**:3
Merritt, Justine
    Brief Entry **1985**:3
Mfume, Kweisi **1996**:3
Michelman, Kate **1998**:4
Michener, James A.
    Obituary **1998**:1
Midler, Bette **1989**:4
Mikulski, Barbara **1992**:4
Milburn, Rodney Jr.
    Obituary **1998**:2
Milland, Ray
    Obituary **1986**:2
Millard, Barbara J.
    Brief Entry **1985**:3
Miller, Arthur **1999**:4
Miller, Bebe **2000**:2
Miller, Dennis **1992**:4
Miller, Nicole **1995**:4
Miller, Rand **1995**:4
Miller, Reggie **1994**:4
Miller, Roger
    Obituary **1993**:2

Miller, Sue **1999**:3
Mills, Wilbur
    Obituary **1992**:4
Minnesota Fats
    Obituary **1996**:3
Minsky, Marvin **1994**:3
Misrach, Richard **1991**:2
Mitchell, Arthur **1995**:1
Mitchell, George J. **1989**:3
Mitchell, John
    Obituary **1989**:2
Mitchell, Joni **1991**:4
Mitchelson, Marvin **1989**:2
Mitchum, Robert
    Obituary **1997**:4
Mizrahi, Isaac **1991**:1
Moby **2000**:1
Mohajer, Dineh **1997**:3
Molinari, Susan **1996**:4
Monaghan, Tom **1985**:1
Mondavi, Robert **1989**:2
Monk, Art **1993**:2
Monroe, Bill
    Obituary **1997**:1
Monroe, Rose Will
    Obituary **1997**:4
Montana, Joe **1989**:2
Montgomery, Elizabeth
    Obituary **1995**:4
Moody, John **1985**:3
Moon, Warren **1991**:3
Moore, Archie
    Obituary **1999**:2
Moore, Clayton
    Obituary **2000**:3
Moore, Demi **1991**:4
Moore, Julianne **1998**:1
Moore, Mary Tyler **1996**:2
Moore, Michael **1990**:3
Morgan, Dodge **1987**:1
Morgan, Robin **1991**:1
Morita, Noriyuki Pat **1987**:3
Moritz, Charles **1989**:3
Morris, Dick **1997**:3
Morris, Mark **1991**:1
Morrison, Sterling
    Obituary **1996**:1
Morrison, Toni **1998**:1
Morrison, Trudi
    Brief Entry **1986**:2
Mosbacher, Georgette **1994**:2
Moss, Cynthia **1995**:2
Moss, Randy **1999**:3
Motherwell, Robert
    Obituary **1992**:1
Mott, William Penn, Jr. **1986**:1
Mourning, Alonzo **1994**:2
Moyers, Bill **1991**:4
Muldowney, Shirley **1986**:1
Mullis, Kary **1995**:3
Mumford, Lewis
    Obituary **1990**:2
Murdoch, Rupert **1988**:4
Murphy, Eddie **1989**:2
Murray, Arthur
    Obituary **1991**:3
Musburger, Brent **1985**:1
Muskie, Edmund S.
    Obituary **1996**:3
Nader, Ralph **1989**:4
Nance, Jack
    Obituary **1997**:3

Napolitano, Janet **1997**:1
Nauman, Bruce **1995**:4
Navratilova, Martina **1989**:1
Neal, James Foster **1986**:2
Nechita, Alexandra **1996**:4
Neiman, LeRoy **1993**:3
Nelson, Harriet
    Obituary **1995**:1
Nelson, Rick
    Obituary **1986**:1
Nelson, Willie **1993**:4
Nemerov, Howard
    Obituary **1992**:1
Neuharth, Allen H. **1986**:1
Nevelson, Louise
    Obituary **1988**:3
Newhouse, Samuel I., Jr. **1997**:1
New Kids on the Block **1991**:2
Newman, Arnold **1993**:1
Newman, Joseph **1987**:1
Newman, Paul **1995**:3
Newton, Huey
    Obituary **1990**:1
Nichols, Mike **1994**:4
Nicholson, Jack **1989**:2
Nipon, Albert
    Brief Entry **1986**:4
Nirvana **1992**:4
Nixon, Pat
    Obituary **1994**:1
Nixon, Richard
    Obituary **1994**:4
Nolan, Lloyd
    Obituary **1985**:4
Nolte, Nick **1992**:4
Noonan, Peggy **1990**:3
North, Alex **1986**:3
North, Oliver **1987**:4
Norton, Edward **2000**:2
Norville, Deborah **1990**:3
Notorious B.I.G.
    Obituary **1997**:3
Noyce, Robert N. **1985**:4
Nunn, Sam **1990**:2
Nussbaum, Karen **1988**:3
Nye, Bill **1997**:2
Nyro, Laura
    Obituary **1997**:3
Oates, Joyce Carol **2000**:1
O'Brien, Conan **1994**:1
O'Connor, Cardinal John **1990**:3
O'Connor, John
    Obituary **2000**:4
O'Connor, Sandra Day **1991**:1
O'Donnell, Rosie **1994**:3
Olajuwon, Akeem **1985**:1
Oldham, Todd **1995**:4
O'Leary, Hazel **1993**:4
Olin, Ken **1992**:3
Oliver, Daniel **1988**:2
Olmos, Edward James **1990**:1
Olsen, Kenneth H. **1986**:4
Olson, Billy **1986**:3
Olson, Johnny
    Obituary **1985**:4
O'Malley, Susan **1995**:2
Onassis, Jacqueline Kennedy
    Obituary **1994**:4
O'Neal, Shaquille **1992**:1
O'Neill, Tip
    Obituary **1994**:3
Ono, Yoko **1989**:2

Orbison, Roy
   Obituary **1989**:2
Ormandy, Eugene
   Obituary **1985**:2
Orr, Kay **1987**:4
Osborne, Joan **1996**:4
Osgood, Charles **1996**:2
O'Steen, Van
   Brief Entry **1986**:3
Ostin, Mo **1996**:2
Otte, Ruth **1992**:4
Ovitz, Michael **1990**:1
Owens, Delia and Mark **1993**:3
Pacino, Al **1993**:4
Packard, David
   Obituary **1996**:3
Page, Geraldine
   Obituary **1987**:4
Pagels, Elaine **1997**:1
Paglia, Camille **1992**:3
Paige, Emmett, Jr.
   Brief Entry **1986**:4
Pakula, Alan
   Obituary **1999**:2
Paley, William S.
   Obituary **1991**:2
Palmer, Jim **1991**:2
Paltrow, Gwyneth **1997**:1
Panetta, Leon **1995**:1
Papp, Joseph
   Obituary **1992**:2
Parker, Colonel Tom
   Obituary **1997**:2
Parker, Sarah Jessica **1999**:2
Parker, Trey and Matt Stone **1998**:2
Parks, Bert
   Obituary **1992**:3
Parsons, David **1993**:4
Parton, Dolly **1999**:4
Pass, Joe
   Obituary **1994**:4
Pastorius, Jaco
   Obituary **1988**:1
Pataki, George **1995**:2
Paterno, Joe **1995**:4
Pauley, Jane **1999**:1
Pauling, Linus
   Obituary **1995**:1
Paulsen, Pat
   Obituary **1997**:4
Paulucci, Jeno
   Brief Entry **1986**:3
Pavin, Corey **1996**:4
Paxton, Bill **1999**:3
Payton, Lawrence
   Obituary **1997**:4
Payton, Walter
   Obituary **2000**:2
Pearl, Minnie
   Obituary **1996**:3
Pearl Jam **1994**:2
Pedersen, William **1989**:4
Peete, Calvin **1985**:4
Pei, I.M. **1990**:4
Peller, Clara
   Obituary **1988**:1
Peltier, Leonard **1995**:1
Pendleton, Clarence M.
   Obituary **1988**:4
Penn, Sean **1987**:2
Penn & Teller **1992**:1
Penske, Roger **1988**:3

Pepper, Claude
   Obituary **1989**:4
Percy, Walker
   Obituary **1990**:4
Perelman, Ronald **1989**:2
Perez, Rosie **1994**:2
Perkins, Anthony
   Obituary **1993**:2
Perkins, Carl
   Obituary **1998**:2
Perlman, Steve **1998**:2
Perot, H. Ross **1992**:4
Perry, Carrie Saxon **1989**:2
Perry, Harold A.
   Obituary **1992**:1
Perry, Luke **1992**:3
Perry, Matthew **1997**:2
Perry, William **1994**:4
Pesci, Joe **1992**:4
Peter, Valentine J. **1988**:2
Peters, Bernadette **2000**:1
Peters, Tom **1998**:1
Petersen, Donald Eugene **1985**:1
Peterson, Cassandra **1988**:1
Peterson, Roger Tory
   Obituary **1997**:1
Petty, Tom **1988**:1
Pfeiffer, Michelle **1990**:2
Phair, Liz **1995**:3
Phelan, John Joseph, Jr. **1985**:4
Philbin, Regis **2000**:2
Phillips, Julia **1992**:1
Phoenix, Joaquin **2000**:4
Phoenix, River **1990**:2
   Obituary **1994**:2
Piazza, Mike **1998**:4
Pierce, David Hyde **1996**:3
Pierce, Frederick S. **1985**:3
Pierce, Mary **1994**:4
Pilatus, Robert
   Obituary **1998**:3
Pincay, Laffit, Jr. **1986**:3
Pinchot, Bronson **1987**:4
Pinker, Steven A. **2000**:1
Pinkett Smith, Jada **1998**:3
Pipher, Mary **1996**:4
Pippen, Scottie **1992**:2
Pirro, Jeanine **1998**:2
Pitt, Brad **1995**:2
Pittman, Robert W. **1985**:1
Plato, Dana
   Obituary **1999**:4
Plotkin, Mark **1994**:3
Poitier, Sidney **1990**:3
Popcorn, Faith
   Brief Entry **1988**:1
Pope, Generoso **1988**:4
Porter, Sylvia
   Obituary **1991**:4
Portman, John **1988**:2
Portman, Natalie **2000**:3
Potok, Anna Maximilian
   Brief Entry **1985**:2
Potts, Annie **1994**:1
Pough, Richard Hooper **1989**:1
Povich, Maury **1994**:3
Powell, Colin **1990**:1
Powell, Lewis F.
   Obituary **1999**:1
Pratt, Jane **1999**:1
Predock, Antoine **1993**:2

Preminger, Otto
   Obituary **1986**:3
Presser, Jackie
   Obituary **1988**:4
Preston, Robert
   Obituary **1987**:3
Price, Vincent
   Obituary **1994**:2
Pride, Charley **1998**:1
Priestly, Jason **1993**:2
Prince **1995**:3
Prince, Faith **1993**:2
Prinze, Freddie, Jr. **1999**:3
Pritzker, A.N.
   Obituary **1986**:2
Proctor, Barbara Gardner **1985**:3
Profet, Margie **1994**:4
Proulx, E. Annie **1996**:1
Prowse, Juliet
   Obituary **1997**:1
Prusiner, Stanley **1998**:2
Pryor, Richard **1999**:3
Public Enemy **1992**:1
Puccio, Thomas P. **1986**:4
Puck, Wolfgang **1990**:1
Puente, Tito
   Obituary **2000**:4
Puzo, Mario
   Obituary **2000**:1
Pynchon, Thomas **1997**:4
Quaid, Dennis **1989**:4
Quayle, Dan **1989**:2
Queen Latifah **1992**:2
Quill, Timothy E. **1997**:3
Quindlen, Anna **1993**:1
Quinlan, Karen Ann
   Obituary **1985**:2
Quinn, Jane Bryant **1993**:4
Quinn, Martha **1986**:4
Quivers, Robin **1995**:4
Rabbitt, Eddie
   Obituary **1998**:4
Radecki, Thomas
   Brief Entry **1986**:2
Radner, Gilda
   Obituary **1989**:4
Radocy, Robert
   Brief Entry **1986**:3
Raimi, Sam **1999**:2
Raimondi, John
   Brief Entry **1987**:4
Raines, Franklin **1997**:4
Raitt, Bonnie **1990**:2
Ramo, Roberta Cooper **1996**:1
Rand, A. Barry **2000**:3
Randi, James **1990**:2
Raphael, Sally Jessy **1992**:4
Rapp, C.J.
   Brief Entry **1987**:3
Rashad, Phylicia **1987**:3
Raskin, Jef **1997**:4
Rauschenberg, Robert **1991**:2
Ray, James Earl
   Obituary **1998**:4
Raye, Martha
   Obituary **1995**:1
Raymond, Lee R. **2000**:3
Reasoner, Harry
   Obituary **1992**:1
Redenbacher, Orville
   Obituary **1996**:1
Redfield, James **1995**:2

Schwinn, Edward R., Jr.
 Brief Entry **1985**:4
Scorsese, Martin **1989**:1
Scott, Gene
 Brief Entry **1986**:1
Scott, George C.
 Obituary **2000**:2
Scott, Randolph
 Obituary **1987**:2
Sculley, John **1989**:4
Secretariat
 Obituary **1990**:1
Sedelmaier, Joe **1985**:3
Seger, Bob **1987**:1
Seidelman, Susan **1985**:4
Seinfeld, Jerry **1992**:4
Selena
 Obituary **1995**:4
Selig, Bud **1995**:2
Serrano, Andres **2000**:4
Sevareid, Eric
 Obituary **1993**:1
Shabazz, Betty
 Obituary **1997**:4
Shakur, Tupac
 Obituary **1997**:1
Shalala, Donna **1992**:3
Shalikashvili, John **1994**:2
Shandling, Garry **1995**:1
Sharkey, Ray
 Obituary **1994**:1
Sharpe, Sterling **1994**:3
Sharpton, Al **1991**:2
Shaw, William **2000**:3
Shawn, Dick
 Obituary **1987**:3
Shawn, William
 Obituary **1993**:3
Sheedy, Ally **1989**:1
Sheehan, Daniel P. **1989**:1
Sheffield, Gary **1998**:1
Sheindlin, Judith **1999**:1
Shepard, Alan
 Obituary **1999**:1
Shepard, Sam **1996**:4
Shepherd, Cybill **1996**:3
Sherman, Cindy **1992**:3
Sherman, Russell **1987**:4
Shields, Brooke **1996**:3
Shilts, Randy **1993**:4
 Obituary **1994**:3
Shimomura, Tsutomu **1996**:1
Shirley, Donna **1999**:1
Shocked, Michelle **1989**:4
Shore, Dinah
 Obituary **1994**:3
Shriver, Maria
 Brief Entry **1986**:2
Shue, Andrew **1994**:4
Shula, Don **1992**:2
Sidney, Ivan
 Brief Entry **1987**:2
Siebert, Muriel **1987**:2
Sigmund, Barbara Boggs
 Obituary **1991**:1
Silber, John **1990**:1
Silverman, Jonathan **1997**:2
Silvers, Phil
 Obituary **1985**:4
Silverstein, Shel
 Obituary **1999**:4
Silverstone, Alicia **1997**:4

Simmons, Adele Smith **1988**:4
Simmons, Ruth **1995**:2
Simon, Paul **1992**:2
Simpson, Wallis
 Obituary **1986**:3
Sinatra, Frank
 Obituary **1998**:4
Sinclair, Mary **1985**:2
Singer, Isaac Bashevis
 Obituary **1992**:1
Singleton, John **1994**:3
Sinise, Gary **1996**:1
Sirica, John
 Obituary **1993**:2
Siskel, Gene
 Obituary **1999**:3
Skelton, Red
 Obituary **1998**:1
Skinner, B.F.
 Obituary **1991**:1
Skinner, Sam **1992**:3
Slater, Christian **1994**:1
Slater, Rodney E. **1997**:4
Slotnick, Barry
 Brief Entry **1987**:4
Smale, John G. **1987**:3
Smiley, Jane **1995**:4
Smith, Buffalo Bob
 Obituary **1999**:1
Smith, Emmitt **1994**:1
Smith, Frederick W. **1985**:4
Smith, Jack **1994**:3
Smith, Jeff **1991**:4
Smith, Jerry
 Obituary **1987**:1
Smith, Kate
 Obituary **1986**:3
Smith, Kevin **2000**:4
Smith, Roger **1990**:3
Smith, Samantha
 Obituary **1985**:3
Smith, Will **1997**:2
Smith, Willi
 Obituary **1987**:3
Smits, Jimmy **1990**:1
Smoot, George F. **1993**:3
Snider, Dee **1986**:1
Snipes, Wesley **1993**:1
Snoop Doggy Dogg **1995**:2
Snow, Hank
 Obituary **2000**:3
Snowe, Olympia **1995**:3
Snyder, Jimmy
 Obituary **1996**:4
Snyder, Mitch
 Obituary **1991**:1
Somers, Suzanne **2000**:1
Sondheim, Stephen **1994**:4
Soren, David
 Brief Entry **1986**:3
Sorvino, Mira **1996**:3
Souter, David **1991**:3
Southern, Terry
 Obituary **1996**:2
Sowell, Thomas **1998**:3
Spacey, Kevin **1996**:4
Spade, David **1999**:2
Spader, James **1991**:2
Spears, Britney **2000**:3
Spector, Phil **1989**:1
Spheeris, Penelope **1989**:2
Spiegelman, Art **1998**:3

Spielberg, Steven **1993**:4 **1997**:4
Spock, Benjamin **1995**:2
 Obituary **1998**:3
Spong, John **1991**:3
Sprewell, Latrell **1999**:4
Stahl, Lesley **1997**:1
Stallings, George A., Jr. **1990**:1
Stallone, Sylvester **1994**:2
Starr, Kenneth **1998**:3
Steel, Danielle **1999**:2
Steel, Dawn **1990**:1
 Obituary **1998**:2
Steele, Shelby **1991**:2
Steger, Will **1990**:4
Steinberg, Leigh **1987**:3
Steinbrenner, George **1991**:1
Steinem, Gloria **1996**:2
Stella, Frank **1996**:2
Stempel, Robert **1991**:3
Stephanopoulos, George **1994**:3
Sterling, Bruce **1995**:4
Stern, David **1991**:4
Stern, Howard **1988**:2 **1993**:3
Stevens, Eileen **1987**:3
Stevenson, McLean
 Obituary **1996**:3
Stewart, Dave **1991**:1
Stewart, Jimmy
 Obituary **1997**:4
Stewart, Martha **1992**:1
Stewart, Payne
 Obituary **2000**:2
Stewart, Potter
 Obituary **1986**:1
Stiller, Ben **1999**:1
Stockton, John Houston **1997**:3
Stofflet, Ty
 Brief Entry **1987**:1
Stokes, Carl
 Obituary **1996**:4
Stone, I.F.
 Obituary **1990**:1
Stone, Irving
 Obituary **1990**:2
Stone, Oliver **1990**:4
Stone, Sharon **1993**:4
Stonesifer, Patty **1997**:1
Strait, George **1998**:3
Strange, Curtis **1988**:4
Strauss, Robert **1991**:4
Streep, Meryl **1990**:2
Street, Picabo **1999**:3
Streisand, Barbra **1992**:2
Stroh, Peter W. **1985**:2
Stroman, Susan **2000**:4
Strug, Kerri **1997**:3
Studi, Wes **1994**:3
Styne, Jule
 Obituary **1995**:1
Suarez, Xavier
 Brief Entry **1986**:2
Sui, Anna **1995**:1
Sullivan, Louis **1990**:4
Sulzberger, Arthur O., Jr. **1998**:3
Sun Ra
 Obituary **1994**:1
Sununu, John **1989**:2
Susskind, David
 Obituary **1987**:2
Swaggart, Jimmy **1987**:3
Swank, Hilary **2000**:3

Swayze, John Cameron
  Obituary **1996**:1
Sweeney, John J. **2000**:3
Swoopes, Sheryl **1998**:2
Szent-Gyoergyi, Albert
  Obituary **1987**:2
Tafel, Richard **2000**:4
Tagliabue, Paul **1990**:2
Tan, Amy **1998**:3
Tandy, Jessica **1990**:4
  Obituary **1995**:1
Tannen, Deborah **1995**:1
Tanny, Vic
  Obituary **1985**:3
Tarantino, Quentin **1995**:1
Tarkenian, Jerry **1990**:4
Tartikoff, Brandon **1985**:2
  Obituary **1998**:1
Taylor, Lawrence **1987**:3
Taylor, Lili **2000**:2
Taylor, Maxwell
  Obituary **1987**:3
Taylor, Paul **1992**:3
Taylor, Susan L. **1998**:2
Tenet, George **2000**:3
Terry, Randall **1991**:4
Tesh, John **1996**:3
Testaverde, Vinny **1987**:2
Thalheimer, Richard
  Brief Entry **1988**:3
Tharp, Twyla **1992**:4
Thiebaud, Wayne **1991**:1
Thomas, Clarence **1992**:2
Thomas, Danny
  Obituary **1991**:3
Thomas, Dave **1986**:2 **1993**:2
Thomas, Debi **1987**:2
Thomas, Derrick
  Obituary **2000**:3
Thomas, Frank **1994**:3
Thomas, Helen **1988**:4
Thomas, Isiah **1989**:2
Thomas, Michael Tilson **1990**:3
Thomas, Michel **1987**:4
Thomas, Thurman **1993**:1
Thompson, Fred **1998**:2
Thompson, Hunter S. **1992**:1
Thompson, John **1988**:3
Thompson, Starley
  Brief Entry **1987**:3
Thornton, Billy Bob **1997**:4
Thurman, Uma **1994**:2
Tiffany **1989**:1
Tillstrom, Burr
  Obituary **1986**:1
Tilly, Jennifer **1997**:2
Tisch, Laurence A. **1988**:2
TLC **1996**:1
Tom and Ray Magliozzi **1991**:4
Tomei, Marisa **1995**:2
Tompkins, Susie
  Brief Entry **1987**:2
Tone-Loc **1990**:3
Toomer, Ron **1990**:1
Toone, Bill
  Brief Entry **1987**:2
Torme, Mel
  Obituary **1999**:4
Torre, Joseph Paul **1997**:1
Totenberg, Nina **1992**:2
Tower, John
  Obituary **1991**:4

Traub, Marvin
  Brief Entry **1987**:3
Travis, Randy **1988**:4
Travolta, John **1995**:2
Treybig, James G. **1988**:3
Tribe, Laurence H. **1988**:1
Tritt, Travis **1995**:1
Trotman, Alex **1995**:4
Trotter, Charlie **2000**:4
Troutt, Kenny A. **1998**:1
Trudeau, Garry **1991**:2
Truitt, Anne **1993**:1
Trump, Donald **1989**:2
Tsongas, Paul Efthemios
  Obituary **1997**:2
Tucker, Chris **1999**:1
Tucker, Forrest
  Obituary **1987**:1
Tune, Tommy **1994**:2
Ture, Kwame
  Obituary **1999**:2
Turner, Janine **1993**:2
Turner, Kathleen **1985**:3
Turner, Lana
  Obituary **1996**:1
Turner, Ted **1989**:1
Turner, Tina **2000**:3
Tutwiler, Margaret **1992**:4
Twitty, Conway
  Obituary **1994**:1
Twombley, Cy **1995**:1
Tyler, Anne **1995**:4
Tyler, Liv **1997**:2
Tyler, Richard **1995**:3
Tyner, Rob
  Obituary **1992**:2
Tyson, Don **1995**:3
Tyson, Laura D'Andrea **1994**:1
Tyson, Mike **1986**:4
Udall, Mo
  Obituary **1999**:2
Unz, Ron **1999**:1
Upshaw, Dawn **1991**:2
Upshaw, Gene **1988**:1
Urich, Robert **1988**:1
Vagelos, P. Roy **1989**:4
Valente, Benita **1985**:3
Van Duyn, Mona **1993**:2
Van Dyken, Amy **1997**:1
Van Halen, Edward **1985**:2
Vanilla Ice **1991**:3
Van Sant, Gus **1992**:2
Van Slyke, Andy **1992**:4
Varney, Jim
  Obituary **2000**:3
Varney, Jim
  Brief Entry **1985**:4
Vaughan, Sarah
  Obituary **1990**:3
Vaughan, Stevie Ray
  Obituary **1991**:1
Vaughn, Mo **1999**:2
Vaughn, Vince **1999**:2
Veeck, Bill
  Obituary **1986**:1
Vega, Suzanne **1988**:1
Ventura, Jesse **1999**:2
Venturi, Robert **1994**:4
Verdi-Fletcher, Mary **1998**:2
Vickrey, William S.
  Obituary **1997**:2
Vidal, Gore **1996**:2

Vincent, Fay **1990**:2
Vinton, Will
  Brief Entry **1988**:1
Violet, Arlene **1985**:3
Vitale, Dick **1988**:4 **1994**:4
Vogel, Paula **1999**:2
Vonnegut, Kurt **1998**:4
von Trapp, Maria
  Obituary **1987**:3
vos Savant, Marilyn **1988**:2
Vreeland, Diana
  Obituary **1990**:1
Wachner, Linda **1988**:3 **1997**:2
Waddell, Thomas F.
  Obituary **1988**:2
Waitt, Ted **1997**:4
Waldron, Hicks B. **1987**:3
Walgreen, Charles III
  Brief Entry **1987**:4
Walker, Alice **1999**:1
Walker, Junior
  Obituary **1996**:2
Walker, Kara **1999**:2
Walker, Nancy
  Obituary **1992**:3
Wallace, George
  Obituary **1999**:1
Wallace, Irving
  Obituary **1991**:1
Wallis, Hal
  Obituary **1987**:1
Walsh, Bill **1987**:4
Walters, Barbara **1998**:3
Walton, Sam **1986**:2
  Obituary **1993**:1
Wang, An **1986**:1
  Obituary **1990**:3
Wapner, Joseph A. **1987**:1
Warhol, Andy
  Obituary **1987**:2
Warner, Kurt **2000**:3
Warren, Robert Penn
  Obituary **1990**:1
Washington, Alonzo **2000**:1
Washington, Denzel **1993**:2
Washington, Grover, Jr. **1989**:1
Washington, Harold
  Obituary **1988**:1
Wasserstein, Wendy **1991**:3
Waters, John **1988**:3
Waters, Maxine **1998**:4
Watson, Elizabeth **1991**:2
Watterson, Bill **1990**:3
Wattleton, Faye **1989**:1
Watts, J.C. **1999**:2
Wayans, Damon **1998**:4
Wayans, Keenen Ivory **1991**:1
Wayne, David
  Obituary **1995**:3
Weaver, Sigourney **1988**:3
Webb, Wellington E. **2000**:3
Webber, Chris **1994**:1
Weber, Pete **1986**:3
Wegman, William **1991**:1
Weicker, Lowell P., Jr. **1993**:1
Weil, Andrew **1997**:4
Weill, Sandy **1990**:4
Weinstein, Bob and Harvey **2000**:4
Weintraub, Jerry **1986**:1
Weitz, Bruce **1985**:4
Welch, Bob **1991**:3
Welch, Jack **1993**:3

Wells, David **1999**:3
Wells, Mary
  Obituary **1993**:1
Wells, Sharlene
  Brief Entry **1985**:1
Wenner, Jann **1993**:1
West, Cornel **1994**:2
West, Dorothy **1996**:1
West, Dottie
  Obituary **1992**:2
Wexler, Nancy S. **1992**:3
Whelan, Wendy **1999**:3
Whitaker, Forest **1996**:2
White, Bill **1989**:3
White, Jaleel **1992**:3
White, Reggie **1993**:4
White, Ryan
  Obituary **1990**:3
Whitestone, Heather **1995**:1
Whitman, Christine Todd **1994**:3
Whitman, Meg **2000**:3
Whitmire, Kathy **1988**:2
Whittle, Christopher **1989**:3
Wiesel, Elie **1998**:1
Wiest, Dianne **1995**:2
Wigand, Jeffrey **2000**:4
Wigler, Michael
  Brief Entry **1985**:1
Wilder, L. Douglas **1990**:3
Wildmon, Donald **1988**:4
Wilkens, Lenny **1995**:2
Williams, Anthony **2000**:4
Williams, Doug **1988**:2
Williams, Edward Bennett
  Obituary **1988**:4
Williams, G. Mennen
  Obituary **1988**:2
Williams, Joe
  Obituary **1999**:4
Williams, Ricky **2000**:2
Williams, Robin **1988**:4
Williams, Serena **1999**:4
Williams, Vanessa L. **1999**:2
Williams, Venus **1998**:2
Williams, Willie L. **1993**:1
Williamson, Marianne **1991**:4
Willis, Bruce **1986**:4
Willson, S. Brian **1989**:3
Wilson, Brian **1996**:1
Wilson, Carl
  Obituary **1998**:2
Wilson, Cassandra **1996**:3
Wilson, Edward O. **1994**:4
Wilson, Flip
  Obituary **1999**:2
Wilson, Jerry
  Brief Entry **1986**:2
Wilson, Pete **1992**:3
Wilson, William Julius **1997**:1
Winans, CeCe **2000**:1
Winfrey, Oprah **1986**:4 **1997**:3
Winger, Debra **1994**:3
Winston, George **1987**:1
Winter, Paul **1990**:2
Witkin, Joel-Peter **1996**:1
Wolf, Naomi **1994**:3
Wolf, Stephen M. **1989**:3
Wolfe, Tom **1999**:2
Wolfman Jack
  Obituary **1996**:1
Wong, B.D. **1998**:1
Woodard, Lynette **1986**:2

Woodruff, Robert Winship
  Obituary **1985**:1
Woods, James **1988**:3
Woods, Tiger **1995**:4
Woodson, Ron **1996**:4
Woodwell, George S. **1987**:2
Worthy, James **1991**:2
Wright, Steven **1986**:3
Wu, Harry **1996**:1
Wyle, Noah **1997**:3
Wynette, Tammy
  Obituary **1998**:3
Wynn, Keenan
  Obituary **1987**:1
Wynn, Stephen A. **1994**:3
Wynonna **1993**:3
Yamaguchi, Kristi **1992**:3
Yamasaki, Minoru
  Obituary **1986**:2
Yankovic, Weird Al **1985**:4
Yankovic, Frank
  Obituary **1999**:2
Yard, Molly **1991**:4
Yeager, Chuck **1998**:1
Yearwood, Trisha **1999**:1
Yetnikoff, Walter **1988**:1
Yoakam, Dwight **1992**:4
Yokich, Stephen P. **1995**:4
York, Dick
  Obituary **1992**:4
Young, Coleman A.
  Obituary **1998**:1
Young, Robert
  Obituary **1999**:1
Young, Steve **1995**:2
Youngblood, Johnny Ray **1994**:1
Youngman, Henny
  Obituary **1998**:3
Zahn, Paula **1992**:3
Zamboni, Frank J.
  Brief Entry **1986**:4
Zamora, Pedro
  Obituary **1995**:2
Zanker, Bill
  Brief Entry **1987**:3
Zanuck, Lili Fini **1994**:2
Zappa, Frank
  Obituary **1994**:2
Zech, Lando W.
  Brief Entry **1987**:4
Ziff, William B., Jr. **1986**:4
Zigler, Edward **1994**:1
Zinnemann, Fred
  Obituary **1997**:3
Zucker, Jeff **1993**:3
Zuckerman, Mortimer **1986**:3
Zwilich, Ellen **1990**:1

ANGOLAN
  Savimbi, Jonas **1986**:2 **1994**:2

ARGENTINIAN
  Bocca, Julio **1995**:3
  Herrera, Paloma **1996**:2
  Maradona, Diego **1991**:3
  Pelli, Cesar **1991**:4
  Sabatini, Gabriela
    Brief Entry **1985**:4
  Timmerman, Jacobo
    Obituary **2000**:3

AUSTRALIAN
  Allen, Peter
    Obituary **1993**:1
  Anderson, Judith
    Obituary **1992**:3
  Bee Gees, The **1997**:4
  Blanchett, Cate **1999**:3
  Bond, Alan **1989**:2
  Clavell, James
    Obituary **1995**:1
  Gibb, Andy
    Obituary **1988**:3
  Gibson, Mel **1990**:1
  Helfgott, David **1997**:2
  Hughes, Robert **1996**:4
  Humphries, Barry **1993**:1
  Hutchence, Michael
    Obituary **1998**:1
  Kidman, Nicole **1992**:4
  Murdoch, Rupert **1988**:4
  Norman, Greg **1988**:3
  Powter, Susan **1994**:3
  Summers, Anne **1990**:2
  Travers, P.L.
    Obituary **1996**:4
  Tyler, Richard **1995**:3
  Webb, Karrie **2000**:4

AUSTRIAN
  Brandauer, Klaus Maria **1987**:3
  Djerassi, Carl **2000**:4
  Drucker, Peter F. **1992**:3
  Falco
    Brief Entry **1987**:2
  Frankl, Viktor E.
    Obituary **1998**:1
  Hrabal, Bohumil
    Obituary **1997**:3
  Lamarr, Hedy
    Obituary **2000**:3
  Lang, Helmut **1999**:2
  Lorenz, Konrad
    Obituary **1989**:3
  Porsche, Ferdinand
    Obituary **1998**:4
  Puck, Wolfgang **1990**:1
  von Karajan, Herbert
    Obituary **1989**:4
  von Trapp, Maria
    Obituary **1987**:3

BANGLADESHI
  Nasrin, Taslima **1995**:1

BELGIAN
  Hepburn, Audrey
    Obituary **1993**:2
  von Furstenberg, Diane **1994**:2

BOSNIAN
  Izetbegovic, Alija **1996**:4

BRAZILIAN
  Cardoso, Fernando Henrique **1996**:4
  Castaneda, Carlos
    Obituary **1998**:4
  Collor de Mello, Fernando **1992**:4
  Fittipaldi, Emerson **1994**:2
  Ronaldo **1999**:2
  Salgado, Sebastiao **1994**:2

Senna, Ayrton **1991**:4
  Obituary **1994**:4
Xuxa **1994**:2

BRITISH

Adamson, George
  Obituary **1990**:2
Baddeley, Hermione
  Obituary **1986**:4
Beckett, Wendy (Sister) **1998**:3
Branson, Richard **1987**:1
Chatwin, Bruce
  Obituary **1989**:2
Cleese, John **1989**:2
Cummings, Sam **1986**:3
Dalton, Timothy **1988**:4
Davison, Ian Hay **1986**:1
Day-Lewis, Daniel **1989**:4 **1994**:4
Dench, Judi **1999**:4
Egan, John **1987**:2
Eno, Brian **1986**:2
Ferguson, Sarah **1990**:3
Fiennes, Ranulph **1990**:3
Foster, Norman **1999**:4
Gift, Roland **1990**:2
Goodall, Jane **1991**:1
Hamilton, Hamish
  Obituary **1988**:4
Harrison, Rex
  Obituary **1990**:4
Hawking, Stephen W. **1990**:1
Hockney, David **1988**:3
Hoskins, Bob **1989**:1
Hounsfield, Godfrey **1989**:2
Howard, Trevor
  Obituary **1988**:2
Ireland, Jill
  Obituary **1990**:4
Knopfler, Mark **1986**:2
Laing, R.D.
  Obituary **1990**:1
Lawrence, Ruth
  Brief Entry **1986**:3
Leach, Robin
  Brief Entry **1985**:4
Lennox, Annie **1985**:4 **1996**:4
Livingstone, Ken **1988**:3
Lloyd Webber, Andrew **1989**:1
Macmillan, Harold
  Obituary **1987**:2
MacMillan, Kenneth
  Obituary **1993**:2
Maxwell, Robert **1990**:1
Michael, George **1989**:2
Milne, Christopher Robin
  Obituary **1996**:4
Moore, Henry
  Obituary **1986**:4
Murdoch, Iris
  Obituary **1999**:4
Norrington, Roger **1989**:4
Oldman, Gary **1998**:1
Olivier, Laurence
  Obituary **1989**:4
Philby, Kim
  Obituary **1988**:3
Rattle, Simon **1989**:4
Redgrave, Vanessa **1989**:2
Rhodes, Zandra **1986**:2
Roddick, Anita **1989**:4
Runcie, Robert **1989**:4
Saatchi, Charles **1987**:3

Steptoe, Patrick
  Obituary **1988**:3
Stevens, James
  Brief Entry **1988**:1
Thatcher, Margaret **1989**:2
Tudor, Antony
  Obituary **1987**:4
Ullman, Tracey **1988**:3
Wilson, Peter C.
  Obituary **1985**:2
Wintour, Anna **1990**:4

BRUNEI

Bolkiah, Sultan Muda Hassanal
  1985:4

BULGARIAN

Christo **1992**:3
Dimitrova, Ghena **1987**:1

BURMESE

Suu Kyi, Aung San **1996**:2

CAMBODIAN

Lon Nol
  Obituary **1986**:1
Pol Pot
  Obituary **1998**:4

CANADIAN

Altman, Sidney **1997**:2
Barenaked Ladies **1997**:2
Black, Conrad **1986**:2
Bouchard, Lucien **1999**:2
Bourassa, Robert
  Obituary **1997**:1
Bourque, Raymond Jean **1997**:3
Burr, Raymond
  Obituary **1994**:1
Campbell, Kim **1993**:4
Campbell, Neve **1998**:2
Campeau, Robert **1990**:1
Candy, John **1988**:2
  Obituary **1994**:3
Carrey, Jim **1995**:1
Cerovsek, Corey
  Brief Entry **1987**:4
Cherry, Don **1993**:4
Chretien, Jean **1990**:4 **1997**:2
Coffey, Paul **1985**:4
Copps, Sheila **1986**:4
Cronenberg, David **1992**:3
Dewhurst, Colleen
  Obituary **1992**:2
Dion, Celine **1995**:3
Eagleson, Alan **1987**:4
Ebbers, Bernie **1998**:1
Egoyan, Atom **2000**:2
Erickson, Arthur **1989**:3
Fonyo, Steve
  Brief Entry **1985**:4
Foster, David **1988**:2
Fox, Michael J. **1986**:1
Frank, Robert **1995**:2
Frye, Northrop
  Obituary **1991**:3
Fuhr, Grant **1997**:3
Garneau, Marc **1985**:1
Gatien, Peter
  Brief Entry **1986**:1
Gilmour, Doug **1994**:3

Graham, Nicholas **1991**:4
Green, Tom **1999**:4
Greene, Graham **1997**:2
Greene, Lorne
  Obituary **1988**:1
Gretzky, Wayne **1989**:2
Haney, Chris
  Brief Entry **1985**:1
Harris, Michael Deane **1997**:2
Hayakawa, Samuel Ichiye
  Obituary **1992**:3
Hextall, Ron **1988**:2
Hull, Brett **1991**:4
Jennings, Peter Charles **1997**:2
Johnson, Pierre Marc **1985**:4
Jones, Jenny **1998**:2
Juneau, Pierre **1988**:3
Jung, Andrea **2000**:2
Keeler, Ruby
  Obituary **1993**:4
Kent, Arthur **1991**:4 **1997**:2
Kielburger, Craig **1998**:1
Lalonde, Marc **1985**:1
Lang, K.D. **1988**:4
Lanois, Daniel **1991**:1
Lemieux, Claude **1996**:1
Lemieux, Mario **1986**:4
Levesque, Rene
  Obituary **1988**:1
Lewis, Stephen **1987**:2
Mandel, Howie **1989**:1
Markle, C. Wilson **1988**:1
McLachlan, Sarah **1998**:4
McLaren, Norman
  Obituary **1987**:2
McLaughlin, Audrey **1990**:3
McTaggart, David **1989**:4
Messier, Mark **1993**:1
Morgentaler, Henry **1986**:3
Morissette, Alanis **1996**:2
Mulroney, Brian **1989**:2
Munro, Alice **1997**:1
Myers, Mike **1992**:3 **1997**:4
O'Donnell, Bill
  Brief Entry **1987**:4
Ondaatje, Philip Michael **1997**:3
Parizeau, Jacques **1995**:1
Peckford, Brian **1989**:1
Peterson, David **1987**:1
Pocklington, Peter H. **1985**:2
Pratt, Christopher **1985**:3
Raffi **1988**:1
Randi, James **1990**:2
Reisman, Simon **1987**:4
Reitman, Ivan **1986**:3
Reuben, Gloria **1999**:4
Richard, Maurice
  Obituary **2000**:4
Roy, Patrick **1994**:2
Rypien, Mark **1992**:3
Sainte-Marie, Buffy **2000**:1
Shaffer, Paul **1987**:1
Short, Martin **1986**:1
Strong, Maurice **1993**:1
Twain, Shania **1996**:3
Vander Zalm, William **1987**:3
Vickrey, William S.
  Obituary **1997**:2
Villeneuve, Jacques **1997**:1
Williams, Lynn **1986**:4
Wilson, Bertha
  Brief Entry **1986**:1

Wood, Sharon
  Brief Entry **1988**:1
Young, Neil **1991**:2
Yzerman, Steve **1991**:2

CHILEAN
  Arrau, Claudio
    Obituary **1992**:1
  Pinochet, Augusto **1999**:2

CHINESE
  Chan, Jackie **1996**:1
  Chen, Joan **2000**:2
  Chen, T.C.
    Brief Entry **1987**:3
  Deng Xiaoping **1995**:1
    Obituary **1997**:3
  Fang Lizhi **1988**:1
  Gong Li **1998**:4
  Hatem, George
    Obituary **1989**:1
  Hou Hsiao-hsien **2000**:2
  Hu Yaobang
    Obituary **1989**:4
  Hwang, David Henry **1999**:1
  Jiang Quing
    Obituary **1992**:1
  Jiang Zemin **1996**:1
  Lee, Ang **1996**:3
  Lee, Henry C. **1997**:1
  Lord, Bette Bao **1994**:1
  Lucid, Shannon **1997**:1
  Wei Jingsheng **1998**:2
  Woo, John **1994**:2
  Wu, Harry **1996**:1
  Ye Jianying
    Obituary **1987**:1
  Yen, Samuel **1996**:4
  Zhao Ziyang **1989**:1

COLOMBIAN
  Botero, Fernando **1994**:3
  Leguizamo, John **1999**:1
  Schroeder, Barbet **1996**:1

CONGOLESE
  Kabila, Laurent **1998**:1
  Mobutu Sese Seko
    Obituary **1998**:4

COSTA RICAN
  Arias Sanchez, Oscar **1989**:3

CROATIAN
  Tudjman, Franjo **1996**:2
  Tudjman, Franjo
    Obituary **2000**:2

CUBAN
  Acosta, Carlos **1997**:4
  Canseco, Jose **1990**:2
  Castro, Fidel **1991**:4
  Cugat, Xavier
    Obituary **1991**:2
  Estefan, Gloria **1991**:4
  Garcia, Andy **1999**:3
  Garcia, Cristina **1997**:4
  Goizueta, Roberto **1996**:1
    Obituary **1998**:1
  Saralegui, Cristina **1999**:2

Zamora, Pedro
  Obituary **1995**:2

CZECH
  Albright, Madeleine **1994**:3
  Hammer, Jan **1987**:3
  Hasek, Dominik **1998**:3
  Havel, Vaclav **1990**:3
  Hingis, Martina **1999**:1
  Hrabal, Bohumil
    Obituary **1997**:3
  Jagr, Jaromir **1995**:4
  Klima, Petr **1987**:1
  Kukoc, Toni **1995**:4
  Maxwell, Robert
    Obituary **1992**:2
  Porizkova, Paulina
    Brief Entry **1986**:4
  Serkin, Rudolf
    Obituary **1992**:1
  Stoppard, Tom **1995**:4
  Trump, Ivana **1995**:2

DANISH
  Kristiansen, Kjeld Kirk **1988**:3
  Lander, Toni
    Obituary **1985**:4

DOMINICAN
  Sosa, Sammy **1999**:1

DUTCH
  de Kooning, Willem **1994**:4
    Obituary **1997**:3
  Parker, Colonel Tom
    Obituary **1997**:2

EGYPTIAN
  Ghali, Boutros Boutros **1992**:3
  Mubarak, Hosni **1991**:4
  Rahman, Sheik Omar Abdel- **1993**:3

ENGLISH
  Altea, Rosemary **1996**:3
  Amanpour, Christiane **1997**:2
  Ambler, Eric
    Obituary **1999**:2
  Amis, Kingsley
    Obituary **1996**:2
  Andrews, Julie **1996**:1
  Ashcroft, Peggy
    Obituary **1992**:1
  Bee Gees, The **1997**:4
  Berners-Lee, Tim **1997**:4
  Blair, Tony **1997**:4
  Bonham Carter, Helena **1998**:4
  Bowie, David **1998**:2
  Brown, Tina **1992**:1
  Burgess, Anthony
    Obituary **1994**:2
  Bush, Kate **1994**:3
  Caine, Michael **2000**:4
  Campbell, Naomi **2000**:2
  Carey, George **1992**:3
  Charles, Prince of Wales **1995**:3
  Clapton, Eric **1993**:3
  Comfort, Alex
    Obituary **2000**:4
  Cook, Peter
    Obituary **1995**:2

Costello, Elvis **1994**:4
Crawford, Michael **1994**:2
Crisp, Quentin
  Obituary **2000**:3
Cushing, Peter
  Obituary **1995**:1
Diana, Princess of Wales **1993**:1
  Obituary **1997**:4
Driver, Minnie **2000**:1
Elliott, Denholm
  Obituary **1993**:2
Everything But The Girl **1996**:4
Faldo, Nick **1993**:3
Fielding, Helen **2000**:4
Fiennes, Ralph **1996**:2
Fonteyn, Margot
  Obituary **1991**:3
Freud, Lucian **2000**:4
Gielgud, John
  Obituary **2000**:4
Grant, Hugh **1995**:3
Greene, Graham
  Obituary **1991**:4
Harvey, Polly Jean **1995**:4
Headroom, Max **1986**:4
Hebard, Caroline **1998**:2
Hill, Benny
  Obituary **1992**:3
Hughes, Ted
  Obituary **1999**:2
Hume, Basil Cardinal
  Obituary **2000**:1
Humphry, Derek **1992**:2
Hurley, Elizabeth **1999**:2
Irons, Jeremy **1991**:4
John, Elton **1995**:4
Lane, Ronnie
  Obituary **1997**:4
Law, Jude **2000**:3
Leach, Penelope **1992**:4
Leakey, Mary Douglas
  Obituary **1997**:2
le Carre, John **2000**:1
LeVay, Simon **1992**:2
Lewis, Lennox **2000**:2
Lupino, Ida
  Obituary **1996**:1
Lyne, Adrian **1997**:2
Major, John **1991**:2
McDowall, Roddy
  Obituary **1999**:1
McKellen, Ian **1994**:1
Mercury, Freddie
  Obituary **1992**:2
Montagu, Ashley
  Obituary **2000**:2
Moss, Kate **1995**:3
Newkirk, Ingrid **1992**:3
Newton-John, Olivia **1998**:4
Nunn, Trevor **2000**:2
Oasis **1996**:3
Ogilvy, David
  Obituary **2000**:1
Osborne, John
  Obituary **1995**:2
Park, Nick **1997**:3
Patten, Christopher **1993**:3
Penrose, Roger **1991**:4
Pleasence, Donald
  Obituary **1995**:3
Redgrave, Lynn **1999**:3
Richards, Keith **1993**:3

Roth, Tim **1998**:2
Saatchi, Maurice **1995**:4
Sacks, Oliver **1995**:4
Seal **1994**:4
Seymour, Jane **1994**:4
Springer, Jerry **1998**:4
Springfield, Dusty
    Obituary **1999**:3
Stewart, Patrick **1996**:1
Sting **1991**:4
Stoppard, Tom **1995**:4
Sullivan, Andrew **1996**:1
Taylor, Elizabeth **1993**:3
Thompson, Emma **1993**:2
Tilberis, Elizabeth **1994**:3
Trotman, Alex **1995**:4
Uchida, Mitsuko **1989**:3
Westwood, Vivienne **1998**:3
Wiles, Andrew **1994**:1
Wilmut, Ian **1997**:3

FIJI ISLANDER
Singh, Vijay **2000**:4

FILIPINO
Aquino, Corazon **1986**:2
Lewis, Loida Nicolas **1998**:3
Marcos, Ferdinand
    Obituary **1990**:1
Natori, Josie **1994**:3
Ramos, Fidel **1995**:2

FINNISH
Kekkonen, Urho
    Obituary **1986**:4
Torvalds, Linus **1999**:3

FRENCH
Adjani, Isabelle **1991**:1
Arnault, Bernard **2000**:4
Baulieu, Etienne-Emile **1990**:1
Besse, Georges
    Obituary **1987**:1
Bourgeois, Louise **1994**:1
Brando, Cheyenne
    Obituary **1995**:4
Calment, Jeanne
    Obituary **1997**:4
Chagall, Marc
    Obituary **1985**:2
Chirac, Jacques **1995**:4
Colbert, Claudette
    Obituary **1997**:1
Cousteau, Jacques-Yves
    Obituary **1998**:2
Cousteau, Jean-Michel **1988**:2
Cresson, Edith **1992**:1
Delors, Jacques **1990**:2
Depardieu, Gerard **1991**:2
Dubuffet, Jean
    Obituary **1985**:4
Duras, Marguerite
    Obituary **1996**:3
Gaultier, Jean-Paul **1998**:1
Godard, Jean-Luc **1998**:1
Grappelli, Stephane
    Obituary **1998**:1
Guillem, Sylvie **1988**:2
Indurain, Miguel **1994**:1
Klarsfeld, Beate **1989**:1
Lefebvre, Marcel **1988**:4

Malle, Louis
    Obituary **1996**:2
Mitterrand, Francois
    Obituary **1996**:2
Petrossian, Christian
    Brief Entry **1985**:3
Picasso, Paloma **1991**:1
Ponty, Jean-Luc **1985**:4
Prost, Alain **1988**:1
Rampal, Jean-Pierre **1989**:2
Reza, Yasmina **1999**:2
Rothschild, Philippe de
    Obituary **1988**:2
Rykiel, Sonia **2000**:3
Thomas, Michel **1987**:4
Villechaize, Herve
    Obituary **1994**:1

GERMAN
Barbie, Klaus
    Obituary **1992**:2
Becker, Boris
    Brief Entry **1985**:3
Beuys, Joseph
    Obituary **1986**:3
Blobel, Gunter **2000**:4
Boyle, Gertrude **1995**:3
Brandt, Willy
    Obituary **1993**:2
Breitschwerdt, Werner **1988**:4
Casper, Gerhard **1993**:1
Dietrich, Marlene
    Obituary **1992**:4
Etzioni, Amitai **1994**:3
Frank, Anthony M. **1992**:1
Graf, Steffi **1987**:4
Grass, Gunter **2000**:2
Hahn, Carl H. **1986**:4
Hess, Rudolph
    Obituary **1988**:1
Honecker, Erich
    Obituary **1994**:4
Kiefer, Anselm **1990**:2
Kinski, Klaus **1987**:2
Klarsfeld, Beate **1989**:1
Kohl, Helmut **1994**:1
Lagerfeld, Karl **1999**:4
Max, Peter **1993**:2
Mengele, Josef
    Obituary **1985**:2
Mutter, Anne-Sophie **1990**:3
Nuesslein-Volhard, Christiane **1998**:1
Pfeiffer, Eckhard **1998**:4
Pilatus, Robert
    Obituary **1998**:3
Polke, Sigmar **1999**:4
Rey, Margret E.
    Obituary **1997**:2
Richter, Gerhard **1997**:2
Sander, Jil **1995**:2
Schily, Otto
    Brief Entry **1987**:4
Schrempp, Juergen **2000**:2
Schroder, Gerhard **1999**:1
Witt, Katarina **1991**:3

GHANIAN
Annan, Kofi **1999**:1

GREEK
Huffington, Arianna **1996**:2
Papandreou, Andrea
    Obituary **1997**:1

GUATEMALAN
Menchu, Rigoberta **1993**:2

GUINEA-BISSAUNI
Makeba, Miriam **1989**:2
Ture, Kwame
    Obituary **1999**:2

HAITIAN
Aristide, Jean-Bertrand **1991**:3
Cedras, Raoul **1994**:4
Preval, Rene **1997**:2

HONG KONGER
Chow Yun-fat **1999**:4
Lee, Martin **1998**:2

HUNGARIAN
Dorati, Antal
    Obituary **1989**:2
Fodor, Eugene
    Obituary **1991**:3
Gabor, Eva
    Obituary **1996**:1
Grove, Andrew S. **1995**:3
Polgar, Judit **1993**:3
Solti, Georg
    Obituary **1998**:1

ICELANDIC
Bjork **1996**:1
Finnbogadottir, Vigdis
    Brief Entry **1986**:2

INDIAN
Chopra, Deepak **1996**:3
Devi, Phoolan **1986**:1
Durrell, Gerald
    Obituary **1995**:3
Gandhi, Indira
    Obituary **1985**:1
Gandhi, Rajiv
    Obituary **1991**:4
Gandhi, Sonia **2000**:2
Gowda, H. D. Deve **1997**:1
Mahesh Yogi, Maharishi **1991**:3
Mehta, Zubin **1994**:3
Mother Teresa **1993**:1
    Obituary **1998**:1
Musharraf, Pervez **2000**:2
Prowse, Juliet
    Obituary **1997**:1
Rajneesh, Bhagwan Shree
    Obituary **1990**:2
Ram, Jagjivan
    Obituary **1986**:4
Rao, P. V. Narasimha **1993**:2
Rushdie, Salman **1994**:1
Vajpayee, Atal Behari **1998**:4
Wahid, Abdurrahman **2000**:3

INDONESIAN
Habibie, Bacharuddin Jusuf **1999**:3
Megawati Sukarnoputri **2000**:1

MOZAMBICAN
Chissano, Joaquim **1987**:4
Dhlakama, Afonso **1993**:3
Machel, Samora
Obituary **1987**:1

NAMIBIAN
Nujoma, Sam **1990**:4

NEW ZEALANDER
Campion, Jane **1991**:4
Crowe, Russell **2000**:4
Shipley, Jenny **1998**:3

NICARAGUAN
Astorga, Nora **1988**:2
Cruz, Arturo **1985**:1
Obando, Miguel **1986**:4
Robelo, Alfonso **1988**:1

NIGERAN
Abacha, Sani **1996**:3
Babangida, Ibrahim Badamosi **1992**:4
Obasanjo, Olusegun **2000**:2
Okoye, Christian **1990**:2
Olajuwon, Akeem **1985**:1
Sade **1993**:2
Saro-Wiwa, Ken
Obituary **1996**:2

NORWEGIAN
Brundtland, Gro Harlem **2000**:1
Cammermeyer, Margarethe **1995**:2
Olav, King of Norway
Obituary **1991**:3

PAKISTANI
Bhutto, Benazir **1989**:4
Zia ul-Haq, Mohammad
Obituary **1988**:4

PALESTINIAN
Arafat, Yasser **1989**:3 **1997**:3
Freij, Elias **1986**:4
Habash, George **1986**:1
Husseini, Faisal **1998**:4
Nidal, Abu **1987**:1
Terzi, Zehdi Labib **1985**:3

PANAMANIAN
Blades, Ruben **1998**:2

PERUVIAN
Fujimori, Alberto **1992**:4
Perez de Cuellar, Javier **1991**:3

POLISH
Begin, Menachem
Obituary **1992**:3
Eisenstaedt, Alfred
Obituary **1996**:1
John Paul II, Pope **1995**:3
Kieslowski, Krzysztof
Obituary **1996**:3
Kinski, Klaus
Obituary **1992**:2
Kosinski, Jerzy
Obituary **1991**:4

Masur, Kurt **1993**:4
Niezabitowska, Malgorzata **1991**:3
Rosten, Leo
Obituary **1997**:3
Sabin, Albert
Obituary **1993**:4
Singer, Isaac Bashevis
Obituary **1992**:1
Walesa, Lech **1991**:2

PORTUGUESE
Saramago, Jose **1999**:1

PUERTO RICAN
Alvarez, Aida **1999**:2
Ferrer, Jose
Obituary **1992**:3
Julia, Raul
Obituary **1995**:1
Martin, Ricky **1999**:4
Novello, Antonia **1991**:2
Trinidad, Felix **2000**:4

ROMANIAN
Ceausescu, Nicolae
Obituary **1990**:2
Codrescu, Andre **1997**:3

RUSSIAN
Brodsky, Joseph
Obituary **1996**:3
Gorbachev, Raisa
Obituary **2000**:2
Gordeeva, Ekaterina **1996**:4
Grinkov, Sergei
Obituary **1996**:2
Kasparov, Garry **1997**:4
Konstantinov, Vladimir **1997**:4
Kournikova, Anna **2000**:3
Lebed, Alexander **1997**:1
Primakov, Yevgeny **1999**:3
Putin, Vladimir **2000**:3
Sarraute, Nathalie
Obituary **2000**:2
Schneerson, Menachem Mendel **1992**:4
Obituary **1994**:4

SALVADORAN
Duarte, Jose Napoleon
Obituary **1990**:3

SCOTTISH
Connery, Sean **1990**:4
McGregor, Ewan **1998**:2
Rowling, J.K. **2000**:1

SOUTH AFRICAN
Blackburn, Molly
Obituary **1985**:4
Buthelezi, Mangosuthu Gatsha **1989**:3
de Klerk, F.W. **1990**:1
Duncan, Sheena
Brief Entry **1987**:1
Fugard, Athol **1992**:3
Hani, Chris
Obituary **1993**:4
Makeba, Miriam **1989**:2
Mandela, Nelson **1990**:3

Mandela, Winnie **1989**:3
Matthews, Dave **1999**:3
Mbeki, Thabo **1999**:4
Paton, Alan
Obituary **1988**:3
Ramaphosa, Cyril **1988**:2
Slovo, Joe **1989**:2
Suzman, Helen **1989**:3
Tambo, Oliver **1991**:3
Treurnicht, Andries **1992**:2

SOVIET
Asimov, Isaac
Obituary **1992**:3
Chernenko, Konstantin
Obituary **1985**:1
Dalai Lama **1989**:1
Dubinin, Yuri **1987**:4
Dzhanibekov, Vladimir **1988**:1
Erte
Obituary **1990**:4
Federov, Sergei **1995**:1
Godunov, Alexander
Obituary **1995**:4
Gorbachev, Mikhail **1985**:2
Grebenshikov, Boris **1990**:1
Gromyko, Andrei
Obituary **1990**:2
Karadzic, Radovan **1995**:3
Milosevic, Slobodan **1993**:2
Molotov, Vyacheslav Mikhailovich
Obituary **1987**:1
Nureyev, Rudolf
Obituary **1993**:2
Sakharov, Andrei Dmitrievich
Obituary **1990**:2
Smirnoff, Yakov **1987**:2
Vidov, Oleg **1987**:4
Yeltsin, Boris **1991**:1
Zhirinovsky, Vladimir **1994**:2

SPANISH
Almodovar, Pedro **2000**:3
Banderas, Antonio **1996**:2
Blahnik, Manolo **2000**:2
Carreras, Jose **1995**:2
Dali, Salvador
Obituary **1989**:2
de Pinies, Jamie
Brief Entry **1986**:3
Domingo, Placido **1993**:2
Juan Carlos I **1993**:1
Lopez de Arriortua, Jose Ignacio **1993**:4
Miro, Joan
Obituary **1985**:1
Moneo, Jose Rafael **1996**:4
Montoya, Carlos
Obituary **1993**:4
Samaranch, Juan Antonio **1986**:2
Segovia, Andres
Obituary **1987**:3
Wences, Senor
Obituary **1999**:4

SRI LANKAN
Ondaatje, Philip Michael **1997**:3

SUDANESE
Turabi, Hassan **1995**:4

SWEDISH
Bergman, Ingmar **1999**:4
Cardigans, The **1997**:4
Garbo, Greta
Obituary **1990**:3
Lindbergh, Pelle
Obituary **1985**:4
Olin, Lena **1991**:2
Palme, Olof
Obituary **1986**:2
Renvall, Johan
Brief Entry **1987**:4

SWISS
Frank, Robert **1995**:2
Vollenweider, Andreas **1985**:2

SYRIAN
Assad, Hafez
Obituary **2000**:4
Assad, Hafez al- **1992**:1
Assad, Rifaat **1986**:3

TAHITIAN
Brando, Cheyenne
Obituary **1995**:4

TAIWANESE
Ho, David **1997**:2
Lee Teng-hui **2000**:1

TANZANIAN
Nyerere, Julius
Obituary **2000**:2

TRINIDADIAN
Ture, Kwame
Obituary **1999**:2

TURKISH
Ocalan, Abdullah **1999**:4

UKRAINIAN
Baiul, Oksana **1995**:3

VENEZUELAN
Herrera, Carolina **1997**:1
Perez, Carlos Andre **1990**:2

VIETNAMESE
Dong, Pham Van
Obituary **2000**:4
Le Duan
Obituary **1986**:4

Le Duc Tho
Obituary **1991**:1

WELSH
Dahl, Roald
Obituary **1991**:2
Hopkins, Anthony **1992**:4
Jones, Tom **1993**:4
Zeta-Jones, Catherine **1999**:4

YUGOSLAVIAN
Filipovic, Zlata **1994**:4
Pogorelich, Ivo **1986**:4
Seles, Monica **1991**:3

ZAIRAN
Mobutu Sese Seko **1993**:4
Obituary **1998**:1

ZAMBIAN
Chiluba, Frederick **1992**:3

ZIMBABWEAN
Mugabe, Robert **1988**:4

2000 Occupation Index

This index lists all newsmakers alphabetically by their occupations or fields of primary activity. Indexes in softbound issues allow access to the current year's entries; indexes in annual hardbound volumes are cumulative, covering the entire *Newsmakers* series.

Listee names are followed by a year and issue number; thus **1996**:3 indicates that an entry on that individual appears in both 1996, Issue 3 and the 1996 cumulation. For access to newsmakers appearing earlier than the current softbound issue, see the previous year's cumulation.

ART AND DESIGN

Adams, Scott **1996**:4
Addams, Charles
  Obituary **1989**:1
Anderson, Laurie **2000**:2
Arman **1993**:1
Armani, Giorgio **1991**:2
Avedon, Richard **1993**:4
Baldessari, John **1991**:4
Banks, Jeffrey **1998**:2
Barbera, Joseph **1988**:2
Barnes, Ernie **1997**:4
Barry, Lynda **1992**:1
Bean, Alan L. **1986**:2
Beuys, Joseph
  Obituary **1986**:3
Blahnik, Manolo **2000**:2
Boone, Mary **1985**:1
Botero, Fernando **1994**:3
Bourgeois, Louise **1994**:1
Bowie, David **1998**:2
Bunshaft, Gordon **1989**:3
  Obituary **1991**:1
Cameron, David
  Brief Entry **1988**:1
Campbell, Ben Nighthorse **1998**:1
Campbell, Naomi **2000**:2
Castelli, Leo
  Obituary **2000**:1
Catlett, Elizabeth **1999**:3
Chagall, Marc
  Obituary **1985**:2
Chast, Roz **1992**:4
Chatham, Russell **1990**:1
Chia, Sandro **1987**:2
Chihuly, Dale **1995**:2
Christo **1992**:3
Claiborne, Liz **1986**:3
Clemente, Francesco **1992**:2
Cooper, Alexander **1988**:4
Crumb, R. **1995**:4
Dali, Salvador
  Obituary **1989**:2
DeCarava, Roy **1996**:3
de Kooning, Willem **1994**:4
  Obituary **1997**:3

Diebenkorn, Richard
  Obituary **1993**:4
Donghia, Angelo R.
  Obituary **1985**:2
Dubuffet, Jean
  Obituary **1985**:4
Eisenman, Peter **1992**:4
Eisenstaedt, Alfred
  Obituary **1996**:1
Ellis, Perry
  Obituary **1986**:3
Engelbreit, Mary **1994**:3
Erickson, Arthur **1989**:3
Erte
  Obituary **1990**:4
Finley, Karen **1992**:4
Fisher, Mary **1994**:3
Ford, Tom **1999**:3
Foster, Norman **1999**:4
Frank, Robert **1995**:2
Frankenthaler, Helen **1990**:1
Freud, Lucian **2000**:4
Gaines, William M.
  Obituary **1993**:1
Gaultier, Jean-Paul **1998**:1
Gehry, Frank O. **1987**:1
Gober, Robert **1996**:3
Goody, Joan **1990**:2
Gould, Chester
  Obituary **1985**:2
Graham, Nicholas **1991**:4
Graham, Robert **1993**:4
Graves, Michael **2000**:1
Graves, Nancy **1989**:3
Groening, Matt **1990**:4
Guccione, Bob **1986**:1
Gund, Agnes **1993**:2
Halston
  Obituary **1990**:3
Handford, Martin **1991**:3
Haring, Keith
  Obituary **1990**:3
Hilfiger, Tommy **1993**:3
Hockney, David **1988**:3
Hughes, Robert **1996**:4
Isozaki, Arata **1990**:2
Jahn, Helmut **1987**:3

Johnson, Betsey **1996**:2
Johnson, Philip **1989**:2
Jordan, Charles M. **1989**:4
Judge, Mike **1994**:2
Kahlo, Frida **1991**:3
Kamali, Norma **1989**:1
Karan, Donna **1988**:1
Kaskey, Ray
  Brief Entry **1987**:2
Katz, Alex **1990**:3
Kelly, Ellsworth **1992**:1
Kelly, Patrick
  Obituary **1990**:2
Kent, Corita
  Obituary **1987**:1
Kiefer, Anselm **1990**:2
Klein, Calvin **1996**:2
Koons, Jeff **1991**:4
Kors, Michael **2000**:4
Kostabi, Mark **1989**:4
Lagerfeld, Karl **1999**:4
Lang, Helmut **1999**:2
Lauren, Ralph **1990**:1
Leibovitz, Annie **1988**:4
Lichtenstein, Roy **1994**:1
  Obituary **1998**:1
Lin, Maya **1990**:3
Longo, Robert **1990**:4
MacNelly, Jeff
  Obituary **2000**:4
Mansion, Gracie
  Brief Entry **1986**:3
Mapplethorpe, Robert
  Obituary **1989**:3
Max, Peter **1993**:2
McCartney, Linda
  Obituary **1998**:4
McFarlane, Todd **1999**:1
Mellinger, Frederick
  Obituary **1990**:4
Miller, Nicole **1995**:4
Miro, Joan
  Obituary **1985**:1
Misrach, Richard **1991**:2
Miyake, Issey **1985**:2
Mizrahi, Isaac **1991**:1
Moneo, Jose Rafael **1996**:4

Moore, Henry
  Obituary **1986**:4
Motherwell, Robert
  Obituary **1992**:1
Mumford, Lewis
  Obituary **1990**:2
Natori, Josie **1994**:3
Nauman, Bruce **1995**:4
Nechita, Alexandra **1996**:4
Neiman, LeRoy **1993**:3
Nevelson, Louise
  Obituary **1988**:3
Newman, Arnold **1993**:1
Nipon, Albert
  Brief Entry **1986**:4
Ogilvy, David
  Obituary **2000**:1
Oldham, Todd **1995**:4
Ono, Yoko **1989**:2
Pedersen, William **1989**:4
Pei, I.M. **1990**:4
Pelli, Cesar **1991**:4
Penn & Teller **1992**:1
Picasso, Paloma **1991**:1
Polke, Sigmar **1999**:4
Portman, John **1988**:2
Potok, Anna Maximilian
  Brief Entry **1985**:2
Pozzi, Lucio **1990**:2
Prada, Miuccia **1996**:1
Pratt, Christopher **1985**:3
Predock, Antoine **1993**:2
Radocy, Robert
  Brief Entry **1986**:3
Raimondi, John
  Brief Entry **1987**:4
Raskin, Jef **1997**:4
Rauschenberg, Robert **1991**:2
Rhodes, Zandra **1986**:2
Richter, Gerhard **1997**:2
Ringgold, Faith **2000**:3
Ritts, Herb **1992**:4
Roberts, Xavier **1985**:3
Roche, Kevin **1985**:1
Rosenberg, Evelyn **1988**:2
Rothenberg, Susan **1995**:3
Rouse, James
  Obituary **1996**:4
Rykiel, Sonia **2000**:3
Saatchi, Charles **1987**:3
Salgado, Sebastiao **1994**:2
Schnabel, Julian **1997**:1
Schulz, Charles
  Obituary **2000**:3
Schulz, Charles M. **1998**:1
Serrano, Andres **2000**:4
Sherman, Cindy **1992**:3
Smith, Willi
  Obituary **1987**:3
Spiegelman, Art **1998**:3
Stella, Frank **1996**:2
Sui, Anna **1995**:1
Tamayo, Rufino
  Obituary **1992**:1
Thiebaud, Wayne **1991**:1
Tompkins, Susie
  Brief Entry **1987**:2
Trudeau, Garry **1991**:2
Truitt, Anne **1993**:1
Twombley, Cy **1995**:1
Tyler, Richard **1995**:3
Venturi, Robert **1994**:4

Versace, Donatella **1999**:1
Versace, Gianni
  Brief Entry **1988**:1
  Obituary **1998**:2
von Furstenberg, Diane **1994**:2
Vreeland, Diana
  Obituary **1990**:1
Walker, Kara **1999**:2
Warhol, Andy
  Obituary **1987**:2
Washington, Alonzo **2000**:1
Watterson, Bill **1990**:3
Wegman, William **1991**:1
Westwood, Vivienne **1998**:3
Wilson, Peter C.
  Obituary **1985**:2
Wintour, Anna **1990**:4
Witkin, Joel-Peter **1996**:1
Yamasaki, Minoru
  Obituary **1986**:2

BUSINESS

Ackerman, Will **1987**:4
Agnelli, Giovanni **1989**:4
Ailes, Roger **1989**:3
Akers, John F. **1988**:3
Akin, Phil
  Brief Entry **1987**:3
Allaire, Paul **1995**:1
Allen, Bob **1992**:4
Allen, John **1992**:1
Alter, Hobie
  Brief Entry **1985**:1
Alvarez, Aida **1999**:2
Amos, Wally **2000**:1
Ancier, Garth **1989**:1
Andreessen, Marc **1996**:2
Annenberg, Walter **1992**:3
Antonini, Joseph **1991**:2
Aoki, Rocky **1990**:2
Aretsky, Ken **1988**:1
Arison, Ted **1990**:3
Arledge, Roone **1992**:2
Arnault, Bernard **2000**:4
Ash, Mary Kay **1996**:1
Aurre, Laura
  Brief Entry **1986**:3
Ballmer, Steven **1997**:2
Banks, Jeffrey **1998**:2
Barad, Jill **1994**:2
Barksdale, James L. **1998**:2
Barrett, Craig R. **1999**:4
Bauer, Eddie
  Obituary **1986**:3
Beals, Vaughn **1988**:2
Beers, Charlotte **1999**:3
Ben & Jerry **1991**:3
Benetton, Luciano **1988**:1
Berlusconi, Silvio **1994**:4
Besse, Georges
  Obituary **1987**:1
Bezos, Jeff **1998**:4
Bieber, Owen **1986**:1
Bikoff, James L.
  Brief Entry **1986**:2
Black, Cathleen **1998**:4
Black, Conrad **1986**:2
Bloch, Henry **1988**:4
Bloch, Ivan **1986**:3
Bloomberg, Michael **1997**:1
Boiardi, Hector
  Obituary **1985**:3

Bolkiah, Sultan Muda Hassanal
  1985:4
Bond, Alan **1989**:2
Bose, Amar
  Brief Entry **1986**:4
Boyer, Herbert Wayne **1985**:1
Boyle, Gertrude **1995**:3
Branson, Richard **1987**:1
Bravo, Ellen **1998**:2
Breitschwerdt, Werner **1988**:4
Brennan, Edward A. **1989**:1
Brennan, Robert E. **1988**:1
Bronfman, Edgar, Jr. **1994**:4
Brooks, Diana D. **1990**:1
Brown, Tina **1992**:1
Buffett, Jimmy **1999**:3
Buffett, Warren **1995**:2
Burnison, Chantal Simone **1988**:3
Burns, Robin **1991**:2
Burr, Donald Calvin **1985**:3
Busch, August A. III **1988**:2
Busch, August Anheuser, Jr.
  Obituary **1990**:2
Bushnell, Nolan **1985**:1
Buss, Jerry **1989**:3
Cain, Herman **1998**:3
Calloway, D. Wayne **1987**:3
Campeau, Robert **1990**:1
Canfield, Alan B.
  Brief Entry **1986**:3
Carter, Billy
  Obituary **1989**:1
Case, Steve **1995**:4 **1996**:4
Chenault, Kenneth I. **1999**:3
Claiborne, Liz **1986**:3
Clark, Jim **1997**:1
Coleman, Sheldon, Jr. **1990**:2
Combs, Sean Puffy **1998**:4
Cooper, Alexander **1988**:4
Coors, William K.
  Brief Entry **1985**:1
Copeland, Al **1988**:3
Covey, Stephen R. **1994**:4
Cox, Richard Joseph
  Brief Entry **1985**:1
Craig, Sid and Jenny **1993**:4
Crandall, Robert L. **1992**:1
Crawford, Cheryl
  Obituary **1987**:1
Cray, Seymour R.
  Brief Entry **1986**:3
  Obituary **1997**:2
Cummings, Sam **1986**:3
D'Alessio, Kitty
  Brief Entry **1987**:3
Davison, Ian Hay **1986**:1
DeBartolo, Edward J., Jr. **1989**:3
Dell, Michael **1996**:2
Deming, W. Edwards **1992**:2
  Obituary **1994**:2
de Passe, Suzanne **1990**:4
Diemer, Walter E.
  Obituary **1998**:2
DiFranco, Ani **1997**:1
Diller, Barry **1991**:1
Disney, Lillian
  Obituary **1998**:3
Disney, Roy E. **1986**:3
Dolby, Ray Milton
  Brief Entry **1986**:1
Doubleday, Nelson, Jr. **1987**:1
Drexler, Millard S. **1990**:3

Morgan, Dodge **1987**:1
Morita, Akio **1989**:4
Morita, Akio
　Obituary **2000**:2
Moritz, Charles **1989**:3
Mosbacher, Georgette **1994**:2
Murdoch, Rupert **1988**:4
Murray, Arthur
　Obituary **1991**:3
Neuharth, Allen H. **1986**:1
Newhouse, Samuel I., Jr. **1997**:1
Nipon, Albert
　Brief Entry **1986**:4
Noyce, Robert N. **1985**:4
Nussbaum, Karen **1988**:3
Olsen, Kenneth H. **1986**:4
Ostin, Mo **1996**:2
Otte, Ruth **1992**:4
Ovitz, Michael **1990**:1
Packard, David
　Obituary **1996**:3
Paulucci, Jeno
　Brief Entry **1986**:3
Peller, Clara
　Obituary **1988**:1
Penske, Roger **1988**:3
Perelman, Ronald **1989**:2
Perot, H. Ross **1992**:4
Peters, Tom **1998**:1
Petersen, Donald Eugene **1985**:1
Petrossian, Christian
　Brief Entry **1985**:3
Pfeiffer, Eckhard **1998**:4
Phelan, John Joseph, Jr. **1985**:4
Pierce, Frederick S. **1985**:3
Pittman, Robert W. **1985**:1
Pocklington, Peter H. **1985**:2
Popcorn, Faith
　Brief Entry **1988**:1
Pope, Generoso **1988**:4
Porizkova, Paulina
　Brief Entry **1986**:4
Porsche, Ferdinand
　Obituary **1998**:4
Porter, Sylvia
　Obituary **1991**:4
Portman, John **1988**:2
Prada, Miuccia **1996**:1
Pratt, Jane **1999**:1
Presser, Jackie
　Obituary **1988**:4
Pritzker, A.N.
　Obituary **1986**:2
Proctor, Barbara Gardner **1985**:3
Puck, Wolfgang **1990**:1
Quinn, Jane Bryant **1993**:4
Radocy, Robert
　Brief Entry **1986**:3
Rand, A. Barry **2000**:3
Rapp, C.J.
　Brief Entry **1987**:3
Raymond, Lee R. **2000**:3
Redenbacher, Orville
　Obituary **1996**:1
Redstone, Sumner **1994**:1
Rhodes, Zandra **1986**:2
Riggio, Leonard S. **1999**:4
Riney, Hal **1989**:1
Riordan, Richard **1993**:4
Roberts, Xavier **1985**:3
Roddick, Anita **1989**:4

Rooney, Art
　Obituary **1989**:1
Roosevelt, Franklin D., Jr.
　Obituary **1989**:1
Ross, Percy
　Brief Entry **1986**:2
Ross, Steven J.
　Obituary **1993**:3
Rothschild, Philippe de
　Obituary **1988**:2
Rothstein, Ruth **1988**:2
Rowland, Pleasant **1992**:3
Saatchi, Maurice **1995**:4
Sagansky, Jeff **1993**:2
Sander, Jil **1995**:2
Sasakawa, Ryoichi
　Brief Entry **1988**:1
Schlessinger, David
　Brief Entry **1985**:1
Schoenfeld, Gerald **1986**:2
Schott, Marge **1985**:4
Schrempp, Juergen **2000**:2
Schultz, Howard **1995**:3
Schwab, Charles **1989**:3
Schwinn, Edward R., Jr.
　Brief Entry **1985**:4
Sculley, John **1989**:4
Sedelmaier, Joe **1985**:3
Siebert, Muriel **1987**:2
Smale, John G. **1987**:3
Smith, Frederick W. **1985**:4
Smith, Jack **1994**:3
Smith, Roger **1990**:3
Spector, Phil **1989**:1
Steel, Dawn **1990**:1
　Obituary **1998**:2
Steinberg, Leigh **1987**:3
Steinbrenner, George **1991**:1
Stempel, Robert **1991**:3
Stern, David **1991**:4
Stewart, Martha **1992**:1
Stonesifer, Patty **1997**:1
Stroh, Peter W. **1985**:2
Strong, Maurice **1993**:1
Sullivan, Andrew **1996**:1
Summers, Anne **1990**:2
Tagliabue, Paul **1990**:2
Tanny, Vic
　Obituary **1985**:3
Tartikoff, Brandon **1985**:2
　Obituary **1998**:1
Thalheimer, Richard
　Brief Entry **1988**:3
Thomas, Dave **1986**:2 **1993**:2
Thomas, Michel **1987**:4
Tilberis, Elizabeth **1994**:3
Tisch, Laurence A. **1988**:2
Tompkins, Susie
　Brief Entry **1987**:2
Toyoda, Eiji **1985**:2
Traub, Marvin
　Brief Entry **1987**:3
Treybig, James G. **1988**:3
Trotman, Alex **1995**:4
Trotter, Charlie **2000**:4
Troutt, Kenny A. **1998**:1
Trump, Donald **1989**:2
Trump, Ivana **1995**:2
Turner, Ted **1989**:1
Tyler, Richard **1995**:3
Tyson, Don **1995**:3
Unz, Ron **1999**:1

Upshaw, Gene **1988**:1
Vagelos, P. Roy **1989**:4
Veeck, Bill
　Obituary **1986**:1
Versace, Donatella **1999**:1
Versace, Gianni
　Brief Entry **1988**:1
　Obituary **1998**:2
Vinton, Will
　Brief Entry **1988**:1
von Furstenberg, Diane **1994**:2
Wachner, Linda **1988**:3 **1997**:2
Waitt, Ted **1997**:4
Waldron, Hicks B. **1987**:3
Walgreen, Charles III
　Brief Entry **1987**:4
Walton, Sam **1986**:2
　Obituary **1993**:1
Wang, An **1986**:1
　Obituary **1990**:3
Weill, Sandy **1990**:4
Weinstein, Bob and Harvey **2000**:4
Weintraub, Jerry **1986**:1
Welch, Jack **1993**:3
Westwood, Vivienne **1998**:3
Whitman, Meg **2000**:3
Whittle, Christopher **1989**:3
Williams, Edward Bennett
　Obituary **1988**:4
Williams, Lynn **1986**:4
Wilson, Jerry
　Brief Entry **1986**:2
Wilson, Peter C.
　Obituary **1985**:2
Wintour, Anna **1990**:4
Wolf, Stephen M. **1989**:3
Woodruff, Robert Winship
　Obituary **1985**:1
Wynn, Stephen A. **1994**:3
Yamamoto, Kenichi **1989**:1
Yetnikoff, Walter **1988**:1
Zamboni, Frank J.
　Brief Entry **1986**:4
Zanker, Bill
　Brief Entry **1987**:3
Ziff, William B., Jr. **1986**:4
Zuckerman, Mortimer **1986**:3

DANCE
Abdul, Paula **1990**:3
Acosta, Carlos **1997**:4
Ailey, Alvin **1989**:2
　Obituary **1990**:2
Allen, Debbie **1998**:2
Astaire, Fred
　Obituary **1987**:4
Baryshnikov, Mikhail Nikolaevich
　1997:3
Bennett, Michael
　Obituary **1988**:1
Bissell, Patrick
　Obituary **1988**:2
Bocca, Julio **1995**:3
Campbell, Neve **1998**:2
Cunningham, Merce **1998**:1
Davis, Sammy, Jr.
　Obituary **1990**:4
Dean, Laura **1989**:4
de Mille, Agnes
　Obituary **1994**:2
Englund, Richard
　Obituary **1991**.3

Fagan, Garth **2000**:1
Farrell, Suzanne **1996**:3
Feld, Eliot **1996**:1
Fenley, Molissa **1988**:3
Ferri, Alessandra **1987**:2
Flatley, Michael **1997**:3
Fonteyn, Margot
  Obituary **1991**:3
Forsythe, William **1993**:2
Fosse, Bob
  Obituary **1988**:1
Garr, Teri **1988**:4
Glover, Savion **1997**:1
Godunov, Alexander
  Obituary **1995**:4
Graham, Martha
  Obituary **1991**:4
Gregory, Cynthia **1990**:2
Guillem, Sylvie **1988**:2
Herrera, Paloma **1996**:2
Hewitt, Jennifer Love **1999**:2
Hines, Gregory **1992**:4
Jackson, Janet **1990**:4
Jamison, Judith **1990**:3
Joffrey, Robert
  Obituary **1988**:3
Jones, Bill T. **1991**:4
Kaye, Nora
  Obituary **1987**:4
Keeler, Ruby
  Obituary **1993**:4
Kelly, Gene
  Obituary **1996**:3
Kistler, Darci **1993**:1
Lander, Toni
  Obituary **1985**:4
MacMillan, Kenneth
  Obituary **1993**:2
Madonna **1985**:2
Marshall, Susan **2000**:4
Miller, Bebe **2000**:2
Mitchell, Arthur **1995**:1
Morris, Mark **1991**:1
Murray, Arthur
  Obituary **1991**:3
North, Alex **1986**:3
Nureyev, Rudolf
  Obituary **1993**:2
Parker, Sarah Jessica **1999**:2
Parsons, David **1993**:4
Perez, Rosie **1994**:2
Prowse, Juliet
  Obituary **1997**:1
Rauschenberg, Robert **1991**:2
Renvall, Johan
  Brief Entry **1987**:4
Robbins, Jerome
  Obituary **1999**:1
Rogers, Ginger
  Obituary **1995**:4
Stroman, Susan **2000**:4
Takei, Kei **1990**:2
Taylor, Paul **1992**:3
Tharp, Twyla **1992**:4
Tudor, Antony
  Obituary **1987**:4
Tune, Tommy **1994**:2
Verdi-Fletcher, Mary **1998**:2
Whelan, Wendy **1999**:3

EDUCATION

Abramson, Lyn **1986**:3
Alexander, Lamar **1991**:2
Bakker, Robert T. **1991**:3
Bayley, Corrine
  Brief Entry **1986**:4
Billington, James **1990**:3
Botstein, Leon **1985**:3
Bush, Millie **1992**:1
Campbell, Bebe Moore **1996**:2
Casper, Gerhard **1993**:1
Cavazos, Lauro F. **1989**:2
Cheek, James Edward
  Brief Entry **1987**:1
Cheney, Lynne V. **1990**:4
Clements, George **1985**:1
Cole, Johnetta B. **1994**:3
Coles, Robert **1995**:1
Commager, Henry Steele
  Obituary **1998**:3
Curran, Charles E. **1989**:2
Davis, Angela **1998**:3
Delany, Sarah
  Obituary **1999**:3
Deming, W. Edwards **1992**:2
  Obituary **1994**:2
Dershowitz, Alan **1992**:1
Dove, Rita **1994**:3
Drucker, Peter F. **1992**:3
Edelman, Marian Wright **1990**:4
Edwards, Harry **1989**:4
Etzioni, Amitai **1994**:3
Feldman, Sandra **1987**:3
Fernandez, Joseph **1991**:3
Folkman, Judah **1999**:1
Fox, Matthew **1992**:2
Fulbright, J. William
  Obituary **1995**:3
Futrell, Mary Hatwood **1986**:1
Futter, Ellen V. **1995**:1
Ghali, Boutros Boutros **1992**:3
Giamatti, A. Bartlett **1988**:4
  Obituary **1990**:1
Goldhaber, Fred
  Brief Entry **1986**:3
Gray, Hanna **1992**:4
Green, Richard R. **1988**:3
Gregorian, Vartan **1990**:3
Gund, Agnes **1993**:2
Hackney, Sheldon **1995**:1
Hair, Jay D. **1994**:3
Hayakawa, Samuel Ichiye
  Obituary **1992**:3
Healy, Bernadine **1993**:1
Healy, Timothy S. **1990**:2
Heaney, Seamus **1996**:2
Heller, Walter
  Obituary **1987**:4
Hill, Anita **1994**:1
Hillegass, Clifton Keith **1989**:4
Hunter, Madeline **1991**:2
Janzen, Daniel H. **1988**:4
Jordan, King **1990**:1
Justiz, Manuel J. **1986**:4
Kemp, Jan **1987**:2
King, Mary-Claire **1998**:3
Kopp, Wendy **1993**:3
Kozol, Jonathan **1992**:1
Lagasse, Emeril **1998**:3
Lamb, Wally **1999**:1
Lang, Eugene M. **1990**:3

Langston, J. William
  Brief Entry **1986**:2
Lawrence, Ruth
  Brief Entry **1986**:3
Laybourne, Geraldine **1997**:1
Leach, Penelope **1992**:4
Lerner, Michael **1994**:2
MacKinnon, Catharine **1993**:2
Malloy, Edward Monk **1989**:4
Marier, Rebecca **1995**:4
McAuliffe, Christa
  Obituary **1985**:4
McMillan, Terry **1993**:2
Morrison, Toni **1998**:1
Mumford, Lewis
  Obituary **1990**:2
Nemerov, Howard
  Obituary **1992**:1
Nye, Bill **1997**:2
Owens, Delia and Mark **1993**:3
Pagels, Elaine **1997**:1
Paglia, Camille **1992**:3
Parizeau, Jacques **1995**:1
Peter, Valentine J. **1988**:2
Riley, Richard W. **1996**:3
Rodin, Judith **1994**:4
Rosendahl, Bruce R.
  Brief Entry **1986**:4
Rowland, Pleasant **1992**:3
Scheck, Barry **2000**:4
Schuman, Patricia Glass **1993**:2
Shalala, Donna **1992**:3
Sherman, Russell **1987**:4
Silber, John **1990**:1
Simmons, Adele Smith **1988**:4
Simmons, Ruth **1995**:2
Smoot, George F. **1993**:3
Sowell, Thomas **1998**:3
Spock, Benjamin **1995**:2
  Obituary **1998**:3
Steele, Shelby **1991**:2
Tannen, Deborah **1995**:1
Thiebaud, Wayne **1991**:1
Thomas, Michel **1987**:4
Tribe, Laurence H. **1988**:1
Tyson, Laura D'Andrea **1994**:1
Unz, Ron **1999**:1
Van Duyn, Mona **1993**:2
Vickrey, William S.
  Obituary **1997**:2
Warren, Robert Penn
  Obituary **1990**:1
West, Cornel **1994**:2
Wexler, Nancy S. **1992**:3
Wiesel, Elie **1998**:1
Wigand, Jeffrey **2000**:4
Wiles, Andrew **1994**:1
Wilson, Edward O. **1994**:4
Wilson, William Julius **1997**:1
Wu, Harry **1996**:1
Zanker, Bill
  Brief Entry **1987**:3
Zigler, Edward **1994**:1

FILM

Abbott, George
  Obituary **1995**:3
Adjani, Isabelle **1991**:1
Affleck, Ben **1999**:1
Aiello, Danny **1990**:4
Alda, Robert
  Obituary **1986**:3

Driver, Minnie **2000**:1
Duchovny, David **1998**:3
Duffy, Karen **1998**:1
Dukakis, Olympia **1996**:4
Duvall, Robert **1999**:3
Eastwood, Clint **1993**:3
Egoyan, Atom **2000**:2
Eisner, Michael **1989**:2
Elliott, Denholm
　Obituary **1993**:2
Ephron, Henry
　Obituary **1993**:2
Ephron, Nora **1992**:3
Epps, Omar **2000**:4
Estevez, Emilio **1985**:4
Fairbanks, Douglas, Jr.
　Obituary **2000**:4
Farley, Chris
　Obituary **1998**:2
Farrow, Mia **1998**:3
Fawcett, Farrah **1998**:4
Fell, Norman
　Obituary **1999**:2
Fellini, Federico
　Obituary **1994**:2
Ferrer, Jose
　Obituary **1992**:3
Fetchit, Stepin
　Obituary **1986**:1
Field, Sally **1995**:3
Fiennes, Ralph **1996**:2
Fishburne, Laurence **1995**:3
Fisher, Carrie **1991**:1
Flanders, Ed
　Obituary **1995**:3
Fleming, Art
　Obituary **1995**:4
Flockhart, Calista **1998**:4
Fonda, Bridget **1995**:1
Ford, Harrison **1990**:2
Fosse, Bob
　Obituary **1988**:1
Foster, Jodie **1989**:2
Fox, Michael J. **1986**:1
Fox, Vivica **1999**:1
Franciscus, James
　Obituary **1992**:1
Frank, Robert **1995**:2
Franz, Dennis **1995**:2
Fraser, Brendan **2000**:1
Freeman, Morgan **1990**:4
Freleng, Friz
　Obituary **1995**:4
Fugard, Athol **1992**:3
Gabor, Eva
　Obituary **1996**:1
Garbo, Greta
　Obituary **1990**:3
Garcia, Andy **1999**:3
Gardenia, Vincent
　Obituary **1993**:2
Gardner, Ava Lavinia
　Obituary **1990**:2
Garofalo, Janeane **1996**:4
Garr, Teri **1988**:4
Garson, Greer
　Obituary **1996**:4
Geffen, David **1985**:3 **1997**:3
Gellar, Sarah Michelle **1999**:3
Gere, Richard **1994**:3
Gibson, Mel **1990**:1

Gielgud, John
　Obituary **2000**:4
Gift, Roland **1990**:2
Gilford, Jack
　Obituary **1990**:4
Gish, Lillian
　Obituary **1993**:4
Gleason, Jackie
　Obituary **1987**:4
Gless, Sharon **1989**:3
Glover, Danny **1998**:4
Gobel, George
　Obituary **1991**:4
Godard, Jean-Luc **1998**:1
Godunov, Alexander
　Obituary **1995**:4
Goldberg, Leonard **1988**:4
Goldberg, Whoopi **1993**:3
Goldblum, Jeff **1988**:1 **1997**:3
Gong Li **1998**:4
Gooding, Cuba, Jr. **1997**:3
Goodman, John **1990**:3
Gordon, Dexter **1987**:1 **1990**:4
Gordon, Gale
　Obituary **1996**:1
Gossett, Louis, Jr. **1989**:3
Graham, Heather **2000**:1
Grant, Cary
　Obituary **1987**:1
Grant, Hugh **1995**:3
Grant, Rodney A. **1992**:1
Greene, Graham **1997**:2
Greene, Lorne
　Obituary **1988**:1
Grier, Pam **1998**:3
Griffith, Melanie **1989**:2
Grodin, Charles **1997**:3
Grusin, Dave
　Brief Entry **1987**:2
Hackman, Gene **1989**:3
Hall, Anthony Michael **1986**:3
Hall, Arsenio **1990**:2
Hamilton, Margaret
　Obituary **1985**:3
Hammer, Jan **1987**:3
Hanks, Tom **1989**:2 **2000**:2
Hannah, Daryl **1987**:4
Harmon, Mark **1987**:1
Harrison, Rex
　Obituary **1990**:4
Harry, Deborah **1990**:1
Hartman, Phil **1996**:2
　Obituary **1998**:4
Harwell, Ernie **1997**:3
Hawke, Ethan **1995**:4
Hawn, Goldie Jeanne **1997**:2
Hayek, Salma **1999**:1
Hayes, Helen
　Obituary **1993**:4
Hayes, Isaac **1998**:4
Hayworth, Rita
　Obituary **1987**:3
Heche, Anne **1999**:1
Heckerling, Amy **1987**:2
Hemingway, Margaux
　Obituary **1997**:1
Henson, Brian **1992**:1
Henson, Jim **1989**:1
　Obituary **1990**:4
Hepburn, Audrey
　Obituary **1993**:2
Hepburn, Katharine **1991**:2

Hershey, Barbara **1989**:1
Heston, Charlton **1999**:4
Hewitt, Jennifer Love **1999**:2
Hill, Lauryn **1999**:3
Hines, Gregory **1992**:4
Holmes, John C.
　Obituary **1988**:3
Hopkins, Anthony **1992**:4
Horne, Lena **1998**:4
Hoskins, Bob **1989**:1
Hou Hsiao-hsien **2000**:2
Houseman, John
　Obituary **1989**:1
Howard, Ron **1997**:2
Howard, Trevor
　Obituary **1988**:2
Hudson, Rock
　Obituary **1985**:4
Humphries, Barry **1993**:1
Hunt, Helen **1994**:4
Hunter, Holly **1989**:4
Hurley, Elizabeth **1999**:2
Hurt, William **1986**:1
Huston, Anjelica **1989**:3
Huston, John
　Obituary **1988**:1
Hutton, Timothy **1986**:3
Ice Cube **1999**:2
Ice-T **1992**:3
Ireland, Jill
　Obituary **1990**:4
Irons, Jeremy **1991**:4
Itami, Juzo
　Obituary **1998**:2
Ives, Burl
　Obituary **1995**:4
Jackson, Samuel L. **1995**:4
Jarmusch, Jim **1998**:3
Jay, Ricky **1995**:1
Jillian, Ann **1986**:4
Johnson, Don **1986**:1
Jolie, Angelina **2000**:2
Jones, Cherry **1999**:3
Jones, Tommy Lee **1994**:2
Jonze, Spike **2000**:3
Jordan, Neil **1993**:3
Judd, Ashley **1998**:1
Julia, Raul
　Obituary **1995**:1
Kahn, Madeline
　Obituary **2000**:2
Kasem, Casey **1987**:1
Katzenberg, Jeffrey **1995**:3
Kavner, Julie **1992**:3
Kaye, Danny
　Obituary **1987**:2
Keaton, Diane **1997**:1
Keaton, Michael **1989**:4
Keeler, Ruby
　Obituary **1993**:4
Keitel, Harvey **1994**:3
Keith, Brian
　Obituary **1997**:4
Kelly, Gene
　Obituary **1996**:3
Kidman, Nicole **1992**:4
Kilmer, Val **1991**:4
King, Stephen **1998**:1
Kinski, Klaus **1987**:2
Kinski, Klaus
　Obituary **1992**:2
Kline, Kevin **2000**:1

2000 Occupation Index

Radner, Gilda
  Obituary **1989**:4
Raimi, Sam **1999**:2
Raye, Martha
  Obituary **1995**:1
Redford, Robert **1993**:2
Redgrave, Lynn **1999**:3
Redgrave, Vanessa **1989**:2
Reed, Donna
  Obituary **1986**:1
Reese, Della **1999**:2
Reeve, Christopher **1997**:2
Reeves, Keanu **1992**:1
Reeves, Steve
  Obituary **2000**:4
Reiner, Rob **1991**:2
Reiser, Paul **1995**:2
Reitman, Ivan **1986**:3
Remick, Lee
  Obituary **1992**:1
Reuben, Gloria **1999**:4
Reubens, Paul **1987**:2
Ricci, Christina **1999**:1
Richards, Michael **1993**:4
Riddle, Nelson
  Obituary **1985**:4
Ringwald, Molly **1985**:4
Robbins, Jerome
  Obituary **1999**:1
Robbins, Tim **1993**:1
Roberts, Julia **1991**:3
Rock, Chris **1998**:1
Rogers, Ginger
  Obituary **1995**:4
Rogers, Roy
  Obituary **1998**:4
Roker, Roxie
  Obituary **1996**:2
Rolle, Esther
  Obituary **1999**:2
Rollins, Howard E., Jr. **1986**:1
Roth, Tim **1998**:2
Rourke, Mickey **1988**:4
Rowan, Dan
  Obituary **1988**:1
Rudner, Rita **1993**:2
Rudnick, Paul **1994**:3
Ruehl, Mercedes **1992**:4
RuPaul **1996**:1
Russo, Rene **2000**:2
Ryan, Meg **1994**:1
Ryder, Winona **1991**:2
Sandler, Adam **1999**:2
Sarandon, Susan **1995**:3
Savage, Fred **1990**:1
Savalas, Telly
  Obituary **1994**:3
Schneider, Rob **1997**:4
Schroeder, Barbet **1996**:1
Schwarzenegger, Arnold **1991**:1
Schwimmer, David **1996**:2
Scorsese, Martin **1989**:1
Scott, George C.
  Obituary **2000**:2
Scott, Randolph
  Obituary **1987**:2
Seidelman, Susan **1985**:4
Seymour, Jane **1994**:4
Shaffer, Paul **1987**:1
Sharkey, Ray
  Obituary **1994**:1

Shawn, Dick
  Obituary **1987**:3
Sheedy, Ally **1989**:1
Shepard, Sam **1996**:4
Shields, Brooke **1996**:3
Shore, Dinah
  Obituary **1994**:3
Short, Martin **1986**:1
Shue, Andrew **1994**:4
Silverman, Jonathan **1997**:2
Silvers, Phil
  Obituary **1985**:4
Silverstone, Alicia **1997**:4
Sinatra, Frank
  Obituary **1998**:4
Singleton, John **1994**:3
Sinise, Gary **1996**:1
Siskel, Gene
  Obituary **1999**:3
Slater, Christian **1994**:1
Smirnoff, Yakov **1987**:2
Smith, Kevin **2000**:4
Smith, Will **1997**:2
Smits, Jimmy **1990**:1
Snipes, Wesley **1993**:1
Sondheim, Stephen **1994**:4
Sorvino, Mira **1996**:3
Southern, Terry
  Obituary **1996**:2
Spacey, Kevin **1996**:4
Spade, David **1999**:2
Spader, James **1991**:2
Spheeris, Penelope **1989**:2
Spielberg, Steven **1993**:4 **1997**:4
Staller, Ilona **1988**:3
Stallone, Sylvester **1994**:2
Steel, Dawn **1990**:1
  Obituary **1998**:2
Stevenson, McLean
  Obituary **1996**:3
Stewart, Jimmy
  Obituary **1997**:4
Stewart, Patrick **1996**:1
Stiller, Ben **1999**:1
Sting **1991**:4
Stone, Oliver **1990**:4
Stone, Sharon **1993**:4
Stoppard, Tom **1995**:4
Streep, Meryl **1990**:2
Streisand, Barbra **1992**:2
Studi, Wes **1994**:3
Styne, Jule
  Obituary **1995**:1
Susskind, David
  Obituary **1987**:2
Swank, Hilary **2000**:3
Tanaka, Tomoyuki
  Obituary **1997**:3
Tandy, Jessica **1990**:4
  Obituary **1995**:1
Tarantino, Quentin **1995**:1
Taylor, Elizabeth **1993**:3
Taylor, Lili **2000**:2
Thiebaud, Wayne **1991**:1
Thompson, Emma **1993**:2
Thompson, Fred **1998**:2
Thornton, Billy Bob **1997**:4
Thurman, Uma **1994**:2
Tilly, Jennifer **1997**:2
Tomei, Marisa **1995**:2
Travolta, John **1995**:2
Tucker, Chris **1999**:1

Tucker, Forrest
  Obituary **1987**:1
Turner, Janine **1993**:2
Turner, Kathleen **1985**:3
Turner, Lana
  Obituary **1996**:1
Tyler, Liv **1997**:2
Ullman, Tracey **1988**:3
Urich, Robert **1988**:1
Vanilla Ice **1991**:3
Van Sant, Gus **1992**:2
Varney, Jim
  Obituary **2000**:3
Vaughn, Vince **1999**:2
Ventura, Jesse **1999**:2
Vidal, Gore **1996**:2
Vidov, Oleg **1987**:4
Villechaize, Herve
  Obituary **1994**:1
Vincent, Fay **1990**:2
Walker, Nancy
  Obituary **1992**:3
Wallis, Hal
  Obituary **1987**:1
Warhol, Andy
  Obituary **1987**:2
Washington, Denzel **1993**:2
Waters, John **1988**:3
Wayans, Damon **1998**:4
Wayans, Keenen Ivory **1991**:1
Wayne, David
  Obituary **1995**:3
Weaver, Sigourney **1988**:3
Wegman, William **1991**:1
Weinstein, Bob and Harvey **2000**:4
Weintraub, Jerry **1986**:1
Whitaker, Forest **1996**:2
Wiest, Dianne **1995**:2
Williams, Robin **1988**:4
Williams, Vanessa L. **1999**:2
Willis, Bruce **1986**:4
Winfrey, Oprah **1986**:4 **1997**:3
Winger, Debra **1994**:3
Wolfman Jack
  Obituary **1996**:1
Wong, B.D. **1998**:1
Woo, John **1994**:2
Woods, James **1988**:3
Wyle, Noah **1997**:3
Wynn, Keenan
  Obituary **1987**:1
Young, Robert
  Obituary **1999**:1
Zanuck, Lili Fini **1994**:2
Zeffirelli, Franco **1991**:3
Zeta-Jones, Catherine **1999**:4

LAW

Abzug, Bella **1998**:2
Achtenberg, Roberta **1993**:4
Allred, Gloria **1985**:2
Angelos, Peter **1995**:4
Archer, Dennis **1994**:4
Astorga, Nora **1988**:2
Babbitt, Bruce **1994**:1
Bailey, F. Lee **1995**:4
Baker, James A. III **1991**:2
Bikoff, James L.
  Brief Entry **1986**:2
Blackmun, Harry A.
  Obituary **1999**:3

Bradley, Tom
Obituary **1999**:1
Brennan, William
Obituary **1997**:4
Breyer, Stephen Gerald **1994**:4
1997:2
Brown, Willie **1996**:4
Brown, Willie L. **1985**:2
Burger, Warren E.
Obituary **1995**:4
Burnison, Chantal Simone **1988**:3
Campbell, Kim **1993**:4
Cantrell, Ed
Brief Entry **1985**:3
Casey, William
Obituary **1987**:3
Casper, Gerhard **1993**:1
Clark, Marcia **1995**:1
Clinton, Bill **1992**:1
Clinton, Hillary Rodham **1993**:2
Cochran, Johnnie **1996**:1
Colby, William E.
Obituary **1996**:4
Cuomo, Mario **1992**:2
Darden, Christopher **1996**:4
Dees, Morris **1992**:1
Dershowitz, Alan **1992**:1
Deutch, John **1996**:4
Dole, Elizabeth Hanford **1990**:1
Dukakis, Michael **1988**:3
Eagleson, Alan **1987**:4
Ehrlichman, John
Obituary **1999**:3
Ervin, Sam
Obituary **1985**:2
Estrich, Susan **1989**:1
Fairstein, Linda **1991**:1
Fehr, Donald **1987**:2
Florio, James J. **1991**:2
Foster, Vincent
Obituary **1994**:1
France, Johnny
Brief Entry **1987**:1
Freeh, Louis J. **1994**:2
Fulbright, J. William
Obituary **1995**:3
Furman, Rosemary
Brief Entry **1986**:4
Garrison, Jim
Obituary **1993**:2
Ginsburg, Ruth Bader **1993**:4
Giuliani, Rudolph **1994**:2
Glasser, Ira **1989**:1
Gore, Albert, Sr.
Obituary **1999**:2
Grisham, John **1994**:4
Harvard, Beverly **1995**:2
Hayes, Robert M. **1986**:3
Hill, Anita **1994**:1
Hills, Carla **1990**:3
Hirschhorn, Joel
Brief Entry **1986**:1
Hoffa, Jim, Jr. **1999**:2
Hyatt, Joel **1985**:3
Ireland, Patricia **1992**:2
Ito, Lance **1995**:3
Janklow, Morton **1989**:3
Kennedy, John F., Jr. **1990**:1
Obituary **1999**:4
Kennedy, Weldon **1997**:3
Kunstler, William
Obituary **1996**:1

Kunstler, William **1992**:3
Kurzban, Ira **1987**:2
Lee, Henry C. **1997**:1
Lee, Martin **1998**:2
Lewis, Loida Nicolas **1998**:3
Lewis, Reginald F. **1988**:4
Obituary **1993**:3
Lightner, Candy **1985**:1
Liman, Arthur **1989**:4
Lipsig, Harry H. **1985**:1
Lipton, Martin **1987**:3
MacKinnon, Catharine **1993**:2
Marshall, Thurgood
Obituary **1993**:3
McCloskey, James **1993**:1
Mitchell, George J. **1989**:3
Mitchell, John
Obituary **1989**:2
Mitchelson, Marvin **1989**:2
Morrison, Trudi
Brief Entry **1986**:2
Nader, Ralph **1989**:4
Napolitano, Janet **1997**:1
Neal, James Foster **1986**:2
O'Connor, Sandra Day **1991**:1
O'Leary, Hazel **1993**:4
O'Steen, Van
Brief Entry **1986**:3
Panetta, Leon **1995**:1
Pirro, Jeanine **1998**:2
Powell, Lewis F.
Obituary **1999**:1
Puccio, Thomas P. **1986**:4
Quayle, Dan **1989**:2
Raines, Franklin **1997**:4
Ramaphosa, Cyril **1988**:2
Ramo, Roberta Cooper **1996**:1
Reno, Janet **1993**:3
Rothwax, Harold **1996**:3
Scalia, Antonin **1988**:2
Scheck, Barry **2000**:4
Schily, Otto
Brief Entry **1987**:4
Sheehan, Daniel P. **1989**:1
Sheindlin, Judith **1999**:1
Sirica, John
Obituary **1993**:2
Skinner, Sam **1992**:3
Slater, Rodney E. **1997**:4
Slotnick, Barry
Brief Entry **1987**:4
Souter, David **1991**:3
Starr, Kenneth **1998**:3
Steinberg, Leigh **1987**:3
Stern, David **1991**:4
Stewart, Potter
Obituary **1986**:1
Strauss, Robert **1991**:4
Tagliabue, Paul **1990**:2
Thomas, Clarence **1992**:2
Thompson, Fred **1998**:2
Tribe, Laurence H. **1988**:1
Vincent, Fay **1990**:2
Violet, Arlene **1985**:3
Wapner, Joseph A. **1987**:1
Watson, Elizabeth **1991**:2
Williams, Edward Bennett
Obituary **1988**:4
Williams, Willie L. **1993**:1
Wilson, Bertha
Brief Entry **1986**:1

MUSIC
Abdul, Paula **1990**:3
Ackerman, Will **1987**:4
Acuff, Roy
Obituary **1993**:2
Aguilera, Christina **2000**:4
Albert, Stephen **1986**:1
Allen, Peter
Obituary **1993**:1
Amos, Tori **1995**:1
Anderson, Marion
Obituary **1993**:4
Andrews, Julie **1996**:1
Andrews, Maxene
Obituary **1996**:2
Anthony, Marc **2000**:3
Arlen, Harold
Obituary **1986**:3
Arnaz, Desi
Obituary **1987**:1
Arrau, Claudio
Obituary **1992**:1
Arrested Development **1994**:2
Astaire, Fred
Obituary **1987**:4
Autry, Gene
Obituary **1999**:1
Badu, Erykah **2000**:4
Baez, Joan **1998**:3
Bailey, Pearl
Obituary **1991**:1
Baker, Anita **1987**:4
Bartoli, Cecilia **1994**:1
Basie, Count
Obituary **1985**:1
Battle, Kathleen **1998**:1
Beastie Boys, The **1999**:1
Beck **2000**:2
Bee Gees, The **1997**:4
Benatar, Pat **1986**:1
Bennett, Tony **1994**:4
Berlin, Irving
Obituary **1990**:1
Bernhard, Sandra **1989**:4
Bernstein, Leonard
Obituary **1991**:1
Bjork **1996**:1
Blades, Ruben **1998**:2
Blakey, Art
Obituary **1991**:1
Blige, Mary J. **1995**:3
Bolton, Michael **1993**:2
Bon Jovi, Jon **1987**:4
Bono **1988**:4
Bono, Sonny **1992**:2
Obituary **1998**:2
Botstein, Leon **1985**:3
Bowie, David **1998**:2
Bowles, Paul
Obituary **2000**:3
Boxcar Willie
Obituary **1999**:4
Boyz II Men **1995**:1
Brandy **1996**:4
Branson, Richard **1987**:1
Braxton, Toni **1994**:3
Brooks, Garth **1992**:1
Brown, James **1991**:4
Buckley, Jeff
Obituary **1997**:4
Buffett, Jimmy **1999**:3
Bush, Kate **1994**:3

Butterfield, Paul
Obituary **1987**:3
Cage, John
Obituary **1993**:1
Calloway, Cab
Obituary **1995**:2
Cardigans, The **1997**:4
Carey, Mariah **1991**:3
Carlisle, Belinda **1989**:3
Carpenter, Mary-Chapin **1994**:1
Carreras, Jose **1995**:2
Carter, Ron **1987**:3
Cash, Johnny **1995**:3
Cerovsek, Corey
Brief Entry **1987**:4
Chapman, Tracy **1989**:2
Cheatham, Adolphus Doc
Obituary **1997**:4
Cher **1993**:1
Clapton, Eric **1993**:3
Clarke, Stanley **1985**:4
Cleveland, James
Obituary **1991**:3
Cliburn, Van **1995**:1
Cobain, Kurt
Obituary **1994**:3
Cole, Natalie **1992**:4
Collins, Albert
Obituary **1994**:2
Combs, Sean Puffy **1998**:4
Connick, Harry, Jr. **1991**:1
Coolio **1996**:4
Copland, Aaron
Obituary **1991**:2
Coppola, Carmine
Obituary **1991**:4
Corea, Chick **1986**:3
Costello, Elvis **1994**:4
Crawford, Michael **1994**:2
Cray, Robert **1988**:2
Crosby, David **2000**:4
Crothers, Scatman
Obituary **1987**:1
Crow, Sheryl **1995**:2
Crowe, Russell **2000**:4
Cugat, Xavier
Obituary **1991**:2
Cyrus, Billy Ray **1993**:1
D'Arby, Terence Trent **1988**:4
Davis, Miles
Obituary **1992**:2
Davis, Sammy, Jr.
Obituary **1990**:4
Day, Dennis
Obituary **1988**:4
Dean, Laura **1989**:4
Denver, John
Obituary **1998**:1
de Passe, Suzanne **1990**:4
DiFranco, Ani **1997**:1
Di Meola, Al **1986**:4
Dimitrova, Ghena **1987**:1
Dion, Celine **1995**:3
Dr. Demento **1986**:1
Dr. Dre **1994**:3
Dolenz, Micky **1986**:4
Domingo, Placido **1993**:2
Dorati, Antal
Obituary **1989**:2
Dorsey, Thomas A.
Obituary **1993**:3

Duncan, Todd
Obituary **1998**:3
Dupri, Jermaine **1999**:1
Dylan, Bob **1998**:1
Eazy-E
Obituary **1995**:3
Eckstine, Billy
Obituary **1993**:4
Edmonds, Kenneth Babyface **1995**:3
Eldridge, Roy
Obituary **1989**:3
Eno, Brian **1986**:2
En Vogue **1994**:1
Enya **1992**:3
Ertegun, Ahmet **1986**:3
Esquivel, Juan **1996**:2
Estefan, Gloria **1991**:4
Etheridge, Melissa **1995**:4
Everything But The Girl **1996**:4
Falco
Brief Entry **1987**:2
Farrell, Perry **1992**:2
Fender, Leo
Obituary **1992**:1
Fitzgerald, Ella
Obituary **1996**:4
Ford, Tennessee Ernie
Obituary **1992**:2
Foster, David **1988**:2
Franklin, Aretha **1998**:3
Franklin, Melvin
Obituary **1995**:3
Garcia, Jerry **1988**:3
Obituary **1996**:1
Geffen, David **1985**:3 **1997**:3
Geldof, Bob **1985**:3
Getz, Stan
Obituary **1991**:4
Gibb, Andy
Obituary **1988**:3
Gifford, Kathie Lee **1992**:2
Gift, Roland **1990**:2
Gill, Vince **1995**:2
Gillespie, Dizzy
Obituary **1993**:2
Glass, Philip **1991**:4
Goodman, Benny
Obituary **1986**:3
Goody, Sam
Obituary **1992**:1
Gordon, Dexter **1987**:1 **1990**:4
Gore, Tipper **1985**:4
Graham, Bill **1986**:4
Obituary **1992**:2
Grant, Amy **1985**:4
Grappelli, Stephane
Obituary **1998**:1
Grebenshikov, Boris **1990**:1
Green Day **1995**:4
Grusin, Dave
Brief Entry **1987**:2
Guccione, Bob, Jr. **1991**:4
Hammer, Jan **1987**:3
Hammer, M. C. **1991**:2
Hammond, John
Obituary **1988**:2
Hancock, Herbie **1985**:1
Harris, Emmylou **1991**:3
Harry, Deborah **1990**:1
Hart, Mary
Brief Entry **1988**:1
Hart, Mickey **1991**:2

Harvey, Polly Jean **1995**:4
Hawkins, Screamin' Jay
Obituary **2000**:3
Hayes, Isaac **1998**:4
Heard, J.C.
Obituary **1989**:1
Heid, Bill
Brief Entry **1987**:2
Heifetz, Jascha
Obituary **1988**:2
Helfgott, David **1997**:2
Helms, Bobby
Obituary **1997**:4
Hewitt, Jennifer Love **1999**:2
Hill, Faith **2000**:1
Hill, Lauryn **1999**:3
Hirt, Al
Obituary **1999**:4
Hoffs, Susanna **1988**:2
Hooker, John Lee **1998**:1
Hootie and the Blowfish **1995**:4
Horne, Lena **1998**:4
Hornsby, Bruce **1989**:3
Horovitz, Adam **1988**:3
Horowitz, Vladimir
Obituary **1990**:1
Houston, Cissy **1999**:3
Houston, Whitney **1986**:3
Hubbard, Freddie **1988**:4
Hutchence, Michael
Obituary **1998**:1
Hynde, Chrissie **1991**:1
Ice Cube **1999**:2
Ice-T **1992**:3
Iglesias, Enrique **2000**:1
Indigo Girls **1994**:4
Ives, Burl
Obituary **1995**:4
Jackson, Cordell **1992**:4
Jackson, Janet **1990**:4
Jackson, Michael **1996**:2
James, Etta **1995**:2
Jarrett, Keith **1992**:4
Jewel **1999**:2
Joel, Billy **1994**:3
John, Elton **1995**:4
Jones, Jenny **1998**:2
Jones, Quincy **1990**:4
Jones, Tom **1993**:4
Kaye, Sammy
Obituary **1987**:4
Kelly, R. **1997**:3
Kendricks, Eddie
Obituary **1993**:2
Kenny G **1994**:4
Kilmer, Val **1991**:4
King, Coretta Scott **1999**:3
Knopfler, Mark **1986**:2
Kravitz, Lenny **1991**:1
Kronos Quartet **1993**:1
Kurzweil, Raymond **1986**:3
Kyser, Kay
Obituary **1985**:3
Lane, Burton
Obituary **1997**:2
Lane, Ronnie
Obituary **1997**:4
Lang, K.D. **1988**:4
Lanois, Daniel **1991**:1
Larson, Jonathan
Obituary **1997**:2
Lauper, Cyndi **1985**:1

Tune, Tommy **1994**:2
Turner, Tina **2000**:3
Twain, Shania **1996**:3
Twitty, Conway
  Obituary **1994**:1
Tyner, Rob
  Obituary **1992**:2
Uchida, Mitsuko **1989**:3
Ullman, Tracey **1988**:3
Upshaw, Dawn **1991**:2
Valente, Benita **1985**:3
Van Halen, Edward **1985**:2
Vanilla Ice **1991**:3
Vaughan, Sarah
  Obituary **1990**:3
Vaughan, Stevie Ray
  Obituary **1991**:1
Vega, Suzanne **1988**:1
Vollenweider, Andreas **1985**:2
von Karajan, Herbert
  Obituary **1989**:4
von Trapp, Maria
  Obituary **1987**:3
Walker, Junior
  Obituary **1996**:2
Washington, Grover, Jr. **1989**:1
Weintraub, Jerry **1986**:1
Wells, Mary
  Obituary **1993**:1
West, Dottie
  Obituary **1992**:2
Williams, Joe
  Obituary **1999**:4
Williams, Vanessa L. **1999**:2
Willis, Bruce **1986**:4
Wilson, Brian **1996**:1
Wilson, Carl
  Obituary **1998**:2
Wilson, Cassandra **1996**:3
Winans, CeCe **2000**:1
Winston, George **1987**:1
Winter, Paul **1990**:2
Wynette, Tammy
  Obituary **1998**:3
Wynonna **1993**:3
Yankovic, Weird Al **1985**:4
Yankovic, Frank
  Obituary **1999**:2
Yearwood, Trisha **1999**:1
Yoakam, Dwight **1992**:4
Young, Neil **1991**:2
Zappa, Frank
  Obituary **1994**:2
Zinnemann, Fred
  Obituary **1997**:3
Zwilich, Ellen **1990**:1

**POLITICS AND
GOVERNMENT--FOREIGN**
Abacha, Sani **1996**:3
Adams, Gerald **1994**:1
Ahern, Bertie **1999**:3
Akihito, Emperor of Japan **1990**:1
Albright, Madeleine **1994**:3
Annan, Kofi **1999**:1
Aquino, Corazon **1986**:2
Arafat, Yasser **1989**:3 **1997**:3
Arens, Moshe **1985**:1
Arias Sanchez, Oscar **1989**:3
Aristide, Jean-Bertrand **1991**:3
Assad, Hafez
  Obituary **2000**:4

Assad, Hafez al- **1992**:1
Assad, Rifaat **1986**:3
Astorga, Nora **1988**:2
Babangida, Ibrahim Badamosi **1992**
  :4
Banda, Hastings **1994**:3
Barak, Ehud **1999**:4
Barbie, Klaus
  Obituary **1992**:2
Begin, Menachem
  Obituary **1992**:3
Berlusconi, Silvio **1994**:4
Berri, Nabih **1985**:2
Bhutto, Benazir **1989**:4
Blair, Tony **1997**:4
Bolkiah, Sultan Muda Hassanal **1985**
  :4
Bouchard, Lucien **1999**:2
Bourassa, Robert
  Obituary **1997**:1
Brandt, Willy
  Obituary **1993**:2
Brundtland, Gro Harlem **2000**:1
Buthelezi, Mangosuthu Gatsha **1989**
  :3
Campbell, Kim **1993**:4
Cardoso, Fernando Henrique **1996**:4
Castro, Fidel **1991**:4
Ceausescu, Nicolae
  Obituary **1990**:2
Cedras, Raoul **1994**:4
Chernenko, Konstantin
  Obituary **1985**:1
Chiluba, Frederick **1992**:3
Chissano, Joaquim **1987**:4
Chretien, Jean **1990**:4 **1997**:2
Collor de Mello, Fernando **1992**:4
Colosio, Luis Donaldo **1994**:3
Copps, Sheila **1986**:4
Cresson, Edith **1992**:1
Cruz, Arturo **1985**:1
Dalai Lama **1989**:1
de Klerk, F.W. **1990**:1
Delors, Jacques **1990**:2
Deng Xiaoping **1995**:1
  Obituary **1997**:3
de Pinies, Jamie
  Brief Entry **1986**:3
Dhlakama, Afonso **1993**:3
Doe, Samuel
  Obituary **1991**:1
Doi, Takako
  Brief Entry **1987**:4
Dong, Pham Van
  Obituary **2000**:4
Duarte, Jose Napoleon
  Obituary **1990**:3
Dubinin, Yuri **1987**:4
Ferguson, Sarah **1990**:3
Finnbogadottir, Vigdis
  Brief Entry **1986**:2
Freij, Elias **1986**:4
Fujimori, Alberto **1992**:4
Galvin, Martin
  Brief Entry **1985**:3
Gandhi, Indira
  Obituary **1985**:1
Gandhi, Rajiv
  Obituary **1991**:4
Gandhi, Sonia **2000**:2
Garneau, Marc **1985**:1
Ghali, Boutros Boutros **1992**:3

Gorbachev, Mikhail **1985**:2
Gorbachev, Raisa
  Obituary **2000**:2
Gowda, H. D. Deve **1997**:1
Gromyko, Andrei
  Obituary **1990**:2
Habash, George **1986**:1
Habibie, Bacharuddin Jusuf **1999**:3
Hani, Chris
  Obituary **1993**:4
Harriman, Pamela **1994**:4
Harris, Michael Deane **1997**:2
Havel, Vaclav **1990**:3
Herzog, Chaim
  Obituary **1997**:3
Hess, Rudolph
  Obituary **1988**:1
Hirohito, Emperor of Japan
  Obituary **1989**:2
Honecker, Erich
  Obituary **1994**:4
Hosokawa, Morihiro **1994**:1
Hume, John **1987**:1
Hussein, Saddam **1991**:1
Husseini, Faisal **1998**:4
Hussein I, King **1997**:3
  Obituary **1999**:3
Hu Yaobang
  Obituary **1989**:4
Izetbegovic, Alija **1996**:4
Jiang Quing
  Obituary **1992**:1
Jiang Zemin **1996**:1
Johnson, Pierre Marc **1985**:4
Juan Carlos I **1993**:1
Jumblatt, Walid **1987**:4
Juneau, Pierre **1988**:3
Kabila, Laurent **1998**:1
Kamel, Hussein **1996**:1
Karadzic, Radovan **1995**:3
Kekkonen, Urho
  Obituary **1986**:4
Khatami, Mohammed **1997**:4
Khomeini, Ayatollah Ruhollah
  Obituary **1989**:4
Kim Dae Jung **1998**:3
Kim Il Sung
  Obituary **1994**:4
Kim Jong Il **1995**:2
King Hassan II
  Obituary **2000**:1
Kohl, Helmut **1994**:1
Lalonde, Marc **1985**:1
Landsbergis, Vytautas **1991**:3
Lebed, Alexander **1997**:1
Le Duan
  Obituary **1986**:4
Le Duc Tho
  Obituary **1991**:1
Lee, Martin **1998**:2
Lee Teng-hui **2000**:1
Levesque, Rene
  Obituary **1988**:1
Levy, David **1987**:2
Lewis, Stephen **1987**:2
Livingstone, Ken **1988**:3
Lon Nol
  Obituary **1986**:1
Machel, Samora
  Obituary **1987**:1
Macmillan, Harold
  Obituary **1987**:2

Major, John **1991**:2
Mandela, Nelson **1990**:3
Mandela, Winnie **1989**:3
Marcos, Ferdinand
    Obituary **1990**:1
Masako, Crown Princess **1993**:4
Mas Canosa, Jorge
    Obituary **1998**:2
Mbeki, Thabo **1999**:4
McGuinness, Martin **1985**:4
McLaughlin, Audrey **1990**:3
Megawati Sukarnoputri **2000**:1
Milosevic, Slobodan **1993**:2
Mitterrand, Francois
    Obituary **1996**:2
Miyazawa, Kiichi **1992**:2
Mobutu Sese Seko
    Obituary **1998**:4
Mobutu Sese Seko **1993**:4
    Obituary **1998**:1
Moi, Daniel arap **1993**:2
Molotov, Vyacheslav Mikhailovich
    Obituary **1987**:1
Mori, Yoshiro **2000**:4
Mubarak, Hosni **1991**:4
Mugabe, Robert **1988**:4
Mulroney, Brian **1989**:2
Musharraf, Pervez **2000**:2
Netanyahu, Benjamin **1996**:4
Nidal, Abu **1987**:1
Niezabitowska, Malgorzata **1991**:3
Nujoma, Sam **1990**:4
Nyerere, Julius
    Obituary **2000**:2
Obando, Miguel **1986**:4
Obasanjo, Olusegun **2000**:2
Obuchi, Keizo
    Obituary **2000**:4
Obuchi, Keizo **1999**:2
Ocalan, Abdullah **1999**:4
Olav, King of Norway
    Obituary **1991**:3
Palme, Olof
    Obituary **1986**:2
Papandreou, Andrea
    Obituary **1997**:1
Parizeau, Jacques **1995**:1
Paton, Alan
    Obituary **1988**:3
Patten, Christopher **1993**:3
Paz, Octavio **1991**:2
Peckford, Brian **1989**:1
Peres, Shimon **1996**:3
Perez, Carlos Andre **1990**:2
Perez de Cuellar, Javier **1991**:3
Peterson, David **1987**:1
Philby, Kim
    Obituary **1988**:3
Pinochet, Augusto **1999**:2
Pol Pot
    Obituary **1998**:4
Preval, Rene **1997**:2
Primakov, Yevgeny **1999**:3
Putin, Vladimir **2000**:3
Qaddhafi, Muammar **1998**:3
Rabin, Yitzhak **1993**:1
    Obituary **1996**:2
Rafsanjani, Ali Akbar Hashemi
    1987:3
Rahman, Sheik Omar Abdel- **1993**:3
Ram, Jagjivan
    Obituary **1986**:4

Ramos, Fidel **1995**:2
Rao, P. V. Narasimha **1993**:2
Reisman, Simon **1987**:4
Robelo, Alfonso **1988**:1
Robinson, Mary **1993**:1
Salinas, Carlos **1992**:1
Sarkis, Elias
    Obituary **1985**:3
Saro-Wiwa, Ken
    Obituary **1996**:2
Savimbi, Jonas **1986**:2 **1994**:2
Schily, Otto
    Brief Entry **1987**:4
Schroder, Gerhard **1999**:1
Shipley, Jenny **1998**:3
Simpson, Wallis
    Obituary **1986**:3
Slovo, Joe **1989**:2
Staller, Ilona **1988**:3
Strauss, Robert **1991**:4
Suu Kyi, Aung San **1996**:2
Suzman, Helen **1989**:3
Tambo, Oliver **1991**:3
Terzi, Zehdi Labib **1985**:3
Thatcher, Margaret **1989**:2
Treurnicht, Andries **1992**:2
Trimble, David **1999**:1
Tudjman, Franjo **1996**:2
Tudjman, Franjo
    Obituary **2000**:2
Turabi, Hassan **1995**:4
Vajpayee, Atal Behari **1998**:4
Vander Zalm, William **1987**:3
Wahid, Abdurrahman **2000**:3
Walesa, Lech **1991**:2
Wei Jingsheng **1998**:2
Wilson, Bertha
    Brief Entry **1986**:1
Ye Jianying
    Obituary **1987**:1
Yeltsin, Boris **1991**:1
Zedillo, Ernesto **1995**:1
Zeroual, Liamine **1996**:2
Zhao Ziyang **1989**:1
Zhirinovsky, Vladimir **1994**:2
Zia ul-Haq, Mohammad
    Obituary **1988**:4
Chirac, Jacques **1995**:4

POLITICS AND GOVERNMENT--U.S.

Abraham, Spencer **1991**:4
Abrams, Elliott **1987**:1
Abzug, Bella **1998**:2
Achtenberg, Roberta **1993**:4
Agnew, Spiro Theodore
    Obituary **1997**:1
Ailes, Roger **1989**:3
Albright, Madeleine **1994**:3
Alexander, Lamar **1991**:2
Alioto, Joseph L.
    Obituary **1998**:3
Alvarez, Aida **1999**:2
Archer, Dennis **1994**:4
Aspin, Les
    Obituary **1996**:1
Atwater, Lee **1989**:4
    Obituary **1991**:4
Babbitt, Bruce **1994**:1
Baker, James A. III **1991**:2
Baldrige, Malcolm
    Obituary **1988**:1
Banks, Dennis J. **1986**:4

Barry, Marion **1991**:1
Barshefsky, Charlene **2000**:4
Begaye, Kelsey **1999**:3
Bennett, William **1990**:1
Benson, Ezra Taft
    Obituary **1994**:4
Bentsen, Lloyd **1993**:3
Berger, Sandy **2000**:1
Berle, Peter A.A.
    Brief Entry **1987**:3
Biden, Joe **1986**:3
Bono, Sonny **1992**:2
    Obituary **1998**:2
Boxer, Barbara **1995**:1
Boyington, Gregory Pappy
    Obituary **1988**:2
Bradley, Bill **2000**:2
Bradley, Tom
    Obituary **1999**:1
Brady, Sarah and James S. **1991**:4
Braun, Carol Moseley **1993**:1
Brennan, William
    Obituary **1997**:4
Brown, Edmund G., Sr.
    Obituary **1996**:3
Brown, Jerry **1992**:4
Brown, Ron **1990**:3
Brown, Ron
    Obituary **1996**:4
Brown, Willie **1996**:4
Brown, Willie L. **1985**:2
Browner, Carol M. **1994**:1
Buchanan, Pat **1996**:3
Bundy, McGeorge
    Obituary **1997**:1
Bush, Barbara **1989**:3
Bush, George W., Jr. **1996**:4
Caliguiri, Richard S.
    Obituary **1988**:3
Campbell, Ben Nighthorse **1998**:1
Campbell, Bill **1997**:1
Carey, Ron **1993**:3
Carter, Billy
    Obituary **1989**:1
Carter, Jimmy **1995**:1
Casey, William
    Obituary **1987**:3
Cavazos, Lauro F. **1989**:2
Chavez, Linda **1999**:3
Chavez-Thompson, Linda **1999**:1
Cheney, Dick **1991**:3
Cheney, Lynne V. **1990**:4
Christopher, Warren **1996**:3
Cisneros, Henry **1987**:2
Clark, J. E.
    Brief Entry **1986**:1
Clinton, Bill **1992**:1
Clinton, Hillary Rodham **1993**:2
Clyburn, James **1999**:4
Cohen, William S. **1998**:1
Collins, Cardiss **1995**:3
Connally, John
    Obituary **1994**:1
Conyers, John, Jr. **1999**:1
Cuomo, Mario **1992**:2
D'Amato, Al **1996**:1
DeLay, Tom **2000**:1
Dinkins, David N. **1990**:2
Dolan, Terry **1985**:2
Dole, Bob **1994**:2
Dole, Elizabeth Hanford **1990**:1
Dukakis, Michael **1988**:3

Tsongas, Paul Efthemios
  Obituary **1997**:2
Tutwiler, Margaret **1992**:4
Tyson, Laura D'Andrea **1994**:1
Udall, Mo
  Obituary **1999**:2
Ventura, Jesse **1999**:2
Violet, Arlene **1985**:3
Wallace, George
  Obituary **1999**:1
Washington, Harold
  Obituary **1988**:1
Waters, Maxine **1998**:4
Watts, J.C. **1999**:2
Webb, Wellington E. **2000**:3
Weicker, Lowell P., Jr. **1993**:1
Whitman, Christine Todd **1994**:3
Whitmire, Kathy **1988**:2
Wilder, L. Douglas **1990**:3
Williams, Anthony **2000**:4
Williams, G. Mennen
  Obituary **1988**:2
Wilson, Pete **1992**:3
Yard, Molly **1991**:4
Young, Coleman A.
  Obituary **1998**:1
Zech, Lando W.
  Brief Entry **1987**:4

RADIO

Albert, Marv **1994**:3
Albom, Mitch **1999**:3
Ameche, Don
  Obituary **1994**:2
Autry, Gene
  Obituary **1999**:1
Backus, Jim
  Obituary **1990**:1
Barber, Red
  Obituary **1993**:2
Bell, Art **2000**:1
Blanc, Mel
  Obituary **1989**:4
Campbell, Bebe Moore **1996**:2
Caray, Harry **1988**:3
  Obituary **1998**:3
Cherry, Don **1993**:4
Codrescu, Andre **1997**:3
Cosell, Howard
  Obituary **1995**:4
Costas, Bob **1986**:4
Day, Dennis
  Obituary **1988**:4
Dr. Demento **1986**:1
Donnellan, Nanci **1995**:2
Durrell, Gerald
  Obituary **1995**:3
Edwards, Bob **1993**:2
Fleming, Art
  Obituary **1995**:4
Ford, Tennessee Ernie
  Obituary **1992**:2
Gobel, George
  Obituary **1991**:4
Goodman, Benny
  Obituary **1986**:3
Gordon, Gale
  Obituary **1996**:1
Graham, Billy **1992**:1
Granato, Cammi **1999**:3
Grange, Red
  Obituary **1991**:3

Greene, Lorne
  Obituary **1988**:1
Gross, Terry **1998**:3
Harmon, Tom
  Obituary **1990**:3
Harvey, Paul **1995**:3
Harwell, Ernie **1997**:3
Houseman, John
  Obituary **1989**:1
Hughes, Cathy **1999**:1
Imus, Don **1997**:1
Ives, Burl
  Obituary **1995**:4
Kasem, Casey **1987**:1
Keyes, Alan **1996**:2
King, Larry **1993**:1
Kyser, Kay
  Obituary **1985**:3
Levesque, Rene
  Obituary **1988**:1
Limbaugh, Rush **1991**:3
Magliozzi, Tom and Ray **1991**:4
Nelson, Harriet
  Obituary **1995**:1
Olson, Johnny
  Obituary **1985**:4
Osgood, Charles **1996**:2
Paley, William S.
  Obituary **1991**:2
Parks, Bert
  Obituary **1992**:3
Porter, Sylvia
  Obituary **1991**:4
Quivers, Robin **1995**:4
Raphael, Sally Jessy **1992**:4
Raye, Martha
  Obituary **1995**:1
Riddle, Nelson
  Obituary **1985**:4
Roberts, Cokie **1993**:4
Saralegui, Cristina **1999**:2
Schlessinger, Laura **1996**:3
Sevareid, Eric
  Obituary **1993**:1
Shore, Dinah
  Obituary **1994**:3
Smith, Buffalo Bob
  Obituary **1999**:1
Smith, Kate
  Obituary **1986**:3
Stern, Howard **1988**:2 **1993**:3
Swayze, John Cameron
  Obituary **1996**:1
Tom and Ray Magliozzi **1991**:4
Totenberg, Nina **1992**:2
Wolfman Jack
  Obituary **1996**:1
Young, Robert
  Obituary **1999**:1

RELIGION

Abernathy, Ralph
  Obituary **1990**:3
Altea, Rosemary **1996**:3
Applewhite, Marshall Herff
  Obituary **1997**:3
Aristide, Jean-Bertrand **1991**:3
Beckett, Wendy (Sister) **1998**:3
Benson, Ezra Taft
  Obituary **1994**:4
Bernardin, Cardinal Joseph **1997**:2
Berri, Nabih **1985**:2

Browning, Edmond
  Brief Entry **1986**:2
Burns, Charles R.
  Brief Entry **1988**:1
Carey, George **1992**:3
Chavis, Benjamin **1993**:4
Chopra, Deepak **1996**:3
Clements, George **1985**:1
Cleveland, James
  Obituary **1991**:3
Coffin, William Sloane, Jr. **1990**:3
Cunningham, Reverend William
  Obituary **1997**:4
Curran, Charles E. **1989**:2
Daily, Bishop Thomas V. **1990**:4
Dalai Lama **1989**:1
Dearden, John Cardinal
  Obituary **1988**:4
Dorsey, Thomas A.
  Obituary **1993**:3
Eilberg, Amy
  Brief Entry **1985**:3
Farrakhan, Louis **1990**:4
Fox, Matthew **1992**:2
Fulghum, Robert **1996**:1
Graham, Billy **1992**:1
Grant, Amy **1985**:4
Hahn, Jessica **1989**:4
Harris, Barbara **1996**:3
Harris, Barbara **1989**:3
Healy, Timothy S. **1990**:2
Huffington, Arianna **1996**:2
Hume, Basil Cardinal
  Obituary **2000**:1
Hunter, Howard **1994**:4
Irwin, James
  Obituary **1992**:1
Jackson, Jesse **1996**:1
John Paul II, Pope **1995**:3
Jumblatt, Walid **1987**:4
Kahane, Meir
  Obituary **1991**:2
Khomeini, Ayatollah Ruhollah
  Obituary **1989**:4
Kissling, Frances **1989**:2
Koresh, David
  Obituary **1993**:4
Krol, John
  Obituary **1996**:3
Lefebvre, Marcel **1988**:4
Levinger, Moshe **1992**:1
Mahesh Yogi, Maharishi **1991**:3
Mahony, Roger M. **1988**:2
Maida, Adam Cardinal **1998**:2
Malloy, Edward Monk **1989**:4
McCloskey, James **1993**:1
Mother Teresa **1993**:1
  Obituary **1998**:1
Obando, Miguel **1986**:4
O'Connor, Cardinal John **1990**:3
O'Connor, John
  Obituary **2000**:4
Perry, Harold A.
  Obituary **1992**:1
Peter, Valentine J. **1988**:2
Rafsanjani, Ali Akbar Hashemi **1987**:3
Rahman, Sheik Omar Abdel- **1993**:3
Rajneesh, Bhagwan Shree
  Obituary **1990**:2
Reed, Ralph **1995**:1
Reese, Della **1999**:2

Waddell, Thomas F.
  Obituary **1988**:2
Weil, Andrew **1997**:4
Wexler, Nancy S. **1992**:3
Wigand, Jeffrey **2000**:4
Wigler, Michael
  Brief Entry **1985**:1
Wiles, Andrew **1994**:1
Wilmut, Ian **1997**:3
Wilson, Edward O. **1994**:4
Woodwell, George S. **1987**:2
Yeager, Chuck **1998**:1
Yen, Samuel **1996**:4
Zech, Lando W.
  Brief Entry **1987**:4

SOCIAL ISSUES

Abbey, Edward
  Obituary **1989**:3
Abernathy, Ralph
  Obituary **1990**:3
Ali, Muhammad **1997**:2
Allred, Gloria **1985**:2
Amory, Cleveland
  Obituary **1999**:2
Anastas, Robert
  Brief Entry **1985**:2
Aristide, Jean-Bertrand **1991**:3
Baez, Joan **1998**:3
Baird, Bill
  Brief Entry **1987**:2
Baldwin, James
  Obituary **1988**:2
Ball, Edward **1999**:2
Banks, Dennis J. **1986**:4
Bayley, Corrine
  Brief Entry **1986**:4
Ben & Jerry **1991**:3
Bergalis, Kimberly
  Obituary **1992**:3
Berresford, Susan V. **1998**:4
Biehl, Amy
  Obituary **1994**:1
Blackburn, Molly
  Obituary **1985**:4
Bly, Robert **1992**:4
Bradshaw, John **1992**:1
Brady, Sarah and James S. **1991**:4
Bravo, Ellen **1998**:2
Bristow, Lonnie **1996**:1
Brooks, Gwendolyn **1998**:1
Brower, David **1990**:4
Brown, Jim **1993**:2
Brown, Judie **1986**:2
Bush, Barbara **1989**:3
Cammermeyer, Margarethe **1995**:2
Caplan, Arthur L. **2000**:2
Carter, Amy **1987**:4
Carter, Rubin **2000**:3
Chavez, Cesar
  Obituary **1993**:4
Chavez-Thompson, Linda **1999**:1
Chavis, Benjamin **1993**:4
Cleaver, Eldridge
  Obituary **1998**:4
Clements, George **1985**:1
Clinton, Hillary Rodham **1993**:2
Coffin, William Sloane, Jr. **1990**:3
Cole, Johnetta B. **1994**:3
Coles, Robert **1995**:1
Connerly, Ward **2000**:2

Coors, William K.
  Brief Entry **1985**:1
Crisp, Quentin
  Obituary **2000**:3
Cruzan, Nancy
  Obituary **1991**:3
Davis, Angela **1998**:3
Dees, Morris **1992**:1
Devi, Phoolan **1986**:1
Dickinson, Brian **1998**:2
Dorris, Michael
  Obituary **1997**:3
Douglas, Marjory Stoneman **1993**:1
  Obituary **1998**:4
Downey, Morton, Jr. **1988**:4
Duncan, Sheena
  Brief Entry **1987**:1
Edelman, Marian Wright **1990**:4
Edwards, Harry **1989**:4
Elders, Joycelyn **1994**:1
Ellison, Ralph
  Obituary **1994**:4
Etzioni, Amitai **1994**:3
Evers-Williams, Myrlie **1995**:4
Falkenberg, Nanette **1985**:2
Faludi, Susan **1992**:4
Farrakhan, Louis **1990**:4
Faubus, Orval
  Obituary **1995**:2
Faulkner, Shannon **1994**:4
Ferrell, Trevor
  Brief Entry **1985**:2
Filipovic, Zlata **1994**:4
Finley, Karen **1992**:4
Fisher, Mary **1994**:3
Fonyo, Steve
  Brief Entry **1985**:4
Foreman, Dave **1990**:3
Friedan, Betty **1994**:2
Galvin, Martin
  Brief Entry **1985**:3
Garcia, Jerry **1988**:3
  Obituary **1996**:1
Gebbie, Kristine **1994**:2
Geldof, Bob **1985**:3
Gertz, Alison
  Obituary **1993**:2
Glaser, Elizabeth
  Obituary **1995**:2
Glasser, Ira **1989**:1
Goetz, Bernhard Hugo **1985**:3
Goldhaber, Fred
  Brief Entry **1986**:3
Goodall, Jane **1991**:1
Gore, Tipper **1985**:4
Grant, Charity
  Brief Entry **1985**:2
Greenberg, Hank
  Obituary **1986**:4
Guyer, David
  Brief Entry **1988**:1
Hackney, Sheldon **1995**:1
Hahn, Jessica **1989**:4
Hale, Clara
  Obituary **1993**:3
Hayes, Robert M. **1986**:3
Healey, Jack **1990**:1
Hebard, Caroline **1998**:2
Hefner, Christie **1985**:1
Hepburn, Audrey
  Obituary **1993**:2

Hoffman, Abbie
  Obituary **1989**:3
Hudson, Rock
  Obituary **1985**:4
Huerta, Dolores **1998**:1
Huffington, Arianna **1996**:2
Hullinger, Charlotte
  Brief Entry **1985**:1
Hume, John **1987**:1
Humphry, Derek **1992**:2
Ireland, Jill
  Obituary **1990**:4
Ireland, Patricia **1992**:2
Jackson, Jesse **1996**:1
Jacobs, Joe **1994**:1
Jordan, King **1990**:1
Jorgensen, Christine
  Obituary **1989**:4
Judkins, Reba
  Brief Entry **1987**:3
Kennedy, Rose
  Obituary **1995**:3
Kevorkian, Jack **1991**:3
Kielburger, Craig **1998**:1
King, Bernice **2000**:2
King, Coretta Scott **1999**:3
Kissling, Frances **1989**:2
Klarsfeld, Beate **1989**:1
Kozol, Jonathan **1992**:1
Kramer, Larry **1991**:2
Krim, Mathilde **1989**:2
Kunstler, William
  Obituary **1996**:1
Kurzban, Ira **1987**:2
LaDuke, Winona **1995**:2
Lang, Eugene M. **1990**:3
Leary, Timothy
  Obituary **1996**:4
LeVay, Simon **1992**:2
Lightner, Candy **1985**:1
Lipkis, Andy
  Brief Entry **1985**:3
Lodge, Henry Cabot
  Obituary **1985**:1
Lord, Bette Bao **1994**:1
MacKinnon, Catharine **1993**:2
Mahony, Roger M. **1988**:2
Makeba, Miriam **1989**:2
Mandela, Nelson **1990**:3
Mandela, Winnie **1989**:3
Mankiller, Wilma P.
  Brief Entry **1986**:2
Maraldo, Pamela J. **1993**:4
Marier, Rebecca **1995**:4
Martinez, Bob **1992**:1
Mathews, Dan **1998**:3
Matlovich, Leonard P.
  Obituary **1988**:4
McCall, Nathan **1994**:4
McCartney, Bill **1995**:3
McCloskey, J. Michael **1988**:2
McGuinness, Martin **1985**:4
McTaggart, David **1989**:4
Menchu, Rigoberta **1993**:2
Mengele, Josef
  Obituary **1985**:2
Menninger, Karl
  Obituary **1991**:1
Merritt, Justine
  Brief Entry **1985**:3
Michelman, Kate **1998**:4

Douglas, Buster **1990**:4
Dravecky, Dave **1992**:1
Drexler, Clyde **1992**:4
Drysdale, Don
   Obituary **1994**:1
Duncan, Tim **2000**:1
Durocher, Leo
   Obituary **1992**:2
Duval, David **2000**:3
Duvall, Camille
   Brief Entry **1988**:1
Dykstra, Lenny **1993**:4
Eagleson, Alan **1987**:4
Edwards, Harry **1989**:4
Elway, John **1990**:3
Esiason, Boomer **1991**:1
Evans, Janet **1989**:1
Ewing, Patrick **1985**:3
Faldo, Nick **1993**:3
Favre, Brett Lorenzo **1997**:2
Federov, Sergei **1995**:1
Fehr, Donald **1987**:2
Ferrari, Enzo **1988**:4
Fielder, Cecil **1993**:2
Fiennes, Ranulph **1990**:3
Firestone, Roy **1988**:2
Fittipaldi, Emerson **1994**:2
Flood, Curt
   Obituary **1997**:2
Flutie, Doug **1999**:2
Foss, Joe **1990**:3
Fuhr, Grant **1997**:3
Garcia, Joe
   Brief Entry **1986**:4
Gardner, Randy **1997**:2
Garnett, Kevin **2000**:3
Gathers, Hank
   Obituary **1990**:3
Gault, Willie **1991**:2
Gerulaitis, Vitas
   Obituary **1995**:1
Giamatti, A. Bartlett **1988**:4
   Obituary **1990**:1
Gibson, Kirk **1985**:2
Gilmour, Doug **1994**:3
Gomez, Lefty
   Obituary **1989**:3
Gooden, Dwight **1985**:2
Gordeeva, Ekaterina **1996**:4
Gordon, Jeff **1996**:1
Graf, Steffi **1987**:4
Granato, Cammi **1999**:3
Grange, Red
   Obituary **1991**:3
Graziano, Rocky
   Obituary **1990**:4
Greenberg, Hank
   Obituary **1986**:4
Gretzky, Wayne **1989**:2
Griffey, Ken Jr. **1994**:1
Grinkov, Sergei
   Obituary **1996**:2
Gumbel, Greg **1996**:4
Gwynn, Tony **1995**:1
Hagler, Marvelous Marvin **1985**:2
Hamilton, Scott **1998**:2
Hamm, Mia **2000**:1
Hanauer, Chip **1986**:2
Hardaway, Anfernee **1996**:2
Harkes, John **1996**:4
Harmon, Tom
   Obituary **1990**:3

Harwell, Ernie **1997**:3
Hasek, Dominik **1998**:3
Hayes, Woody
   Obituary **1987**:2
Hernandez, Willie **1985**:1
Hershiser, Orel **1989**:2
Hextall, Ron **1988**:2
Hill, Grant **1995**:3
Hill, Lynn **1991**:2
Hingis, Martina **1999**:1
Hogan, Ben
   Obituary **1997**:4
Hogan, Hulk **1987**:3
Holtz, Lou **1986**:4
Holyfield, Evander **1991**:3
Howard, Desmond Kevin **1997**:2
Howser, Dick
   Obituary **1987**:4
Hull, Brett **1991**:4
Hunter, Catfish
   Obituary **2000**:1
Indurain, Miguel **1994**:1
Inkster, Juli **2000**:2
Irvin, Michael **1996**:3
Jackson, Bo **1986**:3
Jackson, Phil **1996**:3
Jagr, Jaromir **1995**:4
Jenkins, Sally **1997**:2
Jeter, Derek **1999**:4
Johnson, Earvin Magic **1988**:4
Johnson, Jimmy **1993**:3
Johnson, Kevin **1991**:1
Johnson, Keyshawn **2000**:4
Johnson, Larry **1993**:3
Johnson, Michael **2000**:1
Johnson, Randy **1996**:2
Jones, Jerry **1994**:4
Jones, Marion **1998**:4
Jordan, Michael **1987**:2
Joyner, Florence Griffith **1989**:2
   Obituary **1999**:1
Joyner-Kersee, Jackie **1993**:1
Kallen, Jackie **1994**:1
Kanokogi, Rusty
   Brief Entry **1987**:1
Kasparov, Garry **1997**:4
Kelly, Jim **1991**:4
Kemp, Jack **1990**:4
Kemp, Jan **1987**:2
Kemp, Shawn **1995**:1
Kerrigan, Nancy **1994**:3
King, Don **1989**:1
Kiraly, Karch
   Brief Entry **1987**:1
Kite, Tom **1990**:3
Klima, Petr **1987**:1
Knievel, Robbie **1990**:1
Knight, Bobby **1985**:3
Koch, Bill **1992**:3
Konstantinov, Vladimir **1997**:4
Kournikova, Anna **2000**:3
Kroc, Ray
   Obituary **1985**:1
Krone, Julie **1989**:2
Kruk, John **1994**:4
Krzyzewski, Mike **1993**:2
Kukoc, Toni **1995**:4
Laettner, Christian **1993**:1
LaFontaine, Pat **1985**:1
Lalas, Alexi **1995**:1
Landry, Tom
   Obituary **2000**:3

Lemieux, Claude **1996**:1
Lemieux, Mario **1986**:4
LeMond, Greg **1986**:4
Leonard, Sugar Ray **1989**:4
Leslie, Lisa **1997**:4
Lewis, Lennox **2000**:2
Lewis, Reggie
   Obituary **1994**:1
Leyland, Jim **1998**:2
Lindbergh, Pelle
   Obituary **1985**:4
Lindros, Eric **1992**:1
Lipinski, Tara **1998**:3
Lofton, Kenny **1998**:1
Lopez, Nancy **1989**:3
Louganis, Greg **1995**:3
Lukas, D. Wayne **1986**:2
Madden, John **1995**:1
Maddux, Greg **1996**:2
Majerle, Dan **1993**:4
Malone, Karl **1990**:1 **1997**:3
Mantle, Mickey
   Obituary **1996**:2
Maradona, Diego **1991**:3
Maravich, Pete
   Obituary **1988**:2
Maris, Roger
   Obituary **1986**:1
Martin, Billy **1988**:4
   Obituary **1990**:2
Mattingly, Don **1986**:2
Matuszak, John
   Obituary **1989**:4
McCarron, Chris **1995**:4
McCartney, Bill **1995**:3
McGwire, Mark **1999**:1
McMahon, Jim **1985**:4
McMahon, Vince, Jr. **1985**:4
Messier, Mark **1993**:1
Milburn, Rodney Jr.
   Obituary **1998**:2
Miller, Reggie **1994**:4
Minnesota Fats
   Obituary **1996**:3
Monaghan, Tom **1985**:1
Monk, Art **1993**:2
Montana, Joe **1989**:2
Moon, Warren **1991**:3
Moore, Archie
   Obituary **1999**:2
Morgan, Dodge **1987**:1
Moss, Randy **1999**:3
Mourning, Alonzo **1994**:2
Muldowney, Shirley **1986**:1
Musburger, Brent **1985**:1
Navratilova, Martina **1989**:1
Newman, Paul **1995**:3
Nomo, Hideo **1996**:2
Norman, Greg **1988**:3
O'Donnell, Bill
   Brief Entry **1987**:4
Okoye, Christian **1990**:2
Olajuwon, Akeem **1985**:1
Olson, Billy **1986**:3
O'Malley, Susan **1995**:2
O'Neal, Shaquille **1992**:1
Pak, Se Ri **1999**:4
Palmer, Jim **1991**:2
Paterno, Joe **1995**:4
Pavin, Corey **1996**:4
Payton, Walter
   Obituary **2000**:2

Schroeder, William J.
    Obituary **1986**:4
Sculley, John **1989**:4
Shirley, Donna **1999**:1
Sinclair, Mary **1985**:2
Tom and Ray Magliozzi **1991**:4
Toomer, Ron **1990**:1
Torvalds, Linus **1999**:3
Treybig, James G. **1988**:3
Wang, An **1986**:1
    Obituary **1990**:3
Yamamoto, Kenichi **1989**:1

TELEVISION
Affleck, Ben **1999**:1
Albert, Marv **1994**:3
Albom, Mitch **1999**:3
Alda, Robert
    Obituary **1986**:3
Alexander, Jane **1994**:2
Alexander, Jason **1993**:3
Allen, Debbie **1998**:2
Allen, Tim **1993**:1
Alley, Kirstie **1990**:3
Altman, Robert **1993**:2
Amanpour, Christiane **1997**:2
Ameche, Don
    Obituary **1994**:2
Amsterdam, Morey
    Obituary **1997**:1
Ancier, Garth **1989**:1
Anderson, Gillian **1997**:1
Anderson, Harry **1988**:2
Anderson, Judith
    Obituary **1992**:3
Andrews, Julie **1996**:1
Angelou, Maya **1993**:4
Aniston, Jennifer **2000**:3
Applegate, Christina **2000**:4
Arden, Eve
    Obituary **1991**:2
Arledge, Roone **1992**:2
Arlen, Harold
    Obituary **1986**:3
Arnaz, Desi
    Obituary **1987**:1
Arnold, Tom **1993**:2
Arquette, Rosanna **1985**:2
Autry, Gene
    Obituary **1999**:1
Axthelm, Pete
    Obituary **1991**:3
Aykroyd, Dan **1989**:3 **1997**:3
Bacall, Lauren **1997**:3
Backus, Jim
    Obituary **1990**:1
Bacon, Kevin **1995**:3
Baddeley, Hermione
    Obituary **1986**:4
Bailey, Pearl
    Obituary **1991**:1
Ball, Lucille
    Obituary **1989**:3
Barbera, Joseph **1988**:2
Barkin, Ellen **1987**:3
Barney **1993**:4
Barr, Roseanne **1989**:1
Barrymore, Drew **1995**:3
Basinger, Kim **1987**:2
Bassett, Angela **1994**:4
Bateman, Justine **1988**:4

Baxter, Anne
    Obituary **1986**:1
Beatty, Warren **2000**:1
Belushi, Jim **1986**:2
Belzer, Richard **1985**:3
Bergen, Candice **1990**:1
Bernardi, Herschel
    Obituary **1986**:4
Bernsen, Corbin **1990**:2
Bernstein, Leonard
    Obituary **1991**:1
Berry, Halle **1996**:2
Bialik, Mayim **1993**:3
Bixby, Bill
    Obituary **1994**:2
Blades, Ruben **1998**:2
Blanc, Mel
    Obituary **1989**:4
Blanchett, Cate **1999**:3
Bloodworth-Thomason, Linda **1994**
    :1
Bochco, Steven **1989**:1
Bolger, Ray
    Obituary **1987**:2
Bonet, Lisa **1989**:2
Bono, Sonny **1992**:2
    Obituary **1998**:2
Booth, Shirley
    Obituary **1993**:2
Bradshaw, John **1992**:1
Brandy **1996**:4
Bridges, Llyod
    Obituary **1998**:3
Brokaw, Tom **2000**:3
Brosnan, Pierce **2000**:3
Brown, Les **1994**:3
Buckley, Betty **1996**:2
Bullock, Sandra **1995**:4
Burnett, Carol **2000**:3
Burns, George
    Obituary **1996**:3
Burns, Ken **1995**:2
Burr, Raymond
    Obituary **1994**:1
Butler, Brett **1995**:1
Caine, Michael **2000**:4
Calhoun, Rory
    Obituary **1999**:4
Campbell, Neve **1998**:2
Campion, Jane **1991**:4
Candy, John **1988**:2
    Obituary **1994**:3
Carey, Drew **1997**:4
Carlin, George **1996**:3
Carrey, Jim **1995**:1
Carson, Lisa Nicole **1999**:3
Carter, Chris **2000**:1
Caruso, David **1994**:3
Carvey, Dana **1994**:1
Cassavetes, John
    Obituary **1989**:2
Caulfield, Joan
    Obituary **1992**:1
Chancellor, John
    Obituary **1997**:1
Channing, Stockard **1991**:3
Chase, Chevy **1990**:1
Chavez, Linda **1999**:3
Cher **1993**:1
Cherry, Don **1993**:4
Child, Julia **1999**:4
Cho, Margaret **1995**:2

Chow Yun-fat **1999**:4
Chung, Connie **1988**:4
Clay, Andrew Dice **1991**:1
Cleese, John **1989**:2
Clooney, George **1996**:4
Close, Glenn **1988**:3
Coco, James
    Obituary **1987**:2
Colasanto, Nicholas
    Obituary **1985**:2
Coleman, Dabney **1988**:3
Connery, Sean **1990**:4
Convy, Bert
    Obituary **1992**:1
Cook, Peter
    Obituary **1995**:2
Copperfield, David **1986**:3
Coppola, Francis Ford **1989**:4
Cosby, Bill **1999**:2
Cosell, Howard
    Obituary **1995**:4
Costas, Bob **1986**:4
Couric, Katherine **1991**:4
Cousteau, Jacques-Yves
    Obituary **1998**:2
Cox, Courteney **1996**:2
Cox, Richard Joseph
    Brief Entry **1985**:1
Crawford, Broderick
    Obituary **1986**:3
Crawford, Cindy **1993**:3
Crawford, Michael **1994**:2
Crichton, Michael **1995**:3
Cronkite, Walter Leland **1997**:3
Crothers, Scatman
    Obituary **1987**:1
Crystal, Billy **1985**:3
Curtis, Jamie Lee **1995**:1
Cushing, Peter
    Obituary **1995**:1
Dalton, Timothy **1988**:4
Damon, Matt **1999**:1
Danes, Claire **1999**:4
Daniels, Faith **1993**:3
Daniels, Jeff **1989**:4
Danza, Tony **1989**:1
Davis, Bette
    Obituary **1990**:1
Davis, Geena **1992**:1
Davis, Sammy, Jr.
    Obituary **1990**:4
Day, Dennis
    Obituary **1988**:4
De Cordova, Frederick **1985**:2
DeGeneres, Ellen **1995**:3
Depardieu, Gerard **1991**:2
Depp, Johnny **1991**:3
De Vito, Danny **1987**:1
Dewhurst, Colleen
    Obituary **1992**:2
Diamond, Selma
    Obituary **1985**:2
DiCaprio, Leonardo Wilhelm **1997**:2
Dickerson, Nancy H.
    Obituary **1998**:2
Diller, Barry **1991**:1
Disney, Roy E. **1986**:3
Doherty, Shannen **1994**:2
Dolenz, Micky **1986**:4
Douglas, Michael **1986**:2
Downey, Morton, Jr. **1988**:4
Drescher, Fran **1995**:3

Duchovny, David **1998**:3
Duffy, Karen **1998**:1
Dukakis, Olympia **1996**:4
Duke, Red
   Brief Entry **1987**:1
Durrell, Gerald
   Obituary **1995**:3
Duvall, Robert **1999**:3
Eastwood, Clint **1993**:3
Ebert, Roger **1998**:3
Eisner, Michael **1989**:2
Elfman, Jenna **1999**:4
Ellerbee, Linda **1993**:3
Elliott, Denholm
   Obituary **1993**:2
Engstrom, Elmer W.
   Obituary **1985**:2
Farley, Chris
   Obituary **1998**:2
Fawcett, Farrah **1998**:4
Fell, Norman
   Obituary **1999**:2
Ferrer, Jose
   Obituary **1992**:3
Field, Sally **1995**:3
Firestone, Roy **1988**:2
Fishburne, Laurence **1995**:3
Fisher, Carrie **1991**:1
Flanders, Ed
   Obituary **1995**:3
Fleming, Art
   Obituary **1995**:4
Flockhart, Calista **1998**:4
Fonda, Bridget **1995**:1
Ford, Tennessee Ernie
   Obituary **1992**:2
Fosse, Bob
   Obituary **1988**:1
Foster, Jodie **1989**:2
Foster, Phil
   Obituary **1985**:3
Fox, Michael J. **1986**:1
Fox, Vivica **1999**:1
Foxworthy, Jeff **1996**:1
Foxx, Redd
   Obituary **1992**:2
Franciscus, James
   Obituary **1992**:1
Franz, Dennis **1995**:2
Freeman, Morgan **1990**:4
Freleng, Friz
   Obituary **1995**:4
Funt, Allen
   Obituary **2000**:1
Gabor, Eva
   Obituary **1996**:1
Garcia, Andy **1999**:3
Gardenia, Vincent
   Obituary **1993**:2
Garofalo, Janeane **1996**:4
Gellar, Sarah Michelle **1999**:3
Gere, Richard **1994**:3
Gifford, Kathie Lee **1992**:2
Gilford, Jack
   Obituary **1990**:4
Gillett, George **1988**:1
Gish, Lillian
   Obituary **1993**:4
Gleason, Jackie
   Obituary **1987**:4
Gless, Sharon **1989**:3
Glover, Danny **1998**:4

Gobel, George
   Obituary **1991**:4
Goldberg, Gary David **1989**:4
Goldberg, Leonard **1988**:4
Goldberg, Whoopi **1993**:3
Goldblum, Jeff **1988**:1 **1997**:3
Goodman, John **1990**:3
Gordon, Gale
   Obituary **1996**:1
Goren, Charles H.
   Obituary **1991**:4
Gossett, Louis, Jr. **1989**:3
Graham, Billy **1992**:1
Grammer, Kelsey **1995**:1
Grange, Red
   Obituary **1991**:3
Grant, Rodney A. **1992**:1
Graziano, Rocky
   Obituary **1990**:4
Green, Tom **1999**:4
Greene, Graham **1997**:2
Greene, Lorne
   Obituary **1988**:1
Griffith, Melanie **1989**:2
Grodin, Charles **1997**:3
Groening, Matt **1990**:4
Gumbel, Bryant **1990**:2
Gumbel, Greg **1996**:4
Gunn, Hartford N., Jr.
   Obituary **1986**:2
Hackman, Gene **1989**:3
Haley, Alex
   Obituary **1992**:3
Hall, Anthony Michael **1986**:3
Hall, Arsenio **1990**:2
Hamilton, Margaret
   Obituary **1985**:3
Hamilton, Scott **1998**:2
Hammer, Jan **1987**:3
Hanks, Tom **1989**:2 **2000**:2
Harmon, Mark **1987**:1
Hart, Mary
   Brief Entry **1988**:1
Hartman, Phil **1996**:2
   Obituary **1998**:4
Hawn, Goldie Jeanne **1997**:2
Hayek, Salma **1999**:1
Hayes, Helen
   Obituary **1993**:4
Hayes, Isaac **1998**:4
Headroom, Max **1986**:4
Heche, Anne **1999**:1
Hefner, Christie **1985**:1
Henning, Doug
   Obituary **2000**:3
Henson, Brian **1992**:1
Henson, Jim **1989**:1
   Obituary **1990**:4
Hepburn, Katharine **1991**:2
Hershey, Barbara **1989**:1
Heston, Charlton **1999**:4
Hewitt, Jennifer Love **1999**:2
Hill, Benny
   Obituary **1992**:3
Hill, Lauryn **1999**:3
Hoskins, Bob **1989**:1
Houseman, John
   Obituary **1989**:1
Houston, Cissy **1999**:3
Howard, Ron **1997**:2
Howard, Trevor
   Obituary **1988**:2

Hudson, Rock
   Obituary **1985**:4
Huffington, Arianna **1996**:2
Humphries, Barry **1993**:1
Hunt, Helen **1994**:4
Hunter, Holly **1989**:4
Hurley, Elizabeth **1999**:2
Hurt, William **1986**:1
Huston, Anjelica **1989**:3
Hutton, Timothy **1986**:3
Ireland, Jill
   Obituary **1990**:4
Irons, Jeremy **1991**:4
Itami, Juzo
   Obituary **1998**:2
Jackson, Janet **1990**:4
Jackson, Samuel L. **1995**:4
Jennings, Peter Charles **1997**:2
Jillian, Ann **1986**:4
Johnson, Don **1986**:1
Jones, Cherry **1999**:3
Jones, Jenny **1998**:2
Jones, Tom **1993**:4
Jones, Tommy Lee **1994**:2
Judd, Ashley **1998**:1
Judge, Mike **1994**:2
Julia, Raul
   Obituary **1995**:1
Juneau, Pierre **1988**:3
Kahn, Madeline
   Obituary **2000**:2
Kasem, Casey **1987**:1
Katzenberg, Jeffrey **1995**:3
Kavner, Julie **1992**:3
Kaye, Danny
   Obituary **1987**:2
Kaye, Sammy
   Obituary **1987**:4
Keaton, Michael **1989**:4
Keitel, Harvey **1994**:3
Keith, Brian
   Obituary **1997**:4
Kelley, DeForest
   Obituary **2000**:1
Kent, Arthur **1991**:4 **1997**:2
Kidman, Nicole **1992**:4
King, Larry **1993**:1
King, Stephen **1998**:1
Kinison, Sam
   Obituary **1993**:1
Kloss, Henry E.
   Brief Entry **1985**:2
Knight, Ted
   Obituary **1986**:4
Knight, Wayne **1997**:1
Koplovitz, Kay **1986**:3
Koppel, Ted **1989**:1
Kordich, Jay **1993**:2
Kudrow, Lisa **1996**:1
Kulp, Nancy
   Obituary **1991**:3
Kuralt, Charles
   Obituary **1998**:3
Lagasse, Emeril **1998**:3
Lahti, Christine **1988**:2
Lake, Ricki **1994**:4
Landon, Michael
   Obituary **1992**:1
Lange, Jessica **1995**:4
Lansbury, Angela **1993**:1
Larroquette, John **1986**:2
LaSalle, Eriq **1996**:4

Lawless, Lucy **1997**:4
Lawrence, Martin **1993**:4
Laybourne, Geraldine **1997**:1
Leach, Penelope **1992**:4
Leach, Robin
  Brief Entry **1985**:4
Leary, Denis **1993**:3
Lee, Pamela **1996**:4
Leguizamo, John **1999**:1
Leigh, Jennifer Jason **1995**:2
Lemmon, Jack **1998**:4
Leno, Jay **1987**:1
Letterman, David **1989**:3
Levinson, Barry **1989**:3
Lewis, Juliette **1999**:3
Lewis, Richard **1992**:1
Lewis, Shari **1993**:1
  Obituary **1999**:1
Liberace
  Obituary **1987**:2
Little, Cleavon
  Obituary **1993**:2
Liu, Lucy **2000**:4
LL Cool J **1998**:2
Locklear, Heather **1994**:3
Long, Shelley **1985**:1
Lopez, Jennifer **1998**:4
Lord, Jack
  Obituary **1998**:2
Lords, Traci **1995**:4
Louis-Dreyfus, Julia **1994**:1
Loy, Myrna
  Obituary **1994**:2
Lucci, Susan **1999**:4
Lupino, Ida
  Obituary **1996**:1
Lynch, David **1990**:4
MacMurray, Fred
  Obituary **1992**:2
MacRae, Gordon
  Obituary **1986**:2
Macy, William H. **1999**:3
Madden, John **1995**:1
Maher, Bill **1996**:2
Malkovich, John **1988**:2
Malone, John C. **1988**:3 **1996**:3
Mandel, Howie **1989**:1
Mantegna, Joe **1992**:1
Martin, Dean
  Obituary **1996**:2
Martin, Mary
  Obituary **1991**:2
Martin, Steve **1992**:2
Matlin, Marlee **1992**:2
Matthau, Walter **2000**:3
McCarthy, Jenny **1997**:4
McDormand, Frances **1997**:3
McDowall, Roddy
  Obituary **1999**:1
McGillis, Kelly **1989**:3
McGregor, Ewan **1998**:2
McKee, Lonette **1996**:1
McKellen, Ian **1994**:1
Meadows, Audrey
  Obituary **1996**:3
Meredith, Burgess
  Obituary **1998**:1
Midler, Bette **1989**:4
Milland, Ray
  Obituary **1986**:2
Miller, Dennis **1992**:4

Mitchum, Robert
  Obituary **1997**:4
Montgomery, Elizabeth
  Obituary **1995**:4
Moore, Clayton
  Obituary **2000**:3
Moore, Demi **1991**:4
Moore, Julianne **1998**:1
Moore, Mary Tyler **1996**:2
Morita, Noriyuki Pat **1987**:3
Moyers, Bill **1991**:4
Murdoch, Rupert **1988**:4
Murphy, Eddie **1989**:2
Musburger, Brent **1985**:1
Myers, Mike **1992**:3 **1997**:4
Nance, Jack
  Obituary **1997**:3
Neeson, Liam **1993**:4
Nelson, Harriet
  Obituary **1995**:1
Nelson, Rick
  Obituary **1986**:1
Nelson, Willie **1993**:4
Newton-John, Olivia **1998**:4
Nichols, Mike **1994**:4
Nolan, Lloyd
  Obituary **1985**:4
Nolte, Nick **1992**:4
Norville, Deborah **1990**:3
Nye, Bill **1997**:2
O'Brien, Conan **1994**:1
O'Donnell, Rosie **1994**:3
Oldman, Gary **1998**:1
Olin, Ken **1992**:3
Olivier, Laurence
  Obituary **1989**:4
Olmos, Edward James **1990**:1
Olson, Johnny
  Obituary **1985**:4
Osgood, Charles **1996**:2
O'Sullivan, Maureen
  Obituary **1998**:4
Otte, Ruth **1992**:4
Ovitz, Michael **1990**:1
Paley, William S.
  Obituary **1991**:2
Palmer, Jim **1991**:2
Park, Nick **1997**:3
Parker, Sarah Jessica **1999**:2
Parker, Trey and Matt Stone **1998**:2
Parks, Bert
  Obituary **1992**:3
Pauley, Jane **1999**:1
Paulsen, Pat
  Obituary **1997**:4
Paxton, Bill **1999**:3
Peller, Clara
  Obituary **1988**:1
Penn, Sean **1987**:2
Perez, Rosie **1994**:2
Perry, Luke **1992**:3
Perry, Matthew **1997**:2
Peterson, Cassandra **1988**:1
Pfeiffer, Michelle **1990**:2
Philbin, Regis **2000**:2
Phoenix, River **1990**:2
  Obituary **1994**:2
Pierce, David Hyde **1996**:3
Pierce, Frederick S. **1985**:3
Pinchot, Bronson **1987**:4
Pinkett Smith, Jada **1998**:3
Pitt, Brad **1995**:2

Pittman, Robert W. **1985**:1
Plato, Dana
  Obituary **1999**:4
Pleasence, Donald
  Obituary **1995**:3
Poitier, Sidney **1990**:3
Potts, Annie **1994**:1
Povich, Maury **1994**:3
Powter, Susan **1994**:3
Price, Vincent
  Obituary **1994**:2
Priestly, Jason **1993**:2
Prince, Faith **1993**:2
Prinze, Freddie, Jr. **1999**:3
Pryor, Richard **1999**:3
Quaid, Dennis **1989**:4
Queen Latifah **1992**:2
Quinn, Martha **1986**:4
Quivers, Robin **1995**:4
Radecki, Thomas
  Brief Entry **1986**:2
Radner, Gilda
  Obituary **1989**:4
Raimi, Sam **1999**:2
Randi, James **1990**:2
Raphael, Sally Jessy **1992**:4
Rashad, Phylicia **1987**:3
Raye, Martha
  Obituary **1995**:1
Reasoner, Harry
  Obituary **1992**:1
Redgrave, Lynn **1999**:3
Redgrave, Vanessa **1989**:2
Reed, Donna
  Obituary **1986**:1
Reed, Robert
  Obituary **1992**:4
Reese, Della **1999**:2
Reeve, Christopher **1997**:2
Reiner, Rob **1991**:2
Reiser, Paul **1995**:2
Remick, Lee
  Obituary **1992**:1
Reuben, Gloria **1999**:4
Reubens, Paul **1987**:2
Ricci, Christina **1999**:1
Richards, Michael **1993**:4
Riddle, Nelson
  Obituary **1985**:4
Rivera, Geraldo **1989**:1
Robbins, Tim **1993**:1
Roberts, Cokie **1993**:4
Roberts, Julia **1991**:3
Robertson, Pat **1988**:2
Robinson, Max
  Obituary **1989**:2
Rock, Chris **1998**:1
Roddenberry, Gene
  Obituary **1992**:2
Rogers, Fred **2000**:4
Rogers, Roy
  Obituary **1998**:4
Roker, Roxie
  Obituary **1996**:2
Rolle, Esther
  Obituary **1999**:2
Rollins, Howard E., Jr. **1986**:1
Rose, Charlie **1994**:2
Rourke, Mickey **1988**:4
Rowan, Dan
  Obituary **1988**:1
Rudner, Rita **1993**:2

Russell, Keri **2000**:1
Ryan, Meg **1994**:1
Sagansky, Jeff **1993**:2
Sajak, Pat
  Brief Entry **1985**:4
Sandler, Adam **1999**:2
Saralegui, Cristina **1999**:2
Sarandon, Susan **1995**:3
Savage, Fred **1990**:1
Savalas, Telly
  Obituary **1994**:3
Sawyer, Diane **1994**:4
Schneider, Rob **1997**:4
Schwimmer, David **1996**:2
Scott, Gene
  Brief Entry **1986**:1
Sedelmaier, Joe **1985**:3
Seinfeld, Jerry **1992**:4
Sevareid, Eric
  Obituary **1993**:1
Seymour, Jane **1994**:4
Shaffer, Paul **1987**:1
Shandling, Garry **1995**:1
Sharkey, Ray
  Obituary **1994**:1
Shawn, Dick
  Obituary **1987**:3
Sheedy, Ally **1989**:1
Sheindlin, Judith **1999**:1
Shepherd, Cybill **1996**:3
Shields, Brooke **1996**:3
Shore, Dinah
  Obituary **1994**:3
Short, Martin **1986**:1
Shriver, Maria
  Brief Entry **1986**:2
Shue, Andrew **1994**:4
Silverman, Jonathan **1997**:2
Silvers, Phil
  Obituary **1985**:4
Silverstone, Alicia **1997**:4
Sinise, Gary **1996**:1
Siskel, Gene
  Obituary **1999**:3
Skelton, Red
  Obituary **1998**:1
Slater, Christian **1994**:1
Smirnoff, Yakov **1987**:2
Smith, Buffalo Bob
  Obituary **1999**:1
Smith, Jeff **1991**:4
Smith, Kate
  Obituary **1986**:3
Smits, Jimmy **1990**:1
Snipes, Wesley **1993**:1
Somers, Suzanne **2000**:1
Sondheim, Stephen **1994**:4
Southern, Terry
  Obituary **1996**:2
Spade, David **1999**:2
Spheeris, Penelope **1989**:2
Spielberg, Steven **1993**:4 **1997**:4
Springer, Jerry **1998**:4
Stern, Howard **1988**:2 **1993**:3
Stevenson, McLean
  Obituary **1996**:3
Stewart, Martha **1992**:1
Stewart, Patrick **1996**:1
Stiller, Ben **1999**:1
Stone, Sharon **1993**:4
Stoppard, Tom **1995**:4
Streisand, Barbra **1992**:2

Studi, Wes **1994**:3
Susskind, David
  Obituary **1987**:2
Swaggart, Jimmy **1987**:3
Swayze, John Cameron
  Obituary **1996**:1
Tandy, Jessica **1990**:4
  Obituary **1995**:1
Tartikoff, Brandon **1985**:2
  Obituary **1998**:1
Taylor, Elizabeth **1993**:3
Tesh, John **1996**:3
Thomas, Danny
  Obituary **1991**:3
Thompson, Emma **1993**:2
Thornton, Billy Bob **1997**:4
Tillstrom, Burr
  Obituary **1986**:1
Tilly, Jennifer **1997**:2
Tisch, Laurence A. **1988**:2
Tomei, Marisa **1995**:2
Totenberg, Nina **1992**:2
Travolta, John **1995**:2
Trotter, Charlie **2000**:4
Trudeau, Garry **1991**:2
Tucker, Chris **1999**:1
Tucker, Forrest
  Obituary **1987**:1
Turner, Janine **1993**:2
Turner, Lana
  Obituary **1996**:1
Turner, Ted **1989**:1
Ullman, Tracey **1988**:3
Urich, Robert **1988**:1
Vanilla Ice **1991**:3
Varney, Jim
  Obituary **2000**:3
Varney, Jim
  Brief Entry **1985**:4
Vaughn, Vince **1999**:2
Ventura, Jesse **1999**:2
Vidal, Gore **1996**:2
Villechaize, Herve
  Obituary **1994**:1
Vitale, Dick **1988**:4 **1994**:4
Walker, Nancy
  Obituary **1992**:3
Walters, Barbara **1998**:3
Wapner, Joseph A. **1987**:1
Washington, Denzel **1993**:2
Wayans, Damon **1998**:4
Wayans, Keenen Ivory **1991**:1
Wayne, David
  Obituary **1995**:3
Weitz, Bruce **1985**:4
Whitaker, Forest **1996**:2
White, Jaleel **1992**:3
Whittle, Christopher **1989**:3
Williams, Robin **1988**:4
Williams, Vanessa L. **1999**:2
Willis, Bruce **1986**:4
Wilson, Flip
  Obituary **1999**:2
Winfrey, Oprah **1986**:4 **1997**:3
Winger, Debra **1994**:3
Wolfman Jack
  Obituary **1996**:1
Wong, B.D. **1998**:1
Woods, James **1988**:3
Wright, Steven **1986**:3
Wyle, Noah **1997**:3

Wynn, Keenan
  Obituary **1987**:1
Xuxa **1994**:2
Yetnikoff, Walter **1988**:1
York, Dick
  Obituary **1992**:4
Young, Robert
  Obituary **1999**:1
Youngman, Henny
  Obituary **1998**:3
Zahn, Paula **1992**:3
Zamora, Pedro
  Obituary **1995**:2
Zeta-Jones, Catherine **1999**:4
Zucker, Jeff **1993**:3

THEATER
Abbott, George
  Obituary **1995**:3
Adjani, Isabelle **1991**:1
Albee, Edward **1997**:1
Alda, Robert
  Obituary **1986**:3
Alexander, Jane **1994**:2
Alexander, Jason **1993**:3
Allen, Joan **1998**:1
Allen, Peter
  Obituary **1993**:1
Ameche, Don
  Obituary **1994**:2
Andrews, Julie **1996**:1
Angelou, Maya **1993**:4
Arden, Eve
  Obituary **1991**:2
Ashcroft, Peggy
  Obituary **1992**:1
Aykroyd, Dan **1989**:3 **1997**:3
Bacall, Lauren **1997**:3
Bacon, Kevin **1995**:3
Baddeley, Hermione
  Obituary **1986**:4
Bailey, Pearl
  Obituary **1991**:1
Barkin, Ellen **1987**:3
Barry, Lynda **1992**:1
Bassett, Angela **1994**:4
Bates, Kathy **1991**:4
Beckett, Samuel Barclay
  Obituary **1990**:2
Belushi, Jim **1986**:2
Bening, Annette **1992**:1
Bennett, Joan
  Obituary **1991**:2
Bennett, Michael
  Obituary **1988**:1
Bernardi, Herschel
  Obituary **1986**:4
Bernhard, Sandra **1989**:4
Bernstein, Leonard
  Obituary **1991**:1
Bishop, Andre **2000**:1
Blackstone, Harry Jr.
  Obituary **1997**:4
Blanchett, Cate **1999**:3
Bloch, Ivan **1986**:3
Bogosian, Eric **1990**:4
Bolger, Ray
  Obituary **1987**:2
Bonham Carter, Helena **1998**:4
Booth, Shirley
  Obituary **1993**:2
Bowie, David **1998**:2

Branagh, Kenneth **1992**:2
Brandauer, Klaus Maria **1987**:3
Brynner, Yul
  Obituary **1985**:4
Buckley, Betty **1996**:2
Bullock, Sandra **1995**:4
Burck, Wade
  Brief Entry **1986**:1
Burr, Raymond
  Obituary **1994**:1
Busch, Charles **1998**:3
Byrne, Gabriel **1997**:4
Caesar, Adolph
  Obituary **1986**:3
Cagney, James
  Obituary **1986**:2
Caine, Michael **2000**:4
Candy, John **1988**:2
  Obituary **1994**:3
Carrey, Jim **1995**:1
Carson, Lisa Nicole **1999**:3
Cassavetes, John
  Obituary **1989**:2
Caulfield, Joan
  Obituary **1992**:1
Channing, Stockard **1991**:3
Close, Glenn **1988**:3
Coco, James
  Obituary **1987**:2
Connery, Sean **1990**:4
Convy, Bert
  Obituary **1992**:1
Cook, Peter
  Obituary **1995**:2
Coppola, Carmine
  Obituary **1991**:4
Costner, Kevin **1989**:4
Crawford, Broderick
  Obituary **1986**:3
Crawford, Cheryl
  Obituary **1987**:1
Crawford, Michael **1994**:2
Crisp, Quentin
  Obituary **2000**:3
Culkin, Macaulay **1991**:3
Cusack, John **1999**:3
Cushing, Peter
  Obituary **1995**:1
Dafoe, Willem **1988**:1
Dalton, Timothy **1988**:4
Daniels, Jeff **1989**:4
Day-Lewis, Daniel **1989**:4 **1994**:4
Dench, Judi **1999**:4
De Niro, Robert **1999**:1
Dennis, Sandy
  Obituary **1992**:4
Depardieu, Gerard **1991**:2
Dern, Laura **1992**:3
De Vito, Danny **1987**:1
Dewhurst, Colleen
  Obituary **1992**:2
Diggs, Taye **2000**:1
Douglas, Michael **1986**:2
Dukakis, Olympia **1996**:4
Duncan, Todd
  Obituary **1998**:3
Duvall, Robert **1999**:3
Elliott, Denholm
  Obituary **1993**:2
Ephron, Henry
  Obituary **1993**:2
Fawcett, Farrah **1998**:4

Feld, Kenneth **1988**:2
Ferrer, Jose
  Obituary **1992**:3
Fiennes, Ralph **1996**:2
Fishburne, Laurence **1995**:3
Fisher, Carrie **1991**:1
Flanders, Ed
  Obituary **1995**:3
Flockhart, Calista **1998**:4
Fo, Dario **1998**:1
Fosse, Bob
  Obituary **1988**:1
Freeman, Morgan **1990**:4
Fugard, Athol **1992**:3
Gabor, Eva
  Obituary **1996**:1
Gardenia, Vincent
  Obituary **1993**:2
Garr, Teri **1988**:4
Geffen, David **1985**:3 **1997**:3
Gere, Richard **1994**:3
Gielgud, John
  Obituary **2000**:4
Gilford, Jack
  Obituary **1990**:4
Gleason, Jackie
  Obituary **1987**:4
Glover, Danny **1998**:4
Glover, Savion **1997**:1
Gobel, George
  Obituary **1991**:4
Goldberg, Whoopi **1993**:3
Goldblum, Jeff **1988**:1 **1997**:3
Gossett, Louis, Jr. **1989**:3
Grammer, Kelsey **1995**:1
Grant, Cary
  Obituary **1987**:1
Grant, Hugh **1995**:3
Greene, Graham **1997**:2
Gregory, Dick **1990**:3
Hall, Anthony Michael **1986**:3
Hamilton, Margaret
  Obituary **1985**:3
Harrison, Rex
  Obituary **1990**:4
Havel, Vaclav **1990**:3
Hawke, Ethan **1995**:4
Hayes, Helen
  Obituary **1993**:4
Henning, Doug
  Obituary **2000**:3
Hepburn, Katharine **1991**:2
Hines, Gregory **1992**:4
Hopkins, Anthony **1992**:4
Horne, Lena **1998**:4
Hoskins, Bob **1989**:1
Houseman, John
  Obituary **1989**:1
Houston, Cissy **1999**:3
Humphries, Barry **1993**:1
Hunt, Helen **1994**:4
Hunter, Holly **1989**:4
Hurt, William **1986**:1
Hwang, David Henry **1999**:1
Irons, Jeremy **1991**:4
Irwin, Bill **1988**:3
Itami, Juzo
  Obituary **1998**:2
Ives, Burl
  Obituary **1995**:4
Jackson, Samuel L. **1995**:4
Jay, Ricky **1995**:1

Jillian, Ann **1986**:4
Jones, Cherry **1999**:3
Jones, Tommy Lee **1994**:2
Julia, Raul
  Obituary **1995**:1
Kahn, Madeline
  Obituary **2000**:2
Kavner, Julie **1992**:3
Kaye, Danny
  Obituary **1987**:2
Kaye, Nora
  Obituary **1987**:4
Keeler, Ruby
  Obituary **1993**:4
Keitel, Harvey **1994**:3
Kilmer, Val **1991**:4
Kinski, Klaus **1987**:2
Kline, Kevin **2000**:1
Kramer, Larry **1991**:2
Kushner, Tony **1995**:2
Lahti, Christine **1988**:2
Lane, Burton
  Obituary **1997**:2
Lane, Nathan **1996**:4
Lange, Jessica **1995**:4
Lansbury, Angela **1993**:1
Larson, Jonathan
  Obituary **1997**:2
Lawless, Lucy **1997**:4
Leary, Denis **1993**:3
Leigh, Jennifer Jason **1995**:2
Lithgow, John **1985**:2
Little, Cleavon
  Obituary **1993**:2
Lloyd Webber, Andrew **1989**:1
Loewe, Frederick
  Obituary **1988**:2
Logan, Joshua
  Obituary **1988**:4
Lord, Jack
  Obituary **1998**:2
MacRae, Gordon
  Obituary **1986**:2
Macy, William H. **1999**:3
Maher, Bill **1996**:2
Malkovich, John **1988**:2
Maltby, Richard, Jr. **1996**:3
Mamet, David **1998**:4
Mantegna, Joe **1992**:1
Marshall, Penny **1991**:3
Martin, Mary
  Obituary **1991**:2
McDormand, Frances **1997**:3
McDowall, Roddy
  Obituary **1999**:1
McGillis, Kelly **1989**:3
McGregor, Ewan **1998**:2
McKee, Lonette **1996**:1
McKellen, Ian **1994**:1
Merrick, David
  Obituary **2000**:4
Midler, Bette **1989**:4
Montand, Yves
  Obituary **1992**:2
Montgomery, Elizabeth
  Obituary **1995**:4
Moore, Mary Tyler **1996**:2
Neeson, Liam **1993**:4
Newman, Paul **1995**:3
Nichols, Mike **1994**:4
Nolan, Lloyd
  Obituary **1985**:4

Nolte, Nick **1992**:4
North, Alex **1986**:3
Nunn, Trevor **2000**:2
O'Donnell, Rosie **1994**:3
Oldman, Gary **1998**:1
Olin, Ken **1992**:3
Olin, Lena **1991**:2
Olivier, Laurence
  Obituary **1989**:4
Osborne, John
  Obituary **1995**:2
O'Sullivan, Maureen
  Obituary **1998**:4
Pacino, Al **1993**:4
Page, Geraldine
  Obituary **1987**:4
Papp, Joseph
  Obituary **1992**:2
Paulsen, Pat
  Obituary **1997**:4
Penn, Sean **1987**:2
Penn & Teller **1992**:1
Perkins, Anthony
  Obituary **1993**:2
Peters, Bernadette **2000**:1
Pfeiffer, Michelle **1990**:2
Picasso, Paloma **1991**:1
Pinchot, Bronson **1987**:4
Pleasence, Donald
  Obituary **1995**:3
Poitier, Sidney **1990**:3
Preminger, Otto
  Obituary **1986**:3
Preston, Robert
  Obituary **1987**:3
Price, Vincent
  Obituary **1994**:2
Prince, Faith **1993**:2
Quaid, Dennis **1989**:4
Radner, Gilda
  Obituary **1989**:4
Rashad, Phylicia **1987**:3
Raye, Martha
  Obituary **1995**:1
Redford, Robert **1993**:2
Redgrave, Lynn **1999**:3
Redgrave, Vanessa **1989**:2
Reeves, Keanu **1992**:1
Reitman, Ivan **1986**:3
Reza, Yasmina **1999**:2
Richards, Michael **1993**:4
Robbins, Jerome
  Obituary **1999**:1
Roker, Roxie
  Obituary **1996**:2
Rolle, Esther
  Obituary **1999**:2
Rudner, Rita **1993**:2
Rudnick, Paul **1994**:3
Ruehl, Mercedes **1992**:4
Sarandon, Susan **1995**:3
Schoenfeld, Gerald **1986**:2
Schwimmer, David **1996**:2
Scott, George C.
  Obituary **2000**:2
Seymour, Jane **1994**:4
Shaffer, Paul **1987**:1
Shawn, Dick
  Obituary **1987**:3
Shepard, Sam **1996**:4
Short, Martin **1986**:1

Silvers, Phil
  Obituary **1985**:4
Sinise, Gary **1996**:1
Slater, Christian **1994**:1
Snipes, Wesley **1993**:1
Sondheim, Stephen **1994**:4
Spacey, Kevin **1996**:4
Stewart, Jimmy
  Obituary **1997**:4
Stewart, Patrick **1996**:1
Stiller, Ben **1999**:1
Sting **1991**:4
Stoppard, Tom **1995**:4
Streep, Meryl **1990**:2
Streisand, Barbra **1992**:2
Styne, Jule
  Obituary **1995**:1
Susskind, David
  Obituary **1987**:2
Tandy, Jessica **1990**:4
  Obituary **1995**:1
Taylor, Elizabeth **1993**:3
Taylor, Lili **2000**:2
Thompson, Emma **1993**:2
Tomei, Marisa **1995**:2
Tune, Tommy **1994**:2
Ullman, Tracey **1988**:3
Urich, Robert **1988**:1
Vogel, Paula **1999**:2
Walker, Nancy
  Obituary **1992**:3
Washington, Denzel **1993**:2
Wasserstein, Wendy **1991**:3
Wayne, David
  Obituary **1995**:3
Weaver, Sigourney **1988**:3
Weitz, Bruce **1985**:4
Wences, Senor
  Obituary **1999**:4
Whitaker, Forest **1996**:2
Wiest, Dianne **1995**:2
Willis, Bruce **1986**:4
Wong, B.D. **1998**:1
Woods, James **1988**:3
Wyle, Noah **1997**:3
Youngman, Henny
  Obituary **1998**:3
Zeffirelli, Franco **1991**:3

WRITING

Adams, Scott **1996**:4
Albom, Mitch **1999**:3
Alexie, Sherman **1998**:4
Amanpour, Christiane **1997**:2
Ambler, Eric
  Obituary **1999**:2
Amis, Kingsley
  Obituary **1996**:2
Amory, Cleveland
  Obituary **1999**:2
Angelou, Maya **1993**:4
Angier, Natalie **2000**:3
Asimov, Isaac
  Obituary **1992**:3
Axthelm, Pete
  Obituary **1991**:3
Bacall, Lauren **1997**:3
Bakker, Robert T. **1991**:3
Baldwin, James
  Obituary **1988**:2
Ball, Edward **1999**:2
Baraka, Amiri **2000**:3

Barber, Red
  Obituary **1993**:2
Barry, Dave **1991**:2
Barry, Lynda **1992**:1
Beckett, Samuel Barclay
  Obituary **1990**:2
Bloodworth-Thomason, Linda **1994**:1
Blume, Judy **1998**:4
Bly, Robert **1992**:4
Bombeck, Erma
  Obituary **1996**:4
Bowles, Paul
  Obituary **2000**:3
Bradshaw, John **1992**:1
Branagh, Kenneth **1992**:2
Brodsky, Joseph
  Obituary **1996**:3
Brokaw, Tom **2000**:3
Brooks, Gwendolyn **1998**:1
Brown, Tina **1992**:1
Buffett, Jimmy **1999**:3
Burgess, Anthony
  Obituary **1994**:2
Burroughs, William S.
  Obituary **1997**:4
Burroughs, William S. **1994**:2
Buscaglia, Leo
  Obituary **1998**:4
Busch, Charles **1998**:3
Bush, Millie **1992**:1
Butler, Octavia E. **1999**:3
Byrne, Gabriel **1997**:4
Caen, Herb
  Obituary **1997**:4
Campbell, Bebe Moore **1996**:2
Caplan, Arthur L. **2000**:2
Carcaterra, Lorenzo **1996**:1
Carey, George **1992**:3
Carver, Raymond
  Obituary **1989**:1
Castaneda, Carlos
  Obituary **1998**:4
Castillo, Ana **2000**:4
Chatwin, Bruce
  Obituary **1989**:2
Chavez, Linda **1999**:3
Cheney, Lynne V. **1990**:4
Child, Julia **1999**:4
Chopra, Deepak **1996**:3
Clancy, Tom **1998**:4
Clark, Mary Higgins **2000**:4
Clavell, James
  Obituary **1995**:1
Cleaver, Eldridge
  Obituary **1998**:4
Codrescu, Andre **1997**:3
Cole, Johnetta B. **1994**:3
Coles, Robert **1995**:1
Comfort, Alex
  Obituary **2000**:4
Condon, Richard
  Obituary **1996**:4
Cook, Robin **1996**:3
Cosby, Bill **1999**:2
Covey, Stephen R. **1994**:4
Cowley, Malcolm
  Obituary **1989**:3
Crichton, Michael **1995**:3
Cronenberg, David **1992**:3
Dahl, Roald
  Obituary **1991**:2

2000 Cumulative Subject Index

This index lists all newsmakers alphabetically by their occupations or fields of primary activity. Indexes in softbound issues allow access to the current year's entries; indexes in annual hardbound volumes are cumulative, covering the entire *Newsmakers* series.

Listee names are followed by a year and issue number; thus **1996**:3 indicates that an entry on that individual appears in both 1996, Issue 3 and the 1996 cumulation. For access to newsmakers appearing earlier than the current softbound issue, see the previous year's cumulation.

ABC Television
  Arledge, Roone **1992**:2
  Diller, Barry **1991**:1
  Funt, Allen
    Obituary **2000**:1
  Philbin, Regis **2000**:2
  Pierce, Frederick S. **1985**:3

ABT
  See: American Ballet Theatre

Abortion
  Allred, Gloria **1985**:2
  Baird, Bill
    Brief Entry **1987**:2
  Baulieu, Etienne-Emile **1990**:1
  Brown, Judie **1986**:2
  Falkenberg, Nanette **1985**:2
  Kissling, Frances **1989**:2
  Morgentaler, Henry **1986**:3
  Terry, Randall **1991**:4
  Wattleton, Faye **1989**:1
  Yard, Molly **1991**:4

Abscam
  Neal, James Foster **1986**:2
  Puccio, Thomas P. **1986**:4

Academy Awards
  Affleck, Ben **1999**:1
  Allen, Woody **1994**:1
  Almodovar, Pedro **2000**:3
  Ameche, Don
    Obituary **1994**:2
  Andrews, Julie **1996**:1
  Arlen, Harold
    Obituary **1986**:3
  Arthur, Jean
    Obituary **1992**:1
  Ashcroft, Peggy
    Obituary **1992**:1
  Astor, Mary
    Obituary **1988**:1
  Barbera, Joseph **1988**:2
  Baryshnikov, Mikhail Nikolaevich
    1997:3

Bates, Kathy **1991**:4
Baxter, Anne
  Obituary **1986**:1
Beatty, Warren **2000**:1
Benigni, Roberto **1999**:2
Bergman, Ingmar **1999**:4
Berlin, Irving
  Obituary **1990**:1
Booth, Shirley
  Obituary **1993**:2
Brynner, Yul
  Obituary **1985**:4
Cagney, James
  Obituary **1986**:2
Caine, Michael **2000**:4
Capra, Frank
  Obituary **1992**:2
Cassavetes, John
  Obituary **1989**:2
Cher **1993**:1
Connery, Sean **1990**:4
Copland, Aaron
  Obituary **1991**:2
Coppola, Carmine
  Obituary **1991**:4
Coppola, Francis Ford **1989**:4
Crawford, Broderick
  Obituary **1986**:3
Damon, Matt **1999**:1
Davis, Bette
  Obituary **1990**:1
Davis, Geena **1992**:1
Demme, Jonathan **1992**:4
Dench, Judi **1999**:4
De Niro, Robert **1999**:1
Dennis, Sandy
  Obituary **1992**:4
Diamond, I.A.L.
  Obituary **1988**:3
Douglas, Michael **1986**:2
Duvall, Robert **1999**:3
Eastwood, Clint **1993**:3
Elliott, Denholm
  Obituary **1993**:2
Fellini, Federico
  Obituary **1994**:2

Ferrer, Jose
  Obituary **1992**:3
Field, Sally **1995**:3
Fosse, Bob
  Obituary **1988**:1
Gielgud, John
  Obituary **2000**:4
Gish, Lillian
  Obituary **1993**:4
Goldberg, Whoopi **1993**:3
Gooding, Cuba, Jr. **1997**:3
Gossett, Louis, Jr. **1989**:3
Grant, Cary
  Obituary **1987**:1
Hackman, Gene **1989**:3
Hanks, Tom **1989**:2 **2000**:2
Hawn, Goldie Jeanne **1997**:2
Hayes, Helen
  Obituary **1993**:4
Hayes, Isaac **1998**:4
Hepburn, Audrey
  Obituary **1993**:2
Hepburn, Katharine **1991**:2
Heston, Charlton **1999**:4
Hopkins, Anthony **1992**:4
Houseman, John
  Obituary **1989**:1
Hurt, William **1986**:1
Huston, Anjelica **1989**:3
Huston, John
  Obituary **1988**:1
Hutton, Timothy **1986**:3
Irons, Jeremy **1991**:4
Ives, Burl
  Obituary **1995**:4
Jones, Tommy Lee **1994**:2
Jordan, Neil **1993**:3
Kaye, Danny
  Obituary **1987**:2
Keaton, Diane **1997**:1
Kline, Kevin **2000**:1
Kubrick, Stanley
  Obituary **1999**:3
Kurosawa, Akira **1991**:1
  Obituary **1999**:1
Lange, Jessica **1995**:4
Lemmon, Jack **1998**:4

Levinson, Barry **1989**:3
Lithgow, John **1985**:2
Loy, Myrna
  Obituary **1994**:2
Lucas, George **1999**:4
Malle, Louis
  Obituary **1996**:2
Mancini, Henry
  Obituary **1994**:4
Marvin, Lee
  Obituary **1988**:1
Matlin, Marlee **1992**:2
Matthau, Walter **2000**:3
McDormand, Frances **1997**:3
McDowall, Roddy
  Obituary **1999**:1
McLaren, Norman
  Obituary **1987**:2
Milland, Ray
  Obituary **1986**:2
Newman, Paul **1995**:3
Nichols, Mike **1994**:4
Nicholson, Jack **1989**:2
North, Alex **1986**:3
Pacino, Al **1993**:4
Page, Geraldine
  Obituary **1987**:4
Pakula, Alan
  Obituary **1999**:2
Park, Nick **1997**:3
Pesci, Joe **1992**:4
Phillips, Julia **1992**:1
Poitier, Sidney **1990**:3
Prince **1995**:3
Puzo, Mario
  Obituary **2000**:1
Redford, Robert **1993**:2
Redgrave, Vanessa **1989**:2
Reed, Donna
  Obituary **1986**:1
Riddle, Nelson
  Obituary **1985**:4
Robbins, Jerome
  Obituary **1999**:1
Rogers, Ginger
  Obituary **1995**:4
Rollins, Howard E., Jr. **1986**:1
Ruehl, Mercedes **1992**:4
Sainte-Marie, Buffy **2000**:1
Scott, George C.
  Obituary **2000**:2
Sinatra, Frank
  Obituary **1998**:4
Sorvino, Mira **1996**:3
Spacey, Kevin **1996**:4
Stallone, Sylvester **1994**:2
Streep, Meryl **1990**:2
Streisand, Barbra **1992**:2
Styne, Jule
  Obituary **1995**:1
Swank, Hilary **2000**:3
Tandy, Jessica **1990**:4
  Obituary **1995**:1
Taylor, Elizabeth **1993**:3
Thompson, Emma **1993**:2
Tomei, Marisa **1995**:2
Trudeau, Garry **1991**:2
Vinton, Will
  Brief Entry **1988**:1
Wallis, Hal
  Obituary **1987**:1
Washington, Denzel **1993**:2

Wiest, Dianne **1995**:2
Zanuck, Lili Fini **1994**:2

ACLU
  See: American Civil Liberties Union

Acoustics
  Kloss, Henry E.
    Brief Entry **1985**:2

Acquired Immune Deficiency Syndrome
  Ashe, Arthur
    Obituary **1993**:3
  Bennett, Michael
    Obituary **1988**:1
  Bergalis, Kimberly
    Obituary **1992**:3
  Dolan, Terry **1985**:2
  Eazy-E
    Obituary **1995**:3
  Fisher, Mary **1994**:3
  Gallo, Robert **1991**:1
  Gebbie, Kristine **1994**:2
  Gertz, Alison
    Obituary **1993**:2
  Glaser, Elizabeth
    Obituary **1995**:2
  Halston
    Obituary **1990**:3
  Haring, Keith
    Obituary **1990**:3
  Ho, David **1997**:2
  Holmes, John C.
    Obituary **1988**:3
  Hudson, Rock
    Obituary **1985**:4
  Kramer, Larry **1991**:2
  Krim, Mathilde **1989**:2
  Kushner, Tony **1995**:2
  Liberace
    Obituary **1987**:2
  Louganis, Greg **1995**:3
  Mapplethorpe, Robert
    Obituary **1989**:3
  Matlovich, Leonard P.
    Obituary **1988**:4
  McKinney, Stewart B.
    Obituary **1987**:4
  Mullis, Kary **1995**:3
  Robinson, Max
    Obituary **1989**:2
  Shilts, Randy **1993**:4
    Obituary **1994**:3
  Smith, Jerry
    Obituary **1987**:1
  Taylor, Elizabeth **1993**:3
  Waddell, Thomas F.
    Obituary **1988**:2
  White, Ryan
    Obituary **1990**:3
  Zamora, Pedro
    Obituary **1995**:2

ACT-UP
  See: AIDS Coalition to Unleash Power

Adolph Coors Co.
  Coors, William K.
    Brief Entry **1985**:1

Adoption
  Clements, George **1985**:1

Advertising
  Ailes, Roger **1989**:3
  Beers, Charlotte **1999**:3
  Freeman, Cliff **1996**:1
  Kroll, Alexander S. **1989**:3
  Lazarus, Shelly **1998**:3
  McElligott, Thomas J. **1987**:4
  Ogilvy, David
    Obituary **2000**:1
  O'Steen, Van
    Brief Entry **1986**:3
  Peller, Clara
    Obituary **1988**:1
  Proctor, Barbara Gardner **1985**:3
  Riney, Hal **1989**:1
  Saatchi, Charles **1987**:3
  Saatchi, Maurice **1995**:4
  Sedelmaier, Joe **1985**:3
  Vinton, Will
    Brief Entry **1988**:1
  Whittle, Christopher **1989**:3

AFL-CIO
  See: American Federation of Labor and Congress of Industrial Organizations

African National Congress
  Buthelezi, Mangosuthu Gatsha **1989**:3
  Hani, Chris
    Obituary **1993**:4
  Mandela, Nelson **1990**:3
  Mbeki, Thabo **1999**:4
  Slovo, Joe **1989**:2
  Tambo, Oliver **1991**:3

Agriculture
  Davis, Noel **1990**:3

AIDS
  See: Acquired Immune Deficiency Syndrome

AIDS Coalition to Unleash Power
  Kramer, Larry **1991**:2

AIM
  See: American Indian Movement
  Peltier, Leonard **1995**:1

A.J. Canfield Co.
  Canfield, Alan B.
    Brief Entry **1986**:3

ALA
  See: American Library Association

Albert Nipon, Inc.
  Nipon, Albert
    Brief Entry **1986**:4

Alcohol abuse
  Anastas, Robert
    Brief Entry **1985**:2
  Bradshaw, John **1992**:1

Architecture
Bunshaft, Gordon **1989**:3
  Obituary **1991**:1
Cooper, Alexander **1988**:4
Eisenman, Peter **1992**:4
Erickson, Arthur **1989**:3
Foster, Norman **1999**:4
Gehry, Frank O. **1987**:1
Goody, Joan **1990**:2
Graves, Michael **2000**:1
Isozaki, Arata **1990**:2
Jahn, Helmut **1987**:3
Johnson, Philip **1989**:2
Kiefer, Anselm **1990**:2
Lin, Maya **1990**:3
Moneo, Jose Rafael **1996**:4
Mumford, Lewis
  Obituary **1990**:2
Pedersen, William **1989**:4
Pei, I.M. **1990**:4
Pelli, Cesar **1991**:4
Portman, John **1988**:2
Predock, Antoine **1993**:2
Roche, Kevin **1985**:1
Rouse, James
  Obituary **1996**:4
Venturi, Robert **1994**:4
Yamasaki, Minoru
  Obituary **1986**:2

Argus Corp. Ltd.
Black, Conrad **1986**:2

Arizona state government
Hull, Jane Dee **1999**:2

Arkansas state government
Clinton, Bill **1992**:1

Artificial heart
Jarvik, Robert K. **1985**:1
Schroeder, William J.
  Obituary **1986**:4

Artificial intelligence
Minsky, Marvin **1994**:3

Association of Southeast Asian Nations
Bolkiah, Sultan Muda Hassanal **1985**:4

Astronautics
Bean, Alan L. **1986**:2
Collins, Eileen **1995**:3
Conrad, Pete
  Obituary **2000**:1
Dzhanibekov, Vladimir **1988**:1
Garneau, Marc **1985**:1
Glenn, John **1998**:3
Lucid, Shannon **1997**:1
McAuliffe, Christa
  Obituary **1985**:4

Astronomy
Bopp, Thomas **1997**:3
Geller, Margaret Joan **1998**:2
Hale, Alan **1997**:3
Hawking, Stephen W. **1990**:1
Smoot, George F. **1993**:3

AT&T
Allen, Bob **1992**:4

Atari
Bushnell, Nolan **1985**:1
Kingsborough, Donald
  Brief Entry **1986**:2
Perlman, Steve **1998**:2

Atlanta Braves baseball team
Lofton, Kenny **1998**:1
Maddux, Greg **1996**:2
Sanders, Deion **1992**:4
Turner, Ted **1989**:1

Atlanta Falcons football team
Sanders, Deion **1992**:4

Atlanta Hawks basketball team
Maravich, Pete
  Obituary **1988**:2
McMillen, Tom **1988**:4
Turner, Ted **1989**:1
Wilkens, Lenny **1995**:2

Atlantic Records
Ertegun, Ahmet **1986**:3

Automobile racing
Ferrari, Enzo **1988**:4
Fittipaldi, Emerson **1994**:2
Gordon, Jeff **1996**:1
Muldowney, Shirley **1986**:1
Newman, Paul **1995**:2
Penske, Roger **1988**:3
Porsche, Ferdinand
  Obituary **1998**:4
Prost, Alain **1988**:1
St. James, Lyn **1993**:2
Senna, Ayrton **1991**:4
  Obituary **1994**:4
Villeneuve, Jacques **1997**:1
Zanardi, Alex **1998**:2

Aviation
Burr, Donald Calvin **1985**:3
Dubrof, Jessica
  Obituary **1996**:4
MacCready, Paul **1986**:4
Martin, Dean Paul
  Obituary **1987**:3
Moody, John **1985**:3
Rutan, Burt **1987**:2
Schiavo, Mary **1998**:2
Wolf, Stephen M. **1989**:3
Yeager, Chuck **1998**:1

Avis Rent A Car
Rand, A. Barry **2000**:3

Avon Products, Inc.
Jung, Andrea **2000**:2
Waldron, Hicks B. **1987**:3

Bad Boy Records
Combs, Sean Puffy **1998**:4

Ballet West
Lander, Toni
  Obituary **1985**:4

Ballooning
Aoki, Rocky **1990**:2

Baltimore, Md., city government
Schaefer, William Donald **1988**:1

Baltimore Orioles baseball team
Angelos, Peter **1995**:4
Palmer, Jim **1991**:2
Ripken, Cal, Jr. **1986**:2
Ripken, Cal, Sr.
  Obituary **1999**:4
Robinson, Frank **1990**:2
Williams, Edward Bennett
  Obituary **1988**:4

Band Aid
Geldof, Bob **1985**:3

Bard College
Botstein, Leon **1985**:3

Barnes & Noble, Inc.
Riggio, Leonard S. **1999**:4

Baseball
Abbott, Jim **1988**:3
Ainge, Danny **1987**:1
Barber, Red
  Obituary **1993**:2
Boggs, Wade **1989**:3
Bonds, Barry **1993**:3
Campanella, Roy
  Obituary **1994**:1
Canseco, Jose **1990**:2
Caray, Harry **1988**:3
  Obituary **1998**:3
Carter, Gary **1987**:1
Carter, Joe **1994**:2
Clemens, Roger **1991**:4
Davis, Eric **1987**:4
DiMaggio, Joe
  Obituary **1999**:3
Doubleday, Nelson, Jr. **1987**:1
Dravecky, Dave **1992**:1
Drysdale, Don
  Obituary **1994**:1
Durocher, Leo
  Obituary **1992**:2
Dykstra, Lenny **1993**:4
Edwards, Harry **1989**:4
Fehr, Donald **1987**:2
Fielder, Cecil **1993**:2
Giamatti, A. Bartlett **1988**:4
  Obituary **1990**:1
Gibson, Kirk **1985**:2
Gomez, Lefty
  Obituary **1989**:3
Gooden, Dwight **1985**:2
Greenberg, Hank
  Obituary **1986**:4
Griffey, Ken Jr. **1994**:1
Gwynn, Tony **1995**:1
Hernandez, Willie **1985**:1
Howser, Dick
  Obituary **1987**:4

Hunter, Catfish
  Obituary **2000**:1
Jackson, Bo **1986**:3
Johnson, Randy **1996**:2
Kroc, Ray
  Obituary **1985**:1
Kruk, John **1994**:4
Leyland, Jim **1998**:2
Lofton, Kenny **1998**:1
Maddux, Greg **1996**:2
Mantle, Mickey
  Obituary **1996**:1
Maris, Roger
  Obituary **1986**:1
Martin, Billy **1988**:4
  Obituary **1990**:2
Mattingly, Don **1986**:2
McGwire, Mark **1999**:1
Monaghan, Tom **1985**:1
Nomo, Hideo **1996**:2
Palmer, Jim **1991**:2
Piazza, Mike **1998**:4
Ripken, Cal, Jr. **1986**:2
Robinson, Frank **1990**:2
Rose, Pete **1991**:1
Ryan, Nolan **1989**:4
Saberhagen, Bret **1986**:1
Sanders, Deion **1992**:4
Schembechler, Bo **1990**:3
Schmidt, Mike **1988**:3
Schott, Marge **1985**:4
Selig, Bud **1995**:2
Sheffield, Gary **1998**:1
Sosa, Sammy **1999**:1
Steinbrenner, George **1991**:1
Stewart, Dave **1991**:1
Thomas, Frank **1994**:3
Van Slyke, Andy **1992**:4
Vaughn, Mo **1999**:2
Veeck, Bill
  Obituary **1986**:1
Vincent, Fay **1990**:2
Welch, Bob **1991**:3
Wells, David **1999**:3
White, Bill **1989**:3

Basketball
Ainge, Danny **1987**:1
Barkley, Charles **1988**:2
Bias, Len
  Obituary **1986**:3
Bird, Larry **1990**:3
Chaney, John **1989**:1
Cooper, Cynthia **1999**:1
Drexler, Clyde **1992**:4
Ewing, Patrick **1985**:3
Gathers, Hank
  Obituary **1990**:3
Hardaway, Anfernee **1996**:2
Jackson, Phil **1996**:3
Johnson, Earvin Magic **1988**:4
Johnson, Kevin **1991**:1
Johnson, Larry **1993**:3
Jordan, Michael **1987**:2
Kemp, Shawn **1995**:1
Knight, Bobby **1985**:3
Krzyzewski, Mike **1993**:2
Kukoc, Toni **1995**:4
Laettner, Christian **1993**:1
Leslie, Lisa **1997**:4
Lewis, Reggie
  Obituary **1994**:1

Majerle, Dan **1993**:4
Malone, Karl **1990**:1 **1997**:3
Maravich, Pete
  Obituary **1988**:2
McMillen, Tom **1988**:4
Miller, Reggie **1994**:4
Mourning, Alonzo **1994**:2
Olajuwon, Akeem **1985**:1
O'Malley, Susan **1995**:2
O'Neal, Shaquille **1992**:1
Riley, Pat **1994**:3
Robinson, David **1990**:4
Rodman, Dennis **1991**:3
Stern, David **1991**:4
Stockton, John Houston **1997**:3
Swoopes, Sheryl **1998**:2
Tarkenian, Jerry **1990**:4
Thomas, Isiah **1989**:2
Thompson, John **1988**:3
Vitale, Dick **1988**:4 **1994**:4
Webber, Chris **1994**:1
Wilkens, Lenny **1995**:2
Woodard, Lynette **1986**:2
Worthy, James **1991**:2

Beatrice International
Lewis, Reginald F. **1988**:4
  Obituary **1993**:3

Benetton Group
Benetton, Luciano **1988**:1

Benihana of Tokyo, Inc.
Aoki, Rocky **1990**:2

Berkshire Hathaway, Inc.
Buffett, Warren **1995**:2

Bethlehem, Jordan, city government
Freij, Elias **1986**:4

Bicycling
Armstrong, Lance **2000**:1
Indurain, Miguel **1994**:1
LeMond, Greg **1986**:4
Roberts, Steven K. **1992**:1

Bill T. Jones/Arnie Zane & Company
Jones, Bill T. **1991**:4

Billiards
Minnesota Fats
  Obituary **1996**:3

Biodiversity
Wilson, Edward O. **1994**:4

Bioethics
Bayley, Corrine
  Brief Entry **1986**:4
Caplan, Arthur L. **2000**:2

Biogen, Inc.
Gilbert, Walter **1988**:3

Biosphere 2
Allen, John **1992**:1

Biotechnology
Gilbert, Walter **1988**:3
Haseltine, William A. **1999**:2

Birds
Berle, Peter A.A.
  Brief Entry **1987**:3
Pough, Richard Hooper **1989**:1
Redig, Patrick **1985**:3
Toone, Bill
  Brief Entry **1987**:2

Birth control
Baird, Bill
  Brief Entry **1987**:2
Baulieu, Etienne-Emile **1990**:1
Djerassi, Carl **2000**:4
Falkenberg, Nanette **1985**:2
Morgentaler, Henry **1986**:3
Rock, John
  Obituary **1985**:1
Wattleton, Faye **1989**:1

Black Panther Party
Cleaver, Eldridge
  Obituary **1998**:4
Newton, Huey
  Obituary **1990**:1
Ture, Kwame
  Obituary **1999**:2

Black Sash
Duncan, Sheena
  Brief Entry **1987**:1

Blockbuster Video
Huizenga, Wayne **1992**:1

Bloomingdale's
Campeau, Robert **1990**:1
Traub, Marvin
  Brief Entry **1987**:3

Boat racing
Aoki, Rocky **1990**:2
Conner, Dennis **1987**:2
Copeland, Al **1988**:3
Hanauer, Chip **1986**:2
Turner, Ted **1989**:1

Bodybuilding
Powter, Susan **1994**:3
Reeves, Steve
  Obituary **2000**:4
Schwarzenegger, Arnold **1991**:1

Body Shops International
Roddick, Anita **1989**:4

Boston Bruins hockey team
Bourque, Raymond Jean **1997**:3

Bose Corp.
Bose, Amar
  Brief Entry **1986**:4

Boston Celtics basketball team
Ainge, Danny **1987**:1
Bird, Larry **1990**:3
Lewis, Reggie
  Obituary **1994**:1
Maravich, Pete
  Obituary **1988**:2

Boston, Mass., city government
Flynn, Ray **1989**:1
Frank, Barney **1989**:2

Boston Properties Co.
Zuckerman, Mortimer **1986**:3

Boston Red Sox baseball team
Boggs, Wade **1989**:3
Clemens, Roger **1991**:4
Conigliaro, Tony
Obituary **1990**:3
Vaughn, Mo **1999**:2

Boston University
Silber, John **1990**:1

Bowling
Weber, Pete **1986**:3

Boxing
Abercrombie, Josephine **1987**:2
Armstrong, Henry
Obituary **1989**:1
Bowe, Riddick **1993**:2
Carter, Rubin **2000**:3
Danza, Tony **1989**:1
De La Hoya, Oscar **1998**:2
Douglas, Buster **1990**:4
Graziano, Rocky
Obituary **1990**:4
Hagler, Marvelous Marvin **1985**:2
Holyfield, Evander **1991**:3
Kallen, Jackie **1994**:1
King, Don **1989**:1
Leonard, Sugar Ray **1989**:4
Lewis, Lennox **2000**:2
Moore, Archie
Obituary **1999**:2
Robinson, Sugar Ray
Obituary **1989**:3
Trinidad, Felix **2000**:4
Tyson, Mike **1986**:4

Boys Town
Peter, Valentine J. **1988**:2

BrainReserve
Popcorn, Faith
Brief Entry **1988**:1

Branch Davidians religious sect
Koresh, David
Obituary **1993**:4

Brewing
Busch, August A. III **1988**:2
Coors, William K.
Brief Entry **1985**:1
Stroh, Peter W. **1985**:2

Bridge
Goren, Charles H.
Obituary **1991**:4

British Columbia provincial government
Vander Zalm, William **1987**:3

British royal family
Charles, Prince of Wales **1995**:3
Diana, Princess of Wales **1993**:1
Obituary **1997**:4
Ferguson, Sarah **1990**:3

Broadcasting
Albert, Marv **1994**:3
Allen, Mel
Obituary **1996**:4
Ancier, Garth **1989**:1
Barber, Red
Obituary **1993**:2
Bell, Art **2000**:1
Brown, James **1991**:4
Caray, Harry **1988**:3
Obituary **1998**:3
Cherry, Don **1993**:4
Chung, Connie **1988**:4
Cosell, Howard
Obituary **1995**:4
Costas, Bob **1986**:4
Couric, Katherine **1991**:4
Daniels, Faith **1993**:3
Dickerson, Nancy H.
Obituary **1998**:2
Diller, Barry **1991**:1
Dr. Demento **1986**:1
Donnellan, Nanci **1995**:2
Drysdale, Don
Obituary **1994**:1
Edwards, Bob **1993**:2
Ellerbee, Linda **1993**:3
Firestone, Roy **1988**:2
Gillett, George **1988**:1
Goldberg, Leonard **1988**:4
Grange, Red
Obituary **1991**:3
Gumbel, Bryant **1990**:2
Gunn, Hartford N., Jr.
Obituary **1986**:2
Harvey, Paul **1995**:3
Imus, Don **1997**:1
Jones, Jenny **1998**:2
Kasem, Casey **1987**:1
Kent, Arthur **1991**:4 **1997**:2
King, Larry **1993**:1
Kluge, John **1991**:1
Koppel, Ted **1989**:1
Kuralt, Charles
Obituary **1998**:3
Madden, John **1995**:1
Moyers, Bill **1991**:4
Murdoch, Rupert **1988**:4
Musburger, Brent **1985**:1
Norville, Deborah **1990**:3
Osgood, Charles **1996**:2
Paley, William S.
Obituary **1991**:2
Pauley, Jane **1999**:1
Pierce, Frederick S. **1985**:3
Povich, Maury **1994**:3
Quivers, Robin **1995**:4
Reasoner, Harry
Obituary **1992**:4
Riley, Pat **1994**:3
Rivera, Geraldo **1989**:1
Roberts, Cokie **1993**:4
Robertson, Pat **1988**:2
Sawyer, Diane **1994**:4
Sevareid, Eric
Obituary **1993**:1

Shriver, Maria
Brief Entry **1986**:2
Snyder, Jimmy
Obituary **1996**:4
Stahl, Lesley **1997**:1
Stern, Howard **1988**:2 **1993**:3
Swaggart, Jimmy **1987**:3
Tartikoff, Brandon **1985**:2
Obituary **1998**:1
Totenberg, Nina **1992**:2
Turner, Ted **1989**:1
Vitale, Dick **1988**:4 **1994**:4
Walters, Barbara **1998**:3
Zahn, Paula **1992**:3
Zucker, Jeff **1993**:3

Brokerage
Brennan, Robert E. **1988**:1
Fomon, Robert M. **1985**:3
Phelan, John Joseph, Jr. **1985**:4
Schwab, Charles **1989**:3
Siebert, Muriel **1987**:2

Brooklyn Dodgers baseball team
Campanella, Roy
Obituary **1994**:1
Drysdale, Don
Obituary **1994**:1

Brown University
Gregorian, Vartan **1990**:3

Buddhism
Dalai Lama **1989**:1

Buffalo Bills football team
Flutie, Doug **1999**:2
Kelly, Jim **1991**:4
Thomas, Thurman **1993**:1

Buffalo Sabres
Hasek, Dominik **1998**:3

Cabbage Patch Kids
Roberts, Xavier **1985**:3

Cable Ace Awards
Blades, Ruben **1998**:2
Carey, Drew **1997**:4
Maher, Bill **1996**:2
Rock, Chris **1998**:1

Cable News Network (CNN)
Amanpour, Christiane **1997**:2

Cable television
Cox, Richard Joseph
Brief Entry **1985**:1
Firestone, Roy **1988**:2
Headroom, Max **1986**:4
Hefner, Christie **1985**:1
Johnson, Robert L. **2000**:4
Koplovitz, Kay **1986**:3
Malone, John C. **1988**:3 **1996**:3
Murdoch, Rupert **1988**:4
Otte, Ruth **1992**:4
Pittman, Robert W. **1985**:1
Quinn, Martha **1986**:4
Robertson, Pat **1988**:2

Turner, Ted **1989**:1
Vitale, Dick **1988**:4 **1994**:4

California Angels baseball team
Abbott, Jim **1988**:3
Autry, Gene
Obituary **1999**:1
Conigliaro, Tony
Obituary **1990**:3
Ryan, Nolan **1989**:4

Caldecott Book Awards
Ringgold, Faith **2000**:3

California state government
Brown, Edmund G., Sr.
Obituary **1996**:3
Brown, Jerry **1992**:4
Brown, Willie L. **1985**:2
Roybal-Allard, Lucille **1999**:4
Wilson, Pete **1992**:3

Camping equipment
Bauer, Eddie
Obituary **1986**:3
Coleman, Sheldon, Jr. **1990**:2

Canadian Broadcasting Corp.
Juneau, Pierre **1988**:3

Cancer research
DeVita, Vincent T., Jr. **1987**:3
Folkman, Judah **1999**:1
Fonyo, Steve
Brief Entry **1985**:4
Gale, Robert Peter **1986**:4
Hammond, E. Cuyler
Obituary **1987**:1
King, Mary-Claire **1998**:3
Krim, Mathilde **1989**:2
Love, Susan **1995**:2
Rosenberg, Steven **1989**:1
Szent-Gyoergyi, Albert
Obituary **1987**:2
Wigler, Michael
Brief Entry **1985**:1

Cannes Film Festival
Egoyan, Atom **2000**:2
Hou Hsiao-hsien **2000**:2
Smith, Kevin **2000**:4

Carnival Cruise Lines
Arison, Ted **1990**:3

Car repair
Magliozzi, Tom and Ray **1991**:4

Cartoons
Addams, Charles
Obituary **1989**:1
Barbera, Joseph **1988**:2
Barry, Lynda **1992**:1
Blanc, Mel
Obituary **1989**:4
Chast, Roz **1992**:4
Disney, Roy E. **1986**:3
Freleng, Friz
Obituary **1995**:4

Gaines, William M.
Obituary **1993**:1
Gould, Chester
Obituary **1985**:2
Groening, Matt **1990**:4
Judge, Mike **1994**:2
MacNelly, Jeff
Obituary **2000**:4
Parker, Trey and Matt Stone **1998**:2
Schulz, Charles
Obituary **2000**:3
Schulz, Charles M. **1998**:1
Spiegelman, Art **1998**:3
Trudeau, Garry **1991**:2
Watterson, Bill **1990**:3

Catholic Church
Beckett, Wendy (Sister) **1998**:3
Bernardin, Cardinal Joseph **1997**:2
Burns, Charles R.
Brief Entry **1988**:1
Clements, George **1985**:1
Cunningham, Reverend William
Obituary **1997**:4
Curran, Charles E. **1989**:2
Daily, Bishop Thomas V. **1990**:4
Dearden, John Cardinal
Obituary **1988**:4
Fox, Matthew **1992**:2
Healy, Timothy S. **1990**:2
Hume, Basil Cardinal
Obituary **2000**:1
John Paul II, Pope **1995**:3
Kissling, Frances **1989**:2
Krol, John
Obituary **1996**:3
Lefebvre, Marcel **1988**:4
Mahony, Roger M. **1988**:2
Maida, Adam Cardinal **1998**:2
Obando, Miguel **1986**:4
O'Connor, Cardinal John **1990**:3
O'Connor, John
Obituary **2000**:4
Peter, Valentine J. **1988**:2
Rock, John
Obituary **1985**:1
Stallings, George A., Jr. **1990**:1

CAT Scanner
Hounsfield, Godfrey **1989**:2

Cattle rustling
Cantrell, Ed
Brief Entry **1985**:3

Caviar
Petrossian, Christian
Brief Entry **1985**:3

CBC
See: Canadian Broadcasting Corp.

CBS, Inc.
Cox, Richard Joseph
Brief Entry **1985**:1
Cronkite, Walter Leland **1997**:3
Paley, William S.
Obituary **1991**:2
Reasoner, Harry
Obituary **1992**:1

Sagansky, Jeff **1993**:2
Tisch, Laurence A. **1988**:2
Yetnikoff, Walter **1988**:1

CDF
See: Children's Defense Fund

Center for Equal Opportunity
Chavez, Linda **1999**:3

Centers for Living
Williamson, Marianne **1991**:4

Central America
Astorga, Nora **1988**:2
Cruz, Arturo **1985**:1
Obando, Miguel **1986**:4
Robelo, Alfonso **1988**:1

Central Intelligence Agency
Carter, Amy **1987**:4
Casey, William
Obituary **1987**:3
Colby, William E.
Obituary **1996**:4
Deutch, John **1996**:4
Gates, Robert M. **1992**:2
Inman, Bobby Ray **1985**:1
Tenet, George **2000**:3

Centurion Ministries
McCloskey, James **1993**:1

Cesar Awards
Adjani, Isabelle **1991**:1
Depardieu, Gerard **1991**:2

Chanel, Inc.
D'Alessio, Kitty
Brief Entry **1987**:3
Lagerfeld, Karl **1999**:4

Chantal Pharmacentical Corp.
Burnison, Chantal Simone **1988**:3

Charlotte Hornets basketball team
Bryant, Kobe **1998**:3
Johnson, Larry **1993**:3
Mourning, Alonzo **1994**:2

Chef Boy-ar-dee
Boiardi, Hector
Obituary **1985**:3

Chess
Kasparov, Garry **1997**:4
Polgar, Judit **1993**:3

Chicago Bears football team
McMahon, Jim **1985**:4
Payton, Walter
Obituary **2000**:2

Chicago Bulls basketball team
Jackson, Phil **1996**:3
Jordan, Michael **1987**:2
Kukoc, Toni **1995**:4

Silvers, Phil
  Obituary **1985**:4
Sinatra, Frank
  Obituary **1998**:4
Springer, Jerry **1998**:4
Stiller, Ben **1999**:1
Streep, Meryl **1990**:2
Susskind, David
  Obituary **1987**:2
Tharp, Twyla **1992**:4
Tillstrom, Burr
  Obituary **1986**:1
Vonnegut, Kurt **1998**:4
Walker, Nancy
  Obituary **1992**:3
Walters, Barbara **1998**:3
Weitz, Bruce **1985**:4
Wilson, Flip
  Obituary **1999**:2
Witt, Katarina **1991**:3
Woods, James **1988**:3
Young, Robert
  Obituary **1999**:1

Encore Books
  Schlessinger, David
    Brief Entry **1985**:1

Energy Machine
  Newman, Joseph **1987**:1

Entrepreneurs
  Akin, Phil
    Brief Entry **1987**:3
  Allen, John **1992**:1
  Alter, Hobie
    Brief Entry **1985**:1
  Aoki, Rocky **1990**:2
  Arison, Ted **1990**:3
  Aurre, Laura
    Brief Entry **1986**:3
  Bauer, Eddie
    Obituary **1986**:3
  Ben & Jerry **1991**:3
  Berlusconi, Silvio **1994**:4
  Black, Conrad **1986**:2
  Bloomberg, Michael **1997**:1
  Boiardi, Hector
    Obituary **1985**:3
  Bose, Amar
    Brief Entry **1986**:4
  Branson, Richard **1987**:1
  Buffett, Warren **1995**:2
  Burr, Donald Calvin **1985**:3
  Bushnell, Nolan **1985**:1
  Campeau, Robert **1990**:1
  Clark, Jim **1997**:1
  Covey, Stephen R. **1994**:4
  Craig, Sid and Jenny **1993**:4
  Cray, Seymour R.
    Brief Entry **1986**:3
    Obituary **1997**:2
  Cummings, Sam **1986**:3
  Dell, Michael **1996**:2
  DiFranco, Ani **1997**:1
  Ertegun, Ahmet **1986**:3
  Garcia, Joe
    Brief Entry **1986**:4
  Gates, Bill **1993**:3 **1987**:4
  Gatien, Peter
    Brief Entry **1986**:1

Gillett, George **1988**:1
Graham, Bill **1986**:4
  Obituary **1992**:2
Guccione, Bob **1986**:1
Haney, Chris
  Brief Entry **1985**:1
Herrera, Carolina **1997**:1
Hilbert, Stephen C. **1997**:4
Honda, Soichiro
  Obituary **1986**:1
Hughes, Mark **1985**:3
Hyatt, Joel **1985**:3
Ilitch, Mike **1993**:4
Inatome, Rick **1985**:4
Isaacson, Portia
  Brief Entry **1986**:1
Jacuzzi, Candido
  Obituary **1987**:1
Jones, Arthur A. **1985**:3
Katz, Lillian **1987**:4
Kerkorian, Kirk **1996**:2
Kingsborough, Donald
  Brief Entry **1986**:2
Knight, Philip H. **1994**:1
Koplovitz, Kay **1986**:3
Kurzweil, Raymond **1986**:3
Mahesh Yogi, Maharishi **1991**:3
Markle, C. Wilson **1988**:1
Marriott, J. Willard
  Obituary **1985**:4
McGowan, William **1985**:2
McIntyre, Richard
  Brief Entry **1986**:2
Melman, Richard
  Brief Entry **1986**:1
Monaghan, Tom **1985**:1
Moody, John **1985**:3
Morgan, Dodge **1987**:1
Murdoch, Rupert **1988**:4
Murray, Arthur
  Obituary **1991**:3
Olsen, Kenneth H. **1986**:4
Paulucci, Jeno
  Brief Entry **1986**:3
Penske, Roger **1988**:3
Pocklington, Peter H. **1985**:2
Radocy, Robert
  Brief Entry **1986**:3
Roberts, Xavier **1985**:3
Roddick, Anita **1989**:4
Sasakawa, Ryoichi
  Brief Entry **1988**:1
Schlessinger, David
  Brief Entry **1985**:1
Smith, Frederick W. **1985**:4
Tanny, Vic
  Obituary **1985**:3
Thalheimer, Richard
  Brief Entry **1988**:3
Thomas, Michel **1987**:4
Tompkins, Susie
  Brief Entry **1987**:2
Trump, Donald **1989**:2
Trump, Ivana **1995**:2
Turner, Ted **1989**:1
Waitt, Ted **1997**:4
Wilson, Jerry
  Brief Entry **1986**:2
Wilson, Peter C.
  Obituary **1985**:2
Wynn, Stephen A. **1994**:3

Zanker, Bill
  Brief Entry **1987**:3

Environmentalism
  Ben & Jerry **1991**:3
  Brower, David **1990**:4
  Denver, John
    Obituary **1998**:1
  Douglas, Marjory Stoneman **1993**:1
    Obituary **1998**:4
  Foreman, Dave **1990**:3
  Gore, Albert, Jr. **1993**:2
  Hair, Jay D. **1994**:3
  Ngau, Harrison **1991**:3
  Plotkin, Mark **1994**:3
  Strong, Maurice **1993**:1

Environmental Protection Agency
  Browner, Carol M. **1994**:1

EPA
  See: Environmental Protection
    Agency

Episcopal Church
  Browning, Edmond
    Brief Entry **1986**:2
  Harris, Barbara **1996**:3
  Harris, Barbara **1989**:3
  Spong, John **1991**:3

Espionage
  Philby, Kim
    Obituary **1988**:3

Esprit clothing
  Tompkins, Susie
    Brief Entry **1987**:2

Essence magazine
  Gillespie, Marcia **1999**:4
  Lewis, Edward T. **1999**:4
  Taylor, Susan L. **1998**:2

Estee Lauder
  Burns, Robin **1991**:2
  Lauder, Estee **1992**:2

Ethnobotany
  Plotkin, Mark **1994**:3

European Commission
  Delors, Jacques **1990**:2

Euthanasia
  Cruzan, Nancy
    Obituary **1991**:3
  Humphry, Derek **1992**:2
  Kevorkian, Jack **1991**:3

Excel Communications
  Troutt, Kenny A. **1998**:1

Exploration
  Ballard, Robert D. **1998**:4
  Fiennes, Ranulph **1990**:3
  Steger, Will **1990**:4

ExxonMobil Oil
Raymond, Lee R. **2000**:3

Fabbrica Italiana Automobili Torino SpA
Agnelli, Giovanni **1989**:4

Faith Center Church
Scott, Gene
Brief Entry **1986**:1

Fallon McElligott
McElligott, Thomas J. **1987**:4

Famous Amos Chocolate Chip Cookies
Amos, Wally **2000**:1

Fashion
Armani, Giorgio **1991**:2
Avedon, Richard **1993**:4
Bacall, Lauren **1997**:3
Banks, Jeffrey **1998**:2
Benetton, Luciano **1988**:1
Blahnik, Manolo **2000**:2
Cameron, David
Brief Entry **1988**:1
Claiborne, Liz **1986**:3
Crawford, Cindy **1993**:3
D'Alessio, Kitty
Brief Entry **1987**:3
Ellis, Perry
Obituary **1986**:3
Erte
Obituary **1990**:4
Ford, Tom **1999**:3
Gaultier, Jean-Paul **1998**:1
Gucci, Maurizio
Brief Entry **1985**:4
Haas, Robert D. **1986**:4
Halston
Obituary **1990**:3
Herrera, Carolina **1997**:1
Hilfiger, Tommy **1993**:3
Johnson, Betsey **1996**:2
Kamali, Norma **1989**:1
Karan, Donna **1988**:1
Kelly, Patrick
Obituary **1990**:2
Klein, Calvin **1996**:2
Kors, Michael **2000**:4
Lagerfeld, Karl **1999**:4
Lang, Helmut **1999**:2
Lauren, Ralph **1990**:1
Mellinger, Frederick
Obituary **1990**:4
Mello, Dawn **1992**:2
Miller, Nicole **1995**:4
Miyake, Issey **1985**:2
Mizrahi, Isaac **1991**:1
Natori, Josie **1994**:3
Nipon, Albert
Brief Entry **1986**:4
Oldham, Todd **1995**:4
Picasso, Paloma **1991**:1
Porizkova, Paulina
Brief Entry **1986**:4
Potok, Anna Maximilian
Brief Entry **1985**:2
Prada, Miuccia **1996**:1
Rhodes, Zandra **1986**:2
Rykiel, Sonia **2000**:3

Sander, Jil **1995**:2
Smith, Willi
Obituary **1987**:3
Sui, Anna **1995**:1
Tilberis, Elizabeth **1994**:3
Tompkins, Susie
Brief Entry **1987**:2
Trump, Ivana **1995**:2
Tyler, Richard **1995**:3
Versace, Donatella **1999**:1
Versace, Gianni
Brief Entry **1988**:1
Obituary **1998**:2
von Furstenberg, Diane **1994**:2
Wachner, Linda **1988**:3 **1997**:2
Westwood, Vivienne **1998**:3

FBI
See: Federal Bureau of Investigation

FDA
See: Food and Drug Administration

Federal Bureau of Investigation
Freeh, Louis J. **1994**:2
Kennedy, Weldon **1997**:3

Federal Communications Commission (FCC)
Hundt, Reed Eric **1997**:2

Federal Express Corp.
Smith, Frederick W. **1985**:4

Federal Reserve System
Greenspan, Alan **1992**:2

Federal Trade Commission
Oliver, Daniel **1988**:2

Feminism
See: Women's issues

Fiat
See: Fabbrica Italiana Automobili Torino SpA

Film Criticism
Kael, Pauline **2000**:4

Fire fighting
Adair, Red **1987**:3

Fireworks
Grucci, Felix **1987**:1

First Jersey Securities
Brennan, Robert E. **1988**:1

Florida Marlins baseball team
Leyland, Jim **1998**:2
Sheffield, Gary **1998**:1

Flying
See: Aviation

FOE
See: Friends of the Earth

Food and Drug Administration
Kessler, David **1992**:1

Football
Aikman, Troy **1994**:2
Barnes, Ernie **1997**:4
Bell, Ricky
Obituary **1985**:1
Bledsoe, Drew **1995**:1
Bosworth, Brian **1989**:1
Brown, Jim **1993**:2
Brown, Paul
Obituary **1992**:1
Cunningham, Randall **1990**:1
Davis, Terrell **1998**:2
Elway, John **1990**:3
Esiason, Boomer **1991**:1
Flutie, Doug **1999**:2
Gault, Willie **1991**:2
Grange, Red
Obituary **1991**:3
Hayes, Woody
Obituary **1987**:2
Holtz, Lou **1986**:4
Irvin, Michael **1996**:3
Jackson, Bo **1986**:3
Johnson, Jimmy **1993**:3
Johnson, Keyshawn **2000**:4
Jones, Jerry **1994**:4
Kelly, Jim **1991**:4
Kemp, Jack **1990**:4
Landry, Tom
Obituary **2000**:3
Madden, John **1995**:1
Matuszak, John
Obituary **1989**:4
McMahon, Jim **1985**:4
Monk, Art **1993**:2
Montana, Joe **1989**:2
Moon, Warren **1991**:3
Moss, Randy **1999**:3
Okoye, Christian **1990**:2
Payton, Walter
Obituary **2000**:2
Rice, Jerry **1990**:4
Rypien, Mark **1992**:3
Sanders, Barry **1992**:1
Sanders, Deion **1992**:4
Schembechler, Bo **1990**:3
Sharpe, Sterling **1994**:3
Shula, Don **1992**:2
Smith, Emmitt **1994**:1
Smith, Jerry
Obituary **1987**:1
Tagliabue, Paul **1990**:2
Taylor, Lawrence **1987**:3
Testaverde, Vinny **1987**:2
Thomas, Derrick
Obituary **2000**:3
Thomas, Thurman **1993**:1
Upshaw, Gene **1988**:1
Walsh, Bill **1987**:4
Warner, Kurt **2000**:3
White, Reggie **1993**:4
Williams, Doug **1988**:2
Young, Steve **1995**:2

Hanna-Barbera Productions
Barbera, Joseph **1988**:2

Hard Candy
Mohajer, Dineh **1997**:3

Harlem Globetrotters basketball team
Woodard, Lynette **1986**:2

Harley-Davidson Motor Co., Inc.
Beals, Vaughn **1988**:2

Hartford, Conn., city government
Perry, Carrie Saxon **1989**:2

Hasbro, Inc.
Hassenfeld, Stephen **1987**:4

Hasidism
Schneerson, Menachem Mendel
1992:4
Obituary **1994**:4

Hasty Pudding Theatricals
Beatty, Warren **2000**:1
Burnett, Carol **2000**:3
Hanks, Tom **1989**:2 **2000**:2
Peters, Bernadette **2000**:1

Hearst Magazines
Black, Cathleen **1998**:4

Heisman Trophy
Flutie, Doug **1999**:2
Howard, Desmond Kevin **1997**:2
Jackson, Bo **1986**:3
Testaverde, Vinny **1987**:2
Williams, Ricky **2000**:2

Helmsley Hotels, Inc.
Helmsley, Leona **1988**:1

Hemlock Society
Humphry, Derek **1992**:2

Herbalife International
Hughes, Mark **1985**:3

Hereditary Disease Foundation
Wexler, Nancy S. **1992**:3

Herut Party (Israel)
Levy, David **1987**:2

HEW
See: Department of Health,
Education, and Welfare

Hewlett-Packard
Fiorina, Carleton S. **2000**:1
Packard, David
Obituary **1996**:3

HGS
See: Human Genome Sciences, Inc.

HHR
See: Department of Health and
Human Services

High Flight Foundation
Irwin, James
Obituary **1992**:1

Hitchhiking
Heid, Bill
Brief Entry **1987**:2

Hobie Cat
Alter, Hobie
Brief Entry **1985**:1
Hasek, Dominik **1998**:3

Hockey
Bourque, Raymond Jean **1997**:3
Cherry, Don **1993**:4
Coffey, Paul **1985**:4
Eagleson, Alan **1987**:4
Federov, Sergei **1995**:1
Fuhr, Grant **1997**:3
Gilmour, Doug **1994**:3
Granato, Cammi **1999**:3
Gretzky, Wayne **1989**:2
Hextall, Ron **1988**:2
Hull, Brett **1991**:4
Jagr, Jaromir **1995**:4
Klima, Petr **1987**:1
Konstantinov, Vladimir **1997**:4
LaFontaine, Pat **1985**:1
Lemieux, Claude **1996**:1
Lemieux, Mario **1986**:4
Lindbergh, Pelle
Obituary **1985**:4
Lindros, Eric **1992**:1
Messier, Mark **1993**:1
Pocklington, Peter H. **1985**:2
Richard, Maurice
Obituary **2000**:4
Roy, Patrick **1994**:2
Yzerman, Steve **1991**:2
Zamboni, Frank J.
Brief Entry **1986**:4

Honda Motor Co.
Honda, Soichiro
Obituary **1986**:1

Hong Kong government
Lee, Martin **1998**:2
Patten, Christopher **1993**:3

Horror fiction
King, Stephen **1998**:1
Koontz, Dean **1999**:3

Horse racing
Day, Pat **1995**:2
Desormeaux, Kent **1990**:2
Krone, Julie **1989**:2
Lukas, D. Wayne **1986**:2
McCarron, Chris **1995**:4
Mellon, Paul
Obituary **1999**:3
O'Donnell, Bill
Brief Entry **1987**:4
Pincay, Laffit, Jr. **1986**:3

Secretariat
Obituary **1990**:1

Houston Astros baseball team
Lofton, Kenny **1998**:1
Ryan, Nolan **1989**:4

Houston Oilers football team
Moon, Warren **1991**:3

Houston Rockets basketball team
Olajuwon, Akeem **1985**:1

Houston, Tex., city government
Watson, Elizabeth **1991**:2
Whitmire, Kathy **1988**:2

HUD
See: Department of Housing and
Urban Development

Hustler Magazine
Flynt, Larry **1997**:3

Hugo Awards
Asimov, Isaac
Obituary **1992**:3

Human Genome Sciences, Inc.
Haseltine, William A. **1999**:2

Huntington's disease
Wexler, Nancy S. **1992**:3

Hyatt Legal Services
Bloch, Henry **1988**:4
Hyatt, Joel **1985**:3

Hydroponics
Davis, Noel **1990**:3

IACC
See: International Anticounterfeiting
Coalition

IBM Corp.
See: International Business
Machines Corp.

Ice cream
Ben & Jerry **1991**:3

Ice skating
Baiul, Oksana **1995**:3
Gordeeva, Ekaterina **1996**:4
Grinkov, Sergei
Obituary **1996**:2
Hamilton, Scott **1998**:2
Kerrigan, Nancy **1994**:3
Lipinski, Tara **1998**:3
Thomas, Debi **1987**:2
Witt, Katarina **1991**:3
Yamaguchi, Kristi **1992**:3
Zamboni, Frank J.
Brief Entry **1986**:4

Zech, Lando W.
    Brief Entry **1987**:4

Nuclear Regulatory Commission
Zech, Lando W.
    Brief Entry **1987**:4

NUM
    See: National Union of
    Mineworkers

NWF
    See: National Wildlife Federation

Oakland A's baseball team
Canseco, Jose **1990**:2
Caray, Harry **1988**:3
    Obituary **1998**:3
Stewart, Dave **1991**:1
Welch, Bob **1991**:3

Oakland Raiders football team
Matuszak, John
    Obituary **1989**:4
Upshaw, Gene **1988**:1

Obie Awards
Albee, Edward **1997**:1
Bergman, Ingmar **1999**:4
Close, Glenn **1988**:3
Coco, James
    Obituary **1987**:2
Daniels, Jeff **1989**:4
Dewhurst, Colleen
    Obituary **1992**:2
Dukakis, Olympia **1996**:4
Duvall, Robert **1999**:3
Fo, Dario **1998**:1
Fugard, Athol **1992**:3
Hurt, William **1986**:1
Hwang, David Henry **1999**:1
Irwin, Bill **1988**:3
Kline, Kevin **2000**:1
Leguizamo, John **1999**:1
Miller, Arthur **1999**:4
Pacino, Al **1993**:4
Shepard, Sam **1996**:4
Streep, Meryl **1990**:2
Tune, Tommy **1994**:2
Vogel, Paula **1999**:2
Washington, Denzel **1993**:2
Woods, James **1988**:3

Occidental Petroleum Corp.
Hammer, Armand
    Obituary **1991**:3

Oceanography
Cousteau, Jacques-Yves
    Obituary **1998**:2
Cousteau, Jean-Michel **1988**:2
Fisher, Mel **1985**:4

Office of National Drug Control Policy
Bennett, William **1990**:1
Martinez, Bob **1992**:1

Ogilvy & Mather Advertising
Lazarus, Shelly **1998**:3

Ohio State University football team
Hayes, Woody
    Obituary **1987**:2

Oil
Adair, Red **1987**:3
Aurre, Laura
    Brief Entry **1986**:3
Hammer, Armand
    Obituary **1991**:3
Jones, Jerry **1994**:4

Olympic games
Abbott, Jim **1988**:3
Ali, Muhammad **1997**:2
Armstrong, Lance **2000**:1
Baiul, Oksana **1995**:3
Baumgartner, Bruce
    Brief Entry **1987**:3
Benoit, Joan **1986**:3
Blair, Bonnie **1992**:3
Boitano, Brian **1988**:3
Bradley, Bill **2000**:2
Conner, Dennis **1987**:2
Davenport, Lindsay **1999**:2
De La Hoya, Oscar **1998**:2
DiBello, Paul
    Brief Entry **1986**:4
Drexler, Clyde **1992**:4
Eagleson, Alan **1987**:4
Edwards, Harry **1989**:4
Evans, Janet **1989**:1
Ewing, Patrick **1985**:3
Gault, Willie **1991**:2
Graf, Steffi **1987**:4
Granato, Cammi **1999**:3
Grinkov, Sergei
    Obituary **1996**:2
Hamilton, Scott **1998**:2
Hamm, Mia **2000**:1
Holyfield, Evander **1991**:3
Johnson, Michael **2000**:1
Jordan, Michael **1987**:2
Joyner, Florence Griffith **1989**:2
    Obituary **1999**:1
Joyner-Kersee, Jackie **1993**:1
Kerrigan, Nancy **1994**:3
Kiraly, Karch
    Brief Entry **1987**:1
Knight, Bobby **1985**:3
Laettner, Christian **1993**:1
LaFontaine, Pat **1985**:1
Lalas, Alexi **1995**:1
Leonard, Sugar Ray **1989**:4
Leslie, Lisa **1997**:4
Lewis, Lennox **2000**:2
Lindbergh, Pelle
    Obituary **1985**:4
Lipinski, Tara **1998**:3
Louganis, Greg **1995**:3
Milburn, Rodney Jr.
    Obituary **1998**:2
Retton, Mary Lou **1985**:2
Rudolph, Wilma
    Obituary **1995**:2
Samaranch, Juan Antonio **1986**:2
Street, Picabo **1999**:3
Strug, Kerri **1997**:3
Swoopes, Sheryl **1998**:2
Thomas, Debi **1987**:2
Thompson, John **1988**:3
Tomba, Alberto **1992**:3

Van Dyken, Amy **1997**:1
Waddell, Thomas F.
    Obituary **1988**:2
Witt, Katarina **1991**:3
Woodard, Lynette **1986**:2
Yamaguchi, Kristi **1992**:3

ON Technology
Kapor, Mitch **1990**:3

Ontario provincial government
Eagleson, Alan **1987**:4
Peterson, David **1987**:1

Opera
Anderson, Marion
    Obituary **1993**:4
Bartoli, Cecilia **1994**:1
Battle, Kathleen **1998**:1
Carreras, Jose **1995**:2
Domingo, Placido **1993**:2
Pavarotti, Luciano **1997**:4
Upshaw, Dawn **1991**:2
Zeffirelli, Franco **1991**:3

Operation Rescue
Terry, Randall **1991**:4

Orlando Magic basketball team
Hardaway, Anfernee **1996**:2

Painting
Bean, Alan L. **1986**:2
Botero, Fernando **1994**:3
Chagall, Marc
    Obituary **1985**:2
Chatham, Russell **1990**:1
Chia, Sandro **1987**:2
Dali, Salvador
    Obituary **1989**:2
de Kooning, Willem **1994**:4
    Obituary **1997**:3
Diebenkorn, Richard
    Obituary **1993**:4
Dubuffet, Jean
    Obituary **1985**:4
Frankenthaler, Helen **1990**:1
Freud, Lucian **2000**:4
Graves, Nancy **1989**:3
Haring, Keith
    Obituary **1990**:3
Hockney, David **1988**:3
Kahlo, Frida **1991**:3
Katz, Alex **1990**:3
Kelly, Ellsworth **1992**:1
Kiefer, Anselm **1990**:2
Kostabi, Mark **1989**:4
Lichtenstein, Roy **1994**:1
    Obituary **1998**:1
Longo, Robert **1990**:4
Miro, Joan
    Obituary **1985**:1
Motherwell, Robert
    Obituary **1992**:1
Nechita, Alexandra **1996**:4
Neiman, LeRoy **1993**:3
Ono, Yoko **1989**:2
Polke, Sigmar **1999**:4
Pozzi, Lucio **1990**:2
Pratt, Christopher **1985**:3

Rauschenberg, Robert **1991**:2
Rothenberg, Susan **1995**:3
Schnabel, Julian **1997**:1
Stella, Frank **1996**:2
Tamayo, Rufino
 Obituary **1992**:1
Thiebaud, Wayne **1991**:1
Twombley, Cy **1995**:1
Warhol, Andy
 Obituary **1987**:2
Wegman, William **1991**:1

Pakistan People's Party
Bhutto, Benazir **1989**:4

Paleontology
Bakker, Robert T. **1991**:3
Horner, Jack **1985**:2

Palestine Liberation Organization
Arafat, Yasser **1989**:3 **1997**:3
Habash, George **1986**:1
Husseini, Faisal **1998**:4
Hussein I, King **1997**:3
 Obituary **1999**:3
Redgrave, Vanessa **1989**:2
Terzi, Zehdi Labib **1985**:3

Palimony
Marvin, Lee
 Obituary **1988**:1
Mitchelson, Marvin **1989**:2

Palm Computing
Hawkins, Jeff and Donna Dubinsky
 2000:2

Paralegals
Furman, Rosemary
 Brief Entry **1986**:4

Paramount Pictures
Diller, Barry **1991**:1
Lansing, Sherry **1995**:4
Steel, Dawn **1990**:1
 Obituary **1998**:2

Parents' Music Resource Center
Gore, Tipper **1985**:4
Snider, Dee **1986**:1

Parents of Murdered Children
Hullinger, Charlotte
 Brief Entry **1985**:1

Paris Opera Ballet Company
Guillem, Sylvie **1988**:2

Parkinson's disease
Ali, Muhammad **1997**:2
Langston, J. William
 Brief Entry **1986**:2

Parks
Mott, William Penn, Jr. **1986**:1

Parsons Dance Company
Parsons, David **1993**:4

Parti Quebecois
Johnson, Pierre Marc **1985**:4
Levesque, Rene
 Obituary **1988**:1
Parizeau, Jacques **1995**:1

Paul Taylor Dance Company
Taylor, Paul **1992**:3

PBA
See: Professional Bowlers
 Association

PBS
See: Public Broadcasting Service

Peabody Awards
Child, Julia **1999**:4
Duncan, Todd
 Obituary **1998**:3
Gross, Terry **1998**:3
Kuralt, Charles
 Obituary **1998**:3
Miller, Arthur **1999**:4
Osgood, Charles **1996**:2
Schulz, Charles M. **1998**:1

Peace Corps
Ruppe, Loret Miller **1986**:2

Pennsylvania State University
Paterno, Joe **1995**:4

Penthouse International Ltd.
Guccione, Bob **1986**:1

People Express Airlines
Burr, Donald Calvin **1985**:3

People for the Ethical Treatment of Animals
Mathews, Dan **1998**:3
McCartney, Linda
 Obituary **1998**:4
Newkirk, Ingrid **1992**:3

People Organized and Working for Economic Rebirth
Farrakhan, Louis **1990**:4

People's Choice Awards
Almodovar, Pedro **2000**:3
Applegate, Christina **2000**:4
Burnett, Carol **2000**:3
Somers, Suzanne **2000**:1

Pepsico, Inc.
Calloway, D. Wayne **1987**:3
Sculley, John **1989**:4

Performance art
Beuys, Joseph
 Obituary **1986**:3
Bogosian, Eric **1990**:4
Finley, Karen **1992**:4
Irwin, Bill **1988**:3
Ono, Yoko **1989**:2

Penn & Teller **1992**:1
Pozzi, Lucio **1990**:2

Perry Ellis Award
Cameron, David
 Brief Entry **1988**:1

Persian Gulf War
Amanpour, Christiane **1997**:2
Hussein I, King **1997**:3
 Obituary **1999**:3
Kent, Arthur **1991**:4 **1997**:2
Powell, Colin **1990**:1
Schwarzkopf, Norman **1991**:3

PFLP
See: Popular Front for the
 Liberation of Palestine

PGA
See: Professional Golfers Association

Philadelphia Eagles football team
Cunningham, Randall **1990**:1

Philadelphia Flyers hockey team
Hextall, Ron **1988**:2
Lindbergh, Pelle
 Obituary **1985**:4

Philadelphia Phillies baseball team
Dykstra, Lenny **1993**:4
Kruk, John **1994**:4
Schmidt, Mike **1988**:3
Williams, Ricky **2000**:2

Philadelphia 76ers basketball team
Barkley, Charles **1988**:2
Chamberlain, Wilt
 Obituary **2000**:2

Philanthropy
Annenberg, Walter **1992**:3
Bolkiah, Sultan Muda Hassanal **1985**:4
Duke, Doris
 Obituary **1994**:2
Ferrell, Trevor
 Brief Entry **1985**:2
Haas, Robert D. **1986**:4
Hammer, Armand
 Obituary **1991**:3
Heinz, H.J.
 Obituary **1987**:2
Judkins, Reba
 Brief Entry **1987**:3
Kaye, Danny
 Obituary **1987**:2
Lang, Eugene M. **1990**:3
Marriott, J. Willard
 Obituary **1985**:4
Mellon, Paul
 Obituary **1999**:3
Menuhin, Yehudi
 Obituary **1999**:3
Pritzker, A.N.
 Obituary **1986**:2
Ross, Percy
 Brief Entry **1986**:2

Primerica
Weill, Sandy **1990**:4

Princeton, N.J., city government
Sigmund, Barbara Boggs
Obituary **1991**:1

Pritzker Prize
Bunshaft, Gordon **1989**:3
Obituary **1991**:1
Foster, Norman **1999**:4
Johnson, Philip **1989**:2
Pritzker, A.N.
Obituary **1986**:2
Roche, Kevin **1985**:1
Venturi, Robert **1994**:4

Procter & Gamble Co.
Smale, John G. **1987**:3

Proctor & Gardner Advertising, Inc.
Proctor, Barbara Gardner **1985**:3

Professional Bowlers Association
Weber, Pete **1986**:3

Professional Golfers Association
Azinger, Paul **1995**:2
Chen, T.C.
Brief Entry **1987**:3
Couples, Fred **1994**:4
Norman, Greg **1988**:3
Peete, Calvin **1985**:4
Sarazen, Gene
Obituary **1999**:4
Singh, Vijay **2000**:4
Stewart, Payne
Obituary **2000**:2
Strange, Curtis **1988**:4

Professional Flair
Verdi-Fletcher, Mary **1998**:2

Progress and Freedom Foundation
Huffington, Arianna **1996**:2

Project Head Start
Zigler, Edward **1994**:1

Promise Keepers
McCartney, Bill **1995**:3

Psychedelic drugs
Castaneda, Carlos
Obituary **1998**:4
Leary, Timothy
Obituary **1996**:4
McKenna, Terence **1993**:3

Psychiatry
Bettelheim, Bruno
Obituary **1990**:3
Coles, Robert **1995**:1
Frankl, Viktor E.
Obituary **1998**:1
Laing, R.D.
Obituary **1990**:1

Menninger, Karl
Obituary **1991**:1

Psychology
Pinker, Steven A. **2000**:1

Public Broadcasting Service
Barney **1993**:4
Gunn, Hartford N., Jr.
Obituary **1986**:2
Lewis, Shari **1993**:1
Obituary **1999**:1
Rogers, Fred **2000**:4
Rose, Charlie **1994**:2
Trotter, Charlie **2000**:4

Public relations
Kingsley, Patricia **1990**:2

Publishing
Annenberg, Walter **1992**:3
Black, Conrad **1986**:2
Brown, Tina **1992**:1
Doubleday, Nelson, Jr. **1987**:1
Epstein, Jason **1991**:1
Evans, Joni **1991**:4
Forbes, Malcolm S.
Obituary **1990**:3
Forbes, Steve **1996**:2
Gaines, William M.
Obituary **1993**:1
Graham, Donald **1985**:4
Guccione, Bob **1986**:1
Guccione, Bob, Jr. **1991**:4
Hamilton, Hamish
Obituary **1988**:4
Hefner, Christie **1985**:1
Hillegass, Clifton Keith **1989**:4
Ingersoll, Ralph II **1988**:2
Kennedy, John F., Jr. **1990**:1
Obituary **1999**:4
Lear, Frances **1988**:3
Levin, Gerald **1995**:2
Lewis, Edward T. **1999**:4
Macmillan, Harold
Obituary **1987**:2
Maxwell, Robert **1990**:1
Maxwell, Robert
Obituary **1992**:2
Morgan, Dodge **1987**:1
Morgan, Robin **1991**:1
Murdoch, Rupert **1988**:4
Neuharth, Allen H. **1986**:1
Newhouse, Samuel I., Jr. **1997**:1
Onassis, Jacqueline Kennedy
Obituary **1994**:4
Pope, Generoso **1988**:4
Pratt, Jane **1999**:1
Rowland, Pleasant **1992**:3
Steinem, Gloria **1996**:2
Sullivan, Andrew **1996**:1
Summers, Anne **1990**:2
Tilberis, Elizabeth **1994**:3
Wenner, Jann **1993**:1
Whittle, Christopher **1989**:3
Wintour, Anna **1990**:4
Ziff, William B., Jr. **1986**:4
Zuckerman, Mortimer **1986**:3
Zwilich, Ellen **1990**:1

Pulitzer Prize
Abbott, George
Obituary **1995**:3
Albee, Edward **1997**:1
Albert, Stephen **1986**:1
Angier, Natalie **2000**:3
Barry, Dave **1991**:2
Bennett, Michael
Obituary **1988**:1
Brooks, Gwendolyn **1998**:1
Caen, Herb
Obituary **1997**:4
Coles, Robert **1995**:1
Copland, Aaron
Obituary **1991**:2
Dove, Rita **1994**:3
Ebert, Roger **1998**:3
Faludi, Susan **1992**:4
Geisel, Theodor
Obituary **1992**:2
Haley, Alex
Obituary **1992**:3
Kushner, Tony **1995**:2
Lelyveld, Joseph S. **1994**:4
Logan, Joshua
Obituary **1988**:4
Mailer, Norman **1998**:1
Mamet, David **1998**:4
Marsalis, Wynton **1997**:4
McCourt, Frank **1997**:4
Merrill, James
Obituary **1995**:3
Michener, James A.
Obituary **1998**:1
Miller, Arthur **1999**:4
Morrison, Toni **1998**:1
Papp, Joseph
Obituary **1992**:2
Proulx, E. Annie **1996**:1
Quindlen, Anna **1993**:1
Roth, Philip **1999**:1
Royko, Mike
Obituary **1997**:4
Safire, William **2000**:3
Shepard, Sam **1996**:4
Smiley, Jane **1995**:4
Sondheim, Stephen **1994**:4
Trudeau, Garry **1991**:2
Tyler, Anne **1995**:4
Van Duyn, Mona **1993**:2
Vogel, Paula **1999**:2
Walker, Alice **1999**:1
Wasserstein, Wendy **1991**:3
Wilson, Edward O. **1994**:4

Quebec provincial government
Bouchard, Lucien **1999**:2
Johnson, Pierre Marc **1985**:4
Levesque, Rene
Obituary **1988**:1

Radical Party (Italy)
Staller, Ilona **1988**:3

Radio One, Inc.
Hughes, Cathy **1999**:1

Random House publishers
Evans, Joni **1991**:4

RCA Corp.
Engstrom, Elmer W.
Obituary **1985**:2

Real estate
Bloch, Ivan **1986**:3
Buss, Jerry **1989**:3
Campeau, Robert **1990**:1
Portman, John **1988**:2
Trump, Donald **1989**:2

Reebok U.S.A. Ltd., Inc.
Fireman, Paul
Brief Entry **1987**:2

Renaissance Motion Pictures
Raimi, Sam **1999**:2

RENAMO
Dhlakama, Afonso **1993**:3

Renault, Inc.
Besse, Georges
Obituary **1987**:1

Republican National Committee
Abraham, Spencer **1991**:4
Atwater, Lee **1989**:4
Obituary **1991**:4
Molinari, Susan **1996**:4

Resistancia Nacional Mocambican
See: RENAMO

Restaurants
Aoki, Rocky **1990**:2
Aretsky, Ken **1988**:1
Bushnell, Nolan **1985**:1
Copeland, Al **1988**:3
Fertel, Ruth **2000**:2
Kaufman, Elaine **1989**:4
Kerrey, Bob **1986**:1 **1991**:3
Kroc, Ray
Obituary **1985**:1
Lagasse, Emeril **1998**:3
Melman, Richard
Brief Entry **1986**:1
Petrossian, Christian
Brief Entry **1985**:3
Puck, Wolfgang **1990**:1
Thomas, Dave **1986**:2 **1993**:2

Retailing
Drexler, Millard S. **1990**:3

Reuben Awards
Gould, Chester
Obituary **1985**:2
Schulz, Charles
Obituary **2000**:3

Revlon, Inc.
Duffy, Karen **1998**:1
Perelman, Ronald **1989**:2

Rhode Island state government
Violet, Arlene **1985**:3

Richter Scale
Richter, Charles Francis
Obituary **1985**:4

Ringling Brothers and Barnum & Bailey Circus
Burck, Wade
Brief Entry **1986**:1
Feld, Kenneth **1988**:2

RJR Nabisco, Inc.
Horrigan, Edward, Jr. **1989**:1

Robotics
Kwoh, Yik San **1988**:2

Rock Climbing
Hill, Lynn **1991**:2

Rockman
Scholz, Tom **1987**:2

Roller Coasters
Toomer, Ron **1990**:1

Rolling Stone magazine
Wenner, Jann **1993**:1

Rotary engine
Yamamoto, Kenichi **1989**:1

Running
Benoit, Joan **1986**:3
Joyner, Florence Griffith **1989**:2
Obituary **1999**:1
Knight, Philip H. **1994**:1

Russian Federation
Putin, Vladimir **2000**:3
Yeltsin, Boris **1991**:1

SADD
See: Students Against Drunken
Driving

Sailing
Alter, Hobie
Brief Entry **1985**:1
Conner, Dennis **1987**:2
Koch, Bill **1992**:3
Morgan, Dodge **1987**:1
Turner, Ted **1989**:1

St. Louis Blues hockey team
Fuhr, Grant **1997**:3
Hull, Brett **1991**:4

St. Louis Browns baseball team
Veeck, Bill
Obituary **1986**:1

St. Louis Cardinals baseball team
Busch, August A. III **1988**:2
Busch, August Anheuser, Jr.
Obituary **1990**:2
Caray, Harry **1988**:3
Obituary **1998**:3
McGwire, Mark **1999**:1

St. Louis Rams football team
Warner, Kurt **2000**:3

San Antonio Spurs basketball team
Duncan, Tim **2000**:1
Robinson, David **1990**:4

San Antonio, Tex., city government
Cisneros, Henry **1987**:2

San Diego Chargers football team
Barnes, Ernie **1997**:4
Bell, Ricky
Obituary **1985**:1

San Diego Padres baseball team
Dravecky, Dave **1992**:1
Gwynn, Tony **1995**:1
Kroc, Ray
Obituary **1985**:1
Sheffield, Gary **1998**:1

San Francisco city government
Alioto, Joseph L.
Obituary **1998**:3
Brown, Willie **1996**:4

San Francisco 49ers football team
DeBartolo, Edward J., Jr. **1989**:3
Montana, Joe **1989**:2
Rice, Jerry **1990**:4
Walsh, Bill **1987**:4
Young, Steve **1995**:2

San Francisco Giants baseball team
Bonds, Barry **1993**:3
Dravecky, Dave **1992**:1

SANE/FREEZE
Coffin, William Sloane, Jr. **1990**:3

Save the Children Federation
Guyer, David
Brief Entry **1988**:1

SBA
See: Small Business Administration

Schottco Corp.
Schott, Marge **1985**:4

Schwinn Bicycle Co.
Schwinn, Edward R., Jr.
Brief Entry **1985**:4

Science fiction
Asimov, Isaac
Obituary **1992**:3
Butler, Octavia E. **1999**:3
Kelley, DeForest
Obituary **2000**:1
Lucas, George **1999**:4
Sterling, Bruce **1995**:4

Sculpture
Beuys, Joseph
Obituary **1986**:3
Botero, Fernando **1994**:3
Bourgeois, Louise **1994**:1
Chia, Sandro **1987**:2
Christo **1992**:3

Submarines
Rickover, Hyman
Obituary **1986**:4
Zech, Lando W.
Brief Entry **1987**:4

Sun Microsystems, Inc.
McNealy, Scott **1999**:4

Sunbeam Corp.
Dunlap, Albert J. **1997**:2

Suicide
Applewhite, Marshall Herff
Obituary **1997**:3
Dorris, Michael
Obituary **1997**:3
Hutchence, Michael
Obituary **1998**:1
Quill, Timothy E. **1997**:3

Sundance Institute
Redford, Robert **1993**:2

Sunshine Foundation
Sample, Bill
Brief Entry **1986**:2

Superconductors
Chaudhari, Praveen **1989**:4
Chu, Paul C.W. **1988**:2

Supreme Court of Canada
Wilson, Bertha
Brief Entry **1986**:1

Surfing
Curren, Tommy
Brief Entry **1987**:4

SWAPO
See: South West African People's
Organization

Swimming
Evans, Janet **1989**:1
Van Dyken, Amy **1997**:1

Tampa Bay Buccaneers football team
Bell, Ricky
Obituary **1985**:1
Johnson, Keyshawn **2000**:4
Testaverde, Vinny **1987**:2
Williams, Doug **1988**:2
Young, Steve **1995**:2

Tandem Computers, Inc.
Treybig, James G. **1988**:3

Teach for America
Kopp, Wendy **1993**:3

Tectonics
Rosendahl, Bruce R.
Brief Entry **1986**:4

Teddy Ruxpin
Kingsborough, Donald
Brief Entry **1986**:2

Tele-Communications, Inc.
Malone, John C. **1988**:3 **1996**:3

Televangelism
Graham, Billy **1992**:1
Hahn, Jessica **1989**:4
Robertson, Pat **1988**:2
Rogers, Adrian **1987**:4
Swaggart, Jimmy **1987**:3

Temple University basketball team
Chaney, John **1989**:1

Tennis
Agassi, Andre **1990**:2
Ashe, Arthur
Obituary **1993**:3
Becker, Boris
Brief Entry **1985**:3
Capriati, Jennifer **1991**:1
Courier, Jim **1993**:2
Davenport, Lindsay **1999**:2
Gerulaitis, Vitas
Obituary **1995**:1
Graf, Steffi **1987**:4
Hingis, Martina **1999**:1
Kournikova, Anna **2000**:3
Navratilova, Martina **1989**:1
Pierce, Mary **1994**:4
Riggs, Bobby
Obituary **1996**:2
Sabatini, Gabriela
Brief Entry **1985**:4
Sampras, Pete **1994**:1
Seles, Monica **1991**:3
Williams, Serena **1999**:4
Williams, Venus **1998**:2

Test tube babies
Steptoe, Patrick
Obituary **1988**:3

Texas Rangers baseball team
Ryan, Nolan **1989**:4

Texas State Government
Bush, George W., Jr. **1996**:4
Richards, Ann **1991**:2

Therapeutic Recreation Systems
Radocy, Robert
Brief Entry **1986**:3

Timberline Reclamations
McIntyre, Richard
Brief Entry **1986**:2

Time Warner Inc.
Ho, David **1997**:2
Levin, Gerald **1995**:2
Ross, Steven J.
Obituary **1993**:3

TLC Beatrice International
Lewis, Loida Nicolas **1998**:3

TLC Group L.P.
Lewis, Reginald F. **1988**:4
Obituary **1993**:3

Today Show
Couric, Katherine **1991**:4
Gumbel, Bryant **1990**:2
Norville, Deborah **1990**:3

Tony Awards
Abbott, George
Obituary **1995**:3
Alda, Robert
Obituary **1986**:3
Alexander, Jane **1994**:2
Alexander, Jason **1993**:3
Allen, Debbie **1998**:2
Allen, Joan **1998**:1
Bacall, Lauren **1997**:3
Bailey, Pearl
Obituary **1991**:1
Bennett, Michael
Obituary **1988**:1
Bloch, Ivan **1986**:3
Booth, Shirley
Obituary **1993**:2
Brynner, Yul
Obituary **1985**:4
Buckley, Betty **1996**:2
Burnett, Carol **2000**:3
Channing, Stockard **1991**:3
Close, Glenn **1988**:3
Crawford, Cheryl
Obituary **1987**:1
Crawford, Michael **1994**:2
Dench, Judi **1999**:4
Dennis, Sandy
Obituary **1992**:4
Dewhurst, Colleen
Obituary **1992**:2
Fagan, Garth **2000**:1
Ferrer, Jose
Obituary **1992**:3
Fiennes, Ralph **1996**:2
Fishburne, Laurence **1995**:3
Flanders, Ed
Obituary **1995**:3
Fosse, Bob
Obituary **1988**:1
Gleason, Jackie
Obituary **1987**:4
Glover, Savion **1997**:1
Harrison, Rex
Obituary **1990**:4
Hepburn, Katharine **1991**:2
Hines, Gregory **1992**:4
Hwang, David Henry **1999**:1
Irons, Jeremy **1991**:4
Kahn, Madeline
Obituary **2000**:2
Keaton, Diane **1997**:1
Kline, Kevin **2000**:1
Kushner, Tony **1995**:2
Lane, Nathan **1996**:4
Lansbury, Angela **1993**:1
Lithgow, John **1985**:2
Mantegna, Joe **1992**:1
Matthau, Walter **2000**:3

Cumulative Newsmakers Index

This index lists all newsmakers included in the entire *Newsmakers* series.

Listee names are followed by a year and issue number; thus **1996**:3 indicates that an entry on that individual appears in both 1996, Issue 3 and the 1996 cumulation.

Berger, Sandy 1945- **2000**:1
Bergman, Ingmar 1918- **1999**:4
Berle, Peter A.A.
    Brief Entry **1987**:3
Berlin, Irving 1888-1989
    Obituary **1990**:1
Berlusconi, Silvio 1936(?)- **1994**:4
Bernardi, Herschel 1923-1986
    Obituary **1986**:4
Bernardin, Cardinal Joseph 1928-1996 ....
    1997:2
Berners-Lee, Tim 1955(?)- **1997**:4
Bernhard, Sandra 1955(?)- **1989**:4
Bernsen, Corbin 1955- **1990**:2
Bernstein, Leonard 1918-1990
    Obituary **1991**:1
Berresford, Susan V. 1943- **1998**:4
Berri, Nabih 1939(?)- **1985**:2
Berry, Halle 1968- **1996**:2
Besse, Georges 1927-1986
    Obituary **1987**:1
Bettelheim, Bruno 1903-1990
    Obituary **1990**:3
Beuys, Joseph 1921-1986
    Obituary **1986**:3
Bezos, Jeff 1964- **1998**:4
Bhraonain, Eithne Ni
    See Enya
Bhutto, Benazir 1953- **1989**:4
Bialik, Mayim 1975- **1993**:3
Bias, Len 1964(?)-1986
    Obituary **1986**:3
Bias, Leonard
    See Bias, Len
Biden, Joe 1942- **1986**:3
Biden, Joseph Robinette, Jr.
    See Biden, Joe
Bieber, Owen 1929- **1986**:1
Biehl, Amy 1967(?)-1993
    Obituary **1994**:1
Bigelow, Kathryn 1952(?)- **1990**:4
Bikoff, James L.
    Brief Entry **1986**:2
Billington, James 1929- **1990**:3
Bird, Larry 1956- **1990**:3
Birnbaum, Nathan
    See Burns, George
Bishop, Andre 1948- **2000**:1
Bissell, Patrick 1958-1987
    Obituary **1988**:2
Bissell, Walter Patrick
    See Bissell, Patrick
Bixby, Bill 1934-1993
    Obituary **1994**:2
Bjork 1965- **1996**:1
Black, Cathleen 1944- **1998**:4
Black, Conrad 1944- **1986**:2
Blackburn, Molly 1931(?)-1985
    Obituary **1985**:4
Blackmun, Harry A. 1908-1999
    Obituary **1999**:3
Blackstone, Harry Jr. 1934-1997
    Obituary **1997**:4
Blades, Ruben 1948- **1998**:2
Blahnik, Manolo 1942- **2000**:2
Blair, Anthony Charles Lynton
    See Blair, Tony
Blair, Bonnie 1964- **1992**:3
Blair, Tony 1953- **1997**:4
Blakey, Art 1919-1990
    Obituary **1991**:1

Blanc, Mel 1908-1989
    Obituary **1989**:4
Blanchett, Cate 1969- **1999**:3
Blau, Jeno
    See Ormandy, Eugene
Bledsoe, Drew 1972- **1995**:1
Blige, Mary J. 1971- **1995**:3
Blobel, Gunter 1936- **2000**:4
Bloch, Erich 1925- **1987**:4
Bloch, Henry 1922- **1988**:4
Bloch, Ivan 1940- **1986**:3
Bloodworth-Thomason, Linda 1947- ....
    1994:1
Bloomberg, Michael 1942- **1997**:1
Blount, Herman
    See Sun Ra
Blume, Judy 1936- **1998**:4
Bly, Robert 1926- **1992**:4
Bocca, Julio 1967- **1995**:3
Bochco, Steven 1943- **1989**:1
Boggs, Wade 1958- **1989**:3
Bogosian, Eric 1953- **1990**:4
Boiardi, Hector 1897-1985
    Obituary **1985**:3
Boitano, Brian 1963- **1988**:3
Bolger, Ray 1904-1987
    Obituary **1987**:2
Bolger, Raymond Wallace
    See Bolger, Ray
Bolkiah, Sultan Muda Hassanal 1946- ....
    1985:4
Bollea, Terry Gene
    See Hogan, Hulk
Bolton, Michael 1953(?)- **1993**:2
Bombeck, Erma 1927-1996
    Obituary **1996**:4
Bond, Alan 1938- **1989**:2
Bonds, Barry 1964- **1993**:3
Bonet, Lisa 1967- **1989**:2
Bonham Carter, Helena 1966- **1998**:4
Bonilla, Bobby 1963- **1992**:2
Bonilla, Roberto Martin Antonio
    See Bonilla, Bobby
Bon Jovi, Jon 1962- **1987**:4
Bono 1960- **1988**:4
Bono, Cher
    See Cher
Bono, Salvatore Philip
    See Bono, Sonny
Bono, Sonny 1935-1998 .... **1992**:2
    Obituary **1998**:2
Boone, Mary 1951- **1985**:1
Booth, Shirley 1898-1992
    Obituary **1993**:2
Bopp, Thomas 1949- **1997**:3
Bose, Amar
    Brief Entry **1986**:4
Bosworth, Brian 1965- **1989**:1
Botero, Fernando 1932- **1994**:3
Botstein, Leon 1946- **1985**:3
Bouchard, Lucien 1938- **1999**:2
Bourassa, Robert 1933-1996
    Obituary **1997**:1
Bourgeois, Louise 1911- **1994**:1
Bourque, Raymond Jean 1960- **1997**:3
Boutros Ghali, Boutros
    See Ghali, Boutros Boutros
Bowe, Riddick 1967(?)- **1993**:2
Bowie, David 1947- **1998**:2
Bowles, Paul 1910-1999
    Obituary **2000**:3
Bowman, Scotty 1933- **1998**:4

Boxcar Willie 1931-1999
    Obituary **1999**:4
Boxer, Barbara 1940- **1995**:1
Boyer, Herbert Wayne 1936- **1985**:1
Boyington, Gregory Pappy 1912-1988
    Obituary **1988**:2
Boyle, Gertrude 1924- **1995**:3
Boyz II Men **1995**:1
Bradley, Bill 1943- **2000**:2
Bradley, Tom 1917-1998
    Obituary **1999**:1
Bradshaw, John 1933- **1992**:1
Brady, James S.
    See Brady, Sarah and James S.
Brady, Sarah
    See Brady, Sarah and James S.
Brady, Sarah and James S. **1991**:4
Branagh, Kenneth 1960- **1992**:2
Brandauer, Klaus Maria 1944- **1987**:3
Brando, Cheyenne 1970-1995
    Obituary **1995**:4
Brandt, Willy 1913-1992
    Obituary **1993**:2
Brandy 1979- **1996**:4
Branson, Richard 1951- **1987**:1
Braun, Carol Moseley 1947- **1993**:1
Bravo, Ellen 1944- **1998**:2
Bravo, Miguel Obando y
    See Obando, Miguel
Braxton, Toni 1967- **1994**:3
Breitschwerdt, Werner 1927- **1988**:4
Bremen, Barry 1947- **1987**:3
Brennan, Edward A. 1934- **1989**:1
Brennan, Robert E. 1943(?)- **1988**:1
Brennan, William 1906-1997
    Obituary **1997**:4
Breyer, Stephen Gerald 1938- .. **1994**:4 ..
    1997:2
Bridges, Llyod 1913-1998
    Obituary **1998**:3
Bristow, Lonnie 1930- **1996**:1
Broadus, Calvin
    See Snoop Doggy Dogg
Brodsky, Joseph 1940-1996
    Obituary **1996**:3
Brokaw, Tom 1940- **2000**:3
Bronfman, Edgar, Jr. 1955- **1994**:4
Brooks, Albert 1948(?)- **1991**:4
Brooks, Diana D. 1950- **1990**:1
Brooks, Garth 1962- **1992**:1
Brooks, Gwendolyn 1917- **1998**:1
Brosnan, Pierce 1952- **2000**:3
Brower, David 1912- **1990**:4
Brown, Edmund G., Sr. 1905-1996
    Obituary **1996**:3
Brown, Edmund Gerald, Jr.
    See Brown, Jerry
Brown, James 1928(?)- **1991**:4
Brown, James Nathaniel
    See Brown, Jim
Brown, Jerry 1938- **1992**:4
Brown, Jim 1936- **1993**:2
Brown, Judie 1944- **1986**:2
Brown, Les 1945- **1994**:3
Brown, Leslie Calvin
    See Brown, Les
Brown, Pat
    See Brown, Edmund G., Sr.
Brown, Paul 1908-1991
    Obituary **1992**:1
Brown, Ron 1941- **1990**:3

Major, John 1943- **1991**:2
Makeba, Miriam 1934- **1989**:2
Malkovich, John 1953- **1988**:2
Malle, Louis 1932-1995
  Obituary **1996**:2
Malloy, Edward Monk 1941- **1989**:4
Malone, John C. 1941- ... **1988**:3 ... **1996**:3
Malone, Karl 1963- ...... **1990**:1 ...... **1997**:3
Maltby, Richard, Jr. 1937- **1996**:3
Mamet, David 1947- **1998**:4
Mancini, Henry 1924-1994
  Obituary **1994**:4
Mandel, Howie 1955- **1989**:1
Mandela, Nelson 1918- **1990**:3
Mandela, Winnie 1934- **1989**:3
Mankiller, Wilma P.
  Brief Entry **1986**:2
Mansion, Gracie
  Brief Entry **1986**:3
Manson, Marilyn 1969- **1999**:4
Mantegna, Joe 1947- **1992**:1
Mantle, Mickey 1931-1995
  Obituary **1996**:1
Mapplethorpe, Robert 1946-1989
  Obituary **1989**:3
Maradona, Diego 1961(?)- **1991**:3
Maraldo, Pamela J. 1948(?)- **1993**:4
Maravich, Pete 1948-1988
  Obituary **1988**:2
Marcos, Ferdinand 1917-1989
  Obituary **1990**:1
Marier, Rebecca 1974- **1995**:4
Marin, Cheech 1946- **2000**:1
Maris, Roger 1934-1985
  Obituary **1986**:1
Mark, Marky
  See Marky Mark
Markle, C. Wilson 1938- **1988**:1
Markle, Clarke Wilson
  See Markle, C. Wilson
Marky Mark 1971- **1993**:3
Marley, Ziggy 1968- **1990**:4
Marriott, J. Willard 1900-1985
  Obituary **1985**:4
Marriott, J. Willard, Jr. 1932- **1985**:4
Marriott, John Willard
  See Marriott, J. Willard
Marriott, John Willard, Jr.
  See Marriott, J. Willard, Jr.
Marrow, Tracey
  See Ice-T
Marsalis, Branford 1960- **1988**:3
Marsalis, Wynton 1961- **1997**:4
Marsh, Dorothy Marie
  See West, Dottie
Marshall, Penny 1942- **1991**:3
Marshall, Susan 1958- **2000**:4
Marshall, Thurgood 1908-1993
  Obituary **1993**:3
Martin, Alfred Manuel
  See Martin, Billy
Martin, Billy 1928-1989 .... **1988**:4
  Obituary **1990**:2
Martin, Dean 1917-1995
  Obituary **1996**:2
Martin, Dean Paul 1952(?)-1987
  Obituary **1987**:3
Martin, Judith 1938- **2000**:3
Martin, Lynn 1939- **1991**:4
Martin, Mary 1913-1990
  Obituary **1991**:2
Martin, Ricky 1971- **1999**:4

Martin, Steve 1945- **1992**:2
Martinez, Bob 1934- **1992**:1
Marvin, Lee 1924-1987
  Obituary **1988**:1
Mary Kay
  See Ash, Mary Kay
Masako, Crown Princess 1963- **1993**:4
Mas Canosa, Jorge 1939-1997
  Obituary **1998**:2
Masina, Giulietta 1920-1994
  Obituary **1994**:3
Master P 1970- **1999**:4
Mastroianni, Marcello 1914-1996
  Obituary **1997**:2
Masur, Kurt 1927- **1993**:4
Matalin, Mary 1953- **1995**:2
Mathews, Dan 1965- **1998**:3
Matlin, Marlee 1965- **1992**:2
Matlovich, Leonard P. 1944(?)-1988
  Obituary **1988**:4
Matthau, Walter 1920- **2000**:3
Matthews, Dave 1967- **1999**:3
Mattingly, Don 1961- **1986**:2
Mattingly, Donald Arthur
  See Mattingly, Don
Matuszak, John 1951(?)-1989
  Obituary **1989**:4
Max, Peter 1937- **1993**:2
Maxwell, Hamish 1926- **1989**:4
Maxwell, Robert 1923- **1990**:1
Maxwell, Robert 1923-1991
  Obituary **1992**:2
Maynard, Joyce 1953- **1999**:4
Mbeki, Thabo 1942- **1999**:4
McAuliffe, Christa 1948-1986
  Obituary **1985**:4
McAuliffe, Sharon Christa
  See McAuliffe, Christa
McCain, John S. 1936- **1998**:4
McCall, Nathan 1955- **1994**:4
McCarroll, Tony
  See Oasis
McCarron, Chris 1955- **1995**:4
McCarthy, Carolyn 1944- **1998**:4
McCarthy, Jenny 1972- **1997**:4
McCartney, Bill 1940- **1995**:3
McCartney, Linda 1942-1998
  Obituary **1998**:4
McCary, Michael S.
  See Boyz II Men
McCloskey, J. Michael 1934- **1988**:2
McCloskey, James 1944(?)- **1993**:1
McCloskey, John Michael
  See McCloskey, J. Michael
McCloy, John J. 1895-1989
  Obituary **1989**:3
McColough, C. Peter 1922- **1990**:2
McConaughey, Matthew David 1969- ....
  1997:1
McCourt, Frank 1930- **1997**:4
McCrea, Joel 1905-1990
  Obituary **1991**:1
McCready, Mike
  See Pearl Jam
McDermott, Alice 1953- **1999**:2
McDonnell, Sanford N. 1922- **1988**:4
McDormand, Frances 1957- **1997**:3
McDowall, Roddy 1928-1998
  Obituary **1999**:1
McDuffie, Robert 1958- **1990**:2
McElligott, Thomas J. 1943- **1987**:4
McEntire, Reba 1954- **1987**:3

McEntire, Reba 1954- **1994**:2
McFarlane, Todd 1961- **1999**:1
McFerrin, Bobby 1950- **1989**:1
McGillis, Kelly 1957- **1989**:3
McGowan, William 1927- **1985**:2
McGowan, William G. 1927-1992
  Obituary **1993**:1
McGraw, Tim 1966- **2000**:3
McGregor, Ewan 1971(?)- **1998**:2
McGuigan, Paul
  See Oasis
McGuinness, Martin 1950(?)- **1985**:4
McGwire, Mark 1963- **1999**:1
McIntyre, Joseph
  See New Kids on the Block
McIntyre, Richard
  Brief Entry **1986**:2
McKee, Lonette 1952(?)- **1996**:1
McKellen, Ian 1939- **1994**:1
McKenna, Terence **1993**:3
McKinney, Cynthia A. 1955- **1997**:1
McKinney, Stewart B. 1931-1987
  Obituary **1987**:4
McLachlan, Sarah 1968- **1998**:4
McLaren, Norman 1914-1987
  Obituary **1987**:2
McLaughlin, Audrey 1936- **1990**:3
McMahon, James Robert
  See McMahon, Jim
McMahon, Jim 1959- **1985**:4
McMahon, Vince, Jr. 1945(?)- **1985**:4
McManus, Declan
  See Costello, Elvis
McMillan, Terry 1951- **1993**:2
McMillen, Tom 1952- **1988**:4
McMurtry, James 1962- **1990**:2
McNamara, Robert S. 1916- **1995**:4
McNealy, Scott 1954- **1999**:4
McRae, Carmen 1920(?)-1994
  Obituary **1995**:2
McTaggart, David 1932(?)- **1989**:4
Meadows, Audrey 1925-1996
  Obituary **1996**:3
Megawati Sukarnoputri 1947- **2000**:1
Mehta, Zubin 1938(?)- **1994**:3
Mellinger, Frederick 1924(?)-1990
  Obituary **1990**:4
Mello, Dawn 1938(?)- **1992**:2
Mellon, Paul 1907-1999
  Obituary **1999**:3
Melman, Richard
  Brief Entry **1986**:1
Menchu, Rigoberta 1960(?)- **1993**:2
Meneghel, Maria da Graca
  See Xuxa
Mengele, Josef 1911-1979
  Obituary **1985**:2
Mengers, Sue 1938- **1985**:3
Menninger, Karl 1893-1990
  Obituary **1991**:1
Menuhin, Yehudi 1916-1999
  Obituary **1999**:3
Merchant, Natalie 1963- **1996**:3
Mercury, Freddie 1946-1991
  Obituary **1992**:2
Meredith, Burgess 1909-1997
  Obituary **1998**:1
Merrick, David 1912-2000
  Obituary **2000**:4
Merrill, James 1926-1995
  Obituary **1995**:3